W9-CGM-865

Thirty-fifth issue
Trente-cinquième édition
Trigésima quinta edición

1975 Year Book of Labour Statistics

Annuaire des statistiques du travail

Anuario de Estadísticas del Trabajo

International Labour Office   Geneva
Bureau international du Travail   Genève
Oficina Internacional del Trabajo   Ginebra

BIBLIOTHEQUE DE DROIT
U.d'O.
O.U.
LAW LIBRARY

Copyright © International Labour Office 1975
Copyright © Bureau international du Travail 1975
Copyright © Oficina Internacional del Trabajo 1975

ISBN 92-2-001426-2 (hardback; relié toile; en tela)
ISBN 92-2-001427-0 (paperback; broché; en rústica)

ILO publications can be obtained through major booksellers or ILO local offices in many countries, or direct from ILO Publications, International Labour Office, CH-1211 Geneva 22, Switzerland. A catalogue or list of new publications will be sent free of charge from the above address.

Les publications du BIT peuvent être obtenues dans les principales librairies ou les bureaux locaux du BIT dans de nombreux pays, ou sur demande adressée directement à Publications du BIT, Bureau international du Travail, CH-1211 Genève 22, Suisse, lequel enverra également sur demande un catalogue ou une liste des nouvelles publications.

Las publicaciones de la OIT pueden obtenerse en las principales librerías o en oficinas locales de la OIT en muchos países o pidiéndolas a: Publicaciones de la OIT, Oficina Internacional del Trabajo, CH-1211 Ginebra 22, Suiza, que también puede enviar a quienes lo soliciten un catálogo o una lista de nuevas publicaciones.

Price:
Hardback: 95 Swiss frs.

Prix:
Relié toile: 95 fr. suisses

Precio:
En tela: 95 frs. suizos

PRINTED IN SWITZERLAND   IMPRIMÉ EN SUISSE   IMPRESO EN SUIZA

111489

Contents

Contents

Contents

Table des matières

Table des matières

Table des matières

Indice general

Indice general

Indice general

Preface

The *Year Book of Labour Statistics, 1975*, presents a summary of the principal labour statistics in some 180 countries or territories. Whenever possible, the data cover the last ten years (1965-1974) and, for some tables, one month or one period near the middle of 1975. Texts, headings and notes are given in English, French and Spanish, in order to enable as wide a use as possible of this publication.

The data are drawn from information sent to the Office by the national statistical services, or from official publications. The International Labour Office wishes to express its gratitude to the statistical services of the different countries for their valuable collaboration. It also thanks the Statistical Office of the United Nations, which supplied the data for table 24, and the International Monetary Fund, which provided the data for tables 28 A and 28 B.

Arrangement of material

The various subjects are grouped in ten chapters, each with an introductory note briefly indicating the main characteristics of the different types of series published in the tables.

The countries appear by continent in accordance with the table " Order of arrangement of countries and territories " (see page XIX).

Base period of indices

For the series presented in the form of index numbers, a uniform base (1970 = 100) has been adopted in the *Year Book* in accordance with the practice followed by the statistical services of the United Nations and of the specialised agencies. When data are available only for periods after 1970, indices are shown in *italics*, usually with the first calendar year for which the figures are available as the base period. Whenever a series is interrupted and replaced by a new series the latter is linked to the former if the two series are sufficiently comparable or otherwise it is published on a new base; this break in continuity is indicated by a horizontal or vertical line separating the two series and by an explanatory footnote.

Classifications used in the " Year Book "

Data by division of economic activity, by industry or by occupational groups are arranged, as far as possible, according to international classifications, i.e. the *International Standard Industrial Classification of all Economic Activities* (ISIC) or the *International Standard Classification of Occupations* (ISCO). As of the 1974 issue of the *Year Book*, the international classifications used are those of 1968 (see Appendix); these classifications differ substantially in a number of respects from those of 1958, which were used in previous issues of the *Year Book*, in particular with regard to the divisions of economic activity "Trade, financing, insurance, real estate, restaurants, hotels and services" as well as the occupational groups "miners, quarrymen and related workers, workers in transport and communications".

The code numbers corresponding to the **new** international classifications (ISIC or ISCO 1968) are shown in the tables where data are presented by division of economic activity, by industry or by occupational groups.

References, sources and index

A list of publications of the International Labour Office dealing with the special problems of statistical methodology involved in the compilation of labour statistics is given in Part A of the list of references and sources. Part B lists the main national publications in which current labour statistics are issued.

An Index at the end of the *Year Book* shows the countries and territories for which data are given in each table, with appropriate page references.

**Data published
in the " Bulletin of Labour Statistics "**

Monthly, quarterly or half-yearly data on employment, unemployment, hours of work, wages and consumer prices for the last three years are published in the *Bulletin of Labour Statistics*.

The second quarterly issue of the *Bulletin* also contains the results of an inquiry carried out annually by the ILO on the wages of adult wage earners in 41 occupations, monthly salaries and normal hours of work per week of employees in selected occupations, and retail prices of selected consumer goods, in October each year.

Préface

L'*Annuaire des statistiques du travail, 1975*, présente, pour quelque 180 pays ou territoires, un résumé des principales statistiques du travail. Dans la mesure du possible, les données couvrent les dix dernières années (1965-1974) et, pour certains tableaux, un mois ou une période proche du milieu de l'année 1975. Les textes, en-têtes et notes sont publiés en trois langues (anglais, français et espagnol), de manière à permettre une utilisation aussi large que possible de cet ouvrage.

Les données proviennent de renseignements communiqués au Bureau par les services statistiques nationaux ou de publications officielles. Le Bureau international du Travail tient à exprimer sa gratitude aux services statistiques des différents pays pour leur précieuse collaboration. Il remercie également le Bureau de statistique des Nations Unies qui a fourni les données du tableau 24, et le Fonds monétaire international qui a fourni les données des tableaux 28 A et 28 B.

Disposition des sujets traités

Les différents sujets traités dans cet *Annuaire* sont groupés en dix chapitres dont chacun comprend une note introductive où sont indiquées brièvement les principales caractéristiques des divers types de séries publiées dans les tableaux.

Les pays sont présentés par continent, selon la liste figurant au tableau « Ordre de présentation des pays et territoires » (voir p. XIX).

Période de base des indices

Pour les séries présentées sous forme de nombres-indices, une base uniforme (100 en 1970) a été adoptée dans l'*Annuaire*, conformément à la pratique suivie par les services statistiques des Nations Unies et des institutions spécialisées. Lorsque des données ne sont disponibles que pour des périodes postérieures à 1970, les indices, imprimés en *italique*, sont généralement présentés avec, pour période de base, la première année civile pour laquelle des chiffres sont disponibles. Lorsqu'une série est interrompue et remplacée par une nouvelle série, cette dernière est raccordée à la précédente dans la mesure où ces deux séries sont suffisamment comparables, ou publiée sur une nouvelle base dans le cas contraire; cette discontinuité dans l'homogénéité des séries est indiquée par un trait horizontal ou vertical séparant les deux séries et par une note explicative de bas de page.

Classifications utilisées dans l'« Annuaire »

Les données par branche d'activité économique, par classe d'industrie ou par groupe de professions sont, dans la mesure du possible, présentées selon les classifications internationales, soit respectivement, la *Classification internationale type, par industrie, de toutes les branches d'activité économique* (CITI) ou la *Classification internationale type des professions* (CITP). Dès l'édition de 1974 de l'*Annuaire*, les classifications internationales utilisées sont celles de 1968 (voir annexe); ces classifications comportent d'importantes modifications par rapport à celles de 1958 utilisées dans les précédentes éditions de l'*Annuaire*, en particulier en ce qui concerne les branches d'activité économique « Commerce, banques, assurances, affaires immobilières, restaurants, hôtels et services » ainsi que les groupes de professions « mineurs, carriers et travailleurs assimilés, travailleurs des transports et communications ».

Les numéros de code correspondant aux **nouvelles** classifications internationales (CITI ou CITP 1968) ont été indiqués dans les tableaux où sont présentées les données par branche d'activité économique, par industrie ou par groupes de professions.

Références, sources et index

Une liste des publications du Bureau international du Travail traitant des problèmes particuliers aux méthodes statistiques utilisées pour l'établissement des statistiques du travail est donnée dans la partie A de la liste des références et sources. La partie B fournit la liste des principales publications nationales dans lesquelles sont diffusées les statistiques courantes du travail.

Un index présenté à la fin de l'*Annuaire* permet aux lecteurs de connaître les pays et territoires pour lesquels des données sont présentées dans chaque tableau, ainsi que la page où elles apparaissent.

Données publiées dans le « Bulletin des statistiques du travail »

Des données mensuelles, trimestrielles ou semestrielles sur l'emploi, le chômage, la durée du travail, les salaires et les prix à la consommation pour les trois dernières années sont publiées dans le *Bulletin des statistiques du travail*.

Le deuxième fascicule trimestriel du *Bulletin* contient aussi les résultats d'une enquête menée annuellement par le BIT sur les salaires des ouvriers adultes dans 41 professions, les traitements mensuels et la durée du travail par semaine des employés dans certaines professions et les prix de détail de certains biens de consommation au mois d'octobre de chaque année.

Prefacio

El *Anuario de Estadísticas del Trabajo, 1975,* presenta, para unos 180 países y territorios, un resumen de las principales estadísticas del trabajo. En lo posible, los datos cubren los diez últimos años (1965-1974) y, para ciertos cuadros, un mes o un período próximo de la mitad del año 1975. Los textos, encabezamientos y notas son trilingües (inglés, francés y español), a fin de que esta publicación pueda ser utilizada con la mayor amplitud posible.

Los datos provienen de las informaciones comunicadas a la Oficina por los servicios estadísticos o de publicaciones oficiales de cada país. La Oficina Internacional del Trabajo desea expresar su gratitud a los servicios estadísticos de los diferentes países por su preciosa colaboración. Agradece asimismo a la Oficina de Estadística de las Naciones Unidas, que ha proporcionado los datos del cuadro 24, y al Fondo Monetario Internacional por los datos de los cuadros 28 A y 28 B.

Disposición de los temas tratados

Los diferentes temas tratados en este *Anuario* se hallan agrupados en diez capítulos, cada uno de los cuales comprende una nota de introducción que indica brevemente las principales características de las diversas clases de series publicadas en los cuadros.

Los países se presentan por continentes, según la lista que figura en el cuadro « Orden de presentación de los países y territorios » (véase pág. xx).

Período de base de los índices

Para las series presentadas en forma de números índices, se ha adoptado en el *Anuario* una base uniforme (1970 = 100), de conformidad con la práctica seguida por los servicios estadísticos de las Naciones Unidas y de las instituciones especializadas. Cuando sólo se dispone de datos para períodos posteriores a 1970, los índices, impresos en *itálicas*, se presentan generalmente tomando como período de base el primer año civil para el cual se dispone de cifras. Cuando una serie queda interrumpida y se substituye por otra nueva, esta última serie se enlaza con la anterior en la medida en que esas dos series sean suficientemente comparables o, en caso contrario, se publica sobre una nueva base; esta discontinuidad de la homogeneidad de las series se indica por una raya horizontal o vertical entre las dos series y por una nota explicativa al pie de la página.

Clasificaciones utilizadas en el « Anuario »

Los datos por división de actividad económica, por industria o por grupo de ocupaciones se presentan, en la medida de lo posible, con arreglo a las clasificaciones internacionales, es decir, según la *Clasificación industrial internacional uniforme de todas las actividades económicas* (CIIU) y la *Clasificación internacional uniforme de ocupaciones* (CIUO), respectivamente. A partir de la edición de 1974 del *Anuario*, las clasificaciones internacionales utilizadas son las de 1968 (véase Apéndice); tales clasificaciones encierran importantes modificaciones en relación con las de 1958, utilizadas en las ediciones precedentes del *Anuario*, sobre todo con respecto a las divisiones de actividad económica « Comercio, establecimientos financieros, seguros, bienes inmuebles, restaurantes, hoteles y servicios » y a los grupos de ocupaciones « mineros, canteros y trabajadores asimilados, trabajadores de los transportes y comunicaciones ».

Los números de clave correspondientes a las **nuevas** clasificaciones internacionales (CIIU o CIUO 1968) se indican en los cuadros donde se presentan los datos por división de actividad económica, por industria o por grupo de ocupaciones.

Referencias, fuentes e índice

En la parte A de la lista de referencias y fuentes se presenta una lista de las publicaciones de la Oficina Internacional del Trabajo sobre los problemas particulares de los métodos estadísticos utilizados para la compilación de las estadísticas del trabajo. En la parte B se presenta la lista de las principales publicaciones nacionales en que aparecen las estadísticas ordinarias del trabajo.

El índice, situado al fin del *Anuario*, señala los países y territorios que figuran en los datos presentados en cada cuadro y la página que contiene dichos datos.

Datos publicados en el « Boletín de Estadísticas del Trabajo »

En el *Boletín de Estadísticas del Trabajo* se presentan los datos mensuales, trimestrales y semestrales sobre el empleo, el desempleo, las horas de trabajo, los salarios y los precios del consumo de los tres últimos años.

El fascículo del segundo trimestre del *Boletín* contiene también los resultados de una encuesta que efectúa cada año la OIT sobre los salarios de los obreros adultos en 41 profesiones, los sueldos mensuales y las horas normales de trabajo por semana de los empleados en ciertas profesiones y los precios al por menor de determinados bienes de consumo durante el mes de octubre de cada año.

Order of arrangement of countries and territories
Ordre de présentation des pays et territoires
Orden de presentación de los países y territorios

The countries and territories are listed by continent in the following order: Africa, America, Asia, Europe and Oceania. The designations employed are those in use on 30 June 1975 for statistical and other technical information.

The name of each country appears in English, French or Spanish when the national language of the country, or the language commonly used in it, is one of the three; in other cases the name of the country is given in the language used in official correspondence between the country in question and the ILO.

In the following table the name and order of listing of the countries appear under the heading " **Year Book** " with a reference number for each country. The table also comprises an index in which the countries are arranged in the alphabetical order of their names in each of the three languages; by using the reference numbers the reader can quickly find the name in English, French or Spanish of a country appearing under the heading " **Year Book** " or, starting from its name in any one of these languages, the country designation used in the *Year Book*.

Note: The designations employed (which reflect United Nations practice) and the presentation of the material in this publication do not imply the expression of any opinion whatsoever on the part of the International Labour Office concerning the legal status of any country, territory, city or area or of its authorities, or concerning the delimitation of its frontiers or boundaries; where the designation " country " appears in the headings of tables, it covers countries, territories, cities or areas. Certain data which relate to the Federal Republic of Germany and the German Democratic Republic include the relevant data relating to Berlin for which separate data have not been supplied (such figures are indicated by the symbol « △»). This is without prejudice to any question of status which may be involved.

Les pays et territoires sont présentés par continent dans l'ordre: Afrique, Amérique, Asie, Europe et Océanie. Les désignations utilisées sont celles qui étaient en usage au 30 juin 1975 pour les données statistiques et les autres données techniques.

Le nom de chaque pays figure en français, en anglais ou en espagnol quand la langue nationale de ce pays ou celle qui y est communément utilisée est l'une de ces trois langues; dans les autres cas, le nom du pays figure dans la langue de correspondance officielle de ce pays avec le BIT.

Dans le tableau ci-après, la dénomination et l'ordre de présentation des pays figurent sous la rubrique « **Annuaire** » avec un numéro de référence pour chaque pays. Ce tableau comporte également un index où les pays sont disposés dans l'ordre alphabétique de leur dénomination dans chacune des trois langues; les numéros de référence permettent de retrouver rapidement la dénomination française, anglaise ou espagnole d'un pays figurant sous la rubrique « **Annuaire** » ou, inversement, de retrouver la dénomination d'un pays utilisée dans l'*Annuaire* en partant de sa dénomination dans l'une quelconque de ces langues.

Note: Les désignations utilisées dans cette publication (qui s'inspirent de la pratique des Nations Unies) et la présentation des données n'impliquent de la part du Bureau international du Travail aucune prise de position quant au statut juridique de tel ou tel pays, territoire, ville ou zone ou de ses autorités, ni quant au tracé de ses frontières ou limites; l'appellation « pays » figurant dans certaines rubriques des tableaux désigne des pays, des territoires, des villes ou des zones. Certaines données se rapportant à la République fédérale d'Allemagne et à la République démocratique allemande comprennent, sans par là préjuger des questions de statut qui peuvent se poser à cet égard, les données relatives à Berlin pour lequel des informations séparées n'ont pas été fournies (de telles données sont indiquées par le symbole « △ »).

Order of arrangement of countries and territories *(concl.)*

Ordre de présentation des pays et territoires *(fin)*

Orden de presentación de los países y territorios *(fin)*

Los países y territorios se presentan por continentes en este orden: Africa, América, Asia, Europa y Oceanía. Las designaciones empleadas son las vigentes en 30 de junio de 1975 para informaciones estadísticas y otras informaciones técnicas.

El nombre de cada país figura en español, francés o inglés, cuando su idioma nacional o de uso general es una de estas tres lenguas; en otros casos el nombre del país figura en la lengua que el país utiliza en su correspondencia oficial con la OIT.

En el cuadro siguiente, la denominación y el orden de presentación de los países figuran bajo la rúbrica « **Anuario** », que va acompañada de un número de referencia para cada país. Este cuadro comprende también un índice en que los países se hallan dispuestos en el orden alfabético de su denominación en cada una de las tres lenguas; los números de referencia permiten hallar rápidamente la denominación en español, francés o inglés de un país que figura en la rúbrica « **Anuario** » o, al contrario, hallar la denominación de un país que se utiliza en el *Anuario* partiendo de la denominación en una de estas tres lenguas.

Nota : Las designaciones empleadas en esta publicación (que se inspiran en la práctica seguida en las Naciones Unidas) y la forma en que aparecen presentados los datos no implican juicio alguno, por parte de la OIT, sobre la condición jurídica de ninguno de los países, territorios, ciudades o áreas citados o de sus autoridades, ni respecto de la delimitación de sus fronteras o límites ; con la palabra « país » que figura en los títulos de algunos cuadros se designa a países, territorios, ciudades o áreas. Ciertos datos relativos a la República Federal de Alemania y a la República Democrática Alemana comprenden los datos relativos a Berlín, respecto del cual no se han proporcionado cifras separadas (esos datos se identifican por medio del símbolo « △ »). Tal presentación se hace sin perjuicio de las cuestiones de condición jurídica que puedan plantearse al respecto.

Order of arrangement of countries and territories
Ordre de présentation des pays et territoires
Orden de presentación de los países y territorios

Year Book Annuaire Anuario		Index — Indice		
		English	*Français*	*Español*

<table>
<tr><td colspan="2" align="center">AFRICA — AFRIQUE
AFRICA</td><td></td><td></td><td></td></tr>
<tr><td></td><td></td><td>—</td><td>—</td><td>Alto Volta   (16)</td></tr>
<tr><td>1</td><td>**Algérie**</td><td>Algeria</td><td>Algérie</td><td>*Argelia*</td></tr>
<tr><td>2</td><td>**Angola**</td><td>Angola</td><td>Angola</td><td>Angola</td></tr>
<tr><td></td><td></td><td>—</td><td>—</td><td>Argelia   (1)</td></tr>
<tr><td>3</td><td>**Botswana**</td><td>Botswana</td><td>Botswana</td><td>Botswana</td></tr>
<tr><td>4</td><td>**Burundi**</td><td>Burundi</td><td>Burundi</td><td>Burundi</td></tr>
<tr><td></td><td></td><td>—</td><td>—</td><td>Cabo Verde   (6)</td></tr>
<tr><td>5</td><td>**Cameroun**</td><td>Cameroon</td><td>Cameroun</td><td>Camerún</td></tr>
<tr><td>6</td><td>**Cap-Vert**</td><td>Cape Verde Is.</td><td>Cap-Vert</td><td>*Cabo Verde*</td></tr>
<tr><td>7</td><td>**République centrafricaine**</td><td>Central African Republic</td><td>République centrafricaine</td><td>República Centroafricana</td></tr>
<tr><td>8</td><td>**Congo**</td><td>Chad   (41)
Congo</td><td>—
Congo</td><td>—
Congo</td></tr>
<tr><td>9</td><td>**Côte-d'Ivoire**</td><td>*Ivory Coast*</td><td>Côte-d'Ivoire</td><td>Costa de Marfil</td></tr>
<tr><td></td><td></td><td>—</td><td>—</td><td>Chad   (41)</td></tr>
<tr><td>10</td><td>**Dahomey**</td><td>Dahomey</td><td>Dahomey</td><td>Dahomey</td></tr>
<tr><td>11</td><td>**Egypt**</td><td>Egypt</td><td>Egypte</td><td>Egipto</td></tr>
<tr><td>12</td><td>**Ethiopia**</td><td>Ethiopia</td><td>Ethiopie</td><td>Etiopía</td></tr>
<tr><td>13</td><td>**Gabon**</td><td>Gabon</td><td>Gabon</td><td>Gabón</td></tr>
<tr><td>14</td><td>**Ghana**</td><td>Ghana</td><td>Ghana</td><td>Ghana</td></tr>
<tr><td>15</td><td>**Guinée**</td><td>Guinea</td><td>Guinée</td><td>Guinea</td></tr>
<tr><td>16</td><td>**Haute-Volta**</td><td>*Upper Volta*
Ivory Coast   (9)</td><td>Haute-Volta
—</td><td>*Alto Volta*
—</td></tr>
<tr><td>17</td><td>**Kenya**</td><td>Kenya</td><td>Kenya</td><td>Kenia</td></tr>
<tr><td>18</td><td>**Lesotho**</td><td>Lesotho</td><td>Lesotho</td><td>Lesotho</td></tr>
<tr><td>19</td><td>**Liberia**</td><td>Liberia</td><td>Libéria</td><td>Liberia</td></tr>
<tr><td>20</td><td>**Libyan Arab Republic**</td><td>Libyan Arab Republic</td><td>République arabe libyenne</td><td>República Arabe Libia</td></tr>
<tr><td>21</td><td>**Madagascar**</td><td>Madagascar</td><td>Madagascar</td><td>Madagascar</td></tr>
<tr><td>22</td><td>**Malawi**</td><td>Malawi</td><td>Malawi</td><td>Malawi</td></tr>
<tr><td>23</td><td>**Mali**</td><td>Mali</td><td>Mali</td><td>Malí</td></tr>
<tr><td>24</td><td>**Maroc**</td><td>*Morocco*</td><td>Maroc</td><td>Marruecos</td></tr>
<tr><td></td><td></td><td>—</td><td>Maurice: (26)
Rodrigues</td><td>Mauricio: (26)
Rodrigues</td></tr>
<tr><td>25</td><td>**Mauritanie**</td><td>—
Mauritania</td><td>Mauritanie</td><td>Mauritania</td></tr>
<tr><td>26</td><td>**Mauritius:**
  Rodrigues</td><td>Mauritius:
  Rodrigues</td><td>*Maurice:*
  Rodrigues</td><td>*Mauricio:*
  Rodrigues</td></tr>
<tr><td>27</td><td>**Mozambique**</td><td>Morocco   (24)
Mozambique</td><td>—
Mozambique</td><td>—
Mozambique</td></tr>
<tr><td>28</td><td>**Namibia**</td><td>Namibia</td><td>Namibie</td><td>Namibia</td></tr>
<tr><td>29</td><td>**Niger**</td><td>Niger</td><td>Niger</td><td>Níger</td></tr>
<tr><td>30</td><td>**Nigeria**</td><td>Nigeria</td><td>Nigéria</td><td>Nigeria</td></tr>
<tr><td></td><td></td><td>—</td><td>Ouganda   (44)</td><td>—</td></tr>
<tr><td>31</td><td>**Réunion**</td><td>Réunion</td><td>Réunion</td><td>Reunión</td></tr>
<tr><td>32</td><td>**St. Hélène**</td><td>St. Helena</td><td>Sainte-Hélène</td><td>Santa Elena</td></tr>
<tr><td>33</td><td>**Sénégal**</td><td>Senegal</td><td>Sénégal</td><td>Senegal</td></tr>
<tr><td>34</td><td>**Seychelles**</td><td>Seychelles</td><td>Seychelles</td><td>Seychelles</td></tr>
<tr><td>35</td><td>**Sierra Leone**</td><td>Sierra Leone</td><td>Sierra Leone</td><td>Sierra Leona</td></tr>
<tr><td>36</td><td>**Somalia**</td><td>Somalia</td><td>Somalie</td><td>Somalia</td></tr>
</table>

Order of arrangement of countries and territories
Ordre de présentation des pays et territoires
Orden de presentación de los países y territorios

Year Book Annuaire Anuario	Index — Indice		
	English	Français	Español
	—	Souaziland (39) Soudan (38)	—
37 South Africa, Rep of	South Africa, Rep. of	République sud-africaine	República de Sudáfrica
38 Sudan	Sudan	Soudan	Sudán
39 Swaziland	Swaziland	Souaziland	Swazilandia
40 Tanzania: Tanganyika Zanzibar	Tanzania: Tanganyika Zanzibar	Tanzanie: Tanganyika Zanzibar	Tanzania: Tanganyika Zanzíbar
41 Tchad	Chad	Tchad	Chad
42 Togo	Togo	Togo	Togo
43 Tunisie	Tunisia	Tunisie	Túnez
44 Uganda	Uganda	Ouganda	Uganda
	Upper Volta (16)	—	—
45 Zaïre	Zaire	Zaïre	Zaire
46 Zambia	Zambia	Zambie	Zambia
AMERICA — AMÉRIQUE AMÉRICA			
47 Antigua	Antigua	Antigua	Antigua
48 Antilles néerlandaises	Netherlands Antilles	Antilles néerlandaises	Antillas Neerlandesas
49 Argentina	Argentina	Argentine	Argentina
50 Bahamas	Bahamas	Bahamas	Bahamas
51 Barbados	Barbados	Barbade	Barbados
52 Belize	Belize	Belize	Belize
53 Bermuda	Bermuda	Bermudes	Bermudas
54 Bolivia	Bolivia	Bolivie	Bolivia
55 Brésil	Brazil	Brésil	Brasil
	—	Iles Caïmanes (57)	Islas Caimán (57)
56 Canada	Canada	Canada	Canadá
57 Cayman Is.	Cayman Is.	Iles Caïmanes	Islas Caimán
	Chile (61)	Chili (61)	—
58 Colombia	Colombia	Colombie	Colombia
59 Costa Rica	Costa Rica	Costa Rica	Costa Rica
60 Cuba	Cuba	Cuba	Cuba
61 Chile	Chile	Chili	Chile
62 Dominica	Dominica	Dominique	Dominica
63 República Dominicana	Dominican Republic	République dominicaine	República Dominicana
64 Ecuador	Ecuador	Equateur	Ecuador
65 El Salvador	El Salvador	El Salvador	El Salvador
66 Falkland Is. (Malvinas)	Falkland Is. (Malvinas)	Iles Falkland (Malvinas)	Islas Malvinas (Falkland)
	—	Etats-Unis (92)	Estados Unidos (92)
	—	Iles Falkland (Malvinas) (66)	—
	French Guiana (72)	—	—
	—	Grenade (68)	Granada (68)
67 Greenland	Greenland	Groenland	Groenlandia
68 Grenada	Grenada	Grenade	Granada
69 Guadeloupe	Guadeloupe	Guadeloupe	Guadalupe
70 Guatemala	Guatemala	Guatemala	Guatemala
			Guayana Francesa (72)
71 Guyana	Guyana	Guyane	Guyana
72 Guyane française	French Guiana	Guyane française	Guayana Francesa
73 Haïti	Haiti	Haïti	Haití

Order of arrangement of countries and territories
Ordre de présentation des pays et territoires
Orden de presentación de los países y territorios

Year Book Annuaire Anuario		Index — Indice		
		English	*Français*	*Español*
74	**Honduras**	Honduras	Honduras	Honduras
75	**Jamaica**	Jamaica	Jamaïque	Jamaica
		—	—	Islas Malvinas (Falkland) (66)
76	**Martinique**	Martinique	Martinique	Martinica
77	**México**	Mexico	Mexique	México
78	**Montserrat**	Montserrat	Montserrat	Montserrat
		Netherlands Antilles (48)	—	—
79	**Nicaragua**	Nicaragua	Nicaragua	Nicaragua
80	**Panamá**	Panama	Panama	Panamá
81	**Panama Canal Zone**	Panama Canal Zone	*Zone du Canal de Panama*	*Zona del Canal de Panamá*
82	**Paraguay**	Paraguay	Paraguay	Paraguay
83	**Perú**	Peru	Pérou	Perú
84	**Puerto Rico**	Puerto Rico	Porto Rico	Puerto Rico
85	**St. Kitts**	St. Kitts	Saint-Christophe	San Cristóbal
86	**St. Lucia**	St. Lucia	Sainte-Lucie	*Santa Lucía*
87	**Saint-Pierre-et-Miquelon**	St. Pierre and Miquelon	Saint-Pierre-et-Miquelon	San Pedro y Miquelón
88	**St. Vincent**	St. Vincent	Saint-Vincent	San Vicente
		—	—	Santa Lucía (86)
89	**Surinam**	Surinam	Surinam	Surinam
90	**Trinidad and Tobago**	Trinidad and Tobago	Trinité-et-Tobago	Trinidad y Tabago
91	**Turks and Caicos Is.**	Turks and Caicos Is.	Iles Turques et Caïques	Islas Turcos y Caicos
92	**United States**	United States	*Etats-Unis*	*Estados Unidos*
93	**Uruguay**	Uruguay	Uruguay	Uruguay
94	**Venezuela**	Venezuela	Venezuela	Venezuela
95	**Virgin Is. (Brit.)**	Virgin Is. (Brit.)	Iles Vierges (brit.)	Islas Vírgenes (Brit.)
96	**Virgin Is. (US)**	Virgin Is. (US)	Iles Vierges (E-U)	Islas Vírgenes (EE.UU.)
		—	Zone du Canal de Panama (81)	Zona del Canal de Panamá (81)
	ASIA — ASIE ASIA			
97	**Afghanistan**	Afghanistan	Afghanistan	Afganistán
98	**Bahrain**	Bahrain	Bahrein	Bahrein
99	**Bangladesh**	Bangladesh	Bangladesh	Bangladesh
		—	Birmanie (101)	Birmania (101)
100	**Brunei**	Brunei	Brunéi	Brunéi
101	**Burma**	Burma	*Birmanie*	*Birmania*
102	**Cambodge**	Cambodia	Cambodge	Camboya
		—	—	República de Corea (112)
103	**Cyprus**	Cyprus	Chypre	Chipre
		—	République de Corée (112)	—
		—	—	Filipinas (119)
104	**Hong Kong**	Hong Kong	Hong-kong	Hong Kong
105	**India**	India	Inde	India
106	**Indonesia**	Indonesia	Indonésie	Indonesia
		—	Irak (108)	Irak (108)
107	**Iran**	Iran	Iran	Irán
108	**Iraq**	Iraq	*Irak*	*Irak*
109	**Israel**	Israel	Israël	Israel
110	**Japan**	Japan	Japon	Japón
111	**Jordan**	Jordan	Jordanie	Jordania
112	**Korea, Rep. of**	Korea, Rep. of	*République de Corée*	*República de Corea*
113	**Kuwait**	Kuwait	Koweït	Kuwait

Order of arrangement of countries and territories
Ordre de présentation des pays et territoires
Orden de presentación de los países y territorios

Year Book Annuaire Anuario		Index — Indice		
		English	Français	Español
114	Laos	Laos	Laos	Laos
115	Liban	Lebanon	Liban	Líbano
116	Malaysia:	Malaysia:	Malaisie:	Malasia:
	East Malaysia (Sabah)	East Malaysia (Sabah)	Malaisie orientale (Sabah)	Malasia oriental (Sabah)
	» » (Sarawak)	» » (Sarawak)	» » (Sarawak)	» » (Sarawak)
	West Malaysia	West Malaysia	Malaisie occidentale	Malasia occidental
117	Nepal	Nepal	Népal	Nepal
118	Pakistan	Pakistan	Pakistan	Pakistán
119	Philippines	Philippines	Philippines	*Filipinas*
120	Qatar	Qatar	Qatar	Qatar
121	Singapore	Singapore	Singapour	Singapur
		—	—	República Arabe Siria (124)
		South Viet-Nam, Rep. of (123)	—	—
122	Sri Lanka	Sri Lanka	Sri Lanka	Sri Lanka
123	Sud Viet-Nam, Rép. du	*South Viet-Nam, Rep. of*	Sud Viet-Nam, Rép. du	*Viet-Nam del Sur, Rep. de*
124	République arabe syrienne	Syrian Arab Republic	République arabe syrienne	*República Arabe Siria*
125	Thailand	Thailand	Thailande	Tailandia
		—	—	Viet-Nam del Sur, Rep. de (123)
126	Yemen, People's Dem. Rep. of	Yemen, People's Dem. Rep. of	Yémen, Rép. dém. pop. du	Yemen, Rep. Dem. Pop. del
	EUROPE — EUROPE EUROPA			
127	Albanie	Albania	Albanie	Albania
		—	Rép. dém. allemande (138)	Rep. Dem. Alemana (138)
		—	Allemagne, Rép. féd. d' (139)	Alemania, Rep. Fed. de (139)
		—	Iles Anglo-normandes (131)	Islas Anglonormandas (131)
128	Austria	Austria	Autriche	Austria
129	Belgique	Belgium	Belgique	Bélgica
130	Bulgarie	Bulgaria	Bulgarie	Bulgaria
131	Channel Is.	Channel Is.	*Iles Anglo-normandes*	*Islas Anglonormandas*
132	Czechoslovakia	Czechoslovakia	*Tchécoslovaquie*	Checoslovaquia
133	Denmark	Denmark	Danemark	Dinamarca
134	España	*Spain*	Espagne	España
135	Faeroe Is.	Faeroe Is.	Iles Féroé	Islas Feroé
136	Finland	Finland	Finlande	Finlandia
137	France	France	France	Francia
138	German Democratic Republic	German Democratic Republic	*Rép. dém. allemande*	*Rep. Dem. Alemana*
139	Germany, Fed. Rep. of	Germany, Fed. Rep. of	*Allemagne, Rép. féd. d'*	*Alemania, Rep. Fed. de*
140	Gibraltar	Gibraltar	Gibraltar	Gibraltar
141	Grèce	Greece	Grèce	Grecia
142	Hongrie	Hungary	Hongrie	Hungría
		—	Irlande (144)	Irlanda (144)
143	Iceland	Iceland	Islande	Islandia
144	Ireland	Ireland	*Irlande*	*Irlanda*
145	Isle of Man	Isle of Man	*Ile de Man*	*Isla de Man*
146	Italie	Italy	Italie	Italia
147	Liechtenstein	Liechtenstein	Liechtenstein	Liechtenstein
148	Luxembourg	Luxembourg	Luxembourg	Luxemburgo
149	Malta	Malta	Malte	Malta
		—	Ile de Man (145)	Isla de Man (145)
150	Monaco	Monaco	Monaco	Mónaco
		Netherlands (152)	—	—

Order of arrangement of countries and territories
Ordre de présentation des pays et territoires
Orden de presentación de los países y territorios

Year Book Annuaire Anuario		Index — Indice		
		English	Français	Español
151	Norway	Norway	Norvège	Noruega
152	Pays-Bas	*Netherlands*	Pays-Bas	Países Bajos
153	Pologne	Poland	Pologne	Polonia
154	Portugal	Portugal	Portugal	Portugal
		—	—	Reino Unido (159)
155	Roumanie	Romania	Roumanie	Rumania
		—	Royaume-Uni (159)	—
		—	Suède (157)	Suecia (157)
		Spain (132)	—	—
156	Suisse	*Switzerland*	Suisse	Suiza
157	Sweden	Sweden	*Suède*	*Suecia*
		Switzerland (154)	—	—
		—	Tchécoslovaquie (132)	—
158	Turquie	Turkey	Turquie	Turquía
159	United Kingdom	United Kingdom	*Royaume-Uni*	*Reino Unido*
160	Yugoslavia	Yugoslavia	Yougoslavie	Yugoslavia
	OCEANIA — OCÉANIE OCEANÍA			
161	American Samoa	American Samoa	*Samoa américaines*	*Samoa Americana*
162	Australia	Australia	Australie	Australia
163	Christmas Is.	Christmas Is.	Ile Christmas	*Isla Christmas*
164	Cocos Is.	Cocos Is.	Iles Cocos	Islas Cocos
		—	—	Islas Cook (165)
		—	—	Isla Christmas (163)
165	Cook Is.	Cook Is.	Iles Cook	*Islas Cook*
166	Fiji	Fiji	Fidji	Fiji
		French Polynesia (177)	—	—
167	Gilbert and Ellice Is.	Gilbert and Ellice Is.	Iles Gilbert-et-Ellice	Islas Gilbert y Ellice
168	Guam	Guam	Guam	Guam
169	Nauru	Nauru	Nauru	Nauru
		—	Ile Nioué (172)	Isla Niue (172)
		—	Ile Norfolk (173)	Isla Norfolk (173)
		New Caledonia (174)	Nouvelle-Calédonie (174)	Nueva Caledonia (174)
170	New Hebrides	New Hebrides	Nouvelles-Hébrides	Nuevas Hébridas
171	New Zealand	New Zealand	Nouvelle-Zélande	Nueva Zelandia
172	Niue Is.	Niue Is.	*Ile Nioué*	*Isla Niue*
173	Norfolk Is.	Norfolk Is.	*Ile Norfolk*	*Isla Norfolk*
174	Nouvelle-Calédonie	*New Caledonia*	*Nouvelle-Calédonie*	*Nueva Caledonia*
175	Pacific Is.	Pacific Is.	Iles du Pacifique	Islas del Pacífico
176	Papua New Guinea	Papua New Guinea	Papouasie-Nouvelle-Guinée	Papua-Nueva Guinea
177	Polynésie française	*French Polynesia*	Polynésie française	Polinesia Francesa
178	Solomon Is. (Brit.)	Solomon Is. (Brit.)	Iles Salomon (brit.)	Islas Salomón (Brit.)
179	Tokelau Is.	Tokelau Is.	*Iles Tokélaou*	*Islas Tokelau*
180	Tonga	Tonga	*Tonga*	*Tonga*
		—	Samoa américaines (161)	Samoa Americana (161)
181	Western Samoa	Western Samoa	Samoa-Occidental	Samoa Occidental
		—	Iles Tokélaou (179)	Islas Tokelau (179)
			Tonga (180)	Tonga (180)
182	URSS	USSR	URSS	URSS
183	RSS de Biélorussie	Byelorussian SSR	RSS de Biélorussie	RSS de Bielorrusia
184	RSS d'Ukraine	Ukrainian SSR	RSS d'Ukraine	RSS de Ucrania

Explanation of signs used in the tables

Explication des signes utilisés dans les tableaux

Explicación de los signos que figuran en los cuadros

.   =   not applicable.
... =   not available.
*   =   provisional.
—   =   magnitude not zero but less than half of unit employed.
×   =   division of economic activity represented by only some of its constituent branches.
△   =   See " *Note* ", page XIX.
———— or I = data placed before or after one of these two breaklines are not strictly comparable or a new series begins immediately after the line (see footnotes).
Indices in *italics* = indices based on a year other than **1970.**
In the tables, decimal figures are separated by a period.

.   =   ne s'applique pas.
... =   pas disponible.
*   =   provisoire.
—   =   résultat inférieur à la moitié de l'unité retenue.
×   =   branche d'activité économique représentée seulement par quelques-unes des industries qui la constituent.
△   =   Voir « *Note* », page XIX.
———— ou I = les chiffres placés avant et après l'un de ces deux filets ne sont pas strictement comparables ou une nouvelle série commence immédiatement après le filet (voir les notes de bas de page).
Indices en *italique* = indices ayant comme base une année autre que **1970.**
Dans les tableaux, un point sépare les unités des décimales.

.   =   no se aplica.
... =   no disponible.
*   =   provisional.
—   =   importancia numérica no nula, pero inferior a la mitad de la unidad empleada.
×   =   división de actividad económica representada solamente por algunas de las industrias que la constituyen.
△   =   Véase « *Nota* », página xx.
———— o I = las cifras que figuran antes y después de una de estas dos rayas no son estrictamente comparables o una nueva serie comienza inmediatamente después de la raya (véanse notas al pie de la página correspondiente).
Indices en *itálicas* = índices que no tienen por base el año **1970.**
En los cuadros, un punto separa las unidades de los decimales.

Total and economically active population

Population totale et population active

Población total
            y población económicamente activa

Total and economically active population

The data presented in tables 1, 2 A and 2 B refer to the *economically active* population, i.e. to the total of *employed* persons (including employers, persons working on their own account, salaried employees and wage earners, and, so far as data are available, unpaid family workers) and of *unemployed* persons at the time of the census or survey. The economically active population does not include students, women occupied solely in domestic duties, retired persons, persons living entirely on their own means, and persons wholly dependent upon others. The practice varies between countries as regards the treatment of such groups as armed forces, inmates of institutions, persons living on reservations, persons seeking work for the first time, seasonal workers and persons engaged in part-time economic activities. In some countries, all or part of these groups are included among the economically active while in other countries they are treated as inactive.[1]

The comparability of the data is hampered by the differences between countries—and even within a country—as regards details of the definitions used, age groups and methods of collection and tabulation (population censuses, labour force sample surveys, etc.). For example, the extent to which family workers who assist in family enterprises are included among the enumerated economically active population varies considerably from one country to another. The reference period is an important factor of difference: in some countries census data on the economically active population according to industry, occupation or status (as employer, employee, etc.), refer to the actual position of each individual on the day of the census or survey or during a brief specific period such as the week immediately prior to the census or survey date, while in others the data recorded refer to the usual position of each person, generally without reference to any given period of time. Also, while in some countries only

those persons who have attained a certain minimum age are included in the statistics of the economically active population, in others there is no such age provision in the definition of economic activity.

As of the 1974 issue of the *Year Book*, changes have been made in the presentation of the data shown in certain tables owing to the introduction of the revised 1968 editions of the International Standard Industrial Classification of all Economic Activities (ISIC) and the International Standard Classification of Occupations (ISCO), see " Preface ".

Table 1

Total and economically active population by sex and age group

This table shows the economically active population and its relation to the total population, by sex and age, according to the latest available censuses or surveys.

The table also gives the ratios of the total economically active population to the total population of all ages, or crude activity rates. In interpreting these rates, the effects of differences in the definitions of the economically active population used in the various countries should be taken into account. In particular, the activity rates for females are frequently not comparable internationally, since in many countries relatively large numbers of women assist on farms or in other family enterprises without pay, and there are differences from one country to another in the criteria adopted for determining the extent to which such workers are to be counted among the economically active. Activity rates for young persons should be compared with caution owing to variations among countries in the treatment of family workers, of persons seeking work for the first time, and of students engaged in part-time economic activities. It should also be recalled

---

[1] For a review of the problems concerning definitions, methods of collection and classifications of data on total and economically active population, see United Nations: *Handbook of Population Census Methods*, Vol. II: *Economic Characteristics of the Population* (ST/STAT/ SER.F/5/Rev.1) (New York, 1958).

that the proportions of population of each sex aged under 15 or over 65 years will affect crude activity rates. [1]

Tables 2 A and 2 B

Structure of the economically active population

These tables show the distribution of the economically active population according to *status* (as employers, workers on own account, employees, etc.) cross-classified by *industry* (branch of economic activity) (table 2 A) and by *occupational group* (table 2 B).

Many points of difference arise from country to country with regard to classification by *status*. In most countries managers and directors are classified as salaried employees, but in a few cases they are grouped with employers. Family workers are nearly always counted among the economically active, but the figures are based on a number of different definitions or criteria. Employers and workers on their own account are shown as one group since separate data for these categories are generally not available. For the same reason, salaried employees and wage earners have also been grouped together in these tables. Differences between countries with respect to classification by status are particularly pronounced with regard to the treatment of unemployed persons: in general they are included with salaried employees and wage earners, but in some cases they form the most important part of the group " Others and status unknown ".

As indicated in the tables, most countries have supplied data on the basis of the nomenclature of the *International Standard Industrial Classification of All Economic Activities (ISIC)* and the *International Standard Classification of Occupations (ISCO)* (see Appendix). The classification according to industry (branch of

economic activity) is fundamentally different from that according to occupational group. In the first, all persons employed by manufacturing establishments, for example, are classed under manufacturing, irrespective of their particular occupations. The classification according to occupational group, on the other hand, brings together individuals working in similar occupations, irrespective of the industries or branches of economic activity with which they are connected. Where the data are given according to national classifications, it should be borne in mind that the industrial and occupational classifications employed by the different countries present many points of divergence. The actual content of industrial or occupational groups may differ from one country to another owing to variations in definitions and methods of tabulation. Classification into broad groups may also obscure fundamental differences in the industrial or occupational patterns of the various countries. Where the unemployed are not classified according to the branch of economic activity or occupation in which they are usually, or were most recently engaged, they are frequently included under " Activities not adequately described ". [2]

---

[1] For data by age group relating to years earlier than 1963, see previous issues of the *Year Book*.

[2] For data relating to years earlier than 1963, see previous issues of the *Year Book*.

Population totale
et population active

Les données présentées dans les tableaux 1, 2 A et 2 B se rapportent à la *population active*, c'est-à-dire au total des personnes *occupées* (employeurs, personnes travaillant à leur propre compte, employés et ouvriers et, dans la mesure où des données sont disponibles, travailleurs familiaux non rémunérés) et des personnes *en chômage* à la date du recensement ou de l'enquête. La population active ne comprend pas les étudiants, les femmes occupées exclusivement aux travaux de leur ménage, les retraités, les rentiers et les personnes entièrement à la charge d'autrui. En ce qui concerne les membres des forces armées, les pensionnaires d'institutions, les personnes établies dans des réserves, les personnes qui cherchent pour la première fois un emploi, les travailleurs saisonniers et les personnes qui ont une activité à temps partiel, leur classement varie selon les pays: dans certains, ces groupes sont compris en totalité ou en partie dans la population active; dans d'autres, ils sont considérés comme inactifs [1].

La comparabilité des données est affectée par les différences que présentent, selon les pays — et souvent pour un même pays —, les définitions utilisées, les groupes d'âge et les méthodes de rassemblement et de tabulation employées (recensements de la population, enquêtes par sondage sur la main-d'œuvre, etc.). Ainsi, la mesure dans laquelle les travailleurs familiaux aidant le chef de famille dans l'entreprise familiale sont compris dans la population active diffère très sensiblement d'un pays à un autre. Quant à la période de référence, elle est un important élément de différence: dans certains pays, les données du recensement ou de l'enquête relatives à la population active selon la branche d'activité économique, la profession ou la situation dans la profession se rapportent à la situation effective de chaque individu le jour du recensement ou de l'enquête, ou pendant une brève période déterminée, telle

que la semaine précédant immédiatement la date du recensement ou de l'enquête, tandis que, dans d'autres pays, les données recueillies ont trait à la situation habituelle de chaque personne, sans se rapporter à une période déterminée. De même, alors que, dans certains pays, les statistiques de la population active n'englobent que les personnes ayant atteint un certain âge minimum, dans d'autres, une telle limite d'âge n'est pas prévue dans la définition de la population active.

Dès l'édition de 1974 de l'*Annuaire*, des modifications ont été apportées à la présentation des données de certains tableaux en raison de l'introduction des éditions révisées 1968 de la Classification internationale type par industrie de toutes les branches d'activité économique (CITI) et de la Classification internationale type des professions (CITP), voir « Préface ».

Tableau 1

Population totale et population active par sexe et groupe d'âge

Ce tableau fournit des données sur la population active et son rapport à la population totale, par sexe et par groupe d'âge, d'après les recensements ou enquêtes les plus récents.

Le tableau indique également les rapports de la population active totale à la population totale pour tous les groupes d'âge, soit les taux d'activité bruts. En analysant ces taux, il convient de tenir compte des différences que présente la définition de la population active selon les pays. Les taux d'activité des femmes, notamment, ne se prêtent souvent pas à des comparaisons internationales, car, dans beaucoup de pays, un nombre relativement élevé de femmes aident, sans rémunération, aux travaux de l'exploitation familiale, agricole ou autre, et il existe, entre les pays, des différences dans les critères utilisés pour déterminer dans quelle mesure cette catégorie de travailleuses doit être comptée dans la population active. Il convient de se montrer

---

[1] Pour l'étude des problèmes relatifs aux définitions, aux méthodes de rassemblement et à la classification des données sur la population active et la population totale, voir Nations Unies: *Manuel des méthodes de recensement de la population*, vol. II: *Caractéristiques économiques de la population* (ST/STAT/SER.F/5/Rev.1) (New York, 1958).

5

prudent dans la comparaison des taux d'activité des jeunes gens, étant donné que les travailleurs familiaux, les personnes en quête d'emploi pour la première fois et les étudiants qui ont une activité à temps partiel ne sont pas comptés de la même manière dans les différents pays. Il convient aussi de tenir compte du fait que les proportions de la population de chaque sexe âgée de moins de quinze ans ou de plus de soixante-cinq ans influent sur les taux d'activité bruts [1].

Tableaux 2 A et 2 B

Structure de la population active

Ces tableaux montrent la répartition de la population active distribuée simultanément suivant la *situation dans la profession* (employeurs, personnes travaillant à leur propre compte, employés et ouvriers, etc.), par *branche d'activité économique* (tableau 2 A) et par *groupe de professions* (tableau 2 B).

La classification d'après la *situation dans la profession* présente de nombreuses différences d'un pays à un autre. Dans la plupart des pays, les directeurs et les administrateurs sont classés parmi les employés, alors que, dans quelques cas, ils sont rangés parmi les employeurs. Les travailleurs familiaux sont presque toujours compris dans la population active, mais les données se fondent sur des définitions et des critères différents. Les employeurs et les personnes travaillant à leur propre compte ont été groupés, car on ne dispose généralement pas de données distinctes sur ces deux groupes. Pour la même raison, les employés et les ouvriers ont aussi été groupés dans ces tableaux. Les différences existant, entre les pays, dans les classifications par situation dans la profession sont particulièrement accusées en ce qui concerne les chômeurs: en général, ceux-ci sont comptés avec les employés et les ouvriers; mais, dans certains cas, ils constituent la majeure partie de la rubrique « Autres et situation non définie ».

Comme le montrent les tableaux, les données fournies par la plupart des pays reposent sur la *Classification internationale type, par industrie, de toutes les branches d'activité économique (CITI)* et la *Classification internationale type des professions (CITP)* (voir annexe). La classification d'après la branche d'activité économique est essentiellement différente de la classification par groupe de professions; dans la première, toutes les personnes occupées dans les établissements de l'industrie manufacturière, par exemple, sont classées dans l'industrie manufacturière, quelle que soit leur profession individuelle. Par contre, dans la classification par groupe de professions, toutes les personnes travaillant dans des professions semblables sont réunies sans tenir compte de la branche d'activité économique à laquelle elles sont rattachées. Il convient de ne pas oublier que lorsque les données fournies ont été rassemblées selon les classifications nationales des branches d'activité ou des groupes de professions, celles-ci présentent de nombreuses différences d'un pays à un autre. Le contenu réel des groupes dans lesquels sont rangées les branches d'activité et les professions peut varier selon les pays, en raison des différences dans les définitions et les méthodes de tabulation. De même, les classifications en larges divisions peuvent dissimuler des différences fondamentales dans la structure des branches d'activité ou des professions des divers pays. Les chômeurs qui ne sont pas classés par branche d'activité économique, ou d'après leur profession — qu'il s'agisse de leur profession habituelle ou de celle qu'ils ont exercée en dernier lieu —, sont souvent compris dans « Activités mal désignées » [2].

---

[1] Pour des données par groupe d'âge relatives aux années antérieures à 1963, voir les éditions précédentes de l'*Annuaire*.

[2] Pour des données relatives aux années antérieures à 1963, voir les éditions précédentes de l'*Annuaire*.

Población total y población económicamente activa

Los datos que figuran en los cuadros 1, 2 A y 2 B se refieren a la población *económicamente activa*, es decir, al total de personas *ocupadas* (comprendidos los empleadores, los trabajadores por cuenta propia, los empleados y los obreros, y, en la medida en que se dispone de datos, los trabajadores familiares no remunerados) y las que se encontraban *desempleadas* en la época del censo o encuesta. La población económicamente activa no incluye a los estudiantes, a las mujeres que se ocupan solamente de labores domésticas, a los pensionados, a los rentistas ni a las personas que dependen por completo de otras. La práctica varía según los países en cuanto a la consideración que debe darse a grupos tales como las fuerzas armadas, las personas internadas en distintos establecimientos, los indígenas que viven en reservas, las personas que buscan trabajo por primera vez, los trabajadores estacionales y las personas ocupadas en actividades económicas a tiempo parcial. En algunos países, estos grupos son incluidos, totalmente o en parte, en la población económicamente activa, en tanto que en otros se los considera como población inactiva [1].

La comparabilidad de los datos se encuentra obstaculizada por las diferencias que existen de un país a otro — y a menudo para un mismo país — en lo que respecta a los detalles de las definiciones empleadas, a los grupos de edad y a los métodos de recolección y tabulación (censos de la población, encuestas por muestra sobre la fuerza trabajadora, etc.). Por ejemplo, el grado en que los trabajadores familiares que cooperan en la empresa familiar se encuentran incluidos en la población económicamente activa varía considerablemente de un país a otro. El período de referencia es un importante factor de disparidad: en algunos países, los datos suministrados por el censo, relativos a la población económicamente activa según la industria, la ocupación o la categoría de la ocupación

(como empleador, empleado, etc.), se refieren a la situación efectiva (o de hecho) de cada individuo en el día del censo o encuesta o durante un período breve y específico anterior a la fecha del censo o encuesta, por ejemplo, la semana precedente, en tanto que en otros países los datos obtenidos se refieren a la situación habitual de cada persona, en general sin referencia a un determinado período de tiempo. Asimismo, mientras que en ciertos países las estadísticas de población económicamente activa comprenden solamente a las personas que han sobrepasado cierta edad mínima, en otros no existen estipulaciones de edad en la definición de la actividad económica.

A partir de la edición de 1974 del *Anuario*, se ha modificado la presentación de los datos de ciertos cuadros debido a la introducción de las ediciones revisadas 1968 de la Clasificación industrial internacional uniforme de todas las actividades económicas (CIIU) y de la Clasificación internacional uniforme de ocupaciones (CIUO). Véase « Prefacio ».

Cuadro 1

Población total y población económicamente activa por sexo y grupo de edad

Este cuadro muestra la población económicamente activa y su relación con la población total, por sexo y por edad, según los censos o encuestas más recientes de que se dispone.

El cuadro da también la población económicamente activa total en porcentaje de la población total en todas las edades, es decir, las tasas brutas de actividad. Al interpretar estas tasas deben tenerse en cuenta las diferencias en las definiciones de la población económicamente activa utilizadas en los distintos países. La proporción de mujeres activas, en especial, no es, a menudo, comparable, ya que en muchos países un número relativamente grande de mujeres ayudan en el trabajo agrícola o en otras empresas de tipo familiar sin recibir remuneración, y porque el criterio adoptado para deter-

---

[1] Para proceder a un estudio de los problemas relativos a las definiciones y a los métodos de obtención y clasificación de los datos sobre la población económicamente activa y la población total, véase Naciones Unidas: *Manual de métodos de censos de población*, vol. II: *Características económicas de la población* (ST/STAT/SER.F/ 5/Rev.1) (Nueva York, 1958).

minar la medida en que estas trabajadoras deben ser incluidas en la población económicamente activa varía de un país a otro. Las tasas de actividad correspondientes a los jóvenes deben compararse con precaución a causa de las diferencias que existen de país a país en la consideración del grupo de los trabajadores familiares, de las personas que buscan trabajo por primera vez y de los estudiantes ocupados en actividades económicas a tiempo parcial. Asimismo, las proporciones de población de cada sexo de menos de 15 años o de más de 65 años influirán en las tasas brutas de actividad[1].

Cuadros 2 A y 2 B

Estructura de la población económicamente activa

Estos cuadros muestran la distribución de la población económicamente activa según la *categoría de ocupación* (es decir, según sean empleadores, trabajadores por cuenta propia, empleados, obreros, etc.), clasificada en combinación con la *rama de actividad económica* (cuadro 2A) y con los *grupos de ocupaciones* (cuadro 2 B).

La clasificación según la *categoría de ocupación* presenta numerosas diferencias de un país a otro. En la mayoría de los países se clasifica a los directores y gerentes como empleados, mientras que en otros se los agrega al grupo de los empleadores. Los trabajadores familiares han sido casi siempre comprendidos en la población económicamente activa, pero las cifras se basan en definiciones y criterios diferentes. Los empleadores y los trabajadores por cuenta propia han sido incluidos en un mismo grupo, porque en general no existen datos separados disponibles para estas categorías de trabajadores. Por la misma razón, los empleados y los obreros han sido reunidos en un mismo grupo en este cuadro. Las diferencias que ofrecen, de un país a otro, las clasificaciones según la categoría de ocupación se acentúan particularmente en lo que

respecta al criterio observado en cuanto a las personas desempleadas. En general, éstas se incluyen con los empleados y los obreros, pero en algunos casos constituyen la mayor parte del grupo « Otros y categoría no definida ».

Tal como se indica en los cuadros, la mayoría de los países han suministrado los datos basándose en la nomenclatura de la *Clasificación industrial internacional uniforme de todas las actividades económicas (CIIU)* y de la *Clasificación internacional uniforme de ocupaciones (CIUO)* (véase apéndice). La clasificación por rama de actividad económica es fundamentalmente diferente de la clasificación por grupos de ocupaciones. En la primera, todas las personas ocupadas, por ejemplo, en los establecimientos manufactureros se clasifican dentro de la industria manufacturera, sean cuales fueren sus ocupaciones individuales. Por el contrario, en la clasificación por grupos de ocupaciones, todas las personas que trabajan en ocupaciones similares se reúnen en un mismo grupo, independientemente de las industrias o ramas de actividad económica a las que se hallen vinculadas. Cuando los datos dados están basados en las clasificaciones nacionales, debe tenerse en cuenta que las clasificaciones por ramas de actividad económica y por ocupaciones utilizadas por los diferentes países presentan múltiples divergencias. La significación real de los grupos industriales o de ocupaciones puede variar de un país a otro en razón de las diferencias que existen en los sistemas de definiciones y en los métodos de tabulación. Asimismo, la clasificación en grandes grupos puede encubrir diferencias fundamentales en la estructura industrial o de las ocupaciones de los diversos países. Cuando los desempleados no están clasificados según la rama de actividad económica o la ocupación en que trabajan habitualmente o en la que desempeñaron su última ocupación, a menudo están incluidos en « Actividades no bien especificadas »[2].

---

[1] Para datos por grupo de edad relativos a los años anteriores a 1963, véanse las ediciones precedentes del *Anuario*.

[2] Para datos relativos a los años anteriores a 1963. véanse las ediciones precedentes del *Anuario*.

1 Total and economically active population by sex and age group
Population totale et population active par sexe et groupe d'âge
Población total y población económicamente activa por sexo y grupo de edad

Country and age group *Pays et groupe d'âge* País y grupo de edad	Males — *Hommes* — Hombres			Females — *Femmes* — Mujeres			Total		
	Total population *Population totale* Población total	Economically active population *Population active* Población activa		Total population *Population totale* Población total	Economically active population *Population active* Población activa		Total population *Population totale* Población total	Economically active population *Population active* Población activa	
		Number *Nombre* Número	Per cent *Pour-cent* Por ciento		Number *Nombre* Número	Per cent *Pour-cent* Por ciento		Number *Nombre* Número	Per cent *Pour-cent* Por ciento

AFRICA — AFRIQUE — AFRICA

Algérie (4.IV.66) ‡									
− 15	2 909 497	58 055	*2.0*	2 778 848	15 659	*0.6*	5 688 345	73 714	*1.3*
15-19	540 987	355 310	*65.7*	541 079	20 082	*3.7*	1 082 066	375 392	*34.7*
20-24	343 544	320 747	*93.4*	419 754	15 215	*3.6*	763 298	335 962	*44.0*
25-29	326 396	314 122	*96.2*	411 296	10 908	*2.7*	737 692	325 030	*44.1*
30-44	793 945	761 073	*95.9*	918 198	23 624	*2.6*	1 712 143	784 697	*45.8*
45-49	190 417	178 085	*93.5*	194 450	5 865	*3.0*	384 867	183 950	*47.8*
50-54	171 526	154 990	*90.4*	178 181	5 910	*3.3*	349 707	160 900	*46.0*
55-59	152 234	130 080	*85.4*	141 526	4 515	*3.2*	293 760	134 595	*45.8*
60-64	129 876	95 880	*73.8*	134 426	3 536	*2.6*	264 302	99 416	*37.6*
65 + ...	249 580	83 072	*33.3*	276 342	3 764	*1.4*	525 922	86 836	*16.5*
?	9 143	3 796	*41.5*	10 434	375	*3.6*	19 577	4 171	*21.3*
Total . . .	**5 817 145**	**2 455 210**	*42.2*	**6 004 534**	**109 453**	*1.8*	**11 821 679**	**2 564 663**	*21.7*
Angola (30.XII.60)									
Total . . .	**2 459 015**	**1 310 388**	*53.3*	**2 371 434**	**111 578**	*4.7*	**4 830 449**	**1 421 966**	*29.4*
Botswana (31.VIII.71) ‡									
Total . . .	**298 782**	**135 494**	*45.3*	**321 047**	**158 355**	*49.3*	**619 829**	**293 849**	*47.4*
Burundi (1965) ‡									
Total . . .	**1 584 530**	**782 000**	*49.4*	**1 625 560**	**832 000**	*51.2*	**3 210 090**	**1 614 000**	*50.3*
Cameroun									
Afric. (31.XII.70) ‡									
Total . . .	**2 803 000**	...	...	**3 033 000**	...	...	**5 836 000**	**2 245 000**	*38.5*
Cap-Vert (15.XII.60)									
Total . . .	**92 691**	**44 754**	*48.3*	**107 211**	**60 816**	*56.7*	**199 902**	**105 570**	*52.8*
Rép. centrafricaine (31.XII.62) ‡									
Total . . .	**628 944**	**230 000**	*36.6*	**650 698**	**250 000**	*38.4*	**1 279 642**	**480 000**	*37.5*

‡ For notes, see pp. 272-294.   ‡ *Voir notes pp. 272-294.*   ‡ Véanse las notas en las págs. 272-294.

BIBLIOTHEQUE DE DROIT
U.d'O.

1 Total and economically active population by sex and age group
Population totale et population active par sexe et groupe d'âge
Población total y población económicamente activa por sexo y grupo de edad

Country and age group *Pays et groupe d'âge* País y grupo de edad	Males — *Hommes* — Hombres			Females — *Femmes* — Mujeres			Total		
	Total population *Population totale* Población total	Economically active population		Total population *Population totale* Población total	Economically active population		Total population *Population totale* Población total	Economically active population	
		Population active Población activa			*Population active* Población activa			*Population active* Población activa	
		Number *Nombre* Número	Per cent *Pour- cent* Por ciento		Number *Nombre* Número	Per cent *Pour- cent* Por ciento		Number *Nombre* Número	Per cent *Pour- cent* Por ciento
Côte-d'Ivoire (1970) ‡									
Total . . .	**2 370 000**	**1 319 550**	*55.7*	**2 260 000**	**1 328 810**	*58.8*	**4 630 000**	**2 648 360**	*57.2*
Dahomey (5.X.61) ‡									
Total . . .	**1 020 558**	**553 000**	*54.2*	**1 061 953**	**557 000**	*52.5*	**2 082 511**	**1 110 000**	*53.3*
Egypt (30.V.66*) ‡									
− 15	6 567 353	406 391	*6.2*	6 077 973	78 942	*1.3*	12 645 326	485 333	*3.8*
15-19	1 574 533	922 006	*58.6*	1 435 181	104 460	*7.3*	3 009 714	1 026 466	*34.1*
20-29	1 893 127	1 584 205	*83.7*	2 129 831	166 584	*7.8*	4 022 958	1 750 789	*43.5*
30-49	3 218 095	3 158 544	*98.1*	3 270 921	174 111	*5.3*	6 489 016	3 332 655	*51.4*
50-59	937 431	908 461	*96.9*	915 323	46 876	*5.1*	1 852 754	955 337	*51.6*
60 + ...	866 327	314 121	*36.3*	961 042	16 561	*1.7*	1 827 369	330 682	*18.1*
Total . . .	**15 056 866**	**7 711 840**	*51.2*	**14 790 271**	**621 893**	*4.2*	**29 847 137**	**8 333 733**	*27.9*
» (V.73) ‡									
Total . . .	**17 703 600**	**8 727 800**	*49.3*	**17 388 200**	**539 100**	*3.1*	**35 091 800**	**9 266 900**	*26.4*
Ethiopia (1972-73)‡									
Total . . .	**14 148 700**	**4 951 800**	*35.0*	**13 652 100**	**1 718 100**	*12.6*	**27 800 800**	**9 266 900**	*24.0*
Gabon (31.XII.63) ‡									
− 15	27 000	6 000	*22.2*	38 000	5 000	*13.2*	65 000	11 000	*16.9*
15-19	18 000	12 000	*66.7*	42 000	15 000	*35.7*	60 000	27 000	*45.0*
20-64	143 000	100 000	*69.9*	135 000	75 000	*55.6*	278 000	175 000	*62.9*
65 + ...	3 000	500	*16.7*	5 000	1 000	*20.0*	8 000	1 500	*18.8*
?	15 000	1 500	*10.0*	10 000	4 000	*40.0*	25 000	5 500	*22.0*
Total . . .	**206 000**	**120 000**	*58.3*	**230 000**	**100 000**	*43.5*	**436 000**	**220 000**	*50.5*
Ghana (1.III.70)									
− 15	2 020 809	.	.	1 995 156	.	.	4 015 965	.	.
15-19	399 017	168 829	*42.3*	379 038	148 725	*39.2*	778 055	317 554	*40.8*
20-24	305 586	252 416	*82.6*	375 545	230 641	*61.4*	681 131	483 057	*70.9*
25-29	289 945	276 983	*95.5*	341 481	221 855	*65.0*	631 426	498 838	*79.0*
30-44	659 496	644 582	*97.7*	689 348	509 278	*73.9*	1 348 844	1 153 860	*85.5*
45-49	144 014	140 440	*97.5*	128 052	99 811	*77.9*	272 066	240 251	*88.3*
50-54	119 660	115 559	*96.6*	111 777	88 343	*79.0*	231 437	203 902	*88.1*
55-59	76 473	72 824	*95.2*	66 043	49 834	*75.5*	142 516	122 658	*86.1*
60-64	75 302	68 985	*91.6*	71 076	50 522	*71.1*	146 378	119 507	*81.6*
65 + ...	157 507	118 777	*75.4*	153 988	73 214	*47.5*	311 495	191 991	*61.6*
Total . . .	**4 247 809**	**1 859 395**	*43.8*	**4 311 504**	**1 472 223**	*34.1*	**8 559 313**	**3 331 618**	*38.9*

‡ For notes, see pp. 272-294. ‡ *Voir notes pp. 272-294.* ‡ Véanse las notas en las págs. 272-294.

1 Total and economically active population by sex and age group
Population totale et population active par sexe et groupe d'âge
Población total y población económicamente activa por sexo y grupo de edad

Country and age group / Pays et groupe d'âge / País y grupo de edad	Males — Hommes — Hombres			Females — Femmes — Mujeres			Total		
	Total population / Population totale / Población total	Economically active population / Population active / Población activa		Total population / Population totale / Población total	Economically active population / Population active / Población activa		Total population / Population totale / Población total	Economically active population / Population active / Población activa	
		Number / Nombre / Número	Per cent / Pourcent / Por ciento		Number / Nombre / Número	Per cent / Pourcent / Por ciento		Number / Nombre / Número	Per cent / Pourcent / Por ciento
Haute-Volta (31.XII.72)†									
Total . . .	2 700 727	1 344 981	49.8	2 679 208	1 511 758	56.4	5 379 935	2 856 739	53.1
Lesotho (IV.66)									
Total . . .	367 087	163 529	44.5	482 926	273 167	56.6	850 013	436 696	51.4
Liberia (2.IV.62)†									
Total . . .	503 588	263 560	52.3	512 855	148 234	28.9	1 016 443	411 794	40.5
Libyan Arab Republic (31.VII.64)†									
− 15	344 248	11 764	3.4	323 198	3 123	1.0	667 446	14 887	2.2
15-19	60 424	23 616	39.1	58 104	2 577	4.4	118 528	26 193	22.1
20-24	62 405	49 601	79.5	56 994	2 525	4.4	119 399	52 126	43.7
25-29	62 314	58 110	93.3	61 472	2 405	3.9	123 786	60 515	48.9
30-44	128 161	122 971	96.0	117 004	5 192	4.4	245 165	128 163	52.3
45-54	50 487	47 702	94.5	44 950	2 347	5.2	95 437	50 049	52.4
55-64	37 357	31 608	84.6	29 769	1 094	3.7	67 126	32 702	48.7
65 + ...	42 776	22 225	52.0	34 819	558	1.6	77 595	22 783	29.4
?	485	237	48.9	534	44	8.2	1 019	281	27.6
Total . . .	788 657	367 834	46.6	726 844	19 865	2.7	1 515 501	387 699	25.6
Madagascar (1.I.65)†									
Total . . .	3 123 109	1 570 000	50.3	3 212 701	1 630 000	50.7	6 335 810	3 200 000	50.5
Maroc (20.VII.71)†									
− 15	3 591 476	181 317	5.0	3 405 641	82 074	2.4	6 997 117	263 391	3.8
15-19	744 199	438 546	58.9	705 688	116 977	16.6	1 449 887	555 523	38.3
20-24	498 509	424 588	85.2	546 273	73 568	13.5	1 044 782	498 156	47.7
25-29	401 632	382 215	95.2	502 285	55 481	11.1	903 917	437 696	48.4
30-44	1 124 999	1 088 417	96.7	1 300 104	146 063	11.2	2 425 103	1 234 480	50.9
45-49	265 098	250 606	94.5	229 643	33 901	14.8	494 741	284 507	57.5
50-54	262 754	241 028	91.7	245 455	46 970	19.1	508 209	287 998	56.7
55-59	151 293	134 386	88.8	101 277	22 632	22.4	252 570	157 018	62.2
60-64	175 554	110 522	63.0	194 686	14 748	7.6	370 240	125 270	33.8
65 + ...	370 391	123 738	33.4	336 849	12 741	3.8	707 240	136 479	19.3
Total . . .	7 585 905	3 375 363	44.5	7 567 901	605 155	8.0	15 153 806	3 980 518	26.3

† For notes, see pp. 272-294.   † Voir notes pp. 272-294.   † Véanse las notas en las págs. 272-294.

1 Total and economically active population by sex and age group
Population totale et population active par sexe et groupe d'âge
Población total y población económicamente activa por sexo y grupo de edad

Country and age group *Pays et groupe d'âge* País y grupo de edad	Males — *Hommes* — Hombres			Females — *Femmes* — Mujeres			Total		
	Total population *Population totale* Población total	Economically active population		Total population *Population totale* Población total	Economically active population		Total population *Population totale* Población total	Economically active population	
		Population active Población activa			*Population active* Población activa			*Population active* Población activa	
		Number *Nombre* Número	Per cent *Pour-cent* Por ciento		Number *Nombre* Número	Per cent *Pour-cent* Por ciento		Number *Nombre* Número	Per cent *Pour-cent* Por ciento
Mauritius:									
Mauritius (30.VI.72*)									
− 15	167 383	4 994	*3.0*	163 902	1 129	*0.7*	331 285	6 123	*1.8*
15-19	50 226	32 196	*64.1*	50 430	7 467	*14.8*	100 656	39 663	*39.4*
20-24	40 150	37 911	*94.4*	39 677	8 659	*21.8*	79 827	46 570	*58.3*
25-29	26 204	25 537	*97.5*	26 970	5 373	*19.9*	53 174	30 910	*58.1*
30-44	60 229	58 420	*97.0*	59 646	15 084	*25.3*	119 875	73 504	*61.3*
45-49	20 139	19 165	*95.2*	18 441	5 160	*28.0*	38 580	24 325	*63.1*
50-54	14 535	13 304	*91.5*	13 209	3 659	*27.7*	27 744	16 963	*61.1*
55-59	12 617	10 721	*85.0*	12 464	2 981	*23.9*	25 081	13 702	*54.6*
60-64	9 213	3 818	*41.4*	9 574	1 217	*12.7*	18 787	5 035	*26.8*
65 + ...	12 475	2 710	*21.7*	17 864	913	*5.1*	30 339	3 623	*11.9*
?	409	112	*27.4*	442	72	*16.3*	851	184	*21.6*
Total . . .	**413 580**	**208 888**	*50.5*	**412 619**	**51 714**	*12.5*	**826 199**	**260 602**	*31.5*
Rodrigues (30.VI.72)									
Total . . .	**12 270**	**6 140**	*50.0*	**12 499**	**2 066**	*16.5*	**24 769**	**8 206**	*33.1*
Mozambique (15.XII.70)									
− 15	1 902 019	83 653	*4.4*	1 797 069	24 999	*1.4*	3 699 088	108 652	*2.9*
15-19	311 030	275 377	*88.5*	260 778	84 229	*32.3*	571 808	359 606	*62.9*
20-24	322 527	319 120	*98.9*	344 649	112 585	*32.7*	667 176	431 705	*64.7*
25-29	267 878	266 519	*99.5*	330 850	103 911	*31.4*	598 728	370 430	*61.9*
30-44	718 582	715 236	*99.5*	838 131	258 677	*30.9*	1 556 713	973 913	*62.6*
45-49	159 484	158 490	*99.4*	165 037	57 461	*34.8*	324 521	215 951	*66.5*
50-54	114 507	113 296	*98.9*	131 219	46 541	*35.5*	245 726	159 837	*65.0*
55-59	79 349	78 051	*98.4*	92 025	32 258	*35.1*	171 374	110 309	*64.4*
60-64	83 640	79 490	*95.0*	93 128	31 557	*33.9*	176 768	111 047	*62.8*
65 + ...	79 533	67 282	*84.6*	77 498	18 874	*24.4*	157 031	86 156	*54.9*
Total . . .	**4 038 549**	**2 156 514**	*53.4*	**4 130 384**	**771 092**	*18.7*	**8 168 933**	**2 927 606**	*35.8*
Namibia (6.IX.60)									
Total . . .	**265 312**	**158 713**	*59.8*	**260 692**	**44 610**	*17.1*	**526 004**	**203 323**	*38.7*
Niger (1960) ‡									
Total . . .	**1 297 557**	**687 680**	*53.0*	**1 313 916**	**80 310**	*6.1*	**2 611 473**	**767 990**	*29.4*
Nigeria (4.XI.63)									
− 15	12 325 411	.	.	11 600 175	.	.	23 925 586	.	.
15-19	2 501 434	1 404 182	*56.1*	2 749 750	528 068	*19.2*	5 251 184	1 932 250	*36.8*
20-24	3 153 836	2 704 399	*85.7*	3 769 352	961 747	*25.5*	6 923 188	3 666 146	*53.0*
25-29	2 606 386	2 506 115	*96.2*	2 964 199	866 224	*29.2*	5 570 585	3 372 339	*60.5*
30-44	4 759 917	4 627 429	*97.2*	4 454 271	1 383 368	*31.1*	9 214 188	6 010 797	*65.2*
45-49	682 464	667 895	*97.9*	485 584	170 095	*35.0*	1 168 048	837 990	*71.7*
50-54	682 577	668 007	*97.9*	534 322	187 173	*35.0*	1 216 899	855 180	*70.3*
55-59	277 241	267 762	*96.6*	186 235	63 667	*34.2*	463 476	331 429	*71.5*
60-64	447 156	431 869	*96.6*	338 636	115 769	*34.2*	785 792	547 638	*69.7*
65 + ...	675 430	609 098	*90.2*	475 679	142 943	*30.1*	1 151 109	752 041	*65.3*
Total . . .	**28 111 852**	**13 886 756**	*49.4*	**27 558 203**	**4 419 054**	*16.0*	**55 670 055**	**18 305 810**	*32.9*

‡ For notes, see pp. 272-294. ‡ *Voir notes pp. 272-294.* ‡ Véanse las notas en las págs. 272-294.

1

Total and economically active population by sex and age group
Population totale et population active par sexe et groupe d'âge
Población total y población económicamente activa por sexo y grupo de edad

Country and age group / Pays et groupe d'âge / País y grupo de edad	Males — Hommes — Hombres			Females — Femmes — Mujeres			Total		
	Total population / Population totale / Población total	Economically active population / Population active / Población activa		Total population / Population totale / Población total	Economically active population / Population active / Población activa		Total population / Population totale / Población total	Economically active population / Population active / Población activa	
		Number / Nombre / Número	Per cent / Pour-cent / Por ciento		Number / Nombre / Número	Per cent / Pour-cent / Por ciento		Number / Nombre / Número	Per cent / Pour-cent / Por ciento
Réunion (16.X.67) ‡									
− 15	94 854	.	.	95 143	.	.	189 997	.	.
15-19	20 983	6 038	28.8	21 786	2 407	11.0	42 769	8 445	19.7
20-24	13 712	10 163	74.1	15 016	4 197	28.0	28 728	14 360	50.0
25-29	12 563	10 588	84.3	13 482	3 482	25.8	26 045	14 070	54.0
30-44	32 664	27 878	85.3	33 047	7 737	23.4	65 711	35 615	54.2
45-49	7 843	6 239	79.5	8 015	2 034	25.4	15 858	8 273	52.2
50-54	6 407	4 630	72.3	6 814	1 552	22.8	13 221	6 182	46.8
55-59	5 297	3 346	63.2	5 769	1 076	18.7	11 066	4 422	40.0
60-64	3 713	1 277	34.4	4 530	425	9.4	8 243	1 702	20.7
65 + ...	4 902	629	12.8	8 876	226	2.5	13 778	855	6.2
?	559	298	53.3	550	112	20.4	1 109	410	37.0
Total . . .	**203 497**	**71 086**	**34.9**	**213 028**	**23 248**	**10.9**	**416 525**	**94 334**	**22.6**
St. Helena (24.VII.66) ‡									
Total . . .	**2 661**	**1 635**	**61.4**	**2 464**	**1 407**	**57.1**	**5 125**	**3 042**	**59.4**
Sénégal (1972-73) ‡									
Total . . .	**1 926 356**	**973 027**	**50.5**	**1 995 934**	**674 785**	**33.8**	**3 922 290**	**1 647 812**	**42.0**
Seychelles (5.V.71)									
− 15	11 495	515	4.5	11 361	227	2.0	22 856	742	3.2
15-19	2 508	2 020	80.5	2 271	1 272	56.0	4 779	3 292	68.9
20-24	1 886	1 793	95.1	1 606	876	54.5	3 492	2 669	76.4
25-29	1 464	1 410	96.3	1 299	622	47.9	2 763	2 032	73.5
30-44	3 860	3 716	96.3	4 072	1 817	44.6	7 932	5 533	69.8
45-49	1 111	1 041	93.7	1 130	507	44.9	2 241	1 548	69.1
50-54	931	853	91.6	983	375	38.1	1 914	1 228	64.2
55-59	832	693	83.3	921	339	36.8	1 753	1 032	58.9
60-64	672	500	74.4	747	216	28.9	1 419	716	50.5
65 + ...	1 367	666	48.7	1 962	241	12.3	3 329	907	27.2
?	118	103	87.3	54	25	46.3	172	128	74.4
Total . . .	**26 244**	**13 310**	**50.7**	**26 406**	**6 517**	**24.7**	**52 650**	**19 827**	**37.7**
Sierra Leone (1.IV.63)									
− 15	408 915	25 202	6.2	391 489	15 198	3.9	800 404	40 400	5.0
15-19	82 867	53 187	64.2	111 511	44 809	40.2	194 378	97 996	50.4
20-24	75 528	66 947	88.6	115 256	52 819	45.8	190 784	119 766	62.8
25-29	93 550	86 790	92.8	114 203	54 474	47.7	207 753	141 264	68.0
30-54	306 800	286 914	93.5	272 013	137 458	50.5	578 813	424 372	73.3
55 + ...	113 463	85 133	75.0	94 760	28 806	30.4	208 223	113 939	54.7
Total . . .	**1 081 123**	**604 173**	**55.9**	**1 099 232**	**333 564**	**30.3**	**2 180 355**	**937 737**	**43.0**

‡ For notes, see pp. 272-294.   ‡ Voir notes pp. 272-294.   ‡ Véanse las notas en las págs. 272-294.

1 Total and economically active population by sex and age group
Population totale et population active par sexe et groupe d'âge
Población total y población económicamente activa por sexo y grupo de edad

Country and age group / Pays et groupe d'âge / País y grupo de edad	Males — Hommes — Hombres			Females — Femmes — Mujeres			Total		
	Total population / Population totale / Población total	Economically active population / Population active / Población activa Number / Nombre / Número	Per cent / Pour-cent / Por ciento	Total population / Population totale / Población total	Economically active population / Population active / Población activa Number / Nombre / Número	Per cent / Pour-cent / Por ciento	Total population / Population totale / Población total	Economically active population / Population active / Población activa Number / Nombre / Número	Per cent / Pour-cent / Por ciento
South Africa, Rep. of (6.V.70)‡									
— 20	5 431 180	698 150	12.9	5 495 810	542 630	9.9	10 926 990	1 240 780	11.4
20-24	902 540	836 500	92.7	925 940	538 180	58.1	1 828 480	1 374 680	75.2
25-34	1 441 560	1 399 160	97.1	1 490 090	659 240	44.2	2 931 650	2 058 400	70.2
35-44	1 100 110	1 072 670	97.5	1 112 370	441 910	39.7	2 212 480	1 514 580	68.5
45-54	804 230	776 690	96.6	795 370	283 810	35.7	1 599 600	1 060 500	66.3
55-64	495 740	423 290	85.4	537 830	121 130	22.5	1 033 570	544 420	52.7
65 + ...	371 140	164 940	44.4	498 960	27 920	5.6	870 100	192 860	22.2
Total . . .	**10 546 100**	**5 371 400**	50.9	**10 856 370**	**2 614 820**	24.1	**21 402 470**	**7 986 220**	37.3
Swaziland (24.V.66)									
— 15	85 975	.	.	88 480	.	.	174 455	.	.
15-19	17 848	9 270	51.9	18 928	8 637	45.6	36 776	17 907	48.7
20-24	10 876	9 049	83.2	15 846	8 205	51.8	26 722	17 254	64.6
25-29	12 634	11 695	92.6	15 795	7 800	49.4	28 429	19 495	68.6
30-44	25 941	24 400	94.1	27 750	14 195	51.2	53 691	38 595	71.9
45-49	6 534	6 154	94.2	6 622	3 513	58.3	13 156	9 667	77.0
50-54	5 829	5 432	93.2	5 576	3 003	53.9	11 405	8 435	74.0
55-59	3 647	3 375	92.5	3 474	1 923	55.4	7 121	5 298	74.4
60-64	3 108	2 793	89.9	3 388	1 839	54.3	6 496	4 632	71.3
65 + ...	5 957	4 702	78.9	9 448	4 337	45.9	15 415	9 039	58.6
?	446	385	86.3	459	438	95.4	905	823	90.9
Total . . .	**178 795**	**77 255**	43.2	**195 776**	**53 890**	27.5	**374 571**	**131 145**	35.0
Tanzania:									
Tanganyika (26.VIII.67*)									
— 15	2 639 771	172 559	6.5	2 619 532	171 788	6.6	5 259 303	344 347	6.5
15-19	501 411	297 151	59.3	558 663	365 705	65.5	1 060 074	662 856	62.5
20-24	368 478	309 724	84.1	528 179	385 915	73.1	896 657	695 639	77.6
25-29	447 621	414 867	92.7	556 731	419 723	75.4	1 004 352	834 590	83.1
30-44	889 110	843 913	94.9	941 012	729 703	77.5	1 830 122	1 573 616	86.0
45-49	246 020	235 820	95.9	226 749	181 731	80.1	472 769	417 551	88.3
50-54	170 481	161 928	95.0	176 154	137 170	77.9	346 635	299 098	86.3
55-59	105 399	99 586	94.5	100 450	78 882	78.5	205 849	178 468	86.7
60-64	103 881	93 633	90.1	111 818	62 686	56.1	215 699	156 319	72.5
65 + ...	354 241	282 011	79.6	312 953	131 561	42.0	667 194	413 572	62.0
Total . . .	**5 826 413**	**2 911 192**	50.0	**6 132 241**	**2 664 864**	43.5	**11 958 654**	**5 576 056**	46.6
Zanzibar (26.VIII.67*)									
— 15	77 996	2 107	2.7	74 351	2 359	3.2	152 347	4 466	2.9
15-19	11 246	4 703	41.8	11 932	7 870	66.0	23 178	12 573	54.2
20-24	9 957	8 307	83.4	14 795	12 134	82.0	24 752	20 441	82.6
25-29	13 649	13 005	95.3	15 269	12 809	83.9	28 918	25 814	89.3
30-44	32 535	31 537	96.9	31 859	26 957	84.6	64 394	58 494	90.8
45-49	6 593	6 347	96.3	4 535	3 626	80.0	11 128	9 973	89.6
50-54	7 621	7 252	95.2	7 417	6 276	84.6	15 038	13 528	90.0
55-59	3 593	3 349	93.2	2 182	1 629	74.7	5 775	4 978	86.2
60-64	6 685	5 934	88.8	5 606	3 720	66.4	12 291	9 654	78.5
65 + ...	9 606	7 467	77.7	7 388	3 652	49.4	16 994	11 119	65.4
Total . . .	**179 481**	**90 008**	50.1	**175 334**	**81 032**	46.2	**354 815**	**171 040**	48.2

‡ For notes, see pp. 272-294.   ‡ Voir notes pp. 272-294.   ‡ Véanse las notas en las págs. 272-294.

1 Total and economically active population by sex and age group
Population totale et population active par sexe et groupe d'âge
Población total y población económicamente activa por sexo y grupo de edad

Country and age group *Pays et groupe d'âge* País y grupo de edad	Males — *Hommes* — Hombres			Females — *Femmes* — Mujeres			Total		
	Total population *Population totale* Población total	Economically active population		Total population *Population totale* Población total	Economically active population		Total population *Population totale* Población total	Economically active population	
		Population active Población activa			*Population active* Población activa			*Population active* Población activa	
		Number *Nombre* Número	Per cent *Pour-cent* Por ciento		Number *Nombre* Número	Per cent *Pour-cent* Por ciento		Number *Nombre* Número	Per cent *Pour-cent* Por ciento
Tchad (VI.72) ‡									
Total . . .	**1 802 000**	**979 000**	*54.3*	**1 989 000**	**292 000**	*14.7*	**3 791 000**	**1 271 000**	*33.5*
Togo (1.III-30.IV.70) ‡									
Total . . .	**940 790**	**405 871**	*43.1*	**1 015 126**	**313 437**	*30.9*	**1 955 916**	**719 308**	*36.8*
Tunisie (3.V.66) ‡									
− 15	1 083 833	.	.	1 015 491	.	.	2 099 324	.	.
15-19	192 079	98 677	*51.4*	188 751	16 536	*8.8*	380 830	115 213	*30.3*
20-24	142 290	129 431	*91.0*	151 018	13 090	*8.7*	293 308	142 521	*48.6*
25-29	141 771	136 205	*96.1*	154 431	8 211	*5.3*	296 202	144 416	*48.8*
30-44	373 523	360 870	*96.6*	377 242	16 413	*4.4*	750 765	377 283	*50.3*
45-49	92 258	87 773	*95.1*	83 371	3 860	*4.6*	175 629	91 633	*52.2*
50-54	82 561	76 349	*92.5*	71 983	3 190	*4.4*	154 544	79 539	*51.5*
55-59	70 919	61 540	*86.8*	58 510	2 222	*3.8*	129 429	63 762	*49.3*
60-64	48 749	36 153	*74.2*	43 416	1 486	*3.4*	92 165	37 639	*40.8*
65 + ...	86 329	40 268	*46.6*	74 403	1 461	*2.0*	160 732	41 729	*26.0*
?	107	.	.	316	.	.	423	.	.
Total . . .	**2 314 419**	**1 027 266**	*44.4*	**2 218 932**	**66 469**	*3.0*	**4 533 531**	**1 093 735**	*24.1*
» (I.71) ‡									
Total . . .	**2 537 000**	**1 046 400**	*41.2*	**2 642 000**	**340 300**	*12.9*	**5 179 000**	**1 386 700**	*26.8*
Zambia (22-30.VIII.69) ‡									
− 15	928 630	.	.	930 198	.	.	1 858 828	.	.
15-19	172 676	74 432	*43.1*	183 880	73 154	*39.8*	356 556	147 586	*41.4*
20-24	132 325	105 919	*80.0*	189 445	53 319	*28.1*	321 770	159 238	*49.5*
25-29	125 438	113 322	*90.3*	161 368	39 235	*24.3*	286 806	152 557	*53.2*
30-44	320 471	289 029	*90.2*	347 285	85 529	*24.6*	667 756	374 558	*56.1*
45-49	85 163	74 431	*87.4*	76 410	24 332	*31.8*	161 573	98 763	*61.1*
50-54	59 464	51 649	*86.9*	53 819	21 996	*40.9*	113 283	73 645	*65.0*
55-59	62 980	54 495	*86.5*	40 714	20 088	*49.3*	103 694	74 583	*71.9*
60-64	29 161	19 761	*67.8*	25 638	9 481	*37.0*	54 799	29 242	*53.4*
65 + ...	48 974	22 278	*45.5*	39 699	9 359	*23.6*	88 673	31 637	*35.7*
?	21 729	10 015	*46.1*	21 528	7 874	*36.6*	43 257	17 889	*41.4*
Total . . .	**1 987 011**	**815 331**	*41.0*	**2 069 984**	**344 367**	*16.6*	**4 056 995**	**1 159 698**	*28.6*

‡ For notes, see pp. 272-294.   ‡ *Voir notes pp. 272-294.*   ‡ Véanse las notas en las págs. 272-294.

POPULATION

1 Total and economically active population by sex and age group
Population totale et population active par sexe et groupe d'âge
Población total y población económicamente activa por sexo y grupo de edad

Country and age group / Pays et groupe d'âge / País y grupo de edad	Males — Hommes — Hombres Total population / Population totale / Población total	Males Economically active population / Population active / Población activa Number / Nombre / Número	Males Per cent / Pour-cent / Por ciento	Females — Femmes — Mujeres Total population / Population totale / Población total	Females Economically active population / Population active / Población activa Number / Nombre / Número	Females Per cent / Pour-cent / Por ciento	Total Total population / Population totale / Población total	Total Economically active population / Population active / Población activa Number / Nombre / Número	Total Per cent / Pour-cent / Por ciento
AMERICA — AMÉRIQUE — AMERICA									
Antigua (7.IV.70)									
− 15	14 270	37	0.3	14 253	22	0.2	28 523	59	0.2
15-19	3 485	2 072	59.5	3 616	1 332	36.8	7 101	3 404	47.9
20-24	2 479	2 459	99.2	2 755	1 872	67.9	5 234	4 331	82.7
25-29	1 481	1 476	99.7	1 839	1 117	60.7	3 320	2 593	78.1
30-44	3 291	3 281	99.7	4 463	2 258	50.6	7 754	5 539	71.4
45-49	1 253	1 250	99.8	1 432	659	46.0	2 685	1 909	71.1
50-54	1 171	1 169	99.8	1 343	614	45.7	2 514	1 783	70.9
55-59	1 170	1 158	99.0	1 185	355	30.0	2 355	1 513	64.2
60-64	882	805	91.3	1 033	296	28.7	1 915	1 101	57.5
65 + ...	1 053	537	51.0	2 217	242	10.9	3 270	779	23.8
?	54	31	57.4	69	25	36.2	123	56	45.5
Total . . .	**30 589**	**14 275**	46.7	**34 205**	**8 792**	25.7	**64 794**	**23 067**	35.6
» (XII.73) ‡									
Total . . .	**32 430**	**13 712**	42.3	**36 920**	**8 671**	23.5	**69 350**	**22 383**	32.3
Antilles néerlandaises (1.I.72)									
− 15	42 263	152	0.4	40 704	60	0.1	82 967	212	0.3
15-19	12 255	4 624	37.7	11 979	3 888	32.5	24 234	8 512	35.1
20-24	8 972	7 945	88.6	9 383	6 338	67.5	18 355	14 283	77.8
25-29	7 353	6 935	94.3	8 445	4 433	52.5	15 798	11 368	72.0
30-44	17 344	16 459	94.9	19 174	7 331	38.2	36 518	23 790	65.1
45-49	4 249	3 986	93.8	4 406	1 339	30.4	8 655	5 325	61.5
50-54	3 500	3 106	88.7	3 892	1 037	26.6	7 392	4 143	56.0
55-59	2 981	2 398	80.4	3 407	840	24.7	6 388	3 238	50.7
60-64	2 999	1 584	52.8	3 309	493	14.9	6 308	2 077	32.9
65 + ...	4 728	1 075	22.7	7 047	431	6.1	11 775	1 506	12.8
Total . . .	**106 644**	**48 264**	45.3	**111 746**	**26 190**	23.4	**218 390**	**74 454**	34.1
Argentina (30.IX.70) ‡									
− 15	3 474 300	123 200	3.5	3 379 150	65 100	1.9	6 853 450	188 300	2.7
15-19	1 058 850	643 250	60.7	1 039 850	322 900	31.1	2 098 700	966 150	46.0
20-24	969 950	837 550	86.3	980 550	427 500	43.6	1 950 500	1 265 050	64.9
25-29	842 550	807 250	95.8	860 150	311 750	36.2	1 702 700	1 119 000	65.7
30-44	2 333 200	2 278 650	97.7	2 332 650	682 050	29.2	4 665 850	2 960 700	63.5
45-49	683 550	651 750	95.3	698 950	175 350	25.1	1 382 500	827 100	59.8
50-54	562 300	512 350	91.1	584 800	128 550	22.0	1 147 100	640 900	55.9
55-59	517 800	413 000	79.8	549 250	88 500	16.1	1 067 050	501 500	47.0
60-64	436 050	246 000	56.4	454 750	46 250	10.2	890 800	292 250	32.8
65 + ...	738 450	209 500	28.4	892 950	41 000	4.6	1 631 400	250 500	15.4
Total . . .	**11 617 000**	**6 722 500**	57.9	**11 773 050**	**2 288 950**	19.4	**23 390 050**	**9 011 450**	38.5

‡ For notes, see pp. 272-294.   ‡ Voir notes pp. 272-294.   ‡ Véanse las notas en las págs. 272-294.

16

1

Total and economically active population by sex and age group
Population totale et population active par sexe et groupe d'âge
Población total y población económicamente activa por sexo y grupo de edad

Country and age group *Pays et groupe d'âge* País y grupo de edad	Males — *Hommes* — Hombres			Females — *Femmes* — Mujeres			Total		
	Total population *Population totale* Población total	Economically active population		Total population *Population totale* Población total	Economically active population		Total population *Population totale* Población total	Economically active population	
		Population active Población activa			*Population active* Población activa			*Population active* Población activa	
		Number *Nombre* Número	Per cent *Pour-cent* Por ciento		Number *Nombre* Número	Per cent *Pour-cent* Por ciento		Number *Nombre* Número	Per cent *Pour-cent* Por ciento
Bahamas (7.IV.70)									
− 15	37 194	327	*0.9*	36 407	220	*0.6*	73 601	547	*0.7*
15-19	7 107	4 067	*57.2*	7 509	3 345	*44.5*	14 616	7 412	*50.7*
20-24	6 205	5 919	*95.4*	6 462	4 646	*71.9*	12 667	10 565	*83.4*
25-29	6 847	6 782	*99.1*	6 854	4 460	*65.1*	13 701	11 242	*82.1*
30-44	14 311	14 170	*99.0*	14 021	8 727	*62.2*	28 332	22 897	*80.8*
45-49	3 015	2 947	*97.7*	3 193	1 864	*58.4*	6 208	4 811	*77.5*
50-54	2 852	2 757	*96.7*	3 023	1 709	*56.5*	5 875	4 466	*76.0*
55-59	2 282	2 167	*95.0*	2 256	1 198	*53.1*	4 538	3 365	*74.2*
60-64	1 494	1 289	*86.3*	1 923	841	*43.7*	3 417	2 130	*62.3*
65 + ...	2 354	1 363	*57.9*	3 503	993	*28.3*	5 857	2 356	*40.2*
Total . . .	**83 661**	**41 788**	*49.9*	**85 151**	**28 003**	*32.9*	**168 812**	**69 791**	*41.3*
Barbados (7.IV.70 *) ‡									
− 15	43 768	93	*0.2*	43 422	32	*0.1*	87 190	125	*0.1*
15-19	12 829	5 485	*42.8*	12 879	2 946	*22.9*	25 708	8 431	*32.8*
20-24	9 875	8 610	*87.2*	9 567	5 472	*57.2*	19 442	14 082	*72.4*
25-29	5 724	5 229	*91.4*	6 268	3 519	*56.1*	11 992	8 748	*72.9*
30-44	13 643	12 857	*94.2*	17 887	9 452	*52.8*	31 530	22 309	*70.8*
45-49	4 300	4 062	*94.5*	5 569	2 748	*49.3*	9 869	6 810	*69.0*
50-54	4 786	4 440	*92.8*	6 057	2 770	*45.7*	10 843	7 210	*66.5*
55-59	4 467	3 910	*87.5*	5 531	2 202	*39.8*	9 998	6 112	*61.1*
60 + ...	11 078	5 727	*51.7*	17 579	2 933	*16.7*	28 657	8 660	*30.2*
Total . . .	**110 470**	**50 413**	*45.6*	**124 759**	**32 074**	*25.7*	**235 229**	**82 487**	*35.1*
Belize (7.IV.70*)									
− 20	36 257	4 895	*13.5*	35 689	1 469	*4.1*	71 946	6 364	*8.8*
20-24	4 033	3 900	*96.7*	4 119	1 286	*31.2*	8 152	5 186	*63.6*
25-29	3 008	2 941	*97.8*	3 095	673	*21.7*	6 103	3 614	*59.2*
30-44	7 837	7 663	*97.8*	7 770	1 463	*18.8*	15 607	9 126	*58.5*
45-49	1 986	1 939	*97.6*	1 894	345	*18.2*	3 880	2 284	*58.9*
50-54	1 649	1 570	*95.2*	1 680	295	*17.6*	3 329	1 865	*56.0*
55-59	1 575	1 440	*91.4*	1 627	275	*16.9*	3 202	1 715	*53.6*
60-64	1 301	1 128	*86.7*	1 281	183	*14.3*	2 582	1 311	*50.8*
65 + ...	2 445	1 452	*59.4*	2 688	204	*7.6*	5 133	1 656	*32.3*
Total . . .	**60 091**	**26 928**	*44.8*	**59 843**	**6 193**	*10.3*	**119 934**	**33 121**	*27.6*
Bermuda (25.X.70)									
− 15	7 780	1	*—*	7 740	.	*.*	15 520	1	*—*
15-19	2 073	1 106	*53.4*	2 043	774	*37.9*	4 116	1 880	*45.7*
20-24	2 452	2 350	*95.8*	2 189	1 731	*79.1*	4 641	4 081	*87.9*
25-44	8 046	7 863	*97.7*	7 403	5 225	*70.6*	15 449	13 088	*84.7*
45-54	2 665	2 576	*96.7*	2 669	1 693	*63.4*	5 334	4 269	*80.0*
55-64	1 873	1 697	*90.7*	2 055	1 063	*51.7*	3 928	2 760	*70.3*
65 + ...	1 404	809	*57.6*	1 938	431	*22.2*	3 342	1 240	*37.1*
Total . . .	**26 293**	**16 402**	*62.4*	**26 037**	**10 917**	*41.9*	**52 330**	**27 319**	*52.2*

‡ For notes, see pp. 272-294.   ‡ *Voir notes pp. 272-294.*   ‡ Véanse las notas en las págs. 272-294.

1 Total and economically active population by sex and age group
Population totale et population active par sexe et groupe d'âge
Población total y población económicamente activa por sexo y grupo de edad

Country and age group *Pays et groupe d'âge* País y grupo de edad	Males — *Hommes* — Hombres			Females — *Femmes* — Mujeres			Total		
	Total population *Population totale* Población total	Economically active population *Population active* Población activa		Total population *Population totale* Población total	Economically active population *Population active* Población activa		Total population *Population totale* Población total	Economically active population *Population active* Población activa	
		Number *Nombre* Número	Per cent *Pour-cent* Por ciento		Number *Nombre* Número	Per cent *Pour-cent* Por ciento		Number *Nombre* Número	Per cent *Pour-cent* Por ciento
Brésil (1.IX.70) ‡									
− 15	19 704 106	1 135 959	5.8	19 426 327	376 914	1.9	39 130 433	1 512 873	3.9
15-19	4 995 432	3 104 352	62.1	5 257 851	1 284 616	24.4	10 253 283	4 388 968	42.8
20-24	4 037 135	3 576 454	88.6	4 248 670	1 217 267	28.7	8 285 805	4 793 721	57.9
25-29	3 173 285	2 989 509	94.2	3 330 784	758 607	22.8	6 504 069	3 748 116	57.6
30-44	7 591 040	7 245 935	95.5	7 698 804	1 588 722	20.6	15 289 844	8 834 657	57.8
45-49	1 795 031	1 656 202	92.3	1 751 654	326 624	18.6	3 546 685	1 982 826	55.9
50-54	1 486 365	1 304 052	87.7	1 453 992	240 039	16.5	2 940 357	1 544 091	52.5
55-59	1 160 154	957 718	82.6	1 128 221	159 957	14.2	2 288 375	1 117 675	48.8
60-64	903 253	663 758	73.5	887 874	100 780	11.4	1 791 127	764 538	42.7
65 + & ?	1 485 542	757 838	51.0	1 623 517	111 921	6.9	3 109 059	869 759	28.0
Total . . .	**46 331 343**	**23 391 777**	50.5	**46 807 694**	**6 165 447**	13.2	**93 139 037**	**29 557 224**	31.7
» (X-XII.73) ‡									
Total . . .	**48 541 126**	**26 079 628**	53.7	**49 384 545**	**11 670 610**	23.6	**97 925 671**	**37 750 238**	38.5
Canada (1.VI.71*) ‡									
− 15	3 254 600	.	.	3 123 900	.	.	6 378 500	.	.
15-24	2 018 000	1 316 900	65.3	1 980 600	975 900	49.3	3 998 600	2 292 800	57.3
25-44	2 751 700	2 550 600	92.7	2 668 900	1 180 500	44.2	5 420 600	3 731 100	68.8
45-64	1 988 200	1 707 900	85.9	2 038 200	817 400	40.1	4 026 300	2 525 300	62.7
65 + ...	782 600	184 700	23.6	961 400	79 400	8.3	1 743 900	264 100	15.1
Total . . .	**10 795 000**	**5 760 200**	53.4	**10 773 000**	**3 053 100**	28.3	**21 568 000**	**8 813 300**	40.9
Cayman Is. (7.IV.60)									
Total . . .	**3 974**	**2 229**	56.1	**4 537**	**930**	20.5	**8 511**	**3 159**	37.1
Colombia (15.VII.64)									
− 15	4 129 273	179 534	4.3	4 026 256	48 087	1.2	8 155 529	227 621	2.8
15-19	836 284	554 382	66.3	929 756	203 143	21.8	1 766 040	757 525	42.9
20-24	671 272	602 702	89.8	746 103	195 930	26.3	1 417 375	798 632	56.3
25-29	549 667	527 104	95.9	616 153	132 956	21.6	1 165 820	660 060	56.6
30-44	1 303 316	1 268 236	97.3	1 370 076	271 329	19 8	2 673 392	1 539 565	57.6
45-49	291 251	282 286	96.9	300 973	58 151	19.3	592 224	340 437	57.5
50-54	262 251	249 441	95.1	256 047	46 796	18.3	518 298	296 237	57.2
55-59	167 127	154 524	92.5	164 475	27 068	16.5	331 602	181 592	54.8
60-64	163 818	142 217	86.8	176 149	25 034	14.2	339 967	167 251	49.2
65 + ...	240 393	141 637	58.9	283 868	23 568	8.3	524 261	165 205	31.5
Total . . .	**8 614 652**	**4 102 063**	47.6	**8 869 856**	**1 032 062**	11.6	**17 484 508**	**5 134 125**	29.4
» (VII.70) ‡									
Total . . .	**10 404 800**	**4 574 738**	44.0	**10 713 000**	**1 651 052**	15.4	**21 117 800**	**6 225 800**	29.5

‡ For notes, see pp. 272-294.   ‡ *Voir notes pp. 272-294.*   ‡ Véanse las notas en las págs. 272-294.

1 Total and economically active population by sex and age group
Population totale et population active par sexe et groupe d'âge
Población total y población económicamente activa por sexo y grupo de edad

Country and age group / Pays et groupe d'âge / País y grupo de edad	Males — Hommes — Hombres Total population / Population totale / Población total	Males — Hommes — Hombres Economically active population / Population active / Población activa Number / Nombre / Número	Males — Hommes — Hombres Economically active population Per cent / Pour-cent / Por ciento	Females — Femmes — Mujeres Total population / Population totale / Población total	Females — Femmes — Mujeres Economically active population / Population active / Población activa Number / Nombre / Número	Females — Femmes — Mujeres Economically active population Per cent / Pour-cent / Por ciento	Total Total population / Population totale / Población total	Total Economically active population / Population active / Población activa Number / Nombre / Número	Total Economically active population Per cent / Pour-cent / Por ciento
Costa Rica (14.V.73)									
− 15	418 816	20 614	4.9	405 646	4 001	1.0	824 462	24 615	3.0
15-19	111 239	75 156	67.6	111 413	22 820	20.5	222 652	97 976	44.0
20-24	82 177	73 819	89.8	84 946	25 048	29.5	167 123	98 867	59.2
25-29	60 636	58 857	97.1	63 137	16 843	26.7	123 773	75 700	61.2
30-44	134 485	132 154	98.3	136 577	30 374	22.2	271 062	162 528	60.0
45-49	32 039	31 374	97.9	31 750	5 330	16.8	63 789	36 704	57.5
50-54	27 090	26 115	96.4	27 313	3 679	13.5	54 403	29 794	54.8
55-59	20 234	19 079	94.3	20 169	2 151	10.7	40 403	21 230	52.5
60-64	19 117	16 442	86.0	18 998	1 482	7.8	38 115	17 924	47.0
65 + ...	32 702	18 670	57.1	33 296	1 305	3.9	65 998	19 975	30.3
Total . . .	**938 535**	**472 280**	*50.3*	**933 245**	**113 033**	*12.1*	**1 871 780**	**585 313**	*31.3*
Cuba (6.IX.70*) ‡									
− 15	1 601 778	4 325	0.3	1 548 407	1 530	0.1	3 150 185	5 855	0.2
15-19	390 162	199 095	51.0	377 646	61 959	16.4	767 808	261 054	34.0
20-24	365 458	313 291	85.7	356 491	90 048	25.3	721 949	403 339	55.9
25-29	332 441	307 339	92.4	320 165	77 395	24.2	652 606	384 734	59.0
30-44	737 385	689 610	93.5	717 180	159 102	22.2	1 454 565	848 712	58.3
45-49	191 232	176 069	92.1	182 986	34 605	18.9	374 218	210 674	56.3
50-54	179 344	159 315	88.8	167 410	26 647	15.9	346 754	185 962	53.6
55-59	161 984	133 185	82.2	152 539	18 319	12.0	314 523	151 504	48.2
60-64	141 828	92 825	65.4	121 896	8 229	6.8	263 724	101 054	38.3
65 + ...	273 012	75 998	27.8	234 051	4 423	1.9	507 063	80 421	15.9
Total . . .	**4 374 624**	**2 151 052**	*49.2*	**4 178 771**	**482 257**	*11.5*	**8 553 395**	**2 633 309**	*30.8*
Chile (22.IV.70) ‡									
− 15	1 736 480	14 220	0.8	1 720 220	5 940	0.3	3 456 700	20 160	0.6
15-19	442 640	187 200	42.3	457 960	75 080	16.4	900 600	262 280	29.1
20-24	356 960	296 400	83.0	387 000	123 720	32.0	743 960	420 120	56.5
25-29	294 300	279 940	95.1	319 720	91 380	28.6	614 020	371 320	60.5
30-44	707 020	678 260	95.9	763 720	182 660	23.9	1 470 740	860 920	58.5
45-49	168 040	155 860	92.8	180 840	38 180	21.1	348 880	194 040	55.6
50-54	144 800	126 240	87.2	159 780	29 520	18.5	304 580	155 760	51.1
55-59	124 820	100 780	80.7	138 340	20 420	14.8	263 160	121 200	46.1
60-64	103 580	73 740	71.2	113 240	11 840	10.5	216 820	85 580	39.5
65 + ...	182 440	73 440	40.3	231 420	12 840	5.5	413 860	86 280	20.8
?	60 420	19 740	32.7	59 400	9 960	16.8	119 820	29 700	24.8
Total . . .	**4 321 500**	**2 005 820**	*46.4*	**4 531 640**	**601 540**	*13.3*	**8 853 140**	**2 607 360**	*29.5*
Dominica (7.IV.60)									
Total . . .	**28 167**	**13 328**	*47.3*	**31 749**	**10 081**	*31.8*	**59 916**	**20 409**	*39.1*
Rep. Dominicana (9-10.I.70) ‡									
− 15	959 310	70 840	7.4	945 115	35 233	3.7	1 904 425	106 073	5.6
15-19	211 910	116 846	55.1	235 740	52 906	22.4	447 650	169 752	37.9
20-24	156 130	129 387	82.9	172 585	49 266	28.5	328 715	178 653	54.3
25-29	116 585	107 324	92.1	128 300	36 597	28.5	244 885	143 921	58.8
30-44	298 145	274 077	91.9	291 520	84 236	28.9	589 665	358 313	60.8
45-49	63 170	58 643	92.8	57 980	16 175	27.9	121 150	74 818	61.8
50-54	58 150	52 773	90.8	50 105	14 151	28.2	108 255	66 924	61.8
55-59	35 050	31 500	89.9	29 245	7 848	26.8	64 295	39 348	61.2
60-64	38 220	33 198	86.9	34 475	9 470	27.5	72 695	42 668	58.7
65 + ...	62 320	47 502	76.2	62 350	13 028	20.9	124 670	60 530	48.6
Total . . .	**1 998 990**	**922 090**	*46.1*	**2 007 415**	**318 910**	*15.9*	**4 006 405**	**1 241 000**	*31.0*

‡ For notes, see pp. 272-294.   ‡ Voir notes pp. 272-294.   ‡ Véanse las notas en las págs. 272-294.

19

POPULATION

1 Total and economically active population by sex and age group
Population totale et population active par sexe et groupe d'âge
Población total y población económicamente activa por sexo y grupo de edad

Country and age group Pays et groupe d'âge País y grupo de edad	Males — Hommes — Hombres			Females — Femmes — Mujeres			Total		
	Total population Population totale Población total	Economically active population Population active Población activa		Total population Population totale Población total	Economically active population Population active Población activa		Total population Population totale Población total	Economically active population Population active Población activa	
		Number Nombre Número	Per cent Pour-cent Por ciento		Number Nombre Número	Per cent Pour-cent Por ciento		Number Nombre Número	Per cent Pour-cent Por ciento
Ecuador (25.XI.62) ‡									
Total . . .	**2 236 476**	**1 207 235**	*54.0*	**2 239 531**	**235 356**	*10.5*	**4 476 007**	**1 442 591**	*32.2*
» (XI.74) ‡									
Total . . .	**3 523 326**	**1 754 700**	*49.8*	**3 524 874**	**466 100**	*13.2*	**7 048 200**	**2 220 800**	*31.5*
El Salvador (27.VI.71)									
— 15	831 341	80 394	*9.7*	807 261	69 072	*8.6*	1 638 602	149 466	*9.1*
15-19	175 365	125 193	*71.4*	182 205	96 054	*52.7*	357 570	221 247	*61.9*
20-24	146 529	137 311	*93.7*	152 898	64 708	*42.3*	299 427	202 019	*67.5*
25-29	111 105	109 492	*98.5*	122 745	38 710	*31.5*	233 850	148 202	*63.4*
30-44	264 127	262 597	*99.4*	274 638	70 996	*25.9*	538 765	333 593	*61.9*
45-49	57 903	57 443	*99.2*	62 235	14 142	*22.7*	120 138	71 585	*59.6*
50-54	47 221	46 463	*98.4*	52 086	10 940	*21.0*	99 307	57 403	*57.8*
55-59	34 456	33 774	*98.0*	36 411	6 896	*18.9*	70 867	40 670	*57.4*
60-64	34 157	32 920	*96.4*	34 196	6 424	*18.8*	68 353	39 344	*57.6*
65 + ...	58 414	43 885	*75.1*	63 947	7 443	*11.6*	122 361	51 328	*41.9*
?	.	.	.	20	.	.	20	.	.
Total . . .	**1 760 618**	**929 472**	*52.8*	**1 788 642**	**385 385**	*21.5*	**3 549 260**	**1 314 857**	*37.0*
Falkland Is. (Malvinas) (3.XII.72)									
Total . . .	**1 081**	**813**	*75.2*	**876**	**193**	*22.0*	**1 957**	**1 006**	*51.4*
Greenland (31.XII.70)									
— 15	10 312	116	*1.1*	9 887	73	*0.7*	20 199	189	*0.9*
15-19	1 792	1 396	*77.9*	1 812	1 058	*58.4*	3 604	2 454	*68.1*
20-24	1 804	1 731	*96.0*	1 667	1 086	*65.1*	3 471	2 817	*81.2*
25-29	2 561	2 532	*98.9*	1 916	1 041	*54.3*	4 477	3 573	*79.8*
30-44	4 988	4 933	*98.9*	3 763	1 793	*47.6*	8 751	6 726	*76.9*
45-49	827	809	*97.8*	749	324	*43.3*	1 576	1 133	*71.9*
50-54	691	655	*94.8*	606	224	*37.0*	1 297	879	*67.8*
55-59	527	443	*84.1*	549	155	*28.2*	1 076	598	*55.6*
60-64	376	188	*50.0*	451	62	*13.7*	827	250	*30.2*
65 + ...	538	95	*17.7*	715	27	*3.8*	1 253	122	*9.7*
Total . . .	**24 416**	**12 898**	*52.8*	**22 115**	**5 843**	*26.4*	**46 531**	**18 741**	*40.3*
Grenada (7.IV.70)									
Total . . .	**43 692**	...	...	**49 083**	...	...	**92 775**	**25 868**	*27.9*

‡ For notes, see pp. 272-294.   ‡ *Voir notes pp. 272-294.*   ‡ Véanse las notas en las págs. 272-294.

1 Total and economically active population by sex and age group
Population totale et population active par sexe et groupe d'âge
Población total y población económicamente activa por sexo y grupo de edad

Country and age group *Pays et groupe d'âge* País y grupo de edad	Males — *Hommes* — Hombres			Females — *Femmes* — Mujeres			Total		
	Total population *Population totale* Población total	Economically active population		Total population *Population totale* Población total	Economically active population		Total population *Population totale* Población total	Economically active population	
		Population active Población activa			*Population active* Población activa			*Population active* Población activa	
		Number *Nombre* Número	Per cent *Pour-cent* Por ciento		Number *Nombre* Número	Per cent *Pour-cent* Por ciento		Number *Nombre* Número	Per cent *Pour-cent* Por ciento
Guadeloupe (16.X.67) ‡									
− 15	67 508	.	.	66 135	.	.	133 643	.	.
15-19	17 443	5 219	29.9	17 544	2 231	12.7	34 987	7 450	21.3
20-24	11 071	7 090	64.0	11 241	4 438	39.5	22 312	11 528	51.7
25-29	7 974	7 314	91.7	8 797	3 857	43.8	16 771	11 171	66.6
30-44	22 341	20 747	92.9	24 133	10 381	43.0	46 474	31 128	67.0
45-49	6 522	5 893	90.4	6 579	3 065	46.6	13 101	8 958	68.4
50-54	5 377	4 600	85.5	5 691	2 595	45.6	11 068	7 195	65.0
55-59	4 588	3 663	79.8	4 838	2 024	41.8	9 426	5 687	60.3
60-64	3 525	2 132	60.5	4 085	1 171	28.7	7 610	3 303	43.4
65 + ...	5 879	1 543	26.2	9 110	835	9.2	14 989	2 378	15.9
?	1 234	800	64.8	1 109	382	34.4	2 343	1 182	50.4
Total . . .	**153 462**	**59 001**	**38.4**	**159 262**	**30 979**	**19.5**	**312 724**	**89 980**	**28.8**
» (I.74) ‡									
Total . . .	...	68 000	...	...	53 200	...	**335 100**	**121 200**	**36.2**
Guatemala (26.III.73) ‡									
− 15	1 188 260	94 000	7 9	1 147 380	13 620	1.2	2 335 640	107 620	4.6
15-19	275 100	198 860	72.3	287 060	41 680	14.5	562 160	240 540	42.8
20-24	231 860	210 080	90.6	239 540	40 380	16.9	471 400	250 460	53.1
25-29	168 100	159 380	94.8	179 260	26 260	14.6	347 360	185 640	53.4
30-44	389 480	372 420	95.6	393 880	55 420	14.1	783 360	427 840	54.6
45-49	93 540	89 240	95.4	89 760	11 760	13.1	183 300	101 000	55.1
50-54	75 400	71 260	94.5	73 040	9 320	12.8	148 440	80 580	54.3
55-59	50 860	46 280	91.0	48 300	5 420	11.2	99 160	51 700	52.1
60 + ...	122 700	93 100	75.9	121 880	8 860	7.3	244 580	101 960	41.7
Total . . .	**2 595 300**	**1 334 620**	**51.4**	**2 580 100**	**212 720**	**8.2**	**5 175 400**	**1 547 340**	**29.9**
Guyana (7.IV.60)									
Total . . .	**279 128**	**134 828**	**48.3**	**281 202**	**39 902**	**14.2**	**560 330**	**174 730**	**31.2**
» (20.III.65) ‡									
Total . . .	...	126 895	...	...	47 877	...	**647 100**	**174 772**	**27.0**
Guyane française (16.X.67) ‡									
− 15	8 398	.	.	8 215	.	.	16 613	.	.
15-19	1 995	842	42.2	1 919	309	16.1	3 914	1 151	29.4
20-24	2 989	2 723	91.1	1 272	579	45.5	4 261	3 302	77.5
25-29	1 559	1 472	94.4	1 313	538	41.0	2 872	2 010	70.0
30-44	4 342	4 070	93.7	3 343	1 531	45.8	7 685	5 601	72.9
45-49	1 162	1 070	92.1	931	410	44.0	2 093	1 480	70.7
50-54	967	849	87.8	828	380	45.9	1 795	1 229	68.5
55-59	772	643	83.3	627	245	39.1	1 399	888	63.5
60-64	565	424	75.0	493	173	35.1	1 058	597	56.4
65 + ...	1 106	441	39.9	1 273	140	11.0	2 379	581	24.4
?	223	147	65.9	100	26	26.0	323	173	53.6
Total . . .	**24 078**	**12 681**	**52.7**	**20 314**	**4 331**	**21.3**	**44 392**	**17 012**	**38.3**

‡ For notes, see pp. 272-294.　　　　‡ *Voir notes pp. 272-294.*　　　　‡ Véanse las notas en las págs. 272-294.

1 Total and economically active population by sex and age group
Population totale et population active par sexe et groupe d'âge
Población total y población económicamente activa por sexo y grupo de edad

Country and age group / Pays et groupe d'âge / País y grupo de edad	Males — Hommes — Hombres			Females — Femmes — Mujeres			Total		
	Total population / Population totale / Población total	Economically active population / Population active / Población activa		Total population / Population totale / Población total	Economically active population / Population active / Población activa		Total population / Population totale / Población total	Economically active population / Population active / Población activa	
		Number / Nombre / Número	Per cent / Pour-cent / Por ciento		Number / Nombre / Número	Per cent / Pour-cent / Por ciento		Number / Nombre / Número	Per cent / Pour-cent / Por ciento
Haïti (9.X.71*)									
− 15	924 140	219 440	23.7	899 920	222 300	24.7	1 824 060	441 740	24.2
15-19	237 820	143 040	60.1	247 180	145 740	59.0	485 000	288 780	59.5
20-24	151 000	123 160	81.6	183 260	141 300	77.1	334 260	264 460	79.1
25-29	125 360	113 280	90.4	161 140	129 240	80.2	286 500	242 520	84.6
30-49	420 960	399 940	95.0	473 140	389 200	82.3	894 100	789 140	88.3
50-54	69 740	64 140	92.0	73 000	57 680	79.0	142 740	121 820	85.3
55-64	91 460	82 380	90.1	93 100	68 800	73.9	184 560	151 180	81.9
65 + & ?	85 720	67 340	78.6	103 140	63 060	61.1	188 860	130 400	69.0
Total . . .	**2 106 200**	**1 212 720**	57.6	**2 233 880**	**1 217 320**	54.5	**4 340 080**	**2 430 040**	56.0
Honduras (6.III.74*)									
− 15	...	...	...	...	...	...	1 279 162	52 759	4.1
15-19	...	...	...	...	...	...	286 616	118 150	41.2
20-24	...	...	...	...	...	...	222 924	115 178	51.7
25-29	...	...	...	...	...	...	164 539	90 656	55.1
30-44	...	...	...	...	...	...	371 539	208 062	56.0
45-49	...	...	...	...	...	...	87 577	48 300	55.2
50-54	...	...	...	...	...	...	69 000	37 154	53.8
55-59	...	...	...	...	...	...	50 423	25 265	50.1
60-64	...	...	...	...	...	...	45 116	22 292	49.4
65 + ...	...	...	...	...	...	...	76 961	25 264	32.8
Total . . .	...	...	...	...	...	...	**2 653 857**	**743 080**	28.0
Jamaica (7.IV.70 *)									
Total . . .	**885 878**	**378 288**	42.7	**927 716**	**188 157**	20.3	**1 813 594**	**566 445**	31.2
» (X.74)‡									
− 14	429 900	.	.	425 200	.	.	855 100	.	.
14-24	187 200	120 400	64.3	200 300	99 100	49.5	387 500	219 500	56.6
25-34	89 000	86 000	96.6	103 000	79 400	77.1	192 000	165 400	86.1
35-44	77 200	75 000	97.2	91 500	71 900	78.6	168 700	146 900	87.1
45-54	72 800	70 200	96.4	85 800	60 200	70.2	158 600	130 400	82.2
55-64	64 500	58 800	91.2	68 800	36 000	52.3	133 300	94 800	71.1
65 + ...	61 100	38 800	63.5	74 100	18 700	25.2	135 200	57 500	42.5
Total . . .	**981 700**	**449 200**	45.8	**1 048 700**	**365 300**	34.8	**2 030 400**	**814 500**	40.1

‡ For notes, see pp. 272-294. ‡ Voir notes pp. 272-294. ‡ Véanse las notas en las págs. 272-294.

1 Total and economically active population by sex and age group
Population totale et population active par sexe et groupe d'âge
Población total y población económicamente activa por sexo y grupo de edad

Country and age group Pays et groupe d'âge País y grupo de edad	Males — Hommes — Hombres			Females — Femmes — Mujeres			Total		
	Total population Population totale Población total	Economically active population *Population active* Población activa		Total population Population totale Población total	Economically active population *Population active* Población activa		Total population Population totale Población total	Economically active population *Population active* Población activa	
		Number *Nombre* Número	Per cent *Pour-cent* Por ciento		Number *Nombre* Número	Per cent *Pour-cent* Por ciento		Number *Nombre* Número	Per cent *Pour-cent* Por ciento
Martinique (16.X.67) ‡									
− 15	69 243	.	.	68 463	.	.	137 706	.	.
15-19	17 464	3 946	*22.6*	17 699	2 405	*13.6*	35 163	6 351	*18.1*
20-24	10 590	8 137	*76.8*	10 940	5 336	*48.8*	21 530	13 473	*62.6*
25-29	7 143	6 345	*88.8*	8 890	4 679	*52.6*	16 033	11 024	*68.8*
30-44	23 009	20 655	*89.8*	25 632	11 826	*46.1*	48 641	32 481	*66.7*
45-49	6 520	5 555	*85.2*	6 991	3 149	*45.0*	13 511	8 704	*64.4*
50-54	5 760	4 639	*80.5*	6 046	2 531	*41.9*	11 806	7 170	*60.7*
55-59	4 982	3 487	*70.0*	5 548	2 049	*36.9*	10 530	5 536	*52.6*
60-64	3 888	1 721	*44.3*	4 523	944	*20.9*	8 411	2 665	*31.7*
65 + ...	6 515	1 315	*20.2*	10 033	657	*6.5*	16 548	1 972	*11.9*
?	98	64	*65.3*	53	24	*45.3*	151	88	*58.3*
Total . . .	**155 212**	**55 864**	*36.0*	**164 818**	**33 600**	*20.4*	**320 030**	**89 464**	*28.0*
» (31.XII.70) ‡									
Total . . .	**165 500**	**61 600**	*37.2*	**174 500**	**40 000**	*22.9*	**340 000**	**101 600**	*29.9*
México (28.I.70) ‡									
− 15	11 357 361	245 939	*2.2*	10 929 319	93 676	*0.9*	22 286 680	339 615	*1.5*
15-19	2 491 047	1 244 052	*49.9*	2 563 344	536 720	*20.9*	5 054 391	1 780 772	*35.2*
20-24	1 930 300	1 536 418	*79.6*	2 102 041	505 872	*24.1*	4 032 341	2 042 290	*50.6*
25-29	1 575 414	1 427 290	*90.6*	1 685 004	292 410	*17.4*	3 260 418	1 719 700	*52.7*
30-44	3 480 221	3 264 427	*93.8*	3 561 029	564 465	*15.9*	7 041 250	3 828 892	*54.4*
45-49	829 719	778 971	*93.9*	807 299	132 355	*16.4*	1 637 018	911 326	*55.7*
50-54	589 788	544 203	*92.3*	602 255	95 748	*15.9*	1 192 043	639 951	*53.7*
55-59	501 529	454 437	*90.6*	510 330	77 295	*15.1*	1 011 859	531 732	*52.6*
60-64	451 069	388 344	*86.1*	466 784	65 861	*14.1*	917 853	454 205	*49.5*
65 + ...	859 166	604 719	*70.4*	932 219	101 855	*10.9*	1 791 385	706 574	*39.4*
Total . . .	**24 065 614**	**10 488 800**	*43.6*	**24 159 624**	**2 466 257**	*10.2*	**48 225 238**	**12 955 057**	*26.9*
» (VI.74) ‡									
Total . . .	**29 337 586**	**12 613 765**	*43.0*	**28 780 123**	**3 332 636**	*11.6*	**58 117 709**	**15 946 401**	*27.4*
Montserrat (7.IV.70*)									
− 20	2 826	365	*12.9*	2 805	211	*7.5*	5 631	576	*10.2*
20-24	460	423	*92.0*	433	257	*59.4*	893	680	*76.1*
25-54	1 193	1 096	*91.9*	1 448	621	*42.9*	2 641	1 717	*65.0*
55-64	465	347	*74.6*	591	150	*25.4*	1 056	497	*47.1*
65 + ...	430	224	*52.1*	807	75	*9.3*	1 237	299	*24.2*
Total . . .	**5 374**	**2 455**	*45.7*	**6 084**	**1 314**	*21.6*	**11 458**	**3 769**	*32.9*

‡ For notes, see pp. 272-294.   ‡ *Voir notes pp. 272-294.*   ‡ Véanse las notas en las págs. 272-294.

1 Total and economically active population by sex and age group
Population totale et population active par sexe et groupe d'âge
Población total y población económicamente activa por sexo y grupo de edad

Country and age group Pays et groupe d'âge País y grupo de edad	Males — Hommes — Hombres			Females — Femmes — Mujeres			Total		
	Total population Population totale Población total	Economically active population Population active Población activa		Total population Population totale Población total	Economically active population Population active Población activa		Total population Population totale Población total	Economically active population Population active Población activa	
		Number Nombre Número	Per cent Pour-cent Por ciento		Number Nombre Número	Per cent Pour-cent Por ciento		Number Nombre Número	Per cent Pour-cent Por ciento
Nicaragua (20.IV.71) ‡									
− 15	462 920	25 660	5.5	449 730	5 120	1.1	912 650	30 780	3.4
15-19	99 890	53 550	53.6	107 450	18 570	17.3	207 340	72 120	34.8
20-24	72 860	58 990	81.0	82 130	20 980	25.5	154 990	79 970	51.6
25-29	56 460	49 900	88.4	64 850	15 520	23.9	121 310	65 420	53.9
30-49	156 980	143 640	91.5	169 800	37 020	21.8	326 780	180 660	55.3
50-54	23 530	20 590	87.5	23 940	4 430	18.5	47 470	25 020	52.7
55-59	15 890	13 650	85.9	17 580	3 270	18.6	33 470	16 920	50.6
60-64	15 650	12 670	81.0	17 080	2 070	12.1	32 730	14 740	45.0
65 + ...	25 770	15 650	60.7	32 180	2 960	9.2	57 950	18 610	32.1
Total . . .	**929 950**	**394 300**	*42.4*	**964 740**	**109 940**	*11.4*	**1 894 690**	**504 240**	*26.6*
Panamá (10.V.70) ‡									
− 15	314 053	10 546	3.4	306 084	4 499	1.5	620 137	15 045	2.4
15-19	71 783	43 700	60.9	72 718	22 227	30.6	144 501	65 927	45.6
20-24	62 298	58 164	93.4	62 954	25 394	40.3	125 252	83 558	66.7
25-29	50 941	49 343	96.9	50 815	18 088	35.6	101 756	67 431	66.3
30-44	110 880	107 865	97.3	106 100	34 061	32.1	216 980	141 926	65.4
45-49	28 053	26 951	96.1	25 418	7 398	29.1	53 471	34 349	64.2
50-54	24 858	23 257	93.6	21 985	5 516	25.1	46 843	28 773	61.4
55-59	20 207	18 099	89.6	17 791	3 717	20.9	37 998	21 816	57.4
60-64	14 854	11 476	77.3	13 223	1 965	14.9	28 077	13 441	47.9
65 + ...	26 085	13 931	53.4	26 982	2 138	7.9	53 067	16 069	30.3
Total . . .	**724 012**	**363 332**	*50.2*	**704 070**	**125 003**	*17.8*	**1 428 082**	**488 335**	*34.2*
Panama Canal Zone (1.IV.70)									
− 14	7 164	.	.	6 897	.	.	14 061	.	.
14-17	1 360	203	14.9	1 403	256	18.2	2 763	459	16.6
18-24	5 154	4 587	89.0	2 365	1 021	43.2	7 519	5 608	74.6
25-34	3 497	3 389	96.9	3 293	955	29.0	6 790	4 344	64.0
35-44	3 003	2 952	98.3	2 513	744	29.6	5 516	3 696	67.0
45-64	3 801	3 698	97.3	3 008	1 074	35.7	6 809	4 772	70.1
65 + ...	275	137	49.8	465	33	7.1	740	170	23.0
Total . . .	**24 254**	**14 966**	*61.7*	**19 944**	**4 083**	*20.5*	**44 198**	**19 049**	*43.1*
» » » (1.V.73) ‡									
Total . . .	**23 600**	**14 525**	*61.6*	**19 500**	**3 975**	*20.4*	**43 100**	**18 500**	*42.9*
Paraguay (9.VII.72) ‡									
− 15	539 570	25 560	4.7	515 280	7 390	1.4	1 054 850	32 950	3.1
15-19	128 640	100 140	77.8	130 010	32 190	24.8	258 650	132 330	51.2
20-24	92 510	86 840	93.9	98 490	30 870	31.3	191 000	117 710	61.6
25-29	72 310	70 560	97.6	75 500	20 710	27.4	147 810	91 270	61.7
30-44	166 260	163 690	98.5	174 890	41 840	23.9	341 150	205 530	60.2
45-49	40 450	39 100	96.7	44 210	8 800	19.9	84 660	47 900	56.6
50-54	37 000	35 490	95.9	38 430	7 340	19.1	75 430	42 830	56.8
55-59	26 910	24 980	92.8	28 190	4 840	17.2	55 100	29 820	54.1
60-64	22 660	20 270	89.5	25 410	3 470	13.7	48 070	23 740	49.4
65 + ...	40 540	26 660	65.8	53 060	3 970	7.5	93 600	30 630	32.7
Total . . .	**1 166 850**	**593 290**	*50.8*	**1 183 470**	**161 420**	*13.6*	**2 350 320**	**754 710**	*32.1*

‡ For notes, see pp. 272-294.   ‡ *Voir notes pp. 272-294.*   ‡ Véanse las notas en las págs. 272-294.

1

Total and economically active population by sex and age group
Population totale et population active par sexe et groupe d'âge
Población total y población económicamente activa por sexo y grupo de edad

Country and age group Pays et groupe d'âge País y grupo de edad	Males — Hommes — Hombres			Females — Femmes — Mujeres			Total		
	Total population Population totale Población total	Economically active population Population active Población activa		Total population Population totale Población total	Economically active population Population active Población activa		Total population Population totale Población total	Economically active population Population active Población activa	
		Number Nombre Número	Per cent Pour-cent Por ciento		Number Nombre Número	Per cent Pour-cent Por ciento		Number Nombre Número	Per cent Pour-cent Por ciento
Perú (4.VI.72) ‡									
− 15	3 014 733	48 389	1.6	2 922 531	37 064	1.3	5 937 264	85 453	1.4
15-19	715 127	284 678	39.8	698 185	123 393	17.7	1 413 312	408 071	28.9
20-24	571 969	458 911	80.2	578 620	149 007	25.8	1 150 589	607 918	52.8
25-29	458 049	429 782	93.8	471 501	115 588	24.5	929 550	545 370	58.7
30-44	1 053 388	1 026 090	97.4	1 052 429	223 680	21.3	2 105 817	1 249 770	59.3
45-49	241 742	234 733	97.1	246 223	48 098	19.5	487 965	282 831	58.0
50-54	195 367	186 615	95.5	193 251	34 685	17.9	388 618	221 300	56.9
55-59	149 321	138 552	92.8	150 654	24 180	16.1	299 975	162 732	54.2
60-65	133 330	111 829	83.9	141 240	18 933	13.4	274 570	130 762	47.6
65 + ...	238 375	146 486	61.5	284 110	24 105	8.5	522 485	170 591	32.6
?	13 129	5 333	40.6	14 934	1 482	9.9	28 063	6 815	24.3
Total . . .	**6 784 530**	**3 071 398**	*45.3*	**6 753 678**	**800 215**	*11.8*	**13 538 208**	**3 871 613**	*28.6*
Puerto Rico (1.IV.70) ‡									
− 15	502 120	1 343	0.3	488 800	558	0.1	990 920	1 901	0.2
15-19	143 806	24 877	17.3	147 520	14 022	9.5	291 326	38 899	13.4
20-24	108 077	65 621	60.7	125 799	45 130	35.9	233 876	110 751	47.4
25-29	84 729	64 765	76.4	97 909	36 005	36.8	182 638	100 770	55.2
30-44	203 209	161 984	79.7	227 413	75 991	33 4	430 622	237 975	55.3
45-49	59 437	44 358	74.6	62 529	15 893	25.4	121 966	60 251	49.4
50-54	53 032	37 537	70.8	52 539	10 994	20.9	105 571	48 531	46.0
55-59	49 156	32 240	65.6	47 297	6 965	14.7	96 453	39 205	40.6
60-64	40 673	21 034	51.7	40 911	4 175	10.2	81 584	25 209	30.9
65 + ...	85 710	17 610	20.5	91 367	2 688	2.9	177 077	20 298	11.5
Total . . .	**1 329 949**	**471 369**	*35.4*	**1 382 084**	**212 421**	*15.4*	**2 712 033**	**683 790**	*25.2*
» » (III.75) ‡									
Total . . .	**1 501 701**	**598 940**	*39.9*	**1 576 314**	**270 770**	*17.2*	**3 078 015**	**869 710**	*28.3*
St. Kitts (7.IV.70 *)									
Total . . .	**21 044**	...	...	**23 840**	...	...	**44 884**	**21 809**	*48.6*
St. Lucia (7.IV.60)									
Total . . .	**40 693**	**20 001**	*49.2*	**45 415**	**11 371**	*25.0*	**86 108**	**31 372**	*36.4*

‡ For notes, see pp. 272-294. ‡ Voir notes pp. 272-294. ‡ Véanse las notas en las págs. 272-294.

POPULATION

1 Total and economically active population by sex and age group
Population totale et population active par sexe et groupe d'âge
Población total y población económicamente activa por sexo y grupo de edad

Country and age group Pays et groupe d'âge País y grupo de edad	Males — *Hommes* — Hombres			Females — *Femmes* — Mujeres			Total		
	Total population *Population totale* Población total	Economically active population *Population active* Población activa		Total population *Population totale* Población total	Economically active population *Population active* Población activa		Total population *Population totale* Población total	Economically active population *Population active* Población activa	
		Number *Nombre* Número	Per cent *Pour-cent* Por ciento		Number *Nombre* Número	Per cent *Pour-cent* Por ciento		Number *Nombre* Número	Per cent *Pour-cent* Por ciento
Saint-Pierre-et-Miquelon (12.VI.67)									
− 15	860	.	.	816	.	.	1 676	.	.
15-19	262	124	47.3	270	81	30.0	532	205	38.5
20-24	192	181	94.3	182	86	47.3	374	267	71.4
25-29	204	200	98.0	171	52	30.4	375	252	67.2
30-44	490	486	99.2	445	106	23.8	935	592	63.3
45-49	117	113	96.6	148	25	16.9	265	138	52.1
50-59	246	223	90.7	252	64	25.4	498	287	57.6
60 + ...	222	94	42.3	309	41	13.3	531	135	25.4
Total . . .	**2 593**	**1 421**	*54.8*	**2 593**	**455**	*17.5*	**5 186**	**1 876**	*36.2*
» » » (XII.71)‡									
Total . . .	**2 810**	**1 635**	*58.2*	**2 790**	**460**	*16.5*	**5 600**	**2 095**	*37.4*
St. Vincent (7.IV.60)									
Total . . .	**37 561**	**15 196**	*40.5*	**42 387**	**9 660**	*22.8*	**79 948**	**24 856**	*31.1*
Surinam (31.III.64)‡									
− 15	68 748	148	0.2	66 678	159	0.2	135 426	307	0.2
15-19	13 921	5 706	41.0	13 761	2 366	17.2	27 682	8 072	29.2
20-24	9 866	8 852	89.7	10 550	3 434	32.5	20 416	12 286	60.2
25-29	8 872	8 537	96.2	9 451	2 512	26.6	18 323	11 049	60.3
30-44	21 123	20 472	96.9	21 807	5 664	26.0	42 930	26 136	60.9
45-49	4 271	4 090	95.8	4 431	1 248	28.2	8 702	5 338	61.3
50-54	4 376	4 066	92.9	4 007	1 113	27.8	8 383	5 179	61.8
55-59	3 328	2 925	87.9	3 680	973	26.4	7 008	3 898	55.6
60-64	2 824	2 079	73.6	2 984	595	19.9	5 808	2 674	46.0
65 + ...	5 832	2 726	46.7	6 293	602	9.6	12 125	3 328	27.4
?	2 881	1 595	55.4	2 521	337	13.4	5 402	1 932	35.8
Total . . .	**146 042**	**61 196**	*41.9*	**146 163**	**19 003**	*13.0*	**292 205**	**80 199**	*27.4*
Trinidad and Tobago (7.IV.60)									
Total . . .	**411 580**	**203 732**	*49.5*	**416 377**	**74 415**	*17.9*	**827 957**	**278 147**	*33.6*
» » » (III.71)‡									
Total . . .	**525 100**	**256 100**	*48.8*	**506 800**	**99 900**	*19.7*	**1 031 900**	**356 200**	*34.5*
Turks and Caicos Is. (7.IV.60)									
Total . . .	**2 552**	**1 195**	*46.8*	**3 116**	**913**	*29.3*	**5 668**	**2 108**	*37.2*

‡ For notes, see pp. 272-294.   ‡ *Voir notes pp. 272-294.*   ‡ Véanse las notas en las págs. 272-294.

1 Total and economically active population by sex and age group
Population totale et population active par sexe et groupe d'âge
Población total y población económicamente activa por sexo y grupo de edad

Country and age group / Pays et groupe d'âge / País y grupo de edad	Males — Hommes — Hombres			Females — Femmes — Mujeres			Total		
	Total population / Population totale / Población total	Economically active population / Population active / Población activa		Total population / Population totale / Población total	Economically active population / Population active / Población activa		Total population / Population totale / Población total	Economically active population / Population active / Población activa	
		Number / Nombre / Número	Per cent / Pourcent / Por ciento		Number / Nombre / Número	Per cent / Pourcent / Por ciento		Number / Nombre / Número	Per cent / Pourcent / Por ciento
United States (1.IV.70) ‡									
− 15	29 550 555	251 421	0.9	28 460 924	116 582	0.4	58 011 479	368 003	0.6
15-19	9 716 327	3 916 050	40.3	9 480 843	2 766 261	29.2	19 197 170	6 682 311	34.8
20-24	7 753 863	6 271 281	80.9	8 351 006	4 682 580	56.1	16 104 869	10 953 861	68.0
25-29	6 572 273	6 106 084	92.9	6 823 213	3 098 736	45.4	13 395 486	9 204 820	68.7
30-44	16 864 228	16 005 247	94.9	17 719 054	8 553 544	48.3	34 583 282	24 558 791	71.0
45-49	5 832 820	5 452 272	93.5	6 250 413	3 311 308	53.0	12 083 233	8 763 580	72.5
50-54	5 339 439	4 881 781	91.4	5 735 821	2 980 121	52.0	11 075 260	7 861 902	71.0
55-59	4 779 461	4 147 143	86.8	5 229 509	2 476 916	47.4	10 008 970	6 624 059	66.2
60-64	4 043 919	2 952 888	73.0	4 607 335	1 663 444	36.1	8 651 254	4 616 332	53.4
65 + ...	8 437 630	2 092 496	24.8	11 664 244	1 171 278	10.0	20 101 874	3 263 774	16.2
Total . . .	**98 890 515**	**52 076 663**	*52.7*	**104 322 362**	**30 820 770**	*29.5*	**203 212 877**	**82 897 433**	*40.8*
» » (1974) ‡									
Total . . .	**102 945 000**	**57 349 000**	*55.7*	**108 446 000**	**35 892 000**	*33.1*	**211 390 000**	**93 240 000**	*44.1*
Uruguay (16.X.63)									
− 15	367 848	12 580	3.4	357 361	4 818	1.3	725 209	17 398	2.4
15-19	103 012	72 114	70.0	102 838	30 186	29.4	205 850	102 300	49.7
20-24	95 222	88 830	93.3	97 319	39 004	40.1	192 541	127 834	66.4
25-29	91 398	88 778	97.1	95 542	35 205	36.8	186 940	123 983	66.3
30-44	277 266	269 472	97.2	279 220	97 532	34.9	556 486	367 004	66.0
45-49	73 143	68 751	94.0	73 848	19 816	26.8	146 991	88 567	60.3
50-54	71 973	62 492	86.8	69 976	14 951	21.4	141 949	77 443	54.6
55-59	60 247	43 866	72.8	57 704	8 902	15.4	117 951	52 768	44.7
60-64	51 035	27 104	53.1	51 396	4 818	9.4	102 431	31 922	31.2
65 + ...	88 614	18 699	21.1	107 712	3 511	3.3	196 326	22 210	11.3
?	10 628	7 301	6.9	12 208	3 537	29.0	22 836	10 838	47.5
Total . . .	**1 290 386**	**759 987**	*58.9*	**1 305 124**	**252 280**	*19.3*	**2 595 510**	**1 012 267**	*39.0*
Venezuela (2.XI.71)									
− 15	2 437 645	.	.	2 386 637	.	.	4 824 282	.	.
15-19	601 632	304 155	50.6	618 350	125 825	20.3	1 219 982	429 980	35.2
20-24	468 221	379 539	81.1	494 304	145 047	29.3	962 525	524 586	54.5
25-29	339 379	315 971	93.1	359 572	105 757	29.4	698 951	421 728	60.3
30-44	804 002	773 980	96.3	792 047	200 836	25.4	1 596 049	974 816	61.1
45-54	347 627	322 798	92.9	330 247	62 883	19.0	677 874	385 681	56.9
55-64	209 667	170 596	81.4	214 830	25 477	11.9	424 497	196 073	46.2
65 + ...	141 538	71 571	50.6	175 824	10 239	5.8	317 362	81 810	25.8
Total . . .	**5 349 711**	**2 338 610**	*43.7*	**5 371 811**	**676 064**	*12.6*	**10 721 522**	**3 014 674**	*28.1*

‡ For notes, see pp. 272-294.   ‡ Voir notes pp. 272-294.   ‡ Véanse las notas en las págs. 272-294.

POPULATION

1 Total and economically active population by sex and age group
Population totale et population active par sexe et groupe d'âge
Población total y población económicamente activa por sexo y grupo de edad

Country and age group *Pays et groupe d'âge* País y grupo de edad	Males — *Hommes* — Hombres			Females — *Femmes* — Mujeres			Total		
	Total population *Population totale* Población total	Economically active population *Population active* Población activa		Total population *Population totale* Población total	Economically active population *Population active* Población activa		Total population *Population totale* Población total	Economically active population *Population active* Población activa	
		Number *Nombre* Número	Per cent *Pour-cent* Por ciento		Number *Nombre* Número	Per cent *Pour-cent* Por ciento		Number *Nombre* Número	Per cent *Pour-cent* Por ciento
Virgin Is. (Brit.) (7.IV.70)									
− 15	1 882	.	.	1 906	.	.	3 788	.	.
15-19	498	347	69.7	460	169	36.7	958	516	53.9
20-24	667	654	98.1	413	258	62.5	1 080	912	84.4
25-29	436	415	95.2	345	194	56.2	781	609	78.0
30-44	785	769	98.0	633	281	44.4	1 418	1 050	74.0
45-49	200	193	96.5	168	53	31.5	368	246	66.8
50-54	156	146	93.6	173	51	29.5	329	197	59.9
55-59	144	130	90.3	123	26	21.1	267	156	58.4
60-64	103	90	87.4	76	16	21.1	179	106	59.2
65 + ...	260	152	58.5	244	26	10.7	504	178	35.3
Total . . .	**5 131**	**2 896**	*56.4*	**4 541**	**1 074**	*23.7*	**9 672**	**3 970**	*41.0*
» » (US) (1.IV.70)									
Total . . .	**31 157**	**16 030**	*51.4*	**31 311**	**9 869**	*31.5*	**62 468**	**25 899**	*41.5*

1 **Total and economically active population by sex and age group**
Population totale et population active par sexe et groupe d'âge
Población total y población económicamente activa por sexo y grupo de edad

Country and age group *Pays et groupe d'âge* País y grupo de edad	Males — *Hommes* — Hombres			Females — *Femmes* — Mujeres			Total		
	Total population *Population totale* Población total	Economically active population *Population active* Población activa		Total population *Population totale* Población total	Economically active population *Population active* Población activa		Total population *Population totale* Población total	Economically active population *Population active* Población activa	
		Number *Nombre* Número	Per cent *Pour-cent* Por ciento		Number *Nombre* Número	Per cent *Pour-cent* Por ciento		Number *Nombre* Número	Per cent *Pour-cent* Por ciento

ASIA — ASIE — ASIA

Bahrain (3.IV.71)									
− 15	48 152	284	*0.6*	47 488	6	—	95 640	290	*0.3*
15-19	11 606	4 967	*42.8*	10 583	323	*3.1*	22 189	5 290	*23.8*
20-24	9 590	8 476	*88.4*	6 887	798	*11.6*	16 477	9 274	*56.3*
25-29	9 095	8 882	*97.7*	6 819	695	*10.2*	15 914	9 577	*60.2*
30-44	21 057	20 680	*98.2*	15 357	997	*6.5*	36 414	21 677	*59.5*
45-49	4 979	4 796	*96.3*	3 464	159	*4.6*	8 443	4 955	*58.7*
50-54	4 303	3 954	*91.9*	2 985	117	*3.9*	7 288	4 071	*55.9*
55-59	2 191	1 851	*84.5*	1 497	55	*3.7*	3 688	1 906	*51.7*
60 + ...	5 341	3 162	*59.2*	4 684	99	*2.1*	10 025	3 261	*32.5*
Total . . .	**116 314**	**57 052**	*49.0*	**99 764**	**3 249**	*3.3*	**216 078**	**60 301**	*27.9*
Bangladesh (1.III.74*) ‡									
Total . . .	**37 071 740**	**18 740 364**	*50.6*	**34 407 331**	**6 440 964**	*18.7*	**71 479 071**	**25 181 328**	*35.2*
Brunei (11.VIII.71)									
− 15	30 109	.	.	29 027	.	.	59 136	.	.
15-19	8 315	2 736	*32.9*	7 546	849	*11.3*	15 861	3 585	*22.6*
20-24	7 160	6 197	*86.6*	5 839	1 765	*30.2*	12 999	7 962	*61.3*
25-29	5 340	5 185	*97.1*	3 973	968	*24.4*	9 313	6 153	*66.1*
30-44	11 698	11 425	*97.7*	9 684	1 920	*19.8*	21 382	13 345	*62.4*
45-49	2 709	2 631	*97.1*	1 964	398	*20.3*	4 673	3 029	*64.8*
50-54	2 222	2 108	*94.9*	1 559	336	*21.6*	3 781	2 444	*64.6*
55-59	1 548	1 364	*88.1*	1 016	232	*22.8*	2 564	1 596	*62.2*
60-64	1 391	1 125	*80.9*	1 202	226	*18.8*	2 593	1 351	*52.1*
65 + ...	1 981	1 161	*58.6*	1 664	191	*11.5*	3 645	1 352	*37.1*
?	299	279	*93.3*	10	3	*30.0*	309	282	*91.3*
Total . . .	**72 772**	**34 211**	*47.0*	**63 484**	**6 888**	*10.8*	**136 256**	**41 099**	*30.2*
Cambodge (17.V.62)									
Total . . .	**2 862 939**	**1 449 003**	*50.6*	**2 865 832**	**1 050 732**	*36.7*	**5 728 771**	**2 499 735**	*43.6*
Cyprus (11.XII.60) ‡									
Total . . .	**275 599**	**155 244**	*56.3*	**291 502**	**80 114**	*27.5*	**567 101**	**235 358**	*41.5*
» (1974) ‡									
Total . . .	**316 000**	**191 109**	*60.5*	**323 000**	**78 891**	*24.4*	**639 000**	**270 000**	*42.3*

‡ For notes, see pp. 272-294.   ‡ *Voir notes pp. 272-294.*   ‡ Véanse las notas en las págs. 272-294.

29

1 **Total and economically active population by sex and age group**
Population totale et population active par sexe et groupe d'âge
Población total y población económicamente activa por sexo y grupo de edad

Country and age group *Pays et groupe d'âge* País y grupo de edad	Males — *Hommes* — Hombres			Females — *Femmes* — Mujeres			Total		
	Total population *Population totale* Población total	Economically active population *Population active* Población activa		Total population *Population totale* Población total	Economically active population *Population active* Población activa		Total population *Population totale* Población total	Economically active population *Population active* Población activa	
		Number *Nombre* Número	Per cent *Pourcent* Por ciento		Number *Nombre* Número	Per cent *Pourcent* Por ciento		Number *Nombre* Número	Per cent *Pourcent* Por ciento
Hong Kong (9.III.71)									
− 15	720 120	12 545	*1.7*	687 784	23 380	*3.4*	1 407 904	35 925	*2.6*
15-19	219 657	110 791	*50.4*	208 187	117 402	*56.4*	427 844	228 193	*53.3*
20-24	173 211	156 277	*90.2*	163 142	113 441	*69.5*	336 353	269 718	*80.2*
25-29	107 121	104 879	*97.9*	86 603	37 370	*43.2*	193 724	142 249	*73.4*
30-44	380 215	375 091	*98.7*	333 080	126 664	*38.0*	713 295	501 755	*70.3*
45-49	112 946	110 364	*97.7*	105 424	41 291	*39.2*	218 370	151 655	*69.4*
50-54	100 968	96 306	*95.4*	94 295	36 402	*38.6*	195 263	132 708	*68.0*
55-59	74 933	66 787	*89.1*	75 671	27 258	*36.0*	150 604	94 045	*62.4*
60-64	52 292	40 334	*77.1*	63 409	19 889	*31.4*	115 701	60 223	*52.1*
65 + ...	59 139	23 526	*39.8*	118 433	14 910	*12.6*	177 572	38 436	*21.6*
Total . . .	**2 000 602**	**1 096 900**	*54.8*	**1 936 028**	**558 007**	*28.8*	**3 936 630**	**1 654 907**	*42.0*
India (1.IV.71) ‡									
− 15	118 869 804	7 884 742	*6.6*	111 384 183	2 853 582	*2.6*	230 253 987	10 738 324	*4.7*
15-19	25 210 778	13 926 988	*55.2*	22 236 250	3 445 084	*15.5*	47 447 028	17 372 072	*36.6*
20-24	21 562 684	17 529 831	*81.3*	21 519 694	3 840 492	*17.8*	43 082 378	21 370 323	*49.6*
25-29	20 326 799	19 146 256	*94.2*	20 472 557	4 039 789	*19.7*	40 799 356	23 186 045	*56.8*
30-39	35 539 998	34 504 022	*97.1*	33 517 489	7 185 897	*21.4*	69 057 487	41 689 919	*60.4*
40-49	27 515 109	26 706 779	*97.1*	23 640 000	5 289 722	*22.4*	51 155 109	31 996 501	*62.5*
50-59	17 984 691	16 909 415	*94.0*	15 360 790	2 979 699	*19.4*	33 345 481	19 889 114	*59.6*
60 + ...	16 870 536	12 448 015	*73.8*	15 822 229	1 660 370	*10.5*	32 692 765	14 108 385	*43.2*
?	56 215	19 088	*34.0*	60 003	3 628	*6.0*	116 218	22 716	*19.5*
Total . . .	**283 936 614**	**149 075 136**	*52.5*	**264 013 195**	**31 298 263**	*11.9*	**547 949 809**	**180 373 399**	*32.9*
Indonesia (24.IX.71) ‡									
− 15	26 556 747	1 338 761	*5.0*	25 704 559	995 090	*3.9*	52 261 306	2 333 851	*4.5*
15-19	5 642 791	2 761 730	*48.9*	5 748 375	1 646 081	*28.6*	11 391 346	4 407 811	*38.7*
20-24	3 555 777	2 719 698	*76.5*	4 405 511	1 402 632	*31.8*	7 961 288	4 122 330	*51.8*
25-29	4 033 202	3 648 929	*90.5*	5 009 212	1 710 071	*34.1*	9 042 414	5 359 000	*59.3*
30-44	10 687 107	9 939 931	*93.0*	11 316 937	4 526 314	*40.0*	22 004 044	14 466 245	*65.7*
45-49	2 398 710	2 198 288	*91.6*	2 248 418	992 945	*44.2*	4 647 128	3 191 233	*68.7*
50-54	1 887 607	1 661 887	*88.0*	1 946 969	824 278	*42.3*	3 834 576	2 486 165	*64.8*
55-64	2 107 960	1 709 457	*81.1*	2 250 203	815 349	*36.2*	4 358 163	2 524 806	*57.9*
65 + ...	1 405 110	850 435	*60.5*	1 546 605	352 823	*22.8*	2 951 715	1 203 258	*40.8*
?	3 975	3 285	*82.6*	3 890	2 086	*53.6*	7 865	5 371	*68.3*
Total . . .	**58 279 166**	**26 832 401**	*46.0*	**60 180 679**	**13 267 669**	*22.0*	**118 459 845**	**40 100 070**	*33.9*
Iran (1.XI.66) ‡									
− 15	6 029 262	571 390	*9.5*	5 531 067	201 941	*3.7*	11 560 329	773 331	*6.7*
15-19	1 060 029	720 875	*68.0*	1 069 007	165 966	*15.5*	2 129 036	886 841	*41.7*
20-24	792 896	720 180	*90.8*	889 265	125 899	*14.2*	1 682 161	846 079	*50.3*
25-29	801 665	774 547	*96.6*	848 007	108 083	*12.7*	1 649 672	882 630	*53.5*
30-44	2 365 024	2 310 415	*97.7*	2 042 311	250 893	*12.3*	4 407 335	2 561 308	*58.1*
45-49	479 395	459 871	*95.9*	364 213	43 913	*12.1*	843 608	503 784	*59.7*
50-54	370 469	337 619	*91.2*	370 370	39 920	*10.8*	740 839	377 611	*51.0*
55-59	223 539	193 239	*86.4*	204 362	18 016	*8.8*	427 901	211 255	*49.4*
60-64	344 198	254 957	*74.1*	325 739	24 682	*7.6*	669 937	279 639	*41.7*
65 + ...	515 188	241 092	*46.8*	452 917	20 515	*4.5*	968 105	261 607	*27.0*
Total . . .	**12 981 665**	**6 584 257**	*50.7*	**12 097 258**	**999 828**	*8.3*	**25 078 923**	**7 584 085**	*30.2*

‡ For notes, see pp. 272-294.   ‡ *Voir notes pp. 272-294.*   ‡ Véanse las notas en las págs. 272-294.

1
Total and economically active population by sex and age group
Population totale et population active par sexe et groupe d'âge
Población total y población económicamente activa por sexo y grupo de edad

Country and age group *Pays et groupe d'âge* País y grupo de edad	Males — *Hommes* — Hombres			Females — *Femmes* — Mujeres			Total		
	Total population *Population totale* Población total	Economically active population *Population active* Población activa		Total population *Population totale* Población total	Economically active population *Population active* Población activa		Total population *Population totale* Población total	Economically active population *Population active* Población activa	
		Number *Nombre* Número	Per cent *Pour-cent* Por ciento		Number *Nombre* Número	Per cent *Pour-cent* Por ciento		Number *Nombre* Número	Per cent *Pour-cent* Por ciento
Israel (22.V.61) ‡									
Total . . .	1 106 069	555 670	50.2	1 073 422	196 520	18.3	2 179 491	752 190	34.5
» (1974) ‡									
— 14	541 400	.	.	515 900	.	.	1 057 300	.	.
14-17	132 400	26 000	19.6	123 400	15 700	12.7	255 800	41 700	16.3
18-24	230 400	91 500	39.7	223 300	92 500	41.4	453 700	183 000	40.6
25-34	235 800	201 400	85.4	231 900	94 000	40.5	467 700	295 500	63.2
35-44	164 000	148 000	90.2	172 900	64 500	37.3	336 900	212 600	63.1
45-54	152 400	146 600	96.2	167 700	59 900	35.7	320 100	206 600	64.5
55-64	126 800	105 200	83.0	136 000	29 900	22.0	262 800	135 100	51.4
65 + ...	126 100	39 800	31.6	128.500	7 600	5.9	254 600	47 400	18.6
Total . . .	1 709 300	758 600	44.4	1 699 700	364 100	21.4	3 409 000	1 122 900	32.9
Japan (1.X.70)									
— 15	12 857 389	.	.	12 295 390	.	.	25 152 779	.	.
15-19	4 622 873	1 686 029	36.5	4 544 171	1 622 407	35.7	9 167 044	3 308 436	36.1
20-24	5 344 885	4 465 512	83.5	5 382 751	3 811 925	70.8	10 727 636	8 277 437	77.2
25-29	4 545 780	4 461 872	98.2	4 602 418	2 077 440	45.1	9 148 198	6 539 312	71.5
30-44	12 061 329	11 874 719	98.5	12 046 474	6 672 656	55.4	24 107 803	18 547 375	76.9
45-49	2 696 819	2 644 781	98.1	3 222 878	2 083 330	64.6	5 919 697	4 728 111	79.9
50-54	2 172 383	2 114 375	97.3	2 669 007	1 624 892	60.9	4 841 390	3 739 267	77.2
55-59	2 055 135	1 936 123	94.2	2 400 078	1 288 979	53.7	4 455 213	3 225 102	72.4
60-64	1 766 393	1 515 965	85.8	1 985 726	858 899	43.3	3 752 119	2 374 864	63.3
65 + ...	3 246 191	1 767 229	54.4	4 147 101	813 531	19.6	7 393 292	2 580 760	34.9
Total . . .	51 369 177	32 466 605	63.2	53 295 994	20 854 059	39.1	104 665 171	53 320 664	50.9
» (1974) ‡									
Total . . .	53 860 000	32 780 000	60.9	55 900 000	19 960 000	35.7	109 750 000	52 740 000	48.1
Jordan (18.XI.61)									
Total . . .	867 597	367 926	42.4	838 629	22 052	2.6	1 706 226	389 978	22.9
» (1971) ‡									
Total . . .	1 185 000	510 700	43.1	1 162 000	30 300	2.6	2 347 000	541 000	23.1

‡ For notes, see pp. 272-294.   ‡ *Voir notes pp. 272-294.*   ‡ Véanse las notas en las págs. 272-294.

1 Total and economically active population by sex and age group
Population totale et population active par sexe et groupe d'âge
Población total y población económicamente activa por sexo y grupo de edad

Country and age group / Pays et groupe d'âge / País y grupo de edad	Males — Hommes — Hombres Total population / Population totale / Población total	Males Economically active population / Population active / Población activa Number / Nombre / Número	Males Per cent / Pour-cent / Por ciento	Females — Femmes — Mujeres Total population / Population totale / Población total	Females Economically active population Number / Nombre / Número	Females Per cent / Pour-cent / Por ciento	Total Total population / Population totale / Población total	Total Economically active population Number / Nombre / Número	Total Per cent / Pour-cent / Por ciento
Korea, Rep. of (1.X.70)‡									
− 15	6 852 123	73 630	1.1	6 389 310	70 450	1.1	13 241 433	144 080	1.1
15-19	1 573 179	721 663	45.9	1 514 955	610 690	40.3	3 088 134	1 332 353	43.1
20-24	1 298 687	653 752	50.3	1 224 483	537 755	43.9	2 523 170	1 191 507	47.2
25-29	1 096 819	939 630	85.7	1 107 474	351 572	31.7	2 204 293	1 291 202	58.6
30-44	2 714 984	2 606 280	96.0	2 794 398	1 161 645	41.6	5 509 382	3 767 925	68.4
45-49	628 934	598 972	95.2	655 694	318 302	48.5	1 284 628	917 274	71.4
50-54	506 554	465 417	91.9	517 981	234 273	45.2	1 024 535	699 690	68.3
55-59	407 895	348 165	85.4	447 146	174 946	39.1	855 041	523 111	61.2
60-64	302 362	205 281	67.9	362 896	97 533	26.9	665 258	302 814	45.5
65 + ...	398 078	139 806	35.1	641 300	67 753	10.6	1 039 378	207 559	20.0
Total . . .	**15 779 615**	**6 752 596**	*42.8*	**15 655 637**	**3 624 919**	*23.2*	**31 435 252**	**10 377 515**	*33.0*
» » » (1974)‡									
Total . . .	**16 813 000**	**7 652 000**	*45.5*	**16 646 000**	**4 428 000**	*26.6*	**33 459 000**	**12 080 000**	*36.1*
Kuwait (21.IV.70)									
− 15	163 159	1 479	0.9	156 142	380	0.2	319 301	1 859	0.6
15-19	32 843	13 550	41.3	28 914	1 188	4.1	61 757	14 738	23.9
20-24	41 861	36 995	88.4	31 198	3 419	11.0	73 059	40 414	55.3
25-29	47 344	46 593	98.4	30 591	3 996	13.1	77 935	50 589	64.9
30-44	94 979	94 349	99.3	45 480	5 526	12.2	140 459	99 875	71.1
45-49	14 592	14 350	98.3	6 752	878	13.0	21 344	15 228	71.3
50-54	9 846	9 250	93.9	6 217	647	10.4	16 063	9 897	61.6
55-59	4 875	4 308	88.4	3 021	223	7.4	7 896	4 531	57.4
60-64	4 093	2 861	69.9	3 896	215	5.5	7 989	3 076	38.5
65 + ...	6 149	2 040	33.2	6 517	130	2.0	12 666	2 170	17.1
?	140	124	88.6	53	12	22.6	193	136	70.5
Total . . .	**419 881**	**225 899**	*53.8*	**318 781**	**16 614**	*5.2*	**738 662**	**242 513**	*32 8*
Liban (XI.70)‡									
Total . . .	**1 080 015**	**472 620**	*43.8*	**1 046 310**	**99 135**	*9.5*	**2 126 325**	**571 755**	*26.9*

‡ For notes, see pp. 272-294.   ‡ *Voir notes pp. 272-294.*   ‡ Véanse las notas en las págs. 272-294.

1 Total and economically active population by sex and age group
Population totale et population active par sexe et groupe d'âge
Población total y población económicamente activa por sexo y grupo de edad

Country and age group Pays et groupe d'âge País y grupo de edad	Males — *Hommes* — Hombres			Females — *Femmes* — Mujeres			Total		
	Total population *Population totale* Población total	Economically active population *Population active* Población activa		Total population *Population totale* Población total	Economically active population *Population active* Población activa		Total population *Population totale* Población total	Economically active population *Population active* Población activa	
		Number *Nombre* Número	Per cent *Pour-cent* Por ciento		Number *Nombre* Número	Per cent *Pour-cent* Por ciento		Number *Nombre* Número	Per cent *Pour-cent* Por ciento
Malaysia:									
East Malaysia:									
Sabah (24-25.VIII.70*)									
− 15	158 279	3 860	2.4	150 023	4 408	2.9	308 302	8 268	2.7
15-19	30 324	12 794	42.2	31 359	10 253	32.7	61 683	23 047	37.4
20-24	23 352	19 276	82.5	22 526	9 396	41.7	45 878	28 672	62.5
25-44	84 957	75 442	88.8	74 507	31 284	42.0	159 464	106 726	66.9
45-49	13 024	11 274	86.6	10 840	4 836	44.6	23 864	16 110	67.5
50-54	10 114	8 572	84.8	7 906	3 219	40.7	18 020	11 791	65.4
55-59	7 719	6 201	80.3	6 191	2 358	38.1	13 910	8 559	61.5
60-64	5 041	3 621	71.8	4 039	1 223	30.3	9 080	4 844	53.3
65 + ...	6 904	3 539	51.3	6 499	1 158	17.8	13 403	4 697	35.0
Total . . .	**339 714**	**144 579**	**42.6**	**313 890**	**68 135**	**21.7**	**653 604**	**212 714**	**32.5**
Sarawak (24-25.VIII.70*)									
− 15	253 379	9 748	3.8	242 813	11 181	4.6	496 192	20 929	4.2
15-19	43 381	26 970	62.2	46 615	24 144	51.8	89 996	51 114	56.8
20-24	33 689	30 645	91.0	36 615	20 026	54.7	70 304	50 671	72.1
25-29	29 179	27 369	93.8	29 803	15 959	53.5	58 982	43 328	73.5
30-44	65 213	61 165	93.8	67 900	37 853	55.7	133 113	99 018	74.4
45-49	16 467	15 143	92.0	16 118	9 184	57.0	32 585	24 327	74.7
50-54	15 803	14 049	88.9	14 863	7 883	53.0	30 666	21 932	71.5
55-59	11 395	9 520	83.5	9 332	4 185	44.8	20 727	13 705	66.1
60-64	10 159	7 578	74.6	9 123	3 583	39.3	19 282	11 161	57.9
65 + ...	13 344	7 179	53.8	11 822	2 645	22.4	25 166	9 824	39.0
Total . . .	**492 009**	**209 366**	**42.6**	**485 004**	**136 643**	**28.2**	**977 013**	**346 009**	**35.4**
West Malaysia (24.VIII.70)									
− 15	2 015 027	51 285	2.5	1 929 754	42 842	2.2	3 944 781	94 127	2.4
15-19	481 945	251 829	52.3	491 619	160 865	32.7	973 564	412 694	42.4
20-24	362 318	314 847	86.9	377 423	157 237	41.7	739 741	472 084	63.8
25-29	269 841	251 948	93.4	275 708	105 311	38.2	545 549	357 259	65.5
30-44	650 162	610 401	93.9	669 605	263 729	39.4	1 319 767	874 130	66.2
45-49	151 519	138 463	91.4	157 266	63 697	40.5	308 785	202 160	65.5
50-54	138 938	120 272	86.6	135 541	49 299	36.4	274 479	169 571	61.8
55-59	116 495	87 822	75.4	105 869	30 661	29.0	222 364	118 483	53.3
60-64	100 855	65 531	65.0	93 116	21 867	23.5	193 971	87 398	45.1
65 + ...	144 211	65 890	45.7	134 187	17 153	12.8	278 398	83 043	29.8
Total . . .	**4 431 311**	**1 958 288**	**44.2**	**4 370 088**	**912 661**	**20.9**	**8 801 399**	**2 870 949**	**32.6**
Nepal (22.VI.71)									
− 15	2 379 422	416 521	17.5	2 295 156	238 041	10.4	4 674 578	654 562	14.0
15-19	547 493	414 369	75.7	499 966	230 896	46.2	1 047 459	645 265	61.6
20-24	466 022	418 290	89.8	503 653	197 439	39.2	969 675	615 729	63.5
25-29	456 297	434 000	95.1	473 990	173 426	36.6	930 287	607 426	65.3
30-44	1 074 075	1 042 597	97.1	1 091 575	367 177	33.6	2 165 650	1 409 774	65.1
45-49	245 521	237 772	96.8	215 577	69 958	32.4	461 098	307 730	66.7
50-54	204 304	191 990	94.0	196 530	59 950	30.5	400 834	251 940	62.9
55-59	132 983	120 018	90.3	124 716	34 551	27.7	257 699	154 569	60.0
60-64	138 441	88 784	64.1	155 789	27 939	17.9	294 230	116 723	39.7
65 + ...	172 645	69 947	40.5	181 828	18 859	10.4	354 473	88 806	25.1
Total . . .	**5 817 203**	**3 434 288**	**59.0**	**5 738 780**	**1 418 236**	**24.7**	**11 555 983**	**4 852 524**	**42.0**

POPULATION

1 Total and economically active population by sex and age group
Population totale et population active par sexe et groupe d'âge
Población total y población económicamente activa por sexo y grupo de edad

Country and age group *Pays et groupe d'âge* País y grupo de edad	Males — *Hommes* — Hombres			Females — *Femmes* — Mujeres			Total		
	Total population *Population totale* Población total	Economically active population *Population active* Población activa		Total population *Population totale* Población total	Economically active population *Population active* Población activa		Total population *Population totale* Población total	Economically active population *Population active* Población activa	
		Number *Nombre* Número	Per cent *Pour-cent* Por ciento		Number *Nombre* Número	Per cent *Pour-cent* Por ciento		Number *Nombre* Número	Per cent *Pour-cent* Por ciento
Pakistan (1.II.61) ‡									
Total . . .	**47 516 890**	**26 443 488**	*55.7*	**42 765 784**	**3 762 493**	*8.8*	**90 282 674**	**30 205 981**	*33.5*
» (I.72) ‡									
Total . . .	**32 516 332**	**16 893 460**	*52.0*	**29 177 019**	**1 587 770**	*5.4*	**61 693 351**	**18 481 230**	*30.0*
Philippines (6.V.70) ‡									
− 15	8 092 367	458 408	*5.7*	7 681 275	275 447	*3.6*	15 773 642	733 855	*4.7*
15-19	1 732 927	908 399	*52.4*	1 941 489	610 911	*31.5*	3 674 416	1 519 310	*41.3*
20-24	1 573 616	1 195 826	*76.0*	1 789 833	615 246	*34.4*	3 363 449	1 811 072	*53.8*
25-29	1 420 272	1 243 733	*87.6*	1 452 012	519 044	*35.7*	2 872 284	1 762 777	*61.4*
30-44	2 832 765	2 562 593	*90.5*	2 784 982	1 054 843	*37.9*	5 617 747	3 617 436	*64.4*
45-49	607 271	544 942	*89.7*	671 002	259 621	*38.7*	1 278 273	804 563	*62.9*
50-54	501 626	436 905	*87.1*	569 655	208 009	*36.5*	1 071 281	644 914	*60.2*
55-59	440 867	378 367	*85.8*	484 732	161 650	*33.3*	925 599	540 017	*58.3*
60-64	357 850	283 743	*79.3*	376 668	107 882	*28.6*	734 518	391 625	*53.3*
65 + ...	625 256	353 357	*56.5*	647 184	114 537	*17.7*	1 272 440	467 894	*36.8*
?	3 107	1 578	*50.8*	3 312	1 542	*46.6*	6 419	3 120	*48.6*
Total . . .	**18 187 924**	**8 367 851**	*46.0*	**18 402 144**	**3 928 732**	*21.3*	**36 590 068**	**12 296 583**	*33.6*
Qatar (VII.75) ‡									
Total . . .	...	**78 550**	...	...	**1 753**	...	**170 000**	**80 303**	*47.2*
Singapore (22.VI.70)									
− 15	413 471	5 441	*1.3*	391 365	3 994	*1.0*	804 836	9 435	*1.2*
15-19	126 358	70 331	*55.7*	120 059	51 627	*43.0*	246 417	121 958	*49.5*
20-24	103 181	95 851	*92.9*	100 554	53 939	*53.6*	203 735	149 790	*73.5*
25-29	66 650	65 290	*98.0*	66 095	20 340	*30.8*	132 745	85 630	*64.5*
30-44	180 918	177 743	*98.2*	169 235	34 308	*20.3*	350 153	212 051	*60.6*
45-49	44 148	42 466	*96.2*	37 598	6 589	*17.5*	81 746	49 055	*60.0*
50-54	37 770	33 287	*88.1*	33 453	5 864	*17.5*	71 223	39 151	*55.0*
55-59	34 044	25 152	*73.9*	31 321	5 073	*16.2*	65 365	30 225	*46.2*
60-64	24 998	13 897	*55.6*	23 925	3 216	*13.4*	48 923	17 113	*35.0*
65 + ...	30 589	9 765	*31.9*	38 775	2 503	*6.5*	69 364	12 268	*17.7*
Total . . .	**1 062 127**	**539 223**	*50.8*	**1 012 380**	**187 453**	*18.5*	**2 074 507**	**726 676**	*35.0*
» (V-VI.74) ‡									
Total . . .	**1 120 888**	**582 299**	*51.9*	**1 098 209**	**276 094**	*25.1*	**2 219 099**	**858 393**	*38.7*
Sri Lanka (9.X.71) ‡									
− 15	2 567 513	52 391	*2.0*	2 429 050	32 751	*1.3*	4 996 563	85 142	*1.7*
15-19	687 270	334 017	*48.6*	677 807	178 823	*26.4*	1 365 077	512 840	*37.6*
20-24	613 820	547 463	*89.2*	628 614	265 064	*42.2*	1 242 434	812 527	*65.4*
25-29	461 496	447 006	*96.9*	471 938	185 363	*39.3*	933 434	632 369	*67.7*
30-44	1 038 154	1 010 434	*97.3*	984 885	324 136	*32.9*	2 023 039	1 334 570	*66.0*
45-49	288 238	275 892	*95.7*	259 911	77 441	*29.8*	548 149	353 333	*64.5*
50-54	224 805	207 406	*92.3*	196 829	48 152	*24.5*	421 634	255 558	*60.6*
55-59	195 036	157 841	*80.9*	164 442	27 531	*16.7*	359 478	185 372	*51.6*
60-64	152 410	100 029	*65.6*	119 864	12 560	*10.5*	272 274	112 589	*41.4*
65 + ...	297 206	121 100	*40.7*	251 855	12 788	*5.1*	549 061	133 888	*24.4*
Total . . .	**6 525 948**	**3 253 579**	*49.9*	**6 185 195**	**1 164 609**	*18.8*	**12 711 143**	**4 418 188**	*34.8*

‡ For notes, see pp. 272-294. ‡ *Voir notes pp. 272-294.* ‡ Véanse las notas en las págs. 272-294.

1 Total and economically active population by sex and age group
Population totale et population active par sexe et groupe d'âge
Población total y población económicamente activa por sexo y grupo de edad

	Males — *Hommes* — Hombres			Females — *Femmes* — Mujeres			Total		
		Economically active population			Economically active population			Economically active population	
Country and age group	Total population	*Population active*		Total population	*Population active*		Total population	*Population active*	
		Población activa			Población activa			Población activa	
Pays et groupe d'âge	*Population totale*	Number	Per cent	*Population totale*	Number	Per cent	*Population totale*	Number	Per cent
País y grupo de edad	Población total	*Nombre*	*Pour- cent*	Población total	*Nombre*	*Pour- cent*	Población total	*Nombre*	*Pour- cent*
		Número	Por ciento		Número	Por ciento		Número	Por ciento
Sud Viet-Nam, Rép. du (1973) ‡									
Total . . .	9 687 000	4 034 000	*41.6*	10 213 000	2 997 000	*29.3*	19 900 000	7 031 000	*35.3*
Rép. arabe syrienne (23.IX.70) ‡									
— 15	1 565 344	81 837	*5.2*	1 442 051	32 058	*2.2*	3 007 395	113 895	*3.8*
15-19	296 377	160 079	*54.0*	285 122	32 840	*11.5*	581 499	192 919	*33.2*
20-24	229 781	186 595	*81.2*	213 985	21 756	*10.2*	443 766	208 351	*47.0*
25-29	160 714	152 676	*95.0*	176 209	16 200	*9.2*	336 923	168 876	*50.1*
30-44	436 157	427 511	*98.0*	435 620	36 953	*8.5*	871 777	464 464	*53.3*
45-49	103 687	99 729	*96.2*	93 343	7 456	*8.0*	197 030	107 185	*54.4*
50-54	76 286	71 557	*93.8*	72 314	5 537	*7.7*	148 600	77 094	*51.9*
55-59	59 527	54 025	*90.8*	54 076	3 292	*6.1*	113 603	57 317	*50.5*
60-64	61 628	50 914	*82.6*	63 954	3 555	*5.6*	125 582	54 469	*43.4*
65 + ...	194 462	75 540	*38.8*	133 188	4 197	*3.2*	327 650	79 737	*24.3*
?	350	223	*63.7*	214	22	*10.3*	564	245	*43.4*
Total . . .	3 184 313	1 360 686	*42.7*	2 970 076	163 866	*5.5*	6 154 389	1 524 552	*24.8*
» (IX.73) ‡									
Total . . .	3 494 016	1 344 615	*38.5*	3 455 639	343 960	*10.0*	6 949 655	1 688 575	*24.3*
Thailand (1.IV.70)									
— 15	7 851 655	790 764	*10.1*	7 654 605	897 480	*11.7*	15 506 260	1 688 244	*10.9*
15-19	1 832 177	1 418 783	*77.4*	1 885 371	1 455 529	*77.2*	3 717 548	2 874 312	*77.3*
20-24	1 321 641	1 178 333	*89.2*	1 361 717	1 075 402	*79.0*	2 683 358	2 253 735	*84.0*
25-29	1 098 083	1 047 744	*95.4*	1 143 377	896 868	*78.4*	2 241 460	1 944 612	*86.8*
30-44	2 774 610	2 678 020	*96.5*	2 801 027	2 230 120	*79.6*	5 575 637	4 908 140	*88.0*
45-49	599 118	574 690	*95.9*	597 454	475 505	*79.6*	1 196 572	1 050 195	*87.8*
50-54	472 185	441 659	*93.5*	489 794	361 711	*73.8*	961 979	803 370	*83.5*
55-59	388 328	346 601	*89.3*	401 731	264 855	*65.9*	790 059	611 456	*77.4*
60-64	300 801	224 418	*74.6*	324 223	154 100	*47.5*	625 024	378 518	*60.6*
65 + ...	463 613	206 844	*44.6*	592 387	125 439	*21.2*	1 056 000	332 283	*31.5*
?	21 651	2 904	*13.4*	21 826	2 367	*10.8*	43 477	5 271	*12.1*
Total . . .	17 123 862	8 910 760	*52.0*	17 273 512	7 939 376	*46.0*	34 397 374	16 850 136	*49.0*
» (VII-IX.73) ‡	19 201 320	9 496 280	*49.5*	19 456 750	7 620 270	*39.2*	38 658 070	17 116 550	*44.3*
Yemen, People's Dem. Rep. of (14.V.73) ‡									
Total . . .	787 017	333 954	*42.4*	803 258	75 788	*9.4*	1 590 275	409 742	*25.8*

‡ For notes, see pp. 272-294.   ‡ *Voir notes pp. 272-294.*   ‡ Véanse las notas en las págs. 272-294.

1 Total and economically active population by sex and age group
Population totale et population active par sexe et groupe d'âge
Población total y población económicamente activa por sexo y grupo de edad

Country and age group *Pays et groupe d'âge* País y grupo de edad	Males — *Hommes* — Hombres			Females — *Femmes* — Mujeres			Total		
	Total population *Population totale* Población total	Economically active population		Total population *Population totale* Población total	Economically active population		Total population *Population totale* Población total	Economically active population	
		Population active Población activa			*Population active* Población activa			*Population active* Población activa	
		Number *Nombre* Número	Per cent *Pour-cent* Por ciento		Number *Nombre* Número	Per cent *Pour-cent* Por ciento		Number *Nombre* Número	Per cent *Pour-cent* Por ciento

EUROPE — EUROPE — EUROPA

Albanie (2.X.60)									
Total . . .	**835 294**	**443 254**	*53.1*	**791 021**	**287 508**	*36.3*	**1 626 315**	**730 762**	*44.9*
Austria (12.V.71)									
− 15	932 952	.	.	889 380	.	.	1 822 332	.	.
15-19	259 718	170 252	*65.6*	251 738	150 934	*60.0*	511 456	321 186	*62.8*
20-24	268 441	234 852	*87.5*	260 447	177 118	*68.0*	528 888	411 970	*77.9*
25-29	245 814	232 583	*94.6*	240 501	135 241	*56.2*	486 315	367 824	*75.6*
30-44	683 774	670 253	*98.0*	681 404	351 669	*51.6*	1 365 178	1 021 922	*74.9*
45-49	204 339	195 824	*95.8*	276 570	148 388	*53.7*	480 909	344 212	*71.6*
50-54	141 845	131 545	*92.7*	197 552	95 715	*48.5*	339 397	227 260	*67.0*
55-59	174 921	146 482	*83.7*	238 599	85 480	*35.8*	413 520	231 962	*56.1*
60-64	188 659	84 621	*44.9*	258 179	34 044	*13.2*	446 838	118 665	*26.6*
65 + ...	401 256	31 919	*8.0*	660 314	21 066	*3.2*	1 061 570	52 985	*5.0*
Total . . .	**3 501 719**	**1 898 331**	*54.2*	**3 954 684**	**1 199 655**	*30.3*	**7 456 403**	**3 097 986**	*41.5*
Belgique (31.XII.70)									
− 15	1 161 707	6 487	*0.6*	1 111 052	4 216	*0.4*	2 272 759	10 703	*0.5*
15-19	371 025	153 060	*41.3*	356 728	123 084	*34.5*	727 753	276 144	*37.9*
20-24	369 148	307 641	*83.3*	353 797	215 526	*60.9*	722 945	523 167	*72.4*
25-29	293 822	282 171	*96.0*	282 582	140 320	*49.7*	576 404	422 491	*73.3*
30-44	938 603	903 598	*96.3*	931 784	334 320	*35.9*	1 870 387	1 237 918	*66.2*
45-49	324 392	299 225	*92.2*	330 538	101 775	*30.8*	654 930	401 000	*61.2*
50-54	221 470	197 570	*89.2*	230 305	63 563	*27.6*	451 775	261 133	*57.8*
55-59	261 068	214 981	*82.3*	281 784	56 444	*20.0*	542 852	271 425	*50.0*
60-64	249 036	158 826	*63.8*	286 395	21 845	*7.6*	535 431	180 671	*33.7*
65 + ...	531 595	36 172	*6.8*	764 113	16 994	*2.2*	1 295 708	53 166	*4.1*
Total . . .	**4 721 866**	**2 559 731**	*54.2*	**4 929 078**	**1 078 087**	*21.9*	**9 650 944**	**3 637 818**	*37.7*
» (VI-XII.72) ‡									
Total . . .	**4 759 900**	**2 650 168**	*55.7*	**4 966 900**	**1 318 674**	*26.5*	**9 726 800**	**3 968 842**	*40.8*
Bulgarie (1.XII.65)									
− 15	1 004 111	693	*0.1*	958 036	1 357	*0.1*	1 962 147	2 050	*0.1*
15-19	357 850	127 423	*35.6*	346 473	113 369	*32.7*	704 323	240 792	*34.2*
20-24	294 336	229 486	*78.0*	290 223	209 133	*72.1*	584 559	438 619	*75.0*
25-29	287 514	275 307	*95.8*	284 728	238 515	*83.8*	572 242	513 822	*89.8*
30-44	983 351	961 074	*97.7*	972 194	846 747	*87.1*	1 955 545	1 807 821	*92.4*
45-49	197 307	190 422	*96.5*	197 902	160 492	*81.1*	395 209	350 914	*88.8*
50-54	249 652	232 460	*93.1*	243 457	167 369	*68.7*	493 109	399 829	*81.1*
55-59	234 237	195 868	*83.6*	237 387	83 766	*35.3*	471 624	279 634	*59.3*
60-64	188 450	103 791	*55.1*	193 412	35 374	*18.3*	381 862	139 165	*36.4*
65 + ...	317 359	73 150	*23.0*	389 887	22 002	*5.6*	707 246	95 152	*13.5*
Total . . .	**4 114 167**	**2 389 674**	*58.1*	**4 113 699**	**1 878 124**	*45.7*	**8 227 866**	**4 267 798**	*51.9*

‡ For notes, see pp. 272-294.   ‡ *Voir notes pp. 272-294.*   ‡ Véanse las notas en las págs. 272-294.

1 Total and economically active population by sex and age group
Population totale et population active par sexe et groupe d'âge
Población total y población económicamente activa por sexo y grupo de edad

Country and age group Pays et groupe d'âge País y grupo de edad	Males — *Hommes* — Hombres			Females — *Femmes* — Mujeres			Total		
	Total population *Population totale* Población total	Economically active population *Population active* Población activa		Total population *Population totale* Población total	Economically active population *Population active* Población activa		Total population *Population totale* Población total	Economically active population *Population active* Población activa	
		Number *Nombre* Número	Per cent *Pour-cent* Por ciento		Number *Nombre* Número	Per cent *Pour-cent* Por ciento		Number *Nombre* Número	Per cent *Pour-cent* Por ciento
Channel Is.:									
Jersey (4.IV.71)									
Total . . .	**33 770**	**22 061**	*65.3*	**35 559**	**12 580**	*35.4*	**69 329**	**34 641**	*50.0*
Czechoslovakia (1.XII.70) ‡									
− 15	1 698 268	.	.	1 616 119	.	.	3 314 387	.	.
15-19	658 892	230 338	*35.0*	629 910	263 519	*41.8*	1 288 802	493 857	*38.3*
20-24	639 449	581 145	*90.9*	616 294	487 159	*79.0*	1 255 743	1 068 304	*85.1*
25-29	508 423	500 722	*98.5*	502 229	395 550	*78.8*	1 010 652	896 272	*88.7*
30-44	1 309 146	1 285 842	*98.2*	1 336 350	1 069 074	*80.0*	2 645 496	2 354 916	*89.0*
45-49	474 379	455 292	*96.0*	511 734	395 756	*77.3*	986 113	851 048	*86.3*
50-54	277 799	258 948	*93.2*	302 836	212 324	*70.1*	580 635	471 272	*81.2*
55-59	392 778	333 811	*85.0*	433 986	158 575	*36.5*	826 764	492 386	*59.6*
60-64	381 825	127 056	*33.3*	437 970	79 604	*18.2*	819 795	206 660	*25.5*
65 + ...	643 368	94 157	*14.6*	965 032	49 734	*5.2*	1 608 400	143 891	*8.9*
?	4 385	2 665	*60.8*	3 815	1 231	*32.3*	8 200	3 896	*47.5*
Total . . .	**6 988 712**	**3 869 976**	*55.4*	**7 356 275**	**3 112 526**	*42.3*	**14 344 987**	**6 982 502**	*48.7*
Denmark (9.XI.70)									
− 15	587 202	1 629	*0.3*	558 807	781	*0.1*	1 146 009	2 410	*0.2*
15-19	191 440	106 254	*55.5*	180 672	86 280	*47.8*	372 112	192 534	*51.7*
20-24	211 816	175 308	*82.8*	199 821	134 798	*67.5*	411 637	310 106	*75.3*
25-29	197 202	182 966	*92.8*	186 219	109 272	*58.7*	383 421	292 238	*76.2*
30-44	436 145	425 704	*97.6*	432 021	242 273	*56.1*	868 166	667 977	*76.9*
45-49	149 293	144 119	*96.5*	153 353	85 032	*55.4*	302 646	229 151	*75.7*
50-54	144 015	136 469	*94.8*	147 998	74 728	*50.5*	292 013	211 197	*72.3*
55-59	139 714	127 255	*91.1*	146 243	59 950	*41.0*	285 957	187 205	*65.5*
60-64	126 785	103 140	*81.4*	138 592	36 117	*26.1*	265 377	139 257	*52.5*
65 + ...	267 785	62 900	*23.5*	342 456	18 312	*5.3*	610 241	81 212	*13.3*
Total . . .	**2 451 397**	**1 465 744**	*59.8*	**2 486 182**	**847 543**	*34.1*	**4 937 579**	**2 313 287**	*46.9*
» (X.74) ‡									
Total . . .	**2 505 246**	**1 463 953**	*58.4*	**2 548 557**	**1 014 666**	*39.8*	**5 053 803**	**2 478 619**	*49.0*
España (31.XII.70) ‡									
− 15	4 840 881	106 092	*2.2*	4 618 759	50 447	*1.1*	9 459 640	156 539	*1.7*
15-19	1 372 110	903 985	*65.9*	1 337 224	490 758	*36.7*	2 709 334	1 394 743	*51.5*
20-24	1 287 654	1 043 239	*81.0*	1 261 098	498 911	*39.6*	2 548 752	1 542 150	*60.5*
25-29	1 120 907	1 067 342	*95.2*	1 118 575	232 471	*20.8*	2 239 482	1 299 813	*58.0*
30-44	3 362 296	3 254 961	*96.8*	3 426 861	466 364	*13.6*	6 789 157	3 721 325	*54.8*
45-49	1 050 225	1 003 010	*95.5*	1 083 343	155 664	*14.4*	2 133 568	1 158 674	*54.3*
50-54	807 312	740 935	*91.8*	920 141	138 083	*15.0*	1 727 453	879 018	*50.9*
55-59	751 940	650 139	*86.5*	878 954	128 866	*14.7*	1 630 894	779 005	*47.8*
60-64	692 288	513 880	*74.2*	819 402	96 181	*11.7*	1 511 690	610 061	*40.4*
65 + ...	1 356 134	290 471	*21.4*	1 934 539	76 260	*3.9*	3 290 673	366 731	*11.1*
Total . . .	**16 641 747**	**9 574 054**	*57.5*	**17 398 896**	**2 334 005**	*13.4*	**34 040 643**	**11 908 059**	*35.0*
» (VII-XII.74) ‡									
Total . . .	...	...	...	...	...	...	**35 225 000**	**13 332 200**	*37.8*

‡ For notes, see pp. 272-294.   ‡ *Voir notes pp. 272-294.*   ‡ Véanse las notas en las págs. 272-294.

1 Total and economically active population by sex and age group
Population totale et population active par sexe et groupe d'âge
Población total y población económicamente activa por sexo y grupo de edad

Country and age group / *Pays et groupe d'âge* / País y grupo de edad	Males — *Hommes* — Hombres			Females — *Femmes* — Mujeres			Total		
	Total population / *Population totale* / Población total	Economically active population / *Population active* / Población activa		Total population / *Population totale* / Población total	Economically active population / *Population active* / Población activa		Total population / *Population totale* / Población total	Economically active population / *Population active* / Población activa	
		Number / *Nombre* / Número	Per cent / *Pour-cent* / Por ciento		Number / *Nombre* / Número	Per cent / *Pour-cent* / Por ciento		Number / *Nombre* / Número	Per cent / *Pour-cent* / Por ciento
Faeroe Is. (16.XI.70)									
— 15	6 288	.	.	5 974	.	.	12 262	.	.
15-19	1 710	1 174	68.7	1 600	889	55.6	3 310	2 063	62.3
20-24	1 603	1 421	88.6	1 298	651	50.2	2 901	2 072	71.4
25-44	4 908	4 805	97.9	4 130	1 021	24.7	9 038	5 826	64.5
45-54	2 230	2 140	96.0	2 089	456	21.8	4 319	2 596	60.1
55-59	985	908	92.2	878	195	22.2	1 863	1 103	59.2
60-64	817	687	84.1	718	94	13.1	1 535	781	50.9
65 + ...	1 610	570	35.4	1 774	103	5.8	3 384	673	19.9
Total . . .	**20 151**	**11 705**	58.1	**18 461**	**3 409**	18.5	**38 612**	**15 114**	39.1
Finland (31.XII.70)									
— 15	570 573	225	—	547 977	154	—	1 118 550	379	—
15-19	215 689	94 034	43.6	205 481	69 064	33.6	421 170	163 098	38.7
20-24	228 348	177 928	77.9	216 751	135 686	62.6	445 099	313 614	70.5
25-29	169 075	155 694	92.1	161 956	109 664	67.7	331 031	265 358	80.2
30-44	430 793	414 094	96.1	425 970	288 111	67.6	856 763	702 205	82.0
45-49	130 270	119 545	91.8	148 699	95 483	64.2	278 969	215 028	77.1
50-54	106 252	92 717	87.3	132 245	77 879	58.9	238 497	170 596	71.5
55-59	109 496	85 985	78.5	137 817	68 121	49.4	247 313	154 106	62.3
60-64	100 563	63 449	63.1	132 893	38 765	29.2	233 456	102 214	43.8
65 + ...	158 926	21 995	13.8	268 562	9 664	3.6	427 488	31 659	7.4
Total . . .	**2 219 985**	**1 225 666**	55.2	**2 378 351**	**892 591**	37.5	**4 598 336**	**2 118 257**	46.1
France (1.III.68) ‡									
— 15	6 011 784	.	.	5 779 176	.	.	11 790 960	.	.
15-19	2 146 908	917 940	42.8	2 070 432	648 688	31.3	4 217 340	1 566 628	37.1
20-24	1 934 952	1 598 300	82.6	1 850 840	1 152 936	62.3	3 785 792	2 751 236	72.7
25-29	1 480 552	1 408 236	95.1	1 381 968	700 776	50.7	2 862 520	2 109 012	73.7
30-44	4 973 532	4 825 140	97.0	4 816 360	2 041 720	42.4	9 789 892	6 866 860	70.1
45-49	1 530 404	1 461 108	95.5	1 561 208	710 652	45.5	3 091 612	2 171 760	70.2
50-54	952 944	871 432	91.4	1 006 020	455 732	45.3	1 958 964	1 327 164	67.7
55-59	1 354 184	1 116 624	82.5	1 469 264	620 952	42.3	2 823 448	1 737 576	61.5
60-64	1 248 908	821 068	65.7	1 422 636	460 676	32.4	2 671 544	1 281 744	48.0
65 + ...	2 562 360	494 844	19.3	4 100 124	334 312	8.2	6 662 484	829 156	12.4
Total . . .	**24 196 528**	**13 514 692**	55.9	**25 458 028**	**7 126 444**	28.0	**49 654 556**	**20 641 136**	41.6
» (1.I.75*) ‡									
Total . . .	**25 818 400**	**14 214 100**	55.1	**26 856 400**	**8 199 900**	30.5	**52 674 800**	**22 414 000**	42.6
German Dem. Rep. (1.I.71) △									
— 20	2 710 546	219 323	8.1	2 577 703	183 336	7.1	5 288 249	402 659	7.6
20-24	495 279	430 548	86.9	475 328	354 439	74.6	970 607	784 987	80.9
25-29	556 122	540 068	97.1	548 700	434 994	79.3	1 104 822	975 062	88.3
30-39	1 218 591	1 204 078	98.8	1 199 707	·955 078	79.6	2 418 298	2 159 156	89.3
40-49	818 444	802 336	98.0	1 087 677	868 189	79.8	1 906 121	1 670 525	87.6
50-54	244 818	235 159	96.1	403 208	296 599	73.6	648 026	531 758	82.1
55-59	366 757	339 124	92.5	601 730	376 194	62.5	968 487	715 318	73.9
60-64	438 666	365 983	83.4	664 649	209 183	31.5	1 103 315	575 166	52.1
65 + ...	1 016 042	276 507	27.2	1 644 351	123 113	7.5	2 660 393	399 620	15.0
Total . . .	**7 865 265**	**4 413 126**	56.1	**9 203 053**	**3 801 125**	41.3	**17 068 318**	**8 214 251**	48.1

‡ For notes, see pp. 272-294.   ‡ *Voir notes pp. 272-294.*   ‡ Véanse las notas en las págs. 272-294.

1

Total and economically active population by sex and age group
Population totale et population active par sexe et groupe d'âge
Población total y población económicamente activa por sexo y grupo de edad

	Males — *Hommes* — Hombres			Females — *Femmes* — Mujeres			Total		
		Economically active population			Economically active population			Economically active population	
Country and age group	Total population	*Population active*		Total population	*Population active*		Total population	*Population active*	
		Población activa			Población activa			Población activa	
Pays et groupe d'âge	*Population totale*	Number	Per cent	*Population totale*	Number	Per cent	*Population totale*	Number	Per cent
País y grupo de edad	Población total	*Nombre*	*Pour-cent*	Población total	*Nombre*	*Pour-cent*	Población total	*Nombre*	*Pour-cent*
		Número	Por ciento		Número	Por ciento		Número	Por ciento
Germany, Fed. Rep. of (27.V.70)△‡									
− 15	7 206 600	.	.	6 851 700	.	.	14 058 300	.	.
15-19	2 044 100	1 367 100	66.9	1 951 700	1 256 800	64.4	3 995 800	2 623 900	65.7
20-24	1 905 000	1 652 800	86.8	1 820 100	1 221 900	67.1	3 725 100	2 874 700	77.2
25-29	2 226 700	2 093 800	94.0	2 065 900	1 063 300	51.5	4 292 600	3 157 100	73.5
30-44	6 582 500	6 457 100	98.1	6 226 500	2 881 600	46.3	12 809 000	9 338 700	72.9
45-49	1 622 600	1 560 800	96.2	2 191 800	1 061 800	48.4	3 814 400	2 622 600	68.8
50-54	1 055 800	987 800	93.6	1 468 300	631 700	43.0	2 524 100	1 619 500	64.2
55-59	1 573 800	1 373 700	87.3	2 179 800	756 800	34.7	3 753 600	2 130 500	56.8
60-64	1 562 800	1 084 800	69.4	2 124 400	378 100	17.8	3 687 200	1 463 000	39.7
65 + ...	3 086 800	496 700	16.1	4 903 800	283 300	5.8	7 990 600	780 000	9.8
Total . . .	**28 866 700**	**17 074 700**	*59.2*	**31 783 900**	**9 535 400**	*30.0*	**60 650 600**	**26 610 000**	*43.9*
» » (IV.74) △ ‡									
Total . . .	**29 684 000**	**17 178 000**	*57.9*	**32 376 000**	**10 056 000**	*31.1*	**62 061 000**	**27 234 000**	*43.9*
Gibraltar (6.X.70) ‡									
− 15	2 865	.	.	2 797	.	.	5 662	.	.
15-19	958	700	73.1	786	466	59.3	1 744	1 166	66.9
20-24	1 303	1 261	96.8	830	463	55.8	2 133	1 724	80.8
25-44	4 072	4 009	98.5	2 870	865	30.1	6 942	4 874	70.2
45-49	791	777	98.2	860	215	25.0	1 651	992	60.1
50-54	760	725	95.4	826	235	28.5	1 586	960	60.5
55-59	669	624	93.3	707	178	25.2	1 376	802	58.3
60-64	557	482	86.5	634	123	19.4	1 191	605	50.8
65 + ...	900	474	52.7	1 422	100	7.0	2 322	574	24.7
?	39	39	100.0	26	12	46.2	65	51	78.5
Total . . .	**12 914**	**9 091**	*70.4*	**11 758**	**2 657**	*22.6*	**24 672**	**11 748**	*47.6*
Grèce (14.III.71) ‡									
− 15	1 142 456	40 156	3.5	1 081 448	24 956	2.3	2 223 904	65 112	2.9
15-19	338 544	156 956	46.4	327 552	90 952	27.8	666 096	247 908	37.2
20-24	328 808	159 448	48.5	307 368	112 132	36.5	636 176	271 580	42.7
25-29	245 176	218 504	89.1	259 264	86 684	33.4	504 440	305 188	60.5
30-44	919 068	878 036	95.5	997 808	318 264	31.9	1 916 876	1 196 300	62.4
45-49	243 940	227 752	93.4	259 740	79 072	30.4	503 680	306 824	60.9
50-54	205 876	184 352	89.5	233 920	62 872	26.9	439 796	247 224	56.2
55-59	233 064	191 748	82.3	247 260	55 256	22.3	480 324	247 004	51.4
60-64	211 160	139 068	65.9	228 804	39 260	17.2	439 964	178 328	40.5
65 + ...	418 540	133 568	31.9	538 040	35 960	6.7	956 580	169 528	17.7
?	116	.	.	420	.	.	536	.	.
Total . . .	**4 286 748**	**2 329 588**	*54.3*	**4 481 624**	**905 408**	*20.2*	**8 768 372**	**3 234 996**	*36.9*

‡ For notes, see pp. 272-294.   ‡ *Voir notes pp. 272-294.*   ‡ Véanse las notas en las págs. 272-294.

POPULATION

1 Total and economically active population by sex and age group
Population totale et population active par sexe et groupe d'âge
Población total y población económicamente activa por sexo y grupo de edad

Country and age group / Pays et groupe d'âge / País y grupo de edad	Males — Hommes — Hombres Total population / Population totale / Población total	Males Economically active population / Population active / Población activa Number / Nombre / Número	Males Per cent / Pour-cent / Por ciento	Females — Femmes — Mujeres Total population / Population totale / Población total	Females Economically active population / Population active / Población activa Number / Nombre / Número	Females Per cent / Pour-cent / Por ciento	Total Total population / Population totale / Población total	Total Economically active population / Population active / Población activa Number / Nombre / Número	Total Per cent / Pour-cent / Por ciento
Hongrie (1.I.70) ‡									
− 15	1 119 402	3 739	0.3	1 057 105	9 958	0.9	2 176 507	13 697	0.6
15-19	469 624	214 892	45.8	447 510	219 504	49.1	917 134	434 396	47.4
20-24	395 921	362 217	91.5	383 328	253 572	66.2	779 249	615 789	79.0
25-29	371 769	366 289	98.5	369 096	240 965	65.3	740 865	607 254	82.0
30-44	1 033 581	1 012 420	98.0	1 087 451	757 780	69.7	2 121 032	1 770 200	83.5
45-49	345 653	329 884	95.4	385 543	246 599	64.0	731 196	576 483	78.8
50-54	201 598	185 134	91.8	229 145	129 691	56.6	430 743	314 825	73.1
55-59	309 219	260 963	84.4	356 355	103 952	29.2	665 574	364 915	54.8
60 + ...	756 884	197 946	26.2	1 002 915	93 171	9.3	1 759 799	291 117	16.5
Total . . .	5 003 651	2 933 484	58.6	5 318 448	2 055 192	38.6	10 322 099	4 988 676	48.3
» (I.74) ‡									
Total . . .	5 067 000	2 862 100	56.5	5 382 000	2 211 500	41.1	10 449 000	5 073 600	48.6
Iceland (1.XII.60)									
Total . . .	88 693	49 457	55.8	86 987	18 683	21.5	175 680	68 140	38.8
Ireland (18.IV.71)									
− 15	475 786	2 597	0.5	455 366	2 753	0.6	931 152	5 350	0.6
15-19	136 773	69 308	50.7	130 954	58 781	44.9	267 727	128 089	47.8
20-24	109 961	97 800	88.9	105 290	68 408	65.0	215 251	166 208	77.2
25-29	87 736	84 894	96.8	85 257	29 479	34.6	172 993	114 373	66.1
30-44	228 735	223 462	97.7	224 452	44 714	19.9	453 187	268 176	59.2
45-49	79 533	77 236	97.1	80 591	16 218	20.1	160 124	93 454	58.4
50-54	80 039	76 824	96.0	79 043	16 959	21.5	159 082	93 783	59.0
55-59	78 429	73 730	94.0	76 418	16 638	21.8	154 847	90 368	58.4
60-64	68 131	59 651	87.6	65 935	13 625	20.7	134 066	73 276	54.7
65 + ...	150 637	66 162	43.9	179 182	20 292	11.3	329 819	86 454	26.2
Total . . .	1 495 760	831 664	55.6	1 482 488	287 867	19.4	2 978 248	1 119 531	37.6
» (IV.74) ‡									
Total . . .	1 547 800	…	…	1 537 800	…	…	3 085 600	1 122 000	36.4
Isle of Man (24.IV.66)									
Total . . .	23 226	14 151	60.9	27 197	6 442	23.7	50 423	20 593	40.8
Italie (24.X.71)									
− 15	6 779 523	49 123	0.7	6 448 140	31 737	0.5	13 227 663	80 860	0.6
15-19	1 960 547	1 019 814	52.0	1 888 583	693 334	36.7	3 849 130	1 713 148	44.5
20-24	2 081 281	1 661 210	79.8	2 013 199	900 174	44.7	4 094 480	2 561 384	62.6
25-29	1 755 216	1 644 098	93.7	1 751 830	634 624	36.2	3 507 046	2 278 722	65.0
30-44	5 562 482	5 341 657	96.0	5 667 094	1 726 108	30.5	11 229 576	7 067 765	62.9
45-49	1 757 129	1 617 765	92.1	1 870 856	555 752	29.7	3 627 985	2 173 517	59.9
50-54	1 227 806	1 070 147	87.2	1 356 564	357 303	26.3	2 584 370	1 427 450	55.2
55-59	1 430 225	1 072 053	75.0	1 574 167	265 751	16.9	3 004 392	1 337 804	44.5
60-64	1 370 987	556 971	46.0	1 539 098	152 595	9.9	2 910 085	709 566	24.4
65 + ...	2 551 027	341 908	13.4	3 550 793	113 805	3.2	6 101 820	455 713	7.5
Total . . .	26 476 223	14 374 746	54.3	27 660 324	5 431 183	19.6	54 136 547	19 805 929	36.6
» (IV.75) ‡									
Total . . .	26 778 000	13 984 000	52.2	28 139 000	5 452 000	19.4	54 917 000	19 436 000	35.4

‡ For notes, see pp. 272-294. ‡ Voir notes pp. 272-294. ‡ Véanse las notas en las págs. 272-294.

1 Total and economically active population by sex and age group
Population totale et population active par sexe et groupe d'âge
Población total y población económicamente activa por sexo y grupo de edad

Country and age group *Pays et groupe d'âge* País y grupo de edad	Males — *Hommes* — Hombres			Females — *Femmes* — Mujeres			Total		
	Total population *Population totale* Población total	Economically active population		Total population *Population totale* Población total	Economically active population		Total population *Population totale* Población total	Economically active population	
		Population active Población activa			*Population active* Población activa			*Population active* Población activa	
		Number *Nombre* Número	Per cent *Pour-cent* Por ciento		Number *Nombre* Número	Per cent *Pour-cent* Por ciento		Number *Nombre* Número	Per cent *Pour-cent* Por ciento
Liechtenstein (1.XII.70)									
− 15	3 009	.	.	2 952	1	—	5 961	1	—
15-19	919	663	72.1	884	683	77.3	1 803	1 346	74.7
20-24	973	940	96.6	1 052	784	74.5	2 025	1 724	85.1
25-29	1 024	1 012	98.8	931	431	46.3	1 955	1 443	73.8
30-44	2 052	2 040	99.4	1 914	723	37.8	3 966	2 763	69.7
45-49	591	584	98.8	639	251	39.3	1 230	835	67.9
50-54	481	466	96.9	459	165	35.9	940	631	67.1
55-59	463	429	92.7	470	174	37.0	933	603	64.6
60-64	400	343	85.8	456	131	28.7	856	474	55.4
65 + ...	704	294	41.8	977	137	14.0	1 681	431	25.6
Total . . .	**10 616**	**6 771**	*63.8*	**10 734**	**3 480**	*32.4*	**21 350**	**10 251**	*48.0*
» (XII.73) ‡									
Total . . .	**11 516**	...	...	**11 640**	...	...	**23 156**	**9 979**	*43.1*
Luxembourg (31.XII.70) ‡									
− 15	38 366	.	.	36 801	.	.	75 167	.	.
15-19	12 554	6 895	54.9	12 003	6 627	55.2	24 557	13 522	55.1
20-24	11 569	9 798	84.7	11 286	6 011	53.3	22 855	15 809	69.2
25-29	11 553	11 220	97.1	10 705	3 590	33.5	22 258	14 810	66.5
30-44	37 347	36 717	98.3	35 301	8 503	24.1	72 648	45 220	62.2
45-49	9 680	9 280	95.9	11 630	2 780	23.9	21 310	12 060	56.6
50-54	8 351	7 631	91.4	9 132	2 022	22.1	17 483	9 653	55.2
55-59	9 878	7 837	79.3	10 768	2 008	18.6	20 646	9 845	47.7
60-64	9 366	4 260	45.5	10 712	1 282	12.0	20 078	5 542	27.6
65 + ...	17 886	1 801	10.1	24 953	993	4.0	42 839	2 794	6.5
Total . . .	**166 550**	**95 439**	*57.3*	**173 291**	**33 816**	*19.5*	**339 841**	**129 255**	*38.0*
» (XII.74) ‡									
Total . . .	...	...	...	...	...	...	**357 000**	**150 500**	*42.2*
Malta (26.XI.67)									
− 20	65 116	12 252	18.8	63 305	6 082	9.6	128 421	18 334	14.3
20-29	21 238	20 030	94.3	25 632	7 917	30.9	46 870	27 947	59.6
30-49	32 798	31 513	96.1	38 328	5 244	13.7	71 126	36 757	51.7
50-59	13 269	11 648	87.8	14 182	1 610	11.4	27 451	13 258	48.3
60 + ...	18 177	4 811	26.5	22 171	1 146	5.2	40 348	5 957	14.8
Total . . .	**150 598**	**80 254**	*53.3*	**163 618**	**21 999**	*13.4*	**314 216**	**102 253**	*32.5*
» (XI-XII.72) ‡									
Total . . .	**152 363**	**81 391**	*53.4*	**166 167**	**25 251**	*15.2*	**318 530**	**106 642**	*33.5*

‡ For notes, see pp. 272-294.   ‡ *Voir notes pp. 272-294.*   ‡ Véanse las notas en las págs. 272-294.

1 Total and economically active population by sex and age group
Population totale et population active par sexe et groupe d'âge
Población total y población económicamente activa por sexo y grupo de edad

Country and age group *Pays et groupe d'âge* País y grupo de edad	Males — *Hommes* — Hombres			Females — *Femmes* — Mujeres			Total		
	Total population *Population totale* Población total	Economically active population		Total population *Population totale* Población total	Economically active population		Total population *Population totale* Población total	Economically active population	
		Population active Población activa			*Population active* Población activa			*Population active* Población activa	
		Number *Nombre* Número	Per cent *Pour-cent* Por ciento		Number *Nombre* Número	Per cent *Pour-cent* Por ciento		Number *Nombre* Número	Per cent *Pour-cent* Por ciento
Monaco (1.III.68) ‡									
− 15	1 533	.	.	1 446	.	.	2 979	.	.
15-19	569	108	19.0	585	101	17.3	1 154	209	18.1
20-24	717	416	58.0	811	452	55.7	1 528	868	56.8
25-29	648	568	87.7	696	428	61.5	1 344	996	74.1
30-44	1 992	1 941	97.4	2 255	1 188	52.7	4 247	3 129	73.7
45-49	748	723	96.7	927	498	53.7	1 675	1 221	72.9
50-54	558	505	90.5	715	349	48.8	1 273	854	67.1
55-59	812	708	87.2	1 050	503	47.9	1 862	1 211	65.0
60-64	825	607	73.6	987	380	38.5	1 812	987	54.5
65 + ...	1 997	465	23.3	3 097	363	11.7	5 094	828	16.3
?	25	14	56.0	42	8	19.0	67	22	32.8
Total . . .	**10 424**	**6 055**	*58.1*	**12 611**	**4 270**	*33.9*	**23 035**	**10 325**	*44.8*
Norway (1.XI.70) ‡									
− 16	513 582	.	.	487 437	.	.	1 001 019	.	.
16-19	123 074	44 527	36.2	117 244	34 970	29.8	240 318	79 497	33.1
20-24	161 072	126 044	78.3	150 947	73 066	48.4	312 019	199 110	63.8
25-29	133 457	120 411	90.2	125 555	43 824	34.9	259 012	164 235	63.4
30-44	313 884	301 650	96.1	305 846	85 329	27.9	619 730	386 979	62.4
45-49	125 272	117 874	94.1	124 233	43 255	34.8	249 505	161 129	64.6
50-54	123 336	113 245	91.8	125 539	44 111	35.1	248 875	157 356	63.2
55-59	113 469	99 542	87.7	117 268	37 532	32.0	230 737	137 074	59.4
60-64	98 624	77 900	79.0	107 662	26 393	24.5	206 286	104 293	50.6
65 + ...	220 378	56 572	25.7	286 254	15 914	5.6	506 632	72 486	14.3
Total . . .	**1 926 148**	**1 057 765**	*54.9*	**1 947 985**	**404 394**	*20.8*	**3 874 133**	**1 462 159**	*37.7*
Pays-Bas (28.II.71*)									
− 15	1 843 000	10 000	5.4	1 747 000	6 000	3.4	3 590 000	16 000	4.5
15-19	568 000	239 000	42.1	540 000	266 000	49.3	1 108 000	505 000	45.6
20-24	597 000	501 000	83.9	565 000	314 000	55.6	1 162 000	815 000	70.1
25-34	897 000	861 000	96.0	829 000	209 000	25.2	1 726 000	1 070 000	62.0
35-44	773 000	749 000	96.9	752 000	173 000	23.0	1 525 000	922 000	60.5
45-49	367 000	350 000	95.4	381 000	88 000	23.1	748 000	438 000	58.6
50-54	323 000	299 000	92.6	337 000	72 000	21.4	660 000	371 000	56.2
55-59	299 000	261 000	87.3	322 000	59 000	18.3	621 000	320 000	51.5
60-64	266 000	199 000	74.8	301 000	38 000	12.6	567 000	237 000	41.8
65 + ...	588 000	77 000	13.1	751 000	21 000	2.8	1 339 000	98 000	7.3
Total . . .	**6 521 000**	**3 546 000**	*54.4*	**6 525 000**	**1 246 000**	*19.1*	**13 046 000**	**4 792 000**	*36.7*
Pologne (8.XII.70)									
− 15	4 409 198	.	.	4 218 278	.	.	8 627 476	.	.
15-19	1 771 632	557 875	31.5	1 705 610	436 502	25.6	3 477 242	994 377	28.6
20-24	1 498 807	1 284 493	85.7	1 458 565	1 068 868	73.3	2 957 372	2 353 361	79 6
25-29	948 774	913 264	96.3	939 442	705 413	75.1	1 888 216	1 618 677	85.7
30-44	3 300 327	3 189 876	96.7	3 367 150	2 666 721	79.2	6 667 477	5 856 597	87.8
45-49	914 793	870 240	95.1	1 071 250	848 350	79.2	1 986 043	1 718 590	86.5
50-54	587 441	552 484	94.0	693 634	526 313	75.9	1 281 075	1 078 797	84.2
55-59	674 050	612 914	90.9	827 104	563 164	68.1	1 501 154	1 176 078	78.3
60-64	676 251	561 455	83.0	823 532	420 719	51.1	1 499 783	982 174	65.5
65 + ...	1 062 117	598 759	56.4	1 673 602	552 761	33.0	2 735 719	1 151 520	42.1
?	10 228	7 450	72.8	10 485	6 227	59.4	20 713	13 677	66.0
Total . . .	**15 853 618**	**9 148 810**	*57.7*	**16 788 652**	**7 795 038**	*46.4*	**32 642 270**	**16 943 848**	*51.9*
» (III.74)‡									
Total . . .	**16 312 730**	**9 424 317**	*57.8*	**17 323 203**	**8 082 238**	*46.7*	**33 635 933**	**17 506 555**	*52.0*

‡ For notes, see pp. 272-294.　　　　　　‡ *Voir notes pp. 272-294.*　　　　　　‡ Véanse las notas en las págs. 272-294.

1 Total and economically active population by sex and age group
Population totale et population active par sexe et groupe d'âge
Población total y población económicamente activa por sexo y grupo de edad

País y grupo de edad	Males — Hommes — Hombres			Females — Femmes — Mujeres			Total		
	Total population / Population totale / Población total	Economically active population / Population active / Población activa		Total population / Population totale / Población total	Economically active population / Population active / Población activa		Total population / Population totale / Población total	Economically active population / Population active / Población activa	
Country and age group / Pays et groupe d'âge / País y grupo de edad		Number Nombre Número	Per cent Pour-cent Por ciento		Number Nombre Número	Per cent Pour-cent Por ciento		Number Nombre Número	Per cent Pour-cent Por ciento
Portugal (15.XII.70) ‡									
− 15	1 245 480	69 255	5.6	1 206 370	41 320	3.4	2 451 850	110 575	4.5
15-19	355 490	280 925	79.0	375 410	168 135	44.8	730 900	449 060	61.4
20-24	297 945	277 235	93.0	330 095	150 130	45.5	628 040	427 365	68.0
25-29	241 340	233 375	96.7	277 395	91 875	33.1	518 735	325 250	62.7
30-44	774 060	752 480	97.2	867 050	202 850	23.4	1 641 110	955 330	58.2
45-49	242 785	230 505	94.9	270 445	53 660	19.8	513 230	284 165	55.4
50-54	209 280	193 200	92.3	235 320	41 770	17.8	444 600	234 970	52.8
55-59	206 185	180 300	87.4	233 565	36 175	15.5	439 750	216 475	49.2
60-64	184 055	145 575	79.1	226 095	30 775	13.6	410 150	176 350	43.0
65 + ...	332 545	176 070	52.9	500 215	40 255	8.0	832 760	216 325	26.0
Total . . .	**4 089 165**	**2 538 920**	**62.1**	**4 521 960**	**856 945**	**19.0**	**8 611 125**	**3 395 865**	**39.4**
Roumanie (15.III.66) ‡									
− 15	2 541 975	6 320	0.3	2 426 549	10 725	0.4	4 968 524	17 045	0.3
15-19	810 951	393 211	48.5	779 220	395 967	50.8	1 590 171	789 178	49.6
20-24	639 723	580 836	90.8	628 078	466 885	74.3	1 267 801	1 047 721	82.6
25-29	779 009	757 334	97.2	778 115	611 159	78.5	1 557 124	1 368 493	87.9
30-44	2 200 748	2 160 795	98.2	2 248 668	1 763 323	78.4	4 449 416	3 924 118	88.2
45-49	362 916	350 901	96.7	445 110	334 693	75.2	808 026	685 594	84.8
50-54	498 286	468 493	94.0	580 132	413 742	71.3	1 078 418	882 235	81.8
55-59	488 530	437 967	89.7	538 466	316 810	58.8	1 026 996	754 777	73.5
60-64	401 853	271 448	67.6	445 513	184 933	41.5	847 366	456 381	53.9
65 + ...	620 446	244 093	39.3	872 303	184 038	21.1	1 492 749	428 131	28.7
?	6 638	3 778	56.9	9 934	4 849	48.8	16 572	8 627	52.1
Total . . .	**9 351 075**	**5 675 176**	**60.7**	**9 752 088**	**4 687 124**	**48.1**	**19 103 163**	**10 362 300**	**54.2**
Suisse (1.XII.70)									
− 15	749 714	345	—	716 819	376	0.1	1 466 533	721	—
15-19	230 472	144 848	62.8	220 127	128 590	58.4	450 599	273 438	60.7
20-24	258 567	226 847	87.7	253 148	180 246	71.2	511 715	407 093	79.6
25-29	269 165	258 899	96.2	251 406	127 588	50.7	520 571	386 487	74.2
30-44	647 173	640 120	98.9	620 758	270 545	43.6	1 267 931	910 665	71.8
45-49	185 788	182 829	98.4	192 142	87 092	45.3	377 930	269 921	71.4
50-54	156 207	151 688	97.1	161 519	69 366	42.9	317 726	221 054	69.6
55-59	157 093	149 052	94.9	169 878	66 888	39.4	326 971	215 940	66.0
60-64	145 268	126 778	87.3	170 055	50 774	29.9	315 323	177 552	56.3
65 + ...	289 879	91 882	31.7	424 605	41 024	9.7	714 484	132 906	18.6
Total . . .	**3 089 326**	**1 973 288**	**63.9**	**3 180 457**	**1 022 489**	**32.1**	**6 269 783**	**2 995 777**	**47.8**
Sweden (1.XI.70) ‡									
− 15	855 666	.	.	810 323	.	.	1 665 989	.	.
15-19	281 867	92 798	32.9	269 292	78 794	29.3	551 159	171 592	31.1
20-24	336 406	208 473	62.0	321 093	171 225	53.3	657 499	379 698	57.7
25-29	329 163	279 855	85.0	304 487	149 114	49.0	633 650	428 969	67.7
30-44	716 141	660 737	92.3	690 598	344 017	49.8	1 406 739	1 004 754	71.4
45-49	264 703	245 935	92.9	262 934	144 540	55.0	527 637	390 475	74.0
50-54	261 392	240 291	91.9	260 451	130 951	50.3	521 843	371 242	71.1
55-59	252 886	223 640	88.4	255 709	105 062	41.1	508 595	328 702	64.6
60-64	234 857	177 777	75.7	245 458	63 053	25.7	480 315	240 830	50.1
65 + ...	500 856	76 252	15.2	622 621	20 154	3.2	1 123 477	96 406	8.6
Total . . .	**4 033 937**	**2 205 758**	**54.7**	**4 042 966**	**1 206 910**	**29.9**	**8 076 903**	**3 412 668**	**42.3**

‡ For notes, see pp. 272-294. ‡ Voir notes pp. 272-294. ‡ Véanse las notas en las págs. 272-294.

1 Total and economically active population by sex and age group
Population totale et population active par sexe et groupe d'âge
Población total y población económicamente activa por sexo y grupo de edad

Country and age group *Pays et groupe d'âge* País y grupo de edad	Males — *Hommes* — Hombres			Females — *Femmes* — Mujeres			Total		
	Total population *Population totale* Población total	Economically active population *Population active* Población activa		Total population *Population totale* Población total	Economically active population *Population active* Población activa		Total population *Population totale* Población total	Economically active population *Population active* Población activa	
		Number *Nombre* Número	Per cent *Pour-cent* Por ciento		Number *Nombre* Número	Per cent *Pour-cent* Por ciento		Number *Nombre* Número	Per cent *Pour-cent* Por ciento
Turquie (25.X.70) ‡									
− 15	7 665 800	...	...	7 222 993	...	...	14 888 793	1 294 928	8.7
15-19	1 893 407	...	...	1 807 452	...	...	3 700 859	2 290 764	61.9
20-24	1 532 288	...	...	1 363 088	...	...	2 895 376	2 109 631	72.9
25-29	1 114 435	...	...	1 165 117	...	...	2 279 552	1 685 658	73.9
30-44	3 024 292	...	...	3 123 820	...	...	6 148 112	4 651 613	75.7
45-49	637 290	...	...	581 793	...	...	1 219 083	925 645	75.9
50-54	465 754	...	...	509 664	...	...	975 418	728 131	74.6
55-59	513 288	...	...	448 647	...	...	961 935	682 091	70.9
60-64	483 070	...	...	532 736	...	...	1 015 806	668 351	65.8
65 + ...	715 417	...	...	827 831	...	...	1 543 248	791 836	51.3
?	17 960	...	...	20 407	...	...	38 367	5	—
Total . . .	**18 063 001**	...	...	**17 603 548**	...	...	**35 666 549**	**15 828 653**	44.4
United Kingdom (25.IV.71)									
− 15	6 872 679	.	.	6 514 913	.	.	13 387 592	.	.
15-19	1 960 650	1 191 458	60.8	1 871 618	1 042 837	55 7	3 832 268	2 234 295	58.3
20-24	2 132 008	1 916 133	89.9	2 104 516	1 265 607	60.1	4 236 524	3 181 740	75.1
25-29	1 821 998	1 767 121	97.0	1 787 626	768 603	43.0	3 609 624	2 535 724	70.2
30-44	4 908 747	4 819 943	98.2	4 849 983	2 570 464	53.0	9 758 730	7 390 407	75.7
45-49	1 750 412	1 714 400	97.9	1 793 850	1 103 714	61.5	3 544 262	2 818 114	79.5
50-54	1 590 628	1 545 574	97.2	1 682 533	986 317	58.6	3 273 161	2 531 891	77.4
55-59	1 614 284	1 537 316	95.2	1 746 169	886 111	50.7	3 360 453	2 423 427	72.1
60-64	1 496 946	1 295 166	86.5	1 708 946	478 365	28.0	3 205 892	1 773 531	55.3
65 + ...	2 803 924	541 500	19.3	4 502 170	284 527	6.3	7 306 094	826 027	11.3
Total . . .	**26 952 276**	**16 328 611**	60.6	**28 562 324**	**9 386 545**	32.9	**55 514 600**	**25 715 156**	46.3
Yugoslavia (31.III.71) ‡									
− 15	2 815 305	27 917	1.0	2 684 950	45 075	1.7	5 500 255	72 992	1.3
15-19	1 013 455	418 840	41.3	971 489	369 506	38.0	1 984 944	788 346	39.7
20-24	900 219	737 132	81.9	854 108	476 487	55.8	1 754 327	1 213 619	69.2
25-29	649 334	617 803	95.1	641 884	360 714	56.2	1 291 218	978 517	75.8
30-44	2 302 564	2 227 883	96.8	2 327 793	1 139 172	48.9	4 630 357	3 367 055	72.7
45-49	540 228	475 294	88.0	663 158	281 055	42.4	1 203 386	756 349	62.9
50-54	322 606	273 177	84.7	399 414	141 812	35.5	722 020	414 989	57.5
55-59	383 319	284 243	74.2	464 962	127 419	27.4	848 281	411 662	48.5
60-64	413 884	259 348	62.7	467 119	109 836	23.5	881 003	369 184	41.9
65 + ...	690 779	351 586	50.9	924 123	143 344	15.5	1 614 902	494 930	30.6
?	45 589	13 109	28.8	46 690	9 064	19.4	92 279	22 173	24.0
Total . . .	**10 077 282**	**5 686 332**	56.4	**10 445 690**	**3 203 484**	30.7	**20 522 972**	**8 889 816**	43.3

‡ For notes, see pp. 272-294.   ‡ *Voir notes pp. 272-294.*   ‡ Véanse las notas en las págs. 272-294.

1 Total and economically active population by sex and age group
Population totale et population active par sexe et groupe d'âge
Población total y población económicamente activa por sexo y grupo de edad

Country and age group *Pays et groupe d'âge* País y grupo de edad	Males — *Hommes* — Hombres			Females — *Femmes* — Mujeres			Total		
	Total population *Population totale* Población total	Economically active population *Population active* Población activa		Total population *Population totale* Población total	Economically active population *Population active* Población activa		Total population *Population totale* Población total	Economically active population *Population active* Población activa	
		Number *Nombre* Número	Per cent *Pour-cent* Por ciento		Number *Nombre* Número	Per cent *Pour-cent* Por ciento		Number *Nombre* Número	Per cent *Pour-cent* Por ciento

OCEANIA — OCÉANIE — OCEANIA

American Samoa									
» » (1.IV.70)									
Total . . .	**13 682**	**3 450**	*25.2*	**13 477**	**1 963**	*14.6*	**27 159**	**5 413**	*19.9*
» » (V.72) ‡									
Total . . .	...	...	...	...	...	...	**29 100**	**9 700**	*33.3*
Australia (30.VI.71)									
− 15	1 880 557	.	.	1 789 495	.	.	3 670 052	.	.
15-19	567 960	316 624	*55.8*	542 236	282 297	*52.1*	1 110 196	598 921	*54.0*
20-24	558 166	497 515	*89.1*	538 779	315 597	*58.6*	1 096 945	813 112	*74.1*
25-29	480 748	454 128	*94.5*	452 779	177 048	*39.1*	933 527	631 176	*67.6*
30-44	1 200 963	1 140 387	*95.0*	1 127 521	478 105	*42.4*	2 328 484	1 618 492	*69.5*
45-49	399 611	375 037	*93.9*	381 913	164 625	*43.1*	781 524	539 662	*69.1*
50-54	332 641	306 044	*92.0*	330 295	120 284	*36.4*	662 936	426 328	*64.3*
55-59	301 464	266 417	*88.4*	303 971	86 045	*28.3*	605 435	352 462	*58.2*
60-64	243 740	184 302	*75.6*	257 804	41 125	*16.0*	501 544	225 427	*45.0*
65 + ...	446 861	99 185	*22.2*	618 134	25 723	*4.2*	1 064 995	124 908	*11.7*
Total . . .	**6 412 711**	**3 639 639**	*56.8*	**6 342 927**	**1 690 849**	*26.7*	**12 755 638**	**5 330 488**	*41.8*
Christmas Is. (30.VI.71)									
Total . . .	**1 732**	**1 224**	*70.7*	**959**	**153**	*16.0*	**2 691**	**1 377**	*51.2*
Cocos Is. (30.VI.66)									
Total . . .	**375**	**223**	*59.5*	**309**	**56**	*18.1*	**684**	**279**	*40.8*
Cook Is. (1.IX.66)									
− 15	5 061	.	.	4 922	.	.	9 983	.	.
15-19	969	643	*66.4*	905	361	*39.9*	1 874	1 004	*53.6*
20-24	559	550	*98.4*	715	373	*52.2*	1 274	923	*72.5*
25-34	988	984	*99.6*	978	347	*35.5*	1 966	1 331	*67.7*
35-44	822	813	*98.9*	757	238	*31.4*	1 579	1 051	*66.6*
45-64	1 034	1 003	*97.0*	888	266	*30.0*	1 922	1 269	*66.0*
65 + ...	316	160	*50.6*	333	30	*9.0*	649	190	*29.3*
Total . . .	**9 749**	**4 153**	*42.1*	**9 498**	**1 615**	*17.0*	**19 247**	**5 768**	*30.0*

‡ For notes, see pp. 272-294.   ‡ *Voir notes pp. 272-294.*   ‡ Véanse las notas en las págs. 272-294.

45

1 **Total and economically active population by sex and age group**
Population totale et population active par sexe et groupe d'âge
Población total y población económicamente activa por sexo y grupo de edad

Country and age group / Pays et groupe d'âge / País y grupo de edad	Males — Hommes — Hombres			Females — Femmes — Mujeres			Total		
	Total population / Population totale / Población total	Economically active population / Population active / Población activa		Total population / Population totale / Población total	Economically active population / Population active / Población activa		Total population / Population totale / Población total	Economically active population / Population active / Población activa	
		Number / Nombre / Número	Per cent / Pour-cent / Por ciento		Number / Nombre / Número	Per cent / Pour-cent / Por ciento		Number / Nombre / Número	Per cent / Pour-cent / Por ciento
Fiji (12.IX.66)									
— 15	113 182	.	.	109 557	.	.	222 739	.	.
15-19	25 473	18 503	72.6	25 438	1 609	6.3	50 911	20 112	39.5
20-24	20 677	19 824	95.9	21 128	2 398	11.3	41 805	22 222	53.2
25-29	17 060	16 745	98.2	17 247	1 625	9.4	34 307	18 370	53.5
30-44	35 686	35 134	98.5	33 947	2 440	7.2	69 633	37 574	54.0
45-49	8 819	8 651	98.1	8 072	489	6.1	16 891	9 140	54.1
50-54	7 091	6 825	96.2	6 205	365	5.9	13 296	7 190	54.1
55-59	4 689	4 388	93.6	4 147	219	5.3	8 836	4 607	52.1
60-64	3 527	3 069	87.0	3 111	105	3.4	6 638	3 174	47.8
65 + ...	6 403	3 198	49.9	5 022	110	2.2	11 425	3 308	29.0
?	140	96	68.6	106	16	15.1	246	112	45.5
Total . . .	**242 747**	**116 433**	**48.0**	**233 980**	**9 376**	**4.0**	**476 727**	**125 809**	**26.4**
Gilbert and Ellice Is. (6.XII.68)									
— 15	12 419	.	.	11 776	.	.	24 195	.	.
15-19	2 592	1 826	70.5	2 811	166	5.9	5 403	1 992	36.9
20-24	1 859	1 774	95.2	1 975	212	10.7	3 834	1 986	51.8
25-34	2 855	2 797	98.0	3 261	145	4.5	6 116	2 942	48.1
35-44	2 625	2 577	98.2	2 567	80	3.1	5 192	2 657	51.2
45-64	3 013	2 902	96.3	3 376	69	2.0	6 389	2 971	46.5
65+	968	654	67.6	1 252	13	1.0	2 220	667	30.0
?	73	59	80.8	95	5	5.3	168	64	38.1
Total . . .	**26 404**	**12 589**	**47.7**	**27 113**	**690**	**2.5**	**53 517**	**13 279**	**24.8**
Guam (1.IV.70)									
Total . . .	**47 362**	**25 403**	**53.6**	**37 634**	**7 296**	**19.4**	**84 996**	**32 699**	**38.5**
Nauru (30.VI.66)									
— 15	1 254	.	.	1 166	.	.	2 420	.	.
15-19	195	132	67.7	174	64	36.8	369	196	53.1
20-24	337	330	97.9	135	41	30.4	472	371	78.6
25-29	438	428	97.7	215	33	15.3	653	461	70.6
30-44	1 002	967	96.5	447	51	11.4	1 449	1 018	70.3
45-49	223	220	98.7	79	11	13.9	302	231	76.5
50-54	110	102	92.7	55	14	25.5	165	116	70.3
55-59	66	61	92.4	24	2	8.3	90	63	70.0
60-64	41	33	80.5	26	2	7.7	67	35	52.2
65 + ...	37	11	29.7	33	2	6.1	70	13	18.6
Total . . .	**3 703**	**2 284**	**61.7**	**2 354**	**220**	**9.3**	**6 057**	**2 504**	**41.3**
New Hebrides (28.V.67)									
— 15	18 157	.	.	17 760	.	.	35 917	.	.
15-19	3 961	2 149	54.3	3 598	2 390	66.4	7 559	4 539	60.1
20-24	3 074	2 809	91.4	3 040	2 668	87.8	6 114	5 477	89.6
25-34	5 564	5 415	97.3	5 131	4 509	87.9	10 695	9 924	92.8
35-44	3 988	3 910	98.0	3 351	3 049	91.0	7 339	6 959	94.8
45-64	4 440	4 332	97.6	3 199	2 873	89.8	7 639	7 205	94.3
65 + ...	1 405	784	55.8	843	208	24.7	2 248	992	44.1
?	37	19	51.4	34	18	52.9	71	37	52.1
Total . . .	**40 626**	**19 418**	**47.8**	**36 956**	**15 715**	**42.5**	**77 582**	**35 133**	**45.3**

1 Total and economically active population by sex and age group
Population totale et population active par sexe et groupe d'âge
Población total y población económicamente activa por sexo y grupo de edad

Country and age group Pays et groupe d'âge País y grupo de edad	Males — *Hommes* — Hombres			Females — *Femmes* — Mujeres			Total		
	Total population *Population totale* Población total	Economically active population		Total population *Population totale* Población total	Economically active population		Total population *Population totale* Población total	Economically active population	
		Population active Población activa			*Population active* Población activa			*Population active* Población activa	
		Number *Nombre* Número	Per cent *Pour-cent* Por ciento		Number *Nombre* Número	Per cent *Pour-cent* Por ciento		Number *Nombre* Número	Per cent *Pour-cent* Por ciento
New Zealand (23.III.71) ‡									
— 15	464 512	.	.	445 111	.	.	909 623		
15-19	133 116	75 973	*57.1*	127 673	72 598	*56.9*	260 789	148 571	*57.0*
20-24	119 447	108 686	*91.0*	115 512	63 367	*54.9*	234 959	172 053	*73.2*
25-29	94 622	92 495	*97.8*	92 690	27 421	*29.6*	187 312	119 916	*64.0*
30-44	244 429	241 247	*98.7*	235 146	81 472	*34.6*	479 575	322 719	*67.3*
45-49	80 879	79 281	*98.0*	78 488	31 408	*40.0*	159 367	110 689	*69.5*
50-54	69 141	66 585	*96.3*	71 658	25 254	*35.2*	140 799	91 839	*65.2*
55-59	65 264	60 131	*92.1*	66 919	18 392	*27.5*	132 183	78 523	*59.4*
60-64	55 597	38 479	*69.2*	58 260	9 044	*15.5*	113 857	47 523	*41.7*
65 + ...	103 849	22 092	*21.3*	140 318	4 910	*3.5*	244 167	27 002	*11.1*
Total . . .	**1 430 856**	**784 969**	*54.9*	**1 431 775**	**333 866**	*23.3*	**2 862 631**	**1 118 835**	*39.1*
Niue Is. (28.IX.71)									
Total . . .	**2 507**	**1 011**	*40.3*	**2 483**	**411**	*16.6*	**4 990**	**1 422**	*28.5*
Norfolk Is. (30.VI.71)									
Total . . .	**824**	**516**	*62.6*	**859**	**344**	*40.0*	**1 683**	**860**	*51.1*
Nouvelle-Calédonie (11.III.69) ‡									
— 15	19 753	194	*1.0*	19 544	134	*0.7*	39 297	328	*0.8*
15-19	4 934	2 177	*44.1*	4 411	1 450	*32.9*	9 345	3 627	*38.8*
20-29	8 757	7 481	*85.4*	7 347	3 580	*48.7*	16 104	11 061	*68.7*
30-49	12 130	11 567	*95.4*	10 425	4 861	*46.6*	22 555	16 428	*72.8*
50-59	3 907	3 507	*89.8*	3 106	1 455	*46.8*	7 013	4 962	*70.8*
60 + ...	2 729	1 665	*61.0*	2 796	893	*31.9*	5 525	2 558	*46.3*
?	381	131	*34.4*	359	90	*25.1*	740	221	*29.9*
Total . . .	**52 591**	**26 722**	*50.8*	**47 988**	**12 463**	*26.0*	**100 579**	**39 185**	*39.0*
» » (I.75) ‡									
Total . . .	**69 700**	**40 000**	*57.4*	**64 700**	**20 000**	*31.1*	**134 000**	**60 000**	*44.8*
Pacific Is. (1.IV.70)									
Total . . .	**46 482**	**11 066**	*23.8*	**44 458**	**3 427**	*7.7*	**90 940**	**14 493**	*15.9*
Papua New Guinea (VI-VII.66) ‡									
— 15	484 479	57 043	*11.8*	436 696	61 476	*14.1*	921 175	118 519	*12.9*
15-19	100 080	78 318	*78.3*	88 964	77 059	*86.6*	189 044	155 377	*82.2*
20-24	81 236	77 818	*95.8*	79 432	73 650	*92.7*	160 668	151 468	*94.3*
25-44	309 437	304 242	*98.3*	298 586	285 844	*95.7*	608 023	590 086	*97.0*
45-54	94 889	91 065	*96.0*	84 620	78 885	*93.2*	179 509	169 950	*94.7*
55-64	38 111	33 039	*86.7*	32 247	25 701	*79.7*	70 358	58 740	*83.5*
65 + ...	12 074	7 156	*59.3*	9 466	4 657	*49.2*	21 540	11 813	*54.8*
Total . . .	**1 120 306**	**648 681**	*57.9*	**1 030 011**	**607 272**	*59.0*	**2 150 317**	**1 255 953**	*58.4*

‡ For notes, see pp. 272-294.   ‡ *Voir notes pp. 272-294.*   ‡ Véanse las notas en las págs. 272-294.

1 Total and economically active population by sex and age group
Population totale et population active par sexe et groupe d'âge
Población total y población económicamente activa por sexo y grupo de edad

	Males — Hommes — Hombres			Females — Femmes — Mujeres			Total		
Country and age group *Pays et groupe d'âge* País y grupo de edad	Total population *Population totale* Población total	Economically active population *Population active* Población activa		Total population *Population totale* Población total	Economically active population *Population active* Población activa		Total population *Population totale* Población total	Economically active population *Population active* Población activa	
		Number *Nombre* Número	Per cent *Pour-cent* Por ciento		Number *Nombre* Número	Per cent *Pour-cent* Por ciento		Number *Nombre* Número	Per cent *Pour-cent* Por ciento
Polynésie française (9.XI.67) ‡									
Total . . .	**51 731**	**22 623**	*43.7*	**46 584**	**8 850**	*19.0*	**98 315**	**31 473**	*32.0*
»　　　»　　(XII.70) ‡									
Total . . .	**51 130**	**24 940**	*48.8*	**58 870**	**11 090**	*18.8*	**110 000**	**36 030**	*32.8*
Tokelau Is. (21.II.72 *)									
Total . . .	**737**	**302**	*41.0*	**862**	**57**	*6.6*	**1 599**	**359**	*22.5*
Tonga (30.XI.66)									
− 15	18 609	.	.	17 136	.	.	35 745	.	.
15-19	4 001	1 986	*49.6*	3 824	69	*1.8*	7 825	2 055	*26.3*
20-24	3 118	2 763	*88.6*	3 101	374	*12.1*	6 219	3 137	*50.4*
25-29	2 749	2 671	*97.2*	2 692	253	*9.4*	5 441	2 924	*53.7*
30-44	6 126	6 007	*98.1*	5 891	290	*4.9*	12 017	6 297	*52.4*
45-49	1 427	1 404	*98.4*	1 284	45	*3.5*	2 711	1 449	*53.4*
50-54	1 088	1 078	*99.1*	976	28	*2.9*	2 064	1 106	*53.6*
55-59	773	765	*99.0*	711	21	*3.0*	1 484	786	*53.0*
60 + ...	1 821	1 226	*67.3*	1 936	18	*0.9*	3 757	1 244	*33.1*
?	125	.	.	41	.	.	166	.	.
Total . . .	**39 837**	**17 900**	*44.9*	**37 592**	**1 098**	*2.9*	**77 429**	**18 998**	*24.5*
Western Samoa (7.XI.71)									
− 15	38 684	939	*2.4*	35 156	88	*0.3*	73 840	1 027	*1.4*
15-19	9 144	5 266	*57.6*	7 993	904	*11.3*	17 137	6 170	*36.0*
20-24	5 518	5 147	*93.3*	5 002	1 189	*23.8*	10 520	6 336	*60.2*
25-29	4 081	4 014	*98.4*	3 959	768	*19.4*	8 040	4 782	*59.5*
30-44	9 592	9 477	*98.8*	9 678	1 544	*16.0*	19 270	11 021	*57.2*
45-49	2 519	2 491	*98.9*	2 221	333	*15.0*	4 740	2 824	*59.6*
50-54	2 031	1 976	*97.3*	2 071	252	*12.2*	4 102	2 228	*54.3*
55-59	1 397	1 332	*95.3*	1 323	124	*9.4*	2 720	1 456	*53.5*
60-64	1 125	990	*88.0*	1 095	73	*6.7*	2 220	1 063	*47.9*
65 + ...	1 859	919	*49.4*	2 179	75	*3.4*	4 038	994	*24.6*
Total . . .	**75 950**	**32 551**	*42.9*	**70 677**	**5 350**	*7.6*	**146 627**	**37 901**	*25.8*

‡ For notes, see pp. 272-294.　　　　‡ *Voir notes pp. 272-294.*　　　　‡ Véanse las notas en las págs. 272-294.

1

Total and economically active population by sex and age group
Population totale et population active par sexe et groupe d'âge
Población total y población económicamente activa por sexo y grupo de edad

Country and age group *Pays et groupe d'âge* País y grupo de edad	Males — *Hommes* — Hombres			Females — *Femmes* — Mujeres			Total		
	Total population *Population totale* Población total	Economically active population *Population active* Población activa		Total population *Population totale* Población total	Economically active population *Population active* Población activa		Total population *Population totale* Población total	Economically active population *Population active* Población activa	
		Number *Nombre* Número	Per cent *Pour-cent* Por ciento		Number *Nombre* Número	Per cent *Pour-cent* Por ciento		Number *Nombre* Número	Per cent *Pour-cent* Por ciento
URSS (15.I.70) † *(a)*									
− 20	46 864 610	4 694 380	*10.0*	45 108 588	4 042 860	*9.0*	91 973 198	8 737 240	*9.5*
20-29	15 440 324	13 852 591	*89.7*	15 435 297	13 322 621	*86.3*	30 875 621	27 175 212	*88.0*
30-39	18 548 102	18 102 672	*97.6*	19 190 437	17 790 938	*92.7*	37 738 539	35 893 610	*95.1*
40-49	13 502 168	12 956 244	*96.0*	17 756 475	16 084 532	*90.6*	31 258 643	29 040 776	*92.9*
50-54	3 429 835	3 086 301	*90.0*	5 647 905	4 365 206	*77.3*	9 077 740	7 451 507	*82.1*
55-59	4 273 019	3 417 372	*80.0*	7 740 157	2 045 929	*26.4*	12 013 176	5 463 301	*45.5*
60 + ...	9 210 936	1 846 210	*20.0*	19 303 493	1 358 395	*7.0*	28 514 429	3 204 605	*11.2*
?	130 383	34 558	*26.5*	138 405	26 766	*19.3*	268 788	61 324	*22.8*
Total . . .	**111 399 377**	**57 990 328**	*52.1*	**130 320 757**	**59 037 247**	*45.3*	**241 720 134**	**117 027 575**	*48.4*
RSS de Biélorussie (15.I.70) †									
Total . . .	**4 137 816**	**2 115 241**	*51.1*	**4 864 522**	**2 267 710**	*46.6*	**9 002 338**	**4 382 951**	*48.7*
RSS d'Ukraine (15.I.70) †									
Total . . .	**21 305 320**	**11 585 091**	*54.4*	**25 821 197**	**12 214 781**	*47.3*	**47 126 517**	**23 799 872**	*50.5*

† For notes, see pp. 272-294. † *Voir notes pp. 272-294.* † Véanse las notas en las págs. 272-294.

(a) Incl. Byelorussian SSR and Ukrainian SSR, shown separately in this table.

a) *Y compris les RSS de Biélorussie et d'Ukraine, figurant séparément dans ce tableau.*

(a) Incl. las RSS de Bielorrusia y de Ucrania, que figuran separadamente en este cuadro.

POPULATION

2 Structure of the economically active population
Structure de la population active
Estructura de la población económicamente activa

Industry (Branch of economic activity)	Employers and workers on own account Employeurs et personnes travaillant à leur propre compte Empleadores y trabajadores por cuenta propia			Salaried employees and wage earners Employés et ouvriers Empleados y obreros			Family workers Travailleurs familiaux Trabajadores familiares		
	Males Hommes Hombres	Females Femmes Mujeres	Total	Males Hommes Hombres	Females Femmes Mujeres	Total	Males Hommes Hombres	Females Femmes Mujeres	Total

AFRICA — AFRIQUE — AFRICA

Algérie (4.IV.1966) ╫

(ISIC 1958)

Industry	Males	Females	Total	Males	Females	Total	Males	Females	Total
Agriculture, forestry, hunting and fishing	362 249	3 302	365 551	773 680	7 243	780 923	132 635	12 703	145 338
Mining and quarrying	305	2	307	21 014	402	21 416	40	2	42
Manufacturing	33 229	6 275	39 504	110 331	7 140	117 471	2 857	909	3 766
Construction	13 001	12	13 013	112 056	667	112 723	377	2	379
Electricity, gas, water and sanitary services	550	1	551	9 109	390	9 499	.	.	.
Commerce	92 449	791	93 240	48 547	2 831	51 378	6 771	140	6 911
Transport, storage and communication	16 417	27	16 444	66 945	2 280	69 225	616	4	620
Services	20 296	1 159	21 455	263 648	50 107	313 755	692	203	895
Activities not adequately described	2 631	78	2 709	64 978	1 965	66 943	428	93	521
Persons seeking work for the first time	.	.	.	.	.	.	.	.	.
Total . . .	541 127	11 647	552 774	1 470 308	73 025	1 543 333	144 416	14 056	158 472

Botswana (1964) ╫

(ISIC 1958)

Industry	Males	Females	Total	Males	Females	Total	Males	Females	Total
Agriculture, forestry, hunting and fishing	94 521	115 328	209 849	8 224	1 410	9 634	5 144	2 224	7 368
Mining and quarrying	5	2	7	1 475	51	1 526	.	.	.
Manufacturing	404	38	442	628	10	638	13	.	13
Construction	343	3	346	1 204	14	1 218	6	.	6
Electricity, gas, water and sanitary services	.	.	.	52	.	52	.	.	.
Commerce	539	91	630	897	241	1 138	3	1	4
Transport, storage and communication	50	5	55	1 238	30	1 268	5	.	5
Services	30	32	62	2 530	3 084	5 614	133	401	534
Activities not adequately described	19	5	24	125	10	135	1	2	3
Total . . .	95 911	115 504	211 415	16 373	4 850	21 223	5 305	2 628	7 933

Côte-d'Ivoire (1.I.1964) ╫

(ISIC 1958)

Industry	Males	Females	Total	Males	Females	Total	Males	Females	Total
Agriculture, forestry, hunting and fishing	...	...	1 359 700	...	...	90 300	...	...	150 000
Mining and quarrying	...	...	20	...	...	3 050	...	...	.
Manufacturing	...	...	250	...	...	15 300	...	...	.
Construction	...	...	100	...	...	16 490	...	...	.
Electricity, gas, water and sanitary services	...	...	60	...	...	6 750	...	...	.
Commerce	...	...	106 000	...	...	19 300	...	...	.
Transport, storage and communication	...	...	25 000	...	...	16 870	...	...	.
Services	...	...	.	...	...	40 810	...	...	.
Total . . .	...	...	1 491 130	...	...	208 870	...	...	150 000

╫ For notes, see pp. 272-294.

A **Distribution by status and by industry (branch of economic activity)**
Répartition suivant la situation dans la profession et par branche d'activité économique
Distribución según la categoría de ocupación y por rama de actividad económica

Others and status unknown / Autres et situation non définie / Otros y categoría no definida			TOTAL			%	Branche d'activité économique / Rama de actividad económica	
Males / Hommes / Hombres	Females / Femmes / Mujeres	Total	Males / Hommes / Hombres	Females / Femmes / Mujeres	Total			
							(CITI 1958)	(CIIU 1958)
1 534	67	**1 601**	1 270 098	23 315	**1 293 413**	50.4	Agriculture, sylviculture, chasse et pêche	Agricultura, silvicultura, caza y pesca
97	8	**105**	21 456	414	**21 870**	0.9	Industries extractives	Minas y canteras
2 089	172	**2 261**	148 506	14 496	**163 002**	6.4	Industries manufacturières	Industrias manufactureras
2 578	9	**2 587**	128 012	690	**128 702**	5.0	Construction	Construcción
93	.	**93**	9 752	391	**10 143**	0.4	Electricité, gaz, eau et services sanitaires	Electricidad, gas, agua y servicios sanitarios
733	13	**746**	148 500	3 775	**152 275**	5.9	Com., banq., assur., aff. imm.	Comercio
1 602	5	**1 607**	85 580	2 316	**87 896**	3.4	Transports, entrepôts et communications	Transportes, almacenaje y comunicaciones
1 498	309	**1 807**	286 134	51 778	**337 912**	13.2	Services	Servicios
15 067	519	**15 586**	83 104	2 655	**85 759**	3.3	Activités mal désignées	Actividades no bien especif.
274 068	9 623	**283 691**	274 068	9 623	**283 691**	11.1	Personnes en quête d'emploi pour la première fois	Personas en busca de trabajo por primera vez
299 359	10 725	**310 084**	2 455 210	109 453	**2 564 663**	100.0	Total	Total
							(CITI 1958)	(CIIU 1958)
794	4	**798**	108 683	118 966	**227 649**	90.8	Agriculture, sylviculture, chasse et pêche	Agricultura, silvicultura, caza y pesca
392	15	**407**	1 872	68	**1 940**	0.8	Industries extractives	Minas y canteras
551	776	**1 327**	1 596	824	**2 420**	1.0	Industries manufacturières	Industrias manufactureras
1 125	9	**1 134**	2 678	26	**2 704**	1.1	Construction	Construcción
68	.	**68**	120	.	**120**	—	Electricité, gaz, eau et services sanitaires	Electricidad, gas, agua y servicios sanitarios
578	118	**696**	2 017	451	**2 468**	1.0	Com., banq., assur., aff. imm.	Comercio
967	20	**987**	2 260	55	**2 315**	0.9	Transports, entrepôts et communications	Transportes, almacenaje y comunicaciones
2 414	1 174	**3 588**	5 107	4 691	**9 798**	3.9	Services	Servicios
999	103	**1 102**	1 144	120	**1 264**	0.5	Activités mal désignées	Actividades no bien especif.
7 888	2 219	**10 107**	125 477	125 201	**250 678**	100.0	Total	Total
							(CITI 1958)	(CIIU 1958)
.	.	.	...	...	**1 600 000**	86.4	Agriculture, sylviculture, chasse et pêche	Agricultura, silvicultura, caza y pesca
.	.	.	...	...	**3 070**	0.2	Industries extractives	Minas y canteras
.	.	.	...	...	**15 550**	0.8	Industries manufacturières	Industrias manufactureras
.	.	.	...	...	**16 590**	0.9	Construction	Construcción
.	.	.	...	...	**6 810**	0.4	Electricité, gaz, eau et services sanitaires	Electricidad, gas, agua y servicios sanitarios
.	.	.	...	...	**125 300**	6.8	Com., banq., assur., aff. imm.	Comercio
.	.	.	...	...	**41 870**	2.3	Transports, entrepôts et communications	Transportes, almacenaje y comunicaciones
.	.	.	...	...	**40 810**	2.2	Services	Servicios
.	.	.	979 000	871 000	**1 850 000**	100.0	Total	Total

✝ *Voir notes pp. 272-294.*   ✝ Véanse las notas en las págs. 272-294.

POPULATION

2 Structure of the economically active population
Structure de la population active
Estructura de la población económicamente activa

Industry (Branch of economic activity)	Employers and workers on own account Employeurs et personnes travaillant à leur propre compte Empleadores y trabajadores por cuenta propia			Salaried employees and wage earners Employés et ouvriers Empleados y obreros			Family workers Travailleurs familiaux Trabajadores familiares		
	Males Hommes Hombres	Females Femmes Mujeres	Total	Males Hommes Hombres	Females Femmes Mujeres	Total	Males Hommes Hombres	Females Femmes Mujeres	Total

Egypt (30.V.1966)

1. Agriculture, hunting, forestry and fishing	1 552 064	34 723	**1 586 787**	1 629 285	71 237	**1 700 522**	1 091 642	67 962	**1 159 604**
2. Mining and quarrying	574	.	**574**	16 695	443	**17 138**	.	.	.
3. Manufacturing	194 100	11 666	**205 766**	800 211	35 633	**835 844**	27 164	2 514	**29 678**
4. Electricity, gas and water	1 635	127	**1 762**	48 318	846	**49 164**	155	.	**155**
5. Construction	39 368	148	**39 516**	162 199	1 453	**163 652**	2 310	122	**2 432**
6. Wholesale and retail trade, restaurants and hotels	360 306	22 392	**382 698**	169 755	12 758	**182 513**	31 498	2 311	**33 809**
7. Transport, storage and communication	58 880	195	**59 075**	266 193	6 981	**273 174**	7 418	20	**7 438**
8. Financing, insurance, real estate and business services	115 892	4 302	**120 194**	884 337	223 166	**1 107 503**	13 309	5 325	**18 634**
9. Community, social and personal services									
0. Activities not adequately described . .	42 996	11 024	**54 020**	130 819	30 930	**161 749**	64 717	75 615	**140 332**
Persons seeking work for the first time									
Total . . .	2 365 815	84 577	**2 450 392**	4 107 812	383 447	**4 491 259**	1 238 213	153 869	**1 392 082**

Gabon (31.XII.1963) †

(ISIC 1958)									
Agriculture, forestry, hunting and fishing	7 500	4 500	**12 000**	12 950	430	**13 380**	50 000	60 000	**110 000**
Mining and quarrying	1 000	.	**1 000**	6 400	120	**6 520**	.	.	.
Manufacturing	.	.	.	3 680	515	**4 195**	.	.	.
Construction	100	.	**100**	3 450	110	**3 560**	.	.	.
Electricity, gas, water and sanitary services	.	.	.	120	15	**135**	.	.	.
Commerce	1 500	1 000	**2 500**	4 200	1 460	**5 660**	.	.	.
Transport, storage and communication	200	.	**200**	2 550	100	**2 650**	.	.	.
Services	.	.	.	4 600	2 400	**7 000**	.	.	.
Activities not adequately described .	300	200	**500**	600	300	**900**	.	.	.
Total . . .	10 600	5 700	**16 300**	38 550	5 450	**44 000**	50 000	60 000	**110 000**

Libyan Arab Republic (31.VII.1964) †

(ISIC 1958)									
Agriculture, forestry, hunting and fishing	92 578	424	**93 002**	27 145	357	**27 502**	20 470	2 247	**22 717**
Mining and quarrying	246	1	**247**	11 302	51	**11 353**	9	.	**9**
Manufacturing	5 049	1 783	**6 832**	12 825	622	**13 447**	647	5 368	**6 015**
Construction	1 362	6	**1 368**	28 294	162	**28 456**	55	2	**57**
Electricity, gas, water and sanitary services	156	1	**157**	5 397	74	**5 471**	7	2	**9**
Commerce	19 109	119	**19 228**	5 156	82	**5 238**	309	6	**315**
Transport, storage and communication	4 558	7	**4 565**	16 787	91	**16 878**	50	6	**56**
Services	2 227	177	**2 404**	70 522	4 282	**74 804**	99	105	**204**
Activities not adequately described .	1 176	98	**1 274**	8 864	361	**9 225**	1 367	1 530	**2 897**
Total . . .	126 461	2 616	**129 077**	186 292	6 082	**192 374**	23 013	9 266	**32 279**

† For notes, see pp. 272-294.

A Distribution by status and by industry (branch of economic activity)
Répartition suivant la situation dans la profession et par branche d'activité économique
Distribución según la categoría de ocupación y por rama de actividad económica

Others and status unknown / Autres et situation non définie / Otros y categoría no definida			TOTAL			Branche d'activité économique	Rama de actividad económica
Males / Hommes / Hombres	Females / Femmes / Mujeres	Total	Males / Hommes / Hombres	Females / Femmes / Mujeres	Total		
.	.	.	4 272 991	173 922	**4 446 913**	% 53.3	1. Agriculture, chasse, sylviculture et pêche	1. Agricultura, caza, silvicultura y pesca
.	.	.	17 269	443	**17 712**	0.2	2. Industries extractives	2. Minas y canteras
.	.	.	1 021 475	49 813	**1 071 288**	12.9	3. Industries manufacturières	3. Industrias manufactureras
.	.	.	50 108	973	**51 081**	0.6	4. Electricité, gaz et eau	4. Electricidad, gas y agua
.	.	.	203 877	1 723	**205 600**	2.5	5. Construction	5. Construcción
.	.	.	561 559	37 461	**599 020**	7.2	6. Commerce (gros et détail) ; restaurants, hôtels	6. Comercio (por mayor y por menor); restaurantes, hoteles
.	.	.	332 491	7 196	**339 687**	4.1	7. Transports, entrepôts et communications	7. Transportes, almacenamiento y comunicaciones
.	.	.	1 013 538	232 793	**1 246 331**	14.9	8. Banques, assur., affaires imm., services aux entreprises / 9. Services à la collectivité, services sociaux et personnels	8. Bancos, seguros, bienes inmuebles, servicios para empresas / 9. Servicios comunales, sociales y personales
.	.	.	238 532	117 569	**356 101**	4.3	0. Activités mal désignées / Personnes en quête d'emploi pour la première fois	0. Actividades no bien especif. / Personas en busca de trabajo por primera vez
.	.	.	7 711 840	621 893	**8 333 733**	100.0	Total	Total

						%	(CITI 1958)	(CIIU 1958)
20 850	28 850	**49 700**	91 300	93 780	**185 080**	84.1	Agriculture, sylviculture, chasse et pêche	Agricultura, silvicultura, caza y pesca
.	.	.	7 400	120	**7 520**	3.4	Industries extractives	Minas y canteras
.	.	.	3 680	515	**4 195**	1.9	Industries manufacturières	Industrias manufactureras
.	.	.	3 550	110	**3 660**	1.7	Construction	Construcción
.	.	.	120	15	**135**	0.1	Electricité, gaz, eau et services sanitaires	Electricidad, gas, agua y servicios sanitarios
.	.	.	5 700	2 460	**8 160**	3.7	Com., banq., assur., aff. imm.	Comercio
.	.	.	2 750	100	**2 850**	1.3	Transports, entrepôts et communications	Transportes, almacenaje y comunicaciones
.	.	.	4 600	2 400	**7 000**	3.2	Services	Servicios
.	.	.	900	500	**1 400**	0.6	Activités mal désignées	Actividades no bien especif.
20 850	28 850	**49 700**	120 000	100 000	**220 000**	100.0	Total	Total

						%	(CITI 1958)	(CIIU 1958)
324	8	**332**	140 517	3 036	**143 553**	37.1	Agriculture, sylviculture, chasse et pêche	Agricultura, silvicultura, caza y pesca
18	.	**18**	11 575	52	**11 627**	3.0	Industries extractives	Minas y canteras
242	11	**253**	18 763	7 784	**26 547**	6.8	Industries manufacturières	Industrias manufactureras
165	.	**165**	29 876	170	**30 046**	7.7	Construction	Construcción
11	.	**11**	5 571	77	**5 648**	1.5	Electricité, gaz, eau et services sanitaires	Electricidad, gas, agua y servicios sanitarios
31	2	**33**	24 605	209	**24 814**	6.4	Com., banq., assur., aff. imm.	Comercio
68	.	**68**	21 463	104	**21 567**	5.6	Transports, entrepôts et communications	Transportes, almacenaje y comunicaciones
175	60	**235**	73 023	4 624	**77 647**	20.0	Services	Servicios
31 034	1 820	**32 854**	42 441	3 809	**46 250**	11.9	Activités mal désignées	Actividades no bien especif.
32 068	1 901	**33 969**	367 834	19 865	**387 699**	100.0	Total	Total

‡ Voir notes pp. 272-294.

‡ Véanse las notas en las págs. 272-294.

2 Structure of the economically active population
Structure de la population active
Estructura de la población económicamente activa

Industry (Branch of economic activity)	Employers and workers on own account / Employeurs et personnes travaillant à leur propre compte / Empleadores y trabajadores por cuenta propia			Salaried employees and wage earners / Employés et ouvriers / Empleados y obreros			Family workers / Travailleurs familiaux / Trabajadores familiares		
	Males Hommes Hombres	Females Femmes Mujeres	Total	Males Hommes Hombres	Females Femmes Mujeres	Total	Males Hommes Hombres	Females Femmes Mujeres	Total
Maroc (20.VII.1971) †									
1. Agriculture, hunting, forestry and fishing	...	...	894 033	...	...	418 732	...	...	672 444
2. Mining and quarrying	...	...	3 481	...	...	39 891	...	...	974
3. Manufacturing	...	...	124 085	...	...	214 238	...	...	25 485
4. Electricity, gas and water	...	...	571	...	...	9 946	...	...	122
5. Construction	...	...	29 395	...	...	138 305	...	...	2 752
6. Wholesale and retail trade, restaurants and hotels	...	...	193 284	...	...	78 704	...	...	14 920
7. Transport, storage and communication	...	...	26 968	...	...	71 400	...	...	1 527
8. Financing, insurance, real estate and business services	...	...	2 597	...	...	2 881	...	...	93
9. Community, social and personal services	...	...	34 697	...	...	445 624	...	...	19 036
0. Activities not adequately described	...	...	29 832	...	...	65 173	...	...	6 688
Unemployed	...	...	...	...	...	...	...	...	...
Total ...	...	...	1 338 943	...	...	1 484 894	...	...	744 041
Mauritius									
Mauritius (30.VI.1972*)									
1. Agriculture, hunting, forestry and fishing	...	...	...	...	...	...	...	...	...
2. Mining and quarrying	...	...	...	...	...	...	...	...	...
3. Manufacturing	...	...	...	...	...	...	...	...	...
4. Electricity, gas and water	...	...	...	...	...	...	...	...	...
5. Construction	...	...	...	...	...	...	...	...	...
6. Wholesale and retail trade, restaurants and hotels	...	...	...	...	...	...	...	...	...
7. Transport, storage and communication	...	...	...	...	...	...	...	...	...
8. Financing, insurance, real estate and business services	...	...	...	...	...	...	...	...	...
9. Community, social and personal services	...	...	...	...	...	...	...	...	...
0. Activities not adequately described	...	...	...	...	...	...	...	...	...
Persons seeking work for the first time	.	.	.	.	.	.	.	.	.
Total ...	...	...	...	...	...	...	...	...	...
Mozambique (15.XII.1970) †									
1. Agriculture, hunting, forestry and fishing	817 816	424 309	1 242 125	437 731	34 076	471 807	155 922	264 786	420 708
2. Mining and quarrying	796	34	830	122 363	518	122 881	31	1	32
3. Manufacturing	18 880	658	19 538	125 396	10 648	136 044	365	33	398
4. Electricity, gas and water	35	.	35	2 412	77	2 489	2	1	3
5. Construction	2 665	8	2 673	78 286	438	78 724	60	1	61
6. Wholesale and retail trade, restaurants and hotels	14 899	3 285	18 184	57 879	6 140	64 019	163	104	267
7. Transport, storage and communication	1 397	3	1 400	60 182	1 117	61 299	12	1	13
8. Financing, insurance, real estate and business services	214	20	234	4 181	1 502	5 683	1	.	1
9. Community, social and personal services	4 182	451	4 633	197 755	20 942	218 697	191	25	216
0. Activities not adequately described	251	67	318	198	29	227	16	2	18
Unemployed	...	...	...	...	...	...	...	...	...
Total ...	861 135	428 835	1 289 970	1 086 383	75 487	1 161 870	156 763	264 954	421 717

† For notes, see pp. 272-294.

A Distribution by status and by industry (branch of economic activity)
Répartition suivant la situation dans la profession et par branche d'activité économique
Distribución según la categoría de ocupación y por rama de actividad económica

Others and status unknown / Autres et situation non définie / Otros y categoría no definida			TOTAL				Branche d'activité économique	Rama de actividad económica
Males / Hommes / Hombres	Females / Femmes / Mujeres	Total	Males / Hommes / Hombres	Females / Femmes / Mujeres	Total			
						%		
...	...	2 851	...	...	1 988 060	50.0	1. Agriculture, chasse, sylviculture et pêche	1. Agricultura, caza, silvicultura y pesca
...	...	194	...	...	44 540	1.1	2. Industries extractives	2. Minas y canteras
...	...	5 456	...	...	369 264	9.3	3. Industries manufacturières	3. Industrias manufactureras
...	...	171	...	...	10 810	0.3	4. Electricité, gaz et eau	4. Electricidad, gas y agua
...	...	1 243	...	...	171 695	4.3	5. Construction	5. Construcción
...	...	2 174	...	...	289 082	7.3	6. Commerce (gros et détail); restaurants, hôtels	6. Comercio (por mayor y por menor); restaurantes, hoteles
...	...	530	...	...	100 425	2.5	7. Transports, entrepôts et communications	7. Transportes, almacenamiento y comunicaciones
...	...	31	...	...	5 602	0.1	8. Banques, assur., affaires imm., services aux entreprises	8. Bancos, seguros, bienes inmuebles, servicios para empresas
...	...	2 371	...	...	501 728	12.6	9. Services à la collectivité, services sociaux et personnels	9. Servicios comunales, sociales y personales
...	...	53 719	...	...	155 412	3.9	0. Activités mal désignées	0. Actividades no bien especif.
...	...	343 900	...	...	343 900	8.6	Chômeurs	Desempleados
...	...	412 640	3 375 363	605 155	3 980 518	100.0	Total	Total

Others and status unknown / Autres et situation non définie / Otros y categoría no definida			TOTAL				Branche d'activité économique	Rama de actividad económica
Males / Hommes / Hombres	Females / Femmes / Mujeres	Total	Males / Hommes / Hombres	Females / Femmes / Mujeres	Total			
						%		
...	...	...	56 515	16 571	73 086	28.2	1. Agriculture, chasse, sylviculture et pêche	1. Agricultura, caza, silvicultura y pesca
...	...	...	99	28	127	—	2. Industries extractives	2. Minas y canteras
...	...	...	25 420	4 644	30 064	11.5	3. Industries manufacturières	3. Industrias manufactureras
...	...	...	3 072	91	3 163	1.2	4. Electricité, gaz et eau	4. Electricidad, gas y agua
...	...	...	21 256	159	21 415	8.2	5. Construction	5. Construcción
...	...	...	18 246	2 949	21 195	8.1	6. Commerce (gros et détail); restaurants, hôtels	6. Comercio (por mayor y por menor); restaurantes, hoteles
...	...	...	14 392	387	14 779	5.7	7. Transports, entrepôts et communications	7. Transportes, almacenamiento y comunicaciones
...	...	...	2 274	517	2 791	1.1	8. Banques, assur., affaires imm., services aux entreprises	8. Bancos, seguros, bienes inmuebles, servicios para empresas
...	...	...	35 351	19 215	54 566	20.9	9. Services à la collectivité, services sociaux et personnels	9. Servicios comunales, sociales y personales
...	...	...	1 521	402	1 923	0.7	0. Activités mal désignées	0. Actividades no bien especif.
...	...	...	30 742	6 751	37 493	14.4	Personnes en quête d'emploi pour la première fois	Personas en busca de trabajo por primera vez
...	...	...	208 888	51 714	260 602	100.0	Total	Total

Others and status unknown / Autres et situation non définie / Otros y categoría no definida			TOTAL				Branche d'activité économique	Rama de actividad económica
Males / Hommes / Hombres	Females / Femmes / Mujeres	Total	Males / Hommes / Hombres	Females / Femmes / Mujeres	Total			
						%		
277	55	332	1 411 746	723 226	2 134 972	73.4	1. Agriculture, chasse, sylviculture et pêche	1. Agricultura, caza, silvicultura y pesca
29	.	29	123 219	553	123 772	4.3	2. Industries extractives	2. Minas y canteras
16	.	16	144 657	11 339	155 996	5.4	3. Industries manufacturières	3. Industrias manufactureras
1	.	1	2 450	78	2 528	0.1	4. Electricité, gaz et eau	4. Electricidad, gas y agua
11	.	11	81 022	447	81 469	2.8	5. Construction	5. Construcción
9	3	12	72 950	9 532	82 482	2.8	6. Commerce (gros et détail); restaurants, hôtels	6. Comercio (por mayor y por menor); restaurantes, hoteles
11	1	12	61 602	1 122	62 724	2.2	7. Transports, entrepôts et communications	7. Transportes, almacenamiento y comunicaciones
1	.	1	4 397	1 522	5 919	0.2	8. Banques, assur., affaires imm., services aux entreprises	8. Bancos, seguros, bienes inmuebles, servicios para empresas
216	199	415	202 344	21 617	223 961	7.7	9. Services à la collectivité, services sociaux et personnels	9. Servicios comunales, sociales y personales
980	231	1 211	1 445	329	1 774	0.1	0. Activités mal désignées	0. Actividades no bien especif.
28 993	1 327	30 320	28 993	1 327	30 320	1.0	Chômeurs	Desempleados
30 544	1 816	32 360	2 134 825	771 092	2 905 917	100.0	Total	Total

† Voir notes pp. 272-294

† Véanse las notas en las págs. 272-294.

2 Structure of the economically active population
Structure de la population active
Estructura de la población económicamente activa

Industry (Branch of economic activity)	Employers and workers on own account *Employeurs et personnes travaillant à leur propre compte* Empleadores y trabajadores por cuenta propia			Salaried employees and wage earners *Employés et ouvriers* Empleados y obreros			Family workers *Travailleurs familiaux* Trabajadores familiares		
	Males *Hommes* Hombres	Females *Femmes* Mujeres	Total	Males *Hommes* Hombres	Females *Femmes* Mujeres	Total	Males *Hommes* Hombres	Females *Femmes* Mujeres	Total

Réunion (16.X.1967) †

(ISIC 1958)

Agriculture, forestry, hunting and fishing	7 966	443	8 409	16 839	1 081	17 920	1 364	126	1 490
Mining and quarrying	29	.	29	11	1	12	.	1	1
Manufacturing	762	286	1 048	5 513	536	6 049	23	14	37
Construction	691	9	700	13 183	205	13 388	20	.	20
Electricity, gas, water and sanitary services	3	.	3	570	56	626	.	.	.
Commerce	2 922	1 123	4 045	4 055	1 488	5 543	269	434	703
Transport, storage and communication	730	18	748	4 063	131	4 194	41	7	48
Services	487	173	660	11 140	16 812	27 952	8	11	19
Activities not adequately described	24	5	29	120	26	146	4	4	8
Total	13 614	2 057	15 671	55 494	20 336	75 830	1 729	597	2 326

Seychelles (5.V.1971)

1. Agriculture, hunting, forestry and fishing	1 177	91	1 268	2 485	1 338	3 823	45	31	76
2. Mining and quarrying	4	.	4	119	3	122	.	.	.
3. Manufacturing	296	180	476	389	92	481	11	1	12
4. Electricity, gas and water	8	.	8	92	4	96	.	.	.
5. Construction	172	4	176	3 663	361	4 024	5	.	5
6. Wholesale and retail trade, restaurants and hotels	283	63	346	364	342	706	28	49	77
7. Transport, storage and communication	87	1	88	855	38	893	1	.	1
8. Financing, insurance, real estate and business services	18	1	19	72	21	100	.	.	.
9. Community, social and personal services	125	199	324	1 605	2 760	4 365	4	15	19
0. Activities not adequately described	157	57	214	1 221	803	2 024	24	56	30
Total	2 327	596	2 923	10 865	5 769	16 634	118	152	270

Sierra Leone (1.IV.1963) †

(ISIC 1958)

Agriculture, forestry, hunting and fishing	262 727	28 450	291 177	5 295	221	5 516	136 899	268 464	405 363
Mining and quarrying	17 648	168	17 816	26 186	174	26 360	3 428	45	3 473
Manufacturing	23 956	4 396	28 352	7 544	310	7 854	3 579	1 412	4 991
Construction	3 056	26	3 082	12 403	141	12 544	536	13	549
Electricity, gas, water and sanitary services	64	22	86	2 095	43	2 138	7	15	22
Commerce	22 834	16 533	39 367	6 836	1 008	7 844	1 174	4 740	5 914
Transport, storage and communication	1 723	39	1 762	13 463	333	13 796	600	12	612
Services	2 324	564	2 888	21 466	3 768	25 234	269	213	482
Activities not adequately described	385	17	402	401	69	470	27	26	53
Total	334 717	50 215	384 932	95 689	6 067	101 756	146 519	274 940	421 459

† For notes, see pp. 272-294.

A Distribution by status and by industry (branch of economic activity)
Répartition suivant la situation dans la profession et par branche d'activité économique
Distribución según la categoría de ocupación y por rama de actividad económica

Others and status unknown / Autres et situation non définie / Otros y categoría no definida			TOTAL				Branche d'activité économique	Rama de actividad económica
Males / Hommes / Hombres	Females / Femmes / Mujeres	Total	Males / Hommes / Hombres	Females / Femmes / Mujeres	Total	%		
						%	(CITI 1958)	(CIIU 1958)
36	3	39	26 205	1 653	**27 858**	29.5	*Agriculture, sylviculture, chasse et pêche*	Agricultura, silvicultura, caza y pesca
.	.	.	40	2	**42**	—	*Industries extractives*	Minas y canteras
19	3	22	6 317	839	**7 156**	7.6	*Industries manufacturières*	Industrias manufactureras
17	.	17	13 911	214	**14 125**	15.0	*Construction*	Construcción
.	.	.	573	56	**629**	0.7	*Electricité, gaz, eau et services sanitaires*	Electricidad, gas, agua y servicios sanitarios
5	1	6	7 251	3 046	**10 297**	10.9	*Com., banq., assur., aff. imm.*	Comercio
2	.	2	4 836	156	**4 992**	5.3	*Transports, entrepôts et communications*	Transportes, almacenaje y comunicaciones
76	202	278	11 711	17 198	**28 909**	30.7	*Services*	Servicios
94	49	143	242	84	**326**	0.3	*Activités mal désignées*	Actividades no bien especif.
249	258	507	71 086	23 248	**94 334**	100.0	*Total*	Total
						%		
.	.	.	3 707	1 460	**5 167**	26.1	1. *Agriculture, chasse, sylviculture et pêche*	1. Agricultura, caza, silvicultura y pesca
.	.	.	123	3	**126**	0.6	2. *Industries extractives*	2. Minas y canteras
.	.	.	696	273	**969**	4.9	3 *Industries manufacturières*	3. Industrias manufactureras
.	.	.	100	4	**104**	0 5	4. *Electricité, gaz et eau*	4. Electricidad, gas y agua
.	.	.	3 840	365	**4 205**	21.2	5. *Construction*	5. Construcción
.	.	.	675	454	**1 129**	5.7	6. *Commerce (gros et détail); restaurants, hôtels*	6. Comercio (por mayor y por menor); restaurantes, hoteles
.	.	.	943	39	**982**	5.0	7. *Transports, entrepôts et communications*	7. Transportes, almacenamiento y comunicaciones
.	.	.	90	29	**119**	0.6	8. *Banques, assur., affaires imm., services aux entreprises*	8. Bancos, seguros, bienes inmuebles, servicios para empresas
.	.	.	1 734	2 974	**4 708**	23.7	9. *Services à la collectivité, services sociaux et personnels*	9. Servicios comunales, sociales y personales
.	.	.	1 402	916	**2 318**	11.7	0. *Activités mal désignées*	0. Actividades no bien especif.
.	.	.	13 310	6 517	**19 827**	100.0	*Total*	Total
						%	(CITI 1958)	(CIIU 1958)
...	...	...	404 921	297 135	**702 056**	74.8	*Agriculture, sylviculture, chasse et pêche*	Agricultura, silvicultura, caza y pesca
...	...	...	47 262	387	**47 649**	5.1	*Industries extractives*	Minas y canteras
...	...	...	35 079	6 118	**41 197**	4.4	*Industries manufacturières*	Industrias manufactureras
...	...	...	15 995	180	**16 175**	1.7	*Construction*	Construcción
...	...	...	2 166	80	**2 246**	0.2	*Electricité, gaz, eau et services sanitaires*	Electricidad, gas, agua y servicios sanitarios
...	...	...	30 844	22 281	**53 125**	5.7	*Com., banq., assur., aff. imm.*	Comercio
...	...	...	15 786	384	**16 170**	1.7	*Transports, entrepôts et communications*	Transportes, almacenaje y comunicaciones
...	...	...	24 059	4 545	**28 604**	3.1	*Services*	Servicios
27 248	2 342	**29 590**	28 061	2 454	**30 515**	3.3	*Activités mal désignées*	Actividades no bien especif.
27 248	2 342	**29 590**	604 173	333 564	**937 737**	100.0	*Total*	Total

‡ *Voir notes pp. 272-294.*

‡ Véanse las notas en las págs. 272-294.

POPULATION

2 Structure of the economically active population
Structure de la population active
Estructura de la población económicamente activa

Industry (Branch of economic activity)	Employers and workers on own account Employeurs et personnes travaillant à leur propre compte Empleadores y trabajadores por cuenta propia			Salaried employees and wage earners Employés et ouvriers Empleados y obreros			Family workers Travailleurs familiaux Trabajadores familiares		
	Males Hommes Hombres	Females Femmes Mujeres	Total	Males Hommes Hombres	Females Femmes Mujeres	Total	Males Hommes Hombres	Females Femmes Mujeres	Total

South Africa, Rep. of (6.V.1970) †

1. Agriculture, hunting, forestry and fishing	...	...	...	...	...	...	...	...	...
2. Mining and quarrying	...	...	...	...	...	...	...	...	...
3. Manufacturing	...	...	...	...	...	...	...	...	...
4. Electricity, gas and water	...	...	...	...	...	...	...	...	...
5. Construction	...	...	...	...	...	...	...	...	...
6. Wholesale and retail trade, restaurants and hotels	...	...	...	...	...	...	...	...	...
7. Transport, storage and communication	...	...	...	...	...	...	...	...	...
8. Financing, insurance, real estate and business services	...	...	...	...	...	...	...	...	...
9. Community, social and personal services	...	...	...	...	...	...	...	...	...
0. Activities not adequately described	...	...	...	...	...	...	...	...	...
Unemployed	...	...	...	...	...	...	...	...	...
Total	...	...	...	...	...	...	...	...	...

Tanzania

Tanganyika (26.VIII.1967*)
(ISIC 1958)

Agriculture, forestry, hunting and fishing	1 857 276	2 173 345	4 030 621	142 360	6 421	148 781	483 424	412 203	895 627
Mining and quarrying	693	22	715	4 161	75	4 236	35	.	35
Manufacturing	27 488	5 714	33 202	53 154	2 844	55 998	1 613	442	2 055
Construction	6 406	56	6 462	23 469	162	23 631	240	4	244
Electricity, gas, water and sanitary services	153	6	159	5 242	140	5 382	2	5	7
Commerce	36 304	3 984	40 288	26 795	2 079	28 874	1 994	695	2 689
Transport, storage and communication	2 893	44	2 937	40 768	590	41 358	150	15	165
Services	16 377	5 041	21 418	141 656	28 891	170 547	2 065	3 166	5 231
Activities not adequately described	9 513	8 159	17 672	17 779	2 873	20 652	4 877	4 341	9 218
Total	1 957 103	2 196 371	4 153 474	455 384	44 075	499 459	494 400	420 871	915 271

Zanzibar (26.VIII.1967*)
(ISIC 1958)

Agriculture, forestry, hunting and fishing	55 963	66 507	122 470	1 725	172	1 897	7 917	7 335	15 252
Mining and quarrying	9	.	9	17	.	17	.	.	.
Manufacturing	2 023	3 711	5 734	1 158	182	1 340	94	241	335
Construction	658	1	659	1 900	95	1 995	19	.	19
Electricity, gas, water and sanitary services	25	.	25	254	7	261	6	.	6
Commerce	4 071	768	4 839	1 572	143	1 715	158	31	189
Transport, storage and communication	519	13	532	1 769	49	1 818	14	.	14
Services	1 675	474	2 149	7 627	1 113	8 740	81	28	109
Activities not adequately described	203	76	279	429	41	470	36	26	62
Total	65 146	71 550	136 696	16 451	1 802	18 253	8 325	7 661	15 986

† For notes, see pp. 272-294.

A Distribution by status and by industry (branch of economic activity)
Répartition suivant la situation dans la profession et par branche d'activité économique
Distribución según la categoría de ocupación y por rama de actividad económica

Males Hommes Hombres	Females Femmes Mujeres	Total	Males Hommes Hombres	Females Femmes Mujeres	Total	%	Branche d'activité économique	Rama de actividad económica
...	...	...	1 567 930	671 260	**2 239 190**	*28.0*	1. *Agriculture, chasse, sylviculture et pêche*	1. Agricultura, caza, silvicultura y pesca
...	...	...	670 230	5 910	**676 140**	*8.5*	2. *Industries extractives*	2. Minas y canteras
...	...	...	810 190	213 530	**1 023 720**	*12.8*	3. *Industries manufacturières*	3. Industrias manufactureras
...	...	...	48 140	1 550	**49 690**	*0.6*	4. *Electricité, gaz et eau*	4. Electricidad, gas y agua
...	...	...	437 260	9 100	**446 360**	*5.6*	5. *Construction*	5. Construcción
...	...	...	519 180	196 890	**716 070**	*9.0*	6. *Commerce (gros et détail) ; restaurants, hôtels*	6. Comercio (por mayor y por menor); restaurantes, hoteles
...	...	...	310 850	27 470	**338 320**	*4.2*	7. *Transports, entrepôts et communications*	7. Transportes, almacenamiento y comunicaciones
...	...	...	115 160	75 220	**190 380**	*2.4*	8. *Banques, assur., affaires imm., services aux entreprises*	8. Bancos, seguros, bienes inmuebles, servicios para empresas
...	...	...	590 380	983 610	**1 573 990**	*19.7*	9. *Services à la collectivité, services sociaux et personnels*	9. Servicios comunales, sociales y personales
...	...	...	130 630	172 440	**303 070**	*3.8*	0. *Activités mal désignées*	0. Actividades no bien especif.
...	...	...	171 450	257 840	**429 290**	*5.4*	*Chômeurs*	Desempleados
...	...	...	5 371 400	2 614 820	**7 986 220**	*100.0*	*Total*	Total

Males Hommes Hombres	Females Femmes Mujeres	Total	Males Hommes Hombres	Females Femmes Mujeres	Total	%	(CITI 1958)	(CIIU 1958)
1 016	819	**1 835**	2 484 076	2 592 788	**5 076 864**	*91.2*	*Agriculture, sylviculture, chasse et pêche*	Agricultura silvicultura, caza y pesca
3	2	**5**	4 892	99	**4 991**	*0.1*	*Industries extractives*	Minas y canteras
119	67	**186**	82 374	9 067	**91 441**	*1.6*	*Industries manufacturières*	Industrias manufactureras
54	.	**54**	30 169	222	**30 391**	*0.5*	*Construction*	Construcción
22	.	**22**	5 419	151	**5 570**	*0.1*	*Electricité, gaz, eau et services sanitaires*	Electricidad, gas, agua y servicios sanitarios
173	16	**189**	65 266	6 774	**72 040**	*1.3*	*Com., banq., assur., aff. imm.*	Comercio
.	.	.	43 811	649	**44 460**	*0.8*	*Transports, entrepôts et communications*	Transportes, almacenaje y comunicaciones
196	87	**283**	160 294	37 185	**197 479**	*3.5*	*Services*	Servicios
2 722	2 556	**5 278**	34 891	17 929	**52 820**	*0.9*	*Activités mal désignées*	Actividades no bien especif.
4 305	3 547	**7 852**	2 911 192	2 664 864	**5 576 056**	*100.0*	*Total*	Total

Males Hommes Hombres	Females Femmes Mujeres	Total	Males Hommes Hombres	Females Femmes Mujeres	Total	%	(CITI 1958)	(CIIU 1958)
7	3	**10**	65 612	74 017	**139 629**	*81.6*	*Agriculture, sylviculture, chasse et pêche*	Agricultura silvicultura, caza y pesca
.	.	.	26	.	**26**	*—*	*Industries extractives*	Minas y canteras
10	4	**14**	3 285	4 138	**7 423**	*4.3*	*Industries manufacturières*	Industrias manufactureras
9	.	**9**	2 586	96	**2 682**	*1.6*	*Construction*	Construcción
.	.	.	285	7	**292**	*0.2*	*Electricité, gaz, eau et services sanitaires*	Electricidad, gas, agua y servicios sanitarios
21	.	**21**	5 822	942	**6 764**	*4.0*	*Com., banq., assur., aff. imm.*	Comercio
8	.	**8**	2 310	62	**2 372**	*1.4*	*Transports, entrepôts et communications*	Transportes, almacenaje y comunicaciones
16	3	**19**	9 399	1 618	**11 017**	*6.4*	*Services*	Servicios
15	9	**24**	683	152	**835**	*0.5*	*Activités mal désignées*	Actividades no bien especif.
86	19	**105**	90 008	81 032	**171 040**	*100.0*	*Total*	Total

† *Voir notes pp. 272-294.*

† Véanse las notas en las págs. 272-294.

2 Structure of the economically active population
Structure de la population active
Estructura de la población económicamente activa

Industry (Branch of economic activity)	Employers and workers on own account _Employeurs et personnes travaillant à leur propre compte_ Empleadores y trabajadores por cuenta propia			Salaried employees and wage earners _Employés et ouvriers_ Empleados y obreros			Family workers _Travailleurs familiaux_ Trabajadores familiares		
	Males _Hommes_ Hombres	Females _Femmes_ Mujeres	Total	Males _Hommes_ Hombres	Females _Femmes_ Mujeres	Total	Males _Hommes_ Hombres	Females _Femmes_ Mujeres	Total

Tunisie (3.V.1966) †

(ISIC 1958)									
Agriculture, forestry, hunting and fishing	...	...	...	...	...	...	...	...	...
Mining and quarrying	...	...	...	...	...	...	...	...	...
Manufacturing	...	...	...	...	...	...	...	...	...
Construction	...	...	...	...	...	...	...	...	...
Electricity, gas, water and sanitary services	...	...	...	...	...	...	...	...	...
Commerce	...	...	...	...	...	...	...	...	...
Transport, storage and communication	...	...	...	...	...	...	...	...	...
Services	...	...	...	...	...	...	...	...	...
Activities not adequately described .	...	...	...	...	...	...	...	...	...
Persons seeking work for the first time	.	.	.	.	.	.	.	.	.
Total . . .	263 695	14 639	**278 334**	632 955	42 533	**675 488**	31 480	2 825	**34 305**

Zambia (22-30.VIII.1969 *) †

Agriculture, hunting, forestry and fishing	...	...	...	...	...	...	...	...	...
Mining and quarrying	...	...	...	...	...	...	...	...	...
Manufacturing	...	...	...	...	...	...	...	...	...
Construction	...	...	...	...	...	...	...	...	...
Wholesale and retail trade	...	...	...	...	...	...	...	...	...
Transport and communication	...	...	...	...	...	...	...	...	...
Services	...	...	...	...	...	...	...	...	...
Activities not adequately described . .	...	...	...	...	...	...	...	...	...
Persons seeking work	.	.	.	.	.	.	.	.	...
Total . . .	...	...	...	...	...	...	...	...	...

† For notes, see pp. 272-294.

A Distribution by status and by industry (branch of economic activity)
Répartition suivant la situation dans la profession et par branche d'activité économique
Distribución según la categoría de ocupación y por rama de actividad económica

Others and status unknown / Autres et situation non définie / Otros y categoría no definida			TOTAL				Branche d'activité économique	Rama de actividad económica
Males / Hommes / Hombres	Females / Femmes / Mujeres	Total	Males / Hommes / Hombres	Females / Femmes / Mujeres	Total			
						%	(CITI 1958)	(CIIU 1958)
...	...	...	440 304	7 992	448 296	41.0	Agriculture, sylviculture, chasse et pêche	Agricultura, silvicultura, caza y pesca
...	...	...	23 393	162	23 555	2.2	Industries extractives	Minas y canteras
...	...	...	79 351	24 231	103 582	9.5	Industries manufacturières	Industrias manufactureras
...	...	...	59 058	305	59 363	5.4	Construction	Construcción
...	...	...	16 896	214	17 110	1.6	Electricité, gaz, eau et services sanitaires	Electricidad, gas, agua y servicios sanitarios
...	...	...	71 406	2 099	73 505	6.7	Com., banq., assur., aff. imm.	Comercio
...	...	...	37 546	1 157	38 703	3.5	Transports, entrepôts et communications	Transportes, almacenaje y comunicaciones
...	...	...	191 238	21 934	213 172	19.5	Services	Servicios
...	...	...	71 811	3 794	75 605	6.9	Activités mal désignées	Actividades no bien especif.
...	...	...	36 263	4 581	40 844	3.7	Personnes en quête d'emploi pour la première fois	Personas en busca de trabajo por primera vez
99 136	6 472	105 608	1 027 266	66 469	1 093 735	100.0	Total	Total
						%		
...	...	...	154 721	21 569	176 290	15.2	Agriculture, chasse, sylviculture et pêche	Agricultura, caza, silvicultura y pesca
...	...	...	46 829	2 151	48 980	4.2	Industries extractives	Minas y canteras
...	...	...	28 355	2 319	30 674	2.6	Industries manufacturières	Industrias manufactureras
...	...	...	49 781	1 318	51 099	4.4	Construction	Construcción
...	...	...	30 341	5 183	35 524	3.1	Commerce (gros et détail)	Comercio (por mayor y por menor)
...	...	...	36 250	1 318	37 568	3.2	Transports et communications	Transportes y comunicaciones
...	...	...	140 814	22 142	162 956	14.1	Services	Servicios
...	...	...	120 409	92 756	213 165	18.4	Activités mal désignées	Actividades no bien especif.
...	...	...	207 831	195 611	403 442	34.8	Personnes en quête d'emploi	Personas en busca de trabajo
...	...	...	815 331	344 367	1 159 698	100.0	Total	Total

† Voir notes pp. 272-294.

† Véanse las notas en las págs. 272-294.

POPULATION

2 Structure of the economically active population
Structure de la population active
Estructura de la población económicamente activa

Industry (Branch of economic activity)	Employers and workers on own account / Employeurs et personnes travaillant à leur propre compte / Empleadores y trabajadores por cuenta propia			Salaried employees and wage earners / Employés et ouvriers / Empleados y obreros			Family workers / Travailleurs familiaux / Trabajadores familiares		
	Males Hommes Hombres	Females Femmes Mujeres	Total	Males Hommes Hombres	Females Femmes Mujeres	Total	Males Hommes Hombres	Females Femmes Mujeres	Total

Antigua (7.IV.1970)

Industry									
1. Agriculture, hunting, forestry and fishing	...	...	...	...	...	...	...	...	...
2. Mining and quarrying	...	...	...	...	...	...	...	...	...
3. Manufacturing	...	...	...	...	...	...	...	...	...
4. Electricity, gas and water	...	...	...	...	...	...	...	...	...
5. Construction	...	...	...	...	...	...	...	...	...
6. Wholesale and retail trade, restaurants and hotels	...	...	...	...	...	...	...	...	...
7. Transport, storage and communication	...	...	...	...	...	...	...	...	...
8. Financing, insurance, real estate and business services	...	...	...	...	...	...	...	...	...
9. Community, social and personal services	...	...	...	...	...	...	...	...	...
0. Activities not adequately described	...	...	...	...	...	...	...	...	...
Total ...	2 035	791	**2 826**	10 077	6 051	**16 128**	98	44	**142**

Antilles néerlandaises (1.I.1972) ‡

Industry									
1. Agriculture, hunting, forestry and fishing	...	...	...	...	...	...	...	...	...
2. Mining and quarrying	...	...	...	...	...	...	...	...	...
3. Manufacturing	...	...	...	...	...	...	...	...	...
4. Electricity, gas and water	...	...	...	...	...	...	...	...	...
5. Construction	...	...	...	...	...	...	...	...	...
6. Wholesale and retail trade, restaurants and hotels	...	...	...	...	...	...	...	...	...
7. Transport, storage and communication	...	...	...	...	...	...	...	...	...
8. Financing, insurance, real estate and business services	...	...	...	...	...	...	...	...	...
9. Community, social and personal services	...	...	...	...	...	...	...	...	...
0. Activities not adequately described	...	...	...	...	...	...	...	...	...
Persons seeking work for the first time	.	.	.	.	.	.	.	.	.
Unemployed	...	...	...	...	...	...	...	...	...
Total ...	3 304	679	**3 983**	36 433	17 930	**54 363**	189	510	**699**

‡ For notes, see pp. 272-294.

A Distribution by status and by industry (branch of economic activity)
Répartition suivant la situation dans la profession et par branche d'activité économique
Distribución según la categoría de ocupación y por rama de actividad económica

Others and status unknown / Autres et situation non définie / Otros y categoría no definida			TOTAL				Branche d'activité économique	Rama de actividad económica
Males / Hommes / Hombres	Females / Femmes / Mujeres	Total	Males / Hommes / Hombres	Females / Femmes / Mujeres	Total	%		
...	...	...	1 709	740	2 449	10.6	1. Agriculture, chasse, sylviculture et pêche	1. Agricultura, caza, silvicultura y pesca
...	...	...	52	7	59	0.3	2. Industries extractives	2. Minas y canteras
...	...	...	1 169	511	1 680	7.3	3. Industries manufacturières	3. Industrias manufactureras
...	...	...	385	30	415	1.8	4. Electricité, gaz et eau	4. Electricidad, gas y agua
...	...	...	2 805	67	2 872	12.5	5. Construction	5. Construcción
...	...	...	1 798	1 614	3 412	14.8	6. Commerce (gros et détail) ; restaurants, hôtels	6. Comercio (por mayor y por menor); restaurantes, hoteles
...	...	...	1 695	252	1 947	8.4	7. Transports, entrepôts et communications	7. Transportes, almacenamiento y comunicaciones
...	...	...	621	628	1 249	5.4	8. Banques, assur., affaires imm., services aux entreprises	8. Bancos, seguros, bienes inmuebles, servicios para empresas
...	...	...	2 605	4 003	6 608	28.6	9. Services à la collectivité, services sociaux et personnels	9. Servicios comunales, sociales y personales
...	...	...	1 436	940	2 376	10.3	0. Activités mal désignées	0. Actividades no bien especif.
2 065	1 906	3 971	14 275	8 792	23 067	100.0	Total	Total

Others and status unknown / Autres et situation non définie / Otros y categoría no definida			TOTAL				Branche d'activité économique	Rama de actividad económica
Males / Hommes / Hombres	Females / Femmes / Mujeres	Total	Males / Hommes / Hombres	Females / Femmes / Mujeres	Total	%		
...	...	...	550	38	588	0.8	1. Agriculture, chasse, sylviculture et pêche	1. Agricultura, caza, silvicultura y pesca
...	...	...	421	17	438	0.6	2. Industries extractives	2. Minas y canteras
...	...	...	8 335	2 214	10 549	14.4	3. Industries manufacturières	3. Industrias manufactureras
...	...	...	1 129	82	1 211	1.7	4. Electricité, gaz et eau	4. Electricidad, gas y agua
...	...	...	5 491	214	5 705	7.8	5. Construction	5. Construcción
...	...	...	8 587	6 914	15 501	21.1	6. Commerce (gros et détail) ; restaurants, hôtels	6. Comercio (por mayor y por menor); restaurantes, hoteles
...	...	...	4 523	601	5 124	7.0	7. Transports, entrepôts et communications	7. Transportes, almacenamiento y comunicaciones
...	...	...	1 409	1 082	2 491	3.4	8. Banques, assur., affaires imm., services aux entreprises	8. Bancos, seguros, bienes inmuebles, servicios para empresas
...	...	...	10 648	7 788	18 436	25.1	9. Services à la collectivité, services sociaux et personnels	9. Servicios comunales, sociales y personales
...	...	...	1 044	1 487	2 531	3.5	0. Activités mal désignées	0. Actividades no bien especif.
...	...	...	1 822	2 134	3 956	5.4	Personnes en quête d'emploi pour la première fois	Personas en busca de trabajo por primera vez
...	...	...	3 902	2 838	6 740	9.2	Chômeurs	Desempleados
7 935	6 290	14 225	47 861	25 409	73 270	100.0	Total	Total

✝ *Voir notes pp. 272-294.* ✝ Véanse las notas en las págs. 272-294.

POPULATION

2 Structure of the economically active population
Structure de la population active
Estructura de la población económicamente activa

Industry (Branch of economic activity)	Employers and workers on own account Employeurs et personnes travaillant à leur propre compte Empleadores y trabajadores por cuenta propia			Salaried employees and wage earners Employés et ouvriers Empleados y obreros			Family workers Travailleurs familiaux Trabajadores familiares		
	Males Hommes Hombres	Females Femmes Mujeres	Total	Males Hommes Hombres	Females Femmes Mujeres	Total	Males Hommes Hombres	Females Femmes Mujeres	Total

Argentina (30.IX.1970) ‡

1. Agriculture, hunting, forestry and fishing	416 050	25 650	**441 700**	671 250	36 400	**707 650**	132 200	24 300	**156 500**
2. Mining and quarrying	950	.	**950**	41 050	1 750	**42 800**	100	.	**100**
3. Manufacturing	184 000	93 500	**277 500**	1 139 900	306 500	**1 446 400**	10 150	7 200	**17 350**
4. Electricity, gas and water	1 100	.	**1 100**	88 350	5 650	**94 000**	50	.	**50**
5. Construction	161 000	1 100	**162 100**	518 700	10 850	**529 550**	6 500	100	**6 600**
6. Wholesale and retail trade, restaurants and hotels	480 450	110 250	**590 700**	494 550	192 650	**687 200**	21 750	10 500	**32 250**
7. Transport, storage and communication	109 500	4 500	**114 000**	418 700	45 600	**464 300**	3 250	1 000	**4 250**
8. Financing, insurance, real estate and business services	44 250	7 050	**51 300**	137 800	61 050	**198 850**	350	200	**550**
9. Community, social and personal services	170 950	67 650	**238 600**	781 200	1 016 700	**1 797 900**	5 500	18 850	**24 350**
0. Activities not adequately described	85 050	13 900	**98 950**	328 850	83 000	**411 850**	28 950	14 900	**43 850**
Total . . .	1 653 300	323 600	**1 976 900**	4 620 350	1 760 150	**6 380 500**	208 800	77 050	**285 850**

Bahamas (7.IV.1970 *)

1. Agriculture, hunting, forestry and fishing	2 056	1 013	**3 069**	1 226	373	**1 599**	38	85	**123**
2. Mining and quarrying	6	.	**6**	56	16	**72**	.	.	**.**
3. Manufacturing	267	827	**1 094**	2 215	512	**2 727**	.	3	**3**
4. Electricity, gas and water	76	1	**77**	1 133	117	**1 250**	2	.	**2**
5. Construction	1 146	13	**1 159**	7 043	258	**7 301**	7	2	**9**
6. Wholesale and retail trade, restaurants and hotels	691	538	**1 229**	7 819	7 073	**14 892**	8	28	**36**
7. Transport, storage and communication	809	11	**820**	3 449	1 242	**4 691**	.	1	**1**
8. Financing, insurance, real estate and business services	203	22	**225**	2 787	2 317	**5 104**	.	2	**2**
9. Community, social and personal services	713	631	**1 344**	6 993	8 502	**15 495**	9	25	**34**
0. Activities not adequately described / Unemployed	15	9	**24**	3 020	4 357	**7 377**	1	25	**26**
Total . . .	5 982	3 065	**9 047**	35 741	24 767	**60 508**	65	171	**236**

Barbados (7.IV.1970 *) ‡

1. Agriculture, hunting, forestry and fishing	...	...	...	...	...	...	...	...	...
2. Mining and quarrying	...	...	...	...	...	...	...	...	...
3. Manufacturing	...	...	...	...	...	...	...	...	...
4. Electricity, gas and water	...	...	...	...	...	...	...	...	...
5. Construction	...	...	...	...	...	...	...	...	...
6. Wholesale and retail trade, restaurants and hotels	...	...	...	...	...	...	...	...	...
7. Transport, storage and communication	...	...	...	...	...	...	...	...	...
8. Financing, insurance, real estate and business services / 9. Community, social and personal services	...	...	...	...	...	...	...	...	...
0. Activities not adequately described	...	...	...	...	...	...	...	...	...
Total . . .	...	...	...	...	...	...	...	...	...

‡ For notes, see pp. 272-294.

A Distribution by status and by industry (branch of economic activity)
Répartition suivant la situation dans la profession et par branche d'activité économique
Distribución según la categoría de ocupación y por rama de actividad económica

Others and status unknown / Autres et situation non définie / Otros y categoría no definida			TOTAL				Branche d'activité économique	Rama de actividad económica
Males / Hommes / Hombres	Females / Femmes / Mujeres	Total	Males / Hommes / Hombres	Females / Femmes / Mujeres	Total	%		
23 650	1 600	**25 250**	1 243 150	87 950	**1 331 100**	*14.8*	1. *Agriculture, chasse, sylviculture et pêche*	1. Agricultura, caza, silvicultura y pesca
750	.	**750**	42 850	1 750	**44 600**	*0.5*	2. *Industries extractives*	2. Minas y canteras
23 450	6 550	**30 000**	1 357 500	413 750	**1 771 250**	*19.7*	3. *Industries manufacturières*	3. Industrias manufactureras
1 250	150	**1 400**	90 750	5 800	**96 550**	*1.1*	4. *Electricité, gaz et eau*	4. Electricidad, gas y agua
12 850	200	**13 050**	699 050	12 250	**711 300**	*7.9*	5. *Construction*	5. Construcción
11 750	8 900	**14 650**	1 008 500	316 300	**1 324 800**	*14.7*	6. *Commerce (gros et détail); restaurants, hôtels*	6. Comercio (por mayor y por menor); restaurantes, hoteles
10 000	700	**10 700**	541 450	51 800	**593 250**	*6.6*	7. *Transports, entrepôts et communications*	7. Transportes, almacenamiento y comunicaciones
1 550	400	**1 950**	183 950	68 700	**252 650**	*2.8*	8. *Banques, assur., affaires imm., services aux entreprises*	8. Bancos, seguros, bienes inmuebles, servicios para empresas
15 900	22 000	**37 900**	973 550	1 125 200	**2 098 750**	*23.2*	9. *Services à la collectivité, services sociaux et personnels*	9. Servicios comunales, sociales y personales
138 900	93 650	**232 550**	581 750	205 450	**787 200**	*8.7*	0. *Activités mal désignées*	0. Actividades no bien especif.
240 050	128 150	**368 200**	6 722 500	2 288 950	**9 011 450**	*100.0*	*Total*	Total

Males	Females	Total	Males	Females	Total	%	Branche d'activité économique	Rama de actividad económica
.	.	.	3 320	1 471	**4 791**	*6.9*	1. *Agriculture, chasse, sylviculture et pêche*	1. Agricultura, caza, silvicultura y pesca
.	.	.	62	16	**78**	*0.1*	2. *Industries extractives*	2. Minas y canteras
.	.	.	2 482	1 342	**3 824**	*5.5*	3. *Industries manufacturières*	3. Industrias manufactureras
.	.	.	1 211	118	**1 329**	*1.9*	4. *Electricité, gaz et eau*	4. Electricidad, gas y agua
.	.	.	8 196	273	**8 469**	*12.1*	5. *Construction*	5. Construcción
.	.	.	8 518	7 639	**16 157**	*23.2*	6. *Commerce (gros et détail); restaurants, hôtels*	6. Comercio (por mayor y por menor); restaurantes, hoteles
.	.	.	4 258	1 254	**5 512**	*7.9*	7. *Transports, entrepôts et communications*	7. Transportes, almacenamiento y comunicaciones
.	.	.	2 990	2 341	**5 331**	*7.6*	8. *Banques, assur., affaires imm., services aux entreprises*	8. Bancos, seguros, bienes inmuebles, servicios para empresas
.	.	.	7 715	9 158	**16 873**	*24.2*	9. *Services à la collectivité, services sociaux et personnels*	9. Servicios comunales, sociales y personales
.	.	.	3 036	4 391	**7 427**	*10.6*	{ 0. *Activités mal désignées* / *Chômeurs*	{ 0. Actividades no bien especif. / Desempleados
.	.	.	41 788	28 003	**69 791**	*100.0*	*Total*	Total

Males	Females	Total	Males	Females	Total	%	Branche d'activité économique	Rama de actividad económica
...	...	...	8 553	5 068	**13 621**	*16.2*	1. *Agriculture, chasse, sylviculture et pêche*	1. Agricultura, caza, silvicultura y pesca
...	...	...	283	19	**302**	*0.4*	2. *Industries extractives*	2. Minas y canteras
...	...	...	7 814	4 442	**12 256**	*14.6*	3. *Industries manufacturières*	3. Industrias manufactureras
...	...	...	1 013	100	**1 113**	*1.3*	4. *Electricité, gaz et eau*	4. Electricidad, gas y agua
...	...	...	10 388	290	**10 678**	*12.7*	5. *Construction*	5. Construcción
...	...	...	6 026	6 069	**12 095**	*14.4*	6. *Commerce (gros et détail); restaurants, hôtels*	6. Comercio (por mayor y por menor); restaurantes, hoteles
...	...	...	4 050	567	**4 617**	*5.5*	7. *Transports, entrepôts et communications*	7. Transportes, almacenamiento y comunicaciones
...	...	...	10 567	15 024	**25 591**	*30.5*	{ 8. *Banques, assur., affaires imm., services aux entreprises* / 9. *Services à la collectivité, services sociaux et personnels*	{ 8. Bancos, seguros, bienes inmuebles, servicios para empresas / 9. Servicios comunales, sociales y personales
...	...	...	2 363	1 345	**3 708**	*4.4*	0. *Activités mal désignées*	0. Actividades no bien especif.
...	...	...	51 057	32 924	**83 981**	*100.0*	*Total*	Total

† *Voir notes pp. 272-294.*

† *Véanse las notas en las págs. 272-294.*

2 Structure of the economically active population
Structure de la population active
Estructura de la población económicamente activa

Industry (Branch of economic activity)	Employers and workers on own account Employeurs et personnes travaillant à leur propre compte Empleadores y trabajadores por cuenta propia			Salaried employees and wage earners Employés et ouvriers Empleados y obreros			Family workers Travailleurs familiaux Trabajadores familiares		
	Males Hommes Hombres	Females Femmes Mujeres	Total	Males Hommes Hombres	Females Femmes Mujeres	Total	Males Hommes Hombres	Females Femmes Mujeres	Total

Bermuda (25.X.1970)

(ISIC 1958)

Industry	M	F	T	M	F	T	M	F	T
Agriculture, forestry, hunting and fishing / Mining and quarrying	...	...	...	...	...	...	...	...	...
Manufacturing	...	...	...	...	...	...	...	...	...
Construction	...	...	...	...	...	...	...	...	...
Electricity, gas, water and sanitary services	...	...	...	...	...	...	...	...	...
Commerce	...	...	...	...	...	...	...	...	...
Transport, storage and communication	...	...	...	...	...	...	...	...	...
Services	...	...	...	...	...	...	...	...	...
Activities not adequately described	...	...	...	...	...	...	...	...	...
Total	817	195	**1 012**	15 568	10 685	**26 253**	9	34	**43**

Brésil (1.IX.1970) ✝

Industry	M	F	T	M	F	T	M	F	T
1. Agriculture, hunting, forestry and fishing	6 730 545	448 677	**7 179 222**	3 115 045	214 775	**3 329 820**	1 986 825	594 179	**2 581 004**
2. Mining and quarrying	45 211	779	**45 990**	125 232	2 311	**127 543**	1 833	58	**1 891**
3. Manufacturing	279 366	68 969	**348 335**	2 341 176	536 074	**2 877 250**	12 452	3 768	**16 220**
4. Electricity, gas and water	1 624	14	**1 638**	147 885	8 853	**156 738**	52	.	**52**
5. Construction	351 186	636	**351 822**	1 348 938	14 377	**1 363 315**	4 490	53	**4 543**
6. Wholesale and retail trade, restaurants and hotels	926 439	96 067	**1 022 506**	949 678	267 107	**1 216 785**	17 008	7 209	**24 217**
7. Transport, storage and communication	264 553	693	**265 246**	914 445	60 956	**975 401**	3 645	82	**3 727**
8. Financing, insurance, real estate and business services	26 816	976	**27 792**	329 424	76 704	**406 128**	78	31	**109**
9. Community, social and personal services	581 139	527 600	**1 108 739**	2 304 334	3 046 335	**5 350 669**	30 676	26 202	**56 878**
0. Activities not adequately described	44 206	44 687	**88 893**	319 869	70 034	**389 903**	179 450	46 231	**225 681**
Total	9 251 085	1 189 098	**10 440 183**	11 896 026	4 297 526	**16 193 552**	2 236 509	677 813	**2 914 322**

✝ For notes, see pp. 272-294.

Distribution by status and by industry (branch of economic activity)
Répartition suivant la situation dans la profession et par branche d'activité économique
Distribución según la categoría de ocupación y por rama de actividad económica

Others and status unknown / Autres et situation non définie / Otros y categoría no definida			TOTAL				Branche d'activité économique	Rama de actividad económica
Males / Hommes / Hombres	Females / Femmes / Mujeres	Total	Males / Hommes / Hombres	Females / Femmes / Mujeres	Total	%		
							(CITI 1958)	(CIIU 1958)
...	...	...	404	24	**428**	*1.6*	*Agriculture, sylviculture, chasse et pêche*	Agricultura, silvicultura, caza y pesca
							Industries extractives	Minas y canteras
...	...	...	1 342	423	**1 765**	*6.5*	*Industries manufacturières*	Industrias manufactureras
...	...	...	3 486	78	**3 564**	*13.0*	*Construction*	Construcción
...	...	...	360	87	**447**	*1.6*	*Electricité, gaz, eau et services sanitaires*	Electricidad, gas, agua y servicios sanitarios
...	...	...	2 758	3 198	**5 956**	*21.8*	*Com., banq., assur., aff. imm.*	Comercio
...	...	...	2 116	666	**2 782**	*10.2*	*Transports, entrepôts et communications*	Transportes, almacenaje y comunicaciones
...	...	...	5 835	6 381	**12 216**	*44.7*	*Services*	Servicios
...	...	...	101	60	**161**	*0.6*	*Activités mal désignées*	Actividades no bien especif.
8	3	**11**	16 402	10 917	**27 319**	*100.0*	*Total*	Total

Others and status unknown			TOTAL				Branche d'activité économique	Rama de actividad económica
Males	Females	Total	Males	Females	Total	%		
284	28	**312**	11 832 699	1 257 659	**13 090 358**	*44.3*	*1. Agriculture, chasse, sylviculture et pêche*	1. Agricultura, caza, silvicultura y pesca
.	.	.	172 276	3 148	**175 424**	*0.6*	*2. Industries extractives*	2. Minas y canteras
56	.	**56**	2 633 050	608 811	**3 241 861**	*11.0*	*3. Industries manufacturières*	3. Industrias manufactureras
.	.	.	149 561	8 867	**158 428**	*0.5*	*4. Electricité, gaz et eau*	4. Electricidad, gas y agua
34	.	**34**	1 704 648	15 066	**1 719 714**	*5.8*	*5. Construction*	5. Construcción
27	4	**31**	1 893 152	370 387	**2 263 539**	*7.7*	*6. Commerce (gros et détail) ; restaurants, hôtels*	6. Comercio (por mayor y por menor); restaurantes, hoteles
17	4	**21**	1 182 660	61 735	**1 244 395**	*4.2*	*7. Transports, entrepôts et communications*	7. Transportes, almacenamiento y comunicaciones
11	.	**11**	356 329	77 711	**434 040**	*1.5*	*8. Banques, assur., affaires imm., services aux entreprises*	8. Bancos, seguros, bienes inmuebles, servicios para empresas
31	13	**44**	2 916 180	3 600 150	**6 516 330**	*22.0*	*9. Services à la collectivité, services sociaux et personnels*	9. Servicios comunales, sociales y personales
7 697	961	**8 658**	551 222	161 913	**713 135**	*2.4*	*0. Activités mal désignées*	0. Actividades no bien especif.
8 157	1 010	**9 167**	23 391 777	6 165 447	**29 557 224**	*100.0*	*Total*	Total

† *Voir notes pp. 272-294.*

† Véanse las notas en las págs. 272-294.

2 Structure of the economically active population
Structure de la population active
Estructura de la población económicamente activa

Industry (Branch of economic activity)	Employers and workers on own account — Employeurs et personnes travaillant à leur propre compte — Empleadores y trabajadores por cuenta propia			Salaried employees and wage earners — Employés et ouvriers — Empleados y obreros			Family workers — Travailleurs familiaux — Trabajadores familiares		
	Males Hommes Hombres	Females Femmes Mujeres	Total	Males Hommes Hombres	Females Femmes Mujeres	Total	Males Hommes Hombres	Females Femmes Mujeres	Total
Canada (V.1975) ǂ									
1. Agriculture, hunting, forestry and fishing	301 000	—	310 000	153 000	26 000	179 000	56 000	62 000	119 000
2. Mining and quarrying	—	—	—	125 000	11 000	136 000	—	—	—
3. Manufacturing	31 000	—	34 000	1 452 000	467 000	1 920 000	—	—	—
4. Electricity, gas and water	—	—	—	82 000	14 000	96 000	—	—	—
5. Construction	98 000	—	98 000	461 000	30 000	491 000	—	—	—
6. Wholesale and retail trade, restaurants and hotels	148 000	30 000	178 000	858 000	566 000	1 425 000	—	33 000	38 000
7. Transport, storage and communication	41 000	—	42 000	524 000	125 000	649 000	—	—	—
8. Financing, insurance, real estate and business services	20 000	—	22 000	180 000	277 000	457 000	—	—	—
9. Community, social and personal services	147 000	61 000	208 000	1 345 000	1 605 000	2 950 000	—	16 000	17 000
Persons seeking work for the first time / Unemployed	13 000	—	14 000	445 000	189 000	634 000	.	.	.
Total . . .	801 000	106 000	907 000	5 623 000	3 311 000	8 934 000	64 000	122 000	186 000
Colombia									
(15.VII.1964) (ISIC 1958)									
Agriculture, forestry, hunting and fishing	975 517	53 631	1 029 148	984 892	36 446	1 021 338	343 552	25 715	369 267
Mining and quarrying	12 538	11 520	24 058	44 787	3 144	47 931	3 323	5 429	8 752
Manufacturing	123 700	75 920	199 620	340 945	90 514	431 459	6 793	11 748	18 541
Construction	42 720	.	42 720	168 061	3 428	171 489	1 765	.	1 765
Electricity, gas, water and sanitary services	594	.	594	11 550	1 017	12 567	24	.	24
Commerce	190 627	44 374	235 001	132 289	57 435	189 724	6 603	6 251	12 854
Transport, storage and communication	43 753	626	44 379	131 944	11 497	143 441	1 125	113	1 238
Services	57 022	36 214	93 236	312 734	508 525	821 259	1 525	4 659	6 184
Activities not adequately described	28 575	5 648	34 223	75 757	25 324	101 081	1 268	792	2 060
Total . . .	1 475 046	227 933	1 702 979	2 202 959	737 330	2 940 289	365 978	54 707	420 685
(VII.1970) ǂ									
1. Agriculture, hunting, forestry and fishing	...	...	...	...	...	...	...	...	...
2. Mining and quarrying	...	...	...	...	...	...	...	...	...
3. Manufacturing	...	...	...	...	...	...	...	...	...
4. Electricity, gas and water	...	...	...	...	...	...	...	...	...
5. Construction	...	...	...	...	...	...	...	...	...
6. Wholesale and retail trade, restaurants and hotels	...	...	...	...	...	...	...	...	...
7. Transport, storage and communication	...	...	...	...	...	...	...	...	...
8. Financing, insurance, real estate and business services	...	...	...	...	...	...	...	...	...
9. Community, social and personal services	...	...	...	...	...	...	...	...	...
Total . . .	...	...	...	...	...	...	...	...	...

ǂ For notes, see pp. 272-294.

A Distribution by status and by industry (branch of economic activity)
Répartition suivant la situation dans la profession et par branche d'activité économique
Distribución según la categoría de ocupación y por rama de actividad económica

Others and status unknown / Autres et situation non définie / Otros y categoría no definida			TOTAL				Branche d'activité économique	Rama de actividad económica
Males *Hommes* Hombres	Females *Femmes* Mujeres	Total	Males *Hommes* Hombres	Females *Femmes* Mujeres	Total			
						%		
.	.	.	510 000	97 000	**607 000**	6.0	1. *Agriculture, chasse, sylviculture et pêche*	1. Agricultura, caza, silvicultura y pesca
.	.	.	126 000	11 000	**137 000**	1.4	2. *Industries extractives*	2. Minas y canteras
.	.	.	1 484 000	471 000	**1 955 000**	19.3	3. *Industries manufacturières*	3. Industrias manufactureras
.	.	.	82 000	14 000	**97 000**	1.0	4. *Electricité, gaz et eau*	4. Electricidad, gas y agua
.	.	.	559 000	35 000	**594 000**	5.9	5. *Construction*	5. Construcción
.	.	.	1 012 000	629 000	**1 641 000**	16.3	6. *Commerce (gros et détail) ; restaurants, hôtels*	6. Comercio (por mayor y por menor); restaurantes, hoteles
.	.	.	565 000	128 000	**693 000**	6.9	7. *Transports, entrepôts et communications*	7. Transportes, almacenamiento y comunicaciones
.	.	.	200 000	281 000	**482 000**	4.8	8. *Banques, assur., affaires imm., services aux entreprises*	8. Bancos, seguros, bienes inmuebles, servicios para empresas
.	.	.	1 493 000	1 681 000	**3 175 000**	31.3	9. *Services à la collectivité, services sociaux et personnels*	9. Servicios comunales, sociales y personales
42 000	25 000	**67 000**	42 000	25 000	**67 000**	0.7	*Personnes en quête d'emploi pour la première fois*	Personas en busca de trabajo por primera vez
.	.	.	458 000	190 000	**648 000**	6.4	*Chômeurs*	Desempleados
42 000	25 000	**67 000**	6 530 000	3 564 000	**10 094 000**	100.0	*Total*	Total

						%	(CITI 1958)	(CIIU 1958)
7 097	209	**7 306**	2 311 058	116 001	**2 427 059**	47.2	*Agriculture, sylviculture, chasse et pêche*	Agricultura, silvicultura, caza y pesca
502	36	**538**	61 150	20 129	**81 279**	1.6	*Industries extractives*	Minas y canteras
5 205	1 136	**6 341**	476 643	179 318	**655 961**	12.8	*Industries manufacturières*	Industrias manufactureras
4 688	43	**4 731**	217 234	3 471	**220 705**	4.3	*Construction*	Construcción
80	11	**91**	12 248	1 028	**13 276**	0.3	*Electricité, gaz, eau et services sanitaires*	Electricidad, gas, agua y servicios sanitarios
2 343	598	**2 941**	331 862	108 658	**440 520**	8.6	*Com., banq., assur., aff. imm.*	Comercio
2 663	96	**2 759**	179 485	12 332	**191 817**	3.7	*Transports, entrepôts et communications*	Transportes, almacenaje y comunicaciones
2 911	2 356	**5 267**	374 192	551 754	**925 946**	18.0	*Services*	Servicios
32 591	7 607	**40 198**	138 191	39 371	**177 562**	3.5	*Activités mal désignées*	Actividades no bien especif.
58 080	12 092	**70 172**	4 102 063	1 032 062	**5 134 125**	100.0	*Total*	Total

						%		
...	...	...	2 252 601	147 445	**2 400 046**	38.6	1. *Agriculture, chasse, sylviculture et pêche*	1. Agricultura, caza, silvicultura y pesca
...	...	...	29 278	3 718	**32 996**	0.5	2. *Industries extractives*	2. Minas y canteras
...	...	...	613 472	347 792	**961 264**	15.4	3. *Industries manufacturières*	3. Industrias manufactureras
...	...	...	27 906	3 846	**31 752**	0.5	4. *Electricité, gaz et eau*	4. Electricidad, gas y agua
...	...	...	247 950	11 666	**259 616**	4.2	5. *Construction*	5. Construcción
...	...	...	517 403	331 796	**849 199**	13.6	6. *Commerce (gros et détail) ; restaurants, hôtels*	6. Comercio (por mayor y por menor); restaurantes, hoteles
...	...	...	235 142	24 474	**259 616**	4.2	7. *Transports, entrepôts et communications*	7. Transportes, almacenamiento y comunicaciones
...	...	...	69 079	25 553	**94 632**	1.5	8. *Banques, assur., affaires imm., services aux entreprises*	8. Bancos, seguros, bienes inmuebles, servicios para empresas
...	...	...	581 907	754 772	**1 336 679**	21.5	9. *Services à la collectivité, services sociaux et personnels*	9. Servicios comunales, sociales y personales
...	...	...	4 574 738	1 651 062	**6 225 800**	100.0	*Total*	Total

✝ *Voir notes pp. 272-294.* ✝ Véanse las notas en las págs. 272-294.

2 Structure of the economically active population
Structure de la population active
Estructura de la población económicamente activa

Industry (Branch of economic activity)	Employers and workers on own account Employeurs et personnes travaillant à leur propre compte Empleadores y trabajadores por cuenta propia			Salaried employees and wage earners Employés et ouvriers Empleados y obreros			Family workers Travailleurs familiaux Trabajadores familiares		
	Males Hommes Hombres	Females Femmes Mujeres	Total	Males Hommes Hombres	Females Femmes Mujeres	Total	Males Hommes Hombres	Females Femmes Mujeres	Total

Costa Rica (14.V.1973)

1. Agriculture, hunting, forestry and fishing	55 090	209	55 299	123 253	4 050	127 303	30 299	325	30 624
2. Mining and quarrying	291	1	292	1 156	66	1 222	43	.	43
3. Manufacturing	6 990	2 402	9 392	44 163	15 732	59 895	514	116	630
4. Electricity, gas and water	34	.	34	5 223	273	5 496	1	.	1
5. Construction	3 006	8	3 014	35 624	167	35 791	271	2	273
6. Wholesale and retail trade, restaurants and hotels	17 840	2 548	20 388	30 494	14 664	45 158	1 356	773	2 129
7. Transport, storage and communication	3 656	14	3 670	19 929	1 105	21 034	253	7	260
8. Financing, insurance, real estate and business services	1 222	56	1 278	10 325	2 041	12 366	15	14	29
9. Community, social and personal services	5 496	782	6 278	48 421	63 738	112 159	281	255	536
0. Activities not adequately described	433	26	459	8 515	1 223	9 738	84	4	88
Persons seeking work for the first time	.	.	.	.	.	.	.	.	.
Total ...	94 058	6 046	100 104	327 103	103 059	430 162	33 117	1 496	34 613

Cuba (6.IX.1970*) †

Agriculture, hunting, forestry and fishing	...	...	236 801	...	...	519 212	...	...	34 289
Mining and quarrying									
Manufacturing	...	...	1 759	...	...	531 372	...	...	24
Electricity and gas									
Construction	...	...	948	...	...	156 212	...	...	6
Wholesale and retail trade, restaurants and hotels; storage; personal services	...	...	3 789	...	...	302 107	...	...	29
Transport and communication	...	...	16 552	...	...	144 761	...	...	23
Community and social services; water; financing, insurance, real estate and business services	...	...	774	...	...	646 792	...	...	24
Activities not adequately described	.	.	.	...	...	23 142	.	.	.
Total ...	...	...	260 623	...	...	2 323 598	...	...	34 395

† For notes, see pp. 272-294.

A Distribution by status and by industry (branch of economic activity)
Répartition suivant la situation dans la profession et par branche d'activité économique
Distribución según la categoría de ocupación y por rama de actividad económica

Others and status unknown / *Autres et situation non définie* / Otros y categoría no definida			TOTAL				*Branche d'activité économique*	Rama de actividad económica
Males / *Hommes* / Hombres	Females / *Femmes* / Mujeres	Total	Males / *Hommes* / Hombres	Females / *Femmes* / Mujeres	Total	%		
.	.	.	208 642	4 584	**213 226**	36.4	1. *Agriculture, chasse, sylviculture et pêche*	.1. Agricultura, caza, silvicultura y pesca
.	.	.	1 490	67	**1 557**	0.3	2. *Industries extractives*	2. Minas y canteras
.	.	.	51 667	18 250	**69 917**	11.9	3. *Industries manufacturières*	3. Industrias manufactureras
.	.	.	5 258	273	**5 531**	0.9	4. *Electricité, gaz et eau*	4. Electricidad, gas y agua
.	.	.	38 901	177	**39 078**	6.7	5. *Construction*	5. Construcción
.	.	.	49 690	17 985	**67 675**	11.6	6. *Commerce (gros et détail); restaurants, hôtels*	6. Comercio (por mayor y por menor); restaurantes, hoteles
.	.	.	23 838	1 126	**24 964**	4.3	7. *Transports, entrepôts et communications*	7. Transportes, almacenamiento y comunicaciones
.	.	.	11 562	2 111	**13 673**	2.3	8. *Banques, assur., affaires imm., services aux entreprises*	8. Bancos, seguros, bienes inmuebles, servicios para empresas
.	.	.	54 198	64 775	**118 973**	20.3	9. *Services à la collectivité, services sociaux et personnels*	9. Servicios comunales, sociales y personales
.	.	.	9 032	1 253	**10 285**	1.8	0. *Activités mal désignées*	0. Actividades no bien especif.
18 002	2 432	**20 434**	18 002	2 432	**20 434**	3.5	*Personnes en quête d'emploi pour la première fois*	Personas en busca de trabajo por primera vez
18 002	2 432	**20 434**	472 280	113 033	**585 313**	100.0	*Total*	Total

Males / *Hommes* / Hombres	Females / *Femmes* / Mujeres	Total	Males / *Hommes* / Hombres	Females / *Femmes* / Mujeres	Total	%	*Branche d'activité économique*	Rama de actividad económica
...	...	54	...	...	790 356	30.0	*Agriculture, chasse, sylviculture et pêche*	Agricultura, caza, silvicultura y pesca
...	...	103	...	...	533 258	20.3	{ *Industries extractives* / *Industries manufacturières* / *Electricité et gaz*	{ Minas y canteras / Industrias manufactureras / Electricidad y gas
...	...	16	...	...	157 182	6.0	*Construction*	Construcción
...	...	33	...	...	305 958	11.6	*Commerce (gros et détail); restaurants, hôtels; entrepôts; services personnels*	Comercio (por mayor y por menor); restaurantes, hoteles; almacenamiento; servicios personales
...	...	42	...	...	161 378	6.1	*Transports et communications*	Transportes y comunicaciones
...	...	148	...	...	647 738	24.6	*Services à la collectivité et serv. sociaux; eau; banques, assur., aff. imm., services aux entreprises*	Servicios comunales y sociales; agua; bancos, seguros, bienes inmuebles, servicios para empresas
...	...	14 297	...	...	37 439	1.4	*Activités mal désignées*	Actividades no bien especif.
...	...	14 693	2 151 052	482 257	**2 633 309**	100.0	*Total*	Total

☦ *Voir notes pp. 272-294.*
☦ Véanse las notas en las págs. 272-294.

2 Structure of the economically active population
Structure de la population active
Estructura de la población económicamente activa

Industry (Branch of economic activity)	Employers and workers on own account / Employeurs et personnes travaillant à leur propre compte / Empleadores y trabajadores por cuenta propia			Salaried employees and wage earners / Employés et ouvriers / Empleados y obreros			Family workers / Travailleurs familiaux / Trabajadores familiares		
	Males Hommes Hombres	Females Femmes Mujeres	Total	Males Hommes Hombres	Females Femmes Mujeres	Total	Males Hommes Hombres	Females Femmes Mujeres	Total
Chile (22.IV.1970) ‡									
1. Agriculture, hunting, forestry and fishing	165 600	6 160	**171 760**	332 400	8 940	**341 340**	29 860	2 020	**31 880**
2. Mining and quarrying	5 680	60	**5 740**	66 880	1 080	**67 960**	120	40	**160**
3. Manufacturing	40 080	39 080	**79 160**	257 060	63 980	**321 040**	800	680	**1 480**
4. Electricity, gas, water and sanitary services	680	40	**720**	19 000	1 120	**20 120**	20	.	**20**
5. Construction	14 640	140	**14 780**	128 100	1 960	**130 060**	260	.	**260**
6. Wholesale and retail trade, restaurants and hotels	107 640	42 620	**150 260**	99 720	41 660	**141 380**	1 740	2 040	**3 780**
7. Transport, storage and communication	31 060	640	**31 700**	111 100	7 760	**118 860**	360	20	**380**
8. Financing, insurance, real estate and business services	7 100	980	**8 080**	24 740	8 080	**32 820**	40	60	**100**
9. Community, social and personal services (excl. sanitary services) . . .	72 560	26 000	**98 560**	266 400	285 280	**551 680**	1 000	680	**1 680**
0. Activities not adequately described . .	18 060	3 400	**21 460**	84 480	18 000	**102 480**	2 480	760	**3 240**
Total . . .	463 100	119 120	**582 220**	1 389 880	437 860	**1 827 740**	36 680	6 300	**42 980**
República Dominicana (9–10.I.1970) ‡									
1. Agriculture, hunting, forestry and fishing	203 143	24 232	**227 375**	142 855	20 546	**163 401**	45 824	8 492	**54 316**
2. Mining and quarrying	146	37	**183**	339	84	**423**	80	.	**80**
3. Manufacturing	14 638	6 629	**21 267**	59 509	8 094	**67 603**	650	377	**1 027**
4. Electricity, gas and water	33	11	**44**	1 308	218	**1 526**	.	9	**9**
5. Construction	8 400	1 030	**9 430**	11 746	1 118	**12 864**	142	111	**253**
6. Wholesale and retail trade, restaurants and hotels	34 211	7 077	**41 288**	19 504	5 432	**24 936**	908	582	**1 490**
7. Transport, storage and communication	13 492	883	**14 375**	19 977	2 085	**22 062**	259	133	**392**
8. Financing, insurance, real estate and business services	990	169	**1 159**	14 043	4 056	**18 099**	.	20	**20**
9. Community, social and personal services	15 974	3 485	**19 459**	61 849	56 559	**118 408**	563	528	**1 091**
0. Activities not adequately described . .	18 619	12 179	**30 798**	24 757	19 652	**44 409**	6 564	7 475	**14 039**
Persons seeking work for the first time	.	.	.	.	.	.	.	.	.
Total . . .	309 646	55 732	**365 378**	355 887	117 844	**473 731**	54 990	17 727	**72 717**

‡ For notes, see pp. 272-294.

A Distribution by status and by industry (branch of economic activity)
Répartition suivant la situation dans la profession et par branche d'activité économique
Distribución según la categoría de ocupación y por rama de actividad económica

Others and status unknown — *Autres et situation non définie* — Otros y categoría no definida			TOTAL				Branche d'activité économique	Rama de actividad económica
Males *Hommes* Hombres	Females *Femmes* Mujeres	Total	Males *Hommes* Hombres	Females *Femmes* Mujeres	Total	%	*Branche d'activité économique*	Rama de actividad económica
7 020	340	**7 360**	534 880	17 460	**552 340**	*21.2*	1. *Agriculture, chasse, sylviculture et pêche*	1. Agricultura, caza, silvicultura y pesca
1 360	80	**1 440**	74 040	1 260	**75 300**	*2.9*	2. *Industries extractives*	2. Minas y canteras
8 900	4 860	**13 760**	306 840	108 600	**415 440**	*15.9*	3. *Industries manufacturières*	3. Industrias manufactureras
380	40	**420**	20 080	1 200	**21 280**	*0.8*	4. *Electricité, gaz, eau et services sanitaires*	4. Electricidad, gas, agua y servicios sanitarios
3 380	20	**3 400**	146 380	2 120	**148 500**	*5.7*	5. *Construction*	5. Construcción
5 120	2 560	**7 680**	214 220	88 880	**303 100**	*11.6*	6. *Commerce (gros et détail) ; restaurants, hôtels*	6. Comercio (por mayor y por menor); restaurantes, hoteles
4 400	180	**4 580**	146 920	8 600	**155 520**	*6.0*	7. *Transports, entrepôts et communications*	7. Transportes, almacenamiento y comunicaciones
880	100	**980**	32 760	9 220	**41 980**	*1.6*	8. *Banques, assur., affaires imm., services aux entreprises*	8. Bancos, seguros, bienes inmuebles, servicios para empresas
10 200	5 420	**15 620**	350 160	317 380	**667 540**	*25.6*	9. *Services à la collectivité, services sociaux et personnels (non compris serv. sanitaires)*	9. Servicios comunales, sociales y personales (excl. servicios sanitarios)
74 520	24 660	**99 180**	179 540	46 820	**226 360**	*8.7*	0. *Activités mal désignées*	0. Actividades no bien especif.
116 160	38 260	**154 420**	2 005 820	601 540	**2 607 360**	*100.0*	*Total*	Total

						%		
65 757	38 466	**104 223**	457 579	91 736	**549 315**	*44.3*	1. *Agriculture, chasse, sylviculture et pêche*	1. Agricultura, caza, silvicultura y pesca
126	28	**154**	691	149	**840**	*0.1*	2. *Industries extractives*	2. Minas y canteras
6 740	4 352	**11 092**	81 537	19 452	**100 989**	*8.1*	3. *Industries manufacturières*	3. Industrias manufactureras
118	31	**149**	1 459	269	**1 728**	*0.1*	4. *Electricité, gaz et eau*	4. Electricidad, gas y agua
4 521	1 440	**5 961**	24 809	3 699	**28 508**	*2.3*	5. *Construction*	5. Construcción
6 705	2 645	**9 350**	61 328	15 736	**77 064**	*6.2*	6. *Commerce (gros et détail) ; restaurants, hôtels*	6. Comercio (por mayor y por menor); restaurantes, hoteles
5 457	1 011	**6 468**	39 185	4 112	**43 297**	*3.5*	7. *Transports, entrepôts et communications*	7. Transportes, almacenamiento y comunicaciones
646	156	**802**	15 679	4 401	**20 080**	*1.6*	8. *Banques, assur., affaires imm., services aux entreprises*	8. Bancos, seguros, bienes inmuebles, servicios para empresas
8 801	6 124	**14 925**	87 187	66 696	**153 883**	*12.4*	9. *Services à la collectivité, services sociaux et personnels*	9. Servicios comunales, sociales y personales
77 262	69 492	**146 754**	127 202	108 798	**236 000**	*19.0*	0. *Activités mal désignées Personnes en quête d'emploi pour la première fois*	0. Actividades no bien especif. Personas en busca de trabajo por primera vez
25 434	3 862	**29 296**	25 434	3 862	**29 296**	*2.4*		
201 567	127 607	**329 174**	922 090	318 910	**1 241 000**	*100.0*	*Total*	Total

† *Voir notes pp. 272-294.*

† Véanse las notas en las págs. 272-294.

2 Structure of the economically active population
Structure de la population active
Estructura de la población económicamente activa

Industry (Branch of economic activity)	Employers and workers on own account *Employeurs et personnes travaillant à leur propre compte* Empleadores y trabajadores por cuenta propia			Salaried employees and wage earners *Employés et ouvriers* Empleados y obreros			Family workers *Travailleurs familiaux* Trabajadores familiares		
	Males *Hommes* Hombres	Females *Femmes* Mujeres	Total	Males *Hommes* Hombres	Females *Femmes* Mujeres	Total	Males *Hommes* Hombres	Females *Femmes* Mujeres	Total

El Salvador (27.VI.1971) †

1. Agriculture, hunting, forestry and fishing	...	...	212 652	...	...	309 081	...	...	91 840
2. Mining and quarrying	...	...	141	...	...	742	...	...	20
3. Manufacturing	...	...	33 339	...	...	68 430	...	...	5 240
4. Electricity, gas and water	...	...	181	...	...	3 127	...	...	.
5. Construction	...	...	2 225	...	...	25 182	...	...	340
6. Wholesale and retail trade, restaurants and hotels	...	...	58 274	...	...	35 339	...	...	2 342
7. Transport, storage and communication	...	...	3 293	...	...	28 630	...	...	360
8. Financing, insurance, real estate and business services	...	...	1 103	...	...	8 453	...	...	140
9. Community, social and personal services	...	...	10 238	...	...	156 562	...	...	3 022
0. Activities not adequately described	...	...	390	...	...	1 843	...	...	193 396
Total ...	...	...	321 836	...	...	637 389	...	...	296 700

Greenland (31.XII.1970)

1. Agriculture, hunting, forestry and fishing	2 388	5	2 393	1 091	3	1 094	.	6	6
2. Mining and quarrying	1	.	1	145	8	153	.	.	.
3. Manufacturing	68	9	77	1 566	727	2 293	.	1	1
4. Electricity, gas and water	.	.	.	209	2	211	.	.	.
5. Construction	297	.	297	2 353	102	2 455	.	1	1
6. Wholesale and retail trade, restaurants and hotels	98	32	130	1 284	1 020	2 304	.	27	27
7. Transport, storage and communication	111	4	115	1 603	141	1 744	.	3	3
8. Financing, insurance, real estate and business services	.	.	.	70	43	113	.	.	.
9. Community, social and personal services	36	19	55	1 378	3 543	4 921	.	1	1
0. Activities not adequately described	.	.	.	200	146	346	.	.	.
Total ...	2 999	69	3 068	9 899	5 735	15 634	.	39	39

Guadeloupe (16.X.1967) †

(ISIC 1958)									
Agriculture, forestry, hunting and fishing	10 532	2 187	12 719	9 917	4 576	14 493	662	1 284	1 946
Mining and quarrying	9	.	9	28	12	40	1	1	2
Manufacturing	1 500	1 331	2 831	5 543	833	6 376	39	73	112
Construction	2 801	25	2 826	10 656	235	10 891	54	5	59
Electricity, gas, water and sanitary services	337	149	486	888	1 491	2 379	5	7	12
Commerce	1 482	2 828	4 310	2 824	3 065	5 889	68	431	499
Transport, storage and communication	1 430	27	1 457	3 767	595	4 362	29	4	33
Services	208	171	379	5 191	10 658	15 849	15	42	57
Activities not adequately described	70	26	96	267	171	438	2	3	5
Total ...	18 369	6 744	25 113	39 081	21 636	60 717	875	1 849	2 724

† For notes, see pp. 272-294.

A

Distribution by status and by industry (branch of economic activity)
Répartition suivant la situation dans la profession et par branche d'activité économique
Distribución según la categoría de ocupación y por rama de actividad económica

Table 1

Males / Hommes / Hombres	Females / Femmes / Mujeres	Total	Males / Hommes / Hombres	Females / Femmes / Mujeres	Total	%	Branche d'activité économique	Rama de actividad económica
							1. Agriculture, chasse, sylviculture et pêche	1. Agricultura, caza, silvicultura y pesca
...	...	184	...	...	613 757	46.6	2. Industries extractives	2. Minas y canteras
...	...	.	...	...	903	0.1	3. Industries manufacturières	3. Industrias manufactureras
...	...	843	...	...	107 852	8.2	4. Electricité, gaz et eau	4. Electricidad, gas y agua
...	...	40	...	...	3 348	0.3	5. Construction	5. Construcción
...	...	181	...	...	27 928	2.1	6. Commerce (gros et détail); restaurants, hôtels	6. Comercio (por mayor y por menor); restaurantes, hoteles
...	...	180	...	...	96 135	7.3	7. Transports, entrepôts et communications	7. Transportes, almacenamiento y comunicaciones
...	...	41	...	...	32 324	2.5	8. Banques, assur., affaires imm., services aux entreprises	8. Bancos, seguros, bienes inmuebles, servicios para empresas
...	...	.	...	...	9 696	0.7	9. Services à la collectivité, services sociaux et personnels	9. Servicios comunales, sociales y personales
...	...	1 050	...	...	170 872	13.0	0. Activités mal désignées	0. Actividades no bien especif.
...	...	56 413	...	...	252 042	19.2		
...	...	58 932	929 472	385 385	1 314 857	100.0	Total	Total

Table 2

			Males / Hommes / Hombres	Females / Femmes / Mujeres	Total	%	Branche d'activité économique	Rama de actividad económica
.	.	.	3 479	14	3 493	18.6	1. Agriculture, chasse, sylviculture et pêche	1. Agricultura, caza, silvicultura y pesca
.	.	.	146	8	154	0.8	2. Industries extractives	2. Minas y canteras
.	.	.	1 634	737	2 371	12.7	3. Industries manufacturières	3. Industrias manufactureras
.	.	.	209	2	211	1.1	4. Electricité, gaz et eau	4. Electricidad, gas y agua
.	.	.	2 650	103	2 753	14.7	5. Construction	5. Construcción
.	.	.	1 382	1 079	2 461	13.1	6. Commerce (gros et détail); restaurants, hôtels	6. Comercio (por mayor y por menor); restaurantes, hoteles
.	.	.	1 714	148	1 862	9.9	7. Transports, entrepôts et communications	7. Transportes, almacenamiento y comunicaciones
.	.	.	70	43	113	0.6	8. Banques, assur., affaires imm., services aux entreprises	8. Bancos, seguros, bienes inmuebles, servicios para empresas
.	.	.	1 414	3 563	4 977	26.6	9. Services à la collectivité, services sociaux et personnels	9. Servicios comunales, sociales y personales
.	.	.	200	146	346	1.9	0. Activités mal désignées	0. Actividades no bien especif.
.	.	.	12 898	5 843	18 741	100.0	Total	Total

Table 3

Males / Hommes / Hombres	Females / Femmes / Mujeres	Total	Males / Hommes / Hombres	Females / Femmes / Mujeres	Total	%	(CITI 1958)	(CIIU 1958)
9	3	12	21 120	8 050	29 170	32.4	Agriculture, sylviculture, chasse et pêche	Agricultura, silvicultura, caza y pesca
.	1	1	38	13	51	0.1	Industries extractives	Minas y canteras
5	2	7	7 087	2 239	9 326	10.4	Industries manufacturières	Industrias manufactureras
3	.	3	13 514	265	13 779	15.3	Construction	Construcción
1	1	2	1 231	1 648	2 879	3.2	Electricité, gaz, eau et services sanitaires	Electricidad, gas, agua y servicios sanitarios
5	6	11	4 379	6 330	10 709	11.9	Com., banq., assur., aff. imm.	Comercio
6	.	6	5 232	626	5 858	6.5	Transports, entrepôts et communications	Transportes, almacenaje y comunicaciones
64	40	104	5 478	10 911	16 389	18.2	Services	Servicios
583	697	1 280	922	897	1 819	2.0	Activités mal désignées	Actividades no bien especif.
676	750	1 426	59 001	30 979	89 980	100.0	Total	Total

Column group headers: Others and status unknown / *Autres et situation non définie* / Otros y categoría no definida — and — TOTAL

† *Voir notes pp. 272-294.*

† Véanse las notas en las págs. 272-294.

2 Structure of the economically active population
Structure de la population active
Estructura de la población económicamente activa

Industry (Branch of economic activity)	Employers and workers on own account _Employeurs et personnes travaillant à leur propre compte_ Empleadores y trabajadores por cuenta propia			Salaried employees and wage earners _Employés et ouvriers_ Empleados y obreros			Family workers _Travailleurs familiaux_ Trabajadores familiares		
	Males _Hommes_ Hombres	Females _Femmes_ Mujeres	Total	Males _Hommes_ Hombres	Females _Femmes_ Mujeres	Total	Males _Hommes_ Hombres	Females _Femmes_ Mujeres	Total

Guatemala (26.III.1973) †

(ISIC 1958)

Industry	Males	Females	Total	Males	Females	Total	Males	Females	Total
Agriculture, forestry, hunting and fishing	402 060	2 340	**404 400**	306 260	10 040	**316 300**	...	...	...
Mining and quarrying	420	40	**460**	1 760	.	**1 760**	...	...	...
Manufacturing	60 500	26 820	**87 320**	96 480	15 180	**111 660**	...	...	...
Construction	12 620	.	**12 620**	47 440	260	**47 700**	...	...	...
Electricity, gas, water and sanitary services	200	.	**200**	3 620	100	**3 720**	...	...	...
Commerce	49 360	21 560	**70 920**	26 840	10 640	**37 480**	...	...	...
Transport, storage and communication	7 760	120	**7 880**	28 940	940	**29 880**	...	...	...
Services	10 060	6 460	**16 520**	74 680	100 700	**175 380**	...	...	...
Activities not adequately described . } Persons seeking work for the first time	3 480	780	**4 260**	14 120	4 020	**18 140**	...	...	...
Total . . .	546 460	58 120	**604 580**	600 140	141 880	**742 020**	...	...	...

Guyana (III.1965) †

(ISIC 1958)

Industry	Males	Females	Total	Males	Females	Total	Males	Females	Total
Agriculture, forestry, hunting and fishing	14 578	1 398	**15 976**	20 619	3 090	**23 709**	2 960	1 207	**4 167**
Mining and quarrying	211	.	**211**	4 112	330	**4 442**	.	.	.
Manufacturing	2 944	2 531	**5 475**	15 706	2 705	**18 411**	526	100	**626**
Construction	175	.	**175**	6 551	20	**6 571**	.	.	.
Electricity, gas, water and sanitary services	60	.	**60**	1 899	70	**1 969**	.	.	.
Commerce	3 524	3 707	**7 231**	7 347	2 694	**10 041**	370	1 259	**1 629**
Transport, storage and communication	1 105	.	**1 105**	7 302	590	**7 892**	20	.	**20**
Services	745	1 076	**1 821**	11 799	13 561	**25 360**	.	66	**66**
Activities not adequately described .	21	.	**21**	660	170	**830**	30	.	**30**
Persons seeking work for the first time	.	.	.	.	.	.	.	.	.
Total . . .	23 363	8 712	**32 075**	75 995	23 230	**99 225**	3 906	2 632	**6 538**

Guyane française (16.X.1967) †

Industry	Males	Females	Total	Males	Females	Total	Males	Females	Total
Agriculture, forestry, hunting and fishing	1 512	211	**1 723**	679	113	**792**	146	471	**617**
Mining and quarrying	130	1	**131**	128	5	**133**	2	1	**3**
Manufacturing	211	152	**363**	559	85	**644**	6	17	**23**
Construction	521	1	**522**	2 921	97	**3 018**	8	2	**10**
Electricity, gas and water	.	.	.	124	20	**144**	.	.	.
Commerce	434	253	**687**	727	428	**1 155**	34	124	**158**
Transport, storage and communication	210	7	**217**	463	62	**525**	4	3	**7**
Services (incl. sanitary services) . .	62	110	**172**	3 766	2 096	**5 862**	.	1	**1**
Activities not adequately described .	.	.	.	.	.	.	.	.	.
Total . . .	3 080	735	**3 815**	9 367	2 906	**12 273**	200	619	**819**

† For notes, see pp. 272-294.

A

Distribution by status and by industry (branch of economic activity)
Répartition suivant la situation dans la profession et par branche d'activité économique
Distribución según la categoría de ocupación y por rama de actividad económica

Others and status unknown / Autres et situation non définie / Otros y categoría no definida			TOTAL				Branche d'activité économique	Rama de actividad económica
Males Hommes Hombres	Females Femmes Mujeres	Total	Males Hommes Hombres	Females Femmes Mujeres	Total			

						%	(CITI 1958)	(CIIU 1958)
157 920	2 800	160 720	866 240	15 180	881 420	56.8	Agriculture, sylviculture, chasse et pêche	Agricultura, silvicultura, caza y pesca
120	.	120	2 300	40	2 340	0.2	Industries extractives	Minas y canteras
9 100	4 700	13 800	166 080	46 700	212 780	13.8	Industries manufacturières	Industrias manufactureras
1 900	.	1 900	61 960	260	62 220	4.0	Construction	Construcción
.	.	.	3 820	100	3 920	0.3	Electricité, gaz, eau et services sanitaires	Electricidad, gas, agua y servicios sanitarios
3 840	1 560	5 400	80 040	33 760	113 800	7.4	Com., banq., assur., aff. imm.	Comercio
460	20	480	37 160	1 080	38 240	2.5	Transports, entrepôts et communications	Transportes, almacenaje y comunicaciones
1 180	1 080	2 260	85 920	108 240	194 160	12.5	Services	Servicios
							Activités mal désignées	Actividades no bien especif.
13 500	2 560	16 060	31 100	7 360	38 460	2.5	Personnes en quête d'emploi pour la première fois	Personas en busca de trabajo por primera vez
188 020	12 720	200 740	1 334 620	212 720	1 547 340	100.0	Total	Total

						%	(CITI 1958)	(CIIU 1958)
7 082	880	7 962	45 239	6 575	51 814	29.6	Agriculture, sylviculture, chasse et pêche	Agricultura, silvicultura, caza y pesca
280	.	280	4 603	330	4 933	2.8	Industries extractives	Minas y canteras
1 340	520	1 860	20 516	5 856	26 372	15.1	Industries manufacturières	Industrias manufactureras
2 370	10	2 380	9 096	30	9 126	5.2	Construction	Construcción
216	10	226	2 175	80	2 255	1.3	Electricité, gaz, eau et services sanitaires	Electricidad, gas, agua y servicios sanitarios
786	850	1 636	12 027	8 510	20 537	11.8	Com., banq., assur., aff. imm.	Comercio
880	20	900	9 307	610	9 917	5.7	Transports, entrepôts et communications	Transportes, almacenaje y comunicaciones
700	1 744	2 444	13 244	16 447	29 691	17.0	Services	Servicios
3 217	2 880	6 097	3 928	3 050	6 978	4.0	Activités mal désignées	Actividades no bien especif.
6 760	6 389	13 149	6 760	6 389	13 149	7.5	Personnes en quête d'emploi pour la première fois	Personas en busca de trabajo por primera vez
23 631	13 303	36 934	126 895	47 877	174 772	100.0	Total	Total

						%		
.	.	.	2 337	795	3 132	18.4	Agriculture, sylviculture, chasse et pêche	Agricultura, silvicultura, caza y pesca
.	.	.	260	7	267	1.6	Industries extractives	Minas y canteras
.	.	.	776	254	1 030	6.1	Industries manufacturières	Industrias manufactureras
.	.	.	3 450	100	3 550	20.9	Construction	Construcción
.	.	.	124	20	144	0.8	Electricité, gaz et eau	Electricidad, gas y agua
.	.	.	1 195	805	2 000	11.8	Com., banq., assur., aff. imm.	Comercio
.	.	.	677	72	749	4.4	Transports, entrepôts et communications	Transportes, almacenaje y comunicaciones
33	71	104	3 861	2 278	6 139	36.0	Services (y compris services sanitaires)	Servicios (incl. servicios sanitarios)
1	.	1	1	.	1	—	Activités mal désignées	Actividades no bien especif.
34	71	105	12 681	4 331	17 012	100.0	Total	Total

✝ *Voir notes pp. 272-294.*

✝ Véanse las notas en las págs. 272-294.

POPULATION

Structure of the economically active population
Structure de la population active
Estructura de la población económicamente activa

Industry (Branch of economic activity)	Employers and workers on own account *Employeurs et personnes travaillant à leur propre compte* Empleadores y trabajadores por cuenta propia			Salaried employees and wage earners *Employés et ouvriers* Empleados y obreros			Family workers *Travailleurs familiaux* Trabajadores familiares		
	Males *Hommes* Hombres	Females *Femmes* Mujeres	Total	Males *Hommes* Hombres	Females *Femmes* Mujeres	Total	Males *Hommes* Hombres	Females *Femmes* Mujeres	Total

Honduras (VI.1974) ‡

Industry									
1. Agriculture, hunting, forestry and fishing	...	...	...	...	...	...	...	...	...
2. Mining and quarrying	...	...	...	...	...	...	...	...	...
3. Manufacturing	...	...	...	...	...	...	...	...	...
4. Electricity, gas and water	...	...	...	...	...	...	...	...	...
5. Construction	...	...	...	...	...	...	...	...	...
6. Wholesale and retail trade, restaurants and hotels	...	...	...	...	...	...	...	...	...
7. Transport, storage and communication	...	...	...	...	...	...	...	...	...
8. Financing, insurance, real estate and business services	...	...	...	...	...	...	...	...	...
9. Community, social and personal services									
0. Activities not adequately described									
Total	159 700	86 150	**245 850**	211 400	142 400	**353 800**	16 150	12 900	**29 050**

Jamaica (1973) ‡

(ISIC 1958)

Industry									
Agriculture, forestry, hunting and fishing	...	...	...	...	...	...	...	...	...
Mining and quarrying									
Manufacturing	...	...	...	...	...	...	...	...	...
Construction	...	...	...	...	...	...	...	...	...
Commerce	...	...	...	...	...	...	...	...	...
Electricity, gas, water and sanitary services	...	...	...	...	...	...	...	...	...
Transport, storage and communication									
Services	...	...	...	...	...	...	...	...	...
Activities not adequately described	...	...	...	...	...	...	...	...	...
Persons seeking work for the first time	.	.	.	.	.	.	.	.	.
Total	159 700	86 150	**245 850**	211 400	142 400	**353 800**	16 150	12 900	**29 050**

Martinique (16.X.1967) ‡

(ISIC 1958)

Industry									
Agriculture, forestry, hunting and fishing	6 097	786	**6 883**	10 998	6 607	**17 605**	259	225	**484**
Mining and quarrying	10	.	**10**	165	6	**171**	.	.	**.**
Manufacturing	1 388	923	**2 311**	4 403	1 095	**5 498**	51	43	**94**
Construction	1 624	6	**1 630**	8 307	203	**8 510**	25	1	**26**
Electricity, gas, water and sanitary services	196	63	**259**	1 459	1 897	**3 356**	2	2	**4**
Commerce	1 119	2 423	**3 542**	2 634	4 231	**6 865**	67	366	**433**
Transport, storage and communication	1 445	13	**1 458**	3 257	180	**3 437**	21	5	**26**
Services	484	299	**783**	10 844	13 753	**24 597**	5	8	**13**
Activities not adequately described	75	67	**142**	588	287	**875**	4	2	**6**
Total	12 438	4 580	**17 018**	42 655	28 259	**70 914**	434	652	**1 086**

‡ For notes, see pp. 272-294.

78

A Distribution by status and by industry (branch of economic activity)
Répartition suivant la situation dans la profession et par branche d'activité économique
Distribución según la categoría de ocupación y por rama de actividad económica

Others and status unknown / Autres et situation non définie / Otros y categoría no definida			TOTAL			%	Branche d'activité économique	Rama de actividad económica
Males / Hommes / Hombres	Females / Femmes / Mujeres	Total	Males / Hommes / Hombres	Females / Femmes / Mujeres	Total			
...	...	...	...	...	435 067	56.8	1. Agriculture, chasse, sylviculture et pêche	1. Agricultura, caza, silvicultura y pesca
...	...	...	...	...	2 339	0.3	2. Industries extractives	2. Minas y canteras
...	...	...	...	...	88 604	11.6	3. Industries manufacturières	3. Industrias manufactureras
...	...	...	...	...	2 221	0.3	4. Electricité, gaz et eau	4. Electricidad, gas y agua
...	...	...	...	...	22 770	3.0	5. Construction	5. Construcción
...	...	...	...	...	60 438	7.9	6. Commerce (gros et détail); restaurants, hôtels	6. Comercio (por mayor y por menor); restaurantes, hoteles
...	...	...	...	...	22 573	3.0	7. Transports, entrepôts et communications	7. Transportes, almacenamiento y comunicaciones
...	...	...	...	...	130 921	17.1	8. Banques, assur., affaires imm., services aux entreprises / 9. Services à la collectivité, services sociaux et personnels / 0. Activités mal désignées	8. Bancos, seguros, bienes inmuebles, servicios para empresas / 9. Servicios comunales, sociales y personales / 0. Actividades no bien especif.
...	...	...	...	...	764 933	100.0	Total	Total

Others and status unknown			TOTAL			%	(CITI 1958)	(CIIU 1958)
Males	Females	Total	Males	Females	Total			
...	...	...	174 350	46 700	221 050	27.4	Agriculture, sylviculture, chasse et pêche / Industries extractives	Agricultura, silvicultura, caza y pesca / Minas y canteras
...	...	...	64 900	30 300	95 200	11.8	Industries manufacturières	Industrias manufactureras
...	...	...	53 000	1 850	54 850	6.8	Construction	Construcción
...	...	...	32 000	67 500	99 500	12.3	Com., banq., assur., aff. imm.	Comercio
...	...	...	22 900	6 750	29 650	3.7	Electricité, gaz, eau et services sanitaires / Transports, entrepôts et communications	Electricidad, gas, agua y servicios sanitarios / Transportes, almacenaje y comunicaciones
...	...	...	76 950	164 900	241 850	30.1	Services	Servicios
...	...	...	4 500	3 000	7 500	0.9	Activités mal désignées	Actividades no bien especif.
...	...	...	16 200	40 150	56 350	7.0	Personnes en quête d'emploi pour la première fois	Personas en busca de trabajo por primera vez
57 550	119 700	177 250	444 800	361 150	805 950	100.0	Total	Total

Others and status unknown			TOTAL			%	(CITI 1958)	(CIIU 1958)
Males	Females	Total	Males	Females	Total			
152	26	178	17 506	7 644	25 150	28.1	Agriculture, sylviculture, chasse et pêche	Agricultura, silvicultura, caza y pesca
.	.	.	175	6	181	0.2	Industries extractives	Minas y canteras
5	2	7	5 847	2 063	7 910	8.8	Industries manufacturières	Industrias manufactureras
.	.	.	9 956	210	10 166	11.4	Construction	Construcción
.	.	.	1 657	1 962	3 619	4.0	Electricité, gaz, eau et services sanitaires	Electricidad, gas, agua y servicios sanitarios
.	.	.	3 820	7 020	10 840	12.1	Com., banq., assur., aff. imm.	Comercio
7	.	7	4 730	198	4 928	5.5	Transports, entrepôts et communications	Transportes, almacenaje y comunicaciones
1	1	2	11 334	14 061	25 395	28.5	Services	Servicios
171	80	251	839	436	1 275	1.4	Activités mal désignées	Actividades no bien especif.
336	109	445	55 864	33 600	89 464	100.0	Total	Total

† Voir notes pp. 272-294.

† Véanse las notas en las págs. 272-294.

2 Structure of the economically active population
Structure de la population active
Estructura de la población económicamente activa

Industry (Branch of economic activity)	Employers and workers on own account _Employeurs et personnes travaillant à leur propre compte_ Empleadores y trabajadores por cuenta propia			Salaried employees and wage earners _Employés et ouvriers_ Empleados y obreros			Family workers _Travailleurs familiaux_ Trabajadores familiares		
	Males _Hommes_ Hombres	Females _Femmes_ Mujeres	Total	Males _Hommes_ Hombres	Females _Femmes_ Mujeres	Total	Males _Hommes_ Hombres	Females _Femmes_ Mujeres	Total

México

(28.I.1970) ‡

Agriculture, forestry, hunting and fishing	1 981 587	94 285	**2 075 872**	2 382 125	117 329	**2 499 454**	473 153	55 040	**528 193**
Mining and quarrying	12 526	1 515	**14 041**	151 665	11 560	**163 225**	2 444	465	**2 909**
Manufacturing	319 510	111 640	**431 150**	1 355 801	310 964	**1 666 765**	46 237	24 922	**71 159**
Construction	102 582	2 684	**105 266**	440 349	14 103	**454 452**	10 298	990	**11 288**
Electricity	5 462	556	**6 018**	42 574	4 065	**46 639**	539	89	**628**
Commerce	404 012	129 209	**533 221**	400 452	167 527	**567 979**	58 473	37 205	**95 678**
Transport and communication	97 140	3 155	**100 295**	245 418	13 363	**258 781**	8 866	871	**9 737**
Services (incl. gas, water and sanitary services and storage)	326 774	222 544	**549 318**	1 077 809	864 151	**1 941 960**	33 596	39 908	**73 504**
Activities not adequately described . .	157 969	80 918	**238 887**	315 134	140 433	**455 567**	36 305	16 766	**53 071**
Total . . .	3 407 562	646 506	**4 054 068**	6 411 327	1 643 495	**8 054 822**	669 911	176 256	**846 167**

(VI.1975) ‡

Agriculture, forestry, hunting and fishing	2 571 707	152 167	**2 723 874**	3 159 121	188 122	**3 347 243**	623 858	88 313	**712 171**
Mining and quarrying	16 661	2 507	**19 168**	198 885	18 479	**217 364**	3 253	752	**4 005**
Manufacturing	417 554	187 048	**604 602**	1 764 323	492 241	**2 256 564**	60 004	40 001	**100 005**
Construction	137 189	4 405	**141 594**	577 001	22 490	**599 491**	13 406	1 612	**15 018**
Electricity	7 289	931	**8 220**	55 709	6 553	**62 262**	700	108	**808**
Commerce	529 362	215 984	**745 346**	512 311	261 072	**773 383**	75 753	59 699	**135 452**
Transport and communication	129 900	5 192	**135 092**	320 195	21 416	**341 611**	11 664	1 361	**13 025**
Services (incl. gas, water and sanitary services and storage)	418 985	370 550	**789 535**	1 368 733	1 376 123	**2 744 856**	42 566	64 105	**106 671**
Total . . .	4 228 647	938 784	**5 167 431**	7 956 278	2 386 496	**10 342 774**	831 204	255 951	**1 087 155**

Nicaragua (20.IV.1971 *) ‡

1. Agriculture, hunting, forestry and fishing	84 060	1 440	**85 500**	96 380	4 650	**101 030**	37 120	1 530	**38 650**
2. Mining and quarrying	180	10	**190**	2 660	40	**2 700**	90	10	**100**
3. Manufacturing	11 690	8 950	**20 640**	29 390	7 040	**36 430**	730	460	**1 190**
4. Electricity, gas and water	270	—	**270**	2 320	120	**2 440**	30	—	**30**
5. Construction	2 940	20	**2 960**	14 550	240	**14 790**	190	—	**190**
6. Wholesale and retail trade, restaurants and hotels	12 520	13 500	**26 020**	12 660	7 280	**19 940**	520	490	**1 010**
7. Transport, storage and communication	2 890	60	**2 950**	12 950	710	**13 660**	140	—	**140**
8. Financing, insurance, real estate and business services	920	80	**1 000**	3 940	1 220	**5 160**	10	—	**10**
9. Community, social and personal services	7 010	3 600	**10 610**	32 190	47 700	**79 890**	960	1 540	**2 500**
0. Activities not adequately described . .	700	60	**760**	3 620	1 000	**4 620**	60	—	**60**
Total . . .	123 180	27 720	**150 900**	210 660	70 000	**280 660**	39 850	4 030	**43 880**

‡ For notes, see pp. 272-294.

A Distribution by status and by industry (branch of economic activity)
Répartition suivant la situation dans la profession et par branche d'activité économique
Distribución según la categoría de ocupación y por rama de actividad económica

Others and status unknown / Autres et situation non définie / Otros y categoría no definida			TOTAL				Branche d'activité économique	Rama de actividad económica
Males / Hommes / Hombres	Females / Femmes / Mujeres	Total	Males / Hommes / Hombres	Females / Femmes / Mujeres	Total	%		
.	.	.	4 836 865	266 654	5 103 519	39.5	Agriculture, sylviculture, chasse et pêche	Agricultura, silvicultura, caza y pesca
.	.	.	166 635	13 540	180 175	1.4	Industries extractives	Minas y canteras
.	.	.	1 721 548	447 526	2 169 074	16.7	Industries manufacturières	Industrias manufactureras
.	.	.	553 229	17 777	571 006	4.4	Construction	Construcción
.	.	.	48 575	4 710	53 285	0.4	Electricité	Electricidad
.	.	.	862 937	333 941	1 196 878	9.2	Com., banq., assur., aff. imm.	Comercio
.	.	.	351 424	17 389	368 813	2.8	Transports et communications	Transportes y comunicaciones
.	.	.	1 438 179	1 126 603	2 564 782	19.8	Services (y compris gaz, eau et services sanitaires et entrepôts)	Servicios (incl. gas, agua y servicios sanitarios y almacenaje)
.	.	.	509 408	238 117	747 525	5.8	Activités mal désignées	Actividades no bien especif.
.	.	.	10 488 800	2 466 257	12 955 057	100.0	Total	Total
.	.	.	6 354 686	428 602	6 783 288	40.9	Agriculture, sylviculture, chasse et pêche	Agricultura, silvicultura, caza y pesca
.	.	.	218 799	21 738	240 537	1.4	Industries extractives	Minas y canteras
.	.	.	2 241 881	719 290	2 961 171	17.8	Industries manufacturières	Industrias manufactureras
.	.	.	727 596	28 507	756 103	4.6	Construction	Construcción
.	.	.	63 698	7 592	71 290	0.4	Electricité	Electricidad
.	.	.	1 117 426	536 755	1 654 181	10.0	Com., banq., assur., aff. imm.	Comercio
.	.	.	461 759	27 969	489 728	3.0	Transports et communications	Transportes y comunicaciones
.	.	.	1 830 284	1 810 778	3 641 062	21.9	Services (y compris gaz, eau et services sanitaires et entrepôts)	Servicios (incl. gas, agua y servicios sanitarios y almacenaje)
.	.	.	13 016 129	3 581 231	16 597 360	100.0	Total	Total

Males / Hommes / Hombres	Females / Femmes / Mujeres	Total	Males / Hommes / Hombres	Females / Femmes / Mujeres	Total	%	Branche d'activité économique	Rama de actividad económica
8 360	570	8 930	225 920	8 190	234 110	46.4	1. Agriculture, chasse, sylviculture et pêche	1. Agricultura, caza, silvicultura y pesca
60	—	60	2 990	60	3 050	0.6	2. Industries extractives	2. Minas y canteras
1 750	580	2 330	43 560	17 030	60 590	12.0	3. Industries manufacturières	3. Industrias manufactureras
90	10	100	2 710	130	2 840	0.6	4. Electricité, gaz et eau	4. Electricidad, gas y agua
630	—	630	18 310	260	18 570	3.7	5. Construction	5. Construcción
740	680	1 420	26 440	21 950	48 390	9.6	6. Commerce (gros et détail); restaurants, hôtels	6. Comercio (por mayor y por menor); restaurantes, hoteles
580	20	600	16 560	790	17 350	3.4	7. Transports, entrepôts et communications	7. Transportes, almacenamiento y comunicaciones
150	30	180	5 020	1 330	6 350	1.3	8. Banques, assur., affaires imm., services aux entreprises	8. Bancos, seguros, bienes inmuebles, servicios para empresas
7 910	6 180	14 090	48 070	59 020	107 090	21.2	9. Services à la collectivité, services sociaux et personnels	9. Servicios comunales, sociales y personales
340	120	460	4 720	1 180	5 900	1.2	0. Activités mal désignées	0. Actividades no bien especif.
13 491	8 190	28 800	394 300	109 940	504 240	100.0	Total	Total

✝ *Voir notes pp. 272-294.*　　　　　　　　　　　　　　　　✝ Véanse las notas en las págs. 272-294.

POPULATION

2 Structure of the economically active population
Structure de la population active
Estructura de la población económicamente activa

Industry (Branch of economic activity)	Employers and workers on own account Employeurs et personnes travaillant à leur propre compte Empleadores y trabajadores por cuenta propia			Salaried employees and wage earners Employés et ouvriers Empleados y obreros			Family workers Travailleurs familiaux Trabajadores familiares		
	Males Hommes Hombres	Females Femmes Mujeres	Total	Males Hommes Hombres	Females Femmes Mujeres	Total	Males Hommes Hombres	Females Femmes Mujeres	Total

Panamá (10.V.1970) ‡

1. Agriculture, hunting, forestry and fishing	125 149	2 528	**127 677**	37 681	1 393	**39 074**	16 163	4 987	**21 150**
2. Mining and quarrying	143	3	**146**	456	40	**496**	7	.	**7**
3. Manufacturing	3 700	5 414	**9 114**	22 922	6 358	**29 280**	159	253	**412**
4. Electricity, gas and water	.	.	.	3 640	577	**4 217**	.	.	.
5. Construction	6 041	.	**6 041**	20 990	783	**21 773**	85	10	**95**
6. Wholesale and retail trade, restaurants and hotels	10 194	4 089	**14 283**	27 212	14 812	**42 024**	596	822	**1 418**
7. Transport, storage and communication	6 902	43	**6 945**	7 493	2 451	**9 944**	30	4	**34**
8. Financing, insurance, real estate and business services	634	63	**697**	5 502	3 430	**8 932**	4	16	**20**
9. Community, social and personal services	5 584	5 701	**11 285**	33 902	56 501	**90 403**	103	98	**201**
0. Activities not adequately described . .	543	89	**632**	1 288	680	**1 968**	106	26	**132**
Persons seeking work for the first time	.	.	.	.	.	.	.	.	.
Persons working in the Canal Zone .	101	45	**146**	17 422	4 237	**21 659**	.	.	.
Total . . .	158 991	17 975	**176 966**	178 508	91 262	**269 770**	17 253	6 216	**23 469**

Paraguay (9.VII.1972) ‡

1. Agriculture, hunting, forestry and fishing	209 320	7 480	**216 800**	65 720	2 690	**68 410**	71 740	10 960	**82 700**
2. Mining and quarrying	130	—	**130**	1 020	—	**1 020**	—	—	—
3. Manufacturing	16 240	31 870	**48 110**	43 020	11 250	**54 270**	1 400	1 700	**3 100**
4. Electricity, gas and water	50	—	**50**	1 820	100	**1 920**	—	—	—
5. Construction	9 280	10	**9 290**	17 210	60	**17 270**	200	—	**200**
6. Wholesale and retail trade, restaurants and hotels	21 730	16 400	**38 130**	12 790	6 980	**19 770**	660	750	**1 410**
7. Transport, storage and communication	4 520	20	**4 540**	15 410	1 120	**16 530**	100	—	**100**
8. Financing, insurance, real estate and business services	1 670	120	**1 790**	3 290	730	**4 020**	—	—	—
9. Community, social and personal services	9 520	5 250	**14 770**	48 930	56 660	**105 590**	350	210	**560**
0. Activities not adequately described . .	850	120	**970**	5 480	1 120	**6 600**	140	30	**170**
Unemployed.	...	...	...	...	...	...	...	...	...
Total . . .	273 310	61 270	**334 580**	214 690	80 710	**295 400**	74 590	13 650	**88 240**

‡ For notes, see pp. 272-294.

A Distribution by status and by industry (branch of economic activity)
Répartition suivant la situation dans la profession et par branche d'activité économique
Distribución según la categoría de ocupación y por rama de actividad económica

Others and status unknown / Autres et situation non définie / Otros y categoría no definida			TOTAL				Branche d'activité économique	Rama de actividad económica
Males / Hommes / Hombres	Females / Femmes / Mujeres	Total	Males / Hommes / Hombres	Females / Femmes / Mujeres	Total	%		
44	2	46	179 037	8 910	187 947	38.4	1. Agriculture, chasse, sylviculture et pêche	1. Agricultura, caza, silvicultura y pesca
1	.	1	607	43	650	0.1	2. Industries extractives	2. Minas y canteras
24	17	41	26 805	12 042	38 847	8.0	3. Industries manufacturières	3. Industrias manufactureras
9	.	9	3 649	577	4 226	0.9	4. Electricité, gaz et eau	4. Electricidad, gas y agua
19	18	37	27 135	811	27 946	5.7	5. Construction	5. Construcción
18	8	26	38 020	19 731	57 751	11.8	6. Commerce (gros et détail); restaurants, hôtels	6. Comercio (por mayor y por menor); restaurantes, hoteles
10	1	11	14 435	2 499	16 934	3.5	7. Transports, entrepôts et communications	7. Transportes, almacenamiento y comunicaciones
2	1	3	6 142	3 510	9 652	2.0	8. Banques, assur., affaires imm., services aux entreprises	8. Bancos, seguros, bienes inmuebles, servicios para empresas
7	27	34	39 596	62 327	101 923	20.9	9. Services à la collectivité, services sociaux et personnels	9. Servicios comunales, sociales y personales
436	401	837	2 373	1 196	3 569	0.7	0. Activités mal désignées	0. Actividades no bien especif.
8 010	9 075	17 085	8 010	9 075	17 085	3.5	Personnes en quête d'emploi pour la première fois	Personas en busca de trabajo por primera vez
.	.	.	17 523	4 282	21 805	4.5	Personnes travaillant dans la zone du canal	Empleados en la Zona del Canal
8 580	9 550	18 130	363 332	125 003	488 335	100.0	Total	Total

Others and status unknown			TOTAL				Branche d'activité économique	Rama de actividad económica
Males	Females	Total	Males	Females	Total	%		
130	10	140	346 910	21 140	368 050	48.6	1. Agriculture, chasse, sylviculture et pêche	1. Agricultura, caza, silvicultura y pesca
—	—	—	1 150	—	1 150	0.3	2. Industries extractives	2. Minas y canteras
30	40	70	60 690	44 860	105 550	14.0	3. Industries manufacturières	3. Industrias manufactureras
—	—	—	1 870	100	1 970	0.3	4. Electricité, gaz et eau	4. Electricidad, gas y agua
40	—	40	26 730	70	26 800	3.6	5. Construction	5. Construcción
10	10	20	35 190	24 140	59 330	7.9	6. Commerce (gros et détail); restaurants, hôtels	6. Comercio (por mayor y por menor); restaurantes, hoteles
—	—	—	20 030	1 140	21 170	2.8	7. Transports, entrepôts et communications	7. Transportes, almacenamiento y comunicaciones
—	—	—	4 960	850	5 810	0.8	8. Banques, assur., affaires imm., services aux entreprises	8. Bancos, seguros, bienes inmuebles, servicios para empresas
60	30	90	58 860	62 150	121 010	16.0	9. Services à la collectivité, services sociaux et personnels	9. Servicios comunales, sociales y personales
8 200	1 540	9 740	14 670	2 810	17 480	2.3	0. Activités mal désignées	0. Actividades no bien especif.
22 230	4 160	26 390	22 230	4 160	26 390	3.5	Chômeurs	Desempleados
30 700	5 790	36 490	593 290	161 420	754 710	100.0	Total	Total

† Voir notes pp. 272-294.   † Véanse las notas en las págs. 272-294.

83

2 Structure of the economically active population
Structure de la population active
Estructura de la población económicamente activa

Industry (Branch of economic activity)	Employers and workers on own account Employeurs et personnes travaillant à leur propre compte Empleadores y trabajadores por cuenta propia			Salaried employees and wage earners Employés et ouvriers Empleados y obreros			Family workers Travailleurs familiaux Trabajadores familiares		
	Males Hommes Hombres	Females Femmes Mujeres	Total	Males Hommes Hombres	Females Femmes Mujeres	Total	Males Hommes Hombres	Females Femmes Mujeres	Total

Perú (4.VI.1972) ‡

Industry	Males	Females	Total	Males	Females	Total	Males	Females	Total
1. Agriculture, hunting, forestry and fishing	955 666	60 955	1 016 621	326 179	26 352	352 531	115 186	44 599	159 785
2. Mining and quarrying	1 400	66	1 466	49 835	1 232	51 067	74	37	111
3. Manufacturing	96 663	75 346	172 009	249 971	41 612	291 583	3 966	7 444	11 410
4. Electricity, gas and water	.	.	.	6 842	360	7 202	.	.	.
5. Construction	34 531	256	34 787	132 412	1 321	133 733	489	22	511
6. Wholesale and retail trade, restaurants and hotels	151 304	84 510	235 814	114 590	34 254	148 844	5 041	5 130	10 171
7. Transport, storage and communication	50 650	487	51 137	104 555	6 010	110 565	714	22	736
8. Financing, insurance, real estate and business services	6 159	370	6 529	31 047	7 505	38 552	80	22	102
9. Community, social and personal services	56 370	17 465	73 835	290 093	264 979	555 072	1 352	920	2 272
0. Activities not adequately described	3 710	551	4 261	106 614	29 669	136 283	3 829	2 416	6 245
Persons seeking work for the first time	.	.	.	.	.	.	.	.	.
Total	1 356 453	240 006	1 596 459	1 412 138	413 294	1 825 432	130 731	60 612	191 343

Puerto Rico (III.1975) ‡

Industry	Males	Females	Total	Males	Females	Total	Males	Females	Total
1. Agriculture, hunting, forestry and fishing	20 600	—	21 000	44 400	1 300	45 700	1 100	—	1 300
2. Mining and quarrying	—	—	—	1 800	—	1 900	—	—	—
3. Manufacturing	3 800	—	3 800	88 700	70 400	159 100	—	—	—
4. Electricity, gas and water	—	—	—	13 400	2 000	15 400	—	—	—
5. Construction	6 500	—	6 500	90 900	1 300	92 200	—	—	—
6. Wholesale and retail trade, restaurants and hotels	36 000	7 300	43 300	75 500	29 200	104 700	1 400	5 000	6 400
7. Transport, storage and communication	12 300	—	12 400	23 700	4 200	27 900	—	—	—
8. Financing, insurance, real estate and business services	—	—	1 000	9 800	9 800	19 600	—	—	—
9. Community, social and personal services	18 100	7 000	25 100	144 500	125 100	269 600	—	—	—
0. Activities not adequately described / Persons seeking work for the first time	...	...	...	...	...	...	...	...	...
Total	98 000	15 000	113 100	492 800	243 300	736 100	2 900	5 500	8 400

Saint-Pierre-et-Miquelon (12.VI.1967)

(ISIC 1958)

Industry	Males	Females	Total	Males	Females	Total	Males	Females	Total
Agriculture, forestry, hunting and fishing	132	.	132	69	1	70	10	.	10
Manufacturing	1	.	1	124	42	166	.	.	.
Construction	21	.	21	139	.	139	2	.	2
Electricity, gas, water and sanitary services	8	.	8	26	.	26	.	.	.
Commerce	74	65	139	99	88	187	11	8	19
Transport, storage and communication	24	1	25	128	9	137	.	.	.
Services	5	.	5	471	210	681	.	.	.
Activities not adequately described	10	9	19	66	22	88	1	.	1
Total	275	75	350	1 122	372	1 494	24	8	32

‡ For notes, see pp. 272-294.

A **Distribution by status and by industry (branch of economic activity)**
Répartition suivant la situation dans la profession et par branche d'activité économique
Distribución según la categoría de ocupación y por rama de actividad económica

Others and status unknown / *Autres et situation non définie* / Otros y categoría no definida			TOTAL				Branche d'activité économique	Rama de actividad económica
Males / *Hommes* / Hombres	Females / *Femmes* / Mujeres	Total	Males / *Hommes* / Hombres	Females / *Femmes* / Mujeres	Total	%		
5 521	1 161	**6 682**	1 402 552	133 067	**1 535 619**	*40.6*	1. *Agriculture, chasse, sylviculture et pêche*	1. Agricultura, caza, silvicultura y pesca
268	19	**287**	51 577	1 354	**52 931**	*1.4*	2. *Industries extractives*	2. Minas y canteras
3 554	2 611	**6 165**	354 154	127 013	**481 167**	*12.7*	3. *Industries manufacturières*	3. Industrias manufactureras
29	1	**30**	6 871	361	**7 232**	*0.2*	4. *Electricité, gaz et eau*	4. Electricidad, gas y agua
1 933	32	**1 965**	169 365	1 631	**170 996**	*4.5*	5. *Construction*	5. Construcción
2 533	1 737	**4 270**	273 468	125 631	**399 099**	*10.5*	6. *Commerce (gros et détail); restaurants, hôtels*	6. Comercio (por mayor y por menor); restaurantes, hoteles
2 020	151	**2 171**	157 939	6 670	**164 609**	*4.4*	7. *Transports, entrepôts et communications*	7. Transportes, almacenamiento y comunicaciones
302	123	**425**	37 588	8 020	**45 608**	*1.2*	8. *Banques, assur., affaires imm., services aux entreprises*	8. Bancos, seguros, bienes inmuebles, servicios para empresas
30 275	2 923	**33 198**	378 090	286 287	**664 377**	*17.5*	9. *Services à la collectivité, services sociaux et personnels*	9. Servicios comunales, sociales y personales
33 480	15 688	**49 168**	147 633	48 324	**195 957**	*5.2*	0. *Activités mal désignées*	0. Actividades no bien especif.
43 772	24 793	**68 565**	43 772	24 793	**68 565**	*1.8*	*Personnes en quête d'emploi pour la première fois*	Personas en busca de trabajo por primera vez
123 687	49 239	**172 926**	3 023 009	763 151	**3 786 160**	*100.0*	*Total*	Total

Others and status unknown			TOTAL			%	Branche d'activité économique	Rama de actividad económica
...	...	...	66 100	2 000	**68 100**	*7.8*	1. *Agriculture, chasse, sylviculture et pêche*	1. Agricultura, caza, silvicultura y pesca
...	...	...	1 800	—	**1 900**	*0.2*	2. *Industries extractives*	2. Minas y canteras
...	...	...	92 600	70 600	**163 200**	*18.8*	3. *Industries manufacturières*	3. Industrias manufactureras
...	...	...	13 400	2 000	**15 400**	*1.8*	4. *Electricité, gaz et eau*	4. Electricidad, gas y agua
...	...	...	97 700	1 200	**98 900**	*11.4*	5. *Construction*	5. Construcción
...	...	...	112 900	41 400	**154 400**	*17.8*	6. *Commerce (gros et détail); restaurants, hôtels*	6. Comercio (por mayor y por menor); restaurantes, hoteles
...	...	...	36 000	4 300	**40 300**	*4.6*	7. *Transports, entrepôts et communications*	7. Transportes, almacenamiento y comunicaciones
...	...	...	10 600	9 900	**20 500**	*2.4*	8. *Banques, assur., affaires imm., services aux entreprises*	8. Bancos, seguros, bienes inmuebles, servicios para empresas
...	...	...	162 700	132 100	**295 000**	*33.8*	9. *Services à la collectivité, services sociaux et personnels*	9. Servicios comunales, sociales y personales
5 100	7 000	**12 000**	5 100	7 000	**12 000**	*1.4*	{ 0. *Activités mal désignées* / *Personnes en quête d'emploi pour la première fois*	{ 0. Actividades no bien especif. / Personas en busca de trabajo por primera vez
5 100	7 000	**12 000**	598 900	270 800	**869 700**	*100.0*	*Total*	Total

Others and status unknown			TOTAL			%	(CITI 1958)	(CIIU 1958)
.	.	.	211	1	**212**	*11.3*	*Agriculture, sylviculture, chasse et pêche*	Agricultura, silvicultura, caza y pesca
.	.	.	125	42	**167**	*8.9*	*Industries manufacturières*	Industrias manufactureras
.	.	.	162	.	**162**	*8.6*	*Construction*	Construcción
.	.	.	34	.	**34**	*1.8*	*Electricité, gaz, eau et services sanitaires*	Electricidad, gas, agua y servicios sanitarios
.	.	.	184	161	**345**	*18.4*	*Com., banq., assur., aff. imm.*	Comercio
.	.	.	152	10	**162**	*8.6*	*Transports, entrepôts et communications*	Transportes, almacenaje y comunicaciones
.	.	.	476	210	**686**	*36.6*	*Services*	Servicios
.	.	.	77	31	**108**	*5.8*	*Activités mal désignées*	Actividades no bien especif.
.	.	.	1 421	455	**1 876**	*100.0*	*Total*	Total

‡ *Voir notes pp. 272-294.*　　　　　　　　　　‡ Véanse las notas en las págs. 272-294.

2 Structure of the economically active population
Structure de la population active
Estructura de la población económicamente activa

Industry (Branch of economic activity)	Employers and workers on own account Employeurs et personnes travaillant à leur propre compte Empleadores y trabajadores por cuenta propia			Salaried employees and wage earners Employés et ouvriers Empleados y obreros			Family workers Travailleurs familiaux Trabajadores familiares		
	Males Hommes Hombres	Females Femmes Mujeres	Total	Males Hommes Hombres	Females Femmes Mujeres	Total	Males Hommes Hombres	Females Femmes Mujeres	Total

Surinam (31.III.1964) †

(ISIC 1958)

Industry	M	F	Total	M	F	Total	M	F	Total
Agriculture, forestry, hunting and fishing	10 460	1 117	11 577	2 978	479	3 457	1 936	2 952	4 888
Mining and quarrying	6	.	6	5 372	182	5 554	9	1	10
Manufacturing	1 077	471	1 548	4 984	528	5 512	61	22	83
Construction	328	1	329	1 883	26	1 909	10	2	12
Electricity, gas, water and sanitary services	9	.	9	707	88	795	.	.	.
Commerce	2 146	725	2 871	3 990	1 452	5 442	210	335	545
Transport, storage and communication	633	8	641	1 204	34	1 238	22	5	27
Services	503	351	854	15 107	7 779	22 886	38	65	103
Activities not adequately described	254	39	293	1 302	162	1 464	34	65	99
Unemployed	...	...	...	...	...	...	...	...	...
Total ...	15 416	2 712	18 128	37 527	10 730	48 257	2 320	3 447	5 767

Trinidad and Tobago (1973) †

(ISIC 1958)

Industry	M	F	Total	M	F	Total	M	F	Total
Agriculture, forestry, hunting and fishing	...	...	...	...	...	...	...	...	...
Mining and quarrying	...	...	...	...	...	...	...	...	...
Manufacturing	...	...	...	...	...	...	...	...	...
Construction									
Electricity, gas, water and sanitary services	...	...	...	...	...	...	...	...	...
Commerce	...	...	...	...	...	...	...	...	...
Transport, storage and communication	...	...	...	...	...	...	...	...	...
Services	...	...	...	...	...	...	...	...	...
Activities not adequately described	...	...	...	...	...	...	...	...	...
Persons seeking work for the first time	.	.	.	.	.	.	.	.	.
Total ...	39 900	15 300	55 200	211 400	77 600	289 000	12 900	10 700	23 600

† For notes, see pp. 272-294.

A Distribution by status and by industry (branch of economic activity)
Répartition suivant la situation dans la profession et par branche d'activité économique
Distribución según la categoría de ocupación y por rama de actividad económica

Others and status unknown / Autres et situation non définie / Otros y categoría no definida			TOTAL			%	Branche d'activité économique	Rama de actividad económica
Males / Hommes / Hombres	Females / Femmes / Mujeres	Total	Males / Hommes / Hombres	Females / Femmes / Mujeres	Total		(CITI 1958)	(CIIU 1958)
...	...	...	15 374	4 548	**19 922**	*24.8*	*Agriculture, sylviculture, chasse et pêche*	Agricultura, silvicultura, caza y pesca
...	...	...	5 387	183	**5 570**	*7.0*	*Industries extractives*	Minas y canteras
...	...	...	6 122	1 021	**7 143**	*8.9*	*Industries manufacturières*	Industrias manufactureras
...	...	...	2 221	29	**2 250**	*2.8*	*Construction*	Construcción
...	...	...	716	88	**804**	*1.0*	*Electricité, gaz, eau et services sanitaires*	Electricidad, gas, agua y servicios sanitarios
...	...	...	6 346	2 512	**8 858**	*11.1*	*Com., banq., assur., aff. imm.*	Comercio
...	...	...	1 859	47	**1 906**	*2.4*	*Transports, entrepôts et communications*	Transportes, almacenaje y comunicaciones
...	...	...	15 648	8 195	**23 843**	*29.7*	*Services*	Servicios
...	...	...	1 590	266	**1 856**	*2.3*	*Activités mal désignées*	Actividades no bien especif.
5 933	2 114	**8 047**	5 933	2 114	**8 047**	*10.0*	*Chômeurs*	Desempleados
5 933	2 114	**8 047**	61 196	19 003	**80 199**	*100.0*	*Total*	Total

						%	(CITI 1958)	(CIIU 1958)
...	...	...	42 200	13 200	**55 400**	*14.5*	*Agriculture, sylviculture, chasse et pêche*	Agricultura, silvicultura, caza y pesca
...	...	...	55 400	15 500	**70 900**	*18.5*	*Industries extractives / Industries manufacturières / Construction*	Minas y canteras / Industrias manufactureras / Construcción
...	...	...	55 600	5 400	**61 000**	*15.9*	*Electricité, gaz, eau et services sanitaires*	Electricidad, gas, agua y servicios sanitarios
...	...	...	36 600	28 200	**64 800**	*16.9*	*Com., banq., assur., aff. imm.*	Comercio
...	...	...	26 300	3 000	**29 300**	*7.7*	*Transports, entrepôts et communications*	Transportes, almacenaje y comunicaciones
...	...	...	46 000	38 100	**84 100**	*22.0*	*Services*	Servicios
...	...	...	3 100	1 000	**4 100**	*1.1*	*Activités mal désignées*	Actividades no bien especif.
...	...	...	4 900	8 100	**13 000**	*3.4*	*Personnes en quête d'emploi pour la première fois*	Personas en busca de trabajo por primera vez
5 800	8 900	**14 700**	270 000	112 500	**382 500**	*100.0*	*Total*	Total

† *Voir notes pp. 272-294.*

† Véanse las notas en las págs. 272-294.

2 Structure of the economically active population
Structure de la population active
Estructura de la población económicamente activa

Industry (Branch of economic activity)	Employers and workers on own account Employeurs et personnes travaillant à leur propre compte Empleadores y trabajadores por cuenta propia			Salaried employees and wage earners Employés et ouvriers Empleados y obreros			Family workers Travailleurs familiaux Trabajadores familiares		
	Males Hommes Hombres	Females Femmes Mujeres	Total	Males Hommes Hombres	Females Femmes Mujeres	Total	Males Hommes Hombres	Females Femmes Mujeres	Total

United States (1974) ‡

1. Agriculture, hunting, forestry and fishing	1 666 000	120 000	**1 786 000**	1 277 000	257 000	**1 533 000**	141 000	252 000	**393 000**
2. Mining and quarrying	16 000	—	**16 000**	596 000	62 000	**657 000**	1 000	—	**1 000**
3. Manufacturing	231 000	28 000	**259 000**	15 304 000	6 535 000	**21 839 000**	3 000	26 000	**28 000**
4. Electricity, gas and water	8 000	—	**8 000**	1 078 000	148 000	**1 226 000**	—	—	**1 000**
5. Construction	873 000	15 000	**887 000**	4 752 000	299 000	**5 052 000**	3 000	34 000	**37 000**
6. Wholesale and retail trade, restaurants and hotels	1 247 000	484 000	**1 732 000**	8 992 000	7 337 000	**16 328 000**	30 000	238 000	**267 000**
7. Transport, storage and communication	201 000	9 000	**210 000**	3 355 000	1 080 000	**4 435 000**	1 000	12 000	**12 000**
8. Financing, insurance, real estate and business services	242 000	65 000	**306 000**	2 076 000	2 444 000	**4 520 000**	1 000	15 000	**16 000**
9. Community, social and personal services	1 389 000	872 000	**2 261 000**	11 405 000	14 998 000	**26 405 000**	11 000	110 000	**120 000**
Armed forces	.	.	.	2 162 000	67 000	**2 229 000**	.	.	.
Persons seeking work for the first time	.	.	.	.	.	.	.	.	.
Total . . .	5 872 000	·1 593 000	**7 465 000**	50 996 000	33 228 000	**84 223 000**	190 000	686 000	**876 000**

Uruguay (16.X.1963 *) ‡

(ISIC 1958)									
Agriculture, forestry, hunting and fishing	68 267	1 784	**70 051**	95 428	4 048	**99 476**	12 174	922	**13 096**
Mining and quarrying	348	3	**351**	1 994	19	**2 013**	6	.	**6**
Manufacturing	30 517	23 308	**53 825**	127 729	35 938	**163 667**	509	323	**832**
Construction	10 662	40	**10 702**	43 881	388	**44 269**	84	2	**86**
Electricity, gas, water and sanitary services	39	.	**39**	14 970	1 491	**16 461**	.	.	.
Commerce	36 586	6 776	**43 362**	65 482	18 346	**83 828**	736	827	**1 563**
Transport, storage and communication	9 657	61	**9 718**	45 024	3 388	**48 412**	70	5	**75**
Services	21 158	19 195	**40 353**	111 302	112 924	**224 226**	167	303	**470**
Activities not adequately described	4 477	628	**5 105**	19 434	4 587	**24 021**	321	82	**403**
Persons seeking work for the first time	.	.	.	.	.	.	.	.	.
Total . . .	181 711	51 795	**233 506**	525 244	181 129	**706 373**	14 067	2 464	**16 531**

‡ For notes, see pp. 272-294.

Distribution by status and by industry (branch of economic activity)
Répartition suivant la situation dans la profession et par branche d'activité économique
Distribución según la categoría de ocupación y por rama de actividad económica

Others and status unknown *Autres et situation non définie* Otros y categoría no definida			TOTAL				*Branche d'activité économique*	Rama de actividad económica
Males *Hommes* Hombres	Females *Femmes* Mujeres	Total	Males *Hommes* Hombres	Females *Femmes* Mujeres	Total	%		
.	.	.	3 084 000	629 000	**3 712 000**	4.0	1. *Agriculture, chasse, sylviculture et pêche*	1. Agricultura, caza, silvicultura y pesca
.	.	.	613 000	62 000	**674 000**	0.7	2. *Industries extractives*	2. Minas y canteras
.	.	.	15 538 000	6 589 000	**22 126 000**	23.7	3. *Industries manufacturières*	3. Industrias manufactureras
.	.	.	1 086 000	148 000	**1 235 000**	1.3	4. *Electricité, gaz et eau*	4. Electricidad, gas y agua
.	.	.	5 628 000	348 000	**5 976 000**	6.4	5. *Construction*	5. Construcción
.	.	.	10 268 000	8 059 000	**18 327 000**	19.7	6. *Commerce (gros et détail); restaurants, hôtels*	6. Comercio (por mayor y por menor); restaurantes, hoteles
.	.	.	3 557 000	1 101 000	**4 657 000**	5.0	7. *Transports, entrepôts et communications*	7. Transportes, almacenamiento y comunicaciones
.	.	.	2 319 000	2 524 000	**4 842 000**	5.2	8. *Banques, assur., affaires imm., services aux entreprises*	8. Bancos, seguros, bienes inmuebles, servicios para empresas
.	.	.	12 805 000	15 980 000	**28 786 000**	30.9	9. *Services à la collectivité, services sociaux et personnels*	9. Servicios comunales, sociales y personales
.	.	.	2 162 000	67 000	**2 229 000**	2.4	*Forces armées*	Fuerzas armadas
291 000	385 000	**676 000**	291 000	385 000	**676 000**	0.7	*Personnes en quête d'emploi pour la première fois*	Personas en busca de trabajo por primera vez
291 000	385 000	**676 000**	57 352 000	35 892 000	**93 240 000**	100.0	*Total*	Total

						%	(CITI 1958)	(CIIU 1958)
...	...	...	176 888	6 790	**183 678**	18.1	*Agriculture, sylviculture, chasse et pêche*	Agricultura, silvicultura, caza y pesca
...	...	...	2 366	22	**2 388**	0.2	*Industries extractives*	Minas y canteras
...	...	...	159 758	58 594	**218 352**	21.6	*Industries manufacturières*	Industrias manufactureras
...	...	...	54 964	433	**55 397**	5.5	*Construction*	Construcción
...	...	...	15 053	1 495	**16 548**	1.6	*Electricité, gaz, eau et services sanitaires*	Electricidad, gas, agua y servicios sanitarios
...	...	...	103 352	26 087	**129 439**	12.8	*Com., banq., assur., aff. imm.*	Comercio
...	...	...	55 059	3 459	**58 518**	5.8	*Transports, entrepôts et communications*	Transportes, almacenaje y comunicaciones
...	...	...	134 463	134 976	**269 439**	26.6	*Services*	Servicios
...	...	...	44 747	13 825	**58 572**	5.8	*Activités mal désignées*	Actividades no bien especif.
...	...	...	13 337	6 599	**19 936**	2.0	*Personnes en quête d'emploi pour la première fois*	Personas en busca de trabajo por primera vez
...	...	...	759 987	252 280	**1 012 267**	100.0	*Total*	Total

‡ *Voir notes pp. 272-294.*   ‡ *Véanse las notas en las págs. 272-294.*

2 Structure of the economically active population
Structure de la population active
Estructura de la población económicamente activa

Industry (Branch of economic activity)	Employers and workers on own account *Employeurs et personnes travaillant à leur propre compte* Empleadores y trabajadores por cuenta propia			Salaried employees and wage earners *Employés et ouvriers* Empleados y obreros			Family workers *Travailleurs familiaux* Trabajadores familiares		
	Males *Hommes* Hombres	Females *Femmes* Mujeres	Total	Males *Hommes* Hombres	Females *Femmes* Mujeres	Total	Males *Hommes* Hombres	Females *Femmes* Mujeres	Total

Venezuela (2.XI.1971)

(ISIC 1958)									
Agriculture, forestry, hunting and fishing	...	...	...	...	...	...	...	...	...
Mining and quarrying	...	...	...	...	...	...	...	...	...
Manufacturing	...	...	...	...	...	...	...	...	...
Construction	...	...	...	...	...	...	...	...	...
Electricity, gas, water and sanitary services	...	...	...	...	...	...	...	...	...
Commerce	...	...	...	...	...	...	...	...	...
Transport, storage and communication	...	...	...	...	...	...	...	...	...
Services	...	...	...	...	...	...	...	...	...
Activities not adequately described	...	...	...	...	...	...	...	...	...
Persons seeking work for the first time	.	.	.	.	.	.	.	.	.
Total ...	...	...	...	...	...	...	...	...	...

Virgin Is. (Brit.) (7.IV.1970) †

1. Agriculture, hunting, forestry and fishing	...	...	...	...	...	...	...	...	...
2. Mining and quarrying	...	...	...	...	...	...	...	...	...
3. Manufacturing	...	...	...	...	...	...	...	...	...
4. Electricity, gas and water	...	...	...	...	...	...	...	...	...
5. Construction	...	...	...	...	...	...	...	...	...
6. Wholesale and retail trade	...	...	...	...	...	...	...	...	...
7. Transport, storage and communication	...	...	...	...	...	...			
8. Financing, insurance, real estate and business services							...	...	...
9. Community, social and personal services; restaurants and hotels							...	...	...
0. Activities not adequately described Unemployed	...	...	...	...	...	...	...	...	...
Total ...	446	116	**562**	2 363	860	**3 223**	20	45	**65**

† For notes, see pp. 272-294.

A. Distribution by status and by industry (branch of economic activity)
Répartition suivant la situation dans la profession et par branche d'activité économique
Distribución según la categoría de ocupación y por rama de actividad económica

Others and status unknown / Autres et situation non définie / Otros y categoría no definida			TOTAL			%	Branche d'activité économique	Rama de actividad económica
Males / Hommes / Hombres	Females / Femmes / Mujeres	Total	Males / Hommes / Hombres	Females / Femmes / Mujeres	Total			
						%	(CITI 1958)	(CIIU 1958)
...	...	...	593 385	18 151	**611 536**	*20.3*	*Agriculture, sylviculture, chasse et pêche*	Agricultura, silvicultura, caza y pesca
...	...	...	35 886	2 470	**38 356**	*1.3*	*Industries extractives*	Minas y canteras
...	...	...	322 927	80 177	**403 104**	*13.4*	*Industries manufacturières*	Industrias manufactureras
...	...	...	30 470	3 534	**34 004**	*1.1*	*Construction*	Construcción
...	...	...	154 823	3 799	**158 622**	*5.3*	*Electricité, gaz, eau et services sanitaires*	Electricidad, gas, agua y servicios sanitarios
...	...	...	312 472	66 372	**378 844**	*12.6*	*Com., banq., assur., aff. imm.*	Comercio
...	...	...	115 269	8 948	**124 217**	*4.1*	*Transports, entrepôts et communications*	Transportes, almacenaje y comunicaciones
...	...	...	400 676	375 553	**776 229**	*25.7*	*Services*	Servicios
...	...	...	344 052	109 243	**453 295**	*15.0*	*Activités mal désignées*	Actividades no bien especif.
...	...	...	28 650	7 817	**36 467**	*1.2*	*Personnes en quête d'emploi pour la première fois*	Personas en busca de trabajo por primera vez
...	...	...	2 338 610	676 064	**3 014 674**	*100.0*	*Total*	Total

Others and status unknown / Autres et situation non définie / Otros y categoría no definida			TOTAL			%	Branche d'activité économique	Rama de actividad económica
Males / Hommes / Hombres	Females / Femmes / Mujeres	Total	Males / Hommes / Hombres	Females / Femmes / Mujeres	Total			
						%		
...	...	...	285	13	**298**	*7.5*	1. *Agriculture, chasse, sylviculture et pêche*	1. Agricultura, caza, silvicultura y pesca
...	...	...	4	3	**7**	*0.2*	2. *Industries extractives*	2. Minas y canteras
...	...	...	151	36	**187**	*4.7*	3. *Industries manufacturières*	3. Industrias manufactureras
...	...	...	186	151	**337**	*8.5*	4. *Electricité, gaz et eau*	4. Electricidad, gas y agua
...	...	...	1 168	19	**1 187**	*29.9*	5. *Construction*	5. Construcción
...	...	...	112	72	**184**	*4.6*	6. *Commerce (gros et détail)*	6. Comercio (por mayor y por menor)
...	...	...	288	36	**324**	*8.2*	7. *Transports, entrepôts et communications*	7. Transportes, almacenamiento y comunicaciones
...	...	...	601	677	**1 278**	*32.2*	8. *Banques, assur., affaires imm., services aux entreprises* 9. *Services à la collectivité, services sociaux et personnels; restaurants, hôtels*	8. Bancos, seguros, bienes inmuebles, servicios para empresas 9. Servicios comunales, sociales y personales; restaurantes, hoteles
...	...	...	101	67	**168**	*4.2*	0. *Activités mal désignées* Chômeurs	0. Actividades no bien especif. Desempleados
67	53	**120**	2 896	1 074	**3 970**	*100.0*	*Total*	Total

† *Voir notes pp. 272-294.*

† Véanse las notas en las págs. 272-294.

2 Structure of the economically active population
Structure de la population active
Estructura de la población económicamente activa

Industry (Branch of economic activity)	Employers and workers on own account Employeurs et personnes travaillant à leur propre compte Empleadores y trabajadores por cuenta propia			Salaried employees and wage earners Employés et ouvriers Empleados y obreros			Family workers Travailleurs familiaux Trabajadores familiares		
	Males Hommes Hombres	Females Femmes Mujeres	Total	Males Hommes Hombres	Females Femmes Mujeres	Total	Males Hommes Hombres	Females Femmes Mujeres	Total

Bahrain (3.IV.1971)

ASIA — ASIE — ASIA

1. Agriculture, hunting, forestry and fishing	1 693	1	**1 694**	1 957	2	**1 959**	336	1	**337**
2. Mining and quarrying	56	.	**56**	27	.	**27**	2	.	**2**
3. Manufacturing	1 035	22	**1 057**	7 130	62	**7 192**	127	3	**130**
4. Electricity, gas and water	.	.	**.**	1 701	4	**1 705**	.	.	**.**
5. Construction	947	.	**947**	9 411	40	**9 451**	6	.	**6**
6. Wholesale and retail trade, restaurants and hotels	3 856	27	**3 883**	3 304	113	**3 417**	403	3	**406**
7. Transport, storage and communication	1 841	2	**1 843**	5 774	117	**5 891**	9	.	**9**
8. Financing, insurance, real estate and business services	217	4	**221**	792	71	**863**	.	.	**.**
9. Community, social and personal services	700	53	**753**	14 950	2 679	**17 629**	6	.	**6**
0. Activities not adequately described	13	.	**13**	90	3	**93**	.	.	**.**
Persons seeking work for the first time	.	.	**.**	.	.	**.**	.	.	**.**
Total . . .	10 358	109	**10 467**	45 136	3 091	**48 227**	889	7	**896**

Brunei (11.VIII.1971)

1. Agriculture, hunting, forestry and fishing	...	...	...	...	...	...	...	...	...
2. Mining and quarrying	...	...	...	...	...	...	...	...	...
3. Manufacturing	...	...	...	...	...	...	...	...	...
4. Electricity, gas and water	...	...	...	...	...	...	...	...	...
5. Construction	...	...	...	...	...	...	...	...	...
6. Wholesale and retail trade, restaurants and hotels	...	...	...	...	...	...	...	...	...
7. Transport, storage and communication	...	...	...	...	...	...	...	...	...
8. Financing, insurance, real estate and business services	...	...	...	...	...	...	...	...	...
9. Community, social and personal services	...	...	...	...	...	...	...	...	...
0. Activities not adequately described	...	...	...	...	...	...	...	...	...
Unemployed	...	...	...	...	...	...	...	...	...
Total . . .	5 071	1 547	**6 618**	28 285	4 381	**32 666**	206	522	**728**

A Distribution by status and by industry (branch of economic activity)
Répartition suivant la situation dans la profession et par branche d'activité économique
Distribución según la categoría de ocupación y por rama de actividad económica

Others and status unknown / Autres et situation non définie / Otros y categoría no definida			TOTAL			Branche d'activité économique	Rama de actividad económica
Males / Hommes / Hombres	Females / Femmes / Mujeres	Total	Males / Hommes / Hombres	Females / Femmes / Mujeres	Total		
					%		
.	.	.	3 986	4	3 990	6.6	1. Agriculture, chasse, sylviculture et pêche	1. Agricultura, caza, silvicultura y pesca
.	.	.	85	7	92	0.2	2. Industries extractives	2. Minas y canteras
.	.	.	8 292	80	8 372	13.9	3. Industries manufacturières	3. Industrias manufactureras
.	.	.	1 701	4	1 705	2.8	4. Electricité, gaz et eau	4. Electricidad, gas y agua
.	.	.	10 364	40	10 404	17.3	5. Construction	5. Construcción
.	.	.	7 563	143	7 706	12.8	6. Commerce (gros et détail); restaurants, hôtels	6. Comercio (por mayor y por menor); restaurantes, hoteles
.	.	.	7 624	119	7 743	12.8	7. Transports, entrepôts et communications	7. Transportes, almacenamiento y comunicaciones
.	.	.	1 009	75	1 084	1.8	8. Banques, assur., affaires imm., services aux entreprises	8. Bancos, seguros, bienes inmuebles, servicios para empresas
.	.	.	15 656	2 732	18 388	30.4	9. Services à la collectivité, services sociaux et personnels	9. Servicios comunales, sociales y personales
.	.	.	103	3	106	0.2	0. Activités mal désignées	0. Actividades no bien especif.
669	42	711	669	42	711	1.2	Personnes en quête d'emploi pour la première fois	Personas en busca de trabajo por primera vez
669	42	711	57 052	3 249	60 301	100.0	Total	Total

						%		
...	...	...	3 296	1 480	4 776	11.6	1. Agriculture, chasse, sylviculture et pêche	1. Agricultura, caza, silvicultura y pesca
...	...	...	2 720	195	2 915	7.1	2. Industries extractives	2. Minas y canteras
...	...	...	1 466	285	1 751	4.3	3. Industries manufacturières	3. Industrias manufactureras
...	...	...	1 061	25	1 086	2.6	4. Electricité, gaz et eau	4. Electricidad, gas y agua
...	...	...	7 929	161	8 090	19.7	5. Construction	5. Construcción
...	...	...	3 332	857	4 189	10.2	6. Commerce (gros et détail); restaurants, hôtels	6. Comercio (por mayor y por menor); restaurantes, hoteles
...	...	...	2 034	93	2 127	5.2	7. Transports, entrepôts et communications	7. Transportes, almacenamiento y comunicaciones
...	...	...	527	118	645	1.6	8. Banques, assur., affaires imm., services aux entreprises	8. Bancos, seguros, bienes inmuebles, servicios para empresas
...	...	...	11 146	3 217	14 363	34.9	9. Services à la collectivité, services sociaux et personnels	9. Servicios comunales, sociales y personales
...	...	...	51	19	70	0.2	0. Activités mal désignées	0. Actividades no bien especif.
...	...	...	649	438	1 087	2.6	Chômeurs	Desempleados
649	438	1 087	34 211	6 888	41 099	100.0	Total	Total

POPULATION

2 Structure of the economically active population
Structure de la population active
Estructura de la población económicamente activa

Industry (Branch of economic activity)	Employers and workers on own account Employeurs et personnes travaillant à leur propre compte Empleadores y trabajadores por cuenta propia			Salaried employees and wage earners Employés et ouvriers Empleados y obreros			Family workers Travailleurs familiaux Trabajadores familiares		
	Males Hommes Hombres	Females Femmes Mujeres	Total	Males Hommes Hombres	Females Femmes Mujeres	Total	Males Hommes Hombres	Females Femmes Mujeres	Total

Burma (1973-74) ‡

1. Agriculture, hunting, forestry and fishing	...	...	...	...	...	...	...	...	...
2. Mining and quarrying	...	...	...	...	...	...	...	...	...
3. Manufacturing	...	...	...	...	...	...	...	...	...
4. Electricity, gas and water	...	...	...	...	...	...	...	...	...
5. Construction	...	...	...	...	...	...	...	...	...
6. Wholesale and retail trade, restaurants and hotels	...	...	...	...	...	...	...	...	...
7. Transport, storage and communication	...	...	...	...	...	...	...	...	...
8. Financing, insurance, real estate and business services	...	...	...	...	...	...	...	...	...
9. Community, social and personal services									
0. Activities not adequately described	...	...	...	...	...	...	...	...	...
Total . . .	...	...	...	...	...	...	...	...	...

Cyprus (1974) ‡

(ISIC 1958)

Agriculture, forestry, hunting and fishing	...	...	...	...	...	...	...	...	...
Mining and quarrying	...	...	...	...	...	...	...	...	...
Manufacturing	...	...	...	...	...	...	...	...	...
Construction	...	...	...	...	...	...	...	...	...
Electricity, gas, water and sanitary services	...	...	...	...	...	...	...	...	...
Commerce	...	...	...	...	...	...	...	...	...
Transport, storage and communication	...	...	...	...	...	...	...	...	...
Services	...	...	...	...	...	...	...	...	...
Activities not adequately described	...	...	...	...	...	...	...	...	...
Armed forces									
Unemployed	...	...	...	...	...	...	...	...	...
Total . . .	...	...	...	...	...	...	...	...	...

Hong Kong (9.III.1971) ‡

1. Agriculture, hunting, forestry and fishing	24 203	7 304	31 507	7 460	2 336	9 796	9 192	12 480	21 672
2. Mining and quarrying	182	24	206	3 215	1 083	4 298	7	7	14
3. Manufacturing	37 042	5 147	42 189	399 919	308 589	708 508	2 228	2 609	4 837
4. Electricity, gas and water	73	5	78	8 067	704	8 771	3	18	21
5. Construction	2 772	90	2 862	74 030	6 129	80 159	102	35	137
6. Wholesale and retail trade, restaurants and hotels	55 806	15 678	71 484	136 362	41 013	177 375	1 881	3 185	5 066
7. Transport, storage and communication	7 566	678	8 244	97 403	7 013	104 416	1 024	1 038	2 062
8. Financing, insurance, real estate and business services	1 169	50	1 219	29 427	10 405	39 832	7	14	21
9. Community, social and personal services	10 091	1 347	11 438	127 822	93 519	221 341	201	379	580
0. Activities not adequately described	1 615	635	2 250	10 834	10 519	21 353	286	827	1 113
Persons seeking work for the first time	.	.	.	.	.	.	.	.	.
Total . . .	140 519	30 958	171 477	894 539	481 310	1 375 849	14 931	20 592	35 523

‡ For notes, see pp. 272-294.

A Distribution by status and by industry (branch of economic activity)
Répartition suivant la situation dans la profession et par branche d'activité économique
Distribución según la categoría de ocupación y por rama de actividad económica

Others and status unknown / Autres et situation non définie / Otros y categoría no definida			TOTAL				Branche d'activité économique	Rama de actividad económica
Males / Hommes / Hombres	Females / Femmes / Mujeres	Total	Males / Hommes / Hombres	Females / Femmes / Mujeres	Total	%		
...	...	...	...	...	8 015 418	68.9	1. Agriculture, chasse, sylviculture et pêche	1. Agricultura, caza, silvicultura y pesca
...	...	...	...	...	61 010	0.5	2. Industries extractives	2. Minas y canteras
...	...	...	...	...	829 388	7.1	3. Industries manufacturières	3. Industrias manufactureras
...	...	...	...	...	13 921	0.1	4. Electricité, gaz et eau	4. Electricidad, gas y agua
...	...	...	...	...	173 865	1.5	5. Construction	5. Construcción
...	...	...	...	...	1 034 085	8.9	6. Commerce (gros et détail) ; restaurants, hôtels	6. Comercio (por mayor y por menor); restaurantes, hoteles
...	...	...	...	...	405 825	3.5	7. Transports, entrepôts et communications	7. Transportes, almacenamiento y comunicaciones
...	...	...	...	...	509 614	4.4	8. Banques, assur., affaires imm., services aux entreprises \ 9. Services à la collectivité, services sociaux et personnels	8. Bancos, seguros, bienes inmuebles, servicios para empresas \ 9. Servicios comunales, sociales y personales
...	...	...	...	...	590 711	5.1	0. Activités mal désignées	0. Actividades no bien especif.
...	...	...	...	...	11 633 837	100.0	Total	Total

Others and status unknown			TOTAL			%	(CITI 1958)	(CIIU 1958)
...	...	...	43 369	32 881	76 250	28.2	Agriculture, sylviculture, chasse et pêche	Agricultura, silvicultura, caza y pesca
...	...	...	3 242	147	3 389	1.3	Industries extractives	Minas y canteras
...	...	...	20 498	10 443	30 941	11.5	Industries manufacturières	Industrias manufactureras
...	...	...	20 658	1 381	22 039	8.2	Construction	Construcción
...	...	...	2 413	97	2 510	0.9	Electricité, gaz, eau et services sanitaires	Electricidad, gas, agua y servicios sanitarios
...	...	...	18 322	7 866	26 188	9.7	Com., banq., assur., aff. imm.	Comercio
...	...	...	8 522	1 202	9 724	3.6	Transports, entrepôts et communications	Transportes, almacenaje y comunicaciones
...	...	...	26 901	15 893	42 794	15.8	Services	Servicios
...	...	...	5 384	888	6 272	2.3	Activités mal désignées	Actividades no bien especif.
...	...	...	41 800	8 093	49 893	18.5	Forces armées \ Chômeurs	Fuerzas armadas \ Desempleados
...	...	...	191 109	78 891	270 000	100.0	Total	Total

Others and status unknown			TOTAL			%	Branche d'activité économique	Rama de actividad económica
1 327	428	1 755	42 182	22 548	64 730	3.9	1. Agriculture, chasse, sylviculture et pêche	1. Agricultura, caza, silvicultura y pesca
89	38	127	3 493	1 152	4 645	0.3	2. Industries extractives	2. Minas y canteras
6 245	2 732	8 977	445 434	319 077	764 511	46.2	3. Industries manufacturières	3. Industrias manufactureras
41	20	61	8 184	747	8 931	0.5	4. Electricité, gaz et eau	4. Electricidad, gas y agua
2 131	139	2 270	79 035	6 393	85 428	5.2	5. Construction	5. Construcción
3 034	769	3 803	197 083	60 645	257 728	15.6	6. Commerce (gros et détail) ; restaurants, hôtels	6. Comercio (por mayor y por menor); restaurantes, hoteles
4 540	110	4 650	110 533	8 839	119 372	7.2	7. Transports, entrepôts et communications	7. Transportes, almacenamiento y comunicaciones
242	39	281	30 845	10 508	41 353	2.5	8. Banques, assur., affaires imm., services aux entreprises	8. Bancos, seguros, bienes inmuebles, servicios para empresas
1 517	2 626	4 143	139 631	97 871	237 502	14.4	9. Services à la collectivité, services sociaux et personnels	9. Servicios comunales, sociales y personales
15 723	6 271	21 994	28 458	18 252	46 710	2.8	0. Activités mal désignées	0. Actividades no bien especif.
12 022	11 975	23 997	12 022	11 975	23 997	1.4	Personnes en quête d'emploi pour la première fois	Personas en busca de trabajo por primera vez
46 911	25 147	72 058	1 096 900	558 007	1 654 907	100.0	Total	Total

† Voir notes pp. 272-294.

† Véanse las notas en las págs. 272-294.

2 Structure of the economically active population
Structure de la population active
Estructura de la población económicamente activa

Industry (Branch of economic activity)	Employers and workers on own account *Employeurs et personnes travaillant à leur propre compte* Empleadores y trabajadores por cuenta propia			Salaried employees and wage earners *Employés et ouvriers* Empleados y obreros			Family workers *Travailleurs familiaux* Trabajadores familiares		
	Males *Hommes* Hombres	Females *Femmes* Mujeres	Total	Males *Hommes* Hombres	Females *Femmes* Mujeres	Total	Males *Hommes* Hombres	Females *Femmes* Mujeres	Total

India (1.IV.1971) ‡

Industry	Males	Females	Total	Males	Females	Total	Males	Females	Total
1. Agriculture, hunting, forestry and fishing	1 334 100	144 700	**1 478 800**	1 565 600	528 600	**2 094 200**	614 200	109 700	**723 900**
2. Mining and quarrying	91 400	19 100	**110 500**	696 600	100 600	**797 200**	10 700	4 400	**15 100**
3. Manufacturing (incl. repair services)	4 978 700	688 200	**5 666 900**	7 307 000	712 800	**8 019 800**	2 586 000	794 800	3 380 800
4. Electricity, gas and water	17 900	400	**18 300**	504 900	9 200	**514 100**	.	.	.
5. Construction	838 300	62 100	**900 400**	1 137 400	133 200	**1 270 600**	36 100	8 200	**44 300**
6. Wholesale and retail trade, restaurants and hotels	5 415 000	385 600	**5 800 600**	2 238 000	66 800	**2 304 800**	577 200	65 700	**642 900**
7. Transport, storage and communication	936 700	40 900	**977 600**	3 293 100	103 300	**3 396 400**	25 500	1 700	**27 200**
8. Financing, insurance, real estate and business services	339 500	4 300	**343 800**	893 000	33 200	**926 200**	19 300	600	**19 900**
9. Community, social and personal services (excl. repair services)	2 178 800	349 000	**2 527 800**	9 519 700	1 546 800	**11 066 500**	287 200	136 400	**423 600**
0. Activities not adequately described	724 000	130 200	**854 200**	271 200	47 900	**319 100**	32 800	9 000	**41 800**
Total . . .	16 854 400	1 824 500	**18 678 900**	27 426 500	3 282 400	**30 708 900**	4 189 000	1 130 500	**5 319 500**

Indonesia (24.IX.1971 *) ‡

Industry	Males	Females	Total	Males	Females	Total	Males	Females	Total
1. Agriculture, hunting, forestry and fishing	9 389 215	2 069 006	**11 458 221**	3 931 850	1 852 069	**5 783 919**	3 680 126	4 023 747	**7 703 873**
2. Mining and quarrying	5 715	286	**6 001**	79 735	4 337	**84 072**	774	1 288	**2 062**
3. Manufacturing	399 352	518 313	**917 665**	1 036 960	522 767	**1 559 727**	93 865	381 360	**475 225**
4. Electricity, gas and water	3 190	523	**3 713**	33 182	1 194	**34 376**	243	.	**243**
5. Construction	108 464	867	**109 331**	604 173	8 400	**612 573**	27 141	1 083	**28 224**
6. Wholesale and retail trade, restaurants and hotels	1 721 497	1 322 727	**3 044 224**	429 211	145 716	**574 927**	202 288	330 928	**533 216**
7. Transport, storage and communication	215 721	3 303	**219 024**	676 943	13 312	**690 255**	21 872	1 100	**22 972**
8. Financing, insurance, real estate and business services	3 433	737	**4 170**	76 764	16 460	**93 224**	1 170	228	**1 398**
9. Community, social and personal services	420 407	132 173	**552 580**	2 400 194	868 662	**3 268 856**	83 350	75 516	**158 866**
0. Activities not adequately described	...	...	...	...	...	...	...	...	...
Persons seeking work for the first time	.	.	.	.	.	.	.	.	.
Total . . .	12 266 994	4 047 935	**16 314 929**	9 269 012	3 432 917	**12 701 929**	4 110 829	4 815 250	**8 926 079**

‡ For notes, see pp. 272-294.

A   Distribution by status and by industry (branch of economic activity)
Répartition suivant la situation dans la profession et par branche d'activité économique
Distribución según la categoría de ocupación y por rama de actividad económica

Others and status unknown / *Autres et situation non définie* / Otros y categoría no definida			TOTAL				*Branche d'activité économique*	Rama de actividad económica
Males / *Hommes* / Hombres	Females / *Femmes* / Mujeres	Total	Males / *Hommes* / Hombres	Females / *Femmes* / Mujeres	Total	%		
100 605 200	25 060 900	**125 666 100**	104 119 100	25 843 900	**129 963 000**	*72.0*	1. *Agriculture, chasse, sylviculture et pêche*	1. Agricultura, caza, silvicultura y pesca
·	·	·	798 700	124 100	**922 800**	*0.5*	2. *Industries extractives*	2. Minas y canteras
·	·	·	14 871 700	2 195 800	**17 067 500**	*9.5*	3. *Industries manufacturières (y compris serv. de réparations)*	3. Industrias manufactureras (incl. serv. de reparaciones)
·	·	·	522 800	9 600	**532 400**	*0.3*	4. *Électricité, gaz et eau*	4. Electricidad, gas y agua
·	·	·	2 011 800	203 500	**2 215 300**	*1.2*	5. *Construction*	5. Construcción
·	·	·	8 230 200	518 100	**8 748 300**	*4.9*	6. *Commerce (gros et détail); restaurants, hôtels*	6. Comercio (por mayor y por menor); restaurantes, hoteles
·	·	·	4 255 300	145 900	**4 401 200**	*2.4*	7. *Transports, entrepôts et communications*	7. Transportes, almacenamiento y comunicaciones
·	·	·	1 251 800	38 100	**1 289 900**	*0.7*	8. *Banques, assur., affaires imm., services aux entreprises*	8. Bancos, seguros, bienes inmuebles, servicios para empresas
·	·	·	11 985 700	2 032 200	**14 017 900**	*7.8*	9. *Services à la collectivité, services sociaux et personnels (non compris serv. de réparations)*	9. Servicios comunales, sociales y personales (excl. serv. de reparaciones
·	·	·	1 028 000	187 100	**1 215 100**	*0.7*	0. *Activités mal désignées*	0. Actividades no bien especif.
100 605 200	25 060 900	**125 666 100**	149 075 100	31 298 300	**180 373 400**	*100.0*	*Total*	Total

Others and status unknown			TOTAL				*Branche d'activité économique*	Rama de actividad económica
Males	Females	Total	Males	Females	Total	%		
...	...	...	17 001 191	7 944 822	**24 946 013**	*62.2*	1. *Agriculture, chasse, sylviculture et pêche*	1. Agricultura, caza, silvicultura y pesca
...	...	...	86 224	5 911	**92 135**	*0.2*	2. *Industries extractives*	2. Minas y canteras
...	...	...	1 530 177	1 422 440	**2 952 617**	*7.4*	3. *Industries manufacturières*	3. Industrias manufactureras
...	...	...	36 615	1 717	**38 332**	*0.1*	4. *Électricité, gaz et eau*	4. Electricidad, gas y agua
...	...	...	739 778	10 350	**750 128**	*1.9*	5. *Construction*	5. Construcción
...	...	...	2 352 996	1 799 371	**4 152 367**	*10.4*	6. *Commerce (gros et détail); restaurants, hôtels*	6. Comercio (por mayor y por menor); restaurantes, hoteles
...	...	...	914 536	17 715	**932 251**	*2.3*	7. *Transports, entrepôts et communications*	7. Transportes, almacenamiento y comunicaciones
...	...	...	81 367	17 425	**98 792**	*0.2*	8. *Banques, assur., affaires imm., services aux entreprises*	8. Bancos, seguros, bienes inmuebles, servicios para empresas
...	...	...	2 903 951	1 076 351	**3 980 302**	*9.9*	9. *Services à la collectivité, services sociaux et personnels*	9. Servicios comunales, sociales y personales
885 827	863 335	**1 749 162**	885 827	863 335	**1 749 162**	*4.4*	0. *Activités mal désignées*	0. Actividades no bien especif.
299 739	108 232	**407 971**	299 739	108 232	**407 971**	*1.0*	*Personnes en quête d'emploi pour la première fois*	Personas en busca de trabajo por primera vez
1 185 566	971 567	**2 157 133**	26 832 401	13 267 669	**40 100 070**	*100.0*	*Total*	Total

† *Voir notes pp. 272-294.*

† Véanse las notas en las págs. 272-294.

2 Structure of the economically active population
Structure de la population active
Estructura de la población económicamente activa

Industry (Branch of economic activity	Employers and workers on own account *Employeurs et personnes travaillant à leur propre compte* Empleadores y trabajadores por cuenta propia			Salaried employees and wage earners *Employés et ouvriers* Empleados y obreros			Family workers *Travailleurs familiaux* Trabajadores familiares		
	Males *Hommes* Hombres	Females *Femmes* Mujeres	Total	Males *Hommes* Hombres	Females *Femmes* Mujeres	Total	Males *Hommes* Hombres	Females *Femmes* Mujeres	Total

Iran (1.XI.1966) ╬

(ISIC 1958)									
Agriculture, forestry, hunting and fishing	1 799 166	42 256	1 841 422	733 531	66 679	800 210	424 392	93 905	518 297
Mining and quarrying	1 121	7	1 128	24 646	393	25 039	93	1	94
Manufacturing	198 013	147 983	345 996	543 110	262 674	805 784	15 844	97 087	112 931
Construction	46 864	171	47 035	455 999	1 723	457 722	3 923	176	4 099
Electricity, gas, water and sanitary services	1 012	10	1 022	51 084	682	51 766	28	.	28
Commerce	379 550	3 529	383 079	149 432	4 881	154 313	13 119	485	13 604
Transport, storage and communication	56 918	153	57 071	161 837	2 309	164 146	2 286	86	2 372
Services	112 820	8 104	120 924	631 549	156 557	788 106	14 107	4 762	18 869
Activities not adequately described .	12 566	1 231	13 797	71 918	3 357	75 275	5 353	1 424	6 777
Persons seeking work for the first time	...	...	...	...	...	...	...	...	...
Unemployed									
Total . . .	2 608 030	203 444	2 811 474	2 823 106	499 255	3 322 361	479 145	197 926	677 071

Israel (1974) ╬

1. Agriculture, hunting, forestry and fishing	37 300	5 900	43 200	16 000	3 400	19 400	2 300	6 000	8 200
2. Mining and quarrying . . . . }	36 000	6 800	42 800	177 700	50 900	228 600	600	1 800	2 400
3. Manufacturing . . . . }									
4. Electricity, gas and water	200	—	200	8 800	1 300	10 200	—	—	—
5. Construction	19 200	—	19 200	64 700	3 200	67 900	400	100	400
6. Wholesale and retail trade, restaurants and hotels	45 600	10 000	55 600	39 900	24 300	64 200	1 600	10 100	11 700
7. Transport, storage and communication	22 600	1 700	24 300	48 500	10 500	59 000	100	100	200
8. Financing, insurance, real estate and business services	8 900	1 300	10 200	28 300	30 400	58 800	—	800	900
9. Community, social and personal services	20 500	20 700	41 200	156 600	155 200	311 800	100	1 300	1 500
0. Activities not adequately described . .	700	300	1 000	4 000	2 300	6 300	—	—	—
Persons seeking work for the first time	.	.	.	.	.	.	.	.	.
Unemployed	...	...	...	...	...	...	...	...	...
Total . . .	191 000	47 100	238 000	544 500	281 400	826 000	5 100	20 200	25 300

╬ For notes, see pp. 272-294.

A Distribution by status and by industry (branch of economic activity)
Répartition suivant la situation dans la profession et par branche d'activité économique
Distribución según la categoría de ocupación y por rama de actividad económica

Others and status unknown / *Autres et situation non définie* / Otros y categoría no definida			TOTAL				Branche d'activité économique	Rama de actividad económica
Males / *Hommes* / Hombres	Females / *Femmes* / Mujeres	Total	Males / *Hommes* / Hombres	Females / *Femmes* / Mujeres	Total			
						%	(CITI 1958)	(CIIU 1958)
8 198	388	**8 586**	2 965 287	203 228	**3 168 515**	*41.8*	*Agriculture, sylviculture, chasse et pêche*	Agricultura, silvicultura, caza y pesca
51	.	**51**	25 911	401	**26 312**	*0.3*	*Industries extractives*	Minas y canteras
1 832	1 057	**2 889**	758 799	508 801	**1 267 600**	*16.7*	*Industries manufacturières*	Industrias manufactureras
917	5	**922**	507 703	2 075	**509 778**	*6.7*	*Construction*	Construcción
41	1	**42**	52 165	693	**52 858**	*0.7*	*Electricité, gaz, eau et services sanitaires*	Electricidad, gas, agua y servicios sanitarios
995	32	**1 027**	543 096	8 927	**552 023**	*7.3*	*Com., banq., assur., aff. imm.*	Comercio
490	7	**497**	221 531	2 555	**224 086**	*3.0*	*Transports, entrepôts et communications*	Transportes, almacenaje y comunicaciones
1 242	544	**1 786**	759 718	169 967	**929 685**	*12.2*	*Services*	Servicios
24 366	7 324	**31 690**	114 203	13 336	**127 539**	*1.7*	*Activités mal désignées*	Actividades no bien especif.
635 844	89 845	**725 689**	635 844	89 845	**725 689**	*9.6*	*Personnes en quête d'emploi pour la première fois / Chômeurs*	Personas en busca de trabajo por primera vez / Desempleados
673 976	99 203	**773 179**	6 584 257	999 828	**7 584 085**	*100.0*	*Total*	Total

						%		
200	200	**400**	55 600	15 500	**71 100**	*6.3*	1. *Agriculture, chasse, sylviculture et pêche*	1. Agricultura, caza, silvicultura y pesca
2 500	1 600	**4 100**	216 800	61 100	**278 000**	*24.9*	2. *Industries extractives* / 3. *Industries manufacturières*	2. Minas y canteras / 3. Industrias manufactureras
100	—	**100**	9 100	1 300	**10 400**	*0.9*	4. *Electricité, gaz et eau*	4. Electricidad, gas y agua
2 400	100	**2 500**	86 700	3 500	**90 200**	*8.0*	5. *Construction*	5. Construcción
1 400	800	**2 200**	88 500	45 200	**133 700**	*11.9*	6. *Commerce (gros et détail); restaurants, hôtels*	6. Comercio (por mayor y por menor); restaurantes, hoteles
1 000	200	**1 200**	72 200	12 500	**84 700**	*7.5*	7. *Transports, entrepôts et communications*	7. Transportes, almacenamiento y comunicaciones
400	600	**1 000**	37 600	33 100	**70 900**	*6.3*	8. *Banques, assur., affaires imm., services aux entreprises*	8. Bancos, seguros, bienes inmuebles, servicios para empresas
1 300	1 800	**3 100**	178 500	179 000	**357 500**	*31.9*	9. *Services à la collectivité, services sociaux et personnels*	9. Servicios comunales, sociales y personales
600	800	**1 400**	5 300	3 400	**8 700**	*0.8*	0. *Activités mal désignées*	0. Actividades no bien especif.
8 100	9 300	**17 400**	8 100	9 300	**17 400**	*1.5*	*Personnes en quête d'emploi pour la première fois / Chômeurs*	Personas en busca de trabajo por primera vez / Desempleados
...	...	...	...	...	...			
18 200	15 400	**33 700**	758 600	364 100	**1 122 900**	*100.0*	*Total*	Total

† *Voir notes pp. 272-294.*

† *Véanse las notas en las págs. 272-294.*

2 Structure of the economically active population
Structure de la population active
Estructura de la población económicamente activa

Industry (Branch of economic activity)	Employers and workers on own account *Employeurs et personnes travaillant à leur propre compte* Empleadores y trabajadores por cuenta propia			Salaried employees and wage earners *Employés et ouvriers* Empleados y obreros			Family workers *Travailleurs familiaux* Trabajadores familiares		
	Males *Hommes* Hombres	Females *Femmes* Mujeres	Total	Males *Hommes* Hombres	Females *Femmes* Mujeres	Total	Males *Hommes* Hombres	Females *Femmes* Mujeres	Total

Japan

(1.X.1970) †

Industry	Males	Females	Total	Males	Females	Total	Males	Females	Total
1. Agriculture, hunting, forestry and fishing	3 351 665	942 720	**4 294 385**	400 555	97 615	**498 170**	1 035 525	4 335 600	**5 371 125**
2. Mining and quarrying	7 335	180	**7 515**	189 470	22 130	**211 600**	1 605	1 465	**3 070**
3. Manufacturing	801 825	554 355	**1 356 180**	7 719 680	3 760 335	**11 480 015**	195 030	544 625	**739 655**
4. Electricity, gas and water	215	25	**240**	257 025	33 335	**290 360**	15	20	**35**
5. Construction	714 600	2 905	**717 505**	2 730 310	362 090	**3 092 400**	103 035	65 735	**168 770**
6. Wholesale and retail trade, restaurants and hotels	1 529 475	655 715	**2 185 190**	3 805 640	2 887 085	**6 692 725**	345 045	1 379 540	**1 724 585**
7. Transport, storage and communication	90 915	1 470	**92 385**	2 726 230	392 620	**3 118 850**	10 250	13 650	**23 900**
8. Financing, insurance, real estate and business services	163 485	63 790	**227 275**	1 159 665	748 240	**1 907 905**	10 190	43 075	**53 265**
9. Community, social and personal services	593 675	614 910	**1 208 585**	3 902 440	2 687 975	**6 590 415**	80 425	312 145	**392 570**
0. Activities not adequately described	1 010	280	**1 290**	9 675	6 305	**15 980**	150	590	**740**
Unemployed	...	...	...	...	...	...	...	...	...
Total	7 254 200	2 836 350	**10 090 550**	22 900 690	10 997 730	**33 898 420**	1 781 270	6 696 445	**8 477 715**

(1974) †

Industry	Males	Females	Total	Males	Females	Total	Males	Females	Total
1. Agriculture, hunting, forestry and fishing	2 420 000	840 000	**3 260 000**	370 000	90 000	**470 000**	580 000	2 430 000	**3 000 000**
2. Mining and quarrying	—	—	—	120 000	10 000	**130 000**	—	—	—
3. Manufacturing	800 000	690 000	**1 500 000**	8 030 000	3 900 000	**11 930 000**	170 000	570 000	**740 000**
4. Electricity, gas and water	—	—	—	290 000	40 000	**330 000**	—	—	—
5. Construction	780 000	—	**780 000**	3 090 000	490 000	**3 580 000**	120 000	110 000	**220 000**
6. Wholesale and retail trade, restaurants and hotels	1 600 000	660 000	**2 260 000**	4 030 000	2 840 000	**6 870 000**	330 000	1 440 000	**1 760 000**
7. Transport, storage and communication	150 000	—	**150 000**	2 730 000	360 000	**3 090 000**	10 000	30 000	**40 000**
8. Financing, insurance, real estate and business services	80 000	20 000	**100 000**	830 000	660 000	**1 490 000**	—	20 000	**30 000**
9. Community, social and personal services	730 000	740 000	**1 460 000**	4 890 000	3 300 000	**8 190 000**	90 000	410 000	**500 000**
0. Activities not adequately described	—	—	**10 000**	20 000	—	**20 000**	—	—	—
Unemployed	...	...	...	...	...	...	...	...	...
Total	6 560 000	2 960 000	**9 520 000**	24 400 000	11 710 000	**36 100 000**	1 300 000	5 000 000	**6 300 000**

† For notes, see pp. 272-294.

A **Distribution by status and by industry (branch of economic activity)**
Répartition suivant la situation dans la profession et par branche d'activité économique
Distribución según la categoría de ocupación y por rama de actividad económica

Others and status unknown / *Autres et situation non définie* / Otros y categoría no definida			TOTAL			%	Branche d'activité économique	Rama de actividad económica
Males / *Hommes* / Hombres	Females / *Femmes* / Mujeres	Total	Males / *Hommes* / Hombres	Females / *Femmes* / Mujeres	Total			
...	...	...	4 787 745	5 375 935	**10 163 680**	*19.1*	1. *Agriculture, chasse, sylviculture et pêche*	1. Agricultura, caza, silvicultura y pesca
...	...	...	198 410	23 775	**222 185**	*0.4*	2. *Industries extractives*	2. Minas y canteras
...	...	...	8 716 535	4 859 315	**13 575 850**	*25.6*	3. *Industries manufacturières*	3. Industrias manufactureras
...	...	...	257 255	33 380	**290 635**	*0.5*	4. *Electricité, gaz et eau*	4. Electricidad, gas y agua
...	...	...	3 547 945	430 730	**3 978 675**	*7.5*	5. *Construction*	5. Construcción
...	...	...	5 680 160	4 922 340	**10 602 500**	*19.9*	6. *Commerce (gros et détail) ; restaurants, hôtels*	6. Comercio (por mayor y por menor); restaurantes, hoteles
...	...	...	2 827 395	407 740	**3 235 135**	*6.1*	7. *Transports, entrepôts et communications*	7. Transportes, almacenamiento y comunicaciones
...	...	...	1 333 340	855 105	**2 188 445**	*4.1*	8. *Banques, assur., affaires imm., services aux entreprises*	8. Bancos, seguros, bienes inmuebles, servicios para empresas
...	...	...	4 576 540	3 615 030	**8 191 570**	*15.4*	9. *Services à la collectivité, services sociaux et personnels*	9. Servicios comunales, sociales y personales
310	1 140	**1 450**	11 145	8 315	**19 460**	*—*	0. *Activités mal désignées*	0. Actividades no bien especif.
483 233	244 727	**727 960**	483 233	244 727	**727 960**	*1.4*	*Chômeurs*	Desempleados
483 543	245 867	**729 410**	32 419 703	20 776 392	**53 196 095**	*100.0*	*Total*	Total
—	—	—	3 380 000	3 360 000	**6 730 000**	*12.8*	1. *Agriculture, chasse, sylviculture et pêche*	1. Agricultura, caza, silvicultura y pesca
—	—	—	120 000	10 000	**140 000**	*0.3*	2. *Industries extractives*	2. Minas y canteras
—	—	—	9 010 000	5 170 000	**14 170 000**	*26.8*	3. *Industries manufacturières*	3. Industrias manufactureras
—	—	—	290 000	40 000	**330 000**	*0.6*	4. *Electricité, gaz et eau*	4. Electricidad, gas y agua
—	—	—	3 980 000	600 000	**4 590 000**	*8.7*	5. *Construction*	5. Construcción
—	—	—	5 960 000	4 940 000	**10 900 000**	*20.7*	6. *Commerce (gros et détail) ; restaurants, hôtels*	6. Comercio (por mayor y por menor); restaurantes, hoteles
—	—	—	2 890 000	390 000	**3 280 000**	*6.2*	7. *Transports, entrepôts et communications*	7. Transportes, almacenamiento y comunicaciones
—	—	—	910 000	700 000	**1 620 000**	*3.1*	8. *Banques, assur., affaires imm., services aux entreprises*	8. Bancos, seguros, bienes inmuebles, servicios para empresas
—	—	—	5 710 000	4 440 000	**10 150 000**	*19.2*	9. *Services à la collectivité, services sociaux et personnels*	9. Servicios comunales, sociales y personales
50 000	20 000	**80 000**	70 000	30 000	**100 000**	*0.2*	0. *Activités mal désignées*	0. Actividades no bien especif.
460 000	260 000	**720 000**	460 000	260 000	**720 000**	*1.4*	*Chômeurs*	Desempleados
520 000	290 000	**810 000**	32 780 000	19 960 000	**52 740 000**	*100.0*	*Total*	Total

✝ *Voir notes pp. 272-294.*   ✝ Véanse las notas en las págs. 272-294.

2 Structure of the economically active population
Structure de la population active
Estructura de la población económicamente activa

Industry (Branch of economic activity)	Employers and workers on own account Employeurs et personnes travaillant à leur propre compte Empleadores y trabajadores por cuenta propia			Salaried employees and wage earners Employés et ouvriers Empleados y obreros			Family workers Travailleurs familiaux Trabajadores familiares		
	Males Hommes Hombres	Females Femmes Mujeres	Total	Males Hommes Hombres	Females Femmes Mujeres	Total	Males Hommes Hombres	Females Femmes Mujeres	Total

Korea, Rep. of

(1.X.1970) †

1. Agriculture, hunting, forestry and fishing	1 955 325	318 330	2 273 655	375 741	174 246	549 987	689 273	1 642 413	2 331 686
2. Mining and quarrying	7 104	315	7 419	84 692	5 656	90 348	1 176	602	1 778
3. Manufacturing	176 799	60 161	236 960	719 844	389 827	1 109 671	29 945	68 412	98 357
4. Electricity, gas and water	1 549	93	1 642	27 324	1 713	29 037	83	31	114
5. Construction	55 036	858	55 894	378 996	17 286	396 282	6 370	2 304	8 674
6. Wholesale and retail trade, restaurants and hotels	520 270	224 547	744 817	225 166	126 988	352 154	44 660	137 328	181 988
7. Transport, storage and communication	39 140	741	39 881	263 190	24 032	287 222	1 334	290	1 624
8. Financing, insurance, real estate and business services	26 410	840	27 250	52 850	15 383	68 233	516	230	746
9. Community, social and personal services	106 941	24 962	131 903	739 849	315 808	1 055 657	9 478	10 334	19 812
0. Activities not adequately described . .	424	52	476	2 171	422	2 593	134	143	277
Unemployed	...	...	...	...	...	...	...	...	...
Total . . .	2 888 998	630 899	3 519 897	2 869 823	1 071 361	3 941 184	782 969	1 862 087	2 645 056

(1974) †

1. Agriculture, hunting, forestry and fishing	1 959 000	353 000	2 312 000	475 000	227 000	702 000	832 000	1 738 000	2 570 000
2. Mining and quarrying	3 000	—	3 000	43 000	4 000	47 000	—	—	—
3. Manufacturing	193 000	184 000	377 000	1 058 000	477 000	1 535 000	37 000	63 000	100 000
4. Electricity, gas and water	1 000	—	1 000	33 000	2 000	35 000	—	—	—
5. Construction	23 000	—	23 000	401 000	20 000	421 000	3 000	3 000	6 000
6. Wholesale and retail trade, restaurants and hotels	688 000	393 000	1 081 000	203 000	111 000	314 000	70 000	295 000	365 000
7. Transport, storage and communication	44 000	—	44 000	278 000	32 000	310 000	5 000	—	5 000
8. Financing, insurance, real estate and business services	34 000	3 000	37 000	81 000	29 000	110 000	—	—	—
9. Community, social and personal services	101 000	31 000	132 000	701 000	332 000	1 033 000	9 000	14 000	23 000
Unemployed	...	...	...	...	...	...	...	...	...
Total . . .	3 046 000	964 000	4 010 000	3 273 000	1 234 000	4 507 000	956 000	2 113 000	3 069 000

† For notes, see pp. 272-294.

A Distribution by status and by industry (branch of economic activity)
Répartition suivant la situation dans la profession et par branche d'activité économique
Distribución según la categoría de ocupación y por rama de actividad económica

Others and status unknown / *Autres et situation non définie* / Otros y categoría no definida			TOTAL				Branche d'activité économique	Rama de actividad económica
Males / *Hommes* / Hombres	Females / *Femmes* / Mujeres	Total	Males / *Hommes* / Hombres	Females / *Femmes* / Mujeres	Total	%		
846	805	**1 651**	3 021 185	2 135 794	**5 156 979**	*49.6*	1. *Agriculture, chasse, sylviculture et pêche*	1. Agricultura, caza, silvicultura y pesca
63	.	**63**	93 035	6 573	**99 608**	*1.0*	2. *Industries extractives*	2. Minas y canteras
1 427	1 104	**2 531**	928 015	519 504	**1 447 519**	*13.9*	3. *Industries manufacturières*	3. Industrias manufactureras
41	11	**52**	28 997	1 848	**30 845**	*0.3*	4. *Electricité, gaz et eau*	4. Electricidad, gas y agua
1 094	41	**1 135**	441 496	20 489	**461 985**	*4.5*	5. *Construction*	5. Construcción
750	458	**1 208**	790 846	489 321	**1 280 167**	*12.3*	6. *Commerce (gros et détail) ; restaurants, hôtels*	6. Comercio (por mayor y por menor); restaurantes, hoteles
408	73	**481**	304 072	25 136	**329 208**	*3.2*	7. *Transports, entrepôts et communications*	7. Transportes, almacenamiento y comunicaciones
211	62	**273**	79 987	16 515	**96 502**	*0.9*	8. *Banques, assur., affaires imm., services aux entreprises*	8. Bancos, seguros, bienes inmuebles, servicios para empresas
12 642	2 299	**14 941**	868 910	353 403	**1 222 313**	*11.8*	9. *Services à la collectivité, services sociaux et personnels*	9. Servicios comunales, sociales y personales
18 761	5 718	**24 479**	21 490	6 335	**27 825**	*0.3*	0. *Activités mal désignées*	0. Actividades no bien especif.
174 563	50 001	**224 564**	174 563	50 001	**224 564**	*2.2*	*Chômeurs*	Desempleados
210 806	**60 572**	**271 378**	**6 752 596**	**3 624 919**	**10 377 515**	*100.0*	*Total*	Total
.	.	.	3 266 000	2 318 000	**5 584 000**	*46.2*	1. *Agriculture, chasse, sylviculture et pêche*	1. Agricultura, caza, silvicultura y pesca
.	.	.	46 000	4 000	**50 000**	*0.4*	2. *Industries extractives*	2. Minas y canteras
.	.	.	1 288 000	724 000	**2 012 000**	*16.7*	3. *Industries manufacturières*	3. Industrias manufactureras
.	.	.	34 000	2 000	**36 000**	*0.3*	4. *Electricité, gaz et eau*	4. Electricidad, gas y agua
.	.	.	427 000	23 000	**450 000**	*3.7*	5. *Construction*	5. Construcción
.	.	.	961 000	799 000	**1 760 000**	*14.6*	6. *Commerce (gros et détail) ; restaurants, hôtels*	6. Comercio (por mayor y por menor); restaurantes, hoteles
.	.	.	327 000	32 000	**359 000**	*3.0*	7. *Transports, entrepôts et communications*	7. Transportes, almacenamiento y comunicaciones
.	.	.	115 000	32 000	**147 000**	*1.2*	8. *Banques, assur., affaires imm., services aux entreprises*	8. Bancos, seguros, bienes inmuebles, servicios para empresas
.	.	.	811 000	377 000	**1 188 000**	*9.8*	9. *Services à la collectivité, services sociaux et personnels*	9. Servicios comunales, sociales y personales
377 000	117 000	**494 000**	377 000	117 000	**494 000**	*4.1*	*Chômeurs*	Desempleados
377 000	**117 000**	**494 000**	**7 652 000**	**4 428 000**	**12 080 000**	*100.0*	*Total*	Total

‡ *Voir notes pp. 272-294.*

‡ Véanse las notas en las págs. 272-294.

2 Structure of the economically active population
Structure de la population active
Estructura de la población económicamente activa

Industry (Branch of economic activity)	Employers and workers on own account *Employeurs et personnes travaillant à leur propre compte* Empleadores y trabajadores por cuenta propia			Salaried employees and wage earners *Employés et ouvriers* Empleados y obreros			Family workers *Travailleurs familiaux* Trabajadores familiares		
	Males *Hommes* Hombres	Females *Femmes* Mujeres	Total	Males *Hommes* Hombres	Females *Femmes* Mujeres	Total	Males *Hommes* Hombres	Females *Femmes* Mujeres	Total
Kuwait (21.IV.1970)									
1. Agriculture, hunting, forestry and fishing	342	1	343	3 643	4	3 647	66	4	70
2. Mining and quarrying	583	28	611	5 643	152	5 795	229	536	765
3. Manufacturing	3 538	5	3 543	28 395	110	28 505	40	.	40
4. Electricity, gas and water	2	.	2	7 234	16	7 250	.	.	.
5. Construction	12 691	1	12 692	20 901	67	20 968	11	.	11
6. Wholesale and retail trade, restaurants and hotels	13 639	22	13 661	15 067	296	15 363	248	11	259
7. Transport, storage and communication	2 964	.	2 964	9 032	141	9 173	1	.	1
8. Financing, insurance, real estate and business services	810	.	810	2 674	242	2 916	4	.	4
9. Community, social and personal services	6 283	98	6 381	82 984	14 706	97 690	47	10	57
0. Activities not adequately described . .	196	1	197	309	13	322	3	.	3
Unemployed	...	...	...	...	...	...	...	...	...
Total . . .	41 048	156	41 204	175 882	15 747	191 629	649	561	1 210
Liban (XI.1970) ‡									
1. Agriculture, hunting, forestry and fishing	...	...	43 245	...	...	28 260	...	...	24 780
2. Mining and quarrying	...	...	240	...	...	630	...	...	45
3. Manufacturing	...	...	27 210	...	...	63 570	...	...	3 105
4. Electricity, gas and water	...	...	75	...	...	5 535	.	.	.
5. Construction	...	...	12 615	...	...	21 945	...	...	420
6. Wholesale and retail trade, restaurants and hotels	...	...	49 020	...	...	36 735	...	...	5 220
7. Transport, storage and communication	...	...	12 735	...	...	24 945	...	...	345
8. Financing, insurance, real estate and business services	...	...	4 950	...	...	13 170	...	...	135
9. Community, social and personal services	...	...	19 890	...	...	125 415	...	...	1 515
0. Activities not adequately described . .	...	...	240	...	...	1 740	...	...	105
Unemployed	...	...	...	...	...	...	...	...	...
Total . . .	...	...	170 220	...	...	321 945	...	...	35 670

‡ For notes, see pp. 272-294.

A Distribution by status and by industry (branch of economic activity)
Répartition suivant la situation dans la profession et par branche d'activité économique
Distribución según la categoría de ocupación y por rama de actividad económica

Others and status unknown / Autres et situation non définie / Otros y categoría no definida			TOTAL				Branche d'activité économique	Rama de actividad económica
Males / Hommes / Hombres	Females / Femmes / Mujeres	Total	Males / Hommes / Hombres	Females / Femmes / Mujeres	Total	%		
.	.	.	4 051	9	4 060	1.7	1. Agriculture, chasse, sylviculture et pêche	1. Agricultura, caza, silvicultura y pesca
.	.	.	6 455	716	7 171	3.0	2. Industries extractives	2. Minas y canteras
3	.	3	31 976	115	32 091	13.2	3. Industries manufacturières	3. Industrias manufactureras
.	.	.	7 236	16	7 252	3.0	4. Electricité, gaz et eau	4. Electricidad, gas y agua
1	.	1	33 604	68	33 672	13.9	5. Construction	5. Construcción
.	.	.	28 954	329	29 283	12.1	6. Commerce (gros et détail) ; restaurants, hôtels	6. Comercio (por mayor y por menor); restaurantes, hoteles
.	.	.	11 997	141	12 138	5.0	7. Transports, entrepôts et communications	7. Transportes, almacenamiento y comunicaciones
.	.	.	3 488	242	3 730	1.5	8. Banques, assur., affaires imm., services aux entreprises	8. Bancos, seguros, bienes inmuebles, servicios para empresas
6	2	8	89 320	14 816	104 136	42.9	9. Services à la collectivité, services sociaux et personnels	9. Servicios comunales, sociales y personales
289	16	305	797	30	827	0.3	0. Activités mal désignées	0. Actividades no bien especif.
8 021	132	8 153	8 021	132	8 153	3.4	Chômeurs	Desempleados
8 320	150	8 470	225 899	16 614	242 513	100.0	Total	Total

Others and status unknown / Autres et situation non définie / Otros y categoría no definida			TOTAL				Branche d'activité économique	Rama de actividad económica
Males / Hommes / Hombres	Females / Femmes / Mujeres	Total	Males / Hommes / Hombres	Females / Femmes / Mujeres	Total	%		
...	...	5 475	80 535	21 225	101 760	17.8	1. Agriculture, chasse, sylviculture et pêche	1. Agricultura, caza, silvicultura y pesca
...	...	...	76 890	18 645	915	0.2	2. Industries extractives	2. Minas y canteras
...	...	735			94 620	16.5	3. Industries manufacturières	3. Industrias manufactureras
...	...	...	5 550	60	5 610	1.0	4. Electricité, gaz et eau	4. Electricidad, gas y agua
...	...	75	34 800	255	35 055	6.1	5. Construction	5. Construcción
...	...	645	85 845	5 775	91 620	16.0	6. Commerce (gros et détail) ; restaurants, hôtels	6. Comercio (por mayor y por menor); restaurantes, hoteles
...	...	210	36 375	1 860	38 235	6.7	7. Transports, entrepôts et communications	7. Transportes, almacenamiento y comunicaciones
...	...	165	15 600	2 820	18 420	3.2	8. Banques, assur., affaires imm., services aux entreprises	8. Bancos, seguros, bienes inmuebles, servicios para empresas
...	...	2 970	106 605	43 185	149 790	26.3	9. Services à la collectivité, services sociaux et personnels	9. Servicios comunales, sociales y personales
...	...	300	2 085	300	2 385	0.4	0. Activités mal désignées	0. Actividades no bien especif.
...	...	33 345	28 335	5 010	33 345	5.8	Chômeurs	Desempleados
...	...	43 920	472 620	99 135	571 755	100.0	Total	Total

☨ Voir notes pp. 272-294.

☨ Véanse las notas en las págs. 272-294.

2 Structure of the economically active population
Structure de la population active
Estructura de la población económicamente activa

Industry (Branch of economic activity)	Employers and workers on own account _Employeurs et personnes travaillant à leur propre compte_ Empleadores y trabajadores por cuenta propia			Salaried employees and wage earners _Employés et ouvriers_ Empleados y obreros			Family workers _Travailleurs familiaux_ Trabajadores familiares		
	Males _Hommes_ Hombres	Females _Femmes_ Mujeres	Total	Males _Hommes_ Hombres	Females _Femmes_ Mujeres	Total	Males _Hommes_ Hombres	Females _Femmes_ Mujeres	Total

Malaysia

East Malaysia:

Sabah (24-25.VIII.1970*)

(ISIC 1958)

Agriculture, forestry, hunting and fishing	...	...	...	...	...	...	...	...	...
Mining and quarrying	...	...	...	...	...	...	...	...	...
Manufacturing	...	...	...	...	...	...	...	...	...
Construction	...	...	...	...	...	...	...	...	...
Electricity, gas, water and sanitary services	...	...	...	...	...	...	...	...	...
Commerce	...	...	...	...	...	...	...	...	...
Transport, storage and communication	...	...	...	...	...	...	...	...	...
Services	...	...	...	...	...	...	...	...	...
Activities not adequately described	...	...	...	...	...	...	...	...	...
Total ...	...	...	...	...	...	...	...	...	...

Sarawak (24-25.VIII.1970*)

(ISIC 1958)

Agriculture, forestry, hunting and fishing	...	...	...	...	...	...	...	...	...
Mining and quarrying	...	...	...	...	...	...	...	...	...
Manufacturing	...	...	...	...	...	...	...	...	...
Construction	...	...	...	...	...	...	...	...	...
Electricity, gas, water and sanitary services	...	...	...	...	...	...	...	...	...
Commerce	...	...	...	...	...	...	...	...	...
Transport, storage and communication	...	...	...	...	...	...	...	...	...
Services	...	...	...	...	...	...	...	...	...
Activities not adequately described	...	...	...	...	...	...	...	...	...
Total ...	...	...	...	...	...	...	...	...	...

West Malaysia (24.VIII.1970)

(ISIC 1958)

Agriculture, forestry, hunting and fishing	...	...	...	...	...	...	...	...	...
Mining and quarrying	...	...	...	...	...	...	...	...	...
Manufacturing	...	...	...	...	...	...	...	...	...
Construction	...	...	...	...	...	...	...	...	...
Electricity, gas, water and sanitary services	...	...	...	...	...	...	...	...	...
Commerce	...	...	...	...	...	...	...	...	...
Transport, storage and communication	...	...	...	...	...	...	...	...	...
Services	...	...	...	...	...	...	...	...	...
Activities not adequately described	...	...	...	...	...	...	...	...	...
Persons seeking work for the first time	.	.	.	.	.	.	.	.	.
Total ...	...	...	...	...	...	...	...	...	...

A
Distribution by status and by industry (branch of economic activity)
Répartition suivant la situation dans la profession et par branche d'activité économique
Distribución según la categoría de ocupación y por rama de actividad económica

Males Hommes Hombres	Females Femmes Mujeres	Total	Males Hommes Hombres	Females Femmes Mujeres	Total	%	Branche d'activité économique	Rama de actividad económica
	Others and status unknown / *Autres et situation non définie* / Otros y categoría no definida			TOTAL				

Males Hombres	Females Mujeres	Total	Males Hombres	Females Mujeres	Total	%	Branche d'activité économique	Rama de actividad económica
							(CITI 1958)	(CIIU 1958)
...	...	...	81 997	43 780	**125 777**	*59.1*	*Agriculture, sylviculture, chasse et pêche*	Agricultura silvicultura, caza y pesca
...	...	...	856	33	**889**	*0.4*	*Industries extractives*	Minas y canteras
...	...	...	5 971	1 108	**7 079**	*3.3*	*Industries manufacturières*	Industrias manufactureras
...	...	...	5 803	427	**6 230**	*2.9*	*Construction*	Construcción
...	...	...	1 279	116	**1 395**	*0.7*	*Electricité, gaz, eau et services sanitaires*	Electricidad, gas, agua y servicios sanitarios
...	...	...	9 171	2 599	**11 770**	*5.5*	*Com., banq., assur., aff. imm.*	Comercio
...	...	...	6 527	396	**6 923**	*3.3*	*Transports, entrepôts et communications*	Transportes, almacenaje y comunicaciones
...	...	...	24 560	7 766	**32 326**	*15.2*	*Services*	Servicios
...	...	...	8 415	11 910	**20 325**	*9.6*	*Activités mal désignées*	Actividades no bien especif.
...	...	...	144 579	68 135	**212 714**	*100.0*	*Total*	Total
							(CITI 1958)	(CIIU 1958)
...	...	...	127 187	101 764	**228 951**	*66.2*	*Agriculture, sylviculture, chasse et pêche*	Agricultura silvicultura, caza y pesca
...	...	...	1 029	79	**1 108**	*0.3*	*Industries extractives*	Minas y canteras
...	...	...	13 535	3 468	**17 003**	*4.9*	*Industries manufacturières*	Industrias manufactureras
...	...	...	5 165	176	**5 341**	*1.5*	*Construction*	Construcción
...	...	...	1 343	67	**1 410**	*0.4*	*Electricité, gaz, eau et services sanitaires*	Electricidad, gas, agua y servicios sanitarios
...	...	...	14 163	3 153	**17 316**	*5.0*	*Com., banq., assur., aff. imm.*	Comercio
...	...	...	5 769	321	**6 090**	*1.8*	*Transports, entrepôts et communications*	Transportes, almacenaje y comunicaciones
...	...	...	29 580	8 789	**38 369**	*11.1*	*Services*	Servicios
...	...	...	11 595	18 826	**30 421**	*8.8*	*Activités mal désignées*	Actividades no bien especif.
...	...	...	209 366	136 643	**346 009**	*100.0*	*Total*	Total
							(CITI 1958)	(CIIU 1958)
...	...	...	772 886	451 689	**1 224 575**	*42.6*	*Agriculture, sylviculture, chasse et pêche*	Agricultura silvicultura, caza y pesca
...	...	...	48 203	7 073	**55 276**	*1.9*	*Industries extractives*	Minas y canteras
...	...	...	178 881	73 058	**251 939**	*8.8*	*Industries manufacturières*	Industrias manufactureras
...	...	...	55 624	4 238	**59 862**	*2.1*	*Construction*	Construcción
...	...	...	18 732	1 024	**19 756**	*0.7*	*Electricité, gaz, eau et services sanitaires*	Electricidad, gas, agua y servicios sanitarios
...	...	...	224 993	49 611	**274 604**	*9.6*	*Com., banq., assur., aff. imm.*	Comercio
...	...	...	93 852	4 117	**97 969**	*3.4*	*Transports, entrepôts et communications*	Transportes, almacenaje y comunicaciones
...	...	...	332 158	140 468	**472 626**	*16.5*	*Services*	Servicios
...	...	...	152 417	127 331	**279 748**	*9.7*	*Activités mal désignées*	Actividades no bien especif.
...	...	...	80 542	54 052	**134 594**	*4.7*	*Personnes en quête d'emploi pour la première fois*	Personas en busca de trabajo por primera vez
...	...	...	1 958 288	912 661	**2 870 949**	*100.0*	*Total*	Total

POPULATION

2 Structure of the economically active population
Structure de la population active
Estructura de la población económicamente activa

Industry (Branch of economic activity)	Employers and workers on own account *Employeurs et personnes travaillant à leur propre compte* Empleadores y trabajadores por cuenta propia			Salaried employees and wage earners *Employés et ouvriers* Empleados y obreros			Family workers *Travailleurs familiaux* Trabajadores familiares		
	Males *Hommes* Hombres	Females *Femmes* Mujeres	Total	Males *Hommes* Hombres	Females *Femmes* Mujeres	Total	Males *Hommes* Hombres	Females *Femmes* Mujeres	Total
Nepal (22.VI.1971)									
1. Agriculture, hunting, forestry and fishing	2 846 945	1 253 240	4 100 185	237 550	38 684	276 234	102 812	100 321	203 133
2. Mining and quarrying	4	2	6	26	3	29	1	.	1
3. Manufacturing	17 583	3 392	20 975	26 695	2 709	29 404	1 113	410	1 523
4. Electricity, gas and water	83	2	85	1 478	24	1 502	9	.	9
5. Construction	501	22	523	4 314	97	4 411	61	21	82
6. Wholesale and retail trade, restaurants and hotels	46 925	6 689	53 614	7 255	546	7 801	1 528	617	2 145
7. Transport, storage and communication	924	36	960	8 326	277	8 603	72	2	74
8. Financing, insurance, real estate and business services	194	11	205	3 123	121	3 244	14	3	17
9. Community, social and personal services	13 062	1 485	14 547	112 746	9 305	122 051	944	217	1 161
Total	2 926 221	1 264 879	4 191 100	401 513	51 766	453 279	106 554	101 591	208 145
Pakistan (I.1972) ‡									
1. Agriculture, hunting, forestry and fishing	...	...	5 383 660	...	...	808 027	...	...	4 323 598
2. Mining and quarrying	...	...	30 090	...	...	38 274	...	...	11 005
3. Manufacturing	...	...	1 135 657	...	...	674 248	...	...	412 206
4. Electricity, gas and water	...	...	7 633	...	...	57 463	...	...	...
5. Construction	...	...	429 577	...	...	153 149	...	...	27 648
6. Wholesale and retail trade, restaurants and hotels	...	...	1 288 845	...	...	163 075	...	...	293 794
7. Transport, storage and communication	...	...	433 398	...	...	339 449	...	...	89 134
8. Financing, insurance, real estate and business services	...	...	62 655	...	...	76 460	...	...	10 523
9. Community, social and personal services	...	...	400 941	...	...	758 307	...	...	126 216
0. Activities not adequately described	...	...	225 349	...	...	120 684	...	...	226 399
Unemployed	...	...	...	...	...	...	...	...	...
Total	...	...	9 397 805	...	...	3 189 136	...	...	5 520 523
Philippines (6.V.1970) ‡ (1)									
(ISIC 1958)									
Agriculture, forestry, hunting and fishing	...	...	...	...	...	...	...	...	...
Mining and quarrying	...	...	...	...	...	...	...	...	...
Manufacturing	...	...	...	...	...	...	...	...	...
Construction	...	...	...	...	...	...	...	...	...
Electricity, gas, water and sanitary services	...	...	...	...	...	...	...	...	...
Commerce	...	...	...	...	...	...	...	...	...
Transport, storage and communication	...	...	...	...	...	...	...	...	...
Services	...	...	...	...	...	...	...	...	...
Activities not adequately described	...	...	...	...	...	...	...	...	...
Persons seeking work for the first time	.	.	.	.	.	.	.	.	.
Total	3 572 849	917 090	4 489 939	3 297 251	1 611 785	4 909 036	1 264 350	1 061 669	2 326 019

‡ For notes, see pp. 272-294.

A **Distribution by status and by industry (branch of economic activity)**
Répartition suivant la situation dans la profession et par branche d'activité économique
Distribución según la categoría de ocupación y por rama de actividad económica

Others and status unknown / Autres et situation non définie / Otros y categoría no definida			TOTAL				Branche d'activité économique	Rama de actividad económica
Males / Hommes / Hombres	Females / Femmes / Mujeres	Total	Males / Hommes / Hombres	Females / Femmes / Mujeres	Total	%		
.	.	.	3 187 307	1 392 245	4 579 552	94.4	1. Agriculture, chasse, sylviculture et pêche	1. Agricultura, caza, silvicultura y pesca
.	.	.	31	5	36	—	2. Industries extractives	2. Minas y canteras
.	.	.	45 391	6 511	51 902	1.1	3. Industries manufacturières	3. Industrias manufactureras
.	.	.	1 570	26	1 596	—	4. Electricité, gaz et eau	4. Electricidad, gas y agua
.	.	.	4 876	140	5 016	0.1	5. Construction	5. Construcción
.	.	.	55 708	7 852	63 560	1.3	6. Commerce (gros et détail) ; restaurants, hôtels	6. Comercio (por mayor y por menor); restaurantes, hoteles
.	.	.	9 322	315	9 637	0.2	7. Transports, entrepôts et communications	7. Transportes, almacenamiento y comunicaciones
.	.	.	3 331	135	3 466	0.1	8. Banques, assur., affaires imm., services aux entreprises	8. Bancos, seguros, bienes inmuebles, servicios para empresas
.	.	.	126 752	11 007	137 759	2.8	9. Services à la collectivité, services sociaux et personnels	9. Servicios comunales, sociales y personales
.	.	.	3 434 288	1 418 236	4 852 524	100.0	Total	Total

Males / Hommes / Hombres	Females / Femmes / Mujeres	Total	Males / Hommes / Hombres	Females / Femmes / Mujeres	Total	%	Branche d'activité économique	Rama de actividad económica
...	...	...	...	...	10 515 285	56.9	1. Agriculture, chasse, sylviculture et pêche	1. Agricultura, caza, silvicultura y pesca
...	...	...	...	...	79 369	0.4	2. Industries extractives	2. Minas y canteras
...	...	...	...	...	2 222 111	12.0	3. Industries manufacturières	3. Industrias manufactureras
...	...	...	...	...	65 096	0.4	4. Electricité, gaz et eau	4. Electricidad, gas y agua
...	...	...	...	...	610 374	3.3	5. Construction	5. Construcción
...	...	...	...	...	1 745 714	9.4	6. Commerce (gros et détail) ; restaurants, hôtels	6. Comercio (por mayor y por menor); restaurantes, hoteles
...	...	...	...	...	861 981	4.7	7. Transports, entrepôts et communications	7. Transportes, almacenamiento y comunicaciones
...	...	...	...	...	149 638	0.8	8. Banques, assur., affaires imm., services aux entreprises	8. Bancos, seguros, bienes inmuebles, servicios para empresas
...	...	...	...	...	1 285 464	7.0	9. Services à la collectivité, services sociaux et personnels	9. Servicios comunales, sociales y personales
...	...	...	...	...	572 432	3.1	0. Activités mal désignées	0. Actividades no bien especif.
...	...	373 766	...	...	373 766	2.0	Chômeurs	Desempleados
...	...	373 766	16 893 460	1 587 770	18 481 230	100.0	Total	Total

Males / Hommes / Hombres	Females / Femmes / Mujeres	Total	Males / Hommes / Hombres	Females / Femmes / Mujeres	Total	%	(CITI 1958)	(CIIU 1958)
...	...	...	5 099 809	1 232 262	6 332 071	51.4	Agriculture, sylviculture, chasse et pêche	Agricultura, silvicultura, caza y pesca
...	...	...	49 886	2 783	52 669	0.4	Industries extractives	Minas y canteras
...	...	...	639 383	762 398	1 401 781	11.4	Industries manufacturières	Industrias manufactureras
...	...	...	457 716	3 416	461 132	3.8	Construction	Construcción
...	...	...	32 536	1 341	33 877	0.3	Electricité, gaz, eau et services sanitaires	Electricidad, gas, agua y servicios sanitarios
...	...	...	389 565	472 410	861 975	7.0	Com., banq., assur., aff. imm.	Comercio
...	...	...	500 985	11 298	512 283	4.2	Transports, entrepôts et communications	Transportes, almacenaje y comunicaciones
...	...	...	845 701	1 081 324	1 927 025	15.7	Services	Servicios
...	...	...	141 557	47 301	188 858	1.5	Activités mal désignées	Actividades no bien especif.
...	...	...	210 713	314 199	524 912	4.3	Personnes en quête d'emploi pour la première fois	Personas en busca de trabajo por primera vez
233 401	338 188	571 589	8 367 851	3 928 732	12 296 583	100.0	Total	Total

✝ *Voir notes pp. 272-294.*

✝ Véanse las notas en las págs. 272-294.

2 Structure of the economically active population
Structure de la population active
Estructura de la población económicamente activa

Industry (Branch of economic activity)	Employers and workers on own account *Employeurs et personnes travaillant à leur propre compte* Empleadores y trabajadores por cuenta propia			Salaried employees and wage earners *Employés et ouvriers* Empleados y obreros			Family workers *Travailleurs familiaux* Trabajadores familiares		
	Males *Hommes* Hombres	Females *Femmes* Mujeres	Total	Males *Hommes* Hombres	Females *Femmes* Mujeres	Total	Males *Hommes* Hombres	Females *Femmes* Mujeres	Total

Philippines (V.1974) ‡ (2)

ISIC (1958)

Agriculture, forestry, hunting and fishing	3 482 000	226 000	3 707 000	841 000	256 000	1 097 000	2 083 000	1 350 000	3 433 000
Mining and quarrying	3 000	3 000	3 000	35 000	1 000	36 000	3 000		3 000
Manufacturing	154 000	243 000	398 000	616 000	357 000	973 000	44 000	92 000	136 000
Construction	19 000	—	19 000	380 000	4 000	384 000	1 000	—	1 000
Electricity, gas, water and sanitary services	—	—	—	40 000	3 000	43 000	—	—	—
Commerce	361 000	509 000	870 000	283 000	172 000	455 000	95 000	192 000	288 000
Transport, storage and communication	94 000	4 000	97 000	397 000	14 000	411 000	10 000	—	10 000
Services	79 000	82 000	160 000	752 000	1 126 000	1 878 000	13 000	34 000	47 000
Activities not adequately described	—	2 000	2 000	4 000	1 000	5 000	—	—	—
Persons seeking work for the first time	.	.	.	.	.	.	.	.	.
Total . . .	4 191 000	1 068 000	5 259 000	3 348 000	1 935 000	5 284 000	2 248 000	1 669 000	3 917 000

Singapore

(22.VI. 1970)

1. Agriculture, hunting, forestry and fishing	11 418	1 422	12 840	2 492	397	2 889	3 752	2 977	6 729
2. Mining and quarrying	79	3	82	1 877	202	2 079	7	.	7
3. Manufacturing	11 433	4 156	15 589	82 037	42 906	124 943	1 509	1 059	2 568
4. Electricity, gas and water	23	.	23	7 056	533	7 589	3	.	3
5. Construction	7 840	232	8 072	32 216	2 564	34 780	253	21	274
6. Wholesale and retail trade, restaurants and hotels	53 173	6 464	59 637	63 101	17 598	80 699	7 650	4 924	12 574
7. Transport, storage and communication	17 126	116	17 242	57 769	3 813	61 582	203	14	217
8. Financing, insurance, real estate and business services	1 992	100	2 092	15 702	5 187	20 889	72	18	90
9. Community, social and personal services	10 104	3 396	13 500	107 423	54 949	162 372	652	498	1 150
0. Activities not adequately described	94	14	108	213	41	254	11	8	19
Unemployed	...	...	...	...	...	...	...	...	...
Total . . .	113 282	15 903	129 185	369 886	128 190	498 076	14 112	9 519	23 631

(V-VI.1974) ‡

1. Agriculture, hunting, forestry and fishing	9 762	1 651	11 413	2 186	971	3 157	3 448	3 691	7 139
2. Mining and quarrying	340	.	340	1 117	291	1 408	.	.	.
3. Manufacturing	11 316	6 167	17 483	116 751	97 034	213 785	1 214	1 748	2 962
4. Electricity, gas and water	.	.	.	9 179	1 117	10 296	49	.	49
5. Construction	5 439	146	5 585	32 636	3 837	36 473	437	.	437
6. Wholesale and retail trade, restaurants and hotels	48 469	8 401	56 870	68 380	36 084	104 464	5 634	5 682	11 316
7. Transport, storage and communication	14 958	146	15 104	71 197	11 024	82 221	194	.	194
8. Financing, insurance, real estate and business services	2 962	292	3 254	27 585	15 687	43 272	49	.	49
9. Community, social and personal services	9 859	3 303	13 162	117 237	63 329	180 566	534	874	1 408
0. Activities not adequately described	194	.	194	1 067	681	1 748	.	.	.
Unemployed									
Total . . .	103 299	20 106	123 405	447 335	230 055	677 390	11 559	11 995	23 554

‡ For notes, see pp. 272-294.

A Distribution by status and by industry (branch of economic activity)
Répartition suivant la situation dans la profession et par branche d'activité économique
Distribución según la categoría de ocupación y por rama de actividad económica

Others and status unknown / Autres et situation non définie / Otros y categoría no definida			TOTAL				Branche d'activité économique	Rama de actividad económica
Males / Hommes / Hombres	Females / Femmes / Mujeres	Total	Males / Hommes / Hombres	Females / Femmes / Mujeres	Total			
						%	(CITI 1958)	(CIIU 1958)
110 000	50 000	**159 000**	6 516 000	1 882 000	**8 398 000**	*55.3*	*Agriculture, sylviculture, chasse et pêche*	Agricultura, silvicultura, caza y pesca
2 000	—	**2 000**	42 000	4 000	**46 000**	*0.3*	*Industries extractives*	Minas y canteras
38 000	27 000	**65 000**	853 000	720 000	**1 573 000**	*10.3*	*Industries manufacturières*	Industrias manufactureras
53 000	—	**53 000**	452 000	4 000	**456 000**	*3.0*	*Construction*	Construcción
3 000	—	**3 000**	43 000	3 000	**46 000**	*0.3*	*Electricité, gaz, eau et services sanitaires*	Electricidad, gas, agua y servicios sanitarios
24 000	34 000	**58 000**	764 000	907 000	**1 671 000**	*11.0*	*Com., banq., assur., aff. imm.*	Comercio
30 000	1 000	**31 000**	530 000	19 000	**549 000**	*3.6*	*Transports, entrepôts et communications*	Transportes, almacenaje y comunicaciones
27 000	39 000	**66 000**	870 000	1 281 000	**2 151 000**	*14.2*	*Services*	Servicios
7 000	6 000	**13 000**	11 000	10 000	**20 000**	*0.1*	*Activités mal désignées*	Actividades no bien especif.
158 000	134 000	**292 000**	158 000	134 000	**292 000**	*1.9*	*Personnes en quête d'emploi pour la première fois*	Personas en busca de trabajo por primera vez
454 000	291 000	**744 000**	10 240 000	4 964 000	**15 204 000**	*100.0*	*Total*	Total

Others and status unknown			TOTAL				Branche d'activité économique	Rama de actividad económica
						%		
...	...	...	17 662	4 796	**22 458**	*3.1*	*1. Agriculture, chasse, sylviculture et pêche*	1. Agricultura, caza, silvicultura y pesca
...	...	...	1 963	205	**2 168**	*0.3*	*2. Industries extractives*	2. Minas y canteras
...	...	...	94 979	48 121	**143 100**	*19.7*	*3. Industries manufacturières*	3. Industrias manufactureras
...	...	...	7 082	533	**7 615**	*1.0*	*4. Electricité, gaz et eau*	4. Electricidad, gas y agua
...	...	...	40 309	2 817	**43 126**	*5.9*	*5. Construction*	5. Construcción
...	...	...	123 924	28 986	**152 910**	*21.0*	*6. Commerce (gros et détail); restaurants, hôtels*	6. Comercio (por mayor y por menor); restaurantes, hoteles
...	...	...	75 098	3 943	**79 041**	*10.9*	*7. Transports, entrepôts et communications*	7. Transportes, almacenamiento y comunicaciones
...	...	...	17 766	5 305	**23 071**	*3.2*	*8. Banques, assur., affaires imm., services aux entreprises*	8. Bancos, seguros, bienes inmuebles, servicios para empresas
...	...	...	118 179	58 843	**177 022**	*24.4*	*9. Services à la collectivité, services sociaux et personnels*	9. Servicios comunales, sociales y personales
...	...	...	318	63	**381**	*0.1*	*0. Activités mal désignées*	0. Actividades no bien especif.
41 943	33 841	**75 784**	41 943	33 841	**75 784**	*10.4*	*Chômeurs*	Desempleados
41 943	33 841	**75 784**	539 223	187 453	**726 676**	*100.0*	*Total*	Total
						%		
...	...	...	15 396	6 313	**21 709**	*2.5*	*1. Agriculture, chasse, sylviculture et pêche*	1. Agricultura, caza, silvicultura y pesca
...	...	...	1 457	291	**1 748**	*0.2*	*2. Industries extractives*	2. Minas y canteras
...	...	...	129 281	104 949	**234 230**	*27.3*	*3. Industries manufacturières*	3. Industrias manufactureras
...	...	...	9 228	1 117	**10 345**	*1.2*	*4. Electricité, gaz et eau*	4. Electricidad, gas y agua
...	...	...	38 512	3 983	**42 495**	*5.0*	*5. Construction*	5. Construcción
...	...	...	122 483	50 167	**172 650**	*20.1*	*6. Commerce (gros et détail); restaurants, hôtels*	6. Comercio (por mayor y por menor); restaurantes, hoteles
...	...	...	86 349	11 170	**97 519**	*11.4*	*7. Transports, entrepôts et communications*	7. Transportes, almacenamiento y comunicaciones
...	...	...	30 596	15 979	**46 575**	*5.4*	*8. Banques, assur., affaires imm., services aux entreprises*	8. Bancos, seguros, bienes inmuebles, servicios para empresas
...	...	...	127 630	67 506	**195 136**	*22.7*	*9. Services à la collectivité, services sociaux et personnels*	9. Servicios comunales, sociales y personales
...	...	...	1 261	681	**1 942**	*0.2*	*0. Activités mal désignées*	0. Actividades no bien especif.
20 106	13 938	**34 044**	20 106	13 938	**34 044**	*4.0*	*Chômeurs*	Desempleados
20 106	13 938	**34 044**	582 299	276 094	**858 393**	*100.0*	*Total*	Total

ǂ *Voir notes pp. 272-294.*   ǂ Véanse las notas en las págs. 272-294.

2 Structure of the economically active population
Structure de la population active
Estructura de la población económicamente activa

Industry (Branch of economic activity)	Employers and workers on own account *Employeurs et personnes travaillant à leur propre compte* Empleadores y trabajadores por cuenta propia			Salaried employees and wage earners *Employés et ouvriers* Empleados y obreros			Family workers *Travailleurs familiaux* Trabajadores familiares		
	Males *Hommes* Hombres	Females *Femmes* Mujeres	Total	Males *Hommes* Hombres	Females *Femmes* Mujeres	Total	Males *Hommes* Hombres	Females *Femmes* Mujeres	Total

Sri Lanka (9.X.1971*)

1. Agriculture, hunting, forestry and fishing	661 768	62 558	**724 326**	573 852	357 367	**931 219**	83 599	84 816	**168 415**
2. Mining and quarrying	1 799	61	**1 860**	11 992	1 351	**13 343**	71	31	**102**
3. Manufacturing	48 130	17 632	**65 762**	196 262	80 717	**276 979**	2 692	1 984	**4 676**
4. Electricity, gas and water	280	.	**280**	8 914	248	**9 162**	.	.	.
5. Construction	7 110	20	**7 130**	103 800	1 174	**104 974**	300	10	**310**
6. Wholesale and retail trade, restaurants and hotels	131 527	9 220	**140 747**	184 209	11 356	**195 565**	6 746	2 376	**9 122**
7. Transport, storage and communication	8 295	40	**8 335**	143 050	3 637	**146 687**	234	10	**244**
8. Financing, insurance, real estate and business services	1 464	88	**1 552**	22 904	1 850	**24 754**	41	.	**41**
9. Community, social and personal services	32 561	3 460	**36 021**	319 236	127 534	**446 770**	2 629	2 713	**5 342**
0. Activities not adequately described . .	33 853	5 097	**38 950**	216 605	34 964	**251 569**	3 250	4 495	**7 745**
Persons seeking work for the first time ⎫ ⎬ Unemployed . . . . ⎭	...	...	...	...	...	...	...	...	...
Total . . .	926 787	98 176	**1 024 963**	1 780 824	620 198	**2 401 022**	99 562	96 435	**195 997**

République arabe syrienne (23.IX.1970) ‡ (1)

1. Agriculture, hunting, forestry and fishing	372 291	22 598	**394 889**	115 522	24 009	**139 531**	153 479	60 105	**213 584**
2. Mining and quarrying	899	3	**902**	7 350	201	**7 551**	180	3	**183**
3. Manufacturing	36 316	7 073	**43 389**	119 531	10 227	**129 758**	5 530	2 353	**7 883**
4. Electricity, gas and water	48	1	**49**	7 006	214	**7 220**	14	.	**14**
5. Construction	14 759	19	**14 778**	90 427	578	**91 005**	1 365	8	**1 373**
6. Wholesale and retail trade, restaurants and hotels	90 986	597	**91 583**	37 318	1 248	**38 566**	8 736	107	**8 843**
7. Transport, storage and communication	14 672	1	**14 673**	44 735	809	**45 544**	1 026	1	**1 027**
8. Financing, insurance, real estate and business services	3 246	32	**3 278**	5 022	981	**6 003**	43	1	**44**
9. Community, social and personal services	31 203	844	**32 047**	143 088	24 880	**167 968**	1 893	116	**2 009**
0. Activities not adequately described . .	825	13	**838**	2 563	69	**2 632**	70	3	**73**
Total . . .	565 245	31 181	**596 426**	572 562	63 216	**635 778**	172 336	62 697	**235 033**

‡ For notes, see pp. 272-294.

A Distribution by status and by industry (branch of economic activity)
Répartition suivant la situation dans la profession et par branche d'activité économique
Distribución según la categoría de ocupación y por rama de actividad económica

Others and status unknown / Autres et situation non définie / Otros y categoría no definida			TOTAL				Branche d'activité économique	Rama de actividad económica
Males / Hommes / Hombres	Females / Femmes / Mujeres	Total	Males / Hommes / Hombres	Females / Femmes / Mujeres	Total	%		
...	...	...	1 319 219	504 741	1 823 960	41.4	1. Agriculture, chasse, sylviculture et pêche	1. Agricultura, caza, silvicultura y pesca
...	...	...	13 862	1 443	15 305	0.3	2. Industries extractives	2. Minas y canteras
...	...	...	247 084	100 333	347 417	7.9	3. Industries manufacturières	3. Industrias manufactureras
...	...	...	9 194	248	9 442	0.2	4. Electricité, gaz et eau	4. Electricidad, gas y agua
...	...	...	111 210	1 204	112 414	2.5	5. Construction	5. Construcción
...	...	...	322 482	22 952	345 434	7.8	6. Commerce (gros et détail) ; restaurants, hôtels	6. Comercio (por mayor y por menor); restaurantes, hoteles
...	...	...	151 579	3 687	155 266	3.5	7. Transports, entrepôts et communications	7. Transportes, almacenamiento y comunicaciones
...	...	...	24 409	1 938	26 347	0.6	8. Banques, assur., affaires imm., services aux entreprises	8. Bancos, seguros, bienes inmuebles, servicios para empresas
...	...	...	354 426	133 707	488 133	11.0	9. Services à la collectivité, services sociaux et personnels	9. Servicios comunales, sociales y personales
...	...	...	253 708	44 556	298 264	6.8	0. Activités mal désignées	0. Actividades no bien especif.
446 406	349 800	796 206	446 406	349 800	796 206	18.0	{ Personnes en quête d'emploi pour la première fois / Chômeurs	{ Personas en busca de trabajo por primera vez / Desempleados
446 406	349 800	796 206	3 253 579	1 164 609	4 418 188	100.0	Total	Total

Others and status unknown / Autres et situation non définie / Otros y categoría no definida			TOTAL				Branche d'activité économique	Rama de actividad económica
Males / Hommes / Hombres	Females / Femmes / Mujeres	Total	Males / Hommes / Hombres	Females / Femmes / Mujeres	Total	%		
5	...	5	641 297	106 712	748 009	49.0	1. Agriculture, chasse, sylviculture et pêche	1. Agricultura, caza, silvicultura y pesca
...	...	...	8 429	207	8 636	0.6	2. Industries extractives	2. Minas y canteras
34	2	36	161 411	19 655	181 066	11.9	3. Industries manufacturières	3. Industrias manufactureras
...	...	...	7 068	215	7 283	0.5	4. Electricité, gaz et eau	4. Electricidad, gas y agua
8	...	8	106 559	605	107 164	7.0	5. Construction	5. Construcción
10	...	10	137 050	1 952	139 002	9.1	6. Commerce (gros et détail) ; restaurants, hôtels	6. Comercio (por mayor y por menor); restaurantes, hoteles
12	...	12	60 445	811	61 256	4.0	7. Transports, entrepôts et communications	7. Transportes, almacenamiento y comunicaciones
2	...	2	8 313	1 014	9 327	0.6	8. Banques, assur., affaires imm., services aux entreprises	8. Bancos, seguros, bienes inmuebles, servicios para empresas
11	2	13	176 195	25 842	202 037	13.3	9. Services à la collectivité, services sociaux et personnels	9. Servicios comunales, sociales y personales
50 461	6 768	57 229	53 919	6 853	60 772	4.0	0. Activités mal désignées	0. Actividades no bien especif.
50 543	6 772	57 315	1 360 686	163 866	1 524 552	100.0	Total	Total

✝ Voir notes pp. 272-294.

✝ Véanse las notas en las págs. 272-294.

2 Structure of the economically active population
Structure de la population active
Estructura de la población económicamente activa

Industry (Branch of economic activity)	Employers and workers on own account / Employeurs et personnes travaillant à leur propre compte / Empleadores y trabajadores por cuenta propia			Salaried employees and wage earners / Employés et ouvriers / Empleados y obreros			Family workers / Travailleurs familiaux / Trabajadores familiares		
	Males Hommes Hombres	Females Femmes Mujeres	Total	Males Hommes Hombres	Females Femmes Mujeres	Total	Males Hommes Hombres	Females Femmes Mujeres	Total

République arabe syrienne (IX.1973) ‡ (2)

Industry	Males	Females	Total	Males	Females	Total	Males	Females	Total
1. Agriculture, hunting, forestry and fishing	...	...	387 441	...	...	95 300	...	...	367 491
2. Mining and quarrying	...	...	4 284	...	...	9 694	...	...	381
3. Manufacturing	...	...	45 024	...	...	108 465	...	...	7 691
4. Electricity, gas and water	.	.	.	...	...	7 324	.	.	.
5. Construction	...	...	15 017	...	...	71 548	...	...	1 694
6. Wholesale and retail trade, restaurants and hotels	...	...	110 856	...	...	29 755	...	...	12 868
7. Transport, storage and communication	...	...	17 434	...	...	45 882	...	...	1 210
8. Financing, insurance, real estate and business services	...	...	5 109	...	...	5 031	...	...	...
9. Community, social and personal services	...	...	30 254	...	...	229 113	...	...	2 902
0. Activities not adequately described	...	...	...	...	...	317	...	...	...
Persons seeking work for the first time	.	.	.	.	.	.	.	.	.
Total . . .	...	...	615 419	...	...	602 429	...	...	394 237

Thailand

Industry	Males	Females	Total	Males	Females	Total	Males	Females	Total
(1.IV.1970) (ISIC 1958)									
Agriculture, forestry, hunting and fishing	3 509 726	597 833	4 107 559	318 393	222 284	540 677	2 786 768	5 720 310	8 507 078
Mining and quarrying	6 263	1 793	8 056	51 829	15 675	67 504	3 140	4 597	7 737
Manufacturing	94 068	74 284	168 352	266 109	162 173	428 282	28 827	53 515	82 342
Construction	32 786	1 387	34 173	119 369	23 448	142 817	2 838	915	3 753
Electricity, gas, water and sanitary services	435	29	464	21 540	3 154	24 694	44	14	58
Commerce	230 453	218 931	449 384	106 717	49 736	156 453	62 910	197 516	260 426
Transport, storage and communication	89 339	2 398	91 737	157 836	11 592	169 428	3 528	1 139	4 667
Services	72 174	51 753	123 927	655 775	317 500	973 275	13 702	50 416	64 118
Activities not adequately described	9 220	3 091	12 311	73 166	21 574	94 740	1 637	3 167	4 804
Persons seeking work for the first time	.	.	.	.	.	.	.	.	.
Total . . .	4 044 464	951 499	4 995 963	1 770 734	827 136	2 597 870	2 903 394	6 031 589	8 934 983
(VII-IX.1973) ‡									
Agriculture, forestry, hunting and fishing	3 450 130	752 070	4 202 200	451 010	316 590	767 600	2 668 130	4 628 370	7 296 500
Mining and quarrying	10 750	3 710	14 460	85 930	8 170	94 100	230	2 030	2 260
Manufacturing	204 520	127 790	332 310	491 040	243 760	734 800	39 270	94 450	133 720
Construction	56 000	680	56 680	174 250	25 930	200 180	960	140	1 100
Electricity, gas, water and sanitary services	110	.	110	44 800	3 530	48 330	.	.	.
Commerce	353 690	373 220	726 910	208 890	74 450	283 340	86 170	295 350	381 520
Transport, storage and communication	156 420	370	156 790	209 500	9 650	219 150	4 510	3 370	7 880
Services	105 390	106 210	211 600	619 970	433 860	1 053 830	17 590	92 320	109 910
Activities not adequately described	70	.	70	70	.	70	.	1 590	1 590
Persons seeking work for the first time	.	.	.	.	.	.	.	.	.
Unemployed	.	.	.	.	.	.	.	.	.
Total . . .	4 337 080	1 364 050	5 701 130	2 285 460	1 115 940	3 401 400	2 816 860	5 117 620	7 934 480

‡ For notes, see pp. 272-294.

A **Distribution by status and by industry (branch of economic activity)**
Répartition suivant la situation dans la profession et par branche d'activité économique
Distribución según la categoría de ocupación y por rama de actividad económica

Others and status unknown / Autres et situation non définie / Otros y categoría no definida			TOTAL				Branche d'activité économique	Rama de actividad económica
Males / Hommes / Hombres	Females / Femmes / Mujeres	Total	Males / Hommes / Hombres	Females / Femmes / Mujeres	Total			
						%		
...	...	7 410	...	...	857 642	50.9	1. Agriculture, chasse, sylviculture et pêche	1. Agricultura, caza, silvicultura y pesca
...	...	563	...	...	14 922	0.9	2. Industries extractives	2. Minas y canteras
...	...	4 916	...	...	166 096	9.8	3. Industries manufacturières	3. Industrias manufactureras
...	...	278	...	...	7 602	0.5	4. Electricité, gaz et eau	4. Electricidad, gas y agua
...	...	7 500	...	...	95 759	5.7	5. Construction	5. Construcción
...	...	5 642	...	...	159 121	9.4	6. Commerce (gros et détail); restaurants, hôtels	6. Comercio (por mayor y por menor); restaurantes, hoteles
...	...	2 082	...	...	66 608	3.9	7. Transports, entrepôts et communications	7. Transportes, almacenamiento y comunicaciones
...	...	283	...	...	10 423	0.6	8. Banques, assur., affaires imm., services aux entreprises	8. Bancos, seguros, bienes inmuebles, servicios para empresas
...	...	6 989	...	...	269 258	15.9	9. Services à la collectivité, services sociaux et personnels	9. Servicios comunales, sociales y personales
.	.	.	...	...	317	—	0. Activités mal désignées	0. Actividades no bien especif.
...	...	40 827	...	...	40 827	2.4	Personnes en quête d'emploi pour la première fois	Personas en busca de trabajo por primera vez
...	...	**76 490**	1 344 615	343 960	**1 688 575**	100.0	Total	Total

Males / Hommes / Hombres	Females / Femmes / Mujeres	Total	Males / Hommes / Hombres	Females / Femmes / Mujeres	Total	%	(CITI 1958)	(CIIU 1958)
21 159	25 428	46 587	6 636 046	6 565 855	13 201 901	78.2	Agriculture, sylviculture, chasse et pêche	Agricultura, silvicultura, caza y pesca
2 271	1 079	3 350	63 503	23 144	86 647	0.5	Industries extractives	Minas y canteras
2 426	1 238	3 664	391 430	291 210	682 640	4.1	Industries manufacturières	Industrias manufactureras
574	160	734	155 567	25 910	181 477	1.1	Construction	Construcción
56	15	71	22 075	3 212	25 287	0.2	Electricité, gaz, eau et services sanitaires	Electricidad, gas, agua y servicios sanitarios
3 131	6 404	9 535	403 211	472 587	875 798	5.2	Com., banq., assur., aff. imm.	Comercio
1 744	822	2 566	252 447	15 951	268 398	1.6	Transports, entrepôts et communications	Transportes, almacenaje y comunicaciones
12 201	10 686	22 887	753 852	430 355	1 184 207	7.0	Services	Servicios
22 650	11 407	34 057	106 673	39 239	145 912	0.9	Activités mal désignées	Actividades no bien especif.
125 956	71 913	197 869	125 956	71 913	197 869	1.2	Personnes en quête d'emploi pour la première fois	Personas en busca de trabajo por primera vez
192 168	129 152	**321 320**	8 910 760	7 939 376	**16 850 136**	100.0	Total	Total

Males / Hommes / Hombres	Females / Femmes / Mujeres	Total	Males / Hommes / Hombres	Females / Femmes / Mujeres	Total	%	(CITI 1958)	(CIIU 1958)
110	4 070	4 180	6 569 380	5 701 100	12 270 480	71.8	Agriculture, sylviculture, chasse et pêche	Agricultura, silvicultura, caza y pesca
60	.	60	96 970	13 910	110 880	0.6	Industries extractives	Minas y canteras
240	60	300	735 070	466 060	1 201 130	7.0	Industries manufacturières	Industrias manufactureras
.	.	.	231 210	26 750	257 960	1.5	Construction	Construcción
			44 910	3 530	48 440	0.3	Electricité, gaz, eau et services sanitaires	Electricidad, gas, agua y servicios sanitarios
200	320	520	648 950	743 340	1 392 290	8.1	Com., banq., assur., aff. imm.	Comercio
80	.	80	370 510	13 390	383 900	2.2	Transports, entrepôts et communications	Transportes, almacenaje y comunicaciones
140	120	260	743 090	632 510	1 375 600	8.0	Services	Servicios
60	190	250	200	1 780	1 980	—	Activités mal désignées	Actividades no bien especif.
27 840	15 200	43 040	27 840	15 200	43 040	0.3	Personnes en quête d'emploi pour la première fois	Personas en busca de trabajo por primera vez
28 150	2 700	30 850	28 150	2 700	30 850	0.2	Chômeurs	Desempleados
56 880	22 660	**76 540**	9 496 280	7 620 270	**17 116 550**	100.0	Total	Total

† Voir notes pp. 272-294.

† Véanse las notas en las págs. 272-294.

POPULATION

2 Structure of the economically active population
Structure de la population active
Estructura de la población económicamente activa

Industry (Branch of economic activity)	Employers and workers on own account Employeurs et personnes travaillant à leur propre compte Empleadores y trabajadores por cuenta propia			Salaried employees and wage earners Employés et ouvriers Empleados y obreros			Family workers Travailleurs familiaux Trabajadores familiares		
	Males Hommes Hombres	Females Femmes Mujeres	Total	Males Hommes Hombres	Females Femmes Mujeres	Total	Males Hommes Hombres	Females Femmes Mujeres	Total

Austria

(12.V.1971)									
1. Agriculture, hunting, forestry and fishing	148 006	56 724	**204 730**	40 752	19 829	**60 581**	38 745	122 422	**161 167**
2. Mining and quarrying	286	20	**306**	24 440	2 282	**26 722**	59	61	**120**
3. Manufacturing	49 256	9 116	**58 372**	595 640	302 554	**898 194**	4 584	11 160	**15 744**
4. Electricity, gas and water	1	.	**1**	31 183	4 285	**35 468**	.	1	**1**
5. Construction	12 974	530	**13 504**	232 389	13 400	**245 789**	837	1 976	**2 813**
6. Wholesale and retail trade, restaurants and hotels	53 345	40 989	**94 334**	154 443	206 102	**360 545**	7 059	26 394	**33 453**
7. Transport, storage and communication	8 326	863	**9 189**	157 339	26 593	**183 932**	909	822	**1 731**
8. Financing, insurance, real estate and business services	9 626	2 429	**12 055**	52 004	50 466	**102 470**	207	1 509	**1 716**
9. Community, social and personal services	16 551	8 343	**24 894**	225 803	258 150	**483 953**	815	4 586	**5 401**
0. Activities not adequately described . .	6 148	4 386	**10 534**	24 211	20 059	**44 270**	2 393	3 604	**5 997**
Total . . .	304 519	123 400	**427 919**	1 538 204	903 720	**2 441 924**	55 608	172 535	**228 143**
(1974) ╫									
1. Agriculture, hunting, forestry and fishing	166 000	172 000	**338 000**	38 000	16 000	**54 000**	...	...	...
2. Mining and quarrying	1 000	.	**1 000**	21 000	20 000	**23 000**	...	...	...
3. Manufacturing	49 000	14 000	**63 000**	579 000	274 000	**853 000**	...	...	...
4. Electricity, gas and water	.	.	.	28 000	4 000	**32 000**	...	...	...
5. Construction	16 000	4 000	**20 000**	226 000	18 000	**244 000**	...	...	...
6. Wholesale and retail trade, restaurants and hotels	61 000	63 000	**124 000**	156 000	210 000	**366 000**	...	...	...
7. Transport, storage and communication	9 000	2 000	**11 000**	162 000	29 000	**191 000**	...	...	...
8. Financing, insurance, real estate and business services	10 000	3 000	**13 000**	72 000	75 000	**147 000**	...	...	...
9. Community, social and personal services	16 000	13 000	**29 000**	222 000	243 000	**465 000**	...	...	...
0. Activities not adequately described . .	1 000	2 000	**3 000**	24 000	22 000	**46 000**	...	...	...
Total . . .	329 000	273 000	**602 000**	1 528 000	893 000	**2 421 000**	...	...	...

╫ For notes, see pp. 272-294.

A Distribution by status and by industry (branch of economic activity)
Répartition suivant la situation dans la profession et par branche d'activité économique
Distribución según la categoría de ocupación y por rama de actividad económica

Others and status unknown / *Autres et situation non définie* / Otros y categoría no definida			TOTAL				Branche d'activité économique	Rama de actividad económica
Males / *Hommes* / Hombres	Females / *Femmes* / Mujeres	Total	Males / *Hommes* / Hombres	Females / *Femmes* / Mujeres	Total	%		
.	.	.	227 503	198 975	426 478	13.8	1. *Agriculture, chasse, sylviculture et pêche*	1. Agricultura, caza, silvicultura y pesca
.	.	.	24 785	2 363	27 148	0.9	2. *Industries extractives*	2. Minas y canteras
.	.	.	649 480	322 830	972 310	31.3	3. *Industries manufacturières*	3. Industrias manufactureras
.	.	.	31 184	4 286	35 470	1.1	4. *Electricité, gaz et eau*	4. Electricidad, gas y agua
.	.	.	246 200	15 906	262 106	8.5	5. *Construction*	5. Construcción
.	.	.	214 847	273 485	488 332	15.8	6. *Commerce (gros et détail) ; restaurants, hôtels*	6. Comercio (por mayor y por menor); restaurantes, hoteles
.	.	.	166 574	28 278	194 852	6.3	7. *Transports, entrepôts et communications*	7. Transportes, almacenamiento y comunicaciones
.	.	.	61 837	54 404	116 241	3.8	8. *Banques, assur., affaires imm., services aux entreprises*	8. Bancos, seguros, bienes inmuebles, servicios para empresas
.	.	.	243 169	271 079	514 248	16.5	9. *Services à la collectivité, services sociaux et personnels*	9. Servicios comunales, sociales y personales
.	.	.	32 752	28 049	60 801	2.0	0. *Activités mal désignées*	0. Actividades no bien especif.
.	.	.	**1 898 331**	**1 199 655**	**3 097 986**	*100.0*	*Total*	Total
.	.	.	204 000	188 000	392 000	13.0	1. *Agriculture, chasse, sylviculture et pêche*	1. Agricultura, caza, silvicultura y pesca
.	.	.	22 000	2 000	24 000	0.8	2. *Industries extractives*	2. Minas y canteras
.	.	.	628 000	288 000	916 000	30.3	3. *Industries manufacturières*	3. Industrias manufactureras
.	.	.	28 000	4 000	32 000	1.1	4. *Electricité, gaz et eau*	4. Electricidad, gas y agua
.	.	.	242 000	22 000	264 000	8.7	5. *Construction*	5. Construcción
.	.	.	217 000	273 000	490 000	16.2	6. *Commerce (gros et détail) ; restaurants, hôtels*	6. Comercio (por mayor y por menor); restaurantes, hoteles
.	.	.	171 000	31 000	202 000	6.7	7. *Transports, entrepôts et communications*	7. Transportes, almacenamiento y comunicaciones
.	.	.	82 000	78 000	160 000	5.3	8. *Banques, assur., affaires imm., services aux entreprises*	8. Bancos, seguros, bienes inmuebles, servicios para empresas
.	.	.	238 000	256 000	494 000	16.3	9. *Services à la collectivité, services sociaux et personnels*	9. Servicios comunales, sociales y personales
.	.	.	25 000	24 000	49 000	1.6	0. *Activités mal désignées*	0. Actividades no bien especif.
.	.	.	**1 857 000**	**1 166 000**	**3 023 000**	*100.0*	*Total*	Total

‡ *Voir notes pp. 272-294.*

‡ Véanse las notas en las págs. 272-294.

2 Structure of the economically active population
Structure de la population active
Estructura de la población económicamente activa

Industry (Branch of economic activity)	Employers and workers on own account Employeurs et personnes travaillant à leur propre compte Empleadores y trabajadores por cuenta propia			Salaried employees and wage earners Employés et ouvriers Empleados y obreros			Family workers Travailleurs familiaux Trabajadores familiares		
	Males Hommes Hombres	Females Femmes Mujeres	Total	Males Hommes Hombres	Females Femmes Mujeres	Total	Males Hommes Hombres	Females Femmes Mujeres	Total

Belgique

(31.XII.1970)

1. Agriculture, hunting, forestry and fishing	102 640	13 365	**116 005**	13 891	1 066	**14 957**	16 541	14 546	**31 087**
2. Mining and quarrying	305	24	**329**	48 238	793	**49 031**	24	8	**32**
3. Manufacturing	50 484	5 099	**55 583**	814 616	284 838	**1 099 454**	4 265	5 821	**10 086**
4. Electricity, gas and water	123	6	**129**	31 802	2 238	**34 040**	13	2	**15**
5. Construction	42 659	812	**43 471**	236 755	6 895	**243 650**	3 220	1 172	**4 392**
6. Wholesale and retail trade, restaurants and hotels	139 853	84 968	**224 821**	192 256	128 476	**320 732**	11 974	44 521	**56 495**
7. Transport, storage and communication	12 446	733	**13 179**	196 799	19 905	**216 704**	1 390	2 483	**3 873**
8. Financing, insurance, real estate and business services	19 355	3 924	**23 279**	85 850	51 170	**137 020**	411	2 232	**2 643**
9. Community, social and personal services	31 613	18 622	**50 235**	372 204	318 859	**691 063**	1 369	7 035	**8 404**
0. Activities not adequately described . .	3 166	1 184	**4 350**	41 977	22 727	**64 704**	240	607	**847**
Persons on compulsory military service	.	.	.	.	.	.	.	.	.
Unemployed	...	...	...	...	...	...	...	...	...
Total . . .	402 644	128 737	**531 381**	2 034 388	836 967	**2 871 355**	39 447	78 427	**117 874**

(30.VI.1974) ‡

1. Agriculture, hunting, forestry and fishing	87 604	10 887	**98 491**	11 189	1 226	**12 415**	11 395	17 343	**28 738**
2. Mining and quarrying	309	25	**334**	37 293	659	**37 952**	24	8	**32**
3. Manufacturing	46 220	4 585	**50 805**	828 673	308 206	**1 136 879**	3 915	7 690	**11 605**
4. Electricity, gas and water	123	6	**129**	30 832	1 897	**32 729**	.	.	.
5. Construction	40 486	784	**41 270**	241 799	7 215	**249 014**	3 013	1 680	**4 693**
6. Wholesale and retail trade, restaurants and hotels.	130 020	79 016	**209 036**	248 584	168 409	**416 993**	11 096	61 109	**72 205**
7. Transport, storage and communication	12 194	723	**12 917**	220 876	27 539	**248 415**	1 346	3 658	**5 004**
8. Financing, insurance, real estate and business services	22 183	4 855	**27 038**	115 376	74 961	**190 337**	460	3 771	**4 231**
9. Community, social and personal services	33 745	19 871	**53 616**	404 395	484 769	**889 164**	1 716	12 486	**14 202**
0 Activities not adequately described . .	...	...	...	...	...	...	...	...	...
Persons on compulsory military service	.	.	.	.	.	.	.	.	.
Persons seeking work for the first time . . . . } Unemployed . . . . }	...	...	...	...	...	...	...	...	...
Total . . .	372 884	120 752	**493 636**	2 139 017	1 074 881	**3 213 898**	32 965	107 745	**140 710**

‡ For notes, see pp. 272-294.

A Distribution by status and by industry (branch of economic activity)
Répartition suivant la situation dans la profession et par branche d'activité économique
Distribución según la categoría de ocupación y por rama de actividad económica

Others and status unknown / *Autres et situation non définie* / Otros y categoría no definida			TOTAL				Branche d'activité économique	Rama de actividad económica
Males / *Hommes* / Hombres	Females / *Femmes* / Mujeres	Total	Males / *Hommes* / Hombres	Females / *Femmes* / Mujeres	Total	%		
52	17	69	133 124	28 994	162 118	4.5	1. *Agriculture, chasse, sylviculture et pêche*	1. Agricultura, caza, silvicultura y pesca
17	.	17	48 584	825	49 409	1.4	2. *Industries extractives*	2. Minas y canteras
215	138	353	869 580	295 896	1 165 476	32.0	3. *Industries manufacturières*	3. Industrias manufactureras
18	.	18	31 956	2 246	34 202	0.9	4. *Electricité, gaz et eau*	4. Electricidad, gas y agua
103	6	109	282 737	8 885	291 622	8.0	5. *Construction*	5. Construcción
119	112	231	344 202	258 077	602 279	16.6	6. *Commerce (gros et détail) ; restaurants, hôtels*	6. Comercio (por mayor y por menor); restaurantes, hoteles
139	10	149	210 774	23 131	233 905	6.4	7. *Transports, entrepôts et communications*	7. Transportes, almacenamiento y comunicaciones
32	19	51	105 648	57 345	162 993	4.5	8. *Banques, assur., affaires imm., services aux entreprises*	8. Bancos, seguros, bienes inmuebles, servicios para empresas
362	367	729	405 548	344 883	750 431	20.6	9. *Services à la collectivité, services sociaux et personnels*	9. Servicios comunales, sociales y personales
1 536	687	2 223	46 919	25 205	72 124	2.0	0. *Activités mal désignées*	0. Actividades no bien especif.
32 991	.	32 991	32 991	.	32 991	0.9	*Militaires du contingent*	Personas en servicio militar obligatorio
47 668	32 600	80 268	47 668	32 600	80 268	2.2	*Chômeurs*	Desempleados
83 252	33 956	117 208	2 559 731	1 078 087	3 637 818	100.0	*Total*	Total
...	...	...	110 188	29 456	139 644	3.5	1. *Agriculture, chasse, sylviculture et pêche*	1. Agricultura, caza, silvicultura y pesca
...	...	...	37 626	692	38 318	1.0	2. *Industries extractives*	2. Minas y canteras
...	...	...	878 808	320 481	1 199 289	30.1	3. *Industries manufacturières*	3. Industrias manufactureras
...	...	...	30 955	1 903	32 858	0.8	4. *Electricité, gaz et eau*	4. Electricidad, gas y agua
...	...	...	285 298	9 679	294 977	7.4	5. *Construction*	5. Construcción
...	...	...	389 700	308 534	698 234	17.5	6. *Commerce (gros et détail) ; restaurants, hôtels*	6. Comercio (por mayor y por menor); restaurantes, hoteles
...	...	...	234 416	31 920	266 336	6.7	7. *Transports, entrepôts et communications*	7. Transportes, almacenamiento y comunicaciones
...	...	...	138 019	83 587	221 606	5.6	8. *Banques, assur., affaires imm., services aux entreprises*	8. Bancos, seguros, bienes inmuebles, servicios para empresas
...	...	...	439 856	517 126	956 982	24.0	9. *Services à la collectivité, services sociaux et personnels*	9. Servicios comunales, sociales y personales
1 542	1 042	2 584	1 542	1 042	2 584	0.1	0. *Activités mal désignées*	0. Actividades no bien especif.
40 731	.	40 731	40 731	.	40 731	1.0	*Miliciens (service militaire obligatoire)*	Personas en servicio militar obligatorio
44 413	49 106	93 519	44 413	49 106	93 519	2.3	{ *Personnes en quête d'emploi pour la première fois* { *Chômeurs*	{ Personas en busca de trabajo por primera vez { Desempleados
86 686	50 148	136 834	2 631 552	1 353 526	3 985 078	100.0	*Total*	Total

✝ *Voir notes pp. 272-294.* ✝ Véanse las notas en las págs. 272-294.

POPULATION

2 Structure of the economically active population
Structure de la population active
Estructura de la población económicamente activa

Industry (Branch of economic activity)	Employers and workers on own account *Employeurs et personnes travaillant à leur propre compte* Empleadores y trabajadores por cuenta propia			Salaried employees and wage earners *Employés et ouvriers* Empleados y obreros			Family workers *Travailleurs familiaux* Trabajadores familiares		
	Males *Hommes* Hombres	Females *Femmes* Mujeres	Total	Males *Hommes* Hombres	Females *Femmes* Mujeres	Total	Males *Hommes* Hombres	Females *Femmes* Mujeres	Total
Bulgarie (1.XII.1965) †									
Agriculture and forestry	12 281	9 554	**21 835**	143 335	161 814	**305 149**	...	...	...
Mining and quarrying (incl. ferrous and non-ferrous metallurgy).	.	.	.	113 025	20 544	**133 569**	...	...	...
Manufacturing	13 112	5 207	**18 319**	498 066	335 238	**833 304**	...	...	...
Construction	5 359	37	**5 396**	202 878	24 141	**227 019**	...	...	...
Electricity and steam	.	.	.	14 754	2 905	**17 659**	...	...	...
Commerce	1 776	389	**2 165**	96 513	106 284	**202 797**	...	...	...
Transport, storage and communication	1 481	17	**1 498**	154 279	33 466	**187 745**	...	...	...
Services	1 757	164	**1 921**	27 945	22 500	**50 445**	...	...	...
Activities not adequately described . . .	3 667	686	**4 353**	251 811	235 987	**487 798**	...	...	...
Total . . .	39 433	16 054	**55 487**	1 502 606	942 879	**2 445 485**	...	...	...
Channel Is.									
Jersey (4.IV.1971) †									
1. Agriculture, hunting, forestry and fishing	977	64	**1 041**	1 315	509	**1 824**	.	.	.
2. Mining and quarrying	8	.	**8**	202	7	**209**	.	.	.
3. Manufacturing	289	59	**348**	2 045	1 037	**3 082**	.	.	.
4. Electricity, gas and water	1	.	**1**	587	64	**651**	.	.	.
5. Construction	919	1	**920**	3 150	90	**3 240**	.	.	.
6. Wholesale and retail trade, restaurants and hotels	526	231	**757**	2 368	2 534	**4 902**	.	.	.
7. Transport, storage and communication	284	19	**303**	1 861	538	**2 399**	.	.	.
8. Financing, insurance, real estate and business services	126	36	**162**	732	867	**1 599**	.	.	.
9. Community, social and personal services	1 118	675	**1 793**	5 186	5 541	**10 727**	.	.	.
0. Activities not adequately described . .	25	16	**41**	342	292	**634**	.	.	.
Total . . .	4 273	1 101	**5 374**	17 788	11 479	**29 267**	.	.	.
Czechoslovakia (1.XII.1970) †									
1. Agriculture, hunting, forestry and fishing	28 086	27 573	**55 659**	288 744	160 051	**448 795**	.	.	.
2. Mining and quarrying	.	.	.	174 724	28 770	**203 494**	.	.	.
3. Manufacturing	952	690	**1 642**	1 312 025	1 031 503	**2 343 528**	.	.	.
4. Electricity, gas and water	.	.	.	62 792	21 446	**84 238**	.	.	.
5. Construction	159	.	**159**	483 906	93 732	**577 638**	.	.	.
6. Wholesale and retail trade, restaurants and hotels	80	81	**161**	193 928	435 489	**629 417**	.	.	.
7. Transport, storage and communication	116	10	**126**	343 902	147 437	**491 339**	.	.	.
8. Financing, insurance, real estate and business services	122	64	**186**	25 428	40 526	**65 954**	.	.	.
9. Community, social and personal services	3 150	1 417	**4 567**	521 387	705 108	**1 226 495**	.	.	.
0. Activities not adequately described . .	1 048	619	**1 667**	17 234	6 224	**23 458**	.	.	.
Total . . .	33 713	30 454	**64 167**	3 424 070	2 670 286	**6 094 356**	.	.	.

† For notes, see pp. 272-294.

A   Distribution by status and by industry (branch of economic activity)
Répartition suivant la situation dans la profession et par branche d'activité économique
Distribución según la categoría de ocupación y por rama de actividad económica

Others and status unknown / Autres et situation non définie / Otros y categoría no definida			TOTAL				Branche d'activité économique	Rama de actividad económica
Males / Hommes / Hombres	Females / Femmes / Mujeres	Total	Males / Hommes / Hombres	Females / Femmes / Mujeres	Total			

						%		
701 464	862 950	**1 564 414**	857 080	1 034 318	**1 891 398**	44.4	*Agriculture et sylviculture*	Agricultura y silvicultura
...	...	...	113 025	20 544	**133 569**	3.1	*Industries extractives (y compris métallurgie des métaux ferreux et non ferreux)*	Minas y canteras (incl. metalurgia de metales ferrosos y no ferrosos)
89 267	50 426	**139 693**	600 445	390 871	**991 316**	23.3	*Industries manufacturières*	Industrias manufactureras
47 669	570	**48 239**	255 906	24 748	**280 654**	6.6	*Construction*	Construcción
...	...	...	14 754	2 905	**17 659**	0.4	*Electricité et vapeur*	Electricidad y vapor
218	792	**1 010**	98 507	107 465	**205 972**	4.8	*Com., banq., assur., aff. imm.*	Comercio
...	...	...	155 760	33 483	**189 243**	4.4	*Transports, entrepôts et communications*	Transportes, almacenaje y comunicaciones
6 025	3 096	**9 121**	35 727	25 760	**61 487**	1.4	*Services*	Servicios
2 992	1 357	**4 349**	258 470	238 030	**496 500**	11.6	*Activités mal désignées*	Actividades no bien especif.
847 635	919 191	**1 766 826**	2 389 674	1 878 124	**4 267 798**	100.0	*Total*	Total

						%		
·	·	·	2 292	573	**2 865**	8.3	*1. Agriculture, chasse sylviculture et pêche*	1. Agricultura, caza, silvicultura y pesca
·	·	·	210	7	**217**	0.6	*2. Industries extractives*	2. Minas y canteras
·	·	·	2 334	1 096	**3 430**	9.9	*3. Industries manufacturières*	3. Industrias manufactureras
·	·	·	588	64	**652**	1.9	*4. Electricité, gaz et eau*	4. Electricidad, gas y agua
·	·	·	4 069	91	**4 160**	12.0	*5. Construction*	5. Construcción
·	·	·	2 894	2 765	**5 659**	16.3	*6. Commerce (gros et détail) ; restaurants, hôtels*	6. Comercio (por mayor y por menor); restaurantes, hoteles
·	·	·	2 145	557	**2 702**	7.8	*7. Transports, entrepôts et communications*	7. Transportes, almacenamiento y comunicaciones
·	·	·	858	903	**1 761**	5.1	*8. Banques, assur., affaires imm., services aux entreprises*	8. Bancos, seguros, bienes inmuebles, servicios para empresas
·	·	·	6 304	6 216	**12 520**	36.2	*9. Services à la collectivité, services sociaux et personnels*	9. Servicios comunales, sociales y personales
·	·	·	367	308	**675**	1.9	*0. Activités mal désignées*	0. Actividades no bien especif.
·	·	·	22 061	12 580	**34 641**	100.0	*Total*	Total

						%		
320 508	318 635	**639 143**	637 378	506 259	**1 143 597**	16.4	*1. Agriculture, chasse, sylviculture et pêche*	1. Agricultura, caza, silvicultura y pesca
47	9	**56**	174 771	28 779	**203 550**	2.9	*2. Industries extractives*	2. Minas y canteras
45 681	73 748	**119 429**	1 358 658	1 105 941	**2 464 599**	35.3	*3. Industries manufacturières*	3. Industrias manufactureras
894	1 385	**2 279**	63 686	22 831	**86 517**	1.2	*4. Electricité, gaz et eau*	4. Electricidad, gas y agua
16 589	3 614	**20 203**	500 654	97 346	**598 000**	8.6	*5. Construction*	5. Construcción
823	1 610	**2 433**	194 831	437 180	**632 011**	9.1	*6. Commerce (gros et détail) ; restaurants, hôtels*	6. Comercio (por mayor y por menor); restaurantes, hoteles
157	64	**221**	344 175	147 511	**491 686**	7.0	*7. Transports, entrepôts et communications*	7. Transportes, almacenamiento y comunicaciones
196	156	**352**	25 746	40 746	**66 492**	1.0	*8. Banques, assur., affaires imm., services aux entreprises*	8. Bancos, seguros, bienes inmuebles, servicios para empresas
5 237	7 512	**12 749**	529 774	714 037	**1 243 811**	17.8	*9. Services à la collectivité, services sociaux et personnels*	9. Servicios comunales, sociales y personales
22 061	5 053	**27 114**	40 343	11 896	**52 239**	0.7	*0. Activités mal désignées*	0. Actividades no bien especif.
412 193	411 786	**823 979**	3 869 976	3 112 526	**6 982 502**	100.0	*Total*	Total

† *Voir notes pp. 272-294.*   † Véanse las notas en las págs. 272-294.

2 Structure of the economically active population
Structure de la population active
Estructura de la población económicamente activa

Industry (Branch of economic activity)	Employers and workers on own account Employeurs et personnes travaillant à leur propre compte Empleadores y trabajadores por cuenta propia			Salaried employees and wage earners Employés et ouvriers Empleados y obreros			Family workers Travailleurs familiaux Trabajadores familiares		
	Males Hommes Hombres	Females Femmes Mujeres	Total	Males Hommes Hombres	Females Femmes Mujeres	Total	Males Hommes Hombres	Females Femmes Mujeres	Total

Denmark

(9.XI.1970) †

1. Agriculture, hunting, forestry and fishing	131 019	4 622	**135 641**	57 942	5 236	**63 178**	167	45 421	**45 588**
2. Mining and quarrying	252	9	**261**	2 662	115	**2 777**	1	31	**32**
3. Manufacturing	34 976	3 350	**38 326**	388 419	161 510	**549 929**	89	10 672	**10 761**
4. Electricity, gas and water	144	1	**145**	11 472	1 276	**12 748**	.	3	**3**
5. Construction	28 693	228	**28 921**	169 508	6 437	**175 945**	16	5 608	**5 624**
6. Wholesale and retail trade, restaurants and hotels	58 319	13 400	**71 719**	126 358	123 655	**250 013**	449	22 318	**22 767**
7. Transport, storage and communication	18 390	523	**18 913**	105 686	25 925	**131 611**	18	2 674	**2 692**
8. Financing, insurance, real estate and business services	10 479	1 119	**11 598**	53 653	51 545	**105 198**	16	1 787	**1 803**
9. Community, social and personal services	24 644	11 453	**36 097**	191 336	306 050	**497 386**	82	9 242	**9 324**
0. Activities not adequately described . .	.	.	.	50 924	16 358	**67 282**	.	.	.
Total . . .	306 916	34 705	**341 621**	1 157 960	698 107	**1 856 067**	838	97 756	**98 594**

(X.1974) †

1. Agriculture, hunting, forestry and fishing	121 685	3 074	**124 759**	44 580	7 206	**51 786**	.	51 776	**51 776**
2. Mining and quarrying	193	.	**193**	2 148	87	**2 235**	.	60	**60**
3. Manufacturing	33 797	3 790	**37 587**	382 345	158 231	**540 576**	.	10 674	**10 674**
4. Electricity, gas and water	.	.	.	12 695	1 541	**14 236**	.	.	.
5. Construction	30 887	412	**31 299**	155 027	8 116	**163 143**	.	7 076	**7 076**
6. Wholesale and retail trade, restaurants and hotels	52 332	10 770	**63 102**	129 740	135 186	**264 926**	.	24 372	**24 372**
7. Transport, storage and communication	16 804	705	**17 509**	117 393	31 883	**149 276**	.	4 012	**4 012**
8. Financing, insurance, real estate and business services	10 797	1 630	**12 427**	66 343	67 376	**133 719**	.	1 874	**1 874**
9. Community, social and personal services	23 430	11 264	**34 694**	235 251	447 964	**683 215**	.	6 998	**6 998**
0. Activities not adequately described . .	.	.	.	28 506	18 590	**47 096**	.	.	.
Total . . .	289 925	31 645	**321 570**	1 174 028	876 180	**2 050 208**	.	106 842	**106 842**

† For notes, see pp. 272-294.

 Distribution by status and by industry (branch of economic activity)
Répartition suivant la situation dans la profession et par branche d'activité économique
Distribución según la categoría de ocupación y por rama de actividad económica

Others and status unknown *Autres et situation non définie* Otros y categoría no definida			TOTAL				Branche d'activité économique	Rama de actividad económica
Males *Hommes* Hombres	Females *Femmes* Mujeres	Total	Males *Hommes* Hombres	Females *Femmes* Mujeres	Total	%		
.	.	.	189 128	55 279	**244 407**	*10.6*	1. *Agriculture, chasse, sylviculture et pêche*	1. Agricultura, caza, silvicultura y pesca
.	.	.	2 915	155	**3 070**	*0.1*	2. *Industries extractives*	2. Minas y canteras
.	.	.	423 484	175 532	**599 016**	*25.9*	3. *Industries manufacturières*	3. Industrias manufactureras
.	.	.	11 616	1 280	**12 896**	*0.6*	4. *Electricité, gaz et eau*	4. Electricidad, gas y agua
.	.	.	198 217	12 273	**210 490**	*9.1*	5. *Construction*	5. Construcción
.	.	.	185 126	159 373	**344 499**	*14.9*	6. *Commerce (gros et détail) ; restaurants, hôtels*	6. Comercio (por mayor y por menor); restaurantes, hoteles
.	.	.	124 094	29 122	**153 216**	*6.6*	7. *Transports, entrepôts et communications*	7. Transportes, almacenamiento y comunicaciones
.	.	.	64 148	54 451	**118 599**	*5.1*	8. *Banques, assur., affaires imm., services aux entreprises*	8. Bancos, seguros, bienes inmuebles, servicios para empresas
30	16 975	**17 005**	216 092	243 720	**559 812**	*24.2*	9. *Services à la collectivité, services sociaux et personnels*	9. Servicios comunales, sociales y personales
.	.	.	50 924	16 358	**67 282**	*2.9*	0. *Activités mal désignées*	0. Actividades no bien especif.
30	16 975	**17 005**	1 465 744	847 543	**2 313 287**	*100.0*	*Total*	Total
.	.	.	166 265	62 056	**228 321**	*9.2*	1. *Agriculture, chasse, sylviculture et pêche*	1. Agricultura, caza, silvicultura y pesca
.	.	.	2 341	147	**2 488**	*0.1*	2. *Industries extractives*	2. Minas y canteras
.	.	.	416 142	172 695	**588 837**	*23.8*	3. *Industries manufacturières*	3. Industrias manufactureras
.	.	.	12 695	1 541	**14 236**	*0.6*	4. *Electricité, gaz et eau*	4. Electricidad, gas y agua
.	.	.	185 914	15 604	**201 518**	*8.1*	5. *Construction*	5. Construcción
.	.	.	182 072	170 328	**352 400**	*14.2*	6. *Commerce (gros et détail) ; restaurants, hôtels*	6. Comercio (por mayor y por menor); restaurantes, hoteles
.	.	.	134 197	36 599	**170 796**	*6.9*	7. *Transports, entrepôts et communications*	7. Transportes, almacenamiento y comunicaciones
.	.	.	77 140	70 880	**148 020**	*6.0*	8. *Banques, assur., affaires imm., services aux entreprises*	8. Bancos, seguros, bienes inmuebles, servicios para empresas
.	.	.	258 681	466 226	**724 907**	*29.2*	9. *Services à la collectivité, services sociaux et personnels*	9. Servicios comunales, sociales y personales
.	.	.	28 506	18 590	**47 096**	*1.9*	0. *Activités mal désignées*	0. Actividades no bien especif.
.	.	.	1 463 953	1 014 666	**2 478 619**	*100.0*	*Total*	Total

✝ *Voir notes pp. 272-294.*

✝ Véanse las notas en las págs. 272-294.

2 Structure of the economically active population
Structure de la population active
Estructura de la población económicamente activa

Industry (Branch of economic activity)	Employers and workers on own account *Employeurs et personnes travaillant à leur propre compte* Empleadores y trabajadores por cuenta propia			Salaried employees and wage earners *Employés et ouvriers* Empleados y obreros			Family workers *Travailleurs familiaux* Trabajadores familiares		
	Males *Hommes* Hombres	Females *Femmes* Mujeres	Total	Males *Hommes* Hombres	Females *Femmes* Mujeres	Total	Males *Hommes* Hombres	Females *Femmes* Mujeres	Total

España

(31.XII.1970) ‡

1. Agriculture, hunting, forestry and fishing	1 045 428	66 970	**1 112 398**	1 190 337	70 361	**1 260 698**	393 242	172 382	**565 624**
2. Mining and quarrying	4 673	29	**4 702**	117 394	2 036	**119 430**	727	33	**760**
3. Manufacturing	171 392	43 979	**215 371**	2 098 439	634 361	**2 732 800**	37 102	11 677	**48 779**
4. Electricity, gas and water	1 550	78	**1 628**	79 662	4 383	**84 045**	203	16	**219**
5. Construction	116 917	978	**117 895**	1 050 661	19 538	**1 070 199**	12 383	453	**12 836**
6. Wholesale and retail trade, restaurants and hotels	386 428	98 094	**484 522**	664 532	273 854	**938 386**	44 040	40 111	**84 151**
7. Transport, storage and communication	108 693	792	**109 485**	482 063	52 144	**534 207**	9 730	521	**10 251**
8. Financing, insurance, real estate and business services	22 676	850	**23 526**	215 136	48 338	**263 474**	848	535	**1 383**
9. Community, social and personal services	126 700	36 013	**162 713**	960 141	661 236	**1 621 377**	12 460	7 814	**20 274**
0. Activities not adequately described	12 706	1 438	**14 144**	104 476	27 867	**132 343**	2 062	528	**2 590**
Total	1 997 163	249 221	**2 246 384**	6 962 841	1 794 118	**8 756 959**	512 797	234 070	**746 867**

(X-XII.1974) ‡

1. Agriculture, hunting, forestry and fishing	...	...	...	...	...	...	...	...	...
2. Mining and quarrying	...	...	...	...	...	...	...	...	...
3. Manufacturing	...	...	...	...	...	...	...	...	...
4. Electricity, gas and water	...	...	...	...	...	...	...	...	...
5. Construction	...	...	...	...	...	...	...	...	...
6. Wholesale and retail trade, restaurants and hotels									
7. Transport, storage and communication	...	...	...	...	...	...	...	...	...
8. Financing, insurance, real estate and business services	...	...	...	...	...	...	...	...	...
9. Community, social and personal services									
0. Activities not adequately described	...	...	...	...	...	...	...	...	...
Total	...	...	...	...	...	...	...	...	...

Faeroe Is. (16.XI.1970)

1. Agriculture, hunting, forestry and fishing	600	5	**605**	2 931	10	**2 941**	1	22	**23**
2. Mining and quarrying	3	.	**3**	106	.	**106**	.	.	.
3. Manufacturing	260	26	**286**	2 341	345	**2 686**	.	21	**21**
4. Electricity, gas and water	3	.	**3**	74	7	**81**	.	.	.
5. Construction	221	.	**221**	1 219	21	**1 240**	.	9	**9**
6. Wholesale and retail trade, restaurants and hotels	382	79	**461**	523	745	**1 268**	.	5	**5**
7. Transport, storage and communication	128	2	**130**	1 308	106	**1 414**	1	88	**89**
8. Financing, insurance, real estate and business services	1	.	**1**	128	93	**221**	.	.	.
9. Community, social and personal services	86	67	**157**	861	1 485	**2 346**	.	10	**10**
0. Activities not adequately described	.	.	.	528	263	**791**	.	.	.
Total	1 684	179	**1 863**	10 019	3 075	**13 094**	2	155	**157**

‡ For notes, see pp. 272-294.

A Distribution by status and by industry (branch of economic activity)
Répartition suivant la situation dans la profession et par branche d'activité économique
Distribución según la categoría de ocupación y por rama de actividad económica

Table 1

| Others and status unknown / Autres et situation non définie / Otros y categoría no definida | | | TOTAL | | | % | Branche d'activité économique | Rama de actividad económica |
Males / Hommes / Hombres	Females / Femmes / Mujeres	Total	Males / Hommes / Hombres	Females / Femmes / Mujeres	Total			
17 351	2 655	**20 006**	2 646 358	312 368	**2 958 726**	24.8	1. Agriculture, chasse, sylviculture et pêche	1. Agricultura, caza, silvicultura y pesca
941	58	**999**	123 735	2 156	**125 891**	1.1	2. Industries extractives	2. Minas y canteras
15 614	7 256	**22 870**	2 322 547	697 273	**3 019 820**	25.5	3. Industries manufacturières	3. Industrias manufactureras
595	65	**660**	82 010	4 542	**86 552**	0.7	4. Electricité, gaz et eau	4. Electricidad, gas y agua
15 647	553	**16 200**	1 195 608	21 522	**1 217 130**	10.2	5. Construction	5. Construcción
11 014	4 126	**15 140**	1 106 014	416 185	**1 522 199**	12.8	6. Commerce (gros et détail); restaurants, hôtels	6. Comercio (por mayor y por menor); restaurantes, hoteles
4 722	647	**5 369**	605 208	54 104	**659 312**	5.5	7. Transports, entrepôts et communications	7. Transportes, almacenamiento y comunicaciones
2 068	411	**2 479**	240 728	50 134	**290 862**	2.4	8. Banques, assur., affaires imm., services aux entreprises	8. Bancos, seguros, bienes inmuebles, servicios para empresas
26 455	39 685	**66 140**	1 125 756	744 748	**1 870 504**	15.7	9. Services à la collectivité, services sociaux et personnels	9. Servicios comunales, sociales y personales
6 846	1 140	**7 986**	126 090	30 973	**157 063**	1.3	0. Activités mal désignées	0. Actividades no bien especif.
101 253	56 596	**157 849**	9 574 054	2 334 005	**11 908 059**	100.0	Total	Total

Table 2

Males	Females	Total	Males	Females	Total	%	Branche d'activité économique	Rama de actividad económica
...	...	...	...	...	**3 065 600**	23.0	1. Agriculture, chasse, sylviculture et pêche	1. Agricultura, caza, silvicultura y pesca
...	...	...	...	...	**101 900**	0.8	2. Industries extractives	2. Minas y canteras
...	...	...	...	...	**3 433 800**	25.8	3. Industries manufacturières	3. Industrias manufactureras
...	...	...	...	...	**82 200**	0.6	4. Electricité, gaz et eau	4. Electricidad, gas y agua
...	...	...	...	...	**1 336 300**	10.0	5. Construction	5. Construcción
...	...	...	...	...	**1 748 300**	13.1	6. Commerce (gros et détail); restaurants, hôtels	6. Comercio (por mayor y por menor); restaurantes, hoteles
...	...	...	...	...	**694 500**	5.2	7. Transports, entrepôts et communications	7. Transportes, almacenamiento y comunicaciones
...	...	...	...	...	**271 800**	2.0	8. Banques, assur., affaires imm., services aux entreprises	8. Bancos, seguros, bienes inmuebles, servicios para empresas
...	...	...	...	...	**2 597 800**	19.5	{ 9. Services à la collectivité, services sociaux et personnels / 0. Activités mal désignées	{ 9. Servicios comunales, sociales y personales / 0. Actividades no bien especif.
...	...	...	...	...	**13 332 200**	100.0	Total	Total

Table 3

Males	Females	Total	Males	Females	Total	%	Branche d'activité économique	Rama de actividad económica
.	.	.	3 532	37	**3 569**	23.6	1. Agriculture, chasse, sylviculture et pêche	1. Agricultura, caza, silvicultura y pesca
.	.	.	109	.	**109**	0.7	2. Industries extractives	2. Minas y canteras
.	.	.	2 601	392	**2 993**	19.8	3. Industries manufacturières	3. Industrias manufactureras
.	.	.	77	7	**84**	0.6	4. Electricité, gaz et eau	4. Electricidad, gas y agua
.	.	.	1 440	30	**1 470**	9.7	5. Construction	5. Construcción
.	.	.	905	829	**1 734**	11.5	6. Commerce (gros et détail); restaurants, hôtels	6. Comercio (por mayor y por menor); restaurantes, hoteles
.	.	.	1 437	196	**1 633**	10.8	7. Transports, entrepôts et communications	7. Transportes, almacenamiento y comunicaciones
.	.	.	129	93	**222**	1.5	8. Banques, assur., affaires imm., services aux entreprises	8. Bancos, seguros, bienes inmuebles, servicios para empresas
.	.	.	947	1 562	**2 509**	16.6	9. Services à la collectivité, services sociaux et personnels	9. Servicios comunales, sociales y personales
.	.	.	528	263	**791**	5.2	0. Activités mal désignées	0. Actividades no bien especif.
.	.	.	11 705	3 409	**15 114**	100.0	Total	Total

‡ Voir notes pp. 272-294.

‡ Véanse las notas en las págs. 272-294.

POPULATION

2 Structure of the economically active population
Structure de la population active
Estructura de la población económicamente activa

Industry (Branch of economic activity)	Employers and workers on own account *Employeurs et personnes travaillant à leur propre compte* Empleadores y trabajadores por cuenta propia			Salaried employees and wage earners *Employés et ouvriers* Empleados y obreros			Family workers *Travailleurs familiaux* Trabajadores familiares		
	Males *Hommes* Hombres	Females *Femmes* Mujeres	Total	Males *Hommes* Hombres	Females *Femmes* Mujeres	Total	Males *Hommes* Hombres	Females *Femmes* Mujeres	Total

Finland

(31.XII.1970)									
1. Agriculture, hunting, forestry and fishing	177 112	31 813	**208 925**	71 313	8 539	**79 852**	38 251	101 927	**140 178**
2. Mining and quarrying	98	2	**100**	5 983	885	**6 868**	17	15	**32**
3. Manufacturing	9 033	5 049	**14 082**	316 880	189 885	**506 765**	952	1 629	**2 581**
4. Electricity, gas and water	5	.	**5**	15 402	2 961	**18 363**	.	.	.
5. Construction	8 857	55	**8 912**	154 981	12 016	**166 997**	453	329	**782**
6. Wholesale and retail trade, restaurants and hotels	15 957	12 102	**28 059**	102 601	187 615	**290 216**	1 681	7 954	**9 635**
7. Transport, storage and communication	20 837	451	**21 288**	93 480	33 552	**127 032**	1 304	489	**1 793**
8. Financing, insurance, real estate and business services	2 016	533	**2 549**	25 043	43 747	**68 790**	36	306	**342**
9. Community, social and personal services	8 089	9 332	**17 421**	133 136	231 595	**364 731**	410	1 056	**1 466**
0. Activities not adequately described	674	185	**859**	16 568	6 227	**22 795**	46	52	**98**
Total	242 678	59 522	**302 200**	935 387	717 022	**1 652 409**	43 150	113 757	**156 907**
(1973) ‡									
1. Agriculture, hunting, forestry and fishing	...	...	...	...	...	...	...	...	...
2. Mining and quarrying ⎫ 3. Manufacturing ⎬ 4. Electricity, gas and water ⎭	...	...	...	...	...	...	...	...	...
5. Construction	...	...	...	...	...	...	...	...	...
6. Wholesale and retail trade, restaurants and hotels	...	...	...	...	...	...	...	...	...
7. Transport, storage and communication	...	...	...	...	...	...	...	...	...
8. Financing, insurance, real estate and business services	...	...	...	...	...	...	...	...	...
9. Community, social and personal services	...	...	...	...	...	...	...	...	...
Armed forces	...	...	...	...	...	...	...	...	...
Unemployed	...	...	...	...	...	...	...	...	...
Total	219 000	195 000	**414 000**	952 000	798 000	**1 750 000**	...	...	...

‡ For notes, see pp. 272-294.

A Distribution by status and by industry (branch of economic activity)
Répartition suivant la situation dans la profession et par branche d'activité économique
Distribución según la categoría de ocupación y por rama de actividad económica

Males / Hommes / Hombres	Females / Femmes / Mujeres	Total	Males / Hommes / Hombres	Females / Femmes / Mujeres	Total	%	Branche d'activité économique	Rama de actividad económica
							Others and status unknown / *Autres et situation non définie* / Otros y categoría no definida	**TOTAL**
28	27	**55**	286 704	142 306	**429 010**	*20.3*	1. *Agriculture, chasse, sylviculture et pêche*	1. Agricultura, caza, silvicultura y pesca
7	1	**8**	6 105	903	**7 008**	*0.3*	2. *Industries extractives*	2. Minas y canteras
411	261	**672**	327 276	196 824	**524 100**	*24.7*	3. *Industries manufacturières*	3. Industrias manufactureras
23	7	**30**	15 430	2 968	**18 398**	*0.9*	4. *Electricité, gaz et eau*	4. Electricidad, gas y agua
84	11	**95**	164 375	12 411	**176 786**	*8.3*	5. *Construction*	5. Construcción
102	119	**221**	120 341	207 790	**328 131**	*15.5*	6. *Commerce (gros et détail); restaurants, hôtels*	6. Comercio (por mayor y por menor); restaurantes, hoteles
53	19	**72**	115 674	34 511	**150 185**	*7.1*	7. *Transports, entrepôts et communications*	7. Transportes, almacenamiento y comunicaciones
26	10	**36**	27 121	44 596	**71 717**	*3.4*	8. *Banques, assur., affaires imm., services aux entreprises*	8. Bancos, seguros, bienes inmuebles, servicios para empresas
138	130	**268**	141 773	242 113	**383 886**	*18.1*	9. *Services à la collectivité, services sociaux et personnels*	9. Servicios comunales, sociales y personales
3 579	1 705	**5 284**	20 867	8 169	**29 036**	*1.4*	0. *Activités mal désignées*	0. Actividades no bien especif.
4 451	2 290	**6 741**	1 225 666	892 591	**2 118 257**	*100.0*	*Total*	Total
...	...	...	209 000	160 000	**369 000**	*16.4*	1. *Agriculture, chasse, sylviculture et pêche*	1. Agricultura, caza, silvicultura y pesca
...	...	...	376 000	208 000	**584 000**	*26.1*	2. *Industries extractives* / 3. *Industries manufacturières* / 4. *Electricité, gaz et eau*	2. Minas y canteras / 3. Industrias manufactureras / 4. Electricidad, gas y agua
...	...	...	170 000	15 000	**185 000**	*8.2*	5. *Construction*	5. Construcción
...	...	...	123 000	218 000	**341 000**	*15.2*	6. *Commerce (gros et détail); restaurants, hôtels*	6. Comercio (por mayor y por menor); restaurantes, hoteles
...	...	...	110 000	41 000	**151 000**	*6.7*	7. *Transports, entrepôts et communications*	7. Transportes, almacenamiento y comunicaciones
...	...	...	30 000	58 000	**88 000**	*3.9*	8. *Banques, assur., affaires imm., services aux entreprises*	8. Bancos, seguros, bienes inmuebles, servicios para empresas
...	...	...	142 000	293 000	**435 000**	*19.4*	9. *Services à la collectivité, services sociaux et personnels*	9. Servicios comunales, sociales y personales
...	...	...	41 000	.	**41 000**	*1.8*	*Forces armées*	Fuerzas armadas
...	...	...	29 000	22 000	**51 000**	*2.3*	*Chômeurs*	Desempleados
59 000	22 000	**81 000**	1 230 000	1 015 000	**2 245 000**	*100.0*	*Total*	Total

✝ *Voir notes pp. 272-294.*

✝ Véanse las notas en las págs. 272-294.

POPULATION

2 Structure of the economically active population
Structure de la population active
Estructura de la población económicamente activa

Industry (Branch of economic activity)	Employers and workers on own account — Employeurs et personnes travaillant à leur propre compte — Empleadores y trabajadores por cuenta propia			Salaried employees and wage earners — Employés et ouvriers — Empleados y obreros			Family workers — Travailleurs familiaux — Trabajadores familiares		
	Males Hommes Hombres	Females Femmes Mujeres	Total	Males Hommes Hombres	Females Femmes Mujeres	Total	Males Hommes Hombres	Females Femmes Mujeres	Total

France

(1.III.1968) ‡									
1. Agriculture, hunting, forestry and fishing	...	...	2 485 088	...	...	637 620	...	...	...
2. Mining and quarrying	...	...	3 892	...	...	246 756	...	...	...
3. Manufacturing	...	...	379 768	...	...	4 936 748	...	...	...
4. Electricity, gas and water	...	...	756	...	...	160 200	...	...	...
5. Construction	...	...	295 200	...	...	1 630 676	...	...	...
6. Wholesale and retail trade, restaurants and hotels	...	...	1 038 708	...	...	1 972 652	...	...	...
7. Transport, storage and communication	...	...	67 996	...	...	1 118 036	...	...	...
8. Financing, insurance, real estate and business services	...	...	101 516	...	...	741 872	...	...	...
9. Community, social and personal services	...	...	414 316	...	...	3 730 052	...	...	...
Persons on compulsory military service	.	.	.	...	.	243 160	.	.	.
Unemployed	...	...	...	...	...	...	...	...	...
Total ...	...	...	4 787 240	...	...	15 417 772	...	...	...
(1974*) ‡									
1. Agriculture, hunting, forestry and fishing	...	...	1 943 800	...	...	508 600	...	...	...
2. Mining and quarrying	...	...	2 400	...	...	182 200	...	...	...
3. Manufacturing	...	...	296 700	...	...	5 664 600	...	...	...
4. Electricity, gas and water	...	...	700	...	...	173 500	...	...	...
5. Construction	...	...	289 600	...	...	1 711 600	...	...	...
6. Wholesale and retail trade, restaurants and hotels	...	...	942 900	...	...	2 558 800	...	...	...
7. Transport, storage and communication	...	...	66 300	...	...	1 095 300	...	...	...
8. Financing, insurance, real estate and business services	...	...	100 600	...	...	1 088 000	...	...	...
9. Community, social and personal services	...	...	434 500	...	...	4 399 300	...	...	...
Persons on compulsory military service	.	.	.	...	.	292 800	.	.	.
Unemployed	...	...	...	...	...	...	...	...	...
Total ...	...	...	4 057 500	...	...	17 674 700	...	...	...

‡ For notes, see pp. 272-294.

A

Distribution by status and by industry (branch of economic activity)
Répartition suivant la situation dans la profession et par branche d'activité économique
Distribución según la categoría de ocupación y por rama de actividad económica

Others and status unknown / *Autres et situation non définie* / Otros y categoría no definida			TOTAL				Branche d'activité économique	Rama de actividad económica
Males *Hommes* Hombres	Females *Femmes* Mujeres	Total	Males *Hommes* Hombres	Females *Femmes* Mujeres	Total	%		
...	...	...	...	...	3 122 708	15.1	1. *Agriculture, chasse, sylviculture et pêche*	1. Agricultura, caza, silvicultura y pesca
...	...	...	...	...	250 648	1.2	2. *Industries extractives*	2. Minas y canteras
...	...	...	...	...	5 316 516	25.8	3. *Industries manufacturières*	3. Industrias manufactureras
...	...	...	...	...	160 956	0.8	4. *Electricité, gaz et eau*	4. Electricidad, gas y agua
...	...	...	...	...	1 925 876	9.3	5. *Construction*	5. Construcción
...	...	...	...	...	3 011 360	14.6	6. *Commerce (gros et détail) ; restaurants, hôtels*	6. Comercio (por mayor y por menor); restaurantes, hoteles
...	...	...	...	...	1 186 032	5.7	7. *Transports, entrepôts et communications*	7. Transportes, almacenamiento y comunicaciones
...	...	...	...	...	843 388	4.1	8. *Banques, assur., affaires imm., services aux entreprises*	8. Bancos, seguros, bienes inmuebles, servicios para empresas
...	...	...	...	...	4 144 368	20.1	9. *Services à la collectivité, services sociaux et personnels*	9. Servicios comunales, sociales y personales
.	.	.	...	.	243 160	1.2	*Militaires du contingent*	Personas en servicio militar obligatorio
...	...	436 124	...	...	436 124	2.1	*Chômeurs*	Desempleados
...	...	436 124	13 514 692	7 126 444	20 641 136	100.0	*Total*	Total
...	...	...	...	...	2 452 400	11.0	1. *Agriculture, chasse, sylviculture et pêche*	1. Agricultura, caza, silvicultura y pesca
...	...	...	...	...	184 600	0.8	2. *Industries extractives*	2. Minas y canteras
...	...	...	...	...	5 961 300	26.9	3. *Industries manufacturières*	3. Industrias manufactureras
...	...	...	...	...	174 200	0.8	4. *Electricité, gaz et eau*	4. Electricidad, gas y agua
...	...	...	...	...	1 981 200	8.9	5. *Construction*	5. Construcción
...	...	...	...	...	3 501 700	15.7	6. *Commerce (gros et détail) ; restaurants, hôtels*	6. Comercio (por mayor y por menor); restaurantes, hoteles
...	...	...	...	...	1 161 600	5.2	7. *Transports, entrepôts et communications*	7. Transportes, almacenamiento y comunicaciones
...	...	...	...	...	1 188 600	5.3	8. *Banques, assur., affaires imm., services aux entreprises*	8. Bancos, seguros, bienes inmuebles, servicios para empresas
...	...	...	...	...	4 833 800	21.8	9. *Services à la collectivité, services sociaux et personnels*	9. Servicios comunales, sociales y personales
.	.	.	.	.	292 800	1.3	*Militaires du contingent*	Personas en servicio militar obligatorio
...	...	501 000	...	...	501 000	2.3	*Chômeurs*	Desempleados
...	...	501 000	...	...	22 233 200	100.0	*Total*	Total

‡ *Voir notes pp. 272-294.*   ‡ Véanse las notas en las págs. 272-294.

2 Structure of the economically active population
Structure de la population active
Estructura de la población económicamente activa

Industry (Branch of economic activity)	Employers and workers on own account *Employeurs et personnes travaillant à leur propre compte* Empleadores y trabajadores por cuenta propia			Salaried employees and wage earners *Employés et ouvriers* Empleados y obreros			Family workers *Travailleurs familiaux* Trabajadores familiares		
	Males *Hommes* Hombres	Females *Femmes* Mujeres	Total	Males *Hommes* Hombres	Females *Femmes* Mujeres	Total	Males *Hommes* Hombres	Females *Femmes* Mujeres	Total
German Dem. Rep. (1.I.1971*) △									
1. Agriculture, hunting, forestry and fishing	...	...	...	...	...	...	...	...	...
2. Mining and quarrying	...	...	...	...	...	...	...	...	...
3. Manufacturing	...	...	...	...	...	...	...	...	...
4. Electricity, gas and water	...	...	...	...	...	...	...	...	...
5. Construction	...	...	...	...	...	...	...	...	...
6. Wholesale and retail trade, restaurants and hotels	...	...	...	...	...	...	...	...	...
7. Transport, storage and communication	...	...	...	...	...	...	...	...	...
8. Financing, insurance, real estate and business services	...	...	...	...	...	...	...	...	...
9. Community, social and personal services	...	...	...	...	...	...	...	...	...
0. Activities not adequately described									
Total	...	...	...	...	...	...	...	...	...
Germany, Fed. Rep. of △									
(27.V.1970) ‡									
1. Agriculture, hunting, forestry and fishing	578 500	84 600	**663 100**	227 000	92 400	**319 400**	219 000	789 000	**1 008 000**
2. Mining and quarrying	400	—	**400**	311 100	11 500	**322 600**	—	—	—
3. Manufacturing	360 200	62 200	**422 400**	6 511 300	2 944 700	**9 456 000**	24 900	145 800	**170 700**
4. Electricity, gas and water	800	200	**1 000**	185 800	27 900	**213 700**	—	—	—
5. Construction	172 400	5 700	**178 100**	1 835 200	107 800	**1 943 000**	7 900	35 000	**42 900**
6. Wholesale and retail trade, restaurants and hotels	505 900	272 200	**778 100**	1 284 600	1 670 200	**2 954 800**	39 300	262 600	**301 900**
7. Transport, storage and communication	70 500	6 900	**77 400**	1 108 600	240 400	**1 349 000**	3 700	13 000	**16 700**
8. Financing, insurance, real estate and business services	139 200	20 800	**160 000**	541 300	505 600	**1 046 900**	1 700	26 100	**27 800**
9. Community, social and personal services	212 200	78 600	**290 800**	2 655 000	2 006 000	**4 661 000**	7 900	80 000	**87 900**
Unemployed	...	...	...	...	...	...	...	...	...
Total	2 040 000	531 400	**2 571 400**	14 659 800	7 606 400	**22 266 200**	304 400	1 351 500	**1 655 900**
(IV.1974) ‡									
1. Agriculture, hunting, forestry and fishing	512 000	104 000	**617 000**	178 000	69 000	**248 000**	161 000	773 000	**934 000**
2. Mining and quarrying	—	—	—	310 000	29 000	**339 000**	—	—	—
3. Manufacturing	405 000	55 000	**461 000**	7 081 000	3 058 000	**10 139 000**	12 000	109 000	**121 000**
4. Electricity, gas and water	—	—	—	176 000	16 000	**192 000**	—	—	—
5. Construction	156 000	2 000	**158 000**	1 735 000	116 000	**1 850 000**	2 000	27 000	**29 000**
6. Wholesale and retail trade, restaurants and hotels	487 000	223 000	**710 000**	1 205 000	1 818 000	**3 023 000**	24 000	217 000	**241 000**
7. Transport, storage and communication	71 000	5 000	**76 000**	1 174 000	278 000	**1 452 000**	2 000	11 000	**13 000**
8. Financing, insurance, real estate and business services	143 000	19 000	**162 000**	544 000	590 000	**1 133 000**	—	19 000	**20 000**
9. Community, social and personal services	181 000	84 000	**264 000**	2 615 000	2 384 000	**4 999 000**	4 000	48 000	**52 000**
Total	1 955 000	493 000	**2 448 000**	15 017 000	8 358 000	**23 375 000**	205 000	1 205 000	**1 410 000**

‡ For notes, see pp. 272-294.

A Distribution by status and by industry (branch of economic activity)
Répartition suivant la situation dans la profession et par branche d'activité économique
Distribución según la categoría de ocupación y por rama de actividad económica

Others and status unknown / Autres et situation non définie / Otros y categoría no definida			TOTAL				Branche d'activité économique	Rama de actividad económica
Males / Hommes / Hombres	Females / Femmes / Mujeres	Total	Males / Hommes / Hombres	Females / Femmes / Mujeres	Total	%		
...	...	...	529 254	430 725	**959 979**	11.7	1. Agriculture, chasse, sylviculture et pêche	1. Agricultura, caza, silvicultura y pesca
...	...	...	152 636	45 924	**198 560**	2.4	2. Industries extractives	2. Minas y canteras
...	...	...	1 764 164	1 329 525	**3 093 689**	37.6	3. Industries manufacturières	3. Industrias manufactureras
...	...	...	64 406	26 744	**91 150**	1.1	4. Electricité, gaz et eau	4. Electricidad, gas y agua
...	...	...	524 883	89 121	**614 004**	7.5	5. Construction	5. Construcción
...	...	...	269 616	572 805	**842 421**	10.3	6. Commerce (gros et détail) ; restaurants, hôtels	6. Comercio (por mayor y por menor); restaurantes, hoteles
...	...	...	357 468	197 773	**555 241**	6.8	7. Transports, entrepôts et communications	7. Transportes, almacenamiento y comunicaciones
...	...	...	23 012	64 679	**87 691**	1.1	8. Banques, assur., affaires imm., services aux entreprises	8. Bancos, seguros, bienes inmuebles, servicios para empresas
...	...	...	727 687	1 043 829	**1 771 516**	21.5	9. Services à la collectivité, services sociaux et personnels / 0. Activités mal désignées	9. Servicios comunales, sociales y personales / 0. Actividades no bien especif.
...	...	...	4 413 126	3 801 125	**8 214 251**	100.0	Total	Total
...	...	...	1 024 500	966 000	**1 990 500**	7.5	1. Agriculture, chasse, sylviculture et pêche	1. Agricultura, caza, silvicultura y pesca
...	...	...	311 400	11 500	**322 900**	1.2	2. Industries extractives	2. Minas y canteras
...	...	...	6 896 500	3 153 000	**10 049 500**	37.9	3. Industries manufacturières	3. Industrias manufactureras
...	...	...	186 600	28 100	**214 700**	0.8	4. Electricité, gaz et eau	4. Electricidad, gas y agua
...	...	...	2 015 400	148 400	**2 163 800**	8.1	5. Construction	5. Construcción
...	...	...	1 829 900	2 205 000	**4 034 900**	15.2	6. Commerce (gros et détail) ; restaurants, hôtels	6. Comercio (por mayor y por menor); restaurantes, hoteles
...	...	...	1 182 700	260 000	**1 443 000**	5.4	7. Transports, entrepôts et communications	7. Transportes, almacenamiento y comunicaciones
...	...	...	682 400	552 500	**1 234 900**	4.6	8. Banques, assur., affaires imm., services aux entreprises	8. Bancos, seguros, bienes inmuebles, servicios para empresas
...	...	...	2 874 800	2 164 300	**5 039 100**	18.9	9. Services à la collectivité, services sociaux et personnels	9. Servicios comunales, sociales y personales
70 500	46 100	**116 600**	70 500	46 100	**116 600**	0.4	Chômeurs	Desempleados
70 500	46 100	**116 600**	17 074 700	9 535 200	**26 610 100**	100.0	Total	Total
.	.	.	852 000	947 000	**1 798 000**	6.6	1. Agriculture, chasse, sylviculture et pêche	1. Agricultura, caza, silvicultura y pesca
.	.	.	311 000	29 000	**340 000**	1.2	2. Industries extractives	2. Minas y canteras
.	.	.	7 498 000	3 222 000	**10 720 000**	39.4	3. Industries manufacturières	3. Industrias manufactureras
.	.	.	176 000	17 000	**193 000**	0.7	4. Electricité, gaz et eau	4. Electricidad, gas y agua
.	.	.	1 892 000	146 000	**2 037 000**	7.5	5. Construction	5. Construcción
.	.	.	1 716 000	2 258 000	**3 974 000**	14.6	6. Commerce (gros et détail) ; restaurants, hôtels	6. Comercio (por mayor y por menor); restaurantes, hoteles
.	.	.	1 247 000	294 000	**1 541 000**	5.7	7. Transports, entrepôts et communications	7. Transportes, almacenamiento y comunicaciones
.	.	.	687 000	628 000	**1 315 000**	4.8	8. Banques, assur., affaires imm., services aux entreprises	8. Bancos, seguros, bienes inmuebles, servicios para empresas
.	.	.	2 800 000	2 516 000	**5 316 000**	19.5	9. Services à la collectivité, services sociaux et personnels	9. Servicios comunales, sociales y personales
.	.	.	17 178 000	10 056 000	**27 234 000**	100.0	Total	Total

† *Voir notes pp. 272-294.*

† Véanse las notas en las págs. 272-294.

2 Structure of the economically active population
Structure de la population active
Estructura de la población económicamente activa

Industry (Branch of economic activity)	Employers and workers on own account *Employeurs et personnes travaillant à leur propre compte* Empleadores y trabajadores por cuenta propia			Salaried employees and wage earners *Employés et ouvriers* Empleados y obreros			Family workers *Travailleurs familiaux* Trabajadores familiares		
	Males *Hommes* Hombres	Females *Femmes* Mujeres	Total	Males *Hommes* Hombres	Females *Femmes* Mujeres	Total	Males *Hommes* Hombres	Females *Femmes* Mujeres	Total

Gibraltar (6.X.1970*)

Industry	Males	Females	Total	Males	Females	Total	Males	Females	Total
1. Agriculture, hunting, forestry and fishing	1	.	1	2	.	2	...	...	...
2. Mining and quarrying	.	.	.	.		.	.	.	.
3. Manufacturing	54	7	61	2 370	214	2 584	...	...	...
4. Electricity, gas and water	.	.	.	144	6	150	...	...	...
5. Construction	36	.	36	2 206	59	2 265	...	...	...
6. Wholesale and retail trade, restaurants and hotels	318	78	396	1 534	878	2 412	...	...	...
7. Transport, storage and communication	73	.	73	456	53	509	...	...	...
8. Financing, insurance, real estate and business services	36	5	41	156	114	270	...	...	...
9. Community, social and personal services	51	30	81	1 581	1 177	2 758	...	...	...
0. Activities not adequately described	3	2	5	44	24	68	...	...	...
Total . . .	572	122	694	8 493	2 525	11 018	...	...	...

Grèce (14.III.1971) ‡

Industry	Males	Females	Total	Males	Females	Total	Males	Females	Total
1. Agriculture, hunting, forestry and fishing	623 416	72 352	695 768	44 156	19 212	63 368	162 088	384 088	546 176
2. Mining and quarrying	1 900	40	1 940	17 424	1 484	18 908	116	36	152
3. Manufacturing	127 464	32 936	160 400	267 440	107 220	374 660	7 736	8 828	16 564
4. Electricity, gas and water	292	12	304	21 740	2 616	24 356	12	4	16
5. Construction	50 720	248	50 968	200 904	1 204	202 108	1 932	56	1 988
6. Wholesale and retail trade, restaurants and hotels	178 912	20 192	199 104	96 600	44 028	140 628	8 200	13 004	21 204
7. Transport, storage and communication	59 080	556	59 636	137 168	12 264	149 432	1 268	116	1 384
8. Financing, insurance, real estate and business services	23 324	2 212	25 536	33 580	18 556	52 136	164	236	400
9. Community, social and personal services	33 736	14 068	47 804	191 132	103 592	294 724	1 632	2 520	4 152
0. Activities not adequately described	4 268	2 168	6 436	16 092	33 432	49 524	548	1 268	1 816
Total . . .	1 103 112	144 784	1 247 896	1 026 236	343 608	1 369 844	183 696	410 156	593 852

‡ For notes, see pp. 272-294.

A
Distribution by status and by industry (branch of economic activity)
Répartition suivant la situation dans la profession et par branche d'activité économique
Distribución según la categoría de ocupación y por rama de actividad económica

Others and status unknown / Autres et situation non définie / Otros y categoría no definida			TOTAL				Branche d'activité économique	Rama de actividad económica
Males / Hommes / Hombres	Females / Femmes / Mujeres	Total	Males / Hommes / Hombres	Females / Femmes / Mujeres	Total			

						%		
...	...	...	3	.	3	—	1. Agriculture, chasse, sylviculture et pêche	1. Agricultura, caza, silvicultura y pesca
4	1	5	2 428	222	2 650	22.6	2. Industries extractives	2. Minas y canteras
2	...	2	146	6	152	1.3	3. Industries manufacturières	3. Industrias manufactureras
1	...	1	2 243	59	2 302	19.6	4. Electricité, gaz et eau	4. Electricidad, gas y agua
8	5	13	1 860	961	2 821	24.0	5. Construction	5. Construcción
1	...	1	530	53	583	5.0	6. Commerce (gros et détail) ; restaurants, hôtels	6. Comercio (por mayor y por menor); restaurantes, hoteles
...	...	...	192	119	311	2.6	7. Transports, entrepôts et communications	7. Transportes, almacenamiento y comunicaciones
4	2	6	1 636	1 209	2 845	24.2	8. Banques, assur., affaires imm., services aux entreprises	8. Bancos, seguros, bienes inmuebles, servicios para empresas
6	2	8	53	28	81	0.7	9. Services à la collectivité, services sociaux et personnels	9. Servicios comunales, sociales y personales
							0. Activités mal désignées	0. Actividades no bien especif.
26	10	36	9 091	2 657	11 748	100.0	Total	Total

						%		
4 764	2 524	7 288	834 424	478 176	1 312 600	40.6	1. Agriculture, chasse, sylviculture et pêche	1. Agricultura, caza, silvicultura y pesca
88	8	96	19 528	1 568	21 096	0.7	2. Industries extractives	2. Minas y canteras
1 628	1 128	2 756	404 268	150 112	554 380	17.1	3. Industries manufacturières	3. Industrias manufactureras
116	24	140	22 160	2 656	24 816	0.8	4. Electricité, gaz et eau	4. Electricidad, gas y agua
1 352	8	1 360	254 908	1 516	256 424	7.9	5. Construction	5. Construcción
792	296	1 088	284 504	77 520	362 024	11.2	6. Commerce (gros et détail) ; restaurants, hôtels	6. Comercio (por mayor y por menor); restaurantes, hoteles
1 140	80	1 220	198 656	13 016	211 672	6.5	7. Transports, entrepôts et communications	7. Transportes, almacenamiento y comunicaciones
308	144	452	57 376	21 148	78 524	2.4	8. Banques, assur., affaires imm., services aux entreprises	8. Bancos, seguros, bienes inmuebles, servicios para empresas
1 480	944	2 424	277 980	121 124	349 104	10.8	9. Services à la collectivité, services sociaux et personnels	9. Servicios comunales, sociales y personales
4 876	1 704	6 580	25 784	38 572	64 356	2.0	0. Activités mal désignées	0. Actividades no bien especif.
16 544	6 860	23 404	2 329 588	905 408	3 234 996	100.0	Total	Total

✝ *Voir notes pp. 272-294.*

✝ *Véanse las notas en las págs. 272-294.*

2 Structure of the economically active population
Structure de la population active
Estructura de la población económicamente activa

Industry (Branch of economic activity)	Employers and workers on own account / Employeurs et personnes travaillant à leur propre compte / Empleadores y trabajadores por cuenta propia			Salaried employees and wage earners / Employés et ouvriers / Empleados y obreros			Family workers / Travailleurs familiaux / Trabajadores familiares		
	Males Hommes Hombres	Females Femmes Mujeres	Total	Males Hommes Hombres	Females Femmes Mujeres	Total	Males Hommes Hombres	Females Femmes Mujeres	Total

Hongrie

(1.I.1970) ‡

1. Agriculture, hunting, forestry and fishing	30 924	8 350	**39 274**	233 806	95 696	**329 502**	8 313	132 129	**140 442**
2. Mining and quarrying	.	.	.	140 537	21 579	**162 116**	.	.	.
3. Manufacturing	28 472	12 482	**40 954**	832 692	665 366	**1 498 058**	1 015	1 241	**2 256**
4. Electricity, gas and water	.	.	.	84 593	22 694	**107 287**	.	.	.
5. Construction	13 756	361	**14 117**	268 672	55 046	**323 718**	395	78	**473**
6. Wholesale and retail trade, restaurants and hotels / 8. Financing, insurance, real estate and business services	3 302	4 882	**8 184**	157 999	252 602	**410 601**	496	646	**1 142**
7. Transport, storage and communication	5 823	206	**6 029**	261 001	77 398	**338 399**	226	28	**254**
9. Community, social and personal services / 0. Activities not adequately described	5 370	3 488	**8 858**	306 958	406 832	**713 790**	213	517	**730**
Total	87 647	29 769	**117 416**	2 286 258	1 597 213	**3 883 471**	10 658	134 639	**145 297**

(I.1974) ‡

1. Agriculture, hunting, forestry and fishing	26 100	8 200	**34 300**	310 300	124 200	**434 500**	5 900	130 200	**136 100**
2. Mining and quarrying / 3. Manufacturing / 4. Electricity, gas and water	28 700	11 900	**40 600**	908 900	671 400	**1 580 300**	1 000	1 300	**2 300**
5. Construction / 6. Wholesale and retail trade, restaurants and hotels / 8. Financing, insurance, real estate and business services	17 500	400	**17 900**	291 400	60 500	**351 900**	500	—	**500**
	3 900	7 400	**11 300**	158 400	271 300	**429 700**	400	700	**1 100**
7. Transport, storage and communication	5 400	400	**5 800**	290 100	86 700	**376 800**	300	—	**300**
9. Community, social and personal services / 0. Activities not adequately described	6 800	7 100	**13 900**	320 700	477 800	**798 500**	400	1 100	**1 500**
Total	88 400	35 400	**123 800**	2 279 800	1 691 900	**3 971 700**	8 500	133 300	**141 800**

Ireland (18.IV.1971) ‡

1. Agriculture, hunting, forestry and fishing	165 726	18 677	**184 403**	34 672	870	**35 542**	47 187	5 947	**53 134**
2. Mining and quarrying	104	.	**104**	10 008	303	**10 311**	5	.	**5**
3. Manufacturing	7 246	867	**8 113**	140 127	64 104	**204 231**	344	67	**411**
4. Electricity, gas and water	.	.	.	13 119	1 044	**14 163**	.	.	.
5. Construction	11 377	19	**11 396**	70 907	1 642	**72 549**	572	16	**588**
6. Wholesale and retail trade, restaurants and hotels	27 960	8 786	**36 746**	80 675	50 030	**130 705**	2 401	1 856	**4 257**
7. Transport, storage and communication	4 522	987	**5 509**	45 921	8 495	**54 416**	146	51	**197**
8. Financing, insurance, real estate and business services	4 210	369	**4 579**	18 022	13 524	**31 546**	24	29	**53**
9. Community, social and personal services	5 629	2 239	**7 868**	83 297	97 090	**180 387**	134	120	**254**
0. Activities not adequately described	155	30	**185**	2 007	1 166	**3 173**	10	4	**14**
Total	226 929	31 974	**258 903**	498 755	238 268	**737 023**	50 823	8 090	**58 913**

‡ For notes, see pp. 272-294.

A Distribution by status and by industry (branch of economic activity)
Répartition suivant la situation dans la profession et par branche d'activité économique
Distribución según la categoría de ocupación y por rama de actividad económica

Others and status unknown / Autres et situation non définie / Otros y categoría no definida			TOTAL				Branche d'activité économique	Rama de actividad económica
Males / Hommes / Hombres	Females / Femmes / Mujeres	Total	Males / Hommes / Hombres	Females / Femmes / Mujeres	Total	%		

Males	Females	Total	Males	Females	Total	%	Branche d'activité économique	Rama de actividad económica
478 799	235 208	**714 007**	751 842	471 383	**1 223 225**	24.5	1. Agriculture, chasse, sylviculture et pêche	1. Agricultura, caza, silvicultura y pesca
.	.	.	140 537	21 579	**162 116**	3.2	2. Industries extractives	2. Minas y canteras
36 113	47 858	**83 971**	898 292	726 947	**1 625 239**	32.6	3. Industries manufacturières	3. Industrias manufactureras
.	.	.	84 593	22 694	**107 287**	2.2	4. Electricité, gaz et eau	4. Electricidad, gas y agua
29 862	1 874	**31 736**	312 685	57 359	**370 044**	7.4	5. Construction	5. Construcción
9	8	**17**	161 806	258 138	**419 944**	8.4	{ 6. Commerce (gros et détail) ; restaurants, hôtels 8. Banques, assur., affaires imm., services aux entreprises	{ 6. Comercio (por mayor y por menor); restaurantes, hoteles 8. Bancos, seguros, bienes inmuebles, servicios para empresas
65	41	**106**	267 115	77 673	**344 788**	6.9	7. Transports, entrepôts et communications	7. Transportes, almacenamiento y comunicaciones
4 073	8 582	**12 655**	316 614	419 419	**736 033**	14.8	{ 9. Services à la collectivité, services sociaux et personnels 0. Activités mal désignées	{ 9. Servicios comunales, sociales y personales 0. Actividades no bien especif.
548 921	293 571	**842 492**	2 933 484	2 055 192	**4 988 676**	100.0	Total	Total

Males	Females	Total	Males	Females	Total	%	Branche d'activité économique	Rama de actividad económica
377 800	200 000	**577 800**	720 100	462 600	**1 182 700**	23.3	1. Agriculture, chasse, sylviculture et pêche	1. Agricultura, caza, silvicultura y pesca
63 800	129 100	**192 900**	1 002 400	813 700	**1 816 100**	35.8	{ 2. Industries extractives 3. Industries manufacturières 4. Electricité, gaz et eau	{ 2. Minas y canteras 3. Industrias manufactureras 4. Electricidad, gas y agua
36 900	7 100	**44 000**	346 300	68 000	**414 300**	8.2	5. Construction	5. Construcción
200	300	**500**	162 900	279 700	**442 600**	8.7	{ 6. Commerce (gros et détail) ; restaurants, hôtels 8. Banques, assur., affaires imm., services aux entreprises	{ 6. Comercio (por mayor y por menor); restaurantes, hoteles 8. Bancos, seguros, bienes inmuebles, servicios para empresas
400	—	**400**	296 000	87 100	**383 300**	7.6	7. Transports, entrepôts et communications	7. Transportes, almacenamiento y comunicaciones
6 300	14 400	**20 700**	334 200	500 400	**834 600**	16.4	{ 9. Services à la collectivité, services sociaux et personnels 0. Activités mal désignées	{ 9. Servicios comunales, sociales y personales 0. Actividades no bien especif.
485 400	350 900	**836 300**	2 862 100	2 211 500	**5 073 600**	100.0	Total	Total

Males	Females	Total	Males	Females	Total	%	Branche d'activité économique	Rama de actividad económica
11 437	49	**11 486**	259 022	25 543	**284 565**	25.4	1. Agriculture, chasse, sylviculture et pêche	1. Agricultura, caza, silvicultura y pesca
1 100	3	**1 103**	11 217	306	**11 523**	1.0	2. Industries extractives	2. Minas y canteras
9 617	2 418	**12 035**	157 334	67 456	**224 790**	20.1	3. Industries manufacturières	3. Industrias manufactureras
584	10	**594**	13 703	1 054	**14 757**	1.3	4. Electricité, gaz et eau	4. Electricidad, gas y agua
15 436	70	**15 506**	98 292	1 747	**100 039**	8.9	5. Construction	5. Construcción
5 944	2 173	**8 117**	116 980	62 845	**179 825**	16.1	6. Commerce (gros et détail) ; restaurants, hôtels	6. Comercio (por mayor y por menor); restaurantes, hoteles
3 285	135	**3 420**	53 874	9 668	**63 542**	5.7	7. Transports, entrepôts et communications	7. Transportes, almacenamiento y comunicaciones
262	221	**483**	22 518	14 143	**36 661**	3.3	8. Banques, assur., affaires imm., services aux entreprises	8. Bancos, seguros, bienes inmuebles, servicios para empresas
2 886	3 495	**6 381**	91 946	102 944	**194 890**	17.4	9. Services à la collectivité, services sociaux et personnels	9. Servicios comunales, sociales y personales
4 606	961	**5 567**	6 778	2 161	**8 939**	0.8	0. Activités mal désignées	0. Actividades no bien especif.
55 157	9 535	**64 692**	831 664	287 867	**1 119 531**	100.0	Total	Total

‡ *Voir notes pp. 272-294.*

‡ Véanse las notas en las págs. 272-294.

2 Structure of the economically active population
Structure de la population active
Estructura de la población económicamente activa

Industry (Branch of economic activity	Employers and workers on own account Employeurs et personnes travaillant à leur propre compte Empleadores y trabajadores por cuenta propia			Salaried employees and wage earners Employés et ouvriers Empleados y obreros			Family workers Travailleurs familiaux Trabajadores familiares		
	Males Hommes Hombres	Females Femmes Mujeres	Total	Males Hommes Hombres	Females Femmes Mujeres	Total	Males Hommes Hombres	Females Femmes Mujeres	Total

Isle of Man (24.IV.1966)

(ISIC 1958)

Agriculture, forestry, hunting and fishing	575	17	592	1 254	23	1 277	...	...	...
Mining and quarrying	.	.	.	48	.	48	...	...	...
Manufacturing	93	10	103	2 723	781	3 504	...	...	...
Construction	125	1	126	2 665	14	2 679	...	...	...
Electricity, gas, water and sanitary services	.	.	.	573	11	584	...	...	...
Commerce	315	166	481	1 606	1 219	2 825	...	...	...
Transport, storage and communication	50	.	50	1 544	122	1 666	...	...	...
Services	337	1 102	1 439	1 864	2 894	4 758	...	...	...
Activities not adequately described	3	1	4	62	5	67	...	...	...
Unemployed	.	.	.	.	.	.	...	...	...
Total . . .	1 498	1 297	2 795	12 339	5 069	17 408	...	...	...

Italie

(24.X.1971)

1. Agriculture, hunting, forestry and fishing	1 219 278	263 974	1 483 252	908 489	439 065	1 347 554	171 543	240 272	411 815
2. Mining and quarrying } 3. Manufacturing	651 124	114 753	765 877	3 838 307	1 468 398	5 306 705	50 159	40 932	91 091
4. Electricity, gas and water	414	27	441	148 408	11 038	159 446	174	62	236
5. Construction	240 554	1 955	242 509	1 738 139	32 482	1 770 621	12 079	1 056	13 135
6. Wholesale and retail trade, restaurants and hotels	777 529	335 411	1 112 940	745 314	339 089	1 084 403	96 116	230 786	326 902
7. Transport, storage and communication	129 685	2 063	131 748	769 805	82 740	852 545	6 063	1 349	7 412
8. Financing, insurance, real estate and business services	4 248	600	4 848	225 243	54 776	280 019	454	491	945
9. Community, social and personal services	256 312	83 028	339 340	1 748 814	1 319 416	3 068 230	9 588	19 525	29 113
Persons seeking work for the first time	.	.	.	.	.	.	.	.	.
Total . . .	3 279 144	801 811	4 080 955	10 122 519	3 747 004	13 869 523	346 176	534 473	880 649

(IV. 1975) ✝   (ISIC 1958)

Agriculture, forestry, hunting and fishing	1 065 000	192 000	1 258 000	755 000	358 000	1 113 000	174 000	399 000	573 000
Mining and quarrying } Electricity, gas, water and sanitary services	6 000	—	6 000	327 000	18 000	345 000	1 000	—	1 000
Manufacturing	677 000	142 000	820 000	3 702 000	1 417 000	5 119 000	61 000	62 000	123 000
Construction	257 000	3 000	260 000	1 527 000	18 000	1 545 000	14 000	3 000	17 000
Commerce (excl. banking and insurance)	862 000	300 000	1 162 000	659 000	349 000	1 008 000	129 000	279 000	408 000
Transport, storage and communication	145 000	1 000	146 000	823 000	78 000	901 000	3 000	4 000	7 000
Services (incl. banking and insurance)	261 000	71 000	332 000	2 123 000	1 464 000	3 587 000	14 000	25 000	39 000
Persons seeking work for the first time	.	.	.	.	.	.	.	.	.
Unemployed	...	...	...	...	...	...	...	...	...
Total . . .	3 273 000	710 000	3 982 000	9 916 000	3 702 000	13 618 000	396 000	772 000	1 168 000

✝ For notes, see pp. 272-294.

A Distribution by status and by industry (branch of economic activity)
Répartition suivant la situation dans la profession et par branche d'activité économique
Distribución según la categoría de ocupación y por rama de actividad económica

Others and status unknown / Autres et situation non définie / Otros y categoría no definida			TOTAL				Branche d'activité économique	Rama de actividad económica
Males Hommes Hombres	Females Femmes Mujeres	Total	Males Hommes Hombres	Females Femmes Mujeres	Total	%		
							(CITI 1958)	(CIIU 1958)
...	...	...	1 829	40	**1 869**	9.1	Agriculture, sylviculture, chasse et pêche	Agricultura, silvicultura, caza y pesca
...	...	...	48	.	**48**	0.2	Industries extractives	Minas y canteras
...	...	...	2 816	791	**3 607**	17.5	Industries manufacturières	Industrias manufactureras
...	...	...	2 790	15	**2 805**	13.6	Construction	Construcción
...	...	...	573	11	**584**	2.8	Electricité, gaz, eau et services sanitaires	Electricidad, gas, agua y servicios sanitarios
...	...	...	1 921	1 385	**3 306**	16.1	Com., banq., assur., aff. imm.	Comercio
...	...	...	1 594	122	**1 716**	8.3	Transports, entrepôts et communications	Transportes, almacenaje y comunicaciones
...	...	...	2 201	3 996	**6 197**	30.2	Services	Servicios
...	...	...	65	6	**71**	0.3	Activités mal désignées	Actividades no bien especif.
314	76	390	314	76	**390**	1.9	Chômeurs	Desempleados
314	76	**390**	14 151	6 442	**20 593**	100.0	*Total*	Total
						%		
.	.	.	2 299 310	943 311	**3 242 621**	16.4	1. Agriculture, chasse, sylviculture et pêche	1. Agricultura, caza, silvicultura y pesca
.	.	.	4 539 590	1 624 083	**6 163 673**	31.2	{ 2. Industries extractives / 3. Industries manufacturières	{ 2. Minas y canteras / 3. Industrias manufactureras
.	.	.	148 996	11 127	**160 123**	0.8	4. Electricité, gaz et eau	4. Electricidad, gas y agua
.	.	.	1 990 772	35 493	**2 026 265**	10.2	5. Construction	5. Construcción
.	.	.	1 618 959	905 286	**2 524 245**	12.7	6. Commerce (gros et détail) ; restaurants, hôtels	6. Comercio (por mayor y por menor); restaurantes, hoteles
.	.	.	905 553	86 152	**991 705**	5.0	7. Transports, entrepôts et communications	7. Transportes, almacenamiento y comunicaciones
.	.	.	229 945	55 867	**285 812**	1.4	8. Banques, assur., affaires imm., services aux entreprises	8. Bancos, seguros, bienes inmuebles, servicios para empresas
.	.	.	2 014 714	1 421 969	**3 436 783**	17.4	9. Services à la collectivité, services sociaux et personnels	9. Servicios comunales, sociales y personales
626 907	347 895	**974 802**	626 907	347 895	**974 802**	4.9	Personnes en quête d'emploi pour la première fois	Personas en busca de trabajo por primera vez
626 907	347 895	**974 802**	14 374 746	5 431 183	**19 805 929**	100.0	*Total*	Total
							(CITI 1958)	(CIIU 1958)
						%		
...	...	...	1 994 000	949 000	**2 943 000**	15.1	Agriculture, sylviculture, chasse et pêche	Agricultura, silvicultura, caza y pesca
							Industries extractives	Minas y canteras
...	...	...	334 000	18 000	**352 000**	1.8	Electricité, gaz, eau et services sanitaires	Electricidad, gas, agua y servicios sanitarios
...	...	...	4 440 000	1 622 000	**6 062 000**	31.2	Industries manufacturières	Industrias manufactureras
...	...	...	1 798 000	24 000	**1 822 000**	9.4	Construction	Construcción
...	...	...	1 650 000	928 000	**2 578 000**	13.3	Commerce (non compris banques et assur.)	Comercio (excl. bancos y seguros)
...	...	...	971 000	83 000	**1 054 000**	5.4	Transports, entrepôts et communications	Transportes, almacenaje y comunicaciones
...	...	...	2 398 000	1 560 000	**3 958 000**	20.4	Services (y compris banques et assur.)	Servicios (incl. bancos y seguros)
226 000	190 000	**416 000**	226 000	190 000	**416 000**	2.1	Personnes en quête d'emploi pour la première fois	Personas en busca de trabajo por primera vez
173 000	78 000	**251 000**	173 000	78 000	**251 000**	1.3	Chômeurs	Desempleados
399 000	268 000	**667 000**	13 984 000	5 452 000	**19 436 000**	100.0	*Total*	Total

† *Voir notes pp. 272-294.*

† *Véanse las notas en las págs. 272-294.*

2 Structure of the economically active population
Structure de la population active
Estructura de la población económicamente activa

Industry (Branch of economic activity)	Employers and workers on own account — Employeurs et personnes travaillant à leur propre compte — Empleadores y trabajadores por cuenta propia			Salaried employees and wage earners — Employés et ouvriers — Empleados y obreros			Family workers — Travailleurs familiaux — Trabajadores familiares		
	Males Hommes Hombres	Females Femmes Mujeres	Total	Males Hommes Hombres	Females Femmes Mujeres	Total	Males Hommes Hombres	Females Femmes Mujeres	Total
Luxembourg (31.XII.1970) ‡									
1. Agriculture, hunting, forestry and fishing	5 295	520	**5 815**	921	43	**964**	1 335	1 527	**2 862**
2. Mining and quarrying . . . . . . }	1 489	223	**1 712**	38 155	3 462	**41 617**	7	190	**197**
3. Manufacturing . . . . }									
4. Electricity, gas and water	.	.	.	908	62	**970**	.	.	.
5. Construction	1 084	21	**1 105**	10 422	242	**10 664**	.	1	**1**
6. Wholesale and retail trade, restaurants and hotels	3 783	3 249	**7 032**	8 266	7 192	**15 458**	60	1 011	**1 071**
7. Transport, storage and communication	458	26	**484**	6 609	649	**7 258**	.	1	**1**
8. Financing, insurance, real estate and business services	467	37	**504**	3 196	2 385	**5 581**	.	.	.
9. Community, social and personal services	950	316	**1 266**	11 508	12 126	**23 634**	4	35	**39**
Persons seeking work for the first time	.	.	.	.	.	.	.	.	.
Unemployed	...	...	...	...	...	...	...	...	...
Total . . .	13 526	4 392	**17 918**	79 985	26 161	**106 146**	1 406	2 765	**4 171**
Malta									
(26.XI.1967) (ISIC 1958)									
Agriculture, forestry, hunting and fishing	4 512	440	**4 952**	1 002	160	**1 162**	1 067	437	**1 504**
Mining and quarrying	86	.	**86**	585	1	**586**	9	.	**9**
Manufacturing	2 232	572	**2 804**	15 543	3 489	**19 032**	308	67	**375**
Construction	1 363	1	**1 364**	10 532	98	**10 630**	123	2	**125**
Electricity, gas, water and sanitary services	6	.	**6**	2 051	51	**2 102**	.	.	.
Commerce	4 412	1 451	**5 863**	4 048	1 605	**5 653**	318	215	**533**
Transport, storage and communication	786	10	**796**	4 866	280	**5 146**	74	2	**76**
Services	2 777	2 139	**4 916**	16 984	9 503	**26 487**	95	65	**160**
Unemployed	...	...	...	...	...	...	...	...	...
Total . . .	16 174	4 613	**20 787**	55 611	15 187	**70 798**	1 994	788	**2 782**
(XI.1972) ‡ (ISIC 1958)									
Agriculture, forestry, hunting and fishing	5 267	681	**5 948**	403	100	**503**	...	...	...
Mining and quarrying	89	.	**89**	480	.	**480**	...	...	...
Manufacturing	2 660	790	**3 450**	18 962	8 259	**27 221**	...	...	...
Construction	220	.	**220**	8 324	.	**8 324**	...	...	...
Electricity, gas, water and sanitary services	.	.	.	905	5	**910**	...	...	...
Commerce	5 550	2 758	**8 308**	3 810	1 570	**5 380**	...	...	...
Transport, storage and communication	662	24	**686**	3 550	220	**3 770**	...	...	...
Services	2 183	806	**2 989**	28 200	10 014	**38 214**	...	...	...
Persons seeking work for the first time	69	.	**69**	57	24	**81**	.	.	.
Total . . .	16 700	5 059	**21 759**	64 691	20 192	**84 883**	...	...	...

‡ For notes, see pp. 272-294.

A Distribution by status and by industry (branch of economic activity)
Répartition suivant la situation dans la profession et par branche d'activité économique
Distribución según la categoría de ocupación y por rama de actividad económica

Others and status unknown / Autres et situation non définie / Otros y categoría no definida			TOTAL				Branche d'activité économique	Rama de actividad económica
Males / Hommes / Hombres	Females / Femmes / Mujeres	Total	Males / Hommes / Hombres	Females / Femmes / Mujeres	Total	%		
...	...	...	7 551	2 090	9 641	7.5	1. Agriculture, chasse, sylviculture et pêche	1. Agricultura, caza, silvicultura y pesca
...	...	...	39 651	3 875	43 526	33.6	{ 2. Industries extractives 3. Industries manufacturières	{ 2. Minas y canteras 3. Industrias manufactureras
...	...	...	908	62	970	0.8	4. Electricité, gaz et eau	4. Electricidad, gas y agua
...	...	...	11 506	264	11 770	9.1	5. Construction	5. Construcción
...	...	...	12 109	11 452	23 561	18.2	6. Commerce (gros et détail) ; restaurants, hôtels	6. Comercio (por mayor y por menor); restaurantes, hoteles
...	...	...	7 067	676	7 743	6.0	7. Transports, entrepôts et communications	7. Transportes, almacenamiento y comunicaciones
...	...	...	3 663	2 422	6 085	4.7	8. Banques, assur., affaires imm., services aux entreprises	8. Bancos, seguros, bienes inmuebles, servicios para empresas
...	...	...	12 462	12 477	24 939	19.3	9. Services à la collectivité, services sociaux et personnels	9. Servicios comunales, sociales y personales
115	153	268	115	153	268	0.2	Personnes en quête d'emploi pour la première fois	Personas en busca de trabajo por primera vez
407	345	752	407	345	752	0.6	Chômeurs	Desempleados
522	498	1 020	95 439	33 816	129 255	100.0	Total	Total

Others			TOTAL			%	(CITI 1958)	(CIIU 1958)
...	...	...	6 581	1 037	7 618	7.5	Agriculture, sylviculture, chasse et pêche	Agricultura, silvicultura, caza y pesca
...	...	...	680	1	681	0.7	Industries extractives	Minas y canteras
...	...	...	18 083	4 128	22 211	21.6	Industries manufacturières	Industrias manufactureras
...	...	...	12 018	101	12 119	11.9	Construction	Construcción
...	...	...	2 057	51	2 108	2.1	Electricité, gaz, eau et services sanitaires	Electricidad, gas, agua y servicios sanitarios
...	...	...	8 778	3 271	12 049	11.8	Com., banq., assur., aff. imm.	Comercio
...	...	...	5 726	292	6 018	5.9	Transports, entrepôts et communications	Transportes, almacenaje y comunicaciones
...	...	...	19 856	11 707	31 563	30.8	Services	Servicios
6 475	1 411	7 886	6 475	1 411	7 886	7.7	Chômeurs	Desempleados
6 475	1 411	7 886	80 254	21 999	102 253	100.0	Total	Total

Others			TOTAL			%	(CITI 1958)	(CIIU 1958)
.	.	.	5 670	781	6 451	6.0	Agriculture, sylviculture, chasse et pêche	Agricultura, silvicultura, caza y pesca
.	.	.	569	.	569	0.5	Industries extractives	Minas y canteras
.	.	.	21 622	9 049	30 671	28.8	Industries manufacturières	Industrias manufactureras
.	.	.	8 544	.	8 544	8.0	Construction	Construcción
.	.	.	905	5	910	0.9	Electricité, gaz, eau et services sanitaires	Electricidad, gas, agua y servicios sanitarios
.	.	.	9 360	4 328	13 688	12.8	Com., banq., assur., aff. imm.	Comercio
.	.	.	4 212	244	4 456	4.2	Transports, entrepôts et communications	Transportes, almacenaje y comunicaciones
.	.	.	30 383	10 820	41 203	38.7	Services	Servicios
.	.	.	126	24	150	0.1	Personnes en quête d'emploi pour la première fois	Personas en busca de trabajo por primera vez
.	.	.	81 391	25 251	106 642	100.0	Total	Total

† Voir notes pp. 272-294.

† Véanse las notas en las págs. 272-294.

2 Structure of the economically active population
Structure de la population active
Estructura de la población económicamente activa

Industry (Branch of economic activity)	Employers and workers on own account *Employeurs et personnes travaillant à leur propre compte* Empleadores y trabajadores por cuenta propia			Salaried employees and wage earners *Employés et ouvriers* Empleados y obreros			Family workers *Travailleurs familiaux* Trabajadores familiares		
	Males *Hommes* Hombres	Females *Femmes* Mujeres	Total	Males *Hommes* Hombres	Females *Femmes* Mujeres	Total	Males *Hommes* Hombres	Females *Femmes* Mujeres	Total
Monaco (1.III.1968)									
Agriculture, forestry, hunting and fishing	14	1	**15**	4	.	**4**	.	.	.
Mining and quarrying	.	.	.	3	2	**5**	.	.	.
Manufacturing	281	104	**385**	568	478	**1 046**	6	33	**39**
Construction	145	8	**153**	378	50	**428**	5	10	**15**
Electricity, gas and water	.	.	.	74	25	**99**	.	.	.
Commerce	443	253	**696**	598	466	**1 064**	17	75	**92**
Transport, storage and communication	59	2	**61**	277	82	**359**	1	.	**1**
Services (incl. sanitary services)	539	262	**801**	2 415	2 145	**4 560**	12	76	**88**
Activities not adequately described	36	8	**44**	68	62	**130**	2	6	**8**
Unemployed	...	...	...	...	...	...	...	...	...
Total ...	1 517	638	**2 155**	4 385	3 310	**7 695**	43	200	**243**
Norway									
(1.XI.1970) ‡									
1. Agriculture, hunting, forestry and fishing	93 401	3 255	**96 656**	35 434	2 288	**37 722**	10 738	24 903	**35 641**
2. Mining and quarrying	349	1	**350**	8 562	428	**8 990**	8	2	**10**
3. Manufacturing	16 302	1 172	**17 474**	302 827	69 460	**372 287**	310	829	**1 139**
4. Electricity, gas and water	59	1	**60**	14 450	1 334	**15 784**	2	1	**3**
5. Construction	23 247	39	**32 286**	102 311	3 087	**105 398**	210	227	**437**
6. Wholesale and retail trade, restaurants and hotels	22 944	6 079	**29 023**	100 543	92 897	**193 440**	718	6 631	**7 349**
7. Transport, storage and communication	15 173	199	**15 372**	116 973	24 209	**141 182**	194	172	**366**
8. Financing, insurance, real estate and business services	5 796	531	**6 327**	30 435	24 415	**54 850**	23	198	**221**
9. Community, social and personal services	6 440	3 546	**9 986**	147 964	137 406	**285 370**	34	468	**502**
0. Activities not adequately described	174	6	**180**	1 985	547	**2 532**	4	2	**6**
Total ...	183 885	14 829	**198 714**	861 484	356 071	**1 217 555**	12 241	33 433	**45 674**
(1974) ‡									
1. Agriculture, hunting, forestry and fishing	83 000	7 000	**90 000**	34 000	6 000	**40 000**	6 000	37 000	**43 000**
2. Mining and quarrying 3. Manufacturing 4. Electricity, gas and water }	12 000	2 000	**14 000**	321 000	83 000	**404 000**	1 000	1 000	**2 000**
5. Construction	27 000	—	**27 000**	115 000	4 000	**119 000**	1 000	—	**1 000**
6. Wholesale and retail trade, restaurants and hotels	19 000	6 000	**25 000**	110 000	132 000	**242 000**	1 000	7 000	**8 000**
7. Transport, storage and communication	18 000	—	**18 000**	115 000	28 000	**143 000**	1 000	1 000	**2 000**
8. Financing, insurance, real estate and business services	5 000	—	**5 000**	35 000	31 000	**66 000**	—	—	**—**
9. Community, social and personal services	11 000	8 000	**19 000**	139 000	245 000	**384 000**	—	3 000	**3 000**
0. Activities not adequately described	—	—	**—**	—	—	**1 000**	—	—	**—**
Unemployed	...	...	...	...	...	...	...	...	...
Total ...	175 000	24 000	**199 000**	870 000	529 000	**1 399 000**	10 000	49 000	**59 000**

‡ For notes, see pp. 272-294.

A Distribution by status and by industry (branch of economic activity)
Répartition suivant la situation dans la profession et par branche d'activité économique
Distribución según la categoría de ocupación y por rama de actividad económica

Others and status unknown / *Autres et situation non définie* / Otros y categoría no definida			TOTAL				Branche d'activité économique	Rama de actividad económica
Males / *Hommes* / Hombres	Females / *Femmes* / Mujeres	Total	Males / *Hommes* / Hombres	Females / *Femmes* / Mujeres	Total	%		
...	...	...	18	1	**19**	0.2	Agriculture, sylviculture, chasse et pêche	Agricultura, silvicultura, caza y pesca
...	...	...	3	2	**5**	—	Industries extractives	Minas y canteras
...	...	...	855	615	**1 470**	14.2	Industries manufacturières	Industrias manufactureras
...	...	...	528	68	**596**	5.8	Construction	Construcción
...	...	...	74	25	**99**	1.0	Electricité, gaz et eau	Electricidad, gas y agua
...	...	...	1 058	794	**1 852**	17.9	Com., banq., assur., aff. imm.	Comercio
...	...	...	337	84	**421**	4.1	Transports, entrepôts et communications	Transportes, almacenaje y comunicaciones
...	...	...	2 966	2 483	**5 449**	52.8	Services (y compris services sanitaires)	Servicios (incl. servicios sanitarios)
...	...	...	106	76	**182**	1.8	Activités mal désignées	Actividades no bien especif.
110	122	**232**	110	122	**232**	2.2	Chômeurs	Desempleados
110	122	**232**	6 055	4 270	**10 325**	100.0	Total	Total

						%		
...	...	...	139 573	30 446	**170 019**	11.6	1. Agriculture, chasse, sylviculture et pêche	1. Agricultura, caza, silvicultura y pesca
...	...	...	8 919	431	**9 350**	0.6	2. Industries extractives	2. Minas y canteras
5	1	6	319 444	71 462	**390 906**	26.8	3. Industries manufacturières	3. Industrias manufactureras
...	...	...	14 511	1 336	**15 847**	1.1	4. Electricité, gaz et eau	4. Electricidad, gas y agua
4	...	4	125 772	3 353	**129 125**	8.8	5. Construction	5. Construcción
1	...	1	124 206	105 607	**229 813**	15.7	6. Commerce (gros et détail) ; restaurants, hôtels	6. Comercio (por mayor y por menor); restaurantes, hoteles
4	...	4	132 344	24 580	**156 924**	10.7	7. Transports, entrepôts et communications	7. Transportes, almacenamiento y comunicaciones
...	...	...	36 254	25 144	**61 398**	4.2	8. Banques, assur., affaires imm., services aux entreprises	8. Bancos, seguros, bienes inmuebles, servicios para empresas
...	4	4	154 438	141 424	**295 862**	20.3	9. Services à la collectivité, services sociaux et personnels	9. Servicios comunales, sociales y personales
141	56	197	2 304	611	**2 915**	0.2	0. Activités mal désignées	0. Actividades no bien especif.
155	61	**216**	1 057 765	404 394	**1 462 159**	100.0	Total	Total

						%		
...	...	...	124 000	51 000	**175 000**	10.4	1. Agriculture, chasse, sylviculture et pêche	1. Agricultura, caza, silvicultura y pesca
...	...	...	334 000	86 000	**420 000**	24.9	2. Industries extractives / 3. Industries manufacturières	2. Minas y canteras / 3. Industrias manufactureras
...	...	...	143 000	4 000	**147 000**	8.7	4. Electricité, gaz et eau / 5. Construction	4. Electricidad, gas y agua / 5. Construcción
...	...	...	130 000	145 000	**275 000**	16.3	6. Commerce (gros et détail) ; restaurants, hôtels	6. Comercio (por mayor y por menor); restaurantes, hoteles
...	...	...	134 000	29 000	**163 000**	9.7	7. Transports, entrepôts et communications	7. Transportes, almacenamiento y comunicaciones
...	...	...	40 000	32 000	**72 000**	4.3	8. Banques, assur., affaires imm., services aux entreprises	8. Bancos, seguros, bienes inmuebles, servicios para empresas
...	...	...	150 000	256 000	**406 000**	24.1	9. Services à la collectivité, services sociaux et personnels	9. Servicios comunales, sociales y personales
1 000	—	**1 000**	1 000	—	**1 000**	0.1	0. Activités mal désignées	0. Actividades no bien especif.
11 000	14 000	**25 000**	11 000	14 000	**25 000**	1.5	Chômeurs	Desempleados
12 000	15 000	**27 000**	1 067 000	617 000	**1 684 000**	100.0	Total	Total

✝ *Voir notes pp. 272-294.*   ✝ Véanse las notas en las págs. 272-294.

2 Structure of the economically active population
Structure de la population active
Estructura de la población económicamente activa

Industry (Branch of economic activity)	Employers and workers on own account *Employeurs et personnes travaillant à leur propre compte* Empleadores y trabajadores por cuenta propia			Salaried employees and wage earners *Employés et ouvriers* Empleados y obreros			Family workers *Travailleurs familiaux* Trabajadores familiares		
	Males *Hommes* Hombres	Females *Femmes* Mujeres	Total	Males *Hommes* Hombres	Females *Femmes* Mujeres	Total	Males *Hommes* Hombres	Females *Femmes* Mujeres	Total

Pologne

(8.XII.1970) ✝									
Agriculture, hunting, forestry and fishing (excl. sea fishing)	1 673 989	1 211 796	**2 885 785**	621 186	207 335	**828 521**	662 461	2 166 485	**2 828 946**
Coal mining	.	.	.	331 211	43 859	**375 070**	.	.	.
Other mining and quarrying, manufacturing, gas production and sea fishing . .	85 726	19 784	**105 510**	2 517 926	1 580 600	**4 098 526**	4 053	5 078	**9 131**
Electricity and water	.	.	.	91 003	20 029	**111 032**	.	.	.
Construction	31 717	275	**31 992**	930 237	162 214	**1 092 451**	799	213	**1 012**
Wholesale and retail trade; restaurants	6 694	8 585	**15 279**	318 122	703 970	**1 022 092**	960	1 898	**2 858**
Transport, storage and communication	30 598	325	**30 923**	820 409	216 333	**1 036 742**	179	52	**231**
Financing, insurance, real estate and business services	.	.	.	23 725	61 484	**85 209**	.	.	.
Community, social and personal services; hotels . . . . } Activities not adequately described . . }	14 310	9 565	**23 875**	978 155	1 370 330	**2 348 485**	466	1 604	**2 070**
Total . . .	1 843 034	1 250 330	**3 093 364**	6 631 974	4 366 154	**10 998 128**	668 918	2 175 330	**2 844 248**
(III.1974) ✝									
Agriculture, hunting, forestry and fishing (excl. sea fishing)	2 225 517	2 968 103	**5 193 620**	28 070	227 613	**855 683**	...	...	...
Coal mining . . . . }									
Other mining and quarrying, manufacturing, gas production and sea fishing . . }	92 116	27 030	**119 146**	3 192 738	1 983 477	**5 176 215**	...	...	...
Electricity and water . . . . }									
Construction	36 412	991	**37 403**	985 783	212 273	**1 198 056**	...	...	...
Wholesale and retail trade; restaurants	7 714	11 034	**18 748**	345 575	829 497	**1 175 072**	...	...	...
Transport, storage and communication	6 331	272	**6 603**	765 725	235 911	**1 001 636**	...	...	...
Financing, insurance, real estate and business services	—	—	—	22 288	72 624	**94 912**	...	...	...
Community, social and personal services; hotels . . . . } Activities not adequately described . . }	45 655	10 646	**56 311**	1 070 383	1 502 767	**2 573 150**	...	...	...
Total . . .	2 413 755	3 018 076	**5 431 831**	7 010 562	5 064 162	**12 074 724**	...	...	...

✝ For notes, see pp. 272-294.

A **Distribution by status and by industry (branch of economic activity)**
Répartition suivant la situation dans la profession et par branche d'activité économique
Distribución según la categoría de ocupación y por rama de actividad económica

Others and status unknown / *Autres et situation non définie* / Otros y categoría no definida			TOTAL			*Branche d'activité économique*	Rama de actividad económica
Males / *Hommes* / Hombres	Females / *Femmes* / Mujeres	Total	Males / *Hommes* / Hombres	Females / *Femmes* / Mujeres	Total		
					%		
13	10	23	2 957 649	3 585 626	**6 543 275**	38.6	*Agriculture, chasse, sylviculture et pêche (non compris la pêche maritime)*	Agricultura, caza, silvicultura y pesca (excl. la pesca marítima)
.	.	.	331 211	43 859	**375 070**	2.2	*Mines de charbon*	Minas de carbón
82	74	156	2 607 787	1 605 536	**4 213 323**	24.9	*Autres industries extractives, industries manufacturières, production de gaz et pêche maritime*	Otras minas y canteras, industrias manufactureras, producción del gas y pesca marítima
.	.	.	91 003	20 029	**111 032**	0.7	*Electricité et eau*	Electricidad y agua
47	7	54	962 800	162 709	**1 125 509**	6.6	*Construction*	Construcción
7	29	36	325 783	714 482	**1 040 265**	6.1	*Commerce (gros et détail) ; restaurants*	Comercio (por mayor y por menor); restaurantes
8	2	10	851 194	216 712	**1 067 906**	6.3	*Transports, entrepôts et communications*	Transportes, almacenamiento y comunicaciones
.	.	.	23 725	61 484	**85 209**	0.5	*Banques, assur., aff. imm., services aux entreprises*	Bancos, seguros, bienes inm., servicios para empresas
4 727	3 102	7 829	997 658	1 384 601	**2 382 259**	14.1	{ *Services à la collectivité, services sociaux et personnels ; hôtels* { *Activités mal désignées*	{ Servicios comunales, sociales y personales; hoteles { Actividades no bien especif.
4 884	3 224	8 108	9 148 810	7 795 038	**16 943 848**	100.0	*Total*	Total
.	.	.	2 853 587	3 195 716	**6 049 303**	34.6	*Agriculture, chasse, sylviculture et pêche (non compris la pêche maritime)*	Agricultura, caza, silvicultura y pesca (excl. la pesca marítima)
.	.	.	3 284 854	2 010 507	**5 295 361**	30.2	{ *Mines de charbon* { *Autres industries extractives, industries manufacturières, production de gaz et pêche maritime* { *Electricité et eau*	{ Minas de carbón { Otras minas y canteras, industrias manufactureras, producción del gas y pesca marítima { Electricidad y agua
.	.	.	1 022 195	213 264	**1 235 459**	7.1	*Construction*	Construcción
.	.	.	353 289	840 531	**1 193 820**	6.8	*Commerce (gros et détail) ; restaurants*	Comercio (por mayor y por menor); restaurantes
.	.	.	772 056	236 183	**1 008 239**	5.8	*Transports, entrepôts et communications*	Transportes, almacenamiento y comunicaciones
.	.	.	22 288	72 624	**94 912**	0.5	*Banques, assur., aff. imm., services aux entreprises*	Bancos, seguros, bienes inm., servicios para empresas
.	.	.	1 116 048	1 513 413	**2 629 461**	15.0	{ *Services à la collectivité, services sociaux et personnels ; hôtels* { *Activités mal désignées*	{ Servicios comunales, sociales y personales; hoteles { Actividades no bien especif.
.	.	.	9 424 317	8 082 238	**17 506 555**	100.0	*Total*	Total

✝ *Voir notes pp. 272-294.*

✝ Véanse las notas en las págs. 272-294.

2 Structure of the economically active population
Structure de la population active
Estructura de la población económicamente activa

Industry (Branch of economic activity)	Employers and workers on own account / Employeurs et personnes travaillant à leur propre compte / Empleadores y trabajadores por cuenta propia			Salaried employees and wage earners / Employés et ouvriers / Empleados y obreros			Family workers / Travailleurs familiaux / Trabajadores familiares		
	Males Hommes Hombres	Females Femmes Mujeres	Total	Males Hommes Hombres	Females Femmes Mujeres	Total	Males Hommes Hombres	Females Femmes Mujeres	Total

Portugal (15.XII.1970) †

Industry	Males	Females	Total	Males	Females	Total	Males	Females	Total
1. Agriculture, hunting, forestry and fishing	334 880	43 100	**377 980**	423 490	87 025	**510 515**	61 350	47 480	**108 830**
2. Mining and quarrying	585	.	**585**	11 110	440	**11 550**	50	5	**55**
3. Manufacturing	51 230	15 755	**66 985**	421 665	240 025	**661 690**	3 780	2 930	**6 710**
4. Electricity, gas and water	430	20	**450**	14 010	1 795	**15 805**	25	5	**30**
5. Construction	21 120	150	**21 270**	230 285	2 875	**233 160**	1 220	35	**1 255**
6. Wholesale and retail trade, restaurants and hotels	101 480	22 525	**124 005**	149 360	62 435	**211 795**	2 795	3 245	**6 040**
7. Transport, storage and communication	8 780	295	**9 075**	120 335	17 335	**137 670**	285	70	**355**
8. Financing, insurance, real estate and business services	2 810	250	**3 060**	40 405	14 330	**54 735**	35	50	**85**
9. Community, social and personal services	28 495	11 390	**39 885**	222 025	218 535	**440 560**	700	1 645	**2 345**
0. Activities not adequately described	9 815	2 280	**12 635**	59 425	27 075	**86 500**	1 630	1 560	**3 190**
Persons on compulsory military service	.	.	.	.	.	.	.	.	.
Persons seeking work for the first time Unemployed	...	...	...	...	...	...	...	...	...
Total . . .	559 625	96 305	**655 930**	1 692 110	671 870	**2 363 980**	71 870	57 025	**128 895**

Roumanie (15.III.1966) †

Industry	Males	Females	Total	Males	Females	Total	Males	Females	Total
Agriculture and forestry	267 284	432 600	**699 884**	382 083	82 001	**464 084**	1 881 456	2 874 903	**4 756 359**
Mining and quarrying, manufacturing, hunting and fishing	30 573	19 227	**49 800**	1 380 526	439 522	**1 820 048**	103 485	40 192	**143 677**
Construction	11 244	959	**12 203**	449 758	41 955	**491 713**	32 004	599	**32 603**
Electricity, gas, water and sanitary services	.	.	.	40 957	15 431	**56 388**	.	.	.
Commerce	313	347	**660**	239 215	183 364	**422 579**	94	514	**608**
Transport, storage and communication	7 145	221	**7 366**	368 324	61 476	**429 800**	9	.	**9**
Services	14 869	2 364	**17 233**	445 759	474 085	**919 844**	16 005	14 698	**30 703**
Activities not adequately described	293	317	**610**	2 221	1 209	**3 430**	22	15	**37**
Total . . .	331 721	456 035	**787 756**	3 308 843	1 299 043	**4 607 886**	2 033 075	2 930 921	**4 963 996**

Suisse (1.XII.1970) †

Industry	Males	Females	Total	Males	Females	Total	Males	Females	Total
1. Agriculture, hunting, forestry and fishing	100 306	3 683	**103 989**	42 294	5 823	**48 117**	35 194	43 364	**78 558**
2. Mining and quarrying	340	9	**349**	6 123	265	**6 388**	28	35	**63**
3. Manufacturing	61 018	7 343	**68 361**	738 348	303 396	**1 041 744**	5 005	14 653	**19 658**
4. Electricity, gas and water	1	.	**1**	21 511	1 935	**23 446**	.	.	.
5. Construction	25 766	195	**25 961**	244 487	11 415	**255 902**	1 465	1 823	**3 288**
6. Wholesale and retail trade, restaurants and hotels	44 452	18 484	**62 936**	208 463	224 092	**432 555**	3 596	25 100	**28 696**
7. Transport, storage and communication	7 361	181	**7 542**	131 200	30 030	**161 230**	535	603	**1 138**
8. Financing, insurance, real estate and business services	10 477	1 473	**11 950**	82 559	63 587	**146 146**	121	836	**957**
9. Community, social and personal services	21 957	9 654	**31 611**	176 648	247 272	**423 920**	483	4 438	**4 921**
0. Activities not adequately described	3	.	**3**	3 557	2 790	**6 347**	.	.	.
Total . . .	271 681	41 022	**312 703**	1 655 180	890 615	**2 545 795**	46 427	90 852	**137 279**

† For notes, see pp. 272-294.

A Distribution by status and by industry (branch of economic activity)
Répartition suivant la situation dans la profession et par branche d'activité économique
Distribución según la categoría de ocupación y por rama de actividad económica

Others and status unknown / Autres et situation non définie / Otros y categoría no definida			TOTAL				Branche d'activité économique	Rama de actividad económica
Males / Hommes / Hombres	Females / Femmes / Mujeres	Total	Males / Hommes / Hombres	Females / Femmes / Mujeres	Total	%		
4 335	1 190	5 525	824 055	178 795	1 002 850	29.6	1. Agriculture, chasse, sylviculture et pêche	1. Agricultura, caza, silvicultura y pesca
10	.	10	11 755	445	12 200	0.4	2. Industries extractives	2. Minas y canteras
770	610	1 380	477 445	259 320	736 765	21.7	3. Industries manufacturières	3. Industrias manufactureras
15	5	20	14 480	1 825	16 305	0.5	4. Electricité, gaz et eau	4. Electricidad, gas y agua
385	10	395	253 010	3 070	256 080	7.5	5. Construction	5. Construcción
1 140	485	1 625	254 775	88 690	343 465	10.1	6. Commerce (gros et détail); restaurants, hôtels	6. Comercio (por mayor y por menor); restaurantes, hoteles
185	35	220	129 585	17 735	147 320	4.3	7. Transports, entrepôts et communications	7. Transportes, almacenamiento y comunicaciones
95	45	140	43 345	14 675	58 020	1.7	8. Banques, assur., affaires imm., services aux entreprises	8. Bancos, seguros, bienes inmuebles, servicios para empresas
3 430	1 645	5 075	254 650	233 215	487 865	14.4	9. Services à la collectivité, services sociaux et personnels	9. Servicios comunales, sociales y personales
410	250	660	71 280	31 705	102 985	3.0	0. Activités mal désignées	0. Actividades no bien especif.
141 205	.	141 205	141 205	.	141 205	4.2	Militaires du contingent	Personas en servicio militar obligatorio
47 720	21 475	69 195	47 720	21 475	69 195	2.0	Personnes en quête d'emploi pour la première fois	Personas en busca de trabajo por primera vez
15 615	5 995	21 610	15 615	5 995	21 610	0.6	Chômeurs	Desempleados
215 315	31 745	247 060	2 538 920	856 945	3 395 865	100.0	Total	Total

Others and status unknown			TOTAL				Branche d'activité économique	Rama de actividad económica
Males	Females	Total	Males	Females	Total	%		
...	...	...	2 530 823	3 389 504	5 920 327	57.2	Agriculture et sylviculture	Agricultura y silvicultura
...	...	...	1 514 584	498 941	2 013 525	19.4	Industries extractives et manufacturières, chasse et pêche	Minas y canteras, industrias manufactureras, caza y pesca
...	...	...	493 006	43 513	536 519	5.2	Construction	Construcción
...	...	...	40 957	15 431	56 388	0.5	Electricité, gaz, eau et services sanitaires	Electricidad, gas, agua y servicios sanitarios
...	...	...	239 622	184 225	423 847	4.1	Com., banq., assur., aff. imm.	Comercio
...	...	...	375 478	61 697	437 175	4.2	Transports, entrepôts et communications	Transportes, almacenaje y comunicaciones
...	...	...	476 633	491 147	967 780	9.3	Services	Servicios
1 537	1 125	2 662	4 073	2 666	6 739	0.1	Activités mal désignées	Actividades no bien especif.
1 537	1 125	2 662	5 675 176	4 687 124	10 362 300	100.0	Total	Total

Others and status unknown			TOTAL				Branche d'activité économique	Rama de actividad económica
Males	Females	Total	Males	Females	Total	%		
.	.	.	177 794	52 870	230 664	7.7	1. Agriculture, chasse, sylviculture et pêche	1. Agricultura, caza, silvicultura y pesca
.	.	.	6 491	309	6 800	0.2	2. Industries extractives	2. Minas y canteras
.	.	.	804 371	325 392	1 129 763	37.7	3. Industries manufacturières	3. Industrias manufactureras
.	.	.	21 512	1 935	23 447	0.8	4. Electricité, gaz et eau	4. Electricidad, gas y agua
.	.	.	271 718	13 433	285 151	9.5	5. Construction	5. Construcción
.	.	.	256 511	267 676	524 187	17.5	6. Commerce (gros et détail); restaurants, hôtels	6. Comercio (por mayor y por menor); restaurantes, hoteles
.	.	.	139 096	30 814	169 910	5.7	7. Transports, entrepôts et communications	7. Transportes, almacenamiento y comunicaciones
.	.	.	93 157	65 896	159 053	5.3	8. Banques, assur., affaires imm., services aux entreprises	8. Bancos, seguros, bienes inmuebles, servicios para empresas
.	.	.	199 088	261 364	460 452	15.4	9. Services à la collectivité, services sociaux et personnels	9. Servicios comunales, sociales y personales
.	.	.	3 550	2 800	6 350	0.2	0. Activités mal désignées	0. Actividades no bien especif.
.	.	.	1 973 288	1 022 489	2 995 777	100.0	Total	Total

‡ Voir notes pp. 272-294.

‡ Véanse las notas en las págs. 272-294.

2 Structure of the economically active population
Structure de la population active
Estructura de la población económicamente activa

Industry (Branch of economic activity)	Employers and workers on own account / Employeurs et personnes travaillant à leur propre compte / Empleadores y trabajadores por cuenta propia			Salaried employees and wage earners / Employés et ouvriers / Empleados y obreros			Family workers / Travailleurs familiaux / Trabajadores familiares		
	Males / Hommes / Hombres	Females / Femmes / Mujeres	Total	Males / Hommes / Hombres	Females / Femmes / Mujeres	Total	Males / Hommes / Hombres	Females / Femmes / Mujeres	Total
Sweden									
(1.XI.1970) ‡									
1. Agriculture, hunting, forestry and fishing	121 583	4 364	**125 947**	99 387	51 171	**150 558**	...	...	...
2. Mining and quarrying	420	2	**422**	17 665	1 486	**19 151**	...	...	...
3. Manufacturing	22 264	2 855	**25 119**	731 395	238 884	**970 279**	...	...	...
4. Electricity, gas and water	—	—	**—**	23 071	3 432	**26 503**	...	...	...
5. Construction	32 476	68	**32 544**	286 674	13 246	**299 920**	...	...	...
6. Wholesale and retail trade, restaurants and hotels	36 916	13 360	**50 276**	206 557	232 969	**439 526**	...	...	...
7. Transport, storage and communication	23 478	346	**23 824**	175 564	47 668	**223 232**			
8. Financing, insurance, real estate and business services	7 465	942	**8 407**	89 759	70 941	**160 700**	...	...	...
9. Community, social and personal services	26 164	9 975	**36 139**	298 429	512 962	**811 391**	...	...	...
0. Activities not adequately described	668	57	**725**	5 823	2 182	**8 005**	...	...	...
Total	271 434	31 969	**303 403**	1 934 324	1 174 941	**3 109 265**	...	...	...
(1974) ‡									
1. Agriculture, hunting, forestry and fishing	116 100	8 400	**124 500**	79 500	13 400	**93 000**	4 600	42 300	**46 900**
2. Mining and quarrying	200	—	**200**	17 900	1 800	**19 700**	—	—	
3. Manufacturing	19 000	3 900	**22 900**	811 000	285 100	**1 096 200**	100	1 300	**1 500**
4. Electricity, gas and water	—	—	**—**	27 200	4 000	**31 200**	—	—	
5. Construction	30 400	100	**30 500**	244 600	17 600	**262 100**	100	900	**1 000**
6. Wholesale and retail trade, restaurants and hotels	33 800	15 000	**48 800**	234 000	271 100	**505 100**	400	5 300	**5 700**
7. Transport, storage and communication	21 700	600	**22 300**	181 500	66 300	**247 800**	100	600	**700**
8. Financing, insurance, real estate and business services	7 100	1 400	**8 500**	105 900	97 300	**203 200**	—	100	**100**
9. Community, social and personal services	24 800	13 000	**37 700**	355 500	795 100	**1 150 600**	—	2 100	**2 200**
Total	253 100	42 400	**295 500**	2 057 000	1 551 800	**3 608 800**	5 500	52 600	**58 100**
Turquie (25.X.1970) ‡									
1. Agriculture, hunting, forestry and fishing	...	...	...	...	...	...	...	...	...
2. Mining and quarrying	...	...	...	...	...	...	...	...	...
3. Manufacturing	...	...	...	...	...	...	...	...	...
4. Electricity, gas and water	...	...	...	...	...	...	...	...	...
5. Construction	...	...	...	...	...	...	...	...	...
6. Wholesale and retail trade, restaurants and hotels	...	...	...	...	...	...	...	...	...
7. Transport, storage and communication	...	...	...	...	...	...	...	...	...
8. Financing, insurance, real estate and business services	...	...	...	...	...	...	...	...	...
9. Community, social and personal services	...	...	...	...	...	...	...	...	...
0. Activities not adequately described	...	...	...	...	...	...	...	...	...
Total	...	...	4 291 536	...	...	3 879 029	...	...	7 583 078

‡ For notes, see pp. 272-294.

A Distribution by status and by industry (branch of economic activity)
Répartition suivant la situation dans la profession et par branche d'activité économique
Distribución según la categoría de ocupación y por rama de actividad económica

Others and status unknown / Autres et situation non définie / Otros y categoría no definida			TOTAL				Branche d'activité économique	Rama de actividad económica
Males / Hommes / Hombres	Females / Femmes / Mujeres	Total	Males / Hommes / Hombres	Females / Femmes / Mujeres	Total	%		
.	.	.	220 970	55 535	276 505	8.1	1. Agriculture, chasse, sylviculture et pêche	1. Agricultura, caza, silvicultura y pesca
.	.	.	18 085	1 488	19 573	0.6	2. Industries extractives	2. Minas y canteras
.	.	.	753 659	241 739	995 398	29.1	3. Industries manufacturières	3. Industrias manufactureras
.	.	.	23 071	3 432	26 503	0.8	4. Electricité, gaz et eau	4. Electricidad, gas y agua
.	.	.	319 150	13 314	332 464	9.7	5. Construction	5. Construcción
.	.	.	243 473	246 329	489 802	14.4	6. Commerce (gros et détail); restaurants, hôtels	6. Comercio (por mayor y por menor); restaurantes, hoteles
.	.	.	199 042	48 014	247 056	7.2	7. Transports, entrepôts et communications	7. Transportes, almacenamiento y comunicaciones
.	.	.	97 224	71 883	169 107	5.0	8. Banques, assur., affaires imm., services aux entreprises	8. Bancos, seguros, bienes inmuebles, servicios para empresas
.	.	.	324 593	522 937	847 530	24.8	9. Services à la collectivité, services sociaux et personnels	9. Servicios comunales, sociales y personales
.	.	.	6 491	2 239	8 730	0.3	0. Activités mal désignées	0. Actividades no bien especif.
.	.	.	2 205 758	1 206 910	3 412 668	100.0	Total	Total
.	.	.	200 200	64 200	264 400	6.7	1. Agriculture, chasse, sylviculture et pêche	1. Agricultura, caza, silvicultura y pesca
.	.	.	18 100	1 800	20 000	0.5	2. Industries extractives	2. Minas y canteras
.	.	.	830 200	290 400	1 120 500	28.3	3. Industries manufacturières	3. Industrias manufactureras
.	.	.	27 200	4 000	31 200	0.8	4. Electricité, gaz et eau	4. Electricidad, gas y agua
.	.	.	275 000	18 600	293 700	7.4	5. Construction	5. Construcción
.	.	.	268 200	291 400	559 600	14.1	6. Commerce (gros et détail); restaurants, hôtels	6. Comercio (por mayor y por menor); restaurantes, hoteles
.	.	.	203 300	67 500	270 800	6.8	7. Transports, entrepôts et communications	7. Transportes, almacenamiento y comunicaciones
.	.	.	113 000	98 700	211 700	5.3	8. Banques, assur., affaires imm., services aux entreprises	8. Bancos, seguros, bienes inmuebles, servicios para empresas
.	.	.	380 300	810 200	1 190 500	30.1	9. Services à la collectivité, services sociaux et personnels	9. Servicios comunales, sociales y personales
.	.	.	2 315 600	1 646 800	3 962 400	100.0	Total	Total
...	...	...	...	...	10 914 730	68.9	1. Agriculture, chasse, sylviculture et pêche	1. Agricultura, caza, silvicultura y pesca
...	...	...	...	...	106 670	0.7	2. Industries extractives	2. Minas y canteras
...	...	...	...	...	1 272 511	8.0	3. Industries manufacturières	3. Industrias manufactureras
...	...	...	...	...	15 301	0.1	4. Electricité, gaz et eau	4. Electricidad, gas y agua
...	...	...	...	...	409 029	2.6	5. Construction	5. Construcción
...	...	...	...	...	743 331	4.7	6. Commerce (gros et détail); restaurants, hôtels	6. Comercio (por mayor y por menor); restaurantes, hoteles
...	...	...	...	...	379 016	2.4	7. Transports, entrepôts et communications	7. Transportes, almacenamiento y comunicaciones
...	...	...	...	...	169 574	1.1	8. Banques, assur., affaires imm., services aux entreprises	8. Bancos, seguros, bienes inmuebles, servicios para empresas
...	...	...	...	...	1 680 335	10.6	9. Services à la collectivité, services sociaux et personnels	9. Servicios comunales, sociales y personales
...	...	...	...	...	138 156	0.9	0. Activités mal désignées	0. Actividades no bien especif.
...	...	75 010	...	...	15 828 653	100.0	Total	Total

† *Voir notes pp. 272-294.*

† Véanse las notas en las págs. 272-294.

2 Structure of the economically active population
Structure de la population active
Estructura de la población económicamente activa

Industry (Branch of economic activity)	Employers and workers on own account Employeurs et personnes travaillant à leur propre compte Empleadores y trabajadores por cuenta propia			Salaried employees and wage earners Employés et ouvriers Empleados y obreros			Family workers Travailleurs familiaux Trabajadores familiares		
	Males Hommes Hombres	Females Femmes Mujeres	Total	Males Hommes Hombres	Females Femmes Mujeres	Total	Males Hommes Hombres	Females Femmes Mujeres	Total

United Kingdom (25.IV.1971*) ‡

Industry	Males	Females	Total	Males	Females	Total	Males	Females	Total
1. Agriculture, hunting, forestry and fishing	235 640	30 880	**266 520**	288 970	79 260	**368 230**	...	...	...
2. Mining and quarrying	490	30	**520**	374 250	16 690	**390 940**	...	...	...
3. Manufacturing	99 120	20 660	**119 780**	5 621 400	2 394 610	**8 016 010**	...	...	...
4. Electricity, gas and water	.	.	.	300 900	61 400	**362 300**	...	...	...
5. Construction	319 820	2 350	**322 170**	1 252 210	94 750	**1 346 960**	...	...	...
6. Wholesale and retail trade, restaurants and hotels	396 580	203 880	**600 460**	1 321 120	1 782 930	**3 104 050**			
7. Transport, storage and communication	66 630	3 170	**69 800**	1 231 590	262 530	**1 494 120**	...	...	...
8. Financing, insurance, real estate and business services	100 830	18 330	**119 160**	650 260	614 240	**1 264 500**	...	...	...
9. Community, social and personal services	248 120	89 260	**337 380**	2 439 330	2 932 960	**5 372 290**	...	...	...
0. Activities not adequately described	4 570	2 700	**7 270**	79 720	90 430	**170 150**	...	...	...
Unemployed	...	...	...	...	...	...	...	...	...
Total . . .	1 471 800	371 260	**1 843 060**	13 559 750	8 329 800	**21 889 550**	...	...	...

Yugoslavia (31.III.1971) ‡

Industry	Males	Females	Total	Males	Females	Total	Males	Females	Total
Agriculture, hunting, forestry and fishing	1 395 276	426 267	**1 821 543**	235 920	45 949	**281 869**	638 029	1 222 034	**1 860 063**
Mining and quarrying ⎫ Manufacturing ⎭	.	.	.	1 092 555	481 957	**1 574 512**	.	.	.
Crafts and personal services	122 201	19 383	**141 584**	206 741	72 278	**279 019**	8 139	4 211	**12 350**
Construction	3 619	158	**3 777**	360 301	33 026	**393 327**	479	229	**708**
Trade; restaurants and hotels	10 462	4 496	**14 958**	275 740	230 238	**505 978**	1 132	1 544	**2 676**
Transport, storage and communication	14 685	157	**14 842**	267 457	39 747	**307 204**	365	66	**431**
Services (excl. personal services); banking, social insurance	9 817	1 562	**11 379**	496 936	411 940	**908 876**	341	433	**774**
Activities not adequately described	1 981	414	**2 395**	17 573	6 375	**23 948**	322	317	**639**
Persons working abroad temporarily	...	...	...	...	...	...	...	...	...
Persons seeking work for the first time	1 417	401	**1 818**	76 564	47 709	**124 273**	695	249	**944**
Total . . .	1 559 458	452 838	**2 012 296**	3 029 787	1 369 219	**4 399 006**	649 502	1 229 083	**1 878 585**

‡ For notes, see pp. 272-294.

A Distribution by status and by industry (branch of economic activity)
Répartition suivant la situation dans la profession et par branche d'activité économique
Distribución según la categoría de ocupación y por rama de actividad económica

Others and status unknown / Autres et situation non définie / Otros y categoría no definida			TOTAL			%	Branche d'activité économique	Rama de actividad económica
Males / Hommes / Hombres	Females / Femmes / Mujeres	Total	Males / Hommes / Hombres	Females / Femmes / Mujeres	Total			
...	...	...	524 610	110 140	**634 750**	*2.5*	1. *Agriculture, chasse, sylviculture et pêche*	1. Agricultura, caza, silvicultura y pesca
...	...	...	374 740	16 720	**391 460**	*1.6*	2. *Industries extractives*	2. Minas y canteras
...	...	...	5 720 520	2 415 270	**8 135 790**	*32.6*	3. *Industries manufacturières*	3. Industrias manufactureras
...	...	...	300 900	61 400	**362 300**	*1.4*	4. *Electricité, gaz et eau*	4. Electricidad, gas y agua
...	...	...	1 572 030	97 100	**1 669 130**	*6.7*	5. *Construction*	5. Construcción
...	...	...	1 717 700	1 986 810	**3 704 510**	*14.8*	6. *Commerce (gros et détail); restaurants, hôtels*	6. Comercio (por mayor y por menor); restaurantes, hoteles
...	...	...	1 298 220	265 700	**1 563 920**	*6.3*	7. *Transports, entrepôts et communications*	7. Transportes, almacenamiento y comunicaciones
...	...	...	751 090	632 570	**1 383 660**	*5.5*	8. *Banques, assur., affaires imm., services aux entreprises*	8. Bancos, seguros, bienes inmuebles, servicios para empresas
...	...	...	2 687 450	3 022 220	**5 709 670**	*22.8*	9. *Services à la collectivité, services sociaux et personnels*	9. Servicios comunales, sociales y personales
...	...	...	84 290	93 130	**177 420**	*0.7*	0. *Activités mal désignées*	0. Actividades no bien especif.
852 350	436 120	**1 288 470**	852 350	436 120	**1 288 470**	*5.1*	*Chômeurs*	Desempleados
852 350	436 120	**1 288 470**	15 883 900	9 137 180	**25 021 080**	*100.0*	*Total*	Total

						%		
917	635	**1 552**	2 270 142	1 694 885	**3 965 027**	*44.6*	*Agriculture, chasse, sylviculture et pêche*	Agricultura, caza, silvicultura y pesca
.	.	.	1 092 555	481 957	**1 574 512**	*17.7*	{ *Industries extractives* / *Industries manufacturières*	{ Minas y canteras / Industrias manufactureras
268	430	**698**	337 349	96 302	**433 651**	*4.9*	*Artisanat et serv. personnels*	Artesanado y serv. personales
46	5	**51**	364 445	33 418	**397 863**	*4.5*	*Construction*	Construcción
53	79	**132**	287 387	236 357	**523 744**	*5.9*	*Commerce; restaurants et hôtels*	Comercio; restaurantes y hoteles
53	6	**59**	282 560	39 976	**322 536**	*3.6*	*Transports, entrepôts et communications*	Transportes, almacenamiento y comunicaciones
291	88	**379**	507 385	414 023	**921 408**	*10.4*	*Services (non compris serv. personnels); banques, assurances sociales*	Servicios (excl. servicios personales); bancos, seguros sociales
3 198	2 984	**6 182**	23 074	10 090	**33 164**	*0.4*	*Activités mal désignées*	Actividades no bien especif.
441 756	147 412	**589 168**	441 756	147 412	**589 168**	*6.6*	*Personnes travaillant temporairement à l'étranger*	Personas que trabajan temporalmente en el extranjero
1 003	705	**1 708**	79 679	49 064	**128 743**	*1.4*	*Personnes en quête d'emploi pour la première fois*	Personas en busca de trabajo por primera vez
447 585	152 344	**599 929**	5 686 332	3 203 484	**8 889 816**	*100.0*	*Total*	Total

† *Voir notes pp. 272-294.*

† Véanse las notas en las págs. 272-294.

POPULATION

2 Structure of the economically active population
Structure de la population active
Estructura de la población económicamente activa

Industry (Branch of economic activity)	Employers and workers on own account / Employeurs et personnes travaillant à leur propre compte / Empleadores y trabajadores por cuenta propia			Salaried employees and wage earners / Employés et ouvriers / Empleados y obreros			Family workers / Travailleurs familiaux / Trabajadores familiares		
	Males Hommes Hombres	Females Femmes Mujeres	Total	Males Hommes Hombres	Females Femmes Mujeres	Total	Males Hommes Hombres	Females Femmes Mujeres	Total

Australia — OCEANIA — OCÉANIE — OCEANIA

(30.VI.1971)									
1. Agriculture, hunting, forestry and fishing	191 967	39 070	**231 037**	120 951	19 916	**140 867**	5 300	9 203	**14 503**
2. Mining and quarrying	2 002	136	**2 138**	68 349	5 416	**73 765**	96	24	**120**
3. Manufacturing	26 133	7 503	**33 636**	876 910	304 308	**1 181 218**	231	533	**764**
4. Electricity, gas and water	64	11	**75**	83 685	7 490	**91 175**	1	1	**2**
5. Construction	71 590	4 343	**75 933**	320 024	15 575	**335 599**	194	503	**697**
6. Wholesale and retail trade, restaurants and hotels	120 989	58 961	**179 950**	520 040	397 546	**917 586**	890	3 753	**4 643**
7. Transport, storage and communication	34 267	3 301	**37 568**	282 315	54 874	**337 189**	133	308	**441**
8. Financing, insurance, real estate and business services	30 463	5 791	**36 254**	174 766	151 897	**326 663**	190	311	**501**
9. Community, social and personal services . . !	30 468	15 923	**46 391**	473 974	474 817	**948 791**	1 495	4 544	**6 039**
0. Activities not adequately described . .	10 271	2 244	**12 515**	137 658	62 459	**200 117**	1 110	3 141	**4 251**
Persons seeking work for the first time	.	.	.	.	.	.	.	.	.
Unemployed	...	...	...	...	...	...	...	...	...
Total . . .	518 214	137 283	**655 497**	3 058 672	1 494 298	**4 552 970**	9 640	22 321	**31 961**
(1973) ‡									
1. Agriculture, hunting, forestry and fishing	...	...	...	...	...	...	...	...	...
2. Mining and quarrying	...	...	...	...	...	...	...	...	...
3. Manufacturing . . . . ⎫	...	...	...	...	...	...	...	...	...
4. Electricity, gas and water . . . . . ⎬									
5. Construction . . . . ⎭	...	...	...	...	...	...	...	...	...
6. Wholesale and retail trade, restaurants and hotels	...	...	...	...	...	...	...	...	...
7. Transport, storage and communication	...	...	...	...	...	...	...	...	...
8. Financing, insurance, real estate and business services	...	...	...	...	...	...	...	...	...
9. Community, social and personal services	...	...	...	...	...	...	...	...	...
Armed forces	...	...	...	...	...	...	...	...	...
Unemployed	...	...	...	...	...	...	...	...	...
Total . . .	604 000	166 000	**770 000**	3 168 000	1 685 000	**4 853 000**	5 000	12 000	**17 000**

Fiji (12.IX.1966)

(ISIC 1958)									
Agriculture, forestry, hunting and fishing	...	...	...	...	...	...	...	...	...
Mining and quarrying	...	...	...	...	...	...	...	...	...
Manufacturing	...	...	...	...	...	...	...	...	...
Construction	...	...	...	...	...	...	...	...	...
Electricity, gas, water and sanitary services	...	...	...	...	...	...	...	...	...
Commerce	...	...	...	...	...	...	...	...	...
Transport, storage and communication	...	...	...	...	...	...	...	...	...
Services	...	...	...	...	...	...	...	...	...
Activities not adequately described .	...	...	...	...	...	...	...	...	...
Unemployed	...	...	...	...	...	...	...	...	...
Total . . .	...	...	...	...	...	...	...	...	...

‡ For notes, see pp. 272-294.

A **Distribution by status and by industry (branch of economic activity)**
Répartition suivant la situation dans la profession et par branche d'activité économique
Distribución según la categoría de ocupación y por rama de actividad económica

Others and status unknown / Autres et situation non définie / Otros y categoría no definida			TOTAL				Branche d'activité économique	Rama de actividad económica
Males / Hommes / Hombres	Females / Femmes / Mujeres	Total	Males / Hommes / Hombres	Females / Femmes / Mujeres	Total	%		
						%		
...	...	...	318 218	68 189	**386 407**	7.2	1. *Agriculture, chasse, sylviculture et pêche*	1. Agricultura, caza, silvicultura y pesca
...	...	...	70 447	5 576	**76 023**	1.4	2. *Industries extractives*	2. Minas y canteras
...	...	...	903 274	312 344	**1 215 618**	22.9	3. *Industries manufacturières*	3. Industrias manufactureras
...	...	...	83 750	7 502	**91 252**	1.7	4. *Electricité, gaz et eau*	4. Electricidad, gas y agua
...	...	...	391 808	20 421	**412 229**	7.7	5. *Construction*	5. Construcción
...	...	...	641 919	460 260	**1 102 179**	20.7	6. *Commerce (gros et détail) ; restaurants, hôtels*	6. Comercio (por mayor y por menor); restaurants, hoteles
...	...	...	316 715	58 483	**375 198**	7.0	7. *Transports, entrepôts et communications*	7. Transportes, almacenamiento y comunicaciones
...	...	...	205 419	157 999	**363 418**	6.8	8. *Banques, assur., affaires imm., services aux entreprises*	8. Bancos, seguros, bienes inmuebles, servicios para empresas
...	...	...	505 937	495 284	**1 001 221**	18.8	9. *Services à la collectivité, services sociaux et personnels*	9. Servicios comunales, sociales y personales
...	...	...	149 039	67 844	**216 883**	4.1	0. *Activités mal désignées*	0. Actividades no bien especif.
8 237	7 824	**16 061**	8 237	7 824	**16 061**	0.3	*Personnes en quête d'emploi pour la première fois*	Personas en busca de trabajo por primera vez
44 876	29 123	**73 999**	44 876	29 123	**73 999**	1.4	*Chômeurs*	Desempleados
53 113	36 947	**90 060**	3 639 639	1 690 849	**5 330 488**	100.0	*Total*	Total
...	...	...	337 000	70 000	**407 000**	7.0	1. *Agriculture, chasse, sylviculture et pêche*	1. Agricultura, caza, silvicultura y pesca
...	...	...	64 000	4 000	**68 000**	1.2	2. *Industries extractives*	2. Minas y canteras
...	...	...	1 089 000	353 000	**1 442 000**	24.8	{ 3. *Industries manufacturières* 4. *Electricité, gaz et eau*	{ 3. Industrias manufactureras 4. Electricidad, gas y agua
...	...	...	467 000	24 000	**491 000**	8.4	5. *Construction*	5. Construcción
...	...	...	698 000	468 000	**1 166 000**	20.0	6. *Commerce (gros et détail) ; restaurants, hôtels*	6. Comercio (por mayor y por menor); restaurantes, hoteles
...	...	...	359 000	68 000	**427 000**	7.3	7. *Transports, entrepôts et communications*	7. Transportes, almacenamiento y comunicaciones
...	...	...	215 000	183 000	**398 000**	6.8	8. *Banques, assur., affaires imm., services aux entreprises*	8. Bancos, seguros, bienes inmuebles, servicios para empresas
...	...	...	548 000	693 000	**1 241 000**	21.3	9. *Services à la collectivité, services sociaux et personnels*	9. Servicios comunales, sociales y personales
.·.	.	.	71 000	3 000	**74 000**	1.3	*Forces armées*	Fuerzas armadas
...	...	...	54 000	54 000	**108 000**	1.9	*Chômeurs*	Desempleados
125 000	57 000	**182 000**	3 901 000	1 921 000	**5 822 000**	100.0	*Total*	Total
						%	(CITI 1958)	(CIIU 1958)
...	...	...	66 785	716	**67 501**	53.6	*Agriculture, sylviculture, chasse et pêche*	Agricultura, silvicultura, caza y pesca
...	...	...	1 876	27	**1 903**	1.5	*Industries extractives*	Minas y canteras
...	...	...	8 438	407	**8 845**	7.0	*Industries manufacturières*	Industrias manufactureras
...	...	...	7 272	30	**7 302**	5.8	*Construction*	Construcción
...	...	...	889	7	**896**	0.7	*Electricité, gaz, eau et services sanitaires*	Electricidad, gas, agua y servicios sanitarios
...	...	...	7 520	1 130	**8 650**	6.9	*Com., banq., assur., aff. imm.*	Comercio
...	...	...	6 075	197	**6 272**	5.0	*Transports, entrepôts et communications*	Transportes, almacenaje y comunicaciones
...	...	...	2 491	3 185	**5 676**	4.5	*Services*	Servicios
...	...	...	9 877	3 652	**13 529**	10.8	*Activités mal désignées*	Actividades no bien especif.
...	...	...	5 210	25	**5 235**	4.2	*Chômeurs*	Desempleados
...	...	...	116 433	9 376	**125 809**	100.0	*Total*	Total

‡ *Voir notes pp. 272-294.*

‡ *Véanse las notas en las págs. 272-294.*

2 Structure of the economically active population
Structure de la population active
Estructura de la población económicamente activa

Industry (Branch of economic activity)	Employers and workers on own account *Employeurs et personnes travaillant à leur propre compte* Empleadores y trabajadores por cuenta propia			Salaried employees and wage earners *Employés et ouvriers* Empleados y obreros			Family workers *Travailleurs familiaux* Trabajadores familiares		
	Males *Hommes* Hombres	Females *Femmes* Mujeres	Total	Males *Hommes* Hombres	Females *Femmes* Mujeres	Total	Males *Hommes* Hombres	Females *Femmes* Mujeres	Total

New Zealand

(23.III.1971) ✝

Industry	M	F	Total	M	F	Total	M	F	Total
1. Agriculture, hunting, forestry and fishing	60 792	6 301	**67 093**	48 954	11 589	**60 543**	218	143	**361**
2. Mining and quarrying	176	3	**179**	4 845	171	**5 016**	.	.	.
3. Manufacturing	5 491	1 272	**6 763**	199 970	71 811	**271 781**	2	15	**17**
4. Electricity, gas and water	6	5	**11**	12 048	1 158	**13 206**	.	.	.
5. Construction	17 201	60	**17 261**	72 695	2 934	**75 629**	3	2	**5**
6. Wholesale and retail trade, restaurants and hotels	16 024	7 144	**23 168**	100 366	72 779	**173 145**	7	119	**126**
7. Transport, storage and communication	4 810	172	**4 982**	79 497	17 985	**97 482**	.	.	.
8. Financing, insurance, real estate and business services	7 522	402	**7 924**	30 144	26 293	**56 437**	.	3	**3**
9. Community, social and personal services	9 323	2 746	**12 069**	101 008	101 657	**202 665**	6	42	**48**
0. Activities not adequately described	655	99	**754**	1 972	687	**2 659**	14	29	**43**
Total	122 000	18 204	**140 204**	651 499	307 064	**958 563**	250	353	**603**

(X.1974) ✝

Industry	M	F	Total	M	F	Total	M	F	Total
1. Agriculture, hunting, forestry and fishing	...	...	...	...	...	...	...	...	...
2. Mining and quarrying	...	...	...	...	...	...	...	...	...
3. Manufacturing	...	...	...	...	...	...	...	...	...
4. Electricity, gas and water	...	...	...	...	...	...	...	...	...
5. Construction	...	...	...	...	...	...	...	...	...
6. Wholesale and retail trade, restaurants and hotels	...	...	...	...	...	...	...	...	...
7. Transport, storage and communication	...	...	...	...	...	...	...	...	...
8. Financing, insurance, real estate and business services	...	...	...	...	...	...	...	...	...
9. Community, social and personal services	...	...	...	...	...	...	...	...	...
Armed forces	.	.	.	...	...	...	.	.	.
Unemployed	...	...	...	...	...	...	...	...	...
Total	...	...	...	...	...	...	...	...	...

Nouvelle-Calédonie (11.III.1969) ✝

Industry	M	F	Total	M	F	Total	M	F	Total
Agriculture, forestry, hunting and fishing	...	...	...	...	...	...	...	...	...
Mining and quarrying	...	...	...	...	...	...	...	...	...
Manufacturing	...	...	...	...	...	...	...	...	...
Construction	...	...	...	...	...	...	...	...	...
Electricity and water	...	...	...	...	...	...	...	...	...
Commerce	...	...	...	...	...	...	...	...	...
Transport, storage and communication	...	...	...	...	...	...	...	...	...
Services (incl. sanitary services)	...	...	...	...	...	...	...	...	...
Activities not adequately described	...	...	...	...	...	...	...	...	...
Total	6 497	1 933	**8 430**	17 749	5 508	**23 257**	2 243	4 731	**6 974**

✝ For notes, see pp. 272-294.

A Distribution by status and by industry (branch of economic activity)
Répartition suivant la situation dans la profession et par branche d'activité économique
Distribución según la categoría de ocupación y por rama de actividad económica

Others and status unknown / Autres et situation non définie / Otros y categoría no definida			TOTAL				Branche d'activité économique	Rama de actividad económica
Males / Hommes / Hombres	Females / Femmes / Mujeres	Total	Males / Hommes / Hombres	Females / Femmes / Mujeres	Total	%		
701	196	**897**	110 665	18 229	**128 894**	*11.5*	*1. Agriculture, chasse, sylviculture et pêche*	1. Agricultura, caza, silvicultura y pesca
67	3	**70**	5 088	177	**5 265**	*0.5*	*2. Industries extractives*	2. Minas y canteras
1 625	924	**2 549**	207 088	74 022	**281 110**	*25.1*	*3. Industries manufacturières*	3. Industrias manufactureras
51	5	**56**	12 105	1 168	**13 273**	*1.2*	*4. Electricité, gaz et eau*	4. Electricidad, gas y agua
772	21	**793**	90 671	3 017	**93 688**	*8.4*	*5. Construction*	5. Construcción
840	1 036	**1 876**	117 237	81 078	**198 315**	*17.7*	*6. Commerce (gros et détail); restaurants, hôtels*	6. Comercio (por mayor y por menor); restaurantes, hoteles
554	163	**717**	84 861	18 320	**103 181**	*9.2*	*7. Transports, entrepôts et communications*	7. Transportes, almacenamiento y comunicaciones
145	265	**410**	37 811	26 963	**64 774**	*5.8*	*8. Banques, assur., affaires imm., services aux entreprises*	8. Bancos, seguros, bienes inmuebles, servicios para empresas
550	1 195	**1 745**	110 887	105 640	**216 527**	*19.4*	*9. Services à la collectivité, services sociaux et personnels*	9. Servicios comunales, sociales y personales
5 915	4 437	**10 352**	8 556	5 252	**13 808**	*1.2*	*0. Activités mal désignées*	0. Actividades no bien especif.
11 220	8 245	**19 465**	784 969	333 866	**1 118 835**	*100.0*	*Total*	Total
...	...	...	127 900	16 100	**144 000**	*12.1*	*1. Agriculture, chasse, sylviculture et pêche*	1. Agricultura, caza, silvicultura y pesca
...	...	...	4 300	100	**4 400**	*0.4*	*2. Industries extractives*	2. Minas y canteras
...	...	...	210 200	81 700	**291 900**	*24.6*	*3. Industries manufacturières*	3. Industrias manufactureras
...	...	...	13 400	1 400	**14 800**	*1.2*	*4. Electricité, gaz et eau*	4. Electricidad, gas y agua
...	...	...	89 800	3 200	**93 000**	*7.8*	*5. Construction*	5. Construcción
...	...	...	111 900	81 900	**193 800**	*16.3*	*6. Commerce (gros et détail); restaurants, hôtels*	6. Comercio (por mayor y por menor); restaurantes, hoteles
...	...	...	87 700	19 700	**107 400**	*9.0*	*7. Transports, entrepôts et communications*	7. Transportes, almacenamiento y comunicaciones
...	...	...	42 100	32 500	**74 600**	*6.3*	*8. Banques, assur., affaires imm., services aux entreprises*	8. Bancos, seguros, bienes inmuebles, servicios para empresas
...	...	...	130 200	122 500	**252 700**	*21.3*	*9. Services à la collectivité, services sociaux et personnels*	9. Servicios comunales, sociales y personales
...	...	...	10 400	700	**11 000**	*0.9*	*Forces armées*	Fuerzas armadas
...	...	...	700	300	**1 000**	*0.1*	*Chômeurs*	Desempleados
...	...	...	828 600	360 100	**1 188 700**	*100.0*	*Total*	Total
...	...	...	7 277	6 080	**13 357**	*34.0*	*Agriculture, sylviculture, chasse et pêche*	Agricultura, silvicultura, caza y pesca
...	...	...	3 459	93	**3 552**	*9.1*	*Industries extractives*	Minas y canteras
...	...	...	3 415	328	**3 743**	*9.6*	*Industries manufacturières*	Industrias manufactureras
...	...	...	3 684	93	**3 777**	*9.6*	*Construction*	Construcción
...	...	...	193	27	**220**	*0.6*	*Electricité et eau*	Electricidad y agua
...	...	...	2 492	2 042	**4 534**	*11.6*	*Com., banq., assur., aff. imm.*	Comercio
...	...	...	1 713	229	**1 942**	*5.0*	*Transports, entrepôts et communications*	Transportes, almacenaje y comunicaciones
...	...	...	4 318	3 505	**7 823**	*19.9*	*Services (y compris les services sanitaires)*	Servicios (incl. los servicios sanitarios)
...	...	...	171	66	**237**	*0.6*	*Activités mal désignées*	Actividades no bien especif.
233	291	**524**	26 722	12 463	**39 185**	*100.0*	*Total*	Total

‡ *Voir notes pp. 272-294.*

‡ Véanse las notas en las págs. 272-294.

2 Structure of the economically active population
Structure de la population active
Estructura de la población económicamente activa

Industry (Branch of economic activity)	Employers and workers on own account *Employeurs et personnes travaillant à leur propre compte* Empleadores y trabajadores por cuenta propia			Salaried employees and wage earners *Employés et ouvriers* Empleados y obreros			Family workers *Travailleurs familiaux* Trabajadores familiares		
	Males *Hommes* Hombres	Females *Femmes* Mujeres	Total	Males *Hommes* Hombres	Females *Femmes* Mujeres	Total	Males *Hommes* Hombres	Females *Femmes* Mujeres	Total
Tonga (30.XI.1966)									
(ISIC 1958)									
Agriculture, forestry, hunting and fishing	...	...	...	...	...	...	...	...	...
Mining and quarrying	...	...	...	...	...	...	...	...	...
Manufacturing									
Construction	...	...	...	...	...	...	...	...	...
Electricity, gas, water and sanitary services	...	...	...	...	...	...	...	...	...
Commerce	...	...	...	...	...	...	...	...	...
Transport, storage and communication	...	...	...	...	...	...	...	...	...
Services	...	...	...	...	...	...	...	...	...
Total ...	...	...	...	...	...	...	...	...	...
Western Samoa (7.XI.1971)									
1. Agriculture, hunting, forestry and fishing	14 393	293	**14 686**	1 981	510	**2 491**	7 242	984	**8 226**
2. Mining and quarrying	53	48	**101**	564	154	**718**	.	.	.
3. Manufacturing									
4. Electricity, gas and water	5	.	**5**	244	2	**246**	.	1	**1**
5. Construction	58	1	**59**	1 534	24	**1 558**	.	.	.
6. Wholesale and retail trade, restaurants and hotels	309	171	**480**	1 261	645	**1 906**	1	31	**32**
7. Transport, storage and communication	118	.	**118**	1 055	73	**1 128**	2	.	**2**
8. Financing, insurance, real estate and business services	7	1	**8**	126	89	**215**	.	.	.
9. Community, social and personal services	43	5	**48**	3 453	2 254	**5 707**	.	1	**1**
0. Activities not adequately described	...	...	...	...	...	...	...	...	...
Persons seeking work for the first time	.	.	.	.	.	.	.	.	.
Total ...	14 986	519	**15 505**	10 218	3 751	**13 969**	7 245	1 017	**8 262**

A Distribution by status and by industry (branch of economic activity)
Répartition suivant la situation dans la profession et par branche d'activité économique
Distribución según la categoría de ocupación y por rama de actividad económica

Others and status unknown / *Autres et situation non définie* / Otros y categoría no definida			TOTAL			Branche d'activité économique	Rama de actividad económica
Males / *Hommes* / Hombres	Females / *Femmes* / Mujeres	Total	Males / *Hommes* / Hombres	Females / *Femmes* / Mujeres	Total		
					%	(CITI 1958)	(CIIU 1958)
...	...	...	13 992	72	**14 064**	74.0	*Agriculture, sylviculture, chasse et pêche*	Agricultura, silvicultura, caza y pesca
...	...	...	481	21	**502**	2.6	*Industries extractives*	Minas y canteras
...	...	...	89	.	**89**	0.5	*Industries manufacturières*	Industrias manufactureras
							Construction	Construcción
...	...	...	40	.	**40**	0.2	*Electricité, gaz, eau et services sanitaires*	Electricidad, gas, agua y servicios sanitarios
...	...	...	224	186	**410**	2.2	*Com., banq., assur., aff. imm.*	Comercio
...	...	...	362	10	**372**	2.0	*Transports, entrepôts et communications*	Transportes, almacenaje y comunicaciones
...	...	...	2 712	809	**3 521**	18.5	*Services*	Servicios
...	...	...	17 900	1 098	**18 998**	100.0	*Total*	Total

					%		
...	...	...	23 616	1 787	**25 403**	66.9	1. *Agriculture, chasse, sylviculture et pêche*	1. Agricultura, caza, silvicultura y pesca
...	...	...	617	202	**819**	2.2	2. *Industries extractives*	2. Minas y canteras
...	...	...	249	3	**252**	0.7	3. *Industries manufacturières*	3. Industrias manufactureras
...	...	...	1 592	25	**1 617**	4.3	4. *Electricité, gaz et eau*	4. Electricidad, gas y agua
...	...	...	1 571	847	**2 418**	6.4	5. *Construction*	5. Construcción
...	...	...	1 175	73	**1 248**	3.3	6. *Commerce (gros et détail); restaurants, hôtels*	6. Comercio (por mayor y por menor); restaurantes, hoteles
...	...	...	133	90	**223**	0.6	7. *Transports, entrepôts et communications*	7. Transportes, almacenamiento y comunicaciones
...	...	...	3 496	2 260	**5 756**	15.2	8. *Banques, assur., affaires imm., services aux entreprises*	8. Bancos, seguros, bienes inmuebles, servicios para empresas
3	1	**4**	3	1	**4**	—	9. *Services à la collectivité, services sociaux et personnels*	9. Servicios comunales, sociales y personales
99	62	**161**	99	62	**161**	0.4	0. *Activités mal désignées* / *Personnes en quête d'emploi pour la première fois*	0. Actividades no bien especif. / Personas en busca de trabajo por primera vez
102	63	**165**	32 551	5 350	**37 901**	100.0	*Total*	Total

POPULATION

2 Structure of the economically active population
Structure de la population active
Estructura de la población económicamente activa

URSS (15.I.1970) ‡ [a]

Industry (Branch of economic activity)	Salaried employees and wage earners _Employés et ouvriers_ Empleados y obreros			Workers in kolkhozes _Travailleurs des kolkhozes_ Trabajadores de koljoses			Farmers and handicraftsmen (not organised in co-operatives) _Agriculteurs et artisans (non groupés en coopératives)_ Agricultores y artesanos (no agrupados en cooperativas)		
	Males _Hommes_ Hombres	Females _Femmes_ Mujeres	Total	Males _Hommes_ Hombres	Females _Femmes_ Mujeres	Total	Males _Hommes_ Hombres	Females _Femmes_ Mujeres	Total
PRODUCTIVE SECTORS:									
Agriculture	6 412 958	4 976 088	**11 389 046**	8 034 126	9 196 178	**17 230 304**	43 244	274 999	**318 243**
Industry, construction, transport and communication	31 374 715	20 872 418	**52 247 133**	413 628	71 729	**485 357**	24 249	14 514	**38 763**
Trade, public dining, material-technical supply	2 080 227	5 780 243	**7 860 470**	5 446	18 083	**23 529**	.	.	.
Other productive branches	307 971	329 502	**637 473**	316	163	**479**	89	49	**138**
NON-PRODUCTIVE SECTORS:									
Education, cultural institutions, scientific and research institutes, public health	4 692 579	11 800 366	**16 492 945**	16 678	82 273	**98 951**	.	20	**20**
Administration, communal and housing services, banking and insurance . . .	4 224 851	3 725 321	**7 950 172**	9 682	3 166	**12 848**	1 480	434	**1 914**
ACTIVITIES NOT ADEQUATELY DESCRIBED .	169 642	192 206	**361 848**	15 081	33 289	**48 370**	1 492	4 581	**6 073**
Total . . .	49 262 943	47 676 144	**96 939 087**	8 494 957	9 404 881	**17 899 838**	70 554	294 597	**365 151**

‡ For notes, see pp. 272-294.

(a) Incl. Byelorussian SSR and Ukrainian SSR, shown separately in this table.

A Distribution by status and by industry (branch of economic activity)
Répartition suivant la situation dans la profession et par branche d'activité économique
Distribución según la categoría de ocupación y por rama de actividad económica

Family members of employees of kolkhozes and sovkhozes, working on individual agricultural plots *Membres des familles de salariés des kolkhozes et sovkhozes cultivant des parcelles individuelles* Miembros de las familias de asalariados de koljoses y sovjoses que cultivan parcelas individuales			TOTAL				*Branche d'activité économique*	Rama de actividad económica
Males *Hommes* Hombres	Females *Femmes* Mujeres	Total	Males *Hommes* Hombres	Females *Femmes* Mujeres	Total			
						%	SECTEURS PRODUCTIFS:	SECTORES PRODUCTIVOS:
161 874	1 661 625	**1 823 499**	14 652 202	16 108 890	**30 761 092**	*26.3*	*Agriculture*	Agricultura
.	.	.	31 812 592	20 958 661	**52 771 253**	*45.1*	*Industrie, construction, transports et communications*	Industrias, construcción, transportes y comunicaciones
.	.	.	2 085 673	5 798 326	**7 883 999**	*6.7*	*Commerce, restaurants, cafés, etc., fournitures techniques et matériaux*	Comercio, restaurantes, cafés, etc., suministros técnicos y materiales
.	.	.	308 376	329 714	**638 090**	*0.5*	*Autres branches productives*	Otras ramas productivas
							SECTEURS NON PRODUCTIFS:	SECTORES NO PRODUCTIVOS:
.	.	.	4 709 257	11 882 659	**16 591 916**	*14.2*	*Enseignement, institutions culturelles, instituts d'études et de recherches scientifiques, santé publique*	Enseñanza, instituciones culturales, institutos de estudios e investigaciones científicas, salud pública
.	.	.	4 236 013	3 728 921	**7 964 934**	*6.8*	*Administration, services communaux et de logement, banques et assurances*	Administración, servicios comunales y de alojamiento, bancos y seguros
.	.	.	186 215	230 076	**416 291**	*0.4*	ACTIVITÉS MAL DÉSIGNÉES	ACTIVIDADES NO BIEN ESPECIF.
161 874	1 661 625	**1 823 499**	57 990 328	59 037 247	**117 027 575**	*100.0*	*Total*	Total

† *Voir notes pp. 272-294.*

(a) *Y compris les RSS de Biélorussie et d'Ukraine, figurant séparément dans ce tableau.*

† Véanse las notas en las págs. 272-294.

(a) Incl. las RSS de Bielorrusia y de Ucrania, que figuran separadamente en este cuadro.

POPULATION

2 Structure of the economically active population
Structure de la population active
Estructura de la población económicamente activa

RSS de Biélorussie (15.I.1970) ‡

Industry (Branch of economic activity)	Salaried employees and wage earners *Employés et ouvriers* Empleados y obreros			Workers in kolkhozes *Travailleurs des kolkhozes* Trabajadores de koljoses			Farmers and handicraftsmen (not organised in co-operatives) *Agriculteurs et artisans (non groupés en coopératives)* Agricultores y artesanos (no agrupados en cooperativas)		
	Males *Hommes* Hombres	Females *Femmes* Mujeres	Total	Males *Hommes* Hombres	Females *Femmes* Mujeres	Total	Males *Hommes* Hombres	Females *Femmes* Mujeres	Total
PRODUCTIVE SECTORS:									
Agriculture	291 301	266 101	**557 402**	419 299	522 992	**942 291**	1 971	9 700	**11 671**
Industry, construction, transport and communication	977 604	688 950	**1 666 554**	23 545	2 612	**26 157**	1 122	331	**1 453**
Trade, public dining, material-technical supply	67 323	194 644	**261 967**	148	226	**374**	.	.	.
Other productive branches	11 248	11 755	**23 003**	12	4	**16**	.	.	.
NON-PRODUCTIVE SECTORS:									
Education, cultural institutions, scientific and research institutes, public health	147 630	384 476	**532 106**	594	1 069	**1 663**	.	.	.
Administration, communal and housing services, banking and insurance . .	160 277	104 259	**264 536**	308	125	**433**	44	24	**68**
ACTIVITIES NOT ADEQUATELY DESCRIBED .	3 707	4 330	**8 037**	669	1 202	**1 871**	8	48	**56**
Total . . .	1 659 090	1 654 515	**3 313 605**	444 575	528 230	**972 805**	3 145	10 103	**13 248**

RSS d'Ukraine (15.I.1970) ‡

Industry (Branch of economic activity)	Males *Hommes* Hombres	Females *Femmes* Mujeres	Total	Males *Hommes* Hombres	Females *Femmes* Mujeres	Total	Males *Hommes* Hombres	Females *Femmes* Mujeres	Total
PRODUCTIVE SECTORS:									
Agriculture	864 686	720 675	**1 585 361**	2 437 860	3 067 681	**5 505 541**	10 335	64 827	**75 162**
Industry, construction, transport and communication	6 045 361	3 871 507	**9 916 868**	134 121	22 762	**156 883**	6 559	2 655	**9 214**
Trade, public dining, material-technical supply	409 785	1 148 744	**1 558 529**	1 438	5 818	**7 256**	.	.	.
Other productive branches	53 087	48 645	**101 732**	52	27	**79**	4	.	**4**
NON-PRODUCTIVE SECTORS:									
Education, cultural institutions, scientific and research institutes, public health	798 211	2 088 859	**2 887 070**	4 533	32 144	**36 677**	.	.	.
Administration, communal and housing services, banking and insurance . .	720 742	622 627	**1 343 369**	3 334	880	**4 214**	384	104	**488**
ACTIVITIES NOT ADEQUATELY DESCRIBED .	32 788	33 730	**66 518**	4 496	10 104	**14 600**	352	736	**1 088**
Total . . .	8 924 660	8 534 787	**17 459 447**	2 585 834	3 139 416	**5 725 250**	17 634	68 322	**85 956**

‡ For notes, see pp. 272-294.

A **Distribution by status and by industry (branch of economic activity)**
Répartition suivant la situation dans la profession et par branche d'activité économique
Distribución según la categoría de ocupación y por rama de actividad económica

Family members of employees of kolkhozes and sovkhozes, working on individual agricultural plots *Membres des familles de salariés des kolkhozes et sovkhozes cultivant des parcelles individuelles* Miembros de las familias de asalariados de koljoses y sovjoses que cultivan parcelas individuales			TOTAL				Branche d'activité économique	Rama de actividad económica
Males *Hommes* Hombres	Females *Femmes* Mujeres	Total	Males *Hommes* Hombres	Females *Femmes* Mujeres	Total	%		
8 431	74 862	**83 293**	721 002	873 655	**1 594 657**	*36.4*	SECTEURS PRODUCTIFS: *Agriculture*	SECTORES PRODUCTIVOS: Agricultura
.	.	.	1 002 271	691 893	**1 694 164**	*38.7*	*Industrie, construction, transports et communications*	Industrias, construcción, transportes y comunicaciones
.	.	.	67 471	194 870	**262 341**	*6.0*	*Commerce, restaurants, cafés, etc., fournitures techniques et matériaux*	Comercio, restaurantes, cafés, etc., suministros técnicos y materiales
.	.	.	11 260	11 759	**23 019**	*0.5*	*Autres branches productives*	Otras ramas productivas
.	.	.	148 224	385 545	**533 769**	*12.2*	SECTEURS NON PRODUCTIFS: *Enseignement, institutions culturelles, instituts d'études et de recherches scientifiques, santé publique*	SECTORES NO PRODUCTIVOS: Enseñanza, instituciones culturales, institutos de estudios e investigaciones científicas, salud pública
.	.	.	160 629	104 408	**265 037**	*6.0*	*Administration, services communaux et de logement, banques et assurances*	Administración, servicios comunales y de alojamiento, bancos y seguros
.	.	.	4 384	5 580	**9 964**	*0.2*	ACTIVITÉS MAL DÉSIGNÉES	ACTIVIDADES NO BIEN ESPECIF.
8 431	74 862	**83 293**	2 115 241	2 267 710	**4 382 951**	*100.0*	*Total*	Total

						%		
56 963	472 256	**529 219**	3 369 844	4 325 439	**7 695 283**	*32.3*	SECTEURS PRODUCTIFS: *Agriculture*	SECTORES PRODUCTIVOS: Agricultura
.	.	.	6 186 041	3 896 924	**10 082 965**	*42.4*	*Industrie, construction, transports et communications*	Industrias, construcción, transportes y comunicaciones
.	.	.	411 223	1 154 562	**1 565 785**	*6.6*	*Commerce, restaurants, cafés, etc., fournitures techniques et matériaux*	Comercio, restaurantes, cafés, etc., suministros técnicos y materiales
.	.	.	53 143	48 672	**101 815**	*0.4*	*Autres branches productives*	Otras ramas productivas
.	.	.	802 744	2 121 003	**2 923 747**	*12.3*	SECTEURS NON PRODUCTIFS: *Enseignement, institutions culturelles, instituts d'études et de recherches scientifiques, santé publique*	SECTORES NO PRODUCTIVOS: Enseñanza, instituciones culturales, institutos de estudios e investigaciones científicas, salud pública
.	.	.	724 460	623 611	**1 348 071**	*5.7*	*Administration, services communaux et de logement, banques et assurances*	Administración, servicios comunales y de alojamiento, bancos y seguros
.	.	.	37 636	44 570	**82 206**	*0.3*	ACTIVITÉS MAL DÉSIGNÉES	ACTIVIDADES NO BIEN ESPECIF.
56 963	472 256	**529 219**	11 585 091	12 214 781	**23 799 872**	*100.0*	*Total*	Total

† *Voir notes pp. 272-294.*

† Véanse las notas en las págs. 272-294.

2. Structure of the economically active population
Structure de la population active
Estructura de la población económicamente activa

Algérie (4.IV.1966) †

Occupational group	Employers and workers on own account / Employeurs et personnes travaillant à leur propre compte / Empleadores y trabajadores por cuenta propia			Salaried employees and wage earners / Employés et ouvriers / Empleados y obreros			Family workers / Travailleurs familiaux / Trabajadores familiares		
	Males / Hommes / Hombres	Females / Femmes / Mujeres	Total	Males / Hommes / Hombres	Females / Femmes / Mujeres	Total	Males / Hommes / Hombres	Females / Femmes / Mujeres	Total
Professional, technical and related workers	7 189	341	7 530	60 648	17 726	78 374	...	...	...
Administrative, executive and managerial workers	8 332	310	8 642	10 332	869	11 201	...	...	...
Clerical workers	34	6	40	78 659	10 316	88 975	...	...	...
Sales workers	86 454	697	87 151	27 503	791	28 294	6 041	137	6 178
Farmers, fishermen, hunters, loggers and related workers	362 244	3 262	365 506	756 138	7 123	763 261	132 692	12 702	145 394
Miners, quarrymen and related workers	202	1	203	9 770	6	9 776	30	1	31
Workers in transport and communication occupations	16 509	19	16 528	53 784	924	54 708	738	3	741
Craftsmen, prod.-process workers and labourers not elsewhere classified	54 037	6 417	60 454	285 495	7 119	292 614	3 882	920	4 802
Service, sport and recreation workers	5 789	584	6 373	182 039	27 943	209 982	772	222	994
Members of the armed forces									
Workers not classifiable by occupation	337	10	347	5 940	208	6 148	261	71	332
Persons seeking work for the first time	.	.	.	.	.	.	.	.	.
Total . . .	541 127	11 647	552 774	1 470 308	73 025	1 543 333	144 416	14 056	158 472

Botswana (1964) †

Occupational group	Males	Females	Total	Males	Females	Total	Males	Females	Total
Professional, technical and related workers	...	...	...	...	...	...	...	...	...
Administrative, executive and managerial workers	...	...	...	...	...	...	...	...	...
Clerical workers	...	...	...	...	...	...	...	...	...
Sales workers	...	...	...	...	...	...	...	...	...
Farmers, fishermen, hunters, loggers and related workers	...	...	...	...	...	...	...	...	...
Miners, quarrymen and related workers	...	...	...	...	...	...	...	...	...
Workers in transport and communication occupations	...	...	...	...	...	...	...	...	...
Craftsmen, prod.-process workers and labourers not elsewhere classified	...	...	...	...	...	...	...	...	...
Service, sport and recreation workers	...	...	...	...	...	...	...	...	...
Workers not classifiable by occupation	...	...	...	...	...	...	...	...	...
Total . . .	95 911	115 504	211 415	16 373	4 850	21 223	5 305	2 628	7 933

† For notes, see pp. 272-294.

B **Distribution by status and by occupational group**
Répartition suivant la situation dans la profession et par groupe de professions
Distribución según la categoría de ocupación y por grupo de ocupación

Others and status unknown / *Autres et situation non définie* / Otros y categoría no definida			TOTAL			%	*Groupe de professions*	Grupo de ocupaciones
Males / *Hommes* / Hombres	Females / *Femmes* / Mujeres	Total	Males / *Hommes* / Hombres	Females / *Femmes* / Mujeres	Total			
733	70	803	68 570	18 137	86 707	3.4	*Personnes exerçant une profession libérale, techniciens et assimilés*	Trabajadores profesionales, técnicos y trabajadores asimilados
15	3	18	18 679	1 182	19 861	0.8	*Directeurs et cadres administratifs supérieurs*	Administradores, gerentes y directores
950	102	1 052	79 643	10 424	90 067	3.5	*Employés de bureau*	Empleados de oficina
456	5	461	120 454	1 630	122 084	4.8	*Vendeurs*	Vendedores
1 435	63	1 498	1 252 509	23 150	1 275 659	49.7	*Agriculteurs, pêcheurs, chasseurs, forestiers et travailleurs assimilés*	Agricultores, pescadores, cazadores, trabajadores forestales y asimilados
62	.	62	10 064	8	10 072	0.4	*Mineurs, carriers et travailleurs assimilés*	Mineros, canteros y trabajadores asimilados
2 122	3	2 125	73 153	949	74 102	2.9	*Travailleurs des transports et des communications*	Trabajadores de los transportes y comunicaciones
6 672	190	6 862	350 086	14 646	364 732	14.2	*Artisans, ouvriers de métier, ouvriers à la production et manœuvres non classés ailleurs*	Artesanos y trab. ocupados en los div. procesos de producción y peones no clasif. bajo otros epígrafes
1 007	240	1 247	189 607	28 989	218 596	8.5	*Travailleurs spécialisés dans les services, les sports et les activités récréatives* / *Membres des forces armées*	Trabajadores de los servicios, los deportes y las diversiones / Miembros de las fuerzas armadas
								Trabajadores que no pueden ser clasificados según la ocupación
11 839	426	12 265	18 377	715	19 092	0.7	*Personnes ne pouvant être classées selon la profession*	
274 068	9 623	283 691	274 068	9 623	283 691	11.1	*Personnes en quête d'emploi pour la première fois*	Personas en busca de trabajo por primera vez
299 359	10 725	310 084	2 455 210	109 453	2 564 663	100.0	*Total*	Total
						%		
...	...	...	1 752	1 125	2 877	1.1	*Personnes exerçant une profession libérale, techniciens et assimilés*	Trabajadores profesionales, técnicos y trabajadores asimilados
...	...	...	447	24	471	0.2	*Directeurs et cadres administratifs supérieurs*	Administradores, gerentes y directores
...	...	...	849	196	1 045	0.4	*Employés de bureau*	Empleados de oficina
...	...	...	1 439	333	1 772	0.7	*Vendeurs*	Vendedores
...	...	...	107 847	118 962	226 809	90.6	*Agriculteurs, pêcheurs, chasseurs, forestiers et travailleurs assimilés*	Agricultores, pescadores, cazadores, trabajadores forestales y asimilados
...	...	...	1 480	53	1 533	0.6	*Mineurs, carriers et travailleurs assimilés*	Mineros, canteros y trabajadores asimilados
...	...	...	1 293	35	1 328	0.5	*Travailleurs des transports et des communications*	Trabajadores de los transportes y comunicaciones
...	...	...	7 532	764	8 296	3.3	*Artisans, ouvriers de métier, ouvriers à la production et manœuvres non classés ailleurs*	Artesanos y trab. ocupados en los div. procesos de producción y peones no clasif. bajo otros epígrafes
...	...	...	2 693	3 517	6 210	2.5	*Travailleurs spécialisés dans les services, les sports et les activités récréatives*	Trabajadores de los servicios, los deportes y las diversiones
...	...	...	145	192	337	0.1	*Personnes ne pouvant être classées selon la profession*	Trabajadores que no pueden ser clasificados según la ocupación
7 888	2 219	10 107	125 477	125 201	250 678	100.0	*Total*	Total

✝ *Voir notes pp. 272-294.*
✝ Véanse las notas en las págs. 272-294.

161

2 Structure of the economically active population
Structure de la population active
Estructura de la población económicamente activa

Occupational group	Employers and workers on own account / Employeurs et personnes travaillant à leur propre compte / Empleadores y trabajadores por cuenta propia			Salaried employees and wage earners / Employés et ouvriers / Empleados y obreros			Family workers / Travailleurs familiaux / Trabajadores familiares		
	Males / Hommes / Hombres	Females / Femmes / Mujeres	Total	Males / Hommes / Hombres	Females / Femmes / Mujeres	Total	Males / Hommes / Hombres	Females / Femmes / Mujeres	Total

Egypt (30.V.1966) ‡

Occupational group	Males	Females	Total	Males	Females	Total	Males	Females	Total
Professional, technical and related workers	20 281	1 465	**21 746**	258 132	86 180	**344 312**	875	61	**936**
Administrative, executive and managerial workers	44 294	694	**44 988**	86 515	5 304	**91 819**	424	84	**508**
Clerical workers	5 901	128	**6 029**	368 028	42 360	**410 388**	765	93	**858**
Sales workers	362 068	24 903	**386 971**	63 036	2 764	**65 800**	24 358	2 367	**26 725**
Farmers, fishermen, hunters, loggers and related workers	1 537 909	32 764	**1 570 673**	1 381 801	52 923	**1 434 724**	756 791	40 089	**796 880**
Workers in transport and communication occupations	47 241	110	**47 351**	192 873	1 373	**194 246**	5 442	22	**5 464**
Craftsmen, prod.-process workers and labourers not elsewhere classified; miners, quarrymen and related workers	253 278	12 437	**265 715**	1 049 378	27 539	**1 076 917**	28 201	2 213	**30 414**
Service, sport and recreation workers	73 117	1 571	**74 688**	419 800	75 931	**495 731**	7 564	970	**8 534**
Workers not classifiable by occupation	9 880	8 602	**18 482**	62 464	20 466	**82 930**	20 838	49 458	**70 296**
Total . . .	2 353 969	82 674	**2 436 643**	3 882 027	314 840	**4 196 867**	845 258	95 357	**940 615**

Ghana (1.III.1970*) ‡

Occupational group	Males	Females	Total	Males	Females	Total	Males	Females	Total
0-1. Professional, technical and related workers	10 456	3 520	**13 976**	80 930	24 404	**105 334**	201	169	**370**
2. Administrative and managerial workers	5 332	308	**5 640**	5 382	262	**5 644**	23	16	**39**
3. Clerical and related workers	4 418	134	**4 552**	68 559	13 206	**81 765**	26	18	**44**
4. Sales workers	34 858	338 514	**373 372**	14 025	8 414	**22 339**	1 486	16 213	**17 699**
5. Service workers	4 966	6 372	**11 338**	63 986	13 591	**77 577**	237	1 012	**1 249**
6. Agricultural, animal husbandry and forestry workers, fishermen and hunters	729 271	509 191	**1 238 462**	166 272	12 111	**178 383**	130 987	250 424	**381 411**
7-9. Production and related workers, transport equipment, operators and labourers	136 101	188 426	**324 527**	256 895	22 304	**279 199**	3 517	6 510	**10 027**
Persons seeking work for the first time	.	.	.	.	.	.	.	.	.
Total . . .	925 402	1 046 465	**1 971 867**	656 049	94 292	**750 341**	136 477	274 362	**410 839**

‡ For notes, see pp. 272-294.

B **Distribution by status and by occupational group**
Répartition suivant la situation dans la profession et par groupe de professions
Distribución según la categoría de ocupación y por grupo de ocupación

Others and status unknown / Autres et situation non définie / Otros y categoría no definida			TOTAL				Groupe de professions	Grupo de ocupaciones
Males / Hommes / Hombres	Females / Femmes / Mujeres	Total	Males / Hommes / Hombres	Females / Femmes / Mujeres	Total	%		
...	...	...	279 288	87 706	366 994	4.4	Personnes exerçant une profession libérale, techniciens et assimilés	Trabajadores profesionales, técnicos y trabajadores asimilados
...	...	...	131 233	6 082	137 315	1.6	Directeurs et cadres administratifs supérieurs	Administradores, gerentes y directores
...	...	...	374 694	42 581	417 275	5.0	Employés de bureau	Empleados de oficina
...	...	...	449 462	30 034	479 496	5.8	Vendeurs	Vendedores
...	...	...	3 676 501	125 776	3 802 277	45.6	Agriculteurs, pêcheurs, chasseurs, forestiers et travailleurs assimilés	Agricultores, pescadores, cazadores, trabajadores forestales y asimilados
...	...	...	245 556	1 505	247 061	3.0	Travailleurs des transports et des communications	Trabajadores de los transportes y comunicaciones
...	...	...	1 330 857	42 189	1 373 046	16.5	Artisans, ouvriers de métier, ouvriers à la production et manœuvres non classés ailleurs ; mineurs, carriers et travailleurs assimilés	Artesanos y trab. ocupados en los div. procesos de producción y peones no clasif. bajo otros epígrafes; mineros, canteros y trab. asimilados
...	...	...	500 481	78 472	578 953	6.9	Travailleurs spécialisés dans les services, les sports et les activités récréatives	Trabajadores de los servicios, los deportes y las diversiones
630 586	129 022	**759 608**	723 768	207 548	**931 316**	11.2	Personnes ne pouvant être classées selon la profession	Trabajadores que no pueden ser clasificados según la ocupación
630 586	129 022	**759 608**	7 711 840	621 893	**8 333 733**	100.0	Total	Total

						%		
2 227	558	**2 785**	93 814	28 651	**122 465**	3.7	0-1. Personnel des professions scientif., techn., libérales et assimilées	0-1. Profesionales, técnicos y trabajadores asimilados
197	10	**207**	10 934	596	**11 530**	0.3	2. Directeurs et cadres administratifs supérieurs	2. Directores y funcionarios públicos superiores
1 627	331	**1 958**	74 630	13 689	**88 319**	2.7	3. Personnel administratif et travailleurs assimilés	3. Personal administrativo y trabajadores asimilados
1 126	1 897	**3 023**	51 495	365 038	**416 533**	12.5	4. Personnel commercial et vendeurs	4. Comerciantes y vendedores
825	331	**1 156**	70 014	21 306	**91 320**	2.7	5. Travailleurs des services	5. Trabajadores de los servicios
23 218	2 043	**25 261**	1 049 748	773 369	**1 823 517**	54.7	6. Agriculteurs, éleveurs, forestiers, pêcheurs et chasseurs	6. Trab. agrícolas y forestales, pescadores y cazadores
7 921	1 290	**9 211**	404 434	218 530	**622 964**	18.7	7-9. Ouvriers et manœuvres non agricoles et conducteurs d'engins de transport	7-9. Obreros no agrícolas, conductores de máquinas y vehículos de transporte y trabajadores asimilados
104 326	50 644	**154 970**	104 326	50 644	**154 970**	4.7	Personnes en quête d'emploi pour la première fois	Personas en busca de trabajo por primera vez
141 467	57 104	**198 571**	1 859 395	1 472 223	**3 331 618**	100.0	Total	Total

✝ *Voir notes pp. 272-294.*

✝ *Véanse las notas en las págs. 272-294.*

POPULATION

2 Structure of the economically active population
Structure de la population active
Estructura de la población económicamente activa

Occupational group	Employers and workers on own account / Employeurs et personnes travaillant à leur propre compte / Empleadores y trabajadores por cuenta propia			Salaried employees and wage earners / Employés et ouvriers / Empleados y obreros			Family workers / Travailleurs familiaux / Trabajadores familiares		
	Males / Hommes / Hombres	Females / Femmes / Mujeres	Total	Males / Hommes / Hombres	Females / Femmes / Mujeres	Total	Males / Hommes / Hombres	Females / Femmes / Mujeres	Total

Libyan Arab Republic (31.VII.1964) ‡

Professional, technical and related workers	...	...	...	...	...	...	...	...	...
Administrative, executive and managerial workers	...	...	...	...	...	...	...	...	...
Clerical workers	...	...	...	...	...	...	...	...	...
Sales workers	...	...	...	...	...	...	...	...	...
Farmers, fishermen, hunters, loggers and related workers	...	...	...	...	...	...	...	...	...
Miners, quarrymen and related workers	...	...	...	...	...	...	...	...	...
Workers in transport and communication occupations	...	...	...	...	...	...	...	...	...
Craftsmen, prod.-process workers and labourers not elsewhere classified .	...	...	...	...	...	...	...	...	...
Service, sport and recreation workers	...	...	...	...	...	...	...	...	...
Workers not classifiable by occupation	...	...	...	...	...	...	...	...	...
Total . . .	126 461	2 616	**129 077**	186 292	6 082	**192 374**	23 013	9 266	**32 279**

Maroc (20.VII.1971 *) ‡

0-1. Professional, technical and related workers	...	...	...	...	...	...	...	...	...
2. Administrative and managerial workers . . . . ⎫	...	...	...	...	...	...	...	...	...
3. Clerical and related workers . . . . ⎭									
4. Sales workers	...	...	...	...	...	...	...	...	...
5. Service workers	...	...	...	...	...	...	...	...	...
6. Agricultural, animal husbandry and forestry workers, fishermen and hunters	...	...	...	...	...	...	...	...	...
7-9. Production and related workers, transport equipment, operators and labourers	...	...	...	...	...	...	...	...	...
X. Workers not classifiable by occupation	...	...	...	...	...	...	...	...	...
Total . . .	...	...	...	...	...	...	...	...	...

‡ For notes, see pp. 272-294.

B Distribution by status and by occupational group
Répartition suivant la situation dans la profession et par groupe de professions
Distribución según la categoría de ocupación y por grupo de ocupación

Others and status unknown *Autres et situation non définie* Otros y categoría no definida			TOTAL			*Groupe de professions*	Grupo de ocupaciones
Males *Hommes* Hombres	Females *Femmes* Mujeres	Total	Males *Hommes* Hombres	Females *Femmes* Mujeres	Total		
					%		
...	...	...	10 471	1 359	**11 830**	3.1	*Personnes exerçant une profession libérale, techniciens et assimilés*	Trabajadores profesionales, técnicos y trabajadores asimilados
...	...	...	5 390	30	**5 420**	1.4	*Directeurs et cadres administratifs supérieurs*	Administradores, gerentes y directores
...	...	...	18 240	241	**18 481**	4.8	*Employés de bureau*	Empleados de oficina
...	...	...	23 125	166	**23 291**	6.0	*Vendeurs*	Vendedores
...	...	...	141 893	3 566	**145 459**	37.4	*Agriculteurs, pêcheurs, chasseurs, forestiers et travailleurs assimilés*	Agricultores, pescadores, cazadores, trabajadores forestales y asimilados
...	...	...	6 922	3	**6 925**	1.8	*Mineurs, carriers et travailleurs assimilés*	Mineros, canteros y trabajadores asimilados
...	...	...	19 583	93	**19 676**	5.1	*Travailleurs des transports et des communications*	Trabajadores de los transportes y comunicaciones
...	...	...	64 018	8 439	**72 457**	18.7	*Artisans, ouvriers de métier, ouvriers à la production et manœuvres non classés ailleurs*	Artesanos y trab. ocupados en los div. procesos de producción y peones no clasif. bajo otros epígrafes
...	...	...	36 812	2 283	**39 095**	10.1	*Travailleurs spécialisés dans les services, les sports et les activités récréatives*	Trabajadores de los servicios, los deportes y las diversiones
...	...	...	41 380	3 685	**45 065**	11.6	*Personnes ne pouvant être classées selon la profession*	Trabajadores que no pueden ser clasificados según la ocupación
32 068	1 901	**33 969**	367 834	19 865	**387 699**	100.0	*Total*	Total

Others and status unknown			TOTAL			*Groupe de professions*	Grupo de ocupaciones
					%		
...	...	...	134 233	23 774	**158 007**	4.0	0-1. *Personnel des professions scientif., techn., libérales et assimilées*	0-1. Profesionales, técnicos y trabajadores asimilados
...	...	...	91 400	27 769	**119 169**	3.0	2. *Directeurs et cadres administratifs supérieurs* 3. *Personnel administratif et travailleurs assimilés*	2. Directores y funcionarios públicos superiores 3. Personal administrativo y trabajadores asimilados
...	...	...	212 880	10 101	**222 981**	5.6	4. *Personnel commercial et vendeurs*	4. Comerciantes y vendedores
...	...	...	202 512	124 688	**327 200**	8.2	5. *Travailleurs des services*	5. Trabajadores de los servicios
...	...	...	1 818 761	228 450	**2 047 211**	51.4	6. *Agriculteurs, éleveurs, forestiers, pêcheurs et chasseurs*	6. Trab. agrícolas y forestales, pescadores y cazadores
...	...	...	644 047	118 395	**762 442**	19.2	7-9. *Ouvriers et manœuvres non agricoles et conducteurs d'engins de transport*	7-9. Obreros no agrícolas, conductores de máquinas y vehículos de transporte y trabajadores asimilados
...	...	...	271 530	71 978	**343 508**	8.6	X. *Travailleurs ne pouvant être classés selon la profession*	X. Trabajadores que no pueden ser clasificados según la ocupación
...	...	...	3 375 363	605 155	**3 980 518**	100.0	*Total*	Total

‡ *Voir notes pp. 272-294.*

‡ Véanse las notas en las págs. 272-294.

2 Structure of the economically active population
Structure de la population active
Estructura de la población económicamente activa

Occupational group	Employers and workers on own account *Employeurs et personnes travaillant à leur propre compte* Empleadores y trabajadores por cuenta propia			Salaried employees and wage earners *Employés et ouvriers* Empleados y obreros			Family workers *Travailleurs familiaux* Trabajadores familiares		
	Males *Hommes* Hombres	Females *Femmes* Mujeres	Total	Males *Hommes* Hombres	Females *Femmes* Mujeres	Total	Males *Hommes* Hombres	Females *Femmes* Mujeres	Total

Mauritius

Mauritius (30.VI.1972*)

0-1. Professional, technical and related workers	...	...	...	...	...	...	...	...	...
2. Administrative and managerial workers	...	...	...	...	...	...	...	...	...
3. Clerical and related workers	...	...	...	...	...	...	...	...	...
4. Sales workers	...	...	...	...	...	...	...	...	...
5. Service workers	...	...	...	...	...	...	...	...	...
6. Agricultural, animal husbandry and forestry workers, fishermen and hunters	...	...	...	...	...	...	...	...	...
7-9. Production and related workers, transport equipment, operators and labourers	...	...	...	...	...	...	...	...	...
X. Workers not classifiable by occupation	...	...	...	...	...	...	...	...	...
Persons seeking work for the first time	.	.	.	.	.	.	.	.	.
Total . . .	...	...	...	...	...	...	...	...	...

Nigeria (4.XI.1963)

Professional, technical and related workers	...	...	...	...	...	...	...	...	...
Administrative, executive and managerial workers	...	...	...	...	...	...	...	...	...
Clerical workers	...	...	...	...	...	...	...	...	...
Sales workers	...	...	...	...	...	...	...	...	...
Farmers, fishermen, hunters, loggers and related workers	...	...	...	...	...	...	...	...	...
Miners, quarrymen and related workers	...	...	...	...	...	...	...	...	...
Workers in transport and communication occupations	...	...	...	...	...	...	...	...	...
Craftsmen, prod.-process workers and labourers not elsewhere classified	...	...	...	...	...	...	...	...	...
Service, sport and recreation workers	...	...	...	...	...	...	...	...	...
Workers not classifiable by occupation	...	...	...	...	...	...	...	...	...
Unemployed	...	...	...	...	...	...	...	...	...
Total . . .	...	...	...	...	...	...	...	...	...

B Distribution by status and by occupational group
Répartition suivant la situation dans la profession et par groupe de professions
Distribución según la categoría de ocupación y por grupo de ocupación

Others and status unknown / *Autres et situation non définie* / Otros y categoría no definida			TOTAL				Groupe de professions	Grupo de ocupaciones
Males *Hommes* Hombres	Females *Femmes* Mujeres	Total	Males *Hommes* Hombres	Females *Femmes* Mujeres	Total	%		
...	...	...	8 560	4 967	13 527	5.2	0-1. *Personnel des professions scientif., techn., libérales et assimilées*	0-1. Profesionales, técnicos y trabajadores asimilados
...	...	...	1 132	77	1 209	0.5	2. *Directeurs et cadres administratifs supérieurs*	2. Directores y funcionarios públicos superiores
...	...	...	12 015	2 962	14 977	5.7	3. *Personnel administratif et travailleurs assimilés*	3. Personal administrativo y trabajadores asimilados
...	...	...	14 135	2 097	16 232	6.2	4. *Personnel commercial et vendeurs*	4. Comerciantes y vendedores
...	...	...	12 192	12 919	25 111	9.6	5. *Travailleurs des services*	5. Trabajadores de los servicios
...	...	...	54 564	16 705	71 269	27.4	6. *Agriculteurs, éleveurs, forestiers, pêcheurs et chasseurs*	6. Trab. agrícolas y forestales, pescadores y cazadores
...	...	...	74 026	4 827	78 853	30.3	7-9. *Ouvriers et manœuvres non agricoles et conducteurs d'engins de transport*	7-9. Obreros no agrícolas, conductores de máquinas y vehículos de transporte y trabajadores asimilados
...	...	...	1 522	409	1 931	0.7	X. *Travailleurs ne pouvant être classés selon la profession*	X. Trabajadores que no pueden ser clasificados según la ocupación
...	...	...	30 742	6 751	37 493	14.4	*Personnes en quête d'emploi pour la première fois*	Personas en busca de trabajo por primera vez
...	...	...	208 888	51 714	260 602	100.0	*Total*	Total

						%		
...	...	...	375 064	65 546	440 610	2.4	*Personnes exerçant une profession libérale, techniciens et assimilés*	Trabajadores profesionales, técnicos y trabajadores asimilados
...	...	...	36 736	2 666	39 402	0.2	*Directeurs et cadres administratifs supérieurs*	Administradores, gerentes y directores
...	...	...	206 151	21 865	228 016	1.2	*Employés de bureau*	Empleados de oficina
...	...	...	1 113 890	1 692 176	2 806 066	15.3	*Vendeurs*	Vendedores
...	...	...	9 222 376	978 879	10 201 255	55.7	*Agriculteurs, pêcheurs, chasseurs, forestiers et travailleurs assimilés*	Agricultores, pescadores, cazadores, trabajadores forestales y asimilados
...	...	...	13 594	262	13 856	0.1	*Mineurs, carriers et travailleurs assimilés*	Mineros, canteros y trabajadores asimilados
...	...	...	273 523	5 824	279 347	1.5	*Travailleurs des transports et des communications*	Trabajadores de los transportes y comunicaciones
...	...	...	1 676 286	513 758	2 190 044	12.0	*Artisans, ouvriers de métier, ouvriers à la production et manœuvres non classés ailleurs*	Artesanos y trab. ocupados en los div. procesos de producción y peones no clasif. bajo otros epígrafes
...	...	...	641 665	229 213	870 878	4.8	*Travailleurs spécialisés dans les services, les sports et les activités récréatives*	Trabajadores de los servicios, los deportes y las diversiones
...	...	...	55 296	836 115	891 411	4.9	*Personnes ne pouvant être classées selon la profession*	Trabajadores que no pueden ser clasificados según la ocupación
...	...	...	272 175	72 750	344 925	1.9	*Chômeurs*	Desempleados
...	...	...	13 886 756	4 419 054	18 305 810	100.0	*Total*	Total

2 Structure of the economically active population
Structure de la population active
Estructura de la población económicamente activa

Occupational group	Employers and workers on own account *Employeurs et personnes travaillant à leur propre compte* Empleadores y trabajadores por cuenta propia			Salaried employees and wage earners *Employés et ouvriers* Empleados y obreros			Family workers *Travailleurs familiaux* Trabajadores familiares		
	Males *Hommes* Hombres	Females *Femmes* Mujeres	Total	Males *Hommes* Hombres	Females *Femmes* Mujeres	Total	Males *Hommes* Hombres	Females *Femmes* Mujeres	Total

Seychelles (5.V.1971)

0-1. Professional, technical and related workers	53	34	87	497	732	1 229	1	2	3
2. Administrative and managerial workers	278	58	336	150	22	172	6	8	14
3. Clerical and related workers	3	1	4	374	242	616	1	1	2
4. Sales workers	47	15	62	152	110	262	23	39	62
5. Service workers	37	149	186	908	2 080	2 988	2	12	14
6. Agricultural, animal husbandry and forestry workers, fishermen and hunters	1 092	86	1 178	2 355	1 363	3 718	39	32	71
7-9. Production and related workers, transport equipment, operators and labourers	689	198	887	5 462	507	5 969	21	3	24
X. Workers not classifiable by occupation	128	55	183	967	713	1 680	25	55	80
Total . . .	2 327	596	2 923	10 865	5 769	16 634	118	152	270

Sierra Leone (1.IV.1963)

Professional, technical and related workers	1 868	380	2 248	6 176	2 473	8 649	77	92	169
Administrative, executive and managerial workers	240	11	251	1 924	193	2 117	8	8	16
Clerical workers	373	74	447	5 414	1 018	6 432	55	19	74
Sales workers	22 067	16 523	38 590	2 102	740	2 842	1 041	4 770	5 811
Farmers, fishermen, hunters, loggers and related workers	261 028	28 326	289 354	4 609	253	4 862	137 486	268 472	405 958
Miners, quarrymen and related workers	17 981	159	18 140	21 481	98	21 579	3 150	22	3 172
Workers in transport and communication occupations	1 896	56	1 952	10 618	209	10 827	537	3	540
Craftsmen, prod.-process workers and labourers not elsewhere classified .	28 721	4 476	33 197	30 819	502	31 321	4 023	1 430	5 453
Service, sport and recreation workers	543	210	753	12 546	581	13 127	142	124	266
Persons not at work	...	...	...	...	...	...	...	...	...
Total . . .	334 717	50 215	384 932	95 689	6 067	101 756	146 519	274 940	421 459

B Distribution by status and by occupational group
Répartition suivant la situation dans la profession et par groupe de professions
Distribución según la categoría de ocupación y por grupo de ocupación

Others and status unknown / Autres et situation non définie / Otros y categoría no definida			TOTAL				Groupe de professions	Grupo de ocupaciones
Males / Hommes / Hombres	Females / Femmes / Mujeres	Total	Males / Hommes / Hombres	Females / Femmes / Mujeres	Total	%		
.	.	.	551	768	1 319	6.7	0-1. Personnel des professions scientif., techn., libérales et assimilées	0-1. Profesionales, técnicos y trabajadores asimilados
.	.	.	434	88	522	2.6	2. Directeurs et cadres administratifs supérieurs	2. Directores y funcionarios públicos superiores
.	.	.	378	244	622	3.1	3. Personnel administratif et travailleurs assimilés	3. Personal administrativo y trabajadores asimilados
.	.	.	222	164	386	1.9	4. Personnel commercial et vendeurs	4. Comerciantes y vendedores
.	.	.	947	2 241	3 188	16.1	5. Travailleurs des services	5. Trabajadores de los servicios
.	.	.	3 486	1 481	4 967	25.1	6. Agriculteurs, éleveurs, forestiers, pêcheurs et chasseurs	6. Trab. agrícolas y forestales, pescadores y cazadores
.	.	.	6 172	708	6 880	34.7	7-9. Ouvriers et manœuvres non agricoles et conducteurs d'engins de transport	7-9. Obreros no agrícolas, conductores de máquinas y vehículos de transporte y trabajadores asimilados
.	.	.	1 120	823	1 943	9.8	X. Travailleurs ne pouvant être classés selon la profession	X. Trabajadores que no pueden ser clasificados según la ocupación
.	.	.	13 310	6 517	19 827	100.0	Total	Total

Others and status unknown / Autres et situation non définie / Otros y categoría no definida			TOTAL				Groupe de professions	Grupo de ocupaciones
Males / Hommes / Hombres	Females / Femmes / Mujeres	Total	Males / Hommes / Hombres	Females / Femmes / Mujeres	Total	%		
...	...	...	8 121	2 945	11 066	1.2	Personnes exerçant une profession libérale, techniciens et assimilés	Trabajadores profesionales, técnicos y trabajadores asimilados
...	...	...	2 172	212	2 384	0.3	Directeurs et cadres administratifs supérieurs	Administradores, gerentes y directores
...	...	...	5 842	1 111	6 953	0.7	Employés de bureau	Empleados de oficina
...	...	...	25 210	22 033	47 243	5.0	Vendeurs	Vendedores
...	...	...	403 123	297 051	700 174	74.6	Agriculteurs, pêcheurs, chasseurs, forestiers et travailleurs assimilés	Agricultores, pescadores, cazadores, trabajadores forestales y asimilados
...	...	...	42 612	279	42 891	4.6	Mineurs, carriers et travailleurs assimilés	Mineros, canteros y trabajadores asimilados
...	...	...	13 051	268	13 319	1.4	Travailleurs des transports et des communications	Trabajadores de los transportes y comunicaciones
...	...	...	63 563	6 408	69 971	7.5	Artisans, ouvriers de métier, ouvriers à la production et manœuvres non classés ailleurs	Artesanos y trab. ocupados en los div. procesos de producción y peones no clasif. bajo otros epígrafes
...	...	...	13 231	915	14 146	1.5	Travailleurs spécialisés dans les services, les sports et les activités récréatives	Trabajadores de los servicios, los deportes y las diversiones
27 248	2 342	29 590	27 248	2 342	29 590	3.2	Personnes hors d'activité	Personas fuera de actividad
27 248	2 342	29 590	604 173	333 564	937 737	100.0	Total	Total

2 Structure of the economically active population
Structure de la population active
Estructura de la población económicamente activa

Occupational group	Employers and workers on own account / Employeurs et personnes travaillant à leur propre compte / Empleadores y trabajadores por cuenta propia			Salaried employees and wage earners / Employés et ouvriers / Empleados y obreros			Family workers / Travailleurs familiaux / Trabajadores familiares		
	Males *Hommes* Hombres	Females *Femmes* Mujeres	**Total**	Males *Hommes* Hombres	Females *Femmes* Mujeres	**Total**	Males *Hommes* Hombres	Females *Femmes* Mujeres	**Total**

South Africa, Rep. of (6.V.1970) ‡

0-1. Professional, technical and related workers	...	...	...	...	...	...	...	...	...
2. Administrative and managerial workers	...	...	...	...	...	...	...	...	...
3. Clerical and related workers	...	...	...	...	...	...	...	...	...
4. Sales workers	...	...	...	...	...	...	...	...	...
5. Service workers	...	...	...	...	...	...	...	...	...
6. Agricultural, animal husbandry and forestry workers, fishermen and hunters	...	...	...	...	...	...	...	...	...
7-9. Production and related workers, transport equipment, operators and labourers	...	...	...	...	...	...	...	...	...
X. Workers not classifiable by occupation	...	...	...	...	...	...	...	...	...
Total . . .	...	...	...	...	...	...	...	...	...

Tunisie (3.V.1966) ‡

Professional, technical and related workers	...	...	...	...	...	...	...	...	...
Administrative, executive and managerial workers	...	...	...	...	...	...	...	...	...
Clerical workers	...	...	...	...	...	...	...	...	...
Sales workers	...	...	...	...	...	...	...	...	...
Farmers, fishermen, hunters, loggers and related workers	...	...	...	...	...	...	...	...	...
Miners, quarrymen and related workers	...	...	...	...	...	...	...	...	...
Workers in transport and communication occupations	...	...	...	...	...	...	...	...	...
Craftsmen, prod.-process workers and labourers not elsewhere classified .	...	...	...	...	...	...	...	...	...
Service, sport and recreation workers	...	...	...	...	...	...	...	...	...
Workers not classifiable by occupation	...	...	...	...	...	...	...	...	...
Total . . .	263 695	14 639	**278 334**	632 955	42 533	**675 488**	31 480	2 825	**34 305**

‡ For notes, see pp. 272-294.

B Distribution by status and by occupational group
Répartition suivant la situation dans la profession et par groupe de professions
Distribución según la categoría de ocupación y por grupo de ocupación

Others and status unknown / Autres et situation non définie / Otros y categoría no definida			TOTAL				Groupe de professions	Grupo de ocupaciones
Males / Hommes / Hombres	Females / Femmes / Mujeres	Total	Males / Hommes / Hombres	Females / Femmes / Mujeres	Total	%		
...	...	...	178 270	151 790	330 060	4.1	0-1. *Personnel des professions scientif., techn., libérales et assimilées*	0-1. Profesionales, técnicos y trabajadores asimilados
...	...	...	72 660	3 220	75 880	1.0	2. *Directeurs et cadres administratifs supérieurs*	2. Directores y funcionarios públicos superiores
...	...	...	308 950	270 140	579 090	7.3	3. *Personnel administratif et travailleurs assimilés*	3. Personal administrativo y trabajadores asimilados
...	...	...	240 750	88 990	329 740	4.1	4. *Personnel commercial et vendeurs*	4. Comerciantes y vendedores
...	...	...	412 190	854 660	1 266 850	15.9	5. *Travailleurs des services*	5. Trabajadores de los servicios
...	...	...	1 611 440	668 840	2 280 280	28.5	6. *Agriculteurs, éleveurs, forestiers, pêcheurs et chasseurs*	6. Trab. agrícolas y forestales, pescadores y cazadores
...	...	...	2 303 030	176 880	2 479 910	31.0	7-9. *Ouvriers et manœuvres non agricoles et conducteurs d'engins de transport*	7-9. Obreros no agrícolas, conductores de máquinas y vehículos de transporte y trabajadores asimilados
...	...	...	244 110	400 300	644 410	8.1	X. *Travailleurs ne pouvant être classés selon la profession*	X. Trabajadores que no pueden ser clasificados según la ocupación
...	...	...	5 371 400	2 614 820	7 986 220	100.0	*Total*	Total

Others and status unknown			TOTAL				Groupe de professions	Grupo de ocupaciones
Males	Females	Total	Males	Females	Total	%		
...	...	...	36 302	7 611	43 913	4.0	*Personnes exerçant une profession libérale, techniciens et assimilés*	Trabajadores profesionales, técnicos y trabajadores asimilados
...	...	...	6 970	252	7 222	0.7	*Directeurs et cadres administratifs supérieurs*	Administradores, gerentes y directores
...	...	...	24 434	5 323	29 757	2.7	*Employés de bureau*	Empleados de oficina
...	...	...	58 450	1 032	59 482	5.4	*Vendeurs*	Vendedores
...	...	...	416 839	8 013	424 852	38.9	*Agriculteurs, pêcheurs, chasseurs, forestiers et travailleurs assimilés*	Agricultores, pescadores, cazadores, trabajadores forestales y asimilados
...	...	...	19 537	72	19 609	1.8	*Mineurs, carriers et travailleurs assimilés*	Mineros, canteros y trabajadores asimilados
...	...	...	28 052	575	28 627	2.6	*Travailleurs des transports et des communications*	Trabajadores de los transportes y comunicaciones
...	...	...	323 179	28 177	351 356	32.1	*Artisans, ouvriers de métier, ouvriers à la production et manœuvres non classés ailleurs*	Artesanos y trab. ocupados en los div. procesos de producción y peones no clasif. bajo otros epígrafes
...	...	...	52 417	12 013	64 430	5.9	*Travailleurs spécialisés dans les services, les sports et les activités récréatives*	Trabajadores de los servicios, los deportes y las diversiones
...	...	...	61 086	3 401	64 487	5.9	*Personnes ne pouvant être classées selon la profession*	Trabajadores que no pueden ser clasificados según la ocupación
99 136	6 472	105 608	1 027 266	66 469	1 093 735	100.0	*Total*	Total

† *Voir notes pp. 272-294.*

† Véanse las notas en las págs. 272-294.

2 Structure of the economically active population
Structure de la population active
Estructura de la población económicamente activa

Occupational group	Employers and workers on own account *Employeurs et personnes travaillant à leur propre compte* Empleadores y trabajadores por cuenta propia			Salaried employees and wage earners *Employés et ouvriers* Empleados y obreros			Family workers *Travailleurs familiaux* Trabajadores familiares		
	Males *Hommes* Hombres	Females *Femmes* Mujeres	Total	Males *Hommes* Hombres	Females *Femmes* Mujeres	Total	Males *Hommes* Hombres	Females *Femmes* Mujeres	Total

Zambia (22-30.VIII.1969 *) †

Professional, technical and related workers	...	...	...	...	...	...	...	...	...
Administrative, executive and managerial workers	...	...	...	...	...	...	...	...	...
Clerical workers	...	...	...	...	...	...	...	...	...
Sales workers	...	...	...	...	...	...	...	...	...
Farmers, fishermen, hunters, loggers and related workers	...	...	...	...	...	...	...	...	...
Miners, quarrymen and related workers									
Workers in transport and communication occupations	...	...	...	...	...	...	...	...	...
Craftsmen, prod.-process workers and labourers not elsewhere classified .									
Service, sport and recreation workers	...	...	...	...	...	...	...	...	...
Workers not classifiable by occupation	...	...	...	...	...	...	...	...	...
Persons seeking work	...	...	...	...	...	...	...	...	...
Total . . .	...	...	...	...	...	...	...	...	...

† For notes, see pp. 272-294.

B Distribution by status and by occupational group
Répartition suivant la situation dans la profession et par groupe de professions
Distribución según la categoría de ocupación y por grupo de ocupación

Others and status unknown Autres et situation non définie Otros y categoría no definida			TOTAL				Groupe de professions	Grupo de ocupaciones
Males Hommes Hombres	Females Femmes Mujeres	Total	Males Hommes Hombres	Females Femmes Mujeres	Total			
						%		
...	...	...	37 057	9 802	**46 859**	4.0	Personnes exerçant une profession libérale, techniciens et assimilés	Trabajadores profesionales, técnicos y trabajadores asimilados
...	...	...	7 696	907	**8 603**	0.7	Directeurs et cadres administratifs supérieurs	Administradores, gerentes y directores
...	...	...	20 887	5 710	**26 597**	2.3	Employés de bureau	Empleados de oficina
...	...	...	29 154	4 886	**34 040**	2.9	Vendeurs	Vendedores
...	...	...	154 809	21 523	**176 332**	15.2	Agriculteurs, pêcheurs, chasseurs, forestiers et travailleurs assimilés	Agricultores, pescadores, cazadores, trabajadores forestales y asimilados
...	...	...	187 618	8 079	**195 697**	16.9	Mineurs, carriers et travailleurs assimilés / Travailleurs des transports et des communications / Artisans, ouvriers de métier, ouvriers à la production et manœuvres non classés ailleurs	Mineros, canteros y trabajadores asimilados / Trabajadores de los transportes y comunicaciones / Artesanos y trab. ocupados en los div. procesos de producción y peones no clasif. bajo otros epígrafes
...	...	...	67 210	7 790	**75 000**	6.5	Travailleurs spécialisés dans les services, les sports et les activités récréatives	Trabajadores de los servicios, los deportes y las diversiones
...	...	...	103 069	90 059	**193 128**	16.7	Personnes ne pouvant être classées selon la profession	Trabajadores que no pueden ser clasificados según la ocupación
...	...	...	207 831	195 611	**403 442**	34.8	Personnes en quête d'emploi	Personas en busca de trabajo
...	...	...	815 331	344 367	**1 159 698**	100.0	Total	Total

☩ Voir notes pp. 272-294.

☩ Véanse las notas en las págs. 272-294.

POPULATION

2 Structure of the economically active population
Structure de la population active
Estructura de la población económicamente activa

Occupational group	Employers and workers on own account Employeurs et personnes travaillant à leur propre compte Empleadores y trabajadores por cuenta propia			Salaried employees and wage earners Employés et ouvriers Empleados y obreros			Family workers Travailleurs familiaux Trabajadores familiares		
	Males Hommes Hombres	Females Femmes Mujeres	Total	Males Hommes Hombres	Females Femmes Mujeres	Total	Males Hommes Hombres	Females Femmes Mujeres	Total

Antigua (7.IV.1970)

AMERICA — AMÉRIQUE — AMERICA

0-1. Professional, technical and related workers	...	...	...	...	...	...	...	...	...
2. Administrative and managerial workers	...	...	...	...	...	...	...	...	...
3. Clerical and related workers	...	...	...	...	...	...	...	...	...
4. Sales workers	...	...	...	...	...	...	...	...	...
5. Service workers	...	...	...	...	...	...	...	...	...
6. Agricultural, animal husbandry and forestry workers, fishermen and hunters	...	...	...	...	...	...	...	...	...
7-9. Production and related workers, transport equipment, operators and labourers	...	...	...	...	...	...	...	...	...
X. Workers not classifiable by occupation	...	...	...	...	...	...	...	...	...
Total . . .	2 035	791	**2 826**	10 077	6 051	**16 128**	98	44	**142**

Antilles néerlandaises (1.I.1972) ‡

0-1. Professional, technical and related workers	...	...	...	...	...	...	...	...	...
2. Administrative and managerial workers	...	...	...	...	...	...	...	...	...
3. Clerical and related workers	...	...	...	...	...	...	...	...	...
4. Sales workers	...	...	...	...	...	...	...	...	...
5. Service workers	...	...	...	...	...	...	...	...	...
6. Agricultural, animal husbandry and forestry workers, fishermen and hunters	...	...	...	...	...	...	...	...	...
7-9. Production and related workers, transport equipment, operators and labourers	...	...	...	...	...	...	...	...	...
Persons seeking work for the first time	.	.	.	.	.	.	.	.	.
Unemployed	...	...	...	...	...	...	...	...	...
Total . . .	3 304	679	**3 983**	36 433	17 930	**54 363**	189	510	**699**

‡ For notes, see pp. 272-294.

B
Distribution by status and by occupational group
Répartition suivant la situation dans la profession et par groupe de professions
Distribución según la categoría de ocupación y por grupo de ocupación

Others and status unknown / Autres et situation non définie / Otros y categoría no definida			TOTAL			Groupe de professions	Grupo de ocupaciones
Males / Hommes / Hombres	Females / Femmes / Mujeres	Total	Males / Hommes / Hombres	Females / Femmes / Mujeres	Total		

						%		
...	...	...	925	940	**1 865**	8.1	0-1. Personnel des professions scientif., techn., libérales et assimilées	0-1. Profesionales, técnicos y trabajadores asimilados
...	...	...	185	44	**229**	1.0	2. Directeurs et cadres administratifs supérieurs	2. Directores y funcionarios públicos superiores
...	...	...	1 154	1 510	**2 664**	11.5	3. Personnel administratif et travailleurs assimilés	3. Personal administrativo y trabajadores asimilados
...	...	...	777	518	**1 295**	5.6	4. Personnel commercial et vendeurs	4. Comerciantes y vendedores
...	...	...	1 539	3 804	**5 343**	23.2	5. Travailleurs des services	5. Trabajadores de los servicios
...	...	...	1 702	577	**2 279**	9.9	6. Agriculteurs, éleveurs, forestiers, pêcheurs et chasseurs	6. Trab. agrícolas y forestales, pescadores y cazadores
...	...	...	7 149	659	**7 808**	33.8	7-9. Ouvriers et manœuvres non agricoles et conducteurs d'engins de transport	7-9. Obreros no agrícolas, conductores de máquinas y vehículos de transporte y trabajadores asimilados
...	...	...	844	740	**1 584**	6.9	X. Travailleurs ne pouvant être classés selon la profession	X. Trabajadores que no pueden ser clasificados según la ocupación
2 065	1 906	**3 971**	14 275	8 792	**23 067**	100.0	Total	Total

						%		
...	...	...	3 882	2 910	**6 792**	9.3	0-1. Personnel des professions scientif., techn., libérales et assimilées	0-1. Profesionales, técnicos y trabajadores asimilados
...	...	...	1 022	93	**1 115**	1.5	2. Directeurs et cadres administratifs supérieurs	2. Directores y funcionarios públicos superiores
...	...	...	6 007	4 795	**10 802**	14.7	3. Personnel administratif et travailleurs assimilés	3. Personal administrativo y trabajadores asimilados
...	...	...	2 899	3 333	**6 232**	8.5	4. Personnel commercial et vendeurs	4. Comerciantes y vendedores
...	...	...	4 615	6 596	**11 211**	15.3	5. Travailleurs des services	5. Trabajadores de los servicios
...	...	...	593	24	**617**	0.8	6. Agriculteurs, éleveurs, forestiers, pêcheurs et chasseurs	6. Trab. agrícolas y forestales, pescadores y cazadores
...	...	...	23 119	2 686	**28 805**	35.3	7-9. Ouvriers et manœuvres non agricoles et conducteurs d'engins de transport	7-9. Obreros no agrícolas, conductores de máquinas y vehículos de transporte y trabajadores asimilados
...	...	...	1 822	2 134	**3 956**	5.4	Personnes en quête d'emploi pour la première fois	Personas en busca de trabajo por primera vez
...	...	...	3 902	2 838	**6 740**	9.2	Chômeurs	Desempleados
7 935	6 290	**14 225**	47 861	25 409	**73 270**	100.0	Total	Total

† Voir notes pp. 272-294.

† Véanse las notas en las págs. 272-294.

2 Structure of the economically active population
Structure de la population active
Estructura de la población económicamente activa

Occupational group	Employers and workers on own account *Employeurs et personnes travaillant à leur propre compte* Empleadores y trabajadores por cuenta propia			Salaried employees and wage earners *Employés et ouvriers* Empleados y obreros			Family workers *Travailleurs familiaux* Trabajadores familiares		
	Males *Hommes* Hombres	Females *Femmes* Mujeres	Total	Males *Hommes* Hombres	Females *Femmes* Mujeres	Total	Males *Hommes* Hombres	Females *Femmes* Mujeres	Total
Argentina (30.IX.1970) †									
0-1. Professional, technical and related workers	109 000	38 150	**147 150**	190 500	327 750	**518 250**	1 500	1 000	**2 500**
2. Administrative and managerial workers	65 150	3 400	**68 550**	61 750	5 950	**67 700**	300	50	**350**
3. Clerical and related workers	3 300	500	**3 800**	649 600	360 750	**1 010 350**	500	1 150	**1 650**
4. Sales workers	458 200	107 100	**565 300**	331 400	137 950	**469 350**	18 150	8 950	**27 100**
5. Service workers	53 150	43 900	**97 050**	386 800	603 650	**990 450**	3 550	19 250	**22 800**
6. Agricultural, animal husbandry and forestry workers, fishermen and hunters	415 750	25 400	**441 150**	647 700	27 950	**675 650**	130 500	23 600	**154 100**
7-9. Production and related workers, transport equipment, operators and labourers	510 250	96 000	**606 250**	2 146 550	236 500	**2 383 050**	30 150	9 000	**39 150**
X. Workers not classifiable by occupation	38 500	9 100	**47 650**	206 050	59 650	**265 700**	24 150	14 050	**38 200**
Total . . .	1 653 300	323 600	**1 976 900**	4 620 350	1 760 150	**6 380 500**	208 800	77 050	**285 850**
Bahamas (7.IV.1970 *)									
0-1. Professional, technical and related workers	...	...	...	...	...	...	...	...	...
2. Administrative and managerial workers	...	...	...	...	...	...	...	...	...
3. Clerical and related workers	...	...	...	...	...	...	...	...	...
4. Sales workers	...	...	...	...	...	...	...	...	...
5. Service workers	...	...	...	...	...	...	...	...	...
6. Agricultural, animal husbandry and forestry workers, fishermen and hunters	...	...	...	...	...	...	...	...	...
7-9. Production and related workers, transport equipment, operators and labourers	...	...	...	...	...	...	...	...	...
X. Workers not classifiable by occupation . . . . Unemployed	...	...	...	...	...	...	...	...	...
Total . . .	3 811	1 570	**4 381**	21 636	17 345	**38 981**	13	35	**48**

† For notes, see pp. 272-294.

B Distribution by status and by occupational group
Répartition suivant la situation dans la profession et par groupe de professions
Distribución según la categoría de ocupación y por grupo de ocupación

Others and status unknown / Autres et situation non définie / Otros y categoría no definida			TOTAL				Groupe de professions	Grupo de ocupaciones
Males / Hommes / Hombres	Females / Femmes / Mujeres	Total	Males / Hommes / Hombres	Females / Femmes / Mujeres	Total	%		
5 000	4 600	**9 600**	306 000	371 500	**677 500**	*7.5*	0-1. *Personnel des professions scientif., techn., libérales et assimilées*	0-1. Profesionales, técnicos y trabajadores asimilados
1 150	100	**1 250**	128 350	9 500	**137 850**	*1.5*	2. *Directeurs et cadres administratifs supérieurs*	2. Directores y funcionarios públicos superiores
6 700	2 900	**9 600**	660 100	365 300	**1 025 400**	*11.4*	3. *Personnel administratif et travailleurs assimilés*	3. Personal administrativo y trabajadores asimilados
8 950	2 100	**11 050**	816 700	256 100	**1 072 800**	*11.9*	4. *Personnel commercial et vendeurs*	4. Comerciantes y vendedores
7 800	18 450	**26 250**	451 300	685 250	**1 136 550**	*12.6*	5. *Travailleurs des services*	5. Trabajadores de los servicios
24 200	1 000	**25 200**	1 218 150	77 950	**1 296 100**	*14.4*	6. *Agriculteurs, éleveurs, forestiers, pêcheurs et chasseurs*	6. Trab. agrícolas y forestales, pescadores y cazadores
56 200	6 700	**62 900**	2 743 150	348 200	**3 091 350**	*34.3*	7-9. *Ouvriers et manœuvres non agricoles et conducteurs d'engins de transport*	7-9. Obreros no agrícolas, conductores de máquinas y vehículos de transporte y trabajadores asimilados
130 050	92 300	**222 350**	398 750	175 150	**573 900**	*6.4*	X. *Travailleurs ne pouvant être classés selon la profession*	X. Trabajadores que no pueden ser clasificados según la ocupación
240 050	128 150	**368 200**	6 722 500	2 288 950	**9 011 450**	*100.0*	*Total*	Total

Others and status unknown / Autres et situation non définie / Otros y categoría no definida			TOTAL				Groupe de professions	Grupo de ocupaciones
Males / Hommes / Hombres	Females / Femmes / Mujeres	Total	Males / Hommes / Hombres	Females / Femmes / Mujeres	Total	%		
.	.	.	3 294	2 885	**6 179**	*8.9*	0-1. *Personnel des professions scientif., techn., libérales et assimilées*	0-1. Profesionales, técnicos y trabajadores asimilados
.	.	.	3 112	496	**3 608**	*5.2*	2. *Directeurs et cadres administratifs supérieurs*	2. Directores y funcionarios públicos superiores
.	.	.	2 100	5 709	**7 809**	*11.2*	3. *Personnel administratif et travailleurs assimilés*	3. Personal administrativo y trabajadores asimilados
.	.	.	2 021	1 652	**3 673**	*5.3*	4. *Personnel commercial et vendeurs*	4. Comerciantes y vendedores
.	.	.	6 150	9 193	**15 343**	*22.0*	5. *Travailleurs des services*	5. Trabajadores de los servicios
.	.	.	3 021	1 312	**4 333**	*6.2*	6. *Agriculteurs, éleveurs, forestiers, pêcheurs et chasseurs*	6. Trab. agrícolas y forestales, pescadores y cazadores
.	.	.	19 100	2 402	**21 502**	*30.7*	7-9. *Ouvriers et manœuvres non agricoles et conducteurs d'engins de transport*	7-9. Obreros no agrícolas, conductores de máquinas y vehículos de transporte y trabajadores asimilados
.	.	.	2 990	4 354	**7 344**	*10.5*	X. *Travailleurs ne pouvant être classés selon la profession* / *Chômeurs*	X. Trabajadores que no pueden ser clasificados según la ocupación / Desemplead os
.	.	.	41 788	28 003	**69 791**	*100.0*	*Total*	Total

† *Voir notes pp. 272-294.*   † Véanse las notas en las págs. 272-294.

POPULATION

2 Structure of the economically active population
Structure de la population active
Estructura de la población económicamente activa

Occupational group	Employers and workers on own account			Salaried employees and wage earners			Family workers		
	Employeurs et personnes travaillant à leur propre compte			Employés et ouvriers			Travailleurs familiaux		
	Empleadores y trabajadores por cuenta propia			Empleados y obreros			Trabajadores familiares		
	Males *Hommes* Hombres	Females *Femmes* Mujeres	Total	Males *Hommes* Hombres	Females *Femmes* Mujeres	Total	Males *Hommes* Hombres	Females *Femmes* Mujeres	Total
Barbados (7.IV.1970 *) †									
Professional, technical and related workers	...	...	...	...	...	...	...	...	...
Administrative, executive and managerial workers	...	...	...	...	...	...	...	...	...
Clerical workers	...	...	...	...	...	...	...	...	...
Sales workers	...	...	...	...	...	...	...	...	...
Farmers, fishermen, hunters, loggers and related workers	...	...	...	...	...	...	...	...	...
Workers in transport and communication occupations									
Craftsmen, prod.-process workers and labourers not elsewhere classified .	...	...	...	...	...	...	...	...	...
Service, sport and recreation workers									
Workers not classifiable by occupation	...	...	...	...	...	...	...	...	...
Members of the armed forces	.	.	.	...	.	...	.	.	.
Total . . .	...	...	...	...	...	...	...	...	...
Belize (7.IV.1970*)									
0-1. Professional, technical and related workers	...	...	...	...	...	...	...	...	...
2. Administrative and managerial workers	...	...	...	...	...	...	...	...	...
3. Clerical and related workers	...	...	...	...	...	...	...	...	...
4. Sales workers	...	...	...	...	...	...	...	...	...
5. Service workers	...	...	...	...	...	...	...	...	...
6. Agricultural, animal husbandry and forestry workers, fishermen and hunters	...	...	...	...	...	...	...	...	...
7-9. Production and related workers, transport equipment, operators and labourers	...	...	...	...	...	...	...	...	...
X. Workers not classifiable by occupation	...	...	...	...	...	...	...	...	...
Members of the armed forces . . .	...	...	...	...	...	...	...	...	...
Unemployed	...	...	...	...	...	...	...	...	...
Total . . .	7 566	752	**8 318**	17 045	4 900	**21 945**	857	327	**1 184**

† For notes, see pp. 272-294.

B
Distribution by status and by occupational group
Répartition suivant la situation dans la profession et par groupe de professions
Distribución según la categoría de ocupación y por grupo de ocupación

Others and status unknown / Autres et situation non définie / Otros y categoría no definida			TOTAL			Groupe de professions	Grupo de ocupaciones
Males / Hommes / Hombres	Females / Femmes / Mujeres	Total	Males / Hommes / Hombres	Females / Femmes / Mujeres	Total		
						%		
...	...	...	4 694	3 066	7 760	9.2	Personnes exerçant une profession libérale, techniciens et assimilés	Trabajadores profesionales, técnicos y trabajadores asimilados
...	...	...	1 033	125	1 158	1.4	Directeurs et cadres administratifs supérieurs	Administradores, gerentes y directores
...	...	...	3 114	4 429	7 543	9.0	Employés de bureau	Empleados de oficina
...	...	...	3 139	4 405	7 544	9.0	Vendeurs	Vendedores
...	...	...	8 251	4 767	13 018	15.5	Agriculteurs, pêcheurs, chasseurs, forestiers et travailleurs assimilés	Agricultores, pescadores, cazadores, trabajadores forestales y asimilados
							Travailleurs des transports et des communications	Trabajadores de los transportes y comunicaciones
...	...	...	29 364	15 334	44 698	53.2	Artisans, ouvriers de métier, ouvriers à la production et manœuvres non classés ailleurs	Artesanos y trab. ocupados en los div. procesos de producción y peones no clasif. bajo otros epígrafes
							Travailleurs spécialisés dans les services, les sports et les activités récréatives	Trabajadores de los servicios, los deportes y las diversiones
...	...	...	1 457	798	2 255	2.7	Personnes ne pouvant être classées selon la profession	Trabajadores que no pueden ser clasificados según la ocupación
...	.	...	5	.	5	—	Membres des forces armées	Miembros de las fuerzas armadas
...	...	...	51 057	32 924	83 981	100.0	Total	Total

						%		
...	...	...	1 226	1 418	2 644	8.0	0-1. Personnel des professions scientif., techn., libérales et assimilées	0-1. Profesionales, técnicos y trabajadores asimilados
...	...	...	153	16	169	0.5	2. Directeurs et cadres administratifs supérieurs	2. Directores y funcionarios públicos superiores
...	...	...	993	754	1 747	5.3	3. Personnel administratif et travailleurs assimilés	3. Personal administrativo y trabajadores asimilados
...	...	...	1 549	739	2 288	6.9	4. Personnel commercial et vendeurs	4. Comerciantes y vendedores
...	...	...	1 184	1 720	2 904	8.8	5. Travailleurs des services	5. Trabajadores de los servicios
...	...	...	10 047	483	10 530	31.7	6. Agriculteurs, éleveurs, forestiers, pêcheurs et chasseurs	6. Trab. agrícolas y forestales, pescadores y cazadores
...	...	...	7 082	756	7 838	23.7	7-9. Ouvriers et manœuvres non agricoles et conducteurs d'engins de transport	7-9. Obreros no agrícolas, conductores de máquinas y vehículos de transporte y trabajadores asimilados
...	...	...	3 263	103	3 366	10.2	X. Travailleurs ne pouvant être classés selon la profession	X. Trabajadores que no pueden ser clasificados según la ocupación
...	...	...	6	.	6	—	Membres des forces armées	Miembros de las fuerzas armadas
...	...	...	1 425	204	1 629	4.9	Chômeurs	Desempleados
1 460	214	1 674	26 928	6 193	33 121	100.0	Total	Total

† *Voir notes pp. 272-294.*

† Véanse las notas en las págs. 272-294.

2 Structure of the economically active population
Structure de la population active
Estructura de la población económicamente activa

Occupational group	Employers and workers on own account *Employeurs et personnes travaillant à leur propre compte* Empleadores y trabajadores por cuenta propia			Salaried employees and wage earners *Employés et ouvriers* Empleados y obreros			Family workers *Travailleurs familiaux* Trabajadores familiares		
	Males *Hommes* Hombres	Females *Femmes* Mujeres	Total	Males *Hommes* Hombres	Females *Femmes* Mujeres	Total	Males *Hommes* Hombres	Females *Femmes* Mujeres	Total

Bermuda (25.X.1970 *)

Professional, technical and related workers	...	...	...	...	...	...	...	...	...
Administrative, executive and managerial workers	...	...	...	...	...	...	...	...	...
Clerical workers	...	...	...	...	...	...	...	...	...
Sales workers	...	...	...	...	...	...	...	...	...
Farmers, fishermen, hunters, loggers and related workers	...	...	...	...	...	...	...	...	...
Miners, quarrymen and related workers									
Workers in transport and communication occupations	...	...	...	...	...	...	...	...	...
Craftsmen, prod.-process workers and labourers not elsewhere classified	...	...	...	...	...	...	...	...	...
Service, sport and recreation workers	...	...	...	...	...	...	...	...	...
Workers not classifiable by occupation	...	...	...	...	...	...	...	...	...
Members of the armed forces	.	.	.	...	.	...	.	.	.
Total	817	195	**1 012**	15 568	10 685	**26 253**	9	34	**43**

Brésil (1.IX.1970)

0-1. Professional, technical and related workers	...	...	...	...	...	...	...	...	...
2. Administrative and managerial workers	...	...	...	...	...	...	...	...	...
3. Clerical and related workers	...	...	...	...	...	...	...	...	...
4. Sales workers	...	...	...	...	...	...	...	...	...
5. Service workers	...	...	...	...	...	...	...	...	...
6. Agricultural, animal husbandry and forestry workers, fishermen and hunters	...	...	...	...	...	...	...	...	...
7-9. Production and related workers, transport equipment, operators and labourers	...	...	...	...	...	...	...	...	...
X. Workers not classifiable by occupation	...	...	...	...	...	...	...	...	.
Members of the armed forces	.	.	.	...	...	...	.	.	...
Total	9 251 085	1 189 098	**10 440 183**	11 896 026	4 297 526	**16 193 552**	2 236 509	677 813	**2 914 322**

B Distribution by status and by ocupational group
Répartition suivant la situation dans la profession et par groupe de professions
Distribución según la categoría de ocupación y por grupo de ocupación

Others and status unknown / Autres et situation non définie / Otros y categoría no definida			TOTAL				Groupe de professions	Grupo de ocupaciones
Males / Hommes / Hombres	Females / Femmes / Mujeres	Total	Males / Hommes / Hombres	Females / Femmes / Mujeres	Total	%		
...	...	...	2 225	1 378	3 603	13.2	Personnes exerçant une profession libérale, techniciens et assimilés	Trabajadores profesionales, técnicos y trabajadores asimilados
...	...	...	901	81	982	3.6	Directeurs et cadres administratifs supérieurs	Administradores, gerentes y directores
...	...	...	921	3 781	4 702	17.2	Employés de bureau	Empleados de oficina
...	...	...	1 248	1 261	2 509	9.2	Vendeurs	Vendedores
...	...	...	575	1	576	2.1	Agriculteurs, pêcheurs, chasseurs, forestiers et travailleurs assimilés / Mineurs, carriers et travailleurs assimilés	Agricultores, pescadores, cazadores, trabajadores forestales y asimilados / Mineros, canteros y trabajadores asimilados
...	...	...	130	85	215	0.8	Travailleurs des transports et des communications	Trabajadores de los transportes y comunicaciones
...	...	...	7 531	460	7 991	29.3	Artisans, ouvriers de métier, ouvriers à la production et manœuvres non classés ailleurs	Artesanos y trab. ocupados en los div. procesos de producción y peones no clasificados bajo otros epígrafes
...	...	...	2 754	3 776	6 530	23.9	Travailleurs spécialisés dans les services, les sports et les activités récréatives	Trabajadores de los servicios, los deportes y las diversiones
...	...	...	108	94	202	0.7	Personnes ne pouvant être classées selon la profession	Trabajadores que no pueden ser clasificados según la ocupación
...	.	...	9	.	9	—	Membres des forces armées	Miembros de las fuerzas armadas
8	3	11	16 402	10 917	27 319	100.0	Total	Total

Others and status unknown / Autres et situation non définie / Otros y categoría no definida			TOTAL				Groupe de professions	Grupo de ocupaciones
Males / Hommes / Hombres	Females / Femmes / Mujeres	Total	Males / Hommes / Hombres	Females / Femmes / Mujeres	Total	%		
...	...	...	575 545	835 201	1 410 746	4.8	0-1. Personnel des professions scientif., techn., libérales et assimilées	0-1. Profesionales, técnicos y trabajadores asimilados
...	...	...	440 076	57 021	497 097	1.7	2. Directeurs et cadres administratifs supérieurs	2. Directores y funcionarios públicos superiores
...	...	...	1 035 150	526 528	1 561 678	5.3	3. Personnel administratif et travailleurs assimilés	3. Personal administrativo y trabajadores asimilados
...	...	...	1 873 448	320 213	2 193 661	7.4	4. Personnel commercial et vendeurs	4. Comerciantes y vendedores
...	...	...	868 018	2 192 291	3 060 309	10.4	5. Travailleurs des services	5. Trabajadores de los servicios
...	...	...	11 782 384	1 256 765	13 039 149	44.0	6. Agriculteurs, éleveurs, forestiers, pêcheurs et chasseurs	6. Trab. agrícolas y forestales, pescadores y cazadores
...	...	...	5 560 719	702 852	6 263 571	21.2	7-9. Ouvriers et manœuvres non agricoles et conducteurs d'engins de transport	7-9. Obreros no agrícolas, conductores de máquinas y vehículos de transporte y trabajadores asimilados
...	...	...	912 988	274 320	1 187 308	4.0	X. Travailleurs ne pouvant être classés selon la profession	X. Trabajadores que no pueden ser clasificados según la ocupación
...	...	...	343 449	256	343 705	1.2	Membres des forces armées	Miembros de las fuerzas armadas
8 157	1 010	9 167	23 391 777	6 165 447	29 557 224	100.0	Total	Total

181

2 Structure of the economically active population
Structure de la population active
Estructura de la población económicamente activa

Occupational group	Employers and workers on own account Employeurs et personnes travaillant à leur propre compte Empleadores y trabajadores por cuenta propia			Salaried employees and wage earners Employés et ouvriers Empleados y obreros			Family workers Travailleurs familiaux Trabajadores familiares		
	Males Hommes Hombres	Females Femmes Mujeres	Total	Males Hommes Hombres	Females Femmes Mujeres	Total	Males Hommes Hombres	Females Femmes Mujeres	Total

Canada (V.1975) †

Occupational group	Males	Females	Total	Males	Females	Total	Males	Females	Total
0-1. Professional, technical and related workers	73 000	18 000	**91 000**	665 000	659 000	**1 324 000**	...	...	...
2. Administrative and managerial workers	14 000	—	**16 000**	430 000	86 000	**516 000**	...	...	...
3. Clerical and related workers	—	26 000	**28 000**	407 000	1 198 000	**1 605 000**	...	...	...
4. Sales workers	141 000	54 000	**195 000**	550 000	299 000	**849 000**	...	...	...
5. Service workers	58 000	48 000	**106 000**	503 000	536 000	**1 038 000**	...	...	...
6. Agricultural, animal husbandry and forestry workers, fishermen and hunters	357 000	71 000	**428 000**	178 000	18 000	**197 000**	...	...	...
7-9. Production and related workers, transport equipment, operators and labourers	206 000	10 000	**215 000**	2 446 000	323 000	**2 770 000**	...	...	...
Persons seeking work for the first time Unemployed	13 000	—	**14 000**	445 000	189 000	**634 000**	...	...	...
Total . . .	865 000	227 000	**1 092 000**	5 623 000	3 311 000	**8 934 000**	...	...	...

Colombia (15.VII.1964)

Occupational group	Males	Females	Total	Males	Females	Total	Males	Females	Total
Professional, technical and related workers	31 530	6 511	**38 041**	73 711	87 648	**161 359**	318	562	**880**
Administrative, executive and managerial workers	57 512	10 648	**68 160**	55 033	7 756	**62 789**	1 253	1 482	**2 735**
Clerical workers	5 744	871	**6 615**	144 517	82 324	**226 841**	502	457	**959**
Sales workers	132 716	33 555	**166 271**	75 927	34 823	**110 750**	4 917	4 881	**9 798**
Farmers, fishermen, hunters, loggers and related workers	974 535	53 106	**1 027 641**	994 496	27 728	**1 022 224**	343 652	25 354	**369 006**
Miners, quarrymen and related workers	6 966	7 171	**14 137**	21 856	1 025	**22 881**	1 951	3 334	**5 285**
Workers in transport and communication occupations	41 588	337	**41 925**	107 631	1 372	**109 003**	1 040	1	**1 041**
Craftsmen, prod.-process workers and labourers not elsewhere classified	191 643	89 936	**281 579**	497 127	73 651	**570 778**	10 362	14 888	**25 250**
Service, sport and recreation workers	20 639	22 988	**43 627**	122 997	400 351	**523 348**	1 008	3 242	**4 250**
Workers not classifiable by occupation	12 173	2 810	**14 983**	109 664	20 652	**130 316**	975	506	**1 481**
Total . . .	1 475 046	227 933	**1 702 979**	2 202 959	737 330	**2 940 289**	365 978	54 707	**420 685**

† For notes, see pp. 272-294.

B — Distribution by status and by occupational group
Répartition suivant la situation dans la profession et par groupe de professions
Distribución según la categoría de ocupación y por grupo de ocupación

Others and status unknown / Autres et situation non définie / Otros y categoría no definida			TOTAL				Groupe de professions	Grupo de ocupaciones
Males / Hommes / Hombres	Females / Femmes / Mujeres	Total	Males / Hommes / Hombres	Females / Femmes / Mujeres	Total	%		
.	.	.	738 000	677 000	**1 415 000**	14.0	0-1. *Personnel des professions scientif., techn., libérales et assimilées*	0-1. Profesionales, técnicos y trabajadores asimilados
.	.	.	444 000	88 000	**532 000**	5.3	2. *Directeurs et cadres administratifs supérieurs*	2. Directores y funcionarios públicos superiores
.	.	.	410 000	1 224 000	**1 634 000**	16.2	3. *Personnel administratif et travailleurs assimilés*	3. Personal administrativo y trabajadores asimilados
.	.	.	691 000	353 000	**1 044 000**	10.3	4. *Personnel commercial et vendeurs*	4. Comerciantes y vendedores
.	.	.	560 000	584 000	**1 114 000**	11.3	5. *Travailleurs des services*	5. Trabajadores de los servicios
.	.	.	534 000	89 000	**625 000**	6.2	6. *Agriculteurs, éleveurs, forestiers, pêcheurs et chasseurs*	6. Trab. agrícolas y forestales, pescadores y cazadores
.	.	.	2 653 000	332 000	**2 985 000**	29.6	7-9. *Ouvriers et manœuvres non agricoles et conducteurs d'engins de transport*	7-9. Obreros no agrícolas, conductores de máquinas y vehículos de transporte y trabajadores asimilados
42 000	25 000	**67 000**	42 000	25 000	**67 000**	0.7	*Personnes en quête d'emploi pour la première fois*	Personas en busca de trabajo por primera vez
.	.	.	458 000	190 000	**648 000**	6.4	*Chômeurs*	Desempleados
42 000	25 000	**67 000**	6 530 000	3 564 000	**10 094 000**	100.0	*Total*	Total

Males	Females	Total	Males	Females	Total	%	Groupe de professions	Grupo de ocupaciones
615	529	**1 144**	106 174	95 250	**201 424**	3.9	*Personnes exerçant une profession libérale, techniciens et assimilés*	Trabajadores profesionales, técnicos y trabajadores asimilados
677	59	**736**	114 475	19 945	**134 420**	2.6	*Directeurs et cadres administratifs supérieurs*	Administradores, gerentes y directores
1 684	696	**2 380**	152 447	84 348	**236 795**	4.6	*Employés de bureau*	Empleados de oficina
1 597	438	**2 035**	215 157	73 697	**288 854**	5.6	*Vendeurs*	Vendedores
7 612	216	**7 828**	2 320 295	106 404	**2 426 699**	47.4	*Agriculteurs, pêcheurs, chasseurs, forestiers et travailleurs assimilés*	Agricultores, pescadores, cazadores, trabajadores forestales y asimilados
244	65	**309**	31 017	11 595	**42 612**	0.8	*Mineurs, carriers et travailleurs assimilés*	Mineros, canteros y trabajadores asimilados
2 450	165	**2 615**	152 709	1 875	**154 584**	3.0	*Travailleurs des transports et des communications*	Trabajadores de los transportes y comunicaciones
15 135	3 083	**18 218**	714 267	181 558	**895 825**	17.4	*Artisans, ouvriers de métier, ouvriers à la production et manœuvres non classés ailleurs*	Artesanos y trab. ocupados en los div. procesos de producción y peones no clasif. bajo otros epígrafes
1 539	1 716	**3 255**	146 183	428 297	**574 480**	11.2	*Travailleurs spécialisés dans les services, les sports et les activités récréatives*	Trabajadores de los servicios, los deportes y las diversiones
26 527	5 125	**31 652**	149 339	29 093	**178 432**	3.5	*Personnes ne pouvant être classées selon la profession*	Trabajadores que no pueden ser clasificados según la ocupación
58 080	12 092	**70 172**	4 102 063	1 032 062	**5 134 125**	100.0	*Total*	Total

✝ *Voir notes pp. 272-294.*

✝ Véanse las notas en las págs. 272-294.

2 Structure of the economically active population
Structure de la population active
Estructura de la población económicamente activa

Occupational group	Employers and workers on own account *Employeurs et personnes travaillant à leur propre compte* Empleadores y trabajadores por cuenta propia			Salaried employees and wage earners *Employés et ouvriers* Empleados y obreros			Family workers *Travailleurs familiaux* Trabajadores familiares		
	Males *Hommes* Hombres	Females *Femmes* Mujeres	Total	Males *Hommes* Hombres	Females *Femmes* Mujeres	Total	Males *Hommes* Hombres	Females *Femmes* Mujeres	Total

Costa Rica (14.V.1973)

0-1. Professional, technical and related workers	2 647	293	**2 940**	22 245	21 316	**43 561**	49	72	**121**
2. Administrative and managerial workers	2 783	452	**3 235**	5 775	616	**6 391**	11	34	**45**
3. Clerical and related workers	.	.	.	21 485	11 914	**33 399**	35	123	**158**
4. Sales workers	16 453	2 095	**18 548**	18 147	7 056	**25 203**	1 166	604	**1 770**
5. Service workers	758	480	**1 238**	23 115	43 315	**66 430**	195	241	**436**
6. Agricultural, animal husbandry and forestry workers, fishermen and hunters	55 094	202	**55 296**	119 097	2 755	**121 852**	30 251	310	**30 561**
7-9. Production and related workers, transport equipment, operators and labourers	15 724	2 447	**18 171**	107 491	13 985	**121 476**	1 295	87	**1 382**
X. Workers not classifiable by occupation	599	77	**676**	9 748	2 102	**11 850**	115	25	**140**
Persons seeking work for the first time	.	.	.	.	.	.	.	.	.
Total . . .	94 058	6 046	**100 104**	327 103	103 059	**430 162**	33 117	1 496	**34 613**

Cuba (6.IX.1970 *) ‡

0-1. Professional, technical and related workers	...	...	**752**	...	...	**219 082**	...	...	**24**
2. Administrative and managerial workers	...	...	.	...	...	**112 728**	...	...	.
3. Clerical and related workers	...	...	**75**	...	...	**136 036**	...	...	.
4. Sales workers . . . . }									
5. Service workers . . . . }	...	...	**2 646**	...	...	**561 573**	...	...	**32**
6. Agricultural, animal husbandry and forestry workers, fishermen and hunters	...	...	**236 520**	...	...	**437 253**	...	...	**34 254**
7-9. Production and related workers, transport equipment, operators and labourers	...	...	**20 534**	...	...	**835 612**	...	...	**75**
X. Workers not classifiable by occupation	...	...	**96**	...	...	**21 314**	...	...	**10**
Total . . .	...	...	**260 623**	...	...	**2 323 598**	...	...	**34 395**

‡ For notes, see pp. 272-294.

B

Distribution by status and by occupational group
Répartition suivant la situation dans la profession et par groupe de professions
Distribución según la categoría de ocupación y por grupo de ocupación

Others and status unknown / Autres et situation non définie / Otros y categoría no definida			TOTAL				Groupe de professions	Grupo de ocupaciones
Males *Hommes* Hombres	Females *Femmes* Mujeres	Total	Males *Hommes* Hombres	Females *Femmes* Mujeres	Total	%		
.	.	.	24 941	21 681	**46 622**	*8.0*	0-1. *Personnel des professions scientif., techn., libérales et assimilées*	0-1. Profesionales, técnicos y trabajadores asimilados
.	.	.	8 569	1 102	**9 671**	*1.7*	2. *Directeurs et cadres administratifs supérieurs*	2. Directores y funcionarios públicos superiores
.	.	.	21 520	12 037	**33 557**	*5.7*	3. *Personnel administratif et travailleurs assimilés*	3. Personal administrativo y trabajadores asimilados
.	.	.	35 766	9 755	**45 521**	*7.8*	4. *Personnel commercial et vendeurs*	4. Comerciantes y vendedores
.	.	.	24 068	44 036	**68 104**	*11.6*	5. *Travailleurs des services*	5. Trabajadores de los servicios
.	.	.	204 442	3 267	**207 709**	*35.4*	6. *Agriculteurs, éleveurs, forestiers, pêcheurs et chasseurs*	6. Trab. agrícolas y forestales, pescadores y cazadores
.	.	.	124 510	16 519	**141 029**	*24.1*	7-9. *Ouvriers et manœuvres non agricoles et conducteurs d'engins de transport*	7-9. Obreros no agrícolas, conductores de máquinas y vehículos de transporte y trabajadores asimilados
.	.	.	10 462	2 204	**12 666**	*2.2*	X. *Travailleurs ne pouvant être classés selon la profession*	X. Trabajadores que no pueden ser clasificados según la ocupación
18 002	2 432	**20 434**	18 002	2 432	**20 434**	*3.5*	*Personnes en quête d'emploi pour la première fois*	Personas en busca de trabajo por primera vez
18 002	2 432	**20 434**	472 280	113 033	**585 313**	*100.0*	*Total*	Total

Others and status unknown / Autres et situation non définie / Otros y categoría no definida			TOTAL				Groupe de professions	Grupo de ocupaciones
Males *Hommes* Hombres	Females *Femmes* Mujeres	Total	Males *Hommes* Hombres	Females *Femmes* Mujeres	Total	%		
...	...	440	...	...	**220 298**	*8.4*	0-1. *Personnel des professions scientif., techn., libérales et assimilées*	0-1. Profesionales, técnicos y trabajadores asimilados
...	...	17	...	...	**112 745**	*4.3*	2. *Directeurs et cadres administratifs supérieurs*	2. Directores y funcionarios públicos superiores
...	...	74	...	...	**136 185**	*5.2*	3. *Personnel administratif et travailleurs assimilés*	3. Personal administrativo y trabajadores asimilados
...	...	152	...	...	**564 403**	*21.4*	4. *Personnel commercial et vendeurs* / 5. *Travailleurs des services*	4. Comerciantes y vendedores / 5. Trabajadores de los servicios
...	...	138	...	...	**708 165**	*26.9*	6. *Agriculteurs, éleveurs, forestiers, pêcheurs et chasseurs*	6. Trab. agrícolas y forestales, pescadores y cazadores
...	...	868	...	...	**857 089**	*32.5*	7-9. *Ouvriers et manœuvres non agricoles et conducteurs d'engins de transport*	7-9. Obreros no agrícolas, conductores de máquinas y vehículos de transporte y trabajadores asimilados
...	...	13 004	...	...	**34 424**	*1.3*	X. *Travailleurs ne pouvant être classés selon la profession*	X. Trabajadores que no pueden ser clasificados según la ocupación
...	...	**14 693**	2 151 052	482 257	**2 633 309**	*100.0*	*Total*	Total

† *Voir notes pp. 272-294.* † Véanse las notas en las págs. 272-294.

POPULATION

2 Structure of the economically active population
Structure de la population active
Estructura de la población económicamente activa

Occupational group	Employers and workers on own account *Employeurs et personnes travaillant à leur propre compte* Empleadores y trabajadores por cuenta propia			Salaried employees and wage earners *Employés et ouvriers* Empleados y obreros			Family workers *Travailleurs familiaux* Trabajadores familiares		
	Males *Hommes* Hombres	Females *Femmes* Mujeres	Total	Males *Hommes* Hombres	Females *Femmes* Mujeres	Total	Males *Hommes* Hombres	Females *Femmes* Mujeres	Total

Chile (22.IV.1970) †

Occupational group	Males	Females	Total	Males	Females	Total	Males	Females	Total
Professional, technical and related workers	16 600	5 860	**22 460**	72 280	82 600	**154 880**	100	360	**460**
Administrative, executive and managerial workers	26 220	6 080	**32 300**	14 400	2 100	**16 500**	180	160	**340**
Clerical workers	5 620	1 840	**7 460**	161 400	75 220	**236 620**	180	200	**380**
Sales workers	98 300	38 280	**136 580**	48 180	20 340	**68 520**	1 280	1 740	**3 020**
Farmers, fishermen, hunters, loggers and related workers	167 920	6 080	**174 000**	329 080	7 240	**336 320**	29 960	2 040	**32 000**
Workers in transport and communication occupations	28 060	320	**28 380**	70 920	240	**71 160**	460	.	**460**
Miners, quarrymen and related workers Craftsmen, prod.-process workers and labourers not elsewhere classified .	100 180	38 400	**138 580**	540 960	59 300	**600 260**	2 020	660	**2 680**
Service, sport and recreation workers	7 900	19 780	**27 680**	83 640	186 260	**269 900**	120	420	**540**
Workers not classifiable by occupation	12 300	2 480	**14 780**	69 020	4 560	**73 580**	2 380	720	**3 100**
Total . . .	463 100	119 120	**582 220**	1 389 880	437 860	**1 827 740**	36 680	6 300	**42 980**

República Dominicana (9-10.I.1970) †

Occupational group	Males	Females	Total	Males	Females	Total	Males	Females	Total
0-1. Professional, technical and related workers	4 228	1 386	**5 614**	11 359	11 715	**23 074**	66	232	**298**
2. Administrative and managerial workers	1 053	164	**1 217**	1 760	423	**2 183**	37	10	**47**
3. Clerical and related workers	3 586	676	**4 262**	49 421	21 635	**71 056**	187	244	**431**
4. Sales workers	28 975	6 476	**35 451**	13 918	3 091	**17 009**	790	477	**1 267**
5. Service workers	3 585	1 580	**5 165**	18 180	36 124	**54 304**	75	125	**200**
6. Agricultural, animal husbandry and forestry workers, fishermen and hunters	203 399	24 608	**228 007**	142 971	20 747	**163 718**	46 105	8 616	**54 721**
7-9. Production and related workers, transport equipment, operators and labourers	52 177	12 414	**64 591**	97 386	14 885	**112 271**	2 237	2 089	**4 326**
X. Workers not classifiable by occupation	12 643	8 428	**21 071**	20 892	9 224	**30 116**	5 493	5 934	**11 427**
Persons seeking work for the first time	.	.	.	.	.	.	.	.	.
Total . . .	309 646	55 732	**365 378**	355 887	117 844	**473 731**	54 990	17 727	**72 717**

† For notes, see pp. 272-294.

B

Distribution by status and by occupational group
Répartition suivant la situation dans la profession et par groupe de professions
Distribución según la categoría de ocupación y por grupo de ocupación

Others and status unknown *Autres et situation non définie* Otros y categoría no definida			TOTAL				*Groupe de professions*	Grupo de ocupaciones
Males *Hommes* Hombres	Females *Femmes* Mujeres	Total	Males *Hommes* Hombres	Females *Femmes* Mujeres	Total	%		
4 460	2 800	**7 260**	93 440	91 620	**185 060**	*7.1*	*Personnes exerçant une profession libérale, techniciens et assimilés*	Trabajadores profesionales, técnicos y trabajadores asimilados
500	220	**720**	41 300	8 560	**49 860**	*1.9*	*Directeurs et cadres administratifs supérieurs*	Administradores, gerentes y directores
2 780	1 760	**4 540**	169 980	79 020	**249 000**	*9.5*	*Employés de bureau*	Empleados de oficina
3 700	1 860	**5 560**	151 460	62 220	**213 680**	*8.2*	*Vendeurs*	Vendedores
7 220	320	**7 540**	534 180	15 680	**549 860**	*21.1*	*Agriculteurs, pêcheurs, chasseurs, forestiers et travailleurs assimilés*	Agricultores, pescadores, cazadores, trabajadores forestales y asimilados
3 580	20	**3 600**	103 020	580	**103 600**	*4.0*	*Travailleurs des transports et des communications*	Trabajadores de los transportes y comunicaciones
							Mineurs, carriers et travailleurs assimilés	Mineros, canteros y trabajadores asimilados
20 440	5 320	**25 760**	663 600	103 680	**767 280**	*29.5*	*Artisans, ouvriers de métier, ouvriers à la production et manœuvres non classés ailleurs*	Artesanos y trab. ocupados en los div. procesos de producción y peones no clasif. bajo otros epígrafes
2 480	3 140	**5 620**	94 140	209 600	**303 740**	*11.6*	*Travailleurs spécialisés dans les services, les sports et les activités récréatives*	Trabajadores de los servicios, los deportes y las diversiones
71 000	22 820	**93 820**	154 700	30 580	**185 280**	*7.1*	*Personnes ne pouvant être classées selon la profession*	Trabajadores que no pueden ser clasificados según la ocupación
116 160	38 260	**154 420**	2 005 820	601 540	**2 607 360**	*100.0*	*Total*	Total

						%		
2 274	2 800	**5 074**	17 927	16 133	**34 060**	*2.7*	0-1. *Personnel des professions scientif., techn., libérales et assimilées*	0-1. Profesionales, técnicos y trabajadores asimilados
193	157	**350**	3 043	754	**3 797**	*0.3*	2. *Directeurs et cadres administratifs supérieurs*	2. Directores y funcionarios públicos superiores
3 167	2 277	**5 444**	56 361	24 832	**81 193**	*6.5*	3. *Personnel administratif et travailleurs assimilés*	3. Personal administrativo y trabajadores asimilados
5 573	2 405	**7 978**	49 256	12 449	**61 705**	*5.0*	4. *Personnel commercial et vendeurs*	4. Comerciantes y vendedores
1 824	1 678	**3 502**	23 664	39 507	**63 171**	*5.1*	5. *Travailleurs des services*	5. Trabajadores de los servicios
66 163	39 008	**105 171**	458 638	92 979	**551 617**	*44.4*	6. *Agriculteurs, éleveurs, forestiers, pêcheurs et chasseurs*	6. Trab. agrícolas y forestales, pescadores y cazadores
37 691	22 621	**60 312**	189 491	52 009	**241 500**	*19.5*	7-9. *Ouvriers et manœuvres non agricoles et conducteurs d'engins de transport*	7-9. Obreros no agrícolas, conductores de máquinas y vehículos de transporte y trabajadores asimilados
59 248	52 799	**112 047**	98 276	76 385	**174 661**	*14.1*	X. *Travailleurs ne pouvant être classés selon la profession*	X. Trabajadores que no pueden ser clasificados según la ocupación
25 434	3 862	**29 296**	25 434	3 862	**29 296**	*2.4*	*Personnes en quête d'emploi pour la première fois*	Personas en busca de trabajo por primera vez
201 567	127 607	**329 174**	922 090	318 910	**1 241 000**	*100.0*	*Total*	Total

✝ *Voir notes pp. 272-294.*

✝ Véanse las notas en las págs. 272-294.

2 Structure of the economically active population
Structure de la population active
Estructura de la población económicamente activa

Occupational group	Employers and workers on own account *Employeurs et personnes travaillant à leur propre compte* Empleadores y trabajadores por cuenta propia			Salaried employees and wage earners *Employés et ouvriers* Empleados y obreros			Family workers *Travailleurs familiaux* Trabajadores familiares		
	Males *Hommes* Hombres	Females *Femmes* Mujeres	Total	Males *Hommes* Hombres	Females *Femmes* Mujeres	Total	Males *Hommes* Hombres	Females *Femmes* Mujeres	Total
El Salvador (27.VI.1971) †									
0-1. Professional, technical and related workers	...	...	...	...	...	...	...	...	...
2. Administrative and managerial workers	...	...	...	...	...	...	...	...	...
3. Clerical and related workers	...	...	...	...	...	...	...	...	...
4. Sales workers	...	...	...	...	...	...	...	...	...
5. Service workers	...	...	...	...	...	...	...	...	...
6. Agricultural, animal husbandry and forestry workers, fishermen and hunters	...	...	...	...	...	...	...	...	...
7-9. Production and related workers, transport equipment, operators and labourers	...	...	...	...	...	...	...	...	...
X. Workers not classifiable by occupation	...	...	...	...	...	...	...	...	...
Total . . .	...	...	**321 836**	...	...	**637 389**	...	...	**296 700**
Greenland (31.XII.1970 *) †									
0-1. Professional, technical and related workers	...	...	**31**	...	...	**1 775**	...	...	...
2. Administrative and managerial workers	.	.	.	...	...	**33**	...	...	...
3. Clerical and related workers	...	...	**115**	...	...	**1 569**	...	...	...
4. Sales workers	...	...	**100**	...	...	**1 168**	...	...	...
5. Service workers	...	...	**56**	...	...	**2 886**	...	...	...
6. Agricultural, animal husbandry and forestry workers, fishermen and hunters	...	...	**2 396**	...	...	**1 091**	...	...	...
7-9. Production and related workers, transport equipment, operators and labourers	...	...	**370**	...	...	**6 885**	...	...	...
X. Workers not classifiable by occupation	.	.	.	...	...	**251**	...	...	...
Members of the armed forces . . .	.	.	.	...	...	**12**	.	.	.
Total . . .	2 999	69	**3 068**	9 882	5 788	**15 670**	...	...	...

† For notes, see pp. 272-294.

B Distribution by status and by occupational group

Répartition suivant la situation dans la profession et par groupe de professions

Distribución según la categoría de ocupación y por grupo de ocupación

Others and status unknown / *Autres et situation non définie* / Otros y categoría no definida			TOTAL			*Groupe de professions*	Grupo de ocupaciones
Males / *Hommes* / Hombres	Females / *Femmes* / Mujeres	Total	Males / *Hommes* / Hombres	Females / *Femmes* / Mujeres	Total		

						%		
.							0-1. *Personnel des professions scientif., techn., libérales et assimilées*	0-1. Profesionales, técnicos y trabajadores asimilados
...	...	...	...	...	39 287	3.0		
...	...	...	...	...	2 228	0.2	2. *Directeurs et cadres administratifs supérieurs*	2. Directores y funcionarios públicos superiores
...	...	...	...	...	42 182	3.2	3. *Personnel administratif et travailleurs assimilés*	3. Personal administrativo y trabajadores asimilados
...	...	...	...	...	77 249	5.9	4. *Personnel commercial et vendeurs*	4. Comerciantes y vendedores
...	...	...	...	...	93 642	7.1	5. *Travailleurs des services*	5. Trabajadores de los servicios
...	...	...	...	...	610 647	46.4	6. *Agriculteurs, éleveurs, forestiers, pêcheurs et chasseurs*	6. Trab. agrícolas y forestales, pescadores y cazadores
...	...	...	...	...	190 645	14.5	7-9. *Ouvriers et manœuvres non agricoles et conducteurs d'engins de transport*	7-9. Obreros no agrícolas, conductores de máquinas y vehículos de transporte y trabajadores asimilados
...	...	...	...	...	258 977	19.7	X. *Travailleurs ne pouvant être classés selon la profession*	X. Trabajadores que no pueden ser clasificados según la ocupación
...	...	58 932	929 472	385 385	1 314 857	100.0	*Total*	Total

						%		
.	.	.	...	...	1 806	9.6	0-1. *Personnel des professions scientif., techn., libérales et assimilées*	0-1. Profesionales, técnicos y trabajadores asimilados
.	.	.	...	...	33	0.2	2. *Directeurs et cadres administratifs supérieurs*	2. Directores y funcionarios públicos superiores
.	.	.	...	...	1 684	9.0	3. *Personnel administratif et travailleurs assimilés*	3. Personal administrativo y trabajadores asimilados
.	.	.	...	...	1 268	6.8	4. *Personnel commercial et vendeurs*	4. Comerciantes y vendedores
.	.	.	...	...	2 942	15.7	5. *Travailleurs des services*	5. Trabajadores de los servicios
.	.	.	...	...	3 487	18.6	6. *Agriculteurs, éleveurs, forestiers, pêcheurs et chasseurs*	6. Trab. agrícolas y forestales, pescadores y cazadores
.	.	.	...	...	7 255	38.7	7-9. *Ouvriers et manœuvres non agricoles et conducteurs d'engins de transport*	7-9. Obreros no agrícolas, conductores de máquinas y vehículos de transporte y trabajadores asimilados
.	.	.	...	...	251	1.3	X. *Travailleurs ne pouvant être classés selon la profession*	X. Trabajadores que no pueden ser clasificados según la ocupación
.	.	.	...	.	12	0.1	*Membres des forces armées*	Miembros de las fuerzas armadas
.	.	.	12 881	5 857	18 738	100.0	*Total*	Total

✝ *Voir notes pp. 272-294.*　　　　　　　　　　　　　　　✝ Véanse las notas en las págs. 272-294.

POPULATION

2 Structure of the economically active population
Structure de la population active
Estructura de la población económicamente activa

Occupational group	Employers and workers on own account *Employeurs et personnes travaillant à leur propre compte* Empleadores y trabajadores por cuenta propia			Salaried employees and wage earners *Employés et ouvriers* Empleados y obreros			Family workers *Travailleurs familiaux* Trabajadores familiares		
	Males *Hommes* Hombres	Females *Femmes* Mujeres	Total	Males *Hommes* Hombres	Females *Femmes* Mujeres	Total	Males *Hommes* Hombres	Females *Femmes* Mujeres	Total

Guatemala (26.III.1973) ‡

Professional, technical and related workers	5 220	900	**6 120**	24 860	16 820	**41 680**	...	...	...
Administrative, executive and managerial workers	9 800	4 120	**13 920**	9 060	1 040	**10 100**	...	...	...
Clerical workers	500	60	**560**	27 340	13 480	**40 820**	...	...	...
Sales workers	39 920	20 840	**60 760**	14 760	8 560	**23 320**	...	...	...
Farmers, fishermen, hunters, loggers and related workers	403 100	2 080	**405 180**	300 080	8 020	**308 100**	...	...	...
Miners, quarrymen and related workers	1 380	140	**1 520**	1 440	.	**1 440**	...	...	...
Workers in transport and communication occupations	7 000	40	**7 040**	30 620	180	**30 800**	...	...	...
Craftsmen, prod.-process workers and labourers not elsewhere classified	74 620	25 300	**99 920**	150 280	14 000	**164 280**	...	...	...
Service, sport and recreation workers	2 800	4 140	**6 940**	37 040	78 920	**115 960**	...	...	...
Members of the armed forces Workers not classifiable by occupation Persons seeking work for the first time	2 120	500	**2 620**	4 660	860	**5 520**	...	...	...
Total . . .	546 460	58 120	**604 580**	600 140	141 880	**742 020**	...	...	...

Martinique (16.X.1967) ‡

Professional, technical and related workers	348	94	**442**	2 714	4 051	**6 765**	6	1	**7**
Administrative, executive and managerial workers	235	8	**243**	918	478	**1 396**	3	1	**4**
Clerical workers	10	5	**15**	2 305	3 535	**5 840**	2	24	**26**
Sales workers	1 219	2 471	**3 690**	1 081	2 145	**3 226**	60	361	**421**
Farmers, fishermen, hunters, loggers and related workers	6 092	763	**6 855**	11 281	6 523	**17 804**	259	219	**478**
Miners, quarrymen and related workers	6	.	**6**	472	23	**495**	.	.	**.**
Workers in transport and communication occupations	1 179	6	**1 185**	2 301	11	**2 312**	25	2	**27**
Craftsmen, prod.-process workers and labourers not elsewhere classified	3 018	965	**3 983**	15 904	1 576	**17 480**	68	39	**107**
Service, sport and recreation workers	182	206	**388**	1 862	9 635	**11 497**	1	5	**6**
Workers not classifiable by occupation	14	6	**20**	382	140	**522**	.	1	**1**
Members of the armed forces	.	.	**.**	3 556	.	**3 556**	.	.	**.**
Total . . .	12 303	4 524	**16 827**	42 776	28 117	**70 893**	424	653	**1 077**

‡ For notes, see pp. 272-294.

B Distribution by status and by occupational group
Répartition suivant la situation dans la profession et par groupe de professions
Distribución según la categoría de ocupación y por grupo de ocupación

Others and status unknown / Autres et situation non définie / Otros y categoría no definida			TOTAL			Groupe de professions	Grupo de ocupaciones
Males / Hommes / Hombres	Females / Femmes / Mujeres	Total	Males / Hommes / Hombres	Females / Femmes / Mujeres	Total		
						%		
640	80	720	30 720	17 800	48 520	3.1	Personnes exerçant une profession libérale, techniciens et assimilés	Trabajadores profesionales, técnicos y trabajadores asimilados
200	120	320	19 060	5 280	24 340	1.6	Directeurs et cadres administratifs supérieurs	Administradores, gerentes y directores
300	100	400	28 140	13 640	41 780	2.7	Employés de bureau	Empleados de oficina
3 140	1 840	4 980	57 820	31 240	89 060	5.8	Vendeurs	Vendedores
158 200	2 820	161 020	861 380	12 920	874 300	56.5	Agriculteurs, pêcheurs, chasseurs, forestiers et travailleurs assimilés	Agricultores, pescadores, cazadores, trabajadores forestales y asimilados
120	20	140	2 940	160	3 100	0.2	Mineurs, carriers et travailleurs assimilés	Mineros, canteros y trabajadores asimilados
660	20	680	38 280	240	38 520	2.5	Travailleurs des transports et des communications	Trabajadores de los transportes y comunicaciones
11 720	4 360	16 080	236 620	43 660	280 280	18.1	Artisans, ouvriers de métier, ouvriers à la production et manœuvres non classés ailleurs	Artesanos y trab. ocupados en los div. procesos de producción y peones no clasif. bajo otros epígrafes
440	940	1 380	40 280	84 000	124 280	8.0	Travailleurs spécialisés dans les services, les sports et les activités récréatives	Trabajadores de los servicios, los deportes y las diversiones
							Membres des forces armées	Miembros de las fuerzas armadas
							Personnes ne pouvant être classées selon la profession	Trabajadores que no pueden ser clasificados según la ocupación
12 600	2 420	15 020	19 380	3 780	23 160	1.5	Personnes en quête d'emploi pour la première fois	Personas en busca de trabajo por primera vez
188 020	12 720	200 740	1 334 620	212 720	1 547 340	100.0	Total	Total

Others and status unknown / Autres et situation non définie / Otros y categoría no definida			TOTAL			Groupe de professions	Grupo de ocupaciones
Males / Hommes / Hombres	Females / Femmes / Mujeres	Total	Males / Hommes / Hombres	Females / Femmes / Mujeres	Total		
						%		
14	55	69	3 082	4 201	7 283	8.1	Personnes exerçant une profession libérale, techniciens et assimilés	Trabajadores profesionales, técnicos y trabajadores asimilados
3	2	5	1 159	489	1 648	1.8	Directeurs et cadres administratifs supérieurs	Administradores, gerentes y directores
1	.	1	2 318	3 564	5 882	6.6	Employés de bureau	Empleados de oficina
4	6	10	2 364	4 983	7 347	8.2	Vendeurs	Vendedores
5	.	5	17 637	7 505	25 142	28.2	Agriculteurs, pêcheurs, chasseurs, forestiers et travailleurs assimilés	Agricultores, pescadores, cazadores, trabajadores forestales y asimilados
.	.	.	478	23	501	0.6	Mineurs, carriers et travailleurs assimilés	Mineros, canteros y trabajadores asimilados
8	.	8	3 513	19	3 532	3.9	Travailleurs des transports et des communications	Trabajadores de los transportes y comunicaciones
20	9	29	19 010	2 589	21 599	24.1	Artisans, ouvriers de métier, ouvriers à la production et manœuvres non classés ailleurs	Artesanos y trab. ocupados en los div. procesos de producción y peones no clasif. bajo otros epígrafes
152	160	312	2 197	10 006	12 203	13.6	Travailleurs spécialisés dans les services, les sports et les activités récréatives	Trabajadores de los servicios, los deportes y las diversiones
154	74	228	550	221	771	0.9	Personnes ne pouvant être classées selon la profession	Trabajadores que no pueden ser clasificados según la ocupación
.	.	.	3 556	.	3 556	4.0	Membres des forces armées	Miembros de las fuerzas armadas
361	306	667	55 864	33 600	89 464	100.0	Total	Total

☦ *Voir notes pp. 272-294.*

☦ Véanse las notas en las págs. 272-294.

2 Structure of the economically active population
Structure de la population active
Estructura de la población económicamente activa

Occupational group	Employers and workers on own account *Employeurs et personnes travaillant à leur propre compte* Empleadores y trabajadores por cuenta propia			Salaried employees and wage earners *Employés et ouvriers* Empleados y obreros			Family workers *Travailleurs familiaux* Trabajadores familiares		
	Males *Hommes* Hombres	Females *Femmes* Mujeres	Total	Males *Hommes* Hombres	Females *Femmes* Mujeres	Total	Males *Hommes* Hombres	Females *Femmes* Mujeres	Total

México

(28.I.1970) ✝									
Professional, technical and related workers	140 529	39 723	**180 252**	330 134	201 393	**531 527**	14 605	6 825	**21 430**
Administrative, executive and managerial workers	128 089	25 378	**153 467**	139 688	26 673	**166 361**	.	.	.
Clerical workers	66 001	38 408	**104 409**	503 061	350 750	**853 811**	10 285	8 674	**18 959**
Sales workers	393 747	126 475	**520 222**	247 498	107 515	**355 013**	57 013	35 019	**92 032**
Farmers, fishermen, hunters, loggers and related workers	1 925 262	84 082	**2 009 344**	2 347 287	113 024	**2 460 311**	452 254	30 291	**482 545**
Miners, quarrymen and related workers }	430 887	97 342	**528 229**	1 919 688	234 660	**2 154 348**	65 126	21 077	**86 203**
Craftsmen, prod.-process workers and labourers not elsewhere classified . } Workers in transport and communication occupations . . . . }	183 476	156 991	**340 467**	671 861	499 278	**1 171 139**	20 836	28 172	**49 008**
Service, sport and recreation workers }									
Workers not classifiable by occupation	139 571	78 107	**217 678**	252 110	110 202	**362 312**	49 792	46 198	**95 990**
Total . . .	3 407 562	646 506	**4 054 068**	6 411 327	1 643 495	**8 054 822**	669 911	176 256	**846 167**
(VI.1975) ✝									
0-1. Professional, technical and related workers	183 526	63 854	**247 380**	433 954	314 933	**748 887**	19 524	13 429	**32 953**
2. Administrative and managerial workers	166 475	40 289	**206 764**	183 656	41 721	**225 377**	.	.	.
3. Clerical and related workers	85 776	59 699	**145 475**	621 314	548 501	**1 169 815**	13 797	17 083	**30 880**
4. Sales workers	515 435	212 116	**727 551**	320 270	168 139	**488 409**	66 404	68 903	**135 307**
5. Service workers	229 756	262 683	**492 439**	835 144	778 345	**1 613 489**	22 984	55 473	**78 457**
6. Agricultural, animal husbandry and forestry workers, fishermen and hunters	2 484 347	136 087	**2 620 434**	3 054 921	168 783	**3 223 704**	621 287	59 592	**680 879**
7-9. Production and related workers, transport equipment, operators and labourers	563 332	164 056	**727 388**	2 507 019	366 074	**2 873 093**	87 208	41 471	**128 679**
Total . . .	4 228 647	938 784	**5 167 431**	7 956 278	2 386 496	**10 342 774**	831 204	255 951	**1 087 155**

✝ For notes, see pp. 272-294.

B **Distribution by status and by occupational group**
Répartition suivant la situation dans la profession et par groupe de professions
Distribución según la categoría de ocupación y por grupo de ocupación

Others and status unknown / *Autres et situation non définie* / Otros y categoría no definida			TOTAL			*Groupe de professions*	Grupo de ocupaciones
Males / *Hommes* / Hombres	Females / *Femmes* / Mujeres	Total	Males / *Hommes* / Hombres	Females / *Femmes* / Mujeres	Total		
					%		
.	.	.	485 268	247 941	**733 209**	5.7	*Personnes exerçant une profession libérale, techniciens et assimilés*	Trabajadores profesionales, técnicos y trabajadores asimilados
.	.	.	267 777	52 051	**319 828**	2.5	*Directeurs et cadres administratifs supérieurs*	Administradores, gerentes y directores
.	.	.	579 347	397 832	**977 179**	7.5	*Employés de bureau*	Empleados de oficina
.	.	.	698 258	269 009	**967 267**	7.5	*Vendeurs*	Vendedores
.	.	.	4 724 803	227 397	**4 952 200**	38.2	*Agriculteurs, pêcheurs, chasseurs, forestiers et travailleurs assimilés*	Agricultores, pescadores, cazadores, trabajadores forestales y asimilados
.	.	.	2 415 701	353 079	**2 768 780**	21.4	*Mineurs, carriers et travailleurs assimilés* / *Artisans, ouvriers de métier, ouvriers à la production et manœuvres non classés ailleurs* / *Travailleurs des transports et des communications*	Mineros, canteros y trabajadores asimilados / Artesanos y trab. ocupados en los div. procesos de producción y peones no clasif. bajo otros epígrafes / Trabajadores de los transportes y comunicaciones
.	.	.	876 173	684 441	**1 560 614**	12.0	*Travailleurs spécialisés dans les services, les sports et les activités récréatives*	Trabajadores de los servicios, los deportes y las diversiones
.	.	.	441 473	234 507	**675 980**	5.2	*Personnes ne pouvant être classées selon la profession*	Trabajadores que no pueden ser clasificados según la ocupación
.	.	.	10 488 800	2 466 257	**12 955 057**	100.0	*Total*	Total
.	.	.	637 004	392 216	**1 029 220**	6.2	0-1. *Personnel des professions scientif., techn., libérales et assimilées*	0-1. Profesionales, técnicos y trabajadores asimilados
.	.	.	350 131	82 010	**432 141**	2.6	2. *Directeurs et cadres administratifs supérieurs*	2. Directores y funcionarios públicos superiores
.	.	.	720 887	625 283	**1 346 170**	8.1	3. *Personnel administratif et travailleurs assimilés*	3. Personal administrativo y trabajadores asimilados
.	.	.	902 109	449 158	**1 351 267**	8.1	4. *Personnel commercial et vendeurs*	4. Comerciantes y vendedores
.	.	.	1 087 884	1 096 501	**2 184 385**	13.2	5. *Travailleurs des services*	5. Trabajadores de los servicios
.	.	.	6 160 555	364 462	**6 525 017**	39.3	6. *Agriculteurs, éleveurs, forestiers, pêcheurs et chasseurs*	6. Trab. agrícolas y forestales, pescadores y cazadores
.	.	.	3 157 559	571 601	**3 729 160**	22.5	7-9. *Ouvriers et manœuvres non agricoles et conducteurs d'engins de transport*	7-9. Obreros no agrícolas, conductores de máquinas y vehículos de transporte y trabajadores asimilados
.	.	.	13 016 129	3 581 231	**16 597 360**	100.0	*Total*	Total

‡ *Voir notes pp. 272-294.*

‡ Véanse las notas en las págs. 272-294.

2 Structure of the economically active population
Structure de la population active
Estructura de la población económicamente activa

Occupational group	Employers and workers on own account *Employeurs et personnes travaillant à leur propre compte* Empleadores y trabajadores por cuenta propia			Salaried employees and wage earners *Employés et ouvriers* Empleados y obreros			Family workers *Travailleurs familiaux* Trabajadores familiares		
	Males *Hommes* Hombres	Females *Femmes* Mujeres	Total	Males *Hommes* Hombres	Females *Femmes* Mujeres	Total	Males *Hommes* Hombres	Females *Femmes* Mujeres	Total

Nicaragua (20.IV.1971 *) ‡

0-1. Professional, technical and related workers	2 530	640	**3 170**	11 820	10 010	**21 830**	20	60	**80**
2. Administrative and managerial workers	730	180	**910**	3 240	370	**3 610**	—	—	**—**
3. Clerical and related workers	290	190	**480**	12 520	7 260	**19 780**	70	30	**100**
4. Sales workers	10 980	12 660	**23 640**	6 050	4 260	**10 310**	320	420	**740**
5. Service workers	1 880	2 540	**4 420**	9 770	37 270	**47 040**	90	1 170	**1 260**
6. Agricultural, animal husbandry and forestry workers, fishermen and hunters	84 700	1 490	**86 190**	97 580	3 600	**101 180**	37 340	1 490	**38 830**
7-9. Production and related workers, transport equipment, operators and labourers	21 130	9 600	**30 730**	67 020	6 690	**73 710**	1 380	440	**1 820**
X. Workers not classifiable by occupation	940	420	**1 360**	2 660	540	**3 200**	630	420	**1 050**
Total . . .	123 180	27 720	**150 900**	210 660	70 000	**280 660**	39 850	4 030	**43 880**

Panamá (10.V.1970) ‡

0-1. Professional, technical and related workers	1 821	473	**2 294**	14 388	16 389	**30 777**	6	10	**16**
2. Administrative and managerial workers	1 146	218	**1 364**	7 884	1 060	**8 944**	9	11	**20**
3. Clerical and related workers	62	42	**104**	13 135	20 662	**33 797**	15	81	**96**
4. Sales workers	9 640	3 192	**12 832**	12 477	6 252	**18 729**	540	704	**1 244**
5. Service workers	2 101	5 998	**8 099**	22 630	39 687	**62 317**	78	152	**230**
6. Agricultural, animal husbandry and forestry workers, fishermen and hunters	125 109	2 497	**127 606**	32 418	469	**32 887**	16 182	4 981	**21 163**
7-9. Production and related workers, transport equipment, operators and labourers	18 767	5 437	**24 204**	73 081	6 020	**79 101**	365	246	**611**
X. Workers not classifiable by occupation	345	118	**463**	1 374	713	**2 087**	58	31	**89**
Members of the armed forces . . .	.	.	.	1 121	10	**1 131**	.	.	.
Persons seeking work for the first time	.	.	.	.	.	.	.	.	.
Total . . .	158 991	17 975	**176 966**	178 508	91 262	**269 770**	17 253	6 216	**23 469**

‡ For notes, see pp. 272-294.

B Distribution by status and by occupational group
Répartition suivant la situation dans la profession et par groupe de professions
Distribución según la categoría de ocupación y por grupo de ocupación

Others and status unknown / Autres et situation non définie / Otros y categoría no definida			TOTAL				Groupe de professions	Grupo de ocupaciones
Males / Hommes / Hombres	Females / Femmes / Mujeres	Total	Males / Hommes / Hombres	Females / Femmes / Mujeres	Total	%		
500	460	960	14 870	11 170	26 040	5.2	0-1. Personnel des professions scientif., techn., libérales et assimilées	0-1. Profesionales, técnicos y trabajadores asimilados
190	40	230	4 160	590	4 750	0.9	2. Directeurs et cadres administratifs supérieurs	2. Directores y funcionarios públicos superiores
450	270	720	13 330	7 750	21 080	4.2	3. Personnel administratif et travailleurs assimilés	3. Personal administrativo y trabajadores asimilados
570	580	1 150	17 920	17 920	35 840	7.1	4. Personnel commercial et vendeurs	4. Comerciantes y vendedores
340	2 070	2 410	12 080	43 050	55 130	10.9	5. Travailleurs des services	5. Trabajadores de los servicios
8 460	460	8 920	228 080	7 040	235 120	46.7	6. Agriculteurs, éleveurs, forestiers, pêcheurs et chasseurs	6. Trab. agrícolas y forestales, pescadores y cazadores
3 600	640	4 240	93 130	17 370	110 500	21.9	7-9. Ouvriers et manœuvres non agricoles et conducteurs d'engins de transport	7-9. Obreros no agrícolas, conductores de máquinas y vehículos de transporte y trabajadores asimilados
6 500	3 670	10 170	10 730	5 050	15 780	3.1	X. Travailleurs ne pouvant être classés selon la profession	X. Trabajadores que no pueden ser clasificados según la ocupación
20 610	8 190	28 800	394 300	109 940	504 240	100.0	Total	Total

Males / Hommes / Hombres	Females / Femmes / Mujeres	Total	Males / Hommes / Hombres	Females / Femmes / Mujeres	Total	%	Groupe de professions	Grupo de ocupaciones
29	13	42	16 244	16 885	33 129	6.8	0-1. Personnel des professions scientif., techn., libérales et assimilées	0-1. Profesionales, técnicos y trabajadores asimilados
2	.	2	9 041	1 289	10 330	2.1	2. Directeurs et cadres administratifs supérieurs	2. Directores y funcionarios públicos superiores
18	27	45	13 230	20 812	34 042	7.0	3. Personnel administratif et travailleurs assimilés	3. Personal administrativo y trabajadores asimilados
13	10	23	22 670	10 158	32 828	6.7	4. Personnel commercial et vendeurs	4. Comerciantes y vendedores
17	48	65	24 826	45 885	70 711	14.5	5. Travailleurs des services	5. Trabajadores de los servicios
51	2	53	173 760	7 949	181 709	37.2	6. Agriculteurs, éleveurs, forestiers, pêcheurs et chasseurs	6. Trab. agrícolas y forestales, pescadores y cazadores
82	13	95	92 295	11 716	104 011	21.3	7-9. Ouvriers et manœuvres non agricoles et conducteurs d'engins de transport	7-9. Obreros no agrícolas, conductores de máquinas y vehículos de transporte y trabajadores asimilados
358	362	720	2 135	1 224	3 359	0.7	X. Travailleurs ne pouvant être classés selon la profession	X. Trabajadores que no pueden ser clasificados según la ocupación
.	.	.	1 121	10	1 131	0.2	Membres des forces armées	Miembros de las fuerzas armadas
8 010	9 075	17 085	8 010	9 075	17 085	3.5	Personnes en quête d'emploi pour la première fois	Personas en busca de trabajo por primera vez
8 580	9 550	18 130	363 332	125 003	488 335	100.0	Total	Total

☨ Voir notes pp. 272-294.   ☨ Véanse las notas en las págs. 272-294.

2 Structure of the economically active population
Structure de la population active
Estructura de la población económicamente activa

Occupational group	Employers and workers on own account *Employeurs et personnes travaillant à leur propre compte* Empleadores y trabajadores por cuenta propia			Salaried employees and wage earners *Employés et ouvriers* Empleados y obreros			Family workers *Travailleurs familiaux* Trabajadores familiares		
	Males *Hommes* Hombres	Females *Femmes* Mujeres	Total	Males *Hommes* Hombres	Females *Femmes* Mujeres	Total	Males *Hommes* Hombres	Females *Femmes* Mujeres	Total

Paraguay (9.VII.1972) ‡

0-1. Professional, technical and related workers	...	...	...	...	...	...	...	...	...
2. Administrative and managerial workers	...	...	...	...	...	...	...	...	...
3. Clerical and related workers	...	...	...	...	...	...	...	...	...
4. Sales workers	...	...	...	...	...	...	...	...	...
5. Service workers	...	...	...	...	...	...	...	...	...
6. Agricultural, animal husbandry and forestry workers, fishermen and hunters	...	...	...	...	...	...	...	...	...
7-9. Production and related workers, transport equipment, operators and labourers	...	...	...	...	...	...	...	...	...
X. Workers not classifiable by occupation	...	...	...	...	...	...	...	...	...
Unemployed	...	...	...	...	...	...	...	...	...
Total . . .	273 310	61 270	**334 580**	214 690	80 710	**295 400**	74 590	13 650	**88 240**

Perú (4.VI.1972) ‡

0-1. Professional, technical and related workers	24 473	4 389	**28 862**	141 368	89 914	**231 282**	384	190	**574**
2. Administrative and managerial workers	1 712	103	**1 816**	13 298	752	**14 050**	31	7	**38**
3. Clerical and related workers	2 633	1 149	**3 782**	138 698	76 811	**215 509**	275	262	**537**
4. Sales workers	145 143	73 444	**218 587**	71 878	18 519	**90 392**	4 489	4 430	**8 919**
5. Service workers	13 104	24 264	**37 368**	121 314	150 875	**272 189**	758	1 242	**2 000**
6. Agricultural, animal husbandry and forestry workers, fishermen and hunters	954 819	60 841	**1 015 660**	318 734	25 309	**344 043**	114 737	44 420	**159 157**
7-9. Production and related workers, transport equipment, operators and labourers	214 137	75 728	**289 865**	524 703	33 180	**557 883**	5 935	7 401	**13 336**
X. Workers not classifiable by occupation	432	87	**519**	82 150	17 934	**100 084**	4 122	2 660	**6 782**
Persons seeking work for the first time	.	.	.	.	.	.	.	.	.
Total . . .	1 356 453	240 006	**1 596 459**	1 412 138	413 294	**1 825 432**	130 731	60 612	**191 343**

‡ For notes, see pp. 272-294.

B **Distribution by status and by occupational group**
Répartition suivant la situation dans la profession et par groupe de professions
Distribución según la categoría de ocupación y por grupo de ocupación

Others and status unknown / Autres et situation non définie / Otros y categoría no definida			TOTAL				Groupe de professions	Grupo de ocupaciones
Males / Hommes / Hombres	Females / Femmes / Mujeres	Total	Males / Hommes / Hombres	Females / Femmes / Mujeres	Total	%		
...	...	...	14 170	17 200	**31 370**	4.2	0-1. *Personnel des professions scientif., techn., libérales et assimilées*	0-1. Profesionales, técnicos y trabajadores asimilados
...	...	...	3 940	700	**4 640**	0.6	2. *Directeurs et cadres administratifs supérieurs*	2. Directores y funcionarios públicos superiores
...	...	...	20 090	7 330	**27 420**	3.6	3. *Personnel administratif et travailleurs assimilés*	3. Personal administrativo y trabajadores asimilados
...	...	...	29 430	20 760	**50 190**	6.6	4. *Personnel commercial et vendeurs*	4. Comerciantes y vendedores
...	...	...	28 130	43 990	**72 120**	9.6	5. *Travailleurs des services*	5. Trabajadores de los servicios
...	...	...	346 770	20 800	**367 570**	48.7	6. *Agriculteurs, éleveurs, forestiers, pêcheurs et chasseurs*	6. Trab. agrícolas y forestales, pescadores y cazadores
...	...	...	116 990	44 320	**161 310**	21.4	7-9. *Ouvriers et manœuvres non agricoles et conducteurs d'engins de transport*	7-9. Obreros no agrícolas, conductores de máquinas y vehículos de transporte y trabajadores asimilados
...	...	...	11 540	2 160	**13 700**	1.8	X. *Travailleurs ne pouvant être classés selon la profession*	X. Trabajadores que no pueden ser clasificados según la ocupación
...	...	...	22 230	4 160	**26 390**	3.5	*Chômeurs*	Desempleados
30 700	5 790	**36 490**	593 290	161 420	**754 710**	100.0	*Total*	Total

Others and status unknown / Autres et situation non définie / Otros y categoría no definida			TOTAL				Groupe de professions	Grupo de ocupaciones
Males / Hommes / Hombres	Females / Femmes / Mujeres	Total	Males / Hommes / Hombres	Females / Femmes / Mujeres	Total	%		
25 338	1 043	**26 381**	191 563	95 536	**287 099**	7.6	0-1. *Personnel des professions scientif., techn., libérales et assimilées*	0-1. Profesionales, técnicos y trabajadores asimilados
151	.	**151**	15 192	863	**16 055**	0.4	2. *Directeurs et cadres administratifs supérieurs*	2. Directores y funcionarios públicos superiores
1 294	1 057	**2 351**	142 900	79 279	**222 179**	5.9	3. *Personnel administratif et travailleurs assimilés*	3. Personal administrativo y trabajadores asimilados
1 690	897	**2 587**	223 195	97 290	**320 485**	8.5	4. *Personnel commercial et vendeurs*	4. Comerciantes y vendedores
1 551	1 998	**3 549**	136 727	178 379	**315 106**	8.3	5. *Travailleurs des services*	5. Trabajadores de los servicios
4 435	949	**5 384**	1 392 725	131 519	**1 524 244**	40.2	6. *Agriculteurs, éleveurs, forestiers, pêcheurs et chasseurs*	6. Trab. agrícolas y forestales, pescadores y cazadores
9 851	2 421	**12 272**	754 626	118 730	**873 356**	23.1	7-9. *Ouvriers et manœuvres non agricoles et conducteurs d'engins de transport*	7-9. Obreros no agrícolas, conductores de máquinas y vehículos de transporte y trabajadores asimilados
35 605	16 081	**51 686**	122 309	36 762	**159 071**	4.2	X. *Travailleurs ne pouvant être classés selon la profession*	X. Trabajadores que no pueden ser clasificados según la ocupación
43 772	24 793	**68 565**	43 772	24 793	**68 565**	1.8	*Personnes en quête d'emploi pour la première fois*	Personas en busca de trabajo por primera vez
123 687	49 239	**172 926**	3 023 009	763 151	**3 786 160**	100.0	*Total*	Total

† *Voir notes pp. 272-294.*

† Véanse las notas en las págs. 272-294.

POPULATION

2 Structure of the economically active population
Structure de la population active
Estructura de la población económicamente activa

Occupational group	Employers and workers on own account Employeurs et personnes travaillant à leur propre compte Empleadores y trabajadores por cuenta propia			Salaried employees and wage earners Employés et ouvriers Empleados y obreros			Family workers Travailleurs familiaux Trabajadores familiares		
	Males Hommes Hombres	Females Femmes Mujeres	Total	Males Hommes Hombres	Females Femmes Mujeres	Total	Males Hommes Hombres	Females Femmes Mujeres	Total

Puerto Rico (III.1975) ‡

Occupational group	Males	Females	Total	Males	Females	Total	Males	Females	Total
0-1. Professional, technical and related workers	5 200	1 200	**6 400**	36 500	46 400	**82 800**	—	—	—
2. Administrative and managerial workers ⎫	30 500	5 200	**35 700**	70 900	67 300	**138 200**	—	—	—
3. Clerical and related workers ⎬									
4. Sales workers	10 700	3 000	**13 700**	29 200	10 700	**39 900**	—	3 300	**4 200**
5. Service workers	3 100	4 000	**7 000**	57 500	49 200	**106 700**	—	1 400	**1 500**
6. Agricultural, animal husbandry and forestry workers, fishermen and hunters	19 900	—	**20 300**	40 700	1 100	**41 800**	1 000	—	**1 200**
7-9. Production and related workers, transport equipment, operators and labourers	28 700	1 200	**29 900**	257 900	68 700	**326 700**	—	—	—
X. Workers not classifiable by occupation ⎫	...	...	...	...	...	...	...	...	...
Persons seeking work for the first time ⎭									
Total . . .	98 100	15 000	**113 100**	492 800	243 300	**736 100**	2 900	5 500	**8 400**

Surinam (31.III.1964) ‡

Occupational group	Males	Females	Total	Males	Females	Total	Males	Females	Total
Professional, technical and related workers	...	...	...	...	...	...	...	...	...
Administrative, executive and managerial workers	...	...	...	...	...	...	...	...	...
Clerical workers	...	...	...	...	...	...	...	...	...
Sales workers	...	...	...	...	...	...	...	...	...
Farmers, fishermen, hunters, loggers and related workers	...	...	...	...	...	...	...	...	...
Miners, quarrymen and related workers	...	...	...	...	...	...	...	...	...
Workers in transport and communication occupations	...	...	...	...	...	...	...	...	...
Craftsmen, prod.-process workers and labourers not elsewhere classified	...	...	...	...	...	...	...	...	...
Service, sport and recreation workers	...	...	...	...	...	...	...	...	...
Workers not classifiable by occupation	...	...	...	...	...	...	...	...	...
Total . . .	15 416	2 712	**18 128**	37 527	10 730	**48 257**	2 320	3 447	**5 767**

‡ For notes, see pp. 272-294.

B Distribution by status and by occupational group
Répartition suivant la situation dans la profession et par groupe de professions
Distribución según la categoría de ocupación y por grupo de ocupación

Others and status unknown / Autres et situation non définie / Otros y categoría no definida			TOTAL				Groupe de professions	Grupo de ocupaciones
Males / Hommes / Hombres	Females / Femmes / Mujeres	Total	Males / Hommes / Hombres	Females / Femmes / Mujeres	Total	%		
						%	0-1. *Personnel des professions scientif., techn., libérales et assimilées*	0-1. Profesionales, técnicos y trabajadores asimilados
...	...	...	41 700	47 600	**89 300**	10.3		
...	...	...	101 600	73 200	**174 800**	20.1	2. *Directeurs et cadres administratifs supérieurs*	2. Directores y funcionarios públicos superiores
							3. *Personnel administratif et travailleurs assimilés*	3. Personal administrativo y trabajadores asimilados
...	...	...	40 900	16 900	**57 800**	6.6	4. *Personnel commercial et vendeurs*	4. Comerciantes y vendedores
...	...	...	60 700	54 400	**115 200**	13.2	5. *Travailleurs des services*	5. Trabajadores de los servicios
...	...	...	61 600	1 700	**63 300**	7.3	6. *Agriculteurs, éleveurs, forestiers, pêcheurs et chasseurs*	6. Trab. agrícolas y forestales, pescadores y cazadores
							7-9. *Ouvriers et manœuvres non agricoles et conducteurs d'engins de transport*	7-9. Obreros no agrícolas, conductores de máquinas y vehículos de transporte y trabajadores asimilados
...	...	...	287 300	70 000	**357 300**	41.1		
5 100	7 000	**12 000**	5 100	7 000	**12 000**	1.4	X. *Travailleurs ne pouvant être classés selon la profession* *Personnes en quête d'emploi pour la première fois*	X. Trabajadores que no pueden ser clasificados según la ocupación / Personas en busca de trabajo por primera vez
5 100	7 000	**12 000**	598 900	270 800	**869 700**	100.0	*Total*	Total

						%		
...	...	...	2 783	3 147	**5 930**	7.4	*Personnes exerçant une profession libérale, techniciens et assimilés*	Trabajadores profesionales, técnicos y trabajadores asimilados
...	...	...	2 540	142	**2 682**	3.3	*Directeurs et cadres administratifs supérieurs*	Administradores, gerentes y directores
...	...	...	3 834	2 161	**5 995**	7.5	*Employés de bureau*	Empleados de oficina
...	...	...	3 687	1 830	**5 517**	6.9	*Vendeurs*	Vendedores
...	...	...	13 999	4 406	**18 405**	22.9	*Agriculteurs, pêcheurs, chasseurs, forestiers et travailleurs assimilés*	Agricultores, pescadores, cazadores, trabajadores forestales y asimilados
...	...	...	286	.	**286**	0.4	*Mineurs, carriers et travailleurs assimilés*	Mineros, canteros y trabajadores asimilados
...	...	...	5 457	136	**5 593**	7.0	*Travailleurs des transports et des communications*	Trabajadores de los transportes y comunicaciones
...	...	...	21 172	1 217	**22 389**	27.9	*Artisans, ouvriers de métier, ouvriers à la production et manœuvres non classés ailleurs*	Artesanos y trab. ocupados en los div. procesos de producción y peones no clasif. bajo otros epígrafes
...	...	...	2 737	4 466	**7 203**	9.0	*Travailleurs spécialisés dans les services, les sports et les activités récréatives*	Trabajadores de los servicios, los deportes y las diversiones
...	...	...	4 701	1 498	**6 199**	7.7	*Personnes ne pouvant être classées selon la profession*	Trabajadores que no pueden ser clasificados según la ocupación
5 933	2 114	**8 047**	61 196	19 003	**80 199**	100.0	*Total*	Total

☨ *Voir notes pp. 272-294.*

☨ Véanse las notas en las págs. 272-294.

POPULATION

2

Structure of the economically active population
Structure de la population active
Estructura de la población económicamente activa

Occupational group	Employers and workers on own account *Employeurs et personnes travaillant à leur propre compte* Empleadores y trabajadores por cuenta propia			Salaried employees and wage earners *Employés et ouvriers* Empleados y obreros			Family workers *Travailleurs familiaux* Trabajadores familiares		
	Males *Hommes* Hombres	Females *Femmes* Mujeres	Total	Males *Hommes* Hombres	Females *Femmes* Mujeres	Total	Males *Hommes* Hombres	Females *Femmes* Mujeres	Total

Trinidad and Tobago (1973) ǂ

Occupational group	Males	Females	Total	Males	Females	Total	Males	Females	Total
Professional, technical and related workers	...	...	...	...	...	...	...	...	...
Administrative, executive and managerial workers	...	...	...	...	...	...	...	...	...
Clerical workers									
Sales workers	...	...	...	...	...	...	...	...	...
Farmers, fishermen, hunters, loggers and related workers	...	...	...	...	...	...	...	...	...
Miners, quarrymen and related workers									
Craftsmen, prod.-process workers and labourers not elsewhere classified	...	...	...	...	...	...	...	...	...
Workers in transport and communication occupations	...	...	...	...	...	...	...	...	...
Service, sport and recreation workers	...	...	...	...	...	...	...	...	...
Workers not classifiable by occupation	...	...	...	...	...	...	...	...	...
Persons seeking work for the first time	.	.	.	.	.	.	.	.	.
Total . . .	39 900	15 300	**55 200**	211 400	77 600	**289 000**	12 900	10 700	**23 600**

United States (1.IV.1970 *) ǂ (1)

Occupational group	Males	Females	Total	Males	Females	Total	Males	Females	Total
0-1. Professional, technical and related workers	...	...	...	...	...	...	...	...	...
2. Administrative and managerial workers	...	...	...	...	...	...	...	...	...
3. Clerical and related workers	...	...	...	...	...	...	...	...	...
4. Sales workers	...	...	...	...	...	...	...	...	...
5. Service workers	...	...	...	...	...	...	...	...	...
6. Agricultural, animal husbandry and forestry workers, fishermen and hunters	...	...	...	...	...	...	...	...	...
7-9. Production and related workers, transport equipment, operators and labourers	...	...	...	...	...	...	...	...	...
X. Workers not classifiable by occupation	...	...	...	...	...	...	...	...	...
Members of the armed forces	.	.	.	...	...	...	.	.	.
Total . . .	4 849 994	1 061 210	**5 911 204**	44 607 811	27 628 109	**72 235 920**	118 824	285 386	**404 210**

ǂ For notes, see pp. 272-294.

B Distribution by status and by occupational group
Répartition suivant la situation dans la profession et par groupe de professions
Distribución según la categoría de ocupación y por grupo de ocupación

Oth ...nd status unknown / Autres et situation non définie / Otros y categoría no definida			TOTAL			Groupe de professions	Grupo de ocupaciones
Males / Hommes / Hombres	Females / Femmes / Mujeres	Total	Males / Hommes / Hombres	Females / Femmes / Mujeres	Total		
					%		
...	...	...	16 000	12 400	**28 400**	7.4	*Personnes exerçant une profession libérale, techniciens et assimilés*	Trabajadores profesionales, técnicos y trabajadores asimilados
...	...	...	19 100	18 000	**37 100**	9.7	*Directeurs et cadres administratifs supérieurs*	Administradores, gerentes y directores
							Employés de bureau	Empleados de oficina
...	...	...	21 400	18 000	**39 400**	10.3	*Vendeurs*	Vendedores
...	...	...	37 900	12 000	**49 900**	13.0	*Agriculteurs, pêcheurs, chasseurs, forestiers et travailleurs assimilés*	Agricultores, pescadores, cazadores, trabajadores forestales y asimilados
							Mineurs, carriers et travailleurs assimilés	Mineros, canteros y trabajadores asimilados
...	...	...	121 100	15 900	**137 000**	35.9	*Artisans, ouvriers de métier, ouvriers à la production et manœuvres non classés ailleurs*	Artesanos y trab. ocupados en los div. procesos de producción y peones no clasif. bajo otros epígrafes
...	...	...	19 900	1 500	**21 400**	5.6	*Travailleurs des transports et des communications*	Trabajadores de los transportes y comunicaciones
...	...	...	26 400	25 800	**52 200**	13.6	*Travailleurs spécialisés dans les services, les sports et les activités récréatives*	Trabajadores de los servicios, los deportes y las diversiones
...	...	...	3 300	900	**4 200**	1.1	*Personnes ne pouvant être classées selon la profession*	Trabajadores que no pueden ser clasificados según la ocupación
...	...	...	4 900	8 100	**13 000**	3.4	*Personnes en quête d'emploi pour la première fois*	Personas en busca de trabajo por primera vez
5 800	8 900	**14 700**	270 000	112 600	**382 500**	100.0	*Total*	Total

Oth ...nd status unknown			TOTAL			Groupe de professions	Grupo de ocupaciones
					%		
...	...	...	6 798 887	4 549 927	**11 348 814**	13.8	0-1. *Personnel des professions scientif., techn., libérales et assimilées*	0-1. Profesionales, técnicos y trabajadores asimilados
...	...	...	5 315 768	1 055 381	**6 371 149**	7.8	2. *Directeurs et cadres administratifs supérieurs*	2. Directores y funcionarios públicos superiores
...	...	...	3 640 636	10 104 508	**13 745 144**	16.8	3. *Personnel administratif et travailleurs assimilés*	3. Personal administrativo y trabajadores asimilados
...	...	...	3 302 324	2 140 994	**5 443 318**	6.6	4. *Personnel commercial et vendeurs*	4. Comerciantes y vendedores
...	...	...	3 835 631	4 789 362	**8 624 993**	10.5	5. *Travailleurs des services*	5. Trabajadores de los servicios
...	...	...	2 154 302	225 243	**2 379 545**	2.9	6. *Agriculteurs, éleveurs, forestiers, pêcheurs et chasseurs*	6. Trab. agrícolas y forestales, pescadores y cazadores
...	...	...	22 538 020	4 950 521	**27 488 541**	33.5	7-9. *Ouvriers et manœuvres non agricoles et conducteurs d'engins de transport*	7-9. Obreros no agrícolas, conductores de máquinas y vehículos de transporte y trabajadores asimilados
...	...	...	1 963 671	2 685 871	**4 649 542**	5.7	X. *Travailleurs ne pouvant être classés selon la profession*	X. Trabajadores que no pueden ser clasificados según la ocupación
...	...	...	1 952 875	44 860	**1 997 735**	2.4	*Membres des forces armées*	Miembros de las fuerzas armadas
1 925 485	1 571 962	**3 497 447**	51 502 114	30 546 667	**82 048 781**	100.0	*Total*	Total

† *Voir notes pp. 272-294.*

† Véanse las notas en las págs. 272-294.

POPULATION

2 Structure of the economically active population
Structure de la population active
Estructura de la población económicamente activa

Occupational group	Employers and workers on own account *Employeurs et personnes travaillant à leur propre compte* Empleadores y trabajadores por cuenta propia			Salaried employees and wage earners *Employés et ouvriers* Empleados y obreros			Family workers *Travailleurs familiaux* Trabajadores familiares		
	Males *Hommes* Hombres	Females *Femmes* Mujeres	Total	Males *Hommes* Hombres	Females *Femmes* Mujeres	Total	Males *Hommes* Hombres	Females *Femmes* Mujeres	Total

United States (1974) ‡ (2)

0-1. Professional, technical and related workers	753 000	248 000	**1 001 000**	6 592 000	4 734 000	**11 325 000**	1 000	11 000	**12 000**
2. Administrative and managerial workers	1 456 000	328 000	**1 784 000**	5 834 000	1 298 000	**7 132 000**	2 000	24 000	**26 000**
3. Clerical and related workers	39 000	81 000	**119 000**	3 324 000	11 358 000	**14 682 000**	4 000	238 000	**242 000**
4. Sales workers	385 000	176 000	**561 000**	2 760 000	2 016 000	**4 777 000**	6 000	72 000	**79 000**
5. Service workers	178 000	511 000	**689 000**	4 027 000	6 587 000	**10 614 000**	12 000	58 000	**70 000**
6. Agricultural, animal husbandry and forestry workers, fishermen and hunters	1 523 000	98 000	**1 622 000**	904 000	146 000	**1 050 000**	137 000	239 000	**376 000**
7-9. Production and related workers, transport equipment, operators and labourers	1 479 000	132 000	**1 611 000**	23 075 000	5 020 000	**28 094 000**	28 000	44 000	**71 000**
Members of the armed forces . . .	.	.	.	2 162 000	67 000	**2 229 000**	.	.	.
Persons seeking work for the first time	.	.	.	.	.	.	.	.	.
Total . . .	5 813 000	1 573 000	**7 386 000**	48 678 000	31 225 000	**79 903 000**	190 000	686 000	**876 000**

Uruguay (16.X.1963 *) ‡

Professional, technical and related workers	...	...	...	...	...	...	...	...	...
Administrative, executive and managerial workers	...	...	...	...	...	...	...	...	...
Clerical workers	...	...	...	...	...	...	...	...	...
Sales workers	...	...	...	...	...	...	...	...	...
Farmers, fishermen, hunters, loggers and related workers	...	...	...	...	...	...	...	...	...
Miners, quarrymen and related workers	...	...	...	...	...	...	...	...	...
Workers in transport and communication occupations	...	...	...	...	...	...	...	...	...
Craftsmen, prod.-process workers and labourers not elsewhere classified .	...	...	...	...	...	...	...	...	...
Service, sport and recreation workers	...	...	...	...	...	...	...	...	...
Workers not classifiable by occupation	...	...	...	...	...	...	...	...	...
Members of the armed forces	.	.	.	.	.	.	.	.	.
Persons seeking work for the first time	.	.	.	.	.	.	.	.	.
Total . . .	181 711	51 795	**233 506**	525 244	181 129	**706 373**	14 067	2 464	**16 531**

‡ For notes, see pp. 272-294.

B **Distribution by status and by occupational group**
Répartition suivant la situation dans la profession et par groupe de professions
Distribución según la categoría de ocupación y por grupo de ocupación

Others and status unknown / Autres et situation non définie / Otros y categoría no definida			TOTAL			Groupe de professions	Grupo de ocupaciones
Males / Hommes / Hombres	Females / Femmes / Mujeres	Total	Males / Hommes / Hombres	Females / Femmes / Mujeres	Total		

						%		
							0-1. *Personnel des professions scientif., techn., libérales et assimilées*	0-1. Profesionales, técnicos y trabajadores asimilados
136 000	150 000	**285 000**	7 482 000	5 142 000	**12 623 000**	*13.5*	2. *Directeurs et cadres administratifs supérieurs*	2. Directores y funcionarios públicos superiores
112 000	56 000	**168 000**	7 403 000	1 706 000	**9 109 000**	*9.8*	3. *Personnel administratif et travailleurs assimilés*	3. Personal administrativo y trabajadores asimilados
120 000	605 000	**725 000**	3 486 000	12 281 000	**15 767 000**	*16.9*	4. *Personnel commercial et vendeurs*	4. Comerciantes y vendedores
99 000	141 000	**240 000**	3 251 000	2 406 000	**5 657 000**	*6.1*	5. *Travailleurs des services*	5. Trabajadores de los servicios
269 000	495 000	**764 000**	4 487 000	7 650 000	**12 137 000**	*13.0*	6. *Agriculteurs, éleveurs, forestiers, pêcheurs et chasseurs*	6. Trab. agrícolas y forestales, pescadores y cazadores
62 000	18 000	**79 000**	2 626 000	501 000	**3 127 000**	*3.4*	7-9. *Ouvriers et manœuvres non agricoles et conducteurs d'engins de transport*	7-9. Obreros no agrícolas, conductores de máquinas y vehículos de transporte y trabajadores asimilados
1 580 000	558 000	**2 138 000**	26 161 000	5 753 000	**31 914 000**	*34.2*		Miembros de las fuerzas armadas
.	.	.	2 162 000	67 000	**2 229 000**	*2.4*	*Membres des forces armées*	
291 000	385 000	**676 000**	291 000	385 000	**676 000**	*0.7*	*Personnes en quête d'emploi pour la première fois*	Personas en busca de trabajo por primera vez
2 668 000	2 408 000	**5 076 000**	57 349 000	35 892 000	**93 240 000**	*100.0*	*Total*	Total

						%		
...	...	...	24 245	32 739	**56 984**	*5.6*	*Personnes exerçant une profession libérale, techniciens et assimilés*	Trabajadores profesionales, técnicos y trabajadores asimilados
...	...	...	12 404	709	**13 113**	*1.3*	*Directeurs et cadres administratifs supérieurs*	Administradores, gerentes y directores
...	...	...	92 071	34 935	**127 006**	*12.5*	*Employés de bureau*	Empleados de oficina
...	...	...	75 401	19 355	**94 756**	*9.4*	*Vendeurs*	Vendedores
...	...	...	175 581	3 413	**178 994**	*17.7*	*Agriculteurs, pêcheurs, chasseurs, forestiers et travailleurs assimilés*	Agricultores, pescadores, cazadores, trabajadores forestales y asimilados
...	...	...	2 025	11	**2 036**	*0.2*	*Mineurs, carriers et travailleurs assimilés*	Mineros, canteros y trabajadores asimilados
...	...	...	34 006	168	**34 174**	*3.4*	*Travailleurs des transports et des communications*	Trabajadores de los transportes y comunicaciones
...	...	...	227 880	55 632	**283 512**	*27.9*	*Artisans, ouvriers de métier, ouvriers à la production et manœuvres non classés ailleurs*	Artesanos y trab. ocupados en los div. procesos de producción y peones no clasif. bajo otros epígrafes
...	...	...	52 238	87 222	**139 460**	*13.8*	*Travailleurs spécialisés dans les services, les sports et les activités récréatives*	Trabajadores de los servicios, los deportes y las diversiones
...	...	...	38 661	11 450	**50 111**	*5.0*	*Personnes ne pouvant être classées selon la profession*	Trabajadores que no pueden ser clasificados según la ocupación
.	.	.	12 138	47	**12 185**	*1.2*	*Membres des forces armées*	Miembros de las fuerzas armadas
...	...	...	13 337	6 599	**19 936**	*2.0*	*Personnes en quête d'emploi pour la première fois*	Personas en busca de trabajo por primera vez
...	...	...	759 987	252 280	**1 012 267**	*100.0*	*Total*	Total

† *Voir notes pp. 272-294.*

† Véanse las notas en las págs. 272-294.

2 Structure of the economically active population
Structure de la population active
Estructura de la población económicamente activa

Occupational group	Employers and workers on own account *Employeurs et personnes travaillant à leur propre compte* Empleadores y trabajadores por cuenta propia			Salaried employees and wage earners *Employés et ouvriers* Empleados y obreros			Family workers *Travailleurs familiaux* Trabajadores familiares		
	Males *Hommes* Hombres	Females *Femmes* Mujeres	Total	Males *Hommes* Hombres	Females *Femmes* Mujeres	Total	Males *Hommes* Hombres	Females *Femmes* Mujeres	Total

Venezuela (2.XI.1971)

Professional, technical and related workers	...	...	...	...	...	...	...	...	...
Administrative, executive and managerial workers	...	...	...	...	...	...	...	...	...
Clerical workers	...	...	...	...	...	...	...	...	...
Sales workers	...	...	...	...	...	...	...	...	...
Farmers, fishermen, hunters, loggers and related workers	...	...	...	...	...	...	...	...	...
Miners, quarrymen and related workers									
Workers in transport and communication occupations	...	...	...	...	...	...	...	...	...
Craftsmen, prod.-process workers and labourers not elsewhere classified									
Service, sport and recreation workers	...	...	...	...	...	...	...	...	...
Workers not classifiable by occupation	...	...	...	...	...	...	...	...	...
Persons seeking work for the first time	.	.	.	.	.	.	.	.	.
Total ...	...	...	...	...	...	...	...	...	...

Virgin Is. (Brit.) (7.IV.1970)

0-1. Professional, technical and related workers	...	...	...	...	...	...	...	...	...
2. Administrative and managerial workers	...	...	...	...	...	...	...	...	...
3. Clerical and related workers	...	...	...	...	...	...	...	...	...
4. Sales workers	...	...	...	...	...	...	...	...	...
5. Service workers	...	...	...	...	...	...	...	...	...
6. Agricultural, animal husbandry and forestry workers, fishermen and hunters	...	...	...	...	...	...	...	...	...
7-9. Production and related workers, transport equipment, operators and labourers	...	...	...	...	...	...	...	...	...
X. Workers not classifiable by occupation									
Unemployed	...	...	...	...	...	...	...	...	...
Total ...	446	116	**562**	2 363	860	**3 223**	20	45	**65**

B Distribution by status and by occupational group
Répartition suivant la situation dans la profession et par groupe de profession
Distribución según la categoría de ocupación y por grupo de ocupación

Others and status unknown / Autres et situation non définie / Otros y categoría no definida			TOTAL				Groupe de professions	Grupo de ocupaciones
Males / Hommes / Hombres	Females / Femmes / Mujeres	Total	Males / Hommes / Hombres	Females / Femmes / Mujeres	Total	%		
...	...	...	120 708	113 011	233 719	7.8	Personnes exerçant une profession libérale, techniciens et assimilés	Trabajadores profesionales, técnicos y trabajadores asimilados
...	...	...	67 196	8 765	75 961	2.5	Directeurs et cadres administratifs supérieurs	Administradores, gerentes y directores
...	...	...	135 032	110 621	245 653	8.1	Employés de bureau	Empleados de oficina
...	...	...	263 191	43 722	306 913	10.2	Vendeurs	Vendedores
...	...	...	595 821	15 997	611 818	20.3	Agriculteurs, pêcheurs, chasseurs, forestiers et travailleurs assimilés	Agricultores, pescadores, cazadores, trabajadores forestales y asimilados
...	...	...	698 781	78 573	777 354	25.8	Mineurs, carriers et travailleurs assimilés / Travailleurs des transports et des communications / Artisans, ouvriers de métier, ouvriers à la production et manœuvres non classés ailleurs	Mineros, canteros y trabajadores asimilados / Trabajadores de los transportes y comunicaciones / Artesanos y trab. ocupados en los div. procesos de producción y peones no clasif. bajo otros epígrafes
...	...	...	145 629	216 224	361 853	12.0	Travailleurs spécialisés dans les services, les sports et les activités récréatives	Trabajadores de los servicios, los deportes y las diversiones
...	...	...	283 602	81 334	364 936	12.1	Personnes ne pouvant être classées selon la profession	Trabajadores que no pueden ser clasificados según la ocupación
...	...	...	28 650	7 817	36 467	1.2	Personnes en quête d'emploi pour la première fois	Personas en busca de trabajo por primera vez
...	...	...	2 338 610	676 064	3 014 674	100.0	Total	Total

Males / Hommes / Hombres	Females / Femmes / Mujeres	Total	Males / Hommes / Hombres	Females / Femmes / Mujeres	Total	%	Groupe de professions	Grupo de ocupaciones
...	...	...	250	170	420	10.6	0-1. Personnel des professions scientif., techn., libérales et assimilées	0-1. Profesionales, técnicos y trabajadores asimilados
...	...	...	97	24	121	3.0	2. Directeurs et cadres administratifs supérieurs	2. Directores y funcionarios públicos superiores
...	...	...	108	201	309	7.8	3. Personnel administratif et travailleurs assimilés	3. Personal administrativo y trabajadores asimilados
...	...	...	110	145	255	6.4	4. Personnel commercial et vendeurs	4. Comerciantes y vendedores
...	...	...	219	419	638	16.1	5. Travailleurs des services	5. Trabajadores de los servicios
...	...	...	290	11	301	7.6	6. Agriculteurs, éleveurs, forestiers, pêcheurs et chasseurs	6. Trab. agrícolas y forestales, pescadores y cazadores
...	...	...	1 725	43	1 768	44.5	7-9. Ouvriers et manœuvres non agricoles et conducteurs d'engins de transport	7-9. Obreros no agrícolas, conductores de máquinas y vehículos de transporte y trabajadores asimilados
...	...	...	97	61	158	4.0	X. Travailleurs ne pouvant être classés selon la profession / Chômeurs	X. Trabajadores que no pueden ser clasificados según la ocupación / Desempleados
67	53	120	2 896	1 074	3 970	100.0	Total	Total

2 Structure of the economically active population
Structure de la population active
Estructura de la población económicamente activa

Bahrain (3.IV.1971)

Occupational group	Employers and workers on own account *Employeurs et personnes travaillant à leur propre compte* Empleadores y trabajadores por cuenta propia			Salaried employees and wage earners *Employés et ouvriers* Empleados y obreros			Family workers *Travailleurs familiaux* Trabajadores familiares		
	Males *Hommes* Hombres	Females *Femmes* Mujeres	Total	Males *Hommes* Hombres	Females *Femmes* Mujeres	Total	Males *Hommes* Hombres	Females *Femmes* Mujeres	Total
0-1. Professional, technical and related workers	197	41	**238**	2 950	1 636	**4 586**	.	.	.
2. Administrative and managerial workers	192	.	**192**	771	71	**842**	1	.	**1**
3. Clerical and related workers	30	1	**31**	4 767	397	**5 164**	8	1	**9**
4. Sales workers	3 986	35	**4 021**	813	7	**820**	357	2	**359**
5. Service workers	203	12	**215**	8 815	921	**9 736**	13	.	**13**
6. Agricultural, animal husbandry and forestry workers, fishermen and hunters	1 659	.	**1 659**	2 229	4	**2 233**	337	1	**338**
7-9. Production and related workers, transport equipment, operators and labourers	4 076	19	**4 095**	23 667	53	**23 720**	173	3	**176**
X. Workers not classifiable by occupation	15	1	**16**	165	2	**167**	.	.	.
Members of the armed forces	.	.	.	959	.	**959**	.	.	.
Persons seeking work for the first time	.	.	.	.	.	.	.	.	.
Total	10 358	109	**10 467**	45 136	3 091	**48 227**	889	7	**896**

Brunei (11.VIII.1971)

Occupational group	Males	Females	Total	Males	Females	Total	Males	Females	Total
0-1. Professional, technical and related workers	...	...	...	...	...	...	...	...	...
2. Administrative and managerial workers	...	...	...	...	...	...	...	...	...
3. Clerical and related workers	...	...	...	...	...	...	...	...	...
4. Sales workers	...	...	...	...	...	...	...	...	...
5. Service workers	...	...	...	...	...	...	...	...	...
6. Agricultural, animal husbandry and forestry workers, fishermen and hunters	...	...	...	...	...	...	...	...	...
7-9. Production and related workers, transport equipment, operators and labourers	...	...	...	...	...	...	...	...	...
X. Workers not classifiable by occupation	...	...	...	...	...	...	...	...	...
Members of the armed forces	.	.	.	...	...	...	.	.	.
Unemployed	...	...	...	...	...	...	...	...	...
Total	5 071	1 547	**6 618**	28 285	4 381	**32 666**	206	522	**728**

B Distribution by status and by occupational group
Répartition suivant la situation dans la profession et par groupe de professions
Distribución según la categoría de ocupación y por grupo de ocupación

Others and status unknown / Autres et situation non définie / Otros y categoría no definida			TOTAL				Groupe de professions	Grupo de ocupaciones
Males / Hommes / Hombres	Females / Femmes / Mujeres	Total	Males / Hommes / Hombres	Females / Femmes / Mujeres	Total	%		
.	.	.	3 147	1 677	4 824	8.0	0-1. Personnel des professions scientif., techn., libérales et assimilées	0-1. Profesionales, técnicos y trabajadores asimilados
.	.	.	964	71	1 035	1.7	2. Directeurs et cadres administratifs supérieurs	2. Directores y funcionarios públicos superiores
.	.	.	4 805	399	5 204	8.6	3. Personnel administratif et travailleurs assimilés	3. Personal administrativo y trabajadores asimilados
.	.	.	5 156	44	5 200	8.6	4. Personnel commercial et vendeurs	4. Comerciantes y vendedores
.	.	..	9 031	933	9 964	16.5	5. Travailleurs des services	5. Trabajadores de los servicios
.	.	.	4 225	5	4 230	7.0	6. Agriculteurs, éleveurs, forestiers, pêcheurs et chasseurs	6. Trab. agrícolas y forestales, pescadores y cazadores
.	.	.	27 916	75	27 991	46.5	7-9. Ouvriers et manœuvres non agricoles et conducteurs d'engins de transport	7-9. Obreros no agrícolas, conductores de máquinas y vehículos de transporte y trabajadores asimilados
.	.	.	180	3	183	0.3	X. Travailleurs ne pouvant être classés selon la profession	X. Trabajadores que no pueden ser clasificados según la ocupación
.	.	.	959	.	959	1.6	Membres des forces armées	Miembros de las fuerzas armadas
669	42	711	669	42	711	1.2	Personnes en quête d'emploi pour la première fois	Personas en busca de trabajo por primera vez
669	42	711	57 052	3 249	60 301	100.0	Total	Total

Others and status unknown / Autres et situation non définie / Otros y categoría no definida			TOTAL				Groupe de professions	Grupo de ocupaciones
Males / Hommes / Hombres	Females / Femmes / Mujeres	Total	Males / Hommes / Hombres	Females / Femmes / Mujeres	Total	%		
...	...	...	3 469	1 423	4 892	11.9	0-1. Personnel des professions scientif., techn., libérales et assimilées	0-1. Profesionales, técnicos y trabajadores asimilados
...	...	...	590	16	606	1.5	2. Directeurs et cadres administratifs supérieurs	2. Directores y funcionarios públicos superiores
...	...	...	2 871	834	3 705	9.0	3. Personnel administratif et travailleurs assimilés	3. Personal administrativo y trabajadores asimilados
...	...	...	2 510	600	3 110	7.6	4. Personnel commercial et vendeurs	4. Comerciantes y vendedores
...	...	...	5 829	1 701	7 530	18.3	5. Travailleurs des services	5. Trabajadores de los servicios
...	...	...	3 231	1 466	4 697	11.4	6. Agriculteurs, éleveurs, forestiers, pêcheurs et chasseurs	6. Trab. agrícolas y forestales, pescadores y cazadores
...	...	...	11 904	381	12 285	29.9	7-9. Ouvriers et manœuvres non agricoles et conducteurs d'engins de transport	7-9. Obreros no agrícolas, conductores de máquinas y vehículos de transporte y trabajadores asimilados
...	...	...	45	19	64	0.2	X. Travailleurs ne pouvant être classés selon la profession	X. Trabajadores que no pueden ser clasificados según la ocupación
.	.	.	3 113	10	3 123	7.6	Membres des forces armées	Miembros de las fuerzas armadas
...	...	...	649	438	1 087	2.6	Chômeurs	Desempleados
649	438	1 087	34 211	6 888	41 099	100.0	Total	Total

2 Structure of the economically active population
Structure de la population active
Estructura de la población económicamente activa

Occupational group	Employers and workers on own account			Salaried employees and wage earners			Family workers		
	Employeurs et personnes travaillant à leur propre compte			*Employés et ouvriers*			*Travailleurs familiaux*		
	Empleadores y trabajadores por cuenta propia			Empleados y obreros			Trabajadores familiares		
	Males *Hommes* Hombres	Females *Femmes* Mujeres	Total	Males *Hommes* Hombres	Females *Femmes* Mujeres	Total	Males *Hommes* Hombres	Females *Femmes* Mujeres	Total

Hong Kong (9.III.1971) †

0-1. Professional, technical and related workers	3 126	353	**3 479**	41 341	35 086	**76 427**	31	41	**72**
2. Administrative and managerial workers	19 758	1 415	**21 173**	14 627	1 617	**16 244**	59	112	**171**
3. Clerical and related workers	.	.	.	87 439	40 809	**128 248**	79	147	**226**
4. Sales workers	53 255	16 507	**69 762**	73 494	17 223	**90 717**	1 905	3 102	**5 007**
5. Service workers	5 261	900	**6 161**	146 558	78 347	**224 905**	410	719	**1 129**
6. Agricultural, animal husbandry and forestry workers, fishermen and hunters	23 968	7 212	**31 180**	6 868	2 178	**9 046**	9 153	12 405	**21 558**
7-9. Production and related workers, transport equipment, operators and labourers	32 039	3 728	**35 767**	500 922	292 730	**793 652**	2 886	2 991	**5 877**
X. Workers not classifiable by occupation	3 112	843	**3 955**	15 862	13 105	**28 967**	408	1 075	**1 483**
Members of the armed forces	.	.	.	7 428	215	**7 643**	.	.	.
Persons seeking work for the first time	.	.	.	.	.	.	.	.	.
Total . . .	140 519	30 958	**171 477**	894 539	481 310	**1 375 849**	14 931	20 592	**35 523**

India (1.IV.1971) †

0-1. Professional, technical and related workers	669 000	46 900	**715 900**	3 278 100	805 200	**4 083 300**	29 600	5 500	**35 100**
2. Administrative and managerial workers	512 100	10 500	**522 600**	660 400	9 900	**670 300**	15 500	200	**15 700**
3. Clerical and related workers	132 800	3 900	**136 700**	5 019 900	211 700	**5 231 600**	10 000	100	**10 100**
4. Sales workers	5 051 700	356 800	**5 408 500**	1 569 600	50 800	**1 620 400**	537 700	60 400	**598 100**
5. Service workers	1 454 900	242 100	**1 697 000**	3 038 600	575 900	**3 614 500**	290 900	137 900	**428 800**
6. Agricultural, animal husbandry and forestry workers, fishermen and hunters	1 379 300	133 800	**1 513 100**	1 435 300	523 300	**1 958 600**	617 300	108 100	**725 400**
7-9. Production and related workers, transport equipment, operators and labourers	5 095 700	485 700	**5 581 400**	11 036 100	954 200	**11 990 300**	465 300	84 700	**550 000**
X. Workers not classifiable by occupation	2 699 800	539 500	**3 239 300**	1 141 100	149 400	**1 290 500**	2 329 200	740 900	**3 070 100**
Total . . .	16 995 300	1 819 200	**18 814 500**	27 179 100	3 280 400	**30 459 500**	4 295 500	1 137 800	**5 433 300**

† For notes, see pp. 272-294.

B Distribution by status and by occupational group
Répartition suivant la situation dans la profession et par groupe de professions
Distribución según la categoría de ocupación y por grupo de ocupación

Others and status unknown / Autres et situation non définie / Otros y categoría no definida			TOTAL			Groupe de professions	Grupo de ocupaciones
Males / Hommes / Hombres	Females / Femmes / Mujeres	Total	Males / Hommes / Hombres	Females / Femmes / Mujeres	Total		

						%		
							0-1. *Personnel des professions scientif., techn., libérales et assimilées*	0-1. Profesionales, técnicos y trabajadores asimilados
594	204	**798**	45 092	35 684	**80 776**	4.9		
397	47	**444**	34 841	3 191	**38 032**	2.3	2. *Directeurs et cadres administratifs supérieurs*	2. Directores y funcionarios públicos superiores
412	141	**553**	87 930	41 097	**129 027**	7.8	3. *Personnel administratif et travailleurs assimilés*	3. Personal administrativo y trabajadores asimilados
2 395	606	**3 001**	131 049	37 438	**168 487**	10.2	4. *Personnel commercial et vendeurs*	4. Comerciantes y vendedores
2 106	2 672	**4 778**	154 335	82 638	**236 973**	14.3	5. *Travailleurs des services*	5. Trabajadores de los servicios
1 287	409	**1 696**	41 276	22 204	**63 480**	3.8	6. *Agriculteurs, éleveurs, forestiers, pêcheurs et chasseurs*	6. Trab. agrícolas y forestales, pescadores y cazadores
11 671	2 684	**14 355**	547 518	302 133	**849 651**	51.3	7-9. *Ouvriers et manœuvres non agricoles et conducteurs d'engins de transport*	7-9. Obreros no agrícolas, conductores de máquinas y vehículos de transporte y trabajadores asimilados
15 965	6 384	**22 349**	35 347	21 407	**56 754**	3.4	X. *Travailleurs ne pouvant être classés selon la profession*	X. Trabajadores que no pueden ser clasificados según la ocupación
62	25	**87**	7 490	240	**7 730**	0.5	*Membres des forces armées*	Miembros de las fuerzas armadas
12 022	11 975	**23 997**	12 022	11 975	**23 997**	1.5	*Personnes en quête d'emploi pour la première fois*	Personas en busca de trabajo por primera vez
46 911	25 147	**72 058**	1 096 900	558 007	**1 654 907**	100.0	*Total*	Total

						%		
							0-1. *Personnel des professions scientif., techn., libérales et assimilées*	0-1. Profesionales, técnicos y trabajadores asimilados
.	.	.	3 976 700	857 600	**4 834 300**	2.7		
.	.	.	1 188 000	20 600	**1 208 600**	0.7	2. *Directeurs et cadres administratifs supérieurs*	2. Directores y funcionarios públicos superiores
.	.	.	5 162 700	215 700	**5 378 400**	3.0	3. *Personnel administratif et travailleurs assimilés*	3. Personal administrativo y trabajadores asimilados
.	.	.	7 159 000	468 000	**7 627 000**	4.2	4. *Personnel commercial et vendeurs*	4. Comerciantes y vendedores
.	.	.	4 784 400	955 900	**5 740 300**	3.2	5. *Travailleurs des services*	5. Trabajadores de los servicios
100 605 200	25 060 900	**125 666 100**	104 037 100	25 826 100	**129 863 200**	72.0	6. *Agriculteurs, éleveurs, forestiers, pêcheurs et chasseurs*	6. Trab. agrícolas y forestales, pescadores y cazadores
			16 597 100	1 524 600	**18 121 700**	10.0	7-9. *Ouvriers et manœuvres non agricoles et conducteurs d'engins de transport*	7-9. Obreros no agrícolas, conductores de máquinas y vehículos de transporte y trabajadores asimilados
.	.	.	6 170 100	1 429 800	**7 599 900**	4.2	X. *Travailleurs ne pouvant être classés selon la profession*	X. Trabajadores que no pueden ser clasificados según la ocupación
100 605 200	25 060 900	**125 666 100**	149 075 100	31 298 300	**180 373 400**	100.0	*Total*	Total

† *Voir notes pp. 272-294.*   † Véanse las notas en las págs. 272-294.

2 Structure of the economically active population
Structure de la population active
Estructura de la población económicamente activa

Occupational group	Employers and workers on own account Employeurs et personnes travaillant à leur propre compte Empleadores y trabajadores por cuenta propia			Salaried employees and wage earners Employés et ouvriers Empleados y obreros			Family workers Travailleurs familiaux Trabajadores familiares		
	Males Hommes Hombres	Females Femmes Mujeres	Total	Males Hommes Hombres	Females Femmes Mujeres	Total	Males Hommes Hombres	Females Femmes Mujeres	Total

Indonesia (24.IX.1971 *) ‡

0-1. Professional, technical and related workers	...	...	...	...	...	...	...	...	...
2. Administrative and managerial workers	...	...	...	...	...	...	...	...	...
3. Clerical and related workers	...	...	...	...	...	...	...	...	...
4. Sales workers	...	...	...	...	...	...	...	...	...
5. Service workers	...	...	...	...	...	...	...	...	...
6. Agricultural, animal husbandry and forestry workers, fishermen and hunters	...	...	...	...	...	...	...	...	...
7-9. Production and related workers, transport equipment, operators and labourers	...	...	...	...	...	...	...	...	...
X. Workers not classifiable by occupation	...	...	...	...	...	...	...	...	...
Persons seeking work for the first time	.		.	.		.	.	.	.
Total . . .	12 266 994	4 047 935	**16 314 929**	9 269 012	3 432 917	**12 701 929**	4 110 829	4 815 250	**8 926 079**

Iran (1.XI.1966) ‡

Professional, technical and related workers	19 670	1 988	**21 658**	130 195	49 917	**180 112**	299	140	**439**
Administrative, executive and managerial workers	4 157	64	**4 221**	7 353	315	**7 668**	10	5	**15**
Clerical workers	8 103	297	**8 400**	178 269	13 322	**191 591**	560	57	**617**
Sales workers	383 587	3 590	**387 177**	102 477	1 417	**103 894**	12 634	506	**13 140**
Farmers, fishermen, hunters, loggers and related workers	1 794 296	42 279	**1 836 575**	711 814	64 475	**776 289**	422 880	93 710	**516 590**
Miners, quarrymen and related workers ⎫ Workers in transport and communication occupations . . . . ⎬ Craftsmen, prod.-process workers and labourers not elsewhere classified . ⎭	316 583	148 081	**464 664**	1 180 862	262 219	**1 443 081**	22 472	97 356	**119 828**
Service, sport and recreation workers	71 331	5 975	**77 306**	311 465	101 145	**412 610**	14 991	4 699	**19 690**
Workers not classifiable by occupation	10 303	1 170	**11 473**	200 671	6 445	**207 116**	5 299	1 453	**6 752**
Members of the armed forces . . . . ⎫ Persons seeking work for the first time ⎬ Unemployed . . . . ⎭	...	...	...	...	...	...	...	...	...
Total . . .	2 608 030	203 444	**2 811 474**	2 823 106	499 255	**3 322 361**	479 145	197 926	**677 071**

‡ For notes, see pp. 272-294.

B   Distribution by status and by occupational group
Répartition suivant la situation dans la profession et par groupe de professions
Distribución según la categoría de ocupación y por grupo de ocupación

Others and status unknown / Autres et situation non définie / Otros y categoría no definida			TOTAL			Groupe de professions	Grupo de ocupaciones
Males / Hommes / Hombres	Females / Femmes / Mujeres	Total	Males / Hommes / Hombres	Females / Femmes / Mujeres	Total		
						%		
...	...	...	609 677	274 656	**884 333**	2.2	0-1. Personnel des professions scientif., techn., libérales et assimilées	0-1. Profesionales, técnicos y trabajadores asimilados
...	...	...	1 107 483	265 894	**1 373 377**	3.4	2. Directeurs et cadres administratifs supérieurs	2. Directores y funcionarios públicos superiores
...	...	...	1 120 187	141 642	**1 261 829**	3.1	3. Personnel administratif et travailleurs assimilés	3. Personal administrativo y trabajadores asimilados
...	...	...	2 276 489	1 779 298	**4 055 787**	10.1	4. Personnel commercial et vendeurs	4. Comerciantes y vendedores
...	...	...	865 916	646 917	**1 512 833**	3.8	5. Travailleurs des services	5. Trabajadores de los servicios
...	...	...	16 170 544	7 715 459	**23 886 003**	59.7	6. Agriculteurs, éleveurs, forestiers, pêcheurs et chasseurs	6. Trab. agrícolas y forestales, pescadores y cazadores
...	...	...	3 248 814	1 484 570	**4 733 384**	11.8	7-9. Ouvriers et manœuvres non agricoles et conducteurs d'engins de transport	7-9. Obreros no agrícolas, conductores de máquinas y vehículos de transporte y trabajadores asimilados
...	...	...	1 133 552	851 001	**1 984 553**	4.9	X. Travailleurs ne pouvant être classés selon la profession	X. Trabajadores que no pueden ser clasificados según la ocupación
.	.	.	299 739	108 232	**407 971**	1.0	Personnes en quête d'emploi pour la première fois	Personas en busca de trabajo por primera vez
1 185 566	971 567	**2 157 133**	26 832 401	13 267 669	**40 100 070**	100.0	Total	Total

Others and status unknown / Autres et situation non définie / Otros y categoría no definida			TOTAL			Groupe de professions	Grupo de ocupaciones
Males / Hommes / Hombres	Females / Femmes / Mujeres	Total	Males / Hommes / Hombres	Females / Femmes / Mujeres	Total		
						%		
611	124	**735**	150 775	52 169	**202 944**	2.7	Personnes exerçant une profession libérale, techniciens et assimilés	Trabajadores profesionales, técnicos y trabajadores asimilados
28	5	**33**	11 548	389	**11 937**	0.1	Directeurs et cadres administratifs supérieurs	Administradores, gerentes y directores
494	46	**540**	187 426	13 722	**201 148**	2.7	Employés de bureau	Empleados de oficina
647	20	**667**	499 345	5 533	**504 878**	6.7	Vendeurs	Vendedores
8 040	382	**8 422**	2 937 030	200 846	**3 137 876**	41.3	Agriculteurs, pêcheurs, chasseurs, forestiers et travailleurs assimilés	Agricultores, pescadores, cazadores, trabajadores forestales y asimilados
3 039	969	**4 008**	1 522 956	508 625	**2 031 581**	26.8	Mineurs, carriers et travailleurs assimilés / Travailleurs des transports et des communications / Artisans, ouvriers de métier, ouvriers à la production et manœuvres non classés ailleurs	Mineros, canteros y trabajadores asimilados / Trabajadores de los transportes y comunicaciones / Artesanos y trab. ocupados en los div. procesos de producción y peones no clasif. bajo otros epígrafes
721	454	**1 175**	398 508	112 273	**510 781**	6.7	Travailleurs spécialisés dans les services, les sports et les activités récréatives	Trabajadores de los servicios, los deportes y las diversiones
24 552	7 358	**31 910**	240 825	16 426	**257 251**	3.4	Personnes ne pouvant être classées selon la profession / Membres des forces armées	Trabajadores que no pueden ser clasificados según la ocupación / Miembros de las fuerzas armadas
635 844	89 845	**725 689**	635 844	89 845	**725 689**	9.6	Personnes en quête d'emploi pour la première fois / Chômeurs	Personas en busca de trabajo por primera vez / Desempleados
673 976	99 203	**773 179**	6 584 257	999 828	**7 584 085**	100.0	Total	Total

† Voir notes pp. 272-294.   † Véanse las notas en las págs. 272-294.

2 Structure of the economically active population
Structure de la population active
Estructura de la población económicamente activa

Occupational group	Employers and workers on own account *Employeurs et personnes travaillant à leur propre compte* Empleadores y trabajadores por cuenta propia			Salaried employees and wage earners *Employés et ouvriers* Empleados y obreros			Family workers *Travailleurs familiaux* Trabajadores familiares		
	Males *Hommes* Hombres	Females *Femmes* Mujeres	Total	Males *Hommes* Hombres	Females *Femmes* Mujeres	Total	Males *Hommes* Hombres	Females *Femmes* Mujeres	Total

Israel (1974) ‡

0-1. Professional, technical and related workers	13 700	12 900	**26 800**	88 900	85 900	**174 900**	...	...	...
2. Administrative and managerial workers	9 100	400	**9 500**	22 900	2 500	**25 500**	...	...	...
3. Clerical and related workers	4 100	6 000	**10 100**	79 400	92 100	**171 500**	...	...	...
4. Sales workers	42 000	15 100	**57 100**	19 500	9 300	**28 900**	...	...	...
5. Service workers	11 300	14 300	**25 900**	47 600	52 000	**99 500**	...	...	...
6. Agricultural, animal husbandry and forestry workers, fishermen and hunters	39 100	10 600	**49 500**	17 300	2 400	**19 700**	...	...	...
7-9. Production and related workers, transport equipment, operators and labourers	75 800	7 800	**83 400**	260 300	34 800	**295 100**	...	...	...
X. Workers not classifiable by occupation	1 000	300	**1 400**	8 600	2 400	**10 900**	...	...	...
Persons seeking work for the first time Unemployed	. ...	. ...	. ...	. ...	. ...	. ...	. ...	. ...	. ...
Total . . .	196 100	67 400	**263 400**	544 500	281 400	**826 000**	...	...	...

‡ For notes, see pp. 272-294.

B Distribution by status and by occupational group
Répartition suivant la situation dans la profession et par groupe de professions
Distribución según la categoría de ocupación y por grupo de ocupación

Others and status unknown *Autres et situation non définie* Otros y categoría no definida			TOTAL			Groupe de professions	Grupo de ocupaciones
Males *Hommes* Hombres	Females *Femmes* Mujeres	Total	Males *Hommes* Hombres	Females *Femmes* Mujeres	Total		
					%	0-1. *Personnel des professions scientif., techn., libérales et assimilées*	0-1. Profesionales, técnicos y trabajadores asimilados
...	...	...	102 600	98 800	**201 700**	*18.0*		
						2. *Directeurs et cadres administratifs supérieurs*	2. Directores y funcionarios públicos superiores
...	...	...	32 000	2 900	**35 000**	*3.1*		
						3. *Personnel administratif et travailleurs assimilés*	3. Personal administrativo y trabajadores asimilados
...	...	...	83 500	98 100	**181 600**	*16.1*		
						4. *Personnel commercial et vendeurs*	4. Comerciantes y vendedores
...	...	...	61 500	24 400	**86 000**	*7.7*		
...	...	...	58 900	66 300	**125 400**	*11.2*	5. *Travailleurs des services*	5. Trabajadores de los servicios
						6. *Agriculteurs, éleveurs, forestiers, pêcheurs et chasseurs*	6. Trab. agrícolas y forestales, pescadores y cazadores
...	...	...	56 400	13 100	**69 200**	*6.2*		7-9. Obreros no agrícolas, conductores de máquinas y vehículos de transporte y trabajadores asimilados
						7-9. *Ouvriers et manœuvres non agricoles et conducteurs d'engins de transport*	
...	...	...	336 100	42 600	**378 500**	*33.6*		
						X. *Travailleurs ne pouvant être classés selon la profession*	X. Trabajadores que no pueden ser clasificados según la ocupación
...	...	...	9 600	2 700	**12 300**	*1.1*		
						Personnes en quête d'emploi pour la première fois	Personas en busca de trabajo por primera vez
8 100	9 300	**17 400**	8 100	9 300	**17 400**	*1.6*		
10 100	6 100	**16 200**	10 100	6 100	**16 200**	*1.4*	*Chômeurs*	Desempleados
18 200	15 400	**33 700**	758 600	364 100	**1 122 900**	*100.0*	*Total*	Total

† *Voir notes pp. 272-294.*

† Véanse las notas en las págs. 272-294.

2

Structure of the economically active population
Structure de la population active
Estructura de la población económicamente activa

Occupational group	Employers and workers on own account *Employeurs et personnes travaillant à leur propre compte* Empleadores y trabajadores por cuenta propia			Salaried employees and wage earners *Employés et ouvriers* Empleados y obreros			Family workers *Travailleurs familiaux* Trabajadores familiares		
	Males *Hommes* Hombres	Females *Femmes* Mujeres	Total	Males *Hommes* Hombres	Females *Femmes* Mujeres	Total	Males *Hommes* Hombres	Females *Femmes* Mujeres	Total

Japan

(1.X.1970) ‡									
0-1. Professional, technical and related workers	365 660	129 820	**495 480**	1 907 290	1 092 420	**2 999 710**	20 035	47 025	**67 060**
2. Administrative and managerial workers	44 380	4 875	**49 255**	1 892 520	92 375	**1 984 895**	275	85	**360**
3. Clerical and related workers	17 850	16 775	**34 625**	3 854 885	3 588 935	**7 443 820**	20 405	248 875	**269 280**
4. Sales workers	1 132 170	419 630	**1 551 800**	2 173 910	1 191 560	**3 365 470**	226 745	980 270	**1 207 015**
5. Service workers	422 950	433 335	**856 285**	1 335 250	1 528 750	**2 864 000**	91 140	419 945	**511 085**
6. Agricultural, animal husbandry and forestry workers, fishermen and hunters	3 339 400	942 810	**4 282 210**	332 440	85 605	**418 045**	1 031 985	4 320 405	**5 352 390**
7-9. Production and related workers, transport equipment, operators and labourers	1 930 780	888 825	**2 819 605**	11 394 720	3 411 780	**14 806 500**	390 535	679 250	**1 069 785**
X. Workers not classifiable by occupation	1 010	280	**1 290**	9 675	6 305	**15 980**	150	590	**740**
Unemployed	...	...	...	...	...	...	...	...	...
Total	7 254 200	2 836 350	**10 090 550**	22 900 690	10 997 730	**33 898 420**	1 781 270	6 696 445	**8 477 715**
(1974) ‡									
0-1. Professional, technical and related workers	360 000	150 000	**510 000**	1 590 000	1 250 000	**2 840 000**	10 000	40 000	**50 000**
2. Administrative and managerial workers	10 000	—	**10 000**	1 780 000	110 000	**1 900 000**	—	—	—
3. Clerical and related workers	40 000	30 000	**70 000**	4 160 000	3 710 000	**7 860 000**	10 000	340 000	**350 000**
4. Sales workers	1 340 000	500 000	**1 840 000**	2 800 000	1 240 000	**4 040 000**	220 000	1 020 000	**1 240 000**
5. Service workers	410 000	390 000	**800 000**	1 430 000	1 550 000	**2 980 000**	100 000	480 000	**580 000**
6. Agricultural, animal husbandry and forestry workers, fishermen and hunters	2 410 000	840 000	**3 250 000**	320 000	80 000	**400 000**	580 000	2 420 000	**3 000 000**
7-9. Production and related workers, transport equipment, operators and labourers	2 000 000	1 040 000	**3 040 000**	12 300 000	3 750 000	**16 060 000**	380 000	700 000	**1 080 000**
X. Workers not classifiable by occupation	—	—	—	20 000	10 000	**30 000**	—	—	—
Unemployed	...	...	...	...	...	...	...	...	...
Total	6 560 000	2 960 000	**9 520 000**	24 400 000	11 710 000	**36 100 000**	1 300 000	5 000 000	**6 300 000**

‡ For notes, see pp. 272-294.

B Distribution by status and by occupational group
Répartition suivant la situation dans la profession et par groupe de professions
Distribución según la categoría de ocupación y por grupo de ocupación

Others and status unknown / Autres et situation non définie / Otros y categoría no definida			TOTAL			Groupe de professions	Grupo de ocupaciones
Males / Hommes / Hombres	Females / Femmes / Mujeres	Total	Males / Hommes / Hombres	Females / Femmes / Mujeres	Total		
						%		
...	...	...	2 292 985	1 269 265	3 562 250	6.7	0-1. Personnel des professions scientif., techn., libérales et assimilées	0-1. Profesionales, técnicos y trabajadores asimilados
...	...	...	1 937 175	97 335	2 034 510	3.8	2. Directeurs et cadres administratifs supérieurs	2. Directores y funcionarios públicos superiores
...	...	...	3 893 140	3 854 585	7 747 725	14.6	3. Personnel administratif et travailleurs assimilés	3. Personal administrativo y trabajadores asimilados
...	...	...	3 532 825	2 591 460	6 124 285	11.5	4. Personnel commercial et vendeurs	4. Comerciantes y vendedores
...	...	...	1 849 340	2 382 030	4 231 370	8.0	5. Travailleurs des services	5. Trabajadores de los servicios
...	...	...	4 703 825	5 348 820	10 052 645	18.9	6. Agriculteurs, éleveurs, forestiers, pêcheurs et chasseurs	6. Trab. agrícolas y forestales, pescadores y cazadores
...	...	...	13 716 035	4 979 855	18 695 890	35.1	7-9. Ouvriers et manœuvres non agricoles et conducteurs d'engins de transport	7-9. Obreros no agrícolas, conductores de máquinas y vehículos de transporte y trabajadores asimilados
310	1 140	1 450	11 145	8 315	19 460	—	X. Travailleurs ne pouvant être classés selon la profession	X. Trabajadores que no pueden ser clasificados según la ocupación
483 233	244 727	727 960	483 233	244 727	727 960	1.4	Chômeurs	Desempleados
483 543	245 867	729 410	32 419 703	20 776 392	53 196 095	100.0	Total	Total
...	...	...	1 960 000	1 450 000	3 410 000	6.5	0-1. Personnel des professions scientif., techn., libérales et assimilées	0-1. Profesionales, técnicos y trabajadores asimilados
...	...	...	1 790 000	110 000	1 910 000	3.6	2. Directeurs et cadres administratifs supérieurs	2. Directores y funcionarios públicos superiores
...	...	...	4 210 000	4 080 000	8 280 000	15.7	3. Personnel administratif et travailleurs assimilés	3. Personal administrativo y trabajadores asimilados
...	...	...	4 360 000	2 760 000	7 120 000	13.5	4. Personnel commercial et vendeurs	4. Comerciantes y vendedores
...	...	...	1 940 000	2 430 000	4 360 000	8.3	5. Travailleurs des services	5. Trabajadores de los servicios
...	...	...	3 300 000	3 340 000	6 640 000	12.6	6. Agriculteurs, éleveurs, forestiers, pêcheurs et chasseurs	6. Trab. agrícolas y forestales, pescadores y cazadores
...	...	...	14 690 000	5 480 000	20 190 000	38.2	7-9. Ouvriers et manœuvres non agricoles et conducteurs d'engins de transport	7-9. Obreros no agrícolas, conductores de máquinas y vehículos de transporte y trabajadores asimilados
60 000	30 000	90 000	70 000	30 000	110 000	0.2	X. Travailleurs ne pouvant être classés selon la profession	X. Trabajadores que no pueden ser clasificados según la ocupación
460 000	260 000	720 000	460 000	260 000	720 000	1.4	Chômeurs	Desempleados
510 000	290 000	810 000	32 780 000	19 960 000	52 740 000	100.0	Total	Total

† *Voir notes pp. 272-294.*

† Véanse las notas en las págs. 272-294.

2 Structure of the economically active population
Structure de la population active
Estructura de la población económicamente activa

Occupational group	Employers and workers on own account *Employeurs et personnes travaillant à leur propre compte* Empleadores y trabajadores por cuenta propia			Salaried employees and wage earners *Employés et ouvriers* Empleados y obreros			Family workers *Travailleurs familiaux* Trabajadores familiares		
	Males *Hommes* Hombres	Females *Femmes* Mujeres	Total	Males *Hommes* Hombres	Females *Femmes* Mujeres	Total	Males *Hommes* Hombres	Females *Femmes* Mujeres	Total

Korea, Rep. of

(1.X.1970) ‡

Occupational group	Males	Females	Total	Males	Females	Total	Males	Females	Total
0-1. Professional, technical and related workers	39 979	6 657	**46 636**	207 128	65 122	**272 250**	1 593	1 539	**3 132**
2. Administrative and managerial workers	55 893	2 752	**58 645**	36 103	482	**36 585**	403	113	**516**
3. Clerical and related workers	12 890	1 294	**14 184**	477 052	97 771	**574 823**	2 005	1 390	**3 395**
4. Sales workers	491 996	175 216	**667 212**	151 416	51 936	**203 352**	40 267	116 241	**156 508**
5. Service workers	75 696	67 058	**142 754**	210 011	287 115	**497 126**	7 066	29 279	**36 345**
6. Agricultural, animal husbandry and forestry workers, fishermen and hunters	1 953 749	318 198	**2 271 947**	369 398	173 498	**542 896**	689 287	1 642 182	**2 331 469**
7-9. Production and related workers, transport equipment, operators and labourers	257 905	59 641	**317 546**	1 368 171	394 361	**1 762 532**	42 184	71 199	**113 383**
X. Workers not classifiable by occupation	890	83	**973**	50 544	1 076	**51 620**	164	144	**308**
Unemployed	...	...	...	...	...	...	...	...	...
Total ...	2 888 998	630 899	**3 519 897**	2 869 823	1 071 361	**3 941 184**	782 969	1 862 087	**2 645 056**

(1974) ‡

Occupational group	Males	Females	Total	Males	Females	Total	Males	Females	Total
0-1. Professional, technical and related workers	40 000	9 000	**49 000**	204 000	63 000	**267 000**	3 000	2 000	**5 000**
2. Administrative and managerial workers	41 000	2 000	**43 000**	18 000	—	**18 000**	—	—	—
3. Clerical and related workers	17 000	—	**17 000**	584 000	142 000	**726 000**	2 000	3 000	**5 000**
4. Sales workers	646 000	310 000	**956 000**	143 000	53 000	**196 000**	62 000	245 000	**307 000**
5. Service workers	92 000	104 000	**196 000**	217 000	296 000	**513 000**	12 000	57 000	**69 000**
6. Agricultural, animal husbandry and forestry workers, fishermen and hunters	1 961 000	353 000	**2 314 000**	488 000	229 000	**717 000**	831 000	1 738 000	**2 569 000**
7-9. Production and related workers, transport equipment, operators and labourers	249 000	186 000	**435 000**	1 619 000	451 000	**2 070 000**	46 000	68 000	**114 000**
Unemployed	...	...	...	...	...	...	...	...	...
Total ...	3 046 000	964 000	**4 010 000**	3 273 000	1 234 000	**4 507 000**	956 000	2 113 000	**3 069 000**

‡ For notes, see pp. 272-294.

B Distribution by status and by occupational group
Répartition suivant la situation dans la profession et par groupe de professions
Distribución según la categoría de ocupación y por grupo de ocupación

Others and status unknown			TOTAL			Groupe de professions	Grupo de ocupaciones
Autres et situation non définie							
Otros y categoría no definida							
Males / Hommes / Hombres	Females / Femmes / Mujeres	Total	Males / Hommes / Hombres	Females / Femmes / Mujeres	Total		
					%		
						0-1. *Personnel des professions scientif., techn., libérales et assimilées*	0-1. Profesionales, técnicos y trabajadores asimilados
390	366	**756**	249 089	73 682	**322 771**	*3.1*	
						2. *Directeurs et cadres administratifs supérieurs*	2. Directores y funcionarios públicos superiores
42	10	**52**	92 442	3 357	**95 799**	*0.9*	
						3. *Personnel administratif et travailleurs assimilés*	3. Personal administrativo y trabajadores asimilados
895	178	**1 073**	492 842	100 633	**593 475**	*5.7*	
						4. *Personnel commercial et vendeurs*	4. Comerciantes y vendedores
697	322	**1 019**	684 375	343 715	**1 028 090**	*9.9*	
397	1 994	**2 391**	293 170	385 446	**678 616**	*6.5*	5. *Travailleurs des services*	5. Trabajadores de los servicios
						6. *Agriculteurs, éleveurs, forestiers, pêcheurs et chasseurs*	6. Trab. agrícolas y forestales, pescadores y cazadores
846	795	**1 641**	3 013 281	2 134 674	**5 147 955**	*49.6*	
						7-9. *Ouvriers et manœuvres non agricoles et conducteurs d'engins de transport*	7-9. Obreros no agrícolas, conductores de máquinas y vehículos de transporte y trabajadores asimilados
3 200	1 114	**4 314**	1 671 460	526 314	**2 197 774**	*21.2*	
						X. *Travailleurs ne pouvant être classés selon la profession*	X. Trabajadores que no pueden ser clasificados según la ocupación
29 776	5 792	**35 568**	81 374	7 097	**88 471**	*0.9*	
174 563	50 001	**224 564**	174 563	50 001	**224 564**	*2.2*	*Chômeurs*	Desempleados
210 806	60 572	**271 378**	6 752 596	3 624 919	**10 377 515**	*100.0*	*Total*	Total
						0-1. *Personnel des professions scientif., techn., libérales et assimilées*	0-1. Profesionales, técnicos y trabajadores asimilados
...	...	...	247 000	74 000	**321 000**	*2.7*	
						2. *Directeurs et cadres administratifs supérieurs*	2. Directores y funcionarios públicos superiores
...	...	...	59 000	2 000	**61 000**	*0.5*	
						3. *Personnel administratif et travailleurs assimilés*	3. Personal administrativo y trabajadores asimilados
...	...	...	603 000	145 000	**748 000**	*6.2*	
						4. *Personnel commercial et vendeurs*	4. Comerciantes y vendedores
...	...	...	851 000	608 000	**1 459 000**	*12.1*	
...	...	...	321 000	457 000	**778 000**	*6.4*	5. *Travailleurs des services*	5. Trabajadores de los servicios
						6. *Agriculteurs, éleveurs, forestiers, pêcheurs et chasseurs*	6. Trab. agrícolas y forestales, pescadores y cazadores
...	...	...	3 280 000	2 320 000	**5 600 000**	*46.3*	
						7-9. *Ouvriers et manœuvres non agricoles et conducteurs d'engins de transport*	7-9. Obreros no agrícolas, conductores de máquinas y vehículos de transporte y trabajadores asimilados
...	...	...	1 914 000	705 000	**2 619 000**	*21.7*	
337 000	117 000	**494 000**	377 000	117 000	**494 000**	*4.1*	*Chômeurs*	Desempleados
337 000	117 000	**494 000**	7 652 000	4 428 000	**12 080 000**	*100.0*	*Total*	Total

‡ *Voir notes pp. 272-294.*   ‡ Véanse las notas en las págs. 272-294.

POPULATION

2 Structure of the economically active population
Structure de la population active
Estructura de la población económicamente activa

Occupational group	Employers and workers on own account / Employeurs et personnes travaillant à leur propre compte / Empleadores y trabajadores por cuenta propia			Salaried employees and wage earners / Employés et ouvriers / Empleados y obreros			Family workers / Travailleurs familiaux / Trabajadores familiares		
	Males / Hommes / Hombres	Females / Femmes / Mujeres	Total	Males / Hommes / Hombres	Females / Femmes / Mujeres	Total	Males / Hommes / Hombres	Females / Femmes / Mujeres	Total

Kuwait (21.IV.1970)

Occupational group	Males	Females	Total	Males	Females	Total	Males	Females	Total
0-1. Professional, technical and related workers	496	22	518	17 514	7 458	24 972	3	2	5
2. Administrative and managerial workers	354	1	355	1 411	8	1 419	3	.	3
3. Clerical and related workers	122	.	122	26 451	1 497	27 948	6	1	7
4. Sales workers	13 979	23	14 002	6 675	106	6 781	242	5	247
5. Service workers	1 412	20	1 432	49 531	6 596	56 127	23	3	26
6. Agricultural, animal husbandry and forestry workers, fishermen and hunters	318	1	319	3 372	.	3 372	66	10	76
7-9. Production and related workers, transport equipment, operators and labourers	24 320	89	24 409	70 812	77	70 889	305	540	845
X. Workers not classifiable by occupation	47	.	47	116	5	121	1	.	1
Unemployed	...	...	...	...	...	...	...	...	...
Total	41 048	156	41 204	175 882	15 747	191 629	649	561	1 210

Liban (XI.1970) †

Occupational group	Males	Females	Total	Males	Females	Total	Males	Females	Total
0-1. Professional, technical and related workers	7 215	975	8 190	24 330	18 015	42 345	135	270	405
2. Administrative and managerial workers	6 135	120	6 255	4 020	90	4 110	105	15	120
3. Clerical and related workers	555	30	585	34 260	9 600	43 860	195	75	270
4. Sales workers	42 825	810	43 635	16 380	1 245	17 625	3 180	975	4 155
5. Service workers	8 955	1 050	10 005	31 650	19 605	51 255	720	285	1 005
6. Agricultural, animal husbandry and forestry workers, fishermen and hunters	41 010	1 680	42 690	25 230	3 495	28 725	9 060	15 765	24 825
7-9. Production and related workers, transport equipment, operators and labourers	50 610	7 710	58 320	109 770	9 615	119 385	3 945	870	4 815
X. Workers not classifiable by occupation / Members of the armed forces	360	15	375	14 370	210	14 580	15	.	15
Unemployed	...	...	...	...	...	...	...	...	...
Total	157 665	12 390	170 055	260 010	61 875	321 885	17 355	18 255	35 610

† For notes, see pp. 272-294.

B Distribution by status and by occupational group
Répartition suivant la situation dans la profession et par groupe de professions
Distribución según la categoría de ocupación y por grupo de ocupación

Others and status unknown *Autres et situation non définie* Otros y categoría no definida			TOTAL				Groupe de professions	Grupo de ocupaciones
Males *Hommes* Hombres	Females *Femmes* Mujeres	Total	Males *Hommes* Hombres	Females *Femmes* Mujeres	Total	%		
14	2	**16**	18 027	7 484	**25 511**	*10.5*	0-1. *Personnel des professions scientif., techn., libérales et assimilées*	0-1. Profesionales, técnicos y trabajadores asimilados
...	1	**1**	1 768	10	**1 778**	*0.7*	2. *Directeurs et cadres administratifs supérieurs*	2. Directores y funcionarios públicos superiores
2	...	**2**	26 581	1 498	**28 079**	*11.6*	3. *Personnel administratif et travailleurs assimilés*	3. Personal administrativo y trabajadores asimilados
2	...	**2**	20 898	134	**21 032**	*8.7*	4. *Personnel commercial et vendeurs*	4. Comerciantes y vendedores
1	...	**1**	50 967	6 619	**57 586**	*23.7*	5. *Travailleurs des services*	5. Trabajadores de los servicios
3	...	**3**	3 759	11	**3 770**	*1.6*	6. *Agriculteurs, éleveurs, forestiers, pêcheurs et chasseurs*	6. Trab. agrícolas y forestales, pescadores y cazadores
16	...	**16**	95 453	706	**96 159**	*39.6*	7-9. *Ouvriers et manœuvres non agricoles et conducteurs d'engins de transport*	7-9. Obreros no agrícolas, conductores de máquinas y vehículos de transporte y trabajadores asimilados
261	15	**276**	425	20	**445**	*0.2*	X. *Travailleurs ne pouvant être classés selon la profession*	X. Trabajadores que no pueden ser clasificados según la ocupación
8 021	132	**8 153**	8 021	132	**8 153**	*3.4*	*Chômeurs*	Desempleados
8 320	150	**8 470**	225 899	16 614	**242 513**	*100.0*	*Total*	Total

Others and status unknown *Autres et situation non définie* Otros y categoría no definida			TOTAL				Groupe de professions	Grupo de ocupaciones
Males *Hommes* Hombres	Females *Femmes* Mujeres	Total	Males *Hommes* Hombres	Females *Femmes* Mujeres	Total	%		
1 185	750	**1 935**	32 865	20 010	**52 875**	*9.2*	0-1. *Personnel des professions scientif., techn., libérales et assimilées*	0-1. Profesionales, técnicos y trabajadores asimilados
105	...	**105**	10 365	225	**10 590**	*1.9*	2. *Directeurs et cadres administratifs supérieurs*	2. Directores y funcionarios públicos superiores
180	...	**180**	35 190	9 705	**44 895**	*7.9*	3. *Personnel administratif et travailleurs assimilés*	3. Personal administrativo y trabajadores asimilados
555	...	**555**	62 940	3 030	**65 970**	*11.5*	4. *Personnel commercial et vendeurs*	4. Comerciantes y vendedores
300	225	**525**	41 625	21 165	**62 790**	*11.0*	5. *Travailleurs des services*	5. Trabajadores de los servicios
5 175	300	**5 475**	80 475	21 240	**101 715**	*17.8*	6. *Agriculteurs, éleveurs, forestiers, pêcheurs et chasseurs*	6. Trab. agrícolas y forestales, pescadores y cazadores
945	255	**1 200**	165 270	18 450	**183 720**	*32.1*	7-9. *Ouvriers et manœuvres non agricoles et conducteurs d'engins de transport*	7-9. Obreros no agrícolas, conductores de máquinas y vehículos de transporte y trabajadores asimilados
810	75	**885**	15 555	300	**15 855**	*2.8*	X. *Travailleurs ne pouvant être classés selon la profession*	X. Trabajadores que no pueden ser clasificados según la ocupación Miembros de las fuerzas armadas
28 335	5 010	**33 345**	28 335	5 010	**33 345**	*5.8*	*Membres des forces armées* *Chômeurs*	Desempleados
37 590	6 615	**44 205**	472 620	99 135	**571 755**	*100.0*	*Total*	Total

‡ *Voir notes pp. 272-294.*

‡ Véanse las notas en las págs. 272-294.

2 Structure of the economically active population
Structure de la population active
Estructura de la población económicamente activa

Occupational group	Employers and workers on own account *Employeurs et personnes travaillant à leur propre compte* Empleadores y trabajadores por cuenta propia			Salaried employees and wage earners *Employés et ouvriers* Empleados y obreros			Family workers *Travailleurs familiaux* Trabajadores familiares		
	Males *Hommes* Hombres	Females *Femmes* Mujeres	Total	Males *Hommes* Hombres	Females *Femmes* Mujeres	Total	Males *Hommes* Hombres	Females *Femmes* Mujeres	Total

Malaysia (1)

East Malaysia:

Sabah (24-25.VIII.1970*)

0-1. Professional, technical and related workers	...	...	...	...	...	...	...	...	...
2. Administrative and managerial workers	...	...	...	...	...	...	...	...	...
3. Clerical and related workers	...	...	...	...	...	...	...	...	...
4. Sales workers	...	...	...	...	...	...	...	...	...
5. Service workers	...	...	...	...	...	...	...	...	...
6. Agricultural, animal husbandry and forestry workers, fishermen and hunters	...	...	...	...	...	...	...	...	...
7-9. Production and related workers, transport equipment, operators and labourers	...	...	...	...	...	...	...	...	...
X. Workers not classifiable by occupation	...	...	...	...	...	...	...	...	...
Total	...	...	...	...	...	...	...	...	...

Sarawak (24-25.VIII.1970*)

0-1. Professional, technical and related workers	...	...	...	...	...	...	...	...	...
2. Administrative and managerial workers	...	...	...	...	...	...	...	...	...
3. Clerical and related workers	...	...	...	...	...	...	...	...	...
4. Sales workers	...	...	...	...	...	...	...	...	...
5. Service workers	...	...	...	...	...	...	...	...	...
6. Agricultural, animal husbandry and forestry workers, fishermen and hunters	...	...	...	...	...	...	...	...	...
7-9. Production and related workers, transport equipment, operators and labourers	...	...	...	...	...	...	...	...	...
X. Workers not classifiable by occupation	...	...	...	...	...	...	...	...	...
Total	...	...	...	...	...	...	...	...	...

B
Distribution by status and by occupational group
Répartition suivant la situation dans la profession et par groupe de professions
Distribución según la categoría de ocupación y por grupo de ocupación

Others and status unknown / *Autres et situation non définie* / Otros y categoría no definida			TOTAL			*Groupe de professions*	Grupo de ocupaciones
Males / *Hommes* / Hombres	Females / *Femmes* / Mujeres	Total	Males / *Hommes* / Hombres	Females / *Femmes* / Mujeres	Total		
					%₀		
...	...	...	6 596	2 982	**9 578**	4.5	0-1. *Personnel des professions scien-tif., techn., libérales et assi-milées*	0-1. Profesionales, técnicos y tra-bajadores asimilados
...	...	...	1 671	26	**1 697**	0.8	2. *Directeurs et cadres adminis-tratifs supérieurs*	2. Directores y funcionarios públicos superiores
...	...	...	7 884	2 730	**10 614**	5.0	3. *Personnel administratif et tra-vailleurs assimilés*	3. Personal administrativo y tra-bajadores asimilados
...	...	...	5 729	1 988	**7 717**	3.6	4. *Personnel commercial et vendeurs*	4. Comerciantes y vendedores
...	...	...	10 445	3 090	**13 535**	6.4	5. *Travailleurs des services*	5. Trabajadores de los servicios
...	...	...	76 448	43 516	**119 964**	56.3	6. *Agriculteurs, éleveurs, fores-tiers, pêcheurs et chasseurs*	6. Trab. agrícolas y forestales, pescadores y cazadores
...	...	...	28 133	2 183	**30 316**	14.3	7-9. *Ouvriers et manœuvres non agricoles et conducteurs d'engins de transport*	7-9. Obreros no agrícolas, con-ductores de máquinas y vehí-culos de transporte y traba-jadores asimilados
...	...	...	7 673	11 620	**19 293**	9.1	X. *Travailleurs ne pouvant être classés selon la profession*	X. Trabajadores que no pueden ser clasificados según la ocu-pación
...	...	...	144 579	68 135	**212 714**	100.0	*Total*	Total
...	...	...	7 159	3 096	**10 255**	3.0	0-1. *Personnel des professions scien-tif., techn., libérales et assi-milées*	0-1. Profesionales, técnicos y tra-bajadores asimilados
...	...	...	1 689	34	**1 723**	0.5	2. *Directeurs et cadres adminis-tratifs supérieurs*	2. Directores y funcionarios públicos superiores
...	...	...	8 177	2 725	**10 902**	3.2	3. *Personnel administratif et tra-vailleurs assimilés*	3. Personal administrativo y tra-bajadores asimilados
...	...	...	11 166	2 625	**13 791**	4.0	4. *Personnel commercial et vendeurs*	4. Comerciantes y vendedores
...	...	...	13 353	4 241	**17 594**	5.1	5. *Travailleurs des services*	5. Trabajadores de los servicios
...	...	...	126 613	101 340	**227 953**	65.7	6. *Agriculteurs, éleveurs, fores-tiers, pêcheurs et chasseurs*	6. Trab. agrícolas y forestales, pescadores y cazadores
...	...	...	29 613	3 782	**33 395**	9.7	7-9. *Ouvriers et manœuvres non agricoles et conducteurs d'engins de transport*	7-9. Obreros no agrícolas, con-ductores de máquinas y vehí-culos de transporte y traba-jadores asimilados
...	...	...	11 596	18 800	**30 396**	8.8	X. *Travailleurs ne pouvant être classés selon la profession*	X. Trabajadores que no pueden ser clasificados según la ocu-pación
...	...	...	209 366	136 643	**346 009**	100.0	*Total*	Total

2 Structure of the economically active population
Structure de la population active
Estructura de la población económicamente activa

Occupational group	Employers and workers on own account *Employeurs et personnes travaillant à leur propre compte* Empleadores y trabajadores por cuenta propia			Salaried employees and wage earners *Employés et ouvriers* Empleados y obreros			Family workers *Travailleurs familiaux* Trabajadores familiares		
	Males *Hommes* Hombres	Females *Femmes* Mujeres	Total	Males *Hommes* Hombres	Females *Femmes* Mujeres	Total	Males *Hommes* Hombres	Females *Femmes* Mujeres	Total

Malaysia (2)

West Malaysia (24.VIII.1970)

0-1. Professional, technical and related workers	...	...	...	...	...	...	...	...	...
2. Administrative and managerial workers	...	...	...	...	...	...	...	...	...
3. Clerical and related workers	...	...	...	...	...	...	...	...	...
4. Sales workers	...	...	...	...	...	...	...	...	...
5. Service workers	...	...	...	...	...	...	...	...	...
6. Agricultural, animal husbandry and forestry workers, fishermen and hunters	...	...	...	...	...	...	...	...	...
7-9. Production and related workers, transport equipment, operators and labourers	...	...	...	...	...	...	...	...	...
X. Workers not classifiable by occupation	...	...	...	...	...	...	...	...	...
Persons seeking work for the first time	.	.	.	.	.	.	.	.	.
Total . . .	...	...	...	...	...	...	...	...	...

Nepal (22.VI.1971)

0-1. Professional, technical and related workers	4 472	353	**4 825**	18 626	1 633	**20 259**	211	22	**233**
2. Administrative and managerial workers	114	16	**130**	931	29	**960**	4	1	**5**
3. Clerical and related workers	2 530	280	**2 810**	42 140	1 533	**43 673**	239	18	**257**
4. Sales workers	45 307	6 218	**51 525**	6 124	444	**6 568**	1 477	587	**2 064**
5. Service workers	3 445	1 065	**4 510**	25 121	4 153	**29 274**	300	147	**447**
6. Agricultural, animal husbandry and forestry workers, fishermen and hunters	2 847 118	1 253 272	**4 100 390**	237 138	38 677	**275 815**	102 808	100 322	**203 130**
7-9. Production and related workers, transport equipment, operators and labourers	23 235	3 675	**26 910**	71 433	5 297	**76 730**	1 515	494	**2 009**
Total . . .	2 926 221	1 264 879	**4 191 100**	401 513	51 766	**453 279**	106 554	101 591	**208 145**

B Distribution by status and by occupational group
Répartition suivant la situation dans la profession et par groupe de professions
Distribución según la categoría de ocupación y por grupo de ocupación

Others and status unknown / Autres et situation non définie / Otros y categoría no definida			TOTAL			Groupe de professions	Grupo de ocupaciones
Males / Hommes / Hombres	Females / Femmes / Mujeres	Total	Males / Hommes / Hombres	Females / Femmes / Mujeres	Total		
					%		
...	...	...	84 874	44 562	129 436	4.5	0-1. Personnel des professions scientif., techn., libérales et assimilées	0-1. Profesionales, técnicos y trabajadores asimilados
...	...	...	19 623	685	20 308	0.7	2. Directeurs et cadres administratifs supérieurs	2. Directores y funcionarios públicos superiores
...	...	...	99 682	33 659	133 341	4.6	3. Personnel administratif et travailleurs assimilés	3. Personal administrativo y trabajadores asimilados
...	...	...	194 232	42 444	236 676	8.2	4. Personnel commercial et vendeurs	4. Comerciantes y vendedores
...	...	...	151 168	74 249	225 417	7.9	5. Travailleurs des services	5. Trabajadores de los servicios
...	...	...	824 281	497 852	1 322 133	46.1	6. Agriculteurs, éleveurs, forestiers, pêcheurs et chasseurs	6. Trab. agrícolas y forestales, pescadores y cazadores
...	...	...	448 356	94 408	542 764	18.9	7-9. Ouvriers et manœuvres non agricoles et conducteurs d'engins de transport	7-9. Obreros no agrícolas, conductores de máquinas y vehículos de transporte y trabajadores asimilados
...	...	...	55 530	70 750	126 280	4.4	X. Travailleurs ne pouvant être classés selon la profession	X. Trabajadores que no pueden ser clasificados según la ocupación
...	...	...	80 542	54 052	134 594	4.7	Personnes en quête d'emploi pour la première fois	Personas en busca de trabajo por primera vez
...	...	...	1 958 288	912 661	2 870 949	100.0	Total	Total

Others and status unknown / Autres et situation non définie / Otros y categoría no definida			TOTAL			Groupe de professions	Grupo de ocupaciones
Males / Hommes / Hombres	Females / Femmes / Mujeres	Total	Males / Hommes / Hombres	Females / Femmes / Mujeres	Total		
					%		
.	.	.	23 309	2 008	25 317	0.5	0-1. Personnel des professions scientif., techn., libérales et assimilées	0-1. Profesionales, técnicos y trabajadores asimilados
.	.	.	1 049	46	1 095	—	2. Directeurs et cadres administratifs supérieurs	2. Directores y funcionarios públicos superiores
.	.	.	44 909	1 831	46 740	1.0	3. Personnel administratif et travailleurs assimilés	3. Personal administrativo y trabajadores asimilados
.	.	.	52 908	7 249	60 157	1.2	4. Personnel commercial et vendeurs	4. Comerciantes y vendedores
.	.	.	28 866	5 365	34 231	0.7	5. Travailleurs des services	5. Trabajadores de los servicios
.	.	.	3 187 064	1 392 271	4 579 335	94.4	6. Agriculteurs, éleveurs, forestiers, pêcheurs et chasseurs	6. Trab. agrícolas y forestales, pescadores y cazadores
.	.	.	96 183	9 466	105 649	2.2	7-9. Ouvriers et manœuvres non agricoles et conducteurs d'engins de transport	7-9. Obreros no agrícolas, conductores de máquinas y vehículos de transporte y trabajadores asimilados
.	.	.	3 434 288	1 418 236	4 852 524	100.0	Total	Total

POPULATION

2 Structure of the economically active population
Structure de la population active
Estructura de la población económicamente activa

Occupational group	Employers and workers on own account *Employeurs et personnes travaillant à leur propre compte* Empleadores y trabajadores por cuenta propia			Salaried employees and wage earners *Employés et ouvriers* Empleados y obreros			Family workers *Travailleurs familiaux* Trabajadores familiares		
	Males *Hommes* Hombres	Females *Femmes* Mujeres	Total	Males *Hommes* Hombres	Females *Femmes* Mujeres	Total	Males *Hommes* Hombres	Females *Femmes* Mujeres	Total

Pakistan (I.1972) †

Occupational group	Males	Females	Total	Males	Females	Total	Males	Females	Total
0-1. Professional, technical and related workers	...	...	105 975	...	...	251 514	...	...	13 191
2. Administrative and managerial workers	...	...	31 971	...	...	50 599	...	...	6 039
3. Clerical and related workers	...	...	52 610	...	...	327 928	...	...	18 933
4. Sales workers	...	...	1 436 337	...	...	223 414	...	...	488 253
5. Service workers	...	...	225 344	...	...	345 946	...	...	86 234
6. Agricultural, animal husbandry and forestry workers, fishermen and hunters	...	...	5 368 245	...	...	815 801	...	...	4 315 557
7-9. Production and related workers, transport equipment, operators and labourers	...	...	2 177 323	...	...	1 173 934	...	...	592 316
Unemployed	...	...	...	...	...	...	...	...	...
Total . . .	...	...	9 397 805	...	...	3 189 136	...	...	5 520 523

† For notes, see pp. 272-294.

B

Distribution by status and by occupational group
Répartition suivant la situation dans la profession et par groupe de professions
Distribución según la categoría de ocupación y por grupo de ocupación

| Others and status unknown *Autres et situation non définie* Otros y categoría no definida | | | TOTAL | | | *Groupe de professions* | Grupo de ocupaciones |
Males *Hommes* Hombres	Females *Femmes* Mujeres	Total	Males *Hommes* Hombres	Females *Femmes* Mujeres	Total		
					%		
...	...	...	...	...	370 680	2.0	0-1. *Personnel des professions scientif., techn., libérales et assimilées*	0-1. Profesionales, técnicos y trabajadores asimilados
...	...	...	...	...	88 609	0.5	2. *Directeurs et cadres administratifs supérieurs*	2. Directores y funcionarios públicos superiores
...	...	...	...	...	399 471	2.2	3. *Personnel administratif et travailleurs assimilés*	3. Personal administrativo y trabajadores asimilados
...	...	...	...	...	2 148 004	11.6	4. *Personnel commercial et vendeurs*	4. Comerciantes y vendedores
...	...	...	...	...	657 524	3.6	5. *Travailleurs des services*	5. Trabajadores de los servicios
...	..	...	...	...	10 499 603	56.8	6. *Agriculteurs, éleveurs, forestiers, pêcheurs et chasseurs*	6. Trab. agrícolas y forestales, pescadores y cazadores
...	...	...	...	...	3 943 573	21.3	7-9. *Ouvriers et manœuvres non agricoles et conducteurs d'engins de transport*	7-9. Obreros no agrícolas, conductores de máquinas y vehículos de transporte y trabajadores asimilados
...	...	373 766	...	...	373 766	2.0	*Chômeurs*	Desempleados
...	...	373 766	16 893 460	1 587 770	18 481 230	100.0	*Total*	Total

† *Voir notes pp. 272-294.*

† Véanse las notas en las págs. 272-294.

2 Structure of the economically active population
Structure de la population active
Estructura de la población económicamente activa

Occupational group	Employers and workers on own account Employeurs et personnes travaillant à leur propre compte Empleadores y trabajadores por cuenta propia			Salaried employees and wage earners Employés et ouvriers Empleados y obreros			Family workers Travailleurs familiaux Trabajadores familiares		
	Males Hommes Hombres	Females Femmes Mujeres	Total	Males Hommes Hombres	Females Femmes Mujeres	Total	Males Hommes Hombres	Females Femmes Mujeres	Total
Philippines									
(6.V.1970) †									
Professional, technical and related workers	...	...	...	...	...	...	...	...	...
Administrative, executive and managerial workers	...	...	...	...	...	...	...	...	...
Clerical workers	...	...	...	...	...	...	...	...	...
Sales workers	...	...	...	...	...	...	...	...	...
Farmers, fishermen, hunters, loggers and related workers	...	...	...	...	...	...	...	...	...
Miners, quarrymen and related workers	...	...	...	...	...	...	...	...	...
Workers in transport and communication occupations	...	...	...	...	...	...	...	...	...
Craftsmen, prod.-process workers and labourers not elsewhere classified .	...	...	...	...	...	...	...	...	...
Service, sport and recreation workers	...	...	...	...	...	...	...	...	...
Workers not classifiable by occupation	...	...	...	...	...	...	...	...	...
Persons seeking work for the first time	.	.	.	.	.	.	.	.	.
Total . . .	3 572 849	917 090	**4 489 939**	3 297 251	1 611 785	**4 909 036**	1 264 350	1 061 669	**2 326 019**
(V.1974) †									
Professional, technical and related workers	36 000	23 000	**59 000**	236 000	382 000	**618 000**	1 000	1 000	**2 000**
Administrative, executive and managerial workers	53 000	28 000	**82 000**	64 000	6 000	**70 000**	—	—	—
Clerical workers	—	1 000	**1 000**	267 000	230 000	**497 000**	1 000	8 000	**9 000**
Sales workers	357 000	501 000	**858 000**	172 000	114 000	**286 000**	95 000	190 000	**285 000**
Farmers, fishermen, hunters, loggers and related workers	3 481 000	227 000	**3 708 000**	796 000	248 000	**1 044 000**	2 083 000	1 350 000	**3 432 000**
Miners, quarrymen and related workers									
Workers in transport and communication occupations	241 000	245 000	**485 000**	1 440 000	329 000	**1 770 000**	58 000	91 000	**149 000**
Craftsmen, prod.-process workers and labourers not elsewhere classified .									
Service, sport and recreation workers	22 000	42 000	**64 000**	370 000	624 000	**994 000**	10 000	29 000	**40 000**
Workers not classifiable by occupation	1 000	1 000	**3 000**	3 000	2 000	**4 000**	—	—	—
Persons seeking work for the first time	.	.	.	.	.	.	.	.	.
Total . . .	4 191 000	1 068 000	**5 259 000**	3 348 000	1 935 000	**5 284 000**	2 248 000	1 669 000	**3 917 000**

† For notes, see pp. 272-294.

B Distribution by status and by occupational group
Répartition suivant la situation dans la profession et par groupe de professions
Distribución según la categoría de ocupación y por grupo de ocupación

Others and status unknown / *Autres et situation non définie* / Otros y categoría no definida			TOTAL				*Groupe de professions*	Grupo de ocupaciones
Males / *Hommes* / Hombres	Females / *Femmes* / Mujeres	Total	Males / *Hommes* / Hombres	Females / *Femmes* / Mujeres	Total			
						%		
...	...	...	288 603	379 313	**667 916**	*5.4*	*Personnes exerçant une profession libérale, techniciens et assimilés*	Trabajadores profesionales, técnicos y trabajadores asimilados
...	...	...	99 870	39 852	**139 722**	*1.1*	*Directeurs et cadres administratifs supérieurs*	Administradores, gerentes y directores
...	...	...	237 299	145 327	**382 626**	*3.1*	*Employés de bureau*	Empleados de oficina
...	...	...	344 336	454 392	**798 728**	*6.5*	*Vendeurs*	Vendedores
...	...	...	5 028 361	1 224 381	**6 252 742**	*50.8*	*Agriculteurs, pêcheurs, chasseurs, forestiers et travailleurs assimilés*	Agricultores, pescadores, cazadores, trabajadores forestales y asimilados
...	...	...	33 284	523	**33 807**	*0.3*	*Mineurs, carriers et travailleurs assimilés*	Mineros, canteros y trabajadores asimilados
...	...	...	505 228	7 933	**513 161**	*4.2*	*Travailleurs des transports et des communications*	Trabajadores de los transportes y comunicaciones
...	...	...	976 734	724 348	**1 701 082**	*13.8*	*Artisans, ouvriers de métier, ouvriers à la production et manœuvres non classés ailleurs*	Artesanos y trab. ocupados en los div. procesos de producción y peones no clasif. bajo otros epígrafes
...	...	...	303 554	590 158	**893 712**	*7.3*	*Travailleurs spécialisés dans les services, les sports et les activités récréatives*	Trabajadores de los servicios, los deportes y las diversiones
...	...	...	339 869	48 306	**388 175**	*3.2*	*Personnes ne pouvant être classées selon la profession*	Trabajadores que no pueden ser clasificados según la ocupación
...	...	...	210 713	314 199	**524 912**	*4.3*	*Personnes en quête d'emploi pour la première fois*	Personas en busca de trabajo por primera vez
233 401	338 188	**571 589**	8 367 851	3 928 732	**12 296 583**	*100.0*	*Total*	Total
4 000	3 000	**7 000**	277 000	409 000	**686 000**	*4.5*	*Personnes exerçant une profession libérale, techniciens et assimilés*	Trabajadores profesionales, técnicos y trabajadores asimilados
2 000	—	**2 000**	119 000	35 000	**154 000**	*1.0*	*Directeurs et cadres administratifs supérieurs*	Administradores, gerentes y directores
11 000	12 000	**22 000**	279 000	251 000	**529 000**	*3.5*	*Employés de bureau*	Empleados de oficina
19 000	32 000	**50 000**	643 000	837 000	**1 479 000**	*9.7*	*Vendeurs*	Vendedores
109 000	48 000	**157 000**	6 469 000	1 873 000	**8 341 000**	*55.0*	*Agriculteurs, pêcheurs, chasseurs, forestiers et travailleurs assimilés*	Agricultores, pescadores, cazadores, trabajadores forestales y asimilados
128 000	24 000	**153 000**	1 867 000	688 000	**2 556 000**	*16.8*	*Mineurs, carriers et travailleurs assimilés / Travailleurs des transports et des communications / Artisans, ouvriers de métier, ouvriers à la production et manœuvres non classés ailleurs*	Mineros, canteros y trabajadores asimilados / Trabajadores de los transportes y comunicaciones / Artesanos y trab. ocupados en los div. procesos de producción y peones no clasif. bajo otros epígrafes
16 000	31 000	**47 000**	418 000	726 000	**1 145 000**	*7.5*	*Travailleurs spécialisés dans les services, les sports et les activités récréatives*	Trabajadores de los servicios, los deportes y las diversiones
7 000	6 000	**13 000**	11 000	10 000	**21 000**	*0.1*	*Personnes ne pouvant être classées selon la profession*	Trabajadores que no pueden ser clasificados según la ocupación
158 000	134 000	**292 000**	158 000	134 000	**292 000**	*1.9*	*Personnes en quête d'emploi pour la première fois*	Personas en busca de trabajo por primera vez
454 000	291 000	**744 000**	10 240 000	4 964 000	**15 204 000**	*100.0*	*Total*	Total

† *Voir notes pp. 272-294.*

† Véanse las notas en las págs. 272-294.

2 **Structure of the economically active population**
Structure de la population active
Estructura de la población económicamente activa

Occupational group	Employers and workers on own account *Employeurs et personnes travaillant à leur propre compte* Empleadores y trabajadores por cuenta propia			Salaried employees and wage earners *Employés et ouvriers* Empleados y obreros			Family workers *Travailleurs familiaux* Trabajadores familiares		
	Males *Hommes* Hombres	Females *Femmes* Mujeres	Total	Males *Hommes* Hombres	Females *Femmes* Mujeres	Total	Males *Hommes* Hombres	Females *Femmes* Mujeres	Total
Singapore									
(22.VI.1970)									
0-1. Professional, technical and related workers	3 075	676	**3 751**	30 920	21 087	**52 007**	86	55	**141**
2. Administrative and managerial workers	2 928	142	**3 070**	7 734	488	**8 222**	37	15	**52**
3. Clerical and related workers	341	38	**379**	57 690	25 856	**83 546**	158	135	**293**
4. Sales workers	51 120	6 116	**57 236**	30 975	5 817	**36 792**	7 030	4 500	**11 530**
5. Service workers	5 125	2 918	**8 043**	47 077	32 184	**79 261**	726	782	**1 508**
6. Agricultural, animal husbandry and forestry workers, fishermen and hunters	11 761	1 437	**13 198**	6 453	523	**6 976**	3 779	2 990	**6 769**
7-9. Production and related workers, transport equipment, operators and labourers	38 847	4 562	**43 409**	166 451	41 823	**208 274**	2 277	1 027	**3 304**
X. Workers not classifiable by occupation	85	14	**99**	22 586	412	**22 998**	19	15	**34**
Unemployed	...	...	...	...	...	...	...	...	...
Total . . .	113 282	15 903	**129 185**	369 886	128 190	**498 076**	14 112	9 519	**23 631**
(V-VI..1974) †									
0-1. Professional, technical and related workers	4 177	777	**4 954**	56 384	28 945	**85 329**	146	97	**243**
2. Administrative and managerial workers	6 264	389	**6 653**	9 228	874	**10 102**	97	.	**97**
3. Clerical and related workers	728	243	**971**	74 014	59 298	**133 312**	49	146	**195**
4. Sales workers	49 245	7 819	**57 064**	36 133	12 821	**48 954**	5 585	5 731	**11 316**
5. Service workers	3 983	2 720	**6 703**	41 669	34 530	**76 199**	340	1 068	**1 408**
6. Agricultural, animal husbandry and forestry workers, fishermen and hunters	9 859	1 651	**11 510**	4 516	1 360	**5 876**	3 400	3 691	**7 091**
7-9. Production and related workers, transport equipment, operators and labourers	28 945	6 507	**35 452**	191 106	90 186	**281 292**	1 941	1 263	**3 204**
X. Workers not classifiable by occupation	98	.	**98**	34 286	2 040	**36 326**	.	.	.
Unemployed	...	...	...	...	...	...	...	...	...
Total . . .	103 299	20 106	**123 405**	447 336	230 054	**677 390**	11 558	11 996	**23 554**

† For notes, see pp. 272-294.

B Distribution by status and by occupational group
Répartition suivant la situation dans la profession et par groupe de professions
Distribución según la categoría de ocupación y por grupo de ocupación

Others and status unknown *Autres et situation non définie* Otros y categoría no definida			TOTAL			*Groupe de professions*	Grupo de ocupaciones
Males *Hommes* Hombres	Females *Femmes* Mujeres	Total	Males *Hommes* Hombres	Females *Femmes* Mujeres	Total		
						%	
...	...	...	34 081	21 818	**55 899**	7.7	0-1. *Personnel des professions scientif., techn., libérales et assimilées*	0-1. Profesionales, técnicos y trabajadores asimilados
...	...	...	10 699	645	**11 344**	1.6	2. *Directeurs et cadres administratifs supérieurs*	2. Directores y funcionarios públicos superiores
...	...	...	58 189	26 029	**84 218**	11.6	3. *Personnel administratif et travailleurs assimilés*	3. Personal administrativo y trabajadores asimilados
...	...	...	89 125	16 433	**105 558**	14.5	4. *Personnel commercial et vendeurs*	4. Comerciantes y vendedores
...	...	...	52 928	35 884	**88 812**	12.2	5. *Travailleurs des services*	5. Trabajadores de los servicios
...	...	...	21 993	4 950	**26 943**	3.7	6. *Agriculteurs, éleveurs, forestiers, pêcheurs et chasseurs*	6. Trab. agrícolas y forestales, pescadores y cazadores
...	...	...	207 575	47 412	**254 987**	35.1	7-9. *Ouvriers et manœuvres non agricoles et conducteurs d'engins de transport*	7-9. Obreros no agrícolas, conductores de máquinas y vehículos de transporte y trabajadores asimilados
...	...	...	22 690	441	**23 131**	3.2	X. *Travailleurs ne pouvant être classés selon la profession*	X. Trabajadores que no pueden ser clasificados según la ocupación
41 943	33 841	**75 784**	41 943	33 841	**75 784**	10.4	*Chômeurs*	Desempleados
41 943	33 841	**75 784**	539 223	187 453	**726 676**	100.0	*Total*	Total
...	...	...	60 707	29 819	**90 526**	10.5	0-1. *Personnel des professions scientif., techn., libérales et assimilées*	0-1. Profesionales, técnicos y trabajadores asimilados
...	...	...	15 589	1 263	**16 852**	2.0	2. *Directeurs et cadres administratifs supérieurs*	2. Directores y funcionarios públicos superiores
...	...	...	74 791	59 687	**134 478**	15.7	3. *Personnel administratif et travailleurs assimilés*	3. Personal administrativo y trabajadores asimilados
...	...	...	90 963	26 371	**117 334**	13.7	4. *Personnel commercial et vendeurs*	4. Comerciantes y vendedores
...	...	...	45 992	38 318	**84 310**	9.8	5. *Travailleurs des services*	5. Trabajadores de los servicios
...	...	...	17 775	6 702	**24 477**	2.9	6. *Agriculteurs, éleveurs, forestiers, pêcheurs et chasseurs*	6. Trab. agrícolas y forestales, pescadores y cazadores
...	...	...	221 992	97 956	**319 948**	37.2	7-9. *Ouvriers et manœuvres non agricoles et conducteurs d'engins de transport*	7-9. Obreros no agrícolas, conductores de máquinas y vehículos de transporte y trabajadores asimilados
...	...	...	34 384	2 040	**36 424**	4.2	X. *Travailleurs ne pouvant être classés selon la profession*	X. Trabajadores que no pueden ser clasificados según la ocupación
20 106	13 938	**34 044**	20 106	13 938	**34 044**	4.0	*Chômeurs*	Desempleados
20 106	13 938	**34 044**	582 299	276 094	**858 393**	100.0	*Total*	Total

‡ *Voir notes pp. 272-294.*

‡ Véanse las notas en las págs. 272-294.

2 Structure of the economically active population
Structure de la population active
Estructura de la población económicamente activa

Occupational group	Employers and workers on own account Employeurs et personnes travaillant à leur propre compte Empleadores y trabajadores por cuenta propia			Salaried employees and wage earners Employés et ouvriers Empleados y obreros			Family workers Travailleurs familiaux Trabajadores familiares		
	Males Hommes Hombres	Females Femmes Mujeres	Total	Males Hommes Hombres	Females Femmes Mujeres	Total	Males Hommes Hombres	Females Femmes Mujeres	Total

Sri Lanka (9.X.1971*)

0-1. Professional, technical and related workers	11 181	750	**11 931**	92 195	71 906	**164 101**	167	94	**261**
2. Administrative and managerial workers	1 419	53	**1 472**	10 177	632	**10 809**	21	21	**42**
3. Clerical and related workers	1 005	287	**1 292**	166 104	20 557	**186 661**	309	367	**676**
4. Sales workers	132 969	9 202	**142 171**	120 755	6 064	**126 819**	6 071	2 290	**8 361**
5. Service workers	18 422	2 042	**20 464**	128 694	42 452	**171 146**	2 172	2 244	**4 416**
6. Agricultural, animal husbandry and forestry workers, fishermen and hunters	662 022	62 398	**724 420**	544 645	353 415	**898 060**	83 627	84 792	**168 419**
7-9. Production and related workers, transport equipment, operators and labourers	85 547	20 564	**106 111**	670 329	108 526	**778 855**	4 711	2 530	**7 241**
X. Workers not classifiable by occupation	14 222	2 880	**17 102**	47 925	16 646	**64 571**	2 484	4 097	**6 581**
Persons seeking work for the first time ⎱ Unemployed . . . . ⎰	...	...	...	...	...	...	...	...	...
Total . . .	926 787	98 176	**1 024 963**	1 780 824	620 198	**2 401 022**	99 562	96 435	**195 997**

B **Distribution by status and by occupational group**
Répartition suivant la situation dans la profession et par groupe de professions
Distribución según la categoría de ocupación y por grupo de ocupación

Others and status unknown *Autres et situation non définie* Otros y categoría no definida			TOTAL				*Groupe de professions*	Grupo de ocupaciones
Males *Hommes* Hombres	Females *Femmes* Mujeres	Total	Males *Hommes* Hombres	Females *Femmes* Mujeres	Total	%		
...	...	...	103 543	72 750	**176 293**	*4.0*	0-1. *Personnel des professions scientif., techn., libérales et assimilées*	0-1. Profesionales, técnicos y trabajadores asimilados
...	...	...	11 617	706	**12 323**	*0.3*	2. *Directeurs et cadres administratifs supérieurs*	2. Directores y funcionarios públicos superiores
...	...	...	167 418	21 211	**188 629**	*4.3*	3. *Personnel administratif et travailleurs assimilés*	3. Personal administrativo y trabajadores asimilados
...	...	...	259 795	17 556	**277 351**	*6.3*	4. *Personnel commercial et vendeurs*	4. Comerciantes y vendedores
...	...	...	149 288	46 738	**196 026**	*4.4*	5. *Travailleurs des services*	5. Trabajadores de los servicios
...	...	...	1 290 294	500 605	**1 790 899**	*40.5*	6. *Agriculteurs, éleveurs, forestiers, pêcheurs et chasseurs*	6. Trab. agrícolas y forestales, pescadores y cazadores
...	...	...	760 587	131 620	**892 207**	*20.2*	7-9. *Ouvriers et manœuvres non agricoles et conducteurs d'engins de transport*	7-9. Obreros no agrícolas, conductores de máquinas y vehículos de transporte y trabajadores asimilados
...	...	...	64 631	23 623	**88 254**	*2.0*	X. *Travailleurs ne pouvant être classés selon la profession* { *Personnes en quête d'emploi pour la première fois*	X. Trabajadores que no pueden ser clasificados según la ocupación { Personas en busca de trabajo por primera vez
446 406	349 800	**796 206**	446 406	349 800	**796 206**	*18.0*	{ *Chômeurs*	{ Desempleados
446 406	349 800	**796 206**	3 253 579	1 164 609	**4 418 188**	*100.0*	*Total*	Total

2 Structure of the economically active population
Structure de la population active
Estructura de la población económicamente activa

| | Employers and workers on own account
Employeurs et personnes travaillant à leur propre compte
Empleadores y trabajadores por cuenta propia | | | Salaried employees and wage earners
Employés et ouvriers
Empleados y obreros | | | Family workers
Travailleurs familiaux
Trabajadores familiares | | |
Occupational group	Males *Hommes* Hombres	Females *Femmes* Mujeres	Total	Males *Hommes* Hombres	Females *Femmes* Mujeres	Total	Males *Hommes* Hombres	Females *Femmes* Mujeres	Total
République arabe syrienne									
(23.IX.1970) ǂ									
0-1. Professional, technical and related workers	4 884	609	**5 493**	45 125	14 402	**59 527**	141	33	**174**
2. Administrative and managerial workers	2 902	10	**2 912**	2 360	83	**2 443**	12	.	**12**
3. Clerical and related workers	1 742	4	**1 746**	51 867	5 923	**57 790**	113	5	**118**
4. Sales workers	82 996	499	**83 495**	14 933	108	**15 041**	7 151	85	**7 236**
5. Service workers	20 067	347	**20 414**	40 447	6 070	**46 517**	1 152	84	**1 236**
6. Agricultural, animal husbandry and forestry workers, fishermen and hunters	371 992	22 596	**394 588**	115 028	24 012	**139 040**	153 368	60 103	**213 471**
7-9. Production and related workers, transport equipment, operators and labourers	80 567	7 112	**87 679**	302 078	12 605	**314 683**	10 384	2 386	**12 770**
X. Workers not classifiable by occupation	95	4	**99**	724	13	**737**	15	1	**16**
Total . . .	565 245	31 181	**596 426**	572 562	63 216	**635 778**	172 336	62 697	**235 033**
(IX.1973) ǂ									
0-1. Professional, technical and related workers	...	...	...	...	...	...	...	...	...
2. Administrative and managerial workers	...	...	...	...	...	...	...	...	...
3. Clerical and related workers	...	...	...	...	...	...	...	...	...
4. Sales workers	...	...	...	...	...	...	...	...	...
5. Service workers	...	...	...	...	...	...	...	...	...
6. Agricultural, animal husbandry and forestry workers, fishermen and hunters	...	...	...	...	...	...	...	...	...
7-9. Production and related workers, transport equipment, operators and labourers	...	...	...	...	...	...	...	...	...
X. Workers not classifiable by occupation	...	...	...	...	...	...	...	...	...
Persons seeking work for the first time	.	.	.	.	.	.	.	.	.
Total . . .	...	...	**615 419**	...	...	**602 429**	...	...	**394 237**

ǂ For notes, see pp. 272-294.

B

Distribution by status and by occupational group
Répartition suivant la situation dans la profession et par groupe de professions
Distribución según la categoría de ocupación y por grupo de ocupación

Others and status unknown / Autres et situation non définie / Otros y categoría no definida			TOTAL				Groupe de professions	Grupo de ocupaciones
Males / Hommes / Hombres	Females / Femmes / Mujeres	Total	Males / Hommes / Hombres	Females / Femmes / Mujeres	Total	%		
4	1	5	50 154	15 045	**65 199**	4.3	0-1. *Personnel des professions scientif., techn., libérales et assimilées*	0-1. Profesionales, técnicos y trabajadores asimilados
...	...	...	5 274	93	**5 367**	0.4	2. *Directeurs et cadres administratifs supérieurs*	2. Directores y funcionarios públicos superiores
5	...	5	53 727	5 932	**59 659**	3.9	3. *Personnel administratif et travailleurs assimilés*	3. Personal administrativo y trabajadores asimilados
9	...	9	105 089	692	**105 781**	6.9	4. *Personnel commercial et vendeurs*	4. Comerciantes y vendedores
2	2	4	61 668	6 503	**68 171**	4.5	5. *Travailleurs des services*	5. Trabajadores de los servicios
5	...	5	640 393	106 711	**747 104**	49.0	6. *Agriculteurs, éleveurs, forestiers, pêcheurs et chasseurs*	6. Trab. agrícolas y forestales, pescadores y cazadores
71	2	73	393 100	22 105	**415 205**	27.2	7-9. *Ouvriers et manœuvres non agricoles et conducteurs d'engins de transport*	7-9. Obreros no agrícolas, conductores de máquinas y vehículos de transporte y trabajadores asimilados
50 447	6 767	**57 214**	51 281	6 785	**58 066**	3.8	X. *Travailleurs ne pouvant être classés selon la profession*	X. Trabajadores que no pueden ser clasificados según la ocupación
50 543	6 772	**57 315**	1 360 686	163 866	**1 524 552**	100.0	*Total*	Total
...	...	...	51 579	21 515	**73 094**	4.3	0-1. *Personnel des professions scientif., techn., libérales et assimilées*	0-1. Profesionales, técnicos y trabajadores asimilados
...	...	...	2 569	.	**2 569**	0.2	2. *Directeurs et cadres administratifs supérieurs*	2. Directores y funcionarios públicos superiores
...	...	...	99 275	8 757	**108 032**	6.4	3. *Personnel administratif et travailleurs assimilés*	3. Personal administrativo y trabajadores asimilados
...	...	...	144 765	1 133	**145 898**	8.6	4. *Personnel commercial et vendeurs*	4. Comerciantes y vendedores
...	...	...	29 554	4 820	**34 374**	2.0	5. *Travailleurs des services*	5. Trabajadores de los servicios
...	...	...	578 239	280 031	**858 270**	50.9	6. *Agriculteurs, éleveurs, forestiers, pêcheurs et chasseurs*	6. Trab. agrícolas y forestales, pescadores y cazadores
...	...	...	403 385	22 114	**425 499**	25.2	7-9. *Ouvriers et manœuvres non agricoles et conducteurs d'engins de transport*	7-9. Obreros no agrícolas, conductores de máquinas y vehículos de transporte y trabajadores asimilados
...	...	...	8	4	**12**	—	X. *Travailleurs ne pouvant être classés selon la profession*	X. Trabajadores que no pueden ser clasificados según la ocupación
...	...	...	35 241	5 586	**40 827**	2.4	*Personnes en quête d'emploi pour la première fois*	Personas en busca de trabajo por primera vez
...	...	**76 490**	1 344 615	343 960	**1 688 575**	100.0	*Total*	Total

† *Voir notes pp. 272-294.*

† Véanse las notas en las págs. 272-294.

POPULATION

2 Structure of the economically active population
Structure de la population active
Estructura de la población económicamente activa

Occupational group	Employers and workers on own account *Employeurs et personnes travaillant à leur propre compte* Empleadores y trabajadores por cuenta propia			Salaried employees and wage earners *Employés et ouvriers* Empleados y obreros			Family workers *Travailleurs familiaux* Trabajadores familiares		
	Males *Hommes* Hombres	Females *Femmes* Mujeres	Total	Males *Hommes* Hombres	Females *Femmes* Mujeres	Total	Males *Hommes* Hombres	Females *Femmes* Mujeres	Total

Thailand

(1.IV.1970)									
Professional, technical and related workers	13 864	3 926	**17 790**	151 005	110 961	**261 966**	...	...	...
Administrative, executive and managerial workers	10 552	1 536	**12 088**	217 128	15 389	**232 517**	...	...	...
Clerical workers	.	1	**1**	125 728	60 993	**186 721**	...	...	...
Sales workers	233 873	220 591	**454 464**	72 696	34 401	**107 097**	63 634	199 725	**263 359**
Farmers, fishermen, hunters, loggers and related workers	3 510 760	598 158	**4 108 918**	325 800	226 659	**552 459**	2 787 392	5 721 548	**8 508 940**
Miners, quarrymen and related workers	4 574	1 599	**6 173**	25 181	5 295	**30 476**	2 138	3 314	**5 452**
Workers in transport and communication occupations	89 444	2 297	**91 741**	124 324	3 166	**127 490**	3 685	1 131	**4 816**
Craftsmen, prod.-process workers and labourers not elsewhere classified	123 972	75 855	**199 827**	560 147	241 773	**801 920**	33 029	55 827	**88 856**
Service, sport and recreation workers	57 425	47 536	**104 961**	168 725	128 499	**297 224**	13 516	50 044	**63 560**
Workers not classifiable by occupation	...	...	...	...	...	...	...	...	...
Persons seeking work for the first time	.	.	.	.	.	.	.	.	.
Total . . .	4 044 464	951 499	**4 995 963**	1 770 734	827 136	**2 597 870**	2 903 394	6 031 589	**8 934 983**
(VII-IX.1973) ‡									
Professional, technical and related workers	12 330	4 830	**17 160**	156 130	156 420	**312 550**	640	2 620	**3 260**
Administrative, executive and managerial workers	20 820	1 250	**22 070**	90 810	8 340	**99 150**	390	1 950	**2 340**
Clerical workers	2 280	180	**2 460**	167 110	81 550	**248 660**	170	1 070	**1 240**
Sales workers	400 470	444 490	**844 960**	101 110	43 560	**144 670**	100 360	378 170	**478 530**
Farmers, fishermen, hunters, loggers and related workers	3 447 240	755 780	**4 203 020**	513 030	323 040	**836 070**	2 668 370	4 630 450	**7 298 820**
Miners, quarrymen and related workers / Workers in transport and communication occupations	153 070	230	**153 300**	241 070	4 650	**245 720**	4 870	3 310	**8 180**
Craftsmen, prod.-process workers and labourers not elsewhere classified	284 620	132 030	**416 650**	802 860	305 670	**1 108 530**	41 160	94 080	**135 240**
Service, sport and recreation workers	16 250	25 260	**41 510**	213 270	192 710	**405 980**	900	4 380	**5 280**
Workers not classifiable by occupation	.	.	.	70	.	**70**	.	1 590	**1 590**
Persons seeking work for the first time	.	.	.	.	.	.	.	.	.
Total . . .	4 337 080	1 364 050	**5 701 130**	2 285 460	1 115 940	**3 401 400**	2 816 860	5 117 620	**7 934 480**

B Distribution by status and by occupational group
Répartition suivant la situation dans la profession et par groupe de professions
Distribución según la categoría de ocupación y por grupo de ocupación

Others and status unknown / Autres et situation non définie / Otros y categoría no definida			TOTAL				Groupe de professions	Grupo de ocupaciones
Males / Hommes / Hombres	Females / Femmes / Mujeres	Total	Males / Hommes / Hombres	Females / Femmes / Mujeres	Total	%		
2 047	2 301	4 348	166 916	117 188	284 104	1.7	Personnes exerçant une profession libérale, techniciens et assimilés	Trabajadores profesionales, técnicos y trabajadores asimilados
1 296	690	1 986	228 976	17 615	246 591	1.5	Directeurs et cadres administratifs supérieurs	Administradores, gerentes y directores
2 114	1 402	3 516	127 842	62 396	190 238	1.1	Employés de bureau	Empleados de oficina
2 612	6 075	8 687	372 815	460 792	833 607	4.9	Vendeurs	Vendedores
21 370	25 729	47 099	6 645 322	6 572 094	13 217 416	78.4	Agriculteurs, pêcheurs, chasseurs, forestiers et travailleurs assimilés	Agricultores, pescadores, cazadores, trabajadores forestales y asimilados
339	165	504	32 232	10 373	42 605	0.3	Mineurs, carriers et travailleurs assimilés	Mineros, canteros y trabajadores asimilados
727	430	1 157	218 180	7 024	225 204	1.3	Travailleurs des transports et des communications	Trabajadores de los transportes y comunicaciones
13 355	5 985	19 340	730 503	379 440	1 109 943	6.6	Artisans, ouvriers de métier, ouvriers à la production et manœuvres non classés ailleurs	Artesanos y trab. ocupados en los div. procesos de producción y peones no clasif. bajo otros epígrafes
1 652	4 602	6 254	241 318	230 681	471 999	2.8	Travailleurs spécialisés dans les services, les sports et les activités récréatives	Trabajadores de los servicios, los deportes y las diversiones
20 700	9 860	30 560	20 700	9 860	30 560	0.2	Personnes ne pouvant être classées selon la profession	Trabajadores que no pueden ser clasificados según la ocupación
125 956	71 913	197 869	125 956	71 913	197 869	1.2	Personnes en quête d'emploi pour la première fois	Personas en busca de trabajo por primera vez
192 168	129 152	321 320	8 910 760	7 939 376	16 850 136	100.0	Total	Total
2 160	60	2 220	171 260	163 930	335 190	2.0	Personnes exerçant une profession libérale, techniciens et assimilés	Trabajadores profesionales, técnicos y trabajadores asimilados
2 020	.	2 020	114 040	11 540	125 580	0.7	Directeurs et cadres administratifs supérieurs	Administradores, gerentes y directores
4 000	1 320	5 320	173 560	84 120	257 680	1 5	Employés de bureau	Empleados de oficina
3 440	780	4 220	605 380	867 000	1 472 380	8.6	Vendeurs	Vendedores
350	4 070	4 420	6 628 990	5 713 340	12 342 330	72.0	Agriculteurs, pêcheurs, chasseurs, forestiers et travailleurs assimilés / Mineurs, carriers et travailleurs assimilés	Agricultores, pescadores, cazadores, trabajadores forestales y asimilados / Mineros, canteros y trabajadores asimilados
4 280	.	4 280	403 290	8 190	411 480	2.4	Travailleurs des transports et des communications	Trabajadores de los transportes y comunicaciones
11 980	550	12 530	1 140 620	532 330	1 672 950	9.8	Artisans, ouvriers de métier, ouvriers à la production et manœuvres non classés ailleurs	Artesanos y trab. ocupados en los div. procesos de producción y peones no clasif. bajo otros epígrafes
450	430	880	230 870	222 780	453 650	2.7	Travailleurs spécialisés dans les services, les sports et les activités récréatives	Trabajadores de los servicios, los deportes y las diversiones
360	250	610	430	1 840	2 270	—	Personnes ne pouvant être classées selon la profession	Trabajadores que no pueden ser clasificados según la ocupación
27 840	15 200	43 040	27 840	15 200	43 040	0.3	Personnes en quête d'emploi pour la première fois	Personas en busca de trabajo por primera vez
56 880	22 660	76 540	9 496 280	7 620 270	17 116 550	100.0	Total	Total

2 Structure of the economically active population
Structure de la population active
Estructura de la población económicamente activa

Occupational group	Employers and workers on own account *Employeurs et personnes travaillant à leur propre compte* Empleadores y trabajadores por cuenta propia			Salaried employees and wage earners *Employés et ouvriers* Empleados y obreros			Family workers *Travailleurs familiaux* Trabajadores familiares		
	Males *Hommes* Hombres	Females *Femmes* Mujeres	Total	Males *Hommes* Hombres	Females *Femmes* Mujeres	Total	Males *Hommes* Hombres	Females *Femmes* Mujeres	Total

Austria *EUROPE — EUROPE — EUROPA*

Occupational group	Males	Females	Total	Males	Females	Total	Males	Females	Total
(12.V.1971) ǂ									
0-1. Professional, technical and related workers	24 799	6 879	**31 678**	145 001	92 637	**237 638**	...	...	...
2. Administrative and managerial workers	4 386	2 552	**6 938**	11 627	1 383	**13 010**	...	...	...
3. Clerical and related workers	2 874	9 869	**12 743**	237 361	222 740	**460 101**	...	...	...
4. Sales workers	41 213	42 584	**83 797**	73 520	102 535	**176 055**	...	...	...
5. Service workers	22 053	34 652	**56 705**	84 874	220 886	**305 760**	...	...	...
6. Agricultural, animal husbandry and forestry workers, fishermen and hunters	186 586	178 985	**365 571**	41 701	18 219	**59 920**	...	...	...
7-9. Production and related workers, transport equipment, operators and labourers	69 587	12 366	**81 953**	909 932	224 464	**1 134 396**	...	...	...
X. Workers not classifiable by occupation	8 629	8 048	**16 677**	25 421	20 856	**46 277**	...	...	...
Members of the armed forces . . .	.	.	.	8 767	.	**8 767**	.	.	.
Total . . .	360 127	295 935	**656 062**	1 538 204	903 720	**2 441 924**	...	...	...
(1974) ǂ									
0-1. Professional, technical and related workers									
2. Administrative and managerial workers	18 000	18 000	**36 000**	283 000	268 000	**551 000**	...	...	...
3. Clerical and related workers									
4. Sales workers	40 000	36 000	**76 000**	81 000	118 000	**199 000**	...	...	...
5. Service workers	35 000	37 000	**72 000**	104 000	268 000	**372 000**	...	...	...
6. Agricultural, animal husbandry and forestry workers, fishermen and hunters	165 000	171 000	**336 000**	31 000	15 000	**46 000**	...	...	...
7-9. Production and related workers, transport equipment, operators and labourers	70 000	9 000	**79 000**	1 008 000	214 000	**1 222 000**	...	...	...
X. Workers not classifiable by occupation	1 000	2 000	**3 000**	12 000	10 000	**22 000**	...	...	...
Members of the armed forces . . .	.	.	.	9 000	.	**9 000**	.	.	.
Total . . .	329 000	273 000	**602 000**	1 528 000	893 000	**2 421 000**	...	...	...

ǂ For notes, see pp. 272-294.

B Distribution by status and by occupational group
Répartition suivant la situation dans la profession et par groupe de professions
Distribución según la categoría de ocupación y por grupo de ocupación

Others and status unknown / Autres et situation non définie / Otros y categoría no definida			TOTAL				Groupe de professions	Grupo de ocupaciones
Males / Hommes / Hombres	Females / Femmes / Mujeres	Total	Males / Hommes / Hombres	Females / Femmes / Mujeres	Total	%		
.	.	.	169 800	99 516	**269 316**	8.7	0-1. *Personnel des professions scientif., techn., libérales et assimilées*	0-1. Profesionales, técnicos y trabajadores asimilados
.	.	.	16 013	3 935	**19 948**	0.6	2. *Directeurs et cadres administratifs supérieurs*	2. Directores y funcionarios públicos superiores
.	.	.	240 235	232 609	**472 844**	15.3	3. *Personnel administratif et travailleurs assimilés*	3. Personal administrativo y trabajadores asimilados
.	.	.	114 733	145 119	**259 852**	8.4	4. *Personnel commercial et vendeurs*	4. Comerciantes y vendedores
.	.	.	106 927	255 538	**362 465**	11.7	5. *Travailleurs des services*	5. Trabajadores de los servicios
.	.	.	228 287	197 204	**425 491**	13.7	6. *Agriculteurs, éleveurs, forestiers, pêcheurs et chasseurs*	6. Trab. agrícolas y forestales, pescadores y cazadores
.	.	.	979 519	236 830	**1 216 349**	39.3	7-9. *Ouvriers et manœuvres non agricoles et conducteurs d'engins de transport*	7-9. Obreros no agrícolas, conductores de máquinas y vehículos de transporte y trabajadores asimilados
.	.	.	34 050	28 904	**62 954**	2.0	X. *Travailleurs ne pouvant être classés selon la profession*	X. Trabajadores que no pueden ser clasificados según la ocupación
.	.	.	8 767	.	**8 767**	0.3	*Membres des forces armées*	Miembros de las fuerzas armadas
.	.	.	1 898 331	1 199 655	**3 097 986**	100.0	*Total*	Total
							0-1. *Personnel des professions scientif., techn., libérales et assimilées*	0-1. Profesionales, técnicos y trabajadores asimilados
.	.	.	301 000	286 000	587 000	19.4	2. *Directeurs et cadres administratifs supérieurs*	2. Directores y funcionarios públicos superiores
							3. *Personnel administratif et travailleurs assimilés*	3. Personal administrativo y trabajadores asimilados
.	.	.	121 000	154 000	**275 000**	9.1	4. *Personnel commercial et vendeurs*	4. Comerciantes y vendedores
.	.	.	139 000	305 000	**444 000**	14.7	5. *Travailleurs des services*	5. Trabajadores de los servicios
.	.	.	196 000	186 000	**382 000**	12.7	6. *Agriculteurs, éleveurs, forestiers, pêcheurs et chasseurs*	6. Trab. agrícolas y forestales, pescadores y cazadores
.	.	.	1 078 000	223 000	**1 301 000**	43.0	7-9. *Ouvriers et manœuvres non agricoles et conducteurs d'engins de transport*	7-9. Obreros no agrícolas, conductores de máquinas y vehículos de transporte y trabajadores asimilados
.	.	.	13 000	12 000	**25 000**	0.8	X. *Travailleurs ne pouvant être classés selon la profession*	X. Trabajadores que no pueden ser clasificados según la ocupación
.	.	.	9 000	—	**9 000**	0.3	*Membres des forces armées*	Miembros de las fuerzas armadas
.	.	.	1 857 000	1 166 000	**3 023 000**	100.0	*Total*	Total

† *Voir notes pp. 272-294.*

† Véanse las notas en las págs. 272-294.

2 Structure of the economically active population
Structure de la population active
Estructura de la población económicamente activa

Occupational group	Employers and workers on own account / *Employeurs et personnes travaillant à leur propre compte* / Empleadores y trabajadores por cuenta propia			Salaried employees and wage earners / *Employés et ouvriers* / Empleados y obreros			Family workers / *Travailleurs familiaux* / Trabajadores familiares		
	Males *Hommes* Hombres	Females *Femmes* Mujeres	Total	Males *Hommes* Hombres	Females *Femmes* Mujeres	Total	Males *Hommes* Hombres	Females *Femmes* Mujeres	Total
Belgique (31.XII.1970)									
0-1. Professional, technical and related workers	34 305	6 670	**40 975**	190 110	167 866	**357 976**	650	2 760	**3 410**
2. Administrative and managerial workers	22 323	2 088	**24 411**	126 163	14 130	**140 293**	531	952	**1 483**
3. Clerical and related workers	.	.	.	247 332	213 675	**461 007**	469	5 209	**5 678**
4. Sales workers	113 397	87 243	**200 640**	60 832	60 936	**121 768**	9 306	39 040	**48 346**
5. Service workers	13 307	13 440	**26 747**	77 157	135 347	**212 504**	1 196	4 684	**5 880**
6. Agricultural, animal husbandry and forestry workers, fishermen and hunters	102 347	13 343	**115 690**	17 077	860	**17 937**	16 515	14 487	**31 002**
7-9. Production and related workers, transport equipment, operators and labourers	115 966	5 637	**121 603**	1 256 422	240 691	**1 497 113**	10 683	11 072	**21 755**
X. Workers not classifiable by occupation	999	316	**1 315**	7 310	3 462	**10 772**	97	223	**320**
Members of the armed forces . . .	.	.	.	51 985	.	**51 985**	.	.	.
Persons on compulsory military service	.	.	.	.	.	.	.	.	.
Unemployed	...	...	...	...	...	...	...	...	...
Total . . .	402 644	128 737	**531 381**	2 034 388	836 967	**2 871 355**	39 447	78 427	**117 874**
Bulgarie (1.XII.1965)									
Professional, technical and related workers	219	179	**398**	192 753	147 171	**339 924**	...	...	...
Administrative, executive and managerial workers . . . . }	2 368	279	**2 647**	176 285	118 405	**294 690**	...	...	...
Clerical workers . . . . }									
Sales workers	1 779	389	**2 168**	55 285	79 993	**135 278**	...	...	...
Farmers, fishermen, hunters, loggers and related workers	12 508	9 559	**22 067**	126 356	156 415	**282 771**	...	...	...
Miners, quarrymen and related workers	95	16	**111**	56 469	5 133	**61 602**	...	...	...
Workers in transport and communication occupations	1 535	17	**1 552**	217 168	24 557	**241 725**	...	...	...
Craftsmen, prod.-process workers and labourers not elsewhere classified .	12 592	5 139	**17 731**	420 360	249 693	**670 053**	...	...	...
Service, sport and recreation workers	2 695	364	**3 059**	48 035	98 670	**146 705**	...	...	...
Workers not classifiable by occupation	5 642	112	**5 754**	209 895	62 842	**272 737**	...	...	...
Total . . .	39 433	16 054	**55 487**	1 502 606	942 879	**2 445 485**	...	...	...

B **Distribution by status and by occupational group**
Répartition suivant la situation dans la profession et par groupe de professions
Distribución según la categoría de ocupación y por grupo de ocupación

Others and status unknown / Autres et situation non définie / Otros y categoría no definida			TOTAL				Groupe de professions	Grupo de ocupaciones
Males Hommes Hombres	Females Femmes Mujeres	Total	Males Hommes Hombres	Females Femmes Mujeres	Total	%		
328	240	568	225 393	177 536	402 929	11.1	0-1. Personnel des professions scientif., techn., libérales et assimilées	0-1. Profesionales, técnicos y trabajadores asimilados
20	1	21	149 037	17 171	166 208	4.6	2. Directeurs et cadres administratifs supérieurs	2. Directores y funcionarios públicos superiores
6	6	12	247 807	218 890	466 697	12.8	3. Personnel administratif et travailleurs assimilés	3. Personal administrativo y trabajadores asimilados
119	101	220	183 654	187 320	370 974	10.2	4. Personnel commercial et vendeurs	4. Comerciantes y vendedores
52	189	241	91 712	153 660	245 372	6.7	5. Travailleurs des services	5. Trabajadores de los servicios
51	17	68	135 990	28 707	164 697	4.5	6. Agriculteurs, éleveurs, forestiers, pêcheurs et chasseurs	6. Trab. agrícolas y forestales, pescadores y cazadores
651	156	807	1 383 722	257 556	1 641 278	45.2	7-9. Ouvriers et manœuvres non agricoles et conducteurs d'engins de transport	7-9. Obreros no agrícolas, conductores de máquinas y vehículos de transporte y trabajadores asimilados
1 366	646	2 012	9 772	4 647	14 419	0.4	X. Travailleurs ne pouvant être classés selon la profession	X. Trabajadores que no pueden ser clasificados según la ocupación
.	.	.	51 985	.	51 985	1.4	Membres des forces armées	Miembros de las fuerzas armadas
32 991	.	32 991	32 991	.	32 991	0.9	Militaires du contingent	Personas en servicio militar obligatorio
47 668	32 600	80 268	47 668	32 600	80 268	2.2	Chômeurs	Desempleados
83 252	33 956	117 208	2 559 731	1 078 087	3 637 818	100.0	Total	Total

Others and status unknown / Autres et situation non définie / Otros y categoría no definida			TOTAL				Groupe de professions	Grupo de ocupaciones
Males Hommes Hombres	Females Femmes Mujeres	Total	Males Hommes Hombres	Females Femmes Mujeres	Total	%		
11 648	2 329	13 977	204 620	149 679	354 299	8.3	Personnes exerçant une profession libérale, techniciens et assimilés	Trabajadores profesionales, técnicos y trabajadores asimilados
15 936	10 823	26 759	194 589	129 507	324 096	7.6	{ Directeurs et cadres administratifs supérieurs / Employés de bureau	{ Administradores, gerentes y directores / Empleados de oficina
1 727	3 455	5 182	58 791	83 837	142 628	3.3	Vendeurs	Vendedores
594 374	848 813	1 443 187	733 238	1 014 787	1 748 025	41.0	Agriculteurs, pêcheurs, chasseurs, forestiers et travailleurs assimilés	Agricultores, pescadores, cazadores, trabajadores forestales y asimilados
3 554	28	3 582	60 118	5 177	65 295	1.5	Mineurs, carriers et travailleurs assimilés	Mineros, canteros y trabajadores asimilados
62 597	433	63 030	281 300	25 007	306 307	7.2	Travailleurs des transports et des communications	Trabajadores de los transportes y comunicaciones
75 452	42 252	117 704	508 404	297 084	805 488	18.9	Artisans, ouvriers de métier, ouvriers à la production et manœuvres non classés ailleurs	Artesanos y trab. ocupados en los div. procesos de producción y peones no clasif. bajo otros epígrafes
21 855	5 044	26 899	72 585	104 078	176 663	4.1	Travailleurs spécialisés dans les services, les sports et les activités récréatives	Trabajadores de los servicios, los deportes y las diversiones
60 492	6 014	66 506	276 029	68 968	344 997	8.1	Personnes ne pouvant être classées selon la profession	Trabajadores que no pueden ser clasificados según la ocupación
847 635	919 191	1 766 826	2 389 674	1 878 124	4 267 798	100.0	Total	Total

2 Structure of the economically active population
Structure de la population active
Estructura de la población económicamente activa

Occupational group	Employers and workers on own account _Employeurs et personnes travaillant à leur propre compte_ Empleadores y trabajadores por cuenta propia			Salaried employees and wage earners _Employés et ouvriers_ Empleados y obreros			Family workers _Travailleurs familiaux_ Trabajadores familiares		
	Males _Hommes_ Hombres	Females _Femmes_ Mujeres	Total	Males _Hommes_ Hombres	Females _Femmes_ Mujeres	Total	Males _Hommes_ Hombres	Females _Femmes_ Mujeres	Total

Czechoslovakia (1.XII.1970) ‡

Occupational group	Males	Females	Total	Males	Females	Total	Males	Females	Total
0-1. Professional, technical and related workers	3 672	1 679	**5 351**	750 677	552 740	**1 303 417**	.	.	.
2. Administrative and managerial workers	.	.	.	135 282	22 684	**157 966**	.	.	.
3. Clerical and related workers	.	.	.	83 758	410 642	**494 400**	.	.	.
4. Sales workers	44	61	**105**	137 950	334 447	**472 397**	.	.	.
5. Service workers	104	110	**214**	147 614	424 016	**571 630**	.	.	.
6. Agricultural, animal husbandry and forestry workers, fishermen and hunters	27 985	27 521	**55 506**	150 904	122 427	**273 331**	.	.	.
7-9. Production and related workers, transport equipment, operators and labourers	1 643	893	**2 536**	2 011 050	798 516	**2 809 566**	.	.	.
X. Workers not classifiable by occupation	265	190	**455**	6 835	4 814	**11 649**	.	.	.
Total . . .	33 713	30 454	**64 167**	3 424 070	2 670 286	**6 094 356**	.	.	.

Denmark (9.XI.1970)

Occupational group	Males	Females	Total	Males	Females	Total	Males	Females	Total
Professional, technical and related workers	17 259	4 803	**22 062**	110 786	145 877	**256 663**	34	3 693	**3 727**
Administrative, executive and managerial workers	12 525	980	**13 505**	19 150	1 705	**20 855**	36	3 605	**3 641**
Clerical workers	.	.	.	110 155	187 133	**297 288**	.	.	.
Sales workers	46 070	10 915	**56 985**	75 087	70 730	**145 817**	322	19 194	**19 516**
Farmers, fishermen, hunters, loggers and related workers	130 995	4 617	**135 612**	58 328	4 452	**62 780**	167	45 422	**45 589**
Workers in transport and communication occupations . . . . Craftsmen, prod.-process workers and labourers not elsewhere classified .	76 609	3 338	**79 947**	679 529	121 069	**800 598**	100	18 493	**18 593**
Service, sport and recreation workers	13 132	9 570	**22 702**	48 138	168 165	**216 303**	179	7 349	**7 528**
Workers not classifiable by occupation	.	.	.	51 251	16 388	**67 639**	.	.	.
Members of the armed forces	.	.	.	15 892	45	**15 937**	.	.	.
Total . . .	296 590	34 223	**330 813**	1 168 316	715 564	**1 883 880**	838	97 756	**98 594**

‡ For notes, see pp. 272-294.

B Distribution by status and by occupational group
Répartition suivant la situation dans la profession et par groupe de professions
Distribución según la categoría de ocupación y por grupo de ocupación

Others and status unknown / Autres et situation non définie / Otros y categoría no definida			TOTAL				Groupe de professions	Grupo de ocupaciones
Males / Hommes / Hombres	Females / Femmes / Mujeres	Total	Males / Hommes / Hombres	Females / Femmes / Mujeres	Total	%		
38 147	9 205	47 352	792 496	563 624	1 356 120	19.4	0-1. Personnel des professions scientif., techn., libérales et assimilées	0-1. Profesionales, técnicos y trabajadores asimilados
7 280	117	7 397	142 562	22 801	165 363	2.4	2. Directeurs et cadres administratifs supérieurs	2. Directores y funcionarios públicos superiores
4 097	20 625	24 722	87 855	431 267	519 122	7.4	3. Personnel administratif et travailleurs assimilés	3. Personal administrativo y trabajadores asimilados
9 858	8 257	18 115	147 852	342 765	490 617	7.0	4. Personnel commercial et vendeurs	4. Comerciantes y vendedores
9 279	9 765	19 044	156 997	433 891	590 888	8.5	5. Travailleurs des services	5. Trabajadores de los servicios
216 677	291 965	508 642	395 566	441 913	837 479	12.0	6. Agriculteurs, éleveurs, forestiers, pêcheurs et chasseurs	6. Trab. agrícolas y forestales, pescadores y cazadores
103 297	65 317	168 614	2 115 990	864 726	2 980 716	42.7	7-9. Ouvriers et manœuvres non agricoles et conducteurs d'engins de transport	7-9. Obreros no agrícolas, conductores de máquinas y vehículos de transporte y trabajadores asimilados
23 558	6 535	30 093	30 658	11 539	42 197	0.6	X. Travailleurs ne pouvant être classés selon la profession	X. Trabajadores que no pueden ser clasificados según la ocupación
412 193	411 786	823 979	3 869 976	3 112 526	6 982 502	100.0	Total	Total

						%		
.	.	.	128 079	154 373	282 452	12.2	Personnes exerçant une profession libérale, techniciens et assimilés	Trabajadores profesionales, técnicos y trabajadores asimilados
.	.	.	31 711	6 290	38 001	1.6	Directeurs et cadres administratifs supérieurs	Administradores, gerentes y directores
.	.	.	110 155	187 133	297 288	12.9	Employés de bureau	Empleados de oficina
.	.	.	121 479	100 839	222 318	9.6	Vendeurs	Vendedores
.	.	.	189 490	54 491	243 981	10.5	Agriculteurs, pêcheurs, chasseurs, forestiers et travailleurs assimilés	Agricultores, pescadores, cazadores, trabajadores forestales y asimilados
.	.	.	756 238	142 900	899 138	38.9	Travailleurs des transports et des communications / Artisans, ouvriers de métier, ouvriers à la production et manœuvres non classés ailleurs	Trabajadores de los transportes y comunicaciones / Artesanos y trab. ocupados en los div. procesos de producción y peones no clasif. bajo otros epígrafes
.	.	.	61 449	185 084	246 533	10.7	Travailleurs spécialisés dans les services, les sports et les activités récréatives	Trabajadores de los servicios, los deportes y las diversiones
.	.	.	51 251	16 388	67 639	2.9	Personnes ne pouvant être classées selon la profession	Trabajadores que no pueden ser clasificados según la ocupación
.	.	.	15 892	45	15 937	0.7	Membres des forces armées	Miembros de las fuerzas armadas
.	.	.	1 465 744	847 543	2 313 287	100.0	Total	Total

† Voir notes pp. 272-294.   † Véanse las notas en las págs. 272-294.

241

POPULATION

2 Structure of the economically active population
Structure de la population active
Estructura de la población económicamente activa

Occupational group	Employers and workers on own account *Employeurs et personnes travaillant à leur propre compte* Empleadores y trabajadores por cuenta propia			Salaried employees and wage earners *Employés et ouvriers* Empleados y obreros			Family workers *Travailleurs familiaux* Trabajadores familiares		
	Males *Hommes* Hombres	Females *Femmes* Mujeres	Total	Males *Hommes* Hombres	Females *Femmes* Mujeres	Total	Males *Hommes* Hombres	Females *Femmes* Mujeres	Total

España (31.XII.1970) †

0-1. Professional, technical and related workers	82 810	15 784	**98 594**	336 506	172 736	**509 242**	3 442	2 084	**5 526**
2. Administrative and managerial workers	.	.	.	75 861	3 134	**78 995**	.	.	.
3. Clerical and related workers	1 507	889	**2 396**	755 187	318 083	**1 073 270**	7 302	4 625	**11 927**
4. Sales workers	312 051	81 701	**393 752**	371 196	156 535	**527 731**	29 054	31 437	**60 491**
5. Service workers	100 689	36 963	**137 652**	435 126	493 264	**928 390**	14 829	13 695	**28 524**
6. Agricultural, animal husbandry and forestry workers, fishermen and hunters	1 042 569	66 742	**1 109 311**	1 159 107	65 904	**1 225 011**	391 391	171 830	**563 221**
7-9. Production and related workers, transport equipment, operators and labourers	439 518	43 307	**482 825**	3 585 774	550 082	**4 135 856**	62 874	9 265	**72 139**
X. Workers not classifiable by occupation	18 019	3 835	**21 854**	101 578	34 380	**135 958**	3 905	1 134	**5 039**
Members of the armed forces . . .	.	.	.	142 506	.	**142 506**	.	.	.
Total . . .	1 997 163	249 221	**2 246 384**	6 962 841	1 794 118	**8 756 959**	512 797	234 070	**746 867**

Faeroe Is. (1.IV.1966)

Professional, technical and related workers	.	.	.	369	409	**778**	...	...	...
Administrative, executive and managerial workers	.	.	.	123	20	**143**	...	...	...
Clerical workers	.	.	.	464	476	**940**	...	...	...
Sales workers	340	67	**407**	147	521	**668**	...	...	...
Farmers, fishermen, hunters, loggers and related workers	1 511	16	**1 527**	2 132	14	**2 146**	...	...	...
Miners, quarrymen and related workers	1	.	**1**	117	.	**117**	...	...	...
Workers in transport and communication occupations	174	2	**176**	1 231	82	**1 313**	...	...	...
Craftsmen, prod.-process workers and labourers not elsewhere classified .	414	19	**433**	4 260	311	**4 571**	...	...	...
Service, sport and recreation workers	84	51	**135**	140	1 319	**1 459**	...	...	...
Members of the armed forces	.	.	.	103	.	**103**	.	.	.
Total . . .	2 524	155	**2 679**	9 086	3 152	**12 238**	...	...	...

† For notes, see pp. 272-294.

B Distribution by status and by occupational group
Répartition suivant la situation dans la profession et par groupe de professions
Distribución según la categoría de ocupación y por grupo de ocupación

Others and status unknown / Autres et situation non définie / Otros y categoría no definida			TOTAL				Groupe de professions	Grupo de ocupaciones
Males / Hommes / Hombres	Females / Femmes / Mujeres	Total	Males / Hommes / Hombres	Females / Femmes / Mujeres	Total	%		
18 202	25 953	**44 155**	440 960	216 557	**657 517**	5.5	0-1. *Personnel des professions scientif., techn., libérales et assimilées*	0-1. Profesionales, técnicos y trabajadores asimilados
1 265	287	**1 552**	77 126	3 421	**80 547**	0.7	2. *Directeurs et cadres administratifs supérieurs*	2. Directores y funcionarios públicos superiores
6 378	4 125	**10 503**	770 374	327 722	**1 098 096**	9.2	3. *Personnel administratif et travailleurs assimilés*	3. Personal administrativo y trabajadores asimilados
5 774	2 299	**8 073**	718 075	271 972	**990 047**	8.3	4. *Personnel commercial et vendeurs*	4. Comerciantes y vendedores
6 198	10 586	**16 784**	556 842	554 508	**1 111 350**	9.3	5. *Travailleurs des services*	5. Trabajadores de los servicios
16 407	2 576	**18 983**	2 609 474	307 052	**2 916 526**	24.5	6. *Agriculteurs, éleveurs, forestiers, pêcheurs et chasseurs*	6. Trab. agrícolas y forestales, pescadores y cazadores
35 422	7 452	**42 874**	4 123 588	610 106	**4 733 694**	39.8	7-9. *Ouvriers et manœuvres non agricoles et conducteurs d'engins de transport*	7-9. Obreros no agrícolas, conductores de máquinas y vehículos de transporte y trabajadores asimilados
11 607	3 318	**14 925**	135 109	42 667	**177 776**	1.5	X. *Travailleurs ne pouvant être classés selon la profession*	X. Trabajadores que no pueden ser clasificados según la ocupación
.	.	.	142 506	.	**142 506**	1.2	*Membres des forces armées*	Miembros de las fuerzas armadas
101 253	56 596	**157 849**	9 574 054	2 334 005	**11 908 059**	100.0	*Total*	Total

Others and status unknown			TOTAL				Groupe de professions	Grupo de ocupaciones
Males	Females	Total	Males	Females	Total	%		
.	.	.	369	409	**778**	5.2	*Personnes exerçant une profession libérale, techniciens et assimilés*	Trabajadores profesionales, técnicos y trabajadores asimilados
.	.	.	123	20	**143**	1.0	*Directeurs et cadres administratifs supérieurs*	Administradores, gerentes y directores
.	.	.	464	476	**940**	6.3	*Employés de bureau*	Empleados de oficina
.	.	.	487	588	**1 075**	7.2	*Vendeurs*	Vendedores
.	.	.	3 643	30	**3 673**	24.6	*Agriculteurs, pêcheurs, chasseurs, forestiers et travailleurs assimilés*	Agricultores, pescadores, cazadores, trabajadores forestales y asimilados
.	.	.	118	.	**118**	0.8	*Mineurs, carriers et travailleurs assimilés*	Mineros, canteros y trabajadores asimilados
.	.	.	1 405	84	**1 489**	10.0	*Travailleurs des transports et des communications*	Trabajadores de los transportes y comunicaciones
.	.	.	4 674	330	**5 004**	33.5	*Artisans, ouvriers de métier, ouvriers à la production et manœuvres non classés ailleurs*	Artesanos y trab. ocupados en los div. procesos de producción y peones no clasif. bajo otros epígrafes
.	.	.	224	1 370	**1 594**	10.7	*Travailleurs spécialisés dans les services, les sports et les activités récréatives*	Trabajadores de los servicios, los deportes y las diversiones
.	.	.	103	.	**103**	0.7	*Membres des forces armées*	Miembros de las fuerzas armadas
.	.	.	11 610	3 307	**14 917**	100.0	*Total*	Total

‡ *Voir notes pp. 272-294.*　　　　　　　　　　　　　　　　　　　　　‡ Véanse las notas en las págs. 272-294.

243

2 Structure of the economically active population
Structure de la population active
Estructura de la población económicamente activa

Occupational group	Employers and workers on own account / Employeurs et personnes travaillant à leur propre compte / Empleadores y trabajadores por cuenta propia			Salaried employees and wage earners / Employés et ouvriers / Empleados y obreros			Family workers / Travailleurs familiaux / Trabajadores familiares		
	Males / Hommes / Hombres	Females / Femmes / Mujeres	Total	Males / Hommes / Hombres	Females / Femmes / Mujeres	Total	Males / Hommes / Hombres	Females / Femmes / Mujeres	Total

Finland (31.XII.1970)

Occupational group	Males	Females	Total	Males	Females	Total	Males	Females	Total
Professional, technical and related workers	4 884	3 350	8 234	114 678	128 255	242 933	43	260	303
Administrative, executive and managerial workers ⎫ Clerical workers ⎬	1 110	394	1 504	60 233	146 079	206 312	105	2 019	2 124
Sales workers	15 476	9 553	25 029	55 049	84 979	140 028	1 377	7 071	8 448
Farmers, fishermen, hunters, loggers and related workers	176 845	31 795	208 640	68 977	7 860	76 837	38 263	101 882	140 145
Miners, quarrymen and related workers	438	9	447	6 251	186	6 437	26	5	31
Workers in transport and communication occupations	21 300	432	21 732	98 432	30 464	128 896	1 033	254	1 287
Craftsmen, prod.-process workers and labourers not elsewhere classified	20 838	5 151	25 989	482 720	149 091	631 811	2 136	1 288	3 424
Service, sport and recreation workers	1 637	8 807	10 444	40 862	170 026	210 888	164	976	1 140
Workers not classifiable by occupation	150	31	181	.	.	.	3	2	5
Members of the armed forces	.	.	.	8 185	82	8 267	.	.	.
Total	242 678	59 522	302 200	935 387	717 022	1 652 409	43 150	113 757	156 907

France (1.III.1968) †

Occupational group	Males	Females	Total	Males	Females	Total	Males	Females	Total
0-1. Professional, technical and related workers	153 720	43 720	197 440	1 167 220	956 640	2 123 860	1 520	7 720	9 240
2. Administrative and managerial workers	162 660	18 800	181 460	325 320	43 460	368 780	1 560	3 580	5 140
3. Clerical and related workers	1 000	1 060	2 060	892 420	1 468 900	2 361 320	900	19 800	20 700
4. Sales workers	351 920	205 320	557 240	405 300	365 600	770 900	19 800	208 820	228 620
5. Service workers	114 620	111 900	226 520	388 980	1 038 960	1 427 940	7 740	52 740	60 480
6. Agricultural, animal husbandry and forestry workers, fishermen and hunters	1 248 780	169 600	1 418 380	580 220	61 880	642 100	300 880	766 840	1 067 720
7-9. Production and related workers, transport equipment, operators and labourers	582 260	43 600	625 860	5 398 280	1 000 720	6 399 000	23 880	18 060	41 940
X. Workers not classifiable by occupation	9 580	2 460	12 040	702 320	305 680	1 008 000	1 580	2 440	4 020
Members of the armed forces	.	.	.	235 620	5 860	241 480	.	.	.
Unemployed	...	...	...	...	...	...	...	...	...
Total	2 624 540	596 460	3 221 000	10 095 680	5 247 700	15 343 380	357 860	1 080 000	1 437 860

† For notes, see pp. 272-294.

B Distribution by status and by occupational group
Répartition suivant la situation dans la profession et par groupe de professions
Distribución según la categoría de ocupación y por grupo de ocupación

Others and status unknown / Autres et situation non définie / Otros y categoría no definida			TOTAL				Groupe de professions	Grupo de ocupaciones
Males / Hommes / Hombres	Females / Femmes / Mujeres	Total	Males / Hommes / Hombres	Females / Femmes / Mujeres	Total	%		
...	...	...	119 605	131 865	251 470	11.9	Personnes exerçant une profession libérale, techniciens et assimilés	Trabajadores profesionales, técnicos y trabajadores asimilados
...	...	...	61 448	148 492	209 940	9.9	Directeurs et cadres administratifs supérieurs	Administradores, gerentes y directores
...	...	...	71 902	101 603	173 505	8.2	Employés de bureau	Empleados de oficina
							Vendeurs	Vendedores
...	...	...	284 085	141 537	425 622	20.1	Agriculteurs, pêcheurs, chasseurs, forestiers et travailleurs assimilés	Agricultores, pescadores, cazadores, trabajadores forestales y asimilados
...	...	...	6 715	200	6 915	0.3	Mineurs, carriers et travailleurs assimilés	Mineros, canteros y trabajadores asimilados
...	...	...	120 765	31 150	151 915	7.2	Travailleurs des transports et des communications	Trabajadores de los transportes y comunicaciones
...	...	...	505 694	155 530	661 224	31.2	Artisans, ouvriers de métier, ouvriers à la production et manœuvres non classés ailleurs	Artesanos y trab. ocupados en los div. procesos de producción y peones no clasif. bajo otros epígrafes
...	...	...	42 663	179 809	222 472	10.5	Travailleurs spécialisés dans les services, les sports et les activités récréatives	Trabajadores de los servicios, los deportes y las diversiones
4 451	2 290	6 741	4 604	2 323	6 927	0.3	Personnes ne pouvant être classées selon la profession	Trabajadores que no pueden ser clasificados según la ocupación
.	.	.	8 185	82	8 267	0.4	Membres des forces armées	Miembros de las fuerzas armadas
4 451	2 290	6 741	1 225 666	892 591	2 118 257	100.0	Total	Total

Others and status unknown			TOTAL				Groupe de professions	Grupo de ocupaciones
Males	Females	Total	Males	Females	Total	%		
...	...	...	1 322 460	1 008 080	2 330 540	11.4	0-1. Personnel des professions scientif., techn., libérales et assimilées	0-1. Profesionales, técnicos y trabajadores asimilados
...	...	...	489 540	65 840	555 380	2.7	2. Directeurs et cadres administratifs supérieurs	2. Directores y funcionarios públicos superiores
...	...	...	894 320	1 489 760	2 384 080	11.7	3. Personnel administratif et travailleurs assimilés	3. Personal administrativo y trabajadores asimilados
...	...	...	777 020	779 740	1 556 760	7.6	4. Personnel commercial et vendeurs	4. Comerciantes y vendedores
...	...	...	511 340	1 203 600	1 714 940	8.4	5. Travailleurs des services	5. Trabajadores de los servicios
...	...	...	2 129 880	998 320	3 128 200	15.3	6. Agriculteurs, éleveurs, forestiers, pêcheurs et chasseurs	6. Trab. agrícolas y forestales, pescadores y cazadores
...	...	...	6 004 420	1 062 380	7 066 800	34.6	7-9. Ouvriers et manœuvres non agricoles et conducteurs d'engins de transport	7-9. Obreros no agrícolas, conductores de máquinas y vehículos de transporte y trabajadores asimilados
...	...	...	713 480	310 580	1 024 060	5.0	X. Travailleurs ne pouvant être classés selon la profession	X. Trabajadores que no pueden ser clasificados según la ocupación
...	...	...	235 620	5 860	241 480	1.2	Membres des forces armées	Miembros de las fuerzas armadas
237 560	199 360	436 920	237 560	199 360	436 920	2.1	Chômeurs	Desempleados
237 560	199 360	436 920	13 315 640	7 123 520	20 439 160	100.0	Total	Total

‡ *Voir notes pp. 272-294.*

‡ Véanse las notas en las págs. 272-294.

2 Structure of the economically active population
Structure de la population active
Estructura de la población económicamente activa

Occupational group	Employers and workers on own account Employeurs et personnes travaillant à leur propre compte Empleadores y trabajadores por cuenta propia			Salaried employees and wage earners Employés et ouvriers Empleados y obreros			Family workers Travailleurs familiaux Trabajadores familiares		
	Males Hommes Hombres	Females Femmes Mujeres	Total	Males Hommes Hombres	Females Femmes Mujeres	Total	Males Hommes Hombres	Females Femmes Mujeres	Total

Germany, Fed. Rep. of (27.V.1970 *) △ ☨

Occupational group	Males	Females	Total	Males	Females	Total	Males	Females	Total
0-1. Professional, technical and related workers	241 100	51 900	**293 000**	1 470 700	830 400	**2 301 100**	1 300	12 600	**13 900**
2. Administrative and managerial workers	56 400	15 200	**71 600**	447 900	58 500	**506 400**	2 000	5 500	**7 500**
3. Clerical and related workers	7 600	4 700	**12 300**	2 092 900	2 437 800	**4 530 700**	6 000	94 500	**100 500**
4. Sales workers	401 400	164 100	**565 500**	700 000	932 000	**1 632 000**	15 200	148 400	**163 600**
5. Service workers	135 200	105 100	**240 300**	1 003 700	1 218 600	**2 222 300**	9 600	56 400	**66 000**
6. Agricultural, animal husbandry and forestry workers, fishermen and hunters	576 100	74 500	**650 600**	248 200	69 300	**317 500**	231 800	833 800	**1 065 600**
7-9. Production and related workers, transport equipment, operators and labourers	527 700	39 700	**567 400**	7 393 400	1 580 400	**8 973 800**	27 900	37 800	**65 700**
X. Workers not classifiable by occupation	5 000	2 900	**7 900**	25 800	30 200	**56 000**	...	...	...
Foreign workers	...	...	...	...	...	...	...	...	...
Unemployed	...	...	...	...	...	...	...	...	...
Total	1 950 500	458 100	**2 408 600**	13 382 600	7 157 200	**20 539 800**	293 800	1 189 000	**1 482 800**

Gibraltar (6.X.1970 *)

Occupational group	Males	Females	Total	Males	Females	Total	Males	Females	Total
0-1. Professional, technical and related workers	...	...	...	...	...	...	...	...	...
2. Administrative and managerial workers	...	...	...	...	...	...	...	...	...
3. Clerical and related workers									
4. Sales workers	...	...	...	...	...	...	...	...	...
5. Service workers	...	...	...	...	...	...	...	...	...
6. Agricultural, animal husbandry and forestry workers, fishermen and hunters	.	.	.	.	.	.	.	.	.
7-9. Production and related workers, transport equipment, operators and labourers	...	...	...	...	...	...	...	...	...
Total	572	122	**694**	8 493	2 525	**11 018**	...	...	...

☨ For notes, see pp. 272-294.

B Distribution by status and by occupational group
Répartition suivant la situation dans la profession et par groupe de professions
Distribución según la categoría de ocupación y por grupo de ocupación

Males Hommes Hombres	Females Femmes Mujeres	Total	Males Hommes Hombres	Females Femmes Mujeres	Total	%	Groupe de professions	Grupo de ocupaciones
							0-1. *Personnel des professions scientif., techn., libérales et assimilées*	0-1. Profesionales, técnicos y trabajadores asimilados
...	...	...	1 713 100	894 900	**2 608 000**	*9.8*	2. *Directeurs et cadres administratifs supérieurs*	2. Directores y funcionarios públicos superiores
...	...	...	506 300	79 200	**585 500**	*2.2*	3. *Personnel administratif et travailleurs assimilés*	3. Personal administrativo y trabajadores asimilados
...	...	...	2 106 500	2 537 000	**4 643 500**	*17.5*	4. *Personnel commercial et vendeurs*	
...	...	...	1 116 600	1 244 500	**2 361 100**	*8.9*		4. Comerciantes y vendedores
...	...	...	1 148 500	1 380 100	**2 528 600**	*9.5*	5. *Travailleurs des services*	5. Trabajadores de los servicios
							6. *Agriculteurs, éleveurs, forestiers, pêcheurs et chasseurs*	6. Trab. agrícolas y forestales, pescadores y cazadores
...	...	...	1 056 100	977 600	**2 033 700**	*7.6*		7-9. Obreros no agrícolas, conductores de máquinas y vehículos de transporte y trabajadores asimilados
							7-9. *Ouvriers et manœuvres non agricoles et conducteurs d'engins de transport*	
...	...	...	7 949 000	1 657 900	**9 606 900**	*36.1*		X. Trabajadores que no pueden ser clasificados según la ocupación
							X. *Travailleurs ne pouvant être classés selon la profession*	
20 200	155 300	**175 500**	51 000	188 400	**239 400**	*0.9*		
1 357 200	529 600	**1 886 800**	1 357 200	529 600	**1 886 800**	*7.1*	*Travailleurs étrangers*	Trabajadores extranjeros
70 500	46 100	**116 600**	70 500	46 100	**116 600**	*0.4*	*Chômeurs*	Desempleados
1 447 900	731 000	**2 178 900**	17 074 700	9 535 200	**26 610 100**	*100.0*	*Total*	Total

Males Hommes Hombres	Females Femmes Mujeres	Total	Males Hommes Hombres	Females Femmes Mujeres	Total	%	Groupe de professions	Grupo de ocupaciones
							0-1. *Personnel des professions scientif., techn., libérales et assimilées*	0-1. Profesionales, técnicos y trabajadores asimilados
...	...	...	549	412	**961**	*8.2*	2. *Directeurs et cadres administratifs supérieurs*	2. Directores y funcionarios públicos superiores
...	...	...	1 738	624	**2 362**	*20.1*	3. *Personnel administratif et travailleurs assimilés*	3. Personal administrativo y trabajadores asimilados
							4. *Personnel commercial et vendeurs*	
...	...	...	726	464	**1 190**	*10.1*		4. Comerciantes y vendedores
...	...	...	1 030	958	**1 988**	*16.9*	5. *Travailleurs des services*	5. Trabajadores de los servicios
							6. *Agriculteurs, éleveurs, forestiers, pêcheurs et chasseurs*	6. Trab. agrícolas y forestales, pescadores y cazadores
.	.	.	.	.	.	.		7-9. Obreros no agrícolas, conductores de máquinas y vehículos de transporte y trabajadores asimilados
							7-9. *Ouvriers et manœuvres non agricoles et conducteurs d'engins de transport*	
...	...	...	5 048	199	**5 247**	*44.7*		
26	10	**36**	9 091	2 657	**11 748**	*100.0*	*Total*	Total

† *Voir notes pp. 272-294.*

† Véanse las notas en las págs. 272-294.

2 Structure of the economically active population
Structure de la population active
Estructura de la población económicamente activa

Occupational group	Employers and workers on own account *Employeurs et personnes travaillant à leur propre compte* Empleadores y trabajadores por cuenta propia			Salaried employees and wage earners *Employés et ouvriers* Empleados y obreros			Family workers *Travailleurs familiaux* Trabajadores familiares		
	Males *Hommes* Hombres	Females *Femmes* Mujeres	Total	Males *Hommes* Hombres	Females *Femmes* Mujeres	Total	Males *Hommes* Hombres	Females *Femmes* Mujeres	Total

Grèce (14.III.1971) ‡

0-1. Professional, technical and related workers	36 436	7 836	**44 272**	81 348	54 044	**135 392**	1 068	1 336	**2 404**
2. Administrative and managerial workers	3 488	244	**3 732**	14 684	1 292	**15 976**	28	24	**52**
3. Clerical and related workers	4 212	1 172	**5 384**	156 964	78 652	**235 616**	464	1 168	**1 632**
4. Sales workers	137 616	15 704	**153 320**	43 756	21 096	**64 852**	5 828	8 052	**13 880**
5. Service workers	44 552	12 668	**57 220**	103 144	66 380	**169 524**	2 308	5 345	**7 656**
6. Agricultural, animal husbandry and forestry workers, fishermen and hunters	623 436	72 380	**695 816**	45 084	18 904	**63 988**	162 116	384 100	**546 216**
7-9. Production and related workers, transport equipment, operators and labourers	235 436	33 424	**268 860**	574 660	97 952	**672 612**	11 084	8 808	**19 892**
X. Workers not classifiable by occupation	17 936	1 356	**19 292**	6 596	5 288	**11 884**	800	1 320	**2 120**
Total . . .	1 103 112	144 784	**1 247 896**	1 026 236	343 608	**1 369 844**	183 696	410 156	**593 852**

Hongrie (1.I.1970) ‡

0-1. Professional, technical and related workers	1 467	698	**2 165**	277 555	254 192	**531 747**	.	.	.
2. Administrative and managerial workers	86	4	**90**	22 526	4 223	**26 749**	.	.	.
3. Clerical and related workers	30	52	**82**	173 902	353 338	**527 240**	.	.	.
4. Sales workers	3 256	4 682	**7 938**	61 761	99 468	**161 229**	496	646	**1 142**
5. Service workers	3 181	2 249	**5 430**	75 119	190 086	**265 205**	213	517	**730**
6. Agricultural, animal husbandry and forestry workers, fishermen and hunters	30 888	8 347	**39 235**	103 561	58 099	**161 660**	8 313	132 129	**140 442**
7-9. Production and related workers, transport equipment, operators and labourers	48 739	13 737	**62 476**	1 571 834	637 807	**2 209 641**	1 636	1 347	**2 983**
Total . . .	87 647	29 769	**117 416**	2 286 258	1 597 213	**3 883 471**	10 658	134 639	**145 297**

‡ For notes, see pp. 272-294.

B **Distribution by status and by occupational group**
Répartition suivant la situation dans la profession et par groupe de professions
Distribución según la categoría de ocupación y por grupo de ocupación

Others and status unknown / Autres et situation non définie / Otros y categoría no definida			TOTAL				Groupe de professions	Grupo de ocupaciones
Males / Hommes / Hombres	Females / Femmes / Mujeres	Total	Males / Hommes / Hombres	Females / Femmes / Mujeres	Total	%		
848	564	1 412	119 700	63 780	183 480	5.7	0-1. *Personnel des professions scientif., techn., libérales et assimilées*	0-1. Profesionales, técnicos y trabajadores asimilados
108	12	120	18 308	1 572	19 880	0.6	2. *Directeurs et cadres administratifs supérieurs*	2. Directores y funcionarios públicos superiores
816	560	1 376	162 456	81 552	244 008	7.5	3. *Personnel administratif et travailleurs assimilés*	3. Personal administrativo y trabajadores asimilados
340	116	456	187 540	44 968	232 508	7.2	4. *Personnel commercial et vendeurs*	4. Comerciantes y vendedores
3 864	624	4 488	153 868	85 020	238 888	7.4	5. *Travailleurs des services*	5. Trabajadores de los servicios
4 784	2 532	7 316	835 420	477 916	1 313 336	40.6	6. *Agriculteurs, éleveurs, forestiers, pêcheurs et chasseurs*	6. Trab. agrícolas y forestales, pescadores y cazadores
4 040	1 084	5 124	825 220	141 268	966 488	29.9	7-9. *Ouvriers et manœuvres non agricoles et conducteurs d'engins de transport*	7-9. Obreros no agrícolas, conductores de máquinas y vehículos de transporte y trabajadores asimilados
1 744	1 368	3 112	27 076	9 332	36 408	1.1	X. *Travailleurs ne pouvant être classés selon la profession*	X. Trabajadores que no pueden ser clasificados según la ocupación
16 544	6 860	23 404	2 329 588	905 408	3 234 996	100.0	*Total*	Total

Others and status unknown / Autres et situation non définie / Otros y categoría no definida			TOTAL				Groupe de professions	Grupo de ocupaciones
Males / Hommes / Hombres	Females / Femmes / Mujeres	Total	Males / Hommes / Hombres	Females / Femmes / Mujeres	Total	%		
8 852	2 033	10 885	287 874	256 923	544 797	10.9	0-1. *Personnel des professions scientif., techn., libérales et assimilées*	0-1. Profesionales, técnicos y trabajadores asimilados
1 515	137	1 652	24 127	4 364	28 491	0.6	2. *Directeurs et cadres administratifs supérieurs*	2. Directores y funcionarios públicos superiores
5 407	9 930	15 337	179 339	363 320	542 659	10.9	3. *Personnel administratif et travailleurs assimilés*	3. Personal administrativo y trabajadores asimilados
1 910	1 799	3 709	67 423	106 595	174 018	3.5	4. *Personnel commercial et vendeurs*	4. Comerciantes y vendedores
6 064	10 149	16 213	84 577	203 001	287 578	5.8	5. *Travailleurs des services*	5. Trabajadores de los servicios
345 212	214 111	559 323	487 974	412 686	900 660	18.1	6. *Agriculteurs, éleveurs, forestiers, pêcheurs et chasseurs*	6. Trab. agrícolas y forestales, pescadores y cazadores
179 961	55 412	235 373	1 802 170	708 303	2 510 473	50.2	7-9. *Ouvriers et manœuvres non agricoles et conducteurs d'engins de transport*	7-9. Obreros no agrícolas, conductores de máquinas y vehículos de transporte y trabajadores asimilados
548 921	293 571	842 492	2 933 484	2 055 192	4 988 676	100.0	*Total*	Total

✝ *Voir notes pp. 272-294.*

✝ Véanse las notas en las págs. 272-294.

2 Structure of the economically active population
Structure de la population active
Estructura de la población económicamente activa

Occupational group	Employers and workers on own account Employeurs et personnes travaillant à leur propre compte Empleadores y trabajadores por cuenta propia			Salaried employees and wage earners Employés et ouvriers Empleados y obreros			Family workers Travailleurs familiaux Trabajadores familiares		
	Males Hommes Hombres	Females Femmes Mujeres	Total	Males Hommes Hombres	Females Femmes Mujeres	Total	Males Hommes Hombres	Females Femmes Mujeres	Total

Ireland (18.IV.1971) †

0-1. Professional, technical and related workers	6 877	1 362	8 239	46 246	48 564	94 810	16	39	55
2. Administrative and managerial workers	.	.	.	16 933	887	17 820	.	.	.
3. Clerical and related workers	49	53	102	58 872	69 692	128 564	95	288	383
4. Sales workers	25 262	8 348	33 610	43 896	24 835	68 731	1 978	1 476	3 454
5. Service workers	3 769	2 606	6 375	24 767	44 097	68 864	220	296	516
6. Agricultural, animal husbandry and forestry workers, fishermen and hunters	165 761	18 676	184 437	38 626	653	39 279	47 189	5 943	53 132
7-9. Production and related workers, transport equipment, operators and labourers	25 070	902	25 972	260 102	49 283	309 385	1 320	46	1 366
X. Workers not classifiable by occupation	141	27	168	567	247	814	5	2	7
Members of the armed forces . . .	.	.	.	8 746	10	8 756	.	.	.
Total . . .	226 929	31 974	258 903	498 755	238 268	737 023	50 823	8 090	58 913

Isle of Man (24.IV.1966)

Professional, technical and related workers	89	11	100	727	757	1 484	...	...	...
Administrative, executive and managerial workers	.	.	.	666	20	686	...	...	...
Clerical workers	.	.	.	972	983	1 955	...	...	...
Sales workers	313	166	479	834	862	1 696	...	...	...
Farmers, fishermen, hunters, loggers and related workers	575	17	592	1 254	23	1 277	...	...	...
Miners, quarrymen and related workers	.	.	.	45	.	45	...	...	...
Workers in transport and communication occupations	44	.	44	1 391	121	1 512	...	...	...
Craftsmen, prod.-process workers and labourers not elsewhere classified .	212	11	223	5 218	563	5 781	...	...	...
Service, sport and recreation workers	262	1 091	1 353	1 170	1 735	2 905	...	...	...
Workers not classifiable by occupation	3	1	4	6	1	7	...	...	...
Members of the armed forces	.	.	.	56	4	60	.	.	.
Unemployed	...	...	...	...	...	...	...	...	...
Total . . .	1 498	1 297	2 795	12 339	5 069	17 408	...	...	...

† For notes, see pp. 272-294.

B Distribution by status and by occupational group
Répartition suivant la situation dans la profession et par groupe de professions
Distribución según la categoría de ocupación y por grupo de ocupación

Others and status unknown / Autres et situation non définie / Otros y categoría no definida			TOTAL				Groupe de professions	Grupo de ocupaciones
Males / Hommes / Hombres	Females / Femmes / Mujeres	Total	Males / Hommes / Hombres	Females / Femmes / Mujeres	Total	%		
500	737	**1 237**	53 639	50 702	**104 341**	*9.3*	0-1. *Personnel des professions scientif., techn., libérales et assimilées*	0-1. Profesionales, técnicos y trabajadores asimilados
93	3	**96**	17 026	890	**17 916**	*1.6*	2. *Directeurs et cadres administratifs supérieurs*	2. Directores y funcionarios públicos superiores
1 702	1 379	**3 081**	60 718	71 412	**132 130**	*11.8*	3. *Personnel administratif et travailleurs assimilés*	3. Personal administrativo y trabajadores asimilados
1 982	943	**2 925**	73 118	35 602	**108 720**	*9.7*	4. *Personnel commercial et vendeurs*	4. Comerciantes y vendedores
1 381	3 322	**4 703**	30 137	50 321	**80 458**	*7.2*	5. *Travailleurs des services*	5. Trabajadores de los servicios
11 858	47	**11 905**	263 434	25 319	**288 753**	*25.8*	6. *Agriculteurs, éleveurs, forestiers, pêcheurs et chasseurs*	6. Trab. agrícolas y forestales, pescadores y cazadores
34 615	2 330	**36 945**	321 107	52 561	**373 668**	*33.4*	7-9. *Ouvriers et manœuvres non agricoles et conducteurs d'engins de transport*	7-9. Obreros no agrícolas, conductores de máquinas y vehículos de transporte y trabajadores asimilados
2 985	774	**3 759**	3 698	1 050	**4 748**	*0.4*	X. *Travailleurs ne pouvant être classés selon la profession*	X. Trabajadores que no pueden ser clasificados según la ocupación
41	.	**41**	8 787	10	**8 797**	*0.8*	*Membres des forces armées*	Miembros de las fuerzas armadas
55 157	9 535	**64 692**	831 664	287 867	**1 119 531**	*100.0*	*Total*	Total

Others and status unknown / Autres et situation non définie / Otros y categoría no definida			TOTAL				Groupe de professions	Grupo de ocupaciones
Males / Hommes / Hombres	Females / Femmes / Mujeres	Total	Males / Hommes / Hombres	Females / Femmes / Mujeres	Total	%		
...	...	...	816	768	**1 584**	*7.7*	*Personnes exerçant une profession libérale, techniciens et assimilés*	Trabajadores profesionales, técnicos y trabajadores asimilados
...	...	...	666	20	**686**	*3.3*	*Directeurs et cadres administratifs supérieurs*	Administradores, gerentes y directores
...	...	...	972	983	**1 955**	*9.5*	*Employés de bureau*	Empleados de oficina
...	...	...	1 147	1 028	**2 175**	*10.6*	*Vendeurs*	Vendedores
...	...	...	1 829	40	**1 869**	*9.1*	*Agriculteurs, pêcheurs, chasseurs, forestiers et travailleurs assimilés*	Agricultores, pescadores, cazadores, trabajadores forestales y asimilados
...	...	...	45	.	**45**	*0.2*	*Mineurs, carriers et travailleurs assimilés*	Mineros, canteros y trabajadores asimilados
...	...	...	1 435	121	**1 556**	*7.6*	*Travailleurs des transports et des communications*	Trabajadores de los transportes y comunicaciones
...	...	...	5 430	574	**6 004**	*29.1*	*Artisans, ouvriers de métier, ouvriers à la production et manœuvres non classés ailleurs*	Artesanos y trab. ocupados en los div. procesos de producción y peones no clasif. bajo otros epígrafes
...	...	...	1 432	2 826	**4 258**	*20.6*	*Travailleurs spécialisés dans les services, les sports et les activités récréatives*	Trabajadores de los servicios, los deportes y las diversiones
...	...	...	9	2	**11**	*0.1*	*Personnes ne pouvant être classées selon la profession*	Trabajadores que no pueden ser clasificados según la ocupación
.	.	.	56	4	**60**	*0.3*	*Membres des forces armées*	Miembros de las fuerzas armadas
314	76	390	314	76	**390**	*1.9*	*Chômeurs*	Desempleados
314	76	390	14 151	6 442	**20 593**	*100.0*	*Total*	Total

† *Voir notes pp. 272-294.*

† *Véanse las notas en las págs. 272-294.*

POPULATION

2 Structure of the economically active population
Structure de la population active
Estructura de la población económicamente activa

Occupational group	Employers and workers on own account *Employeurs et personnes travaillant à leur propre compte* Empleadores y trabajadores por cuenta propia			Salaried employees and wage earners *Employés et ouvriers* Empleados y obreros			Family workers *Travailleurs familiaux* Trabajadores familiares		
	Males *Hommes* Hombres	Females *Femmes* Mujeres	Total	Males *Hommes* Hombres	Females *Femmes* Mujeres	Total	Males *Hommes* Hombres	Females *Femmes* Mujeres	Total

Italie (1965) †

Professional, technical and related workers	169 000	18 000	**187 000**	497 000	372 000	**869 000**	1 000	3 000	**4 000**
Administrative, executive and managerial workers . . . . } Clerical workers . . . . }	106 000	13 000	**119 000**	959 000	497 000	**1 456 000**	11 000	11 000	**22 000**
Sales workers	831 000	295 000	**1 126 000**	530 000	221 000	**751 000**	153 000	280 000	**433 000**
Farmers, fishermen, hunters, loggers and related workers	1 673 000	250 000	**1 923 000**	1 086 000	435 000	**1 521 000**	598 000	896 000	**1 494 000**
Miners, quarrymen and related workers	3 000	—	**3 000**	93 000	1 000	**94 000**	—	—	—
Workers in transport and communication occupations	169 000	1 000	**170 000**	704 000	11 000	**715 000**	4 000	1 000	**5 000**
Craftsmen, prod.-process workers and labourers not elsewhere classified .	836 000	220 000	**1 056 000**	4 768 000	1 149 000	**5 917 000**	120 000	71 000	**191 000**
Service, sport and recreation workers	71 000	45 000	**116 000**	182 000	412 000	**594 000**	5 000	1 000	**6 000**
Workers not classifiable by occupation	16 000	50 000	**66 000**	684 000	146 000	**830 000**	1 000	—	**1 000**
Persons seeking work for the first time	.	.	.	.	.	.	.	.	.
Total . . .	3 874 000	892 000	**4 766 000**	9 503 000	3 244 000	**12 747 000**	893 000	1 263 000	**2 156 000**

Luxembourg (31.XII.1970) †

0-1. Professional, technical and related workers	1 099	146	**1 245**	6 851	3 706	**10 557**	.	.	.
2. Administrative and managerial workers	376	49	**425**	818	58	**876**	.	.	.
3. Clerical and related workers	.	.	.	14 667	7 864	**22 531**	.	3	**3**
4. Sales workers	2 056	1 841	**3 897**	2 013	3 728	**5 741**	34	871	**905**
5. Service workers	1 153	1 618	**2 771**	2 594	8 745	**11 339**	36	365	**401**
6. Agricultural, animal husbandry and forestry workers, fishermen and hunters	5 293	519	**5 812**	1 163	44	**1 207**	1 336	1 526	**2 862**
7-9. Production and related workers, transport equipment, operators and labourers	3 549	219	**3 768**	51 302	2 016	**53 318**	.	.	.
X. Workers not classifiable by occupation	.	.	.	1	.	**1**	.	.	.
Members of the armed forces	.	.	.	576	.	**576**	.	.	.
Total . . .	13 526	4 392	**17 918**	79 985	26 161	**106 146**	1 406	2 765	**4 171**

† For notes, see pp. 272-294.

B — Distribution by status and by occupational group
Répartition suivant la situation dans la profession et par groupe de professions
Distribución según la categoría de ocupación y por grupo de ocupación

Others and status unknown / Autres et situation non définie / Otros y categoría no definida			TOTAL				Groupe de professions	Grupo de ocupaciones
Males / Hommes / Hombres	Females / Femmes / Mujeres	Total	Males / Hommes / Hombres	Females / Femmes / Mujeres	Total	%		
...	...	...	667 000	393 000	**1 060 000**	*5.3*	Personnes exerçant une profession libérale, techniciens et assimilés	Trabajadores profesionales, técnicos y trabajadores asimilados
...	...	...	1 076 000	521 000	**1 597 000**	*8.0*	Directeurs et cadres administratifs supérieurs	Administradores, gerentes y directores
...	...	...	1 514 000	796 000	**2 310 000**	*11.6*	Employés de bureau / Vendeurs	Empleados de oficina / Vendedores
...	...	...	3 357 000	1 581 000	**4 938 000**	*24.8*	Agriculteurs, pêcheurs, chasseurs, forestiers et travailleurs assimilés	Agricultores, pescadores, cazadores, trabajadores forestales y asimilados
...	...	...	96 000	1 000	**97 000**	*0.5*	Mineurs, carriers et travailleurs assimilés	Mineros, canteros y trabajadores asimilados
...	...	...	877 000	13 000	**890 000**	*4.5*	Travailleurs des transports et des communications	Trabajadores de los transportes y comunicaciones
...	...	...	5 724 000	1 440 000	**7 164 000**	*35.9*	Artisans, ouvriers de métier, ouvriers à la production et manœuvres non classés ailleurs	Artesanos y trab. ocupados en los div. procesos de producción y peones no clasif. bajo otros epígrafes
...	...	...	258 000	458 000	**716 000**	*3.6*	Travailleurs spécialisés dans les services, les sports et les activités récréatives	Trabajadores de los servicios, los deportes y las diversiones
...	...	...	701 000	196 000	**897 000**	*4.5*	Personnes ne pouvant être classées selon la profession	Trabajadores que no pueden ser clasificados según la ocupación
150 000	101 000	**251 000**	150 000	101 000	**251 000**	*1.3*	Personnes en quête d'emploi pour la première fois	Personas en busca de trabajo por primera vez
150 000	101 000	**251 000**	14 420 000	5 500 000	**19 920 000**	*100.0*	*Total*	Total

Others and status unknown			TOTAL				Groupe de professions	Grupo de ocupaciones
Males	Females	Total	Males	Females	Total	%		
21	24	**45**	7 971	3 876	**11 847**	*9.2*	0-1. Personnel des professions scientif., techn., libérales et assimilées	0-1. Profesionales, técnicos y trabajadores asimilados
3	.	**3**	1 197	107	**1 304**	*1.0*	2. Directeurs et cadres administratifs supérieurs	2. Directores y funcionarios públicos superiores
57	83	**140**	14 724	7 950	**22 674**	*17.5*	3. Personnel administratif et travailleurs assimilés	3. Personal administrativo y trabajadores asimilados
17	71	**88**	4 120	6 511	**10 631**	*8.2*	4. Personnel commercial et vendeurs	4. Comerciantes y vendedores
24	125	**149**	3 807	10 853	**14 660**	*11.3*	5. Travailleurs des services	5. Trabajadores de los servicios
8	.	**8**	7 800	2 089	**9 889**	*7.7*	6. Agriculteurs, éleveurs, forestiers, pêcheurs et chasseurs	6. Trab. agrícolas y forestales, pescadores y cazadores
273	36	**309**	55 124	2 271	**57 395**	*44.4*	7-9. Ouvriers et manœuvres non agricoles et conducteurs d'engins de transport	7-9. Obreros no agrícolas, conductores de máquinas y vehículos de transporte y trabajadores asimilados
119	159	**278**	120	159	**279**	*0.2*	X. Travailleurs ne pouvant être classés selon la profession	X. Trabajadores que no pueden ser clasificados según la ocupación
.	.	.	576	.	**576**	*0.5*	Membres des forces armées	Miembros de las fuerzas armadas
522	498	**1 020**	95 439	33 816	**129 255**	*100.0*	*Total*	Total

† *Voir notes pp. 272-294.*   † Véanse las notas en las págs. 272-294.

2 Structure of the economically active population
Structure de la population active
Estructura de la población económicamente activa

Occupational group	Employers and workers on own account *Employeurs et personnes travaillant à leur propre compte* Empleadores y trabajadores por cuenta propia			Salaried employees and wage earners *Employés et ouvriers* Empleados y obreros			Family workers *Travailleurs familiaux* Trabajadores familiares		
	Males *Hommes* Hombres	Females *Femmes* Mujeres	Total	Males *Hommes* Hombres	Females *Femmes* Mujeres	Total	Males *Hommes* Hombres	Females *Femmes* Mujeres	Total

Malta (26.XI.1967)

Professional, technical and related workers	1 831	1 911	**3 742**	4 165	2 984	**7 149**	9	7	**16**
Administrative, executive and managerial workers	3 913	1 292	**5 205**	1 675	120	**1 795**	146	96	**242**
Clerical workers	138	59	**197**	5 927	2 224	**8 151**	20	10	**30**
Sales workers	935	169	**1 104**	1 180	790	**1 970**	146	105	**251**
Farmers, fishermen, hunters, loggers and related workers	4 477	438	**4 915**	792	125	**917**	1 063	436	**1 499**
Miners, quarrymen and related workers	24	.	**24**	571	2	**573**	9	.	**9**
Workers in transport and communication occupations	765	9	**774**	6 367	125	**6 492**	86	1	**87**
Craftsmen, prod.-process workers and labourers not elsewhere classified .	3 489	595	**4 084**	23 972	3 013	**26 985**	453	81	**534**
Service, sport and recreation workers	602	140	**742**	8 931	5 804	**14 735**	62	52	**114**
Members of the armed forces	.	.	.	2 031	.	**2 031**	.	.	.
Unemployed	...	...	...	...	...	...	...	...	...
Total . . .	16 174	4 613	**20 787**	55 611	15 187	**70 798**	1 994	788	**2 782**

B Distribution by status and by occupational group
Répartition suivant la situation dans la profession et par groupe de professions
Distribución según la categoría de ocupación y por grupo de ocupación

Others and status unknown *Autres et situation non définie* Otros y categoría no definida			TOTAL				Groupe de professions	Grupo de ocupaciones
Males *Hommes* Hombres	Females *Femmes* Mujeres	Total	Males *Hommes* Hombres	Females *Femmes* Mujères	Total	%		
...	...	...	6 005	4 902	**10 907**	*10.7*	*Personnes exerçant une profession libérale, techniciens et assimilés*	Trabajadores profesionales, técnicos y trabajadores asimilados
...	...	...	5 734	1 508	**7 242**	*7.1*	*Directeurs et cadres administratifs supérieurs*	Administradores, gerentes y directores
...	...	...	6 085	2 293	**8 378**	*8.2*	*Employés de bureau*	Empleados de oficina
...	...	...	2 261	1 064	**3 325**	*3.3*	*Vendeurs*	Vendedores
...	...	...	6 332	999	**7 331**	*7.2*	*Agriculteurs, pêcheurs, chasseurs, forestiers et travailleurs assimilés*	Agricultores, pescadores, cazadores, trabajadores forestales y asimilados
...	...	...	604	2	**606**	*0.6*	*Mineurs, carriers et travailleurs assimilés*	Mineros, canteros y trabajadores asimilados
...	...	...	7 218	135	**7 353**	*7.2*	*Travailleurs des transports et des communications*	Trabajadores de los transportes y comunicaciones
...	...	...	27 914	3 689	**31 603**	*30.8*	*Artisans, ouvriers de métier, ouvriers à la production et manœuvres non classés ailleurs*	Artesanos y trab. ocupados en los div. procesos de producción y peones no clasif. bajo otros epígrafes
...	...	...	9 595	5 996	**15 591**	*15.2*	*Travailleurs spécialisés dans les services, les sports et les activités récréatives*	Trabajadores de los servicios, los deportes y las diversiones
.	.	.	2 031	.	**2 031**	*2.0*	*Membres des forces armées*	Miembros de las fuerzas armadas
6 475	1 411	**7 886**	6 475	1 411	**7 886**	*7.7*	*Chômeurs*	Desempleados
6 475	1 411	**7 886**	80 254	21 999	**102 253**	*100.0*	*Total*	Total

2 Structure of the economically active population
Structure de la population active
Estructura de la población económicamente activa

Occupational group	Employers and workers on own account *Employeurs et personnes travaillant à leur propre compte* Empleadores y trabajadores por cuenta propia			Salaried employees and wage earners *Employés et ouvriers* Empleados y obreros			Family workers *Travailleurs familiaux* Trabajadores familiares		
	Males *Hommes* Hombres	Females *Femmes* Mujeres	Total	Males *Hommes* Hombres	Females *Femmes* Mujeres	Total	Males *Hommes* Hombres	Females *Femmes* Mujeres	Total

Norway

(1.XI.1970) †

Occupational group	Males	Females	Total	Males	Females	Total	Males	Females	Total
Professional, technical and related workers	8 882	1 559	**10 441**	97 173	71 319	**168 492**	20	174	**194**
Administrative, executive and managerial workers	10 992	1 039	**12 031**	36 999	2 805	**39 804**	35	41	**76**
Clerical workers	618	145	**763**	52 096	86 493	**138 589**	55	1 442	**1 497**
Sales workers	19 518	4 823	**24 341**	50 543	48 219	**98 762**	517	5 289	**5 806**
Farmers, fishermen, hunters, loggers and related workers	93 353	3 257	**96 610**	35 593	2 238	**37 831**	10 730	24 898	**35 628**
Miners, quarrymen and related workers	286	.	**286**	7 086	13	**7 099**	7	.	**7**
Workers in transport and communication occupations	14 392	108	**14 500**	110 637	15 491	**126 128**	204	99	**303**
Craftsmen, prod.-process workers and labourers not elsewhere classified	33 207	985	**34 192**	400 437	49 480	**449 917**	564	496	**1 060**
Service, sport and recreation workers	2 531	2 905	**5 436**	36 768	79 422	**116 190**	106	992	**1 098**
Workers not classifiable by occupation	106	8	**114**	1 796	591	**2 387**	3	2	**5**
Members of the armed forces	.	.	.	32 356	.	**32 356**	.	.	.
Total	183 885	14 829	**198 714**	861 484	356 071	**1 217 555**	12 241	33 433	**45 674**

(1974) †

Occupational group	Males	Females	Total	Males	Females	Total	Males	Females	Total
Professional, technical and related workers	9 000	3 000	**12 000**	117 000	113 000	**230 000**	—	—	—
Administrative, executive and managerial workers	9 000	1 000	**10 0C0**	56 000	8 000	**64 000**	—	—	—
Clerical workers	1 000	—	**1 000**	53 000	115 000	**168 000**	—	2 000	**2 000**
Sales workers	14 000	5 000	**16 000**	54 000	73 000	**127 000**	1 000	6 000	**7 000**
Farmers, fishermen, hunters, loggers and related workers	83 000	6 000	**89 000**	32 000	5 000	**37 000**	6 000	38 000	**44 000**
Miners, quarrymen and related workers; craftsmen, prod.-process workers and labourers not elsewhere classified	40 000	2 000	**42 000**	398 000	52 000	**450 000**	2 000	1 000	**3 000**
Workers in transport and communication occupations	16 000	—	**16 000**	115 000	18 000	**133 000**	1 000	—	**1 000**
Service, sport and recreation workers	3 000	7 000	**10 000**	37 000	145 000	**182 000**	—	2 000	**2 000**
Workers not classifiable by occupation	—	—	—	8 000	—	**8 000**	—	—	—
Unemployed	...	...	...	...	...	...	...	...	...
Total	175 000	24 000	**199 000**	870 000	529 000	**1 399 000**	10 000	49 000	**59 000**

† For notes, see pp. 272-294.

B
Distribution by status and by occupational group
Répartition suivant la situation dans la profession et par groupe de professions
Distribución según la categoría de ocupación y por grupo de ocupación

Others and status unknown / Autres et situation non définie / Otros y categoria no definida			TOTAL				Groupe de professions	Grupo de ocupaciones
Males / Hommes / Hombres	Females / Femmes / Mujeres	Total	Males / Hommes / Hombres	Females / Femmes / Mujeres	Total	%		
2	2	4	106 077	73 054	179 131	12.3	Personnes exerçant une profession libérale, techniciens et assimilés	Trabajadores profesionales, técnicos y trabajadores asimilados
2	.	2	48 028	3 885	51 913	3.6	Directeurs et cadres administratifs supérieurs	Administradores, gerentes y directores
2	.	2	52 771	88 080	140 851	9.6	Employés de bureau	Empleados de oficina
1	.	1	70 579	58 331	128 910	8.8	Vendeurs	Vendedores
.	.	.	139 676	30 393	170 069	11.6	Agriculteurs, pêcheurs, chasseurs, forestiers et travailleurs assimilés	Agricultores, pescadores, cazadores, trabajadores forestales y asimilados
.	.	.	7 379	13	7 392	0.5	Mineurs, carriers et travailleurs assimilés	Mineros, canteros y trabajadores asimilados
2	.	2	125 235	15 698	140 933	9.6	Travailleurs des transports et des communications	Trabajadores de los transportes y comunicaciones
6	1	7	434 214	50 962	485 176	33.2	Artisans, ouvriers de métier, ouvriers à la production et manœuvres non classés ailleurs	Artesanos y trab. ocupados en los div. procesos de producción y peones no clasif. bajo otros epígrafes
.	2	2	39 405	83 321	122 726	8.4	Travailleurs spécialisés dans les services, les sports et les activités récréatives	Trabajadores de los servicios, los deportes y las diversiones
140	56	196	2 045	657	2 702	0.2	Personnes ne pouvant être classées selon la profession	Trabajadores que no pueden ser clasificados según la ocupación
.	.	.	32 356	.	32 356	2.2	Membres des forces armées	Miembros de las fuerzas armadas
155	61	216	1 057 765	404 394	1 462 159	100.0	Total	Total
...	...	...	126 000	116 000	242 000	14.4	Personnes exerçant une profession libérale, techniciens et assimilés	Trabajadores profesionales, técnicos y trabajadores asimilados
...	...	...	65 000	9 000	74 000	4.4	Directeurs et cadres administratifs supérieurs	Administradores, gerentes y directores
...	...	...	54 000	117 000	171 000	10.2	Employés de bureau	Empleados de oficina
...	...	...	69 000	84 000	153 000	9.1	Vendeurs	Vendedores
...	...	...	121 000	50 000	171 000	10.2	Agriculteurs, pêcheurs, chasseurs, forestiers et travailleurs assimilés	Agricultores, pescadores, cazadores, trabajadores forestales y asimilados
...	...	...	440 000	55 000	495 000	29.3	Mineurs, carriers et travailleurs assimilés ; artisans, ouvriers de métier, ouvriers à la production et manœuvres non classés ailleurs	Mineros, canteros y trabajadores asimilados; artesanos y trab. ocupados en los div. procesos de producción y peones no clasif. bajo otros epígrafes
...	...	...	132 000	18 000	150 000	8.9	Travailleurs des transports et des communications	Trabajadores de los transportes y comunicaciones
...	...	...	40 000	154 000	194 000	11.5	Travailleurs spécialisés dans les services, les sports et les activités récréatives	Trabajadores de los servicios, los deportes y las diversiones
...	...	...	9 000	—	9 000	0.5	Personnes ne pouvant être classées selon la profession	Trabajadores que no pueden ser clasificados según la ocupación
11 000	14 000	25 000	11 000	14 000	25 000	1.5	Chômeurs	Desempleados
11 000	14 000	25 000	1 067 000	617 000	1 684 000	100.0	Total	Total

† *Voir notes pp. 272-294.*   † Véanse las notas en las págs. 272-294.

2 Structure of the economically active population
Structure de la population active
Estructura de la población económicamente activa

Occupational group	Employers and workers on own account *Employeurs et personnes travaillant à leur propre compte* Empleadores y trabajadores por cuenta propia			Salaried employees and wage earners *Employés et ouvriers* Empleados y obreros			Family workers *Travailleurs familiaux* Trabajadores familiares		
	Males *Hommes* Hombres	Females *Femmes* Mujeres	Total	Males *Hommes* Hombres	Females *Femmes* Mujeres	Total	Males *Hommes* Hombres	Females *Femmes* Mujeres	Total

Pologne (8.XII.1970) ✝

Occupational group	Males	Females	Total	Males	Females	Total	Males	Females	Total
0-1. Professional, technical and related workers	4 092	1 789	**5 881**	661 813	658 206	**1 320 019**	...	...	...
2. Administrative and managerial workers	221	56	**277**	118 762	44 096	**162 858**	...	...	...
3. Clerical and related workers	1 124	871	**1 995**	594 923	903 136	**1 498 059**	...	...	...
4. Sales workers	6 041	9 536	**15 577**	44 416	271 211	**315 627**	...	...	...
5. Service workers	7 237	7 727	**14 964**	220 947	715 814	**936 761**	...	...	...
6. Agricultural, animal husbandry and forestry workers, fishermen and hunters	2 337 263	3 378 277	**5 715 540**	348 454	127 817	**476 271**	...	...	...
7-9. Production and related workers, transport equipment, operators and labourers	147 301	23 493	**170 794**	4 037 387	1 350 059	**5 387 446**	...	...	...
X. Workers not classifiable by occupation	8 673	3 911	**12 584**	605 272	295 815	**901 087**	...	...	...
Total . . .	2 511 952	3 425 660	**5 937 612**	6 631 974	4 366 154	**10 998 128**	...	...	...

Portugal (15.XII.1970) ✝

Occupational group	Males	Females	Total	Males	Females	Total	Males	Females	Total
0-1. Professional, technical and related workers	12 175	2 510	**14 685**	50 660	52 380	**103 040**	125	155	**280**
2. Administrative and managerial workers	4 495	205	**4 700**	6 190	595	**6 785**	20	25	**45**
3. Clerical and related workers	2 225	770	**2 995**	172 650	89 840	**262 490**	250	295	**545**
4. Sales workers	84 880	19 415	**104 295**	92 215	33 650	**125 865**	2 255	2 685	**4 940**
5. Service workers	17 340	6 605	**23 945**	81 380	144 290	**225 670**	360	1 445	**1 805**
6. Agricultural, animal husbandry and forestry workers, fishermen and hunters	334 785	42 980	**377 765**	417 420	84 785	**502 205**	61 220	47 405	**108 625**
7-9. Production and related workers, transport equipment, operators and labourers	91 325	20 685	**112 010**	784 595	234 690	**1 019 285**	5 950	3 380	**9 330**
X. Workers not classifiable by occupation	12 295	3 135	**15 430**	71 380	31 580	**102 960**	1 685	1 635	**3 320**
Members of the armed forces . . .	105	.	**105**	15 620	60	**15 680**	5	.	**5**
Persons on compulsory military service	.	.	.	.	.	.	.	.	.
Persons seeking work for the first time Unemployed	...	...	...	...	...	...	...	...	...
Total . . .	559 625	96 305	**655 930**	1 692 110	671 870	**2 363 980**	71 870	57 025	**128 895**

✝ For notes, see pp. 272-294.

B **Distribution by status and by occupational group**
Répartition suivant la situation dans la profession et par groupe de professions
Distribución según la categoría de ocupación y por grupo de ocupación

Others and status unknown / Autres et situation non définie / Otros y categoría no definida			TOTAL				Groupe de professions	Grupo de ocupaciones
Males / Hommes / Hombres	Females / Femmes / Mujeres	Total	Males / Hommes / Hombres	Females / Femmes / Mujeres	Total	%		
...	...	...	665 905	659 995	**1 325 900**	*7.8*	0-1. *Personnel des professions scientif., techn., libérales et assimilées*	0-1. Profesionales, técnicos y trabajadores asimilados
...	...	...	118 983	44 152	**163 135**	*1.0*	2. *Directeurs et cadres administratifs supérieurs*	2. Directores y funcionarios públicos superiores
...	...	...	596 047	904 007	**1 500 054**	*8.9*	3. *Personnel administratif et travailleurs assimilés*	3. Personal administrativo y trabajadores asimilados
...	...	...	50 457	280 747	**331 204**	*2.0*	4. *Personnel commercial et vendeurs*	4. Comerciantes y vendedores
...	...	...	228 184	723 541	**951 725**	*5.6*	5. *Travailleurs des services*	5. Trabajadores de los servicios
...	...	...	2 685 717	3 506 094	**6 191 811**	*36.5*	6. *Agriculteurs, éleveurs, forestiers, pêcheurs et chasseurs*	6. Trab. agrícolas y forestales, pescadores y cazadores
...	...	...	4 184 688	1 373 552	**5 558 240**	*32.8*	7-9. *Ouvriers et manœuvres non agricoles et conducteurs d'engins de transport*	7-9. Obreros no agrícolas, conductores de máquinas y vehículos de transporte y trabajadores asimilados
...	...	...	618 829	302 950	**921 779**	*5.4*	X. *Travailleurs ne pouvant être classés selon la profession*	X. Trabajadores que no pueden ser clasificados según la ocupación
4 884	3 224	**8 108**	9 148 810	7 795 038	**16 943 848**	*100.0*	*Total*	Total

Others and status unknown / Autres et situation non définie / Otros y categoría no definida			TOTAL				Groupe de professions	Grupo de ocupaciones
Males / Hommes / Hombres	Females / Femmes / Mujeres	Total	Males / Hommes / Hombres	Females / Femmes / Mujeres	Total	%		
2 450	605	**3 055**	65 410	55 650	**121 060**	*3.6*	0-1. *Personnel des professions scientif., techn., libérales et assimilées*	0-1. Profesionales, técnicos y trabajadores asimilados
175	20	**195**	10 880	845	**11 725**	*0.3*	2. *Directeurs et cadres administratifs supérieurs*	2. Directores y funcionarios públicos superiores
300	170	**470**	175 425	91 075	**266 500**	*7.8*	3. *Personnel administratif et travailleurs assimilés*	3. Personal administrativo y trabajadores asimilados
800	370	**1 170**	180 150	56 120	**236 270**	*7.0*	4. *Personnel commercial et vendeurs*	4. Comerciantes y vendedores
495	870	**1 365**	99 575	153 210	**252 785**	*7.4*	5. *Travailleurs des services*	5. Trabajadores de los servicios
4 300	1 200	**5 500**	817 725	176 370	**994 095**	*29.3*	6. *Agriculteurs, éleveurs, forestiers, pêcheurs et chasseurs*	6. Trab. agrícolas y forestales, pescadores y cazadores
1 430	780	**2 210**	883 300	259 535	**1 142 835**	*33.7*	7-9. *Ouvriers et manœuvres non agricoles et conducteurs d'engins de transport*	7-9. Obreros no agrícolas, conductores de máquinas y vehículos de transporte y trabajadores asimilados
470	260	**730**	85 830	36 610	**122 440**	*3.6*	X. *Travailleurs ne pouvant être classés selon la profession*	X. Trabajadores que no pueden ser clasificados según la ocupación
355	.	**355**	16 085	60	**16 145**	*0.5*	*Membres des forces armées*	Miembros de las fuerzas armadas
141 205	.	**141 205**	141 205	.	**141 205**	*4.2*	*Militaires du contingent*	Personas en servicio militar obligatorio
47 720	21 475	**69 195**	47 720	21 475	**69 195**	*2.0*	*Personnes en quête d'emploi pour la première fois*	Personas en busca de trabajo por primera vez
15 615	5 995	**21 610**	15 615	5 995	**21 610**	*0.6*	*Chômeurs*	Desempleados
215 315	31 745	**247 060**	2 538 920	856 945	**3 395 865**	*100.0*	*Total*	Total

† *Voir notes pp. 272-294.*

† Véanse las notas en las págs. 272-294.

2 Structure of the economically active population
Structure de la population active
Estructura de la población económicamente activa

Occupational group	Employers and workers on own account *Employeurs et personnes travaillant à leur propre compte* Empleadores y trabajadores por cuenta propia			Salaried employees and wage earners *Employés et ouvriers* Empleados y obreros			Family workers *Travailleurs familiaux* Trabajadores familiares		
	Males *Hommes* Hombres	Females *Femmes* Mujeres	Total	Males *Hommes* Hombres	Females *Femmes* Mujeres	Total	Males *Hommes* Hombres	Females *Femmes* Mujeres	Total

Roumanie (15.III.1966) ‡

Professional, technical and related workers	...	...	...	...	...	...	...	...	...
Administrative, executive and managerial workers	...	...	...	...	...	...	...	...	...
Clerical workers									
Sales workers	...	...	...	...	...	...	...	...	...
Farmers, fishermen, hunters, loggers and related workers	...	...	...	...	...	...	...	...	...
Miners, quarrymen and related workers	...	...	...	...	...	...	...	...	...
Workers in transport and communication occupations	...	...	...	...	...	...	...	...	...
Craftsmen, prod.-process workers and labourers not elsewhere classified	...	...	...	...	...	...	...	...	...
Service, sport and recreation workers	...	...	...	...	...	...	...	...	...
Workers not classifiable by occupation	...	...	...	...	...	...	...	...	...
Total . . .	331 721	456 035	**787 756**	3 308 843	1 299 043	**4 607 886**	20 330 751	2 930 921	**4 963 996**

Suisse (1.XII.1970) ‡

0-1. Professional, technical and related workers	31 959	6 031	**37 990**	218 970	106 217	**325 187**	...	...	...
2. Administrative and managerial workers	12 818	825	**13 643**	46 043	1 937	**47 980**	...	...	...
3. Clerical and related workers	4 033	219	**4 252**	273 496	258 714	**532 210**	...	...	...
4. Sales workers	29 711	10 571	**40 282**	75 557	118 128	**193 685**	...	...	...
5. Service workers	20 439	12 830	**33 269**	81 167	219 986	**301 153**	...	...	...
6. Agricultural, animal husbandry and forestry workers, fishermen and hunters	100 419	3 900	**104 319**	83 082	50 356	**133 438**	...	...	...
7-9. Production and related workers, transport equipment, operators and labourers	72 302	6 646	**78 948**	901 469	200 252	**1 101 721**	...	...	...
X. Workers not classifiable by occupation	.	.	.	19 546	25 877	**45 423**	...	...	...
Members of the armed forces	.	.	.	2 277	.	**2 277**	.	.	.
Total . . .	271 681	41 022	**312 703**	1 701 607	981 467	**2 683 074**	...	...	...

‡ For notes, see pp. 272-294.

B
Distribution by status and by occupational group
Répartition suivant la situation dans la profession et par groupe de professions
Distribución según la categoría de ocupación y por grupo de ocupación

Others and status unknown / *Autres et situation non définie* / Otros y categoría no definida			TOTAL				Groupe de professions	Grupo de ocupaciones
Males *Hommes* Hombres	Females *Femmes* Mujeres	Total	Males *Hommes* Hombres	Females *Femmes* Mujeres	Total	%		
...	...	...	527 732	422 113	**949 845**	9.2	Personnes exerçant une profession libérale, techniciens et assimilés	Trabajadores profesionales, técnicos y trabajadores asimilados
...	...	...	191 894	130 351	**322 245**	3.1	Directeurs et cadres administratifs supérieurs	Administradores, gerentes y directores
...	...	...	107 293	73 785	**181 078**	1.7	Employés de bureau / Vendeurs	Empleados de oficina / Vendedores
...	...	...	2 377 537	3 367 282	**5 744 819**	55.4	Agriculteurs, pêcheurs, chasseurs, forestiers et travailleurs assimilés	Agricultores, pescadores, cazadores, trabajadores forestales y asimilados
...	...	...	160 149	4 619	**164 768**	1.6	Mineurs, carriers et travailleurs assimilés	Mineros, canteros y trabajadores asimilados
...	...	...	420 674	46 690	**467 364**	4.5	Travailleurs des transports et des communications	Trabajadores de los transportes y comunicaciones
...	...	...	1 625 901	393 597	**2 019 498**	19.5	Artisans, ouvriers de métier, ouvriers à la production et manœuvres non classés ailleurs	Artesanos y trab. ocupados en los div. procesos de producción y peones no clasif. bajo otros epígrafes
...	...	...	261 558	246 880	**508 438**	4.9	Travailleurs spécialisés dans les services, les sports et les activités récréatives	Trabajadores de los servicios, los deportes y las diversiones
...	...	...	2 438	1 807	**4 245**	0.1	Personnes ne pouvant être classées selon la profession	Trabajadores que no pueden ser clasificados según la ocupación
1 537	1 125	**2 662**	5 675 176	4 687 124	**10 362 300**	100.0	Total	Total

Others and status unknown			TOTAL				Groupe de professions	Grupo de ocupaciones
						%		
.	.	.	250 929	112 248	**363 177**	12.1	0-1. Personnel des professions scientif., techn., libérales et assimilées	0-1. Profesionales, técnicos y trabajadores asimilados
.	.	.	58 861	2 762	**61 623**	2.1	2. Directeurs et cadres administratifs supérieurs	2. Directores y funcionarios públicos superiores
.	.	.	277 529	258 933	**536 462**	17.9	3. Personnel administratif et travailleurs assimilés	3. Personal administrativo y trabajadores asimilados
.	.	.	105 268	128 699	**233 967**	7.8	4. Personnel commercial et vendeurs	4. Comerciantes y vendedores
.	.	.	101 606	232 816	**334 422**	11.2	5. Travailleurs des services	5. Trabajadores de los servicios
.	.	.	183 501	54 256	**237 757**	7.9	6. Agriculteurs, éleveurs, forestiers, pêcheurs et chasseurs	6. Trab. agrícolas y forestales, pescadores y cazadores
.	.	.	973 771	206 898	**1 180 669**	39.4	7-9. Ouvriers et manœuvres non agricoles et conducteurs d'engins de transport	7-9. Obreros no agrícolas, conductores de máquinas y vehículos de transporte y trabajadores asimilados
.	.	.	19 546	25 877	**45 423**	1.5	X. Travailleurs ne pouvant être classés selon la profession	X. Trabajadores que no pueden ser clasificados según la ocupación
.	.	.	2 247	.	**2 277**	0.1	Membres des forces armées	Miembros de las fuerzas armadas
.	.	.	1 973 288	1 022 489	**2 995 777**	100.0	Total	Total

† *Voir notes pp. 272-294.*

† Véanse las notas en las págs. 272-294.

2 **Structure of the economically active population**
Structure de la population active
Estructura de la población económicamente activa

Occupational group	Employers and workers on own account *Employeurs et personnes travaillant à leur propre compte* Empleadores y trabajadores por cuenta propia			Salaried employees and wage earners *Employés et ouvriers* Empleados y obreros			Family workers *Travailleurs familiaux* Trabajadores familiares		
	Males *Hommes* Hombres	Females *Femmes* Mujeres	Total	Males *Hommes* Hombres	Females *Femmes* Mujeres	Total	Males *Hommes* Hombres	Females *Femmes* Mujeres	Total

Sweden

(1.XI.1970) ǂ									
0-1. Professional, technical and related workers	16 770	3 242	**20 012**	363 035	272 061	**635 096**	...	...	...
2. Administrative and managerial workers	2 412	228	**2 640**	64 843	11 575	**76 418**	...	...	...
3. Clerical and related workers	24 030	768	**24 798**	246 532	313 390	**559 922**	...	...	...
4. Sales workers	34 015	10 842	**44 857**	125 797	134 876	**260 673**	...	...	...
5. Service workers	8 683	9 337	**18 020**	82 172	226 259	**308 431**	...	...	...
6. Agricultural, animal husbandry and forestry workers, fishermen and hunters	121 139	4 359	**125 498**	97 380	49 426	**146 806**	...	...	...
7-9. Production and related workers, transport equipment, operators and labourers	64 140	3 167	**67 307**	934 168	165 201	**1 099 369**	...	...	...
X. Workers not classifiable by occupation	245	26	**271**	3 695	2 153	**5 848**	...	...	...
Members of the armed forces . . .	.	.	.	16 702	.	**16 702**	.	.	.
Total . . .	271 434	31 969	**303 403**	1 934 324	1 174 941	**3 109 265**	...	...	...
(1974) ǂ									
0-1. Professional, technical and related workers	15 100	4 600	**19 700**	418 500	398 000	**816 500**	—	—	—
2. Administrative and managerial workers	2 200	—	**2 200**	69 400	7 300	**76 700**	—	—	—
3. Clerical and related workers	1 400	1 700	**3 000**	100 900	361 300	**462 200**	—	2 300	2 300
4. Sales workers	31 300	12 800	**44 100**	151 000	140 600	**291 600**	100	5 700	5 800
5. Service workers	8 400	11 100	**19 500**	102 000	395 200	**497 300**	200	1 300	1 500
6. Agricultural, animal husbandry and forestry workers, fishermen and hunters	115 100	8 300	**123 400**	88 000	12 200	**100 300**	4 500	41 800	46 300
7-9. Production and related workers, transport equipment, operators and labourers	79 600	3 800	**85 500**	1 109 900	236 900	**1 346 900**	700	1 500	2 000
Members of the armed forces . . .	.	.	.	17 300	.	**17 300**	.	.	.
Total . . .	253 100	42 400	**295 500**	2 057 000	1 551 800	**3 608 800**	5 500	52 600	58 100

ǂ For notes, see pp. 272-294.

B **Distribution by status and by occupational group**
Répartition suivant la situation dans la profession et par groupe de professions
Distribución según la categoría de ocupación y por grupo de ocupación

| Others and status unknown / Autres et situation non définie / Otros y categoría no definida | | | TOTAL | | | % | Groupe de professions | Grupo de ocupaciones |
Males / Hommes / Hombres	Females / Femmes / Mujeres	Total	Males / Hommes / Hombres	Females / Femmes / Mujeres	Total			
.	.	.	379 805	275 303	**655 108**	19.2	0-1. *Personnel des professions scientif., techn., libérales et assimilées*	0-1. Profesionales, técnicos y trabajadores asimilados
.	.	.	67 255	11 803	**79 058**	2.3	2. *Directeurs et cadres administratifs supérieurs*	2. Directores y funcionarios públicos superiores
.	.	.	270 562	314 158	**584 720**	17.1	3. *Personnel administratif et travailleurs assimilés*	3. Personal administrativo y trabajadores asimilados
.	.	.	159 812	145 718	**305 530**	9.0	4. *Personnel commercial et vendeurs*	4. Comerciantes y vendedores
.	.	.	90 855	235 596	**326 451**	9.6	5. *Travailleurs des services*	5. Trabajadores de los servicios
.	.	.	218 519	53 785	**272 304**	8.0	6. *Agriculteurs, éleveurs, forestiers, pêcheurs et chasseurs*	6. Trab. agrícolas y forestales, pescadores y cazadores
.	.	.	998 308	168 368	**1 166 676**	34.1	7-9. *Ouvriers et manœuvres non agricoles et conducteurs d'engins de transport*	7-9. Obreros no agrícolas, conductores de máquinas y vehículos de transporte y trabajadores asimilados
.	.	.	3 940	2 179	**6 119**	0.2	X. *Travailleurs ne pouvant être classés selon la profession*	X. Trabajadores que no pueden ser clasificados según la ocupación
.	.	.	16 702	.	**16 702**	0.5	*Membres des forces armées*	Miembros de las fuerzas armadas
.	.	.	2 205 758	1 206 910	**3 412 668**	100.0	*Total*	Total
.	.	.	433 600	402 700	**836 300**	21.1	0-1. *Personnel des professions scientif., techn., libérales et assimilées*	0-1. Profesionales, técnicos y trabajadores asimilados
.	.	.	71 600	7 400	**78 900**	2.0	2. *Directeurs et cadres administratifs supérieurs*	2. Directores y funcionarios públicos superiores
.	.	.	102 300	365 300	**467 600**	11.8	3. *Personnel administratif et travailleurs assimilés*	3. Personal administrativo y trabajadores asimilados
.	.	.	182 400	159 200	**341 600**	8.6	4. *Personnel commercial et vendeurs*	4. Comerciantes y vendedores
.	.	.	110 600	407 600	**518 200**	13.1	5. *Travailleurs des services*	5. Trabajadores de los servicios
.	.	.	207 700	62 400	**270 100**	6.8	6. *Agriculteurs, éleveurs, forestiers, pêcheurs et chasseurs*	6. Trab. agrícolas y forestales, pescadores y cazadores
.	.	.	1 190 200	242 300	**1 432 400**	36.2	7-9. *Ouvriers et manœuvres non agricoles et conducteurs d'engins de transport*	7-9. Obreros no agrícolas, conductores de máquinas y vehículos de transporte y trabajadores asimilados
.	.	.	17 300	.	**17 300**	0.4	*Membres des forces armées*	Miembros de las fuerzas armadas
.	.	.	2 315 600	1 646 800	**3 962 400**	100.0	*Total*	Total

‡ *Voir notes pp. 272-294.*

‡ Véanse las notas en las págs. 272-294.

2 Structure of the economically active population
Structure de la population active
Estructura de la población económicamente activa

Occupational group	Employers and workers on own account *Employeurs et personnes travaillant à leur propre compte* Empleadores y trabajadores por cuenta propia			Salaried employees and wage earners *Employés et ouvriers* Empleados y obreros			Family workers *Travailleurs familiaux* Trabajadores familiares		
	Males *Hommes* Hombres	Females *Femmes* Mujeres	Total	Males *Hommes* Hombres	Females *Femmes* Mujeres	Total	Males *Hommes* Hombres	Females *Femmes* Mujeres	Total

Turquie (25.X.1970) ‡

Occupational group									
0-1. Professional, technical and related workers	...	...	...	...	...	...	...	...	...
2. Administrative and managerial workers	...	...	...	...	...	...	...	...	...
3. Clerical and related workers	...	...	...	...	...	...	...	...	...
4. Sales workers	...	...	...	...	...	...	...	...	...
5. Service workers	...	...	...	...	...	...	...	...	...
6. Agricultural, animal husbandry and forestry workers, fishermen and hunters	...	...	...	...	...	...	...	...	...
7-9. Production and related workers, transport equipment, operators and labourers	...	...	...	...	...	...	...	...	...
X. Workers not classifiable by occupation	...	...	...	...	...	...	...	...	...
Total . . .	...	...	**4 291 536**	...	...	**3 879 029**	...	...	**7 583 078**

United Kingdom (25.IV.1971) ‡

Occupational group									
0-1. Professional, technical and related workers	183 500	40 530	**224 030**	1 501 990	1 007 180	**2 509 170**	...	...	...
2. Administrative and managerial workers	.	.	.	829 870	77 240	**907 110**	...	...	...
3. Clerical and related workers	8 850	23 370	**32 220**	1 707 370	2 635 730	**4 343 100**	...	...	...
4. Sales workers	313 440	146 780	**460 220**	833 160	897 470	**1 730 630**	...	...	...
5. Service workers	145 430	97 620	**243 050**	710 470	1 898 540	**2 609 010**	...	...	...
6. Agricultural, animal husbandry and forestry workers, fishermen and hunters	245 750	32 620	**278 370**	377 600	62 310	**439 910**	...	...	...
7-9. Production and related workers, transport equipment, operators and labourers	570 540	26 880	**597 420**	7 264 190	1 633 980	**8 898 170**	...	...	...
X. Workers not classifiable by occupation	4 290	3 460	**7 750**	95 310	105 340	**200 650**	...	...	...
Members of the armed forces . . .	.	.	.	239 790	12 010	**251 800**	...	...	...
Total . . .	1 471 800	371 260	**1 843 060**	13 559 750	8 329 800	**21 889 550**	...	...	...

‡ For notes, see pp. 272-294.

B Distribution by status and by occupational group
Répartition suivant la situation dans la profession et par groupe de professions
Distribución según la categoría de ocupación y por grupo de ocupación

Others and status unknown *Autres et situation non définie* Otros y categoría no definida			TOTAL				*Groupe de professions*	Grupo de ocupaciones
Males *Hommes* Hombres	Females *Femmes* Mujeres	Total	Males *Hommes* Hombres	Females *Femmes* Mujeres	Total			
						%	0-1. *Personnel des professions scientif., techn., libérales et assimilées*	0-1. Profesionales, técnicos y trabajadores asimilados
...	...	...	...	...	501 130	3.2		
							2. *Directeurs et cadres administratifs supérieurs*	2. Directores y funcionarios públicos superiores
...	...	...	...	...	68 450	0.4		
							3. *Personnel administratif et travailleurs assimilés*	3. Personal administrativo y trabajadores asimilados
...	...	...	...	...	351 808	2.2		
							4. *Personnel commercial et vendeurs*	4. Comerciantes y vendedores
...	...	...	...	...	461 367	2.9		
...	...	...	...	...	570 183	3.6	5. *Travailleurs des services*	5. Trabajadores de los servicios
							6. *Agriculteurs, éleveurs, forestiers, pêcheurs et chasseurs*	6. Trab. agrícolas y forestales, pescadores y cazadores
...	...	...	...	...	10 910 869	69.0		7-9. Obreros no agrícolas, conductores de máquinas y vehículos de transporte y trabajadores asimilados
							7-9. *Ouvriers et manœuvres non agricoles et conducteurs d'engins de transport*	
...	...	...	...	...	2 285 685	14.4		
							X. *Travailleurs ne pouvant être classés selon la profession*	X. Trabajadores que no pueden ser clasificados según la ocupación
...	...	...	...	...	679 161	4.3		
...	...	75 010	...	...	15 828 653	100.0	*Total*	Total

Others and status unknown			TOTAL				*Groupe de professions*	Grupo de ocupaciones
Males	Females	Total	Males	Females	Total			
						%	0-1. *Personnel des professions scientif., techn., libérales et assimilées*	0-1. Profesionales, técnicos y trabajadores asimilados
34 070	19 800	53 870	1 719 560	1 067 510	2 787 070	11.1		
							2. *Directeurs et cadres administratifs supérieurs*	2. Directores y funcionarios públicos superiores
16 440	870	17 310	846 310	78 110	924 420	3.7		
							3. *Personnel administratif et travailleurs assimilés*	3. Personal administrativo y trabajadores asimilados
59 380	40 050	99 430	1 775 600	2 699 150	4 474 750	17.9		
							4. *Personnel commercial et vendeurs*	4. Comerciantes y vendedores
36 180	20 220	56 400	1 182 780	1 064 470	2 247 250	9.0		
45 810	39 920	85 730	901 710	2 036 080	2 937 790	11.7	5. *Travailleurs des services*	5. Trabajadores de los servicios
							6. *Agriculteurs, éleveurs, forestiers, pêcheurs et chasseurs*	6. Trab. agrícolas y forestales, pescadores y cazadores
19 690	1 840	21 530	643 040	96 770	739 810	3.0		7-9. Obreros no agrícolas, conductores de máquinas y vehículos de transporte y trabajadores asimilados
							7-9. *Ouvriers et manœuvres non agricoles et conducteurs d'engins de transport*	
464 200	47 160	511 360	8 298 930	1 708 020	10 006 950	40.0		
							X. *Travailleurs ne pouvant être classés selon la profession*	X. Trabajadores que no pueden ser clasificados según la ocupación
176 580	266 260	442 840	276 180	375 060	651 240	2.6		
.	.	.	239 790	12 010	251 800	1.0	*Membres des forces armées*	Miembros de las fuerzas armadas
852 350	436 120	1 288 470	15 883 900	9 137 180	25 021 080	100.0	*Total*	Total

✝ *Voir notes pp. 272-294.*　　　　　　　　　　　　　✝ Véanse las notas en las págs. 272-294.

2 Structure of the economically active population
Structure de la population active
Estructura de la población económicamente activa

Occupational group	Employers and workers on own account *Employeurs et personnes travaillant à leur propre compte* Empleadores y trabajadores por cuenta propia			Salaried employees and wage earners *Employés et ouvriers* Empleados y obreros			Family workers *Travailleurs familiaux* Trabajadores familiares		
	Males *Hommes* Hombres	Females *Femmes* Mujeres	Total	Males *Hommes* Hombres	Females *Femmes* Mujeres	Total	Males *Hommes* Hombres	Females *Femmes* Mujeres	Total

Yugoslavia (31.III.1971) †

Professional, technical and related workers	11 493	1 707	**13 200**	352 389	311 557	**663 946**	440	457	**897**
Administrative, executive and managerial workers.	.	.	.	84 004	8 132	**92 136**	.	.	.
Clerical workers	124	107	**231**	269 288	262 192	**531 480**	40	61	**101**
Sales workers	2 175	592	**2 767**	176 237	101 981	**278 218**	337	407	**744**
Farmers, fishermen, hunters, loggers and related workers	1 393 725	425 497	**1 819 222**	116 985	23 609	**140 594**	637 439	1 221 469	**1 858 908**
Miners, quarrymen and related workers	173	10	**183**	63 125	894	**64 019**	17	16	**33**
Workers in transport and communication occupations. . . . . ⎤ Craftsmen, prod.-process workers and labourers not elsewhere classified . ⎦	130 961	12 810	**143 771**	1 629 320	371 053	**2 000 373**	8 970	3 741	**12 711**
Service, sport and recreation workers	15 589	10 359	**25 948**	244 320	243 140	**487 460**	1 088	1 997	**3 085**
Workers not classifiable by occupation	5 218	1 756	**6 974**	94 119	46 661	**140 780**	1 171	935	**2 106**
Persons working abroad temporarily .	...	...	...	...	...	...	...	...	...
Total . . .	1 559 458	452 838	**2 012 296**	3 029 787	1 369 219	**4 399 006**	649 502	1 229 083	**1 878 585**

† For notes, see pp. 272-294.

B Distribution by status and by occupational group
Répartition suivant la situation dans la profession et par groupe de professions
Distribución según la categoría de ocupación y por grupo de ocupación

Others and status unknown *Autres et situation non définie* Otros y categoría no definida			TOTAL				Groupe de professions	Grupo de ocupaciones
Males *Hommes* Hombres	Females *Femmes* Mujeres	Total	Males *Hommes* Hombres	Females *Femmes* Mujeres	Total			
						%		
431	179	610	364 753	313 900	678 653	7.6	Personnes exerçant une profession libérale, techniciens et assimilés	Trabajadores profesionales, técnicos y trabajadores asimilados
.	.	.	84 004	8 132	92 136	1.0	Directeurs et cadres administratifs supérieurs	Administradores, gerentes y directores
29	43	72	269 481	262 403	531 884	6.0	Employés de bureau	Empleados de oficina
40	41	81	178 789	103 021	281 810	3.2	Vendeurs	Vendedores
884	619	1 503	2 149 033	1 671 194	3 820 227	43.0	Agriculteurs, pêcheurs, chasseurs, forestiers et travailleurs assimilés	Agricultores, pescadores, cazadores, trabajadores forestales y asimilados
27	.	27	63 342	920	64 262	0.7	Mineurs, carriers et travailleurs assimilés	Mineros, canteros y trabajadores asimilados
1 086	430	1 516	1 770 337	388 034	2 158 371	24.3	Travailleurs des transports et des communications / Artisans, ouvriers de métier, ouvriers à la production et manœuvres non classés ailleurs	Trabajadores de los transportes y comunicaciones / Artesanos y trab. ocupados en los div. procesos de producción y peones no clasif. bajo otros epígrafes
80	552	632	261 077	256 048	517 125	5.8	Travailleurs spécialisés dans les services, les sports et les activités récréatives	Trabajadores de los servicios, los deportes y las diversiones
3 252	3 068	6 320	103 760	52 420	156 180	1.8	Personnes ne pouvant être classées selon la profession	Trabajadores que no pueden ser clasificados según la ocupación
441 756	147 412	589 168	441 756	147 412	589 168	6.6	Personnes travaillant temporairement à l'étranger	Personas que trabajan temporalmente en el extranjero
447 585	152 344	599 929	5 686 332	3 203 484	8 889 816	100.0	Total	Total

† *Voir notes pp. 272-294.*   † Véanse las notas en las págs. 272-294.

2 Structure of the economically active population
Structure de la population active
Estructura de la población económicamente activa

Occupational group	Employers and workers on own account *Employeurs et personnes travaillant à leur propre compte* Empleadores y trabajadores por cuenta propia			Salaried employees and wage earners *Employés et ouvriers* Empleados y obreros			Family workers *Travailleurs familiaux* Trabajadores familiares		
	Males *Hommes* Hombres	Females *Femmes* Mujeres	Total	Males *Hommes* Hombres	Females *Femmes* Mujeres	Total	Males *Hommes* Hombres	Females *Femmes* Mujeres	Total

Australia (30.VI.1971)

OCEANIA — OCÉANIE — OCEANIA

Occupational group	Males	Females	Total	Males	Females	Total	Males	Females	Total
Professional, technical and related workers	35 095	8 072	**43 167**	273 002	215 844	**488 846**	1 232	3 263	**4 495**
Administrative, executive and managerial workers	96 639	19 493	**116 132**	210 044	22 388	**232 432**	159	151	**310**
Clerical workers	1 299	18 192	**19 491**	299 289	509 211	**808 500**	124	2 293	**2 417**
Sales workers	37 710	36 749	**74 459**	179 720	164 642	**344 362**	561	2 504	**3 065**
Farmers, fishermen, hunters, loggers and related workers	194 484	38 553	**233 037**	141 299	15 303	**156 602**	5 345	8 922	**14 267**
Miners, quarrymen and related workers	1 538	43	**1 581**	32 171	40	**32 211**	88	7	**95**
Workers in transport and communication occupations	36 930	1 563	**38 493**	213 950	38 118	**252 068**	153	76	**229**
Craftsmen, prod.-process workers and labourers not elsewhere classified .	96 294	4 148	**100 442**	1 359 986	219 357	**1 579 343**	570	336	**906**
Service, sport and recreation workers	13 029	9 028	**22 057**	131 068	232 588	**363 656**	274	1 575	**1 849**
Workers not classifiable by occupation	5 196	1 442	**6 638**	155 538	74 216	**229 754**	1 134	3 194	**4 328**
Members of the armed forces	.	.	.	62 605	2 591	**65 196**	.	.	.
Persons seeking work for the first time Unemployed	...	...	...	...	...	...	...	...	...
Total . . .	518 214	137 283	**655 497**	3 058 672	1 494 298	**4 552 970**	9 640	22 321	**31 961**

New Zealand (23.III.1971) ‡

Occupational group	Males	Females	Total	Males	Females	Total	Males	Females	Total
0-1. Professional, technical and related workers	10 201	1 242	**11 443**	71 385	55 605	**126 990**	2	3	**5**
2. Administrative and managerial workers	2 139	192	**2 331**	25 164	860	**26 024**	.	.	.
3. Clerical and related workers	566	615	**1 181**	69 213	108 456	**177 669**	.	18	**18**
4. Sales workers	12 273	4 797	**17 070**	63 858	33 352	**97 210**	6	96	**102**
5. Service workers	5 054	3 727	**8 781**	26 250	41 122	**67 372**	.	53	**53**
6. Agricultural, animal husbandry and forestry workers, fishermen and hunters	61 138	6 324	**67 462**	50 340	10 589	**60 929**	222	142	**364**
7-9. Production and related workers, transport equipment, operators and labourers	30 118	1 239	**31 357**	332 649	55 901	**388 550**	6	14	**20**
X. Workers not classifiable by occupation	511	68	**579**	1 868	524	**2 392**	14	27	**41**
Members of the armed forces	.	.	.	10 772	655	**11 427**	.	.	.
Total . . .	122 000	18 204	**140 204**	651 499	307 064	**958 563**	250	353	**603**

‡ For notes, see pp. 272-294.

B Distribution by status and by occupational group
Répartition suivant la situation dans la profession et par groupe de professions
Distribución según la categoría de ocupación y por grupo de ocupación

Others and status unknown / *Autres et situation non définie* / Otros y categoría no definida			TOTAL				Groupe de professions	Grupo de ocupaciones
Males / *Hommes* / Hombres	Females / *Femmes* / Mujeres	Total	Males / *Hommes* / Hombres	Females / *Femmes* / Mujeres	Total			
						%		
...	...	...	309 329	227 179	**536 508**	*10.1*	*Personnes exerçant une profession libérale, techniciens et assimilés*	Trabajadores profesionales, técnicos y trabajadores asimilados
...	...	...	306 842	42 032	**348 874**	*6.5*	*Directeurs et cadres administratifs supérieurs*	Administradores, gerentes y directores
...	...	...	300 712	529 696	**830 408**	*15.6*	*Employés de bureau*	Empleados de oficina
...	...	...	217 991	203 895	**421 886**	*7.9*	*Vendeurs*	Vendedores
...	...	...	341 128	62 778	**403 906**	*7.6*	*Agriculteurs, pêcheurs, chasseurs, forestiers et travailleurs assimilés*	Agricultores, pescadores cazadores, trabajadores forestales y asimilados
...	...	...	33 797	90	**33 887**	*0.6*	*Mineurs, carriers et travailleurs assimilés*	Mineros, canteros y trabajadores asimilados
...	...	...	251 033	39 757	**290 790**	*5.5*	*Travailleurs des transports et des communications*	Trabajadores de los transportes y comunicaciones
...	...	...	1 456 850	223 841	**1 680 691**	*31.5*	*Artisans, ouvriers de métier, ouvriers à la production et manœuvres non classés ailleurs*	Artesanos y trab. ocupados en los div. procesos de producción y peones no clasif. bajo otros epígrafes
...	...	...	144 371	243 191	**387 562**	*7.3*	*Travailleurs spécialisés dans les services, les sports et les activités récréatives*	Trabajadores de los servicios, los deportes y las diversiones
...	...	...	161 868	78 852	**240 720**	*4.5*	*Personnes ne pouvant être classées selon la profession*	Trabajadores que no pueden ser clasificados según la ocupación
.	.	.	62 605	2 591	**65 196**	*1.2*	*Membres des forces armées*	Miembros de las fuerzas armadas
8 237	7 824	**16 061**	8 237	7 824	**16 061**	*0.3*	*Personnes en quête d'emploi pour la première fois*	Personas en busca de trabajo por primera vez
44 876	29 123	**73 999**	44 876	29 123	**73 999**	*1.4*	*Chômeurs*	Desempleados
53 113	36 947	**90 060**	3 639 639	1 690 849	**5 330 488**	*100.0*	*Total*	Total

Others and status unknown			TOTAL				Groupe de professions	Grupo de ocupaciones
Males	Females	Total	Males	Females	Total	%		
362	590	**952**	81 950	57 440	**139 390**	*12.5*	0-1. *Personnel des professions scientif., techn., libérales et assimilées*	0-1. Profesionales, técnicos y trabajadores asimilados
45	3	**48**	27 348	1 055	**28 403**	*2.5*	2. *Directeurs et cadres administratifs supérieurs*	2. Directores y funcionarios públicos superiores
255	1 258	**1 513**	70 034	110 347	**180 381**	*16.1*	3. *Personnel administratif et travailleurs assimilés*	3. Personal administrativo y trabajadores asimilados
406	438	**844**	76 543	38 683	**115 226**	*10.3*	4. *Personnel commercial et vendeurs*	4. Comerciantes y vendedores
375	800	**1 175**	31 679	45 702	**77 381**	*6.9*	5. *Travailleurs des services*	5. Trabajadores de los servicios
715	180	**895**	112 415	17 235	**129 650**	*11.6*	6. *Agriculteurs, éleveurs, forestiers, pêcheurs et chasseurs*	6. Trab. agrícolas y forestales, pescadores y cazadores
3 395	805	**4 200**	366 168	57 959	**424 127**	*38.0*	7-9. *Ouvriers et manœuvres non agricoles et conducteurs d'engins de transport*	7-9. Obreros no agrícolas, conductores de máquinas y vehículos de transporte y trabajadores asimilados
5 633	4 165	**9 798**	8 026	4 784	**12 810**	*1.1*	X. *Travailleurs ne pouvant être classés selon la profession*	X. Trabajadores que no pueden ser clasificados según la ocupación
34	6	**40**	10 806	661	**11 467**	*1.0*	*Membres des forces armées*	Miembros de las fuerzas armadas
11 220	8 245	**19 465**	784 969	333 866	**1 118 835**	*100.0*	*Total*	Total

☦ *Voir notes pp. 272-294.*   ☦ Véanse las notas en las págs. 272-294.

POPULATION

2 Structure of the economically active population
Structure de la population active
Estructura de la población económicamente activa

Occupational group	Employers and workers on own account *Employeurs et personnes travaillant à leur propre compte* Empleadores y trabajadores por cuenta propia			Salaried employees and wage earners *Employés et ouvriers* Empleados y obreros			Family workers *Travailleurs familiaux* Trabajadores familiares		
	Males *Hommes* Hombres	Females *Femmes* Mujeres	Total	Males *Hommes* Hombres	Females *Femmes* Mujeres	Total	Males *Hommes* Hombres	Females *Femmes* Mujeres	Total

Nouvelle-Calédonie (11.III.1969) †

Professional, technical and related workers	144	24	**168**	1 426	1 003	**2 429**	3	4	7
Administrative, executive and managerial workers	133	4	**137**	236	14	**250**	.	.	.
Clerical workers	16	8	**24**	1 333	1 526	**2 859**	3	3	6
Sales workers	523	281	**804**	982	787	**1 769**	22	95	117
Farmers, fishermen, hunters, loggers and related workers	4 351	1 417	**5 768**	687	46	**733**	2 178	4 592	6 770
Miners, quarrymen and related workers	47	.	**47**	2 581	24	**2 605**	.	.	.
Workers in transport and communication occupations	380	9	**389**	1 760	67	**1 827**	6	1	7
Craftsmen, prod.-process workers and labourers not elsewhere classified .	743	100	**843**	6 329	117	**6 446**	19	8	27
Service, sport and recreation workers	79	60	**139**	662	1 855	**2 517**	9	14	23
Workers not classifiable by occupation	81	30	**111**	264	66	**330**	3	14	17
Members of the armed forces	.	.	.	1 489	3	**1 492**	.	.	.
Total . . .	6 497	1 933	**8 430**	17 749	5 508	**23 257**	2 243	4 731	**6 974**

Western Samoa (7.XI.1971)

0-1. Professional, technical and related workers	...	...	...	...	...	...	...	...	...
2. Administrative and managerial workers	...	...	...	...	...	...	...	...	...
3. Clerical and related workers	...	...	...	...	...	...	...	...	...
4. Sales workers	...	...	...	...	...	...	...	...	...
5. Service workers	...	...	...	...	...	...	...	...	...
6. Agricultural, animal husbandry and forestry workers, fishermen and hunters	...	...	...	...	...	...	...	...	...
7-9. Production and related workers, transport equipment, operators and labourers	...	...	...	...	...	...	...	...	...
Persons seeking work for the first time	.	.	.	.	.	.	.	.	.
Total . . .	14 986	519	**15 505**	10 218	3 751	**13 969**	7 245	1 017	**8 262**

† For notes, see pp. 272-294.

B Distribution by status and by occupational group
Répartition suivant la situation dans la profession et par groupe de professions
Distribución según la categoría de ocupación y por grupo de ocupación

Others and status unknown / Autres et situation non définie / Otros y categoría no definida			TOTAL				Groupe de professions	Grupo de ocupaciones
Males / Hommes / Hombres	Females / Femmes / Mujeres	Total	Males / Hommes / Hombres	Females / Femmes / Mujeres	Total	%		
182	258	**440**	1 755	1 289	**3 044**	7.8	Personnes exerçant une profession libérale, techniciens et assimilés	Trabajadores profesionales, técnicos y trabajadores asimilados
2	.	**2**	371	18	**389**	1.0	Directeurs et cadres administratifs supérieurs	Administradores, gerentes y directores
1	2	**3**	1 353	1 539	**2 892**	7.4	Employés de bureau	Empleados de oficina
2	1	**3**	1 529	1 164	**2 693**	6.9	Vendeurs	Vendedores
4	.	**4**	7 220	6 055	**13 275**	33.8	Agriculteurs, pêcheurs, chasseurs, forestiers et travailleurs assimilés	Agricultores, pescadores, cazadores, trabajadores forestales y asimilados
2	.	**2**	2 630	24	**2 654**	6.8	Mineurs, carriers et travailleurs assimilés	Mineros, canteros y trabajadores asimilados
1	.	**1**	2 147	77	**2 224**	5.7	Travailleurs des transports et des communications	Trabajadores de los transportes y comunicaciones
9	.	**9**	7 100	225	**7 325**	18.7	Artisans, ouvriers de métier, ouvriers à la production et manœuvres non classés ailleurs	Artesanos y trab. ocupados en los div. procesos de producción y peones no clasif. bajo otros epígrafes
2	2	**4**	752	1 931	**2 683**	6.8	Travailleurs spécialisés dans les services, les sports et les activités récréatives	Trabajadores de los servicios, los deportes y las diversiones
28	28	**56**	376	138	**514**	1.3	Personnes ne pouvant être classées selon la profession	Trabajadores que no pueden ser clasificados según la ocupación
.	.	.	1 489	3	**1 492**	3.8	Membres des forces armées	Miembros de las fuerzas armadas
233	291	**524**	26 722	12 463	**39 185**	100.0	*Total*	Total

						%		
.	.	.	...	...	**3 250**	8.6	0-1. Personnel des professions scientif., techn, libérales et assimilées	0-1. Profesionales, técnicos y trabajadores asimilados
.	.	.	...	...	**256**	0.7	2. Directeurs et cadres administratifs supérieurs	2. Directores y funcionarios públicos superiores
.	.	.	...	...	**1 393**	3.7	3. Personnel administratif et travailleurs assimilés	3. Personal administrativo y trabajadores asimilados
.	.	.	...	...	**1 244**	3.3	4. Personnel commercial et vendeurs	4. Comerciantes y vendedores
.	.	.	...	...	**1 338**	3.5	5. Travailleurs des services	5. Trabajadores de los servicios
.	.	.	...	...	**25 003**	65.9	6. Agriculteurs, éleveurs, forestiers, pêcheurs et chasseurs	6. Trab. agrícolas y forestales, pescadores y cazadores
.	.	.	...	...	**5 256**	13.9	7-9. Ouvriers et manœuvres non agricoles et conducteurs d'engins de transport	7-9. Obreros no agrícolas, conductores de máquinas y vehículos de transporte y trabajadores asimilados
...	...	...	...	...	**161**	0.4	Personnes en quête d'emploi pour la première fois	Personas en busca de trabajo por primera vez
102	63	**165**	32 551	5 350	**37 901**	100.0	*Total*	Total

† *Voir notes pp. 272-294.*   † Véanse las notas en las págs. 272-294.

271

POPULATION

AFRICA — AFRIQUE — AFRICA

Algérie

Tables 1, 2 A, 2 B:

Excl. military personnel in barracks and 274,668 nationals abroad (256,062 males and 18,606 females) of whom 229,020 are economically active (226,999 males and 2,021 females).

Economically active population figures do not include about 1,200,000 females mainly occupied in agriculture.

Tableaux 1, 2 A, 2 B:

Non compris les militaires dans les casernes, ni 274 668 nationaux à l'étranger (256 062 hommes et 18 606 femmes) dont 229 020 sont économiquement actifs (226 999 hommes et 2 021 femmes).

Les chiffres de la population active ne comprennent pas environ 1 200 000 femmes principalement occupées dans l'agriculture.

Cuadros 1, 2 A, 2 B:

Excl. el personal militar acuartelado y 274 668 nacionales que viven en el extranjero (256 062 hombres y 18 606 mujeres), de los cuales 229 020 son económicamente activos (226 999 hombres y 2 021 mujeres).

Las cifras de la población económicamente activa no incluyen cerca de 1 200 000 mujeres principalmente ocupadas en la agricultura.

Botswana

Table 1:

De jure population. Excl. nomad population (about 11,650 persons).

Tableau 1:

Population de jure. *Non compris la population nomade (environ 11 650 personnes).*

Cuadro 1:

Población *de jure.* Excl. la población nómada (alrededor de 11 650 personas).

Tables 2 A, 2 B:

Excl. nomads (total population estimated at 14,050 persons) and workers abroad.

Tableaux 2 A, 2 B:

Non compris les nomades dont la population totale est estimée à 14 050 personnes, ni les travailleurs à l'étranger.

Cuadros 2 A, 2 B:

Excl. los nómadas, que tienen una población total estimada en 14 050 personas, y los trabajadores en el extranjero.

Burundi

Table 1:

Official estimates.

Tableau 1:

Evaluations officielles.

Cuadro 1:

Estimaciones oficiales.

Cameroun

Table 1:

African population: official estimates.

Tableau 1:

Population africaine : *évaluations officielles.*

Cuadro 1:

Población africana : estimaciones oficiales.

République centrafricaine

Table 1:

Official estimates.

Tableau 1:

Evaluations officielles.

Cuadro 1:

Estimaciones oficiales.

Côte-d'Ivoire

Tables 1, 2 A:

Official estimates.

Tableaux 1, 2 A:

Evaluations officielles.

Cuadros 1, 2 A:

Estimaciones oficiales.

Dahomey

Table 1:

Estimates based on the results of a sample survey.

Tableau 1:

Evaluations fondées sur les résultats d'une enquête par sondage.

Cuadro 1:

Estimaciones basadas en los resultados de una encuesta por muestra.

Notes to tables 1 to 2 B (indicated by the symbol ǂ)
Notes relatives aux tableaux 1 à 2 B (indiquées par le symbole ǂ)
Notas relativas a los cuadros 1 a 2 B (indicadas por medio del símbolo ǂ)

Egypt

Table 1:

1966: economically active population figures by age group do not include persons less than 12 and more than 64 years of age, who appear only in the totals.

1973: estimates based on the results of a labour force sample survey.

Table 2 B:

The group " Others and status unknown " relates to persons less than 15 years of age.

Tableau 1:

1966: *les chiffres de la population active par groupe d'âge ne comprennent pas les personnes âgées de moins de 12 et de plus de 64 ans, qui figurent uniquement dans les totaux.*

1973: *évaluations fondées sur les résultats d'une enquête par sondage sur la main-d'œuvre.*

Tableau 2 B:

La rubrique « Autres et situation non définie » se réfère aux personnes âgées de moins de 15 ans.

Cuadro 1:

1966: las cifras de la población económicamente activa por grupo de edad no incluyen las personas de menos de 12 y de más de 64 años de edad, que aparecen solamente en los totales.

1973: estimaciones basadas en los resultados de una encuesta por muestra sobre la fuerza trabajadora.

Cuadro 2 B:

El grupo « Otros y categoría no definida » se refiere a las personas de menos de 15 años de edad.

Ethiopia

Table 1:

Estimates based on the results of a sample survey.

Tableau 1:

Evaluations fondées sur les résultats d'une enquête par sondage.

Cuadro 1:

Estimaciones basadas en los resultados de una encuesta por muestra.

Gabon

Tables 1, 2 A:

Official estimates.

Tableaux 1, 2 A:

Evaluations officielles.

Cuadros 1, 2 A:

Estimaciones oficiales.

Ghana

Table 2 B:

The group " Employers and workers on own account " includes 6,427 members of producers' co-operatives (6,094 males and 333 females).

The group " Others and status unknown " relates to unemployed.

Tableau 2 B:

La rubrique « Employeurs et personnes travaillant à leur propre compte » comprend 6 427 membres de coopératives de producteurs (6 094 hommes et 333 femmes).

La rubrique « Autres et situation non définie » se réfère aux chômeurs.

Cuadro 2 B:

El grupo « Empleadores y trabajadores por cuenta propia » incluye 6 427 miembros de cooperativas de producción (6 094 hombres y 333 mujeres).

El grupo « Otros y categoría no definida » se refiere a los desempleados.

Haute-Volta

Table 1:
Official estimates.

Tableau 1:
Evaluations officielles.

Cuadro 1:
Estimaciones oficiales.

Liberia

Tables 1, 2 A, 2 B:

Economically active population figures do not include armed forces.

Tableaux 1, 2 A, 2 B:

Les chiffres de la population active ne comprennent pas les forces armées.

Cuadros 1, 2 A, 2 B:

Las cifras de la población económicamente activa no incluyen las fuerzas armadas.

Libyan Arab Republic

Tables 1, 2 A, 2 B:

Data relate to Libyan citizens only; total population at the date of the census numbered 1,564,369 persons (813,386 males and 750,983 females).

Tables 2 A, 2 B:

The group " Others and status unknown " includes 33,596 persons seeking work (31,717 males and 1,879 females).

Tableaux 1, 2 A, 2 B:

Les données se rapportent aux citoyens libyens seulement ; à la date du recensement, la population totale comptait 1 564 369 personnes (813 386 hommes et 750 983 femmes).

Tableaux 2 A, 2 B:

La rubrique « Autres et situation non définie » comprend 33 596 personnes en quête d'emploi (31 717 hommes et 1 879 femmes).

Cuadros 1, 2 A, 2 B:

Los datos se refieren a los ciudadanos libios solamente; en la fecha del censo, la población total era de 1 564 369 personas (813 386 hombres y 750 983 mujeres).

Cuadros 2 A, 2 B:

El grupo « Otros y categoría no definida » incluye 33 596 personas en busca de trabajo (31 717 hombres y 1 879 mujeres).

POPULATION

Notes to tables **1 to 2 B** (indicated by the symbol ✝)
Notes relatives aux tableaux **1 à 2 B** (indiquées par le symbole ✝)
Notas relativas a los cuadros **1 a 2 B** (indicadas por medio del símbolo ✝)

Madagascar

Table 1:
Official estimates.

Tableau 1:
Evaluations officielles.

Cuadro 1:
Estimaciones oficiales.

Maroc

Tables 1, 2 A, 2 B:
De jure population. Figures based on a 10 per cent sample tabulation of census returns.

Female economically active population figures do not include unreported family helpers in agriculture.

Tableaux 1, 2 A, 2 B:
Population de jure. Chiffres fondés sur la tabulation d'un échantillon de 10 pour cent des bulletins de recensement.

Les chiffres de la population active féminine ne comprennent pas les aides familiales non déclarées dans l'agriculture.

Cuadros 1, 2 A, 2 B:
Población *de jure*. Cifras basadas en la tabulación de una muestra del 10 por ciento de los boletines del censo.

Las cifras de la población femenina económicamente activa no incluyen las ayudantes familiares no declaradas en la agricultura.

Mozambique

Table 2 A:
Male economically active population figures do not include 21,689 persons on compulsory military service.

Tableau 2 A:
Les chiffres de la population active masculine ne comprennent pas 21 689 personnes effectuant leur service militaire obligatoire (militaires du contingent).

Cuadro 2 A:
Las cifras de la población económicamente activa masculina no incluyen 21 689 personas en servicio militar obligatorio.

Niger

Table 1:
Estimates based on the results of a sample survey.

Excl. population of Niamey City (about 30,000 inhabitants), nomad populations (about 234,000 persons) and foreigners.

Tableau 1:
Evaluations fondées sur les résultats d'une enquête par sondage.

Non compris la population de la ville de Niamey (environ 30 000 habitants), ni les populations nomades (environ 234 000 personnes), ni les étrangers.

Cuadro 1:
Estimaciones basadas en los resultados de una encuesta por muestra.

Excl. la población de la ciudad de Niamey (cerca de 30 000 habitantes), las poblaciones nómadas (cerca de 234 000 personas) y los extranjeros.

Réunion

Tables 1, 2 A:
Economically active population figures do not include unemployed.

Tableaux 1, 2 A:
Les chiffres de la population active ne comprennent pas les chômeurs.

Cuadros 1, 2 A:
Las cifras de la población económicamente activa no incluyen los desempleados.

St. Helena

Table 1:
Incl. figures for Ascension.

Tableau 1:
Y compris les chiffres pour Ascension.

Cuadro 1:
Incl. las cifras para Ascensión.

Sénégal

Table 1:
Official estimates.

Tableau 1:
Evaluations officielles.

Cuadro 1:
Estimaciones oficiales.

Sierra Leone

Table 2 A:
The group " Others and status unknown " relates to persons not at work at the time of the census.

Tableau 2 A:
La rubrique « Autres et situation non définie » se réfère aux personnes hors d'activité à la date du recensement.

Cuadro 2 A:
El grupo « Otros y categoría no definida » se refiere a las personas fuera de actividad en la fecha del censo.

Notes to tables 1 to 2 B   (indicated by the symbol ‡)

Notes relatives aux tableaux 1 à 2 B   (indiquées par le symbole ‡)

Notas relativas a los cuadros 1 a 2 B   (indicadas por medio del símbolo ‡)

South Africa, Rep. of

Tables 1, 2 A, 2 B:

Figures based on a sample tabulation of census returns.

Tableaux 1, 2 A, 2 B:

Chiffres fondés sur la tabulation d'un échantillon des bulletins de recensement.

Cuadros 1, 2 A, 2 B:

Cifras basadas en la tabulación de una muestra de los boletines del censo.

Tchad

Table 1:

Official estimates.

Tableau 1:

Evaluations officielles.

Cuadro 1:

Estimaciones oficiales.

Togo

Table 1:

Economically active population figures do not include unemployed.

Tableau 1:

Les chiffres de la population active ne comprennent pas les chômeurs.

Cuadro 1:

Las cifras de la población económicamente activa no incluyen los desempleados.

Tunisie

Tables 1 (1966), 2 A, 2 B:

Female economically active population figures do not include about 250,000 family helpers.

Tableaux 1 (1966), 2 A, 2 B:

Les chiffres de la population féminine active ne comprennent pas environ 250 000 aides familiales.

Cuadros 1 (1966), 2 A, 2 B:

Las cifras de la población femenina económicamente activa no incluyen cerca de 250 000 ayudantes familiares.

Table 1:

1971: official estimates.

Tableau 1:

1971: *évaluations officielles.*

Cuadro 1:

1971: estimaciones oficiales.

Tables 2 A, 2 B:

The group " Others and status unknown " includes 14,403 members of producers' co-operatives (14,249 males and 154 females) and persons seeking work for the first time.

Tableaux 2A, 2 B:

La rubrique « Autres et situation non définie » comprend 14 403 membres de coopératives de producteurs (14 249 hommes et 154 femmes) ainsi que les personnes en quête d'emploi pour la première fois.

Cuadros 2 A, 2 B:

El grupo « Otros y categoría no definida » incluye 14 403 miembros de cooperativas de producción (14 249 hombres y 154 mujeres) así como las personas en busca de trabajo por primera vez.

Zambia

Tables 1, 2 A, 2 B:

Provisional figures. Data have not been adjusted for under-enumeration and *(table 1)* for misreporting of ages.

Tableaux 1, 2 A, 2 B:

Chiffres provisoires. Les données n'ont pas été ajustées pour compenser les lacunes d'enregistrement et (tableau 1) *les erreurs relatives aux déclarations d'âge.*

Cuadros 1, 2 A, 2 B:

Cifras provisionales. No se han ajustado los datos para compensar los casos no registrados y *(cuadro 1)* los errores en las declaraciones de edad.

*

*   *

POPULATION

Notes to tables 1 to 2 B (indicated by the symbol ‡)
Notes relatives aux tableaux 1 à 2 B (indiquées par le symbole ‡)
Notas relativas a los cuadros 1 a 2 B (indicadas por medio del símbolo ‡)

AMERICA — AMÉRIQUE — AMERICA

Antigua

Table 1:
1973: official estimates.

Tableau 1:
1973: *évaluations officielles.*

Cuadro 1:
1973: estimaciones oficiales.

Antilles néerlandaises

Tables 2 A, 2 B:
Excl. 1,184 persons (403 males and 781 females) working less than 15 hours per week.

Tableaux 2 A, 2 B:
Non compris 1 184 personnes (403 hommes et 781 femmes) travaillant moins de 15 heures par semaine.

Cuadros 2 A, 2 B:
Excl. 1 184 personas (403 hombres y 781 mujeres) que trabajan menos de 15 horas por semana.

Argentina

Tables 1, 2 A, 2 B:
Figures based on a sample tabulation of census returns.

Tableaux 1, 2 A, 2 B:
Chiffres fondés sur la tabulation d'un échantillon des bulletins de recensement.

Cuadros 1, 2 A, 2 B:
Cifras basadas en la tabulación de una muestra de los boletines del censo.

Table 2 B:
The occupational group " Service workers " includes members of the armed forces.

Tableau 2 B:
Le groupe de professions « Travailleurs des services » comprend les membres des forces armées.

Cuadro 2 B:
El grupo de ocupación « Trabajadores de los servicios » incluye los miembros de las fuerzas armadas.

Barbados

Tables 1, 2 A, 2 B:
Economically active population figures relate to persons who worked during the twelve months preceding the census day, regardless of the duration of work.

Tableaux 1, 2 A, 2 B:
Les chiffres de la population active se réfèrent aux personnes qui ont exercé une activité au cours des douze mois précédant le jour du recensement, quelle que soit la durée de cette activité.

Cuadros 1, 2 A, 2 B:
Las cifras de la población económicamente activa se refieren a las personas que ejercieron una actividad económica durante los doce meses que preceden al día del censo, sin consideración a la duración del trabajo.

Belize

Table 1:
1968: official estimates.

Tableau 1:
1968: *évaluations officielles.*

Cuadro 1:
1968: estimaciones oficiales.

Brésil

Tables 1 (1970), 2 A, 2 B:
De jure population. Economically active population figures are based on a 25 per cent sample tabulation of census returns.

Tableaux 1 (1970), 2 A, 2 B:
Population de jure. *Les chiffres de la population active sont fondés sur la tabulation d'un échantillon de 25 pour cent des bulletins de recensement.*

Cuadros 1 (1970), 2 A, 2 B:
Población *de jure.* Las cifras de la población económicamente activa están basadas en la tabulación de una muestra de 25 por ciento de los boletines del censo.

Table 1:
1973: estimates based on the results of a household survey.

Tableau 1:
1973: *évaluations fondées sur les résultats d'une enquête auprès des ménages.*

Cuadro 1:
1973: estimaciones basadas en los resultados de una encuesta de hogares.

Table 2 A:
The branch " Activities not adequately described " includes 218,757 persons seeking work for the first time (173,712 males and 45,045 females).

Tableau 2 A:
La branche « Activités mal désignées » comprend 218 757 personnes en quête d'emploi pour la première fois (173 712 hommes et 45 045 femmes).

Cuadro 2 A:
La rama « Actividades no bien especificadas » incluye 218 757 personas en busca de trabajo por primera vez (173 712 hombres y 45 045 mujeres).

Notes to tables 1 to 2 B (indicated by the symbol ‡)
Notes relatives aux tableaux 1 à 2 B (indiquées par le symbole ‡)
Notas relativas a los cuadros 1 a 2 B (indicadas por medio del símbolo ‡)

Canada

Table 1:

As each figure is rounded off, in some cases the sum of the entries may differ from the totals shown.

Tables 2 A, 2 B:

Estimates based on the results of a labour force sample survey.

Excl. Yukon, Northwest Territories, armed forces and Indians living on reserves.

Figures of less than 10,000 are indicated by a dash. Consequently, in some cases, the sum of the entries may differ from the total shown.

Table 2 B:

The group "Employers and workers on own account" includes unpaid family workers.

Tableau 1:

Chaque nombre étant arrondi, dans quelques cas les totaux indiqués peuvent différer de la somme de leurs parties composantes.

Tableaux 2 A, 2 B:

Evaluations fondées sur les résultats d'une enquête par sondage sur la main-d'œuvre.

Non compris le Yukon, les Territoires du Nord-Ouest, les forces armées et les Indiens vivant dans les réserves.

Les chiffres représentant moins de 10 000 personnes sont désignés par un tiret. En conséquence, dans quelques cas, les totaux indiqués peuvent différer de la somme de leurs parties composantes.

Tableau 2 B:

La rubrique « Employeurs et personnes travaillant à leur propre compte » comprend les travailleurs familiaux non rémunérés.

Cuadro 1:

Como cada cifra ha sido redondeada, en algunos casos la suma de los guarismos anotados puede diferir del total respectivo.

Cuadros 2 A, 2 B:

Estimaciones basadas en los resultados de una encuesta por muestra sobre la fuerza trabajadora.

Excl. el Yukón, los Territorios del Noroeste, las fuerzas armadas y los indios que viven en las reservas indígenas.

Las cifras inferiores a 10 000 personas están indicadas por un guión. En consecuencia, en algunos casos la suma de los guarismos anotados puede diferir del total respectivo.

Cuadro 2 B:

El grupo « Empleadores y trabajadores por cuenta propia » incluye los trabajadores familiares no remunerados.

Colombia

Tables 1, 2 A:

Estimates based on the results of a household survey.

Tableaux 1, 2 A:

Evaluations fondées sur les résultats d'une enquête auprès des ménages.

Cuadros 1, 2 A:

Estimaciones basadas en los resultados de una encuesta de hogares.

Cuba

Tables 1, 2 A, 2 B:

Economically active population figures do not include domestic servants.

Tables 2 A, 2 B:

The group "Employers and workers on own account" includes 230,525 members of agricultural producers' co-operatives.

Tableaux 1, 2 A, 2 B:

Les chiffres de la population active ne comprennent pas les gens de maison.

Tableaux 2 A, 2 B:

La rubrique « Employeurs et personnes travaillant à leur propre compte » comprend 230 525 membres de coopératives agricoles de producteurs.

Cuadros 1, 2 A, 2 B:

Las cifras de la población económicamente activa no incluyen los empleados domésticos.

Cuadros 2 A, 2 B:

El grupo « Empleadores y trabajadores por cuenta propia » incluye 230 525 miembros de cooperativas agrícolas de producción.

Chile

Tables 1, 2 A, 2 B:

Figures based on a 5 per cent sample tabulation of census returns.

Tableaux 1, 2 A, 2 B:

Chiffres fondés sur la tabulation d'un échantillon de 5 pour cent des bulletins de recensement.

Cuadros 1, 2 A, 2 B:

Cifras basadas en la tabulación de una muestra de 5 por ciento de los boletines del censo.

República Dominicana

Tables 1, 2 A, 2 B:

Figures based on a sample tabulation of census returns.

Table 2 B:

The occupational group "Workers not classifiable by occupation" includes members of the armed forces.

Tableaux 1, 2 A, 2 B:

Chiffres fondés sur la tabulation d'un échantillon des bulletins de recensement.

Tableau 2 B:

Le groupe de professions « Travailleurs ne pouvant être classés selon la profession » comprend les membres des forces armées.

Cuadros 1, 2 A, 2 B:

Cifras basadas en la tabulación de una muestra de los boletines del censo.

Cuadro 2 B:

El grupo de ocupación « Trabajadores que no pueden ser clasificados según la ocupación » incluye los miembros de las fuerzas armadas.

POPULATION

Ecuador

Table 1:

Excl. Indian jungle population

1974: official estimates.

Tableau 1:

Non compris les Indiens sylvicoles.

1974: *évaluations officielles.*

Cuadro 1:

Excl. la población india silvícola.

1974: estimaciones oficiales.

El Salvador

Tables 2 A, 2 B:

The group " Others and status unknown " includes apprentices and persons seeking work for the first time.

Tableaux 2 A, 2 B:

La rubrique « Autres et situation non définie » comprend les apprentis et les personnes en quête d'emploi pour la première fois.

Cuadros 2 A, 2 B:

El grupo « Otros y categoría no definida » incluye los aprendices y las personas en busca de trabajo por primera vez.

Greenland

Table 2 B:

The group " Salaried employees and wage earners " includes family workers.

Tableau 2 B:

La rubrique « Employés et ouvriers » comprend les travailleurs familiaux.

Cuadro 2 B:

El grupo « Empleados y obreros » incluye los trabajadores familiares.

Guadeloupe

Tables 1, 2 A:

Economically active population figures do not include unemployed.

Tableaux 1, 2 A:

Les chiffres de la population active ne comprennent pas les chômeurs.

Cuadros 1, 2 A:

Las cifras de la población económicamente activa no incluyen los desempleados.

Table 1:

1974: official estimates.

Tableau 1:

1974: *évaluations officielles.*

Cuadro 1:

1974: estimaciones oficiales.

Guatemala

Tables 1, 2 A, 2 B:

Figures based on a 5 per cent sample tabulation of census returns. Excl. institutional households.

Economically active population figures do not include unemployed.

Tableaux 1, 2 A, 2 B:

Chiffres fondés sur la tabulation d'un échantillon de 5 pour cent des bulletins de recensement. Non compris les ménages collectifs.

Les chiffres de la population active ne comprennent pas les chômeurs.

Cuadros 1, 2 A, 2 B:

Cifras basadas en la tabulación de una muestra de 5 por ciento de los boletines del censo. Excl. los hogares colectivos.

Las cifras de la población económicamente activa no incluyen los desempleados.

Tables 2 A, 2 B:

The group " Others and status unknown " includes unpaid family workers.

Tableaux 2 A, 2 B:

La rubrique « Autres et situation non définie » comprend les travailleurs familiaux non rémunérés.

Cuadros 2 A, 2 B:

El grupo « Otros y categoría no definida » incluye los trabajadores familiares no remunerados.

Guyana

Tables 1, 2 A:

1965: estimates based on the results of a labour force sample survey.

Tableaux 1, 2 A:

1965: *évaluations fondées sur les résultats d'une enquête par sondage sur la main-d'œuvre.*

Cuadros 1, 2 A:

1965: estimaciones basadas en los resultados de una encuesta por muestra sobre la fuerza trabajadora.

Table 2 A:

1965: the group " Others and status unknown " includes 36,644 persons not at work at the time of the census (23,361 males and 13,283 females).

Tableau 2 A:

1965: *la rubrique « Autres et situation non définie » comprend 36 644 personnes hors d'activité à la date du recensement (23 361 hommes et 13 283 femmes).*

Cuadro 2 A:

1965: el grupo « Otros y categoría no definida » incluye 36 644 personas fuera de actividad en la fecha del censo (23 361 hombres y 13 283 mujeres).

Notes to tables 1 to 2 B (indicated by the symbol ‡)

Notes relatives aux tableaux 1 à 2 B (indiquées par le symbole ‡)

Notas relativas a los cuadros 1 a 2 B (indicadas por medio del símbolo ‡)

Guyane française

Tables 1, 2 A:

Economically active population figures do not include unemployed.

Tableaux 1, 2 A:

Les chiffres de la population active ne comprennent pas les chômeurs.

Cuadros 1, 2 A:

Las cifras de la población económicamente activa no incluyen los desempleados.

Honduras

Table 2 A:

Official estimates.

Tableau 2 A:

Evaluations officielles.

Cuadro 2 A:

Estimaciones oficiales.

Jamaica

Tables 1 (1974), 2 A:

Estimates based on the results of labour force sample surveys.

Tableaux 1 (1974), 2 A:

Evaluations fondées sur les résultats d'enquêtes par sondage sur la main-d'œuvre.

Cuadros 1 (1974), 2 A:

Estimaciones basadas en los resultados de encuestas por muestra sobre la fuerza trabajadora.

Martinique

Tables 1, 2 A, 2 B:

Economically active population figures do not include unemployed.

Tableaux 1, 2 A, 2 B:

Les chiffres de la population active ne comprennent pas les chômeurs.

Cuadros 1, 2 A, 2 B:

Las cifras de la población económicamente activa no incluyen los desempleados.

Table 1:

1970: official estimates.

Tableau 1:

1970: *évaluations officielles.*

Cuadro 1:

1970: estimaciones oficiales.

México

Tables 1, 2 A, 2 B:

1970: economically active population figures relate to persons who worked during 1969, regardless of the duration of work.

Tableaux 1, 2 A, 2 B:

1970: *les chiffres de la population active se réfèrent aux personnes qui ont exercé une activité en 1969, quelle que soit la durée de cette activité.*

Cuadros 1, 2 A, 2 B:

1970: las cifras de la población económicamente activa se refieren a las personas que ejercieron una actividad económica en 1969, sin consideración a la duración del trabajo.

Tables 1 (1974), 2 A, 2 B (1975):

Official estimates.

Tableaux 1 (1974), 2 A, 2 B (1975):

Evaluations officielles.

Cuadros 1 (1974), 2 A, 2 B (1975):

Estimaciones oficiales.

Montserrat

Table 1:

Economically active population figures do not include unemployed.

Tableau 1:

Les chiffres de la population active ne comprennent pas les chômeurs.

Cuadro 1:

Las cifras de la población económicamente activa no incluyen los desempleados.

Nicaragua

Tables 1, 2 A, 2 B:

Provisional figures based on a 10 per cent sample tabulation of census returns.

Tableaux 1, 2 A, 2 B:

Chiffres provisoires fondés sur la tabulation d'un échantillon de 10 pour cent des bulletins de recensement.

Cuadros 1, 2 A, 2 B:

Cifras provisionales basadas en la tabulación de una muestra de 10 por ciento de los boletines del censo.

Panamá

Tables 1, 2 A, 2 B:

Incl. residents of the Republic of Panama working in the Canal Zone.

Tableaux 1, 2 A, 2 B:

Y compris les résidents de la République de Panama qui travaillent dans la Zone du canal.

Cuadros 1, 2 A, 2 B:

Incl. los residentes de la República de Panamá que trabajan en la Zona del Canal.

POPULATION

Notes to tables 1 to 2 B (indicated by the symbol ‡)

Notes relatives aux tableaux 1 à 2 B (indiquées par le symbole ‡)

Notas relativas a los cuadros 1 a 2 B (indicadas por medio del símbolo ‡)

Panama Canal Zone

Table 1:

1973: official estimates.

Tableau 1:

1973: *évaluations officielles.*

Cuadro 1:

1973: estimaciones oficiales.

Paraguay

Tables 1, 2 A, 2 B:

Figures based on a 10 per cent sample tabulation of census returns.

Tableaux 1, 2 A, 2 B:

Chiffres fondés sur la tabulation d'un échantillon de 10 pour cent des bulletins de recensement.

Cuadros 1, 2 A, 2 B:

Cifras basadas en la tabulación de una muestra de 10 por ciento de los boletines del censo.

Perú

Tables 1, 2 A, 2 B:

Population actually enumerated, i.e. excl. Indian jungle population; excl. an adjustment for underenumeration.

Economically active population figures relate to persons 6 years of age and over *(table 1)* and 15 years of age and over *(tables 2 A, 2 B).*

Tableaux 1, 2 A, 2 B:

Population effectivement dénombrée, c'est-à-dire non compris les Indiens sylvicoles ni un ajustement pour compenser les lacunes d'enregistrement.

Les chiffres de la population active se réfèrent aux personnes âgées de 6 ans et plus (tableau 1) *et 15 ans et plus* (tableaux 2 A, 2 B).

Cuadros 1, 2 A, 2 B:

Población efectivamente enumerada, es decir, excl. la población india silvícola; excl. un ajuste para compensar la subenumeración.

Las cifras de la población económicamente activa se refieren a las personas de 6 años y más de edad *(cuadro 1)* y 15 años y más de edad *(cuadros 2 A, 2 B).*

Puerto Rico

Tables 1 (1975), 2 A, 2 B:

Estimates based on the results of a labour force sample survey.

Tableaux 1 (1975), 2 A, 2 B:

Evaluations fondées sur les résultats d'une enquête par sondage sur la main-d'œuvre.

Cuadros 1 (1975), 2 A, 2 B:

Estimaciones basadas en los resultados de una encuesta por muestra sobre la fuerza trabajadora.

Table 1:

1970: economically active population figures do not include unemployed.

Tableau 1:

1970: *les chiffres de la population active ne comprennent pas les chômeurs.*

Cuadro 1:

1970: las cifras de la población económicamente activa no incluyen los desempleados.

Tables 2 A, 2 B:

Figures of less than 1,000 are indicated by a dash; other figures are rounded off to the nearest 100. Consequently, in some cases the sum of the entries may differ from the totals shown.

Tableaux 2 A, 2 B:

Les chiffres représentant moins de 1 000 personnes sont désignés par un tiret ; les autres chiffres sont arrondis au multiple de 100 le plus proche. En conséquence, dans quelques cas, les totaux indiqués peuvent différer de la somme de leurs parties composantes.

Cuadros 2 A, 2 B:

Las cifras inferiores a 1 000 personas están indicadas por un guión; otras cifras estan redondeadas al múltiplo de 100 más próximo. En consecuencia, en algunos casos la suma de los guarismos anotados puede diferir del total respectivo.

Saint-Pierre-et-Miquelon

Table 1:

1971: official estimates.

Tableau 1:

1971: *évaluations officielles.*

Cuadro 1:

1971: estimaciones oficiales.

Surinam

Tables 1, 2 A, 2 B:

Excl. Indian and Negro populations living in tribes.

Economically active population figures do not include armed forces.

Tableaux 1, 2 A, 2 B:

Non compris les populations indiennes et noires vivant en tribus.

Les chiffres de la population active ne comprennent pas les forces armées.

Cuadros 1, 2 A, 2 B:

Excl. las poblaciones indias y negras que viven en tribus.

Las cifras de la población económicamente activa no incluyen las fuerzas armadas.

Tables 2 A, 2 B:

The group " Salaried employees and wage earners " includes 5,396 casual workers (4,802 males and 594 females).

Tableaux 2 A, 2 B:

La rubrique « Employés et ouvriers » comprend 5 396 travailleurs occasionnels (4 802 hommes et 594 femmes).

Cuadros 2 A, 2 B:

El grupo « Empleados y obreros » incluye 5 396 trabajadores ocasionales (4 802 hombres y 594 mujeres).

Table 2 B:

The group " Others and status unknown " relates to unemployed.

Tableau 2 B:

La rubrique « Autres et situation non définie » se réfère aux chômeurs.

Cuadro 2 B:

El grupo « Otros y categoría no definida » se refiere a los desempleados.

Notes to tables 1 to 2 B (indicated by the symbol ✝)

Notes relatives aux tableaux 1 à 2 B (indiquées par le symbole ✝)

Notas relativas a los cuadros 1 a 2 B (indicadas por medio del símbolo ✝)

Trinidad and Tobago

Tables 1 (1971), 2 A, 2 B:

Estimates based on the results of a labour force sample survey.

As each figure is rounded off to the nearest 100, in some cases the sum of the entries may differ from the totals shown.

Tableaux 1 (1971), 2 A, 2 B:

Evaluations fondées sur les résultats d'une enquête par sondage sur la main-d'œuvre.

Chaque nombre étant arrondi au multiple de 100 le plus proche, dans quelques cas les totaux indiqués peuvent différer de la somme de leurs parties composantes.

Cuadros 1 (1971), 2 A, 2 B:

Estimaciones basadas en los resultados de una encuesta por muestra sobre la fuerza trabajadora.

Como cada cifra ha sido redondeada al múltiplo de 100 más próximo, en algunos casos la suma de los guarismos anotados puede diferir del total respectivo.

United States

Tables 1, 2 A, 2 B:

1974: estimates based on the results of labour force sample surveys.

As each figure is rounded off to the nearest 1,000, in some cases the sum of the entries may differ from the totals shown.

Tableaux 1, 2 A, 2 B:

1974: *évaluations fondées sur les résultats d'enquêtes par sondage sur la main-d'œuvre.*

Chaque nombre étant arrondi au multiple de 1 000 le plus proche, dans quelques cas les totaux indiqués peuvent différer de la somme de leurs parties composantes.

Cuadros 1, 2 A, 2 B:

1974: estimaciones basadas en los resultados de encuestas por muestra sobre la fuerza trabajadora.

Como cada cifra ha sido redondeada al múltiplo de 1 000 más próximo, en algunos casos la suma de los guarismos anotados puede diferir del total respectivo.

Table 1:

1974: total population figures are based on mid-year estimates.

Tableau 1:

1974: *les chiffres de la population totale sont fondés sur des estimations au milieu de l'année.*

Cuadro 1:

1974: las cifras de la población total están basadas en estimaciones a mediados del año.

Tables 1, 2 B:

1970: figures based on a sample tabulation of census returns.
De jure population; excl. armed forces overseas.

Economically active population figures relate to persons 14 years of age and over *(table 1)* and 16 years of age and over *(table 2 B).*

Tableaux 1, 2 B:

1970: *chiffres fondés sur la tabulation d'un échantillon des bulletins de recensement.*
Population de jure; *non compris les forces armées stationnées outre-mer.*

Les chiffres de la population active se réfèrent aux personnes âgées de 14 ans et plus (tableau 1) *et de 16 ans et plus* (tableau 2 B).

Cuadros 1, 2 B:

1970: cifras basadas en la tabulación de una muestra de los boletines del censo.
Población *de jure ;* excl. las fuerzas armadas en ultramar.

Las cifras de la población económicamente activa se refieren a las personas de 14 años y más de edad *(cuadro 1)* y de 16 años y más de edad *(cuadro 2 B).*

Table 2 B:

The group " Others and status unknown " relates to unemployed.

Tableau 2 B:

La rubrique « Autres et situation non définie » se réfère aux chômeurs.

Cuadro 2 B:

El grupo « Otros y categoría no definida » se refiere a los desempleados.

Uruguay

Tables 2 A, 2 B:

Figures relating to the group " Others and status unknown " cannot be given; consequently, the sum of the entries does not agree with the total shown.

Tableaux 2 A, 2 B:

Les chiffres de la rubrique « Autres et situation non définie » ne peuvent pas être présentés ; en conséquence, le total indiqué ne correspond pas à la somme de ses parties composantes.

Cuadros 2 A, 2 B:

No pueden darse las cifras relativas al grupo « Otros y categoría no definida »; por consiguiente, el total no corresponde a la suma de las diferentes partidas.

Virgin Is. (Brit.)

Tables 2 A, 2 B:

The group " Employers and workers on own account " includes paid family workers.

Tableaux 2 A, 2 B:

La rubrique « Employeurs et personnes travaillant à leur propre compte » comprend les travailleurs familiaux rémunérés.

Cuadros 2 A, 2 B:

El grupo « Empleadores y trabajadores por cuenta propia » incluye los trabajadores familiares remunerados.

*

*　　*

POPULATION

ASIA — ASIE — ASIA

Bangladesh

Table 1:

Data have not been adjusted for under-enumeration.

Tableau 1:

Les données n'ont pas été ajustées pour compenser les lacunes d'enregistrement.

Cuadro 1:

No se han ajustado los datos para compensar los casos no registrados.

Burma

Table 2 A:

Official estimates.

Tableau 2 A:

Evaluations officielles.

Cuadro 2 A:

Estimaciones oficiales.

Cyprus

Tables 1 (1974), 2 A:

Official estimates.

Tableaux 1 (1974), 2 A:

Evaluations officielles.

Cuadros 1 (1974), 2 A:

Estimaciones oficiales.

Table 1:

1960: excl. 6,465 members of foreign armed forces (6,384 males and 81 females) but incl. their families and dependants (about 15,000 persons).

Tableau 1:

1960: *non compris 6 465 membres des forces armées étrangères (6 384 hommes et 81 femmes), mais y compris leurs familles et personnes à charge (environ 15 000 personnes).*

Cuadro 1:

1960: excl. 6 465 miembros de las fuerzas armadas extranjeras (6 384 hombres y 81 mujeres), pero incl. sus familias y personas a su cargo (cerca de 15 000 personas).

Hong Kong

Tables 2 A, 2 B:

The group "Others and status unknown" relates to unemployed.

Tableaux 2 A, 2 B:

La rubrique « Autres et situation non définie » se réfère aux chômeurs.

Cuadros 2 A, 2 B:

El grupo « Otros y categoría no definida » se refiere a los desempleados.

India

Tables 1, 2 A, 2 B:

Excl. Sikkim.

Economically active population figures do not include persons seeking work for the first time and unemployed.

Tableaux 1, 2 A, 2 B:

Non compris le Sikkim.

Les chiffres de la population active ne comprennent ni les personnes en quête d'emploi pour la première fois ni les chômeurs.

Cuadros 1, 2 A, 2 B:

Excl. el Sikkim.

Las cifras de la población económicamente activa no incluyen las personas en busca de trabajo por primera vez y los desempleados.

Tables 2 A, 2 B:

Estimates based on a 1 per cent sample tabulation of census returns.

As each figure is rounded off to the nearest 100, the totals do not agree with those shown in *table 1*.

The group "Others and status unknown" relates to cultivators and agricultural labourers.

Tableaux 2 A, 2 B:

Evaluations fondées sur la tabulation d'un échantillon de 1 pour cent des bulletins de recensement.

Chaque nombre étant arrondi au multiple de 100 le plus proche, les totaux ne concordent pas avec ceux indiqués au tableau 1.

La rubrique « Autres et situation non définie » se réfère à des cultivateurs et manœuvres agricoles.

Cuadros 2 A, 2 B:

Estimaciones basadas en la tabulación de una muestra de 1 por ciento de los boletines del censo.

Como cada cifra ha sido redondeada al múltiplo de 100 más próximo, los totales no concuerdan con los que aparecen en el *cuadro 1*.

El grupo « Otros y categoría no definida » se refiere a cultivadores y obreros agrícolas no calificados.

Indonesia

Tables 1, 2 A, 2 B:

Figures based on a sample tabulation of census returns.

Tableaux 1, 2 A, 2 B:

Chiffres fondés sur la tabulation d'un échantillon des bulletins de recensement.

Cuadros 1, 2 A, 2 B:

Cifras basadas en la tabulación de una muestra de los boletines del censo.

Iran

Tables 1, 2 A, 2 B:

Excl. unsettled population (127,953 males and 116,188 females).

Tableaux 1, 2 A, 2 B:

Non compris la population sans domicile fixe (127 953 hommes et 116 188 femmes).

Cuadros 1, 2 A, 2 B:

Excl. la población sin residencia fija (127 953 hombres y 116 188 mujeres).

Notes to tables 1 to 2 B (indicated by the symbol ‡)
Notes relatives aux tableaux 1 à 2 B (indiquées par le symbole ‡)
Notas relativas a los cuadros 1 a 2 B (indicadas por medio del símbolo ‡)

Israel

Tables 1, 2 A, 2 B:

Economically active population figures do not include armed forces.

1974: economically active population figures are based on the results of a labour force sample survey.

Incl. data relating to certain territories under occupation by Israeli military forces since June 1967.

As each figure is rounded off to the nearest 100, in some cases the sum of the entries may differ from the totals shown.

Table 1:

1961: economically active population figures are based on a 20 per cent sample tabulation of census returns.

Table 2 A:

The group " Others and status unknown " relates to unemployed.

Tables 2 A, 2 B:

The group " Employers and workers on own account " includes members of producers' co-operatives and members of communal farms *(kibbutzim)*.

Table 2 B:

The group " Employers and workers on own account " includes 25,300 unpaid family workers (5,100 males and 20.200 females).

Tableaux 1, 2 A, 2 B:

Les chiffres de la population active ne comprennent pas les forces armées.

1974: *les chiffres de la population active sont fondés sur les résultats d'une enquête par sondage sur la main-d'œuvre.*

Y compris les données relatives à certains territoires occupés par les forces armées israéliennes depuis juin 1967.

Chaque nombre étant arrondi au multiple de 100 le plus proche, dans quelques cas les totaux indiqués peuvent différer de la somme de leurs parties composantes.

Tableau 1:

1961: *les chiffres de la population active sont fondés sur un échantillon de 20 pour cent des bulletins de recensement.*

Tableau 2 A:

La rubrique « Autres et situation non définie » se réfère aux chômeurs.

Tableaux 2 A, 2 B:

La rubrique « Employeurs et personnes travaillant à leur propre compte » comprend les membres de coopératives de producteurs et les membres des fermes communautaires (kibboutzim).

Tableau 2 B:

La rubrique « Employeurs et personnes travaillant à leur propre compte » comprend 25 300 travailleurs familiaux non rémunérés (5 100 hommes et 20 200 femmes).

Cuadros 1, 2 A, 2 B:

Las cifras de la población económicamente activa no incluyen las fuerzas armadas.

1974: las cifras de la población económicamente activa están basadas en los resultados de una encuesta por muestra sobre la fuerza trabajadora.

Incl. las cifras relativas a ciertos territorios ocupados por las fuerzas armadas israelíes desde junio de 1967.

Como cada cifra ha sido redondeada al múltiplo de 100 más próximo, en algunos casos la suma de los guarismos anotados puede diferir del total respectivo.

Cuadro 1:

1961: las cifras de la población económicamente activa están basadas en una muestra de 20 por ciento de los boletines del censo.

Cuadro 2 A:

El grupo « Otros y categoría no definida » se refiere a los desempleados.

Cuadros 2 A, 2 B:

El grupo « Empleadores y trabajadores por cuenta propia » incluye los miembros de cooperativas de producción y los miembros de granjas comunales *(qibbuzim)*.

Cuadro 2 B:

El grupo « Empleadores y trabajadores por cuenta propia » incluye 25 300 trabajadores familiares no remunerados (5 100 hombres y 20 200 mujeres).

Japan

Tables 1, 2 A, 2 B:

1974: estimates based on the results of labour force sample surveys.

As each figure is rounded off to the nearest 10,000, in some cases the sum of the entries may differ from the totals shown.

Tables 2 A, 2 B:

The group " Salaried employees and wage earners " includes members of producers' co-operatives.

The group " Family workers " includes paid and unpaid family workers.

The branch " Community, social and personal services " includes restaurants and hotels and business services.

1970: figures based on a 20 per cent sample tabulation of census returns.

Tableaux 1, 2 A, 2 B:

1974: *évaluations fondées sur les résultats d'enquêtes par sondage sur la main-d'œuvre.*

Chaque nombre étant arrondi au multiple de 10 000 le plus proche, dans quelques cas les totaux indiqués peuvent différer de la somme de leurs parties composantes.

Tableaux 2 A, 2 B:

La rubrique « Employés et ouvriers » comprend les membres de coopératives de producteurs.

La rubrique « Travailleurs familiaux » comprend les travailleurs familiaux rémunérés et non rémunérés.

La branche « Services à la collectivité, services sociaux et personnels » comprend les restaurants et hôtels et les services aux entreprises.

1970: *chiffres fondés sur la tabulation d'un échantillon de 20 pour cent des bulletins de recensement.*

Cuadros 1, 2 A, 2 B:

1974: estimaciones basadas en los resultados de encuestas por muestra sobre la fuerza trabajadora.

Como cada cifra ha sido redondeada al múltiplo de 10 000 más próximo, en algunos casos la suma de los guarismos anotados puede diferir del total respectivo.

Cuadros 2 A, 2 B:

El grupo « Empleados y obreros » incluye los miembros de cooperativas de producción.

El grupo « Trabajadores familiares » incluye los trabajadores familiares remunerados y no remunerados.

La rama « Servicios comunales, sociales y personales » incluye los restaurantes y hoteles y los servicios para las empresas.

1970: cifras basadas en la tabulación de una muestra de 20 por ciento de los boletines del censo.

POPULATION

Notes to tables 1 to 2 B (indicated by the symbol ‡)

Notes relatives aux tableaux 1 à 2 B (indiquées par le symbole ‡)

Notas relativas a los cuadros 1 a 2 B (indicadas por medio del símbolo ‡)

Jordan

Table 1:

1971: official estimates.

Tableau 1:

1971: *évaluations officielles.*

Cuadro 1:

1971: estimaciones oficiales.

Korea, Rep. of

Tables 1, 2 A, 2 B:

1970: figures based on a 10 per cent sample tabulation of census returns.

Economically active population figures do not include persons seeking work for the first time and armed forces.

1974: estimates based on the results of a labour force sample survey. Excl. armed forces.

Tableaux 1, 2 A, 2 B:

1970: *chiffres fondés sur la tabulation d'un échantillon de 10 pour cent des bulletins de recensement.*

Les chiffres de la population active ne comprennent ni les personnes en quête d'emploi pour la première fois ni les forces armées.

1974: *évaluations fondées sur les résultats d'une enquête par sondage sur la main-d'œuvre. Non compris les forces armées.*

Cuadros 1, 2 A, 2 B:

1970: cifras basadas en la tabulación de una muestra de 10 por ciento de los boletines del censo.

Las cifras de la población económicamente activa no incluyen las personas en busca de trabajo por primera vez y las fuerzas armadas.

1974: estimaciones basadas en los resultados de una encuesta por muestra sobre la fuerza trabajadora. Excl. las fuerzas armadas.

Liban

Tables 1, 2 A, 2 B:

Estimates based on the results of a labour force sample survey.

Tableaux 1, 2 A, 2 B:

Evaluations fondées sur les résultats d'une enquête par sondage sur la main-d'œuvre.

Cuadros 1, 2 A, 2 B:

Estimaciones basadas en los resultados de una encuesta por muestra sobre la fuerza trabajadora.

Pakistan

Tables 1, 2 A, 2 B:

Excl. Jammu and Kashmir (the final status of which has not yet been determined), Gilgit and Baltistan, Junagardh and Manavadar.

1972: estimates based on the results of a labour force survey.

Excl. institutional households.

Table 1:

1961: incl. the area now known as Bangladesh, for which separate data are given in these tables.

Population actually enumerated, i.e. excl. 3,437,939 persons (1,791,755 males and 1,646,184 females) living in certain frontier regions of West Pakistan, 111,369 foreigners (64,824 males and 46,545 females) and an 8.3 per cent adjustment for under-enumeration.

Economically active population figures do not include armed forces.

Tableaux 1, 2 A, 2 B:

Non compris le Jammu et Cachemire (dont le statut définitif n'a pas encore été déterminé), le Gilgit et Baltistan, le Junagardh et le Manavadar.

1972: *évaluations fondées sur les résultats d'une enquête sur la main-d'œuvre.*

Non compris les ménages collectifs.

Tableau 1:

1961: *y compris le territoire maintenant dénommé Bangladesh, pour lequel des données sont présentées séparément dans ces tableaux.*

Population effectivement dénombrée, c'est-à-dire non compris 3 437 939 personnes (1 791 755 hommes et 1 646 184 femmes) résidant dans certaines régions frontières du Pakistan occidental, ni 111 369 étrangers (64 824 hommes et 46 545 femmes), ni un ajustement de 8,3 pour cent pour compenser les lacunes d'enregistrement.

Les chiffres de la population active ne comprennent pas les forces armées.

Cuadros 1, 2 A, 2 B:

Excl. el Jammu y Cachemira (para los cuales el estatuto definitivo no ha sido por ahora determinado), el Gilgit y Baltistan, el Junagardh y el Manavadar.

1972: estimaciones basadas en los resultados de una encuesta sobre la fuerza trabajadora.

Excl. los hogares colectivos.

Cuadro 1:

1961: incl. el territorio ahora llamado Bangladesh, cuyos datos están presentados separadamente en estos cuadros.

Población efectivamente enumerada, es decir, excl. 3 437 939 personas (1 791 755 hombres y 1 646 184 mujeres) que viven en ciertas regiones fronteras del Pakistán Occidental, 111 369 extranjeros (64 824 hombres y 46 545 mujeres) y 8,3 por ciento de ajuste para compensar la subenumeración.

Las cifras de la población económicamente activa no incluyen las fuerzas armadas.

Philippines

Tables 1, 2 A, 2 B:

Economically active population figures do not include armed forces and institutional households.

Tables 2 A, 2 B:

1974: the group " Others and status unknown " includes 725,000 unemployed (441,000 males and 284,000 females).

As each figure is rounded off to the nearest 1,000, in some cases the sum of the entries may differ from the totals shown.

Tableaux 1, 2 A, 2 B:

Les chiffres de la population active ne comprennent ni les forces armées ni les ménages collectifs.

Tableaux 2 A, 2 B:

1974: *la rubrique « Autres et situation non définie » comprend 725 000 chômeurs (441 000 hommes et 284 000 femmes).*

Chaque nombre étant arrondi au multiple de 1 000 le plus proche, dans quelques cas les totaux indiqués peuvent différer de la somme de leurs parties composantes.

Cuadros 1, 2 A, 2 B:

Las cifras de la población económicamente activa no incluyen las fuerzas armadas y los hogares colectivos.

Cuadros 2 A, 2 B:

1974: el grupo « Otros y categoría no definida » incluye 725 000 desempleados (441 000 hombres y 284 000 mujeres).

Como cada cifra ha sido redondeada al múltiplo de 1 000 más próximo, en algunos casos la suma de los guarismos anotados puede diferir del total respectivo.

Notes to tables 1 to 2 B (indicated by the symbol ♱)

Notes relatives aux tableaux 1 à 2 B (indiquées par le symbole ♱)

Notas relativas a los cuadros 1 a 2 B (indicadas por medio del símbolo ♱)

Qatar

Table 1:
Official estimates.

Tableau 1:
Evaluations officielles.

Cuadro 1:
Estimaciones oficiales.

Singapore

Tables 1, 2 A, 2 B:
1974: estimates based on the results of a household survey.

Tableaux 1, 2 A, 2 B:
1974: évaluations fondées sur les résultats d'une enquête auprès des ménages.

Cuadros 1, 2 A, 2 B:
1974: estimaciones basadas en los resultados de una encuesta de hogares.

Sri Lanka

Tables 1, 2 A, 2 B:
Figures based on a 10 per cent sample tabulation of census returns.

Tableaux 1, 2 A, 2 B:
Chiffres fondés sur la tabulation d'un échantillon de 10 pour cent des bulletins de recensement.

Cuadros 1, 2 A, 2 B:
Cifras basadas en la tabulación de una muestra de 10 por ciento de los boletines del censo.

Sud Viet-Nam, Rép. du

Table 1:
Official estimates.

Tableau 1:
Evaluations officielles.

Cuadro 1:
Estimaciones oficiales.

République arabe syrienne

Tables 1, 2 A, 2 B:
1970: Syrian population only.

1973: estimates based on the results of a labour force sample survey.

Tableaux 1, 2 A, 2 B:
1970: population syrienne seulement.

1973: évaluations fondées sur les résultats d'une enquête par sondage sur la main-d'œuvre.

Cuadros 1, 2 A, 2 B:
1970: población siria solamente.

1973: estimaciones basadas en los resultados de una encuesta por muestra sobre la fuerza trabajadora.

Tables 2 A, 2 B:
1970: the branch " Activities not adequately described " and the occupational group " Workers not classifiable by occupation " include 56,095 persons seeking work for the first time (49,399 males and 6,696 females).

The group " Salaried employees and wage earners " includes 3,296 unpaid apprentices (2,132 males and 1,164 females).

1973: the group " Others and status unknown " relates to unemployed.

Tableaux 2 A, 2 B:
1970: la branche « Activités mal désignées » et le groupe de professions « Travailleurs ne pouvant être classés selon la profession » comprennent 56 095 personnes en quête d'emploi pour la première fois (49 399 hommes et 6 696 femmes).

La rubrique « Employés et ouvriers » comprend 3 296 apprentis non rémunérés (2 132 hommes et 1 164 femmes).

1973: la rubrique « Autres et situation non définie » se réfère aux chômeurs.

Cuadros 2 A, 2 B:
1970: la rama « Actividades no bien especificadas » y el grupo de ocupación « Trabajadores que no pueden ser clasificados según la ocupación » incluyen 56 095 personas en busca de trabajo por primera vez (49 399 hombres y 6 696 mujeres).

El grupo « Empleados y obreros » incluye 3 296 aprendices no remunerados (2 132 hombres y 1 164 mujeres).

1973: el grupo « Otros y categoría no definida » se refiere a los desempleados.

Thailand

Tables 1, 2 A, 2 B:
1973: estimates based on the results of a labour force sample survey.

Tableaux 1, 2 A, 2 B:
1973: évaluations fondées sur les résultats d'une enquête par sondage sur la main-d'œuvre.

Cuadros 1, 2 A, 2 B:
1973: estimaciones basadas en los resultados de una encuesta por muestra sobre la fuerza trabajadora.

Yemen, People's Dem. Rep. of

Table 1:
Figures based on a sample tabulation of census returns.

Tableau 1:
Chiffres fondés sur la tabulation d'un échantillon des bulletins de recensement.

Cuadro 1:
Cifras basadas en la tabulación de una muestra de los boletines del censo.

*

*   *

POPULATION

Notes to tables 1 to 2 B (indicated by the symbol †)
Notes relatives aux tableaux 1 à 2 B (indiquées par le symbole †)
Notas relativas a los cuadros 1 a 2 B (indicadas por medio del símbolo †)

EUROPE — EUROPE — EUROPA

Austria

Tables 2 A, 2 B:

1974: estimates based on the results of labour force sample surveys.

Tables 2 A (1974), 2 B:

The group " Employers and workers on own account " includes unpaid family workers.

Tableaux 2 A, 2 B:

1974: évaluations fondées sur les résultats d'enquêtes par sondage sur la main-d'œuvre.

Tableaux 2 A (1974), 2 B:

Le groupe « Employeurs et personnes travaillant à leur propre compte » comprend les travailleurs familiaux non rémunérés.

Cuadros 2 A, 2 B:

1974: estimaciones basadas en los resultados de encuestas por muestra sobre la fuerza trabajadora.

Cuadros 2 A (1974), 2 B:

El grupo « Empleadores y trabajadores por cuenta propia » incluye los trabajadores familiares no remunerados.

Belgique

Tables 1 (1972), 2 A (1974):

Official estimates.

Table 2 A:

1974: the branch " Activities not adequately described " relates to workers in vocational training.

Tableaux 1 (1972), 2 A (1974):

Evaluations officielles.

Tableau 2 A:

1974: la branche « Activités mal désignées » se réfère aux travailleurs en formation professionnelle.

Cuadros 1 (1972), 2 A (1974):

Estimaciones oficiales.

Cuadro 2 A:

1974: la rama « Actividades no bien especificadas » se refiere a los trabajadores en formación profesional.

Bulgarie

Tables 2 A, 2 B:

The group " Others and status unknown " includes 1,763,980 members of producers' co-operatives (845,147 males and 918,833 females).

Tableaux 2 A, 2 B:

La rubrique « Autres et situation non définie » comprend 1 763 980 membres de coopératives de producteurs (845 147 hommes et 918 833 femmes).

Cuadros 2 A, 2 B:

El grupo « Otros y categoría no definida » incluye 1 763 980 miembros de cooperativas de producción (845 147 hombres y 918 833 mujeres).

Channel Is.

Table 2 A:

The branch " Community, social and personal services " includes restaurants and hotels and certain financial services.

Tableau 2 A:

La branche « Services à la collectivité, services sociaux et personnels » comprend les restaurants et hôtels et certains services financiers.

Cuadro 2 A:

La rama « Servicios comunales, sociales y personales » incluye los restaurantes y hoteles así como ciertos servicios financieros.

Czechoslovakia

Tables 1, 2 A, 2 B:

Economically active population figures do not include unpaid family workers.

Tables 2 A, 2 B:

The group " Others and status unknown " includes 794,978 members of producers' co-operatives (389,024 males and 405,954 females).

Tableaux 1, 2 A, 2 B:

Les chiffres de la population active ne comprennent pas les travailleurs familiaux non rémunérés.

Tableaux 2 A, 2 B:

La rubrique « Autres et situation non définie » comprend 794 978 membres de coopératives de producteurs (389 024 hommes et 405 954 femmes).

Cuadros 1, 2 A, 2 B:

Las cifras de la población económicamente activa no incluyen los trabajadores familiares no remunerados.

Cuadros 2 A, 2 B:

El grupo « Otros y categoría no definida » incluye 794 978 miembros de cooperativas de producción (389 024 hombres y 405 954 mujeres).

Denmark

Tables 1, 2 A:

1974: estimates based on the results of a labour force sample survey.

Economically active population figures relate to persons 15 to 74 years of age.

Table 2 A:

1970: the group " Others and status unknown " includes housemaids living at the place of work.

Tableaux 1, 2 A:

1974: évaluations fondées sur les résultats d'enquêtes par sondage sur la main-d'œuvre.

Les chiffres de la population active se réfèrent aux personnes âgées de 15 à 74 ans.

Tableau 2 A:

1970: la rubrique « Autres et situation non définie » comprend des aides familiaux habitant le lieu du travail.

Cuadros 1, 2 A:

1974: estimaciones basadas en los resultados de encuestas por muestra sobre la fuerza trabajadora.

Las cifras de la población económicamente activa se refieren a las personas de 15 a 74 años de edad.

Cuadro 2 A:

1970: el grupo « Otros y categoría no definida » incluye ayudantes familiares que habitan en el lugar de trabajo.

Notes to tables 1 to 2 B (indicated by the symbol ⊬)
Notes relatives aux tableaux 1 à 2 B (indiquées par le symbole ⊬)
Notas relativas a los cuadros 1 a 2 B (indicadas por medio del símbolo ⊬)

España

Tables 1, 2 A, 2 B:

1970: figures based on a 25 per cent sample tabulation of census returns. Incl. non-metropolitan territories.

Tables 1, 2 A:

1974: estimates based on the results of a labour force sample survey.

Tableaux 1, 2 A, 2 B:

1970: *chiffres fondés sur la tabulation d'un échantillon de 25 pour cent des bulletins de recensement. Y compris les territoires non métropolitains.*

Tableaux 1, 2 A:

1974: *évaluations fondées sur les résultats d'une enquête par sondage sur la main-d'œuvre.*

Cuadros 1, 2 A, 2 B:

1970: cifras basadas en la tabulación de una muestra de 25 por ciento de los boletines del censo. Incl. los territorios no metropolitanos.

Cuadros 1, 2 A:

1974: estimaciones basadas en los resultados de una encuesta por muestra sobre la fuerza trabajadora.

Finland

Table 2 A:

1973: estimates based on the results of a labour force sample survey.

Data relate to persons 16 to 74 years of age.

Tableau 2 A:

1973: *évaluations fondées sur les résultats d'une enquête par sondage sur la main-d'œuvre.*

Les données se réfèrent aux personnes âgées de 16 à 74 ans.

Cuadro 2 A:

1973: estimaciones basadas en los resultados de una encuesta por muestra sobre la fuerza trabajadora.

Los datos se refieren a las personas de 16 a 74 años de edad.

France

Tables 1, 2 A:

1968: figures based on a 25 per cent sample tabulation of census returns.

Table 1:

1975: official estimates.

Table 2 A:

1968 and **1974:** the group " Employers and workers on own account " includes family workers.

1974: official estimates.

Table 2 B:

Figures based on a 5 per cent sample tabulation of census returns. Excl. persons on compulsory military service.

Tableaux 1, 2 A:

1968: *chiffres fondés sur la tabulation d'un échantillon de 25 pour cent des bulletins de recensement.*

Tableau 1:

1975: *évaluations officielles.*

Tableau 2 A:

1968 et **1974:** *la rubrique « Employeurs et personnes travaillant à leur propre compte » comprend les travailleurs familiaux.*

1974: *évaluations officielles.*

Tableau 2 B:

Chiffres fondés sur la tabulation d'un échantillon de 5 pour cent des bulletins de recensement. Non compris les personnes effectuant leur service militaire obligatoire (militaires du contingent).

Cuadros 1, 2 A:

1968: cifras basadas en la tabulación de una muestra de 25 por ciento de los boletines del censo.

Cuadro 1:

1975: estimaciones oficiales.

Cuadro 2 A:

1968 y **1974:** el grupo « Empleadores y trabajadores por cuenta propia » incluye los trabajadores familiares.

1974: estimaciones oficiales.

Cuadro 2 B:

Cifras basadas en la tabulación de una muestra de 5 por ciento de los boletines del censo. Excl. las personas en servicio militar obligatorio.

Germany, Fed. Rep. of

Tables 1, 2 A, 2 B:

As each figure is rounded off, in some cases the sum of the entries may differ from the totals shown.

1970: figures based on a sample tabulation of census returns.

Tables 1, 2 A:

1974: estimates based on the results of a labour force sample survey.

Tableaux 1, 2 A, 2 B:

Chaque nombre étant arrondi, dans quelques cas les totaux indiqués peuvent différer de la somme de leurs parties composantes.

1970: *chiffres fondés sur la tabulation d'un échantillon des bulletins de recensement.*

Tableaux 1, 2 A:

1974: *évaluations fondées sur les résultats d'une enquête par sondage sur la main-d'œuvre.*

Cuadros 1, 2 A, 2 B:

Como cada cifra ha sido redondeada, en algunos casos la suma de los guarismos anotados puede diferir del total respectivo.

1970: cifras basadas en la tabulación de una muestra de los boletines del censo.

Cuadros 1, 2 A:

1974: estimaciones basadas en los resultados de una encuesta por muestra sobre la fuerza trabajadora.

POPULATION

Gibraltar

Tables 1, 2 A, 2 B:

Excl. military personnel garrisoned in the area and their families.

Tableaux 1, 2 A, 2 B:

Non compris les militaires en garnison sur le territoire et leurs familles.

Cuadros 1, 2 A, 2 B:

Excl. el personal militar en guarnición en la zona y sus familias.

Grèce

Tables 1, 2 A, 2 B:

Figures based on a 25 per cent sample tabulation of census returns.

Economically active population figures do not include persons seeking work for the first time and persons on compulsory military service.

Table 2 B:

The occupational group " Service workers " includes armed forces.

Tableaux 1, 2 A, 2 B:

Chiffres fondés sur la tabulation d'un échantillon de 25 pour cent des bulletins de recensement.

Les chiffres de la population active ne comprennent ni les personnes en quête d'emploi pour la première fois ni les personnes effectuant leur service militaire obligatoire (militaires du contingent).

Tableau 2 B:

Le groupe de professions « Travailleurs des services » comprend les forces armées.

Cuadros 1, 2 A, 2 B:

Cifras basadas en la tabulación de una muestra de 25 por ciento de los boletines del censo.

Las cifras de la población económicamente activa no incluyen las personas en busca de trabajo por primera vez y las personas en servicio militar obligatorio.

Cuadro 2 B:

El grupo de ocupación « Trabajadores de los servicios » incluye las fuerzas armadas.

Hongrie

Tables 1, 2 A, 2 B:

Economically active population figures do not include persons seeking work for the first time.

1970: economically active population figures do not include 214,893 apprentices (163,919 males and 50,974 females).

Tables 1, 2 A :

1974: official estimates.

Tables 2 A, 2 B:

The group " Others and status unknown " relates to members of producers' co-operatives.

Table 2 B:

The group " Family workers " includes 98,703 family workers of agricultural producers' co-operatives (5,977 males and 92,726 females).

Tableaux 1, 2 A, 2 B:

Les chiffres de la population active ne comprennent pas les personnes en quête d'emploi pour la première fois.

1970: *les chiffres de la population active ne comprennent pas 214 893 apprentis (163 919 hommes et 50 974 femmes).*

Tableaux 1, 2 A:

1974: *évaluations officielles.*

Tableaux 2 A, 2 B:

La rubrique « Autres et situation non définie » se réfère aux membres de coopératives de producteurs.

Tableau 2 B:

La rubrique « Travailleurs familiaux » comprend 98 703 travailleurs familiaux des coopératives agricoles de producteurs (5 977 hommes et 92 726 femmes).

Cuadros 1, 2 A, 2 B:

Las cifras de la población económicamente activa no incluyen las personas en busca de trabajo por primera vez.

1970: las cifras de la población económicamente activa no incluyen 214 893 aprendices (163 919 hombres y 50 974 mujeres).

Cuadros 1, 2 A:

1974: estimaciones oficiales.

Cuadros 2 A, 2 B:

El grupo « Otros y categoría no definida » se refiere a los miembros de cooperativas de producción.

Cuadro 2 B:

El grupo « Trabajadores familiares » incluye 98 703 trabajadores familiares de las cooperativas agrícolas de producción (5 977 hombres y 92 726 mujeres).

Ireland

Tables 1, 2 A, 2 B:

Economically active population figures do not include persons seeking work for the first time.

Tables 2 A, 2 B:

The group " Others and status unknown " relates to unemployed.

Table 1:

1974: official estimates.

Tableaux 1, 2 A, 2 B:

Les chiffres de la population active ne comprennent pas les personnes en quête d'emploi pour la première fois.

Tableaux 2 A, 2 B:

La rubrique « Autres et situation non définie » se réfère aux chômeurs.

Tableau 1:

1974: *évaluations officielles.*

Cuadros 1, 2 A, 2 B:

Las cifras de la población económicamente activa no incluyen las personas en busca de trabajo por primera vez.

Cuadros 2 A, 2 B:

El grupo « Otros y categoría no definida » se refiere a los desempleados.

Cuadro 1:

1974: estimaciones oficiales.

Italie

Tables 1, 2 A (1975), 2 B:

Estimates based on the results of labour force sample surveys.

Tableaux 1, 2 A (1975), 2 B:

Evaluations fondées sur les résultats d'enquêtes par sondage sur la main-d'œuvre.

Cuadros 1, 2 A (1975), 2 B:

Estimaciones basadas en los resultados de encuestas por muestra sobre la fuerza trabajadora.

Notes to tables 1 to 2 B   (indicated by the symbol ‡)
Notes relatives aux tableaux 1 à 2 B   (indiquées par le symbole ‡)
Notas relativas a los cuadros 1 a 2 B   (indicadas por medio del símbolo ‡)

Liechtenstein

Table 1:
1973: official estimates.

Tableau 1:
1973: *évaluations officielles.*

Cuadro 1:
1973: estimaciones oficiales.

Luxembourg

Tables 1, 2 A, 2 B:
De jure population.

Table 1:
1974: official estimates.

Table 2 B:
The group " Others and status unknown " relates to unemployed.

Tableaux 1, 2 A, 2 B:
Population de jure.

Tableau 1:
1974: *évaluations officielles.*

Tableau 2 B:
La rubrique « Autres et situation non définie » se réfère aux chômeurs.

Cuadros 1, 2 A, 2 B:
Población *de jure.*

Cuadro 1:
1974: estimaciones oficiales

Cuadro 2 B:
El grupo « Otros y categoría no definida » se refiere a los desempleados.

Malta

Tables 1, 2 A:
1972: estimates based on the results of a labour force survey.

Table 2 A:
1972: the group " Salaried employees and wage earners " includes unpaid family workers.

Tableaux 1, 2 A:
1972: *évaluations fondées sur les résultats d'une enquête sur la main-d'œuvre.*

Tableau 2 A:
1972: *la rubrique « Employés et ouvriers » comprend les travailleurs familiaux non rémunérés.*

Cuadros 1, 2 A:
1972: estimaciones basadas en los resultados de una encuesta sobre la fuerza trabajadora.

Cuadro 2 A:
1972: el grupo « Empleados y obreros » incluye los trabajadores familiares no remunerados.

Monaco

Tables 1, 2 A:
De jure population.

Tableaux 1, 2 A:
Population de jure.

Cuadros 1, 2 A:
Población *de jure.*

Norway

Tables 1, 2 A, 2 B:
1970: *de jure* population.

Economically active population figures do not include persons seeking work for the first time.

Tables 2 A, 2 B:
1974: estimates based on the results of a labour force sample survey.

Economically active population figures do not include persons on compulsory military service.

As each figure is rounded off to the nearest 1,000, in some cases the sum of the entries may differ from the totals shown.

Tableaux 1, 2 A, 2 B:
1970: *population* de jure.

Les chiffres de la population active ne comprennent pas les personnes en quête d'emploi pour la première fois.

Tableaux 2 A, 2 B:
1974: *évaluations fondées sur les résultats d'une enquête par sondage sur la main-d'oeuvre.*

Les chiffres de la population active ne comprennent pas les personnes effectuant leur service militaire obligatoire (militaires du contingent).

Chaque nombre étant arrondi au multiple de 1 000 le plus proche, dans quelques cas les totaux indiqués peuvent différer de la somme de leurs parties composantes.

Cuadros 1, 2 A, 2 B:
1970: población *de jure.*

Las cifras de la población económicamente activa no incluyen las personas en busca de trabajo por primera vez.

Cuadros 2 A, 2 B:
1974: estimaciones basadas en los resultados de una encuesta por muestra sobre la fuerza trabajadora.

Las cifras de la población económicamente activa no incluyen las personas en servicio militar obligatorio.

Como cada cifra ha sido redondeada al múltiplo de 1 000 más próximo, en algunos casos la suma de los guarismos anotados puede diferir del total respectivo.

Notes to tables 1 to 2 B (indicated by the symbol ‡)
Notes relatives aux tableaux 1 à 2 B (indiquées par le symbole ‡)
Notas relativas a los cuadros 1 a 2 B indicadas por medio del símbolo ‡)

Pologne

Tables 1, 2 A:

1974: figures based on the results of a microcensus.

Tables 2 A, 2 B:

The group "Salaried employees and wage earners" includes members of producers' co-operatives.

Tables 2 A (1974), 2 B:

The group "Employers and workers on own account" includes unpaid family workers.

Tableaux 1, 2 A:

1974: chiffres fondés sur les résultats d'un micro-recensement.

Tableaux 2 A, 2 B:

La rubrique « Employés et ouvriers » comprend les membres de coopératives de producteurs.

Tableaux 2 A (1974), 2 B:

La rubrique « Employeurs et personnes travaillant à leur propre compte » comprend les travailleurs familiaux non rémunérés.

Cuadros 1, 2 A:

1974: cifras basadas en los resultados de un microcenso.

Cuadros 2 A, 2 B:

El grupo « Empleados y obreros » incluye los miembros de cooperativas de producción.

Cuadros 2 A (1974), 2 B:

El grupo « Empleadores y trabajadores por cuenta propia » incluye los trabajadores familiares no remunerados.

Portugal

Tables 1, 2 A, 2 B:

Incl. the Azores and Madeira Islands.

Figures based on a 20 per cent sample tabulation of census returns.

Economically active population figures relate to persons who have worked at least 15 hours during the week preceding the date of the census.

Tableaux 1, 2 A, 2 B:

Y compris les îles Açores et Madère.

Chiffres fondés sur la tabulation d'un échantillon de 20 pour cent des bulletins de recensement.

Les chiffres de la population active se réfèrent aux personnes qui ont travaillé au moins 15 heures au cours de la semaine précédant la date du recensement.

Cuadros 1, 2 A, 2 B:

Incl. las islas Azores y Madera.

Cifras basadas en la tabulación de una muestra de 20 por ciento de los boletines del censo.

Las cifras de la población económicamente activa se refieren a las personas que han trabajado 15 horas o más durante la semana que precede la fecha del censo.

Roumanie

Tables 1, 2 A, 2 B:

Economically active population figures do not include persons seeking work for the first time.

Tables 2 A, 2 B:

The group "Employers and workers on own account" includes unpaid family workers.

The group "Family workers" relates to members of producers' co-operatives.

Tableaux 1, 2 A, 2 B:

Les chiffres de la population active ne comprennent pas les personnes en quête d'emploi pour la première fois.

Tableaux 2 A, 2 B:

La rubrique « Employeurs et personnes travaillant à leur propre compte » comprend les travailleurs familiaux non rémunérés.

La rubrique « Travailleurs familiaux » se réfère aux membres de coopératives de producteurs.

Cuadros 1, 2 A, 2 B:

Las cifras de la población económicamente activa no incluyen las personas en busca de trabajo por primera vez.

Cuadros 2 A, 2 B:

El grupo « Empleadores y trabajadores por cuenta propia » incluye los trabajadores familiares no remunerados.

El grupo « Trabajadores familiares » se refiere a los miembros de cooperativas de producción.

Suisse

Table 2 A:

The group "Family workers" includes paid and unpaid family workers.

The branch "Activities not adequately described" includes 5,256 unemployed and persons seeking work for the first time (3,039 males and 2,217 females).

Table 2 B:

The group "Salaried employees and wage earners" includes unpaid family workers.

Tableau 2 A:

La rubrique « Travailleurs familiaux » comprend les travailleurs familiaux rémunérés et non rémunérés.

La branche « Activités mal désignées » comprend 5 256 chômeurs et personnes en quête d'emploi pour la première fois (3 039 hommes et 2 217 femmes).

Tableau 2 B:

La rubrique « Employés et ouvriers » comprend les travailleurs familiaux non rémunérés.

Cuadro 2 A:

El grupo « Trabajadores familiares » incluye los trabajadores familiares remunerados y no remunerados.

La rama « Actividades no bien especificadas » incluye 5 256 desempleados y personas en busca de trabajo por primera vez (3 039 hombres y 2 217 mujeres).

Cuadro 2 B:

El grupo « Empleados y obreros » incluye los trabajadores familiares no remunerados.

Notes to tables 1 to 2 B (indicated by the symbol ╪)

Notes relatives aux tableaux 1 à 2 B (indiquées par le symbole ╪)

Notas relativas a los cuadros 1 a 2 B (indicadas por medio del símbolo ╪)

Sweden

Tables 1, 2 A, 2 B:

Economically active population figures do not include persons on compulsory military service and persons seeking work for the first time.

1970: economically active population figures do not include unemployed who have never worked during the four months preceding the census date.

Tables 2 A, 2 B:

1970: the group " Salaried employees and wage earners " includes unpaid family workers.

1974: estimates based on the results of labour force sample surveys.

Data relate to persons 16 to 74 years of age.

As each figure is rounded off to the nearest 100, in some cases the sum of the entries may differ from the totals shown.

Tableaux 1, 2 A, 2 B:

Les chiffres de la population active ne comprennent ni les personnes effectuant leur service militaire obligatoire ni les personnes en quête d'emploi pour la première fois.

1970: *les chiffres de la population active ne comprennent pas les chômeurs qui n'ont jamais travaillé au cours des quatre mois précédant la date du recensement.*

Tableaux 2 A, 2 B:

1970: *la rubrique « Employés et ouvriers » comprend les travailleurs familiaux non rémunérés.*

1974: *évaluations fondées sur les résultats d'enquêtes par sondage sur la main-d'œuvre.*

Les données se réfèrent aux personnes âgées de 16 à 74 ans.

Chaque nombre étant arrondi au multiple de 100 le plus proche, dans quelques cas les totaux indiqués peuvent différer de la somme de leurs parties composantes.

Cuadros 1, 2 A, 2 B:

Las cifras de la población económicamente activa no incluyen las personas en servicio militar obligatorio y las personas en busca de trabajo por primera vez.

1970: las cifras de la población económicamente activa no incluyen los desempleados que no han trabajado nunca durante los cuatro meses que preceden la fecha del censo.

Cuadros 2 A, 2 B:

1970: el grupo « Empleados y obreros » incluye los trabajadores familiares no remunerados.

1974: estimaciones basadas en los resultados de encuestas por muestra sobre la fuerza trabajadora.

Los datos se refieren a las personas de 16 a 74 años de edad.

Como cada cifra ha sido redondeada al múltiplo de 100 más próximo, en algunos casos la suma de los guarismos anotados puede diferir del total respectivo.

Turquie

Tables 1, 2 A, 2 B:

Figures based on a 1 per cent sample tabulation of census returns.

Economically active population figures do not include unemployed.

Tableaux 1, 2 A, 2 B:

Chiffres fondés sur la tabulation d'un échantillon de 1 pour cent des bulletins de recensement.

Les chiffres de la population active ne comprennent pas les chômeurs.

Cuadros 1, 2 A, 2 B:

Cifras basadas en la tabulación de una muestra de 1 por ciento de los boletines del censo.

Las cifras de la población económicamente activa no incluyen los desempleados.

United Kingdom

Tables 2 A, 2 B:

Excl. Northern Ireland (411,745 males and 200,495 females). Figures based on a 10 per cent sample tabulation of census returns.

Table 2 B:

The group " Others and status unknown " relates to persons out of employment at the time of the census.

Tableaux 2 A, 2 B:

Non compris l'Irlande du Nord (411 745 hommes et 200 495 femmes). Chiffres fondés sur la tabulation d'un échantillon de 10 pour cent des bulletins de recensement.

Tableau 2 B:

La rubrique « Autres et situation non définie » se réfère aux personnes hors d'activité à la date du recensement.

Cuadros 2 A, 2 B:

Excl. Irlanda del Norte (411 745 hombres y 200 495 mujeres). Cifras basadas en la tabulación de una muestra de 10 por ciento de los boletines del censo.

Cuadro 2 B:

El grupo « Otros y categoría no definida » se refiere a las personas fuera de actividad en la fecha del censo.

POPULATION

Notes to tables 1 to 2 B (indicated by the symbol ‡)

Notes relatives aux tableaux 1 à 2 B (indiquées par le symbole ‡)

Notas relativas a los cuadros 1 a 2 B (indicadas por medio del símbolo ‡)

Yugoslavia

Tables 1, 2 A, 2 B:

Economically active population figures do not include certain unemployed and persons seeking work for the first time who, at the date of the census, declared themselves as being dependents.

Tables 2 A, 2 B:

The group " Salaried employees and wage earners " includes members of producers' co-operatives.

Table 2 B:

The occupational group " Professional, technical and related workers " includes also certain workers in transport and communication occupations.

Tableaux 1, 2 A, 2 B:

Les chiffres de la population active ne comprennent pas un certain nombre de chômeurs et de personnes en quête d'emploi pour la première fois qui, à la date du recensement, se sont déclarées personnes à charge.

Tableaux 2 A, 2 B:

La rubrique « Employés et ouvriers » comprend les membres de coopératives de producteurs.

Tableau 2 B:

Le groupe de professions « Personnes exerçant une profession libérale, techniciens et assimilés » comprend également un certain nombre de travailleurs des transports et des communications.

Cuadros 1, 2 A, 2 B:

Las cifras de la población económicamente activa no incluyen ciertos desempleados y personas en busca de trabajo por primera vez que, en la fecha del censo, se declararon dependientes.

Cuadros 2 A, 2 B:

El grupo « Empleados y obreros » incluye los miembros de cooperativas de producción.

Cuadro 2 B:

El grupo de ocupaciones « Trabajadores profesionales, técnicos y trabajadores asimilados » incluye igualmente ciertos trabajadores de los transportes y comunicaciones.

*
*   *

Notes to tables 1 to 2 B (indicated by the symbol ⴕ)

Notes relatives aux tableaux 1 à 2 B (indiquées par le symbole ⴕ)

Notas relativas a los cuadros 1 a 2 B (indicadas por medio del símbolo ⴕ)

OCEANIA — OCÉANIE — OCEANIA

American Samoa

Table 1:
1972: official estimates.

Tableau 1:
1972: *évaluations officielles.*

Cuadro 1:
1972: estimaciones oficiales.

Australia

Table 2 A:
1973: official estimates.
As each figure is rounded off to the nearest 1,000, in some cases the sum of the entries may differ from the totals shown.

Tableau 2 A:
1973: *évaluations officielles.*
Chaque nombre étant arrondi au multiple de 1 000 le plus proche, dans quelques cas les totaux indiqués peuvent différer de la somme de leurs parties composantes.

Cuadro 2 A:
1973: estimaciones oficiales.
Como cada cifra ha sido redondeada al múltiplo de 1 000 más próximo, en algunos casos la suma de los guarismos anotados puede diferir del total respectivo.

Fiji

Table 2 B:
The group " Salaried employees and wage earners " includes family workers.

Tableau 2 B:
La rubrique « Employés et ouvriers » comprend les travailleurs familiaux.

Cuadro 2 B:
El grupo « Empleados y obreros » incluye los trabajadores familiares.

New Zealand

Tables 1, 2 A, 2 B:
Incl. Maoris.
Excl. armed forces overseas.

Tableaux 1, 2 A, 2 B:
Y compris les Maoris.
Non compris les forces armées stationnées outre-mer.

Cuadros 1, 2 A, 2 B:
Incl. los maoríes.
Excl. las fuerzas armadas en ultramar.

Tables 2 A (1971), 2 B:
The group " Others and status unknown " includes 16,168 unemployed (8,757 males and 7,411 females).

Tableaux 2 A (1971), 2 B:
La rubrique « Autres et situation non définie » comprend 16 168 chômeurs (8 757 hommes et 7 411 femmes).

Cuadros 2 A (1971), 2 B:
El grupo « Otros y categoría no definida » incluye 16 168 desempleados (8 757 hombres y 7 411 mujeres).

Table 2 A:
1974: official estimates.

Tableau 2 A:
1974: *évaluations officielles.*

Cuadro 2 A:
1974: estimaciones oficiales.

Nouvelle-Calédonie

Tables 1, 2 A, 2 B:
Economically active population figures do not include unemployed.

Tableaux 1, 2 A, 2 B:
Les chiffres de la population active ne comprennent pas les chômeurs.

Cuadros 1, 2 A, 2 B:
Las cifras de la población económicamente activa no incluyen los desempleados.

Table 1:
1975: official estimates.

Tableau 1:
1975: *évaluations officielles.*

Cuadro 1:
1975: estimaciones oficiales.

Papua New Guinea

Table 1:
Indigenous population.

Tableau 1:
Population indigène.

Cuadro 1:
Población indígena

POPULATION

Notes to tables **1 to 2 B** (indicated by the symbol ǂ)
Notes relatives aux tableaux **1 à 2 B** (indiquées par le symbole ǂ)
Notas relativas a los cuadros **1 a 2 B** (indicadas por medio del símbolo ǂ)

Polynésie française

Table 1:

Economically active population figures do not include unemployed.

1970: official estimates.

Tableau 1:

Les chiffres de la population active ne comprennent pas les chômeurs.

1970: *évaluations officielles.*

Cuadro 1:

Las cifras de la población económicamente activa no incluyen los desempleados.

1970: estimaciones oficiales.

*
*   *

URSS, RSS de Biélorussie, RSS d'Ukraine

Tables 1, 2 A:

De jure population.

Tableaux 1, 2 A:

Population de jure.

Cuadros 1, 2 A:

Población *de jure.*

Employment

Emploi

Empleo

Employment

Employment is defined as follows in the Resolution concerning statistics of the labour force, employment and unemployment, adopted by the Eighth International Conference of Labour Statisticians (Geneva, 1954) [1]:

(1) Persons in employment consist of all persons above a specified age in the following categories:

(a) at work: persons who performed some work for pay or profit during a specified brief period, either one week or one day;

(b) with a job but not at work: persons who, having already worked in their present job, were temporarily absent during the specified period because of illness or injury, industrial dispute, vacation or other leave of absence, absence without leave, or temporary disorganisation of work due to such reasons as bad weather or mechanical breakdown.

(2) Employers and workers on own account should be included among the employed and may be classified as " at work " or " not at work " on the same basis as other employed persons.

(3) Unpaid family workers currently assisting in the operation of a business or farm are considered as employed if they worked for at least one-third of the normal working time during the specified period.

(4) The following categories of persons are *not* considered as employed:

(a) workers who during the specified period were on temporary or indefinite lay-off without pay;

(b) persons without jobs or businesses or farms who had arranged to start a new job or business or farm at a date subsequent to the period of reference;

(c) unpaid members of the family who worked for less than one-third of the normal working time during the specified period in a family business or farm.

The statistics on employment presented in this chapter are of various types, as indicated below in the table headings and, in general, a certain element of estimation is involved in their com-

[1] See ILO: *The International Recommendations on Labour Statistics* (Geneva, 1976).

pilation.[2] The scope of the series therefore varies from one country to another.

In certain countries, the data relate to employed persons in all *status* groups (employers, own-account workers, employees, unpaid family workers, members of producers' co-operatives), whereas in other countries the data relate only to employees (wage earners and salaried employees). The data generally relate to the total number of persons at work on a specified day or during a specified week in each month or quarter, but sometimes to the average number at work for a given period. Usually, no distinction is made between persons employed full time and those working less than full time. Members of the armed forces are not included in the figures shown.

Where the employment series refer only to employees (wage earners and salaried employees), which group in many cases tends to become an increasingly large proportion of the total labour force, the series will show a rising trend on this account. Also, where series refer only to establishments above a given size, a shift of employment from small to large establishments will be reflected in a rising trend in the series.

The data in this chapter are based on statistics of the following types (indicated in the table headings by the codes I, II and III):

I. *Labour force sample surveys* are a source of regular information on the total civilian labour force, including employers, unpaid family workers, seasonal workers and own-account workers—groups which are often not covered by other types of employment statistics. When based on adequate sampling methods, labour force sample surveys provide statistics with a known degree of reliability.

II. *Statistics of compulsory social insurance* relate to the working population covered by sickness, accident or unemployment insurance

[2] For the descriptions of the various national series, their scope, methods of compilation used, etc., see ILO: *Technical Guide 1976* (description of general series published in the *Bulletin* and the *Year Book of Labour Statistics*), Vol. II, " Employment—Unemployment—Hours of Work—Wages " (Geneva, 1976).

schemes, or the like. The number of contributors or of contributions paid provides a measure of the number of insured persons in employment (unemployed persons being exempt from the obligation to pay contributions). Persons working a very short time or receiving a very low pay are sometimes excluded from these statistics. In addition to changes in the actual number of persons employed, employment statistics based on social insurance records may also reflect changes in coverage of particular industrial, occupational or status groups. More generally, the provisions relating to social insurance schemes determine the scope of the statistics derived from their operation.

III. *Statistics of establishments* show the number of workers on establishment payrolls and may also show the total number of hours worked during a specific pay period. In general, there are two types of statistics of establishments.

The first type covers *all establishments of a given importance*, i.e. fulfilling certain conditions, such as having more than a certain number of employees, having an annual output of more than a certain value, etc. The data thus obtained may be subject to some bias owing to the exclusion of establishments which are below the minimum size fixed for the series; provided, however, that this minimum is small, the scope of such series is usually very wide and they furnish a close approximation of the fluctuations in employment.

The second type of statistics relate to a *sample of establishments*. The chief difficulty with such statistics is to ensure that the sample of establishments remains representative of the whole. For example, changes in industrial structure, the growth and decline of individual establishments, general population movements and pronounced changes in the levels of activity in some sectors of the economy tend to introduce a cumulative bias in this sample which may become appreciable after several years.

In certain countries where statistics of all establishments are available only at annual or longer intervals, they may be combined either by chaining or by interpolation with statistics relating to samples of establishments which are available more frequently.

As of the 1974 issue of the *Year Book*, changes have been made in the presentation of the data shown in certain tables owing to the introduction of the revised 1968 edition of the International Standard Industrial Classification of All Economic Activities (ISIC); see " Preface ".

Table 3

Persons Employed in Major Divisions of Economic Activity

This table presents absolute figures on the distribution of the employed civilian labour force by branch of economic activity *(Industry)*. Industrial groups are arranged, so far as possible, according to the International Standard Industrial Classification of All Economic Activities (see Appendix). The statistics are of various types as indicated in the headings and in general a certain element of estimation is involved in their compilation. In certain cases, the figures refer only to the number of employees (wage earners and salaried employees).

Table 4

General Level of Employment

The indices of employment shown in this table refer to the number of employees (wage earners and salaried employees) in all divisions of economic activity *(Industry)*. In certain cases, the statistics may also cover other *status* groups (employers, own-account workers, etc.). In addition, for certain series the component industries such as " Agriculture, forestry, hunting and fishing " and " Services " are not fully represented or are represented only by certain of the groups composing them.

Table 5

Employment in Non-Agricultural Sectors

The indices shown in this table cover non-agricultural employment only, i.e. employment in all divisions of economic activity except the division "Agriculture, forestry, hunting and fishing". Remarks made on table 4 pertaining to coverage also apply to this table.

Table 6

Employment in Manufacturing

The indices of numbers employed (wage earners and salaried employees) in manufacturing industries given in table 6 A (All Industries) and table 6 B (by Industry) usually form a component part of the corresponding general series of table 4. The different manufacturing industries given in table 6 B have been arranged in so far as possible according to the International Standard Industrial Classification of All Economic Activities (see Appendix), with the corresponding code number of the different industrial major groups. Indices shown in table 6 C relate to total hours worked in manufacturing and are based on aggregate man-hours of work performed during a specified period (usually a month) by wage earners or, in a few cases by all persons employed in the establishments covered. Such series give a measure of variations in the total "volume" of employment.

Table 7

Employment in Mining and Quarrying

Table 8

Employment in Construction

Table 9

Employment in Transport, Storage and Communication

The indices of numbers employed (wage earners and salaried employees) in the major divisions of economic activity *(Industry)* given in tables 7, 8 and 9 usually form component parts of the corresponding general series in table 4.

Emploi

L'emploi est défini de la manière suivante dans la résolution concernant les statistiques de la main-d'œuvre, de l'emploi et du chômage, adoptée par la huitième Conférence internationale des statisticiens du travail (Genève, 1954)[1]:

(1) Les personnes pourvues d'un emploi sont toutes les personnes qui, ayant dépassé un âge spécifié, rentrent dans une des catégories suivantes:

a) personnes au travail: personnes qui ont effectué un travail rémunéré durant une courte période spécifiée, qui peut être soit une semaine, soit un jour;

b) personnes qui ont un emploi mais ne sont pas au travail: personnes qui, ayant déjà travaillé dans leur emploi actuel, en sont temporairement absentes durant la période spécifiée pour cause de maladie ou d'accident, conflit du travail, vacances ou autre forme de congés, absence volontaire ou empêchement temporaire de travailler dû à des causes telles que conditions climatiques défavorables ou incidents techniques.

(2) Les employeurs et les personnes travaillant à leur propre compte doivent rentrer dans la catégorie des personnes pourvues d'un emploi et peuvent être classées comme « étant au travail » ou « n'étant pas au travail », sur la même base que les autres personnes pourvues d'un emploi.

(3) Les travailleurs familiaux non rémunérés qui collaborent de façon habituelle au fonctionnement d'une exploitation agricole ou d'une entreprise sont considérés comme pourvus d'un emploi s'ils ont travaillé pendant une durée au moins égale au tiers de la durée normale du travail pendant la période spécifiée.

(4) Ne sont *pas* considérés comme personnes pourvues d'un emploi:

a) les travailleurs qui, durant la période spécifiée, sont mis à pied temporairement ou pour une durée indéfinie, sans rémunération;

b) les personnes qui n'ont ni emploi, ni exploitation agricole, ni entreprise, et qui ont pris leurs dispositions en vue de commencer à travailler dans un nouvel emploi ou d'ouvrir une exploitation agricole ou une entreprise à une date postérieure à la période de référence;

c) les membres de la famille non rémunérés qui ont travaillé dans l'entreprise ou l'exploitation familiale pendant une durée inférieure au tiers de la durée normale du travail pendant la période spécifiée.

Les statistiques de l'emploi présentées dans ce chapitre sont de types différents, comme on le verra ci-après dans les en-têtes; leur calcul implique souvent des évaluations[2]. En conséquence, la portée des séries varie d'un pays à un autre.

Dans certains pays, les données se rapportent aux personnes occupées dans les différents groupes professionnels et classées suivant la situation dans la profession (employeurs, travailleurs à leur propre compte, salariés, travailleurs familiaux non rémunérés, membres de coopératives de production), alors que dans d'autres pays elles ne concernent que les salariés (ouvriers et employés). Les statistiques se rapportent en général au nombre total des personnes travaillant pendant un jour ou une semaine donnés de chaque mois ou trimestre ou parfois au nombre moyen des personnes employées durant une période déterminée. Aucune distinction n'est généralement faite entre les personnes travaillant à temps complet et celles qui travaillent à horaire réduit. Les forces armées ne sont pas comprises dans les chiffres présentés.

Lorsque les séries relatives à l'emploi se rapportent seulement aux ouvriers et aux employés qui, dans la plupart des cas, ont tendance à former une proportion de plus en plus grande de la population active, les séries peuvent présenter, de ce fait, une tendance ascendante. De même, lorsque les données se rapportent uniquement à des entreprises d'une importance déterminée, le mouvement de l'emploi de petites entreprises vers d'importants établissements se reflétera par une tendance ascendante des séries.

Les données dans ce chapitre sont fondées sur les statistiques des types suivants (indiqués dans les en-têtes des tableaux par les codes I, II et III):

I. *Enquêtes par sondage sur la main-d'œuvre.* Ces enquêtes constituent une source d'information régulière concernant la main-d'œuvre

---

[1] Voir BIT: *Recommandations internationales sur les statistiques du travail* (Genève, 1975).

[2] Pour les descriptions des diverses séries nationales, de leur portée, des méthodes de calcul utilisées, etc., voir BIT: *Guide technique 1976* (description des séries générales publiées dans le *Bulletin* et l'*Annuaire des statistiques du travail*), vol. II, « Emploi — Chômage — Durée du travail — Salaires » (Genève, 1976).

civile totale, y compris les employeurs, les travailleurs familiaux non rémunérés, les travailleurs saisonniers et les travailleurs à leur propre compte, groupes qui sont rarement couverts par les autres types de statistiques de l'emploi. Lorsqu'elles sont fondées sur des méthodes d'échantillonnage adéquates, ces enquêtes par sondage sur la main-d'œuvre fournissent des statistiques que l'on sait être sûres.

II. *Statistiques d'assurances sociales obligatoires.* Ces statistiques concernent la population active couverte par l'assurance-maladie, accidents ou chômage, ou par un régime analogue. Le nombre des cotisants ou des cotisations versées fournit une mesure des effectifs assurés et occupés (les chômeurs étant dispensés du paiement de leur cotisation). Les personnes travaillant durant une très courte période ou qui sont très peu rémunérées sont quelquefois omises de ces statistiques. Outre les changements intervenant dans le nombre effectif des personnes occupées, les statistiques de l'emploi fondées sur les archives des assurances sociales peuvent également refléter des modifications de portée pour certains groupes classés selon la branche d'activité économique, la profession ou la situation dans la profession. De façon plus générale, les dispositions relatives au régime d'assurances sociales déterminent la portée des statistiques tirées de son application.

III. *Statistiques d'établissements.* Ces statistiques fournissent le nombre des travailleurs inscrits sur les bordereaux de salaires et peuvent indiquer également le nombre total des heures effectuées au cours d'une période de paie déterminée. En général, on distingue deux types de statistiques d'établissements :

Le premier type de statistiques englobe *tous les établissements d'une importance déterminée*, c'est-à-dire ceux qui répondent à certains critères (par exemple, les entreprises qui occupent plus d'un certain nombre d'ouvriers; celles dont la production annuelle est supérieure à une certaine valeur, etc.). Ces données ainsi rassemblées

peuvent être sujettes à des écarts systématiques provenant de l'élimination d'établissements qui n'atteignent pas la limite minimum fixée pour ces séries; toutefois, lorsque ce minimum est fixé assez bas, la portée de telles séries est généralement très étendue et ces statistiques reflètent assez fidèlement les fluctuations de l'emploi.

Les statistiques du second type reposent sur un *échantillon d'établissements.* Dans de telles séries, la difficulté principale consiste à conserver aux établissements sélectionnés un caractère représentatif. Par exemple, des variations de la structure industrielle, le développement ou le déclin d'établissements particuliers, le mouvement général de la population ou des changements marqués dans l'activité de certains secteurs économiques ont tendance à introduire un écart systématique cumulatif dans l'échantillon qui, au bout de quelques années, peut devenir sensible.

Dans certains pays où les statistiques de l'ensemble des établissements ne sont disponibles que tous les ans ou à des intervalles plus longs, celles-ci sont combinées soit par enchaînement, soit par interpolation, avec les statistiques relatives à un échantillon d'établissements, plus fréquemment disponibles.

Dès l'édition de 1974 de l'*Annuaire***, des modifications ont été apportées à la présentation des données de certains tableaux en raison de l'introduction de la version révisée 1968 de la Classification internationale type, par industrie, de toutes les branches d'activité économique (CITI); voir « Préface ».**

Tableau 3

Personnes occupées dans les principales branches d'activité économique

Ce tableau présente des chiffres absolus relatifs à la distribution par branche d'activité économique de la main-d'œuvre civile occupée. Les groupes d'activité économique sont présentés, autant que possible, selon la Classification internationale type, par industrie, de toutes les branches d'activité économique (voir annexe). Les statistiques sont de types différents, comme l'indiquent les en-têtes, et, en général, leur calcul implique des évaluations. Dans certains cas, les chiffres se rapportent seulement au nombre de salariés (ouvriers et employés).

Tableau 4

Niveau général de l'emploi

Les indices de l'emploi présentés dans ce tableau correspondent au nombre de salariés (ouvriers et employés) dans toutes les branches d'activité économique. Dans certains cas, les statistiques peuvent également couvrir d'autres groupes professionnels classés selon la situation dans la profession (employeurs, travailleurs à leur propre compte, etc.). En outre, il arrive que les industries composantes (telles que: « Agriculture, sylviculture, chasse et pêche » et « Services ») ne soient pas toutes représentées, ou ne le soient que par une partie seulement des classes qui les composent.

Tableau 5

Emploi dans les secteurs non agricoles

Les indices présentés dans ce tableau couvrent seulement l'emploi non agricole, c'est-à-dire l'emploi dans l'ensemble des branches d'activité économique à l'exception de la branche « Agriculture, sylviculture, chasse et pêche ». Les remarques relatives au tableau 4 concernant les groupes professionnels couverts par les statistiques s'appliquent également au tableau 5.

Tableau 6

Emploi dans les industries manufacturières

Les indices de l'effectif employé (ouvriers et employés) dans les industries manufacturières,

fournis dans le tableau 6 A (ensemble des industries) et le tableau 6 B (par industrie) forment en général des éléments constitutifs des séries générales du tableau 4. Les différentes industries manufacturières figurant au tableau 6 B ont été ordonnées autant que possible conformément à la Classification internationale type, par industrie, de toutes les branches d'activité économique (voir annexe), avec indication du numéro de code correspondant aux différentes classes d'industries. Le tableau 6 C fournit des indices du total des heures de travail effectuées dans les industries manufacturières; ils sont fondés sur le nombre total des heures de travail effectuées durant une certaine période (généralement un mois) par le personnel ouvrier ou, dans quelques cas, par toutes les personnes occupées dans les établissements couverts par les statistiques. De telles séries fournissent une mesure des variations du « volume » total de l'emploi.

Tableau 7

Emploi dans les industries extractives

Tableau 8

Emploi dans la construction

Tableau 9

Emploi dans les transports, les entrepôts et les communications

Les indices de l'effectif employé (ouvriers et employés) dans les principales branches d'activité économique fournis dans les tableaux 7, 8 et 9 forment en général des éléments constitutifs des séries générales du tableau 4.

Empleo

El empleo se halla definido de la manera siguiente en la resolución sobre estadísticas de la fuerza del trabajo, del empleo y del desempleo adoptada por la octava Conferencia Internacional de Estadígrafos del Trabajo (Ginebra, 1954) [1]:

1) Las personas comprendidas en el empleo son todas aquellas que tengan más de cierta edad especificada y que estén dentro de las categorías siguientes:

a) que estén trabajando; es decir, las personas que realizan algún trabajo remunerado durante un breve período especificado, ya sea durante una semana o un día;

b) que tengan un empleo, pero que no estén trabajando, o sea, las personas que hayan trabajado ya en su empleo actual, pero que se hallen temporalmente ausentes del trabajo en el curso del período especificado debido a enfermedad o accidente, conflicto de trabajo, vacaciones u otra clase de permiso, ausencia sin permiso, interrupción del trabajo a causa de determinados motivos, como, por ejemplo, el mal tiempo o averías producidas en las máquinas.

2) Los empleadores y los trabajadores por cuenta propia deberían ser incluidos en la categoría de las personas con empleo y se podrían clasificar como « trabajando » o « sin trabajar » sobre la misma base que las demás personas empleadas.

3) Se considerará que los trabajadores familiares no remunerados que ordinariamente exploten o ayuden a explotar un negocio cualquiera o una explotación agrícola tienen un empleo si han trabajado por lo menos un tercio del tiempo normal de trabajo durante el período especificado.

4) *No* se considerarán como empleadas las personas comprendidas en las categorías siguientes:

a) los trabajadores que durante el período especificado hayan sido suspendidos temporal o indefinidamente, sin goce de remuneración;

b) las personas que no tengan ningún empleo o que no exploten un negocio cualquiera o una explotación agrícola, pero que hayan obtenido un nuevo empleo, negocio o explotación agrícola que haya de comenzar en una fecha subsiguiente al período de referencia;

c) los trabajadores familiares no remunerados que trabajen menos de un tercio del tiempo normal de trabajo durante el período especificado en un negocio o explotación agrícola familiar.

Tal como se indica en los encabezamientos, las estadísticas del empleo que se presentan en este capítulo son de varias clases y su compilación implica a menudo ciertas estimaciones [2]. Por lo tanto, el alcance de las series varía de un país a otro.

En ciertos países, los datos se refieren a las personas empleadas en todos los grupos *profesionales* (empleadores, trabajadores por cuenta propia, asalariados, trabajadores familiares no remunerados, miembros de cooperativas de productores), mientras que en otros países se refieren sólo a los asalariados (obreros y empleados). Las estadísticas del empleo comprenden generalmente el total de trabajadores ocupados en determinado día o durante una determinada semana de cada mes o trimestre; a veces se refieren al promedio de las personas empleadas durante un período dado. Por lo general, no se hace ninguna distinción entre las personas ocupadas a horario completo y las que trabajan a horario reducido. Los miembros de las fuerzas armadas no están incluidos en las estadísticas.

Cuando las series se refieren sólo a los asalariados (obreros y empleados), los cuales tienden a constituir en la mayoría de los casos una proporción cada vez mayor del total de la fuerza de trabajo, las series pueden presentar cierta tendencia a aumentar por la misma razón. Asimismo, cuando las series se refieren solamente a establecimientos que exceden de una determinada dimensión, el cambio de las personas empleadas de los pequeños a los grandes establecimientos se reflejará en una tendencia al aumento de las series.

Los datos que figuran en este capítulo se basan en estadísticas de los siguientes tipos (indicados en los encabezamientos de los cuadros por las claves I, II y III):

---

[1] Véase OIT: *Recomendaciones internacionales sobre estadísticas del trabajo* (Ginebra, 1975).

[2] Para las descripciones de las diversas series nacionales, su alcance, métodos de compilación utilizados, etc., véase OIT: *Guía Técnica 1976* (descripciones de las series generales publicadas en el *Boletín* y el *Anuario de Estadísticas del Trabajo*), vol. II, « Empleo — Desempleo — Horas de trabajo — Salarios » (Ginebra, 1976).

I. *Encuestas por muestra sobre la fuerza tra-bajadora.* Este método permite reunir regular-mente datos sobre el total de la fuerza de tra-bajo civil, comprendidos los empleadores, los trabajadores familiares no remunerados, los tra-bajadores de temporada y los trabajadores por cuenta propia, grupos éstos que suelen quedar fuera de los cálculos en otros tipos de estadísticas del empleo. Dicha técnica, cuando se basa en métodos de muestras apropiados, permite obte-ner estadísticas fidedignas.

II. *Estadísticas del seguro social obligatorio,* relativas a la población activa que tiene un seguro de enfermedad, accidente o desempleo. El número de contribuyentes o de contribuciones pagadas sirve para determinar el número de per-sonas ocupadas aseguradas (ya que los des-empleados están exentos de pagar contribucio-nes). A veces se excluye de estas estadísticas a las personas que trabajan durante períodos muy breves o que reciben una remuneración muy baja. Además de los cambios en el número actual de personas ocupadas, las estadísticas del empleo basadas en los registros del seguro social pueden también reflejar cambios en el alcance de deter-minados grupos de actividades económicas, de ocupación o profesionales. Más generalmente, las disposiciones reglamentarias de los seguros sociales determinan el alcance de las estadísticas basadas en los datos de su funcionamiento.

III. *Estadísticas de establecimientos.* Estas esta-dísticas indican el número de trabajadores que figuran en las nóminas de salarios de los estable-cimientos, y también pueden proporcionar el total de horas trabajadas durante un período de pago determinado. En general, existen dos tipos de estadísticas de establecimientos.

El primer tipo se refiere a *todos los estable-cimientos de una importancia determinada,* es decir, a aquellos que responden a ciertos crite-rios, por ejemplo, establecimientos que ocupan más de cierto número de obreros, estableci-mientos cuya producción anual es superior a cierto valor, etc. Los datos obtenidos pueden estar sujetos a errores sistemáticos debidos a la eliminación de los establecimientos que no alcanzan los límites fijados como criterio mínimo de inclusión en la serie. Sin embargo, y a con-dición de que esos mínimos sean bajos, el alcance de estas series es generalmente muy amplio y refleja con bastante exactitud las fluctuaciones del empleo.

El segundo tipo de estadísticas se refiere a *muestras de establecimientos.* La principal difi-cultad en dichas estadísticas consiste en man-tener el carácter representativo de la muestra de establecimientos. Por ejemplo, los cambios en la estructura industrial, el crecimiento o la declinación de determinados establecimientos, el movimiento general de la población y otras modificaciones importantes del nivel de actividad de ciertos sectores de la economía tienden a introducir un error en la muestra que, al acumu-larse, puede llegar a ser apreciable al cabo de algunos años.

En ciertos países en que se dispone de esta-dísticas de todos los establecimientos solamente a intervalos anuales o aun mayores, los datos pueden combinarse con estadísticas basadas en muestras de establecimientos de las que se dispone con mayor frecuencia, utilizando el método de enlace o por interpolación.

A partir de la edición de 1974 del *Anuario* se ha modificado la presentación de los datos de ciertos cuadros debido a la introducción de la edición revisada 1968 de la Clasificación industrial internacional uniforme de todas las actividades económicas (CIIU). Véase « Prefacio ».

Cuadro 3

Personas ocupadas en las divisiones mayores de la actividad económica

Este cuadro presenta las cifras absolutas de la distribución por ramas de actividad económica *(industria)* de la fuerza de trabajo civil ocu-pada. Los grupos de actividades han sido orde-nados, en la medida de lo posible, según la Clasificación industrial internacional uniforme de todas las actividades económicas (véase Apéndice). Como se indica en los encabezamientos, las estadísticas son de varias clases y su compilación implica por lo general cierto grado de estimación. En algunos casos, las cifras se refieren sólo al número de asalariados (obreros y empleados).

Cuadro 4

Nivel general del empleo

Los índices del empleo que figuran en este cuadro se refieren al número de asalariados (obreros y empleados) en todas las ramas de la actividad económica *(industria)*. En ciertos casos, las estadísticas pueden comprender también otros grupos *profesionales* (empleadores, trabajadores por cuenta propia, etc.). Además, en ciertas series, las actividades correspondientes, tales como « Agricultura, silvicultura, caza y pesca » y « Servicios », no se hallan todas representadas, o están representadas solamente por una parte de los grupos que las componen.

Cuadro 5

Empleo en los sectores no agrícolas

Los índices que se presentan en este cuadro comprenden sólo el empleo no agrícola, es decir, el empleo en todas las ramas de la actividad económica, exceptuada la rama « Agricultura, silvicultura, caza y pesca ». Las observaciones del cuadro 4 relativas al alcance se aplican también a este cuadro.

Cuadro 6

Empleo en las industrias manufactureras

Los índices de las personas ocupadas (obreros y empleados) en las industrias manufactureras que figuran en el cuadro 6 A (todas las industrias) y el cuadro 6 B (por industria) normalmente forman parte de las series generales correspondientes del cuadro 4. Las diversas industrias manufactureras que figuran en el cuadro 6 B han sido ordenadas, en la medida de lo posible, según la Clasificación industrial internacional uniforme de todas las actividades económicas (véase Apéndice), con indicación del número de código correspondiente de las diferentes industrias. Los índices que se presentan en el cuadro 6 C se refieren al total de horas trabajadas en las industrias manufactureras y se basan en la suma de las horas-hombre de trabajo efectuadas durante un período especificado (ordinariamente, un mes) por los obreros o, en unos pocos casos, por todas las personas empleadas en los establecimientos cubiertos por las estadísticas. Estas series proporcionan una medida de las variaciones del « volumen » del empleo.

Cuadro 7

Empleo en minas y canteras

Cuadro 8

Empleo en la construcción

Cuadro 9

Empleo en los transportes, almacenaje y comunicaciones

Los índices de las personas ocupadas (obreros y empleados) en las principales divisiones de la actividad económica *(industria)* presentados en los cuadros 7, 8 y 9, por lo común forman parte de las series generales correspondientes del cuadro 4.

EMPLOYMENT

3 Persons employed in major divisions of economic activity
Personnes occupées dans les principales branches d'activité économique
Personas ocupadas en las divisiones mayores de la actividad económica

AFRICA — AFRIQUE — AFRICA

Egypt

Civilian labour force employed *(Official estimates)*
Main-d'œuvre civile occupée *(Evaluations officielles)*
Fuerza trabajadora civil ocupada *(Estimaciones oficiales)*

(Thousands — *Milliers* — Millares)

Date [1] *Date [1]* Fecha [1]	Total	1 Agriculture, forestry, fishing *Agriculture, sylviculture, pêche* Agricultura, silvicultura, pesca	2 Mining, quarrying *Industries extractives* Minas, canteras	3 Manufacturing *Industries manufacturières* Industrias manufactureras	4 Electricity, gas, water *Electricité, gaz, eau* Electricidad, gas, agua	5 Construction *Construction* Construcción	6 Trade, restaurants and hotels *Commerce, restaurants et hôtels* Comercio, restaurantes y hoteles	7 Transport, storage, communication *Transports, entrepôts, communications* Transportes, almacenaje, comunicaciones	8 Financing, insurance, real estate, business services *Banques, assurances, aff. imm., serv. aux entreprises* Bancos, seguros, bienes inm., serv. para empresas	9 Commu-social, and pers. services *Services à collectivité, services sociaux et pers.* Servicios comunales, sociales y personales	0 Others *Autres* Otros
1971	8 405.6	4 471.5	7.2	1 038.0	25.8	194.9	803.4	323.9	83.5	1 273.2	184.2
1972	8 816.6	4 655.7	19.8	1 113.6	39.2	206.9	849.0	340.7	79.9	1 329.2	182.6
1973	8 712.4	4 400.3	15.4	1 210.4	43.9	242.4	835.0	354.2	87.6	1 359.1	164.1

[1] May of each year.   [1] *Mai de chaque année.*   [1] Mayo de cada año.

Gabon

Number of employees *(Statistics of compulsory social insurance)*
Nombre de salariés *(Statistiques d'assurances sociales obligatoires)*
Número de asalariados *(Estadísticas del seguro social obligatorio)*

(ISIC — CITI — CIIU 1958)

(Thousands — *Milliers* — Millares)

Date *Date* Fecha	Total	Agriculture, forestry, fishing *Agriculture, sylviculture, pêche* Agricultura, silvicultura, pesca	Mining, quarrying *Industries extractives* Minas, canteras	Manufacturing *Industries manufacturières* Industrias manufactureras	Construction *Construction* Construcción	Electricity, gas, water *Electricité, gaz, eau* Electricidad, gas, agua	Commerce *Commerce* Comercio	Transport, storage, communication *Transports, entrepôts, communications* Transportes, almacenaje, comunicaciones	Services [1] *Services [1]* Servicios [1]	Others *Autres* Otros
1965	45.4	10.3	4.1	4.1	4.1	0.6	4.0	2.2	10.5	5.5
1966	47.4	10.4	5.4	3.8	7.7	0.7	5.2	2.5	10.6	1.1
1967	51.8	10.2	4.8	4.4	7.0	1.4	7.1	1.9	13.6	1.4
1968	55.2	9.5	4.9	6.0	9.3	0.4	5.8	3.8	15.3	0.2
1969	59.9	10.1	5.0	6.7	10.8	0.6	6.4	4.5	15.7	0.2
1970	63.0	11.5	5.3	9.3	11.8	0.7	6.7	4.6	13.1	0.1
1971 *	65.0	11.2	6.1	9.2	6.1	1.1	11.5	5.1	14.7	—
1972 *	68.5	12.5	7.0	9.1	10.0	1.7	7.3	6.2	14.7	—

[1] Excl. domestic services.   [1] *Non compris les services domestiques.*   [1] Excl. los servicios domésticos.

3 Persons employed in major divisions of economic activity
Personnes occupées dans les principales branches d'activité économique
Personas ocupadas en las divisiones mayores de la actividad económica

Kenya

Number of employees *(Statistics of establishments)*[1]
Nombre de salariés *(Statistiques d'établissements)*[1]
Número de asalariados *(Estadísticas de establecimientos)*[1]

(Thousands — *Milliers* — Millares)

Date [2] / *Date* [2] / Fecha [2]	Total [3]	1	2	3	4	5	6	7	8	9
		Agriculture, forestry, fishing [4] / *Agriculture, sylviculture, pêche* [4] / Agricultura, silvicultura, pesca [4]	Mining, quarrying / *Industries extractives* / Minas, canteras	Manufacturing / *Industries manufacturières* / Industrias manufactureras	Electricity, gas, water / *Electricité, gaz, eau* / Electricidad, gas, agua	Construction / *Construction* / Construcción	Trade, restaurants and hotels / *Commerce, restaurants et hôtels* / Comercio, restaurantes y hoteles	Transport, storage, communication / *Transports, entrepôts, communications* / Transportes, almacenaje, comunicaciones	Financing, insurance, real estate, business services / *Banques, assurances, aff. imm., serv. aux entreprises* / Bancos, seguros, bienes inm., serv. para empresas	Community, social, and pers. services / *Services à collectivité, services sociaux et pers.* / Servicios comunales, sociales y personales
1972	719.8	246.9	3.2	84.8	5.1	37.6	47.6	45.3	17.5	231.8
1973	761.7	265.4	3.1	94.5	5.4	41.2	46.6	44.4	20.3	240.9

[1] For figures prior to 1972, see previous editions of the *Year Book*. [2] June of each year. [3] Excl. employment in rural areas (except for large enterprises) estimated at between 300,000 and 500,000 employees. [4] Large farms only.

[1] *Pour les données avant 1972, voir les précédentes éditions de* l'Annuaire. [2] *Juin de chaque année.* [3] *Non compris l'emploi dans les zones rurales (à l'exception des grandes entreprises) évalué entre 300 000 et 500 000 salariés.* [4] *Grandes exploitations agricoles seulement.*

[1] Para los datos antes de 1972 véanse las precedentes ediciones del *Anuario*. [2] Junio de cada año. [3] Excl. el empleo en las zonas rurales (con excepción de las grandes empresas), estimado entre 300 000 y 500 000 trabajadores. [4] Grandes explotaciones agrícolas solamente.

Malawi

Number of employees *(Statistics of establishments)* [1]
Nombre de salariés *(Statistiques d'établissements)* [1]
Número de asalariados *(Estadísticas de establecimientos)* [1]

(Thousands — *Milliers* — Millares)

Date / *Date* / Fecha	Total	1	2	3	4	5	6	7	8	9 ×
		Agriculture, forestry, fishing / *Agriculture, sylviculture, pêche* / Agricultura, silvicultura, pesca	Mining, quarrying / *Industries extractives* / Minas, canteras	Manufacturing / *Industries manufacturières* / Industrias manufactureras	Electricity, gas, water / *Electricité, gaz, eau* / Electricidad, gas, agua	Construction / *Construction* / Construcción	Trade, restaurants and hotels / *Commerce, restaurants et hôtels* / Comercio, restaurantes y hoteles	Transport, storage, communication / *Transports, entrepôts, communications* / Transportes, almacenaje, comunicaciones	Financing, insurance, real estate, business services / *Banques, assurances, aff. imm., serv. aux entreprises* / Bancos, seguros, bienes inm., serv. para empresas	Community, social, and pers. services [2] / *Services à collectivité, services sociaux et pers.* [2] / Servicios comunales, sociales y personales [2]
1970	159.6	53.8	0.5	19.5	1.7	18.6	12.3	8.5	1.2	43.5
1971	170.2	57.5	0.6	21.8	2.2	17.8	13.1	9.0	1.2	47.1
1972	189.9	63.9	0.8	23.2	2.4	18.2	15.9	9.8	1.4	54.3
1973	215.7	76.4	0.8	25.7	2.9	21.1	18.4	10.5	1.9	58.0
1974	227.3	80.6	0.9	26.8	2.5	22.9	20.8	11.4	2.3	59.2

[1] Establishments with 20 or more persons employed. Incl. working proprietors and unpaid family workers. [2] Excl. domestic services.

[1] *Etablissements occupant 20 personnes et plus. Y compris les propriétaires-exploitants et les travailleurs familiaux non rémunérés.* [2] *Non compris les services domestiques.*

[1] Establecimientos con 20 y más trabajadores. Incl. los empresarios propietarios y los trabajadores familiares no remunerados. [2] Excl. los servicios domésticos.

EMPLOYMENT

3 Persons employed in major divisions of economic activity
Personnes occupées dans les principales branches d'activité économique
Personas ocupadas en las divisiones mayores de la actividad económica

Mauritius

Number of employees *(Statistics of establishments)*
Nombre de salariés *(Statistiques d'établissements)*
Número de asalariados *(Estadísticas de establecimientos)*

(Thousands — *Milliers* — Millares)

Date [1] *Date* [1] Fecha [1]	Total [2]	1 Agriculture, forestry, fishing [3] *Agriculture, sylviculture, pêche* [3] Agricultura, silvicultura, pesca [3]	2 Mining, quarrying *Industries extractives* Minas, canteras	3 Manufac-turing [4] *Industries manufactu-rières* [4] Industrias manufac-tureras [4]	4 Electricity, gas, water *Electricité, gaz, eau* Electricidad, gas, agua	5 Construction *Construction* Construcción	6 Trade, restaurants and hotels *Commerce, restaurants et hôtels* Comercio, restaurantes y hoteles	7 Transport, storage, communica-tion *Transports, entrepôts, communi-cations* Transportes, almacenaje, comunica-ciones	8 Financing, insurance, real estate, business services *Banques, assurances, aff. imm., serv. aux entreprises* Bancos, seguros, bienes inm., serv. para empresas	9 Community, social, and pers. services *Services à collectivité, services sociaux et pers.* Servicios comunales, sociales y perso-nales
1966	104.0	56.2	0.2	6.9	1.3	2.6	3.1	4.5	...	29.3
1967	105.3	55.3	0.2	7.4	1.3	2.8	3.2	4.4	...	30.8
1968	110.0	59.0	0.2	7.7	1.3	2.0	3.5	4.8	...	31.6
1969	109.7	56.2	0.2	7.9	1.3	2.0	4.0	5.0	...	33.1
1970	112.6	57.2	0.2	8.2	1.3	1.9	4.2	5.3	...	34.3
1971	117.6	57.6	0.2	9.3	1.3	2.1	4.3	5.8	1.7	35.3
1972	126.5	60.0	0.1	10.9	1.3	2.8	5.3	6.6	1.9	37.5
1973	136.8	60.5	0.1	14.6	2.7	4.0	6.0	7.4	2.2	39.4
1974	146.4	59.9	0.1	19.6	2.9	4.8	6.6	8.6	2.5	41.3

[1] March and Sep. of each year.   [2] Excl. relief workers (about 17,100 in 1973).   [3] Incl. sugar and tea factories.   [4] Excl. sugar and tea factories.

[1] *Mars et sept. de chaque année.*   [2] *Non compris les personnes occupées à des travaux publics de secours (environ 17 100 en 1973).*   [3] *Y compris les fabriques de sucre et de thé.*   [4] *Non compris les fabriques de sucre et de thé.*

[1] Marzo y sept. de cada año.   [2] Excl. las personas ocupadas en trabajos públicos de socorro (alrededor de 17 100 en 1973).   [3] Incl. las fábricas de azúcar y té.   [4] Excl. las fábricas de azúcar y té.

Swaziland

Number of employees *(Statistics of establishments)*
Nombre de salariés *(Statistiques d'établissements)*
Número de asalariados *(Estadísticas de establecimientos)*

(Thousands — *Milliers* — Millares)

Date [1] *Date* [1] Fecha [1]	Total	1 Agriculture, forestry, fishing *Agriculture, sylviculture, pêche* Agricultura, silvicultura, pesca	2 Mining, quarrying *Industries extractives* Minas, canteras	3 Manufac-turing *Industries manufactu-rières* Industrias manufac-tureras	4 Electricity, gas, water *Electricité, gaz, eau* Electricidad, gas, agua	5 Construction *Construction* Construcción	6 Trade, restaurants and hotels *Commerce, restaurants et hôtels* Comercio, restaurantes y hoteles	7 Transport, storage, communica-tion *Transports, entrepôts, communi-cations* Transportes, almacenaje, comunica-ciones	8 Financing, insurance, real estate, business services *Banques, assurances, aff. imm., serv. aux entreprises* Bancos, seguros, bienes inm., serv. para empresas	9 Community, social, and pers. services *Services à collectivité, services sociaux et pers.* Servicios comunales, sociales y perso-nales
1970	42.4	18.3	2.9	5.4	0.5	2.3	3.4	1.9	0.3	7.3
1971	47.1	20.8	2.9	5.8	0.5	2.5	3.8	2.1	0.4	8.1
1972	53.9	24.3	3.0	6.5	0.5	3.6	3.8	2.3	0.6	9.2
1973	57.0	23.7	2.9	7.4	0.6	4.0	4.0	2.7	0.6	11.3

[1] Sep. of each year.

[1] *Sept. de chaque année.*

[1] Sept. de cada año.

3 Persons employed in major divisions of economic activity
Personnes occupées dans les principales branches d'activité économique
Personas ocupadas en las divisiones mayores de la actividad económica

Tunisie

Civilian labour force employed *(Official estimates)*
Main-d'œuvre civile occupée *(Evaluations officielles)*
Fuerza trabajadora civil ocupada *(Estimaciones oficiales)*

(ISIC — CITI — CIIU 1958)

(Thousands — *Milliers* — Millares)

Date / *Date* / Fecha	Total	Agriculture, forestry, fishing / *Agriculture, sylviculture, pêche* / Agricultura, silvicultura, pesca	Mining, quarrying / *Industries extractives* / Minas, canteras	Manufacturing / *Industries manufacturières* / Industrias manufactureras	Construction / *Construction* / Construcción	Commerce / *Commerce* / Comercio	Transport, storage, communication / *Transports, entrepôts, communications* / Transportes, almacenaje, comunicaciones	Services / *Services* / Servicios
1968	1 242	766	21	131	56	76	34	159
1969	1 251	766	21	139	48	71	34	172
1970	1 276	767	22	143	49	77	37	181
1971	1 312	770	23	157	54	80	40	188
1972	1 387	800	25	171	59	83	43	206
1973	1 417	800	25	181	65	85	44	217
1974	1 456	800	24	197	73	88	46	227

Uganda

Number of employees *(Statistics of establishments)*
Nombre de salariés *(Statistiques d'établissements)*
Número de asalariados *(Estadísticas de establecimientos)*

(ISIC — CITI — CIIU 1958)

(Thousands — *Milliers* — Millares)

Date [1] / *Date* [1] / Fecha [1]	Total	Agriculture, forestry, fishing / *Agriculture, sylviculture, pêche* / Agricultura, silvicultura, pesca	Mining, quarrying / *Industries extractives* / Minas, canteras	Manufacturing [2] / *Industries manufacturières* [2] / Industrias manufactureras [2]	Construction [3] / *Construction* [3] / Construcción [3]	Commerce [4] / *Commerce* [4] / Comercio [4]	Transport, storage, communication / *Transports, entrepôts, communications* / Transportes, almacenaje, comunicaciones	Services [5] / *Services* [5] / Servicios [5]
1965	241.7	51.0	6.4	37.8	32.5	12.5	10.2	91.2
1966	246.0	52.9	6.4	42.7	29.2	14.2	9.8	90.8
1967	256.8	54.6	6.7	44.2	32.4	14.0	10.7	94.1
1968	281.8	55.9	7.9	49.6	42.0	13.7	11.1	101.7
1969	295.0	56.3	6.3	54.1	42.4	14.7	11.8	109.5
1970	312.4	54.9	7.9	54.0	47.7	14.1	12.6	121.1
1971	324.5	57.7	7.4	54.9	47.4	17.6	13.2	126.4
1972	329.8	60.1	5.8	53.2	43.3	17.1	12.5	137.7
1973	347.6	61.2	5.3	53.6	44.4	17.0	11.9	154.3

[1] June of each year. [2] Incl. electricity. [3] Incl. water. [4] Private sector only. [5] Incl. commerce of public sector.

[1] *Juin de chaque année.* [2] *Y compris l'électricité.* [3] *Y compris l'eau.* [4] *Secteur privé seulement.* [5] *Y compris le commerce du secteur public.*

[1] Junio de cada año. [2] Incl. la electricidad. [3] Incl. el agua. [4] Sector privado solamente. [5] Incl. el comercio del sector público.

EMPLOYMENT

3
Persons employed in major divisions of economic activity
Personnes occupées dans les principales branches d'activité économique
Personas ocupadas en las divisiones mayores de la actividad económica

Zambia

Number of employees *(Statistics of establishments)*
Nombre de salariés *(Statistiques d'établissements)*
Número de asalariados *(Estadísticas de establecimientos)*

(Thousands — *Milliers* — Millares)

Date [1] *Date* [1] Fecha [1]	Total	1 Agriculture, forestry, fishing *Agriculture, sylviculture, pêche* Agricultura, silvicultura, pesca	2 Mining, quarrying *Industries extractives* Minas, canteras	3 Manufac-turing *Industries manufactu-rières* Industrias manufac-tureras	4 Electricity, gas, water *Electricité, gaz, eau* Electricidad, gas, agua	5 Construction *Construction* Construcción	6 Trade, restaurants and hotels *Commerce, restaurants et hôtels* Comercio, restaurantes y hoteles	7 Transport, storage, communica-tion *Transports, entrepôts, communi-cations* Transportes, almacenaje, comunica-ciones	8 Financing, insurance, real estate, business services *Banques, assurances, aff. imm., serv. aux entreprises* Bancos, seguros, bienes inm., serv. para empresas	9 Community, social, and pers. services *Services à collectivité, services sociaux et pers.* Servicios comunales, sociales y perso-nales
1967	307.9	35.8	54.9	31.8	3.0	65.3	31.2	19.8	6.5	59.5
1968	319.2	35.0	54.8	33.6	3.3	67.1	32.3	22.6	7.4	63.0
1969	324.9	37.4	55.6	35.1	3.2	61.1	34.0	22.9	8.3	67.2
1970	340.4	34.3	57.1	37.5	3.1	69.1	33.1	22.8	9.1	74.3
1971	362.0	38.6	58.1	41.3	4.1	68.0	35.9	22.4	10.4	83.2
1972	366.2	37.0	57.9	41.7	4.8	69.7	37.0	26.2	11.7	80.3
1973	380.7	36.6	62.0	41.5	5.8	75.8	36.2	25.8	13.6	83.4
1974 [2]	386.1	36.6	64.0	43.0	5.4	74.8	35.5	26.5	14.6	85.6

[1] June and Dec. of each year.   [2] June.   [1] *Juin et déc. de chaque année.*   [2] *Juin.*   [1] Junio y dic. de cada año.   [2] Junio.

3 **Persons employed in major divisions of economic activity**
Personnes occupées dans les principales branches d'activité économique
Personas ocupadas en las divisiones mayores de la actividad económica

AMERICA — AMÉRIQUE — AMERICA

Belize

Number of employees *(Statistics of establishments)*
Nombre de salariés *(Statistiques d'établissements)*
Número de asalariados *(Estadísticas de establecimientos)*

(ISIC — CITI — CIIU 1958) (Thousands — *Milliers* — Millares)

Date [1] / *Date* [1] / Fecha [1]	Total	Agriculture forestry, fishing / *Agriculture, sylviculture, pêche* / Agricultura, silvicultura, pesca	Mining, quarrying / *Industries extractives* / Minas, canteras	Manufacturing / *Industries manufacturières* / Industrias manufactureras	Construction / *Construction* / Construcción	Commerce / *Commerce* / Comercio	Transport, storage, communication / *Transports, entrepôts, communications* / Transportes, almacenaje, comunicaciones	Services [2] / *Services* [2] / Servicios [2]
1965	14.1	4.7	0.1	2.1	1.6	1.4	0.4	3.8
1966	14.7	4.4	0.1	2.4	1.9	1.5	0.4	4.0
1967	15.0	4.3	—	2.7	1.3	1.5	0.6	4.6
1968	16.4	4.3	0.1	2.8	2.5	1.5	0.6	4.6
1969	17.8	5.0	0.1	2.9	2.8	1.6	0.6	4.8

[1] March of each year. [2] Incl. electricity, gas, water and sanitary services.

[1] *Mars de chaque année.* [2] *Y compris l'électricité, le gaz, l'eau et les services sanitaires.*

[1] Marzo de cada año. [2] Incl. la electricidad, el gas, el agua y los servicios sanitarios.

Canada

Civilian labour force employed *(Labour force sample surveys)* [1]
Main-d'œuvre civile occupée *(Enquêtes par sondage sur la main-d'œuvre)* [1]
Fuerza trabajadora civil ocupada *(Encuestas por muestra sobre la fuerza trabajadora)* [1]

(ISIC — CITI — CIIU 1958) (Thousands — *Milliers* — Millares)

Date / *Date* / Fecha	Total	Agriculture, forestry, fishing / *Agriculture, sylviculture, pêche* / Agricultura, silvicultura, pesca	Mining, quarrying / *Industries extractives* / Minas, canteras	Manufacturing / *Industries manufacturières* / Industrias manufactureras	Construction / *Construction* / Construcción	Electricity, gas, water / *Electricité, gaz, eau* / Electricidad, gas, agua	Commerce / *Commerce* / Comercio	Transport, storage, communication / *Transports, entrepôts, communications* / Transportes, almacenaje, comunicaciones	Services / *Services* / Servicios
1965	6 862	694	134	1 636	463	77	1 425	540	1 892
1966	7 152	646	121	1 744	499	77	1 482	543	2 041
1967	7 379	663	114	1 756	475	80	1 536	580	2 175
1968	7 537	650	117	1 754	470	90	1 587	582	2 288
1969	7 780	636	116	1 819	482	93	1 642	600	2 392
1970	7 879	603	125	1 790	471	89	1 685	603	2 511
1971	8 079	605	129	1 795	495	87	1 715	615	2 638
1972	8 329	574	124	1 857	501	93	1 795	637	2 747
1973	8 759	572	123	1 968	549	99	1 908	674	2 866
1974	9 137	579	127	2 024	598	96	2 021	694	2 998

[1] Persons aged 14 years and over.

[1] *Personnes âgées de 14 ans et plus.*

[1] Personas de 14 años y más.

311

EMPLOYMENT

3 Persons employed in major divisions of economic activity
Personnes occupées dans les principales branches d'activité économique
Personas ocupadas en las divisiones mayores de la actividad económica

Jamaica

Civilian labour force employed (*Labour force sample surveys*) [1]
Main-d'œuvre civile occupée (*Enquêtes par sondage sur la main-d'œuvre*) [1]
Fuerza trabajadora civil ocupada (*Encuestas por muestra sobre la fuerza trabajadora*) [1]

(ISIC — CITI — CIIU 1958)

(Thousands — *Milliers* — Millares)

Date [2] / *Date* [2] / Fecha [2]	Total	Agriculture, forestry, fishing / *Agriculture, sylviculture, pêche* / Agricultura, silvicultura, pesca	Manufacturing / *Industries manufacturières* / Industrias manufactureras	Construction / *Construction* / Construcción	Commerce / *Commerce* / Comercio	Electricity, gas, water, transport, storage, communication / *Electricité, gaz, eau, transports, entrepôts, communications* / Electricidad, gas, agua, transportes, almacenaje, comunicaciones	Services / *Services* / Servicios	Others / *Autres* / Otros
1968 [3]	582.4	220.5	64.8	39.4	67.6	25.7	163.1	2.7
1969	617.4	236.9	69.3	43.8	76.6	18.9	171.9	—
1972	611.3	204.4	76.9	40.2	83.7	26.2	176.6	3.4
1973	629.6	208.8	79.6	41.6	88.6	26.5	179.8	4.8
1974 [4]	648.0	233.4	79.0	40.1	75.5	24.7	195.3	—

[1] Persons aged 14 years and over. [2] April and Oct. of each year. [3] July and Oct. [4] Oct.

[1] *Personnes âgées de 14 ans et plus.* [2] *Avril et oct. de chaque année.* [3] *Juillet et oct.* [4] *Oct.*

[1] Personas de 14 años y más. [2] Abril y oct. de cada año. [3] Julio y oct. [4] Oct.

Panamá

Civilian labour force employed (*Labour force sample surveys*) [1]
Main-d'œuvre civile occupée (*Enquêtes par sondage sur la main-d'œuvre*) [1]
Fuerza trabajadora civil ocupada (*Encuestas por muestra sobre la fuerza trabajadora*) [1]

(Thousands — *Milliers* — Millares)

Date / *Date* / Fecha	Total	1 Agriculture, forestry, fishing / *Agriculture, sylviculture, pêche* / Agricultura, silvicultura, pesca	2 Mining, quarrying / *Industries extractives* / Minas, canteras	3 Manufacturing / *Industries manufacturières* / Industrias manufactureras	4 Electricity, gas, water / *Electricité, gaz, eau* / Electricidad, gas, agua	5 Construction / *Construction* / Construcción	6 Trade, restaurants and hotels / *Commerce, restaurants et hôtels* / Comercio, restaurantes y hoteles	7 Transport, storage, communication / *Transports, entrepôts, communications* / Transportes, almacenaje, comunicaciones	8 Financing, insurance, real estate, business services / *Banques, assurances, aff. imm., serv. aux entreprises* / Bancos, seguros, bienes inm., serv. para empresas	9 Community, social, and pers. services / *Services à collectivité, services sociaux et pers.* / Servicios comunales, sociales y personales	Canal Zone / *Zone du canal* / Zona del Canal
1965	349.9	165.0	0.1	26.1	2.7	15.0	38.9	11.0	6.0	65.1	20.0
1966	371.7	168.0	0.1	32.4	2.6	16.0	42.0	12.3	6.1	70.2	22.0
1967	384.7	155.3	0.1	35.8	3.2	20.8	50.3	13.2	8.0	78.0	20.0
1968	404.1	157.8	0.6	45.7	3.3	19.3	51.0	14.7	7.2	81.6	22.9
1969	420.3	157.4	0.4	41.5	3.0	20.3	58.7	15.8	8.6	92.3	22.3
1970	432.9	158.2	0.5	42.5	3.8	23.5	61.2	16.3	9.1	95.4	22.4
1971	435.6	150.8	0.6	42.1	4.6	26.0	59.2	18.0	9.6	101.1	23.6
1972	449.4	152.5	0.4	43.0	5.2	30.6	63.5	17.7	10.6	103.4	22.5

[1] Persons aged 15 years and over.

[1] *Personnes âgées de 15 ans et plus.*

[1] Personas de 15 años y más.

3 Persons employed in major divisions of economic activity
Personnes occupées dans les principales branches d'activité économique
Personas ocupadas en las divisiones mayores de la actividad económica

Puerto Rico

Civilian labour force employed *(Labour force sample surveys)* [1]
Main-d'œuvre civile occupée *(Enquêtes par sondage sur la main-d'œuvre)* [1]
Fuerza trabajadora civil ocupada *(Encuestas por muestra sobre la fuerza trabajadora)* [1]

(Thousands — *Milliers* — Millares)

		1	3	4	5	6 ×	7	8 ×	6 × ; 8 × ; 9
Date *Date* Fecha	Total	Agriculture, forestry, fishing *Agriculture, sylviculture, pêche* Agricultura, silvicultura, pesca	Manufacturing *Industries manufacturières* Industrias manufactureras	Electricity, gas, water *Electricité, gaz, eau* Electricidad, gas, agua	Construction *Construction* Construcción	Trade *Commerce* Comercio	Transport storage, communication *Transports, entrepôts, communications* Transportes, almacenaje, comunicaciones	Financing, insurance, real estate *Banques, assurances, affaires immobilières* Bancos, seguros, bienes immobiliarios	Community, social, and pers. services [2] *Services à collectivité, services sociaux et pers.* [2] Servicios comunales, sociales y personales [2]
1965	616	103	116	9	57	112	30	11	177
1966	642	95	121	11	61	116	33	11	194
1967	650	88	124	12	63	120	33	12	198
1968	661	81	133	12	66	120	33	12	204
1969	684	74	136	12	71	126	33	14	218
1970	694	66	132	12	78	131	34	16	224
1971	719	59	137	12	83	135	35	17	240
1972	747	54	140	14	77	140	36	18	269
1973	768	50	146	14	81	148	37	20	271
1974	764	52	147	15	77	144	38	19	272

[1] Persons aged 14 years and over. [2] Incl. hotels, restaurants and business services.

[1] *Personnes âgées de 14 ans et plus.* [2] *Y compris les restaurants, les hôtels et les services fournis aux entreprises.*

[1] Personas de 14 años y más. [2] Incl. los restaurantes, los hoteles y los servicios prestados a las empresas.

Trinidad and Tobago

Civilian labour force employed *(Labour force sample surveys)* [1]
Main-d'œuvre civile occupée *(Enquêtes par sondage sur la main-d'œuvre)* [1]
Fuerza trabajadora civil ocupada *(Encuestas por muestra sobre la fuerza trabajadora)* [1]

(ISIC — CITI — CIIU 1958)

(Thousands — *Milliers* — Millares)

Date *Date* Fecha	Total	Agriculture, forestry, fishing *Agriculture, sylviculture, pêche* Agricultura, silvicultura, pesca	Mining, quarrying, manufacturing *Industries extractives, industries manufacturières* Minas, canteras, industrias manufactureras	Construction, electricity, gas, water *Construction, électricité, gaz, eau* Construcción, electricidad, gas, agua	Commerce *Commerce* Comercio	Transport, storage, communication *Transports, entrepôts, communications* Transportes, almacenaje, comunicaciones	Services *Services* Servicios
1965	299.5	71.6	57.5	34.7	49.1	22.8	63.8
1966	302.3	65.4	57.0	35.2	49.7	22.8	72.2
1967	312.3	68.6	63.0	35.1	48.8	22.6	74.2
1968	307.9	69.7	54.4	36.3	48.3	21.5	75.7
1969	316.6	74.6	56.7	40.9	46.5	22.7	75.1
1970	317.2	77.8	65.7	41.8	44.8	20.6	66.5
1971 [2]	321.4	71.8	64.0	47.8	44.3	21.1	72.5
1972	.	.	.	.	.	.	.
1973 *	323.6	53.0	64.3	46.4	58.1	27.2	75.6

[1] Persons aged 15 years and over. [2] First semester.

[1] *Personnes âgées de 15 ans et plus.* [2] *Premier semestre.*

[1] Personas de 15 años y más. [2] Primer semestre.

EMPLOYMENT

3 Persons employed in major divisions of economic activity
Personnes occupées dans les principales branches d'activité économique
Personas ocupadas en las divisiones mayores de la actividad económica

United States

Civilian labour force employed and number of employees
Main-d'œuvre civile occupée et nombre de salariés
Fuerza trabajadora civil ocupada y número de asalariados

(ISIC — CITI — CIIU 1958)

(Thousands — *Milliers* — Millares)

Date / *Date* / Fecha	Civilian labour force [1] *(Labour force sample surveys)* Main-d'œuvre civile [1] *(Enquêtes par sondage sur la main-d'œuvre)* Fuerza trabajadora civil [1] *(Encuestas por muestra sobre la fuerza trabajadora)*			Wage earners and salaried employees *(Statistics of establishments)* Ouvriers et employés *(Statistiques d'établissements)* Obreros y empleados *(Estadísticas de establecimientos)*	Private sector — *Secteur privé* — Sector privado						Government [3] *Gouvernement* [3] Gobierno [3]
	Total	Agricultural *Agricole* Agrícola	Non-agricultural *Non agricole* No agrícola	Total	Mining, quarrying *Industries extractives* Minas, canteras	Manufacturing *Industries manufacturières* Industrias manufactureras	Construction *Construction* Construcción	Electricity, gas, water, transport *Electricité, gaz, eau, transports* Electricidad, gas, agua, transportes	Commerce, services [2] *Commerce, services* [2] Comercio, servicios [2]	Finance *Finance* Finanzas	
1965	71 088	4 361	66 726	60 815	632	18 062	3 186	4 036	21 803	3 023	10 074
1966	72 895	3 979	68 915	63 955	627	19 214	3 275	4 151	22 796	3 100	10 792
1967	74 372	3 844	70 527	65 857	613	19 447	3 208	4 261	23 705	3 225	11 398
1968	75 920	3 817	72 103	67 951	606	19 781	3 306	4 311	24 721	3 381	11 845
1969	77 902	3 606	74 296	70 442	619	20 167	3 525	4 435	25 932	3 562	12 202
1970	78 627	3 462	75 165	70 920	623	19 349	3 536	4 504	26 621	3 687	12 561
1971	79 120	3 387	75 732	71 216	603	18 572	3 639	4 457	27 255	3 802	12 887
1972	81 702	3 472	78 230	73 711	622	19 090	3 831	4 517	28 367	3 943	13 340
1973	84 409	3 452	80 957	76 833	638	20 054	4 028	4 646	29 651	4 075	13 742
1974	85 936	3 492	82 443	78 338	672	20 017	3 985	4 699	30 519	4 161	14 286

[1] Persons aged 16 years and over. [2] Excl. domestic servants. [3] Total number employed in federal, state and local government.

[1] *Personnes âgées de 16 ans et plus.* [2] *Non compris les gens de maison.* [3] *Nombre total des personnes occupées dans les services du gouvernement fédéral, des Etats et des autorités locales.*

[1] Personas de 16 años y más. [2] Excl. el personal del servicio doméstico. [3] Número total de las personas ocupadas en los servicios del Gobierno federal, de los Estados y de los municipios.

3

Persons employed in major divisions of economic activity
Personnes occupées dans les principales branches d'activité économique
Personas ocupadas en las divisiones mayores de la actividad económica

ASIA — ASIE — ASIA

Brunei

Number of employees *(Statistics of establishments)* [1]
Nombre de salariés *(Statistiques d'établissements)* [1]
Número de asalariados *(Estadísticas de establecimientos)* [1]

(Thousands — *Milliers* — Millares)

Date [2] / *Date* [2] / Fecha [2]	Total	1 Agriculture, forestry, fishing / *Agriculture, sylviculture, pêche* / Agricultura, silvicultura, pesca	2 Mining, quarrying / *Industries extractives* / Minas, canteras	3 Manufacturing / *Industries manufacturières* / Industrias manufactureras	4 Electricity, gas, water / *Electricité, gaz, eau* / Electricidad, gas, agua	5 Construction / *Construction* / Construcción	6 Trade, restaurants and hotels / *Commerce, restaurants et hôtels* / Comercio, restaurantes y hoteles	7 Transport, storage, communication / *Transports, entrepôts, communications* / Transportes, almacenaje, comunicaciones	8 Financing, insurance, real estate, business services / *Banques, assurances, aff. imm., serv. aux entreprises* / Bancos, seguros, bienes inm., serv. para empresas	9 Community, social, and pers. services / *Services à collectivité, services sociaux et pers.* / Servicios comunales, sociales y personales
1971	...	0.6	2.7	1.5	...	5.4	1.9	...	0.5	...
1972	27.6	0.9	2.9	1.6	0.8	7.3	2.2	1.1	0.7	10.1
1973	30.3	0.3	3.1	2.0	0.9	6.3	2.9	1.6	0.5	12.7
1974	30.5	0.3	3.3	1.9	0.9	5.6	2.7	1.7	0.6	13.4

[1] Incl. employers and workers on own account.
[2] June of each year.

[1] *Y compris les employeurs et les personnes travaillant à leur propre compte.* [2] *Juin de chaque année.*

[1] Incl. los empleadores y los trabajadores por cuenta propia. [2] Junio de cada año.

Cyprus

Civilian labour force employed *(Official estimates)*
Main-d'œuvre civile occupée *(Evaluations officielles)*
Fuerza trabajadora civil ocupada *(Estimaciones oficiales)*

(ISIC — CITI — CIIU 1958)

(Thousands — *Milliers* — Millares)

Date / *Date* / Fecha	Total	Agriculture, forestry, fishing / *Agriculture, sylviculture, pêche* / Agricultura, silvicultura, pesca	Mining, quarrying / *Industries extractives* / Minas, canteras	Manufacturing / *Industries manufacturières* / Industrias manufactureras	Construction / *Construction* / Construcción	Electricity, gas, water / *Electricité, gaz, eau* / Electricidad, gas, agua	Commerce / *Commerce* / Comercio	Transport, storage, communication / *Transports, entrepôts, communications* / Transportes, almacenaje, comunicaciones	Services / *Services* / Servicios	Others / *Autres* / Otros
1965	227.5	97.5	4.6	31.1	19.9	1.2	18.3	9.6	36.3	9.0
1966	232.9	97.6	5.1	31.2	21.7	1.2	20.5	9.7	37.4	8.5
1967	235.8	97.6	5.1	31.8	23.4	1.1	21.9	10.0	38.6	6.3
1968	241.2	97.3	5.2	33.2	24.3	1.1	22.8	10.5	40.4	6.4
1969	245.1	96.8	4.9	34.1	25.2	1.2	23.6	11.2	41.9	6.2
1970	248.4	96.2	4.9	35.4	25.5	1.3	23.7	11.3	43.7	6.4
1971	252.1	96.2	4.2	36.3	26.0	1.3	24.2	11.4	46.1	6.4
1972	254.8	95.5	3.9	37.3	25.3	2.5	24.1	11.4	48.6	6.2
1973	258.9	93.5	3.8	37.6	27.2	2.6	30.4	11.5	46.1	6.2
1974*	220.1	76.3	3.4	30.9	22.0	2.5	26.2	9.7	42.8	6.3

EMPLOYMENT

3 Persons employed in major divisions of economic activity
Personnes occupées dans les principales branches d'activité économique
Personas ocupadas en las divisiones mayores de la actividad económica

Israel

Civilian labour force employed *(Labour force sample surveys)* [1]
Main-d'œuvre civile occupée *(Enquêtes par sondage sur la main-d'œuvre)* [1]
Fuerza trabajadora civil ocupada *(Encuestas por muestra sobre la fuerza trabajadora)* [1]

(Thousands — *Milliers* — Millares)

Date / *Date* / Fecha	Total	1 Agriculture, forestry, fishing / *Agriculture, sylviculture, pêche* / Agricultura, silvicultura, pesca	2; 3 Mining, quarrying, manufacturing / *Industries extractives, industries manufacturières* / Minas, canteras, industrias manufactureras	4 Electricity, gas, water / *Electricité, gaz, eau* / Electricidad, gas, agua	5 Construction / *Construction* / Construcción	6 Trade, restaurants and hotels / *Commerce, restaurants et hôtels* / Comercio, restaurantes y hoteles	7 Transport, storage, communication / *Transports, entrepôts, communications* / Transportes, almacenaje, comunicaciones	8 Financing, insurance, real estate, business services / *Banques, assurances, aff. imm., serv. aux entreprises* / Bancos, seguros, bienes inm., serv. para empresas	9 Community, social and pers. services / *Services à collectivité, services sociaux et pers.* / Servicios comunales, sociales y personales	0 Others / *Autres* / Otros
1968	910.9	94.3	217.6	11.6	72.9	120.4	68.4	44.5	278.7	2.5
1969	945.8	91.3	226.1	10.6	75.9	125.0	74.7	48.5	290.3	3.4
1970	963.2	84.8	233.3	11.3	80.1	125.0	72.2	49.7	303.8	3.0
1971	997.1	84.5	239.6	11.0	88.3	126.4	74.0	56.7	314.1	2.5
1972	1 047.0	83.4	248.3	8.8	99.3	137.0	76.9	60.2	328.7	4.4
1973	1 088.2	81.4	269.8	10.4	96.0	138.9	78.8	68.0	341.6	3.3
1974	1 089.5	70.7	273.9	10.4	87.7	131.6	83.5	70.0	354.3	7.3

[1] Persons aged 14 years and over. Data cover also certain territories under occupation by Israeli military forces since June 1967.

[1] *Personnes âgées de 14 ans et plus. Les données couvrent aussi certains territoires occupés par les forces armées israéliennes depuis juin 1967.*

[1] Personas de 14 años y más. Los datos cubren también ciertos territorios ocupados por las fuerzas armadas israelíes desde junio de 1967.

Japan

Civilian labour force employed *(Labour force sample surveys)* [1]
Main-d'œuvre civile occupée *(Enquêtes par sondage sur la main-d'œuvre)* [1]
Fuerza trabajadora civil ocupada *(Encuestas por muestra sobre la fuerza trabajadora)* [1]

(Thousands — *Milliers* — Millares)

Date / *Date* / Fecha	Total	1 Agriculture, forestry, fishing / *Agriculture, sylviculture, pêche* / Agricultura, silvicultura, pesca	2 Mining, quarrying / *Industries extractives* / Minas, canteras	3 Manufacturing / *Industries manufacturières* / Industrias manufactureras	4 Electricity, gas, water / *Electricité, gaz, eau* / Electricidad, gas, agua	5 Construction / *Construction* / Construcción	6 × Trade / *Commerce* / Comercio	7 Transport, storage, communication / *Transports, entrepôts, communications* / Transportes, almacenaje, comunicaciones	8 × Financing, insurance, real estate, business services [2] / *Banques, assurances, aff. imm., serv. aux entreprises* [2] / Bancos, seguros, bienes inm., serv. para empresas [2]	6 ×; 8 ×; 9 Community, social, and pers. services [3] / *Services à collectivité, services sociaux et pers.* [3] / Servicios comunales, sociales y personales [3]	0 Others / *Autres* / Otros
1967	49 200	10 360	260	12 520	270	3 590	9 470	2 890	1 360	8 460	20
1968	50 020	9 880	270	13 050	270	3 700	9 820	3 020	1 280	8 670	60
1969	50 400	9 460	240	13 450	270	3 710	10 010	3 110	1 320	8 780	50
1970	50 940	8 860	200	13 770	280	3 940	10 120	3 240	1 320	9 120	70
1971	51 140	8 140	190	13 810	290	4 130	10 330	3 320	1 450	9 410	70
1972	51 090	7 540	160	13 780	290	4 310	10 470	3 250	1 490	9 720	80
1973	52 330	7 030	130	14 360	340	4 640	10 800	3 350	1 560	10 010	100
1974	52 010	6 730	140	14 170	330	4 590	10 900	3 280	1 620	10 150	100

[1] Persons aged 15 years and over. [2] Excl. business services. [3] Incl. restaurants, hotels and business services.

[1] *Personnes âgées de 15 ans et plus.* [2] *Non compris les services fournis aux entreprises.* [3] *Y compris les restaurants, les hôtels et les services fournis aux entreprises.*

[1] Personas de 15 años y más. [2] Excl. los servicios para empresas. [3] Incl. los restaurantes, los hoteles y los servicios para empresas.

3 Persons employed in major divisions of economic activity
Personnes occupées dans les principales branches d'activité économique
Personas ocupadas en las divisiones mayores de la actividad económica

Korea, Rep. of

Civilian labour force employed *(Labour force sample surveys)* [1]
Main-d'œuvre civile occupée *(Enquêtes par sondage sur la main-d'œuvre)* [1]
Fuerza trabajadora civil ocupada *(Encuestas por muestra sobre la fuerza trabajadora)* [1]

(Thousands — *Milliers* — Millares)

Date / *Date* / Fecha	Total	1 Agriculture, forestry, fishing / *Agriculture, sylviculture, pêche* / Agricultura, silvicultura, pesca	2 Mining, quarrying / *Industries extractives* / Minas, canteras	3 Manufacturing / *Industries manufacturières* / Industrias manufactureras	4 Electricity, gas, water / *Electricité, gaz, eau* / Electricidad, gas, agua	5 Construction / *Construction* / Construcción	6 Trade, restaurants and hotels / *Commerce, restaurants et hôtels* / Comercio, restaurantes y hoteles	7 Transport, storage, communication / *Transports, entrepôts, communications* / Transportes, almacenaje, comunicaciones	8 Financing, insurance, real estate, business services / *Banques, assurances, aff. imm., serv. aux entreprises* / Bancos, seguros, bienes inm., serv. para empresas	9 Community, social, and pers. services / *Services à collectivité, services sociaux et pers.* / Servicios comunales, sociales y personales
1971	10 066	4 866	92	1 336	25	348	1 575	369	132	1 313
1972	10 559	5 346	54	1 445	45	392	1 588	355	103	1 231
1973	11 139	5 569	47	1 774	35	371	1 633	360	128	1 222
1974	11 586	5 584	50	2 012	35	450	1 760	360	147	1 188

[1] Persons aged 14 years and over.   [1] *Personnes âgées de 14 ans et plus.*   [1] Personas de 14 años y más.

Pakistan

Civilian labour force employed *(Labour force sample surveys)* [1]
Main-d'œuvre civile occupée *(Enquêtes par sondage sur la main-d'œuvre)* [1]
Fuerza trabajadora civil ocupada *(Encuestas por muestra sobre la fuerza trabajadora)* [1]

(Thousands — *Milliers* — Millares)

Date / *Date* / Fecha	Total	1 Agriculture, forestry, fishing / *Agriculture, sylviculture, pêche* / Agricultura, silvicultura, pesca	2 Mining, quarrying / *Industries extractives* / Minas, canteras	3 Manufacturing [2] / *Industries manufacturières [2]* / Industrias manufactureras [2]	4 Electricity, gas, water [3] / *Electricité, gaz, eau [3]* / Electricidad, gas, agua [3]	5 Construction / *Construction* / Construcción	6 Trade, restaurants and hotels [4] / *Commerce, restaurants et hôtels [4]* / Comercio, restaurantes y hoteles [4]	7 Transport, storage, communication / *Transports, entrepôts, communications* / Transportes, almacenaje, comunicaciones	8 Financing, insurance, real estate, business services / *Banques, assurances, aff. imm., serv. aux entreprises* / Bancos, seguros, bienes inm., serv. para empresas	9 Community, social, and pers. services [5] / *Services à collectivité, services sociaux et pers. [5]* / Servicios comunales, sociales y personales [5]	0 Others / *Autres* / Otros
1969	16 499.7	9 432.7	4.6	2 518.8	55.3	593.5	1 629.8	776.5	.	1 457.5	31.0
1970	17 470.3	10 275.7	20.7	2 609.6	66.4	668.8	1 632.9	787.1	.	1 368.8	40.3
1971	18 025.7	10 641.7	48.2	2 629.0	42.1	633.6	1 875.5	853.5	.	1 271.3	30.6
1972	18 107.5	10 515.3	79.4	2 222.1 *	65.1	610.4	1 745.7	862.0	149.6	1 285.5	...

[1] Persons aged 10 years and over.   [2] 1969-71: incl. repair services.   [3] 1969-71: incl. sanitary services.   [4] 1969-71: incl. banks, insurance and other financial institutions; excl. restaurants and hotels.   [5] 1969-71: excl. repair services, sanitary services, banks, insurance and other financial institutions; incl. restaurants and hotels.

[1] *Personnes âgées de 10 ans et plus.*   [2] *1969-1971: y compris les services de réparation.*   [3] *1969-1971: y compris les services sanitaires.*   [4] *1969-1971: y compris les banques, les assurances et les autres établissements financiers; non compris les restaurants et les hôtels.*   [5] *1969-1971: non compris les services de réparation, les services sanitaires, les banques, les assurances et les autres établissements financiers; y compris les restaurants et les hôtels.*

[1] Personas de 10 años y más.   [2] 1969-1971: incl. los servicios de reparación.   [3] 1969-1971: incl. los servicios de saneamiento.   [4] 1969-1971: incl. los bancos, los seguros y los otros establecimientos financieros; excl. los restaurantes y hoteles.   [5] 1969-1971: excl. los servicios de reparación, los servicios de saneamiento, los bancos, los seguros y los otros establecimientos financieros; incl. los restaurantes y hoteles.

EMPLOYMENT

3 Persons employed in major divisions of economic activity
Personnes occupées dans les principales branches d'activité économique
Personas ocupadas en las divisiones mayores de la actividad económica

Philippines

Civilian labour force employed *(Labour force sample surveys)* [1]
Main-d'œuvre civile occupée *(Enquêtes par sondage sur la main-d'œuvre)* [1]
Fuerza trabajadora civil ocupada *(Encuestas por muestra sobre la fuerza trabajadora)* [1]

(ISIC — CITI — CIIU 1958)

(Thousands — *Milliers* — Millares)

Date [2] / *Date* [2] / Fecha [2]	Total	Agriculture, forestry, fishing / *Agriculture, sylviculture, pêche* / Agricultura, silvicultura, pesca	Mining, quarrying / *Industries extractives* / Minas, canteras	Manufacturing / *Industries manufacturières* / Industrias manufactureras	Construction / *Construction* / Construcción	Electricity, gas, water / *Electricité, gaz, eau* / Electricidad, gas, agua	Commerce / *Commerce* / Comercio	Transport, storage, communication / *Transports, entrepôts, communications* / Transportes, almacenaje, comunicaciones	Services / *Services* / Servicios	Others / *Autres* / Otros
1965	10 543	6 052	28	1 221	299	22	1 120	367	1 426	8
1966	11 032	6 275	28	1 331	323	25	1 197	387	1 413	53
1967	12 185	6 993	52	1 389	347	33	1 352	385	1 614	20
1968	12 481	7 202	46	1 387	378	27	1 379	380	1 624	58
1969	11 235	6 325	51	1 291	349	29	1 109	383	1 658	40
1970	.	.	.	.	.	.	.	.	.	.
1971	12 584	6 440	56	1 472	467	58	1 531	518	2 013	29
1972	13 217	7 160	58	1 467	456	40	1 674	479	1 863	20
1973	13 262	7 016	62	1 418	522	37	1 660	505	2 013	29
1974	14 479	8 245	44	1 508	403	44	1 613	518	2 085	19

[1] Persons aged 10 years and over. [2] May of each year.   [1] *Personnes âgées de 10 ans et plus.* [2] *Mai de chaque année.*   [1] Personas de 10 años y más. [2] Mayo de cada año.

Singapore

Civilian labour force employed *(Labour force sample surveys)* [1]
Main-d'œuvre civile occupée *(Enquêtes par sondage sur la main-d'œuvre)* [1]
Fuerza trabajadora civil ocupada *(Encuestas por muestra sobre la fuerza trabajadora)* [1]

(Thousands — *Milliers* — Millares)

Date [2] / *Date* [2] / Fecha [2]	Total	1 Agriculture, forestry, fishing / *Agriculture, sylviculture, pêche* / Agricultura, silvicultura, pesca	2 Mining, quarrying / *Industries extractives* / Minas, canteras	3 Manufacturing / *Industries manufacturières* / Industrias manufactureras	4 Electricity, gas, water / *Electricité, gaz, eau* / Electricidad, gas, agua	5 Construction / *Construction* / Construcción	6 Trade, restaurants and hotels / *Commerce, restaurants et hôtels* / Comercio, restaurantes y hoteles	7 Transport, storage, communication / *Transports, entrepôts, communications* / Transportes, almacenaje, comunicaciones	8 Financing, insurance, real estate, business services / *Banques, assurances, aff. imm., serv. aux entreprises* / Bancos, seguros, bienes inm., serv. para empresas	9 Community, social, and pers. services [3] / *Services à collectivité, services sociaux et pers.* [3] / Servicios comunales, sociales y personales [3]	0 Others / *Autres* / Otros
1969	392.3	1.7	1.5	102.9	12.5	20.1	88.9	39.2	21.1	104.3	.
1970	432.0	2.0	1.7	127.8	13.7	21.9	95.9	40.8	23.7	104.5	.
1971	477.2	2.4	1.8	148.7	14.7	24.4	108.7	45.9	27.7	102.9	.
1972	531.2	2.5	2.0	181.2	15.5	29.1	117.0	50.0	31.8	102.1	.
1973	595.5	2.5	1.9	214.2	16.0	36.1	126.3	54.6	37.0	106.9	.
1974	824.4	21.7	1.8	234.2	10.3	42.5	172.7	97.5	46.6	195.1	1.9

[1] Persons aged 10 years and over. 1969-73: number of employees (incl. workers on own account and unpaid family workers), persons aged 12 years and over; statistics of establishments. [2] June. 1969-73: March and Sep. of each year. [3] 1969-73: excl. domestic services.

[1] *Personnes âgées de 10 ans et plus. 1969-1973: nombre de salariés (y compris les personnes travaillant à leur compte et les travailleurs familiaux non rémunérés), personnes âgées de 12 ans et plus; statistiques d'établissements.* [2] *Juin. 1969-1973: mars et sept. de chaque année.* [3] *1969-1973: non compris les services domestiques.*

[1] Personas de 10 años y más. 1969-1973: número de asalariados (incl. los trabajadores por cuenta propia y los trabajadores familiares no remunerados), personas de 12 años y más; estadísticas de establecimientos. [2] Junio. 1969-1973: marzo y sept. de cada año. [3] 1969-1973: excl. los servicios domésticos.

3 Persons employed in major divisions of economic activity
Personnes occupées dans les principales branches d'activité économique
Personas ocupadas en las divisiones mayores de la actividad económica

République arabe syrienne

Civilian labour force employed *(Labour force sample surveys)* [1]
Main-d'œuvre civile occupée *(Enquêtes par sondage sur la main-d'œuvre)* [1]
Fuerza trabajadora civil ocupada *(Encuestas por muestra sobre la fuerza trabajadora)* [1]

(Thousands — *Milliers* — Millares)

		1	2	3	4	5	6	7	8	9	0
Date [2] *Date* [2] Fecha [2]	Total	Agriculture, forestry, fishing *Agriculture, sylviculture, pêche* Agricultura, silvicultura, pesca	Mining, quarrying *Industries extractives* Minas, canteras	Manufacturing *Industries manufacturières* Industrias manufactureras	Electricity, gas, water *Electricité, gaz, eau* Electricidad, gas, agua	Construction *Construction* Construcción	Trade, restaurants and hotels *Commerce, restaurants et hôtels* Comercio, restaurantes y hoteles	Transport, storage, communication *Transports, entrepôts, communications* Transportes, almacenaje, comunicaciones	Financing, insurance, real estate, business services *Banques, assurances, aff. imm., serv. aux entreprises* Bancos, seguros, bienes inm., serv. para empresas	Community, social, and pers. services *Services à collectivité, services sociaux et pers.* Servicios comunales, sociales y personales	Others *Autres* Otros
1971	1 522.3	891.8	1.6	172.3	7.0	70.6	140.8	45.9	9.9	182.0	0.5
1972	1 634.2	907.7	3.2	181.2	19.1	99.7	136.9	63.4	8.7	214.3	—
1973	1 612.1	850.2	14.4	161.2	7.3	88.3	153.6	64.5	10.1	262.5	—

[1] Persons aged 10 years and over.   [2] Sep. of each year.   [1] *Personnes âgées de 10 ans et plus.*   [2] *Sept. de chaque année.*   [1] Personas de 10 años y más.   [2] Sept. de cada año.

Thailand

Civilian labour force employed *(Labour force sample surveys)* [1]
Main-d'œuvre civile occupée *(Enquêtes par sondage sur la main-d'œuvre)* [1]
Fuerza trabajadora civil ocupada *(Encuestas por muestra sobre la fuerza trabajadora)* [1]

(ISIC — CITI — CIIU 1958)

(Thousands — *Milliers* — Millares)

		Agriculture, forestry, fishing *Agriculture, sylviculture, pêche* Agricultura, silvicultura, pesca	Mining, quarrying *Industries extractives* Minas, canteras	Manufacturing *Industries manufacturières* Industrias manufactureras	Construction *Construction* Construcción	Electricity, gas, water *Electricité, gaz, eau* Electricidad, gas, agua	Commerce *Commerce* Comercio	Transport, storage, communication *Transports, entrepôts, communications* Transportes, almacenaje, comunicaciones	Services *Services* Servicios	Others *Autres* Otros
Date [2] *Date* [2] Fecha [2]	Total									
1972	16 129.5	11 642.1	118.4	1 239.5	256.7	24.0	1 230.4	313.6	1 302.7	2.1
1973	17 042.7	12 270.5	110.9	1 201.1	258.0	48.4	1 392.3	383.9	1 375.6	2.0

[1] Persons aged 11 years and over.   [2] July-Sep. of each year.   [1] *Personnes âgées de 11 ans et plus.*   [2] *Juillet-sept. de chaque année.*   [1] Personas de 11 años y más.   [2] Julio-dic. de cada año.

EMPLOYMENT

3 Persons employed in major divisions of economic activity
Personnes occupées dans les principales branches d'activité économique
Personas ocupadas en las divisiones mayores de la actividad económica

Albanie [1]

(ISIC — CITI — CIIU 1958)

Number of employees — Nombre de salariés — Número de asalariados

(Thousands — *Milliers* — Millares)

Date / Date / Fecha	Total [2]	Agriculture, forestry, fishing [2] / Agriculture, sylviculture, pêche [2] / Agricultura, silvicultura, pesca [2]	Mining, quarrying, manufacturing [3] / Industries extractives, industries manufacturières [3] / Minas, canteras, industrias manufactureras [3]	Construction / Construction / Construcción	Commerce [4] / Commerce [4] / Comercio [4]	Transport, communication / Transports, communications / Transportes, comunicaciones	Services / Services / Servicios	Others / Autres / Otros
1965	268.4	52.7	83.3	38.7	29.3	11.8	48.4	4.1
1966	285.3	59.3	91.7	38.3	30.5	11.6	50.8	4.5
1967	312.4	64.4	105.3	40.1	32.6	12.0	51.7	6.3
1968	345.2	71.1	120.7	42.2	35.4	13.2	54.9	7.7
1969	369.1	72.7	128.9	48.0	37.2	13.9	62.4	6.1
1970	392.3	75.7	137.1	48.6	39.7	14.9	68.4	7.7
1971	418.6	80.0	142.6	50.5	40.5	18.0	79.2	7.8

[1] Socialised sector. [2] Excl. agricultural co-operatives (about 427,000 persons employed in 1967). [3] Incl. gas and electricity. [4] Incl. storage.

[1] *Secteur socialisé.* [2] *Non compris les coopératives agricoles (environ 427 000 personnes employées en 1967).* [3] *Y compris le gaz et l'électricité.* [4] *Y compris les entrepôts.*

[1] Sector socializado. [2] Excl. las cooperativas agrícolas (alrededor de 427 000 personas empleadas en 1967). [3] Incl. el gas y la electricidad. [4] Incl. el almacenaje.

Austria

Civilian labour force employed *(Labour force sample surveys)*
Main-d'œuvre civile occupée *(Enquêtes par sondage sur la main-d'œuvre)*
Fuerza trabajadora civil ocupada *(Encuestas por muestra sobre la fuerza trabajadora)*

(Thousands — *Milliers* — Millares)

Date [1] / Date [1] / Fecha [1]	Total	1 — Agriculture, forestry, fishing / Agriculture, sylviculture, pêche / Agricultura, silvicultura, pesca	2 — Mining, quarrying / Industries extractives / Minas, canteras	3 — Manufacturing / Industries manufacturières / Industrias manufactureras	4 — Electricity, gas, water / Electricité, gaz, eau / Electricidad, gas, agua	5 — Construction / Construction / Construcción	6 — Trade, restaurants and hotels / Commerce, restaurants et hôtels / Comercio, restaurantes y hoteles	7 — Transport, storage, communication / Transports, entrepôts, communications / Transportes, almacenaje, comunicaciones	8 — Financing, insurance, real estate, business services / Banques, assurances, aff. imm., serv. aux entreprises / Bancos, seguros, bienes inm., serv. para empresas	9 — Community, social, and pers. services / Services à collectivité, services sociaux et pers. / Servicios comunales, sociales y personales	0 — Others / Autres / Otros
1969	3 017	577	33	882	32	257	435	192	86	500	23
1970	3 002	577	32	885	33	258	424	188	92	485	28
1971	3 001	525	30	875	33	264	449	183	108	494	40
1972	3 019	495	32	903	35	269	470	190	120	488	17
1973	3 042	487	28	890	36	263	469	197	145	471	56
1974	3 023	392	24	916	32	264	490	202	160	494	49

[1] Sep. of each year.   [1] *Sept. de chaque année.*   [1] Sept. de cada año.

3

Persons employed in major divisions of economic activity
Personnes occupées dans les principales branches d'activité économique
Personas ocupadas en las divisiones mayores de la actividad económica

Belgique

Civilian labour force employed *(Estimates based on compulsory social insurance statistics)* [1]
Main-d'œuvre civile occupée *(Evaluations fondées sur les statistiques d'assurances sociales obligatoires)* [1]
Fuerza trabajadora civil ocupada *(Estimaciones basadas en las estadísticas del seguro social obligatorio)* [1]

(Thousands — *Milliers* — Millares)

Date [2] / *Date* [2] / Fecha [2]	Total	Agriculture, forestry, fishing / *Agriculture, sylviculture, pêche* / Agricultura, silvicultura, pesca	Mining, quarrying / *Industries extractives* / Minas, canteras	Manufacturing / *Industries manufacturières* / Industrias manufactureras	Electricity, gas, water / *Electricité, gaz, eau* / Electricidad, gas, agua	Construction / *Construction* / Construcción	Trade, restaurants and hotels / *Commerce, restaurants et hôtels* / Comercio, restaurantes y hoteles	Transport, storage, communication / *Transports, entrepôts, communications* / Transportes, almacenaje, comunicaciones	Financing, insur., real est., business serv. / *Banques, assur., aff. imm., serv. aux entreprises* / Bancos, seguros, bienes inm., serv. para empresas	Community, social, and pers. services / *Services à collectivité, serv. sociaux et pers.* / Servicios comunales, sociales y personales
1970	3 665.0	173.8	51.9	1 199.0	31.4	302.2	678.4	237.6	185.1	805.6
1971	3 701.5	161.7	49.0	1 197.4	32.7	302.3	683.8	246.1	198.9	829.6
1972	3 695.5	151.0	46.8	1 179.8	32.7	290.4	685.6	252.3	202.6	854.3
1973	3 744.5	144.2	42.1	1 190.3	32.9	288.3	693.8	260.8	209.6	882.5
1974	3 798.7	139.6	38.3	1 199.3	32.9	295.0	698.2	266.3	221.6	907.5

[1] Incl. persons working abroad (about 52,100 in 1974, of which 36,800 in manufacturing). [2] June of each year.

[1] *Y compris les travailleurs à l'étranger (environ 52 100 en 1974, dont 36 800 dans les industries manufacturières).* [2] *Juin de chaque année.*

[1] Incl. las personas que trabajan en el extranjero (alrededor de 52 100 en 1974, de las cuales 36 800 en las industrias manufactureras). [2] Junio de cada año.

Bulgarie [1]

Number of employees *(Statistics of establishments)*
Nombre de salariés *(Statistiques d'établissements)*
Número de asalariados *(Estadísticas de establecimientos)*

(ISIC — CITI — CIIU 1958)

(Thousands — *Milliers* — Millares)

Date / *Date* / Fecha	Total	Agriculture, forestry [2] / *Agriculture, sylviculture* [2] / Agricultura, silvicultura [2]	Mining, quarrying, manufacturing [3] / *Industries extractives, industries manufacturières* [3] / Minas, canteras, industrias manufactureras [3]	Construction / *Construction* / Construcción	Commerce / *Commerce* / Comercio	Transport, storage, communication / *Transports, entrepôts, communications* / Transportes, almacenaje, comunicaciones	Services [4] / *Services* [4] / Servicios [4]	Others / *Autres* / Otros
1965	2 196.6	214.0	953.9	224.5	200.5	180.5	402.9	20.2
1966	2 404.0	286.5	1 043.2	251.1	190.6	189.7	421.7	21.2
1967	2 516.7	285.7	1 095.6	275.5	201.7	198.1	438.3	21.8
1968	2 559.5	275.7	1 100.2	280.1	211.7	210.4	459.2	22.2
1969	2 648.4	286.2	1 132.1	284.3	221.0	214.1	487.4	23.3
1970	2 748.7	292.9	1 156.0	303.8	232.1	226.6	512.5	24.8
1971	2 864.7	311.1	1 183.6	311.1	267.9	234.7	529.9	26.4
1972	2 993.4	358.2	1 210.3	315.3	283.1	240.3	558.2	28.0
1973	3 273.1	569.6	1 242.8	315.1	285.7	248.9	580.8	30.2
1974*	3 415.4	634.5	1 279.9	323.2	291.5	260.3	594.1	31.9

[1] Socialised sector. [2] State agricultural undertakings. [3] Incl. electricity. [4] Incl. water supply.

[1] *Secteur socialisé.* [2] *Entreprises agricoles d'Etat.* [3] *Y compris l'électricité.* [4] *Y compris la distribution de l'eau.*

[1] Sector socializado. [2] Empresas agrícolas de Estado. [3] Incl. la electricidad. [4] Incl. abastecimiento de agua.

3 Persons employed in major divisions of economic activity
Personnes occupées dans les principales branches d'activité économique
Personas ocupadas en las divisiones mayores de la actividad económica

Czechoslovakia

Civilian labour force employed *(Statistics of establishments)* [1]
Main-d'œuvre civile occupée *(Statistiques d'établissements)* [1]
Fuerza trabajadora civil ocupada *(Estadísticas de establecimientos)* [1]

(Thousands — *Milliers* — Millares)

Date / *Date* / Fecha	Total	1 — Agriculture, forestry, fishing / *Agriculture, sylviculture, pêche* / Agricultura, silvicultura, pesca	2; 3; 4 × — Mining, quarrying, manufacturing [2] / *Industries extractives, industries manufacturières* [2] / Minas, canteras, industrias manufactureras [2]	5 — Construction / *Construction* / Construcción	6 — Trade, restaurants and hotels / *Commerce, restaurants et hôtels* / Comercio, restaurantes y hoteles	7 — Transport, storage, communication / *Transports, entrepôts, communications* / Transportes, almacenaje, comunicaciones	8 — Financing, insurance, real estate, business services / *Banques, assurances, aff. imm., serv. aux entreprises* / Bancos, seguros, bienes inm., serv. para empresas	4 × ; 9 — Community, social, and pers. services [3] / *Services à collectivité, services sociaux et pers.* [3] / Servicios comunales, sociales y personales [3]	0 — Others / *Autres* / Otros
1965	6 477	1 366	2 480	521	547	418	34	1 073	38
1966	6 608	1 360	2 549	541	550	427	34	1 108	39
1967	6 686	1 333	2 570	557	555	436	33	1 163	39
1968	6 794	1 310	2 605	576	590	445	34	1 192	42
1969	6 919	1 296	2 626	585	624	470	34	1 242	42
1970	7 033	1 287	2 670	605	637	478	35	1 272	49
1971	7 115	1 270	2 694	624	668	479	36	1 295	49
1972	7 179	1 196	2 758	639	700	479	36	1 315	56
1973	7 254	1 165	2 799	659	724	483	37	1 334	53
1974	7 358	1 156	2 828	675	744	486	36	1 368	65

[1] Excl. family workers and apprentices. [2] Incl. gas and electricity. [3] Incl. water supply.

[1] *Non compris les travailleurs familiaux et les apprentis.* [2] *Y compris le gaz et l'électricité.* [3] *Y compris la distribution de l'eau.*

[1] Excl. los trabajadores familiares y los aprendices. [2] Incl. el gas y la electricidad. [3] Incl. abastecimientos de agua.

Denmark

Civilian labour force employed *(Labour force sample surveys)* [1]
Main-d'œuvre civile occupée *(Enquêtes par sondage sur la main-d'œuvre)* [1]
Fuerza trabajadora civil ocupada *(Encuestas por muestra sobre la fuerza trabajadora)* [1]

(Thousands — *Milliers* — Millares)

Date [2] / *Date* [2] / Fecha [2]	Total	1 — Agriculture, forestry, fishing / *Agriculture, sylviculture, pêche* / Agricultura, silvicultura, pesca	2 — Mining, quarrying / *Industries extractives* / Minas, canteras	3 — Manufacturing / *Industries manufacturières* / Industrias manufactureras	4 — Electricity, gas, water / *Electricité, gaz, eau* / Electricidad, gas, agua	5 — Construction / *Construction* / Construcción	6 — Trade, restaurants and hotels / *Commerce, restaurants et hôtels* / Comercio, restaurantes y hoteles	7 — Transport, storage, communication / *Transports, entrepôts, communications* / Transportes, almacenaje, comunicaciones	8 — Financing, insurance, real estate, business services / *Banques, assurances, aff. imm., serv. aux entreprises* / Bancos, seguros, bienes inm., serv. para empresas	9 — Community, social, and pers. services / *Services à collectivité, services sociaux et pers.* / Servicios comunales, sociales y personales	0 — Others / *Autres* / Otros
1972	2 355.4	229.7	2.6	586.9	14.3	202.6	352.2	159.0	138.7	658.1	11.3
1973	2 385.2	227.3	2.4	588.7	13.4	201.3	360.8	165.7	140.4	673.2	12.0
1974 [3]	2 354.6	226.8	2.5	555.7	14.2	188.0	344.4	166.9	144.3	698.1	13.7

[1] Persons aged 15 to 74 years. [2] Nov. of each year. [3] Oct.

[1] *Personnes âgées de 15 à 74 ans.* [2] *Nov. de chaque année.* [3] *Oct.*

[1] Personas de 15 a 74 años. [2] Nov. de cada año. [3] Oct.

3 Persons employed in major divisions of economic activity
Personnes occupées dans les principales branches d'activité économique
Personas ocupadas en las divisiones mayores de la actividad económica

España [1]

Civilian labour force employed *(Official estimates)*
Main-d'œuvre civile occupée *(Evaluations officielles)*
Fuerza trabajadora civil ocupada *(Estimaciones oficiales)*

(Thousands — *Milliers* — Millares)

		1	2	3	4	5	6 ×	7	6 ×; 8; 9 ×	
Date [2] *Date [2]* Fecha [2]	Total	Agriculture, forestry, fishing *Agriculture, sylviculture, pêche* Agricultura, silvicultura, pesca	Mining, quarrying *Industries extractives* Minas, canteras	Manufacturing [3] *Industries manufacturières [3]* Industrias manufactureras [3]	Electricity, gas, water *Electricité, gaz, eau* Electricidad, gas, agua	Construction *Construction* Construcción	Trade [4] *Commerce [4]* Comercio [4]	Transport, storage, communication *Transports, entrepôts, communications* Transportes, almacenaje, comunicaciones	Financing, insurance, real estate, business services *Banques, assurances, aff. imm., serv. aux entreprises* Bancos, seguros, bienes inm., serv. para empresas	Community, social, and pers. services [5] *Services à collectivité, services sociaux et pers. [5]* Servicios comunales, sociales y personales [5]
1965	11 993.9	3 968.8	147.0	3 074.5	84.6	933.9	1 017.2	588.5	2 179.4	
1966	12 118.0	3 910.5	136.1	3 136.0	85.8	983.5	1 057.8	601.4	2 206.9	
1967	12 173.5	3 867.8	128.9	3 144.4	86.8	999.9	1 110.4	611.9	2 223.4	
1968	12 280.0	3 849.9	124.1	3 172.7	88.2	1 016.9	1 122.7	624.3	2 281.2	
1969	12 410.0	3 754.3	120.1	3 285.8	89.1	1 049.3	1 149.7	633.8	2 327.9	
1970	12 539.3	3 662.3	117.3	3 374.9	90.9	1 042.0	1 206.5	642.3	2 403.1	
1971	12 608.7	3 552.9	112.9	3 433.8	91.6	1 026.1	1 252.8	658.2	2 480.4	
1972	12 781.5	3 490.1	111.8	3 489.8	92.1	1 077.3	1 285.6	669.0	2 565.8	
1973	12 986.2	3 405.8	108.1	3 540.6	92.6	1 136.8	1 355.0	676.0	2 671.3	
1974	12 864.8	3 042.2	98.0	3 376.9	81.4	1 266.3	1 738.6	689.7	2 571.7	

[1] Excl. Ceuta and Melilla. [2] Fourth quarter of each year. [3] Incl. repair services. [4] Excl. restaurants and hotels. [5] Excl. repair services. Incl. restaurants and hotels.

[1] *Non compris Ceuta et Melilla.* [2] *Quatrième trimestre de chaque année.* [3] *Y compris les services de réparation.* [4] *Non compris les restaurants et les hôtels.* [5] *Non compris les services de réparation. Y compris les restaurants et les hôtels.*

[1] Excl. Ceuta y Melilla. [2] Cuarto trimestre de cada año. [3] Incl. servicios de reparación. [4] Excl. los restaurantes y los hoteles. [5] Excl. los servicios de reparación. Incl. los restaurantes y los hoteles.

Finland

Civilian labour force employed *(Labour force sample surveys)* [1]
Main-d'œuvre civile occupée *(Enquêtes par sondage sur la main-d'œuvre)* [1]
Fuerza trabajadora civil ocupada *(Encuestas por muestra sobre la fuerza trabajadora)* [1]

(Thousands — *Milliers* — Millares)

		1	2; 3; 4	5	6	7	8	9
Date *Date* Fecha	Total	Agriculture, forestry, fishing *Agriculture, sylviculture, pêche* Agricultura, silvicultura, pesca	Mining, quarrying, manufacturing [2] *Industries extractives, industries manufacturières [2]* Minas, canteras, industrias manufactureras [2]	Construction *Construction* Construcción	Trade, restaurants and hotels *Commerce, restaurants et hôtels* Comercio, restaurantes y hoteles	Transport, storage, communication *Transports, entrepôts, communications* Transportes, almacenaje, comunicaciones	Financing, insurance, real estate, business services *Banques, assurances, aff. imm., serv. aux entreprises* Bancos, seguros, bienes inm., serv. para empresas	Community, social, and pers. services *Services à collectivité, services sociaux et pers.* Servicios comunales, sociales y personales
1970	2 126	481	563	187	312	149	.	.
1971	2 123	448	560	184	314	144	74	399
1972	2 118	399	570	180	320	150	79	419
1973	2 164	369	584	185	341	151	88	446
1974	2 229	362	613	187	350	154	99	464

[1] Persons aged 15 to 74 years. [2] Incl. electricity, gas and water.

[1] *Personnes âgées de 15 à 74 ans.* [2] *Y compris l'électricité, le gaz et l'eau.*

[1] Personas de 15 a 74 años. [2] Incl. la electricidad, el gas y el agua.

EMPLOYMENT

3 Persons employed in major divisions of economic activity
Personnes occupées dans les principales branches d'activité économique
Personas ocupadas en las divisiones mayores de la actividad económica

France

Civilian labour force employed *(Official estimates)*
Main-d'œuvre civile occupée *(Evaluations officielles)*
Fuerza trabajadora civil ocupada *(Estimaciones oficiales)*

(Thousands — *Milliers* — Millares)

Date / *Date* / Fecha	Total	1 Agriculture, forestry, fishing / *Agriculture, sylviculture, pêche* / Agricultura, silvicultura, pesca	2 Mining, quarrying / *Industries extractives* / Minas, canteras	3 Manufacturing / *Industries manufacturières* / Industrias manufactureras	4 Electricity, gas, water / *Electricité, gaz, eau* / Electricidad, gas, agua	5 Construction / *Construction* / Construcción	6 Trade, restaurants and hotels / *Commerce, restaurants et hôtels* / Comercio, restaurantes y hoteles	7 Transport, storage, communication / *Transports, entrepôts, communications* / Transportes, almacenaje, comunicaciones	8 Financing, insurance, real estate, business services / *Banques, assurances, aff. imm., serv. aux entreprises* / Bancos, seguros, bienes inm., serv. para empresas	9 Community, social, and pers. services / *Services à collectivité, services sociaux et pers.* / Servicios comunales, sociales y personales
1965	19 544	3 468	287	5 405	154	1 846	2 870	1 175	713	3 626
1966	19 684	3 340	276	5 433	156	1 886	2 932	1 184	753	3 724
1967	19 753	3 216	261	5 405	159	1 903	2 988	1 194	801	3 826
1968	19 749	3 098	242	5 312	162	1 924	3 020	1 204	855	3 932
1969	20 094	3 024	245	5 547	164	1 984	3 150	1 099	899	3 982
1970	20 394	2 907	232	5 670	165	1 999	3 233	1 113	954	4 121
1971	20 510	2 791	219	5 733	165	1 975	3 283	1 112	1 002	4 230
1972	20 662	2 673	209	5 782	167	1 968	3 343	1 115	1 111	4 294
1973	20 939	2 559	197	5 892	170	1 981	3 451	1 131	1 115	4 443
1974*	21 165	2 452	185	5 961	174	1 981	3 502	1 162	1 189	4 559

German Dem. Rep. △

Number of employees — Nombre de salariés — Número de asalariados

(Thousands — *Milliers* — Millares)

Date / *Date* / Fecha	Total	Agriculture, forestry / *Agriculture, sylviculture* / Agricultura, silvicultura	Mining, quarrying, manufacturing [1] / *Industries extractives, industries manufacturières* [1] / Minas, canteras, industrias manufactureras [1]	Construction / *Construction* / Construcción	Commerce / *Commerce* / Comercio	Transport, storage, communication / *Transports, entrepôts, communications* / Transportes, almacenaje, comunicaciones	Others / *Autres* / Otros
1965	6 507.9	305.5	3 085.8	401.0	824.1	563.9	1 327.7
1966	6 573.0	297.6	3 116.7	402.0	828.6	564.4	1 363.9
1967	6 663.5	287.3	3 158.2	414.8	839.8	565.1	1 398.2
1968	6 736.2	279.3	3 166.6	455.3	838.4	562.8	1 433.6
1969	6 805.0	277.1	3 179.6	487.2	826.4	575.8	1 458.9
1970	6 874.4	281.0	3 170.7	505.8	824.9	592.8	1 499.3
1971	6 963.1	277.0	3 212.2	513.5	806.0	599.7	1 554.5
1972	7 136.6	266.9	3 343.1	524.1	812.1	602.2	1 588.3
1973	7 238.7	276.1	3 373.5	528.9	813.7	606.6	1 640.0
1974*	7 324.3	281.9	3 378.5	536.9	829.3	615.3	1 682.5

[1] Incl. electricity and water.   [1] *Y compris l'électricité et l'eau.*   [1] Incl. electricidad y agua.

3 Persons employed in major divisions of economic activity
Personnes occupées dans les principales branches d'activité économique
Personas ocupadas en las divisiones mayores de la actividad económica

Germany, Fed. Rep. of △

Civilian labour force employed *(Official estimates)*
Main-d'œuvre civile occupée *(Evaluations officielles)*
Fuerza trabajadora civil ocupada *(Estimaciones oficiales)*

(Thousands — *Milliers* — Millares)

Date / Date / Fecha	Total	1 Agriculture, forestry, fishing *Agriculture, sylviculture, pêche* Agricultura, silvicultura, pesca	2 Mining, quarrying *Industries extractives* Minas, canteras	3; 9 × Manufacturing [1] *Industries manufacturières [1]* Industrias manufactureras [1]	4 Electricity, gas, water *Electricité, gaz, eau* Electricidad, gas, agua	5 Construction *Construction* Construcción	6 Trade, restaurants and hotels *Commerce, restaurants et hôtels* Comercio, restaurantes y hoteles	7 Transport, storage, communication *Transports, entrepôts, communications* Transportes, almacenaje, comunicaciones	8 Financing, insurance, real estate, business services *Banques, assurances, aff. imm., serv. aux entreprises* Bancos, seguros, bienes inm., serv. para empresas	9 × Community, social, and pers. services [2] *Services à collectivité, services sociaux et pers. [2]* Servicios comunales, sociales y personales [2]
1965	26 418	2 876	450	10 392	256	2 206	3 838	1 580	945	3 875
1966	26 320	2 790	418	10 344	236	2 174	3 911	1 552	969	3 926
1967	25 461	2 638	382	9 846	216	1 993	3 887	1 519	1 014	3 966
1968	25 491	2 523	353	9 933	200	2 034	3 852	1 491	1 038	4 067
1969	25 871	2 395	340	10 361	193	2 066	3 831	1 476	1 060	4 149
1970	26 169	2 262	336	10 607	191	2 066	3 844	1 480	1 100	4 283
1971	26 225	2 144	335	10 530	191	2 087	3 847	1 534	1 169	4 388
1972	26 126	2 038	326	10 365	184	2 091	3 932	1 571	1 203	4 416
1973	26 202	1 954	320	10 423	182	2 058	3 941	1 589	1 219	4 516
1974 *	25 705	1 932	317	10 199	179	1 853	3 851	1 592	1 237	4 545

[1] Incl. repair of motor vehicles. [2] Excl. repair of motor vehicles.

[1] *Y compris la réparation des véhicules à moteur.* [2] *Non compris la réparation des véhicules à moteur.*

[1] Incl. la reparación de vehículos de motor. [2] Excl. la reparación de vehículos de motor.

Hongrie

Civilian labour force employed *(Statistics of establishments)*
Main-d'œuvre civile occupée *(Statistiques d'établissements)*
Fuerza trabajadora civil ocupada *(Estadísticas de establecimientos)*

(ISIC — CITI — CIIU 1958)

(Thousands — *Milliers* — Millares)

Date / Date / Fecha	Total	Agriculture, forestry *Agriculture, sylviculture* Agricultura, silvicultura	Mining, quarrying, manufacturing [1] *Industries extractives, industries manufacturières [1]* Minas, canteras, industrias manufactureras [1]	Construction *Construction* Construcción	Commerce *Commerce* Comercio	Transport, communication *Transports, communications* Transportes, comunicaciones	Others [2] *Autres [2]* Otros [2]
1965	4 657.4	1 365.2	1 599.3	298.1	340.5	320.4	733.9
1966	4 687.9	1 346.2	1 615.9	321.3	343.5	321.9	739.1
1967	4 738.8	1 342.1	1 651.0	330.7	350.9	324.5	739.6
1968	4 827.2	1 332.6	1 723.3	333.8	369.1	330.8	737.6
1969	4 933.6	1 314.1	1 795.4	346.9	392.0	338.2	747.0
1970	4 995.3	1 290.6	1 812.9	373.3	409.9	344.2	764.4
1971	5 024.4	1 274.9	1 776.1	394.8	423.9	372.8	781.9
1972	5 049.9	1 247.3	1 786.8	406.2	429.1	379.6	800.9
1973	5 067.4	1 207.8	1 806.5	411.0	436.5	383.0	822.6
1974 *	5 086.8	1 171.4	1 819.6	417.6	447.8	386.1	844.3

[1] Incl. electricity and water. [2] Incl. sanitary services, gas and services.

[1] *Y compris l'électricité et l'eau.* [2] *Y compris les services sanitaires, le gaz et les services.*

[1] Incl. electricidad y agua. [2] Incl. los servicios sanitarios, el gas y los servicios.

EMPLOYMENT

3 Persons employed in major divisions of economic activity
Personnes occupées dans les principales branches d'activité économique
Personas ocupadas en las divisiones mayores de la actividad económica

Iceland

Civilian labour force employed *(Statistics of compulsory social insurance)*
Main-d'œuvre civile occupée *(Statistiques d'assurances sociales obligatoires)*
Fuerza trabajadora civil ocupada *(Estadísticas del seguro social obligatorio)*

(Thousands — *Milliers* — Millares)

Date / *Date* / Fecha	Total	1 Agriculture, forestry, fishing / *Agriculture, sylviculture, pêche* / Agricultura, silvicultura, pesca	2; 3 Mining, quarrying, manufacturing / *Industries extractives, industries manufacturières* / Minas, canteras, industrias manufactureras	4 Electricity, gas, water / *Electricité, gaz, eau* / Electricidad, gas, agua	5 Construction / *Construction* / Construcción	6 Trade, restaurants and hotels / *Commerce, restaurants et hôtels* / Comercio, restaurantes y hoteles	7 Transport, storage, communication / *Transports, entrepôts, communications* / Transportes, almacenaje, comunicaciones	8 Financing, insurance, real estate, business services / *Banques, assurances, aff. imm., serv. aux entreprises* / Bancos, seguros, bienes inm., serv. para empresas	9 Community, social and pers. services / *Services à collectivité, services sociaux et pers.* / Servicios comunales, sociales y personales	0 Others / *Autres* / Otros
1965	78.5	17.0	20.1	0.4	9.0	10.8	7.2	1.8	11.2	1.0
1966	80.1	17.2	19.8	0.4	9.4	11.0	7.3	2.0	12.0	1.0
1967	80.1	17.3	18.4	0.4	10.4	11.2	7.2	2.1	12.5	0.6
1968	80.4	17.4	17.9	0.4	10.6	10.9	7.0	2.2	13.4	0.6
1969	80.3	17.4	19.2	0.4	8.7	10.6	6.9	2.3	14.1	0.7
1970	84.1	18.0	20.7	0.4	8.7	11.0	6.9	2.4	15.3	0.7
1971	87.9	17.4	22.0	0.5	9.6	11.8	7.3	2.5	16.1	0.7
1972	90.2	17.0	22.6	0.5	9.7	12.2	7.7	2.7	17.1	0.7
1973	92.6	16.9	22.6	0.7	10.8	12.7	7.7	2.8	17.7	0.7

Ireland

Civilian labour force employed *(Official estimates)*
Main-d'œuvre civile occupée *(Evaluations officielles)*
Fuerza trabajadora civil ocupada *(Estimaciones oficiales)*

(Thousands — *Milliers* — Millares)

Date[1] / *Date*[1] / Fecha[1]	Total	1 Agriculture, forestry, fishing / *Agriculture, sylviculture, pêche* / Agricultura, silvicultura, pesca	2 Mining, quarrying / *Industries extractives* / Minas, canteras	3 Manufacturing / *Industries manufacturières* / Industrias manufactureras	4 Electricity, gas, water / *Electricité, gaz, eau* / Electricidad, gas, agua	5 Construction / *Construction* / Construcción	6 Trade, restaurants and hotels / *Commerce, restaurants et hôtels* / Comercio, restaurantes y hoteles	7 Transport, storage, communication / *Transports, entrepôts, communications* / Transportes, almacenaje, comunicaciones	8 Financing, insurance, real estate, business services / *Banques, assurances, aff. imm., serv. aux entreprises* / Bancos, seguros, bienes inm., serv. para empresas	9 Community, social, and pers. services / *Services à collectivité, services sociaux et pers.* / Servicios comunales, sociales y personales	0 Others / *Autres* / Otros
1965	1 061	340	10	197	12	77	168	57	17	179	4
1966	1 058	334	9	198	12	74	168	57	18	183	5
1967	1 052	320	10	200	12	75	169	58	20	184	4
1968	1 055	310	10	204	13	78	169	59	21	187	4
1969	1 058	298	10	211	13	81	171	59	22	189	4
1970	1 045	283	10	213	13	76	171	60	23	193	3
1971	1 047	273	10	214	14	85	171	60	24	193	3
1972	1 037	267	10	212	14	78	171	61	25	196	3
1973	1 041	260	10	217	14	79	172	61	26	199	3
1974	1 047	254	10	222	14	80	172	62	27	203	3

[1] April of each year.　　　[1] *Avril de chaque année.*　　　[1] Abril de cada año.

3 Persons employed in major divisions of economic activity
Personnes occupées dans les principales branches d'activité économique
Personas ocupadas en las divisiones mayores de la actividad económica

Italie

Civilian labour force employed *(Labour force sample surveys)* [1]
Main-d'œuvre civile occupée *(Enquêtes par sondage sur la main-d'œuvre)* [1]
Fuerza trabajadora civil ocupada *(Encuestas por muestra sobre la fuerza trabajadora)* [1]

(ISIC — CITI — CIIU 1958) (Thousands — *Milliers* — Millares)

Date / *Date* / Fecha	Total	Agriculture, forestry, fishing / *Agriculture, sylviculture, pêche* / Agricultura, silvicultura, pesca	Mining, quarrying [2] / *Industries extractives* [2] / Minas, canteras [2]	Manufacturing / *Industries manufacturières* / Industrias manufactureras	Construction / *Construction* / Construcción	Commerce, services / *Commerce, services* / Comercio, servicios	Transport, storage, communication / *Transports, entrepôts, communications* / Transportes, almacenaje, comunicaciones
1965	19 003	4 898	280	5 435	1 944	5 448	998
1966	18 637	4 589	279	5 380	1 873	5 513	1 003
1967	18 846	4 480	271	5 517	1 904	5 679	995
1968	18 800	4 173	288	5 613	1 896	5 862	968
1969	18 611	3 951	302	5 703	1 950	5 725	980
1970	18 693	3 613	292	5 868	1 957	5 974	989
1971	18 645	3 588	287	5 913	1 954	5 916	987
1972	18 331	3 298	310	5 831	1 895	5 985	1 012
1973	18 500	3 192	318	5 897	1 836	6 235	1 022
1974	18 898	3 111	312	6 104	1 840	6 478	1 053

[1] Persons aged 14 years and over. [2] Incl. electricity, gas and water.

[1] *Personnes âgées de 14 ans et plus.* [2] *Y compris l'électricité, le gaz et l'eau.*

[1] Personas de 14 años y más. [2] Incl. la electricidad, el gas y el agua.

Malta

Civilian labour force employed *(Statistics of establishments)* [1]
Main-d'œuvre civile occupée *(Statistiques d'établissements)* [1]
Fuerza trabajadora civil ocupada *(Estadísticas de establecimientos)* [1]

(ISIC — CITI — CIIU 1958) (Thousands — *Milliers* — Millares)

Date [2] / *Date* [2] / Fecha [2]	Total	Agriculture, forestry, fishing / *Agriculture, sylviculture, pêche* / Agricultura, silvicultura, pesca	Mining, quarrying / *Industries extractives* / Minas, canteras	Manufacturing / *Industries manufacturières* / Industrias manufactureras	Construction / *Construction* / Construcción	Electricity, gas, water / *Electricité, gaz, eau* / Electricidad, gas, agua	Commerce / *Commerce* / Comercio	Transport, storage, communication / *Transports, entrepôts, communications* / Transportes, almacenaje, comunicaciones	Services / *Services* / Servicios
1964	84.1	7.4	0.6	17.4	5.7	0.7	12.8	4.3	35.2
1965	85.4	7.1	0.5	18.1	6.9	0.7	13.0	4.1	35.0
1966	88.3	7.0	0.5	18.9	9.2	0.8	12.8	4.0	35.1
1967	90.9	6.9	0.6	19.7	9.7	0.8	12.8	4.0	36.4
1968	93.5	6.5	0.6	20.3	10.0	0.9	13.3	4.3	37.5
1969	98.4	6.3	0.6	22.8	11.8	0.9	13.7	4.5	37.9
1970	99.5	5.9	0.6	24.8	12.6	0.9	13.5	4.5	37.5
1971	101.3	6.2	0.5	25.5	10.5	1.0	14.2	4.6	38.9
1972	98.9	6.4	0.5	27.0	6.6	0.9	13.7	4.5	39.1
1973 *	101.6	6.8	0.5	30.8	3.9	1.1	13.3	4.4	40.8

[1] Excl. family workers. [2] Nov. of each year. 1965-71: Dec.

[1] *Non compris les travailleurs familiaux.* [2] *Nov. de chaque année. 1965-1971: déc.*

[1] Excl. los trabajadores familiares. [2] Nov. de cada año. 1965-1971: dic.

EMPLOYMENT

3 Persons employed in major divisions of economic activity
Personnes occupées dans les principales branches d'activité économique
Personas ocupadas en las divisiones mayores de la actividad económica

Norway

Civilian labour force employed *(Labour force sample surveys)* [1]
Main-d'œuvre civile occupée *(Enquêtes par sondage sur la main-d'œuvre)* [1]
Fuerza trabajadora civil ocupada *(Encuestas por muestra sobre la fuerza trabajadora)* [1]

(Thousands — *Milliers* — Millares)

Date / Date / Fecha	Total	1 Agriculture, forestry, fishing / Agriculture, sylviculture, pêche / Agricultura, silvicultura, pesca	2 Mining, quarrying / Industries extractives / Minas, canteras	3 Manufacturing / Industries manufacturières / Industrias manufactureras	4 Electricity, gas, water / Electricité, gaz, eau / Electricidad, gas, agua	5 Construction / Construction / Construcción	6 Trade, restaurants and hotels / Commerce, restaurants et hôtels / Comercio, restaurantes y hoteles	7 Transport, storage, communication / Transports, entrepôts, communications / Transportes, almacenaje, comunicaciones	8 Financing, insurance, real estate, business services / Banques, assurances, aff. imm., serv. aux entreprises / Bancos, seguros, bienes inm., serv. para empresas	9 Community, social, and pers. services / Services à collectivité, services sociaux et pers. / Servicios comunales, sociales y personales	0 Others / Autres / Otros
1965	1 117	33	7	344	14	108	180	136	47	248	—
1966	1 135	32	8	349	14	110	183	136	49	254	—
1967	1 151	29	7	349	15	113	189	136	52	261	—
1968	1 162	28	8	347	15	110	193	134	55	272	—
1969	1 190	27	8	354	15	114	198	132	58	284	—
1970	1 224	25	9	364	15	116	204	130	63	298	—
1971	.	.	.	.	.	.	.	.	.	.	.
1972	1 649	201	10	392	17	145	264	162	65	392	1
1973	1 654	189	12	389	17	142	270	163	66	405	1
1974	1 659	175	10	392	18	147	275	163	72	406	1

[1] Persons aged 16 to 74 years. 1965-70: compulsory health insurance statistics; employees only.

[1] *Personnes âgées de 16 à 74 ans. 1965-1970 : statistiques de l'assurance-maladie obligatoire ; salariés seulement.*

[1] Personas de 16 a 74 años. 1965-1970: estadísticas del seguro obligatorio de enfermedad; asalariados solamente.

Pays-Bas

Civilian labour force employed—Number of man-years *(Official estimates)* [1]
Main-d'œuvre civile occupée — Nombre d'années-homme *(Evaluations officielles)* [1]
Fuerza trabajadora civil ocupada — Número de años-hombre *(Estimaciones oficiales)* [1]

(Thousands — *Milliers* — Millares)

Date / Date / Fecha	Total	1 Agriculture, forestry, fishing / Agriculture, sylviculture, pêche / Agricultura, silvicultura, pesca	2 Mining, quarrying / Industries extractives / Minas, canteras	3 Manufacturing / Industries manufacturières / Industrias manufactureras	4 Electricity, gas, water / Electricité, gaz, eau / Electricidad, gas, agua	5 Construction / Construction / Construcción	6 Trade, restaurants and hotels / Commerce, restaurants et hôtels / Comercio, restaurantes y hoteles	7 Transport, storage, communication / Transports, entrepôts, communications / Transportes, almacenaje, comunicaciones	8 Financing, insurance real estate, business services / Banques, assurances, aff. imm., serv. aux entreprises / Bancos, seguros, bienes inm., serv. para empresas	9 Community, social, and pers. services / Services à collectivité, services sociaux et pers. / Servicios comunales, sociales y personales
1969	4 493	339	25	1 199	43	493	830	302	237	1 025
1970	4 554	329	21	1 203	43	505	827	305	258	1 063
1971	4 581	320	19	1 186	43	495	834	309	270	1 105
1972	4 538	315	16	1 146	44	473	827	305	276	1 136
1973 *	4 553	309	13	1 127	44	472	827	307	285	1 169
1974 *	4 550	304	10	1 118	44	453	824	306	293	1 198

[1] Excl. civil personnel employed by the Ministry of Defence.

[1] *Non compris le personnel civil employé par le ministère de la Défense.*

[1] Excl. el personal civil empleado por el Ministerio de la Defensa.

3

Persons employed in major divisions of economic activity
Personnes occupées dans les principales branches d'activité économique
Personas ocupadas en las divisiones mayores de la actividad económica

Pologne

Civilian labour force employed *(Statistics of establishments)*
Main-d'œuvre civile occupée *(Statistiques d'établissements)*
Fuerza trabajadora civil ocupada *(Estadísticas de establecimientos)*

(Thousands — *Milliers* — Millares)

		1	2	3	4	5	6	7	8	9	0
Date *Date* Fecha	Total	Agriculture, forestry, fishing *Agriculture, sylviculture, pêche* Agricultura, silvicultura, pesca	Mining, quarrying *Industries extractives* Minas, canteras	Manufac-turing *Industries manufactu-rières* Industrias manufac-tureras	Electricity, gas, water *Electricité, gaz, eau* Electri-cidad, gas, agua	Construc-tion *Construc-tion* Construc-ción	Trade, restaurants and hotels *Commerce, restaurants et hôtels* Comercio, restaurantes y hoteles	Transport, storage, communi-cation *Transports, entrepôts, communi-cations* Trans-portes, almacenaje, comunica-ciones	Financing, insurance, real estate, business services *Banques, assurances, aff. imm., serv. aux entreprises* Bancos, seguros, bienes inm., serv. para empresas	Com-munity, social, and pers. services *Services à collectivité, services sociaux et pers.* Servicios comunales, sociales y perso-nales	Others *Autres* Otros
1970	15 604	5 424	481	3 842	136	1 061	1 067	1 063	135	2 343	52
1971	15 955	5 381	487	3 979	136	1 118	1 058	1 097	142	2 492	65
1972	16 455	5 432	500	4 119	146	1 191	1 136	1 138	149	2 580	64
1973	16 940	5 451	503	4 255	154	1 314	1 197	1 156	159	2 681	70
1974	17 376	5 467	506	4 370	157	1 412	1 264	1 197	165	2 776	62

Roumanie

Civilian labour force employed *(Statistics of establishments)*
Main-d'œuvre civile occupée *(Statistiques d'établissements)*
Fuerza trabajadora civil ocupada *(Estadísticas de establecimientos)*

(ISIC — CITI — CIIU 1958)

(Thousands — *Milliers* — Millares)

Date *Date* Fecha	Total	Agriculture, forestry *Agriculture, sylviculture* Agricultura, silvicultura	Mining, quarrying, manufacturing [1] *Industries extractives, industries manufacturières [1]* Minas, canteras, industrias manufactureras [1]	Construction *Construction* Construcción	Commerce *Commerce* Comercio	Transport, storage, communication *Transports, entrepôts, communications* Transportes, almacenaje, comunicaciones	Services *Services* Servicios	Others *Autres* Otros
1965	9 684	5 495	1 863	609	386	349	885	97
1966	9 786	5 404	1 932	654	399	363	929	105
1967	9 854	5 312	1 975	701	410	376	972	108
1968	9 869	5 233	2 036	713	407	374	995	111
1969	9 895	5 070	2 161	731	425	389	1 001	118
1970	9 875	4 868	2 277	768	427	414	1 012	109
1971	9 939	4 623	2 457	801	469	429	1 046	114
1972	9 971	4 403	2 601	840	509	440	1 066	112
1973	10 021	4 229	2 798	826	516	455	1 080	117
1974	10 070	4 036	2 983	813	542	459	1 107	130

[1] Incl. electricity, gas, water and sanitary services.

[1] *Y compris l'électricité, le gaz l,'eau et les services sanitaires.*

[1] Incl. la electricidad, el gas, el agua y los servicios sanitarios.

3 **Persons employed in major divisions of economic activity**
Personnes occupées dans les principales branches d'activité économique
Personas ocupadas en las divisiones mayores de la actividad económica

Sweden

Civilian labour force employed *(Labour force sample surveys)* [1]
Main-d'œuvre civile occupée *(Enquêtes par sondage sur la main-d'œuvre)* [1]
Fuerza trabajadora civil ocupada *(Encuestas por muestra sobre la fuerza trabajadora)* [1]

(Thousands — *Milliers* — Millares)

Date / Date / Fecha	Total [2]	1 Agriculture, forestry, fishing / Agriculture, sylviculture, pêche / Agricultura, silvicultura, pesca	2 Mining, quarrying / Industries extractives / Minas, canteras	3 Manufacturing / Industries manufacturières / Industrias manufactureras	4 Electricity, gas, water / Electricité, gaz, eau / Electricidad, gas, agua	5 Construction / Construction / Construcción	6 Trade, restaurants and hotels / Commerce, restaurants et hôtels / Comercio, restaurantes y hoteles	7 Transport, storage, communication / Transports, entrepôts, communications / Transportes, almacenaje, comunicaciones	8 Financing, insurance, real estate, business services / Banques, assurances, aff. imm., serv. aux entreprises / Bancos, seguros, bienes inm., serv. para empresas	9 Community, social, and pers. services [2] / Services à collectivité, services sociaux et pers. [2] / Servicios comunales, sociales y personales [2]
1965	3 698	418	22	1 200	34	328	554	263	146	734
1966	3 733	373	19	1 165	36	336	584	279	178	762
1967	3 695	366	16	1 135	34	341	550	267	187	799
1968	3 737	340	22	1 139	37	339	541	280	188	851
1969	3 782	323	22	1 137	31	343	542	291	187	905
1970	3 854	314	21	1 064	24	371	557	266	192	1 046
1971	3 860	300	18	1 054	27	352	558	268	201	1 082
1972	3 862	287	19	1 046	26	331	546	268	206	1 134
1973	3 879	276	18	1 066	27	316	545	269	207	1 153
1974	3 962	264	20	1 121	31	294	560	271	212	1 191

[1] Persons aged 16 to 74 years.   [2] Incl. certain categories of military personnel.

[1] *Personnes âgées de 16 à 74 ans.*   [2] *Y compris certaines catégories de personnel militaire.*

[1] Personas de 16 a 74 años.   [2] Incl. ciertas categorías de personal militar.

3 Persons employed in major divisions of economic activity
Personnes occupées dans les principales branches d'activité économique
Personas ocupadas en las divisiones mayores de la actividad económica

United Kingdom

Civilian labour force employed *(Statistics of establishments)* [1]
Main-d'œuvre civile occupée *(Statistiques d'établissements)* [1]
Fuerza trabajadora civil ocupada *(Estadísticas de establecimientos)* [1]

(Thousands — *Milliers* — Millares)

		1	2	3	4	5	6 ×	7	8	6 × ; 9
Date [2] *Date [2]* Fecha [2]	Total	Agriculture, forestry, fishing *Agriculture, sylviculture, pêche* Agricultura, silvicultura, pesca	Mining, quarrying *Industries extractives* Minas, canteras	Manufac-turing *Industries manufactu-rières* Industrias manufac-tureras	Electricity, gas, water *Electricité, gaz, eau* Electricidad, gas, agua	Construction *Construction* Construcción	Trade *Commerce* Comercio	Transport, storage, communica-tion *Transports, entrepôts, communi-cations* Transportes, almacenaje, comunica-ciones	Financing, insurance, real estate, business services *Banques, assurances, aff. imm., serv. aux entreprises* Bancos, seguros, bienes inm., serv. para empresas	Community, social, and pers. services [3] *Services à collectivité, services sociaux et pers. [3]* Servicios comunales, sociales y perso-nales [3]
1965	25 324	846	628	9 133	418	1 913	3 505	1 702	664	6 512
1966	25 470	812	580	9 162	431	1 947	3 504	1 677	667	6 691
1967	25 081	786	555	8 988	433	1 842	3 333	1 682	678	6 783
1968	24 920	760	489	8 903	421	1 830	3 299	1 666	696	6 854
1969	24 961	730	444	9 035	405	1 790	3 248	1 635	724	6 948
1970	24 786	695	418	9 033	391	1 681	3 183	1 660	1 011	6 715
1971	24 032	736	397	8 179	377	1 593	3 089	1 639	1 025	6 999
1972	24 056	720	379	7 910	356	1 673	3 108	1 617	1 045	7 249
1973	24 641	722	363	7 956	344	1 823	3 204	1 598	1 109	7 521
1974 *	24 767	704	349	7 999	347	1 771	3 221	1 580	1 167	7 630

[1] Prior to 1971: National insurance statistics. [2] June of each year. [3] Incl. restaurants and hotels.

[1] *Avant 1971: statistiques de l'assurance nationale.* [2] *Juin de chaque année.* [3] *Y compris les restaurants et les hôtels.*

[1] Antes de 1971: estadísticas del Seguro Nacional. [2] Junio de cada año. [3] Incl. los restaurantes y los hoteles.

EMPLOYMENT

3 Persons employed in major divisions of economic activity
Personnes occupées dans les principales branches d'activité économique
Personas ocupadas en las divisiones mayores de la actividad económica

Yugoslavia [1]

Number of employees *(Statistics of establishments)*
Nombre de salariés *(Statistiques d'établissements)*
Número de asalariados *(Estadísticas de establecimientos)*

(Thousands — *Milliers* — Millares)

		1	2	3	4	5	6	7	8	9
Date [2] *Date* [2] Fecha [2]	Total	Agriculture, forestry, fishing *Agriculture, sylviculture, pêche* Agricultura, silvicultura, pesca	Mining, quarrying *Industries extractives* Minas, canteras	Manufac-turing *Industries manufactu-rières* Industrias manufac-tureras	Electricity, gas, water *Electricité, gaz, eau* Electricidad, gas, agua	Construction *Construction* Construcción	Trade, restaurants and hotels *Commerce, restaurants et hôtels* Comercio, restaurantes y hoteles	Transport, storage, communica-tion *Transports, entrepôts, communi-cations* Transportes, almacenaje, comunica-ciones	Financing, insurance, real estate, business services *Banques, assurances, aff. imm., serv. aux entreprises* Bancos, seguros, bienes inm., serv. para empresas	Community, social, and pers. services *Services à collectivité, services sociaux et pers.* Servicios comunales, sociales y perso-nales
1965	3 583	400	172	1 300	104	397	348	251	46	565
1966	3 491	371	168	1 273	103	372	349	246	45	564
1967	3 466	344	159	1 273	108	366	362	249	42	563
1968	3 487	319	156	1 266	113	384	374	255	42	578
1969	3 622	314	155	1 322	118	406	402	260	43	602
1970	3 765	308	156	1 376	129	424	433	269	45	625
1971	3 944	309	162	1 446	137	435	473	280	48	654
1972	4 115	312	166	1 522	142	440	507	292	52	682
1973	4 213	315	166	1 568	146	429	532	298	55	704
1974	4 423	325	174	1 654	153	453	562	306	61	735

[1] Socialised sector. [2] March and Sep. of each year.   [1] *Secteur socialisé.* [2] *Mars et sept. de chaque année.*   [1] Sector socializado. [2] Marzo y sept. de cada año.

3

Persons employed in major divisions of economic activity
Personnes occupées dans les principales branches d'activité économique
Personas ocupadas en las divisiones mayores de la actividad económica

OCEANIA — OCÉANIE — OCEANIA

Australia

Civilian labour force employed *(Labour force sample surveys)* [1]
Main-d'œuvre civile occupée *(Enquêtes par sondage sur la main-d'œuvre)* [1]
Fuerza trabajadora civil ocupada *(Encuestas por muestra sobre la fuerza trabajadora)* [1]

(Thousands — *Milliers* — Millares)

		1	2	3-4	5	6 ×	7	8	6 × ; 9
Date *Date* Fecha	Total	Agriculture, forestry, fishing *Agriculture, sylviculture, pêche* Agricultura, silvicultura, pesca	Mining, quarrying *Industries extractives* Minas, canteras	Manufac- turing [2] *Industries manufactu- rières* [2] Industrias manufac- tureras [2]	Construction *Construction* Construcción	Trade *Commerce* Comercio	Transport, storage, communi- cation *Transports, entrepôts, communi- cations* Transportes, almacenaje, comunica- ciones	Financing, insurance, real estate, business services [3] *Banques, assurances, aff. imm., serv. aux entreprises* [3] Bancos, seguros, bienes inm., serv. para empresas [3]	Community, social, and pers. services [4] *Services à collectivité, services sociaux et pers.* [4] Servicios comunales, sociales y perso- nales [4]
1965	4 628	458	53	1 401	394	826	358	170	967
1966	4 761	448	55	1 416	409	856	375	186	1 017
1967	4 880	450	58	1 458	406	863	377	192	1 075
1968	5 001	446	64	1 468	426	887	390	199	1 121
1969	5 151	437	68	1 493	448	898	404	219	1 183
1970	5 329	441	74	1 531	464	927	412	232	1 248
1971	5 425	433	79	1 560	468	957	415	240	1 273
1972	5 489	439	73	1 532	476	993	414	243	1 319
1972 [5]	5 489	429	77	1 415	468	1 124	413	393	1 171
1973	5 640	407	69	1 442	491	1 166	427	398	1 241
1974	5 756	395	71	1 445	510	1 155	440	420	1 319

[1] Persons aged 15 years and over. [2] Incl. electricity, gas and water. 1965-72 (former classification): incl. repair services and sanitary services. [3] 1965-72 (former classification): excl. business services. [4] Incl. restaurants and hotels. 1965-72 (former classification): incl. business services. Excl. repair services and sanitary services. [5] New industrial classification.

[1] *Personnes âgées de 15 ans et plus.* [2] *Y compris l'électricité, le gaz et l'eau. 1965-1972 (ancienne classification) : y compris les services de réparation et les services sanitaires.* [3] *1965-1972 (ancienne classification) : non compris les services fournis aux entreprises.* [4] *Y compris les restaurants et les hôtels. 1965-1972 (ancienne classification) : y compris les services fournis aux entreprises. Non compris les services de réparation et les services sanitaires.* [5] *Nouvelle classification industrielle.*

[1] Personas de 15 años y más. [2] Incl. la electricidad, el gas y el agua. 1965-1972 (clasificación precedente): incl. los servicios de reparación y los servicios de saneamiento. [3] 1965-1972 (clasificación precedente): excl. los servicios para empresas. [4] Incl. los restaurantes y los hoteles. 1965-1972 (clasificación precedente): incl. los servicios para empresas. Excl. los servicios de reparación y los servicios de saneamiento. [5] Nueva clasificación industrial.

EMPLOYMENT

3

Persons employed in major divisions of economic activity
Personnes occupées dans les principales branches d'activité économique
Personas ocupadas en las divisiones mayores de la actividad económica

Fiji

Number of employees *(Statistics of establishments)*
Nombre de salariés *(Statistiques d'établissements)*
Número de asalariados *(Estadísticas de establecimientos)*

(Thousands — *Milliers* — Millares)

Date[1] / *Date*[1] / Fecha[1]	Total	1 Agriculture, forestry, fishing *Agriculture, sylviculture, pêche* Agricultura, silvicultura, pesca	2 Mining, quarrying *Industries extractives* Minas, canteras	3 Manufacturing *Industries manufacturières* Industrias manufactureras	4 Electricity, gas, water *Electricité, gaz, eau* Electricidad, gas, agua	5 Construction *Construction* Construcción	6 Trade, restaurants and hotels *Commerce, restaurants et hôtels* Comercio, restaurantes y hoteles	7 Transport, storage, communication *Transports, entrepôts, communications* Transportes, almacenaje, comunicaciones	8 Financing, insurance, real estate, business services *Banques, assurances, aff. imm., serv. aux entreprises* Bancos, seguros, bienes inm., serv. para empresas	9 Community, social, and pers. services *Services à collectivité, services sociaux et pers.* Servicios comunales, sociales y personales
1969	46.4	2.0	1.9	9.5	1.0	7.8	7.8	3.0	1.7	11.7
1970	51.6	3.8	2.1	9.1	1.1	7.4	8.7	3.9	1.5	14.0
1971	56.2	3.8	1.9	10.0	1.2	8.2	9.1	4.6	1.7	15.6
1972	58.4	2.8	1.7	9.8	1.4	8.2	9.9	5.2	2.0	17.2
1973	61.5	3.4	1.7	10.1	1.7	9.5	9.7	4.9	2.6	17.8

[1] June of each year.   [1] *Juin de chaque année.*   [1] Junio de cada año.

New Zealand

Civilian labour force employed *(Statistics of establishments)* [1]
Main-d'œuvre civile occupée *(Statistiques d'établissements)* [1]
Fuerza trabajadora civil ocupada *(Estadísticas de establecimientos)* [1]

(Thousands — *Milliers* — Millares)

Date[2] / *Date*[2] / Fecha[2]	Total	1 Agriculture, forestry, fishing *Agriculture, sylviculture, pêche* Agricultura, silvicultura, pesca	2 Mining, quarrying *Industries extractives* Minas, canteras	3 Manufacturing *Industries manufacturières* Industrias manufactureras	4 Electricity, gas, water *Electricité, gaz, eau* Electricidad, gas, agua	5 Construction *Construction* Construcción	6 Trade, restaurants and hotels *Commerce, restaurants et hôtels* Comercio, restaurantes y hoteles	7 Transport, storage, communication *Transports, entrepôts, communications* Transportes, almacenaje, comunicaciones	8 Financing, insurance, real estate, business services *Banques, assurances, aff. imm., serv. aux entreprises* Bancos, seguros, bienes inm., serv. para empresas	9 Community, social, and pers. services *Services à collectivité, services sociaux et pers.* Servicios comunales, sociales y personales
1971	1 094	138	5	269	14	86	187	103	66	226
1972	1 103	139	4	269	14	87	187	103	67	233
1973	1 141	141	4	283	14	90	191	104	72	242
1974	1 178	142	4	295	15	93	195	107	75	252

[1] Excl. unpaid family workers and members of producers' co-operatives.   [2] April and Oct. of each year.   [1] *Non compris les travailleurs familiaux non rémunérés et les membres de coopératives de producteurs.*   [2] *Avril et oct. de chaque année.*   [1] Excl. los trabajadores familiares no remunerados y los miembros de cooperativas de producción.   [2] Abril y oct. de cada año.

3 Persons employed in major divisions of economic activity
Personnes occupées dans les principales branches d'activité économique
Personas ocupadas en las divisiones mayores de la actividad económica

URSS [1]

Number of employees *(Statistics of establishments)* [2]
Nombre de salariés *(Statistiques d'établissements)* [2]
Número de asalariados *(Estadísticas de establecimientos)* [2]

(Thousands — *Milliers* — Millares)

Date *Date* Fecha	Total	Agriculture, forestry, fishing [3] *Agriculture, sylviculture, pêche* [3] Agricultura, silvicultura, pesca [3]	Mining, quarrying [4] *Industries extractives* [4] Minas, canteras [4]	Total	Manuf., electr., etc.			Construc- tion [8] *Construc- tion* [8] Construc- ción [8]	Com- merce [9] *Com- merce* [9] Comercio [9]	Transport, commu- nication *Transports, communi- cations* Trans- portes, comunica- ciones	Services [10] *Services* [10] Servicios [10]	Others [11] *Autres* [11] Otros [11]
					Manu- facturing [5] *Industries manufac- turières* [5] Industrias manufac- tureras [5]	Electricity, gas [6] *Electricité, gaz* [6] Electri- cidad, gas [6]	Others [7] *Autres* [7] Otros [7]					
1965	95 568	27 759	2 170	25 277	*23 093*	543	*1 641*	7 301	4 832	8 259	18 825	1 145
1966	97 937	27 531	2 204	26 310	*24 091*	584	*1 635*	7 549	5 037	8 437	19 635	1 234
1967	100 279	27 253	2 220	27 228	*24 969*	605	*1 654*	7 880	5 265	8 590	20 531	1 312
1968	102 823	27 043	2 211	28 217	*25 906*	628	*1 683*	8 149	5 542	8 793	21 548	1 320
1969	104 868	26 455	2 168	28 991	*26 661*	638	*1 692*	8 572	5 771	9 063	22 475	1 373
1970	106 773	26 200	2 141	29 452	*27 125*	636	*1 691*	9 052	5 942	9 315	23 261	1 410
1971	108 874	26 006	2 119	29 911	*27 578*	648	*1 685*	9 549	6 152	9 597	24 098	1 442
1972	111 092	25 940	2 076	30 385	*28 041*	657	*1 687*	9 986	6 372	9 881	24 963	1 489
1973	113 152	26 015	2 051	30 824	*28 465*	661	*1 698*	10 091	6 594	10 170	25 842	1 565
1974	115 280	26 050	2 017	31 416	*29 036*	674	*1 706*	10 260	6 803	10 480	26 654	1 600

[1] Incl. Byelorussian SSR and Ukrainian SSR, shown separately in this table. Socialised sector. [2] Incl. members of collective farms (kolkhozes). [3] Incl. members of collective farms engaged in non-agricultural sectors (industry, construction, commerce, services); excl. members of families working on personal agricultural plots. [4] Excl. geological survey. [5] Excl. publishing. [6] Excl. gas distribution. [7] Incl. industrial sea-fishing and water supply. [8] Incl. capital repairs and geological survey. [9] Incl. state supplies of finished and semi-finished products. [10] Incl. gas distribution. [11] Incl. publishing.

[1] *Y compris les RSS de Biélorussie et d'Ukraine, figurant séparément dans ce tableau. Secteur socialisé.* [2] *Y compris les membres des fermes collectives (kolkhozes).* [3] *Y compris les membres des fermes collectives occupés à des activités dans les secteurs non agricoles (industrie, construction, commerce, services); non compris les membres des familles qui cultivent des parcelles agricoles personnelles.* [4] *Non compris les recherches géologiques.* [5] *Non compris l'édition.* [6] *Non compris la distribution du gaz.* [7] *Y compris la pêche maritime industrielle et la distribution publique de l'eau.* [8] *Y compris l'entretien des biens d'équipement et les recherches géologiques.* [9] *Y compris la fourniture par l'Etat de produits finis et semi-finis.* [10] *Y compris la distribution du gaz.* [11] *Y compris l'édition.*

[1] Incl. las RSS de Bielorrusia y de Ucrania, que figuran separadamente en este cuadro. Sector socializado. [2] Incl. los miembros de haciendas colectivas (koljoses). [3] Incl. los miembros de haciendas colectivas ocupados en los sectores no agrícolas (industria, construcción, comercio, servicios); excl. los miembros de familias que trabajan en parcelas agrícolas personales. [4] Excl. las investigaciones geológicas. [5] Excl. las editoriales, etc. [6] Excl. la distribución de gas. [7] Incl. la pesca marítima industrial y el abastecimiento de agua. [8] Incl. la conservación de los bienes de producción y las investigaciones geológicas. [9] Incl. el suministro por parte del Estado de productos terminados y semiterminados. [10] Incl. la distribución de gas. [11] Incl. las editoriales.

3 — Persons employed in major divisions of economic activity
Personnes occupées dans les principales branches d'activité économique
Personas ocupadas en las divisiones mayores de la actividad económica

Number of employees *(Statistics of establishments)* [1]
Nombre de salariés *(Statistiques d'établissements)* [1]
Número de asalariados *(Estadísticas de establecimientos)* [1]

(Thousands — *Milliers* — Millares)

Date / *Date* / Fecha	Total	Agriculture, forestry, fishing [2] / *Agriculture, sylviculture, pêche* [2] / Agricultura, silvicultura, pesca [2]	Mining, quarrying [3] / *Industries extractives* [3] / Minas, canteras [3]	Manuf., electr., etc. — Total	Manufacturing [4] / *Industries manufacturières* [4] / Industrias manufactureras [4]	Electricity, gas [5] / *Electricité, gaz* [5] / Electricidad, gas [5]	Others [6] / *Autres* [6] / Otros [6]	Construction [7] / *Construction* [7] / Construcción [7]	Commerce [8] / *Commerce* [8] / Comercio [8]	Transport, communication / *Transports, communications* / Transportes, comunicaciones	Services [9] / *Services* [9] / Servicios [9]	Others [10] / *Autres* [10] / Otros [10]

RSS de Biélorussie [11]

Date	Total	Agr.	Mining	Total	Manuf.	Elec.	Others	Constr.	Comm.	Transp.	Serv.	Others
1965	3 561.1	1 553.7	21.4	759.2	*710.5*	*14.8*	*33.9*	210.0	153.9	246.5	571.1	45.3
1966	3 670.6	1 539.7	21.5	820.4	*770.1*	*17.2*	*33.1*	231.6	163.3	255.1	596.4	42.6
1967	3 779.9	1 529.2	23.6	868.6	*816.8*	*19.7*	*32.1*	248.9	174.0	262.3	629.7	43.6
1968	3 913.7	1 534.2	24.5	926.0	*874.1*	*19.9*	*32.0*	263.4	183.1	274.7	665.4	42.4
1969	4 007.9	1 504.8	25.1	966.6	*912.2*	*20.7*	*33.7*	285.4	191.7	287.9	701.2	45.3
1970	4 076.8	1 466.0	26.0	1 004.0	*951.1*	*22.0*	*30.9*	306.3	199.0	298.0	730.2	47.3
1971	4 171.3	1 451.9	26.2	1 042.4	*989.2*	*23.0*	*31.3*	324.0	204.0	307.5	766.2	48.0
1972	4 263.9	1 442.6	26.6	1 078.9	*1 015.3*	*23.2*	*40.6*	338.9	210.8	318.7	798.7	48.5
1973	4 365.7	1 455.3	26.3	1 105.4	*1 041.2*	*23.2*	*41.0*	347.5	219.0	328.6	832.3	51.3
1974	4 438.1	1 442.2	25.2	1 134.7	*1 069.6*	*23.0*	*42.1*	355.1	224.7	337.0	866.1	53.1

RSS d'Ukraine [11]

Date	Total	Agr.	Mining	Total	Manuf.	Elec.	Others	Constr. [12]	Comm.	Transp.	Serv.	Others
1965	19 341	7 127	756	4 291	*4 106*	*80*	*105*	1 301	912	1 474	3 285	195
1966	19 846	7 068	769	4 522	*4 318*	*91*	*113*	1 369	957	1 521	3 431	209
1967	20 300	6 950	771	4 736	*4 519*	*99*	*118*	1 453	1 012	1 567	3 595	216
1968	20 852	6 904	765	4 977	*4 754*	*104*	*119*	1 508	1 081	1 617	3 783	217
1969	21 174	6 684	758	5 163	*4 929*	*106*	*128*	1 567	1 126	1 678	3 968	230
1970	21 524	6 576	759	5 277	*5 009*	*103*	*165*	1 658	1 148	1 743	4 123	240
1971	21 944	6 527	743	5 400	*5 144*	*101*	*155*	1 744	1 197	1 808	4 278	247
1972	22 362	6 514	734	5 500	*5 249*	*103*	*148*	1 811	1 240	1 862	4 441	260
1973	22 650	6 439	710	5 626	*5 379*	*96*	*151*	1 811	1 287	1 899	4 606	272
1974	22 988	6 421	705	5 749	*5 497*	*100*	*152*	1 836	1 321	1 927	4 739	290

[1] Incl. members of collective farms (kolkhozes). [2] Incl. members of collective farms engaged in non-agricultural sectors (industry, construction, commerce, services); excl. members of families working on personal agricultural plots. [3] Excl. geological survey. [4] Excl. publishing. [5] Excl. gas distribution. [6] Incl. industrial sea-fishing and water supply. [7] Incl. capital repairs and geological survey. [8] Incl. state supplies of finished and semi-finished products. [9] Incl. gas distribution. [10] Incl. publishing. [11] Socialised sector. [12] Workers engaged in actual construction and erection processes.

[1] *Y compris les membres des fermes collectives (kolkhozes).* [2] *Y compris les membres des fermes collectives occupés à des activités dans les secteurs non agricoles (industrie, construction, commerce, services); non compris les membres des familles qui cultivent des parcelles agricoles personnelles.* [3] *Non compris les recherches géologiques.* [4] *Non compris l'édition.* [5] *Non compris la distribution du gaz.* [6] *Y compris la pêche maritime industrielle et la distribution publique de l'eau.* [7] *Y compris l'entretien des biens d'équipement et les recherches géologiques.* [8] *Y compris la fourniture par l'Etat de produits finis et semi-finis.* [9] *Y compris la distribution du gaz.* [10] *Y compris l'édition.* [11] *Secteur socialisé.* [12] *Travailleurs effectivement occupés à la construction.*

[1] Incl. los miembros de haciendas colectivas (koljoses). [2] Incl. los miembros de haciendas colectivas ocupados en los sectores no agrícolas (industria, construcción, comercio, servicios); excl. los miembros de familias que trabajan en parcelas agrícolas personales. [3] Excl. las investigaciones geológicas. [4] Excl. las editoriales, etc. [5] Excl. la distribución de gas. [6] Incl. la pesca marítima industrial y el abastecimiento de agua. [7] Incl. la conservación de los bienes de producción y las investigaciones geológicas. [8] Incl. el suministro por parte del Estado de productos terminados y semiterminados. [9] Incl. la distribución de gas. [10] Incl. las editoriales. [11] Sector socializado. [12] Trabajadores ocupados efectivamente en la construcción.

4 General level of employment
Niveau général de l'emploi
Nivel general del empleo

(Indices: 1970 = 100)

Country — *Pays* — País	Code *Code* Clave	1965	1966	1967	1968	1969	1970	1971	1972	1973	1974	1975 (VI)
AFRICA — AFRIQUE **ÁFRICA**												
Cameroun	III	73.0	75.7	67.3	79.9	81.1	**100.0**	85.6	84.2	124.4	...	.
Egypt [1]	. [2]	.	.	.	96.4	99.8	**100.0**	102.0	107.0	105.7	...	.
Gabon [3]	II	72.1	75.2	82.1	87.6	95.0	**100.0**	103.2 *	108.7 *	...	...	.
Ghana [4]	III	99.5	90.8	90.8	98.3	100.7	**100.0**	100.9	99.3 [5] *	...	...	.
Kenya [6]	III [7]	90.3	90.8	92.7	94.1	97.3	**100.0**	107.2	111.7	118.2	128.2 *	.
Malawi [8]	III	.	.	.	84.2	91.8	**100.0**	108.1	118.7	134.9	142.0	148.6 [20]
Mauritius [9]	III	.	92.3	93.5	97.7	97.4	**100.0**	104.5	112.3	121.5	130.0	.
Swaziland [10]	III	.	.	.	.	.	**100.0**	110.9	126.9	134.4	...	.
Tanzania (Tanganyika) [6]	III	89.5	90.2	92.8	94.0	98.1	**100.0**	101.7	...	...	...	.
Tunisie	. [2]	.	.	.	97.3	98.0	**100.0**	102.8	108.6	111.0	114.0	.
Uganda [11]	III	77.4	78.8	82.2	90.2	94.4	**100.0**	103.9	105.6	111.3	...	.
Zambia [12]	III	76.7	85.3	90.5	93.8	95.4	**100.0**	106.3	107.6	111.9	...	...
AMERICA — AMÉRIQUE **AMÉRICA**												
Belize [13]	III	*79.1*	*82.3*	*84.1*	*92.4*	**100.0**	...	...	...	...	...	.
Canada [14]	I	87.1	90.8	93.7	95.7	98.7	**100.0**	102.5	105.7	111.2	116.0	122.3
Jamaica [14]	I [15]	.	.	.	*94.3* [16]	**100.0**	.	.	*99.0*	*102.0*	104.5	.
Panamá [17]	I	80.8	85.7	88.7	93.3	97.0	**100.0**	101.8	105.1	107.2	112.6	.
Puerto Rico [14]	I	88.8	92.5	93.7	95.2	98.6	**100.0**	103.6	107.6	110.7	110.1	104.3 [21]
Trinidad and Tobago [17]	I	94.4	95.3	98.4	97.1	99.8	**100.0**	101.3 [18]	.	102.0 *	...	...
United States [19]	I	90.4	92.7	94.6	96.6	99.1	**100.0**	100.6	103.9	107.4	109.3	108.7

EXPLANATORY NOTES AND CODES: See p. 297.

1 May of each year. 2 Civilian labour force employed (official estimates). 3 Excl. domestic services. 4 Dec. of each year. 5 Sep. 6 June of each year. 7 Excl. employment in rural areas (except for large enterprises). 8 Incl. working proprietors and unpaid family workers. Excl. domestic services. 9 March and Sep. of each year. Excl. relief workers. 10 Sep. of each year. 11 June of each year. 12 Excl. domestic services. Beginning 1967: June and Dec. 13 March of each year. 14 Persons aged 14 years and over. 15 April and Oct. of each year. 16 July and Oct. 17 Persons aged 15 years and over. 18 First semester. 19 Persons aged 16 years and over. 20 First quarter. 21 March.

NOTES EXPLICATIVES ET CODES: Voir p. 300.

1 *Mai de chaque année.* 2 *Main-d'œuvre civile occupée (évaluations officielles).* 3 *Non compris les services domestiques.* 4 *Déc. de chaque année.* 5 *Sept.* 6 *Juin de chaque année.* 7 *Non compris l'emploi dans les zones rurales (à l'exception des grandes entreprises).* 8 *Y compris les propriétaires-exploitants et les travailleurs familiaux non rémunérés. Non compris les services domestiques.* 9 *Mars et sept. de chaque année. Non compris les personnes occupées à des travaux publics de secours.* 10 *Sept. de chaque année.* 11 *Juin de chaque année.* 12 *Non compris les services domestiques. A partir de 1967: juin et déc.* 13 *Mars de chaque année.* 14 *Personnes âgées de 14 ans et plus.* 15 *Avril et oct. de chaque année.* 16 *Juillet et oct.* 17 *Personnes âgées de 15 ans et plus.* 18 *Premier semestre.* 19 *Personnes âgées de 16 ans et plus.* 20 *Premier trimestre.* 21 *Mars.*

NOTAS EXPLICATIVAS Y CLAVES: Véase pág. 303.

1 Mayo de cada año. 2 Fuerza trabajadora civil ocupada (estimaciones oficiales). 3 Excl. los servicios domésticos. 4 Dic. de cada año. 5 Sept. 6 Junio de cada año. 7 Excl. el empleo en las zonas rurales (con excepción de las grandes empresas). 8 Incl. los empresarios propietarios y los trabajadores familiares no remunerados. Excl. los servicios domésticos. 9 Marzo y sept. de cada año. Excl. las personas ocupadas en planes de asistencia. 10 Sept. de cada año. 11 Junio de cada año. 12 Excl. los servicios domésticos. A partir de 1967: junio y dic. 13 Marzo de cada año. 14 Personas de 14 años y más. 15 Abril y oct. de cada año. 16 Julio y oct. 17 Personas de 15 años y más. 18 Primer semestre. 19 Personas de 16 años y más. 20 Primer trimestre. 21 Marzo.

4 General level of employment
Niveau général de l'emploi
Nivel general del empleo

(Indices: 1970 = 100)

Country — Pays — País	Code / Code / Clave	1965	1966	1967	1968	1969	1970	1971	1972	1973	1974	1975 (VI)
ASIA — ASIE / ASIA												
Brunei [1]	III [2]	.	.	.	.	.	.	.	100.0	109.5	110.2	...
Cyprus	. [3]	91.6	93.8	94.9	97.1	98.7	100.0	101.5	102.6	104.2	88.6	.
Israel	II	82.5	82.1	79.8	87.0 [4]	95.0	100.0	105.7	110.0	112.2 *	113.4	115.4 * [27]
Japan [5]	I	92.9	94.9	96.6 [4]	98.2	99.0	100.0	100.4	100.3	102.0	101.4	103.2
Korea, Rep. of [6]	I	84.2	86.4	89.5	93.9	96.6	100.0	103.3	108.4	114.3	118.9	118.8 [28]
East Malaysia												
Sabah [7]	III	.	105.6	103.2	99.6	94.9	100.0	104.8	109.6	121.2	132.3	
Pakistan [8]	I	.	.	.	.	94.4	100.0	103.2	103.6	...	...	
Philippines [9]	I	83.8	87.7	96.8	99.2	89.3	.	100.0	105.0	105.4	115.1	
Singapore [10]	III	.	.	.	.	90.8	100.0	110.5	123.0	137.9	...	.
République arabe syrienne [11]	I	68.5 [12]	72.3	83.0	87.1	100.0	.	80.7 [13]	86.7 [13]	85.5 [13]	...	
Thailand [14]	I [15]	.	.	.	.	.	.	100.0	97.1	102.6	...	
EUROPE — EUROPE / EUROPA												
Albanie [16]	.	68.4	72.7	79.6	88.0	94.1	100.0	106.7	...	...	...	.
Austria	I [17]	.	.	.	.	100.5	100.0	100.0	100.6	101.3	100.7	110.9
Belgique [1]	II [18]	.	.	.	.	.	100.0	101.0	100.8	102.2	103.6	...
Bulgarie [19]	III	79.9	87.5	91.6	93.1	96.4	100.0	104.2	108.9	119.1	124.3 *	.
Czechoslovakia [20]	III	92.1	94.0	95.1	96.6	98.4	100.0	101.2	102.1	103.1	104.6	
Denmark [21]	I [22]	.	.	.	.	.	.	.	100.0	101.3	100.0 [23]	
España [24]	. [3]	95.7	96.6	97.1	97.9	99.0	100.0	100.6	101.9	103.6	102.6	.
Finland [25]	I	100.8	101.3	99.5	97.5	98.8	100.0 [4]	99.9	99.6	101.8	104.8	112.9
France	. [3]	95.8	96.5	96.9	96.8	98.5	100.0	100.6	101.3	102.7	103.8 *	.
German Democratic Republic Δ	.	94.7	95.6	96.9	98.0	99.0	100.0	101.3	103.8	105.3	106.5 *	.
Germany, Fed. Rep. of Δ	. [26]	101.0	100.6	97.3	97.4	98.9	100.0	100.2	99.8	100.1	98.2 *	.

EXPLANATORY NOTES AND CODES: See p. 297

[1] June of each year. [2] Incl. employers and workers on own account. [3] Official estimates. [4] Series linked to former series. [5] Persons aged 15 years and over. [6] Persons aged 14 years and over. [7] Sep. and Dec. of each year. [8] Persons aged 10 years and over. [9] Persons aged 10 years and over. May of each year. [10] Persons aged 12 years and over, excl. domestic services. March and Sep. of each year. [11] Persons aged 12 years and over. Nov. of each year. [12] May and Nov. [13] Sep. [14] Persons aged 11 years and over. [15] July-Sep. of each year. [16] Socialised sector. [17] Sep. of each year. [18] Civilian labour force employed. [19] Socialised sector; excl. agricultural cooperatives. [20] Civilian labour force employed; excl. family workers and apprentices. [21] Persons aged 15 to 74 years. [22] Nov. of each year. [23] Oct. [24] Excl. Ceuta and Melilla. Fourth quarter of each year. [25] Persons aged 15 to 74 years. 1965-69: 15 years and over. [26] Civilian labour force employed (official estimates). [27] April. [28] March.

NOTES EXPLICATIVES ET CODES: Voir p. 300.

[1] *Juin de chaque année.* [2] *Y compris les employeurs et les personnes travaillant à leur propre compte.* [3] *Evaluations officielles.* [4] *Série enchaînée à la précédente.* [5] *Personnes âgées de 15 ans et plus.* [6] *Personnes âgées de 14 ans et plus.* [7] *Sept. et déc. de chaque année.* [8] *Personnes âgées de 10 ans et plus.* [9] *Personnes âgées de 10 ans et plus. Mai de chaque année.* [10] *Personnes âgées de 12 ans et plus, non compris les services domestiques. Mars et sept. de chaque année.* [11] *Personnes âgées de 12 ans et plus. Nov. de chaque qnnée.* [12] *Mai et nov.* [13] *Sept.* [14] *Personnes âgées de 11 ans et plus.* [15] *Juillet-sept. de chaque année.* [16] *Secteur socialisé.* [17] *Sept. de chaque année.* [18] *Main-d'œuvre civile occupée.* [19] *Secteur socialisé; non compris les coopératives agricoles.* [20] *Main-d'œuvre civile occupée; non compris les travailleurs familiaux et les apprentis.* [21] *Personnes âgées de 15 à 74 ans.* [22] *Nov. de chaque année.* [23] *Oct.* [24] *Non compris Ceuta et Melilla. Quatrième trimestre de chaque année.* [25] *Personnes âgées de 15 à 74 ans. 1965-1969: 15 ans et plus.* [26] *Main-d'œuvre civile occupée (évaluations officielles).* [27] *Avril.* [28] *Mars.*

NOTAS EXPLICATIVAS Y CLAVES: Véase pág. 303.

[1] Junio de cada año. [2] Incl. los empleadores y los trabajadores por cuenta propia. [3] Estimaciones oficiales. [4] Serie enlazada con la anterior. [5] Personas de 15 años y más. [6] Personas de 14 años y más. [7] Sept. y dic. de cada año. [8] Personas de 10 años y más. [9] Personas de 10 años y más. Mayo de cada año. [10] Personas de 12 años y más, excl. los servicios domésticos. Marzo y sept. de cada año. [11] Personas de 12 años y más. Nov. de cada año. [12] Mayo y nov. [13] Sept. [14] Personas de 11 años y más. [15] Julio-sept. de cada año. [16] Sector socializado. [17] Sept. de cada año. [18] Fuerza trabajadora civil ocupada. [19] Sector socializado; excl. las cooperativas agrícolas. [20] Fuerza trabajadora civil ocupada; excl. los trabajadores familiares y los aprendices. [21] Personas de 15 a 74 años. [22] Nov. de cada año. [23] Oct. [24] Excl. Ceuta y Melilla. Cuarto trimestre de cada año. [25] Personas de 15 a 74 años. 1965-1969: 15 años y más. [26] Fuerza trabajadora civil ocupada (estimaciones oficiales). [27] Abril. [28] Marzo.

4 General level of employment
Niveau général de l'emploi
Nivel general del empleo

(Indices: 1970 = 100)

Country — Pays — Pais	Code Code Clave	1965	1966	1967	1968	1969	1970	1971	1972	1973	1974	1975 (VI)
Hongrie [1]	III	93.2	93.8	94.9	96.6	98.8	**100.0**	100.6	101.1	101.4	101.8 *	.
Iceland	II	93.3	95.2	95.2	95.6	95.5	**100.0**	104.5	107.3	110.1	...	.
Ireland [2]	. [3]	101.5	101.2	100.7	101.0	101.2	**100.0**	100.2	99.2	99.6	100.2	.
Italie [4]	I	101.7	99.7	100.8	100.6	99.6	**100.0**	99.7	98.1	99.0	101.1	100.4 [21]
Malta [5]	III	85.8	88.7	91.4	93.9	98.9	**100.0**	101.8	99.4	99.2	99.3	.
Norway	I [6]	91.3	92.5	94.5	95.3	97.1	**100.0**	.	100.0 [7]	100.3	100.6	103.8 [22]
Pays-Bas [8]	. [9]	95.5	96.2	95.8	96.9	98.7	**100.0**	100.6	99.6	100.0 *	99.9 *	.
Pologne [10]	III	84.9	88.0	91.5	94.7	98.1	**100.0**	103.1	107.6	111.8	115.9	117.3 [23]
Roumanie [11]	III	84.3	88.0	91.6	93.7	97.0	**100.0**	105.2	110.2	114.1	117.9	.
Sweden [12]	I	96.0	96.9	95.9	97.0	98.1	**100.0**	100.2	100.2	100.7	102.8	106.7
United Kingdom [13]	III [14]	102.2	102.8	101.2	100.5	100.7	**100.0**	98.5 [15]	98.6	101.0	101.5 *	...
Yugoslavia [16]	III	95.2	92.7	92.1	92.6	96.2	**100.0**	104.8	109.3	111.9	117.5	124.1
OCEANIA — OCÉANIE OCEANÍA												
Australia [17]	I	86.8	89.3	91.6	93.8	96.7	**100.0**	101.8	103.0	105.8	108.0	107.6 [24]
Fiji [18]	III	.	.	.	.	90.0	**100.0**	109.0	113.2	119.2	...	.
New Zealand	. [3]	91.4	94.4	95.5	94.8	97.1	**100.0**	101.6	102.5	106.0	109.4	.
URSS [19, 20]	III	89.5	91.7	93.9	96.3	98.2	**100.0**	102.0	104.0	106.0	108.0	.
RSS de Biélorussie [20]	III	87.4	90.0	92.7	96.0	98.3	**100.0**	102.3	104.6	107.1	108.9	.
RSS d'Ukraine [20]	III	89.9	92.2	94.3	96.9	98.4	**100.0**	102.0	103.9	105.2	106.8	.

EXPLANATORY NOTES AND CODES: See p. 297.

[1] Civilian labour force employed. [2] April of each year. [3] Civilian labour force employed (official estimates.) [4] Persons aged 14 years and over. [5] Civilian labour force employed; excl. family workers. Dec. of each year. [6] Persons aged 16 to 74 years. 1965-70: compulsory health insurance statistics; employees only. [7] Series replacing former series. [8] Civilian labour force employed, excl. civil personnel employed by the Ministry of Defence; number of man-years. [9] Official estimates. [10] Socialised sector. Excl. apprentices. Figures include full-time equivalent of part-time workers. [11] Socialised sector. [12] Persons aged 16 to 74 years. Incl. certain categories of military personnel. [13] Civilian labour force employed. June of each year. [14] Prior to 1971: National insurance statistics. [15] Series linked to former series. [16] Socialised sector. March and Sep. of each year. [17] Persons aged 15 years and over. [18] June of each year. [19] Incl. Byelorussian SSR and Ukrainian SSR, shown separately in this table. [20] Socialised sector. Incl. members of collective farms (kolkhozes). [21] April. [22] Second quarter. [23] First quarter. [24] May.

NOTES EXPLICATIVES ET CODES: Voir p. 300.

[1] Main-d'œuvre civile occupée. [2] Avril de chaque année. [3] Main-d'œuvre civile occupée (évaluations officielles). [4] Personnes âgées de 14 ans et plus. [5] Main-d'œuvre civile occupée ; non compris les travailleurs familiaux. Déc. de chaque année. [6] Personnes âgées de 16 à 74 ans. 1965-1970 : statistiques de l'assurance-maladie obligatoire ; salariés seulement. [7] Série remplaçant la précédente. [8] Main-d'œuvre civile occupée, non compris le personnel civil employé par le ministère de la Défense ; nombre d'années-homme. [9] Evaluations officielles. [10] Secteur socialisé. Non compris les apprentis. Les personnes employées à temps partiel sont converties en unité de travail à temps complet. [11] Secteur socialisé. [12] Personnes âgées de 16 à 74 ans. Y compris certaines catégories de personnel militaire. [13] Main-d'œuvre civile occupée. Juin de chaque année. [14] Avant 1971 : statistiques de l'assurance nationale. [15] Série enchaînée à la précédente. [16] Secteur socialisé. Mars et sept. de chaque année. [17] Personnes âgées de 15 ans et plus. [18] Juin de chaque année. [19] Y compris les RSS de Biélorussie et d'Ukraine, figurant séparément dans ce tableau. [20] Secteur socialisé. Y compris les membres des fermes collectives (kolkhozes). [21] Avril. [22] Deuxième trimestre. [23] Premier trimestre. [24] Mai.

NOTAS EXPLICATIVAS Y CLAVES: Véase pág. 303.

[1] Fuerza trabajadora civil ocupada. [2] Abril de cada año. [3] Fuerza trabajadora civil ocupada (estimaciones oficiales). [4] Personas de 14 años y más. [5] Fuerza trabajadora civil ocupada; excl. los trabajadores familiares. Dic. de cada año. [6] Personas de 16 a 74 años. 1965-1970: estadísticas del seguro obligatorio de enfermedad; asalariados solamente. [7] Serie que substituye a la anterior. [8] Fuerza trabajadora civil ocupada, excl. el personal civil empleado por el Ministerio de la Defensa; número de años-hombre. [9] Estimaciones oficiales. [10] Sector socializado. Excl. los aprendices. Las personas empleadas a tiempo parcial son convertidas en unidad de trabajo a pleno tiempo. [11] Sector socializado. [12] Personas de 16 a 74 años. Incl. ciertas categorías de personal militar. [13] Fuerza trabajadora civil ocupada. Junio de cada año. [14] Antes de 1971: estadísticas del Seguro Nacional. [15] Serie enlazada con la anterior. [16] Sector socializado. Marzo y sept. de cada año. [17] Personas de 15 años y más. [18] Junio de cada año. [19] Incl. las RSS de Bielorrusia y de Ucrania, que figuran separadamente en este cuadro. [20] Sector socializado. Incl. los miembros de las haciendas colectivas (koljoses). [21] Abril. [22] Segundo trimestre. [23] Primer trimestre. [24] Mayo.

EMPLOYMENT

5 Employment in non-agricultural sectors
Emploi dans les secteurs non agricoles
Empleo en los sectores no agrícolas

(Indices: 1970 = 100)

Country — Pays — País	Code Code Clave	1965	1966	1967	1968	1969	1970	1971	1972	1973	1974	1975 (VI)
AFRICA — AFRIQUE AFRICA												
Cameroun	III	81.1	84.0	75.8	91.9	92.9	**100.0**	95.3	84.3	93.2	...	.
Egypt [1]	. [2]	.	.		90.8	97.6	**100.0**	95.4	100.9	104.6	...	.
Gabon [3]	II	68.3	71.9	80.7	88.8	96.7	**100.0**	104.6 *	108.8 *	...	...	.
Ghana [4]	III	97.3	89.5	91.0	98.5	101.5	**100.0**	102.0	98.8 [5*]	...	...	.
Kenya [6]	III [7]	.	.	92.6	94.6	98.2	**100.0**	109.1	❘112.4 [8]	118.0	...	.
Malawi [9]	III	.	.	.	85.5	93.0	**100.0**	108.9	119.3	131.6	138.6	135.7 [24]
Mauritius [10]	III	.	86.3	90.3	92.0	96.5	**100.0**	108.3	119.9	137.8	156.0	.
Sierra Leone [4]	III	101.4	101.8	98.4	97.6	100.5	**100.0**	101.3	100.4	100.4	96.8	...
South Africa, Rep. of ... Total	III [11]	81.3	85.1	86.9	89.6	93.9	**100.0**	102.5	102.7	106.6	109.1	...
» » » » [12]	III [11]	87.9	92.7	94.3	95.2	97.8	**100.0**	101.1	100.7	100.8	102.6	...
Swaziland [13]	III	.	.	.	.	.	**100.0**	108.7	122.5	138.5	...	.
Tanzania (Tanganyika) [6]	III	74.5	79.7	85.6	86.4	90.5	**100.0**	96.1	...	...	...	
Tunisie	. [2]	.	.	.	93.5	95.1	**100.0**	106.4	115.2	121.2	128.8	.
Uganda [6]	III	74.5	75.1	79.1	87.9	92.6	**100.0**	103.6	95.0	111.7	...	.
Zambia [3]	III	75.0	83.9	❘88.9 [14]	92.8	93.9	**100.0**	105.7	107.6	112.4	...	...
AMERICA — AMÉRIQUE AMÉRICA												
Belize [15]	III	*73.6*	*80.4*	*84.0*	*94.9*	**100.0**	...	...	...	...	...	.
Canada [16]	I	85.1	89.7	92.6	94.9	98.3	**100.0**	102.7	106.5	112.5	117.6	123.6
El Salvador [17]	III	103.1	111.7	115.5	107.3	107.0	**100.0**	101.1	107.3	109.0	115.6	...
Jamaica [18]	I [19]	.	.	.	*95.1* [20]	**100.0**	.	.	*107.0*	*110.6*	*108.3*	
Panamá [21]	I	67.3	73.8	83.3	89.5	95.6	**100.0**	103.6	108.0	...	...	.
Puerto Rico [18]	I	81.7	87.1	89.5	92.4	97.1	**100.0**	105.1	110.5	114.2	113.4	106.1 [25]
Trinidad and Tobago [21]	I	95.2	99.0	101.8	99.5	101.1	**100.0**	104.3 [22]	.	113.0 *	...	...
United States [23]	I	88.8	91.7	93.8	95.9	98.8	**100.0**	100.8	104.1	107.7	109.7	108.5

EXPLANATORY NOTES AND CODES: See p. 297.

¹ May of each year. ² Civilian labour force employed (official estimates). ³ Excl. domestic services. ⁴ Dec. of each year. ⁵ Sep. ⁶ June of each year. ⁷ Excl. employment in rural areas (except for large enterprises). ⁸ Series linked to former series. ⁹ Incl. working proprietors and unpaid family workers. Excl. domestic services. ¹⁰ March and Sep. of each year. Excl. relief workers. Excl. sugar and tea factories. ¹¹ Excl. commerce and services. ¹² White population. ¹³ Sep. of each year. ¹⁴ Beginning 1967: June and Dec. 1965-66: excl. veterinary services; series linked to former series. ¹⁵ March of each year. ¹⁶ Persons aged 14 years and over. Incl. forestry, fishing and trapping. ¹⁷ Area of San Salvador. Excl. mining. ¹⁸ Persons aged 14 years and over. ¹⁹ April and Oct. of each year. ²⁰ July and Oct. ²¹ Persons aged 15 years and over. ²² First semester. ²³ Persons aged 16 yeards and over. ²⁴ First quarter. ²⁵ March.

NOTES EXPLICATIVES ET CODES: Voir p. 300.

¹ Mai de chaque année. ² Main-d'œuvre civile occupée (évaluations officielles). ³ Non compris les services domestiques. ⁴ Déc. de chaque année. ⁵ Sept. ⁶ Juin de chaque année. ⁷ Non compris l'emploi dans les zones rurales (à l'exception des grandes entreprises). ⁸ Série enchaînée à la précédente. ⁹ Y compris les propriétaires-exploitants et les travailleurs familiaux non rémunérés. Non compris les services domestiques. ¹⁰ Mars et sept. de chaque année. Non compris les personnes occupées à des travaux publics de secours. Non compris les fabriques de sucre et de thé. ¹¹ Non compris le commerce et les services. ¹² Population blanche. ¹³ Sept. de chaque année. ¹⁴ A partir de 1967 : juin et déc. 1965-66 : non compris les services vétérinaires ; série enchaînée à la précédente. ¹⁵ Mars de chaque année. ¹⁶ Personnes âgées de 14 ans et plus. Y compris la sylviculture, la pêche et le piégeage. ¹⁷ Zone de San Salvador. Non compris les mines. ¹⁸ Personnes âgées de 14 ans et plus. ¹⁹ Avril et oct. de chaque année. ²⁰ Juillet et oct. ²¹ Personnes âgées de 15 ans et plus. ²² Premier semestre. ²³ Personnes âgées de 16 ans et plus. ²⁴ Premier trimestre. ²⁵ Mars.

NOTAS EXPLICATIVAS Y CLAVES: Véase pág. 303.

¹ Mayo de cada año. ² Fuerza trabajadora civil ocupada (estimaciones oficiales). ³ Excl. los servicios domésticos. ⁴ Dic. de cada año. ⁵ Sept. ⁶ Junio de cada año. ⁷ Excl. el empleo en las zonas rurales (con excepción de las grandes empresas). ⁸ Serie enlazada con la anterior. ⁹ Incl. los empresarios propietarios y los trabajadores familiares no remunerados. Excl. los servicios domésticos. ¹⁰ Marzo y sept. de cada año. Excl. las personas ocupadas en planes de asistencia. Excl. las fábricas ocupadas en planes de asistencia. Excl. las fábricas de azúcar y de té. ¹¹ Excl. el comercio y los servicios. ¹² Población blanca. ¹³ Sept. de cada año. ¹⁴ A partir de 1967: junio y dic. 1965-66: excl. los servicios veterinarios; serie enlazada con la anterior. ¹⁵ Marzo de cada año. ¹⁶ Personas de 14 años y más. Incl. la silvicultura, la pesca y la caza. ¹⁷ Zona de San Salvador. Excl. las minas. ¹⁸ Personas de 14 años y más. ¹⁹ Abril y oct. de cada año. ²⁰ Julio y oct. ²¹ Personas de 15 años y más. ²² Primer semestre. ²³ Personas de 16 años y más. ²⁴ Primer trimestre. ²⁵ Marzo.

5 Employment in non-agricultural sectors
Emploi dans les secteurs non agricoles
Empleo en los sectores no agrícolas

(Indices: 1970 = 100)

Country — Pays — País	Code / Code / Clave	1965	1966	1967	1968	1969	1970	1971	1972	1973	1974	1975 (VI)
ASIA — ASIE / ASIA												
Brunei[1]	III[2]	.	.	.	.	.	.	.	100.0	112.1	112.7	...
Cyprus	.[3]	85.4	88.9	90.8	94.5	97.4	100.0	101.1	105.6	108.4	94.5	.
India[4]	III	89.8	92.0[5]	92.7	93.5	95.7	100.0	101.1				
Israel	II	80.9	80.9	78.6	86.0[5]	94.8	100.0	106.0	111.0	114.2 *	115.6	117.7 *[26]
Japan[6]	I	85.9	89.3	92.3[5]	95.4	97.3	100.0	102.2	103.5	106.9	106.9	107.3
Korea (Rep. of)[7]	I	70.3	73.5	80.9	90.2	95.0	100.0	107.5	108.0	115.3	124.3	132.2[27]
East Malaysia												
Sabah[8]	III	.	74.0	76.3	83.6	93.0	100.0	106.0	120.8	107.6	124.3	.
Pakistan[9]	I	.	.	.	.	98.2	100.0	102.6	105.5	...	...	.
Philippines[10]	III	73.1	77.4	84.5	85.9	79.9	.	100.0	98.6	101.7	101.3	.
Singapore[11]	III	.	.	.	.	90.7	100.0	110.4	123.0	137.9	...	.
République arabe syrienne[12]	I	99.4[13]	100.1	104.8	95.3	100.0	.	109.1[14]	125.7[14]	131.8[14]	...	.
Thailand[15]	I[16]	.	.	.	.	.	.	100.0	129.7	137.9	...	.
EUROPE — EUROPE / EUROPA												
Albanie[17]	.	68.1	71.4	78.3	86.6	93.6	100.0	107.0	...	...	...	.
Austria	I[18]	.	.	.	.	100.6	100.0	102.1	104.1	105.4	108.5	.
Belgique[1]	II[19]	.	.	.	.	.	100.0	101.4	101.5	103.1	104.6	...
Bulgarie[17]	III	80.7	86.2	90.8	93.0	96.2	100.0	104.0	107.3	110.1	113.2 *	.
Czechoslovakia[20]	III	88.9	91.3	93.2	95.4	97.9	100.0	101.7	104.1	106.0	107.9	.
Denmark[21]	I[22]	.	.	.	.	.	.	.	100.0	101.5	100.1[23]	.
España	II	90.2	96.9	99.6	93.4	96.3	100.0	102.7	107.9	115.0	119.9	.
Finland[24]	I	91.5	93.4	94.2	93.4	96.5	100.0[5]	101.8	104.5	109.1	113.5	124.5
France	.[3]	91.9	93.5	94.6	95.2	97.6	100.0	101.3	102.9	105.1	107.2 *	.
German Democratic Republic		94.1	95.2	96.7	97.9	99.0	100.0	101.4	104.2	105.6	106.8 *	.
Germany, Fed. Rep. of	.[25]	98.5	98.4	95.5	96.1	98.2	100.0	100.7	100.8	101.4	99.6 *	.

EXPLANATORY NOTES AND CODES: See p. 297.

1 June of each year. 2 Incl. employers and workers on own account. 3 Official estimates. 4 Incl. working proprietors. 5 Series linked to former series. 6 Persons aged 15 years and over. 7 Persons aged 14 years and over. 8 Sep. and Dec. of each year. 9 Persons aged 10 years and over. 10 Persons aged 10 years and over. May of each year. 11 Persons aged 12 years and over; excl. domestic services. March and Sep. of each year. 12 Persons aged 12 years and over. Nov. of each year. 13 May and Nov. 14 Sep. 15 Persons aged 11 years and over. 16 July-Sep. of each year. 17 Socialised sector. 18 Sep. of each year. 19 Civilian labour force employed. 20 Civilian labour force employed; excl. family workers and apprentices. 21 Persons aged 15 to 74 years. 22 Nov. of each year. 23 Oct. 24 Persons aged 15 to 74 years. 1965-69: 15 years and over. 25 Civilian labour force employed (official estimates). 26 April. 27 March.

NOTES EXPLICATIVES ET CODES: Voir p. 300.

1 Juin de chaque année. 2 Y compris les employeurs et les personnes travaillant à leur compte. 3 Evaluations officielles. 4 Y compris les propriétaires-exploitants. 5 Série enchaînée à la précédente. 6 Personnes âgées de 15 ans et plus. 7 Personnes âgées de 14 ans et plus. 8 Sept. et déc. de chaque année. 9 Personnes âgées de 10 ans et plus. 10 Personnes âgées de 10 ans et plus. Mai de chaque année. 11 Personnes âgées de 12 ans et plus; non compris les services domestiques. Mars et sept. de chaque année. 12 Personnes âgées de 12 ans et plus. Nov. de chaque année. 13 Mai et nov. 14 Sept. 15 Personnes âgées de 11 ans et plus. 16 Juillet-sept. de chaque année. 17 Secteur socialisé. 18 Sept. de chaque année. 19 Main-d'œuvre civile occupée. 20 Main-d'œuvre civile occupée; non compris les travailleurs familiaux et les apprentis. 21 Personnes âgées de 15 à 74 ans. 22 Nov. de chaque année. 23 Oct. 24 Personnes âgées de 15 à 74 ans. 1965-1969: 15 ans et plus. 25 Main-d'œuvre civile occupée (évaluations officielles). 26 Avril. 27 Mars.

NOTAS EXPLICATIVAS Y CLAVES: Véase pág. 303.

1 Junio de cada año. 2 Incl. los empleadores y los trabajadores por cuenta propia. 3 Estimaciones oficiales. 4 Incl. los empresarios propietarios. 5 Serie enlazada con la anterior. 6 Personas de 15 años y más. 7 Personas de 14 años y más. 8 Sept. y dic. de cada año. 9 Personas de 10 años y más. 10 Personas de 10 años y más. Mayo de cada año. 11 Personas de 12 años y más; excl. los servicios domésticos. Marzo y sept. de cada año. 12 Personas de 12 años y más. Nov. de cada año. 13 Mayo y nov. 14 Sept. 15 Personas de 11 años y más. 16 Julio-sept. de cada año. 17 Sector socializado. 18 Sept. de cada año. 19 Fuerza trabajadora civil ocupada. 20 Fuerza trabajadora civil ocupada; excl. los trabajadores familiares y los aprendices. 21 Personas de 15 a 74 años. 22 Nov. de cada año. 23 Oct. 24 Personas de 15 a 74 años. 1965-1969: 15 años y más. 25 Fuerza trabajadora civil ocupada (estimaciones oficiales). 26 Abril. 27 Marzo.

5 Employment in non-agricultural sectors
Emploi dans les secteurs non agricoles
Empleo en los sectores no agrícolas

(Indices: 1970 = 100)

Country — Pays — País	Code Code Clave	1965	1966	1967	1968	1969	1970	1971	1972	1973	1974	1975 (VI)
Hongrie [1]	III	88.9	90.2	91.7	94.3	97.7	100.0	101.2	102.6	104.2	105.7 *	.
Iceland	II	93.0	95.2	95.0	95.3	95.2	100.0	106.7	110.7	114.5	...	.
Ireland [2]	. [3]	94.6	95.1	96.1	97.8	99.7	100.0	101.6	101.0	102.5	104.1	.
Italie [4]	I	93.5	93.1	95.3	97.0	97.2	100.0	99.8	99.7	101.5	104.7	104.9 [24]
Luxembourg [5]	III	98.0	96.9	92.2	92.3	94.7	100.0	103.3	107.6	108.9	108.2	105 5 *
Malta [6]	III	83.6	86.9	89.7	92.9	98.5	100.0	101.7	98.8	...	...	.
Norway	I [7]	90.3	91.8	93.9	95.0	97.0	100.0	.	|100.0 [8]	101.2	102.5	106.1 [25]
Pays-Bas [9]	. [10]	94.2	95.2	95.0	96.5	| 98.3 [11]	100.0	100.9	100.0	100.4 *	100.5 *	.
Pologne [12]	III	85.2	88.2	91.9	95.1	98.3	100.0	103.3	108.1	112.6	116.7	118.6 [26]
Roumanie [13]	III	83.0	86.6	90.9	93.6	97.0	100.0	105.2	110.3	114.1	118.8	.
Sweden [14]	I	92.6	94.9	94.0	96.0	97.7	100.0	100.5	101.0	101.8	104.5	108.4
Turquie [15]	II	68.2	75.5	81.4	91.8	96.1	100.0	107.0	116.1	125.6	137.0	.
United Kingdom [16]	III [17]	101.6	102.6	100.8	100.3	100.6	100.0	| 98.6 [11]	98.8	101.3	101.9 *	.
Yugoslavia [18]	III	92.1	90.3	90.3	91.7	95.7	100.0	105.2	110.0	112.8	118.6	125.0
OCEANIA — OCÉANIE OCEANÍA												
Australia [19]	I	85.4	88.3	90.7	93.3	96.4	100.0	102.1	|103.4 [11]	106.9	109.5	109.2 [27]
Fiji [20]	III	.	.	.	.	92.9	100.0	109.6	116.3	121.4	...	.
New Zealand [21]	III	90.4	93.5	94.6	94.0	96.7	100.0	102.1	103.1	106.1	109.9	112.5 [24]
URSS [22, 23]	III	84.2	87.4	90.6	94.1	97.3	100.0	102.8	105.7	108.1	110.7	.
RSS de Biélorussie [23]	III	76.9	81.6	86.2	91.1	95.9	100.0	104.2	108.1	111.5	114.7	.
RSS d'Ukraine [23]	III	81.7	85.5	89.3	93.3	96.9	100.0	103.1	106.0	108.4	110.8	.

EXPLANATORY NOTES AND CODES: See p. 297.

[1] Civilian labour force employed. [2] April of each year. [3] Civilian labour force employed (official estimates). [4] Persons aged 14 years and over. [5] Excl. workshops of the Luxembourg railways, services and part of commerce. [6] Civilian labour force employed; excl. family workers. Dec. of each year. [7] Persons aged 16 to 74 years. 1965-70: compulsory health insurance statistics; employees only. [8] Series replacing former series. [9] Civilian labour force employed, excl. civil personnel employed by the Ministry of Defense; number of man-years. [10] Official estimates. [11] Series linked to former series. [12] Socialised sector. [13] Persons aged 16 to 74 years. Incl. certain categories of military personnel. [15] Sep. of each year. Excl. air transport and government services. [16] Excl. Northern Ireland. Civilian labour force employed. June of each year. [17] Prior to 1971: National insurance statistics. [18] Socialised sector. March and Sep. of each year. [19] Persons aged 15 years and over. [20] June of each year. [21] Incl. forestry and logging. [22] Byelorussian SSR and Ukrainian SSR, shown separately in this table. [23] Socialised sector. Incl. industrial sea-fishing. [24] April. [25] Second quarter. [26] First quarter. [27] May.

NOTES EXPLICATIVES ET CODES: Voir p. 300.

[1] Main-d'œuvre civile occupée. [2] Avril de chaque année. [3] Main-d'œuvre civile occupée (évaluations officielles). [4] Personnes âgées de 14 ans et plus. [5] Non compris les ateliers des chemins de fer luxembourgeois, les services et une partie du commerce. [6] Main-d'œuvre civile occupée; non compris les travailleurs familiaux. Déc. de chaque année. [7] Personnes âgées de 16 à 74 ans. 1965-1970: statistique de l'assurance-maladie obligatoire; salariés seulement. [8] Série remplaçant la précédente. [9] Main-d'œuvre civile occupée, non compris le personnel civil employé par le ministère de la Défense; nombre d'années-homme. [10] Evaluations officielles. [11] Série enchaînée à la précédente. [12] Secteur socialisé. Y compris la pêche maritime. Non compris les apprentis. Les personnes employées à temps partiel sont converties en unité de travail à temps complet. [13] Secteur socialisé. [14] Personnes âgées de 16 à 74 ans. Y compris certaines catégories de personnel militaire. [15] Sept. de chaque année. Non compris les transports aériens et les services gouvernementaux. [16] Non compris l'Irlande du Nord. Main-d'œuvre civile occupée. Juin de chaque année. [17] Avant 1971: statistiques de l'assurance nationale. [18] Secteur socialisé. Mars et sept. de chaque année. [19] Personnes âgées de 15 ans et plus. [20] Juin de chaque année. [21] Y compris la sylviculture et l'exploitation forestière. [22] Y compris les RSS de Biélorussie et d'Ukraine, figurant séparément dans ce tableau. [23] Secteur socialisé. Y compris la pêche maritime industrielle. [24] Avril. [25] Deuxième trimestre. [26] Premier trimestre. [27] Mai.

NOTAS EXPLICATIVAS Y CLAVES: Véase pág. 303.

[1] Fuerza trabajadora civil ocupada. [2] Abril de cada año. [3] Fuerza trabajadora civil ocupada (estimaciones oficiales). [4] Personas de 14 años y más. [5] Excl. los talleres de los ferrocarriles luxemburgueses, los servicios y parte del comercio. [6] Fuerza trabajadora civil ocupada; excl. los trabajadores familiares. Dic. de cada año. [7] Personas de 16 a 74 años. 1965-1970: estadísticas del seguro obligatorio de enfermedad; asalariados solamente. [8] Serie que substituye a la anterior. [9] Fuerza trabajadora civil ocupada, excl. el personal civil empleado por el Ministerio de la Defensa; número de años-hombre. [10] Estimaciones oficiales. [11] Serie enlazada con la anterior. [12] Sector socializado. Incl. la pesca marítima. Excl. los aprendices. Las personas empleadas a tiempo parcial son convertidas en unidad de trabajo a pleno tiempo. [13] Sector socializado. [14] Personas de 16 a 74 años. Incl. ciertas categorías de personal militar. [15] Sept. de cada año. Excl. el transporte aéreo y los servicios gubernamentales. [16] Excl. Irlanda del Norte. Fuerza trabajadora civil ocupada. Junio de cada año. [17] Antes de 1971: estadísticas del Seguro Nacional. [18] Sector socializado. Marzo y sept. de cada año. [19] Personas de 15 años y más. [20] Junio de cada año. [21] Incl. la silvicultura y la explotación de la madera. [22] Incl. las RSS de Bielorrusia y de Ucrania, que figuran separadamente en este cuadro. [23] Sector socializado. Incl. la pesca marítima industrial. [24] Abril. [25] Segundo trimestre. [26] Primer trimestre. [27] Mayo.

6 Employment in manufacturing
Emploi dans les industries manufacturières
Empleo en las industrias manufactureras

A All industries
Ensemble des industries
Todas las industrias

(Indices: 1970 = 100)

Country — Pays — País	Code Code Clave	1965	1966	1967	1968	1969	1970	1971	1972	1973	1974	1975 (VI)
AFRICA — AFRIQUE ÁFRICA												
Cameroun	III	39.2	47.9	63.3	88.7	66.7	100.0	112.6	114.9	170.2	...	.
Egypt [1]	. [2]	.	.	.	90.8	95.1	100.0	84.2	90.3	98.1	...	.
Ethiopia [3]	III	97.5	112.1	120.0	.	96.8	100.0	104.9	108.3	...	...	.
Gabon	II	44.2	40.9	47.3	64.7	72.1	100.0	98.5 *	97.9 *	...	...	.
Ghana [4]	III	61.5	67.9	78.0	85.0	100.2	100.0	107.3	96.4 [5]	...	...	.
Kenya [6]	III [7]	.	.	83.0	85.9	88.3	100.0	112.8	ǀ115.8 [8]	128.9	...	...
Malawi [9]	III	.	.	.	88.6	90.7	100.0	111.8	119.0	131.7	137.4	144.7 [21]
Mauritius [10]	III	.	.	89.2	93.1	96.1	100.0	112.3	132.7	177.2	237.5	.
Nigeria	III [11]	.	.	.	63.6	80.7	100.0	114.5	131.8	...	...	...
Sierra Leone [4]	III	120.8	109.9	116.6	116.9	118.9	100.0	93.2	103.7	102.5	103.6	...
South Africa, Rep. of . . . Total	III	79.2	83.1	86.4	88.5	94.1	100.0	103.3	105.5	109.0	113.1	115.5 [22]
» » » » [12]	III	83.9	89.3	92.1	93.6	97.0	100.0	100.7	101.8	102.7	103.3	...
Swaziland [11]	III	.	.	.	.	.	100.0	108.4	121.0	136.7	...	.
Tanzania (Tanganyika) [6]	III	58.0	67.3	71.1	80.5	91.4	100.0	129.4	...	...	...	.
Uganda [6]	III	70.1	79.2	82.0	91.8	100.3	100.0	101.7	98.6	99.3	...	.
Zambia	III [13]	.	78.2	84.7	89.7	93.7	100.0	110.2	111.2	110.8	...	...
AMERICA — AMÉRIQUE AMÉRICA												
Belize [14]	III	74.3	82.7	94.6	96.6	100.0	...	...	...	...	...	.
Canada	III	95.4	100.6	100.2	99.4	102.0	100.0	99.0	100.7	105.8 *	109.0 *	106.4 *
Colombia	III	.	.	.	.	.	.	100.0	105.9	109.1	111.9	...
Chile [15]	III	105.9	104.3	104.3	103.7	99.0	100.0	95.2	105.3	106.0	...	.
República Dominicana	III	73.1	84.5	94.3	87.0	85.9	100.0	103.0	112.3	124.5	...	.
Ecuador	III	99.0	101.8	100.0	98.9	ǀ 97.1 [8]	100.0	100.9	102.5	108.0	...	...
El Salvador [16]	III	97.0	99.2	100.1	97.6	98.1	100.0	99.8	106.9	115.4	118.5	...
Guatemala (Guatemala) [17]	III	91.5	91.2	91.8	95.0	95.2	100.0	100.7	100.6	110.4	120.2	...
Panamá [18]	II	63.9	70.9	77.2	84.3	89.9	100.0	107.3	110.6	123.8 [19]	...	.
Perú	. [20]	87.0	89.3	86.0	95.6	94.3	100.0	106.0	113.1	...	...	.
Puerto Rico	III	81.6	87.2	91.7	98.9	101.7	100.0	101.5	106.1	112.1	111.7	95.9

EXPLANATORY NOTES AND CODES: See p. 297.

[1] May of each year. [2] Civilian labour force employed (official estimates). Incl. mining and quarrying. [3] Year ending in Sep. of the year indicated. [4] Dec. of each year. [5] Sep. [6] June of each year. [7] Excl. employment in rural areas (except for large enterprises). [8] Series linked to former series. [9] Incl. working proprietors and unpaid family workers. [10] March and Sep. of each year. Excl. relief workers. Excl. sugar and tea factories. [11] Sep. of each year. [12] White population. [13] June and Dec. of each year. [14] March of each year. [15] Wage earners only. April of each year. [16] Area of San Salvador. [17] Wage earners only. [18] Aug. of each year. [19] March. [20] Official estimates. [21] First quarter. [22] April.

NOTES EXPLICATIVES ET CODES: Voir p. 300.

[1] Mai de chaque année. [2] Main-d'œuvre civile occupée (évaluations officielles). Y compris les industries extractives. [3] Année se terminant en sept. de l'année indiquée. [4] Déc. de chaque année. [5] Sept. [6] Juin de chaque année. [7] Non compris l'emploi dans les zones rurales (à l'exception des grandes entreprises). [8] Série enchaînée à la précédente. [9] Y compris les propriétaires-exploitants et les travailleurs familiaux non rémunérés. [10] Mars et sept. de chaque année. Non compris les personnes occupées à des travaux publics de secours. Non compris les fabriques de sucre et de thé. [11] Sept. de chaque année. [12] Population blanche. [13] Juin et déc. de chaque année. [14] Mars de chaque année. [15] Ouvriers seulement. Avril de chaque année. [16] Zone de San Salvador. [17] Ouvriers seulement. [18] Août de chaque année. [19] Mars. [20] Evaluations officielles. [21] Premier trimestre. [22] Avril.

NOTAS EXPLICATIVAS Y CLAVES: Véase pág. 303.

[1] Mayo de cada año. [2] Fuerza trabajadora civil ocupada (estimaciones oficiales). Incl. las minas y canteras. [3] Año que se termina en sept. del año indicado. [4] Dic. de cada año. [5] Sept. [6] Junio de cada año. [7] Excl. el empleo en las zonas rurales (con excepción de las grandes empresas). [8] Serie enlazada con la anterior. [9] Incl. los empresarios propietarios y los trabajadores familiares no remunerados. [10] Marzo y sept. de cada año. Excl. las personas ocupadas en planes de asistencia. Excl. las fábricas de azúcar y de té. [11] Sept. de cada año. [12] Población blanca. [13] Junio y dic. de cada año. [14] Marzo de cada año. [15] Obreros solamente. Abril de cada año. [16] Zona de San Salvador. [17] Obreros solamente. [18] Agosto de cada año. [19] Marzo. [20] Estimaciones oficiales. [21] Primer trimestre. [22] Abril.

6 Employment in manufacturing
Emploi dans les industries manufacturières
Empleo en las industrias manufactureras

A All industries
Ensemble des industries
Todas las industrias

(Indices: 1970 = 100)

Country — *Pays* — País	Code *Code* Clave	1965	1966	1967	1968	1969	1970	1971	1972	1973	1974	1975 (VI)
Trinidad and Tobago [1]	III	.	.	.	.	93.6	**100.0**	119.1	106.8	...	...	.
United States	III	93.3	99.3	100.5	102.2	104.2	**100.0**	95.8	97.9	102.4	103.4	94.2
Venezuela	III	96.1	98.2	94.2	96.9	| 98.7 [2]	**100.0**	101.1	102.4	106.6	114.1 *	...
ASIA — ASIE ASIA												
Brunei [3]	III [4]	.	.	.	.	.	.	.	*100.0*	*123.7*	*118.9*	...
Cyprus	. [5]	.	.	85.6	91.8	95.9	**100.0**	105.2	107.3	108.9 *	76.7 *	.
Hong Kong	III	61.0	67.1	74.8	| 82.8 [6]	93.9	**100.0**	104.1	105.2	107.0	| 100.7 [6]	100.6
India	III	94.6	94.2	95.3	95.2	96.2	**100.0**	104.1 *	109.5 *	...	...	
Israel	III	80.0	78.4	74.1	| 85.2 [7]	94.0	**100.0**	103.7	108.3	109.4	113.8	111.6 [16]
Japan	I	87.1	88.9	| 92.4 [6]	95.3	97.6	**100.0**	100.9	100.6	104.4	104.1	97.6
Jordan [8]	III	*91.3*	*92.1*	*83.7*	*90.4*	**100.0**	...	...	...	...	...	
Korea, Rep. of	I	.	61.0	77.9	92.7	96.7	**100.0**	96.4	115.8	145.3	173.1	...
Philippines	III	80.5	86.5	91.0	96.5	105.5	**100.0**	109.4	105.8	109.1	114.9 *	...
Singapore [9]	III	.	.	.	.	81.0	**100.0**	117.0	143.8	169.9	...	...
République arabe syrienne [10]	I	*96.0* [11]	*103.2*	*101.5*	**100.0**	*95.2* [12]	.	...	*133.4* [13]	...	...	
EUROPE — EUROPE EUROPA												
Albanie [14]	.	60.7	66.9	76.8	88.0	94.0	**100.0**	104.0	...	...	...	.
Austria [12]	III	99.3	98.9	95.6	93.9	96.9	**100.0**	| 103.0 [6]	105.2	107.5	107.0	101.1
Belgique [4]	II	.	.	.	.	.	**100.0**	100.1	98.9	100.1	101.2	...
Bulgarie [14]	III	81.6	89.2	93.8	94.9	97.9	**100.0**	102.2	104.4	106.9	109.2 *	...
Czechoslovakia [14]	III	93.3	95.7	96.6	97.9	98.7	**100.0**	100.9	103.7	105.4	106.5	.
Denmark	III	95.7	| 94.0 [6]	94.6	94.3	98.4	| 100.0 [6]	96.7	98.4	101.4	98.6	88.9 [16]
España	II	87.0	92.5	92.7	93.5	99.8	**100.0**	101.3	105.3	110.9	114.8	.
Finland [15]	III	88.0	89.0	88.6	88.4	92.5	**100.0**	103.1	101.6	102.8	110.5 *	119.2

EXPLANATORY NOTES AND CODES: See p. 297.

[1] Excl. sugar distilleries and petroleum refineries. [2] Beginning 1969: establishments with 10 or more workers (prior to 1969 all establishments); series linked to former series. [3] Incl. employers and workers on own account. [4] June of each year. [5] Official estimates. [6] Series linked to former series. [7] Series linked to former series. Beginning 1968: incl. mining and quarrying. [8] Incl. workers on own account and unpaid family workers. [9] March and Sep. of each year. [10] Nov. of each year. [11] May and Nov. [12] Incl. mining and quarrying [13] Sep. [14] Socialised sector; incl. mining and quarrying. [15] Wage earners only. Incl. mining and quarrying. [16] May.

NOTES EXPLICATIVES ET CODES: Voir p. 300.

[1] *Non compris les distilleries du sucre et les raffineries du pétrole.* [2] *A partir de 1969 : établissements occupant 10 travailleurs et plus (avant 1969 tous les établissements) ; série enchaînée à la précédente.* [3] *Y compris les personnes travaillant à leur propre compte.* [4] *Juin de chaque année.* [5] *Evaluations officielles.* [6] *Série enchaînée à la précédente.* [7] *Série enchaînée à la précédente. A partir de 1968 : y compris les industries extractives.* [8] *Y compris les personnes travaillant à leur propre compte et les travailleurs familiaux non rémunérés.* [9] *Mars et sept. de chaque année.* [10] *Nov. de chaque année.* [11] *Mai et nov.* [12] *Y compris les industries extractives.* [13] *Sept.* [14] *Secteur socialisé ; y compris les industries extractives.* [15] *Ouvriers seulement. Y compris les industries extractives.* [16] *Mai.*

NOTAS EXPLICATIVAS Y CLAVES: Véase pág. 303.

[1] Excl. las destilerías de azúcar y las refinerías de petróleo. [2] A partir de 1969: establecimientos con 10 trabajadores y más (antes de 1969 todos los establecimientos); serie enlazada con la anterior. [3] Incl. los trabajadores por cuenta propia. [4] Junio de cada año. [5] Estimaciones oficiales. [6] Serie enlazada con la anterior. [7] Serie enlazada con la anterior. A partir de 1968: incl. las minas y canteras. [8] Incl. los trabajadores por cuenta propia y los trabajadores familiares no remunerados. [9] Marzo y sept. de cada año. [10] Nov. de cada año. [11] Mayo y nov. [12] Incl. las minas y canteras. [13] Sept. [14] Sector socializado, incl. las minas y canteras. [15] Obreros solamente. Incl. las minas y canteras. [16] Mayo.

6 Employment in manufacturing
Emploi dans les industries manufacturières
Empleo en las industrias manufactureras

A All industries
Ensemble des industries
Todas las industrias

(Indices: 1970 = 100)

Country — Pays — País	Code / Code / Clave	1965	1966	1967	1968	1969	1970	1971	1972	1973	1974	1975 (VI)
France	III	99.8	99.9	98.7	96.5	98.3	**100.0**	100.5	101.2	103.0	103.4	101.0
German Democratic Republic Δ[1] . .	.	97.3	98.3	99.6	99.9	100.3	**100.0**	101.3	105.4	106.4	106.0	.
Germany, Fed. Rep. of Δ	.[2]	96.7	96.7	92.0	93.2	97.5	**100.0**	99.3	97.7	98.3	95.9 *	.
Grèce	III	90.6	93.3	92.7	92.1	95.5	**100.0**	106.1	110.5	117.0	118.3	119.9
Hongrie[3]	III	.	.	.	96.4	99.6	**❘100.0**[4]	99.8	99.8	101.6	102.5 *	...
Ireland[5]	III	87.9	89.3	90.0	94.6	98.6	**100.0**	98.8	99.8	102.6 *	103.1 *	98.2 *[19]
Italie	I	88.7	88.6	91.6	93.5	96.6	**100.0**	102.0	101.1	102.8	107.0	105.5 [20]
Luxembourg	III	98.7	98.7	96.4	95.7	98.1	**100.0**	102.9	104.7	...	...	.
Malta[6]	III	71.5	75.0	79.7	82.3	93.9	**100.0**	105.6	110.8	...	...	.
Norway	I[7]	93.6	95.2	96.4	95.9	97.0	**100.0**	.	❘100.0[8]	98.9	100.8	106.1 [21]
Pays-Bas	III	103	102	100	99	100	**❘100**[8]	99	94	93	93	90 [22]
Pologne[9]	III	84.9	88.0	91.6	94.9	98.4	**100.0**	103.1	107.2	110.3	112.9 *	114.4 *[22]
Roumanie[10]	III	81.1	83.9	87.1	90.8	95.8	**100.0**	106.6	112.5	120.3	128.8	.
Suisse[11]	III	104.9	102.8	101.6	100.8	100.6	**100.0**	98.6	96.1	94.7	94.4	87.0
Sweden[12]	III	103.8	102.1	❘ 97.7 [4]	95.8	98.0	**100.0**	97.3	95.7	97.9	...	...
Turquie[13]	II	69.1	74.9	81.6	94.2	95.7	**100.0**	107.7	119.8	130.9	124.6	.
United Kingdom[14]	III[15]	102.7	❘103.0 [4]	99.8	98.8	❘100.1 [4]	**100.0**	❘ 96.6 [4]	93.3	93.9	94.4 *	90.5 *
Yugoslavia[16]	III	94.7	93.4	93.0	92.8	96.2	**100.0**	105.3	111.0	114.5	120.8	126.8
OCEANIA — OCÉANIE OCEANÍA												
Australia	III	91.1	❘ 91.8 [4]	93.4	95.3	97.8	**100.0**	101.0	99.6	100.5	102.6	94.6
Fiji[14]	III	.	.	.	.	103.5	**100.0**	109.9	107.6	110.7	...	.
New Zealand	III	86.5	89.9	90.1	88.4	92.8	**❘ 97.7** [4]	100.0	99.9	104.2	108.0	108.4 [20]
URSS [17, 18]	III	85.1	88.8	92.1	95.5	98.3	**100.0**	101.7	103.4	104.9	107.0	.
RSS de Biélorussie[18]	III	74.7	81.0	85.9	91.9	96.9	**100.0**	104.0	106.8	109.5	112.5	.
RSS d'Ukraine[18]	III	82.0	86.2	90.2	94.9	98.4	**100.0**	102.7	104.8	107.4	109.7	.

EXPLANATORY NOTES AND CODES: See p. 297.　　NOTES EXPLICATIVES ET CODES: Voir p. 300.　　NOTAS EXPLICATIVAS Y CLAVES: Véase pág. 303.

1 Incl. mining and quarrying. 2 Official estimates. 3 State industry. 4 Series linked to former series. 5 Incl. working proprietors. Oct. of each year except for 1969-72: Sep. 6 Dec. of each year. 7 1965-70: compulsory health insurance statistics. 8 Series replacing former series. 9 Socialised sector. Incl. mining, quarrying and sea fishing. Excl. apprentices. Figures include full-time equivalent of part-time workers. 10 Socialised sector. Incl. mining and quarrying. 11 Wage earners only. 12 Wage earners only. 1965-66: incl. mining and quarrying. 13 Sep. of each year. 14 June of each year. 15 Prior to 1971: National insurance statistics. 16 Socialised sector. Incl. mining and quarrying. March and Sep. of each year. 17 Incl. Byelorussian SSR and Ukrainian SSR shown separately in this table. 18 Socialised sector. Excl. publishing. 19 March. 20 April. 21 Second quarter. 22 First quarter.

1 Y compris les industries extractives. 2 Evaluations officielles. 3 Industrie d'Etat. 4 Série enchaînée à la précédente. 5 Y compris les propriétaires-exploitants. Oct. de chaque année, sauf pour 1969-1972: sept. 6 Déc. de chaque année. 7 1965-1970: statistique de l'assurance-maladie obligatoire. 8 Série remplaçant la précédente. 9 Secteur socialisé. Y compris les industries extractives et la pêche maritime. Non compris les apprentis. Les personnes employées à temps partiel sont converties en unité de travail à temps complet. 10 Secteur socialisé. Y compris les industries extractives. 11 Ouvriers seulement. 12 Ouvriers seulement. 1965-1966: y compris les industries extractives. 13 Sept. de chaque année. 14 Juin de chaque année. 15 Avant 1971: statistique de l'assurance nationale. 16 Secteur socialisé. Y compris les industries extractives. Mars et sept. de chaque année. 17 Y compris les RSS de Biélorussie et d'Ukraine, figurant séparément dans ce tableau. 18 Secteur socialisé. Non compris l'édition. 19 Mars. 20 Avril. 21 Deuxième trimestre. 22 Premier trimestre.

1 Incl. las minas y canteras. 2 Estimaciones oficiales. 3 Industria de Estado. 4 Serie enlazada con la anterior. 5 Incl. los empresarios propietarios. Oct. de cada año, salvo 1969-1972: sept. 6 Dic. de cada año. 7 1965-1970: estadísticas del seguro obligatorio de enfermedad. 8 Serie que substituye a la anterior. 9 Sector socializado. Incl. las minas, las canteras y la pesca marítima. Excl. los aprendices. Las personas empleadas a tiempo parcial son convertidas en unidad de trabajo a pleno tiempo. 10 Sector socializado. Incl. las minas y canteras. 11 Obreros solamente. 12 Obreros solamente. 1965-1966: incl. las minas y canteras. 13 Sept. de cada año. 14 Junio de cada año. 15 Antes de 1971: estadísticas del Seguro Nacional. 16 Sector socializado. Incl. las minas y canteras. 17 Incl. las RSS de Bielorrusia y de Ucrania, que figuran separadamente en este cuadro. 18 Sector socializado. Excl. las editoriales. 19 Marzo. 20 Abril. 21 Segundo trimestre. 22 Primer trimestre.

EMPLOYMENT

6 **Employment in manufacturing**
Emploi dans les industries manufacturières
Empleo en las industrias manufactureras

B **By industry**
Par industrie
Por industria

AFRICA — AFRIQUE — AFRICA

Ethiopia

Indices of numbers employed: wage earners and salaried employees *(Statistics of establishments)*
Indices de l'effectif employé: ouvriers et employés *(Statistiques d'établissements)*
Indices de trabajadores ocupados: obreros y empleados *(Estadísticas de establecimientos)*

(1970 = 100)

	311-312	313-314	321	323	331	342	351-352	369	381
Date [1] *Date [1]* Fecha [1]	Food *Aliments* Alimentos	Beverages tobacco *Boissons, tabac* Bebidas, tabaco	*Textiles*	Leather, leather products *Cuir, articles en cuir* Cuero, artículos de cuero	Wood *Bois* Madera	Printing, publishing *Imprimerie, édition* Imprentas, editoriales	Chemicals *Industrie chimique* Productos químicos	Other non-metallic mineral products *Autres produits minéraux non métalliques* Otros productos minerales no metálicos	Metal products *Produits métalliques* Productos metálicos
1969	88.3	108.1	100.2	92.4	94.8	107.2	90.8	93.2	91.0
1970	**100.0**	**100.0**	**100.0**	**100.0**	**100.0**	**100.0**	**100.0**	**100.0**	**100.0**
1971	104.4	100.3	103.4	100.6	122.4	105.1	110.7	94.3	123.2
1972	105.8	103.0	109.0	99.5	124.6	105 0	116.0	97.4	119.3

[1] Year ending in Sep. of the year indicated.   [1] *Année se terminant en sept. de l'année indiquée.*   [1] Año que se termina en sept. del año indicado.

6 Employment in manufacturing
Emploi dans les industries manufacturières
Empleo en las industrias manufactureras

B By industry
Par industrie
Por industria

Ghana

Indices of numbers employed: wage earners and salaried employees *(Statistics of establishments)*
Indices de l'effectif employé: ouvriers et employés *(Statistiques d'établissements)*
Indices de trabajadores ocupados: obreros y empleados *(Estadísticas de establecimientos)*

(1970 = 100)

Date / Date / Fecha	311-312 Food / Aliments / Alimentos	313 Beverages / Boissons / Bebidas	314 Tobacco / Tabac / Tabaco	321 Textiles	322 Clothing / Habillement / Vestido	323-324 Leather, leather products, footwear / Cuir, articles en cuir, chaussures / Cuero, artículos de cuero, calzado	331 Wood / Bois / Madera	332 Furniture / Ameublement / Mobiliario	341 Paper, paper products / Papier, articles en papier / Papel, artículos de papel
1967	80.2	74.8	149.5	35.7	47.1	33.7	80.5	106.2	74.3
1968	90.1	75.5	131.9	49.4	65.6	99.3	91.2	91.1	103.9
1969	.	.	.	.	.	.	.	.	.
1970	100.0	100.0	100.0	100.0	100.0	100.0	100.0	100.0	100.0
1971	.	.	.	.	.	.	.	.	.
1972	126.2	118.5	.	108.6	.	84.2	95.6	95.2	109.1

Date / Date / Fecha	342 Printing, publishing / Imprimerie, édition / Imprentas, editoriales	351-352 Chemicals / Industrie chimique / Productos químicos	353-354 Refineries and products of petroleum and coal / Raffineries et dérivés du pétrole et du charbon / Refinerías y derivados del petróleo y del carbón	362 Glass / Verre / Vidrio	369 Other non-metallic mineral products / Autres produits minéraux non métalliques / Otros productos minerales no metálicos	371 Iron and steel basic industries / Sidérurgie / Industrias básicas de hierro y acero	381 Metal products / Produits métalliques / Productos metálicos	383 Electrical machinery and apparatus / Machines et appareils électriques / Maquinaria y aparatos eléctricos	384 Transport equipment / Matériel de transport / Material de transporte
1967	70.3	86.3	94.3	89.8	67.2	60.3	54.6	25.5	276.7
1968	82.3	104.5	96.1	95.3	90.0	50.6	73.4	51.6	287.9
1969	.	.	.	.	.	.	.	.	.
1970	100.0	100.0	100.0	100.0	100.0	100.0	100.0	100.0	100.0
1971	.	.	.	.	.	.	.	.	.
1972	101.9	104.7	101.8	113.6	95.2	91.2	114.7	117.6	105.0

EMPLOYMENT

6 | Employment in manufacturing
Emploi dans les industries manufacturières
Empleo en las industrias manufactureras

B | By industry
Par industrie
Por industria

Kenya

Indices of numbers employed: wage earners and salaried employees *(Statistics of establishments)* [1]
Indices de l'effectif employé: ouvriers et employés *(Statistiques d'établissements)* [1]
Indices de trabajadores ocupados: obreros y empleados *(Estadísticas de establecimientos)* [1]

(1970 = 100)

	311-312	313-314	321	322	323	324	331	332	341	342
Date [2]	Food	Beverages, tobacco		Clothing	Leather, leather products	Footwear [3]	Wood	Furniture	Paper, paper products	Printing, publishing
Date [2]	*Aliments*	*Boissons, tabac*	Textiles	*Habillement*	*Cuir, articles en cuir*	*Chaussures* [3]	*Bois*	*Ameublement*	*Papier, articles en papier*	*Imprimerie, édition*
Fecha [2]	Alimentos	Bebidas, tabaco		Vestido	Cuero, artículos de cuero	Calzado [3]	Madera	Mobiliario	Papel, artículos de papel	Imprentas, editoriales
1968	100.7	83.6	105.8	94.2	113.9	114.1	86.5	97.6	81.2	85.5
1969	99.9	90.8	103.9	93.3	99.6	83.6	90.2	103.0	89.6	83.2
1970	100.0	100.0	100.0	100.0	100.0	100.0	100.0	100.0	100.0	100.0
1971	116.1	108.1	119.3	131.6	164.7	105.0	112.1	117.6	148.2	110.0
1972	107.2	110.1	131.0	129.8	158.3	85.0 [4]	114.1	116.5	166.5	98.2
1973	120.2	111.2	156.4	130.0	181.9	118.0	117.9	143.7	217.1	101.6

	35 ×	355	36 ×	362	37; 381	382	383	384	390
Date [2]	Chemicals, refineries and products of petroleum and coal, plastics [5]	Rubber products	Non-metallic mineral products [6]	Glass	Metal industries	Machinery (non-electrical)	Electrical machinery and apparatus	Transport equipment [3]	Other manufacturing industries
Date [2]	*Industrie chimique, raffineries et dérivés du pétrole et du charbon, plastique* [5]	*Produits en caoutchouc*	*Produits minéraux non métalliques* [6]	*Verre*	*Industrie métallurgique*	*Machines (non électriques)*	*Machines et appareils électriques*	*Matériel de transport* [3]	*Autres industries manufacturières*
Fecha [2]	Productos químicos, refinerías y derivados del petróleo y del carbón, plástico [5]	Productos de caucho	Productos minerales no metálicos [6]	Vidrio	Industrias metalúrgicas	Maquinaria (no eléctrica)	Maquinaria y aparatos eléctricos	Material de transporte [3]	Otras industrias manufactureras
1968	117.3	73.7	97.5	81.8	90.6	.	.	59.2	67.1
1969	95.5	81.0	98.5	94.6	87.2	99.1	85.5	67.8	98.7
1970	100.0	100.0	100.0	100.0	100.0	100.0	100.0	100.0	100.0
1971	111.6	115.4	123.9	93.7	149.1	85.1	93.0	103.2	130.4
1972	135.4	141.1	143.0	99.7	143.2	102.1	94.1	110.8	159.0
1973	149.3	157.0	155.4	58.1	161.4	88.0	...	128.2	113.4

[1] Excl. employment in rural areas (except for large enterprises). [2] June of each year. [3] 1968-71: incl. repair services. [4] Series linked to former series. [5] Excl. rubber products. [6] Excl. glass.

[1] *Non compris l'emploi dans les zones rurales (à l'exception des grandes entreprises).* [2] *Juin de chaque année.* [3] *1968-1971 : y compris les services de réparation.* [4] *Série enchaînée à la précédente.* [5] *Non compris les produits en caoutchouc.* [6] *Non compris le verre.*

[1] Excl. el empleo en las zonas rurales (con excepción de las grandes empresas). [2] Junio de cada año. [3] 1968-1971: incl. los servicios de reparación. [4] Serie enlazada con la anterior. [5] Excl. los productos de caucho. [6] Excl. el vidrio.

Employment in manufacturing
Emploi dans les industries manufacturières
Empleo en las industrias manufactureras

B

By industry
Par industrie
Por industria

Libyan Arab Republic

Indices of numbers employed: wage earners and salaried employees *(Statistics of establishments)*
Indices de l'effectif employé: ouvriers et employés *(Statistiques d'établissements)*
Indices de trabajadores ocupados: obreros y empleados *(Estadísticas de establecimientos)*

(1970 = 100)

Date / Date / Fecha	311-312 Food / Aliments / Alimentos	313 Beverages / Boissons / Bebidas	314 Tobacco / Tabac / Tabaco	321 Textiles	342 Printing, publishing / Imprimerie, édition / Imprentas, editoriales	351-352 Chemicals / Industrie chimique / Productos químicos	369 Non-metallic mineral products [1] / Produits minéraux non métalliques [1] / Productos minerales no metálicos [1]	381 Metal products [2] / Produits métalliques [2] / Productos metálicos [2]
1967	106.8	92.6	105.2	97.8	115.0	72.4	70.3	79.0
1968	102.4	95.8	98.9	92.0	112.1	96.5	76.0	99.5
1969	91.9	111.4	99.5	104.2	112.4	90.7	84.7	104.0
1970	100.0	100.0	100.0	100.0	100.0	100.0	100.0	100.0
1971	120.1	111.8	103.7	127.9	107.7	102.4	110.0	96.6

[1] Excl. pottery, china, earthenware and glass. [2] Excl. metal furniture.

[1] *Non compris le grès, les porcelaines, les faïences et le verre.* [2] *Non compris les meubles en métal.*

[1] Excl. el barro, la loza, la porcelana y el vidrio. [2] Excl. los muebles metálicos.

Malawi

Indices of numbers employed: wage earners and salaried employees *(Statistics of establishments)*
Indices de l'effectif employé: ouvriers et employés *(Statistiques d'établissements)*
Indices de trabajadores ocupados: obreros y empleados *(Estadísticas de establecimientos)*

(1970 = 100)

Date / Date / Fecha	311-312 Food / Aliments / Alimentos	313 Beverages / Boissons / Bebidas	314 Tobacco / Tabac / Tabaco	321 Textiles	322-324 Clothing, leather, leather products, footwear / Habillement, cuir, articles en cuir, chaussures / Vestido cuero, artículos de cuero, calzado	33 Wood, furnutire / Bois, ameublement / Madera, mobiliario	34 Paper, printing, publishing / Papier, imprimerie, édition / Papel, imprentas, editoriales	351-352; 355-356 Chemicals, rubber and plastic products / Industrie chimique, produits en caoutchouc et en plastique / Productos químicos, de caucho y plástico	369 Non-metallic mineral products [1] / Produits minéraux non métalliques [1] / Productos minerales no metálicos [1]	38 × Metal products machinery, etc. [2] / Produits métalliques, machines, etc. [2] / Productos metálicos, maquinaria, etc. [2]
1970	100.0	100.0	100.0	100.0	100.0	100.0	100.0	100.0	100.0	100.0
1971	104.4	101.2	121.9	107.1	119.0	106.5	118.3	106.2	113.6	131.5
1972	109.9	107.8	135.2	113.3	104.1	117.2	101.4	132.8	121.3	170.6
1973	124.8	119.2	147.0	126.2	126.4	145.4	129.2	120.0	120.2	185.3
1974	149.4	124.4	126.3	133.8	148.0	137.9	139.0	175.4	137.9	211.5

[1] Excl. pottery, china, earthenware and glass. [2] Excl. scientific, measuring, optical, etc., equipment.

[1] *Non compris le grès, les porcelaines, les faïences et le verre.* [2] *Non compris le matériel scientifique, de précision, d'optique, etc.*

[1] Excl. el barro, la loza, la porcelana y el vidrio. [2] Excl. el equipo científico, de medida, de óptica, etc.

6 **Employment in manufacturing**
Emploi dans les industries manufacturières
Empleo en las industrias manufactureras

B **By industry**
Par industrie
Por industria

Mauritius

Indices of numbers employed: wage earners and salaried employees *(Statistics of establishments)* [1]
Indices de l'effectif employé: ouvriers et employés *(Statistiques d'établissements)* [1]
Indices de trabajadores ocupados: obreros y empleados *(Estadísticas de establecimientos)* [1]

(1970 = 100)

	311-312	313-314	321	322	323-324; 355	33
Date [2]	Food [3]	Beverages, tobacco		Clothing	Leather, leather products, footwear, rubber	Wood, furniture
Date [2] Fecha [2]	*Aliments* [3]	*Boissons, tabac*	Textiles	*Habillement*	*Cuir, articles en cuir, chaussures, caoutchouc*	*Bois, ameublement*
	Alimentos [3]	Bebidas, tabaco		Vestido	Cuero, artículos de cuero, calzado, caucho	Madera, mobiliario
1968	72.5	102.1	129.9	59.6	72.3	76.9
1969	90.4	103.2	115.9	90.6	74.2	81.3
1970	**100.0**	**100.0**	**100.0**	**100.0**	**100.0**	**100.0**
1971	107.0	107.6	116.7	279.1	130.8	130.1
1972	163.5	119.2	94.7	594.1	148.7	191.0
1973	204.8	123.8	87.7	1 071.4	210.6	279.3
1974	245.2	142.1	105.6	1 771.4	202.2	305.4

	342	351-352	369	381-383	384	390
Date [2]	Printing, publishing	Chemicals	Non-metallic mineral products [4]	Metal products, machinery	Transport equipment	Other manufacturing industries
Date [2] Fecha [2]	*Imprimerie, édition*	*Industrie chimique*	*Produits minéraux non métalliques* [4]	*Produits métalliques, machines*	*Matériel de transport*	*Autres industries manufacturières*
	Imprentas, editoriales	Productos químicos	Productos minerales no metálicos [4]	Productos metálicos, maquinaria	Material de transporte	Otras industrias manufactureras
1968	93.7	107.2	96.8	103.4	84.5	66.0
1969	97.0	98.0	100.9	100.2	75.8	85.7
1970	**100.0**	**100.0**	**100.0**	**100.0**	**100.0**	**100.0**
1971	111.7	110.7	103.0	107.5	79.0	237.4
1972	111.7	138.9	111.7	125.6	94.9	225.7
1973	137.0	140.3	148.2	203.3	118.4	259.7
1974	151.6	174.1	159.4	317.6	121.7	285.7

[1] Excl. relief workers. [2] Sep. of each year. [3] Excl. sugar and tea factories. [4] Excl. pottery, china, earthenware and glass.

[1] *Non compris les personnes occupées à des travaux publics de secours.* [2] *Sept. de chaque année.* [3] *Non compris les industries du sucre et du thé.* [4] *Non compris le grès, les porcelaines, les faïences et le verre.*

[1] Excl. las personas ocupadas en planes de asistencia. [2] Sept. de cada año. [3] Excl. las industrias del azúcar y del té. [4] Excl. el barro, la loza, la porcelana y el vidrio.

6 Employment in manufacturing
Emploi dans les industries manufacturières
Empleo en las industrias manufactureras

B By industry
Par industrie
Por industria

Mozambique

Indices of numbers employed: wage earners and salaried employees *(Statistics of establishments)*
Indices de l'effectif employé: ouvriers et employés *(Statistiques d'établissements)*
Indices de trabajadores ocupados: obreros y empleados *(Estadísticas de establecimientos)*

(1970 = 100)

	311-312	313	314	321	322	323-324	331	332	34	351
Date [1] Date [1] Fecha [1]	Food *Aliments* Alimentos	Beverages *Boissons* Bebidas	Tobacco *Tabac* Tabaco	Textiles	Clothing *Habillement* Vestido	Leather, leather products, footwear *Cuir, articles en cuir, chaussures* Cuero, artículos de cuero, calzado	Wood *Bois* Madera	Furniture *Ameublement* Mobiliario	Paper, printing, publishing *Papier, imprimerie, édition* Papel, imprentas, editoriales	Industrial chemicals *Chimie industrielle* Química industrial
1967	78.9	69.7	91.5	94.6	80.4	83.4	81.6	73.8	74.2	58.5
1968	77.5	91.3	93.0	95.5	102.7	92.4	83.4	85.7	84.3	74.8
1969	79.9	99.0	81.1	82.0	110.0	106.8	92.7	92.6	90.7	81.8
1970	**100.0**	**100.0**	**100.0**	**100.0**	**100.0**	**100.0**	**100.0**	**100.0**	**100.0**	**100.0**
1971	105.0	128.1	99.6	92.1	126.0	115.2	86.7	114.5	113.0	72.8

	352	353	355-356	362	369	371	381	382-383	384
Date [1] Date [1] Fecha [1]	Other chemical products *Autres produits chimiques* Otros productos químicos	Petroleum refineries *Raffineries de pétrole* Refinerías de petróleo	Rubber and plastic products *Produits en caoutchouc et en plastique* Productos de caucho y de plástico	Glass, and glass products *Verre* Vidrio	Other non-metallic mineral products *Autres produits minéraux non métalliques* Otros productos minerales no metálicos	Iron and steel basic industries *Sidérurgie* Industrias básicas de hierro y acero	Metal products *Produits métalliques* Productos metálicos	Machinery *Machines* Maquinaria	Transport equipment *Matériel de transport* Material de transporte
1967	98.2	92.0	94.6	90.8	98.4	40.1	69.4	.	.
1968	97.8	119.0	104.5	102.2	91.4	57.0	76.4	.	.
1969	99.7	99.7	112.4	114.5	95.0	57.7	95.3	97.4	80.0
1970	**100.0**	**100.0**	**100.0**	**100.0**	**100.0**	**100.0**	**100.0**	**100.0**	**100.0**
1971	.	91.5	136.0	96.9	93.1	.	117.6	.	77.3

[1] Dec. of each year.   [1] *Déc. de chaque année.*   [1] Dic. de cada año.

6   **Employment in manufacturing**
    Emploi dans les industries manufacturières
    Empleo en las industrias manufactureras

B   **By industry**
    Par industrie
    Por industria

Nigeria

Indices of numbers employed: wage earners and salaried employees *(Statistics of establishments)*
Indices de l'effectif employé: ouvriers et employés *(Statistiques d'établissements)*
Indices de trabajadores ocupados: obreros y empleados *(Estadísticas de establecimientos)*

(1970 = 100)

	311-312	313	314	321	322	323	324	331	332
Date [1] *Date* [1] Fecha [1]	Food *Aliments* Alimentos	Beverages *Boissons* Bebidas	Tobacco *Tabac* Tabaco	Textiles	Clothing *Habillement* Vestido	Leather, leather products *Cuir, articles en cuir* Cuero, artículos de cuero	Footwear *Chaussures* Calzado	Wood *Bois* Madera	Furniture *Ameublement* Mobiliario
1969	67.5	80.0	73.5	81.4	51.6	90.8	69.5	90.9	88.7
1970	**100.0**	**100.0**	**100.0**	**100.0**	**100.0**	**100.0**	**100.0**	**100.0**	**100.0**
1971	110.4	100.7	133.4	113.8	76.2	115.7	103.7	115.1	169.5
1972	141.5	128.6	132.1	133.1	97.0	117.1	85.6	107.3	183.7

	341	342	351-352	355	356	361-362	369	381	382	383
Date [1] *Date* [1] Fecha [1]	Paper, paper products *Papier, articles en papier* Papel, artículos de papel	Printing, publishing *Imprimerie, édition* Imprentas, editoriales	Chemicals [2] *Industrie chimique* [2] Productos químicos [2]	Rubber products *Produits en caoutchouc* Productos de caucho	Plastic products *Articles en matière plastique* Productos plásticos	Pottery, china, earthenware and glass *Grès, porcelaines, faïences et verre* Barro, loza, porcelana y vidrio	Other non-metallic mineral products *Autres produits minéraux non métalliques* Otros productos minerales no metálicos	Metal [3] products *Produits métalliques* [3] Productos metálicos [3]	Machinery (non-electrical) *Machines (non électriques)* Maquinaria (no eléctrica)	Electrical machinery and apparatus *Machines et appareils électriques* Maquinaria y aparatos eléctricos
1969	89.2	81.2	87.2	71.2	77.9	56.8	77.3	90.3	116.1	83.3
1970	**100.0**	**100.0**	**100.0**	**100.0**	**100.0**	**100.0**	**100.0**	**100.0**	**100.0**	**100.0**
1971	138.3	105.2	110.1	70.2	137.5	113.6	140.7	132.7	83.0	99.7
1972	150.0	132.5	139.6	89.4	184.0	104.3	165.3	141.5	94.1	135.8

[1] Sep. of each year.   [2] Incl. products of petroleum and coal.   [3] Incl. non-ferrous metal.

[1] *Sept. de chaque année.*   [2] *Y compris les dérivés du pétrole et du charbon.*   [3] *Y compris les métaux non ferreux.*

[1] Sept. de cada año.   [2] Incl. los derivados del petróleo y del carbón.   [3] Incl. los metales no ferrosos.

6 **Employment in manufacturing**
Emploi dans les industries manufacturières
Empleo en las industrias manufactureras

B **By industry**
Par industrie
Por industria

South Africa, Rep. of

Indices of numbers employed: wage earners and salaried employees *(Statistics of establishments)*
Indices de l'effectif employé: ouvriers et employés *(Statistiques d'établissements)*
Indices de trabajadores ocupados: obreros y empleados *(Estadísticas de establecimientos)*

(1970 = 100)

Date [1] / Date [1] / Fecha [1]	Food / Aliments / Alimentos	Beverages / Boissons / Bebidas	Tobacco / Tabac / Tabaco	Textiles	Clothing / Habillement / Vestido	Wood / Bois / Madera	Furniture / Ameublement / Mobiliario	Paper, paper products / Papier, articles en papier / Papel, artículos de papel	Printing, publishing / Imprimerie, édition / Imprentas, editoriales
1965	88.6	81.1	102.3	74.2	76.1	83.1	74.1	92.8	81.1
1966	92.1	85.7	100.0	78.0	79.1	89.5	75.3	95.5	81.7
1967	90.9	83.4	97.7	88.1	83.9	87.7	80.5	100.3	83.8
1968	92.7	93.1	95.5	86.0	87.0	87.7	84.0	100.3	90.9
1969	98.3	94.9	95.5	94.3	94.2	92.6	93.3	103.4	95.6
1970	100.0	100.0	100.0	100.0	100.0	100.0	100.0	100.0	100.0
1971	101.9	112.9	93.2	104.0	103.7	107.8	104.1	104.5	102.9
1972	101.3	114.7	93.2	107.4	107.6	112.3	105.8	106.5	105.3
1973	105.1	118.4	93.2	113.7	109.9	118.7	108.4	110.6	106.5

Date [1] / Date [1] / Fecha [1]	Leather, leather products / Cuir, articles en cuir / Cuero, artículos de cuero	Rubber products / Industrie du caoutchouc / Productos de caucho	Chemicals / Industrie chimique / Productos químicos	Non-metallic mineral products / Produits minéraux non métalliques / Productos minerales no metálicos	Basic metal industries / Industrie métallurgique de base / Industrias metalúrgicas básicas	Metal products / Produits métalliques / Productos metálicos	Machinery (non-electrical) / Machines (non électriques) / Maquinaria (no eléctrica)	Electrical machinery / Machines électriques / Maquinaria eléctrica	Transport equipment / Matériel de transport / Material de transporte
1965	83.3	77.3	89.7	85.7	84.3	78.9	76.0	75.0	65.4
1966	86.4	79.8	90.2	85.4	82.3	83.7	83.3	84.7	68.7
1967	97.0	85.7	93.6	84.7	87.3	87.3	86.9	80.4	78.5
1968	98.5	89.2	93.6	88.6	89.3	89.7	90.6	84.2	77.8
1969	101.5	94.1	95.7	93.9	96.9	93.2	94.0	93.2	87.3
1970	100.0	100.0	100.0	100.0	100.0	100.0	100.0	100.0	100.0
1971	106.1	105.9	103.9	103.2	103.2	104.3	101.9	101.9	105.2	102.7
1972	109.1	109.4	108.2	105.0	106.5	104.2	102.8	103.8	102.1
1973	109.1	113.8	111.6	107.3	114.0	106.4	105.3	107.9	98.2

[1] June of each year.   [1] *Juin de chaque année.*   [1] Junio de cada año.

EMPLOYMENT

6 **Employment in manufacturing**
Emploi dans les industries manufacturières
Empleo en las industrias manufactureras

B By industry
Par industrie
Por industria

AMERICA — AMÉRIQUE — AMERICA

Canada (1)

Indices of numbers employed: wage earners and salaried employees *(Statistics of establishments)*
Indices de l'effectif employé: ouvriers et employés *(Statistiques d'établissements)*
Indices de trabajadores ocupados: obreros y empleados *(Estadísticas de establecimientos)*

(1970 = 100)

	311-312	313	314	321	322	323	324	331	332	341
Date / *Date* / Fecha	Food / *Aliments* / Alimentos	Beverages / *Boissons* / Bebidas	Tobacco / *Tabac* / Tabaco	Textiles	Clothing / *Habillement* / Vestido	Leather, leather products / *Cuir, articles en cuir* / Cuero, artículos de cuero	Footwear / *Chaussures* / Calzado	Wood / *Bois* / Madera	Furniture / *Ameublement* / Mobiliario	Paper, paper products / *Papier, articles en papier* / Papel, artículos de papel
1969	99.5	101.1	102.1	105.3	100.1	108.6	109.2	104.4	105.0	100.3
1970	**100.0**	**100.0**	**100.0**	**100.0**	**100.0**	**100.0**	**100.0**	**100.0**	**100.0**	**100.0**
1971	99.7	100.4	99.0	100.9	99.5	100.4	100.6	106.6	100.6	98.6
1972	99.0	99.3	96.9	106.9	100.8	98.1	95.4	111.4	107.9	98.3
1973	100.8	103.9	95.8	111.7	104.5	100.7	95.4	122.3	116.8	99.8
1974 *	101.4	106.1	97.9	110.4	103.5	100.4	95.4	121.9	121.8	108.6

	342	351	352	353	354	355	356	361	362
Date / *Date* / Fecha	Printing, publishing / *Imprimerie, édition* / Imprentas, editoriales	Industrial chemicals / *Chimie industrielle* / Química industrial	Other chemical products / *Autres produits chimiques* / Otros productos químicos	Petroleum refineries / *Raffineries de pétrole* / Refinerías de petróleo	Products of petroleum and coal / *Dérivés du pétrole et du charbon* / Derivados del petróleo y del carbón	Rubber products / *Industrie du caoutchouc* / Productos de caucho	Plastic products / *Articles en matière plastique* / Productos plásticos	Pottery, china, earthenware [1] / *Grès, porcelaines, faïences* [1] / Barro, loza, porcelana [1]	Glass and glass products / *Verre* / Vidrio
1969	99.3	98.5	99.9	98.0	98.2	110.3	88.5	103.8	102.5
1970	**100.0**	**100.0**	**100.0**	**100.0**	**100.0**	**100.0**	**100.0**	**100.0**	**100.0**
1971	97.4	94.0	96.4	99.0	100.0	99.6	101.6	92.3	94.1
1972	96.3	88.4	95.0	96.0	98.8	100.0	109.3	86.5	100.0
1973	100.0	87.4	97.8	96.0	98.8	111.9	123.1	92.3	108.4
1974 *	105.0	92.0	102.9	106.9	106.0	108.2	120.3	90.2	109.2

[1] Incl. structural clay products.   [1] *Y compris les matériaux de construction en terre cuite.*   [1] Incl. los productos de arcilla para construcción.

6 Employment in manufacturing / Emploi dans les industries manufacturières / Empleo en las industrias manufactureras — B By industry / Par industrie / Por industria

Canada (2)

Indices of numbers employed: wage earners and salaried employees *(Statistics of establishments)*
Indices de l'effectif employé: ouvriers et employés *(Statistiques d'établissements)*
Indices de trabajadores ocupados: obreros y empleados *(Estadísticas de establecimientos)*

(1970 = 100)

Date / Date / Fecha	369 Other non-metallic mineral products [1] / Autres produits minéraux non métalliques [1] / Otros productos minerales no metálicos [1]	371 Iron and steel / Sidérurgie / Hierro y acero	372 Non-ferrous metal / Métaux non ferreux / Metales no ferrosos	381 Metal products / Produits métalliques / Productos metálicos	382 Machinery (non-electrical) / Machines (non électriques) / Maquinaria (no eléctrica)	383 Electrical machinery and apparatus / Machines et appareils électriques / Maquinaria y aparatos eléctricos	384 Transport equipment / Matériel de transport / Material de transporte	385 Scientific, measuring, optical, etc., equipment / Matériel scientifique, de précision, d'optique, etc. / Equipo científico, de medida, de óptica, etc.	390 Other manufacturing industries / Autres industries manufacturières / Otras industrias manufactureras
1969	103.3	94.6	104.5	101.3	101.2	104.1	109.9	101.7	98.6
1970	100.0	100.0	100.0	100.0	100.0	100.0	100.0	100.0	100.0
1971	98.7	99.0	97.7	97.7	96.3	95.3	101.9	98.3	100.2
1972	103.3	98.0	101.5	99.5	93.5	96.1	107.7	100.6	103.8
1973	110.9	101.7	102.3	106.0	102.9	101.2	116.0	102.3	112.2
1974 *	115.9	106.2	100.0	111.0	111.5	109.3	114.4	108.7	116.1

[1] Excl. structural clay products.
[1] *Non compris les matériaux de construction en terre cuite.*
[1] Excl. los productos de arcilla para construcción.

6 Employment in manufacturing
Emploi dans les industries manufacturières
Empleo en las industrias manufactureras

B By industry
Par industrie
Por industria

Chile

Indices of numbers employed: wage earners *(Statistics of establishments)*
Indices de l'effectif employé: ouvriers *(Statistiques d'établissements)*
Indices de trabajadores ocupados: obreros *(Estadísticas de establecimientos)*

(1970 = 100)

Date [1] Date [1] Fecha [1]	Food *Aliments* Alimentos	Beverages *Boissons* Bebidas	Tobacco *Tabac* Tabaco	Textiles	Clothing *Habillement* Vestido	Wood *Bois* Madera	Furniture *Ameublement* Mobiliario	Paper, paper products *Papier, articles en papier* Papel, artículos de papel	Printing, publishing *Imprimerie, édition* Imprentas, editoriales	Leather, leather products *Cuir, articles en cuir* Cuero, artículos de cuero
1965	98.4	100.9	97.2	98.4	109.4	124.9	75.9	101.9	87.6	114.8
1966	101.9	102.6	100.8	97.2	110.4	141.7	65.4	99.6	93.7	115.5
1967	105.2	90.0	111.8	102.7	109.9	132.7	74.1	99.1	97.5	112.3
1968	105.1	92.1	111.9	102.5	106.1	135.8	83.4	109.9	99.2	117.4
1969	101.3	99.7	107.4	102.1	100.3	101.7	91.1	102.0	96.6	104.4
1970	**100.0**	**100.0**	**100.0**	**100.0**	**100.0**	**100.0**	**100.0**	**100.0**	**100.0**	**100.0**
1971	101.6	97.3	102.5	100.5	96.9	99.6	71.3	100.3	97.0	94.5
1972	111.9	112.6	134.4	121.6	98.1	115.0	71.3	101.2	111.0	113.3

Date [1] Date [1] Fecha [1]	Rubber products *Industrie du caoutchouc* Productos de caucho	Chemicals *Industrie chimique* Productos químicos	Products of petroleum and coal *Dérivés du pétrole et du charbon* Derivados del petróleo y del carbón	Non-metallic mineral products *Produits minéraux non métalliques* Productos minerales no metálicos	Basic metal industries *Industrie métallurgi- que de base* Industrias metalúrgicas básicas	Metal products *Produits métalliques* Productos metálicos	Machinery (non- electrical) *Machines (non élec- triques)* Maquinaria (no eléctrica)	Electrical machinery *Machines électriques* Maquinaria eléctrica	Transport equipment *Matériel de transport* Material de transporte	Miscellaneous manufactur- ing *Industries manufactu- rières diverses* Industrias manufactu- reras diversas
1965	61.4	78.4	110.9	114.9	92.3	102.6	90.4	71.7	85.8	95.4
1966	65.9	76.9	107.9	117.5	96.5	95.6	93.6	68.6	101.2	105.6
1967	73.9	77.4	109.5	123.6	95.7	102.1	93.6	87.5	89.3	109.5
1968	85.4	85.2	106.9	116.5	97.3	100.2	89.9	96.9	79.2	112.9
1969	89.6	86.2	105.6	114.5	97.0	100.6	86.7	117.6	81.6	106.6
1970	**100.0**	**100.0**	**100.0**	**100.0**	**100.0**	**100.0**	**100.0**	**100.0**	**100.0**	**100.0**
1971	96.6	100.4	99.8	103.9	100.2	92.5	84.7	93.5	86.6	89.2
1972	115.1	117.7	98.7	115.2	108.7	103.7	89.7	93.6	81.2	83.8

[1] April of each year.   [1] *Avril de chaque année.*   [1] Abril de cada año.

Employment in manufacturing
Emploi dans les industries manufacturières
Empleo en las industrias manufactureras

B By industry
Par industrie
Por industria

República Dominicana

Indices of numbers employed: wage earners and salaried employees *(Statistics of establishments)*
Indices de l'effectif employé: ouvriers et employés *(Statistiques d'établissements)*
Indices de trabajadores ocupados: obreros y empleados *(Estadísticas de establecimientos)*

(1970 = 100)

	311-312	313	314	321	322	323-324	33	341
Date *Date* Fecha	Food *Aliments* Alimentos	Beverages *Boissons* Bebidas	Tobacco *Tabac* Tabaco	Textiles	Clothing *Habillement* Vestido	Leather, leather products, footwear *Cuir, articles en cuir, chaussures* Cuero, artículos de cuero, calzado	Wood, furniture *Bois, ameublement* Madera, mobiliario	Paper, paper products *Papier, articles en papier* Papel, artículos de papel
1967	95.1	88.0	92.4	82.3	112.6	101.1	121.7	73.4
1968	86.5	93.5	88.4	85.4	146.6	99.8	.	68.8
1969	85.2	99.3	85.8	97.7	94.8	92.6	107.3	85.0
1970	**100.0**	**100.0**	**100.0**	**100.0**	**100.0**	**100.0**	**100.0**	**100.0**
1971	102.9	101.0	95.2	97.7	108.9	98.7	109.9	94.1
1972	109.2	110.8	187.3 *	110.3	129.0	130.1	136.6	114.4
1973	119.7	110.5	127.3	191.8	161.4	126.2	152.9	138.1

	342	351	352	355	356	36 ×	37	38 ×
Date *Date* Fecha	Printing, publishing *Imprimerie, édition* Imprentas, editoriales	Industrial chemicals *Chimie industrielle* Química industrial	Other chemical products *Autres produits chimiques* Otros productos químicos	Rubber products *Produits en caoutchouc* Productos de caucho	Plastic products *Articles en matière plastique* Productos plásticos	Non-metallic mineral products [1] *Produits minéraux non métalliques* [1] Productos minerales no metálicos [1]	Basic metal industries *Industrie métallurgique de base* Industrias metalúrgicas básicas	Metal products, machinery, etc. [2] *Produits métalliques, machines, etc.* [2] Productos metálicos, maquinaria, etc. [2]
1967	74.3	77.4	77.5	89.7	53.5	84.7	.	.
1968	90.0	67.8	88.8	111.2	53.5	86.5	.	.
1969	92.3	87.7	95.3	107.8	81.1	99.7	.	88.3
1970	**100.0**	**100.0**	**100.0**	**100.0**	**100.0**	**100.0**	**100.0**	**100.0**
1971	103.1	106.8	110.6	105.8	109.7	102.2	104.2	123.8
1972	124.3	114.3	141.1	154.7	127.6	144.9	107.9	163.7
1973	155.6	129.8	122.9	175.6	160.0	176.9	119.6	194.2

[1] Excl. pottery, china, earthenware. [2] Excl. transport equipment.

[1] *Non compris le grès, les porcelaines et les faïences.*
[2] *Non compris le matériel de transport.*

[1] Excl. el barro, la loza y la porcelana. [2] Excl. el material de transporte.

EMPLOYMENT

 6 Employment in manufacturing
Emploi dans les industries manufacturières
Empleo en las industrias manufactureras

B By industry
Par industrie
Por industria

Ecuador

Indices of numbers employed: wage earners and salaried employees *(Statistics of establishments)*
Indices de l'effectif employé: ouvriers et employés *(Statistiques d'établissements)*
Indices de trabajadores ocupados: obreros y empleados *(Estadísticas de establecimientos)*

(1970 = 100)

Date / Date / Fecha	Food / Aliments / Alimentos	Beverages / Boissons / Bebidas	Tobacco / Tabac / Tabaco	Textiles	Clothing / Habillement / Vestido	Wood / Bois / Madera	Paper, paper products / Papier, articles en papier / Papel, artículos de papel	Printing, publishing / Imprimerie, édition / Imprentas, editoriales
1965	77.7	82.5	106.5	90.7	83.9	79.1	73.2	83.2
1966	81.0	85.4	100.5	92.8	83.3	81.4	79.8	82.4
1967	77.2	87.4	101.9	91.6	82.3	87.6	81.4	84.0
1968	75.0	93.2	97.4	92.8	80.9	88.5	84.9	85.7
1969	98.8	98.8	102·3	96.4	100.7	99.2	83.2	98.5
1970	**100.0**	**100.0**	**100.0**	**100.0**	**100.0**	**100.0**	**100.0**	**100.0**
1971	100.5	98.3	102.8	108.0	102.9	98.2	99.7	100.1
1972	100.0	102.6	102.4	109.4	111.2	100.6	96.2	105.2
1973	106.8	110.7	102.8	111.5	115.3	103.2	96.6	112.6

Date / Date / Fecha	Leather, leather products / Cuir, articles en cuir / Cuero, artículos de cuero	Rubber products / Industrie du caoutchouc / Productos de caucho	Non-metallic mineral products / Produits minéraux non métalliques / Productos minerales no metálicos	Metal products / Produits métalliques / Productos metálicos	Machinery (non-electrical) / Machines (non électriques) / Maquinaria (no eléctrica)	Electrical machinery / Machines électriques / Maquinaria eléctrica	Transport equipment / Matériel de transport / Material de transporte	Miscellaneous manufacturing / Industries manufacturières diverses / Industrias manufactureras diversas
1965	84.5	94.3	84.2	83.1	78.5	83.0	83.8	58.9
1966	74.4	83.0	90.1	80.5	93.6	96.3	76.1	61.9
1967	71.9	80.3	87.0	91.7	103.7	91.9	71.0	65.0
1968	89.7	.	88.7	91.7	126.8	80.8	75.4	67.7
1969	108.6	97.7	96.0	96.8	100.7	101.3	98.6	90.2
1970	**100.0**	**100.0**	**100.0**	**100.0**	**100.0**	**100.0**	**100.0**	**100.0**
1971	99.3	102.1	104.4	99.2	104.3	107.2	93.2	107.4
1972	110.6	104.9	110.1	97.3	115.6	117.7	90.3	111.0
1973	109.7	112.7	119.3	110.1	118.8	143.3	85.2	124.9

6 Employment in manufacturing / Emploi dans les industries manufacturières / Empleo en las industrias manufactureras

B By industry / Par industrie / Por industria

El Salvador [1]

Indices of numbers employed: wage earners and salaried employees *(Statistics of establishments)*
Indices de l'effectif employé: ouvriers et employés *(Statistiques d'établissements)*
Indices de trabajadores ocupados: obreros y empleados *(Estadísticas de establecimientos)*

(1970 = 100)

Date / Date / Fecha	Food / Aliments / Alimentos	Beverages / Boissons / Bebidas	Textiles	Clothing / Habillement / Vestido	Furniture / Ameublement / Mobiliario	Paper, printing, publishing / Papier, imprimerie, édition / Papel, imprentas, editoriales	Non-metallic mineral products / Produits minéraux non métalliques / Productos minerales no metálicos	Metal industries, machinery / Industrie métallurgique, machines / Industrias metalúrgicas, maquinaria	Transport equipment / Matériel de transport / Material de transporte	Other manufacturing / Autres industries manufacturières / Otras industrias manufactureras
1965	93.6	99.7	106.9	104.1	87.2	88.8	112.1	107.5	90.0	74.3
1966	90.9	104.1	103.9	106.6	113.7	93.7	133.3	106.4	94.2	75.4
1967	93.8	107.6	98.2	107.4	116.5	99.6	121.8	101.4	101.5	87.6
1968	90.9	102.5	96.5	97.6	110.3	100.9	110.6	103.0	101.1	91.7
1969	96.3	96.7	100.6	96.8	97.4	96.8	103.5	99.5	92.5	97.5
1970	**100.0**	**100.0**	**100.0**	**100.0**	**100.0**	**100.0**	**100.0**	**100.0**	**100.0**	**100.0**
1971	100.9	107.7	96.5	100.0	102.3	102.9	100.1	106.6	92.1	98.5
1972	106.4	119.6	94.0	117.7	105.0	106.2	104.4	181.2	89.1	101.6
1973	114.0	134.2	96.1	132.3	124.7	110.2	115.5	225.2	83.2	107.9
1974	113.0	134.9	97.7	145.2	116.2	115.6	133.3	221.8	92.2	109.2

[1] Area of San Salvador.   [1] Zone de San Salvador.   [1] Zona de San Salvador.

Guatemala (Guatemala)

Indices of numbers employed: wage earners *(Statistics of establishments)*
Indices de l'effectif employé: ouvriers *(Statistiques d'établissements)*
Indices de trabajadores ocupados: obreros *(Estadísticas de establecimientos)*

Date / Date / Fecha	Food / Aliments / Alimentos	Beverages, tobacco / Boissons, tabac / Bebidas, tabaco	Textiles	Clothing / Habillement / Vestido	Wood, furniture / Bois, ameublement / Madera, mobiliario	Printing, publishing / Imprimerie, édition / Imprentas, editoriales	Rubber products, chemicals / Caoutchouc, industrie chimique / Caucho, productos químicos	Non-metallic mineral products / Produits minéraux non métalliques / Productos minerales no metálicos	Metal industries, machinery, etc. / Industrie métallurgique, machines, etc. / Industrias metalúrgicas, maquinaria, etc.
1965	100.1	94.0	79.1	69.4	94.0	104.5	96.0	104.9	102.3
1966	103.7	101.3	81.5	69.1	80.7	107.0	85.3	103.9	108.1
1967	99.0	104.0	88.1	68.3	84.0	110.0	80.3	108.2	103.8
1968	98.6	101.7	87.9	88.0	102.3	111.8	79.2	103.4	93.4
1969	96.2	103.1	91.1	90.8	93.7	104.5	85.8	100.3	96.0
1970	**100.0**	**100.0**	**100.0**	**100.0**	**100.0**	**100.0**	**100.0**	**100.0**	**100.0**
1971	93.5	100.9	98.4	100.0	103.8	96.1	108.7	104.8	99.2
1972	91.5	100.9	105.6	102.0	93.1	77.3	118.0	103.5	97.9
1973 *	89.4	101.1	113.3	104.0	80.2	62.0	128.0	102.3	97.0
1974 *	127.7	108.2	112.1	113.1	100.5	78.6	135.5	...	96.0

6 **Employment in manufacturing**
Emploi dans les industries manufacturières
Empleo en las industrias manufactureras

B **By industry**
Par industrie
Por industria

Panamá

Indices of numbers employed: wage earners and salaried employees *(Compulsory social insurance statistics)*
Indices de l'effectif employé: ouvriers et employés *(Statistiques d'assurances sociales obligatoires)*
Indices de trabajadores ocupados: obreros y empleados *(Estadísticas del seguro social obligatorio)*

(1970 = 100)

	311-312	313-314	321-322	323-324	33	341	342
Date [1]	Food	Beverages, tobacco	Textiles, clothing	Leather, leather products, footwear	Wood, furniture	Paper, paper products	Printing, publishing
Date [1]	*Aliments*	*Boissons, tabac*	*Textiles, habillement*	*Cuir, articles en cuir, chaussures*	*Bois, ameublement*	*Papier, articles en papier*	*Imprimerie, édition*
Fecha [1]	Alimentos	Bebidas, tabaco	Textiles, vestido	Cuero, artículos de cuero, calzado	Madera, mobiliario	Papel, artículos de papel	Imprentas, editoriales
1970	100.0	100.0	100.0	100.0	100.0	100.0	100.0
1971	96.2	116.1	131.1	100.8	127.8	112.0	83.2
1972	91.7	133.8	132.6	100.3	104.7	109.8	99.3
1973 [2] *	111.6	145.5	144.7	108.3	115.2	107.8	100.8

	351-352	353	354-356	36	37; 381	382-385; 390
Date [1]	Chemicals	Petroleum refineries	Products of petroleum and coal [3]	Non-metallic mineral products	Metal industries	Miscellaneous manufacturing [4]
Date [1]	*Industrie chimique*	*Raffineries de pétrole*	*Dérivés du pétrole et du charbon [3]*	*Produits minéraux non métalliques*	*Industrie métallurgique*	*Industries manufacturières diverses [4]*
Fecha [1]	Productos químicos	Refinerías de petróleo	Derivados del petróleo y del carbón [3]	Productos minerales no metálicos	Industrias metalúrgicas	Industrias manufactureras diversas [4]
1970	100.0	100.0	100.0	100.0	100.0	100.0
1971	124.1	102.4	163.4	121.5	103.1	46.1
1972	118.0	108.7	225.1	142.8	116.4	59.1
1973 [2] *	129.4	120.6	261.7	172.1	120.8	93.5

[1] Aug. of each year. [2] March. [3] Incl. rubber and plastic products. [4] Incl. machinery, transport equipment, etc.

[1] *Août de chaque année.* [2] *Mars.* [3] *Y compris les produits en caoutchouc et en plastique.* [4] *Y compris les machines, le matériel de transport, etc.*

[1] Agosto de cada año. [2] Marzo. [3] Incl. productos de caucho y de plástico. [4] Incl. maquinaria, material de transporte, etc.

6 Employment in manufacturing
Emploi dans les industries manufacturières
Empleo en las industrias manufactureras

B By industry
Par industrie
Por industria

Perú

Indices of numbers employed: wage earners and salaried employees *(Official estimates)*
Indices de l'effectif employé: ouvriers et employés *(Evaluations officielles)*
Indices de trabajadores ocupados: obreros y empleados *(Estimaciones oficiales)*

(1970 = 100)

Date / Date / Fecha	Food / Aliments / Alimentos	Beverages / Boissons / Bebidas	Tobacco / Tabac / Tabaco	Textiles	Clothing / Habillement / Vestido	Wood / Bois / Madera	Furniture / Ameublement / Mobiliario	Paper, paper products / Papier, articles en papier / Papel, artículos de papel	Printing, publishing / Imprimerie, édition / Imprentas, editoriales	Leather, leather products / Cuir, articles en cuir / Cuero, artículos de cuero
1967	88.7	98.9	137.5	98.4	80.7	76.9	62.8	80.5	84.9	92.6
1968	96.9	105.3	137.5	100.8	87.7	96.2	85.1	85.4	102.2	100.0
1969	93.6	103.2	125.0	98.8	88.9	96.2	69.1	100.0	98.9	88.9
1970	**100.0**	**100.0**	**100.0**	**100.0**	**100.0**	**100.0**	**100.0**	**100.0**	**100.0**	**100.0**

Date / Date / Fecha	Rubber products / Industrie du caoutchouc / Productos de caucho	Chemicals / Industrie chimique / Productos químicos	Products of petroleum and coal / Dérivés du pétrole et du charbon / Derivados del petróleo y del carbón	Non-metallic mineral products / Produits minéraux non métalliques / Productos minerales no metálicos	Basic metal industries / Industrie métallurgique de base / Industrias metalúrgicas básicas	Metal products / Produits métalliques / Productos metálicos	Machinery (non-electrical) / Machines (non électriques) / Maquinaria (no eléctrica)	Electrical machinery / Machines électriques / Maquinaria eléctrica	Transport equipment / Matériel de transport / Material de transporte	Miscellaneous manufacturing / Industries manufacturières diverses / Industrias manufactureras diversas
1967	83.3	87.1	43.5	92.9	67.0	74.5	71.6	69.4	81.8	68.0
1968	87.5	87.1	95.7	97.6	73.6	86.3	86.5	81.6	100.0	79.6
1969	100.0	95.9	87.0	92.1	75.8	85.3	91.9	99.8	93.9	81.6
1970	**100.0**	**100.0**	**100.0**	**100.0**	**100.0**	**100.0**	**100.0**	**100.0**	**100.0**	**100.0**

6 Employment in manufacturing
Emploi dans les industries manufacturières
Empleo en las industrias manufactureras

B By industry
Par industrie
Por industria

Puerto Rico

Indices of numbers employed: wage earners *(Statistics of establishments)*
Indices de l'effectif employé: ouvriers *(Statistiques d'établissements)*
Indices de trabajadores ocupados: obreros *(Estadísticas de establecimientos)*

(1970 = 100)

Date [1] / Fecha [1]	311-313 Food, beverages / Aliments, boissons / Alimentos, bebidas	314 Tobacco / Tabac / Tabaco	321 Textiles	322 Clothing / Habillement / Vestido	323 Leather, leather products / Cuir, articles en cuir / Cuero, artículos de cuero	324 Footwear / Chaussures / Calzado	33 Wood, furniture / Bois, ameublement / Madera, mobiliario	341 Paper, paper products / Papier, articles en papier / Papel, artículos de papel	342 Printing, publishing / Imprimerie, édition / Imprentas, editoriales	351 Industrial chemicals / Chimie industrielle / Química industrial
1968	98.1	111.2	91.7	109.5	121.4	149.5	99.7	99.3	97.0	96.8
1969	100.1	96.4	97.3	110.2	104.7	111.0	99.2	107.9	95.0	108.6
1970	100.0	100.0	100.0	100.0	100.0	100.0	100.0	100.0	100.0	100.0
1971	108.0	89.0	74.9	98.5	95.6	64.2	102.3	111.1	97.7	150.2
1972	121.0	88.2	86.3	106.5	68.3	77.0	103.2	91.8	105.8	202.2
1973	120.7	87.2	79.5	108.8	67.8	89.4	98.4	90.0	103.7	227.1
1974	123.7	83.1	79.7	102.0	59.5	86.5	83.5	82.1	115.6	257.4

Date [1] / Fecha [1]	353 Petroleum refineries / Raffineries de pétrole / Refinerías de petróleo	361 Pottery, china, earthenware / Grès, porcelaines, faïences / Barro, loza, porcelana	362 Glass / Verre / Vidrio	369 Other non-metallic mineral products / Autres produits minéraux non métalliques / Otros productos minerales no metálicos	381 Metal products / Produits métalliques / Productos metálicos	382 Machinery (non-electrical) / Machines (non électriques) / Maquinaria (no eléctrica)	383 Electrical machinery and apparatus / Machines et appareils électriques / Maquinaria y aparatos eléctricos	384 Transport equipment / Matériel de transport / Material de transporte	385 Scientific, measuring, optical, etc., equipment / Matériel scientifique, de précision, d'optique, etc. / Equipo científico, de medida, de óptica, etc.	390 Other manufacturing industries / Autres industries manufacturières / Otras industrias manufactureras
1968	92.5	75.5	113.9	104.4	82.1	89.2	86.6	139.9	72.5	89.8
1969	101.8	79.3	109.8	101.7	93.6	91.4	99.6	101.7	78.9	98.7
1970	100.0	100.0	100.0	100.0	100.0	100.0	100.0	100.0	100.0	100.0
1971	101.3	92.6	108.8	108.7	104.2	108.7	117.6	99.3	119.2	85.3
1972	100.2	98.3	117.8	112.2	115.1	101.4	114.2	77.9	145.4	77.9
1973	94.5	97.9	125.0	96.7	120.3	89.6	126.4	105.2	150.9	71.2
1974	94.9	100.0	145.1	97.0	110.7	248.4 *	110.9	84.3	174.6	58.8

[1] Oct. of each year.   [1] *Oct. de chaque année.*   [1] Oct. de cada año.

6 B

Employment in manufacturing
Emploi dans les industries manufacturières
Empleo en las industrias manufactureras

By industry
Par industrie
Por industria

United States (1)

Indices of numbers employed: wage earners *(Statistics of establishments)*
Indices de l'effectif employé: ouvriers *(Statistiques d'établissements)*
Indices de trabajadores ocupados: obreros *(Estadísticas de establecimientos)*

(1970 = 100)

Date / Date / Fecha	311-312 Food / Aliments / Alimentos	313 Beverages / Boissons / Bebidas	314 Tobacco / Tabac / Tabaco	321 Textiles	322 Clothing / Habillement / Vestido	323 Leather, leather products / Cuir, articles en cuir / Cuero, artículos de cuero	324 Footwear [1] / Chaussures [1] / Calzado [1]	331 Wood [2] / Bois [2] / Madera [2]	332 Furniture [3] / Ameublement [3] / Mobiliario [3]
1965	.	.	108.7	96.6	100.8	.	.	107.9	94.2
1966	.	.	104.3	100.4	104.2	.	.	108.7	101.1
1967	.	.	107.2	99.3	103.4	.	.	105.3	98.9
1968	99.2	100.0	104.3	102.9	103.7	117.2	109.7	105.7	102.9
1969	100.0	100.8	101.4	103.3	103.5	111.5	105.9	106.7	106.1
1970	**100.0**	**100.0**	**100.0**	**100.0**	**100.0**	**100.0**	**100.0**	**100.0**	**100.0**
1971	98.8	97.5	91.3	98.1	98.4	96.6	93.5	102.2	100.0
1972	98.0	96.6	89.9	102.0	100.3	100.0	92.5	108.7	84.4
1973	97.4	95.0	94.2	105.7	101.8	98.9	88.7	111.8	90.3
1974	98.4	91.6	94.2	102.2	96.7	98.9	84.9	109.3	87.8

Date / Date / Fecha	341 Paper, paper products / Papier, articles en papier / Papel, artículos de papel	342 Printing, publishing / Imprimerie, édition / Imprentas, editoriales	351 Industrial chemicals / Chimie industrielle / Química industrial	352 Other chemical products / Autres produits chimiques / Otros productos químicos	353 Petroleum refineries / Raffineries de pétrole / Refinerías de petróleo	354 Products of petroleum and coal / Dérivés du pétrole et du charbon / Derivados del petróleo y del carbón	355 Rubber products / Produits en caoutchouc / Productos de caucho	356 Plastic products [4] / Articles en matière plastique [4] / Productos plásticos [4]	361 Pottery, china, earthenware / Grès, porcelaines, faïences / Barro, loza, porcelana
1965	91.7	91.6	.	.	.	.	.	.	.
1966	95.4	95.3	.	.	.	.	.	.	.
1967	96.9	97.6	.	.	.	.	.	.	.
1968	98.7	98.4	100.9	102.0	102.2	100.0	105.2	91.8	102.8
1969	101.5	100.6	102.3	104.8	94.4	103.8	107.5	101.3	105.6
1970	**100.0**	**100.0**	**100.0**	**100.0**	**100.0**	**100.0**	**100.0**	**100.0**	**100.0**
1971	96.1	96.6	97.7	94.8	100.0	111.5	102.8	100.0	97.2
1972	97.8	97.5	98.0	95.6	100.0	119.2	106.6	113.0	102.8
1973	100.4	98.7	101.4	98.4	100.0	123.1	113.2	127.7	111.1
1974	100.4	98.5	104.6	99.2	104.4	115.4	112.3	128.6	113.9

[1] Incl. footwear wholly of wood. [2] Excl. footwear wholly of wood. [3] Incl. furniture and fixtures primarily of metal, and plastic furniture. [4] Excl. plastic furniture.

[1] *Y compris les chaussures faites entièrement en bois.* [2] *Non compris les chaussures faites entièrement en bois.* [3] *Y compris les meubles et accessoires faits principalement en métal et les meubles en matière plastique.* [4] *Non compris les meubles en matière plastique.*

[1] Incl. el calzado totalmente de madera. [2] Excl. el calzado totalmente de madera. [3] Incl. los muebles y accesorios principalmente metálicos y los muebles de material plástico. [4] Excl. los muebles de material plástico.

6 Employment in manufacturing
Emploi dans les industries manufacturières
Empleo en las industrias manufactureras

B By industry
Par industrie
Por industria

United States (2)

Indices of numbers employed: wage earners *(Official estimates)*
Indices de l'effectif employé: ouvriers *(Evaluations officielles)*
Indices de trabajadores ocupados: obreros *(Estimaciones oficiales)*

(1970 = 100)

Date / Date / Fecha	362 Glass / Verre / Vidrio	369 Other non-metallic mineral products / Autres produits minéraux non métalliques / Otros productos minerales no metálicos	371 Iron and steel / Sidérurgie / Hierro y acero	372 Non-ferrous metal / Métaux non ferreux / Metales no ferrosos	382 Machinery (non-electrical) / Machines (non électriques) / Maquinaria (no eléctrica)	383 Electrical machinery and apparatus / Machines et appareils électriques / Maquinaria y aparatos eléctricos	384 Transport equipment / Matériel de transport / Material de transporte	385 Scientific, measuring, optical, etc., equipment / Matériel scientifique, de précision, d'optique, etc. / Equipo científico, de medida, de óptica, etc.	390 Other manufacturing industries / Autres industries manufacturières / Otras industrias manufactureras
1965	.	.	107.4	96.7	91.8	90.2	100.0	89.2	.
1966	.	.	106.0	105.0	101.6	104.7	110.1	98.9	.
1967	.	.	101.8	101.5	103.5	104.5	110.5	101.4	.
1968	99.8	101.6	101.0	99.6	101.5	104.3	116.1	102.5	115.7
1969	103.2	104.1	102.6	105.7	104.5	106.4	117.1	105.8	114.3
1970	**100.0**	**100.0**	**100.0**	**100.0**	**100.0**	**100.0**	**100.0**	**100.0**	**100.0**
1971	98.9	99.7	91.2	94.5	89.3	92.7	98.6	93.9	89.8
1972	103.4	104.4	91.0	98.2	94.8	98.4	102.1	99.6	93.5
1973	108.5	109.7	96.8	106.5	106.7	109.6	109.5	110.8	96.7
1974	108.0	110.7	97 0	107.2	112.1	108.5	101.5	118.0	94.8

6 Employment in manufacturing
Emploi dans les industries manufacturières
Empleo en las industrias manufactureras

B By industry
Par industrie
Por industria

Venezuela

Indices of numbers employed: wage earners and salaried employees *(Statistics of establishments)*
Indices de l'effectif employé: ouvriers et employés *(Statistiques d'établissements)*
Indices de trabajadores ocupados: obreros y empleados *(Estadísticas de establecimientos)*

(1970 = 100)

Date / Date / Fecha	Food / Aliments / Alimentos	Beverages / Boissons / Bebidas	Tobacco / Tabac / Tabaco	Textiles, clothing / Textiles, habillement / Textiles, vestido	Footwear / Chaussures / Calzado	Sawmills, furniture / Scieries, ameublement / Aserraderos, mobiliario	Paper, paper products / Papier, articles en papier / Papel, artículos de papel	Printing, publishing / Imprimerie, édition / Imprentas, editoriales
1965	109.8	87.1	97.7	95.2	97.3	82.2	95.7	90.5
1966	110.9	87.0	96.2	95.3	95.3	94.3	100.5	95.2
1967	93.8	89.5	96.4	92.7	92.6	100.3	98.4	93.6
1968	94.7	92.9	99.6	95.3	93.1	103.8	95.2	94.7
1969 [1]	96.6	97.0	100.5	98.0	95.5	105.5	97.3	97.5
1970	**100.0**	**100.0**	**100.0**	**100.0**	**100.0**	**100.0**	**100.0**	**100.0**
1971	98.1	96.4	98.5	102.8	96.8	107.5	106.7	101.7
1972	99.4	96.4	97.0	105.0	98.0	86.1	110.3	105.7
1973	100.4	102.1	99.9	105.9	81.3	84.0	117.4	114.3
1974	106.6	106.3	108.6	108.7	96.4	83.2	121.9	116.6

Date / Date / Fecha	Rubber products / Industrie du caoutchouc / Productos de caucho	Chemicals / Industrie chimique / Productos químicos	Building materials / Matériaux de construction / Materiales de construcción	Cement / Ciment / Cemento	Basic metal industries / Industrie métallurgique de base / Industrias metalúrgicas básicas	Metal products / Produits métalliques / Productos metálicos	Manufacture of motor vehicles / Construction de véhicules automobiles / Construcción de vehículos automóviles	Repair of motor vehicles / Réparation de véhicules automobiles / Reparación de vehículos automóviles
1965	86.7	89.5	92.4	108.3	97.0	92.0	86.1	96.9
1966	90.6	92.9	93.1	109.4	97.9	94.6	98.3	95.9
1967	88.3	91.4	92.1	107.2	90.5	92.5	95.8	94.0
1968	96.7	91.4	95.0	101.8	98.4	96.2	99.4	92.2
1969 [1]	101.7	95.5	93.4	105.4	98.0	96.5	106.4	97.3
1970	**100.0**	**100.0**	**100.0**	**100.0**	**100.0**	**100.0**	**100.0**	**100.0**
1971	100.0	98.6	106.0	93.5	101.5	104.9	99.6	109.7
1972	102.7	101.5	108.4	94.2	101.4	105.5	102.7	108.5
1973	114.7	104.3	116.1	99.4	109.1	112.7	117.5	103.9
1974	126.4	108.3	115.9	101.7	125.1	112.5	132.5	103.8

[1] Beginning 1969: establishments with 10 or more workers (prior to 1969: all establishments); new series linked to former series.

[1] A partir de 1969: établissements occupant 10 travailleurs et plus (avant 1969: tous les établissements); nouvelle série enchaînée à la série précédente.

[1] A partir de 1969: establecimientos con 10 y más trabajadores (antes de 1969: todos los establecimientos); nueva serie enlazada con la anterior.

EMPLOYMENT

6 Employment in manufacturing
Emploi dans les industries manufacturières
Empleo en las industrias manufactureras

B By industry
Par industrie
Por industria

ASIA — ASIE — ASIA

Cyprus

Indices of numbers employed: wage earners and salaried employees *(Official estimates)* [1]
Indices de l'effectif employé: ouvriers et employés *(Evaluations officielles)* [1]
Indices de trabajadores ocupados: obreros y empleados *(Estimaciones oficiales)* [1]

(1970 = 100)

Date / *Date* / Fecha	311-312 Food / *Aliments* / Alimentos	313 Beverages / *Boissons* / Bebidas	314 Tobacco / *Tabac* / Tabaco	321 Textiles	322 Clothing / *Habillement* / Vestido	323-324 Leather, leather products, footwear / *Cuir, articles en cuir, chaussures* / Cuero, artículos de cuero, calzado	331 Wood / *Bois* / Madera	332 Furniture / *Ameublement* / Mobiliario
1965	76.2	82.6	119.8	55.5	87.4	113.4	68.0	89.5
1966	81.1	88.2	118.9	66.8	93.9	91.6	71.5	90.4
1967	85.5	90.0	109.0	79.9	95.3	80.1	76.4	85.7
1968	92.4	93.5	109.0	84.4	99.5	87.5	86.7	89.9
1969	95.0	96.4	111.5	90.1	99.7	92.8	90.6	94.7
1970	**100.0**	**100.0**	**100.0**	**100.0**	**100.0**	**100.0**	**100.0**	**100.0**
1971	106.7	101.4	85.7	106.6	102.6	106.5	100.1	102.8
1972	100.8	105.1	78.6	151.6	100.9	104.4	87.5	102.2
1973	100.1	104.9	78.4	151.9	103.5	100.9	106.0	100.6

Date / *Date* / Fecha	34 Paper, printing, publishing / *Papier, imprimerie, édition* / Papel, imprentas, editoriales	351-352 Chemicals [2] / *Industrie chimique* [2] / Productos químicos [2]	355-356 Rubber and plastic products / *Produits en caoutchouc et en plastique* / Productos de caucho y de plástico	36 Non-metallic mineral products / *Produits minéraux non métalliques* / Productos minerales no metálicos	381 Metal products / *Produits métalliques* / Productos metálicos	382-384 Machinery; transport equipment / *Machines; matériel de transport* / Maquinaria; material de transporte	385; 390 Other manufacturing industries [3] / *Autres industries manufacturières* [3] / Otras industrias manufactureras [3]
1965	80.5	70.7	...	74.9	64.4	82.7	...
1966	84.7	79.3	61.7	86.0	70.9	88.2	85.7
1967	87.9	84.8	68.6	91.1	87.7	97.1	90.5
1968	92.3	87.1	78.5	...	92.2	99.7	85.0
1969	95.9	94.4	94.7	95.9	97.3	101.2	97.2
1970	**100.0**	**100.0**	**100.0**	**100.0**	**100.0**	**100.0**	**100.0**
1971	108.6	106.5	109.4	99.5	103.2	99.8	105.0
1972	117.1	139.7	125.5	105.1	103.2	122.8	119.7
1973	116.5	141.5	147.0	106.4	106.0	135.3	124.2

[1] Incl. working proprietors, unpaid family workers and apprentices. [2] Beginning 1972: incl. petroleum refineries. [3] Incl. scientific, measuring, optical, etc., equipment.

[1] *Y compris les propriétaires-exploitants, les travailleurs familiaux non rémunérés et les apprentis.* [2] *A partir de 1972: y compris les raffineries de pétrole.* [3] *Y compris le matériel scientifique, de précision, d'optique, etc.*

[1] Incl. los empresarios propietarios, los trabajadores familiares no remunerados y los aprendices. [2] A partir de 1972: incl. refinerías de petróleo. [3] Incl. el equipo científico, de medida, de óptica, etc.

6 Employment in manufacturing
Emploi dans les industries manufacturières
Empleo en las industrias manufactureras

B By industry
Par industrie
Por industria

Hong Kong (1)

Indices of numbers employed: wage earners and salaried employees *(Statistics of establishments)*
Indices de l'effectif employé: ouvriers et employés *(Statistiques d'établissements)*
Indices de trabajadores ocupados: obreros y empleados *(Estadísticas de establecimientos)*

(1970 = 100)

	311-312	313	314	321	322	323	324	331
Date *Date* Fecha	Food *Aliments* Alimentos	Beverages *Boissons* Bebidas	Tobacco *Tabac* Tabaco	Textiles	Clothing *Habillement* Vestido	Leather, leather products *Cuir, articles en cuir* Cuero, artículos de cuero	Footwear *Chaussures* Calzado	Wood *Bois* Madera
1965	89.3	92.0	141.7	70.8	56.7	50.9	36.7	81.2
1966	88.8	98.4	136.8	78.2	61.4	78.4	37.4	81.8
1967	89.1	95.4	127.2	83.9	69.7	90.1	50.0	84.8
1968	90.0	83.5	113.9	90.1	78.8	105.9	67.0	81.8
1969	92.9	84.7	108.9	98.5	92.5	115.1	85.7	90.9
1970	100.0	100.0	100.0	100.0	100.0	100.0	100.0	100.0
1971	103.1	99.6	95.0	104.0	117.9	153.4	118.2	104.5
1972	105.9	117.0	90.7	97.1	130.7	176.5	119.5	107.1
1973	110.9	119.5	78.5	95.3	137.7	184.2	108.8	102.0
1974	106.4	118.6	74.5	88.8	134.2	182.5	89.9	83.6

	332	341	342	351	352	355	356	361-362
Date *Date* Fecha	Furniture *Ameublement* Mobiliario	Paper, paper products *Papier, articles en papier* Papel, artículos de papel	Printing, publishing *Imprimerie, édition* Imprentas, editoriales	Industrial chemicals *Chimie industrielle* Química industrial	Other chemical products *Autres produits chimiques* Otros productos químicos	Rubber products *Produits en caoutchouc* Productos de caucho	Plastic products *Articles en matière plastique* Productos plásticos	Pottery, china, earthenware and glass *Grès, porcelaines, faïences et verre* Barro, loza, porcelana y vidrio
1965	66.7	45.8	80.0	77.0	77.8	71.8	60.7	62.8
1966	70.4	49.0	84.3	89.7	83.0	77.7	67.2	68.0
1967	78.7	59.9	85.7	91.8	88.3	89.6	75.6	78.9
1968	83.1	70.8	86.8	93.1	88.4	105.1	86.7	85.2
1969	92.0	84.9	93.5	88.1	91.6	110.1	98.2	91.9
1970	100.0	100.0	100.0	100.0	100.0	100.0	100.0	100.0
1971	115.5	106.1	104.6	97.8	96.2	96.3	99.1	105.6
1972	138.7	112.1	105.3	104.6	110.6	80.7	99.9	113.2
1973	164.4	121.2	102.9	114.4	120.2	60.7	99.3	118.2
1974	146.9	110.2	99.4	108.0	118.6	55.6	82.6	99.4

EMPLOYMENT

6 Employment in manufacturing
Emploi dans les industries manufacturières
Empleo en las industrias manufactureras

B By industry
Par industrie
Por industria

Hong Kong (2)

Indices of numbers employed: wage earners and salaried employees *(Statistics of establishments)*
Indices de l'effectif employé: ouvriers et employés *(Statistiques d'établissements)*
Indices de trabajadores ocupados: obreros y empleados *(Estadísticas de establecimientos)*

(1970 = 100)

Date / Date / Fecha	369 Other non-metallic mineral products *Autres produits minéraux non métalliques* Otros productos minerales no metálicos	371 Basic metal industries *Industrie métallurgique de base* Industrias metalúrgicas básicas Iron and steel *Sidérurgie* Hierro y acero	372 Non-ferrous metal *Métaux non ferreux* Metales no ferrosos	381 Metal products *Produits métalliques* Productos metálicos	382 Machinery (non-electrical) *Machines (non électriques)* Maquinaria (no eléctrica)	383 Electrical machinery and apparatus *Machines et appareils électriques* Maquinaria y aparatos eléctricos	384 Transport equipment *Matériel de transport* Material de transporte	385 Scientific, measuring, optical, etc., equipment *Matériel scientifique, de précision, d'optique, etc.* Equipo científico, de medida, de óptica, etc.
1965	131.7	142.2	86.9	72.7	79.9	34.9	107.2	46.5
1966	133.1	105.3	82.6	74.5	86.2	53.9	103.0	54.7
1967	111.6	95.0	86.9	83.5	88.0	65.5	105.8	61.6
1968	115.5	98.4	84.7	90.0	93.4	75.4	104.9	73.6
1969	109.2	104.0	90.2	95.2	100.7	95.9	107.2	88.9
1970	**100.0**	**100.0**	**100.0**	**100.0**	**100.0**	**100.0**	**100.0**	**100.0**
1971	94.3	90.6	114.3	99.3	109.9	103.7	118.4	101.0
1972	92.7	82.4	127.9	104.1	120.9	118.8	117.6	109.6
1973	81.7	83.5	107.1	108.7	133.6	138.0	107.1	123.5
1974	75.8	74.3	93.7	104.9	130.8	136.8	103.7	143.1

India (1)

Indices of numbers employed: wage earners and salaried employees *(Statistics of establishments)*
Indices de l'effectif employé: ouvriers et employés *(Statistiques d'établissements)*
Indices de trabajadores ocupados: obreros y empleados *(Estadísticas de establecimientos)*

(1970 = 100)

Date / Date / Fecha	311-312 Food *Aliments* Alimentos	313 Beverages *Boissons* Bebidas	314 Tobacco *Tabac* Tabaco	321 Textiles	322 Clothing *Habillement* Vestido	323 Leather, leather products *Cuir, articles en cuir* Cuero, artículos de cuero	324 Footwear *Chaussures* Calzado	331 Wood *Bois* Madera	332 Furniture *Ameublement* Mobiliario
1965	91.3	61.1	138.0	104.9	110.3	112.5	114.3	86.2	122.2
1966	89.0	66.7	132.2	101.0	103.4	108.3	128.6	85.1	122.2
1967	88.9	72.2	139.7	101.3	93.1	104.2	128.6	87.4	122.2
1968	91.3	83.3	132.2	98.4	93.1	104.2	100.0	93.1	116.7
1969	94.1	88.9	114.9	97.0	93.1	108.3	100.0	88.5	100.0
1970	**100.0**	**100.0**	**100.0**	**100.0**	**100.0**	**100.0**	**100.0**	**100.0**	**100.0**
1971 *	101.0	105.9	105.0	111.7	103.4	100.0	...	96.6	77.8
1972 *	105.5	133.3	133.1	119.2	72.4	104.2	...	95.5	77.8

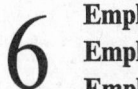

6 **Employment in manufacturing**
Emploi dans les industries manufacturières
Empleo en las industrias manufactureras

B **By industry**
Par industrie
Por industria

India (2)

Indices of numbers employed: wage earners and salaried employees *(Statistics of establishments)*
Indices de l'effectif employé: ouvriers et employés *(Statistiques d'établissements)*
Indices de trabajadores ocupados: obreros y empleados *(Estadísticas de establecimientos)*

(1970 = 100)

Date / Date / Fecha	341 Paper, paper products / Papier, articles en papier / Papel, artículos de papel	342 Printing, publishing / Imprimerie, édition / Imprentas, editoriales	351-352 Chemicals / Industrie chimique / Productos químicos	353 Petroleum refineries / Raffineries de pétrole / Refinerías de petróleo	354 Products of petroleum and coal / Dérivés du pétrole et du charbon / Derivados del petróleo y del carbón	355 Rubber products / Produits en caoutchouc / Productos de caucho	356 Plastic products / Articles en matière plastique / Productos plásticos	361 Pottery, china, earthenware / Grès, porcelaines, faïences / Barro, loza, porcelana	362 Glass / Verre / Vidrio
1965	80.0	91.9	80.1	109.1	58.3	87.1	70.6	81.5	100.0
1966	84.3	91.9	83.7	109.1	66.7	82.9	70.6	81.5	92.7
1967	88.6	92.6	86.2	109.1	75.0	84.3	70.6	81.5	100.0
1968	88.6	96.3	91.9	100.0	83.3	90.0	70.6	96.3	92.7
1969	92.9	97.0	96.7	109.1	100.0	94.3	88.2	92.6	92.7
1970	**100.0**	**100.0**	**100.0**	**100.0**	**100.0**	**100.0**	**100.0**	**100.0**	**100.0**
1971 *	102.9	100.7	109.3	63.6	100.0	88.6	158.8	88.9	96.4
1972 *	107.1	107.4	118.7	63.6	116.7	90.0	176.5	92.6	100.0

Date / Date / Fecha	369 Other non-metallic mineral products / Autres produits minéraux non métalliques / Otros productos minerales no metálicos	371 Basic metal industries — Industrie métallurgique de base — Industrias metalúrgicas básicas / Iron and steel / Sidérurgie / Hierro y acero	372 Non-ferrous metal / Métaux non ferreux / Metales no ferrosos	381 Metal products / Produits métalliques / Productos metálicos	382 Machinery (non-electrical) / Machines (non électriques) / Maquinaria (no eléctrica)	383 Electrical machinery and apparatus / Machines et appareils électriques / Maquinaria y aparatos eléctricos	384 Transport equipment / Matériel de transport / Material de transporte	385 Scientific, measuring, optical, etc., equipment / Matériel scientifique, de précision, d'optique, etc. / Equipo científico, de medida, de óptica, etc.	390 Other manufacturing industries / Autres industries manufacturières / Otras industrias manufactureras
1965	90.4	89.6	89.5	96.2	90.3	75.0	88.5	84.2	102.2
1966	91.6	91.2	94.7	95.3	95.8	77.9	91.5	94.7	98.5
1967	92.7	91.2	94.7	96.7	95.8	84.8	92.7	94.7	100.7
1968	93.3	92.8	89.5	96.7	92.5	86.3	94.7	100.0	94.2
1969	96.1	94.4	97.4	97.6	95.6	90.2	97.0	100.0	97.1
1970	**100.0**	**100.0**	**100.0**	**100.0**	**100.0**	**100.0**	**100.0**	**100.0**	**100.0**
1971 *	109.6	112.4	118.4	87.7	102.8	105.4	87.0	110.5	116.8
1972 *	111.8	119.3	123.7	96.2	101.7	112.7	90.3	110.5	109.5

6 Employment in manufacturing
Emploi dans les industries manufacturières
Empleo en las industrias manufactureras

B By industry
Par industrie
Por industria

Israel

Indices of numbers employed: wage earners and salaried employees *(Statistics of establishments)*
Indices de l'effectif employé: ouvriers et employés *(Statistiques d'établissements)*
Indices de trabajadores ocupados: obreros y empleados *(Estadísticas de establecimientos)*

(1970 = 100)

	31	321	322	323	33	341	342	351-353
Date *Date* Fecha	Food, beverages, tobacco *Aliments, boissons, tabac* Alimentos, bebidas, tabaco	Textiles	Clothing *Habillement* Vestido	Leather, leather products [1] *Cuir, articles en cuir [1]* Cuero, artículos de cuero [1]	Wood, furniture *Bois, ameublement* Madera, mobiliario	Paper *Papier* Papel	Printing *Imprimerie* Imprentas	Chemicals, petroleum refineries [2] *Industrie chimique, raffineries de pétrole [2]* Productos químicos, refinerías de petróleo [2]
1968	94.1	91.3	82.8	91.2	91.8	85.8	94.1	85.8
1969	96.3	98.5	92.1	95.6	96.5	91.2	98.5	94.3
1970	100.0	100.0	100.0	100.0	100.0	100.0	100.0	100.0
1971	103.4	97.9	105.2	90.5	100.7	109.5	100.6	105.1
1972	107.9	101.6	115.8	90.3	105.8	112.5	101.6	114.0
1973	108.1	110.9	116.2	88.9	106.8	113.3	104.9	118.3
1974	109.2	106.9	107.9	84.5	107.5	121.9	110.0	132.6

	355-356	36 ×	37	381	382	383	384	390
Date *Date* Fecha	Rubber and plastic products *Produits en caoutchouc et en plastique* Productos de caucho, de plástico	Non-metallic mineral products [3] *Produits minéraux non métalliques [3]* Productos minerales no metálicos [3]	Basic metal industries *Industrie métallurgique de base* Industrias metalúrgicas básicas	Metal products *Produits métalliques* Productos metálicos	Machinery (non-electrical) *Machines (non électriques)* Maquinaria (no eléctrica)	Electrical machinery *Machines électriques* Maquinaria eléctrica	Transport equipment *Matériel de transport* Material de transporte	Other manufacturing industries *Autres industries manufacturières* Otras industrias manufactureras
1968	86.1	91.6	88.6	80.3	81.9	68.1	63.4	80.3
1969	92.5	95.6	96.8	91.3	93.7	86.8	83.4	86.3
1970	100.0	100.0	100.0	100.0	100.0	100.0	100.0	100.0
1971	106.2	108.9	102.2	108.0	102.5	112.3	104.8	106.7
1972	113.7	118.9	106.1	114.4	107.0	125.3	107.4	109.2
1973	120.2	114.6	112.9	108.4	103.1	135.9	113.7	92.5
1974	115.8	115.4	120.6	112.5	109.6	150.8	126.3	91.6

[1] Incl. footwear. [2] Incl. products of petroleum and coal. [3] Excl. pottery, china and earthenware.

[1] *Y compris la chaussure.* [2] *Y compris les dérivés du pétrole et du charbon.* [3] *Non compris le grès, les porcelaines et les faïences.*

[1] Incl. el calzado. [2] Incl. los derivados del petróleo y del carbón. [3] Excl. el barro, la loza y la porcelana.

6 Employment in manufacturing
Emploi dans les industries manufacturières
Empleo en las industrias manufactureras

B By industry
Par industrie
Por industria

Japan

Indices of numbers employed: wage earners and salaried employees *(Statistics of establishments)*
Indices de l'effectif employé: ouvriers et employés *(Statistiques d'établissements)*
Indices de trabajadores ocupados: obreros y empleados *(Estadísticas de establecimientos)*

(1970 = 100)

Date / Date / Fecha	31 Food, beverages, tobacco / Aliments, boissons, tabac / Alimentos, bebidas, tabaco	321 Textiles	322 Clothing / Habillement / Vestido	323-324 Leather, leather products, footwear / Cuir, articles en cuir, chaussures / Cuero, artículos de cuero, calzado	331 Wood / Bois / Madera	332 Furniture / Ameublement / Mobiliario	341 Paper, paper products / Papier, articles en papier / Papel, artículos de papel	342 Printing, publishing / Imprimerie, édition / Imprentas, editoriales	351-352 Chemicals / Industrie chimique / Productos químicos	353-354 Refineries and products of petroleum and coal / Raffineries et dérivés du pétrole et du charbon / Refinerías y derivados del petróleo y del carbón
1965	93.7	112.6	74.6	109.8	92.3	77.0	103.0	93.6	93.5	71.9
1966	97.7	108.4	81.4	112.8	97.1	83.4	103.0	96.4	91.9	74.9
1967	99.6	104.5	84.4	106.3	99.0	87.8	101.8	96.4	92.9	82.3
1968	101.8	102.7	89.3	99.1	98.0	93.4	101.0	95.9	96.2	90.2
1969	101.2	100.5	93.2	99.5	99.0	94.9	99.7	95.8	98.8	95.2
1970	**100.0**	**100.0**	**100.0**	**100.0**	**100.0**	**100.0**	**100.0**	**100.0**	**100.0**	**100.0**
1971	97.5	97.6	109.2	100.6	97.7	101.4	100.8	103.4	101.0	108.0
1972	95.3	91.4	110.3	98.6	94.1	101.8	101.0	105.1	98.3	111.9
1973	94.9	88.2	113.9	92.3	93.8	105.6	96.9	104.3	97.9	113.6
1974	95.9	83.8	116.5	91.4	91.4	103.1	95.7	100.0	97.7	116.6

Date / Date / Fecha	355 Rubber products / Produits en caoutchouc / Productos de caucho	36 Non-metallic mineral products / Produits minéraux non métalliques / Productos minerales no metálicos	371 Basic metal industries / Industrie métallurgique de base / Industrias metalúrgicas básicas — Iron and steel / Sidérurgie / Hierro y acero	372 Non-ferrous metal / Métaux non ferreux / Metales no ferrosos	381 Metal products / Produits métalliques / Productos metálicos	382 Machinery (non-electrical) / Machines (non électriques) / Maquinaria (no eléctrica)	383 Electrical machinery and apparatus / Machines et appareils électriques / Maquinaria y aparatos eléctricos	384 Transport equipment / Matériel de transport / Material de transporte	385 Scientific, measuring, optical, etc., equipment / Matériel scientifique, de précision, d'optique, etc. / Equipo científico, de medida, de óptica, etc.	390 Other manufacturing industries / Autres industries manufacturières / Otras industrias manufactureras
1965	86.7	87.1	95.8	89.2	83.2	82.9	64.7	77.3	85.2	82.4
1966	87.8	89.4	93.5	88.8	85.7	80.1	65.0	79.5	83.0	86.0
1967	92.0	93.2	95.4	91.4	89.1	83.9	71.4	84.5	84.7	91.0
1968	95.2	95.5	97.1	82.4	93.3	90.6	79.9	90.2	87.4	93.1
1969	97.6	96.8	98.1	94.7	97.1	97.6	91.6	92.4	91.0	98.2
1970	**100.0**	**100.0**	**100.0**	**100.0**	**100.0**	**100.0**	**100.0**	**100.0**	**100.0**	**100.0**
1971	100.9	98.9	100.9	100.1	102.4	100.1	97.8	105.9	105.7	99.3
1972	98.5	96.6	97.4	98.6	102.1	96.2	94.8	109.7	105.7	95.9
1973	96.9	95.3	96.2	98.6	102.3	96.6	97.0	113.5	105.8	94.6
1974	96.1	92.5	96.5	100.0	103.0	98.1	96.5	115.0	104.6	90.3

EMPLOYMENT

6 **Employment in manufacturing**
Emploi dans les industries manufacturières
Empleo en las industrias manufactureras

B **By industry**
Par industrie
Por industria

Korea, Rep. of (1)

Indices of numbers employed: wage earners and salaried employees *(Statistics of establishments)*
Indices de l'effectif employé: ouvriers et employés *(Statistiques d'établissements)*
Indices de trabajadores ocupados: obreros y empleados *(Estadísticas de establecimientos)*

(1972 = 100)

Date / *Date* / Fecha	311-312	313	314	321	322	323-324	331	332	341
	Food	Beverages	Tobacco		Clothing	Leather, leather products, footwear	Wood	Furniture	Paper, paper products
	Aliments	*Boissons*	*Tabac*	Textiles	*Habillement*	*Cuir, articles en cuir, chaussures*	*Bois*	*Ameublement*	*Papier, articles en papier*
	Alimentos	Bebidas	Tabaco		Vestido	Cuero, artículos de cuero, calzado	Madera	Mobiliario	Papel, artículos de papel
1972	**100.0**	**100.0**	**100.0**	**100.0**	**100.0**	**100.0**	**100.0**	**100.0**	**100.0**
1973	*106.9*	*85.1*	*141.2*	*95.1*	*131.8*	*137.2*	*143.4*	*100.3*	*109.8*
1974	*138.4*	*87.7*	*...*	*109.1*	*120.5*	*161.6*	*188.5*	*78.0*	*133.9*

Date / *Date* / Fecha	342	351	352	353	354	355	356	361	362
	Printing, publishing	Industrial chemicals	Other chemical products	Petroleum refineries	Products of petroleum and coal	Rubber products	Plastic products	Pottery, china, earthenware	Glass and glass products
	Imprimerie, édition	*Chimie industrielle*	*Autres produits chimiques*	*Raffineries de pétrole*	*Dérivés du pétrole et du charbon*	*Industrie du caoutchouc*	*Articles en matière plastique*	*Grès, porcelaines, faïences*	*Verre*
	Imprentas, editoriales	Química industrial	Otros productos químicos	Refinerías de petróleo	Derivados del petróleo y del carbón	Productos de caucho	Productos plásticos	Barro, loza, porcelana	Vidrio
1972	**100.0**	**100.0**	**100.0**	**100.0**	**100.0**	**100.0**	**100.0**	**100.0**	**100.0**
1973	*106.9*	*89.9*	*107.1*	*92.2*	*89.8*	*134.7*	*121.9*	*111.5*	*120.2*
1974	*92.6*	*125.4*	*109.5*	*129.0*	*91.7*	*168.7*	*162.2*	*168.1*	*132.6*

6 B

6 Employment in manufacturing
Emploi dans les industries manufacturières
Empleo en las industrias manufactureras

B By industry
Par industrie
Por industria

Korea, Rep. of (2)

Indices of numbers employed: wage earners and salaried employees *(Statistics of establishments)*
Indices de l'effectif employé: ouvriers et employés *(Statistiques d'établissements)*
Indices de trabajadores ocupados: obreros y empleados *(Estadísticas de establecimientos)*

(1972 = 100)

Date / Date / Fecha	369 Other non-metallic mineral products / *Autres produits minéraux non métalliques* / Otros productos minerales no metálicos	37 Basic metal industries / *Industrie métallurgique de base* / Industrias metalúrgicas básicas	381 Metal products / *Produits métalliques* / Productos metálicos	382 Machinery (non-electrical) / *Machines (non électriques)* / Maquinaria (no eléctrica)	383 Electrical machinery and apparatus / *Machines et appareils électriques* / Maquinaria y aparatos eléctricos	384 Transport equipment / *Matériel de transport* / Material de transporte	385 Scientific, measuring, optical, etc., equipment / *Matériel scientifique, de précision, d'optique, etc.* / Equipo científico, de medida, de óptica, etc.	390 Other manufacturing industries / *Autres industries manufacturières* / Otras industrias manufactureras
1972	**100.0**	**100.0**	**100.0**	**100.0**	**100.0**	**100.0**	**100.0**	**100.0**
1973	*103.6*	*134.7*	*117.6*	*119.4*	*170.1*	*128.7*	*143.3*	*117.9*
1974	*124.3*	*180.8*	*135.8*	*141.5*	*219.3*	*208.8*	*148.9*	*114.6*

Philippines (1)

Indices of numbers employed: wage earners and salaried employees *(Statistics of establishments)*
Indices de l'effectif employé: ouvriers et employés *(Statistiques d'établissements)*
Indices de trabajadores ocupados: obreros y empleados *(Estadísticas de establecimientos)*

(1970 = 100)

Date / Date / Fecha	311-312 Food / *Aliments* / Alimentos	313 Beverages / *Boissons* / Bebidas	314 Tobacco / *Tabac* / Tabaco	321 Textiles	322 Clothing / *Habillement* / Vestido	323 Leather, leather products / *Cuir, articles en cuir* / Cuero, artículos de cuero	324 Footwear / *Chaussures* / Calzado	331 Wood / *Bois* / Madera	332 Furniture / *Ameublement* / Mobiliario
1968	98.5	84.8	82.7	100.3	76.0	129.4	147.2	101.0	108.3
1969	97.9	99.3	91.6	109.4	51.5	82.4	130.6	96.9	111.7
1970	**100.0**	**100.0**	**100.0**	**100.0**	**100.0**	**100.0**	**100.0**	**100.0**	**100.0**
1971	104.9	105.3	93.8	116.1	110.8	105.9	83.3	107.3	88.3
1972	109.9	100.1	86.3	98.3	110.4	69.4	67.0	146.1	128.4

EMPLOYMENT

6 Employment in manufacturing
Emploi dans les industries manufacturières
Empleo en las industrias manufactureras

B By industry
Par industrie
Por industria

Philippines (2)

Indices of numbers employed: wage earners and salaried employees *(Statistics of establishments)*
Indices de l'effectif employé: ouvriers et employés *(Statistiques d'établissements)*
Indices de trabajadores ocupados: obreros y empleados *(Estadísticas de establecimientos)*

(1970 = 100)

Date / Date / Fecha	341 Paper, paper products *Papier, articles en papier* Papel, artículos de papel	342 Printing, publishing *Imprimerie, édition* Imprentas, editoriales	351 Industrial chemicals *Chimie industrielle* Química industrial	352 Other chemical products *Autres produits chimiques* Otros productos químicos	353 Petroleum refineries *Raffineries de pétrole* Refinerías de petróleo	355 Rubber products *Produits en caoutchouc* Productos de caucho	356 Plastic products *Articles en matière plastique* Productos plásticos	361-362 Pottery, china, earthenware and glass *Grès, porcelaines, faïences et verre* Barro, loza, porcelana y vidrio
1968	86.4	92.9	100.0	99.4	73.3	105.8	60.9	79.2
1969	88.6	95.5	107.5	103.8	126.7	97.7	73.4	90.9
1970	**100.0**	**100.0**	**100.0**	**100.0**	**100.0**	**100.0**	**100.0**	**100.0**
1971	117.0	89.0	107.5	110.8	120.0	105.8	103.1	107.8
1972	193.6	70.9	127.1	119.7	66.3	112.9	133.0	93.8

Date / Date / Fecha	369 Other non-metallic mineral products *Autres produits minéraux non métalliques* Otros productos minerales no metálicos	371 Basic metal industries / *Industrie métallurgique de base* / Industrias metalúrgicas básicas Iron and steel *Sidérurgie* Hierro y acero	372 Non-ferrous metal *Métaux non ferreux* Metales no ferrosos	381 Metal products *Produits métalliques* Productos metálicos	382 Machinery (non-electrical) [1] *Machines (non électriques)* [1] Maquinaria (no eléctrica) [1]	383 Electrical machinery and apparatus [2] *Machines et appareils électriques* [2] Maquinaria y aparatos eléctricos [2]	384 Transport equipment *Matériel de transport* Material de transporte	385; 390 Other manufacturing industries [3] *Autres industries manufacturières* [3] Otras industrias manufactureras [3]
1968	95.1	72.5	94.4	145.7	86.2	97.0	109.1	136.0
1969	96.1	71.3	94.4	144.5	89.2	91.0	113.6	108.0
1970	**100.0**	**100.0**	**100.0**	**100.0**	**100.0**	**100.0**	**100.0**	**100.0**
1971	126.2	106.6	105.6	112.2	100.0	110.5	110.0	124.0
1972	117.2	99.3	...	100.1	155.2	100.7	152.8	194.0

[1] Excl. refrigerators. [2] Incl. refrigerators. [3] Incl. scientific, measuring, optical, etc., equipment.

[1] *Non compris les réfrigérateurs.* [2] *Y compris les réfrigérateurs.* [3] *Y compris le matériel scientifique, de précision, d'optique, etc.*

[1] Excl. los refrigeradores. [2] Incl. los refrigeradores. [3] Incl. el equipo científico, de medida, de óptica, etc.

6 Employment in manufacturing   B   By industry
Emploi dans les industries manufacturières   Par industrie
Empleo en las industrias manufactureras   Por industria

Singapore (1)

Indices of numbers employed: wage earners and salaried employees *(Statistics of establishments)*
Indices de l'effectif employé: ouvriers et employés *(Statistiques d'établissements)*
Indices de trabajadores ocupados: obreros y empleados *(Estadísticas de establecimientos)*

(1971 = 100)

	311-312	313	314	321	322	323	324	331
Date [1]	Food	Beverages	Tobacco		Clothing	Leather, leather products	Footwear	Wood
Date [1]	*Aliments*	*Boissons*	*Tabac*	Textiles	*Habillement*	*Cuir, articles en cuir*	*Chaussures*	*Bois*
Fecha [1]	Alimentos	Bebidas	Tabaco		Vestido	Cuero, artículos de cuero	Calzado	Madera
1971	**100.0**	**100.0**	**100.0**	**100.0**	**100.0**	**100.0**	**100.0**	**100.0**
1972	*103.4*	*100.8*	*96.3*	*128.0*	*155.6*	*94.4*	*100.4*	*113.7*
1973	*105.0*	*105.8*	*94.6*	*148.0*	*160.6*	*120.4*	*76.7*	*118.5*

	332	341	342	351-352	353-354	355	356	361-362
Date [1]	Furniture	Paper, paper products	Printing, publishing	Chemicals	Refineries and products of petroleum and coal	Rubber products	Plastic products	Pottery, china, earthenware and glass
Date [1]	*Ameublement*	*Papier, articles en papier*	*Imprimerie, édition*	*Industrie chimique*	*Raffineries et dérivés du pétrole et du charbon*	*Produits en caoutchouc*	*Articles en matière plastique*	*Grès, porcelaines, faïences et verre*
Fecha [1]	Mobiliario	Papel, artículos de papel	Imprentas, editoriales	Productos químicos	Refinerías y derivados del petróleo y del carbón	Productos de caucho	Productos plásticos	Barro, loza, porcelana y vidrio
1971	**100.0**	**100.0**	**100.0**	**100.0**	**100.0**	**100.0**	**100.0**	**100.0**
1972	*106.8*	*109.6*	*101.8*	*117.9*	*116.9*	*88.5*	*140.7*	*93.4*
1973	*157.1*	*150.4*	*105.8*	*123.5*	*115.4*	*81.5*	*171.9*	*95.1*

[1] Sep. of each year.   [1] *Sept. de chaque année.*   [1] Sept. de cada año.

6 Employment in manufacturing
Emploi dans les industries manufacturières
Empleo en las industrias manufactureras

B By industry
Par industrie
Por industria

Singapore (2)

Indices of numbers employed: wage earners and salaried employees *(Statistics of establishments)*
Indices de l'effectif employé: ouvriers et employés *(Statistiques d'établissements)*
Indices de trabajadores ocupados: obreros y empleados *(Estadísticas de establecimientos)*

(1971 = 100)

	369	37	381	382	383	384	385	390
Date [1] *Date [1]* Fecha [1]	Other non-metallic mineral products *Autres produits minéraux non métalliques* Otros productos minerales no metálicos	Basic metal industries *Industrie métallurgique de base* Industrias metalúrgicas básicas	Metal products *Produits métalliques* Productos metálicos	Machinery (non-electrical) *Machines (non électriques)* Maquinaria (no eléctrica)	Electrical machinery and apparatus *Machines et appareils électriques* Maquinaria y aparatos eléctricos	Transport equipment *Matériel de transport* Material de transporte	Scientific, measuring, optical, etc., equipment *Matériel scientifique, de précision, d'optique, etc.* Equipo científico, de medida, de óptica, etc.	Other manufacturing industries *Autres industries manufacturières* Otras industrias manufactureras
1971	**100.0**	**100.0**	**100.0**	**100.0**	**100.0**	**100.0**	**100.0**	**100.0**
1972	*103.7*	*135.1*	*106.4*	*131.2*	*155.9*	*116.8*	*360.5*	*81.6*
1973	*112.6*	*99.4*	*120.1*	*179.4*	*218.8*	*128.6*	*584.5*	*79.6*

[1] Sep. of each year   [1] *Sept. de chaque année.*   [1] Sept. de cada año.

6 **Employment in manufacturing**
Emploi dans les industries manufacturières
Empleo en las industrias manufactureras

B **By industry**
Par industrie
Por industria

EUROPE — EUROPE — EUROPA

Austria

Indices of numbers employed: wage earners and salaried employees *(Compulsory social insurance statistics)*
Indices de l'effectif employé: ouvriers et employés *(Statistiques d'assurances sociales obligatoires)*
Indices de trabajadores ocupados: obreros y empleados *(Estadísticas del seguro social obligatorio)*

(1971 = 100)

	31	32	33	34	35	36	37	38	39
Date [1] *Date [1]* Fecha [1]	Food, beverages, tobacco *Aliments, boissons, tabac* Alimentos, bebidas, tabaco	Textiles, clothing, leather *Textiles, habillement, cuir* Textiles, vestido, cuero	Wood, furniture *Bois, ameublement* Madera, mobiliario	Paper, printing, publishing *Papier, imprimerie, édition* Papel, imprentas, editoriales	Chemicals *Industrie chimique* Productos químicos	Non-metallic mineral products *Produits minéraux non métalliques* Productos minerales no metálicos	Basic metal industries *Industrie métallurgique de base* Industrias metalúrgicas básicas	Metal products, machinery, etc. *Produits métalliques, machines, etc.* Productos metálicos, maquinaria, etc.	Other manufacturing industries *Autres industries manufacturières* Otras industrias manufactureras
1971	**100.0**	**100.0**	**100.0**	**100.0**	**100.0**	**100.0**	**100.0**	**100.0**	**100.0**
1972	*99.5*	*100.7*	*99.0*	*103.1*	*105.0*	*95.7*	*92.8*	*103.7*	*96.7*
1973	*102.2*	*99.7*	*105.8*	*105.6*	*107.2*	*97.2*	*92.6*	*111.0*	*95.0*
1974	*100.6*	*93.9*	*107.7*	*106.0*	*108.0*	*97.2*	*98.8*	*111.6*	*100.0*

[1] July of each year.   [1] *Juillet de chaque année.*   [1] Julio de cada año.

6 **Employment in manufacturing**
Emploi dans les industries manufacturières
Empleo en las industrias manufactureras

B **By industry**
Par industrie
Por industria

Belgique

Indices of numbers employed: wage earners and salaried employees *(Compulsory social insurance statistics)*
Indices de l'effectif employé: ouvriers et employés *(Statistiques d'assurances sociales obligatoires)*
Indices de trabajadores ocupados: obreros y empleados *(Estadísticas del seguro social obligatorio)*

(1970 = 100)

	311-312	313	314	321	322	323	324	33	341	342
Date [1]	Food	Beverages	Tobacco		Clothing	Leather, leather products	Footwear	Wood, furniture	Paper, paper products	Printing, publishing
Date [1] / Fecha [1]	*Aliments*	*Boissons*	*Tabac*	Textiles	*Habillement*	*Cuir, articles en cuir*	*Chaussures*	*Bois, ameublement*	*Papier, articles en papier*	*Imprimerie, édition*
	Alimentos	Bebidas	Tabaco		Vestido	Cuero, artículos de cuero	Calzado	Madera, mobiliario	Papel, artículos de papel	Imprentas, editoriales
1965	89.6	110.9	121.3	112.8	95.1	108.8	152.9	93.5	96.5	88.8
1966	92.4	108.8	116.3	112.8	100.0	103.2	150.7	95.0	95.4	91.2
1967	93.6	105.4	110.0	104.0	95.5	95.2	136.9	93.6	92.7	90.7
1968	92.1	101.9	105.8	99.8	94.0	95.9	123.4	92.3	93.1	92.1
1969	92.9	100.2	102.4	100.0	98.0	96.7	111.9	97.8	98.1	95.8
1970	**100.0**	**100.0**	**100.0**	**100.0**	**100.0**	**100.0**	**100.0**	**100.0**	**100.0**	**100.0**
1971	100.2	98.1	101.4	96.2	102.8	92.0	94.6	100.4	97.1	101.0
1972	98.6	96.2	105.3	93.8	107.9	90.4	88.2	100.5	95.5	102.1

	351-352	354	355	362	369	371	381	383	385	390
Date [1]	Chemicals	Products of petroleum and coal	Rubber products	Glass, and glass products	Other non-metallic mineral products	Iron and steel basic industries	Metal products	Electrical machinery and apparatus	Scientific, measuring, optical, etc. equipment	Other manufacturing industries
Date [1] / Fecha [1]	*Industrie chimique*	*Dérivés du pétrole et du charbon*	*Produits en caoutchouc*	*Verre*	*Autres produits minéraux non métalliques*	*Sidérurgie*	*Produits métalliques*	*Machines et appareils électriques*	*Matériel scientifique, de précision, d'optique, etc.*	*Autres industries manufacturières*
	Productos químicos	Derivados del petróleo y del carbón	Productos de caucho	Vidrio	Otros productos minerales no metálicos	Industrias básicas de hierro y acero	Productos metálicos	Maquinaria y aparatos eléctricos	Equipo científico, de medida, de óptica, etc.	Otras industrias manufactureras
1965	94.2	93.6	98.6	97.8	117.1	102.6	96.7	86.6	97.8	66.8
1966	94.0	91.3	93.2	94.5	110.6	98.4	96.8	86.7	103.4	68.2
1967	93.4	90.6	88.9	90.5	106.7	94.5	92.5	84.9	108.5	75.1
1968	93.8	96.4	92.4	92.1	101.5	92.9	92.2	84.8	103.1	79.7
1969	95.1	97.1	98.0	96.8	98.9	95.8	98.3	91.0	101.4	93.2
1970	**100.0**	**100.0**	**100 0**	**100.0**	**100.0**	**100.0**	**100.0**	**100 0**	**100.0**	**100.0**
1971	99.3	103.0	105.0	96.0	97.8	100.9	100.5	102.7	93.7	106.1
1972	100.6	101.7	101.6	92.6	91.8	98.8	96.3	101.3	90.2	111.7

[1] June of each year.   [1] *Juin de chaque année.*   [1] Junio de cada año.

Employment in manufacturing
Emploi dans les industries manufacturières
Empleo en las industrias manufactureras

B By industry
Par industrie
Por industria

Bulgarie [1]

Indices of numbers employed: wage earners and salaried employees *(Statistics of establishments)*
Indices de l'effectif employé: ouvriers et employés *(Statistiques d'établissements)*
Indices de trabajadores ocupados: obreros y empleados *(Estadísticas de establecimientos)*

(1970 = 100)

Date / Date / Fecha	Food, beverages, tobacco / Aliments, boissons, tabac / Alimentos, bebidas, tabaco	Textiles	Clothing [2] / Habillement [2] / Vestido [2]	Wood, furniture [3] / Bois, ameublement [3] / Madera, mobiliario [3]	Paper, paper products / Papier, articles en papier / Papel, artículos de papel	Printing, publishing / Imprimerie, édition / Imprentas, editoriales	Leather, leather products [4] / Cuir, articles en cuir [4] / Cuero, artículos de cuero [4]
1965	85.3	80.3	77.2	100.6	78.8	80.0	72.7
1966	102.4	85.9	90.9	102.1	86.7	87.1	83.6
1967	102.5	88.1	96.6	104.2	92.7	93.4	88.6
1968	98.8	91.1	101.3	104.0	96.0	97.0	92.9
1969	99.6	97.0	105.1	104.5	99.2	99.0	99.0
1970	**100.0**	**100.0**	**100.0**	**100.0**	**100.0**	**100.0**	**100.0**
1971	90.7	107.7	107.4	106.4	109.4	96.0	110.6
1972	91.7	109.6	108.3	105.6	113.6	95.3	112.3
1973	92.8	111.5	112.2	107.0	122.0	108.2	114.3
1974 *	103.5	115.0	110.8	101.3	136.3	113.2	120.2

Date / Date / Fecha	Rubber products, chemicals / Caoutchouc, industrie chimique / Caucho, productos químicos	Building materials / Matériaux de construction / Materiales de construcción	Glass, china, earthenware / Verre, porcelaine, faïence / Vidrio, porcelana, loza	Primary iron and steel [5] / Sidérurgie [5] / Siderurgia [5]	Non-ferrous metals [6] / Métaux non ferreux [6] / Metales no ferrosos [6]	Metal products, machinery, etc. / Produits métalliques, machines, etc. / Productos metálicos, maquinaria, etc.	Other industries / Autres industries / Otras industrias
1965	61.1	95.9	79.6	73.3	108.9	71.7	83.4
1966	65.8	98.7	86.1	80.2	109.5	80.0	88.3
1967	73.6	102.6	93.1	91.5	109.0	90.3	89.1
1968	80.3	102.9	97.8	93.6	104.1	92.3	89.7
1969	85.8	102.9	99.9	97.9	99.1	95.2	98.2
1970	**100.0**	**100.0**	**100.0**	**100.0**	**100.0**	**100.0**	**100.0**
1971	110.1	104.1	103.3	100.3	98.2	110.2	105.8
1972	116.7	111.7	103.8	101.0	...	115.5	112.8
1973	122.1	110.7	106.2	103.5	...	121.0	...
1974 *	120.0	119.7	99.4	103.8	...	119.3	...

[1] State industry. Excl. industrial co-operatives. [2] Excl. footwear. [3] Incl. logging. [4] Incl. footwear. [5] Incl. ore mining. [6] Mining, production and primary transformation.

[1] *Industrie d'Etat. Non compris les coopératives industrielles.* [2] *Non compris la chaussure.* [3] *Y compris l'exploitation forestière.* [4] *Y compris la chaussure.* [5] *Y compris l'extraction des minerais.* [6] *Extraction, production et première transformation.*

[1] Industria de Estado. Excl. las cooperativas industriales. [2] Excl. el calzado. [3] Incl. la explotación de la madera. [4] Incl. el calzado. [5] Incl. la extracción de minerales. [6] Extracción, producción y primera transformación.

6 **Employment in manufacturing**
  Emploi dans les industries manufacturières
  Empleo en las industrias manufactureras

B **By industry**
  Par industrie
  Por industria

Czechoslovakia (1)

Indices of numbers employed: wage earners *(Statistics of establishments)*
Indices de l'effectif employé: ouvriers *(Statistiques d'établissements)*
Indices de trabajadores ocupados: obreros *(Estadísticas de establecimientos)*

(1970 = 100)

Date / *Date* / Fecha	311-312 Food / *Aliments* / Alimentos	313 Beverages / *Boissons* / Bebidas	314 Tobacco / *Tabac* / Tabaco	321 Textiles	322 Clothing / *Habillement* / Vestido	323 Leather, leather products / *Cuir, articles en cuir* / Cuero, artículos de cuero	324 Footwear / *Chaussures* / Calzado	331 Wood / *Bois* / Madera	332 Furniture / *Ameublement* / Mobiliario
1965	92.8	99.2	84.4	97.5	92.1	77.6	95.0	112.6	97.7
1966	95.6	102.5	90.6	100.8	94.2	86.8	97.6	105.3	96.5
1967	94.6	107.4	93.8	102.0	91.9	97.7	98.3	101.0	97.5
1968	95.8	109.0	96.9	100.8	92.9	101.4	99.5	101.1	98.8
1969	97.6	103.7	100.0	100.3	100.2	100.0	101.0	104.0	97.3
1970	**100.0**	**100.0**	**100.0**	**100.0**	**100.0**	**100.0**	**100.0**	**100.0**	**100.0**
1971	101.3	101.6	103.1	100.5	99.5	100.5	102.2	100.2	99.8
1972	101.2	102.5	103.1	100.4	97.7	100.9	103.8	100.6	99.2
1973	101.6	102.5	103.1	99.8	96.8	100.0	104.0	102.1	99.2
1974	101.9	102.0	106.3	99.5	94.4	99.1	102.2	102.7	100.0

Date / *Date* / Fecha	341 Paper, paper products / *Papier, articles en papier* / Papel, artículos de papel	342 Printing, publishing / *Imprimerie, édition* / Imprentas, editoriales	351 Industrial chemicals / *Chimie industrielle* / Química industrial	352 Other chemical products / *Autres produits chimiques* / Otros productos químicos	353 Petroleum refineries / *Raffineries de pétrole* / Refinerías de petróleo	354 Products of petroleum and coal / *Dérivés du pétrole et du charbon* / Derivados del petróleo y del carbón	355 Rubber products / *Produits en caoutchouc* / Productos de caucho	361 Pottery, china, earthenware / *Grès, porcelaines, faïences* / Barro, loza, porcelana	362 Glass / *Verre* / Vidrio
1965	90.7	83.3	76.6	152.8	.	.	90.8	120.0	92.6
1966	91.3	93.5	81.8	121.1	110.9	109.4	117.9	96.5	91.2
1967	96.1	110.2	87.4	99.4	100.0	103.1	124.0	101.2	92.1
1968	98.5	114.0	90.3	98.3	101.4	96.9	127.0	105.9	94.3
1969	99.1	138.6	98.8	103.9	100.7	100.0	100.0	103.5	97.1
1970	**100.0**	**100.0**	**100.0**	**100.0**	**100.0**	**100.0**	**100.0**	**100.0**	**100.0**
1971	101.5	101.4	103.1	111.7	100.7	96.9	92.9	100.0	101.4
1972	101.2	100.0	103.9	113.9	100.0	96.9	95.9	98.8	100.7
1973	101.2	102.3	106.3	112.8	97.1	96.9	98.5	98.8	101.6
1974	103.0	100.5	107.3	113.9	98.6	96.9	100.0	97.6	102.3

6 Employment in manufacturing
Emploi dans les industries manufacturières
Empleo en las industrias manufactureras

B By industry
Par industrie
Por industria

Czechoslovakia (2)

Indices of numbers employed: wage earners *(Statistics of establishments)*
Indices de l'effectif employé: ouvriers *(Statistiques d'établissements)*
Indices de trabajadores ocupados: obreros *(Estadísticas de establecimientos)*

(1970 = 100)

Date / Date / Fecha	369 Other non-metallic mineral products / *Autres produits minéraux non métalliques* / Otros productos minerales no metálicos	371 Basic metal industries / *Industrie métallurgique de base* / Industrias metalúrgicas básicas — Iron and steel / *Sidérurgie* / Hierro y acero	372 Non-ferrous metal / *Métaux non ferreux* / Metales no ferrosos	381 Metal products / *Produits métalliques* / Productos metálicos	382 Machinery (non-electrical) / *Machines (non électriques)* / Maquinaria (no eléctrica)	383 Electrical machinery and apparatus / *Machines et appareils électriques* / Maquinaria y aparatos eléctricos	384 Transport equipment / *Matériel de transport* / Material de transporte	385 Scientific, measuring, optical, etc., equipment / *Matériel scientifique, de précision, d'optique, etc.* / Equipo científico, de medida, de óptica, etc.	390 Other manufacturing industries / *Autres industries manufacturières* / Otras industrias manufactureras
1965	95.8	94.4	.	96.2	97.9	80.7	99.4	69.1	.
1966	96.7	98.7	72.4	78.5	104.4	90.8	102.1	81.7	59.5
1967	98.3	100.0	76.5	83.7	105.2	92.2	105.2	85.4	68.7
1968	98.5	100.2	69.4	86.7	107.3	95.5	106.6	88.4	69.4
1969	98.9	100.4	71.1	95.9	100.6	99.1	109.9	95.8	71.1
1970	**100.0**	**100.0**	**100.0**	**100.0**	**100.0**	**100.0**	**100.0**	**100.0**	**100.0**
1971	101.4	100.1	101.0	102.9	100.0	100.4	100.0	100.8	101.0
1972	97.7	99.9	107.1	102.4	100.6	100.8	100.9	103.0	107.1
1973	95.8	100.0	106.8	102.3	101.3	100.4	100.6	104.0	106.8
1974	95.3	100.0	94.9	100.3	102.3	100.8	100.7	103.5	105.4

EMPLOYMENT

6 Employment in manufacturing
Emploi dans les industries manufacturières
Empleo en las industrias manufactureras

B By industry
Par industrie
Por industria

Denmark (1)

Indices of numbers employed: wage earners and salaried employees *(Statistics of establishments)*
Indices de l'effectif employé: ouvriers et employés *(Statistiques d'établissements)*
Indices de trabajadores ocupados: obreros y empleados *(Estadísticas de establecimientos)*

(1970 = 100)

Date / Date / Fecha	311-312 Food / Aliments / Alimentos	313 Beverages / Boissons / Bebidas	314 Tobacco / Tabac / Tabaco	321 Textiles	322 Clothing / Habillement / Vestido	323 Leather, leather products / Cuir, articles en cuir / Cuero, artículos de cuero	324 Footwear / Chaussures / Calzado	331 Wood / Bois / Madera	332 Furniture / Ameublement / Mobiliario
1970	100.0	100.0	100.0	100.0	100.0	100.0	100.0	100.0	100.0
1971	102.7	100.6	91.7	93.4	89.2	95.2	91.9	94.4	92.4
1972	103.1	103.8	86.8	96.1	90.4	92.4	96.8	97.7	100.5
1973	104.4	108.9	82.9	94.2	86.9	82.3	90.8	101.0	106.8
1974 *	102.2	105.5	75.5	82.5	71.6	75.3	77.7	92.5	91.5

Date / Date / Fecha	341 Paper, paper products / Papier, articles en papier / Papel, artículos de papel	342 Printing, publishing / Imprimerie, édition / Imprentas, editoriales	351 Industrial chemicals / Chimie industrielle / Química industrial	352 Other chemical products / Autres produits chimiques / Otros productos químicos	353 Petroleum refineries / Raffineries de pétrole / Refinerías de petróleo	354 Products of petroleum and coal / Dérivés du pétrole et du charbon / Derivados del petróleo y del carbón	355 Rubber products / Produits en caoutchouc / Productos de caucho	356 Plastic products / Articles en matière plastique / Productos plásticos	361 Pottery, china, earthenware / Grès, porcelaines, faïences / Barro, loza, porcelana
1970	100.0	100.0	100.0	100.0	100.0	100.0	100.0	100.0	100.0
1971	95.3	100.6	96.5	98.4	97.8	98.2	89.5	102.8	103.7
1972	94.1	98.4	95.2	101.3	96.8	98.2	92.2	111.0	110.1
1973	99.6	99.7	105.1	101.2	92.5	84.6	89.1	120.4	113.2
1974 *	99.1	97.9	108.0	102.6	91.8	84.1	84.0	111.6	113.4

6 Employment in manufacturing
Emploi dans les industries manufacturières
Empleo en las industrias manufactureras

B By industry
Par industrie
Por industria

Denmark (2)

Indices of numbers employed: wage earners and salaried employees *(Statistics of establishments)*
Indices de l'effectif employé: ouvriers et employés *(Statistiques d'établissements)*
Indices de trabajadores ocupados: obreros y empleados *(Estadísticas de establecimientos)*

(1970 = 100)

Date / Date / Fecha	362 Glass / Verre / Vidrio	369 Other non-metallic mineral products / Autres produits minéraux non métalliques / Otros productos minerales no metálicos	Basic metal industries / Industrie métallurgique de base / Industrias metalúrgicas básicas 371 Iron and steel / Sidérurgie / Hierro y acero	372 Non-ferrous metal / Métaux non ferreux / Metales no ferrosos	381 Metal products / Produits métalliques / Productos metálicos	382 Machinery (non-electrical) / Machines (non électriques) / Maquinaria (no eléctrica)	383 Electrical machinery and apparatus / Machines et appareils électriques / Maquinaria y aparatos eléctricos	384 Transport equipment / Matériel de transport / Material de transporte	385 Scientific, measuring, optical, etc., equipment / Matériel scientifique, de précision, d'optique, etc. / Equipo científico, de medida, de óptica, etc.	390 Other manufacturing industries / Autres industries manufacturières / Otras industrias manufactureras
1970	**100.0**	**100.0**	**100.0**	**100.0**	**100.0**	**100.0**	**100.0**	**100.0**	**100.0**	**100.0**
1971	98.3	98.2	99.4	92.0	96.0	97.1	88.2	100.5	96.6	90.5
1972	107.7	101.1	89.0	89.8	99.9	97.6	87.3	103.6	96.2	94.2
1973	116.1	105.0	89.5	100.1	104.3	106.7	95.9	105.6	105.1	98.9
1974 *	116.3	93.4	96.5	107.9	99.0	111.0	94.8	106.7	115.4	92.7

EMPLOYMENT

6 Employment in manufacturing
Emploi dans les industries manufacturières
Empleo en las industrias manufactureras

B By industry
Par industrie
Por industria

España

Indices of numbers employed: wage earners and salaried employees *(Social insurance statistics)*
Indices de l'effectif employé: ouvriers et employés *(Statistiques d'assurances sociales)*
Indices de trabajadores ocupados: obreros y empleados *(Estadísticas del seguro social)*

(1970 = 100)

Date *Date* Fecha	31 Food, beverages, tobacco *Aliments, boissons, tabac* Alimentos, bebidas, tabaco	321 Textiles	322 Clothing *Habillement* Vestido	323-324 Leather, leather products, footwear *Cuir, articles en cuir, chaussures* Cuero, artículos de cuero, calzado	33 Wood, furniture *Bois, ameublement* Madera, mobiliario	34 Paper, printing, publishing *Papier, imprimerie, édition* Papel, imprentas, editoriales	35 Chemicals, refineries, products of petroleum and coal, rubber, plastics *Industrie chimique, raffineries et dérivés du pétrole et du charbon, caoutchouc, plastique* Productos químicos, refinerías y derivados del petróleo y del carbón, caucho, plástico	36 Non-metallic mineral products *Produits minéraux non métalliques* Productos minerales no metálicos	37-38 Metal industries, machinery, etc. *Industrie métallurgique, machines, etc.* Industrias metalúrgicas, maquinaria, etc.
1965	116.9	108.5	70.8	75.6	84.7	84.1	80.0	97.3	79.3
1966	124.7	106.8	78.5	78.4	90.8	88.3	85.5	98.6	86.9
1967	93.2	103.8	84.6	82.5	95.1	91.2	90.7	99.9	90.9
1968	96.1	99.8	86.1	86.7	95.6	93.7	92.9	100.1	91.6
1969	99.8	99.4	144.6	96.1	98.5	97.7	96.3	100.2	96.9
1970	100.0	100.0	100.0	100.0	100.0	100.0	100.0	100.0	100.0
1971	100.5	97.5	103.9	103.8	103.9	103.0	104.5	96.8	101.3
1972	103.6	98.4	109.6	111.6	110.1	110.5	109.0	98.0	105.2
1973	104.6	100.3	120.6	117.0	115.6	111.3	116.2	101.8	112.5
1974	107.3	98.6	123.5	117.6	120.9	113.4	122.3	106.7	117.9

6 **Employment in manufacturing**
Emploi dans les industries manufacturières
Empleo en las industrias manufactureras

B **By industry**
Par industrie
Por industria

Finland (1)

Indices of numbers employed: wage earners and salaried employees *(Statistics of establishments)*
Indices de l'effectif employé: ouvriers et employés *(Statistiques d'établissements)*
Indices de trabajadores ocupados: obreros y empleados *(Estadísticas de establecimientos)*

(1970 = 100)

Date / Date / Fecha	311-312 Food / Aliments / Alimentos	313 Beverages / Boissons / Bebidas	314 Tobacco / Tabac / Tabaco	321 Textiles	322 Clothing / Habillement / Vestido	323 Leather, leather products / Cuir, articles en cuir / Cuero, artículos de cuero	324 Footwear / Chaussures / Calzado	331 Wood / Bois / Madera	332 Furniture / Ameublement / Mobiliario
1965	89.0	65.7	114.6	93.4	83.6	87.9	94.5	93.4	83.0
1966	91.9	70.6	113.8	93.8	86.6	86.0	93.7	88.0	84.6
1967	93.2	76.3	111.0	93.0	88.9	89.2	94.1	82.8	87.4
1968	92.8	77.1	102.0	92.8	86.2	86.6	92.9	85.3	86.3
1969	94.4	90.8	100.5	98.1	102.1	89.4	95.7	93.9	92.5
1970	100.0	100.0	100.0	100.0	100.0	100.0	100.0	100.0	100.0
1971	100.0	99.1	100.4	93.3	125.6	99.3	98.2	116.9	68.2
1972	103.4	100.7	100.2	93.2	129.4	100.8	96.5	116.5	77.8
1973	106.0	103.5	104.9	96.3	136.7	101.4	87.4	119.9	79.0
1974 *	108.7	101.6	104.9	95.1	138.1	99.5	81.2	116.9	78.4

Date / Date / Fecha	341 Paper, paper products / Papier, articles en papier / Papel, artículos de papel	342 Printing, publishing / Imprimerie, édition / Imprentas, editoriales	351 Industrial chemicals / Chimie industrielle / Química industrial	352 Other chemical products / Autres produits chimiques / Otros productos químicos	353 Petroleum refineries / Raffineries de pétrole / Refinerías de petróleo	354 Products of petroleum and coal / Dérivés du pétrole et du charbon / Derivados del petróleo y del carbón	355 Rubber products / Produits en caoutchouc / Productos de caucho	356 Plastic products / Articles en matière plastique / Productos plásticos	361 Pottery, china, earthenware / Grès, porcelaines, faïences / Barro, loza, porcelana
1965	92.8	89.6	80.7	108.4	74.9	72.7	82.6	47.8	90.9
1966	92.4	93.1	84.0	112.5	80.0	69.7	89.3	53.1	91.4
1967	91.2	97.5	84.2	109.4	84.7	68.0	88.3	62.6	90.0
1968	92.7	100.7	87.6	110.1	84.7	66.6	86.3	68.4	91.1
1969	96.1	98.7	88.8	111.2	87.4	98.2	92.9	85.6	93.0
1970	100.0	100.0	100.0	100.0	100.0	100.0	100.0	100.0	100.0
1971	103.4	101.1	140.9	111.5	110.2	97.2	78.8	76.4	99.6
1972	102.6	101.3	150.9	114.0	123.1	113.5	79.9	82.9	101.1
1973	105.7	107.5	156.4	120.3	134.1	107.6	86.1	90.3	99.9
1974 *	110.0	111.9	156.6	120.4	137.1	110.7	88.5	84.5	93.1

EMPLOYMENT

6 Employment in manufacturing
Emploi dans les industries manufacturières
Empleo en las industrias manufactureras

B By industry
Par industrie
Por industria

Finland (2)

Indices of numbers employed: wage earners and salaried employees *(Statistics of establishments)*
Indices de l'effectif employé: ouvriers et employés *(Statistiques d'établissements)*
Indices de trabajadores ocupados: obreros y empleados *(Estadísticas de establecimientos)*

(1970 = 100)

Date / Date / Fecha	362 Glass / Verre / Vidrio	369 Other non-metallic mineral products / Autres produits minéraux non métalliques / Otros productos minerales no metálicos	371 Iron and steel / Sidérurgie / Hierro y acero	372 Non-ferrous metal / Métaux non ferreux / Metales no ferrosos	381 Metal products / Produits métalliques / Productos metálicos	382 Machinery (non-electrical) / Machines (non électriques) / Maquinaria (no eléctrica)	383 Electrical machinery and apparatus / Machines et appareils électriques / Maquinaria y aparatos eléctricos	384 Transport equipment / Matériel de transport / Material de transporte	385 Scientific, measuring, optical, etc., equipment / Matériel scientifique, de précision, d'optique, etc. / Equipo científico, de medida, de óptica, etc.	390 Other manufacturing industries / Autres industries manufacturières / Otras industrias manufactureras
1965	84.2	88.2	92.8	55.9	81.3	77.9	79.1	87.6	67.8	48.2
1966	87.2	91.9	91.6	61.4	84.0	81.0	79.2	89.0	71.5	51.9
1967	88.2	90.9	87.1	74.4	82.4	80.5	79.5	91.1	70.5	53.4
1968	88.7	88.9	89.5	79.0	82.2	82.0	80.2	89.0	69.9	85.7
1969	92.3	93.1	95.1	87.3	88.7	90.9	84.0	93.3	84.9	60.2
1970	**100.0**	**100.0**	**100.0**	**100.0**	**100.0**	**100.0**	**100.0**	**100.0**	**100.0**	**100.0**
1971	100.6	102.5	128.1	89.0	85.1	128.9	103.9	104.7	104.6	131.5
1972	99.7	111.8	136.4	95.1	88.9	132.1	112.7	119.9	109.6	138.2
1973	101.6	115.6	128.1	109.3	96.6	134.9	121.6	113 3	180.6	152.0
1974 *	105.2	131.5	138.4	115.0	104.1	138.2	145.6	117.2	203.0	132.5

France

Indices of numbers employed: wage earners and salaried employees *(Official estimates)*
Indices de l'effectif employé: ouvriers et employés *(Evaluations officielles)*
Indices de trabajadores ocupados: obreros y empleados *(Estimaciones oficiales)*

(1971 = 100)

Date / Date / Fecha	31 Food, beverages, tobacco / Aliments, boissons, tabac / Alimentos, bebidas, tabaco	32 Textiles, clothing, leather / Textiles, habillement, cuir / Textiles, vestido, cuero	33 Wood, furniture / Bois, ameublement / Madera, mobiliario	34 Paper, printing, publishing / Papier, imprimerie, édition / Papel, imprentas, editoriales	35 Chemicals [1] / Industrie chimique [1] / Productos químicos [1]	36 Non-metallic mineral products / Produits minéraux non métalliques / Productos minerales no metálicos	37 Basic metal industries / Industrie métallurgique de base / Industrias metalúrgicas básicas	38 Metal products, machinery, etc. / Produits métalliques, machines, etc. / Productos metálicos, maquinaria, etc.	39 Other manufacturing industries / Autres industries manufacturières / Otras industrias manufactureras
1971	**100.0**	**100.0**	**100.0**	**100.0**	**100.0**	**100.0**	**100.0**	**100.0**	**100.0**
1972	*99.4*	*101.4*	*101.8*	*100.8*	*102.3*	*101.2*	*99.0*	*101.3*	*103.1*
1973	*100.4*	*99.8*	*106.2*	*101.9*	*104.7*	*103.2*	*101.0*	*105.2*	*108.3*
1974 *	*100.4*	*97.7*	*108.9*	*101.1*	*107.5*	*105.7*	*104.0*	*108.1*	*109.4*

[1] Incl. refineries, products of petroleum and coal, rubber and plastic products.

[1] *Y compris les raffineries et dérivés du pétrole et du charbon, et les produits en caoutchouc et en plastique.*

[1] Incl. las refinerías y derivados del petróleo y del carbón, y los productos de caucho y de plástico.

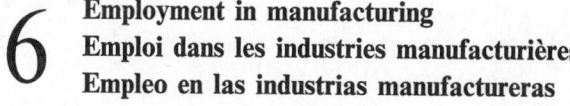

6 Employment in manufacturing
Emploi dans les industries manufacturières
Empleo en las industrias manufactureras

B By industry
Par industrie
Por industria

German Democratic Republic △

Indices of numbers employed: wage earners and salaried employees *(Official estimates)*
Indices de l'effectif employé: ouvriers et employés *(Evaluations officielles)*
Indices de trabajadores ocupados: obreros y empleados *(Estimaciones oficiales)*

(1970 = 100)

	31	321	35	362-369	37	38 ×	383	322-324; 33; 34; 361
Date *Date* Fecha	Food, beverages, tobacco *Aliments, boissons, tabac* Alimentos, bebidas, tabaco	Textiles	Chemicals, refineries and products of petroleum and coal, rubber, plastics [1] *Industrie chimique, raffineries et dérivés du pétrole et du charbon, caoutchouc, plastique [1]* Productos químicos, refinerías y derivados del petróleo y del carbón, caucho, plástico [1]	Non-metallic mineral products [2] *Produits minéraux non métalliques [2]* Productos minerales no metálicos [2]	Basic metal industries [3] *Industrie métallurgique de base [3]* Industrias metalúrgicas básicas [3]	Metal products, machinery [4] *Produits métalliques, machines [4]* Productos metálicos, maquinaria [4]	Electrical machinery and apparatus *Machines et appareils électriques* Maquinaria y aparatos eléctricos	Miscellaneous manufacturing *Industries manufacturières diverses* Industrias manufactureras diversas
1967	93.1	107.6	99.4	95.7	99.2	98.3	91.2	100.9
1968	96.8	105.2	100.6	95.7	100.0	99.6	94.0	101.1
1969	99.1	103.2	100.9	95.7	100.0	99.4	98.4	101.3
1970	**100.0**	**100.0**	**100.0**	**100.0**	**100.0**	**100.0**	**100.0**	**100.0**
1971	102.8	100.0	100.3	98.9	102.5	100.0	103.3	100.4
1972	107.4	103.2	101.9	104.3	102.5	105.8	111.0	108.4

[1] Incl. petroleum and gas extraction. [2] Excl. pottery, china, and earthenware. Incl. ore mining. [3] Incl. metal ore mining. [4] Excl. electrical machinery apparatus and appliances.

[1] *Y compris l'extraction du pétrole et du gaz.* [2] *Non compris le grès, les porcelaines et les faïences. Y compris l'extraction des minerais.* [3] *Y compris l'extraction des minerais métalliques.* [4] *Non compris les machines et appareils électriques.*

[1] Incl. la extracción del petróleo y del gas. [2] Excl. el barro, la loza y la porcelana. Incl. la extracción de los minerales. [3] Incl. la extracción de minerales metálicos. [4] Excl. las maquinarias y aparatos eléctricos.

Germany, Fed. Rep. of △

Indices of numbers employed: wage earners and salaried employees *(Official estimates)*
Indices de l'effectif employé: ouvriers et employés *(Evaluations officielles)*
Indices de trabajadores ocupados: obreros y empleados *(Estimaciones oficiales)*

(1970 = 100)

	31	32	33	34	35	36	37	38	39
Date *Date* Fecha	Food, beverages, tobacco *Aliments, boissons, tabac* Alimentos, bebidas, tabaco	Textiles, clothing, leather *Textiles, habillement, cuir* Textiles, vestido, cuero	Wood, furniture *Bois, ameublement* Madera, mobiliario	Paper, printing, publishing *Papier, imprimerie, édition* Papel, imprentas, editoriales	Chemicals *Industrie chimique* Productos químicos	Non-metallic mineral products *Produits minéraux non métalliques* Productos minerales no metálicos	Basic metal industries *Industrie métallurgique de base* Industrias metalúrgicas básicas	Metal products, machinery, etc. *Produits métalliques, machines, etc.* Productos metálicos maquinaria, etc.	Other manufacturing industries *Autres industries manufacturières* Otras industrias manufactureras
1970	**100.0**	**100.0**	**100.0**	**100.0**	**100.0**	**100.0**	**100.0**	**100.0**	**100.0**
1971	98.5	91.8	100.8	86.6	102.0	98.0	103.1	101.4	98.4
1972	99.1	92.4	102.5	82.9	99.1	110.3	98.0	101.1	91.5
1973	97.1	89.6	103.2	85.4	101.0	109.3	100.0	100.2	96.1
1974 *	93.9	81.2	100.3	75.0	101.2	100.8	103.1	99.0	94.6

6 **Employment in manufacturing**
Emploi dans les industries manufacturières
Empleo en las industrias manufactureras

B **By industry**
Par industrie
Por industria

Grèce (1)

Indices of numbers employed: wage earners and salaried employees *(Statistics of establishments)*
Indices de l'effectif employé: ouvriers et employés *(Statistiques d'établissements)*
Indices de trabajadores ocupados: obreros y empleados *(Estadísticas de establecimientos)*

(1970 = 100)

	311-312	313	314	321	322	323	324	331	332
Date *Date* Fecha	Food *Aliments* Alimentos	Beverages *Boissons* Bebidas	Tobacco *Tabac* Tabaco	Textiles	Clothing *Habillement* Vestido	Leather, leather products *Cuir, articles en cuir* Cuero, artículos de cuero	Footwear *Chaussures* Calzado	Wood *Bois* Madera	Furniture [1] *Ameublement* [1] Mobiliario [1]
1970	100.0	100.0	100.0	100.0	100.0	100.0	100.0	100.0	100.0
1971	104.8	110.6	96.9	106.5	110.7	99.5	105.7	106.1	101.3
1972	105.5	117.8	87.6	113.2	122.3	86.6	118.6	117.3	105.9

	341	342	351	352	353	354	355	356	361
Date *Date* Fecha	Paper, paper products *Papier, articles en papier* Papel, artículos de papel	Printing, publishing *Imprimerie, édition* Imprentas, editoriales	Industrial chemicals *Chimie industrielle* Química industrial	Other chemical products *Autres produits chimiques* Otros productos químicos	Petroleum refineries *Raffineries de pétrole* Refinerías de petróleo	Products of petroleum and coal *Dérivés du pétrole et du charbon* Derivados del petróleo y del carbón	Rubber products *Produits en caoutchouc* Productos de caucho	Plastic products *Articles en matière plastique* Productos plásticos	Pottery, china, earthenware *Grès, porcelaines, faïences* Barro, loza, porcelana
1970	100.0	100.0	100.0	100.0	100.0	100.0	100.0	100.0	100.0
1971	118.6	105.8	102.5	102.1	98.9	93.8	100.5	112.2	116.9
1972	119.7	106.4	108.0	117.3	128.3	92.4	99.0	128.1	125.4

[1] Incl. metal furniture.   [1] *Y compris les meubles métalliques.*   [1] Incl. los muebles metálicos.

6 Employment in manufacturing
Emploi dans les industries manufacturières
Empleo en las industrias manufactureras

B By industry
Par industrie
Por industria

Grèce (2)

Indices of numbers employed: wage earners and salaried employees *(Statistics of establishments)*
Indices de l'effectif employé: ouvriers et employés *(Statistiques d'établissements)*
Indices de trabajadores ocupados: obreros y empleados *(Estadísticas de establecimientos)*

(1970 = 100)

Date / Date / Fecha	362	369	371	372	381	382	383	384	385	390
	Glass / Verre / Vidrio	Other non-metallic mineral products / Autres produits minéraux non métalliques / Otros productos minerales no metálicos	Basic metal industries / Industrie métallurgique de base / Industrias metalúrgicas básicas — Iron and steel / Sidérurgie / Hierro y acero	Non-ferrous metal / Métaux non ferreux / Metales no ferrosos	Metal products [1] / Produits métalliques [1] / Productos metálicos [1]	Machinery (non-electrical) / Machines (non électriques) / Maquinaria (no eléctrica)	Electrical machinery and apparatus / Machines et appareils électriques / Maquinaria y aparatos eléctricos	Transport equipment / Matériel de transport / Material de transporte	Scientific, measuring, optical, etc. equipment / Matériel scientifique, de précision, d'optique, etc. / Equipo científico, de medida, de óptica, etc.	Other manufacturing industries / Autres industries manufacturières / Otras industrias manufactureras
1970	100.0	100.0	100.0	100.0	100.0	100.0	100.0	100.0	100.0	100.0
1971	112.5	101.2	108.6	104.6	104.1	103.3	117.7	122.7	97.0	110.0
1972	111.4	101.2	119.6	108.9	112.6	105.3	130.1	136.2	100.4	120.2

[1] Excl. metal furniture.   [1] *Non compris les meubles métalliques.*   [1] Excl. los muebles metálicos.

Hongrie [1] (1)

Indices of numbers employed: wage earners and salaried employees *(Statistics of establishments)*
Indices de l'effectif employé: ouvriers et employés *(Statistiques d'établissements)*
Indices de trabajadores ocupados: obreros y empleados *(Estadísticas de establecimientos)*

(1970 = 100)

Date / Date / Fecha	311-312	313	314	321	322	323	324	331	332
	Food / Aliments / Alimentos	Beverages / Boissons / Bebidas	Tobacco / Tabac / Tabaco	Textiles	Clothing / Habillement / Vestido	Leather, leather products / Cuir, articles en cuir / Cuero, artículos de cuero	Footwear / Chaussures / Calzado	Wood / Bois / Madera	Furniture / Ameublement / Mobiliario
1968	91.5	98.7	96.5	102.8	93.5	95.9	97.4	103.6	90.3
1969	98.3	98.9	101.0	102.6	96.1	98.8	100.4	104.2	95.2
1970	100.0	100.0	100.0	100.0	100.0	100.0	100.0	100.0	100.0
1971	100.6	100.0	99.5	97.7	101.4	95.7	98.1	94.0	100.0
1972	102.4	102.6	102.0	96.6	100.7	96.0	95.6	91.6	99.0
1973	104.7	106.4	98.5	97.6	103.5	97.3	97.9	92.5	102.1
1974 *	106.7	108.3	96.4	96.4	104.9	98.2	101.1	115.4	101.4

[1] State industry.   [1] *Industrie d'Etat.*   [1] Industria de Estado.

6 Employment in manufacturing
Emploi dans les industries manufacturières
Empleo en las industrias manufactureras

B By industry
Par industrie
Por industria

Hongrie [1] (2)

Indices of numbers employed: wage earners and salaried employees *(Statistics of establishments)*
Indices de l'effectif employé: ouvriers et employés *(Statistiques d'établissements)*
Indices de trabajadores ocupados: obreros y empleados *(Estadísticas de establecimientos)*

(1970 = 100)

Date / Date / Fecha	341 Paper, paper products / *Papier, articles en papier* / Papel, artículos de papel	342 Printing, publishing / *Imprimerie, édition* / Imprentas, editoriales	351 Industrial chemicals / *Chimie industrielle* / Química industrial	352 Other chemical products / *Autres produits chimiques* / Otros productos químicos	353 Petroleum refineries / *Raffineries de pétrole* / Refinerías de petróleo	355 Rubber products / *Produits en caoutchouc* / Productos de caucho	356 Plastic products / *Articles en matière plastique* / Productos plásticos	361 Pottery, china, earthenware / *Grès, porcelaines, faïences* / Barro, loza, porcelana	362 Glass / *Verre* / Vidrio
1968	93.2	92.2	94.4	88.3	87.6	89.4	94.8	79.3	93.7
1969	97.0	97.7	102.8	91.2	95.4	98.3	99.1	95.9	97.7
1970	100.0	100.0	100.0	100.0	100.0	100.0	100.0	100.0	100.0
1971	98.3	102.3	101.4	101.7	103.5	98.8	101.7	100.4	101.9
1972	99.2	101.8	105.0	103.2	105.2	99.8	100.6	101.4	104.7
1973	101.1	102.5	108.9	107.2	106.0	101.3	101.0	106.7	109.4
1974 *	99.7	102.8	110.8	108.3	108.9	100.7	100.7	112.9	114.6

Date / Date / Fecha	369 Other non-metallic mineral products / *Autres produits minéraux non métalliques* / Otros productos minerales no metálicos	371 Basic metal industries / *Industrie métallurgique de base* / Industrias metalúrgicas básicas — Iron and steel / *Sidérurgie* / Hierro y acero	372 Non-ferrous metal / *Métaux non ferreux* / Metales no ferrosos	381 Metal products / *Produits métalliques* / Productos metálicos	382 Machinery (non-electrical) / *Machines (non électriques)* / Maquinaria (no eléctrica)	383 Electrical machinery and apparatus / *Machines et appareils électriques* / Maquinaria y aparatos eléctricos	384 Transport equipment / *Matériel de transport* / Material de transporte	385 Scientific, measuring, optical, etc. equipment / *Matériel scientifique, de précision, d'optique, etc.* / Equipo científico, de medida, de óptica, etc.	390 Other manufacturing industries / *Autres industries manufacturières* / Otras industrias manufactureras
1968	105.3	98.9	90.0	92.3	102.7	92.2	97.9	95.4	96.6
1969	102.8	101.6	97.5	98.2	102.5	99.8	99.1	95.2	98.7
1970	100.0	100.0	100.0	100.0	100.0	100.0	100.0	100.0	100.0
1971	100.9	101.4	103.7	98.3	99.1	100.7	98.5	101.5	96.9
1972	101.6	99.9	105.8	90.3	96.0	105.2	100.4	103.0	94.7
1973	100.7	100.7	106.1	92.3	94.3	109.2	99.5	107.2	91.1
1974 *	97.3	100.5	105.7	91.9	94.9	111.4	98.9	109.9	90.6

[1] State industry.   [1] *Industrie d'Etat.*   [1] Industria de Estado.

Employment in manufacturing
Emploi dans les industries manufacturières
Empleo en las industrias manufactureras

B By industry
Par industrie
Por industria

Ireland

Indices of numbers employed: wage earners and salaried employees *(Statistics of establishments)* [1]
Indices de l'effectif employé: ouvriers et employés *(Statistiques d'établissements)* [1]
Indices de trabajadores ocupados: obreros y empleados *(Estadísticas de establecimientos)* [1]

(1970 = 100)

	311-312	313	314	321	322	323	324	331	332
Date / Date / Fecha	Food / Aliments / Alimentos	Beverages / Boissons / Bebidas	Tobacco / Tabac / Tabaco	Textiles	Clothing / Habillement / Vestido	Leather, leather products / Cuir, articles en cuir / Cuero, artículos de cuero	Footwear / Chaussures / Calzado	Wood / Bois / Madera	Furniture / Ameublement / Mobiliario
1969	97.7	102.2	97.1	101.7	100.0	96.5	104.2	99.7	99.8
1970	**100.0**	**100.0**	**100.0**	**100.0**	**100.0**	**100.0**	**100.0**	**100.0**	**100.0**
1971	99.1	100.0	95.8	94.2	97.2	102.0	91.5	97.4	100.0
1972	98.4	96.2	91.7	87.9	93.9	98.0	88.1	102.6	97.6
1973 *	100.7	94.9	95.8	87.9	92.8	100.0	84.7	102.6	102.4
1974 *	102.5	94.9	100.0	85.2	89.0	100.0	81.4	107.9	102.4

	341	342	351-352	361-362	369	37; 381	382	383	384	353-356; 385; 390
Date / Date / Fecha	Paper, paper products / Papier, articles en papier / Papel, artículos de papel	Printing, publishing / Imprimerie, édition / Imprentas, editoriales	Chemicals / Industrie chimique / Productos químicos	Pottery, china, earthenware and glass / Grès, porcelaines, faïences et verre / Barro, loza, porcelana y vidrio	Other non-metallic mineral products / Autres produits minéraux non métalliques / Otros productos minerales no metálicos	Metal industries / Industrie métallurgique / Industrias metalúrgicas	Machinery (non-electrical) / Machines (non électriques) / Maquinaria (no eléctrica)	Electrical machinery and apparatus / Machines et appareils électriques / Maquinaria y aparatos eléctricos	Transport equipment / Matériel de transport / Material de transporte	Miscellaneous manufacturing [2] / Industries manufacturières diverses [2] / Industrias manufactureras diversas [2]
1969	97.9	93.0	95.9	88.8	109.8	100.2	92.1	99.0	94.5	88.8
1970	**100.0**	**100.0**	**100.0**	**100.0**	**100.0**	**100.0**	**100.0**	**100.0**	**100.0**	**100.0**
1971	100.0	99.1	100.0	102.5	124.0	101.6	103.2	93.3	102.3	104.7
1972	100.0	98.2	104.9	117.5	126.0	113.9	119.4	99.0	103.1	109.4
1973 *	100.0	97.3	112.3	122.5	134.0	122.1	129.0	112.4	106.2	122.4
1974 *	105.3	96.4	119.8	127.5	138.0	122.1	138.7	114.3	106.9	130.6

[1] Incl. working proprietors. [2] Incl. petroleum refineries, products of petroleum and coal, etc.

[1] *Y compris les propriétaires-exploitants.* [2] *Y compris les raffineries de pétrole, les dérivés du pétrole et du charbon, etc.*

[1] Incl. los empresarios propietarios. [2] Incl. las refinerías de petróleo, los derivados del petróleo y del carbón, etc.

6 Employment in manufacturing
Emploi dans les industries manufacturières
Empleo en las industrias manufactureras

B By industry
Par industrie
Por industria

Italie

Indices of numbers employed: wage earners *(Statistics of establishments)*
Indices de l'effectif employé: ouvriers *(Statistiques d'établissements)*
Indices de trabajadores ocupados: obreros *(Estadísticas de establecimientos)*

(1970 = 100)

Date / Date / Fecha	Food / Aliments / Alimentos	Beverages / Boissons / Bebidas	Tobacco / Tabac / Tabaco	Textiles	Clothing / Habillement / Vestido	Wood / Bois / Madera	Furniture / Ameublement / Mobiliario	Paper, paper products / Papier, articles en papier / Papel, artículos de papel	Printing, publishing / Imprimerie, édition / Imprentas, editoriales	Leather, leather products / Cuir, articles en cuir / Cuero, artículos de cuero
1965	97.8	100.4	60.2	102.6	66.4	91.7	73.3	94.3	89.7	88.7
1966	98.4	104.9	95.3	100.4	73.1	91.0	79.3	94.3	91.0	90.4
1967	98.2	104.6	119.1	100.0	79.6	92.8	87.1	95.9	93.9	92.8
1968	98.5	101.6	120.9	97.1	86.4	97.2	93.9	95.3	97.7	96.8
1969	100.6	100.6	105.1	99.6	96.3	100.2	99.8	97.5	98.9	103.2
1970	**100.0**	**100.0**	**100.0**	**100.0**	**100.0**	**100.0**	**100.0**	**100.0**	**100.0**	**100.0**
1971	97.8	97.7	97.0	94.7	99.4	101.2	101.4	98.1	99.8	97.6
1972	99.7	97.8	92.3	89.2	98.6	97.9	102.9	97.8	100.3	97.4
1973	101.4	95.7	89.0	88.4	100.6	98.9	104.7	98.9	103.7	94.8

Date / Date / Fecha	Rubber products / Industrie du caoutchouc / Productos de caucho	Chemicals / Industrie chimique / Productos químicos	Products of petroleum and coal / Dérivés du pétrole et du charbon / Derivados del petróleo y del carbón	Non-metallic mineral products / Produits minéraux non métalliques / Productos minerales no metálicos	Basic metal industries / Industrie métallurgique de base / Industrias metalúrgicas básicas	Foundries (2nd smelting) / Fonderie (2me fusion) / Fundición (2.ª fusión)	Machinery (non-electrical) / Machines (non électriques) / Maquinaria (no eléctrica)	Electrical machinery / Machines électriques / Maquinaria eléctrica	Transport equipment / Matériel de transport / Material de transporte	Miscellaneous manufacturing / Industries manufacturières diverses / Industrias manufactureras diversas
1965	74.1	93.1	106.5	93.0	86.7	88.6	78.5	64.9	79.8	64.2
1966	75.9	94.7	109.3	90.1	86.3	90.2	81.0	68.9	81.4	70.7
1967	82.2	96.8	109.2	91.7	89.0	96.0	85.5	75.1	87.2	75.7
1968	86.1	97.4	100.5	95.1	89.2	96.6	89.8	79.8	88.5	82.7
1969	94.3	97.6	100.3	99.9	90.8	98.9	95.9	90.0	97.7	95.5
1970	**100.0**	**100.0**	**100.0**	**100.0**	**100.0**	**100.0**	**100.0**	**100.0**	**100.0**	**100.0**
1971	105.8	101.5	98.4	96.5	104.0	98.6	99.1	102.5	103.5	102.3
1972	105.6	99.9	99.0	92.2	107.8	93.0	98.6	105.4	107.1	101.9
1973	107.5	100.9	100.5	93.1	112.1	95.3	101.5	113.1	115.9	108.3

6 Employment in manufacturing
Emploi dans les industries manufacturières
Empleo en las industrias manufactureras

B By industry
Par industrie
Por industria

Luxembourg

Indices of numbers employed: wage earners and salaried employees *(Statistics of establishments)*
Indices de l'effectif employé: ouvriers et employés *(Statistiques d'établissements)*
Indices de trabajadores ocupados: obreros y empleados *(Estadísticas de establecimientos)*

(1970 = 100)

Date / Date / Fecha	Food, tobacco / Aliments tabac / Alimentos, tabaco	Beverages / Boissons / Bebidas	Wood, furniture / Bois, ameublement / Madera, mobiliario	Printing, publishing / Imprimerie, édition / Imprentas, editoriales	Rubber products, chemicals / Caoutchouc, industrie chimique / Caucho, productos químicos	Non-metallic mineral products / Produits minéraux non métalliques / Productos minerales no metálicos	Primary iron and steel / Sidérurgie / Siderurgia	Non-ferrous metals / Métaux non ferreux / Metales no ferrosos	Metal products / Produits métalliques / Productos metálicos
1965	102.6	88.5	300.0	72.2	79.8	100.7	106.5	...	79.3
1966	109.6	90.4	284.6	79.2	87.6	99.5	106.3	...	81.1
1967	107.3	91.0	182.8	83.7	88.5	98.5	104.4	...	77.6
1968	100.0	86.7	165.1	84.5	96.0	99.5	102.1	...	78.7
1969	105.1	86.5	178.7	83.8	104.2	98.7	102.7	...	85.0
1970	100.0	100.0	100.0	100.0	100.0	100.0	100.0	100.0	100.0
1971	...	...	91.7	111.0	108.3	107.2	99.2	90.6	117.1
1972	...	...	123.7	100.8	117.0	107.0	98.0	98.6	126.6

Malta

Indices of numbers employed: wage earners and salaried employees *(Statistics of establishments)*
Indices de l'effectif employé: ouvriers et employés *(Statistiques d'établissements)*
Indices de trabajadores ocupados: obreros y empleados *(Estadísticas de establecimientos)*

(1970 = 100)

Date [1] / Date [1] / Fecha [1]	Food / Aliments / Alimentos	Beverages, tobacco / Boissons, tabac / Bebidas, tabaco	Textiles, clothing / Textiles, habillement / Textiles, vestido	Wood, furniture / Bois, ameublement / Madera, mobiliario	Paper, leather / Papier, cuir / Papel, cuero	Rubber products, chemicals [2] / Caoutchouc, industrie chimique [2] / Caucho, productos químicos [2]	Non-metallic mineral products / Produits minéraux non métalliques / Productos minerales no metálicos	Metal products, machinery / Produits métalliques, machines / Productos metálicos, maquinaria	Transport equipment / Matériel de transport / Material de transporte
1965	90.8	72.8	59.5	71.6	67.5	47.8	78.5	36.9	92.4
1966	85.4	71.4	67.1	74.3	65.0	47.1	89.2	38.3	97.8
1967	86.9	81.6	67.9	82.6	82.9	51.4	112.9	47.2	97.2
1968	98.5	82.3	71.9	100.9	94.3	62.3	78.5	56.5	94.6
1969	81.5	88.4	92.9	106.4	102.4	91.3	102.2	71.5	100.0
1970	100.0	100.0	100.0	100.0	100.0	100.0	100.0	100.0	100.0
1971	98.5	89.1	111.2	133.0	127.5	111.6	86.0	118.2	94.0
1972	93.1	102.7	120.5	140.4	124.4	122.5	86.0	133.6	95.0

[1] Dec. of each year. [2] Incl. products of petroleum and coal. [1] Déc. de chaque année. [2] Y compris les dérivés du pétrole et du charbon. [1] Dic. de cada año. [2] Incl. los derivados del petróleo y del carbón.

6 **Employment in manufacturing**
Emploi dans les industries manufacturières
Empleo en las industrias manufactureras

B **By industry**
Par industrie
Por industria

Norway

Indices of numbers employed: civilian labour force employed *(Labour force sample surveys)* [1]
Indices de l'effectif employé: main-d'œuvre civile occupée *(Enquêtes par sondage sur la main-d'œuvre)* [1]
Indices de trabajadores ocupados: fuerza trabajadora civil ocupada *(Encuestas por muestra sobre la fuerza trabajadora)* [1]

(1972 = 100) [2]

Date / Date / Fecha	311-312 Food / Aliments / Alimentos	313 Beverages [3] / Boissons [3] / Bebidas [3]	314 Tobacco / Tabac / Tabaco	321 Textiles	322 Clothing / Habillement / Vestido	323 Leather, leather products / Cuir, articles en cuir / Cuero, artículos de cuero	324 Footwear / Chaussures / Calzado	331 Wood / Bois / Madera	332 Furniture / Ameublement / Mobiliario	341 Paper, paper products / Papier, articles en papier / Papel, artículos de papel
1965	95.5	93.4	.	121.6	116.1	119.1	.	83.7	92.1	103.3
1966	98.5	93.7	.	119.5	112.7	116.0	.	84.2	91.6	101.5
1967	97.6	93.7	.	116.9	110.8	112.6	.	87.7	93.3	98.9
1968	97.1	96.3	.	106.8	105.4	108.2	.	89.6	93.6	98.6
1969	98.7	98.6	.	102.3	103.1	105.2	.	94.3	95.8	98.8
1970	100.0	100.0	.	100.0	100.0	100.0	.	100.0	100.0	100.0
1971	.	.	.	.	.	.	.	.	.	.
1972 [4]	100.0	100.0	100.0	100.0	100.0	100.0	100.0	100.0	100.0	100.0
1973	98.0	100.0	100.0	77.8	100.0	66.7	100.0	96.7	128.6	106.3
1974	84.3	120.0	100.0	61.1	100.0	100.0	50.0	100.0	128.6	118.8

Date / Date / Fecha	342 Printing, publishing / Imprimerie, édition / Imprentas, editoriales	371 Basic metal industries / Industrie métallurgique de base / Industrias metalúrgicas básicas — Iron and steel / Sidérurgie / Hierro y acero	372 Non-ferrous metal / Métaux non ferreux / Metales no ferrosos	381 Metal products / Produits métalliques / Productos metálicos	382 Machinery (non-electrical) / Machines (non électriques) / Maquinaria (no eléctrica)	383 Electrical machinery and apparatus / Machines et appareils électriques / Maquinaria y aparatos eléctricos	384 Transport equipment / Matériel de transport / Material de transporte	385 Scientific, measuring, optical, etc. equipment / Matériel scientifique, de précision, d'optique, etc. / Equipo científico, de medida, de óptica, etc.	390 Other manufacturing industries / Autres industries manufacturières / Otras industrias manufactureras
1965	93.9	89.3	95.2	87.0	84.9	79.7	87.1	.	74.9
1966	94.6	91.5	95.5	87.7	87.9	83.9	91.6	.	75.4
1967	95.1	93.7	97.2	91.2	90.8	88.6	93.6	.	80.0
1968	95.1	93.8	97.5	94.3	89.6	88.8	93.5	.	84.6
1969	97.4	96.7	98.7	94.4	92.6	91.4	95.6	.	89.7
1970	100.0	100.0	100.0	100.0	100.0	100.0	100.0	.	100.0
1971	.	.	.	.	.	.	.	.	.
1972 [4]	100.0	100.0	100.0	100.0	100.0	100.0	100.0	100.0	100.0
1973	100.0	96.3	83.3	87.9	100.0	100.0	129.5	150.0	57.1
1974	103.8	92.6	133.3	97.0	164.3	85.2	131.8	...	42.9

[1] Persons aged 16 to 74 years. 1965-70: compulsory health insurance statistics, wage earners and salaried employees. [2] 1965-71: 1970 = 100. [3] 1965-70: incl. tobacco. [4] Series replacing former series.

[1] *Personnes âgées de 16 à 74 ans. 1965-1970: statistique de l'assurance-maladie obligatoire, ouvriers et employés.* [2] *1965-1971: 100 en 1970.* [3] *1965-1970: y compris le tabac.* [4] *Série remplaçant la précédente.*

[1] Personas de 16 a 74 años. 1965-1970: estadísticas del seguro obligatorio de enfermedad, obreros y empleados. [2] 1965-1971: 1970 = 100. [3] 1965-1970: incl. el tabaco. [4] Serie que substituye a la anterior.

6 **Employment in manufacturing**
Emploi dans les industries manufacturières
Empleo en las industrias manufactureras

B By industry
Par industrie
Por industria

Pays-Bas

Indices of numbers employed: wage earners and salaried employees *(Official estimates)* [1]
Indices de l'effectif employé: ouvriers et employés *(Evaluations officielles)* [1]
Indices de trabajadores ocupados: obreros y empleados *(Estimaciones oficiales)* [1]

(1970 = 100)

Date / Date / Fecha	311-312 Food / Aliments / Alimentos	313-314 Beverages, tobacco / Boissons, tabac / Bebidas, tabaco	321 Textiles	322 Clothing / Habillement / Vestido	323 Leather, leather products [2] / Cuir, articles en cuir [2] / Cuero, artículos de cuero [2]	33 Wood, furniture / Bois, ameublement / Madera, mobiliario
1969	100.0	100.0	106.3	106.5	114.3	101.7
1970	**100.0**	**100.0**	**100.0**	**100.0**	**100.0**	**100.0**
1971	99.3	100.0	93.7	91.9	92.9	98.3
1972	98.0	96.4	84.8	85.5	78.6	96.6
1973 *	96.6	96.4	79.7	75.8	71.4	94.8
1974 *	95.9	96.4	75.9	64.5	71.4	94.8

Date / Date / Fecha	341 Paper, paper products / Papier, articles en papier / Papel, artículos de papel	342 Printing, publishing / Imprimerie, édition / Imprentas, editoriales	351-352; 355-356 Chemicals, rubber and plastic products / Industrie chimique, produits en caoutchouc et en plastique / Productos químicos, de caucho y plástico	353-354 Refineries and products of petroleum and coal / Raffineries et dérivés du pétrole et du charbon / Refinerías y derivados del petróleo y del carbón	36 Non-metallic mineral products / Produits minéraux non métalliques / Productos minerales no metálicos	37-38-390 Metal industries, machinery, transport equipment, other industries / Industrie métallurgique, machines, matériel de transport, autres industries / Industrias metálicas, maquinarias, material de transporte, otras industrias
1969	100.0	97.5	97.5	90.9	100.0	97.8
1970	**100.0**	**100.0**	**100.0**	**100.0**	**100.0**	**100.0**
1971	94.1	100.0	99.2	100.0	98.0	100.0
1972	91.2	97.5	96.7	100.0	94.1	97.2
1973 *	91.2	96.3	95.9	100.0	92.2	97.0
1974 *	94.1	96.3	96.7	100.0	90.2	97.4

[1] Number of man-years. [2] Incl. footwear.   [1] *Nombre d'années-homme.* [2] *Y compris la chaussure.*   [1] Número de años-hombre. [2] Incl. el calzado.

EMPLOYMENT

6 Employment in manufacturing / Emploi dans les industries manufacturières / Empleo en las industrias manufactureras

B By industry / Par industrie / Por industria

Pologne (1)

Indices of numbers employed: wage earners and salaried employees *(Statistics of establishments)* [1]
Indices de l'effectif employé: ouvriers et employés *(Statistiques d'établissements)* [1]
Indices de trabajadores ocupados: obreros y empleados *(Estadísticas de establecimientos)* [1]

(1970 = 100)

Date / Date / Fecha	311-312 Food / Aliments / Alimentos	313 Beverages / Boissons / Bebidas	314 Tobacco / Tabac / Tabaco	321 Textiles	322 Clothing / Habillement / Vestido	323 Leather, leather products / Cuir, articles en cuir / Cuero, artículos de cuero	324 Footwear / Chaussures / Calzado	331 Wood / Bois / Madera	332 Furniture / Ameublement / Mobiliario
1967	93.4	100.4	87.8	94.9	90.7	88.4	93.1	85.1	95.5
1968	95.3	104.3	95.5	96.5	93.8	93.9	97.3	85.6	99.8
1969	97.4	105.4	100.5	98.4	98.6	98.6	101.8	90.6	101.8
1970	**100.0**	**100.0**	**100.0**	**100.0**	**100.0**	**100.0**	**100.0**	**100.0**	**100.0**
1971	105.5	101.0	105.7	101.6	104.0	101.3	103.3	103.2	100.7
1972	108.5	103.2	105.7	105.1	112.2	106.6	110.0	106.5	104.3
1973	112.8	109.7	95.3	107.8	116.0	115.6	112.9	108.4	108.1
1974 *	117.6	111.2	94.6	110.1	116.8	118.6	116.1	110.0	110.5

Date / Date / Fecha	341 Paper, paper products / Papier, articles en papier / Papel, artículos de papel	342 Printing, publishing / Imprimerie, édition / Imprentas, editoriales	351 Industrial chemicals / Chimie industrielle / Química industrial	352 Other chemical products / Autres produits chimiques / Otros productos químicos	353 Petroleum refineries / Raffineries de pétrole / Refinerías de petróleo	354 Products of petroleum and coal / Dérivés du pétrole et du charbon / Derivados del petróleo y del carbón	355 Rubber products / Produits en caoutchouc / Productos de caucho	356 Plastic products / Articles en matière plastique / Productos plásticos	361 Pottery, china, earthenware / Grès, porcelaines, faïences / Barro, loza, porcelana
1967	94.6	92.9	92.5	90.8	82.9	92.2	91.5	92.6	99.8
1968	96.5	95.3	96.4	94.5	89.5	92.9	95.7	91.3	102.1
1969	99.0	98.4	99.9	97.9	95.8	93.7	99.6	97.7	105.3
1970	**100.0**	**100.0**	**100.0**	**100.0**	**100.0**	**100.0**	**100.0**	**100.0**	**100.0**
1971	103.2	103.6	100.1	108.7	102.7	99.6	100.9	124.0	105.7
1972	107.8	107.2	101.6	128.0	110.9	100.0	107.5	123.6	108.4
1973	109.0	110.2	103.2	125.0	128.1	101.4	111.6	138.5	109.2
1974 *	109.3	114.7	107.0	126.8	140.3	102.3	113.6	147.0	113.7

[1] Socialised sector. Excl. apprentices. Figures include full-time equivalent of part-time workers.

[1] *Secteur socialisé. Non compris les apprentis. Les personnes employées à temps partiel sont converties en unité de travail à temps complet.*

[1] Sector socializado. Excl. los aprendices. Las personas empleadas a tiempo parcial son convertidas en unidad de trabajo a pleno tiempo.

6 Employment in manufacturing
Emploi dans les industries manufacturières
Empleo en las industrias manufactureras

B By industry
Par industrie
Por industria

Pologne (2)

Indices of numbers employed: wage earners and salaried employees *(Statistics of establishments)* [1]
Indices de l'effectif employé: ouvriers et employés *(Statistiques d'établissements)* [1]
Indices de trabajadores ocupados: obreros y empleados *(Estadísticas de establecimientos)* [1]

(1970 = 100)

Date / Date / Fecha	362 Glass / Verre / Vidrio	369 Other non-metallic mineral products / Autres produits minéraux non métalliques / Otros productos minerales no metálicos	371 Iron and steel / Sidérurgie / Hierro y acero	372 Non-ferrous metal / Métaux non ferreux / Metales no ferrosos	381 Metal products / Produits métalliques / Productos metálicos	382 Machinery (non-electrical) / Machines (non électriques) / Maquinaria (no eléctrica)	383 Electrical machinery and apparatus / Machines et appareils électriques / Maquinaria y aparatos eléctricos	384 Transport equipment / Matériel de transport / Material de transporte	385 Scientific, measuring, optical, etc. equipment / Matériel scientifique, de précision, d'optique, etc. / Equipo científico, de medida, de óptica, etc.	390 Other manufacturing industries / Autres industries manufacturières / Otras industrias manufactureras
1967	95.5	94.3	91.6	92.0	88.4	86.7	84.3	87.7	80.0	85.5
1968	98.4	98.9	93.5	102.5	93.8	92.2	88.5	94.3	89.2	93.4
1969	101.5	100.5	97.4	98.3	98.4	97.3	95.1	99.5	93.0	99.4
1970	**100.0**	**100.0**	**100.0**	**100.0**	**100.0**	**100.0**	**100.0**	**100.0**	**100.0**	**100.0**
1971	104.6	99.2	102.4	107.0	104.0	103.6	109.0	102.9	102.9	108.7
1972	110.2	101.4	105.1	113.1	107.4	107.6	114.3	106.4	117.4	121.5
1973	114.8	100.9	106.4	116.0	116.4	111.5	121.1	109.0	117.4	125.4
1974 *	117.7	101.3	109.0	123.8	116.0	114.5	132.6	109.9	125.1	131.6

Note: Columns 371 and 372 are subcolumns of "Basic metal industries / Industrie métallurgique de base / Industrias metalúrgicas básicas".

[1] Socialised sector. Excl. apprentices. Figures include full-time equivalent of part-time workers.

[1] *Secteur socialisé. Non compris les apprentis. Les personnes employées à temps partiel sont converties en unité de travail à temps complet.*

[1] Sector socializado. Excl. los aprendices. Las personas empleadas a tiempo parcial son convertidas en unidad de trabajo a pleno tiempo.

Portugal

Indices of numbers employed: wage earners and salaried employees *(Statistics of establishments)*
Indices de l'effectif employé: ouvriers et employés *(Statistiques d'établissements)*
Indices de trabajadores ocupados: obreros y empleados *(Estadísticas de establecimientos)*

(1970 = 100)

Date / Date / Fecha	Food / Aliments / Alimentos	Beer / Bière / Cerveza	Tobacco / Tabac / Tabaco	Cotton / Coton / Algodón	Wool / Laine / Lana	Cork / Liège / Corcho	Paper / Papier / Papel	Rubber products / Industrie du caoutchouc / Productos de caucho	Matches / Allumettes / Cerillas	Non-metallic mineral products / Produits minéraux non métalliques / Productos minerales no metálicos
1964	120.8	81.8	187.8	97.1	87.3	93.1	91.1	91.9	120.3	85.0
1965	112.2	77.3	103.8	106.2	91.6	103.1	99.5	94.8	120.4	89.7
1966	114.4	73.2	95.8	103.9	94.1	95.5	100.0	101.6	113.7	89.5
1967	115.2	81.0	99.2	104.0	94.3	94.8	104.2	95.4	109.2	88.1
1968	117.0	94.4	99.9	143.3	96.5	105.5	104.9	91.5	65.6	67.3
1969	106.5	93.6	107.9	101.7	96.3	105.9	105.7	103.2	101.7	99.1
1970	**100.0**	**100.0**	**100.0**	**100.0**	**100.0**	**100.0**	**100.0**	**100.0**	**100.0**	**100.0**

6 | Employment in manufacturing
Emploi dans les industries manufacturières
Empleo en las industrias manufactureras

B | By industry
Par industrie
Por industria

Roumanie [1]

Indices of numbers employed: wage earners and salaried employees *(Statistics of establishments)*
Indices de l'effectif employé: ouvriers et employés *(Statistiques d'établissements)*
Indices de trabajadores ocupados: obreros y empleados *(Estadísticas de establecimientos)*

(1970 = 100)

Date *Date* Fecha	Food *Aliments* Alimentos	Textiles	Clothing [2] *Habillement [2]* Vestido [2]	Leather, fur, footwear *Cuir, fourrure, chaussure* Cuero, piel, calzado	Wood [3] *Bois [3]* Madera [3]	Cellulose, paper *Cellulose, papier* Celulosa, papel	Printing, publishing *Imprimerie, édition* Imprentas, editoriales
1965	86.3	78.4	69.8	76.2	92.1	85.5	102.4
1966	89.9	82.1	73.9	80.0	91.2	91.0	102.9
1967	92.4	86.1	82.3	84.8	91.7	95.8	101.9
1968	95.8	89.9	87.8	90.4	93.8	99.7	101.9
1969	100.9	94.9	93.7	96.1	97.6	101.0	102.9
1970	**100.0**	**100.0**	**100.0**	**100.0**	**100.0**	**100.0**	**100.0**
1971	106.3	111.9	110.2	108.2	101.7	102.8	102.4
1972	111.8	123.5	121.2	113.7	102.5	106.6	103.3

Date *Date* Fecha	Chemicals *Industrie chimique* Productos químicos	Non-metallic mineral products [4] *Produits minéraux non métalliques [4]* Productos minerales no metálicos [4]	Glass, china, earthenware *Verre, porcelaine, faïence* Vidrio, porcelana, loza	Building materials *Matériaux de construction* Materiales de construcción	Primary iron and steel [4] *Sidérurgie [4]* Siderurgia [4]	Metal products, machinery, etc. *Produits métalliques, machines, etc.* Productos metálicos, maquinaria, etc.	Other industries *Autres industries* Otras industrias
1965	67.1	88.1	80.4	83.9	86.3	74.3	71.7
1966	72.6	95.6	80.1	82.0	86.6	77.9	83.3
1967	79.5	92.6	82.2	83.8	90.3	82.4	85.0
1968	83.6	91.5	82.9	91.7	94.8	87.5	91.7
1969	92.1	93.3	89.2	95.5	97.9	94.4	95.8
1970	**100.0**	**100.0**	**100.0**	**100.0**	**100.0**	**100.0**	**100.0**
1971	107.0	104.7	111.5	103.6	101.2	109.7	80.8
1972	111.2	106.7	119.9	105.1	103.0	119.3	81.7

[1] Socialised sector. [2] Excl. footwear. [3] Incl. exploitation. [4] Incl. ore mining.

[1] *Secteur socialisé.* [2] *Non compris la chaussure.* [3] *Y compris l'exploitation.* [4] *Y compris l'extraction des minerais.*

[1] Sector socializado. [2] Excl. el calzado. [3] Incl. la explotación. [4] Incl. la extracción de minerales.

6 **Employment in manufacturing**
Emploi dans les industries manufacturières
Empleo en las industrias manufactureras

B **By industry**
Par industrie
Por industria

Suisse

Indices of numbers employed: wage earners and salaried employees *(Statistics of establishments)* [1]
Indices de l'effectif employé: ouvriers et employés *(Statistiques d'établissements)* [1]
Indices de trabajadores ocupados: obreros y empleados *(Estadísticas de establecimientos)* [1]

(1970 = 100)

Date [2] / Date [2] / Fecha [2]	Food / Aliments / Alimentos	Beverages / Boissons / Bebidas	Tobacco / Tabac / Tabaco	Textiles	Clothing / Habillement / Vestido	Wood, furniture / Bois, ameublement / Madera, mobiliario	Paper, paper products / Papier, articles en papier / Papel, artículos de papel	Printing, publishing / Imprimerie, édition / Imprentas, editoriales	Leather, leather products / Cuir, articles en cuir / Cuero, artículos de cuero	Rubber products / Industrie du caoutchouc / Productos de caucho
1966	97.3	83.2	100.6	114.0	114.6	105.0	107.6	94.4	115.5	96.1
1967	101.0	103.1	103.4	109.7	110.9	103.7	105.5	97.1	110.5	93.6
1968	100.7	103.8	104.1	107.4	107.4	102.3	102.7	97.3	103.4	100.1
1969	102.2	101.8	103.0	105.6	105.4	100.2	101.4	98.3	103.6	98.3
1970	**100.0**	**100.0**	**100.0**	**100.0**	**100.0**	**100.0**	**100.0**	**100.0**	**100.0**	**100.0**
1971	99.1	101.6	94.1	95.7	95.6	99.6	98.7	99.3	94.6	97.5
1972	98.8	100.8	92.8	90.4	91.7	99.7	96.3	102.9	90.0	98.0
1973	96.6	96.9	87.0	84.7	84.8	93.9	94.3	100.7	84.1	91.3
1974	95.3	92.5	80.9	80.1	77.5	87.3	93.9	98.0	78.5	91.4

Date [2] / Date [2] / Fecha [2]	Chemicals / Industrie chimique / Productos químicos	Products of petroleum and coal / Dérivés du pétrole et du charbon / Derivados del petróleo y del carbón	Non-metallic mineral products / Produits minéraux non métalliques / Productos minerales no metálicos	Basic metal industries / Industrie métallurgique de base / Industrias metalúrgicas básicas	Metal products / Produits métalliques / Productos metálicos	Machinery / Machines / Maquinaria	Transport equipment / Matériel de transport / Material de transporte	Watchmaking industries / Industrie horlogère / Industria relojera	Other industries / Autres industries / Otras industrias
1966	84.6	108.4	107.7	102.1	99.1	95.9	124.5	85.0	111.0
1967	86.5	105.7	106.9	98.3	99.1	95.9	123.8	101.0	81.2
1968	90.6	116.2	103.2	99.0	98.7	95.0	116.9	100.3	92.7
1969	95.1	103.1	101.8	100.5	99.5	97.2	109.7	100.2	99.1
1970	**100.0**	**100.0**	**100.0**	**100.0**	**100.0**	**100.0**	**100.0**	**100.0**	**100.0**
1971	103.1	104.3	99.7	100.7	100.8	101.5	96.7	95.4	101.1
1972	104.8	104.9	99.8	96.6	99.4	98.5	93.2	88.6	93.1
1973	101.0	98.8	98.2	92.5	...	...	...	88.0	...
1974	102.6	97.7	92.9	87.0	...	...	...	88.7	...

[1] Incl. working proprietors. [2] Sep. of each year.   [1] *Y compris les propriétaires-exploitants.* [2] *Sept. de chaque année.*   [1] Incl. los empresarios propietarios. [2] Sept. de cada año.

EMPLOYMENT

6 Employment in manufacturing
Emploi dans les industries manufacturières
Empleo en las industrias manufactureras

B By industry
Par industrie
Por industria

Sweden (1)

Indices of numbers employed: wage earners *(Statistics of establishments)*
Indices de l'effectif employé: ouvriers *(Statistiques d'établissements)*
Indices de trabajadores ocupados: obreros *(Estadísticas de establecimientos)*

(1970 = 100)

Date / Date / Fecha	311-312	313	314	321	322	323	324	331	332
	Food / Aliments / Alimentos	Beverages / Boissons / Bebidas	Tobacco / Tabac / Tabaco	Textiles	Clothing / Habillement / Vestido	Leather, leather products / Cuir, articles en cuir / Cuero, artículos de cuero	Footwear / Chaussures / Calzado	Wood / Bois / Madera	Furniture / Ameublement / Mobiliario
1968	97.5	105.9	101.6	105.3	.	117.5	.	96.8	98.6
1969	98.1	106.7	103.6	105.1	.	100.0	.	98.7	101.9
1970	**100.0**	**100.0**	**100.0**	**100.0**	**100.0**	**100.0**	**100.0**	**100.0**	**100.0**
1971	98.0	97.7	105.4	90.4	86.8	88.0	81.6	96.4	91.6
1972	95.9	84.0	104.6	84.6	81.9	81.9	78.4	95.7	95.9
1973	96.4	79.8	105.5	85.2	79.9	74.0	78.9	99.3	100.4

Date / Date / Fecha	341	342	351	352	353	354	355	356	361
	Paper, paper products / Papier, articles en papier / Papel, artículos de papel	Printing, publishing / Imprimerie, édition / Imprentas, editoriales	Industrial chemicals / Chimie industrielle / Química industrial	Other chemical products / Autres produits chimiques / Otros productos químicos	Petroleum refineries / Raffineries de pétrole / Refinerías de petróleo	Products of petroleum and coal / Dérivés du pétrole et du charbon / Derivados del petróleo y del carbón	Rubber products / Produits en caoutchouc / Productos de caucho	Plastic products / Articles en matière plastique / Productos plásticos	Pottery, china, earthenware / Grès, porcelaines, faïences / Barro, loza, porcelana
1968	100.2	98.0	.	.	.	.	87.1	.	.
1969	99.7	99.0	.	.	.	.	94.4	.	.
1970	**100.0**	**100.0**	**100.0**	**100.0**	**100.0**	**100.0**	**100.0**	**100.0**	**100.0**
1971	96.4	96.6	98.9	98.7	103.9	102.9	101.0	98.9	91.2
1972	97.7	93.8	100.8	100.1	113.2	87.7	95.2	105.7	96.1
1973	99.3	92.6	104.8	101.8	110.2	82.0	96.3	119.4	100.1

6 Employment in manufacturing
Emploi dans les industries manufacturières
Empleo en las industrias manufactureras

B By industry
Par industrie
Por industria

Sweden (2)

Indices of numbers employed: wage earners *(Statistics of establishments)*
Indices de l'effectif employé: ouvriers *(Statistiques d'établissements)*
Indices de trabajadores ocupados: obreros *(Estadísticas de establecimientos)*

(1970 = 100)

Date / Date / Fecha	362 Glass / Verre / Vidrio	369 Other non-metallic mineral products / Autres produits minéraux non métalliques / Otros productos minerales no metálicos	371 Iron and steel / Sidérurgie / Hierro y acero	372 Non-ferrous metal / Métaux non ferreux / Metales no ferrosos	381 Metal products / Produits métalliques / Productos metálicos	382 Machinery (non-electrical) / Machines (non électriques) / Maquinaria (no eléctrica)	383 Electrical machinery and apparatus / Machines et appareils électriques / Maquinaria y aparatos eléctricos	384 Transport equipment / Matériel de transport / Material de transporte	385 Scientific, measuring, optical, etc. equipment / Matériel scientifique, de précision, d'optique, etc. / Equipo científico, de medida, de óptica, etc.	390 Other manufacturing industries / Autres industries manufacturières / Otras industrias manufactureras
1968	.	.	.	.	91.4	91.9	86.0	89.2	.	.
1969	.	.	.	.	94.6	94.1	92.0	97.1	.	.
1970	100.0	100.0	100.0	100.0	100.0	100.0	100.0	100.0	100.0	100.0
1971	90.4	90.4	97.3	102.9	98.2	97.5	104.0	103.5	95.1	97.6
1972	86.7	83.7	94.9	104.6	96.5	95.1	100.3	106.0	84.1	96.6
1973	88.2	80.8	96.6	112.0	99.9	97.6	102.1	110.6	95.0	107.8

Turquie (1)

Indices of numbers employed: wage earners and salaried employees *(Compulsory social insurance statistics)*
Indices de l'effectif employé: ouvriers et employés *(Statistiques d'assurances sociales obligatoires)*
Indices de trabajadores ocupados: obreros y empleados *(Estadísticas del seguro social obligatorio)*

(1970 = 100)

Date[1] / Date[1] / Fecha[1]	Food / Aliments / Alimentos	Beverages / Boissons / Bebidas	Tobacco / Tabac / Tabaco	Textiles[2]	Clothing / Habillement / Vestido	Wood / Bois / Madera	Furniture / Ameublement / Mobiliario	Paper, paper products / Papier, articles en papier / Papel, artículos de papel	Printing, publishing / Imprimerie, édition / Imprentas, editoriales
1965	68.0	53.7	122.1	83.9	49.3	55.8	60.0	98.0	61.3
1966	80.5	59.4	95.3	92.5	65.9	69.8	71.5	101.0	67.4
1967	80.3	64.5	108.0	97.7	70.0	78.6	81.3	104.5	72.4
1968	89.3	74.5	105.0	100.3	96.4	86.9	92.7	106.5	78.5
1969	90.6	85.5	96.0	95.8	97.1	96.3	98.8	104.1	87.8
1970	100.0	100.0	100.0	100.0	100.0	100.0	100.0	100.0	100.0
1971	103.3	91.9	88.3	104.1	158.6	122.7	141.9	106.8	116.3
1972	117.3	102.5	105.2	115.9	170.0	143.5	167.7	121.9	120.9

[1] Sep. of each year. [2] Incl. preparation of cotton.   [1] *Sept. de chaque année.* [2] *Y compris la préparation du coton.*   [1] Sept. de cada año. [2] Incl. la preparación del algodón.

6 **Employment in manufacturing**
Emploi dans les industries manufacturières
Empleo en las industrias manufactureras

B **By industry**
Par industrie
Por industria

Turquie (2)

Indices of numbers employed: wage earners and salaried employees *(Compulsory social insurance statistics)*
Indices de l'effectif employé: ouvriers et employés *(Statistiques d'assurances sociales obligatoires)*
Indices de trabajadores ocupados: obreros y empleados *(Estadísticas del seguro social obligatorio)*

(1970 = 100)

Date [1] Date [1] Fecha [1]	Leather, leather products *Cuir, articles en cuir* Cuero, artículos de cuero	Rubber products *Industrie du caoutchouc* Productos de caucho	Chemicals; products of petroleum and coal *Industrie chimique; dérivés du pétrole et du charbon* Productos químicos; derivados del petróleo y del carbón	Non-metallic mineral products *Produits minéraux non métalliques* Productos minerales no metálicos	Basic metal industries *Industrie métallurgique de base* Industrias metalúrgicas básicas	Metal products *Produits métalliques* Productos metálicos	Machinery *Machines* Maquinaria	Transport equipment *Matériel de transport* Material de transporte	Miscellaneous manufacturing *Industries manufacturières diverses* Industrias manufactureras diversas
1965	65.1	74.1	56.6	68.7	62.7	48.3	52.2	52.2	54.7
1966	74.3	94.4	63.8	67.9	69.4	54.7	63.3	59.2	53.6
1967	75.2	98.4	70.8	81.1	76.2	66.2	68.1	68.6	68.1
1968	78.3	103.8	108.4	89.4	85.8	87.4	96.2	93.5	87.5
1969	89.1	104.7	85.1	99.0	92.4	94.7	105.2	102.1	97.5
1970	**100.0**	**100.0**	**100.0**	**100.0**	**100.0**	**100.0**	**100.0**	**100.0**	**100.0**
1971	131.9	101.0	110.2	108.3	104.1	110.6	123.3	100.5	138.2
1972	157.1	115.2	117.1	115.3	110.8	118.8	144.1	108.2	161.5

[1] Sep. of each year.   [1] *Sept. de chaque année.*   [1] Sept. de cada año.

United Kingdom (1)

Indices of numbers employed: wage earners and salaried employees *(Statistics of establishments)* [1]
Indices de l'effectif employé: ouvriers et employés *(Statistiques d'établissements)* [1]
Indices de trabajadores ocupados: obreros y empleados *(Estadísticas de establecimientos)* [1]

(1970 = 100)

Date [2] Date [2] Fecha [2]	311-312 Food *Aliments* Alimentos	313 Beverages *Boissons* Bebidas	314 Tobacco *Tabac* Tabaco	321 Textiles	322 Clothing *Habillement* Vestido	323 Leather, leather products *Cuir, articles en cuir* Cuero, artículos de cuero	324 Footwear *Chaussures* Calzado	331 Wood *Bois* Madera	332 Furniture *Ameublement* Mobiliario
1969	98.8	97.5	97.8	103.9	105.7	107.4	104.0	103.3	104.8
1970	**100.0**	**100.0**	**100.0**	**100.0**	**100.0**	**100.0**	**100.0**	**100.0**	**100.0**
1971 [3]	86.9	82.9	91.3	86.9	90.0	87.0	93.0	86.3	93.2
1972	85.3	81.6	89.1	83.4	89.8	85.2	90.0	86.3	97.3
1973	85.2	81.6	87.0	83.0	88.0	83.3	88.0	90.2	104.8
1974 *	85.7	86.1	89.1	81.7	84.8	81.7	86.0	88.9	100.0

[1] Prior to 1971: National insurance statistics. [2] June of each year. [3] Series linked to former series.

[1] *Avant 1971: statistiques de l'assurance nationale.* [2] *Juin de chaque année.* [3] *Série enchaînée à la précédente.*

[1] Antes de 1971: estadísticas del Seguro Nacional. [2] Junio de cada año. [3] Serie enlazada con la anterior.

6 Employment in manufacturing
Emploi dans les industries manufacturières
Empleo en las industrias manufactureras

B By industry
Par industrie
Por industria

United Kingdom (2)

Indices of numbers employed: wage earners and salaried employees *(Statistics of establishments)* [1]
Indices de l'effectif employé: ouvriers et employés *(Statistiques d'établissements)* [1]
Indices de trabajadores ocupados: obreros y empleados *(Estadísticas de establecimientos)* [1]

(1970 = 100)

	341	342	351	352	353	354	355	356	361	362
Date [2]	Paper, paper products	Printing, publishing	Industrial chemicals	Other chemical products	Petroleum refineries	Products of petroleum and coal	Rubber products	Plastic products	Pottery, china, earthenware	Glass
Date [2]	*Papier, articles en papier*	*Imprimerie, édition*	*Chimie industrielle*	*Autres produits chimiques*	*Raffineries de pétrole*	*Dérivés du pétrole et du charbon*	*Produits en caoutchouc*	*Articles en matière plastique*	*Grès, porcelaines, faïences*	*Verre*
Fecha [2]	Papel, artículos de papel	Imprentas, editoriales	Química industrial	Otros productos químicos	Refinerías de petróleo	Derivados del petróleo y del carbón	Productos de caucho	Productos plásticos	Barro, loza, porcelana	Vidrio
1969	99.6	98.8	101.3	98.3	86.5	103.8	100.0	98.1	101.7	100.0
1970	**100.0**	**100.0**	**100.0**	**100.0**	**100.0**	**100.0**	**100.0**	**100.0**	**100.0**	**100.0**
1971[3]	96.6	87.9	85.8	98.7	62.2	84.6	93.8	102.8	90.0	93.8
1972	96.1	84.1	83.3	96.2	59.5	76.9	90.1	105.6	90.0	90.1
1973	94.4	83.9	81.1	98.7	56.8	76.9	94.6	114.8	95.0	91.4
1974 *	98.3	85.1	82.0	101.3	54.1	73.1	96.2	118.5	100.0	90.1

	369	371	372	381	382	383	384	385	390
	Other non-metallic mineral products	Basic metal industries		Metal products	Machinery (non-electrical)	Electrical machinery and apparatus	Transport equipment	Scientific, measuring, optical, etc. equipment	Other manufacturing industries
Date [2]		*Industrie métallurgique de base*							
Date [2]		Industrias metalúrgicas básicas							
Date [2]	*Autres produits minéraux non métalliques*	Iron and steel	Non-ferrous metal	*Produits métalliques*	*Machines (non électriques)*	*Machines et appareils électriques*	*Matériel de transport*	*Matériel scientifique, de précision, d'optique, etc.*	*Autres industries manufacturières*
Fecha [2]	Otros productos minerales no metálicos	*Sidérurgie* / Hierro y acero	*Métaux non ferreux* / Metales no ferrosos	Productos metálicos	Maquinaria (no eléctrica)	Maquinaria y aparatos eléctricos	Material de transporte	Equipo científico, de medida, de óptica, etc.	Otras industrias manufactureras
1969	104.0	98.9	98.6	98.7	98.4	100.4	99.3	97.4	101.4
1970	**100.0**	**100.0**	**100.0**	**100.0**	**100.0**	**100.0**	**100.0**	**100.0**	**100.0**
1971[3]	88.5	95.0	91.2	89.4	86.4	89.0	96.8	107.1	90.6
1972	87.0	87.8	85.1	86.3	80.2	86.8	93.2	101.3	88.5
1973	87.5	87.6	87.2	88.1	79.5	88.6	94.5	103.9	89.9
1974 *	84.0	85.8	84.5	89.9	80.3	92.4	93.9	103.9	91.4

[1] Prior to 1971: National insurance statistics. [2] June of each year. [3] Series linked to former series.

[1] *Avant 1971: statistiques de l'assurance nationale.* [2] *Juin de chaque année.* [3] *Série enchaînée à la précédente.*

[1] Antes de 1971: estadísticas del Seguro Nacional. [2] Junio de cada año. [3] Serie enlazada con la anterior.

6 Employment in manufacturing
Emploi dans les industries manufacturières
Empleo en las industrias manufactureras

B By industry
Par industrie
Por industria

Yugoslavia [1] (1)

Indices of numbers employed: wage earners and salaried employees *(Statistics of establishments)*
Indices de l'effectif employé: ouvriers et employés *(Statistiques d'établissements)*
Indices de trabajadores ocupados: obreros y empleados *(Estadísticas de establecimientos)*

(1970 = 100)

	311-312	313	314	321	322	323	324	331	332
Date [2] Date [2] Fecha [2]	Food *Aliments* Alimentos	Beverages *Boissons* Bebidas	Tobacco *Tabac* Tabaco	Textiles	Clothing *Habillement* Vestido	Leather, leather products *Cuir, articles en cuir* Cuero, artículos de cuero	Footwear *Chaussures* Calzado	Wood *Bois* Madera	Furniture *Ameublement* Mobiliario
1965	94.3	75.0	143.8	95.0	77.1	106.3	90.0	105.9	108.5
1966	88.6	75.0	125.0	97.2	81.2	106.3	80.0	107.4	98.3
1967	92.4	91.7	106.3	97.8	81.2	100.0	86.7	104.4	93.2
1968	92.4	91.7	106.3	96.7	81.2	100.0	90.0	95.6	94.9
1969	96.2	91.7	100.0	98.3	91.7	100.0	96.7	95.6	93.2
1970	**100.0**	**100.0**	**100.0**	**100.0**	**100.0**	**100.0**	**100.0**	**100.0**	**100.0**
1971	105.7	108.3	100.0	103.3	108.3	112.5	106.7	105.9	106.8
1972	116.2	133.3	100.0	108.9	127.1	118.8	120.0	104.4	120.3
1973	120.0	150.0	106.3	112.8	141.7	131.3	126.7	107.4	125.4
1974	127.6	175.0	106.3	116.7	152.1	131.3	133.3	116.2	128.8

	341	342	351; 356	352	353	354	355	361	362
Date [2] Date [2] Fecha [2]	Paper, paper products *Papier, articles en papier* Papel, artículos de papel	Printing, publishing *Imprimerie, édition* Imprentas, editoriales	Industrial chemicals [3] *Chimie industrielle [3]* Química industrial [3]	Other chemical products *Autres produits chimiques* Otros productos químicos	Petroleum refineries *Raffineries de pétrole* Refinerías de petróleo	Products of petroleum and coal *Dérivés du pétrole et du charbon* Derivados del petróleo y del carbón	Rubber products *Produits en caoutchouc* Productos de caucho	Pottery, china, earthenware *Grès, porcelaines, faïences* Barro, loza, porcelana	Glass *Verre* Vidrio
1965	86.2	87.8	85.7	75.0	54.5	133.3	77.8	100.0	86.7
1966	93.1	87.8	88.6	79.2	54.5	133.3	83.3	88.9	93.3
1967	89.7	87.8	100.0	77.1	63.6	100.0	88.9	88.9	93.3
1968	93.1	91.8	88.6	87.5	54.5	100.0	88.9	88.9	93.3
1969	96.6	95.9	94.3	93.7	72.7	100.0	94.4	100.0	93.3
1970	**100.0**	**100.0**	**100.0**	**100.0**	**100.0**	**100.0**	**100.0**	**100.0**	**100.0**
1971	103.4	104.1	102.9	108.3	81.8	100.0	105.6	111.1	100.0
1972	106.9	106.1	105.7	116.7	109.1	100.0	111.1	100.0	106.7
1973	110.3	110.2	111.4	120.8	118.2	100.0	116.7	111.1	106.7
1974	117.2	116.3	117.1	127.1	127.3	100.0	127.8	111.1	106.7

[1] Socialised sector. [2] March and Sep. of each year.
[3] Incl. plastic products.

[1] *Secteur socialisé.* [2] *Mars et sept. de chaque année.*
[3] *Y compris les articles en matière plastique.*

[1] Sector socializado. [2] Marzo y sept. de cada año.
[3] Incl. productos plásticos.

6 Employment in manufacturing
Emploi dans les industries manufacturières
Empleo en las industrias manufactureras

B By industry
Par industrie
Por industria

Yugoslavia [1] (2)

Indices of numbers employed: wage earners and salaried employees *(Statistics of establishments)*
Indices de l'effectif employé: ouvriers et employés *(Statistiques d'établissements)*
Indices de trabajadores ocupados: obreros y empleados *(Estadísticas de establecimientos)*

(1970 = 100)

	369	371	372	381	382	383	384	385	390
		Basic metal industries		Metal products	Machinery (non-electrical)	Electrical machinery and apparatus	Transport equipment	Scientific, measuring, optical, etc. equipment	Other manufacturing industries
Date [2]	Other non-metallic mineral products	*Industrie métallurgique de base*							
		Industrias metalúrgicas básicas							
Date [2]	*Autres produits minéraux non métalliques*			*Produits métalliques*	*Machines (non électriques)*	*Machines et appareils électriques*	*Matériel de transport*	*Matériel scientifique, de précision, d'optique, etc.*	*Autres industries manufacturières*
Fecha [2]		Iron and steel	Non-ferrous metal						
	Otros productos minerales no metálicos	*Sidérurgie*	*Métaux non ferreux*	Productos metálicos	Maquinaria (no eléctrica)	Maquinaria y aparatos eléctricos	Material de transporte	Equipo científico, de medida, de óptica, etc.	Otras industrias manufactureras
		Hierro y acero	Metales no ferrosos						
1965	107.4	93.6	73.0	115.8	81.5	88.8	88.3	150.0	133.3
1966	101.9	95.7	75.7	110.5	80.0	85.4	86.7	150.0	116.7
1967	100.0	95.7	81.1	89.5	85.4	86.5	90.6	125.0	116.7
1968	98.1	93.6	97.3	81.6	88.5	86.5	92.2	87.5	100.0
1969	100.0	95.7	97.3	89.5	93.8	94.4	95.3	100.0	100.0
1970	**100.0**	**100.0**	**100.0**	**100.0**	**100.0**	**100.0**	**100.0**	**100.0**	**100.0**
1971	105.6	106.4	102.7	110.5	106.2	106.7	104.7	112.5	100.0
1972	113.0	112.8	78.4	115.8	110.0	113.5	108.6	137.5	83.3
1973	116.7	117.0	83.8	121.1	109.2	116.9	115.6	112.5	100.0
1974	120.4	121.3	89.2	126.3	116.2	124.7	123.4	125.0	83.3

[1] Socialised sector. [2] March and Sep. of each year.   [1] *Secteur socialisé.* [2] *Mars et sept. de chaque année.*   [1] Sector socializado. [2] Marzo y sept. de cada año.

6 B

Employment in manufacturing
Emploi dans les industries manufacturières
Empleo en las industrias manufactureras

By industry
Par industrie
Por industria

OCEANIA — OCÉANIE — OCEANIA

Australia (1)

Indices of numbers employed: wage earners and salaried employees *(Statistics of establishments)*
Indices de l'effectif employé: ouvriers et employés *(Statistiques d'établissements)*
Indices de trabajadores ocupados: obreros y empleados *(Estadísticas de establecimientos)*

(1970 = 100)

	311-312	313	314	321	322	323	324	331	332	341
Date [1] *Date* [1] Fecha [1]	Food *Aliments* Alimentos	Beverages *Boissons* Bebidas	Tobacco *Tabac* Tabaco	Textiles	Clothing *Habillement* Vestido	Leather, leather products *Cuir, articles en cuir* Cuero, artículos de cuero	Footwear *Chaussures* Calzado	Wood *Bois* Madera	Furniture *Ameublement* Mobiliario	Paper, paper products *Papier, articles en papier* Papel, artículos de papel
1969	96.0	98.5	96.2	98.2	100.3	97.9	102.6	104.8	96.3	100.6
1970	**100.0**	**100.0**	**100.0**	**100.0**	**100.0**	**100.0**	**100.0**	**100.0**	**100.0**	**100.0**
1971	.	.	.	.	.	.	.	.	.	.
1972	104.9	107.1	101.5	94.3	95.7	90.0	72.8	97.3	105.6	105.2
1973	105.4	108.6	100.7	92.5	92.6	83.2	65.2	97.9	111.2	103.4

	342	351	352	353	354	355	356	361	362
Date [1] *Date* [1] Fecha [1]	Printing, publishing *Imprimerie, édition* Imprentas, editoriales	Industrial chemicals *Chimie industrielle* Química industrial	Other chemical products *Autres produits chimiques* Otros productos químicos	Petroleum refineries *Raffineries de pétrole* Refinerías de petróleo	Products of petroleum and coal *Dérivés du pétrole et du charbon* Derivados del petróleo y del carbón	Rubber products *Produits en caoutchouc* Productos de caucho	Plastic products *Articles en matière plastique* Productos plásticos	Pottery, china, earthenware *Grès, porcelaines, faïences* Barro, loza, porcelana	Glass *Verre* Vidrio
1969	95.2	95.0	97.0	111.2	85.7	99.0	93.5	100.1	98.5
1970	**100.0**	**100.0**	**100.0**	**100.0**	**100.0**	**100.0**	**100.0**	**100.0**	**100.0**
1971	.	.	.	.	.	.	.	.	.
1972	99.8	98.0	100.9	99.7	98.3	96.1	110.7	98.2	92.0
1973	100.0	98.0	100.5	101.7	95.2	95.0	119.9	102.2	88.7

[1] Year ending in June of year indicated.   [1] *Année se terminant en juin de l'année indiquée.*   [1] Año que termina en junio del año indicado.

6 Employment in manufacturing
Emploi dans les industries manufacturières
Empleo en las industrias manufactureras

B By industry
Par industrie
Por industria

Australia (2,

Indices of numbers employed: wage earners and salaried employees *(Statistics of establishments)*
Indices de l'effectif employé: ouvriers et employés *(Statistiques d'établissements)*
Indices de trabajadores ocupados: obreros y empleados *(Estadísticas de establecimientos)*

(1970 = 100)

	369	371	372	381	382	383	384	385	390
		Basic metal industries		Metal products	Machinery (non-electrical)	Electrical machinery and apparatus	Transport equipment	Scientific, measuring, optical, etc. equipment	Other manufacturing industries
Date [1]	Other non-metallic mineral products	*Industrie métallurgique de base*							
Date [1]		Industrias metalúrgicas básicas		*Produits métalliques*	*Machines (non électriques)*	*Machines et appareils électriques*	*Matériel de transport*	*Matériel scientifique, de précision, d'optique, etc.*	*Autres industries manufacturières*
Fecha [1]	*Autres produits minéraux non métalliques*	Iron and steel	Non-ferrous metal						
	Otros productos minerales no metálicos	*Sidérurgie* Hierro y acero	*Métaux non ferreux* Metales no ferrosos	Productos metálicos	Maquinaria (no eléctrica)	Maquinaria y aparatos eléctricos	Material de transporte	Equipo científico, de medida, de óptica, etc.	Otras industrias manufactureras
1969	97.2	97.0	95.4	95.1	98.3	96.4	97.7	99.5	94.0
1970	**100.0**	**100.0**	**100.0**	**100.0**	**100.0**	**100.0**	**100.0**	**100.0**	**100.0**
1971	.	.	.	.	.	.	.	.	.
1972	99.5	101.8	101.3	101.4	96.6	100.0	102.4	112.4	104.7
1973	104.3	102.7	106.2	97.5	95.5	95.6	103.0	115.6	107.1

[1] Year ending in June of year indicated.   [1] *Année se terminant en juin de l'année indiquée.*   [1] Año que termina en junio del año indicado.

Fiji (1)

Indices of numbers employed: wage earners and salaried employees *(Statistics of establishments)*
Indices de l'effectif employé: ouvriers et employés *(Statistiques d'établissements)*
Indices de trabajadores ocupados: obreros y empleados *(Estadísticas de establecimientos)*

(1970 = 100)

	311-312	313-314	322; 324	331	332
Date [1]	Food	Beverages, tobacco	Clothing, footwear	Wood	Furniture
Date [1]	*Aliments*	*Boissons, tabac*	*Habillement, chaussure*	*Bois*	*Ameublement*
Fecha [1]	Alimentos	Bebidas, tabaco	Vestido, calzado	Madera	Mobiliario
1970	**100.0**	**100.0**	**100.0**	**100.0**	**100.0**
1971	105.9	94.1	112.2	124.7	109.1
1972	103.4	105.5	115.5	132.5	112.0
1973	110.0	114.5	105.9	119.9	115.9

[1] June of each year.   [1] *Juin de chaque année.*   [1] Junio de cada año.

EMPLOYMENT

 6 Employment in manufacturing
Emploi dans les industries manufacturières
Empleo en las industrias manufactureras

B By industry
Par industrie
Por industria

Fiji (2)

Indices of numbers employed: wage earners and salaried employees *(Statistics of establishments)*
Indices de l'effectif employé: ouvriers et employés *(Statistiques d'établissements)*
Indices de trabajadores ocupados: obreros y empleados *(Estadísticas de establecimientos)*

(1970 = 100)

Date [1] Date [1] Fecha [1]	34 Paper, printing, publishing *Papier, imprimerie, édition* Papel, imprentas, editoriales	369 × Cement, cement products *Ciment, produits en ciment* Cemento, productos de cemento	381-383 Metal products, machinery *Produits métalliques, machines* Productos metálicos, maquinaria	384 Transport equipment *Matériel de transport* Material de transporte	352; 355-356; 390 Miscellaneous manufacturing *Industries manufacturières diverses* Industrias manufactureras diversas
1970	**100.0**	**100.0**	**100.0**	**100.0**	**100.0**
1971	101.3	121.9	116.1	113.3	122.4
1972	108.1	117.9	110.3	85.6	110.3
1973	120.3	98.6	112.0	90.8	123.0

[1] June of each year.   [1] *Juin de chaque année.*   [1] Junio de cada año.

New Zealand (1)

Indices of numbers employed: wage earners and salaried employees *(Statistics of establishments)*
Indices de l'effectif employé: ouvriers et employés *(Statistiques d'établissements)*
Indices de trabajadores ocupados: obreros y empleados *(Estadísticas de establecimientos)*

(1970 = 100)

Date [1] Date [1] Fecha [1]	311-312 Food *Aliments* Alimentos	313 Beverages *Boissons* Bebidas	314 Tobacco *Tabac* Tabaco	321 Textiles	322 Clothing *Habillement* Vestido	323 Leather, leather products *Cuir, articles en cuir* Cuero, artículos de cuero	324 Footwear *Chaussures* Calzado	331 Wood *Bois* Madera	332 Furniture *Ameublement* Mobiliario
1969	96.8	94.4	98.1	97.2	94.0	95.9	99.4	100.1	100.6
1970	**100.0**	**100.0**	**100.0**	**100.0**	**100.0**	**100.0**	**100.0**	**100.0**	**100.0**
1971	103.2	105.3	102.7	99.3	98.9	103.7	98.6	97.3	103.4
1972	105.4	110.5	101.9	96.5	96.0	105.5	92.8	99.1	111.5

[1] Year ending in March of the following year.   [1] *Année se terminant en mars de l'année suivante.*   [1] Año que termina en marzo del año siguiente.

6 **Employment in manufacturing**
   Emploi dans les industries manufacturières
   Empleo en las industrias manufactureras

B By industry
   Par industrie
   Por industria

New Zealand (2)

Indices of numbers employed: wage earners and salaried employees *(Statistics of establishments)*
Indices de l'effectif employé: ouvriers et employés *(Statistiques d'établissements)*
Indices de trabajadores ocupados: obreros y empleados *(Estadísticas de establecimientos)*

(1970 = 100)

	341	342	351-352	354	355	356	361	362
Date [1] *Date [1]* Fecha [1]	Paper, paper products *Papier, articles en papier* Papel, artículos de papel	Printing, publishing *Imprimerie, édition* Imprentas, editoriales	Chemicals *Industrie chimique* Productos químicos	Products of petroleum and coal *Dérivés du pétrole et du charbon* Derivados del petróleo y del carbón	Rubber products *Produits en caoutchouc* Productos de caucho	Plastic products *Articles en matière plastique* Productos plásticos	Pottery, china, earthenware *Grès, porcelaines, faïences* Barro, loza, porcelana	Glass *Verre* Vidrio
1969	95.9	97.1	97.0	96.5	104.1	92.8	103.2	93.0
1970	**100.0**	**100.0**	**100.0**	**100.0**	**100.0**	**100.0**	**100.0**	**100.0**
1971	99.5	99.1	104.3	98.8	97.7	114.7	100.0	108.7
1972	103.0	100.3	104.4	95.5	96.6	117.3	97.8	100.0

	369	37	381	382	383	384	385	390
Date [1] *Date [1]* Fecha [1]	Other non-metallic mineral products *Autres produits minéraux non métalliques* Otros productos minerales no metálicos	Basic metal industries *Industrie métallurgique de base* Industrias metalúrgicas básicas	Metal products *Produits métalliques* Productos metálicos	Machinery (non-electrical) *Machines (non électriques)* Maquinaria (no eléctrica)	Electrical machinery and apparatus *Machines et appareils électriques* Maquinaria y aparatos eléctricos	Transport equipment *Matériel de transport* Material de transporte	Scientific, measuring, optical, etc., equipment *Matériel scientifique, de précision, d'optique, etc.* Equipo científico, de medida, de óptica, etc.	Other manufac- turing industries *Autres industries manufac- turières* Otras industrias manufac- tureras
1969	101.5	83.2	85.8	107.2	92.0	90.0	83.0	96.2
1970	**100.0**	**100.0**	**100.0**	**100.0**	**100.0**	**100.0**	**100.0**	**100.0**
1971	95.7	116.8	103.3	96.7	99.8	106.9	96.4	103.8
1972	93.7	127.3	108.6	102.0	103.2	108.7	106.4	98.1

[1] Year ending in March of the following year.   [1] *Année se terminant en mars de l'année suivante.*   [1] Año que termina en marzo del año siguiente.

6 **Employment in manufacturing**
Emploi dans les industries manufacturières
Empleo en las industrias manufactureras

B **By industry**
Par industrie
Por industria

URSS [1]

Indices of numbers employed: wage earners and salaried employees *(Statistics of establishments)*
Indices de l'effectif employé: ouvriers et employés *(Statistiques d'établissements)*
Indices de trabajadores ocupados: obreros y empleados *(Estadísticas de establecimientos)*

(1970 = 100)

	311-312	313-314	321	322	323	324	331	332	341
Date / Date / Fecha	Food / *Aliments* / Alimentos	Beverages, tobacco / *Boissons, tabac* / Bebidas, tabaco	Textiles	Clothing / *Habillement* / Vestido	Leather, leather products / *Cuir, articles en cuir* / Cuero, artículos de cuero	Footwear / *Chaussures* / Calzado	Wood / *Bois* / Madera	Furniture / *Ameublement* / Mobiliario	Paper, paper products / *Papier, articles en papier* / Papel, artículos de papel
1965	88.6	83.8	92.2	78.1	91.1	85.3	100.5	92.1	81.9
1966	91.4	88.9	94.7	83.4	95.8	87.6	101.4	93.9	90.7
1967	95.1	91.9	97.0	88.2	95.8	91.5	97.4	97.4	94.6
1968	98.8	96.4	99.0	93.6	98.4	94.0	98.6	100.4	97.3
1969	99.8	99.4	100.0	97.2	100.0	98.3	99.1	100.9	98.5
1970	**100.0**	**100.0**	**100.0**	**100.0**	**100.0**	**100.0**	**100.0**	**100.0**	**100.0**
1971	100.0	101.7	100.0	100.8	101.0	100.9	97.9	104.6	100.4
1972	100.9	102.8	99.7	101.3	100.0	99.6	96.5	108.1	101.2
1973	101.3	102.8	100.4	101.2	100.0	99.6	95.3	112.3	101.9
1974	103.3	106.4	101.0	101.8	100.5	99.8	94.1	114.2	103.1

	351	352-354	355	356	361	362	369	371	38 ×	383
Date / Date / Fecha	Industrial chemicals / *Chimie industrielle* / Química industrial	Other chemical products, petroleum refineries [2] / *Autres produits chimiques, raffineries de pétrole* [2] / Otros productos químicos, refinerías de petróleo [2]	Rubber products / *Produits en caoutchouc* / Productos de caucho	Plastic products / *Articles en matière plastique* / Productos plásticos	Pottery, china, earthenware / *Grès, porcelaines, faïences* / Barro, loza, porcelana	Glass / *Verre* / Vidrio	Other non-metallic mineral products / *Autres produits minéraux non métalliques* / Otros productos minerales no metálicos	Iron and steel basic industries / *Sidérurgie* / Industrias básicas de hierro y acero	Metal products, machinery and equipment [3] / *Produits métalliques, machines et matériel* [3] / Productos metálicos, maquinaria y equipo [3]	Electrical machinery and apparatus / *Machines et appareils électriques* / Maquinaria y aparatos eléctricos
1965	82.8	79.8	84.5	51.7	93.6	85.8	84.2	91.4	82.5	86.4
1966	89.4	82.8	88.7	65.5	95.2	89.4	88.3	92.8	86.8	87.1
1967	93.3	86.6	92.1	78.2	97.3	92.9	91.2	94.9	90.4	91.7
1968	94.0	96.8	95.8	85.1	98.9	100.0	95.2	98.1	93.9	96.6
1969	97.4	98.0	98.3	93.1	100.5	102.7	98.1	100.2	97.4	99.0
1970	100.0	100.0	100.0	100.0	100.0	100.0	100.0	100.0	100.0	100.0
1971	101.0	100.0	101.7	113.8	101.6	105.3	102.2	100.7	102.8	102.1
1972	104.1	100.6	103.8	117.2	105.9	106.2	103.9	101.0	106.7	104.1
1973	105.9	103.8	109.6	127.6	109.1	108.0	105.0	102.0	109.2	106.5
1974	108.9	103.6	114.6	131.0	112.8	108.9	106.0	102.5	111.4	109.1

[1] Incl. Byelorussian SSR and Ukrainian SSR, shown separately in this table. Socialised sector. [2] Incl. products of petroleum and coal. [3] Excl. electrical machinery.

[1] *Y compris les RSS de Biélorussie et d'Ukraine, figurant séparément dans ce tableau. Secteur socialisé.* [2] *Y compris les dérivés du pétrole et du charbon.* [3] *Non compris les machines électriques.*

[1] Incl. las RSS de Bielorrusia y de Ucrania, que figuran separadamente en este cuadro. Sector socializado. [2] Incl. los derivados del petróleo y del carbón. [3] Excl. las maquinarias eléctricas.

6 B

Employment in manufacturing
Emploi dans les industries manufacturières
Empleo en las industrias manufactureras

By industry
Par industrie
Por industria

RSS de Biélorussie [1]

Indices of numbers employed: wage earners and salaried employees *(Statistics of establishments)*
Indices de l'effectif employé: ouvriers et employés *(Statistiques d'établissements)*
Indices de trabajadores ocupados: obreros y empleados *(Estadísticas de establecimientos)*

(1970 = 100)

	311-312	313-314	321	322	323	324	331	332
Date *Date* Fecha	Food *Aliments* Alimentos	Beverages, tobacco *Boissons, tabac* Bebidas, tabaco	Textiles	Clothing *Habillement* Vestido	Leather, leather products *Cuir, articles en cuir* Cuero, artículos de cuero	Footwear *Chaussures* Calzado	Wood *Bois* Madera	Furniture *Ameublement* Mobiliario
1965	84.2	93.4	72.2	73.2	73.7	88.4	100.3	93.8
1966	87.6	100.7	82.1	80.1	82.8	93.2	97.9	96.5
1967	91.5	94.2	88.3	87.6	83.8	93.6	100.5	97.3
1968	96.2	97.1	93.6	94.2	88.9	96.8	104.2	102.3
1969	98.1	98.5	97.1	96.6	92.9	99.2	101.9	98.5
1970	**100.0**	**100.0**	**100.0**	**100.0**	**100.0**	**100.0**	**100.0**	**100.0**
1971	101.6	102.9	101.0	102.2	98.0	100.4	82.2	125.1
1972	102.5	108.8	103.4	105.4	103.0	97.2	84.1	121.6
1973	101.5	110.2	104.1	106.3	108.1	99.6	88.1	124.7
1974	101.3	110.9	105.7	108.6	108.1	96.4	87.3	129.0

	341	355	36 ×	362	371	38 ×	383
Date *Date* Fecha	Paper, paper products *Papier, articles en papier* Papel, artículos de papel	Rubber products *Produits en caoutchouc* Productos de caucho	Non-metallic mineral products [2] *Produits minéraux non métalliques* [2] Productos minerales no metálicos	Glass *Verre* Vidrio	Iron and steel basic industries *Sidérurgie* Industrias básicas de hierro y acero	Metal products, machinery and equipment [3] *Produits métalliques, machines et matériel* [3] Productos metálicos, maquinaria y equipo [3]	Electrical machinery and apparatus *Machines et appareils électriques* Maquinaria y aparatos eléctricos
1965	88.5	82.2	73.6	85.7	66.7	70.6	61.7
1966	89.7	87.7	81.1	88.2	69.4	77.3	66.2
1967	89.7	91.8	87.1	92.4	66.7	82.3	76.1
1968	94.9	97.3	92.1	95.8	91.7	88.4	88.1
1969	100.0	100.0	97.9	97.5	97.2	94.6	95.0
1970	**100.0**	**100.0**	**100.0**	**100.0**	**100.0**	**100.0**	**100.0**
1971	102.6	108.2	105.2	98.3	102.8	105.9	106.0
1972	103.8	123.3	101.8	99.2	91.7	109.5	110.0
1973	103.8	173.8	100.7	98.3	94.4	112.9	119.4
1974	106.4	201.4	104.2	101.7	97.2	117.5	121.9

[1] Socialised sector. [2] Excl. glass. [3] Excl. electrical machinery.

[1] Secteur socialisé. [2] Non compris le verre. [3] Non compris les machines électriques.

[1] Sector socializado. [2] Excl. el vidrio. [3] Excl. las maquinarias eléctricas.

EMPLOYMENT

6 Employment in manufacturing
Emploi dans les industries manufacturières
Empleo en las industrias manufactureras

B By industry
Par industrie
Por industria

RSS d'Ukraine [1]

Indices of numbers employed: wage earners and salaried employees *(Statistics of establishments)*
Indices de l'effectif employé: ouvriers et employés *(Statistiques d'établissements)*
Indices de trabajadores ocupados: obreros y empleados *(Estadísticas de establecimientos)*

(1970 = 100)

Date / Date / Fecha	311-312 Food / Aliments / Alimentos	313-314 Beverages, tobacco / Boissons, tabac / Bebidas, tabaco	321 Textiles	322 Clothing / Habillement / Vestido	323 Leather, leather products / Cuir, articles en cuir / Cuero, artículos de cuero	324 Footwear / Chaussures / Calzado	331 Wood / Bois / Madera	332 Furniture / Ameublement / Mobiliario	341 Paper, paper products / Papier, articles en papier / Papel, artículos de papel
1965	85.5	81.6	76.3	74.5	80.0	72.8	90.2	97.2	62.5
1966	88.4	85.5	82.2	80.6	80.0	75.7	87.0	97.2	87.5
1967	90.6	92.1	87.7	86.7	91.4	81.6	87.0	100.0	91.7
1968	96.0	96.1	92.8	92.0	94.3	86.4	93.5	105.6	95.8
1969	98.0	100.0	95.8	96.8	97.1	93.2	96.7	103.7	95.8
1970	**100.0**	**100.0**	**100.0**	**100.0**	**100.0**	**100.0**	**100.0**	**100.0**	**100.0**
1971	99.3	102.6	103.4	101.0	105.7	101.9	92.7	110.3	104.2
1972	99.5	103.9	105.9	101.7	108.6	100.0	84.6	120.6	104.2
1973	101.5	105.3	108.5	101.2	105.7	100.0	83.7	121.5	104.2
1974	104.0	107.9	110.2	101.0	105.7	101.0	80.5	124.3	104.2

Date / Date / Fecha	351 Industrial chemicals / Chimie industrielle / Química industrial	352-354 Other chemical products, petroleum refineries [2] / Autres produits chimiques, raffineries de pétrole [2] / Otros productos químicos, refinerías de petróleo [2]	355 Rubber products / Produits en caoutchouc / Productos de caucho	356 Plastic products / Articles en matière plastique / Productos plásticos	361 Pottery, china, earthenware / Grès, porcelaines, faïences / Barro, loza, porcelana	362 Glass / Verre / Vidrio	369 Other non-metallic mineral products / Autres produits minéraux non métalliques / Otros productos minerales no metálicos	371 Iron and steel basic industries / Sidérurgie / Industrias básicas de hierro y acero	38 × Metal products, machinery and equipment [3] / Produits métalliques, machines et matériel [3] / Productos metálicos, maquinaria y equipo [3]	383 Electrical machinery and apparatus / Machines et appareils électriques / Maquinaria y aparatos eléctricos
1965	65.0	101.2	56.7	44.0	83.7	76.9	84.9	87.3	79.4	83.3
1966	71.8	100.0	67.0	56.0	87.8	76.9	88.3	90.6	83.1	84.0
1967	87.7	102.4	80.0	64.0	89.8	80.8	92.8	94.2	88.2	91.7
1968	92.0	100.0	86.7	76.0	91.8	100.0	97.3	99.0	92.8	94.9
1969	96.3	100.0	96.7	88.0	95.9	100.0	100.2	101.0	96.9	98.1
1970	**100.0**	**100.0**	**100.0**	**100.0**	**100.0**	**100.0**	**100.0**	**100.0**	**100.0**	**100.0**
1971	104.3	98.8	103.3	108.0	102.0	103.8	104.5	100.3	103.4	105.8
1972	105.5	100.0	103.3	112.0	106.1	107.7	105.6	99.7	107.1	105.8
1973	108.0	100.0	123.3	112.0	110.2	107.7	106.1	100.6	110.7	110.3
1974	110.4	98.8	136.7	112.0	114.3	107.7	106.8	100.6	114.6	114.7

[1] Socialised sector. [2] Incl. products of petroleum and coal. [3] Excl. electrical machinery.

[1] *Secteur socialisé.* [2] *Y compris les dérivés du pétrole et du charbon.* [3] *Non compris les machines électriques.*

[1] Sector socializado. [2] Incl. los derivados del petróleo y del carbón. [3] Excl. las maquinarias eléctricas.

6 Employment in manufacturing
Emploi dans les industries manufacturières
Empleo en las industrias manufactureras

C Total hours worked
Total des heures de travail effectuées
Total de horas de trabajo efectuadas

(Indices: 1970 = 100)

Country — Pays — País	Code Code Clave	1965	1966	1967	1968	1969	1970	1971	1972	1973	1974	1975 (VI)
AFRICA — AFRIQUE AFRICA												
Malawi [1]	III	.	.	.	.	.	100.0	107.5	117.1	123.4	148.5	...
AMERICA — AMÉRIQUE AMÉRICA												
El Salvador [2]	III	.	107.8	102.4	99.3	97.8	**100.0**	99.0	102.4	112.7	119.2	.
Guatemala (Guatemala)	III	91.9	91.3	92.1	95.4	95.9	**100.0**	101.6	102.1	114.3	128.0 *	...
Puerto Rico	III	83.0	89.5	94.7	101.7	103.3	**100.0**	102.7	106.7	110.3	111.6	96.1 [13]
United States	III	99.1	105.8	104.9	105.8	107.4	**100.0**	96.2	101.4	107.5	104.7	91.6 *
Venezuela	III	98.1	97.6	97.2	100.5	‖99.0 [3]	**100.0**	95.4	94.7	97.8	102.3	.
ASIA — ASIE ASIA												
India	III	96.3	95.2	96.6	95.1	97.0	**100.0**	101.8 *	106.5 *	...	...	
Israel [1]	III	80.5	78.2	71.6	‖85.7 [4]	95.6	**100.0**	105.1	111.6	108.1	108.8	110.0 [14]
Japan [5]	III	88.6	89.7	93.0	96.3	98.1	**100.0**	99.0	96.5	96.1	91.1	85.7 [14]
Korea, Rep. of	I	63.8	69.3	83.0	97.4	100.3	**100.0**	105.0	117.1	148.5	173.4	.
EUROPE — EUROPE EUROPA												
Austria [6]	III	105.6	104.2	98.6	96.8	100.0	**100.0**	100.9	100.3	100.6	98.4	88.3
Czechoslovakia [6,7]	III	103.2	102.6	102.1	101.4	98.0	**100.0**	102.2	102.1	101.7	101.1	.
Denmark	III	112.6	‖106.6 [8]	100.2	‖96.0 [8]	99.5	‖100.0 [8]	95.0	94.1	92.7	90.2 *	81.4 *
Finland [6]	III	96.1	95.7	92.9	94.6	94.6	**100.0**	99.8	102.4	103.1 *	103.6 *	.
France [5]	. [9]	101.5	102.3	100.1	97.6	99.6	**100.0**	99.8	‖*100.0* [10]	*101.1*	*101.1* *	.
Germany, Fed. Rep. of Δ [11]	III	103.3	99.8	89.7	92.5	97.5	**100.0**	95.8	91.5	91.0	85.3	74.8 *
Hongrie [12]	III	.	.	.	103.9	100.9	‖100.0 [8]	98.9	98.5	99.0	99.2 *	95.4 *

EXPLANATORY NOTES AND CODES: See p. 297.

[1] Index of number of man-days worked. [2] Area of San Salvador. [3] Beginning 1969: establishments with 10 or more workers (prior to 1969, all establishments); series linked to former series. [4] Series linked to former series. Beginning 1968: incl. mining and quarrying. [5] Incl. salaried employees. [6] Incl. mining and quarrying. [7] Socialised sector. [8] Series linked to former series. [9] Official estimates. 1965-71: statistics of establishments. [10] Series (base 1971 = 100) replacing former series. [11] Incl. mining. [12] State industry. [13] March. [14] April.

NOTES EXPLICATIVES ET CODES: Voir p. 300.

[1] Indice du nombre de journées-homme effectuées. [2] Zone de San Salvador. [3] A partir de 1969: établissements occupant 10 travailleurs et plus (avant 1969 tous les établissements); série enchaînée à la précédente. [4] Série enchaînée à la précédente. A partir de 1968: y compris les industries extractives. [5] Y compris les employés. [6] Y compris les industries extractives. [7] Secteur socialisé. [8] Série enchaînée à la précédente. [9] Evaluations officielles. 1965-71: statistiques d'établissements. [10] Série (base 100 en 1971) remplaçant la précédente. [11] Y compris les mines. [12] Industrie d'Etat. [13] Mars. [14] Avril.

NOTAS EXPLICATIVAS Y CLAVES: Véase pág. 303.

[1] Indice del total de días-hombre trabajados. [2] Zona de San Salvador. [3] A partir de 1969: establecimientos con 10 trabajadores y más (antes de 1969 todos los establecimientos); serie enlazada con la anterior. [4] Serie enlazada con la anterior. A partir de 1968: incl. las minas y canteras. [5] Incl. los empleados. [6] Incl. las minas y canteras. [7] Sector socializado. [8] Serie enlazada con la anterior. [9] Estimaciones oficiales. 1965-1970: estadísticas de establecimientos. [10] Serie (base 1971 = 100) que substituye a la anterior. [11] Incl. las minas. [12] Industria de Estado. [13] Marzo. [14] Abril.

413

6 Employment in manufacturing
Emploi dans les industries manufacturières
Empleo en las industrias manufactureras

C Total hours worked
Total des heures de travail effectuées.
Total de horas de trabajo efectuadas

(Indices: 1970 = 100)

Country — Pays — País	Code Code Clave	1965	1966	1967	1968	1969	1970	1971	1972	1973	1974	1975 (VI)
Ireland [1]	III	91.8	92.6	91.5	96.1	99.0	**100.0**	97.1	98.0	100.2 *	98.3 *	90.1 * [9]
Italie	III	84.8	89.3	93.5	96.2	97.3	**100.0**	95.6	92.0	91.5	93.9 *	.
Luxembourg	III	*101.2*	*98.8*	*103.8*	*98.0*	**100.0**	‖**100.0** [2]	100.1	103.4	...	...	.
Norway	III	107.9	109.9	108.9	104.8	103.1	**100.0**	96.5	94.7	95.2	...	.
Pologne [3]	III	89.5	92.1	94.0	97.1	99.0	**100.0**	102.9	105.7	107.7	108.3	109.5* [10]
Sweden	III	111.2	109.3	‖102.8 [4]	98.5	98.5	**100.0**	95.6	91.0	91.1	...	.
United Kingdom [5]	II	110.6	‖107.9 [4]	102.4	101.4	102.4	**100.0**	93.5	90.1	92.0 *	88.5 *	86.4 *
Yugoslavia [6]	III	103.5	99.5	95.5	94.8	98.3	**100.0**	104.2	109.2	112.6	118.9 *	.
OCEANIA — OCÉANIE OCEANÍA												
New Zealand [7]	III	88.1	91.9	91.0	88.8	94.7	**100.0**	‖100.8 [4]	100.2	107.2	112.2	110.2 [11]
URSS [8]	III	83.5	86.4	91.8	96.5	99.6	**100.0**	102.2	103.4	104.5	106.9	.
RSS d'Ukraine [8]	III	81.2	83.5	87.4	92.2	92.2	**100.0**	101.6	101.9	104.1	104.8	.

EXPLANATORY NOTES AND CODES: See p. 297.

NOTES EXPLICATIVES ET CODES: Voir p. 300.

NOTAS EXPLICATIVAS Y CLAVES: Véase pág. 303.

[1] Oct. of each year, except for 1969-73: Sep. [2] Series replacing former series. [3] Socialised sector; incl. mining, quarrying and sea fishing. [4] Series linked to former series. [5] Excl. Northern Ireland. [6] Socialised sector. Incl. salaried employees. Incl. mining and quarrying. [7] Incl. salaried employees. April and Oct. of each year. [8] Socialised sector. Incl. salaried employees. [9] March. [10] First quarter. [11] April.

[1] *Oct. de chaque année, sauf pour 1969-1973: sept.* [2] *Série remplaçant la précédente.* [3] *Secteur socialisé; y compris les industries extractives et la pêche maritime.* [4] *Série enchaînée à la précédente.* [5] *Non compris l'Irlande du Nord.* [6] *Secteur socialisé. Y compris les employés. Y compris les industries extractives.* [7] *Y compris les employés. Avril et oct. de chaque année.* [8] *Secteur socialisé. Y compris les employés.* [9] *Mars.* [10] *Premier trimestre.* [11] *Avril.*

[1] Oct. de cada año, salvo para 1969-1973; sept. [2] Serie que substituye a la anterior. [3] Sector socializado; incl. las minas y canteras y la pesca marítima. [4] Serie enlazada con la anterior. [5] Excl. Irlanda del Norte. [6] Sector socializado. Incl. los empleados. Incl. las minas y canteras. [7] Incl. los empleados. Abril y oct. de cada año. [8] Sector socializado. Incl. los empleados. [9] Marzo. [10] Primer trimestre. [11] Abril.

7 Employment in mining and quarrying
Emploi dans les industries extractives
Empleo en las minas y canteras

(Indices: 1970 = 100)

Date / Date / Fecha	AFRICA — AFRIQUE — AFRICA					
	Gabon	Ghana [1]	Kenya	Malawi [5]	Nigeria [6]	Sierra Leone
	II	III	III	III	III	III
		[2]	[4]			[2]
1965	77.0	105.9	.	.	104.1	69.7
1966	103.2	101.2	.	.	106.0	75.6
1967	91.0	104.2	83.8	46.1	100.4	77.8
1968	92 3	103.9	99.7	98.4	96.8	88.1
1969	95.4	102.8	90.3	167.7	94.9	96.2
1970	**100.0**	**100.0**	**100.0**	**100.0**	**100.0**	**100.0**
1971	116.4	95.6	103.9	122.0	99.6	97.5
1972	133.6	99.3 * [3]	112.4	155.3	...	88.3
1973	...	...	110.3	155.1	...	82.1
1974	...	...	...	175.8	...	95.8

Date / Date / Fecha	AFRICA — AFRIQUE — AFRICA						AMERICA AMÉRIQUE AMÉRICA
	South Africa, Rep. of		Swaziland	Tanzania (Tanganyika)	Uganda	Zambia	Canada
	Total	7					
	III		III [8]	III	III	III	III
				[4]	[4]	[9]	
1965	95.7	105.1	.	123.1	80.8	91.7	90.8
1966	96.4	105.3	.	102.7	81.6	94.2	92.5
1967	93.7	102.1	.	104.6	85.4	96.2	94.3
1968	95.7	100.9	.	97.9	98.7	96.1	94.9
1969	95.6	100.2	.	98.2	79.7	97.5	93.3
1970	**100.0**	**100.0**	**100.0**	**100.0**	**100.0**	**100.0**	**100.0**
1971	98.6	97.4	100.7	104.0	93.7	101.7	99.2
1972	95.5	96.2	101.5	...	73.4	101.4	95.4
1973	102.6	97.9	100.6	...	67.1	108.6	96.3 *
1974	...	...	...	...	...	112.2 [10]	99.9 *

Date / Date / Fecha	AMERICA — AMÉRIQUE — AMÉRICA						
	Colombia [11]	Chile	Rep. Dominicana	Ecuador	Perú	Puerto Rico	Trinidad and Tobago [16]
	III	III	III	III	. [15]	III	III
	[13]						
1965	*141.7*	101.5	84.5	132.4	88.2	112.5	.
1966	*131.5*	99.0	84.5	122.0	89.6	112.5	.
1967	*122.4*	91.2	96.2	118.0	94.4	112.5	.
1968	*105.6*	92.2	92.2	109.2	95.0	112.5	.
1969	**100.0**	98.2	102.0	109.2 [14]	100.8	112.5	95.9
1970	.	**100.0**	**100.0**	**100.0**	**100.0**	**100.0**	**100.0**
1971	**100.0** [12]	101.9	97.0	99.3	99.2	112.5	108.3
1972	*119.6*	107.8	...	105.0	100.4	125.0	122.8 *
1973	*111.3*	115.0	...	99.9	...	125.0	...
1974	...	...	...	...	...	...	...

EXPLANATORY NOTES AND CODES: See p. 297.

[1] Gold, diamond, manganese and bauxite mining. [2] Dec. of each year. [3] Sep. [4] June of each year. [5] Incl. working proprietors and unpaid family workers. [6] Metal mining. [7] White population. [8] Sep. of each year. [9] Beginning 1967: June and Dec. [10] June. [11] Extraction of crude oil only. [12] Series replacing former series. June of each year. [13] April of each year. [14] Series linked to former series. [15] Official estimates. [16] Mining and refining of oil and asphalt.

NOTES EXPLICATIVES ET CODES: Voir p. 300.

[1] *Mines d'or, de diamant, de manganèse et de bauxite,* [2] *Déc. de chaque année.* [3] *Sept.* [4] *Juin de chaque année.* [5] *Y compris les propriétaires-exploitants et les travailleurs familiaux non rémunérés.* [6] *Extraction de minerais métalliques.* [7] *Population blanche.* [8] *Sept. de chaque année.* [9] *A partir de 1967: juin et déc.* [10] *Juin.* [11] *Extraction du pétrole brut seulement.* [12] *Série remplaçant la précédente. Juin de chaque année.* [13] *Avril de chaque année.* [14] *Série enchaînée à la précédente.* [15] *Evaluations officielles.* [16] *Extraction et raffinage de pétrole et d'asphalte.*

NOTAS EXPLICATIVAS Y CLAVES: Véase pág. 303.

[1] Minas de oro, de diamante, de manganeso y de bauxita. [2] Dic. de cada año. [3] Sept. [4] Junio de cada año. [5] Incl. los empresarios propietarios y los trabajadores familiares no remunerados. [6] Extracción de minerales metálicos. [7] Población blanca. [8] Sept. de cada año. [9] A partir de 1967: junio y dic. [10] Junio. [11] Extracción de petróleo crudo solamente. [12] Serie que substituye a la anterior. Junio de cada año. [13] Abril de cada año. [14] Serie enlazada con la anterior. [15] Estimaciones oficiales. [16] Extracción y refinación de petróleo y asfalto.

EMPLOYMENT

7 Employment in mining and quarrying
Emploi dans les industries extractives
Empleo en las minas y canteras

(Indices: 1970 = 100)

Date / Date / Fecha	AMERICA — AMÉRIQUE — AMÉRICA		ASIA — ASIE — ASIA				
	United States	Venezuela [1]	Brunei [2]	Cyprus	Hong Kong	India	Israel
	III	III	III [3]	. [5]	III	III	III
1965	101.4	135.6	. [4]	.	223.1	108.3	91.7
1966	100.6	124.6	.	.	207.6	109.6	89.3
1967	98.4	114.2	.	.	160.9	105.2	84.4
1968	97.3	107.0	.	.	141.3	100.9	89.3 [6]
1969	99.4	102.7	.	100.1	111.0	100.2	96.4
1970	100.0	100.0	.	100.0	100.0	100.0	100.0
1971	96.8	98.0	.	85.0	119.1	98.9	99.1
1972	99.8	95.8	100.0	77.9	107.6	103.2	99.1
1973	102.4	93.4	106.7	75.0 *	99.5	113.3 *	100.0
1974	107.9	...	112.8	70.5 *	86.1	...	105.4

Date / Date / Fecha	ASIA — ASIE — ASIA					
	Japan	Jordan [7]	Korea, Rep. of	Malaysia — West Malaysia [8]	Philippines	Singapore
	I	III	I	III	III	III
1965	168.7	94.9	.	100.0 [9]	.	. [10]
1966	153.8	91.4	.	110.1	84.0	.
1967	138.9 [6]	104.8	.	107.8	90.9	.
1968	138.9	116.3	.	107.3	95.8	.
1969	116.7	100.0	.	99.1	98.8	90.5
1970	100.0	...	100.0	100.0	100.0	100.0
1971	100.0	...	76.6	93.2	101.3	108.3
1972	83.3	...	47.7	90.6	108.1	116.3
1973	72.2	...	42.1	84.0	117.9	111.5
1974	72.2	...	43.9	86.9	122.3	...

Date / Date / Fecha	EUROPE — EUROPE — EUROPA						
	Austria	Belgique	España	France	Germany, Fed. Rep. of △	Grèce	Hongrie [12]
	II	II	II	. [5]	. [5]	III	III
1965	125.5	. [4]	.	144.3	134.0	.	108.6
1966	119.6	.	.	138.8	124.2	.	107.2
1967	112.0	.	.	130.8	113.7	93.6	103.9
1968	102.4	.	.	120.4	105.1	92.3	103.3
1969	97.6	.	.	106.1 [11]	101.5	96.7	102.6
1970	100.0	100.0	100.0	100.0	100.0	100.0	100.0
1971	95.8	94.2	94.0	94.7	100.0	100.4	97.4
1972	94.6	90.1	91.5	90.4	97.0	101.7	93.4
1973	90.1	80.9	86.9	85.1	95.5	100.9	92.1
1974	88.9	73.5	84.7	79.8 *	94.3	...	91.4

EXPLANATORY NOTES AND CODES: See p. 297.

1 Iron ore and prospecting, extraction and refining of crude oil. 2 Extraction of crude oil and gas only. 3 Incl. employers and workers on own account. 4 June of each year. 5 Official estimates. 6 Series linked to former series. 7 Incl. workers on own account and unpaid family workers. 8 Excl. quarrying. 9 July of each year. 10 March and Sep. of each year. 11 Series replacing former series. 12 State industry.

NOTES EXPLICATIVES ET CODES: Voir p. 300.

1 Minerai de fer et prospection, exploitation et raffinage du pétrole brut. 2 Extraction du pétrole brut et du gaz seulement. 3 Y compris les employeurs et les personnes travaillant à leur propre compte. 4 Juin de chaque année. 5 Evaluations officielles. 6 Série enchaînée à la précédente. 7 Y compris les personnes travaillant à leur propre compte et les travailleurs familiaux non rémunérés. 8 Non compris les carrières. 9 Juillet de chaque année. 10 Mars et sept. de chaque année. 11 Série remplaçant la précédente. 12 Industrie d'Etat.

NOTAS EXPLICATIVAS Y CLAVES: Véase pág. 303.

1 Mineral de hierro y exploración, explotación y refinación del petróleo crudo. 2 Extracción del petróleo crudo y del gas solamente. 3 Incl. los empleadores y los trabajadores por cuenta propia. 4 Junio de cada año. 5 Estimaciones oficiales. 6 Serie enlazada con la anterior. 7 Incl. los trabajadores por cuenta propia y los trabajadores familiares no remunerados. 8 Excl. las canteras. 9 Julio de cada año. 10 Marzo y sept. de cada año. 11 Serie que substituye a la anterior. 12 Industria de Estado.

7 **Employment in mining and quarrying**
Emploi dans les industries extractives
Empleo en las minas y canteras

(Indices: 1970 = 100)

Date / Date / Fecha	EUROPE — EUROPE — EUROPA					
	Ireland	Italie	Luxembourg	Malta	Norway	Pays-Bas [5]
	III	I	III	III	I [3]	. [6]
	1			2		
1965	90.7	95.4	152.5	89.4	86.9	238.1
1966	109.4	95.7	138.9	87.2	87.9	209.5
1967	96.2	94.0	123.5	100.0	88.6	171.4
1968	91.1	100.0	118.8	102.1	94.2	138.1
1969	98.2	103.9	116.5	104.3	95.7	119.0
1970	100.0	100.0	100.0	100.0	100.0	100.0
1971	98.2	99.6	97.2	87.2	.	90.5
1972	100.0	107.1	92.7	112.8	100.0 [4]	76.2
1973	97.2	109.9	...	...	110.0	61.9 *
1974	99.1	108.2	...	...	100.0	47.6 *

Date / Date / Fecha	EUROPE — EUROPE — EUROPA						
	Pologne [7]	Portugal	Roumanie [8]	Sweden [9]	Turquie	United Kingdom [12]	Yugoslavia [15]
	III	III	III	III	II	III [13]	III
					11	14	16
1965	95.7	87.4	100.7	117.3	108.3	155.6	110.1
1966	96.3	98.7	103.1	115.6	97.4	142.7 [10]	107.6
1967	97.7	99.8	101.0	106.8 [10]	111.6	135.7	102.2
1968	97.2	99.5	98.7	100.5	96.1	118.9	99.9
1969	99.2	97.2	97.4	100.7	97.8	106.6	99.7
1970	100.0	100.0	100.0	100.0	100.0	100.0	100.0
1971	101.2	...	100.5	99.3	120.1	96.9 [10]	103.7
1972	103.0	...	100.3	96.8	104.4	92.4	106.2
1973	102.1	...	...	99.8	106.5	88.3	106.0
1974	102.2 *	...	...	...	120.8	83.9	111.3

Date / Date / Fecha	OCEANIA — OCÉANIE — OCEANÍA			URSS [18, 19]	RSS de Biélorussie [19]	RSS d'Ukraine [19]
	Australia	Fiji	New Zealand			
	III	III	III	III	III	III
	14	14	17			
1965	72.4	.	117.6	101.4	82.3	99.6
1966	76.7 [10]	.	119.6	102.9	82.7	101.3
1967	79.1	.	116.3	103.7	90.8	101.6
1968	83.6	.	109.6	103.3	94.2	100.8
1969	90.5	90.5	102.9	101.3	96.5	99.9
1970	100.0	100.0	100.0	100.0	100.0	100.0
1971	106.9	86.8	92.0	99.0	100.8	97.9
1972	107.3	81.7	85.3	97.0	102.3	96.7
1973	107.6	81.9	84.7	95.8	101.2	93.5
1974	110.1	...	86.4	94.2	96.9	92.9

EXPLANATORY NOTES AND CODES: See p. 297.

1 Oct. of each year, except for 1969-72: Sep. 2 Dec. of each year. 3 1965-1970: compulsory health insurance statistics. 4 Series replacing former series. 5 Number of man-years. 6 Official estimates. 7 Socialised sector. Excl. apprentices. Figures include full-time equivalent of part-time workers. Excl. quarrying. 8 Socialised sector. Extraction of coal, oil and gas only. 9 Wage earners only. 10 Series linked to former series. 11 Sep. of each year. 12 Excl. Northern Ireland. Coal mining. 13 Prior to 1971: National insurance statistics. 14 June of each year. 15 Socialised sector. 16 March and Sep. of each year. 17 April and Oct. of each year. 18 Incl. Byelorussian SSR and Ukrainian SSR, shown separately in this table. 19 Socialised sector. Excl. geological surveys.

NOTES EXPLICATIVES ET CODES: Voir p. 300.

1 Oct. de chaque année, sauf pour 1969-1972: sept. 2 Déc. de chaque année. 3 1965-1970: statistiques de l'assurance-maladie obligatoire. 4 Série remplaçant la précédente. 5 Nombre d'années-homme. 6 Evaluations officielles. 7 Secteur socialisé. Non compris les apprentis. Les personnes employées à temps partiel sont converties en unité de travail à temps complet. Non compris les carrières. 8 Secteur socialisé. Extraction de charbon, pétrole et gaz seulement. 9 Ouvriers seulement. 10 Série enchaînée à la précédente. 11 Sept. de chaque année. 12 Non compris l'Irlande du Nord. Mines de charbon. 13 Avant 1971: statistiques de l'assurance nationale. 14 Juin de chaque année. 15 Secteur socialisé. 16 Mars et sept. de chaque année. 17 Avril et oct. de chaque année. 18 Y compris les RSS de Biélorussie et d'Ukraine, figurant séparément dans le tableau. 19 Secteur socialisé. Non compris les recherches géologiques.

NOTAS EXPLICATIVAS Y CLAVES: Véase pág. 303.

1 Oct. de cada año, salvo 1969-1972: sept. 2 Dic. de cada año. 3 1965-1970: estadísticas del seguro obligatorio de enfermedad. 4 Serie que substituye a la anterior. 5 Número de años-hombre. 6 Estimaciones oficiales. 7 Sector socializado. Excl. los aprendices. Las personas empleadas a tiempo parcial son convertidas en unidad de trabajo a pleno tiempo. Excl. las canteras. 8 Sector socializado. Extracción de carbón, petróleo y gas solamente. 9 Obreros solamente. 10 Serie enlazada con la anterior. 11 Sept. de cada año. 12 Excl. Irlanda del Norte. Minas de carbón. 13 Antes de 1971: estadísticas del Seguro Nacional. 14 Junio de cada año. 15 Sector socializado. 16 Marzo y sept. de cada año. 17 Abril y oct. de cada año. 18 Incl. las RSS de Bielorrusia y de Ucrania, que figuran separadamente en este cuadro. 19 Sector socializado. Excl. las investigaciones geológicas.

8 Employment in construction
Emploi dans la construction
Empleo en la construcción

(Indices: 1970 = 100)

Date / Date / Fecha	AFRICA — AFRIQUE — AFRICA					
	Cameroun	Egypt [1]	Gabon	Ghana	Kenya	Malawi [7]
	III	. [2]	II	III	III [5]	III
				[3]	[6]	
1965	102.5	.	35.1	145.9	.	.
1966	127.7	.	65.0	93.0	.	.
1967	133.9	.	59.1	95.6	97.0	28.5
1968	116.3	99.4 *	78.5	109.6	103.5	82.5
1969	100.5	96.1	91.2	115.0	93.9	93.6
1970	**100.0**	**100.0**	**100.0**	**100.0**	**100.0**	**100.0**
1971	100.6	101.4	52.1	88.7	112.9	95.9
1972	96.6	107.6	84.6	96.1 * [4]	114.5	98.2
1973	152.1	126.1	...	...	125.5	114.0
1974	...	...	...	...	...	123.3

Date / Date / Fecha	AFRICA — AFRIQUE — AFRICA						
	Sierra Leone	South Africa, Rep. of		Swaziland	Tanzania (Tanganyika)	Uganda	Zambia
		Total	. [8]				
	III	III		III [9]	III	III	III
	[3]	[6]	[6]		[6]	[6]	[10]
1965	175.8	50.7	61.2	.	68.8	68.2	65.6
1966	146.7	62.8	73.9	.	64.3	61.1	90.7
1967	119.9	70.4	82.3	.	73.8	67.9	94.5
1968	99.7	76.5	84.9	.	71.9	88.1	97.0
1969	105.7	87.3	91.3	.	73.3	88.9	88.4
1970	**100.0**	**100.0**	**100.0**	**100.0**	**100.0**	**100.0**	**100.0**
1971	108.5	107.7	101.3	109.0	...	99.4	98.4
1972	103.7	107.9	98.3	155.9	...	90.8	100.8
1973	84.2	109.3	99.2	169.7	...	93.1	109.7
1974	93.6	...	...	...	...	...	108.2 [11]

Date / Date / Fecha	AMERICA — AMÉRIQUE — AMÉRICA					
	Belize	Canada	El Salvador [13]	Puerto Rico	Trinidad and Tobago	United States
	III	III	III	I	III	III
	[12]					
1965	57.5	104.0	164.0	.	.	90.1
1966	69.3	113.2	186.9	.	.	92.6
1967	47.0	107.6	175.5	.	.	90.7
1968	89.3	104.8	123.9	.	.	93.5
1969	**100.0**	104.6	125.1	91.1	91.1	99.7
1970	...	**100.0**	**100.0**	**100.0**	**100.0**	**100.0**
1971	...	101.4	103.2	105.1	105.4	102.9
1972	...	96.3	100.7	96.2	107.1 *	108.3
1973	...	96.5 *	93.4	102.5	...	113.9
1974	...	102.8 *	119.7	91.1	...	112.7

EXPLANATORY NOTES AND CODES: See p. 297.

[1] Civilian labour force employed (official estimates).
[2] May of each year. [3] Dec. of each year. [4] Sep.
[5] Excl. employment in rural areas (except for large enterprises). [6] June of each year. [7] Incl. working proprietors and unpaid family workers. [8] White population.
[9] Sep. of each year. [10] Beginning 1967: June and Dec.
[11] June. [12] March of each year. [13] Area of San Salvador.

NOTES EXPLICATIVES ET CODES: Voir p. 300.

[1] Main-d'œuvre civile occupée (évaluations officielles).
[2] Mai de chaque année. [3] Déc. de chaque année. [4] Sept.
[5] Non compris l'emploi dans les zones rurales (à l'exception des grandes entreprises). [6] Juin de chaque année.
[7] Y compris les propriétaires-exploitants et les travailleurs familiaux non rémunérés. [8] Population blanche. [9] Sept. de chaque année. [10] A partir de 1967: juin et déc.
[11] Juin. [12] Mars de chaque année. [13] Zone de San Salvador.

NOTAS EXPLICATIVAS Y CLAVES: Véase pág. 303.

[1] Fuerza trabajadora civil ocupada (estimaciones oficiales). [2] Mayo de cada año. [3] Dic. de cada año.
[4] Sept. [5] Excl. el empleo en las zonas rurales (con excepción de las grandes empresas). [6] Junio de cada año.
[7] Incl. los empresarios propietarios y los trabajadores familiares no remunerados. [8] Población blanca.
[9] Sept. de cada año. [10] A partir de 1967: junio y dic.
[11] Junio. [12] Marzo de cada año. [13] Zona de San Salvador.

8 Employment in construction
Emploi dans la construction
Empleo en la construcción

(Indices: 1970 = 100)

Date / Date / Fecha	ASIA — ASIE — ASIA						
	Brunei	Cyprus	Israel	Japan	Korea, Rep. of	Philippines	Singapore
	III [1]	. [3]	II	I	I	III	III
	[2]						[5]
1965	.	.	111.6	86.8	.	.	.
1966	.	.	94.6	92.8	.	119.1	.
1967	.	90.1	73.8	96.4 [4]	.	130.7	.
1968	.	94.1	80.1 [4]	96.7	.	137.9	.
1969	.	98.5	89.0	94.8	.	167.5	93.5
1970	.	100.0	100.0	100.0	100.0	100.0	100.0
1971	.	102.5	110.7	105.9	142.8	97.7	107.9
1972	100.0	104.0	120.0	111.8	163.5	83.9	127.9
1973	86.4	111.9 *	118.0	119.3	156.8	60.6	155.4
1974	76.8	90.6 *	114.2	117.4	189.6	64.2	...

Date / Date / Fecha	EUROPE — EUROPE — EUROPA					
	Albanie [6]	Austria	Belgique	Bulgarie [6]	Czechoslovakia [6]	Denmark [7]
	.	II	II	III	III	III
			[2]			
1965	79.6	103.3	.	73.9	86.7	92.5
1966	78.7	106.2	.	82.7	90.3	90.2
1967	82.5	104.9	.	90.7	92.3	94.4
1968	86.8	98.9	.	92.2	95.2	93.1 [4]
1969	98.8	96.0	.	93.6	96.8	99.7
1970	100.0	100.0	100.0	100.0	100.0	100.0
1971	104.0	102.6	101.0	102.4	103.2	99.1
1972	...	107.0	96.6	103.8	105.7	95.2
1973	...	113.1	95.6	103.7	109.7	94.8
1974	...	113.2	98.6	106.4 *	112.3	89.8

Date / Date / Fecha	EUROPE — EUROPE — EUROPA					
	España	Finland	France	German Democratic Rep. △	Germany, Fed. Rep. of △	Hongrie [9]
	II	I	. [3]	.	. [3]	III
1965	.	.	91.9	79.3	106.6	80.8
1966	.	.	94.2	79.5	105.0	82.8
1967	.	.	95.1	82.0	95.4	84.7
1968	.	.	95.7	90.0	98.2	91.2
1969	.	100.6	98.7 [8]	96.3	100.1	97.3
1970	100.0	100.0	100.0	100.0	100.0	100.0
1971	100.6	97.7	99.0	101.5	101.1	104.6
1972	103.7	96.0	98.8	103.6	101.4	108.8
1973	109.3	96.0	99.6	104.6	99.7	111.1
1974	111.5	...	99.8 *	106.1	88.9	112.6

EXPLANATORY NOTES AND CODES: See p. 297.

[1] Incl. employers and workers on own account. [2] June of each year. [3] Official estimates. [4] Series linked to former series. [5] March and Sep. of each year. [6] Socialised sector. [7] Wage earners only. May of each year, except for 1969: June. [8] Series replacing former series. [9] State industry.

NOTES EXPLICATIVES ET CODES: Voir p. 300.

[1] Y compris les employeurs et les personnes travaillant à leur propre compte. [2] Juin de chaque année. [3] Evaluations officielles. [4] Série enchaînée à la précédente. [5] Mars et sept. de chaque année. [6] Secteur socialisé. [7] Ouvriers seulement. Mai de chaque année, sauf pour 1969 : juin. [8] Série remplaçant la précédente. [9] Industrie d'Etat.

NOTAS EXPLICATIVAS Y CLAVES: Véase pág. 303.

[1] Incl. los empleadores y los trabajadores por cuenta propia. [2] Junio de cada año. [3] Estimaciones oficiales. [4] Serie enlazada con la anterior. [5] Marzo y sept. de cada año. [6] Sector socializado. [7] Obreros solamente. Mayo de cada año, salvo 1969: junio. [8] Serie que substituye a la anterior. [9] Industria de Estado.

EMPLOYMENT

8 Employment in construction
Emploi dans la construction
Empleo en la construcción

(Indices: 1970 = 100)

Date / Date / Fecha	EUROPE — EUROPE — EUROPA					
	Ireland	Italie	Luxembourg	Malta	Norway	Pays-Bas [5]
	II	I	III	III	I [3]	. [6]
				[2]		
1965	107.6	102.0	94.6	51.0	91.6	90.7
1966	100.6	96.5	91.6	73.0	92.4	91.8
1967	95.3	98.3	78.6	77.2	96.9	89.1
1968	100.4	96.8	76.9	79.0	95.2	93.0
1969	101.1	100.0	86.5	93.7	97.3	97.3
1970	92.4	100.0	100.0	100.0	100.0	100 0
1971	100.0	100.5	127.5	83.4	.	98.0
1972	101.0	96.8	129.5	53.4	100.0 [4]	93.4
1973	101.8	92.8	...	...	99.2	93.4 *
1974	...	92.9	...	...	103.4	89.6 *

Date / Date / Fecha	EUROPE — EUROPE — EUROPA					
	Pologne [7]	Roumanie [8]	Suisse [9]	Turquie	United Kingdom	Yugoslavia [8]
	III	III	III	II	III [11]	III
				[10]	[12]	[14]
1965	85.4	75.1	106.1	62.0	121.4	95.5
1966	87.7	80.3	105.7	70.6	123.2 [13]	89.2
1967	92.5	89.2	102.7	74.5	116.5	88.2
1968	96.4	92.9	99.8	87.7	113.9	91.1
1969	100.3	94.9	98.8	94.8	109.2 [13]	95.8
1970	100.0	100.0	100.0	100.0	100.0	100.0
1971	105.0	104.6	105.8	97.6	94.5 [13]	102.7
1972	111.8	109.3	110.6	108.0	97.3	104.0
1973	123.1 *	108.4	107.4	116.4	103.3	101.8
1974	...	104.8	98.5	129.9	99.5	108.0

Date / Date / Fecha	OCEANIA — OCÉANIE — OCEANÍA			URSS [8, 16]	RSS de Biélorussie [8]	RSS d'Ukraine [18]
	Australia	Fiji	New Zealand			
	III	III	III	III	III	III
	[12]	[12]	[15]	[17]	[17]	[17]
1965	90.7	.	102.2	80.7	68.6	78.5
1966	94.2 [13]	.	105.4	83.4	75.6	82.6
1967	92.0	.	103.9	87.1	81.3	87.6
1968	95.2	.	96.7	90.0	86.0	91.0
1969	97.7	105.8	97.9	94.7	93.2	94.5
1970	100.0	100.0	100.0	100.0	100.0	100.0
1971	103.2	111.1	100.6	105.5	105.8	105.2
1972	104.5	111.3	102.0	110.3	110.6	109.2
1973	105.2	127.7	105.4	111.5	113.5	109.2
1974	106.8	...	109.1	113.3	115.9	110.7

EXPLANATORY NOTES AND CODES: See p. 297.

[1] Oct. of each year, except for 1969-70: Sep. [2] Dec. of each year. [3] 1965-70: compulsory health insurance statistics. [4] Series replacing former series. [5] Number of man-years. [6] Official estimates. [7] Socialised sector. Excl. apprentices. Figures include full-time equivalent of part-time workers. [8] Socialised sector. [9] Wage earners only. [10] Sep. of each year. [11] Prior to 1971: National insurance statistics. [12] June of each year. [13] Series linked to former series. [14] March and Sep. of each year. [15] April and Oct. of each year. [16] Incl. Byelorussian SSR and Ukrainian SSR, shown separately in this table. [17] Incl. capital repairs and geological survey. [18] Socialised sector. Workers engaged in actual construction and erection processes.

NOTES EXPLICATIVES ET CODES: Voir p. 300.

[1] Oct. de chaque année, sauf pour 1969-1970: sept. [2] Déc. de chaque année. [3] 1965-1970: statistiques de l'assurance-maladie obligatoire. [4] Série remplaçant la précédente. [5] Nombre d'années-homme. [6] Evaluations officielles. [7] Secteur socialisé. Non compris les apprentis. Les personnes employées à temps partiel sont converties en unité de travail à temps complet. [8] Secteur socialisé. [9] Ouvriers seulement. [10] Sept. de chaque année. [11] Avant 1971: statistiques de l'assurance nationale. [12] Juin de chaque année. [13] Série enchaînée à la précédente. [14] Mars et sept. de chaque année. [15] Avril et oct. de chaque année. [16] Y compris les RSS de Biélorussie et d'Ukraine, figurant séparément dans ce tableau. [17] Y compris l'entretien des biens d'équipement et les recherches géologiques. [18] Secteur socialisé. Travailleurs effectivement occupés à la construction.

NOTAS EXPLICATIVAS Y CLAVES: Véase pág. 303.

[1] Oct. de cada año, salvo 1969-70: sept. [2] Dic. de cada año. [3] 1965-1970: estadísticas del seguro obligatorio de enfermedad. [4] Serie que substituye a la anterior. [5] Número de años-hombre. [6] Estimaciones oficiales. [7] Sector socializado. Excl. los aprendices. Las personas empleadas a tiempo parcial son convertidas en unidad de trabajo a pleno tiempo. [8] Sector socializado. [9] Obreros solamente. [10] Sept. de cada año. [11] Antes de 1971: estadísticas del Seguro Nacional. [12] Junio de cada año. [13] Serie enlazada con la anterior. [14] Marzo y sept. de cada año. [15] Abril y oct. de cada año. [16] Incl. las RSS de Bielorrusia y de Ucrania, que figuran separadamente en este cuadro. [17] Incl. la conservación de los bienes de producción y las investigaciones geológicas. [18] Sector socializado. Trabajadores ocupados efectivamente en la construcción.

9 Employment in transport, storage and communication
Emploi dans les transports, entrepôts et communications
Empleo en los transportes, almacenaje y comunicaciones

(Indices: 1970 = 100)

Date / Date / Fecha	AFRICA — AFRIQUE — AFRICA						
	Cameroun	Egypt [1]	Gabon	Ghana	Kenya	Malawi [7]	Mauritius [8]
	III	. [2]	II	III	III [5]	III	III
				3	6		
1965	75.8	.	48.0	93.5	.	.	.
1966	75.2	.	55.1	96.9	.	.	.
1967	93.6	.	41.7	92.1	103.6	74.1	84.0
1968	142.3	80.1	83.2	111.8	114.2	96.2	89.6
1969	144.6	92.9	97.8	90.9	115.3	98.4	93.9
1970	100.0	100.0	100.0	100.0	100.0	100.0	100.0
1971	66.6	88.3	112.1	98.5	101.5	105.5	108.3
1972	64.6	92.9	134.9	99.3 * [4]	101.5	115.0	123.6
1973	100.8	96.5	...	...	103.3	123.7	137.9
1974	...	...	...	...	...	134.0	160.7

Date / Date / Fecha	AFRICA — AFRIQUE — AFRICA						
	Sierra Leone	South Africa, Rep. of [9]		Swaziland	Tanzania (Tanganyika)	Uganda	Zambia
		Total	. [10]				
	III	III		III [11]	III	III	III
	3				6	6	12
1965	99.8	97.0	98.3	.	66.1	81.2	65.3
1966	118.3	97.0	100.3	.	76.8	78.0	89.2
1967	102.9	96.1	99.4	.	93.0	84.7	87.1
1968	102.2	97.4	100.0	.	88.8	87.3	99.4
1969	98.1	98.8	100.3	.	100.0	93.7	100.5
1970	100.0	100.0	100.0	100.0	100.0	100.0	100.0
1971	116.3	103.2	102.9	109.2	...	104.8	98.3
1972	109.4	103.5	101.7	121.5	...	99.2	115.2
1973	114.2	104.7	101.0	143.2	...	94.4	113.4
1974	96.3	...	...	...	...	...	116.3 [13]

Date / Date / Fecha	AMERICA — AMÉRIQUE — AMÉRICA						
	Belize	Canada	El Salvador [15]	Panamá	Puerto Rico	Trinidad and Tobago	United States
	III	III	III	II	I	III	III
	14			16			
1965	59.2	93.1	79.3	66.8	.	.	89.6
1966	67.4	95.5	85.4	71.0	.	.	92.2
1967	94.2	98.5	113.6	81.6	.	.	94.6
1968	96.0	97.2	109.8	88.0	.	.	95.7
1969	100.0	99.4	107.8	90.1	100.0	90.6	98.5
1970	...	100.0	100.0	100.0	100.0	100.0	100.0
1971	...	101.8	97.0	105.7	102.6	130.7	99.0
1972	...	103.0	102.2	108.2	107.9	124.0 *	100.3
1973	...	104.8 *	98.1	112.0 [17]	110.5	...	103.2
1974	...	110.7 *	97.6	...	107.9	...	104.3

EXPLANATORY NOTES AND CODES: See p. 297.

[1] Civilian labour force employed (official estimates). [2] May of each year. [3] Dec. of each year. [4] Sep. [5] Excl. employment in rural areas (except for large enterprises). [6] June of each year. [7] Incl. working proprietors and unpaid family workers. [8] March and Sep. of each year. Excl. relief workers. [9] Excl. storage. [10] White population. [11] Sep. of each year. [12] Beginning 1967: June and Dec. [13] June. [14] March of each year. [15] Area of San Salvador. [16] Aug. of each year. [17] March.

NOTES EXPLICATIVES ET CODES: Voir p. 300.

[1] Main-d'œuvre civile occupée (évaluations officielles). [2] Mai de chaque année. [3] Déc. de chaque année. [4] Sept. [5] Non compris l'emploi dans les zones rurales (à l'exception des grandes entreprises). [6] Juin de chaque année. [7] Y compris les propriétaires-exploitants et les travailleurs familiaux non rémunérés. [8] Mars et sept. de chaque année. Non compris les personnes occupées à des travaux publics de secours. [9] Non compris les entrepôts. [10] Population blanche. [11] Sept. de chaque année. [12] A partir de 1967 : juin et déc. [13] Juin. [14] Mars de chaque année. [15] Zone de San Salvador. [16] Août de chaque année. [17] Mars.

NOTAS EXPLICATIVAS Y CLAVES: Véase pág. 303.

[1] Fuerza trabajadora civil ocupada (estimaciones oficiales). [2] Mayo de cada año. [3] Dic. de cada año. [4] Sept. [5] Excl. el empleo en las zonas rurales (con excepción de las grandes empresas). [6] Junio de cada año. [7] Incl. los empresarios propietarios y los trabajadores no remunerados. [8] Marzo y sept. de cada año. Excl. las personas ocupadas en planes de asistencia. [9] Excl. el almacenaje. [10] Población blanca. [11] Sept. de cada año. [12] A partir de 1967: junio y dic. [13] Junio. [14] Marzo de cada año. [15] Zona de San Salvador. [16] Agosto de cada año. [17] Marzo.

EMPLOYMENT

9 Employment in transport, storage and communication
Emploi dans les transports, entrepôts et communications
Empleo en los transportes, almacenaje y comunicaciones

(Indices: 1970 = 100)

Date / Date / Fecha	ASIA — ASIE — ASIA						
	Brunei	Cyprus	Hong Kong	India[4]	Israel	Japan[7]	Korea, Rep. of
	III[1]	.[3]	III	III	II	I	I
	[2]			[5]			
1965	.	.	89.4	93.3	83.3	83.5	.
1966	.	.	97.0	96.1	84.0	88.3	.
1967	.	80.9	86.6	97.6	83.0	90.9[6]	.
1968	.	88.2	89.2	98.1	88.4[6]	93.8	.
1969	.	98.5	92.1	98.4	97.6	95.9	.
1970	.	100.0	100.0	100.0	100.0	100.0	100.0
1971	.	100.9	103.1	102.4	106.4	102.4	113.7
1972	100.0	102.4	103.2	104.0	109.1	99.7	102.0
1973	150.5	102.8 *	106.8	105.1	110.5	103.5	105.7
1974	160.9	86.8 *	112.2	107.3	112.5	100.6	103.3

Date / Date / Fecha	ASIA — ASIE — ASIA			EUROPE — EUROPE — EUROPA		
	Malaysia / West Malaysia	Philippines	Singapore	Albanie[10]	Austria	Belgique
	III	III	III	.	II	II
	[8]		[9]			[2]
1965	92.9	.	.	79.0	90.8	.
1966	94.2	93.1	.	77.7	92.1	.
1967	.	92.6	.	80.5	90.8	.
1968	.	95.3	.	88.1	90.6	.
1969	.	96.6	96.2	92.7	103.4	.
1970	.	100.0	100.0	100.0	100.0	100.0
1971	100.0	99.3	112.0	120.4	98.3	104.1
1972	100.6	117.9	121.9	...	102.3	107.1
1973	103.9	133.7	132.8	...	105.7	110.8
1974	106.4	135.0	...	...	...	113.5

Date / Date / Fecha	EUROPE — EUROPE — EUROPA					
	Bulgarie[11]	Czechoslovakia[11]	España[12]	Finland	France	German Democratic Rep. △
	III	III	II	I	.[3]	.
1965	79.7	87.8	.	.	93.4	95.1
1966	83.7	89.5	.	.	94.4	95.2
1967	87.4	91.4	.	.	95.4	95.3
1968	92.8	93.1	.	.	96.6	94.9
1969	94.5	98.5	.	96.2	98.7[13]	97.1
1970	100.0	100.0	100.0	100.0	100.0	100.0
1971	103.5	100.6	103.1	95.4	100.0	101.2
1972	106.0	100.4	109.5	100.8	100.3	101.6
1973	109.8	101.3	134.8	100.0	101.8	102.3
1974	114.8 *	101.9	137.9	...	104.8 *	103.8

EXPLANATORY NOTES AND CODES: See p. 297.

[1] Incl. employers and workers on own account. [2] June of each year. [3] Official estimates. [4] Posts, telegraphs and railways. [5] March of each year. [6] Series linked to former series. [7] Incl. electricity, gas, water and sanitary services. [8] July of each year. [9] March and Sep. of each year. [10] Socialised sector. Excl. storage. [11] Socialised sector. [12] Excl. some enterprises not affiliated to the national social security system. [13] Series replacing former series.

NOTES EXPLICATIVES ET CODES: Voir p. 300.

[1] Y compris les employeurs et les personnes travaillant à leur propre compte. [2] Juin de chaque année. [3] Evaluations officielles. [4] Postes, télégraphes et chemins de fer. [5] Mars de chaque année. [6] Série enchaînée à la précédente. [7] Y compris l'électricité, le gaz, l'eau et les services sanitaires. [8] Juillet de chaque année. [9] Mars et sept. de chaque année. [10] Secteur socialisé. Non compris les entrepôts. [11] Secteur socialisé. [12] Non compris certaines entreprises non affiliées aux caisses nationales de sécurité sociale. [13] Série remplaçant la précédente.

NOTAS EXPLICATIVAS Y CLAVES: Véase pág. 303.

[1] Incl. los empleadores y los trabajadores por cuenta propia. [2] Junio de cada año. [3] Estimaciones oficiales. [4] Correo, telégrafo y ferrocarriles. [5] Marzo de cada año. [6] Serie enlazada con la anterior. [7] Incl. la electricidad, el gas, el agua y los servicios sanitarios. [8] Julio de cada año. [9] Marzo y sept. de cada año. [10] Sector socializado. Excl. el almacenaje. [11] Sector socializado. [12] Excl. ciertas empresas no afiliadas a las cajas de seguridad social. [13] Serie que substituye a la anterior.

9 Employment in transport, storage and communication
Emploi dans les transports, entrepôts et communications
Empleo en los transportes, almacenaje y comunicaciones

(Indices 1970 = 100)

Date / Date / Fecha	EUROPE — EUROPE — EUROPA					
	Germany, Fed. Rep. of △	Hongrie 2	Ireland		Italie	Malta
			Railways / Chemins de fer / Ferrocarriles	Road transport / Transports par route / Transportes por carretera		
	. 1	III	III		I	III
			3	4		5
1965	106.8	94.9	105.5	86.7	99.3	89.3
1966	104.7	94.4	102.2	88.0	99.6	88.1
1967	102.8	94.4	105.9	89.2	98.8	85.9
1968	100.7	95.8	103.0	94.3	97.0	92.0
1969	99.7	96.3	104.6	94.4	99.4	95.9
1970	**100.0**	**100.0**	**100.0**	**100.0**	**100.0**	**100.0**
1971	103.6	101.7	102.2	102.4	100.7	97.6
1972	106.1	102.3	98.9	106.6	103.9	91.7
1973	107.4	103.7	95.3	107.4	105.3	...
1974	107.7	105.1	...	...	109.6	...

Date / Date / Fecha	EUROPE — EUROPE — EUROPA						
	Norway	Pays-Bas 8	Pologne 9	Roumanie 10	Turquie 11	United Kingdom	Yugoslavia 10
	I 6	. 1	III	III	II	III 13	III
					12	14	16
1965	104.9	98.5	84.5	85.4	69.4	104.9	93.2
1966	104.3	99.6	89.7	88.9	92.1	103.2 15	91.4
1967	104.0	98.9	91.6	92.5	82.0	102.8	92.5
1968	103.7	98.2	94.2	92.7	93.3	101.6	94.6
1969	101.9	98.5	97.7	94.1	99.1	99.2 15	96.7
1970	**100.0**	**100.0**	**100.0**	**100.0**	**100.0**	**100.0**	**100.0**
1971	.	101.5	102.9	102.4	112.2	99.8 15	104.0
1972	*100.0 7*	100.0	106.3	105.5	128.6	98.2	108.4
1973	*100.0*	100.7 *	107.3	109.5	128.2	97.0	110.6
1974	*99.1*	100.4 *	...	109.5	148.5	95.9	113.6

Date / Date / Fecha	OCEANIA — OCÉANIE — OCEANÍA			URSS 18, 19	RSS de Biélorussie 19	RSS d'Ukraine 19
	Australia	Fiji	New Zealand			
	III	III	III	III	III	III
	14	14	17			
1965	88.6	.	96.9	88.7	82.9	84.6
1966	90.9 15	.	98.0	90.6	85.8	87.3
1967	92.4	.	98.9	92.2	88.2	89.9
1968	94.8	.	98.2	94.4	92.4	92.8
1969	96.6	78.6	98.2	97.3	96.8	96.3
1970	**100.0**	**100.0**	**100.0**	**100.0**	**100.0**	**100.0**
1971	102.3	119.2	105.2	103.0	103.4	103.7
1972	102.3	134.6	105.6	106.1	107.2	106.8
1973	104.1	126.4	107.8	110.5	109.2	109.0
1974	108.3	...	111.7	112.5	115.9	110.6

EXPLANATORY NOTES AND CODES: See p. 297.

1 Official estimates. 2 State industry. 3 March of each year. 4 Feb. of each year. Incl. working proprietors. 5 Dec. of each year. 6 1965-70: compulsory health insurance statistics. 7 Series replacing former series. 8 Number of man-years. 9 Socialised sector. Excl. apprentices. Figures include full-time equivalent of part-time workers. 10 Socialised sector. 11 Excl. air transport. 12 Sep. of each year. 13 Prior to 1971: National insurance statistics. 14 June of each year. 15 Series linked to former series. 16 March and Sep. of each year. 17 April and Oct. of each year. 18 Incl. Byelorussian SSR and Ukrainian SSR, shown separately in this table. 19 Socialised sector. Excl. storage.

NOTES EXPLICATIVES ET CODES: Voir p. 300.

1 Evaluations officielles. 2 Industrie d'Etat. 3 Mars de chaque année. 4 Fév. de chaque année. Y compris les propriétaires-exploitants. 5 Déc. de chaque année. 6 1965-1970 : statistiques de l'assurance-maladie obligatoire. 7 Série remplaçant la précédente. 8 Nombre d'années-homme. 9 Secteur socialisé. Non compris les apprentis. Les personnes employées à temps partiel sont converties en unité de travail à temps complet. 10 Secteur socialisé. 11 Non compris les transports aériens. 12 Sept. de chaque année. 13 Avant 1971 : statistique de l'assurance nationale. 14 Juin de chaque année. 15 Série enchaînée à la précédente. 16 Mars et sept. de chaque année. 17 Avril et oct. de chaque année. 18 Y compris les RSS de Biélorussie et d'Ukraine, figurant séparément dans ce tableau. 19 Secteur socialisé. Non compris les entrepôts.

NOTAS EXPLICATIVAS Y CLAVES: Véase pág. 303.

1 Estimaciones oficiales. 2 Industria de Estado. 3 Marzo de cada año. 4 Febr. de cada año. Incl. los propietarios que trabajan. 5 Dic. de cada año. 6 1965-1970: estadísticas del seguro obligatorio de enfermedad. 7 Serie que substituye a la anterior. 8 Número de años-hombre. 9 Sector socializado. Excl. los aprendices Las personas empleadas a tiempo parcial son convertidas en unidad de trabajo a pleno tiempo. 10 Sector socializado. 11 Excl. el transporte aéreo. 12 Sept. de cada año. 13 Antes de 1971: estadísticas del Seguro Nacional. 14 Junio de cada año. 15 Serie enlazada con la anterior. 16 Marzo y sept. de cada año. 17 Abril y oct. de cada año. 18 Incl. las RSS de Bielorrusia y de Ucrania, que figuran separadamente en este cuadro. 19 Sector socializado. Excl. el almacenaje.

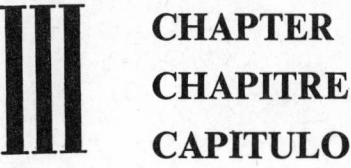

CHAPTER
CHAPITRE
CAPITULO

Unemployment

Chômage

Desempleo

Unemployment

Unemployment is defined as follows in the Resolution concerning statistics of the labour force, employment and unemployment, adopted by the Eighth International Conference of Labour Statisticians (Geneva, 1954) [1]:

(1) Persons in unemployment consist of all persons above a specified age who, on the specified day or for a specified week, were in the following categories:

(a) workers available for employment whose contract of employment had been terminated or temporarily suspended and who were without a job and seeking work for pay or profit;

(b) persons who were available for work (except for minor illness) during the specified period and were seeking work for pay or profit, who were never previously employed or whose most recent status was other than that of employee (i.e. former employers, etc.), or who had been in retirement;

(c) persons without a job and currently available for work who had made arrangements to start a new job at a date subsequent to the specified period;

(d) persons on temporary or indefinite lay-off without pay.

(2) The following categories of persons are not considered to be unemployed:

(a) persons intending to establish their own business or farm, but who had not yet arranged to do so, who were not seeking work for pay or profit;

(b) former unpaid family workers not at work and not seeking work for pay or profit.

In general, the statistics on unemployment shown in this chapter relate to the wholly unemployed, i.e. to persons out of work and seeking employment, either on a particular day or during a relatively short period (e.g. one week). Persons who have not worked owing to sickness, accident or industrial disputes are usually excluded, but partially unemployed persons are sometimes included.

In most cases, the series on unemployment presented in this chapter relate to the entire geographical area of a country but rural areas are often less well covered than other areas in most unemployment statistics.

In some cases, the statistics cover all members of the labour force or all employees; however, usually the data refer only to wage earners and lower-paid salaried employees. Persons employed in mining and manufacturing are more fully covered than persons employed in other non-agricultural industries.

For various reasons, the definitions of " unemployed " adopted in the national statistical series often differ from the recommended international standard definition. The national definitions used vary from one country to another as regards in particular age limits, reference periods, criteria for seeking work, minimum limits of time worked, treatment of persons temporarily laid off, and treatment of first-time job seekers. [2]

Four main types of unemployment statistics may be distinguished (indicated in the table headings by the codes I, II, III and IV).

I. *Labour force sample surveys.* When based on adequate sampling methods, labour force sample surveys have proved in practice to be a satisfactory and reliable method of estimating unemployment. This technique generally yields the best over-all statistics on employment since, in particular, it includes groups of persons who are not covered in unemployment statistics obtained by other methods (e.g. persons seeking jobs for the first time); also changes in legislation, administrative regulations and the like do not affect the continuity of the series. It should be noted that the definition of unemployment used for this type of statistics differs fundamentally from the definitions appli-

---

[1] See ILO: *International Recommendations on Labour Statistics* (Geneva, 1976).

[2] For the descriptions of the various national series, their scope, methods of compilation used, etc., see ILO: *Technical Guide 1976* (description of general series published in the *Bulletin* and the *Year Book of Labour Statistics*), Vol. II, " Employment — Unemployment — Hours of work — Wages " (Geneva, 1976).

For a general discussion of problems associated with the compilation of unemployment statistics see ILO: *Employment, Unemployment and Labour Force Statistics, A Study of Methods*, Studies and Reports, New Series, No. 7, Part I (Geneva, 1948).

cable in the case of the other types of statistics described below. This follows from the procedure of counting as employed persons who have performed any work for pay or profit during the survey week. The percentages of unemployment have been calculated by relating the estimated numbers of persons unemployed to the civilian labour force (employed plus unemployed) derived from the same surveys.

II. *Compulsory unemployment insurance statistics.* These statistics, as a rule, have a broad industrial coverage. Their scope is laid down by the insurance legislation and administrative regulations; in general, the data relate to wage earners and salaried employees or to wage earners only. The percentages of unemployment are computed by comparing the number of insured unemployed to the total number of insured workers. The comparability of the percentages from country to country is affected by differences in scope of the insurance legislation, as well as by differences in administrative regulations in force. The comparability of the percentages over a period of time within the same country is subject to reservations if important changes have taken place in the insurance legislation or in administrative regulations governing the registration of the unemployed.

III. *Statistics of trade union benefit funds.* The scope of these statistics is determined by the degree of development of trade unions, the rules for admission of members to the unions and to the union benefit fund, and by the number of unions reporting. The fluctuations in the number and percentages of unemployed reported are influenced by the growth and contraction of the various trade unions and of their benefit funds. The extent to which statistics of this type are representative of the general state of unemployment in a country is therefore difficult and frequently impossible to ascertain.

IV. *Employment office statistics.* These series usually refer to the numbers of applicants for work on the registers at the end of each month. They may include, in addition to persons without a job, persons on strike, or temporarily ill and unable to work and persons engaged on an employment relief project. In principle, these statistics do not include persons who, although in employment, wish to change their job and are therefore registered at employment offices; such persons are however covered by certain series.

The value of these statistics varies widely. In cases where the employment offices function in close connection with unemployment insurance, registration being a qualifying condition for the receipt of unemployment benefits, they are comparable in reliability to insurance statistics. Employment offices operating in close connection with large unemployment relief schemes may also provide reasonably satisfactory figures during the currency of such schemes. However, where registration is entirely voluntary, and especially where the employment offices function only in the more populous regions of a country or are not widely patronised by employees seeking work or by employers seeking workers, the data are generally very incomplete and do not give a reliable indication of the extent of unemployment. The scope of the figures is determined partly by the manner in which the system of exchanges is organised and the advantages which registration brings, and partly by the extent to which workers are accustomed to register. In many cases persons employed in the mining and manufacturing industries utilise the offices to a greater degree than those engaged in transport, commerce and services, while persons engaged in agriculture and living in less populous areas may scarcely be represented in the statistics at all. The scope of employment exchange statistics is therefore most difficult to ascertain, and in very few cases can satisfactory percentages of unemployment be calculated. In general, these statistics are not comparable from country to country, though their fluctuations within a country may reflect changes in the prevalence of unemployment.

As of the 1974 issue of the *Year Book*, changes have been made in the presentation of the data shown in certain tables owing to the introduction

of the revised 1968 editions of the International Standard Industrial Classification of all Economic Activities (ISIC) and of the International Standard Classification of Occupations (ISCO); see " Preface ".

Table 10

General level of unemployment

As far as possible, the statistics in this table are presented in absolute numbers (in thousands), and in percentages. The *numbers* indicate the size of the problem of unemployment within the fields covered by the respective series. Fluctuations in numbers unemployed reflect not only seasonal and other variations in economic activity but also, over a period, the effects of changes in the size of the population and its industrial and social structure; depending on the type of series used, they may also be influenced by changes in legislation or administrative organisation.

The *percentages* illustrate the severity of unemployment within the fields covered by the respective series. They are calculated by relating the number of workers in the given group who are unemployed during the reference period (usually a particular day or a given week) to the total of employed and unemployed persons in the group at the same date.

Table 11

Unemployment by industrial or occupational groups

This table presents the numbers of persons unemployed (in some cases, applicants for work) in the different industrial or occupational groups.

The remarks made on the general series in table 10 apply here also.

Chômage

La résolution concernant les statistiques de la main-d'œuvre, de l'emploi et du chômage, adoptée par la huitième Conférence internationale des statisticiens du travail (Genève, 1954)[1], donne du chômage la définition suivante:

1) Les personnes en chômage sont toutes les personnes qui ont dépassé un âge spécifié, et qui, un jour spécifié ou une semaine spécifiée, rentrent dans les catégories suivantes:

a) travailleurs à même de prendre un emploi et dont le contrat d'emploi a pris fin ou a été temporairement interrompu, et qui se trouvent sans emploi et en quête de travail rémunéré;

b) personnes à même de travailler (sauf maladies bénignes) durant la période spécifiée et en quête de travail rémunéré, qui n'ont jamais eu d'emploi auparavant, ou dont la dernière position dans la profession n'était pas celle de salarié (c'est-à-dire les anciens employeurs, etc.) ou qui avaient cessé de travailler;

c) personnes sans emploi qui sont normalement à même de travailler immédiatement et ont pris leurs dispositions en vue de commencer à travailler dans un nouvel emploi à une date postérieure à la période spécifiée;

d) personnes mises à pied temporairement ou pour une durée indéfinie, sans rémunération;

2) Ne sont pas considérées comme personnes en chômage:

a) les personnes qui ont l'intention d'ouvrir une entreprise ou une exploitation agricole à leur propre compte, mais qui n'ont pas encore pris leurs dispositions pour ce faire et qui ne sont pas en quête de travail rémunéré;

b) les travailleurs familiaux non rémunérés qui ont cessé leur activité et ne sont pas en quête de travail rémunéré.

Les statistiques relatives au chômage qui figurent dans le présent chapitre se rapportent dans l'ensemble aux chômeurs complets, c'est-à-dire aux personnes sans travail et qui sont en quête d'un emploi, soit un jour donné, soit durant une période relativement courte (une semaine, par exemple). Les personnes n'ayant pas travaillé par suite de maladie, d'accident ou de conflit du travail sont généralement exclues des statistiques du chômage; les chômeurs partiels sont quelquefois compris dans les données.

Les séries sur le chômage présentées dans ce chapitre se rapportent, le plus souvent, à l'ensemble du territoire national d'un pays donné, mais, dans la plupart des statistiques sur le chômage, les données relatives aux zones rurales sont fréquemment moins complètes que celles qui concernent d'autres régions.

Les statistiques ne couvrent tous les effectifs de main-d'œuvre ou tous les salariés que dans quelques cas; dans l'ensemble, elles sont limitées aux ouvriers et aux employés dont la rémunération est peu élevée. Elles sont plus complètes pour les travailleurs des entreprises minières et manufacturières que pour ceux qui sont occupés dans d'autres secteurs non agricoles.

Pour diverses raisons, la définition du mot « chômeur » donnée dans les séries nationales de statistiques s'écarte souvent de la définition normalisée internationale qui est recommandée. Les définitions nationales varient d'un pays à un autre en ce qui concerne notamment les limites d'âge, les périodes de référence, les critères retenus en matière de quête d'emploi, la durée minimum fixée pour la période de travail, le traitement des données concernant les personnes qui ont été mises à pied temporairement ou qui cherchent du travail pour la première fois[2].

On distingue quatre principaux types de statistiques (indiqués dans les en-têtes du tableau par les codes I, II, III et IV).

I. *Enquêtes par sondage sur la main-d'œuvre.* Lorsqu'ils sont fondés sur des méthodes d'échantillonnage adéquates, les sondages de main-d'œuvre se sont révélés en pratique une méthode satisfaisante et sûre pour obtenir une évaluation du chômage. Cette technique fournit générale-

---

[1] Voir BIT: *Recommandations internationales sur les statistiques du travail* (Genève, 1975).

[2] Pour les descriptions des diverses séries nationales, de leur portée, des méthodes de calcul utilisées, etc., voir BIT: *Guide technique 1976* (descriptions des séries générales publiées dans le *Bulletin* et l'*Annuaire des statistiques du travail*), vol. II, « Emploi — Chômage — Durée du travail — Salaires » (Genève, 1976).

Les problèmes que soulève le rassemblement des données sur le chômage sont discutés dans BIT: *Statistiques de l'emploi, du chômage et de la main-d'œuvre, Etudes méthodologiques*, Etudes et documents, nouvelle série, nº 7, partie 1 (Genève, 1948).

ment les meilleures statistiques d'ensemble sur le chômage, car elle permet en particulier de couvrir les groupes de personnes qui ne sont pas compris dans les statistiques du chômage obtenues par d'autres méthodes (tels que les personnes en quête d'emploi pour la première fois); en outre, les changements intervenus dans la législation ou les règlements administratifs n'influent pas sur la continuité des séries. Il faut cependant remarquer que la définition du chômage adoptée pour ce type de statistiques diffère fondamentalement des définitions applicables aux autres types de statistiques décrits ci-dessous. Cela provient du procédé utilisé, qui consiste à compter comme occupée toute personne qui a effectué un travail rémunéré ou rémunérateur quelconque au cours de la semaine de l'enquête. Les pourcentages de chômage ont été calculés en rapportant le nombre évalué des personnes en chômage à l'effectif de la main-d'œuvre civile (personnes occupées, plus chômeurs) dérivé des mêmes enquêtes.

II. *Statistiques de l'assurance-chômage obligatoire.* Ces statistiques ont ordinairement une vaste portée industrielle, définie par la législation nationale en matière d'assurance et les règlements administratifs. En général, les données portent sur les ouvriers et les employés ou sur les ouvriers seulement. Le pourcentage de chômage est calculé en comparant le nombre des chômeurs assurés et le nombre total des travailleurs assurés. La comparabilité des pourcentages d'un pays à un autre peut être compromise par des différences dans la portée de la législation sur l'assurance, de même que par les prescriptions administratives en vigueur. Dans un même pays, la comparabilité des pourcentages pendant une période donnée est sujette à des réserves lorsque d'importantes modifications sont intervenues dans la législation de l'assurance ou dans les dispositions administratives régissant l'inscription des chômeurs.

III. *Statistiques des caisses syndicales.* La portée de ces statistiques dépend du degré de développement des syndicats, des conditions réglant l'affiliation aux syndicats ou à la caisse syndicale et du nombre des syndicats fournis-sant des données aux autorités. Les fluctuations du nombre et du pourcentage des chômeurs inscrits sont influencées par l'accroissement ou la diminution de l'importance des syndicats et de leurs caisses. Il est difficile et souvent même impossible de déterminer jusqu'à quel point les statistiques de ce type peuvent être considérées comme donnant une indication exacte de la situation générale du chômage dans un pays.

IV. *Statistiques des bureaux de placement.* Ces statistiques donnent généralement le nombre de demandeurs d'emploi figurant sur les registres à la fin de chaque mois. Elles peuvent comprendre, outre les personnes sans travail, des personnes en grève ou dans l'incapacité temporaire de travailler par suite de maladie et des personnes occupées à des travaux entrepris pour secourir les chômeurs. En principe, ces statistiques ne comprennent pas les personnes qui, bien que pourvues d'un emploi, sont désireuses d'en changer et sont, en conséquence, inscrites dans des bureaux de placement; ces personnes sont cependant couvertes par certaines séries.

La valeur de ces statistiques est très variable. Lorsque les bureaux de placement fonctionnent en rapport étroit avec une assurance-chômage, l'inscription étant une des conditions mises à l'octroi des indemnités, les données sont aussi fiables que celles des statistiques d'assurance. Quand les bureaux sont en étroite relation avec des régimes d'assistance publique d'une large portée, les chiffres relevés peuvent également fournir des données satisfaisantes durant l'existence de tels régimes. Toutefois, lorsque les inscriptions sont purement volontaires et surtout lorsque les bureaux de placement ne fonctionnent que dans les régions à forte densité de population ou ne sont pas utilisés largement par les salariés en quête de travail ou par les employeurs qui cherchent des travailleurs, les statistiques sont en général très incomplètes et ne fournissent pas une indication sûre du niveau du chômage. La portée des données dépend donc, d'une part, de l'organisation du réseau des bureaux et, d'autre part, de l'habitude qu'ont les travailleurs de s'y inscrire et de l'intérêt qu'ils ont à le faire. Dans bien des cas, les personnes travaillant dans les mines et les industries manufacturières ont davantage recours aux services des bureaux de placement que les travailleurs des transports, du commerce et des services en général; les personnes occupées dans l'agriculture et habitant des régions à population moins dense sont parfois à peine couvertes par les statistiques. La portée des statistiques des bureaux de placement est de ce fait très difficile à préciser et il est très rare que les données permettent de calculer des pourcentages de chômage satisfaisants. En général, ces statistiques ne seront donc pas comparables d'un pays à un autre, bien que leurs fluctuations au sein d'un même pays puissent indiquer les variations dans l'étendue du chômage.

Dès l'édition de 1974 de l'*Annuaire*, des modifications ont été apportées à la présentation des données de certains tableaux en raison de l'introduction des versions révisées 1968 de la Classification internationale type par industrie de toutes les branches d'activité économique (CITI) et de la Classification internationale type des professions (CITP); voir « Préface ».

Tableau 10

Niveau général du chômage

Dans la mesure du possible, les statistiques sont présentées en chiffres absolus (en milliers) et en pourcentages. Les *nombres* indiquent l'étendue du problème du chômage dans les limites couvertes par les diverses séries. Les fluctuations du nombre des chômeurs reflètent, non seulement les variations saisonnières et autres de l'activité économique, mais aussi l'effet des changements dans une période donnée de l'importance numérique de la population et de sa structure sociale et industrielle; elles peuvent aussi être influencées par des changements intervenus dans la législation ou dans l'organisation administrative, selon le genre de séries utilisées.

Les *pourcentages* font ressortir la gravité du chômage, dans les limites couvertes par les diverses séries. Ils sont calculés en rapportant le nombre de travailleurs d'un certain groupe qui se trouvaient en chômage pendant la période de référence (en général, un jour donné ou une semaine donnée) au nombre total des personnes occupées et des chômeurs dans ce groupe à la même date.

Tableau 11

Chômage par groupes d'activité économique ou de professions

Ce tableau montre le nombre de personnes en chômage (dans certains cas, les personnes en quête d'emploi) dans les différents groupe d'activité économique ou de professions.

Les observations concernant les séries géné rales du tableau 10 s'appliquent également a tableau 11.

Desempleo

El desempleo se halla definido en la forma siguiente en la resolución sobre estadísticas de la fuerza del trabajo, del empleo y del desempleo, adoptada por la octava Conferencia Internacional de Estadígrafos del Trabajo (Ginebra, 1954) [1]:

1) Las personas comprendidas en el desempleo serán todas aquellas que tengan más de cierta edad especificada y que, en un día especificado o en una semana especificada, se hallen en las siguientes categorías:

a) los trabajadores disponibles para el empleo cuyo contrato de trabajo haya expirado o esté suspendido temporalmente, que estén sin empleo y busquen trabajo remunerado durante un breve período especificado, con preferencia una semana;

b) las personas que no hayan estado empleadas nunca y aquellas cuya categoría de ocupación más reciente sea distinta de la de asalariado (es decir, antiguos empleadores, etc.) en unión de las que estén jubiladas, cuyas personas se hallen disponibles para trabajar (salvo los casos de enfermedad benigna) en el curso del período especificado y estén buscando trabajo remunerado;

c) las personas sin empleo que en el momento de que se trate se hallen disponibles para trabajar y hayan logrado un nuevo empleo que deba empezar en una fecha subsiguiente al período especificado;

d) las personas que hayan sido suspendidas temporal o indefinidamente, sin goce de remuneración.

2) No se considerará desempleadas a las personas comprendidas en las categorías siguientes:

a) las que tengan el propósito de establecer por su cuenta un negocio cualquiera o explotación agrícola, pero que no hayan tomado medidas en esa dirección y que no estén buscando trabajo remunerado;

b) los antiguos trabajadores familiares no remunerados que no estén trabajando ni buscando trabajo remunerado.

Las estadísticas de desempleo presentadas en este capítulo se refieren generalmente a los desempleados completos, es decir, a las personas sin trabajo y en busca de ocupación, bien un día determinado, bien durante un período relativa-mente breve (una semana, por ejemplo). Las personas que no hayan trabajado a causa de enfermedad, accidente o conflicto del trabajo se excluyen generalmente de las estadísticas de desempleo; los datos comprenden a veces a los desempleados parciales.

En la mayoría de los casos, las estadísticas de desempleo que figuran en este capítulo se refieren a toda una área geográfica de un país determinado, pero, con frecuencia, las regiones rurales no se hallan comprendidas en el mismo grado que otras regiones en la mayoría de las estadísticas de desempleo.

En algunos casos, las estadísticas comprenden todos los sectores de la fuerza trabajadora o todos los asalariados; sin embargo, las cifras se refieren generalmente sólo a los obreros y a los empleados de baja remuneración. Las personas empleadas en las minas y en las industrias manufactureras están incluidas en mayor grado que las personas ocupadas en otras actividades no agrícolas.

Por varias razones, las definiciones de las personas « desempleadas », adoptadas por las estadísticas nacionales, difieren a menudo de la definición recomendada por la Clasificación internacional uniforme. Las definiciones nacionales varían de un país a otro respecto de los límites de edad, los períodos de referencia, los criterios para determinar que una persona está buscando trabajo, los límites mínimos del tiempo trabajado, los criterios para determinar que una persona se halla temporalmente suspendida, y aquellos que buscan por primera vez un empleo [2].

Pueden distinguirse cuatro grandes tipos de estadísticas de desempleo (indicados en los

---

[1] Véase OIT: *Recomendaciones internacionales sobre estadísticas del trabajo* (Ginebra, 1975).

[2] Para las descripciones de las diversas series nacionales, su alcance, métodos de compilación utilizados, etc., véase OIT: *Guía Técnica 1976* (descripciones de las series generales publicadas en el *Boletín* y el *Anuario de Estadísticas del Trabajo*), vol. II, « Empleo — Desempleo — Horas de trabajo — Salarios » (Ginebra, 1976).

Como estudio general de los problemas relativos a la compilación de las estadísticas del desempleo, véase OIT: *Estadísticas del empleo, del desempleo y de la mano de obra, Estudio metodológico*, Estudios y documentos, nueva serie, núm. 7, primera parte (Ginebra, 1948).

encabezamientos de los cuadros por las claves I, II, III y IV).

I. *Encuestas por muestra sobre la fuerza de trabajo.* Estas encuestas, cuando se basan en métodos adecuados, han demostrado ser satisfactorias y fidedignas para la estimación del desempleo. Esta técnica proporciona generalmente las mejores cifras de conjunto sobre el desempleo, porque comprende grupos de individuos no incluidos por las estadísticas de desempleo obtenidas por otros métodos (tales como las personas en busca de ocupación por primera vez); por otra parte, los cambios en la legislación o en los reglamentos administrativos no influyen en la continuidad de las series. Es preciso observar, sin embargo, que la definición del desempleo utilizada en este tipo de estadísticas difiere fundamentalmente de otros tipos de estadísticas descritos más adelante. Esto se debe al procedimiento según el cual se considera como empleada toda persona que haya efectuado un trabajo remunerado cualquiera durante la semana de la encuesta. Los porcentajes de desempleo han sido calculados relacionando el número estimado de personas desempleadas con el conjunto de la fuerza de trabajo civil (personas empleadas más personas desempleadas).

II. *Estadísticas del seguro obligatorio de desempleo.* Estas estadísticas tienen ordinariamente un vasto alcance industrial. Su alcance se establece según la legislación nacional en materia de seguros y según los reglamentos administrativos; en general, los datos se refieren a obreros y a empleados o a obreros solamente. El porcentaje del desempleo se ha calculado comparando el número de desempleados inscritos en el seguro con el número total de trabajadores asegurados. La comparabilidad de los porcentajes de un país a otro puede verse comprometida por diferencias en el alcance de la legislación de seguros, así como por las prescripciones administrativas en vigor. En un país dado, la comparabilidad de los porcentajes, durante un período determinado, está sujeta a reservas, cuando se han introducido importantes modificaciones en la legislación de seguros o en las disposiciones administrativas que rigen la inscripción de los desempleados.

III. *Estadísticas de las cajas de los sindicatos.* El alcance de estas estadísticas depende del grado de desarrollo de los sindicatos, de las reglas que rigen la afiliación a los sindicatos y a las cajas sindicales y del número de sindicatos que facilitan informaciones. Las fluctuaciones del número y del porcentaje de las personas desempleadas se hallan influidas por el desarrollo o la disminución de los sindicatos o de sus cajas sindicales. Por lo tanto, es difícil, y a menudo imposible, definir hasta qué punto puede considerarse que las estadísticas de los sindicatos facilitan una indicación exacta de la situación general del desempleo en un país.

IV. *Estadísticas de las oficinas de colocación.* Estas estadísticas generalmente se refieren al número de solicitantes de empleo que figuran en los registros al fin de cada mes. Las mismas pueden comprender, además de las personas sin trabajo, a las personas en huelga o en incapacidad temporal de trabajar por causa de enfermedad y a las ocupadas en trabajos creados como medio de auxilio a los desempleados. En principio, dichas estadísticas no abarcan a las personas que, aunque ya poseen un empleo, desean cambiarlo y, en consecuencia, se hallan inscritas en las oficinas de colocación; sin embargo, ciertas series incluyen a estas últimas personas.

El valor de dichas estadísticas es muy variable. Cuando las oficinas de colocación funcionan en íntima relación con un seguro de desempleo, siendo la inscripción una de las condiciones exigidas para la concesión de indemnizaciones de desempleo, los datos son tan fiables como los de las estadísticas del seguro. Cuando las oficinas de colocación están en relación íntima con sistemas amplios de asistencia pública, las cifras recogidas pueden proporcionar también datos satisfactorios durante la vigencia de tales sistemas. Sin embargo, cuando las inscripciones son totalmente voluntarias y, sobre todo, cuando las oficinas de colocación no funcionan sino en las regiones de gran densidad de población de un país, o no son utilizadas ampliamente por los obreros en busca de trabajo o por los empleadores en demanda de mano de obra, las estadísticas son generalmente muy incompletas y no proporcionan una indicación fidedigna de la extensión del desempleo. El alcance de los datos depende, pues, por una parte, de la organización de la red de oficinas y, por otra, de las ventajas que proporciona el registro y de la costumbre que tengan los trabajadores de inscribirse en ellas. Con frecuencia sucede que las personas empleadas en las minas o en las industrias manufactureras recurren más a los servicios de colocación que los trabajadores del transporte, el comercio y los servicios, mientras que las personas que trabajan en la agricultura y que viven en territorios de población poco densa pueden no estar englobadas en las estadísticas. El alcance de las estadísticas de las oficinas de colocación es, por esto, muy difícil de precisar, y sólo raramente sus datos permiten calcular porcentajes satisfactorios de desempleo. En general, dichas estadísticas no son comparables de un país a otro, aunque sus fluctuaciones dentro de un mismo país pueden indicar las variaciones en la extensión del desempleo.

A partir de la edición de 1974 del *Anuario*, **se ha modificado la presentación de los datos de ciertos cuadros debido a la introducción de las ediciones revisadas 1968 de la Clasificación industrial internacional uniforme de todas las actividades económicas (CIIU) y de la Clasificación internacional uniforme de ocupaciones (CIUO). Véase « Prefacio ».**

Cuadro 10

Nivel general del desempleo

En la medida de lo posible, las estadísticas de este cuadro presentan cifras absolutas (millares) y porcentajes. Las *cifras* indican la extensión del problema del desempleo en las actividades comprendidas en las respectivas series. Las fluctuaciones de las personas desempleadas

reflejan no sólo variaciones estacionales y otros cambios de la actividad económica, sino también los efectos en las modificaciones del volumen de la población y su composición industrial y social, dentro de un período determinado, todo lo cual depende del tipo de estadísticas utilizadas; pueden hallarse influidas también por cambios de la legislación y la organización administrativa.

Los *porcentajes* hacen resaltar la gravedad del desempleo dentro de los límites que abarcan las diversas series. Se calculan relacionando el número de trabajadores de cierto grupo, que se encuentran desempleados en un período determinado (generalmente un día o una semana), con el conjunto de las personas empleadas y desempleadas de ese grupo en la misma fecha.

Cuadro 11

Desempleo por grupos de actividad económica o de ocupaciones

Este cuadro presenta el número de personas desempleadas (en ciertos casos, solicitantes de trabajo) en los diferentes grupos de actividad económica o de ocupaciones.

Las observaciones formuladas respecto a las series generales del cuadro 10 se aplican también en este caso.

UNEMPLOYMENT

10   General level of unemployment · Niveau général du chômage · Nivel general del desempleo

(Thousands — *Milliers* — Millares)

Country — *Pays* — País	Code *Code* Clave	1965	1966	1967	1968	1969	1970	1971	1972	1973	1974	1975 (VI)
AFRICA — AFRIQUE AFRICA												
Cameroun[1]	IV	.	0.45	1.60	3.48	2.42	2.17	2.38	2.94	4.04	...	...
République centrafricaine (Bangui)	IV	.	.	.	.	.	.	0.32	0.16	0.36	0.49	...
Egypt[2]	I	.	.	.	244.4	218.9	198.0	153.1	134.6	145.1	...	...
» . . . . (%)					(3.1)	(2.7)	(2.4)	(1.8)	(1.5)	(1.6)	...	...
Ghana	IV	11.3	11.5	16.7	17.6	15.0	16.5	18.4	31.2	26.3	28.3	30.2
Haute-Volta[3]	IV	.	0.36	0.35	0.61	0.72	0.99	0.74	0.66	...	...	...
Libyan Arab Republic	IV	.	.	0.68	0.46	0.42	2.58	1.34	5.31	...	...	...
Madagascar	IV	0.84	0.74	0.87	0.85	0.69	0.72	0.92	0.80[4]	1.47	1.12	...
Malawi	IV	1.20	1.61	1.82	1.74	1.25	1.84	1.43	1.96	1.92	2.11	...
Mali[5]	IV	0.13	0.10	0.20	0.40	0.46	0.53	0.45	0.61	0.39	0.48	...
Maroc[6]	IV	18.6	23.7	23.7	22.9	27.4	31.6	26.3	29.8	29.1	26.3	25.6[18]
Mauritius	IV	8.3	14.1	14.2	9.1	14.3	21.0	30.7	34.5	27.2	21.2	20.6[18]
Mozambique	IV	.	2.09	2.09	2.14	2.20	2.14	2.10	2.08	1.95	...	...
Niger (Niamey)	IV	0.08	0.11	0.09	0.09	0.19	0.13	0.22	0.29	0.66	...	...
Nigeria	IV	20.9	26.6	20.1	12.9	12.2	13.5	14.4	15.4	19.1	20.5	20.4[19]
Sénégal (Dakar)	IV	1.94	1.58	1.54	1.80	1.79	2.03	3.29	2.35	3.50	2.90	...
Sierra Leone	IV[7]	6.81	7.97	8.50	8.63	9.11	9.51	8.03	6.80	5.75	5.56	6.19
» »	IV[8]	4.75	4.93	5.19	5.48	5.62	5.76	5.75	5.92	5.90	6.31	6.84
South Africa, Rep. of[9]	IV	11.7	13.5	13.9	13.7	10.9	8.5	8.6	12.2	10.8	8.3	10.6[19]
Sudan	IV	.	.	.	.	.	4.79	4.95	4.08	4.06	4.42	...
Tchad (Fort-Lamy)	IV	0.20[10]	0.20	0.15	0.21	0.22	...	...	...	...	...	...
Tunisie	IV	26.1	42.1	48.3	.	51.3	63.7	52.5	31.9	37.0	32.4	32.7[18]
Zambia	IV	17.6	16.4	12.3	12.9	15.3	10.3	10.2	12.6	9.3	10.6	12.0
AMERICA — AMÉRIQUE AMÉRICA												
Argentina (Gran Buenos Aires) . .	I	167.4	172.7	198.7	153.3	140.3	158.0	196.5[11]	221.5[12]	160.5	121.6	...
» » » » (%)		(5.3)	(5.6)	(6.4)	(5.0)	(4.3)	(4.8)	(6.0)	(6.6)	(5.6)	(3.4)	...
Barbados	IV	1.16	1.61	1.42	0.82	0.69	0.23	0.13	0.21	0.42	0.19	...
Brésil[13]	I	.	.	.	710.0	698.0	725.0[14]	723.0[15]	1 033.9[16]	968.0[16]	...	...
Canada	I	280.0	267.0	315.0	382.0	382.0	495.0	552.0	562.0	520.0	525.0	704.0
» . . . . (%)		(3.9)	(3.6)	(4.1)	(4.8)	(4.7)	(5.9)	(6.4)	(6.3)	(5.6)	(5.4)	(6.8)
Chile	I	.	159.4[16]	132.5[17]	137.2	127.5	101.0	113.4	93.1[18]	...	...	...
» . . . . (%)			(5.7)	(4.7)	(4.8)	(4.7)	(3.4)	(3.8)	(3.1)	...	...	...
» (Gran Santiago)	I	45.7	46.6	55.6	57.1	61.2	73.6	58.9	41.2	54.2	118.4	...
» » » . . . (%)		(5.4)	(5.4)	(6.1)	(6.0)	(6.2)	(7.1)	(5.5)	(3.7)	(4.7)	(9.7)	...
Guadeloupe	IV	.	.	.	.	0.60	0.65	0.59	0.74	0.78	1.01	0.76

EXPLANATORY NOTES: See p. 427.

Codes: See p. 439.

[1] Douala, Yaoundé, Nkongsamba and Garoua. [2] May of each year. [3] Ouagadougou and Bobo-Dioulasso. [4] Jan.-Aug. [5] Bamako, Gao, Kayes, Mopti, Segou and Sikasso. [6] Excl. unemployed who do not re-register after 90 days; 1965-67: excl. unemployed who do not re-register after 30 days. [7] Excl. persons registered at the Maritime Pool. [8] Applicants for work registered at the Maritime Pool. [9] Non-indigenous population. [10] Jan.-Sep. [11] April and July. [12] April and Oct. [13] Data relate to Rio de Janeiro, Guanabara, São Paulo and to other areas varying according to the surveys. [14] First quarter. [15] Fourth quarter. [16] Aug. and Dec. [17] April, Aug. and Dec. [18] March. [19] May.

NOTES EXPLICATIVES: Voir p. 430.

Codes: Voir p. 439.

[1] Douala, Yaoundé, Nkongsamba et Garoua. [2] Mai de chaque année. [3] Ouagadougou et Bobo-Dioulasso. [4] Janv.-août. [5] Bamako, Gao, Kayes, Mopti, Segou et Sikasso. [6] Non compris les chômeurs qui ne se représentent pas après le quatre-vingt-dixième jour de leur inscription ; 1965-1967 : non compris les chômeurs qui ne se représentent pas après le trentième jour de leur inscription. [7] Non compris les demandeurs d'emploi enregistrés au bureau de placement maritime. [8] Demandeurs d'emploi enregistrés au bureau de placement maritime. [9] Population non indigène. [10] Janv.-sept. [11] Avril et juillet. [12] Avril et oct. [13] Les données se réfèrent à Rio de Janeiro, Guanabara, São Paulo, ainsi qu'à d'autres régions variant suivant les enquêtes. [14] Premier trimestre. [15] Quatrième trimestre. [16] Août et déc. [17] Avril, août et déc. [18] Mars. [19] Mai.

NOTAS EXPLICATIVAS: Véase pág. 433.

Claves: Véase pág. 439.

[1] Duala, Yaundé, Nkongsamba y Garoua. [2] Mayo de cada año. [3] Uagadugu y Bobo-Diulasso. [4] Enero-agosto. [5] Bamako, Gao, Kayes, Mopti, Segú y Sikasso. [6] Excl. los desempleados que no vuelven a presentarse en los 90 días que siguen a su inscripción; 1965-1967: excl. los desempleados que no vuelven a presentarse en los 30 días que siguen a su inscripción. [7] Excl. los solicitantes de trabajo registrados en la oficina de colocación marítima. [8] Solicitantes de trabajo registrados en la oficina de colocación marítima. [9] Población no indígena. [10] Enero-sept. [11] Abril y julio. [12] Abril y oct. [13] Los datos se refieren a Río de Janeiro, Guanabara, São Paulo y a otras áreas que varían según las encuestas. [14] Primer trimestre. [15] Cuarto trimestre. [16] Agosto y dic. [17] Abril, agosto y dic. [18] Marzo. [19] Mayo.

10 General level of unemployment
Niveau général du chômage
Nivel general del desempleo

(Thousands — *Milliers* — Millares)

Country — *Pays* — País	Code *Code* Clave	1965	1966	1967	1968	1969	1970	1971	1972	1973	1974	1975 (VI)
Guatemala [1]	IV	0.08	0.19	0.33	0.65	0.74	0.66	0.66	0.62	0.57	0.44	...
Guyana [2]	IV	12.34	12.06	8.94	7.65	6.40	5.18	4.45	3.39	...	...	...
Guyane française [3]	IV	0.01	0.03	0.05	0.07	0.11	0.22	0.29	0.71	0.53	0.68	...
Jamaica	I	.	.	.	144.7	131.7	.	.	184.5	176.4	172.3	...
Panamá	I	29.0	20.0	25.0	31.0	30.0	33.3	36.3	32.2	34.9	30.0	...
» .... (%)		*(7.6)*	*(5.1)*	*(6.2)*	*(7.0)*	*(6.6)*	*(7.1)*	*(7.6)*	*(6.8)*	*(7.0)*	*(5.8)*	...
Perú [4]	I	.	.	.	.	243.2	201.2	195.7	194.0	199.8	195.7	...
Puerto Rico	I [5]	.	86.0	87.0	83.0	76.0	84.0	95.0	101.0	102.0	117.0	145.0 [12]
» » ....(%)		.	*(11.8)*	*(11.7)*	*(11.1)*	*(10.0)*	*(10.8)*	*(11.6)*	*(11.9)*	*(11.7)*	*(13.3)*	*(16.7)*
Surinam	IV	3.04	2.62	2.46	2.46	2.07	2.25	0.96	0.86	1.97	2.20	2.30 [21]
Trinidad and Tobago	I	48.4	48.8	53.7	54.0	48.0	46.4	46.4 [6]	.	58.9	...	...
» » » ....(%)		*(14.0)*	*(14.0)*	*(15.0)*	*(15.0)*	*(13.5)*	*(12.5)*	*(12.6)*	.	*(15.4)*	...	...
United States	I	3 366.0	2 875.0	2 975.0	2 817.0	2 831.0	4 088.0	4 993.0	4 840.0	4 304.0	5 076.0	8 569.0
» » ....(%)		*(4.5)*	*(3.8)*	*(3.8)*	*(3.6)*	*(3.5)*	*(4.9)*	*(5.9)*	*(5.6)*	*(4.9)*	*(5.6)*	*(9.1)*
Uruguay (Montevideo)	I	.	.	.	43.3 [7]	44.9	39.3	41.2	41.7 [8]	49.4 [9]	...	...
» ....(%)		.	.	.	*(8.4)*	*(8.7)*	*(7.5)*	*(7.6)*	*(7.7)*	*(8.9)*	...	...
Venezuela	I	.	.	217.4 [10]	181.6 [11]	191.8 [12]	198.8 [13]	195.2 [14]	...	...	...	...
» ....(%)		.	.	*(7.7)*	*(6.3)*	*(6.5)*	*(6.3)*	*(6.0)*	...	...	...	...
ASIA — *ASIE* ASIA												
Burma [15]	IV	.	71.6	89.4	70.1	72.8	76.4	90.0	108.2	122.6	118.2	115.9 [12]
Cyprus	IV	4.03	3.48	2.86	3.17	2.70	2.81	2.85	2.52	3.31	11.2	22.4
» ....(%)		.	.	*(1.1)*	*(1.2)*	*(1.1)*	*(1.1)*	*(1.1)*	*(0.9)*	*(1.2)*	*(4.1)*	*(8.1)*
India	IV	2 527.0	2 609.8	2 706.3	2 902.8	3 203.9	3 725.7	4 602.3	5 927.6	7 713.8	8 378.3	8 791.0
Indonesia	IV	90.4	71.8	30.5	36.2	38.0	30.7	37.1	90.5	84.3	89.1	...
Iraq	IV	1.96	2.15	2.67	3.98	3.92	5.18	5.03	8.02	9.99	9.03	...
Israel [16]	I	33.2	69.5	96.2	59.0	44.3	38.3	35.7	29.1	29.5	33.7	35.0 [22]
» ....(%)		*(3.6)*	*(7.4)*	*(10.4)*	*(6.1)*	*(4.5)*	*(3.8)*	*(3.5)*	*(2.7)*	*(2.6)*	*(3.0)*	*(3.2)*
Japan	I	390.0	440.0	630.0 [17]	590.0	570.0	590.0	640.0	730.0	670.0	720.0	920.0
» ....(%)		*(0.8)*	*(0.9)*	*(1.3)*	*(1.2)*	*(1.1)*	*(1.2)*	*(1.2)*	*(1.4)*	*(1.3)*	*(1.4)*	*(1.7)*
Korea, Rep. of	I	.	.	578.0	492.0	474.0	454.0	476.0	499.0	461.0	494.0	742.0 [12]
» » » ......(%)		.	.	*(6.2)*	*(5.1)*	*(4.8)*	*(4.5)*	*(4.5)*	*(4.5)*	*(4.0)*	*(4.1)*	*(6.1)*
Malaysia : West Malaysia	IV	93.0	105.8	117.0	127.6	140.4	169.3	157.1	160.7	154.7	134.5	133.7
Pakistan	IV	182.9	179.6	184.1	181.3	215.6	228.8	188.4 [18]	157.4	167.6	189.6	...
Philippines [19]	I	947.0	855.0	1 090.0	1 053.0	812.0	941.6 [20]	636.0	983.0	624.0	725.0	...
» ....(%)		*(8.2)*	*(7.2)*	*(8.2)*	*(7.8)*	*(6.7)*	.	*(4.8)*	*(6.9)*	*(4.4)*	*(4.8)*	...

EXPLANATORY NOTES: See p. 427.

Codes: See p. 439.

1 Guatemala City, Quezaltenango, Escuintla and Puerto Barrios; 1965-72: Guatemala City only. 2 Georgetown and New Amsterdam districts. 3 Cayenne and Kourou. 4 Urban areas. 5 Excl. persons temporarily laid off. 6 First semester. 7 Oct.-Dec. 8 Jan.-May. 9 Feb.-June. 10 April and Aug. 11 March, July and Nov. 12 March. 13 April and Dec. 14 April and July. 15 Greater Rangoon (Rangoon, Insein, Kamayut, Okkalapa) and Mandalay. 16 Incl. persons who did not work in the country during the previous 12 months. Beginning 1968, data cover also certain territories under occupation by Israeli military forces since June 1967. 17 Revised series (sampling design revised). 18 Beginning Sep. 1971; geographical scope revised. 19 May of each year. 20 Census figure. 21 April. 22 First quarter.

NOTES EXPLICATIVES: Voir p. 430.

Codes: Voir p. 439.

1 *Ville de Guatemala, Quezaltenango, Escuintla et Puerto Barrios ; 1965-1972 : ville de Guatemala seulement.* 2 *Districts de Georgetown et de New Amsterdam.* 3 *Cayenne et Kourou.* 4 *Zones urbaines.* 5 *Non compris les personnes temporairement mises à pied.* 6 *Premier semestre.* 7 *Oct.-déc.* 8 *Janv.-mai.* 9 *Fév.-juin.* 10 *Avril et août.* 11 *Mars, juillet et nov.* 12 *Mars.* 13 *Avril et déc.* 14 *Avril et juillet.* 15 *Grand Rangoon (Rangoon, Insein, Kamayut, Okkalapa) et Mandalay.* 16 *Y compris les personnes qui n'ont pas travaillé dans le pays pendant les 12 mois précédents. A partir de 1968, les données couvrent aussi certains territoires occupés par les forces armées israéliennes depuis juin 1967.* 17 *Série révisée (plan d'échantillonnage révisé).* 18 *A partir de sept. 1971 : portée géographique révisée.* 19 *Mai de chaque année.* 20 *Chiffre de recensement.* 21 *Avril.* 22 *Premier trimestre.*

NOTAS EXPLICATIVAS: Véase pág. 433.

Claves: Véase pág. 439.

1 Ciudad de Guatemala, Quezaltenango, Escuintla y Puerto Barrios; 1965-1972: Ciudad de Guatemala solamente. 2 Distritos de Georgetown y de Nueva Amsterdam. 3 Cayena y Kourou. 4 Zonas urbanas. 5 Excl. las personas temporalmente despedidas. 6 Primer semestre. 7 Oct.-dic. 8 Enero-mayo. 9 Febr.-junio. 10 Abril y agosto. 11 Marzo, julio y nov. 12 Marzo. 13 Abril y dic. 14 Abril y julio. 15 Gran Rangún (Rangún, Insein, Kamayut, Okkalapa) y Mandalay. 16 Incl. las personas que no trabajaron en el país en los 12 meses precedentes. A partir de 1968, los datos cubren también ciertos territorios ocupados por las fuerzas armadas israelíes desde junio de 1967. 17 Serie revisada (diseño de la muestra revisado). 18 A partir de sept. 1971: alcance geográfico revisado. 19 Mayo de cada año. 20 Cifra del censo. 21 Abril. 22 Primer trimestre.

10 General level of unemployment
Niveau général du chômage
Nivel general del desempleo

(Thousands — *Milliers* — Millares)

Country — *Pays* — País	Code *Code* Clave	1965	1966	1967	1968	1969	1970	1971	1972	1973	1974	1975 (VI)
Singapore . . . . . , ...	IV	54.4	65.4	77.0	65.4	59.2	50.5	37.8	36.2	35.7	32.5	43.1
Sri Lanka	IV	181.1	224.7	249.5	265.6	306.0	381.0	419.7	440.3	457.7	489.3	521.7
République arabe syrienne	I	104.1 [1]	79.6 [1]	88.2 [2]	131.0 [2]	85.3 [2]	100.3 [3]	123.4 [5]	80.9 [4]	76.5 [4]	...	...
» » » . . (%)	I	(7.4)	(5.5)	(5.3)	(7.4)	(4.3)	(6.4)	(7.5)	(4.7)	(4.5)	...	...
Thailand [5]	I	.	.	.	.	.	.	.	85.5	73.9	...	...
EUROPE — EUROPE EUROPA												
Austria	IV	65.5	61.4	64.6	70.8	67.1	58.4	52.0	49.1	41.3	41.3	37.1
» . . . . (%)		(2.7)	(2.5)	(2.7)	(2.9)	(2.8)	(2.4)	(2.1)	(1.9)	(1.6)	(1.5)	(1.4)
Belgique	IV [6]	55.4	61.5	85.3	102.7	85.3	71.3	70 9	86.8	91.7	104.7	162.0
» . . . . (%)		(2.4)	(2.7)	(3.7)	(4.5)	(3.6)	(2.9)	(2.9)	(3.4)	(3.6)	(4.0)	(6.1)
»	IV [7]	36.8	35.7	45.9	40.0	35.2	31.5	37.0	34.2	32.0	39.4	89.1 [17]
» . . . . (%)		(1.6)	(1.6)	(2.0)	(1.7)	(1.5)	(1.3)	(1.5)	(1.4)	(1.3)	(1.5)	(3.5)
Denmark	III [8]	16.1	18.3	21.8	38.7	31.2	23.9	30.0	29.9	20.1	44.4	83.7
» . . . . (%)		(2.0)	(2.3)	(2.7)	(5.0)	(3.9)	(2.9)	(3.7)	(3.6)	(2.4)	(5.2)	(9.1)
España	IV	147.1	123.2	146.3	182.0	158.9	145.6	190.3	190.9	149.6	150.3	243.7
» . . . . (%)		.	.	.	(1.5)	(1.3)	(1.1)	(1.5)	(1.5)	(1.1)	(1.1)	...
Finland [9] . . . . . , . . .	I	31.0	35.0	63.0	88.0	62.0	| 41.0	49.0	55.0	51.0	39.0	45.0
» . . . . (%)		(1.4)	(1.6)	(2.9)	(4.0)	(2.8)	(1.9)	(2.3)	(2.5)	(2.3)	(1.7)	(1.8)
France [10] . . . . °	IV	142.1	147.7	196.0	253.8	223.0	262.1	338.2	| 383.5	393.9	497.7	738.3
Germany, Fed. Rep. of △	IV	147.4	161.1	459.5	323.5	178.6	148.8	185.1	246.4	273.5	582.5	1 002.1
» » » . . (%)		(0.6)	(0.7)	(2.1)	(1.5)	(0.9)	(0.7)	(0.8)	(1.1)	(1.2)	(2.6)	(4.4)
Gibraltar	IV	0.06	0.07	0.07	0.07	0.04	0.04	0.04	0.05	0.04	0.06	0.12 [17]
Grèce	IV [11]	64.3	64.8	83.5	73.7	66.5	48.7	30.3	23.8	21.4	27.1	26.4
»	IV [12]	5.21	4.91	5.99	4.37	4.17	3.42	4.46 [13]	.	.	.	.
Iceland	IV	.	.	.	.	1.95	1.10	0.57	0.46	0.37	0.37	...
» . . . . (%)		.	.	.	.	(2.5)	(1.3)	(0.7)	(0.5)	(0.4)	(0.4)	...
Ireland	II [14]	.	31.8	36.2	37.3	36.1	41.6	42.4	48.2	44.0	48.1	74.4
» . . . . (%)		.	(6.1)	(6.7)	(6.7)	(6.4)	(7.2)	(7.2)	(8.1)	(7.2)	(7.9)	(12.1)
»	IV [15]	.	47.7	55.0	58.3	57.3	64.9	62.0	71.8	66.8	71.4	101.9
Isle of Man [16]	IV	0.36	0.36	0.35	0.37	0.33	0.37	0.39	| 0.50	0.38	0.35	0.30
Italie	I	714.0	759.0	679.0	684.0	655.0	609.0	609.0	697.0	668.0	560.0	667.0 [17]
» . . . . (%)		(3.6)	(3.9)	(3.5)	(3.5)	(3.4)	(3.2)	(3.2)	(3.7)	(3.5)	(2.9)	(3.4)
Luxembourg	IV	0.05	0.02	0.17	0.09	0.04	0.04	0.02	0.04	0.05	0.06	0.10
Malta	IV	8.20	7.77	5.74	4.77	3.79	3.93	5.34	6.88	6.64	5.85	4.32

EXPLANATORY NOTES: See p. 427.

Codes: See p. 439.

[1] May and Nov. [2] Nov. [3] Sep. (census figure). [4] Sep. [5] July-Sep. [6] Wholly inemployed receiving insurance benefits. [7] Daily average of controlled partially unemployed. [8] Unemployment among insured members of trade union funds. [9] Persons aged 15 to 74 years (1965-69: 15 years and over). [10] Beginning June 1972: excl. certain unemployed over 60 years of age (recipients of " income maintenance benefits "). [11] Excl. unemployed seamen. [12] Unemployed seamen. [13] Jan.-Nov. [14] Excl. agriculture, fishing and private domestic service. [15] Applicants for work on the " live " register. [16] 1965-71: males only. [17] April.

NOTES EXPLICATIVES: Voir p. 430.

Codes: Voir p. 439.

[1] *Mai et nov.* [2] *Nov.* [3] *Sept. (chiffre de recensement).* [4] *Sept.* [5] *Juillet-sept.* [6] *Chômeurs complets indemnisés.* [7] *Moyenne journalière du nombre de chômeurs partiels contrôlés.* [8] *Chômage parmi les membres assurés des caisses syndicales.* [9] *Personnes âgées de 15 à 74 ans (1965-1969: 15 ans et plus).* [10] *A partir de juin 1972: non compris certains chômeurs de plus de 60 ans (bénéficiaires de la « garantie de ressources »).* [11] *Non compris les gens de mer en chômage.* [12] *Gens de mer en chômage.* [13] *Janv.-nov.* [14] *Non compris l'agriculture, la pêche et les services domestiques privés.* [15] *Demandeurs d'emploi restant inscrits.* [16] *1965-1971: hommes seulement.* [17] *Avril.*

NOTAS EXPLICATIVAS: Véase pág. 433.

Claves: Véase pág. 439.

[1] Mayo y nov. [2] Nov. [3] Sept. (cifra del censo). [4] Sept. [5] Julio-sept. [6] Desempleados completos que reciben prestaciones. [7] Promedio diario de desempleados parciales controlados. [8] Desempleo entre los afiliados a las cajas sindicales. [9] Personas de 15 a 74 años (1965-1969: 15 años y más). [10] A partir de junio de 1972: excl. ciertos desempleados de más de 60 años (beneficiarios de la « garantía de recursos »). [11] Excl. los marineros desempleados. [12] Marineros desempleados. [13] Enero-nov. [14] Excl. la agricultura, la pesca y el servicio doméstico particular. [15] Solicitantes de trabajo que continúan inscritos. [16] 1965-1971: hombres solamente. [17] Abril.

10 General level of unemployment
Niveau général du chômage
Nivel general del desempleo

(Thousands — *Milliers* — Millares)

Country — *Pays* — País	Code Code Clave	1965	1966	1967	1968	1969	1970	1971	1972	1973	1974	1975 (VI)
Norway	I	.	.	.	.	.	.	.	28.0	26.0	25.0	40.0[8]
» . . . . (%)		.	.	.	.	.	.	.	(1.7)	(1.5)	(1.5)	(2.3)
»	IV	13.4	11.9	11.4	16.5	15.6	12.5	12.2	14.8	12.8	10.7	11.9
» . . . . (%)		(0.9)	(0.8)	(0.8)	(1.1)	(1.0)	(0.8)	(0.8)	(1.0)	(0.8)	(0.7)	(0.8)
Pays-Bas	IV	26.7	37.3	78.5	71.9[1]	52.9	46.4	62.0	107.9	109.9	134.9	176.5
» . . . . (%)		(0.7)	(1.0)	(2.0)	(1.9)	(1.4)	(1.1)	(1.6)	(2.7)	(2.7)	(4.4)	(4.3)
Suisse	IV	0.30	0.30	0.26	0.30	0.18	0.10	0.10	0.11	0.08	0.22	7.53
Sweden	I[2]	44.0	59.0	80.0	85.0	73.0	59.0	101.0	107.0	98.0	80.0	63.1
» . . . . (%)		(1.2)	(1.6)	(2.1)	(2.2)	(1.9)	(1.5)	(2.5)	(2.7)	(2.5)	(2.0)	(1.5)
»	IV[3]	16.6	22.2	28.8	33.4	29.9	29.5	45.3	48.2	46.0	39.0	29.7
» . . . . (%)		(1.1)	(1.4)	(1.7)	(2.0)	(1.7)	(1.4)	(2.0)	(2.0)	(1.9)	(1.5)	(1.1)
Turquie	IV	.	23.5	26.8	33.0	39.0	43.8	44.9	43.9	44.8	81.7	133.1[9]
United Kingdom	IV[4]	347.1	361.0	558.8	586.0	580.9	618.0	799.1	885.5	630.3	630.9[5]	869.8
» » . . . . . (%)		(1.5)	(1.5)	(2.3)	(2.5)	(2.5)	(2.6)	(3.4)	(3.8)	(2.7)	(2.7)	(3.7)
» »	IV[6]	12.7	29.9	40.3	15.3	16.2	21.9	49.4	79.2	11.6	207.4[7]	81.1
» » . . . . . (%)		(0.1)	(0.1)	(0.2)	(0.1)	(0.1)	(0.1)	(0.2)	(0.3)	(0.1)	(0.9)	...
Yugoslavia	IV	237.0	257.6	269.1	311.0	330.6	319.6	291.3	315.3	381.6	448.6	501.6
» . . . . (%)		(6.1)	(6.7)	(7.0)	(8.0)	(8.2)	(7.7)	(6.7)	(7.0)	(8.1)	(9.0)	(9.5)
OCEANIA — OCÉANIE OCEANÍA												
Australia	I	60.7	71.5	79.1	77.8	80.0	74.7	87.6	125.9	107.7	133.2	230.0[10]
» . . . . (%)		(1.3)	(1.5)	(1.6)	(1.5)	(1.5)	(1.4)	(1.6)	(2.3)	(1.9)	(2.3)	(3.9)
Fiji	IV	0.13	0.18	0.32	.	0.19	0.22	0.13	...	...		...
New Zealand	IV	0.51	0.46	3.85	6.88	2.93	1.60	3.11	5.68	2.32	0.96	5.16

EXPLANATORY NOTES: See p. 427.　　　　NOTES EXPLICATIVES: Voir p. 430.　　　　NOTAS EXPLICATIVAS: Véase pág. 433.

I: Labour force sample surveys.

II: Compulsory unemployment insurance statistics.

III: Statistics of trade unions and union benefit fund statistics.

IV: Employment office statistics.

I: *Enquêtes par sondage sur la main-d'œuvre.*

II: *Statistiques de l'assurance-chômage obligatoire.*

III: *Statistiques des syndicats et des caisses syndicales.*

IV: *Statistiques des bureaux de placement.*

I: Encuestas por muestra sobre la fuerza trabajadora.

II: Estadísticas del seguro obligatorio de desempleo.

III: Estadísticas de los sindicatos y de las cajas sindicales.

IV: Estadísticas de las oficinas de colocación.

[1] Beginning 1968: incl. married women who are not breadwinners. [2] Persons aged 16 to 74 years. [3] Unemployment among members of unemployment insurance funds. [4] Excl. persons temporarily laid off. [5] Jan.-Nov. [6] Persons temporarily laid off. [7] Jan.-Sep. [8] Second quarter. [9] April. [10] May.

[1] *A partir de 1968 : y compris les femmes mariées qui ne sont pas soutien de famille.* [2] *Personnes âgées de 16 à 74 ans.* [3] *Chômage parmi les membres des caisses d'assurance-chômage.* [4] *Non compris les personnes temporairement mises à pied.* [5] *Janv.-nov.* [6] *Personnes temporairement mises à pied.* [7] *Janv.-sept.* [8] *Deuxième trimestre.* [9] *Avril.* [10] *Mai.*

[1] A partir de 1968: incl. las mujeres casadas que no son sostén de familia. [2] Personas de 16 a 74 años. [3] Desempleo entre los afiliados a las cajas de seguro de desempleo. [4] Excl. las personas temporalmente despedidas. [5] Enero-nov. [6] Personas temporalmente despedidas. [7] Enero-sept. [8] Segundo trimestre. [9] Abril. [10] Mayo.

UNEMPLOYMENT

11 Unemployment by industrial or occupational groups
Chômage par groupes d'activité économique ou de professions
Desempleo por grupos de actividad económica o de ocupaciones

AFRICA — AFRIQUE — AFRICA

Cameroun [1]

(ISIC — CITI — CIIU 1958)

Industrial groups *(Employment office statistics)*
Groupes d'activité économique *(Statistiques des bureaux de placement)*
Grupos de actividad económica *(Estadísticas de las oficinas de colocación)*

Date / Date / Fecha	Total	Agriculture, forestry, fishing / *Agriculture, sylviculture, pêche* / Agricultura, silvicultura pesca	Mining, quarrying / *Industries extractives* / Minas, canteras	Manufacturing / *Industries manufacturières* / Industrias manufactureras	Construction / *Construction* / Construcción	Electricity, gas, water and sanitary services / *Electricité, gaz, eau et services sanitaires* / Electricidad, gas, agua y servicios sanitarios	Commerce / *Commerce* / Comercio	Transport, storage, communication / *Transports, entrepôts, communications* / Transportes, almacenaje, comunicaciones	Services / *Services* / Servicios	Activities not adequately described [2] / *Activités mal désignées* [2] / Actividades no bien especificadas [2]
1966	450	13	—	16	59	2	36	26	58	240
1967	1 603	56	12	51	264	31	107	117	173	792
1968	3 476	71	29	68	378	26	224	144	239	2 297
1969	2 418	109	23	39	334	13	102	129	148	1 521
1970	2 167	37	10	56	323	14	174	98	164	1 291
1971	2 383	75	12	44	408	17	252	147	86	1 342
1972	2 938	74	8	48	541	41	267	292	197	1 470
1973	4 040	84	11	53	896	19	378	417	313	1 869

[1] Douala, Yaoundé, Nkongsamba and Garoua.
[2] Incl. persons seeking work for the first time.

[1] *Douala, Yaoundé, Nkongsamba et Garoua.* [2] *Y compris les personnes en quête d'emploi pour la première fois.*

[1] Duala, Yaundé, Nkongsamba y Garoua. [2] Incl. las personas en busca de trabajo por primera vez.

11 Unemployment by industrial or occupational groups
Chômage par groupes d'activité économique ou de professions
Desempleo por grupos de actividad económica o de ocupaciones

Egypt

A Industrial groups *(Labour force sample surveys)*
Groupes d'activité économique *(Enquêtes par sondage sur la main-d'œuvre)*
Grupos de actividad económica *(Encuestas por muestra sobre la fuerza trabajadora)*

Date [1] / *Date* [1] / Fecha [1]	Total	1 Agriculture, forestry, fishing / *Agriculture, sylviculture, pêche* / Agricultura, silvicultura, pesca	2 Mining, quarrying / *Industries extractives* / Minas, canteras	3 Manufacturing / *Industries manufacturières* / Industrias manufactureras	4 Electricity, gas, water / *Electricité, gaz, eau* / Electricidad, gas, agua	5 Construction / *Construction* / Construcción	6 Trade, restaurants and hotels / *Commerce, restaurants et hôtels* / Comercio, restaurantes y hoteles	7 Transport, storage, communication / *Transports, entrepôts, communications* / Transportes, almacenaje, comunicaciones	8 Financing, insur., real est., business serv. / *Banques, assur., aff. imm., serv. aux entreprises* / Bancos, seguros, bienes inm., serv. para empresas	9 Community, social, and pers. services / *Services à collectivité, serv. sociaux et pers.* / Servicios comunales, sociales y personales	0 Activities not adequately described [2] / *Activités mal désignées* [2] / Actividades no bien especificadas [2]
1971	153 100	2 000	—	7 800	—	1 700	6 000	800	300	4 500	130 000
1972	134 600	2 300	—	5 000	—	1 100	2 700	1 600	300	2 100	119 500
1973	145 100	1 000	—	2 000	100	100	1 700	1 100	100	1 200	137 800

B Occupational groups *(Labour force sample surveys)*
Groupes de professions *(Enquêtes par sondage sur la main-d'œuvre)*
Grupos de ocupaciones *(Encuestas por muestra sobre la fuerza trabajadora)*

Date [1] / *Date* [1] / Fecha [1]	Total	0/1 Professional, technical and related workers / *Personnel des professions scientifiques, techniques, libérales et assimilées* / Profesionales, técnicos y trabajadores asimilados	2 Administrative and managerial workers / *Directeurs et cadres administratifs supérieurs* / Directores y funcionarios públicos superiores	3 Clerical and related workers / *Personnel administratif et travailleurs assimilés* / Personal administrativo y trabajadores asimilados	4 Sales workers / *Personnel commercial et vendeurs* / Comerciantes y vendedores	5 Service workers / *Travailleurs spécialisés dans les services* / Trabajadores de los servicios	6 Agricultural, animal husbandry and forestry workers, fishermen and hunters / *Agriculteurs, éleveurs, forestiers, pêcheurs et chasseurs* / Trabajadores agrícolas y forestales, pescadores y cazadores	7/8/9 Production and related workers, transport equipment, operators and labourers / *Ouvriers et manœuvres non agricoles et conducteurs d'engins de transport* / Obreros no agrícolas, conductores de máquinas y vehículos de transp. y trabaj. asimilados	X Workers not classifiable by occupation [2] / *Travailleurs ne pouvant être classés selon la profession* [2] / Trabajadores que no pueden ser clasificados según la ocupación [2]
1970	198 000	2 600	600	3 300	4 200	6 500	10 000	42 100	128 700
1971	153 100	3 300	1 200	1 200	1 800	1 300	2 800	11 300	130 200
1972	134 600	3 100	300	1 000	1 400	1 300	2 500	9 500	115 500
1973	145 100	1 400	—	2 800	600	1 800	600	5 200	132 700

[1] May of each year. [2] Incl. persons seeking work for the first time.

[1] *Mai de chaque année.* [2] *Y compris les personnes en quête d'emploi pour la première fois.*

[1] Mayo de cada año. [2] Incl. las personas en busca de trabajo por primera vez.

11 Unemployment by industrial or occupational groups
Chômage par groupes d'activité économique ou de professions
Desempleo por grupos de actividad económica o de ocupaciones

Ghana

A Industrial groups *(Employment office statistics)*
Groupes d'activité économique *(Statistiques des bureaux de placement)*
Grupos de actividad económica *(Estadísticas de las oficinas de colocación)*

Date [1] / Date [1] / Fecha [1]	Total	1 — Agriculture, forestry, fishing / Agriculture, sylviculture, pêche / Agricultura, silvicultura, pesca	2 — Mining, quarrying / Industries extractives / Minas, canteras	3 — Manufacturing [2] / Industries manufacturières [2] / Industrias manufactureras [2]	4 — Electricity, gas, water / Electricité, gaz, eau / Electricidad, gas, agua	5 — Construction / Construction / Construcción	6× — Trade [3] / Commerce [3] / Comercio [3]	7 — Transport, storage, communication / Transports, entrepôts, communications / Transportes, almacenaje, comunicaciones	8 — Financing, insur., real est., business serv. / Banques, assur., aff. imm., serv. aux entreprises / Bancos, seguros, bienes inm., serv. para empresas	6× ; 9× — Community, social, and pers. services [4] / Services à collectivité, serv. sociaux et pers. [4] / Servicios comunales, sociales y personales [4]	0 — Activities not adequately described [5] / Activités mal désignées [5] / Actividades no bien especificadas [5]
1969	15 460	629	257	1 069	178	2 530	363	472	242	947	8 773
1970	15 763	731	227	1 044	256	2 802	296	415	197	1 232	8 563
1971	18 866	2 263	281	1 097	357	3 096	382	417	256	152	10 565
1972	31 961	2 885	587	1 374	412	5 615	62	709	42	2 434	17 841
1973	25 173	2 523	639	1 719	30	4 014	412	635	275	2 044	12 882
1974	28 752	1 959	749	1 656	1 336	2 355	1 072	780	768	1 769	16 308

[1] March, June, Sep. and Dec. of each year. [2] Incl. repair services. [3] Excl. restaurants and hotels. [4] Excl. repair services. Incl. restaurants and hotels. [5] Incl. persons seeking work for the first time.

[1] Mars, juin, sept. et déc. de chaque année. [2] Y compris les services de réparation. [3] Non compris les restaurants et les hôtels. [4] Non compris les services de réparation. Y compris les restaurants et les hôtels. [5] Y compris les personnes en quête d'emploi pour la première fois.

[1] Marzo, junio, sept. y dic. de cada año. [2] Incl. los servicios de reparación. [3] Excl. los restaurantes y los hoteles. [4] Excl. los servicios de reparación. Incl. los restaurantes y los hoteles. [5] Incl. las personas en busca de trabajo por primera vez.

B Occupational groups *(Employment office statistics)*
Groupes de professions *(Statistiques des bureaux de placement)*
Grupos de ocupaciones *(Estadísticas de las oficinas de colocación)*

Date [1] / Date [1] / Fecha [1]	Total	0/1 — Professional, technical and related workers / Personnel des professions scientifiques, techniques, libérales et assimilées / Profesionales, técnicos y trabajadores asimilados	2 — Administrative and managerial workers / Directeurs et cadres administratifs supérieurs / Directores y funcionarios públicos superiores	3 — Clerical and related workers / Personnel administratif et travailleurs assimilés / Personal administrativo y trabajadores asimilados	4 — Sales workers / Personnel commercial et vendeurs / Comerciantes y vendedores	5 — Service workers / Travailleurs spécialisés dans les services / Trabajadores de los servicios	6 — Agricultural, animal husbandry and forestry workers, fishermen and hunters / Agriculteurs, éleveurs, forestiers, pêcheurs et chasseurs / Trabajadores agrícolas y forestales, pescadores y cazadores	7/8/9 — Production and related workers, transport equipment, operators and labourers / Ouvriers et manœuvres non agricoles et conducteurs d'engins de transport / Obreros no agrícolas, conductores de máquinas y vehículos de transp. y trabaj. asimilados	X — Workers not classifiable by occupation [2] / Travailleurs ne pouvant être classés selon la profession [2] / Trabajadores que no pueden ser clasificados según la ocupación [2]
1969	15 460	76	3	103	38	644	80	6 820	7 696
1970	15 763	76	2	1 136	29	690	80	7 507	6 243
1971	18 866	125	2	986	31	691	58	8 585	8 388
1972	31 961	67	2	1 602	37	1 225	69	13 265	15 694
1973	25 173	64	2	1 425	89	934	83	9 846	12 730
1974	28 752	110	12	1 191	124	1 046	56	10 198	15 589
1975: VI	30 191	73	1	962	108	985	68	12 393	15 601

[1] March, June, Sep. and Dec. of each year. [2] Incl. persons seeking work for the first time.

[1] Mars, juin, sept. et déc. de chaque année. [2] Y compris les personnes en quête d'emploi pour la première fois.

[1] Marzo, junio, sept. y dic. de cada año. [2] Incl. las personas en busca de trabajo por primera vez.

11 Unemployment by industrial or occupational groups
Chômage par groupes d'activité économique ou de professions
Desempleo por grupos de actividad económica o de ocupaciones

Malawi

Occupational groups *(Employment office statistics)* [1]
Groupes de professions *(Statistiques des bureaux de placement)* [1]
Grupos de ocupaciones *(Estadísticas de las oficinas de colocación)* [1]

Date / Date / Fecha	Total	0/1 Professional, technical and related workers / Personnel des professions scientifiques, techniques, libérales et assimilées / Profesionales, técnicos y trabajadores asimilados	2 Administrative and managerial workers / Directeurs et cadres administratifs supérieurs / Directores y funcionarios públicos superiores	3 Clerical and related workers / Personnel administratif et travailleurs assimilés / Personal administrativo y trabajadores asimilados	4 Sales workers / Personnel commercial et vendeurs / Comerciantes y vendedores	5 Service workers / Travailleurs spécialisés dans les services / Trabajadores de los servicios	6 Agricultural, animal husbandry and forestry workers, fishermen and hunters / Agriculteurs, éleveurs, forestiers, pêcheurs et chasseurs / Trabajadores agrícolas y forestales, pescadores y cazadores	7/8/9 Production and related workers, transport equipment, operators and labourers / Ouvriers et manœuvres non agricoles et conducteurs d'engins de transport / Obreros no agrícolas, conductores de máquinas y vehículos de transp. y trabaj. asimilados	X Workers not classifiable by occupation / Travailleurs ne pouvant être classés selon la profession / Trabajadores que no pueden ser clasificados según la ocupación
1973	1 916	4	—	250	50	287	—	1 248	77
1974	2 113	6	5	154	31	195	73	1 572	77

[1] For figures prior to 1973, see previous editions of the *Year Book*.

[1] *Pour les données avant 1973, voir les précédentes éditions de l'*Annuaire.

[1] Para los datos antes de 1973, véanse las precedentes ediciones del *Anuario.*

Mauritius

(ISCO — CITP — CIUO 1958)

Occupational groups *(Employment office statistics)*
Groupes de professions *(Statistiques des bureaux de placement)*
Grupos de ocupaciones *(Estadísticas de las oficinas de colocación)*

Date / Date / Fecha	Total	Professional, technical and related workers / Professions libérales, techniciens et assimilés / Profesiones liberales, técnicos y asimilados	Administrative, executive, managerial workers / Directeurs, cadres administratifs supérieurs / Administradores, gerentes, directores	Clerical workers / Employés de bureau / Empleados de oficina	Sales workers / Vendeurs / Vendedores	Farmers, fishermen and related workers / Agriculteurs, pêcheurs et assimilés / Agricultores, pescadores y asimilados	Miners, quarrymen and related workers / Mineurs, carriers et assimilés / Mineros, canteros y asimilados	Workers in transport and communication occupations / Travailleurs dans les professions des transports et des communications / Trabajadores de los transportes y comunicaciones	Craftsmen, prod. process workers, labourers not elsewhere classified / Artisans, ouvriers de métier et à la production, manœuvres non classés ailleurs / Artesanos, trabaj. ocupados en los div. procesos de prod., peones no clasif. bajo otros epígr.	Service workers / Travailleurs spécialisés dans les services / Trabajadores de los servicios	Workers not classifiable by occupation / Personnes ne pouvant être classées selon la profession / Trabajadores que no pueden ser clasificados según la ocupación
1965	8 333	81	—	205	173	1 762	9	459	2 894	354	2 396
1966	14 129	105	2	204	444	3 774	18	671	4 516	509	3 886
1967	14 178	114	1	179	540	4 152	29	586	4 433	616	3 528
1968	9 084	117	1	130	365	1 810	19	379	3 330	664	2 269
1969	14 284	126	1	147	473	3 430	19	499	4 803	1 025	3 761
1970	20 993	149	1	172	656	5 787	18	598	6 023	1 070	6 519
1971	30 659	196	—	211	974	8 567	29	727	7 547	1 198	11 210
1972	34 463	198	2	196	975	9 577	38	716	7 640	1 116	14 003
1973	27 217	148	1	212	731	6 576	20	475	5 478	911	12 698
1974	21 157	126	—	209	589	5 613	10	325	4 359	681	9 245

11 Unemployment by industrial or occupational groups
Chômage par groupes d'activité économique ou de professions
Desempleo por grupos de actividad económica o de ocupaciones

Nigeria

Occupational groups *(Employment office statistics)*
Groupes de professions *(Statistiques des bureaux de placement)*
Grupos de ocupaciones *(Estadísticas de las oficinas de colocación)*

Date / Date / Fecha	Total	0/1 Professional, technical and related workers / *Personnel des professions scientifiques, techniques, libérales et assimilées* / Profesionales, técnicos y trabajadores asimilados	2 Administrative and managerial workers / *Directeurs et cadres administratifs supérieurs* / Directores y funcionarios públicos superiores	3 Clerical and related workers / *Personnel administratif et travailleurs assimilés* / Personal administrativo y trabajadores asimilados	4 Sales workers / *Personnel commercial et vendeurs* / Comerciantes y vendedores	5 Service workers / *Travailleurs spécialisés dans les services* / Trabajadores de los servicios	6 Agricultural, animal husbandry and forestry workers, fishermen and hunters / *Agriculteurs, éleveurs, forestiers, pêcheurs et chasseurs* / Trabajadores agrícolas y forestales, pescadores y cazadores	7/8/9 Production and related workers, transport equipment, operators and labourers / *Ouvriers et manœuvres non agricoles et conducteurs d'engins de transport* / Obreros no agrícolas, conductores de máquinas y vehículos de transp. y trabaj. asimilados	X Workers not classifiable occupation [1] / *Travailleurs ne pouvant être classés selon la profession* [1] / Trabajadores que no pueden ser clasificados según la ocupación [1]
1967	20 049	368	—	1 343	178	709	99	7 860	9 492
1968	12 929	291	5	1 027	129	642	131	6 730	3 974
1969	12 166	118	1	774	103	624	111	6 493	3 942
1970	13 507	104	1	857	107	587	61	7 362	4 428
1971	14 410	104	1	844	163	589	73	7 818	4 818
1972	15 371	96	—	823	177	1 189	50	8 113	4 923
1973	19 096	93	—	1 078	188	1 451	87	10 046	6 153
1974	20 471	58	2	821	173	862	44	11 944	6 567

[1] Incl. persons seeking work for the first time.
[1] *Y compris les personnes en quête d'emploi pour la première fois.*
[1] Incl. las personas en busca de trabajo por primera vez.

Sierra Leone

Occupational groups *(Employment office statistics)* [1]
Groupes de professions *(Statistiques des bureaux de placement)* [1]
Grupos de ocupaciones *(Estadísticas de las oficinas de colocación)* [1]

Date / Date / Fecha	Total	0/1 Professional, technical and related workers / *Personnel des professions scientifiques, techniques, libérales et assimilées* / Profesionales, técnicos y trabajadores asimilados	2 Administrative and managerial workers / *Directeurs et cadres administratifs supérieurs* / Directores y funcionarios públicos superiores	3 Clerical and related workers / *Personnel administratif et travailleurs assimilés* / Personal administrativo y trabajadores asimilados	4 Sales workers / *Personnel commercial et vendeurs* / Comerciantes y vendedores	5 Service workers / *Travailleurs spécialisés dans les services* / Trabajadores de los servicios	6 Agricultural, animal husbandry and forestry workers, fishermen and hunters / *Agriculteurs, éleveurs, forestiers, pêcheurs et chasseurs* / Trabajadores agrícolas y forestales, pescadores y cazadores	7/8/9 Production and related workers, transport equipment, operators and labourers / *Ouvriers et manœuvres non agricoles et conducteurs d'engins de transport* / Obreros no agrícolas, conductores de máquinas y vehículos de transp. y trabaj. asimilados	X Workers not classifiable by occupation / *Travailleurs ne pouvant être classés selon la profession* / Trabajadores que no pueden ser clasificados según la ocupación
1973	5 746	5	—	1 040	378	509	8	1 121	2 685
1974	5 559	5	—	1 015	390	322	14	746	3 067

[1] Excl. persons registered at the Maritime Pool (6,312 in 1974).
[1] *Non compris les demandeurs d'emploi enregistrés au bureau de placement maritime (6 312 en 1974).*
[1] Excl. los solicitantes de trabajo registrados en la oficina de colocación marítima (6 312 en 1974).

11 Unemployment by industrial or occupational groups
Chômage par groupes d'activité économique ou de professions
Desempleo por grupos de actividad económica o de ocupaciones

South Africa, Rep. of [1]

Occupational groups *(Employment office statistics)*
Groupes de professions *(Statistiques des bureaux de placement)*
Grupos de ocupaciones *(Estadísticas de las oficinas de colocación)*

Date / Date / Fecha	Total	Civil and clerical workers / Fonctionnaires et employés de bureau / Funcionarios y oficinistas	Commercial employees / Employés de commerce / Empleados de comercio	Professional and semi-professional workers / Professions libérales et semi-libérales / Profesiones liberales y semiliberales	Transport, storage, communication, personnel services / Transports, entrepôts, communications, services personnels / Transportes, almacenaje, comunicaciones, servicios personales	Skilled workers / Ouvriers qualifiés / Obreros calificados	Semi-skilled and unskilled workers / Ouvriers semi-qualifiés et non qualifiés / Obreros semicalificados y no calificados
1965	11 653	2 512	1 152	151	1 408	670	5 760
1966	13 534	2 838	1 176	128	1 566	879	6 947
1967	13 899	2 890	1 206	158	1 763	1 007	6 875
1968	13 668	2 898	1 177	183	1 736	950	6 724
1969	10 893	2 471	981	132	1 390	630	5 289
1970	8 489	1 943	751	101	997	437	4 259
1971	8 577	2 105	753	78	936	538	4 167
1972	12 200	3 047	997	100	1 319	1 184	5 553
1973	10 785	2 636	930	124	1 048	929	5 118
1974	8 350	2 126	772	110	836	631	3 875
1975: III	10 445	2 571	930	139	1 016	1 130	4 659

[1] Non-indigenous population.   [1] *Population non indigène.*   [1] Población no indígena.

Tunisie

(ISCO — CITP — CIUO 1958)

Occupational groups *(Employment office statistics)*
Groupes de professions *(Statistiques des bureaux de placement)*
Grupos de ocupaciones *(Estadísticas de las oficinas de colocación)*

Date / Date / Fecha	Total	Professional, technical and related workers / Professions libérales, techniciens et assimilés / Profesiones liberales, técnicos y asimilados	Administrative, executive, managerial workers / Directeurs, cadres administratifs supérieurs / Administradores, gerentes, directores	Clerical workers / Employés de bureau / Empleados de oficina	Sales workers / Vendeurs / Vendedores	Farmers, fishermen and related workers / Agriculteurs, pêcheurs et assimilés / Agricultores, pescadores y asimilados	Miners, quarrymen and related workers / Mineurs, carriers et assimilés / Mineros, canteros y asimilados	Workers in transport and communication occupations / Travailleurs dans les professions des transports et des communications / Trabajadores de los transportes y comunicaciones	Craftsmen, prod. process workers, labourers not elsewhere classified / Artisans, ouvriers de métier et à la prod., manœuvres non classés ailleurs / Artesanos, trabaj. ocupados en los div. procesos de prod., peones no clasif. bajo otros epígr.	Service workers / Travailleurs spécialisés dans les services / Trabajadores de los servicios	Persons seeking work for the first time [1] / Personnes en quête d'emploi pour la première fois [1] / Personas en busca de trabajo por primera vez [1]
1970	63 683	33	5	646	39	10 440	28	630	41 652	1 746	8 464
1971	52 476	42	2	597	37	9 456	31	778	31 597	1 870	8 066
1972	31 929	49	2	481	38	4 892	35	458	17 529	1 306	7 139
1973	36 971	58	3	432	41	6 132	26	439	21 029	835	7 976

[1] Incl. workers not classifiable by occupation.   [1] *Y compris les personnes ne pouvant être classées selon la profession.*   [1] Incl. los trabajadores que no pueden ser clasificados según la ocupación.

11 Unemployment by industrial or occupational groups
Chômage par groupes d'activité économique ou de professions
Desempleo por grupos de actividad económica o de ocupaciones

AMERICA — AMÉRIQUE — AMERICA

Canada

(ISIC — CITI — CIIU 1958)

A Industrial groups *(Labour force sample surveys)*
Groupes d'activité économique *(Enquêtes par sondage sur la main-d'œuvre)*
Grupos de actividad económica *(Encuestas por muestra sobre la fuerza trabajadora)*

Date / Date / Fecha	Total	Agriculture, forestry, fishing / Agriculture, sylviculture, pêche / Agricultura, silvicultura, pesca	Mining, quarrying / Industries extractives / Minas, canteras	Manufacturing / Industries manufacturières / Industrias manufactureras	Construction / Construction / Construcción	Commerce / Commerce / Comercio	Electricity, gas, water, sanitary services, transport, storage, communication / Electricité, gaz, eau, services sanitaires, transports, entrepôts, communications / Electricidad, gas, agua, servicios sanitarios, transportes, almacenaje, comunicaciones	Services[1] / Services[1] / Servicios[1]	Persons seeking work for the first time / Personnes en quête d'emploi pour la première fois / Personas en busca de trabajo por primera vez
1965	280 000	36 000		57 000	53 000	30 000	25 000	53 000	26 000
1966	267 000	31 000		58 000	51 000	29 000	23 000	50 000	26 000
1967	315 000	31 000		74 000	59 000	34 000	29 000	57 000	32 000
1968	382 000	38 000		85 000	68 000	44 000	31 000	76 000	40 000
1969	382 000	38 000		84 000	62 000	45 000	31 000	76 000	46 000
1970	495 000	44 000		114 000	85 000	58 000	35 000	96 000	63 000
1971	552 000	46 000		125 000	85 000	67 000	38 000	118 000	74 000
1972	562 000	40 000		124 000	88 000	70 000	38 000	139 000	63 000
1973	520 000	36 000		109 000	80 000	67 000	36 000	138 000	54 000
1974	525 000	42 000		116 000	81 000	63 000	36 000	138 000	49 000

[1] Incl. finance, insurance and real estate.
[1] *Y compris les établissements financiers, les assurances et les affaires immobilières.*
[1] Incl. los establecimientos financieros, los seguros y los bienes inmuebles.

B Occupational groups *(Labour force sample surveys)*
Groupes de professions *(Enquêtes par sondage sur la main-d'œuvre)*
Grupos de ocupaciones *(Encuestas por muestra sobre la fuerza trabajadora)*

(ISCO — CITP — CIUO 1958)

Date / Date / Fecha	Total	Professional, technical and related workers / Professions libérales, techniciens et assimilés / Profesiones liberales, técnicos y asimilados	Administrative, executive, managerial workers / Directeurs, cadres administratifs supérieurs / Administradores, gerentes, directores	Clerical workers / Employés de bureau / Empleados de oficina	Sales workers / Vendeurs / Vendedores	Farmers, fishermen and related workers / Agriculteurs, pêcheurs et assimilés / Agricultores, pescadores y asimilados	Miners, quarrymen and related workers / Mineurs, carriers et assimilés / Mineros, canteros y asimilados	Workers in transport occupations / Travailleurs dans les professions des transports / Trabajadores de los transportes	Craftsmen, prod. process workers, labourers not elsewhere classified / Artisans, ouvriers de métier et à la production, manœuvres non classés ailleurs / Artesanos, trabaj. ocupados en los div. procesos de produc., peones no clasif. bajo otros epígr.	Service workers / Travailleurs spécialisés dans les services / Trabajadores de los servicios	Persons seeking work for the first time / Personnes en quête d'emploi pour la première fois / Personas en busca de trabajo por primera vez
1965	280 000	40 000 [1]				31 000		20 000	134 000	29 000	26 000
1966	267 000	42 000				28 000		16 000	129 000	26 000	26 000
1967	315 000	52 000				27 000		20 000	153 000	31 000	32 000
1968	382 000	66 000				34 000		21 000	179 000	40 000	40 000
1969	382 000	70 000				33 000		22 000	169 000	42 000	46 000
1970	495 000	96 000				37 000		29 000	224 000	46 000	63 000
1971	552 000	110 000				39 000		33 000	237 000	60 000	74 000
1972	562 000	122 000				38 000		32 000	242 000	66 000	63 000
1973	520 000	125 000				36 000		31 000	212 000	63 000	54 000
1974	525 000	132 000				43 000		26 000	208 000	66 000	49 000

[1] Incl. workers in communication occupations.
[1] *Y compris les travailleurs des communications.*
[1] Incl. los trabajadores de las comunicaciones.

11 Unemployment by industrial or occupational groups
Chômage par groupes d'activité économique ou de professions
Desempleo por grupos de actividad económica o de ocupaciones

Chile

(ISIC — CITI — CIIU 1958)

A Industrial groups *(Labour force sample surveys)*
Groupes d'activité économique *(Enquêtes par sondage sur la main-d'œuvre)*
Grupos de actividad económica *(Encuestas por muestra sobre la fuerza trabajadora)*

Date / Date / Fecha	Total	Agriculture, forestry, fishing / Agriculture, sylviculture, pêche / Agricultura, silvicultura, pesca	Mining, quarrying / Industries extractives / Minas, canteras	Manufacturing / Industries manufacturières / Industrias manufactureras	Construction / Construction / Construcción	Commerce / Commerce / Comercio	Electricity, gas, water, sanitary services, transport, storage, communication / Electricité, gaz, eau, services sanitaires, transports, entrepôts, communications / Electricidad, gas, agua, servicios sanitarios, transportes, almacenaje, comunicaciones	Services / Services / Servicios	Activities not adequately described / Activités mal désignées / Actividades no bien especificadas	Persons seeking work for the first time / Personnes en quête d'emploi pour la première fois / Personas en busca de trabajo por primera vez
1966 [1]	159 400	10 000	2 800	28 500	29 200	13 700	12 400	23 000	3 000	36 800
1967 [2]	132 500	12 200	2 500	27 600	29 000	12 500	9 600	17 100	200	21 800
1968 [3]	158 000	10 700	4 000	31 700	35 900	16 900	6 700	22 000	—	30 000
1969 [4]	111 400	6 700	2 800	23 700	19 400	13 000	9 200	11 500	—	25 100
1970 [3]	105 700	10 100	1 400	21 400	25 000	9 100	9 700	8 800	—	20 300
1971	113 400	8 400	1 900	21 500	21 500	10 400	9 100	13 600	1 700	25 300
1972 [5]	93 100	5 000	2 100	17 200	14 600	7 800	9 000	10 800	1 300	25 200

[1] Aug. and Dec. [2] April, Aug. and Dec. [3] Oct. [4] Sep. [5] March.

[1] Août et déc. [2] Avril, août et déc. [3] Oct. [4] Sept. [5] Mars.

[1] Agosto y dic. [2] Abril, agosto y dic. [3] Oct. [4] Sept. [5] Marzo.

B Occupational groups *(Labour force sample surveys)*
Groupes de professions *(Enquêtes par sondage sur la main-d'œuvre)*
Grupos de ocupaciones *(Encuestas por muestra sobre la fuerza trabajadora)*

(ISCO — CITP — CIUO 1958)

Date / Date / Fecha	Total	Professional, technical and related workers / Professions libérales, techniciens et assimilés / Profesiones liberales, técnicos y asimilados	Administrative, executive, managerial workers / Directeurs, cadres administratifs supérieurs / Administradores, gerentes, directores	Clerical workers / Employés de bureau / Empleados de oficina	Sales workers / Vendeurs / Vendedores	Farmers, fishermen and related workers / Agriculteurs, pêcheurs et assimilés / Agricultores, pescadores y asimilados	Miners, quarrymen and related workers / Mineurs, carriers et assimilés / Mineros, canteros y asimilados	Workers in transport and communication occupations / Travailleurs dans les professions des transports et des communications / Trabajadores de los transportes y comunicaciones	Craftsmen, prod. process workers, labourers not elsewhere classified / Artisans, ouvriers de métier et à la production, manœuvres non classés ailleurs / Artesanos, trabaj. ocupados en los div. procesos de prod., peones no clasif. bajo otros epígr.	Service workers / Travailleurs spécialisés dans les services / Trabajadores de los servicios	Persons seeking work for the first time [6] / Personnes en quête d'emploi pour la première fois [6] / Personas en busca de trabajo por primera vez [6]
1966 [1]	159 400	3 300	400	8 700	6 600	10 100	2 200	8 200	64 400	17 700	37 800
1967 [2]	132 500	1 600	500	9 300	6 300	11 800	2 300	7 700	59 100	11 100	22 800
1968 [3]	158 000	1 300	1 200	9 300	8 800	10 500	2 700	4 600	73 000	16 500	30 200
1969 [4]	111 400	1 600	200	5 400	6 200	6 800	2 500	4 600	51 300	7 700	25 100
1970 [3]	105 700	1 000	200	6 600	4 200	10 400	1 400	5 700	51 400	4 600	20 300
1971	113 400	1 100	400	8 300	4 900	8 100	1 600	6 500	48 800	7 000	26 700
1972 [5]	93 100	1 700	600	7 400	4 400	4 900	1 400	6 500	35 500	5 000	26 200

[1] Aug. and Dec. [2] April, Aug. and Dec. [3] Oct. [4] Sep. [5] March. [6] Incl. workers not classifiable by occupation.

[1] Août et déc. [2] Avril, août et déc. [3] Oct. [4] Sept. [5] Mars. [6] Y compris les personnes ne pouvant être classées selon la profession.

[1] Agosto y dic. [2] Abril, agosto y dic. [3] Oct. [4] Sept. [5] Marzo. [6] Incl. los trabajadores que no pueden ser clasificados según la ocupación.

447

11 **Unemployment by industrial or occupational groups**
Chômage par groupes d'activité économique ou de professions
Desempleo por grupos de actividad económica o de ocupaciones

Jamaica

(ISIC — CITI — CIIU 1958)

A Industrial groups *(Labour force sample surveys)*
Groupes d'activité économique *(Enquêtes par sondage sur la main-d'œuvre)*
Grupos de actividad económica *(Encuestas por muestra sobre la fuerza trabajadora)*

Date / Date / Fecha	Total	Agriculture, forestry, fishing and mining / *Agriculture, sylviculture, pêche et mines* / Agricultura, silvicultura, pesca y minas	Manufacturing / *Industries manufacturières* / Industrias manufactureras	Construction / *Construction* / Construcción	Electricity, gas, water, sanitary services, transport and communication / *Electricité, gaz, eau, services sanitaires, transports et communications* / Electricidad, gas, agua, servicios sanitarios, transportes y comunicaciones	Commerce / *Commerce* / Comercio	Services / *Services* / Servicios	Activities not adequately described / *Activités mal désignées* / Actividades no bien especificadas	Persons seeking work for the first time / *Personnes en quête d'emploi pour la première fois* / Personas en busca de trabajo por primera vez
1968	144 650	16 700	13 650	11 150	3 000	10 300	45 500	1 100	43 300
1969	131 650	9 300	12 300	11 150	2 550	7 950	44 100	—	44 300
1972	184 500	13 600	13 650	12 000	3 050	10 000	49 400	3 950	78 850
1973	176 400	12 250	15 600	13 250	3 200	10 900	62 100	2 750	56 350
1974	172 250	13 550	16 850	11 500	3 700	11 000	57 150		58 500

B Occupational groups *(Labour force sample surveys)*
Groupes de professions *(Enquêtes par sondage sur la main-d'œuvre)*
Grupos de ocupaciones *(Encuestas por muestra sobre la fuerza trabajadora)*

Date / Date / Fecha	Total	Professional, technical and related workers [1] / *Professions libérales, techniciens et assimilés* [1] / Profesiones liberales, técnicos y trabajadores asimilados [1]	Administrative, executive and managerial workers / *Directeurs et cadres administratifs supérieurs* / Administradores, gerentes y directores	Clerical workers / *Employés de bureau* / Empleados de oficina	Sales workers / *Vendeurs* / Vendedores	Workers on own account / *Personnes travaillant à leur propre compte* / Trabajadores por cuenta propia	Craftsmen, prod. process workers, labourers not elsewhere classified / *Artisans, ouvriers de métier et à la production, manœuvres non classés ailleurs* / Artesanos, trabaj. ocupados en los div. procesos de prod., peones no clasif. bajo otros epígr.	Service workers / *Travailleurs spécialisés dans les services* / Trabajadores de los servicios	Workers not classifiable by occupation / *Personnes ne pouvant être classées selon la profession* / Trabajadores que no pueden ser clasificados según la ocupación	Persons seeking work for the first time / *Personnes en quête d'emploi pour la première fois* / Personas en busca de trabajo por primera vez
1972	184 500	1 650		11 800		8 100	44 050	37 500	2 550	78 850
1973	176 400	2 450		14 600		11 800	48 150	42 350	700	56 350
1974	172 250	2 100		14 150		10 700	46 500	39 300	1 000	58 500

[1] Excl. workers on own account.

[1] *Non compris les personnes travaillant à leur propre compte.*

[1] Excl. los trabajadores por cuenta propia.

11

Unemployment by industrial or occupational groups
Chômage par groupes d'activité économique ou de professions
Desempleo por grupos de actividad económica o de ocupaciones

Panamá

Industrial groups *(Labour force sample surveys)* [1]
Groupes d'activité économique *(Enquêtes par sondage sur la main-d'œuvre)* [1]
Grupos de actividad económica *(Encuestas por muestra sobre la fuerza trabajadora)* [1]

Date / Date / Fecha	Total	1 Agriculture, forestry, fishing / Agriculture, sylviculture, pêche / Agricultura, silvicultura, pesca	3 Manufacturing / Industries manufacturières / Industrias manufactureras	4 Electricity, gas, water / Electricité, gaz, eau / Electricidad, gas, agua	5 Construction / Construction / Construcción	6 Trade, restaurants and hotels / Commerce, restaurants et hôtels / Comercio, restaurantes y hoteles	7 Transport, storage, communication / Transports, entrepôts, communications / Transportes, almacenaje, comunicaciones	8 Financing, insur., real est., business serv. / Banques, assur., aff. imm., serv. aux entreprises / Bancos, seguros, bienes inm., serv. para empresas	9 Community, social, and pers. services / Services à collectivité, serv. sociaux et pers. / Servicios comunales, sociales y personales	0 Canal zone / Zone du canal / Zona del Canal	Persons seeking work for the first time / Personnes en quête d'emploi pour la première fois / Personas en busca de trabajo por primera vez
1971	36 300	1 500	2 900	—	4 000	4 200	1 900	500	10 600	2 100	8 000
1972	32 200	1 500	2 200	200	2 900	3 700	900	300	5 800	500	14 800

[1] Data for industrial groups are provisional.

[1] *Les données par groupes d'activité économique sont provisoires.*

[1] Los datos por grupos de actividad económica son provisionales.

Puerto Rico (1)

A

Industrial groups *(Labour force sample surveys)* [1]
Groupes d'activité économique *(Enquêtes par sondage sur la main-d'œuvre)* [1]
Grupos de actividad económica *(Encuestas por muestra sobre la fuerza trabajadora)* [1]

Date / Date / Fecha	Total [2]	1 Agriculture, forestry, fishing / Agriculture, sylviculture, pêche / Agricultura, silvicultura, pesca	3 Manufacturing / Industries manufacturières / Industrias manufactureras	5 Construction / Construction / Construcción	6 × Trade [3] / Commerce [3] / Comercio [3]	7 Transport, storage, communication / Transports, entrepôts, communications / Transportes, almacenaje, comunicaciones	6 × ; 8 × ; 9 Community, social, and pers. services [4] / Services à collectivité, serv. sociaux et pers. [4] / Servicios comunales, sociales y personales [4]	0 Activities not adequately described [5] / Activités mal désignées [5] / Actividades no bien especificadas [5]
1967	87 000	15 000	19 000	17 000	9 000	3 000	15 000	8 000
1968	83 000	14 000	20 000	16 000	8 000	3 000	13 000	7 000
1969	76 000	11 000	19 000	15 000	8 000	3 000	13 000	6 000
1970	84 000	11 000	24 000	16 000	9 000	3 000	13 000	8 000
1971	95 000	10 000	27 000	19 000	11 000	3 000	16 000	9 000
1972	101 000	8 000	27 000	22 000	13 000	3 000	17 000	10 000
1973	102 000	7 000	26 000	22 000	12 000	4 000	20 000	9 000
1974	117 000	9 000	27 000	26 000	13 000	4 000	23 000	12 000

[1] Excl. persons temporarily laid off. [2] Incl. industrial groups not specified in the table. [3] Excl. restaurants and hotels. [4] Incl. restaurants and hotels and business services. [5] Incl. persons seeking work for the first time.

[1] *Non compris les personnes temporairement mises à pied.* [2] *Y compris des groupes d'activité économique non spécifiés dans le tableau.* [3] *Non compris les restaurants et les hôtels.* [4] *Y compris les restaurants et les hôtels et les services fournis aux entreprises.* [5] *Y compris les personnes en quête d'emploi pour la première fois.*

[1] Excl. las personas temporalmente despedidas. [2] Incl. grupos de actividad económica no especificados en el cuadro. [3] Excl. los restaurantes y los hoteles. [4] Incl. los restaurantes y los hoteles y los servicios prestados a las empresas. [5] Incl. las personas en busca de trabajo por primera vez.

11 Unemployment by industrial or occupational groups
Chômage par groupes d'activité économique ou de professions
Desempleo por grupos de actividad económica o de ocupaciones

Puerto Rico (2)

B

Occupational groups *(Labour force sample surveys)* [1]
Groupes de professions *(Enquêtes par sondage sur la main-d'œuvre)* [1]
Grupos de ocupaciones *(Encuestas por muestra sobre la fuerza trabajadora)* [1]

Date / Date / Fecha	Total	0/1 Professional, technical and related workers / *Personnel des professions scientifiques, techniques, libérales et assimilées* / Profesionales, técnicos y trabajadores asimilados	2 Administrative and managerial workers / *Directeurs et cadres administratifs supérieurs* / Directores y funcionarios públicos superiores	3 Clerical and related workers / *Personnel administratif et travailleurs assimilés* / Personal administrativo y trabajadores asimilados	4 Sales workers / *Personnel commercial et vendeurs* / Comerciantes y vendedores	5 Service workers / *Travailleurs spécialisés dans les services* / Trabajadores de los servicios	6 Agricultural, animal husbandry and forestry workers, fishermen and hunters / *Agriculteurs, éleveurs, forestiers, pêcheurs et chasseurs* / Trabajadores agrícolas y forestales, pescadores y cazadores	7/8/9 Production and related workers, transport equipment, operators and labourers / *Ouvriers et manœuvres non agricoles et conducteurs d'engins de transport* / Obreros no agrícolas, conductores de máquinas y vehículos de transp. y trabaj. asimilados	X Workers not classifiable by occupation [2] / *Travailleurs ne pouvant être classés selon la profession* [2] / Trabajadores que no pueden ser clasificados según la ocupación [2]
1966	86 000	—	—	4 000	4 000	8 000	14 000	45 000	9 000
1967	87 000	—	—	4 000	3 000	8 000	15 000	47 000	8 000
1968	83 000	—	—	4 000	3 000	7 000	13 000	46 000	7 000
1969	76 000	—	—	4 000	3 000	7 000	11 000	43 000	6 000
1970	84 000	—	—	4 000	3 000	7 000	10 000	48 000	8 000
1971	95 000	—	—	5 000	4 000	8 000	9 000	56 000	9 000
1972	101 000	2 000	—	7 000	5 000	8 000	7 000	61 000	10 000
1973	102 000	3 000	2 000	7 000	5 000	9 000	7 000	61 000	9 000
1974	117 000	3 000	2 000	9 000	5 000	11 000	8 000	67 000	12 000

[1] Excl. persons temporarily laid off. Figures of less than 1,000 persons are indicated by a dash. [2] Incl. persons seeking work for the first time.

[1] *Non compris les personnes temporairement mises à pied. Les chiffres inférieurs à 1 000 personnes sont désignés par un tiret.* [2] *Y compris les personnes en quête d'emploi pour la première fois.*

[1] Excl. las personas temporalmente despedidas. Las cifras inferiores a 1 000 personas están indicadas con un guión. [2] Incl. las personas en busca de trabajo por primera vez.

11 Unemployment by industrial or occupational groups
Chômage par groupes d'activité économique ou de professions
Desempleo por grupos de actividad económica o de ocupaciones

Trinidad and Tobago

(ISIC — CITI — CIIU 1958)

A Industrial groups *(Labour force sample surveys)*
Groupes d'activité économique *(Enquêtes par sondage sur la main-d'œuvre)*
Grupos de actividad económica *(Encuestas por muestra sobre la fuerza trabajadora)*

Date / Date / Fecha	Total	Agriculture, forestry, fishing / Agriculture, sylviculture, pêche / Agricultura, silvicultura, pesca	Mining, quarrying, manufacturing / Industries extractives, industries manufacturières / Minas, canteras, industrias manufactureras	Construction [1] / Construction [1] / Construcción [1]	Commerce / Commerce / Comercio	Transport, storage, communication / Transports, entrepôts, communications / Transportes, almacenaje, comunicaciones	Services / Services / Servicios	Activities not adequately described / Activités mal désignées / Actividades no bien especificadas	Persons seeking work for the first time / Personnes en quête d'emploi pour la première fois / Personas en busca de trabajo por primera vez
1965	48 400	4 400	5 800	11 800	4 600	2 200	8 600	.	11 000
1966	48 800	3 200	9 800	11 600	5 600	1 200	6 800	.	10 600
1967	53 700	4 600	8 200	14 000	5 300	2 800	9 500	.	9 200
1968	54 000	5 000	8 300	13 400	4 900	2 400	10 100	.	10 000
1969	48 000	4 200	7 400	11 100	4 200	2 000	8 700	.	10 300
1970	46 400	4 600	8 000	11 200	3 900	1 900	6 400	.	10 400
1971 [2]	46 400	3 500	7 500	12 800	3 400	2 400	6 600	.	10 200
1972	.	.	.	.	.	.	.	.	.
1973	58 900	2 400	9 100	14 500	6 800	2 000	8 600	2 600	13 000

[1] Incl. electricity, gas, water and sanitary services.
[2] First semester.

[1] Y compris l'électricité, le gaz, l'eau et les services sanitaires. [2] Premier semestre.

[1] Incl. la electricidad, el gas, el agua y los servicios sanitarios. [2] Primer semestre.

B Occupational groups *(Labour force sample surveys)*
Groupes de professions *(Enquêtes par sondage sur la main-d'œuvre)*
Grupos de ocupaciones *(Encuestas por muestra sobre la fuerza trabajadora)*

(ISCO — CITP — CIUO 1958)

Date / Date / Fecha	Total	Professional, technical and related workers / Professions libérales, techniciens et assimilés / Profesiones liberales, técnicos y asimilados	Administrative, executive, managerial, clerical and related workers / Directeurs, cadres adm. sup., employés de bureau et assimilés / Administradores, gerentes, directores, empleados de oficina y asimilados	Sales workers / Vendeurs / Vendedores	Farmers, fishermen and related workers / Agriculteurs, pêcheurs et assimilés / Agricultores, pescadores y asimilados	Craftsmen, prod. process workers, labourers not elsewhere classified [1] / Artisans, ouvriers de métier et à la production, manœuvres non classés ailleurs [1] / Artesanos, trabaj. ocupados en los div. procesos de prod., peones no clasif. bajo otros epígr. [1]	Workers in transport and communication occupations / Travailleurs des transports et des communications / Trabajadores de los transportes y comunicaciones	Service workers / Travailleurs spécialisés dans les services / Trabajadores de los servicios	Workers not classifiable by occupation / Personnes ne pouvant être classées selon la profession / Trabajadores que no pueden ser clasificados según la ocupación	Persons seeking work for the first time / Personnes en quête d'emploi pour la première fois / Personas en busca de trabajo por primera vez
1965	48 400	400	2 500	2 400	4 000	17 100	2 800	8 400	.	11 000
1966	48 800	400	1 900	3 100	3 200	21 300	2 000	6 400	.	10 600
1967	53 700	1 000	3 000	3 700	4 200	23 500	2 200	7 000	.	9 200
1968	54 000	800	2 600	3 000	4 800	23 600	2 000	7 200	.	10 000
1969	48 000	400	2 200	2 500	4 200	19 200	2 200	6 900	.	10 300
1970	46 400	200	2 400	2 400	4 400	19 900	2 100	4 700	.	10 400
1971 [2]	46 400	300	2 100	1 600	3 400	21 900	1 700	5 300	.	10 200
1972	.	.	.	.	.	.	.	.	.	.
1973	58 900	1 500	3 300	4 000	2 000	24 200	1 200	6 900	2 700	13 000

[1] Incl. miners, quarrymen and related workers.
[2] First semester.

[1] Y compris les mineurs, carriers et travailleurs assimilés.
[2] Premier semestre.

[1] Incl. los mineros, canteros y trabajadores asimilados.
[2] Primer semestre.

11 Unemployment by industrial or occupational groups
Chômage par groupes d'activité économique ou de professions
Desempleo por grupos de actividad económica o de ocupaciones

United States

(ISIC — CITI — CIIU 1958)

A Industrial groups *(Labour force sample surveys)* [1]
Groupes d'activité économique *(Enquêtes par sondage sur la main-d'œuvre)* [1]
Grupos de actividad económica *(Encuestas por muestra sobre la fuerza trabajadora)* [1]

Date / Date / Fecha	Total [2]	Wage earners and salaried employees — *Ouvriers et employés* — Obreros y empleados						
		Agriculture, forestry, fishing / *Agriculture, sylviculture, pêche* / Agricultura, silvicultura, pesca	Mining, quarrying / *Industries extractives* / Minas, canteras	Manufacturing / *Industries manufacturières* / Industrias manufactureras	Construction / *Construction* / Construcción	Commerce / *Commerce* / Comercio	Transport, storage, communication [3] / *Transports, entrepôts, communications* [3] / Transportes, almacenaje, comunicaciones [3]	Services / *Services* / Servicios
1965	3 456 000	122 000	29 000	778 000	378 000	663 000	127 000	651 000
1966	2 976 000	99 000	20 000	654 000	298 000	599 000	95 000	587 000
1967	2 975 000	102 000	19 000	780 000	271 000	605 900	108 000	606 000
1968	2 817 000	92 000	16 000	697 000	259 000	592 000	96 000	603 000
1969	2 831 000	79 000	15 000	709 000	234 000	610 000	107 000	619 000
1970	4 088 000	100 000	16 000	1 197 000	394 000	842 000	163 000	811 000
1971	4 993 000	108 000	23 000	1 404 000	447 000	1 081 000	191 000	1 026 000
1972	4 840 000	108 000	19 000	1 155 000	466 000	1 134 000	183 000	1 021 000
1973	4 304 000	99 000	18 000	932 000	417 000	1 011 000	152 000	963 000
1974	5 076 000	115 000	19 000	1 247 000	499 000	1 197 000	174 000	942 000

[1] Persons aged 16 years and over (1965-66: 14 years and over). [2] Incl. casual workers. Incl. industrial groups not specified in the table. [3] Incl. electricity, gas, water and sanitary services.

[1] *Personnes âgées de 16 ans et plus (1965-66 : 14 ans et plus).* [2] *Y compris les travailleurs occasionnels. Y compris des groupes d'activité économique non spécifiés dans le tableau.* [3] *Y compris l'électricité, le gaz, l'eau et les services sanitaires.*

[1] Personas de 16 años y más (1965-66: 14 años y más). [2] Incl. los trabajadores ocasionales. Incl. grupos de actividad económica no especificados en el cuadro. [3] Incl. la electricidad, el gas, el agua y los servicios sanitarios.

B Occupational groups *(Labour force sample surveys)* [1]
Groupes de professions *(Enquêtes par sondage sur la main-d'œuvre)* [1]
Grupos de ocupaciones *(Encuestas por muestra sobre la fuerza trabajadora)* [1]

(ISCO — CITP — CIUO 1958)

Date / Date / Fecha	Total [2]	Professional, technical and related workers / *Professions libérales, techniciens et assimilés* / Profesiones liberales, técnicos y trabajadores asimilados	Farmers, farm managers / *Agriculteurs, directeurs d'exploitations agric.* / Agricultores, directores de empresas agrícolas	Executive and managerial workers [3] / *Directeurs et cadres adm. supérieurs* [3] / Administradores, gerentes y directores [3]	Clerical and related workers / *Employés de bureau et assimilés* / Empleados de oficina y asimilados	Sales workers / *Vendeurs* / Vendedores	Craftsmen, foremen and related workers [4] / *Artisans, contremaîtres et assimilés* [4] / Artesanos, contramaestres y asimilados [4]	Operative and related workers / *Ouvriers spécialisés et assimilés* / Operarios especializados y asimilados	Housekeeping service workers / *Personnel domestique* / Trabajadores del servicio doméstico	Service workers [5] / *Travailleurs dans les services* [5] / Trabajadores de los servicios [5]	Farm labourers and foremen / *Ouvriers et contremaîtres agricoles* / Obreros y contramaestres agrícolas	Labourers not elsewhere classified / *Ouvriers non classés ailleurs* / Obreros no clasificados en otras partes
1965	3 456 000	133 000	10 000	84 000	375 000	162 000	343 000	774 000	99 000	411 000	103 000	352 000
1966	2 976 000	124 000	9 000	76 000	347 000	133 000	280 000	631 000	85 000	372 000	77 000	290 000
1967	2 975 000	134 000	4 000	70 000	399 000	152 000	249 000	728 000	76 000	366 000	81 000	290 000
1968	2 817 000	126 000	4 000	76 000	391 000	132 000	245 000	653 000	71 000	366 000	69 000	276 000
1969	2 831 000	144 000	2 000	76 000	420 000	140 000	226 000	663 000	61 000	359 000	61 000	265 000
1970	4 088 000	227 000	4 000	112 000	579 000	195 000	398 000	1 057 000	69 000	472 000	79 000	391 000
1971	4 993 000	333 000	5 000	145 000	683 000	225 000	507 000	1 182 000	69 000	650 000	76 000	488 000
1972	4 840 000	282 000	3 000	145 000	704 000	238 000	482 000	1 009 000	60 000	677 000	80 000	483 000
1973	4 304 000	260 000	2 000	123 000	630 000	205 000	434 000	857 000	62 000	612 000	76 000	397 000
1974	5 076 000	285 000	4 000	168 000	725 000	240 000	523 000	1 123 000	56 000	708 000	75 000	492 000

[1] Persons aged 16 years and over (1965-66: 14 years and over). [2] Incl. casual workers. [3] Excl. farm managers. [4] Excl. farm foremen. [5] Excl. house-keeping service workers.

[1] *Personnes âgées de 16 ans et plus (1965-66 : 14 ans et plus).* [2] *Y compris les travailleurs occasionnels.* [3] *Non compris les directeurs d'exploitations agricoles.* [4] *Non compris les contremaîtres agricoles.* [5] *Non compris le personnel domestique.*

[1] Personas de 16 años y más (1965-66: 14 años y más). [2] Incl. los trabajadores ocasionales. [3] Excl. los directores de empresas agrícolas. [4] Excl. los contramaestres agrícolas. [5] Excl. los trabajadores del servicio doméstico.

11 Unemployment by industrial or occupational groups
Chômage par groupes d'activité économique ou de professions
Desempleo por grupos de actividad económica o de ocupaciones

Uruguay (Montevideo)

(ISIC — CITI — CIIU 1958)

A Industrial groups *(Labour force sample surveys)*
Groupes d'activité économique *(Enquêtes par sondage sur la main-d'œuvre)*
Grupos de actividad económica *(Encuestas por muestra sobre la fuerza trabajadora)*

Date / Date / Fecha	Total	Agriculture, forestry, fishing / Agriculture, sylviculture, pêche / Agricultura, silvicultura, pesca	Manufacturing / Industries manufacturières / Industrias manufactureras	Construction / Construction / Construcción	Electricity, gas, water and sanitary services / Electricité, gaz, eau et services sanitaires / Electricidad, gas, agua y servicios sanitarios	Commerce / Commerce / Comercio	Transport, storage, communication / Transports, entrepôts, communications / Transportes, almacenaje, comunicaciones	Services / Services / Servicios	Activities not adequately described / Activités mal désignées / Actividades no bien especificadas	Persons seeking work for the first time / Personnes en quête d'emploi pour la première fois / Personas en busca de trabajo por primera vez
1968 [1]	43 300	200	12 300	4 100	—	5 100	1 300	6 700	—	13 600
1969	44 850	700	14 600	4 000	100	4 700	600	5 300	1 000	13 850
1970	39 250	350	11 650	2 350	100	4 300	850	5 200	1 050	13 400
1971	41 200	250	13 900	2 300	200	4 450	1 400	6 500	500	11 700
1972 [2]	41 700	400	13 500	2 200	100	6 100	2 200	5 900	—	11 300
1973 [3]	49 400	300	14 700	3 600	300	6 000	1 500	8 600	500	13 900

[1] Oct.-Dec. [2] Jan.-May. [3] Feb.-June.   [1] *Oct.-déc.* [2] *Janv.-mai.* [3] *Fév.-juin.*   [1] Oct.-dic.. [2] Enero-mayo. [3] Febr.-junio.

B Occupational groups *(Labour force sample surveys)*
Groupes de professions *(Enquêtes par sondage sur la main-d'œuvre)*
Grupos de ocupaciones *(Encuestas por muestra sobre la fuerza trabajadora)*

(ISCO — CITP — CIUO 1958)

Date / Date / Fecha	Total	Professional, technical and related workers / Professions libérales, techniciens et assimilés / Profesiones liberales, técnicos y asimilados	Administrative, executive, managerial workers / Directeurs, cadres administratifs supérieurs / Administradores, gerentes, directores	Clerical workers / Employés de bureau / Empleados de oficina	Sales workers / Vendeurs / Vendedores	Farmers, fishermen and related workers / Agriculteurs, pêcheurs et assimilés / Agricultores, pescadores y asimilados	Workers in transport occupations / Travailleurs dans les professions des transports / Trabajadores de los transportes	Craftsmen, prod. process workers, labourers not elsewhere classified / Artisans, ouvriers de métier et à la production, manœuvres non classés ailleurs / Artesanos, trabaj. ocupados en los div. procesos de produc., peones no clasif. bajo otros epígr.	Service workers / Travailleurs spécialisés dans les services / Trabajadores de los servicios	Persons seeking work for the first time [4] / Personnes en quête d'emploi pour la première fois [4] / Personas en busca de trabajo por primera vez [4]
1968 [1]	43 300	2 500	—	3 800	3 900	400	1 300	13 600	4 200	13 600
1969	44 850	900	100	2 800	2 950	550	700	18 550	3 450	14 850
1970	39 250	550	50	2 700	3 050	1 200	400	13 450	3 600	14 250
1971	41 200	1 200	200	3 550	3 000	300	1 250	14 950	3 700	13 050
1972 [2]	41 700	1 500	200	3 100	3 300	500	1 000	12 600	4 000	15 500
1973 [3]	49 400	1 800	300	4 500	3 500	500	1 100	18 300	4 400	15 000

[1] Oct.-Dec. [2] Jan.-May. [3] Feb.-June. [4] Incl. workers not classifiable by occupation.   [1] *Oct.-déc.* [2] *Janv.-mai.* [3] *Fév.-juin.* [4] *Y compris les personnes ne pouvant être classées selon la profession.*   [1] Oct.-dic. [2] Enero-mayo. [3] Febr.-junio. [4] Incl. los trabajadores que no pueden ser clasificados según la ocupación.

UNEMPLOYMENT

11 Unemployment by industrial or occupational groups
Chômage par groupes d'activité économique ou de professions
Desempleo por grupos de actividad económica o de ocupaciones

Venezuela

(ISIC — CITI — CIIU 1958)

A Industrial groups *(Labour force sample surveys)*
Groupes d'activité économique *(Enquêtes par sondage sur la main-d'œuvre)*
Grupos de actividad económica *(Encuestas por muestra sobre la fuerza trabajadora)*

Date / Date / Fecha	Total [1]	Agriculture, forestry, fishing / Agriculture, sylviculture, pêche / Agricultura, silvicultura, pesca	Mining, quarrying / Industries extractives / Minas, canteras	Manufacturing / Industries manufacturières / Industrias manufactureras	Construction / Construction / Construcción	Electricity, gas, water and sanitary services / Electricité, gaz, eau et services sanitaires / Electricidad, gas, agua y servicios sanitarios	Commerce / Commerce / Comercio	Transport, storage, communication / Transports, entrepôts, communications / Transportes, almacenaje, comunicaciones	Services / Services / Servicios	Activities not adequately described / Activités mal désignées / Actividades no bien especificadas
1967 [2]	217 372	14 844	4 020	30 775	30 595	2 378	20 693	8 034	42 723	11 822
1968 [3]	181 568	16 256	3 626	26 912	30 377	2 858	22 207	10 532	31 309	2 010
1969 [4]	191 822	12 780	2 922	34 802	31 850	2 707	26 175	10 473	32 988	231
1970 [5]	198 847	17 329	4 842	33 213	30 089	3 419	24 020	12 454	36 089	407
1971 [6]	195 161	15 538	3 566	39 674	29 817	2 832	25 207	14 271	32 663	209

[1] Incl. persons seeking work for the first time. [2] April and Aug. [3] March, July and Nov. [4] March. [5] April and Dec. [6] April and July.

[1] Y compris les personnes en quête d'emploi pour la première fois. [2] Avril et août. [3] Mars, juillet et nov. [4] Mars. [5] Avril et déc. [6] Avril et juillet.

[1] Incl. las personas en busca de trabajo por primera vez. [2] Abril y agosto. [3] Marzo, julio y nov. [4] Marzo. [5] Abril y dic. [6] Abril y julio.

(ISCO — CITP — CIUO 1958)

B Occupational groups *(Labour force sample surveys)*
Groupes de professions *(Enquêtes par sondage sur la main-d'œuvre)*
Grupos de ocupaciones *(Encuestas por muestra sobre la fuerza trabajadora)*

Date / Date / Fecha	Total [1]	Professional, technical and related workers / Professions libérales, techniciens et assimilés / Profesiones liberales, técnicos y asimilados	Administrative, executive, managerial workers / Directeurs, cadres administratifs supérieurs / Administradores, gerentes, directores	Clerical workers / Employés de bureau / Empleados de oficina	Sales workers / Vendeurs / Vendedores	Farmers, fishermen and related workers / Agriculteurs, pêcheurs et assimilés / Agricultores, pescadores y asimilados	Miners, quarrymen and related workers / Mineurs, carriers et assimilés / Mineros, canteros y asimilados	Workers in transport and communication occupations / Travailleurs dans les professions des transports et des communications / Trabajadores de los transportes y comunicaciones	Craftsmen, prod. process workers, labourers not elsewhere classified / Artisans, ouvriers de métier et à la production, manœuvres non classés ailleurs / Artesanos, trabaj. ocupados en los div. procesos de prod., peones no clasif. bajo otros epígr.	Service workers / Travailleurs spécialisés dans les services / Trabajadores de los servicios	Workers not classifiable by occupation / Personnes ne pouvant être classées selon la profession / Trabajadores que no pueden ser clasificados según la ocupación
1967 [2]	217 372	8 148	2 188	21 338	12 962	14 418	1 933	11 622	57 855	23 282	12 138
1968 [3]	181 568	7 738	990	17 102	15 685	13 652	1 431	14 798	56 711	16 057	1 923
1969 [4]	191 822	8 442	2 307	23 300	15 994	10 427	1 600	15 363	61 116	15 687	692
1970 [5]	198 847	10 869	3 316	19 075	16 139	14 185	2 017	14 296	64 725	17 140	100
1971 [6]	195 161	8 296	1 788	18 688	16 493	11 972	2 201	15 837	71 908	16 385	209

[1] Incl. persons seeking work for the first time. [2] April and Aug. [3] March, July and Nov. [4] March. [5] April and Dec. [6] April and July.

[1] Y compris les personnes en quête d'emploi pour la première fois. [2] Avril et août. [3] Mars, juillet et nov. [4] Mars. [5] Avril et déc. [6] Avril et juillet.

[1] Incl. las personas en busca de trabajo por primera vez. [2] Abril y agosto. [3] Marzo, julio y nov. [4] Marzo. [5] Abril y dic. [6] Abril y julio.

11 Unemployment by industrial or occupational groups
Chômage par groupes d'activité économique ou de professions
Desempleo por grupos de actividad económica o de ocupaciones

ASIA — ASIE — ASIA

Cyprus

(ISIC — CITI — CIIU 1958)

A Industrial groups *(Employment office statistics)*
Groupes d'activité économique *(Statistiques des bureaux de placement)*
Grupos de actividad económica *(Estadísticas de las oficinas de colocación)*

Date / Date / Fecha	Total	Agriculture, forestry, fishing / Agriculture, sylviculture, pêche / Agricultura, silvicultura, pesca	Mining, quarrying / Industries extractives / Minas, canteras	Manufactur-ing / Industries manufac-turières / Industrias manufactu-reras	Construction / Construction / Construcción	Electricity, gas, water and sanitary services / Electricité, gaz, eau et services sanitaires / Electricidad, gas, agua y servicios sanitarios	Commerce / Commerce / Comercio	Transport, storage, communica-tion / Transports, entrepôts, communica-itons / Transportes, almacenaje, comunica-ciones	Services / Services / Servicios	Activities not adequately described [1] / Activités mal désignées [1] / Actividades no bien especificadas [1]
1965	4 030	238	117	164	1 594	27	104	148	477	1 161
1966	3 484	226	91	163	1 060	27	135	110	492	1 180
1967	2 857	174	127	210	559	29	173	74	491	1 020
1968	3 174	166	99	231	614	38	209	87	543	1 187
1969	2 703	153	115	202	436	35	188	68	428	1 078
1970	2 810	144	67	237	489	37	212	81	433	1 110
1971	2 846	104	108	254	436	20	208	101	399	1 216
1972	2 524	119	43	208	310	21	121	112	371	1 219
1973	3 314	379	66	255	417	24	165	103	490	1 415
1974	11 206	1 206	239	2 339	2 493	51	1 068	503	1 989	1 318
1975: VI	22 380	3 145	525	4 478	6 371	99	2 014	1 278	3 244	1 226

[1] Incl. persons seeking work for the first time.   [1] *Y compris les personnes en quête d'emploi pour la première fois.*   [1] Incl. las personas en busca de trabajo por primera vez.

B Occupational groups *(Employment office statistics)* [1]
Groupes de professions *(Statistiques des bureaux de placement)* [1]
Grupos de ocupaciones *(Estadísticas de las oficinas de colocación)* [1]

(ISCO — CITP — CIUO 1958)

Date / Date / Fecha	Total	Profes-sional, technical and related workers / Professions libérales, techniciens et assimilés / Profesiones liberales, técnicos y asimilados	Adminis-trative, executive, managerial workers / Directeurs, cadres adminis-tratifs supérieurs / Adminis-tradores, gerentes, directores	Clerical workers / Employés de bureau / Empleados de oficina	Sales workers / Vendeurs / Vende-dores	Farmers, fishermen and related workers / Agricul-teurs, pêcheurs et assimilés / Agricul-tores, pescadores y asimilados	Miners, quarrymen and related workers / Mineurs, carriers et assimilés / Mineros, canteros y asimi-lados	Workers in transport and commu-nication occupations / Travailleurs dans les professions des trans-ports et des communi-cations / Trabaja-dores de los trans-portes y comunica-ciones	Craftsmen, prod. process workers, labourers not elsewhere classified / Artisans, ouvriers de métier et à la production, manœuvres non classés ailleurs / Artesanos, trabaj. ocupados en los div. procesos de produc., peones no clasif. bajo otros epígr.	Service workers / Travailleurs spécialisés dans les services / Trabaja-dores de los servicios	Workers not classifiable by occupation [3] / Personnes ne pouvant être classées selon la profession [3] / Trabaja-dores que no pueden ser clasifica-dos según la ocupación [3]
1965 [2]	4 030	50	1	759	64	56	104	200	2 019	354	—
1966 [2]	3 484	46	1	416	57	28	74	174	1 590	319	688
1967	2 857	45	1	368	57	24	97	141	1 103	271	750
1968	3 174	59	1	407	80	16	56	160	1 249	328	818
1969	2 703	78	4	329	57	15	62	134	963	253	808
1970	2 810	107	14	306	57	18	21	186	1 021	247	833
1971	2 846	183	16	329	52	16	24	158	999	241	828
1972	2 524	296	16	284	42	18	12	134	729	226	767
1973	3 314	453	20	386	48	30	1	160	1 173	248	795
1974	11 206	571	51	1 123	491	184	9	749	6 081	1 257	690
1975: VI	22 380	506	102	1 817	1 128	1 199	20	1 594	13 246	2 238	530

[1] Applicants for work on the "live" register. [2] 1965-66: data for occupational groups relate to March, June, Sep. and Dec. of each year. [3] Incl. certain persons seeking work for the first time.

[1] *Demandeurs d'emploi restant inscrits.* [2] *1965-66: les données par groupes de professions se réfèrent à mars, juin, sept. et déc. de chaque année.* [3] *Y compris certaines personnes en quête d'emploi pour la première fois.*

[1] Solicitantes de trabajo que continúan inscritos. [2] 1965-66: los datos por grupos de ocupaciones se refieren a marzo, junio, sept. y dic. de cada año. [3] Incl. ciertas personas en busca de trabajo por primera vez.

11 Unemployment by industrial or occupational groups
Chômage par groupes d'activité économique ou de professions
Desempleo por grupos de actividad económica o de ocupaciones

India

Occupational groups *(Employment office statistics)* [1]
Groupes de professions *(Statistiques des bureaux de placement)* [1]
Grupos de ocupaciones *(Estadísticas de las oficinas de colocación)* [1]

		0/1	2	3	4	5	6	7/8/9	X
Date [2] *Date* [2] Fecha [2]	Total	Professional, technical and related workers *Personnel des professions scientifiques, techniques, libérales et assimilées* Profesionales, técnicos y trabajadores asimilados	Administrative and managerial workers *Directeurs et cadres administratifs supérieurs* Directores y funcionarios públicos superiores	Clerical and related workers *Personnel administratif et travailleurs assimilés* Personal administrativo y trabajadores asimilados	Sales workers *Personnel commercial et vendeurs* Comerciantes y vendedores	Service workers *Travailleurs spécialisés dans les services* Trabajadores de los servicios	Agricultural, animal husbandry and forestry workers, fishermen and hunters *Agriculteurs, éleveurs, forestiers, pêcheurs et chasseurs* Trabajadores agrícolas y forestales, pescadores y cazadores	Production and related workers, transport equipment, operators and labourers *Ouvriers et manœuvres non agricoles et conducteurs d'engins de transport* Obreros no agrícolas, conductores de máquinas y vehículos de transp. y trabaj. asimilados	Workers not classifiable by occupation [4] *Travailleurs ne pouvant être classés selon la profession* [4] Trabajadores que no pueden ser clasificados según la ocupación [4]
1965	2 542 960	137 516	2 901	75 330		86 805	9 107	343 488	1 887 813
1966	2 611 717	152 417	3 720	90 100		96 932	9 667	348 249	1 910 632
1967	2 728 168	194 002	4 104	109 086		106 284	9 711	386 444	1 918 537
1968	2 945 692	248 219	5 180	128 520		117 894	11 482	416 225	2 018 172
1969	3 286 402	284 885	6 460	147 454		119 910	13 258	417 227	2 297 208
1970	3 844 927	319 078	6 994	163 945		144 578	14 901	473 079	2 722 352
1971	4 797 248	335 781	7 271	203 445		177 610	17 408	391 122	3 664 611
1972	6 292 108	381 277	8 607	271 996		218 685	21 426	538 532	4 851 585
1973	7 906 805	404 120	9 309	348 675		264 022	23 242	689 232	6 168 205
1974 [3]	8 432 869	442 534	8 783	468 068	2 091	227 096	25 722	915 220	6 343 355

[1] Applicants for work on the " live " register. [2] 1965-73: June and Dec. of each year. [3] Dec. New classification. [4] Incl. persons seeking work for the first time.

[1] *Demandeurs d'emploi restant inscrits.* [2] *1965-1973: juin et déc. de chaque année.* [3] *Déc. Nouvelle classification.* [4] *Y compris les personnes en quête d'emploi pour la première fois.*

[1] Solicitantes de trabajo que continúan inscritos. [2] 1965-1973: junio y dic. de cada año. [3] Dic. Nueva clasificación. [4] Incl. las personas en busca de trabajo por primera vez.

11 Unemployment by industrial or occupational groups
Chômage par groupes d'activité économique ou de professions
Desempleo por grupos de actividad económica o de ocupaciones

Indonesia

(ISCO — CITP — CIUO 1958)

Occupational groups *(Employment office statistics)* [1]
Groupes de professions *(Statistiques des bureaux de placement)* [1]
Grupos de ocupaciones *(Estadísticas de las oficinas de colocación)* [1]

Date [2] / Date [2] / Fecha [2]	Total	Professional, technical and related workers / *Professions libérales, techniciens et assimilés* / Profesiones liberales, técnicos y asimilados	Administrative, executive, managerial workers / *Directeurs, cadres administratifs supérieurs* / Administradores, gerentes, directores	Clerical workers / *Employés de bureau* / Empleados de oficina	Sales workers / *Vendeurs* / Vendedores	Farmers, fishermen and related workers / *Agriculteurs, pêcheurs et assimilés* / Agricultores, pescadores y asimilados	Miners, quarrymen and related workers / *Mineurs, carriers et assimilés* / Mineros, canteros y asimilados	Workers in transport and communication occupations / *Travailleurs dans les professions des transports et des communications* / Trabajadores de los transportes y comunicaciones	Craftsmen, prod. process workers, labourers not elsewhere classified / *Artisans, ouvriers de métier et à la production, manœuvres non classés ailleurs* / Artesanos, trabaj. ocupados en los div. procesos de prod., peones no clasif. bajo otros epígr.	Service workers / *Travailleurs spécialisés dans les services* / Trabajadores de los servicios	Persons seeking work for the first time [3] / *Personnes en quête d'emploi pour la première fois* [3] / Personas en busca de trabajo por primera vez [3]
1965	83 353	1 548	21	3 909	114	5 783	13	2 465	3 297	395	65 808
1966	46 729	1 062	12	2 240	91	2 674	26	1 064	2 472	292	36 796
1967	30 333	344	60	1 422	49	2 690	26	701	1 205	156	23 680
1968	45 837	872	131	3 057	112	2 428	30	1 716	1 972	239	35 280
1969	44 247	792	84	6 249	74	2 925	25	1 108	1 901	190	30 899
1970	13 252	619	68	664	27	11	19	293	274	47	11 230
1971	64 116	2 008	276	3 409	352	868	1 497	117	5 195	458	49 936
1972	90 832	3 325	220	5 063	323	1 146	238	2 665	5 213	556	72 083

[1] Applicants for work. [2] Dec. of each year except for 1972: Nov. [3] Incl. workers not classifiable by occupation.

[1] *Demandeurs d'emploi.* [2] *Déc. de chaque année, sauf pour 1972 : nov.* [3] *Y compris les personnes ne pouvant être classées selon la profession.*

[1] Solicitantes de trabajo. [2] Dic. de cada año, salvo 1972: nov. [3] Incl. los trabajadores que no pueden ser clasificados según la ocupación.

UNEMPLOYMENT

11 Unemployment by industrial or occupational groups
Chômage par groupes d'activité économique ou de professions
Desempleo por grupos de actividad económica o de ocupaciones

Israel

A
Industrial groups *(Labour force sample surveys)* [1]
Groupes d'activité économique *(Enquêtes par sondage sur la main-d'œuvre)* [1]
Grupos de actividad económica *(Encuestas por muestra sobre la fuerza trabajadora)* [1]

Date / Date / Fecha	Total	1 — Agriculture, forestry, fishing / Agriculture, sylviculture, pêche / Agricultura, silvicultura, pesca	2-3 — Mining, quarrying, manufacturing / Industries extractives, industries manufacturières / Minas, canteras, industrias manufactureras	4 — Electricity, gas, water / Electricité, gaz, eau / Electricidad, gas, agua	5 — Construction / Construction / Construcción	6 — Trade, restaurants and hotels / Commerce, restaurants et hôtels / Comercio, restaurantes y hoteles	7 — Transport, storage, communication / Transports, entrepôts, communications / Transportes, almacenaje, comunicaciones	8 — Financing, insur., real est., business serv. / Banques, assur., aff. imm., serv. aux entreprises / Bancos, seguros, bienes inm., serv. para empresas	9 — Community, social, and pers. services / Services à collectivité, serv. sociaux et pers. / Servicios comunales, sociales y personales	0 — Activities not adequately described / Activités mal désignées / Actividades no bien especificadas
1970	18 600	1 600	5 500	100	2 700	2 300	1 200	1 000	4 200	—
1971	18 900	1 200	5 100	200	2 500	2 900	1 600	800	4 600	—
1972	15 300	800	4 700	100	2 300	2 100	1 100	500	3 700	—
1973	16 300	300	4 600	100	3 100	2 300	1 000	800	3 800	300
1974	16 200	400	4 100	100	2 500	2 200	1 200	1 000	4 500	200

B
Occupational groups *(Labour force sample surveys)* [1]
Groupes de professions *(Enquêtes par sondage sur la main-d'œuvre)* [1]
Grupos de ocupaciones *(Encuestas por muestra sobre la fuerza trabajadora)* [1]

Date / Date / Fecha	Total	0/1 — Professional, technical and related workers / Personnel des professions scientifiques, techniques, libérales et assimilées / Profesionales, técnicos y trabajadores asimilados	2 — Administrative and managerial workers / Directeurs et cadres administratifs supérieurs / Directores y funcionarios públicos superiores	3 — Clerical and related workers / Personnel administratif et travailleurs assimilés / Personal administrativo y trabajadores asimilados	4 — Sales workers / Personnel commercial et vendeurs / Comerciantes y vendedores	5 — Service workers / Travailleurs spécialisés dans les services / Trabajadores de los servicios	6 — Agricultural, animal husbandry and forestry workers, fishermen and hunters / Agriculteurs, éleveurs, forestiers, pêcheurs et chasseurs / Trabajadores agrícolas y forestales, pescadores y cazadores	7/8/9 — Production and related workers, transport equipment, operators and labourers / Ouvriers et manœuvres non agricoles et conducteurs d'engins de transport / Obreros no agrícolas, conductores de máquinas y vehículos de transp. y trabaj. asimilados	X — Workers not classifiable by occupation / Travailleurs ne pouvant être classés selon la profession / Trabajadores que no pueden ser clasificados según la ocupación
1972	15 300	1 400	100	2 000	600	2 400	700	7 700	400
1973	16 300	1 900	—	2 900	800	2 100	400	8 100	100
1974	16 200	1 800	200	2 600	700	2 700	400	7 500	200

[1] Excl. persons who did not work in the country during the previous 12 months. Data cover also certain territories under occupation by Israeli military forces since June 1967.

[1] *Non compris les personnes qui n'ont pas travaillé dans le pays pendant les 12 mois précédents. Les données couvrent aussi certains territoires occupés par les forces armées israéliennes depuis juin 1967.*

[1] Excl. las personas que no trabajaron en el país en los 12 meses precedentes. Los datos cubren también ciertos territorios ocupados por las fuerzas armadas israelíes desde junio de 1967.

11 Unemployment by industrial or occupational groups
Chômage par groupes d'activité économique ou de professions
Desempleo por grupos de actividad económica o de ocupaciones

Korea, Rep. of

A Industrial groups *(Labour force sample surveys)*
Groupes d'activité économique *(Enquêtes par sondage sur la main-d'œuvre)*
Grupos de actividad económica *(Encuestas por muestra sobre la fuerza trabajadora)*

Date / Date / Fecha	Total	1 — Agriculture, forestry, fishing / Agriculture, sylviculture, pêche / Agricultura, silvicultura, pesca	2 — Mining, quarrying / Industries extractives / Minas, canteras	3 — Manufacturing / Industries manufacturières / Industrias manufactureras	4 — Electricity, gas, water / Electricité, gaz, eau / Electricidad, gas, agua	5 — Construction / Construction / Construcción	6 — Trade, restaurants and hotels / Commerce, restaurants et hôtels / Comercio, restaurantes y hoteles	7 — Transport, storage, communication / Transports, entrepôts, communications / Transportes, almacenaje, comunicaciones	8 — Financing, insur., real est., business serv. / Banques, assur., aff. imm., serv. aux entreprises / Bancos, seguros, bienes inm., serv. para empresas	9 — Community, social, and pers. services / Services à collectivité, serv. sociaux et pers. / Servicios comunales, sociales y personales	0 — Activities not adequately described [1] / Activités mal désignées [1] / Actividades no bien especificadas [1]
1971	476 000	31 000	4 000	54 000	3 000	17 000	35 000	19 000	4 000	39 000	270 000
1972	499 000	23 000	2 000	82 000	3 000	44 000	53 000	24 000	5 000	51 000	212 000
1973	461 000	19 000	4 000	91 000	3 000	35 000	62 000	20 000	6 000	49 000	172 000
1974	494 000	35 000	1 000	106 000	1 000	34 000	62 000	23 000	8 000	48 000	176 000

[1] Incl. persons seeking work for the first time. [1] *Y compris les personnes en quête d'emploi pour la première fois.* [1] Incl. las personas en busca de trabajo por primera vez.

B Occupational groups *(Labour force sample surveys)*
Groupes de professions *(Enquêtes par sondage sur la main-d'œuvre)*
Grupos de ocupaciones *(Encuestas por muestra sobre la fuerza trabajadora)*

Date / Date / Fecha	Total	0/1 — Professional, technical and related workers / Personnel des professions scientifiques, techniques, libérales et assimilées / Profesionales, técnicos y trabajadores asimilados	2 — Administrative and managerial workers / Directeurs et cadres administratifs supérieurs / Directores y funcionarios públicos superiores	3 — Clerical and related workers / Personnel administratif et travailleurs assimilés / Personal administrativo y trabajadores asimilados	4 — Sales workers / Personnel commercial et vendeurs / Comerciantes y vendedores	5 — Service workers / Travailleurs spécialisés dans les services / Trabajadores de los servicios	6 — Agricultural, animal husbandry and forestry workers, fishermen and hunters / Agriculteurs, éleveurs, forestiers, pêcheurs et chasseurs / Trabajadores agrícolas y forestales, pescadores y cazadores	7/8/9 — Production and related workers, transport equipment, operators and labourers / Ouvriers et manœuvres non agricoles et conducteurs d'engins de transport / Obreros no agrícolas, conductores de máquinas y vehículos de transp. y trabaj. asimilados	X — Workers not classifiable by occupation [1] / Travailleurs ne pouvant être classés selon la profession [1] / Trabajadores que no pueden ser clasificados según la ocupación [1]
1969	474 000	3 000	4 000	13 000	21 000	16 000	26 000	87 000	304 000
1970	454 000	5 000	1 000	27 000	24 000	21 000	31 000	67 000	278 000
1971	476 000	7 000	3 000	30 000	35 000	17 000	27 000	88 000	269 000
1972	499 000	7 000	2 000	32 000	46 000	18 000	23 000	156 000	215 000
1973	461 000	7 000	3 000	40 000	52 000	18 000	19 000	150 000	172 000
1974	494 000	10 000	3 000	40 000	54 000	25 000	34 000	152 000	176 000

[1] Incl. persons seeking work for the first time. [1] *Y compris les personnes en quête d'emploi pour la première fois.* [1] Incl. las personas en busca de trabajo por primera vez.

UNEMPLOYMENT

11 Unemployment by industrial or occupational groups
Chômage par groupes d'activité économique ou de professions
Desempleo por grupos de actividad económica o de ocupaciones

Malaysia:
West Malaysia

Occupational groups *(Employment office statistics)* [1]
Groupes de professions *(Statistiques des bureaux de placement)* [1]
Grupos de ocupaciones *(Estadísticas de las oficinas de colocación)* [1]

Date [2] / Date [2] / Fecha [2]	Total	0/1 Professional, technical and related workers / *Personnel des professions scientifiques, techniques, libérales et assimilées* / Profesionales, técnicos y trabajadores asimilados	2 Administrative and managerial workers / *Directeurs et cadres administratifs supérieurs* / Directores y funcionarios públicos superiores	3 Clerical and related workers / *Personnel administratif et travailleurs assimilés* / Personal administrativo y trabajadores asimilados	4 Sales workers / *Personnel commercial et vendeurs* / Comerciantes y vendedores	5 Service workers / *Travailleurs spécialisés dans les services* / Trabajadores de los servicios	6 Agricultural, animal husbandry and forestry workers, fishermen and hunters / *Agriculteurs, éleveurs, forestiers, pêcheurs et chasseurs* / Trabajadores agrícolas y forestales, pescadores y cazadores	7/8/9 Production and related workers, transport equipment, operators and labourers / *Ouvriers et manœuvres non agricoles et conducteurs d'engins de transport* / Obreros no agrícolas, conductores de máquinas y vehículos de transp. y trabaj. asimilados
1970	157 705	9 405	43	37 721	866	17 932	6 470	85 268
1971	155 902	9 976	9	34 225	633	14 810	6 862	89 387
1972	162 420	9 316	69	32 656	683	16 718	7 728	95 250
1973	140 157	6 030	73	27 947	481	12 438	7 436	85 752
1974	128 637	4 979	122	25 350	521	9 784	6 550	81 331
1975: VI	133 689	6 096	293	31 958	621	10 391	6 275	78 055

[1] Applicants for work on the " live " register. [2] Dec. of each year.
[1] *Demandeurs d'emploi restant inscrits.* [2] *Déc. de chaque année.*
[1] Solicitantes de trabajo que continúan inscritos. [2] Dic. de cada año.

Pakistan (1)

(ISIC — CITI — CIIU 1958)

A Industrial groups *(Employment office statistics)* [1]
Groupes d'activité économique *(Statistiques des bureaux de placement)* [1]
Grupos de actividad económica *(Estadísticas de las oficinas de colocación)* [1]

Date [2] / Date [2] / Fecha [2]	Total	Agriculture, forestry, fishing / *Agriculture, sylviculture, pêche* / Agricultura, silvicultura, pesca	Mining, quarrying / *Industries extractives* / Minas, canteras	Manufacturing / *Industries manufacturières* / Industrias manufactureras	Construction / *Construction* / Construcción	Electricity, gas, water and sanitary services / *Électricité, gaz, eau et services sanitaires* / Electricidad, gas, agua y servicios sanitarios	Commerce / *Commerce* / Comercio	Transport, storage, communication / *Transports, entrepôts, communications* / Transportes, almacenaje, comunicaciones	Services / *Services* / Servicios	Activities not adequately described / *Activités mal désignées* / Actividades no bien especificadas
1965	185 477	14 828	487	20 367	8 021	873	2 639	7 024	35 339	95 899
1966	184 318	15 874	471	21 446	8 633	1 168	3 576	6 675	35 581	90 894
1967	184 056	13 181	490	19 502	6 450	677	2 120	8 139	33 187	100 310
1968	183 127	13 223	336	17 974	5 771	653	2 179	7 968	37 961	97 062
1969	223 904	13 977	663	15 982	11 273	869	2 772	10 288	43 568	124 512

[1] Applicants for work on the " live " register. [2] Dec. of each year.
[1] *Demandeurs d'emploi restant inscrits.* [2] *Déc. de chaque année.*
[1] Solicitantes de trabajo que continúan inscritos. [2] Dic. de cada año.

11 Unemployment by industrial or occupational groups
Chômage par groupes d'activité économique ou de professions
Desempleo por grupos de actividad económica o de ocupaciones

Pakistan (2)

(ISCO — CITP — CIUO 1958)

B Occupational groups *(Employment office statistics)* [1]
Groupes de professions *(Statistiques des bureaux de placement)* [1]
Grupos de ocupaciones *(Estadísticas de las oficinas de colocación)* [1]

Date [2] Date [2] Fecha [2]	Total	Professional, technical and related workers *Professions libérales, techniciens et assimilés* Profesiones liberales, técnicos y asimilados	Administrative, executive, managerial workers *Directeurs, cadres administratifs supérieurs* Administradores, gerentes, directores	Clerical workers *Employés de bureau* Empleados de oficina	Sales workers *Vendeurs* Vendedores	Farmers, fishermen and related workers *Agriculteurs, pêcheurs et assimilés* Agricultores, pescadores y asimilados	Miners, quarrymen and related workers *Mineurs, carriers et assimilés* Mineros, canteros y asimilados	Workers in transport and communication occupations *Travailleurs dans les professions des transports et des communications* Trabajadores de los transportes y comunicaciones	Craftsmen, prod. process workers, labourers not elsewhere classified *Artisans, ouvriers de métier et à la production, manœuvres non classés ailleurs* Artesanos, trabaj. ocupados en los div. procesos de prod., peones no clasif. bajo otros epígr.	Service workers *Travailleurs spécialisés dans les services* Trabajadores de los servicios	Workers not classifiable by occupation *Personnes ne pouvant être classées selon la profession* Trabajadores que no pueden ser clasificados según la ocupación
1965	185 477	9 810	1 633	47 642	206	1 821	40	7 613	67 449	48 363	900
1966	184 318	11 181	4 685	55 043	188	1 003	43	8 612	56 381	45 835	1 347
1967	184 056	11 879	2 467	57 298	242	1 664	104	8 238	56 867	43 854	1 443
1968	183 127	13 866	1 738	62 398	299	1 487	23	7 771	49 703	44 779	1 063
1969	223 904	11 385	2 129	64 428	297	2 123	337	14 348	76 153	51 822	882

[1] Applicants for work on the "live" register. [2] Dec. of each year. [1] *Demandeurs d'emploi restant inscrits.* [2] *Déc. de chaque année.* [1] Solicitantes de trabajo que continúan inscritos. [2] Dic. de cada año.

Philippines (1)

(ISIC — CITI — CIIU 1958)

A Industrial groups *(Labour force sample surveys)*
Groupes d'activité économique *(Enquêtes par sondage sur la main-d'œuvre)*
Grupos de actividad económica *(Encuestas por muestra sobre la fuerza trabajadora)*

Date [1] Date [1] Fecha [1]	Total	Agriculture, forestry, fishing *Agriculture, sylviculture, pêche* Agricultura, silvicultura, pesca	Mining, quarrying *Industries extractives* Minas, canteras	Manufacturing *Industries manufacturières* Industrias manufactureras	Construction *Construction* Construcción	Electricity, gas, water and sanitary services *Electricité, gaz, eau et services sanitaires* Electricidad, gas, agua y servicios sanitarios	Commerce *Commerce* Comercio	Transport, storage, communication *Transports, entrepôts, communications* Transportes, almacenaje, comunicaciones	Services *Services* Servicios	Activities not adequately described *Activités mal désignées* Actividades no bien especificadas	Persons seeking work for the first time *Personnes en quête d'emploi pour la première fois* Personas en busca de trabajo por primera vez
1966	855 000	127 000	1 000	31 000	24 000	—	32 000	19 000	30 000	5 000	586 000
1967	1 090 000	186 000	—	36 000	31 000	1 000	45 000	17 000	47 000	5 000	712 000
1968	1 053 000	169 000	1 000	39 000	20 000	1 000	43 000	14 000	57 000	11 000	698 000
1969	812 000	159 000	2 000	44 000	26 000	1 000	53 000	13 000	74 000	10 000	430 000
1970	.	.	.	.	.	.	.	.	.	.	.
1971	636 000	84 000	1 000	44 000	33 000	3 000	36 000	22 000	54 000	6 000	353 000
1972	983 000	123 000	4 000	52 000	46 000	1 000	54 000	22 000	90 000	5 000	586 000
1973	624 000	85 000	1 000	61 000	55 000	5 000	39 000	24 000	58 000	3 000	293 000
1974	725 000	152 000	3 000	65 000	53 000	2 000	58 000	31 000	66 000	2 000	292 000

[1] May of each year. [1] *Mai de chaque année.* [1] Mayo de cada año.

UNEMPLOYMENT

11 Unemployment by industrial or occupational groups
Chômage par groupes d'activité économique ou de professions
Desempleo por grupos de actividad económica o de ocupaciones

Philippines (2)

B Occupational groups *(Labour force sample surveys)*
Groupes de professions *(Enquêtes par sondage sur la main-d'œuvre)*
Grupos de ocupaciones *(Encuestas por muestra sobre la fuerza trabajadora)*

Date [1] / Date [1] / Fecha [1]	Total	0/1 Professional, technical and related workers / Personnel des professions scientifiques, techniques, libérales et assimilées / Profesionales, técnicos y trabajadores asimilados	2 Administrative and managerial workers / Directeurs et cadres administratifs supérieurs / Directores y funcionarios públicos superiores	3 Clerical and related workers / Personnel administratif et travailleurs assimilés / Personal administrativo y trabajadores asimilados	4 Sales workers / Personnel commercial et vendeurs / Comerciantes y vendedores	5 Service workers / Travailleurs spécialisés dans les services / Trabajadores de los servicios	6 Agricultural, animal husbandry and forestry workers, fishermen and hunters / Agriculteurs, éleveurs, forestiers, pêcheurs et chasseurs / Trabajadores agrícolas y forestales, pescadores y cazadores	7/8/9 Production and related workers, transport equipment, operators and labourers / Ouvriers et manœuvres non agricoles et conducteurs d'engins de transport / Obreros no agrícolas, conductores de máquinas y vehículos de transp. y trabaj. asimilados	X Workers not classifiable by occupation / Travailleurs ne pouvant être classés selon la profession / Trabajadores que no pueden ser clasificados según la ocupación	Persons seeking work for the first time / Personnes en quête d'emploi pour la première fois / Personas en busca de trabajo por primera vez
1969	812 000	12 000	2 000	18 000	51 000	47 000	160 000	66 000	26 000	430 000
1970	.	.	.							
1971	636 000	7 000	—	14 000	35 000	38 000	83 000	84 000	22 000	353 000
1972	983 000	23 000	1 000	27 000	46 000	50 000	117 000	108 000	25 000	586 000
1973	624 000	13 000	1 000	26 000	33 000	34 000	85 000	106 000	33 000	293 000
1974	725 000	7 000	2 000	22 000	50 000	46 000	150 000	117 000	37 000	292 000

[1] May of each year.   [1] *Mai de chaque année.*   [1] Mayo de cada año.

Sri Lanka

Occupational groups *(Employment office statistics)* [1]
Groupes de professions *(Statistiques des bureaux de placement)* [1]
Grupos de ocupaciones *(Estadísticas de las oficinas de colocación)* [1]

Date / Date / Fecha	Total	Professional, technical and clerical workers / Professions libérales, techniciens et employés de bureau / Profesiones liberales, técnicos y empleados de oficina	Skilled workers / Ouvriers qualifiés / Obreros calificados	Semi-skilled workers / Ouvriers semi-qualifiés / Obreros semicalificados	Unskilled workers / Ouvriers non qualifiés / Obreros no calificados
1965	181 128	48 050	18 856	43 193	71 029
1966	224 737	62 362	20 906	55 709	85 760
1967	249 467	70 523	22 456	64 673	91 815
1968	265 627	73 703	24 055	69 353	98 516
1969	305 950	80 159	27 852	78 237	119 702
1970	380 962	93 228	34 636	94 509	158 589
1971	419 679	96 156	39 764	96 730	187 029
1972	440 342	91 429	43 087	100 576	205 250
1973	457 671	86 425	43 402	105 188	222 657
1974	489 348	89 087	44 818	112 574	242 869

[1] Applicants for work.   [1] *Demandeurs d'emploi.*   [1] Solicitantes de trabajo.

11 Unemployment by industrial or occupational groups
Chômage par groupes d'activité économique ou de professions
Desempleo por grupos de actividad económica o de ocupaciones

République arabe syrienne

A
Industrial groups *(Labour force sample surveys)*
Groupes d'activité économique *(Enquêtes par sondage sur la main-d'œuvre)*
Grupos de actividad económica *(Encuestas por muestra sobre la fuerza trabajadora)*

		1	2	3	4	5	6	7	8	9	0
Date [1] *Date* [1] Fecha [1]	Total	Agriculture, forestry, fishing *Agriculture, sylviculture, pêche* Agricultura, silvicultura, pesca	Mining, quarrying *Industries extractives* Minas, canteras	Manufacturing *Industries manufacturières* Industrias manufactureras	Electricity, gas, water *Electricité, gaz, eau* Electricidad, gas, agua	Construction *Construction* Construcción	Trade, restaurants and hotels *Commerce, restaurants et hôtels* Comercio, restaurantes y hoteles	Transport, storage, communication *Transports, entrepôts, communications* Transportes, almacenaje, comunicaciones	Financing, insur., real est., business serv. *Banques, assur., aff. imm., serv. aux entreprises* Bancos, seguros, bienes inm., serv. para empresas	Community, social, and pers. services *Services à collectivité, serv. sociaux et pers.* Servicios comunales, sociales y personales	Activities not adequately described [2] *Activités mal désignées* [2] Actividades no bien especificadas [2]
1971	123 387	34 364	556	9 605	205	7 102	7 619	2 060	207	8 045	53 624
1972	80 907	17 641	93	4 182	281	5 986	3 532	1 986	379	4 663	42 164
1973	76 489	7 410	563	4 916	278	7 500	5 642	2 082	283	6 988	40 827

B
Occupational groups *(Labour force sample surveys)*
Groupes de professions *(Enquêtes par sondage sur la main-d'œuvre)*
Grupos de ocupaciones *(Encuestas por muestra sobre la fuerza trabajadora)*

		0/1	2	3	4	5	6	7/8/9	X
Date [1] *Date* [1] Fecha [1]	Total	Professional, technical and related workers *Personnel des professions scientifiques, techniques, libérales et assimilées* Profesionales, técnicos y trabajadores asimilados	Administrative and managerial workers *Directeurs et cadres administratifs supérieurs* Directores y funcionarios públicos superiores	Clerical and related workers *Personnel administratif et travailleurs assimilés* Personal administrativo y trabajadores asimilados	Sales workers *Personnel commercial et vendeurs* Comerciantes y vendedores	Service workers *Travailleurs spécialisés dans les services* Trabajadores de los servicios	Agricultural, animal husbandry and forestry workers, fishermen and hunters *Agriculteurs, éleveurs, forestiers, pêcheurs et chasseurs* Trabajadores agrícolas y forestales, pescadores y cazadores	Production and related workers, transport equipment, operators and labourers *Ouvriers et manœuvres non agricoles et conducteurs d'engins de transport* Obreros no agrícolas, conductores de máquinas y vehículos de transp. y trabaj. asimilados	Workers not classifiable by occupation [2] *Travailleurs ne pouvant être classés selon la profession* [2] Trabajadores que no pueden ser clasificados según la ocupación [2]
1971	123 387	2 637	104	1 398	5 490	2 348	34 646	23 140	53 624
1972	80 907	1 388	—	650	3 540	930	17 926	14 309	42 164
1973	76 489	1 134	—	2 170	4 888	1 609	7 599	18 262	40 827

[1] Sep. of each year. [2] Incl. persons seeking work for the first time.

[1] *Sept. de chaque année.* [2] *Y compris les personnes en quête d'emploi pour la première fois.*

[1] Sept. de cada año. [2] Incl. las personas en busca de trabajo por primera vez.

UNEMPLOYMENT

11 Unemployment by industrial or occupational groups
Chômage par groupes d'activité économique ou de professions
Desempleo por grupos de actividad económica o de ocupaciones

Thailand

(ISCO — CITP — CIUO 1958)

Occupational groups *(Labour force sample surveys)* [1]
Groupes de professions *(Enquêtes par sondage sur la main-d'œuvre)* [1]
Grupos de ocupaciones *(Encuestas por muestra sobre la fuerza trabajadora)* [1]

Date [2] / Date [2] / Fecha [2]	Total	Professional, technical and related workers / *Professions libérales, techniciens et assimilés* / Profesiones liberales, técnicos y asimilados	Administrative, executive, managerial workers / *Directeurs, cadres administratifs supérieurs* / Administradores, gerentes, directores	Clerical workers / *Employés de bureau* / Empleados de oficina	Sales workers / *Vendeurs* / Vendedores	Farmers, fishermen and related workers / *Agriculteurs, pêcheurs et assimilés* / Agricultores, pescadores y asimilados	Workers in transport occupations / *Travailleurs dans les professions des transports* / Trabajadores de los transportes	Craftsmen, prod. process workers, labourers not elsewhere classified / *Artisans, ouvriers de métier et à la production, manœuvres non classés ailleurs* / Artesanos, trabaj. ocupados en los div. procesos de prod., peones no clasif. bajo otros epígr.	Service workers / *Travailleurs spécialisés dans les services* / Trabajadores de los servicios	Workers not classifiable by occupation / *Travailleurs ne pouvant être classés selon la profession* / Trabajadores que no pueden ser clasificados según la ocupación	Persons seeking work for the first time / *Personnes en quête d'emploi pour la première fois* / Personas en busca de trabajo por primera vez
1972	85 470	2 080	450	3 030	5 250	5 290	4 520	20 510	3 260	1 150	39 930
1973	73 890	2 160	1 950	5 320	3 770	190	4 120	12 220	760	360	43 040

[1] Persons 11 years of age and over. [2] July-Sep. of each year.

[1] *Personnes âgées de 11 ans et plus.* [2] *Juillet-sept. de chaque année.*

[1] Personas de 11 años de edad y más. [2] Julio-sept. de cada año.

11

Unemployment by industrial or occupational groups
Chômage par groupes d'activité économique ou de professions
Desempleo por grupos de actividad económica o de ocupaciones

EUROPE — EUROPE — EUROPA

Austria

Occupational or industrial groups *(Employment office statistics)*
Groupes d'activité économique ou de professions *(Statistiques des bureaux de placement)*
Grupos de actividad económica o de ocupaciones *(Estadísticas de las oficinas de colocación)*

Date / Date / Fecha	Total [1]	Agriculture, forestry / Agriculture, sylviculture / Agricultura, silvicultura	Mining / Mines / Minas	Stone, glass, ceramics / Pierre, verre, céramique / Piedra, vidrio, cerámica	Food, beverages, tobacco / Aliments, boissons, tabac / Alimentos, bebidas, tabaco	Textiles	Clothing [2] / Habillement [2] / Vestido [2]	Leather / Cuir / Cuero	Paper / Papier / Papel
1965	65 515	8 525	154	1 847	1 205	2 117	3 953	242	576
1966	61 439	7 079	174	1 684	1 188	1 997	3 973	284	556
1967	64 590	6 750	244	1 700	1 234	2 101	4 511	279	520
1968	70 817	6 867	583	1 837	1 291	1 836	4 324	229	458
1969	67 120	6 410	569	1 725	1 044	1 507	4 048	196	424
1970	58 444	5 683	514	1 371	802	1 399	3 880	175	358
1971	52 020	4 724	450	973	756	1 424	3 843	163	374
1972	49 135	4 102	394	750	698	1 262	3 780	154	361
1973	41 327	3 472	159	569	521	1 014	3 619	153	252
1974	41 306	3 100	115	649	540	977	3 180	135	225
1975: III	60 569	6 073	116	1 379	919	1 467	3 017	373	279

Date / Date / Fecha	Printing / Impression / Imprentas	Chemicals, rubber / Produits chimiques, caoutchouc / Productos químicos, caucho	Wood / Bois / Madera	Metal and electrical workers / Electriciens, ouvriers sur métaux / Electricistas, obreros metalúrgicos	Construction / Construction / Construcción	Hotels, restaurants / Hôtels, restaurants / Hoteles, restaurantes	Transport, communication / Transports, communications / Transportes, comunicaciones	Unskilled workers [3] / Ouvriers non qualifiés [3] / Obreros no calificados [3]	Commercial employees and clerical workers / Employés de commerce et de bureau / Empleados de comercio y de oficina
1965	326	496	1 221	3 302	13 124	6 660	1 172	5 260	8 100
1966	294	562	1 169	3 398	10 813	6 452	1 065	5 232	8 077
1967	260	605	1 271	3 670	11 900	6 612	1 147	5 238	8 741
1968	288	598	1 354	4 356	14 808	6 878	1 467	5 333	10 045
1969	245	526	1 257	3 581	14 715	6 529	1 460	4 896	10 133
1970	227	518	1 040	2 882	10 862	6 185	1 194	4 372	9 718
1971	233	546	843	2 779	6 869	6 167	950	4 419	10 354
1972	256	551	795	2 810	5 095	6 377	898	4 217	9 575
1973	193	452	460	1 997	3 980	6 038	629	2 791	9 037
1974	198	490	589	2 397	4 487	6 425	752	2 907	8 456
1975: III	252	830	1 507	6 411	12 076	4 801	1 912	4 679	8 262

[1] Incl. occupational groups not specified in the table. [2] Incl. shoemakers. [3] Incl. semi-skilled workers of certain occupations.

[1] *Y compris des groupes de professions non spécifiés dans le tableau.* [2] *Y compris les cordonniers.* [3] *Y compris les ouvriers semi-qualifiés de certains métiers.*

[1] Incl. grupos de ocupaciones no especificados en el cuadro. [2] Incl. los zapateros. [3] Incl. obreros semicalificados de ciertas ocupaciones.

11 Unemployment by industrial or occupational groups
Chômage par groupes d'activité économique ou de professions
Desempleo por grupos de actividad económica o de ocupaciones

Belgique

Industrial groups *(Employment office statistics)* [1]
Groupes d'activité économique *(Statistiques des bureaux de placement)* [1]
Grupos de actividad económica *(Estadísticas de las oficinas de colocación)* [1]

Date / Date / Fecha	Total	Agriculture, forestry, fishing / Agriculture, sylviculture, pêche / Agricultura, silvicultura, pesca	Mining, quarrying / Industries extractives / Minas, canteras	Manufacturing / Industries manufacturières / Industrias manufactureras	Electricity, gas, water / Electricité, gaz, eau / Electricidad, gas, agua	Construction / Construction / Construcción	Trade, financing, insurance / Commerce, banques, assurances / Comercio, bancos, seguros	Transport, storage, communication / Transports, entrepôts, communications / Transportes, almacenaje, comunicaciones	Restaurants and hotels / Restaurants et hôtels / Restaurantes y hoteles	Services / Services / Servicios	Activities not adequately described / Activités mal désignées / Actividades no bien especificadas
1966	61 498	2 059	3 821	29 546	118	10 435	4 232	2 362	2 766	5 310	849
1967	85 318	2 012	4 821	43 046	135	15 474	5 941	2 809	3 045	6 738	1 297
1968	102 730	2 091	5 389	50 729	147	19 065	7 942	3 129	3 460	8 620	2 158
1969	85 343	1 723	5 008	41 222	113	12 473	7 836	2 620	3 136	8 747	2 465
1970	71 261	1 277	4 128	35 026	99	8 880	6 705	2 090	2 628	8 478	1 950
1971	80 876	1 185	3 610	34 020	90	10 098	6 625	1 954	2 572	8 579	2 143
1972	86 822	1 177	3 734	41 148	98	13 106	8 511	2 276	2 817	10 735	3 220
1973	91 702	1 085	3 569	43 167	119	10 373	10 284	2 321	3 044	13 245	4 495
1974	104 720	1 057	3 636	48 588	125	9 708	12 477	2 568	3 389	16 418	6 754
1975: VI	162 000	1 266	3 634	84 112	205	17 031	17 684	3 874	3 312	22 380	8 502

[1] Wholly unemployed receiving insurance benefits.   [1] *Chômeurs complets indemnisés.*   [1] Desempleados completos que reciben prestaciones.

Industrial groups *(Employment office statistics)* [1]
Groupes d'activité économique *(Statistiques des bureaux de placement)* [1]
Grupos de actividad económica *(Estadísticas de las oficinas de colocación)* [1]

Date / Date / Fecha	Total	Agriculture, forestry, fishing / Agriculture, sylviculture, pêche / Agricultura, silvicultura, pesca	Mining, quarrying / Industries extractives / Minas, canteras	Manufacturing / Industries manufacturières / Industrias manufactureras	Electricity, gas, water / Electricité, gaz, eau / Electricidad, gas, agua	Construction / Construction / Construcción	Trade, financing, insurance / Commerce, banques, assurances / Comercio, bancos, seguros	Transport, storage, communication / Transports, entrepôts, communications / Transportes, almacenaje, comunicaciones	Restaurants and hotels / Restaurants et hôtels / Restaurantes y hoteles	Services / Services / Servicios	Activities not adequately described / Activités mal désignées / Actividades no bien especificadas
1967	45 870	786	812	24 625	30	15 964	59	2 899	92	383	220
1968	40 008	798	269	16 784	34	19 157	73	2 183	104	426	180
1969	35 250	829	255	10 033	19	21 433	41	2 112	96	390	42
1970	31 507	724	179	11 725	21	16 382	47	1 917	90	401	21
1971	37 030	627	157	14 412	32	18 485	19	2 653	99	462	84
1972	34 187	571	141	14 302	36	15 617	27	2 748	117	527	101
1973	32 042	372	191	12 600	27	16 561	11	1 564	125	522	69
1974	39 386	611	52	22 909	36	13 073	36	1 582	183	743	161

[1] Daily average of controlled partially unemployed.   [1] *Moyenne journalière du nombre de chômeurs partiels contrôlés.*   [1] Promedio diario de desempleados parciales controlados.

11 Unemployment by industrial or occupational groups
Chômage par groupes d'activité économique ou de professions
Desempleo por grupos de actividad económica o de ocupaciones

Denmark

Industrial groups *(Trade union fund statistics)* [1]
Groupes d'activité économique *(Statistiques des caisses syndicales)* [1]
Grupos de actividad económica *(Estadísticas de las cajas sindicales)* [1]

Date *Date* Fecha	Total	Agriculture, forestry, fishing *Agriculture, sylviculture, pêche* Agricultura, silvicultura, pesca	Mining, quarrying *Industries extractives* Minas, canteras	Manufacturing *Industries manufacturières* Industrias manufactureras	Electricity, gas, water *Electricité, gaz, eau* Electricidad, gas, agua	Construction *Construction* Construcción	Trade, restaurants and hotels [2] *Commerce, restaurants et hôtels* [2] Comercio, restaurantes y hoteles [2]	Transport, storage, communication *Transports, entrepôts, communications* Transportes, almacenaje, comunicaciones	Services *Services* Servicios
1969	34 944	2 393	150	11 485	140	12 526	4 403	2 841	1 006
1970	28 981	2 095	141	8 257	115	11 992	3 325	2 229	827
1971	33 910	1 863	121	11 536	109	12 746	3 922	2 638	975
1972	31 801	1 662	93	10 576	112	11 346	4 323	2 608	1 081
1973	23 784	1 366	63	7 577	83	8 109	3 310	2 042	1 234
1974	46 976	1 726	79	19 467	115	14 808	5 475	3 204	2 102

[1] Data by industrial groups represent the monthly average of counts taken on the last Wednesday of the month. [2] Incl. financing, insurance and real estate.

[1] *Les données par groupes d'activité économique représentent la moyenne des relevés effectués le dernier mercredi du mois.* [2] *Y compris les banques, assurances et affaires immobilières.*

[1] Los datos por grupos de actividad económica representan el promedio mensual de los informes obtenidos el último miércoles del mes. [2] Incl. los bancos, seguros y bienes inmuebles.

11 Unemployment by industrial or occupational groups
Chômage par groupes d'activité économique ou de professions
Desempleo por grupos de actividad económica o de ocupaciones

España

A Industrial groups *(Employment office statistics)*
Groupes d'activité économique *(Statistiques des bureaux de placement)*
Grupos de actividad económica *(Estadísticas de las oficinas de colocación)*

		1	2	3	4	5	6 ×	7	6 ×; 8; 9 ×		0
Date / *Date* / Fecha	Total	Agriculture, forestry, fishing / *Agriculture, sylviculture, pêche* / Agricultura, silvicultura, pesca	Mining, quarrying / *Industries extractives* / Minas, canteras	Manufacturing [1] / *Industries manufacturières* [1] / Industrias manufactureras [1]	Electricity, gas. water / *Electricité, gaz, eau* / Electricidad, gas, agua	Construction / *Construction* / Construcción	Trade [2] / *Commerce* [2] / Comercio [2]	Transport, storage, communication / *Transports, entrepôts, communications* / Transportes, almacenaje, comunicaciones	Financing, insur., real est., business serv. / *Banques, assur., aff. imm., serv. aux entreprises* / Bancos, seguros, bienes inm., serv. para empresas	Community, social, and pers. services [3] / *Services à collectivité, services sociaux et pers.* [3] / Servicios comunales, sociales y personales [3]	Activities not adequately described [4] / *Activités mal désignées* [4] / Actividades no bien especificadas [4]
1965	147 074	54 263	3 341	41 360	377	26 112	4 598	3 133	6 570		7 320
1966	123 225	40 120	5 207	34 645	405	21 828	4 390	4 774	6 171		5 685
1967	146 341	40 653	5 307	42 845	647	31 209	5 372	5 730	8 273		6 305
1968	182 019	42 794	5 950	58 674	831	42 645	5 904	6 181	11 016		8 024
1969	158 885	28 449	5 583	56 144	739	38 166	4 843	7 159	11 143		6 659
1970	145 646	19 303	3 921	53 940	622	41 749	4 858	5 358	11 660		4 235
1971	190 272	21 374	3 317	64 594	966	68 435	6 428	5 185	15 164		4 809
1972	190 910	18 743	3 771	61 453	1 063	66 634	8 801	5 035	18 835		6 575
1973	149 559	17 532	3 645	48 857	638	47 438	7 692	3 612	15 805		4 340
1974	150 273	17 214	3 356	47 539	712	48 612	8 517	3 763	15 980		4 580

[1] Incl. repair services. [2] Excl. restaurants and hotels.
[3] Excl. repair services. Incl. restaurants and hotels.
[4] Incl. persons seeking work for the first time.

[1] *Y compris les services de réparation.* [2] *Non compris les restaurants et les hôtels.* [3] *Non compris les services de réparation. Y compris les restaurants et les hôtels.* [4] *Y compris les personnes en quête d'emploi pour la première fois.*

[1] Incl. los servicios de reparación. [2] Excl. los restaurantes y los hoteles. [3] Excl. los servicios de reparación. Incl. los restaurantes y los hoteles. [4] Incl. las personas en busca de trabajo por primera vez.

B Occupational groups *(Employment office statistics)*
Groupes de professions *(Statistiques des bureaux de placement)*
Grupos de ocupaciones *(Estadísticas de las oficinas de colocación)*

(ISCO — CITP — CIUO 1958)

Date / *Date* / Fecha	Total	Professional, technical and related workers / *Professions libérales, techniciens et assimilés* / Profesiones liberales, técnicos y asimilados	Administrative, executive, managerial workers / *Directeurs, cadres administratifs supérieurs* / Administradores, gerentes, directores	Clerical workers / *Employés de bureau* / Empleados de oficina	Sales workers / *Vendeurs* / Vendedores	Farmers, fishermen and related workers / *Agriculteurs, pêcheurs et assimilés* / Agricultores, pescadores y asimilados	Miners, quarrymen and related workers / *Mineurs, carriers et assimilés* / Mineros, canteros y asimilados	Workers in transport and communication occupations / *Travailleurs dans les professions des transports et des communications* / Trabajadores de los transportes y comunicaciones	Craftsmen, prod. process workers, labourers not elsewhere classified / *Artisans, ouvriers de métier et à la production, manœuvres non classés ailleurs* / Artesanos, trabaj. ocupados en los div. procesos de prod., peones no clasif. bajo otros epígr.	Service workers / *Travailleurs spécialisés dans les services* / Trabajadores de los servicios	Workers not classifiable by occupation / *Personnes ne pouvant être classées selon la profession* / Trabajadores que no pueden ser clasificados según la ocupación
1965	147 074	660	95	3 957	1 898	54 738	2 923	2 607	72 319	6 460	1 417
1966	123 225	755	104	3 247	1 915	40 088	4 004	4 231	61 286	5 876	1 719
1967	146 341	1 137	165	3 941	2 721	40 322	4 614	5 298	78 906	7 342	1 895
1968	182 019	1 822	238	5 837	4 189	42 706	5 244	5 845	104 247	9 843	2 048
1969	158 885	1 455	258	5 532	2 814	28 411	5 030	6 877	97 700	8 808	2 000
1970	145 646	1 231	212	5 351	2 844	19 341	3 747	5 100	97 456	8 515	1 849
1971	190 272	1 702	263	8 698	4 064	20 716	6 040	6 052	126 298	13 072	3 367
1972	190 910	2 202	287	9 457	6 055	18 632	8 554	5 906	117 375	17 483	4 959
1973	149 559	1 620	293	7 135	5 651	17 557	6 746	4 413	88 378	14 479	3 287
1974	150 273	2 145	345	7 898	6 822	18 468	6 206	4 372	86 120	15 583	2 314

11 Unemployment by industrial or occupational groups
Chômage par groupes d'activité économique ou de professions
Desempleo por grupos de actividad económica o de ocupaciones

Finland

A Industrial groups *(Labour force sample surveys)* [1]
Groupes d'activité économique *(Enquêtes par sondage sur la main-d'œuvre)* [1]
Grupos de actividad económica *(Encuestas por muestra sobre la fuerza trabajadora)* [1]

Date / Date / Fecha	Total	1 Agriculture, forestry, fishing / *Agriculture, sylviculture, pêche* / Agricultura, silvicultura, pesca	2 Mining, quarrying / *Industries extractives* / Minas, canteras	3 Manufacturing / *Industries manufacturières* / Industrias manufactureras	4 Electricity, gas, water / *Electricité, gaz, eau* / Electricidad, gas, agua	5 Construction / *Construction* / Construcción	6 Trade, restaurants and hotels / *Commerce, restaurants et hôtels* / Comercio, restaurantes y hoteles	7 Transport, storage, communication / *Transports, entrepôts, communications* / Transportes, almacenaje, comunicaciones	8 Financing, insur., real est., business serv. / *Banques, assur., aff. imm., serv. aux entreprises* / Bancos, seguros, bienes inm., serv. para empresas	9 Community, social, and pers. services / *Services à collectivité, services sociaux et pers.* / Servicios comunales, sociales y personales	0 Activities not adequately described / *Activités mal désignées* / Actividades no bien especificadas
1971	49 000	8 000		6 000		12 000	4 000	2 000	—	5 000	12 000
1972	55 000	8 000		8 000		12 000	4 000	2 000	—	6 000	15 000
1973	51 000	7 000		8 000		9 000	5 000	2 000	1 000	5 000	14 000
1974	39 000	4 000		7 000		6 000	6 000	2 000	—	5 000	9 000

B Occupational groups *(Labour force sample surveys)* [1]
Groupes de professions *(Enquêtes par sondage sur la main-d'œuvre)* [1]
Grupos de ocupaciones *(Encuestas por muestra sobre la fuerza trabajadora)* [1]

Date / Date / Fecha	Total	0/1 Professional, technical and related workers / *Personnel des professions scientifiques, techniques, libérales et assimilées* / Profesionales, técnicos y trabajadores asimilados	2 Administrative and managerial workers / *Directeurs et cadres administratifs supérieurs* / Directores y funcionarios públicos superiores	3 Clerical and related workers / *Personnel administratif et travailleurs assimilés* / Personal administrativo y trabajadores asimilados	4 Sales workers / *Personnel commercial et vendeurs* / Comerciantes y vendedores	5 Service workers / *Travailleurs spécialisés dans les services* / Trabajadores de los servicios	6 Agricultural, animal husbandry and forestry workers, fishermen and hunters / *Agriculteurs, éleveurs, forestiers, pêcheurs et chasseurs* / Trabajadores agrícolas y forestales, pescadores y cazadores	7/8/9 Production and related workers, transport equipment, operators and labourers / *Ouvriers et manœuvres non agricoles et conducteurs d'engins de transport* / Obreros no agrícolas, conductores de máquinas y vehículos de transp. y trabaj. asimilados	X Workers not classifiable occupation / *Travailleurs ne pouvant être classés selon la profession* / Trabajadores que no pueden ser clasificados según la ocupación
1971	49 000	3 000	—	1 000	2 000	4 000	8 000	19 000	12 000
1972	55 000	3 000	—	1 000	2 000	4 000	9 000	21 000	15 000
1973	51 000	2 000	—	2 000	2 000	5 000	8 000	19 000	13 000
1974	39 000	2 000	—	2 000	2 000	6 000	5 000	13 000	9 000

[1] Persons aged 15 to 74 years.   [1] *Personnes âgées de 15 à 74 ans.*   [1] Personas de 15 a 74 años.

11 Unemployment by industrial or occupational groups
Chômage par groupes d'activité économique ou de professions
Desempleo por grupos de actividad económica o de ocupaciones

France

Occupational groups *(Employment office statistics)* [1]
Groupes de professions *(Statistiques des bureaux de placement)* [1]
Grupos de ocupaciones *(Estadísticas de las oficinas de colocación)* [1]

Date [2] / Date [2] / Fecha [2]	Total	Materials handling and warehousing / Manutention et stockage / Transporte de materiales y almacenaje	Fishing and water transport / Pêche et navigation / Pesca y transporte por agua	Agriculture, forestry / Agriculture, sylviculture / Agricultura, silvicultura	Earthworks and mining / Terrassement et extraction / Terraplenes y minas	Metal workers / Ouvriers sur métaux / Obreros metalúrgicos	Electricity / Electricité / Electricidad	Building, construction / Bâtiment, construction / Edificación y construcción	Food, beverages / Aliments, boissons / Alimentos, bebidas	Textiles
1965	141 255	33 282	1 104	4 271	1 197	10 790	1 995	8 253	3 508	10 350
1966	147 098	34 258	1 007	4 351	1 217	11 208	2 110	11 252	3 632	7 487
1967	196 033	44 984	916	4 570	1 480	15 646	3 087	18 096	4 496	10 709
1968	253 789	55 390	1 098	5 466	1 844	21 264	4 356	23 349	5 571	15 494
1969	223 020	46 568	1 097	5 926	1 348	15 717	3 296	14 805	4 694	12 567
1970	262 085	54 262	851	5 406	1 403	16 856	3 957	17 108	4 891	15 636
1971	338 159	67 215	881	5 892	1 726	23 097	5 441	23 144	5 698	15 966
1972	383 465	70 518	812	5 891	1 679	26 891	6 104	21 832	6 392	14 598
1973	393 900	66 334	783	5 431	1 227	24 279	5 773	17 125	6 496	14 759
1974	497 711	78 583	943	5 898	1 371	32 666	8 435	21 537	8 104	18 413
1975: IV	757 284	121 744	1 406	9 180	3 187	66 075	17 559	56 083	10 988	24 908

Date [2] / Date [2] / Fecha [2]	Skins, leather / Peaux, cuir / Pieles, cuero	Wood / Bois / Madera	Printing / Arts graphiques / Imprentas	Drivers / Conducteurs d'automobiles / Conductores de automóviles	Commercial employees / Employés de commerce / Empleados de comercio	Domestic personnel / Personnel domestique / Personal doméstico	Clerical workers / Employés de bureau / Empleados de oficina	Professional, executive and managerial workers / Professions libérales, directeurs et cadres adm. sup. / Profesiones liberales, administradores, gerentes y directores	Entertainment / Emplois artistiques et du spectacle / Diversiones	Others / Autres / Otros
1965	1 826	1 320	969	2 654	8 162	14 648	21 257	5 748	2 669	7 252
1966	1 450	1 495	1 009	2 825	8 526	15 190	23 140	6 668	2 684	7 589
1967	2 100	2 221	1 411	4 148	11 149	18 941	31 044	8 765	2 793	9 477
1968	2 866	2 944	2 023	5 409	15 126	24 485	38 375	12 443	3 261	13 025
1969	2 282	2 302	1 836	4 227	16 055	24 196	35 534	13 260	3 496	13 814
1970	2 412	2 665	1 988	5 306	21 410	27 966	44 739	16 650	2 497	16 082
1971	2 576	3 143	2 767	7 250	27 540	34 748	62 298	25 399	3 314	20 064
1972	2 217	2 857	3 361	8 088	32 919	39 180	78 225	33 718	4 775	23 408
1973	2 281	2 417	3 113	7 405	38 671	42 161	88 165	36 617	5 394	25 469
1974	2 201	3 317	4 070	10 015	50 656	50 513	115 098	44 347	6 745	34 799
1975: IV	2 684	6 822	6 551	20 195	70 064	68 789	150 347	64 113	8 168	48 421

[1] Beginning June 1972: excl. certain unemployed over 60 years of age (recipients of " income maintenance benefits "). [2] 1965-66: weighted average of 13 months.

[1] *A partir de juin 1972 : non compris certains chômeurs de plus de 60 ans (bénéficiaires de la « garantie de ressources »).* [2] *1965-66 : moyenne pondérée de 13 mois.*

[1] A partir de junio de 1972: excl. ciertos desempleados de más de 60 años (beneficiarios de la « garantía de recursos »). [2] 1965-66: promedio ponderado de 13 meses.

11

Unemployment by industrial or occupational groups
Chômage par groupes d'activité économique ou de professions
Desempleo por grupos de actividad económica o de ocupaciones

Germany, Fed. Rep. of △

Occupational groups *(Employment office statistics)*
Groupes de professions *(Statistiques des bureaux de placement)*
Grupos de ocupaciones *(Estadísticas de las oficinas de colocación)*

Date / Date / Fecha	Total	0/1 Professional, technical and related workers — *Personnel des professions scientifiques, techniques, libérales et assimilées* — Profesionales, técnicos y trabajadores asimilados	2 Administrative and managerial workers — *Directeurs et cadres administratifs supérieurs* — Directores y funcionarios públicos superiores	3 Clerical and related workers — *Personnel administratif et travailleurs assimilés* — Personal administrativo y trabajadores asimilados	4 Sales workers — *Personnel commercial et vendeurs* — Comerciantes y vendedores	5 Service workers — *Travailleurs spécialisés dans les services* — Trabajadores de los servicios	6 Agricultural, animal husbandry and forestry workers, fishermen and hunters — *Agriculteurs, éleveurs, forestiers, pêcheurs et chasseurs* — Trabajadores agrícolas y forestales, pescadores y cazadores	7/8/9 Production and related workers, transport equipment, operators and labourers — *Ouvriers et manœuvres non agricoles et conducteurs d'engins de transport* — Obreros no agrícolas, conductores de máquinas y vehículos de transp. y trabaj. asimilados	X Workers not classifiable by occupation — *Travailleurs ne pouvant être classés selon la profession* — Trabajadores que no pueden ser clasificados según la ocupación
1965	147 352	6 821	14 568		5 825	11 887	11 510	93 060	3 681
1966	161 059	7 396	13 859		5 950	12 566	9 386	108 596	3 306
1967	459 489	17 466	28 916		16 833	28 356	15 191	346 299	6 428
1968	323 480	16 669	26 065		15 747	24 943	12 842	221 813	5 401
1969	178 579	11 475	16 806		10 265	15 205	10 561	110 720	3 547
1970	148 846	10 897	14 676		9 502	12 823	10 048	88 049	2 851
1971	185 072	13 752	18 975		11 869	16 325	6 922	113 574	3 655
1972	246 433	20 072	27 872		16 622	22 326	7 851	146 601	5 089
1973	273 498	26 541	36 306		23 086	25 745	8 114	147 769	5 937
1974	582 481	48 070	69 206		51 042	45 199	8 439	347 595	12 930

Grèce

(ISCO — CITP — CIUO 1958)

Occupational groups *(Employment office statistics)* [1]
Groupes de professions *(Statistiques des bureaux de placement)* [1]
Grupos de ocupaciones *(Estadísticas de las oficinas de colocación)* [1]

Date / Date / Fecha	Total	Professional, technical and related workers — *Professions libérales, techniciens et assimilés* — Profesiones liberales, técnicos y trabajadores asimilados	Administrative, executive and managerial workers — *Directeurs et cadres administratifs supérieurs* — Administradores, gerentes y directores	Clerical workers — *Employés de bureau* — Empleados de oficina	Sales workers — *Vendeurs* — Vendedores	Farmers, fishermen and related workers — *Agriculteurs, pêcheurs et assimilés* — Agricultores, pescadores y asimilados	Miners, quarrymen and related workers — *Mineurs, carriers et assimilés* — Mineros, canteros y asimilados	Workers in transport and communication occupations — *Travailleurs des transports et des communications* — Trabajadores de los transportes y comunicaciones	Craftsmen, prod. process workers, labourers not elsewhere classified — *Artisans, ouvriers de métier et à la prod., manœuvres non classés ailleurs* — Artesanos, trabaj. ocupados en los div. procesos de produc., peones no clasif. bajo otros epígr.	Service workers and workers not classifiable by occupation — *Travailleurs des services et personnes ne pouvant être classées selon la prof.* — Trabajadores de los servicios y trab. que no pueden ser clasif. según la ocupación
1965	64 289	1 454	30	5 452	2 039	1 744	758	1 904	43 258	7 650
1966	64 795	1 399	30	6 227	2 019	1 925	911	1 873	42 878	7 533
1967	83 506	1 447	42	5 561	2 096	2 004	1 044	2 188	59 719	9 405
1968	73 718	1 567	43	5 710	2 295	1 304	848	2 212	51 260	8 479
1969	66 501	1 447	42	6 089	2 521	1 230	687	1 698	45 154	7 633
1970	48 687	1 240	43	4 508	1 957	996	552	1 380	32 643	5 368
1971	30 317	912	31	2 746	1 144	658	401	929	20 064	3 432
1972	23 833	747	36	1 938	849	615	365	640	15 692	2 951
1973	21 445	712	49	1 847	649	478	301	503	13 983	2 923
1974	27 101	950	80	2 132	749	503	385	810	17 654	3 838
1975: V	33 774	1 088	99	2 499	1 073	314	413	1 135	24 811	2 342

[1] Excl. unemployed seamen.   [1] *Non compris les gens de mer en chômage.*   [1] Excl. los marineros desempleados.

11 Unemployment by industrial or occupational groups
Chômage par groupes d'activité économique ou de professions
Desempleo por grupos de actividad económica o de ocupaciones

Ireland

(ISIC — CITI — CIIU 1958)

Industrial groups *(Employment office statistics)* [1]
Groupes d'activité économique *(Statistiques des bureaux de placement)* [1]
Grupos de actividad económica *(Estadísticas de las oficinas de colocación)* [1]

Date / Date / Fecha	Total	Agriculture, forestry, fishing / Agriculture, sylviculture, pêche / Agricultura, silvicultura, pesca	Mining, quarrying / Industries extractives / Minas, canteras	Manufacturing / Industries manufacturières / Industrias manufactureras	Construction / Construction / Construcción	Electricity, gas, water and sanitary services / Electricité, gaz, eau et services sanitaires / Electricidad, gas, agua y servicios sanitarios	Commerce / Commerce / Comercio	Transport, storage, communication / Transports, entrepôts, communications / Transportes, almacenaje, comunicaciones	Services / Services / Servicios	Activities not adequately described / Activités mal désignées / Actividades no bien especificadas
1966	47 722	14 793	250	9 108	9 246	295	4 754	3 203	5 079	994
1967	55 035	17 381	267	10 923	10 308	311	5 213	3 519	5 844	1 269
1968	58 316	19 185	272	10 727	10 557	338	5 737	3 530	5 485	1 475
1969	57 349	19 215	355	10 520	10 018	361	5 389	3 523	6 381	1 587
1970	64 865	20 826	492	12 150	12 799	443	5 832	3 562	6 900	1 861
1971	61 988	17 369	434	13 723	11 816	383	5 839	3 405	7 186	1 833
1972 [2]	71 527	20 722	435	15 296	13 968	447	6 550	3 609	8 075	2 425
1973	66 785	20 004	409	13 464	12 465	394	6 177	3 457	7 839	2 576
1974	71 392	19 923	453	16 002	13 484	434	6 523	3 487	8 325	2 761
1975: III	102 924	23 057	644	30 563	19 887	594	9 519	4 154	10 924	3 582

[1] Applicants for work on the "live" register. [2] Jan.-March and May-Dec.

[1] *Demandeurs d'emploi restant inscrits.* [2] *Janv.-mars et mai-déc.*

[1] Solicitantes de trabajo que continúan inscritos. [2] Enero-marzo y mayo-dic.

Italie

(ISIC — CITI — CIIU 1958)

Industrial groups *(Labour force sample surveys)*
Groupes d'activité économique *(Enquêtes par sondage sur la main-d'œuvre)*
Grupos de actividad económica *(Encuestas por muestra sobre la fuerza trabajadora)*

Date / Date / Fecha	Total	Agriculture, forestry, fishing / Agriculture, sylviculture, pêche / Agricultura, silvicultura, pesca	Mining, quarrying / Industries extractives / Minas, canteras	Manufacturing / Industries manufacturières / Industrias manufactureras	Construction / Construction / Construcción	Electricity, gas, water and sanitary services / Electricité, gaz, eau et services sanitaires / Electricidad, gas, agua y servicios sanitarios	Commerce / Commerce / Comercio	Transport, storage, communication / Transports, entrepôts, communications / Transportes, almacenaje, comunicaciones	Services / Services / Servicios	Persons seeking work for the first time / Personnes en quête d'emploi pour la première fois / Personas en busca de trabajo por primera vez
1965	714 000	53 000		311 000				101 000		249 000
1966	759 000	55 000		298 000				115 000		291 000
1967	679 000	52 000		230 000				103 000		294 000
1968	689 000	46 000		208 000				104 000		326 000
1969	655 000	39 000		165 000				100 000		351 000
1970	609 000	33 000		144 000				92 000		340 000
1971	609 000	30 000		162 000				87 000		330 000
1972	697 000	29 000		152 000				81 000		435 000
1973	668 000	35 000		135 000				78 000		420 000
1974	560 000	23 000		105 000				66 000		366 000
1975: IV	667 000	29 000		147 000				75 000		416 000

11

Unemployment by industrial or occupational groups
Chômage par groupes d'activité économique ou de professions
Desempleo por grupos de actividad económica o de ocupaciones

Norway

Occupational groups *(Employment office statistics)*
Groupes de professions *(Statistiques des bureaux de placement)*
Grupos de ocupaciones *(Estadísticas de las oficinas de colocación)*

Date / Date / Fecha	Total	0/1 Professional, technical and related workers / *Personnel des professions scientifiques, techniques, libérales et assimilées* / Profesionales, técnicos y trabajadores asimilados	2 Administrative and managerial workers / *Directeurs et cadres administratifs supérieurs* / Directores y funcionarios públicos superiores	3 Clerical and related workers / *Personnel administratif et travailleurs assimilés* / Personal administrativo y trabajadores asimilados	4 Sales workers / *Personnel commercial et vendeurs* / Comerciantes y vendedores	5 Service workers / *Travailleurs spécialisés dans les services* / Trabajadores de los servicios	6 Agricultural, animal husbandry and forestry workers, fishermen and hunters / *Agriculteurs, éleveurs, forestiers, pêcheurs et chasseurs* / Trabajadores agrícolas y forestales, pescadores y cazadores	7/8/9 Production and related workers, transport equipment, operators and labourers / *Ouvriers et manœuvres non agricoles et conducteurs d'engins de transport* / Obreros no agrícolas, conductores de máquinas y vehículos de transp. y trabaj. asimilados	X Workers not classifiable by occupation / *Travailleurs ne pouvant être classés selon la profession* / Trabajadores que no pueden ser clasificados según la ocupación
1969	15 605	646	10	575	495	1 135	1 471	10 323	950
1970	12 458	398	15	483	475	915	1 042	8 161	969
1971	12 193	338	14	486	469	959	1 041	7 895	991
1972	14 812	580	29	658	602	1 278	1 282	9 153	1 230
1973	12 811	594	35	637	627	1 300	975	7 508	1 135
1974	10 662	533	33	664	626	1 238	707	5 761	1 100

11 Unemployment by industrial or occupational groups
Chômage par groupes d'activité économique ou de professions
Desempleo por grupos de actividad económica o de ocupaciones

Pays-Bas

Occupational groups *(Employment office statistics)* [1]
Groupes de professions *(Statistiques des bureaux de placement)* [1]
Grupos de ocupaciones *(Estadísticas de las oficinas de colocación)* [1]

Date / Date / Fecha	Total [3]	Agriculture, hunting, fishing / Agriculture, chasse, pêche / Agricultura, caza, pesca	Mining, quarrying / Industries extractives / Minas, canteras	Pottery, glass, stone / Poterie, verre, pierre / Alfarería, vidrio, piedra	Diamonds / Diamants / Diamantes	Printing / Impression / Imprentas	Textiles	Clothing, cleaning / Habillement, nettoyage / Vestido, limpieza	Wood / Bois / Madera
1965	32 602	2 010	190	45	10	80	137	346	77
1966	42 869	2 098	213	93	2	115	181	350	173
1967	83 464	2 912	408	277	2	252	1 026	974	592
1968 [2]	71 813	2 267	374	194	5	370	801	1 109	439
1969	52 940	1 820	160	85	1	285	342	947	242
1970	46 414	1 608	115	63	18	279	307	930	188
1971	61 999	1 984	105	66	14	494	301	1 085	314
1972	107 930	2 616	139	115	11	932	548	1 407	593
1973	109 891	2 372	127	109	9	957	517	1 642	451
1974	134 905	2 651	136	138	3	1 037	438	2 456	633
1975: III	190 280	4 174	196	259	13	1 347	673	3 428	1 236

Date / Date / Fecha	Leather, rubber / Cuir, caoutchouc / Cuero, caucho	Food, beverages, tobacco / Aliments, boissons, tabac / Alimentos, bebidas, tabaco	Metal workers / Ouvriers sur métaux / Obreros metalúrgicos	Building / Bâtiment / Edificación	Commerce / Commerce / Comercio	Transport / Transports / Transportes	Hotels / Hôtels / Hoteles	Clerical workers / Employés de bureau / Empleados de oficina	Unskilled workers / Ouvriers non qualifiés / Obreros no calificados
1965	71	246	1 522	4 707	1 352	1 825	1 513	2 167	3 741
1966	108	319	2 342	9 131	1 728	2 184	1 576	2 754	5 669
1967	290	516	7 002	21 860	3 169	4 233	2 479	4 900	12 780
1968 [2]	304	556	6 490	13 854	3 908	3 894	3 389	6 501	11 140
1969	243	433	3 722	7 535	3 557	2 671	3 261	5 926	7 075
1970	255	377	3 005	6 382	3 562	2 123	2 933	5 761	5 882
1971	194	420	5 149	11 259	4 501	3 061	2 998	7 660	8 315
1972	322	704	12 681	22 356	5 718	5 352	4 119	13 477	14 591
1973	308	783	11 588	20 295	7 532	4 761	4 801	15 605	13 004
1974	283	806	12 761	31 089	9 310	5 073	5 331	18 099	15 691
1975: III	402	1 309	18 742	48 280	11 738	7 981	7 086	20 947	25 520

[1] 1965-67: Incl. persons employed in social relief works. [2] Beginning 1968: incl. married women who are not breadwinners. [3] Incl. occupational groups not specified in the table.

[1] 1965-1967 : y compris les personnes employées à des travaux sociaux de secours aux chômeurs. [2] A partir de 1968 : y compris les femmes mariées qui ne sont pas soutien de famille. [3] Y compris des groupes de professions non spécifiés dans le tableau.

[1] 1965-1967: incl. las personas ocupadas en trabajos sociales de socorro para desempleados. [2] A partir de 1968: incl. las mujeres casadas que no son sostén de familia. [3] Incl. grupos de ocupaciones no especificados en el cuadro.

11 Unemployment by industrial or occupational groups
Chômage par groupes d'activité économique ou de professions
Desempleo por grupos de actividad económica o de ocupaciones

Suisse

Occupational groups *(Employment office statistics)*
Groupes de professions *(Statistiques des bureaux de placement)*
Grupos de ocupaciones *(Estadísticas de las oficinas de colocación)*

Date / Date / Fecha	Total	Agriculture / *Agriculture* / Agricultura	Food, beverages, tobacco / *Aliments, boissons, tabac* / Alimentos, bebidas, tabaco	Clothing / *Habillement* / Vestido	Leather, rubber / *Cuir, caoutchouc* / Cuero, caucho	Building / *Bâtiment* / Edificación	Wood, cork / *Bois, liège* / Madera, corcho	Textiles	Printing, publishing / *Impression, édition* / Imprentas, editoriales
1965	299	4	1	5	—	104	5	1	1
1966	296	3	2	5	1	115	4	1	1
1967	256	—	1	4	—	70	3	2	1
1968	303	1	2	6	—	100	6	2	2
1969	175	2	—	4	—	43	2	1	1
1970	104	1	1	1	—	26	1	—	—
1971	100	—	—	1	—	14	1	1	2
1972	106	—	1	4	—	4	1	1	1
1973	81	1	—	2	—	6	1	1	1
1974	221	1	2	3	—	26	3	1	20

Date / Date / Fecha	Metal industries, machinery / *Industrie métallurgique, machines* / Industria metalúrgica, maquinaria	Watchmaking, jewellery / *Horlogerie, bijouterie* / Relojería, joyería	Commerce, administration / *Commerce, administration* / Comercio, administración	Hotels, restaurants / *Hôtels, restaurants* / Hoteles, restaurantes	Transport, communication / *Transports, communications* / Transportes, comunicaciones	Professional workers / *Professions libérales* / Profesiones liberales	Domestic workers / *Personnel domestique* / Personal doméstico	Labourers / *Manœuvres* / Peones	Others / *Autres* / Otros
1965	9	3	39	17	6	26	3	31	44
1966	9	3	34	17	7	26	3	29	36
1967	7	4	43	16	3	29	4	35	34
1968	13	6	37	18	7	26	4	37	36
1969	5	3	27	13	2	16	3	25	28
1970	2	1	15	7	2	11	2	18	16
1971	4	16	18	5	1	9	2	10	16
1972	4	21	23	6	1	7	3	15	14
1973	4	3	20	5	2	6	2	15	12
1974	22	4	43	9	7	34	1	28	17

11 Unemployment by industrial or occupational groups
Chômage par groupes d'activité économique ou de professions
Desempleo por grupos de actividad económica o de ocupaciones

Sweden

A Industrial groups *(Labour force sample surveys)* [1]
Groupes d'activité économique *(Enquêtes par sondage sur la main-d'œuvre)* [1]
Grupos de actividad económica *(Encuestas por muestra sobre la fuerza trabajadora)*

Date / Date / Fecha	Total	1 Agriculture, forestry, fishing / Agriculture, sylviculture, pêche / Agricultura, silvicultura, pesca	2 Mining, quarrying / Industries extractives / Minas, canteras	3 Manufacturing / Industries manufacturières / Industrias manufactureras	4 Electricity, gas, water / Electricité, gaz, eau / Electricidad, gas, agua	5 Construction / Construction / Construcción	6 Trade, restaurants and hotels / Commerce, restaurants et hôtels / Comercio, restaurantes y hoteles	7 Transport, storage, communication / Transports, entrepôts, communications / Transportes, almacenaje, comunicaciones	8 Financing, insur., real est., business serv. / Banques, assur., aff. imm., serv. aux entreprises / Bancos, seguros, bienes inm., serv. para empresas	9 Community, social, and pers. services / Services à collectivité, services sociaux et pers. / Servicios comunales, sociales y personales	0 Activities not adequately described / Activités mal désignées / Actividades no bien especificadas
1965	44 000	4 000	—	11 000	—	7 000	7 000	2 000	1 000	7 000	5 000
1966	59 000	3 000	1 000	14 000	—	10 000	9 000	4 000	1 000	9 000	9 000
1967	80 000	6 000	1 000	22 000	—	14 000	12 000	4 000	2 000	12 000	6 000
1968	85 000	8 000	1 000	22 000	—	18 000	11 000	4 000	2 000	13 000	6 000
1969	73 000	5 000	—	21 000	1 000	14 000	9 000	4 000	1 000	12 000	5 000
1970	59 000	4 000	—	14 000	—	11 000	9 000	3 000	2 000	12 000	4 000
1971	101 000	5 000	—	25 000	—	21 000	15 000	4 000	2 000	20 000	7 000
1972	107 000	7 000	—	28 000	1 000	20 000	17 000	6 000	4 000	25 000	—
1973	98 000	6 000	—	26 000	—	17 000	17 000	5 000	3 000	24 000	—
1974	80 000	4 000	—	22 000	—	11 000	14 000	4 000	2 000	22 000	—

[1] Persons aged 16 to 74 years.   [1] *Personnes âgées de 16 à 74 ans.*   [1] Personas de 16 a 74 años.

B Occupational groups *(Labour force sample surveys)* [1]
Groupes de professions *(Enquêtes par sondage sur la main-d'œuvre)* [1]
Grupos de ocupaciones *(Encuestas por muestra sobre la fuerza trabajadora)* [1]

(ISCO — CITP — CIUO 1958)

Date / Date / Fecha	Total	Professional, technical and related workers [2] / Professions libérales, techniciens et assimilés [2] / Profesiones liberales, técnicos y asimilados [2]	Clerical workers / Employés de bureau / Empleados de oficina	Sales workers / Vendeurs / Vendedores	Farmers, fishermen and related workers / Agriculteurs, pêcheurs et assimilés / Agricultores, pescadores y asimilados	Workers in transport and communication occupations / Travailleurs dans les professions des transports et des communications / Trabajadores de los transportes y comunicaciones	Craftsmen, prod. process workers, labourers not elsewhere classified [3] / Artisans, ouvriers de métier et à la production, manœuvres non classés ailleurs [3] / Artesanos, trabaj. ocupados en los div. procesos de produc., peones no clasif. bajo otros epígr.[3]	Service workers / Travailleurs spécialisés dans les services / Trabajadores de los servicios	Workers not classifiable by occupation / Personnes ne pouvant être classées selon la profession / Trabajadores que no pueden ser clasificados según la ocupación
1965	45 000	4 000	3 000	3 000	4 000	2 000	18 000	6 000	6 000
1966	61 000	5 000	3 000	4 000	3 000	2 000	26 000	9 000	10 000
1967	82 000	7 000	5 000	5 000	6 000	4 000	36 000	10 000	8 000
1968	86 000	7 000	5 000	6 000	7 000	5 000	41 000	10 000	7 000
1969	73 000	9 000	4 000	6 000	6 000	4 000	31 000	9 000	5 000
1970	59 000	7 000	4 000	5 000	4 000	3 000	24 000	8 000	4 000
1971	101 000	10 000	8 000	7 000	6 000	4 000	45 000	14 000	7 000
1972	107 000	12 000	9 000	8 000	8 000	6 000	47 000	17 000	—
1973	98 000	13 000	9 000	8 000	6 000	5 000	42 000	15 000	—
1974	80 000	10 000	9 000	6 000	5 000	4 000	32 000	15 000	—

[1] Persons aged 16 to 74 years (1965-69: 14 years and over).   [2] Incl. administrative, executive and managerial workers.   [3] Incl. miners, quarrymen and related workers.

[1] *Personnes âgées de 16 à 74 ans (1965-1969: 14 ans et plus).*   [2] *Y compris les directeurs et les cadres administratifs supérieurs.*   [3] *Y compris les mineurs, carriers et travailleurs assimilés.*

[1] Personas de 16 a 74 años (1965-1969: 14 años y más).   [2] Incl. los administradores, gerentes y directores.   [3] Incl. los mineros, canteros y trabajadores asimilados.

11 Unemployment by industrial or occupational groups
Chômage par groupes d'activité économique ou de professions
Desempleo por grupos de actividad económica o de ocupaciones

United Kingdom [1]

Industrial groups *(National Insurance Scheme statistics)* [2]
Groupes d'activité économique *(Statistiques du régime d'assurance nationale)* [2]
Grupos de actividad económica *(Estadísticas del seguro nacional)* [2]

Date / Date / Fecha	Total [3]	1 Agriculture, forestry, fishing / Agriculture, sylviculture, pêche / Agricultura, silvicultura, pesca	2 Mining, quarrying / Industries extractives / Minas, canteras	3 Manufacturing / Industries manufacturières / Industrias manufactureras	4 Electricity, gas, water / Electricité, gaz, eau / Electricidad, gas, agua	5 Construction / Construction / Construcción	6 Trade, restaurants and hotels / Commerce, restaurants et hôtels / Comercio, restaurantes y hoteles	7 Transport, storage, communication / Transports, entrepôts, communications / Transportes, almacenaje, comunicaciones	8 Financing, insur., real est., business serv. / Banques, assur., aff. imm., serv. aux entreprises / Bancos, seguros, bienes inm., serv. para empresas	9 Community, social, and pers. services / Services à collectivité, services sociaux et pers. / Servicios comunales, sociales y personales	0 Activities not adequately described / Activités mal désignées / Actividades no bien especificadas
1973	630 251	12 758	18 198	174 757	7 046	97 297	84 421	40 007	15 464	87 436	98 399
1974 [4]	630 942	12 504	16 404	161 987	5 971	112 432	81 551	35 141	16 141	88 673	106 705

[1] For figures prior to 1973, see previous editions of the *Year Book*. [2] Excl. persons temporarily laid off. [3] Totals represent the average of the final (adjusted) monthly figures; data for industrial groups are unadjusted figures. [4] Jan.-Nov.

[1] *Pour les données avant 1973, voir les précédentes éditions de l'Annuaire.* [2] *Non compris les personnes temporairement mises à pied.* [3] *Les totaux représentent la moyenne des chiffres définitifs (ajustés) de chaque mois; les données par groupes d'activité économique ne sont pas ajustées.* [4] *Janv.-nov.*

[1] Para los datos antes de 1973, véanse las precedentes ediciones del *Anuario*. [2] Excl. las personas temporalmente despedidas. [3] Los totales representan el promedio de las cifras definitivas (ajustadas) de cada mes; los datos por grupos de actividad económica no han sido ajustados. [4] Enero-nov.

Industrial groups *(National Insurance Scheme statistics)* [1]
Groupes d'activité économique *(Statistiques du régime d'assurance nationale)* [1]
Grupos de actividad económica *(Estadísticas del seguro nacional)* [1]

Date [2] / Date [2] / Fecha [2]	Total [2]	1 Agriculture, forestry, fishing / Agriculture, sylviculture, pêche / Agricultura, silvicultura, pesca	2 Mining, quarrying / Industries extractives / Minas, canteras	3 Manufacturing / Industries manufacturières / Industrias manufactureras	4 Electricity, gas, water / Electricité, gaz, eau / Electricidad, gas, agua	5 Construction / Construction / Construcción	6 Trade, restaurants and hotels / Commerce, restaurants et hôtels / Comercio, restaurantes y hoteles	7 Transport, storage, communication / Transports, entrepôts, communications / Transportes, almacenaje, comunicaciones	8 Financing, insur., real est., business serv. / Banques, assur., aff. imm., serv. aux entreprises / Bancos, seguros, bienes inm., serv. para empresas	9 Community, social, and pers. services / Services à collectivité, services sociaux et pers. / Servicios comunales, sociales y personales	0 Activities not adequately described / Activités mal désignées / Actividades no bien especificadas
1973	11 580	1 819	4	8 276	65	425	127	115	7	114	—
1974 [3]	207 429	2 237	304	194 920	15	1 284	1 375	540	570	42	8 343

[1] Persons temporarily laid off. [2] Totals represent the average of the final (adjusted) monthly figures; data for industrial groups are unadjusted figures. [3] Jan.-Sep.

[1] *Personnes temporairement mises à pied.* [2] *Les totaux représentent la moyenne des chiffres définitifs (ajustés) de chaque mois; les données par groupes d'activité économique ne sont pas ajustées.* [3] *Janv.-sept.*

[1] Personas temporalmente despedidas. [2] Los totales representan el promedio de las cifras definitivas (ajustadas) de cada mes; los datos por grupos de actividad económica no han sido ajustados. [3] Enero-sept.

UNEMPLOYMENT

11 Unemployment by industrial or occupational groups
Chômage par groupes d'activité économique ou de professions
Desempleo por grupos de actividad económica o de ocupaciones

Yugoslavia

A — Industrial groups (Employment office statistics) [1]
Groupes d'activité économique (Statistiques des bureaux de placement) [1]
Grupos de actividad económica (Estadísticas de las oficinas de colocación) [1]

Date [2] Date [2] Fecha [2]	Total	1 Agriculture, forestry, fishing Agriculture, sylviculture, pêche Agricultura, silvicultura, pesca	2-3 Mining, quarrying, manufacturing Industries extractives, industries manufacturières Minas, canteras, industrias manufactureras	4 Electricity, gas, water Electricité, gaz, eau Electricidad, gas, agua	5 Construction Construction Construcción	6 Trade, restaurants and hotels Commerce, restaurants et hôtels Comercio, restaurantes y hoteles	7 Transport, storage, communication Transports, entrepôts, communications Transportes, almacenaje, comunicaciones	8 Financing, insur., real est., business serv. Banques, assur., aff. imm., serv. aux entreprises Bancos, seguros, bienes inm., serv. para empresas	9 Community, social, and pers. services Services à collectivité, services sociaux et pers. Servicios comunales, sociales y personales	0 Activities not adequately described Activités mal désignées Actividades no bien especificadas
1966	177 863	37 903	51 207	8 306	39 806	13 571	5 478	20 063		1 529
1967	198 706	42 344	57 207	9 280	44 471	15 161	6 120	22 414		1 709
1968	196 970	41 974	56 708	9 198	44 082	15 029	6 067	22 218		1 694
1969	169 960	36 218	48 932	7 937	38 037	12 968	5 235	19 171		1 462
1970	141 451	30 143	40 724	6 606	31 657	10 793	4 356	15 956		1 216
1971	143 867	30 658	41 420	6 719	32 197	10 977	4 431	16 228		1 237
1972	153 764	32 767	44 269	7 181	34 412	11 732	4 736	17 345		1 322
1973	178 320	38 000	51 338	8 328	39 908	13 606	5 492	20 114		1 534
1974	194 082	41 359	55 876	9 064	43 436	14 808	5 978	21 892		1 669

[1] Excl. persons seeking work for the first time. [2] Dec. of each year.

[1] Non compris les personnes en quête d'emploi pour la première fois. [2] Déc. de chaque année.

[1] Excl. las personas en busca de trabajo por primera vez. [2] Dic. de cada año.

B — Occupational groups (Employment office statistics)
Groupes de professions (Statistiques des bureaux de placement)
Grupos de ocupaciones (Estadísticas de las oficinas de colocación)

(ISCO — CITP — CIUO 1958)

Date [1] Date [1] Fecha [1]	Total	Professional, technical and related workers Professions libérales, techniciens et assimilés Profesiones liberales, técnicos y asimilados	Administrative, executive, managerial workers Directeurs, cadres administratifs supérieurs Administradores, gerentes, directores	Clerical workers Employés de bureau Empleados de oficina	Sales workers Vendeurs Vendedores	Farmers, fishermen and related workers Agriculteurs, pêcheurs et assimilés Agricultores, pescadores y asimilados	Miners, quarrymen and related workers Mineurs, carriers et assimilés Mineros, canteros y asimilados	Workers in transport and communication occupations Travailleurs dans les professions des transports et des communications Trabajadores de los transportes y comunicaciones	Craftsmen, prod. process workers, labourers not elsewhere classified Artisans, ouvriers de métier et à la production, manœuvres non classés ailleurs Artesanos, trabaj. ocupados en los div. procesos de produc., peones no clasif. bajo otros epígr.	Service workers Travailleurs spécialisés dans les services Trabajadores de los servicios	Workers not classifiable by occupation [2] Personnes ne pouvant être classées selon la profession [2] Trabajadores que no pueden ser clasificados según la ocupación [2]
1966	265 264	11 877	13	20 933	4 353	3 912	671	5 557	30 321	4 839	182 788
1967	291 530	18 862	19	29 397	5 727	2 532	1 061	4 892	37 984	4 918	186 138
1968	326 789	28 466	6	29 953	5 498	3 415	1 279	5 617	38 213	5 599	208 743
1969	315 572	26 212	7	29 194	4 911	2 696	951	4 023	34 639	4 986	207 953
1970	294 096	21 060	1	23 344	4 782	2 428	900	4 204	30 422	3 888	203 067
1971	264 050	11 388	—	14 955	5 813	3 289	453	2 379	27 374	1 950	196 449
1972	288 878	13 577	—	14 267	7 706	3 122	463	2 395	32 702	2 569	212 077
1973	353 881	17 796	—	16 484	11 746	3 856	558	3 705	46 066	3 250	250 420
1974	417 765	20 333	—	20 986	17 013	4 492	547	5 349	59 839	4 245	284 961

[1] June of each year except for 1966-69: Dec. [2] Incl. persons seeking work for the first time.

[1] Juin de chaque année, sauf pour 1966-1969: déc. [2] Y compris les personnes en quête d'emploi pour la première fois.

[1] Junio de cada año salvo 1966-1969: dic. [2] Incl. las personas en busca de trabajo por primera vez.

11

Unemployment by industrial or occupational groups
Chômage par groupes d'activité économique ou de professions
Desempleo por grupos de actividad económica o de ocupaciones

OCEANIA — OCÉANIE — OCEANIA

Australia

A — Industrial groups *(Labour force sample surveys)*
Groupes d'activité économique *(Enquêtes par sondage sur la main-d'œuvre)*
Grupos de actividad económica *(Encuestas por muestra sobre la fuerza trabajadora)*

		1	3	4	5	6 ×	7	8	6 × ; 9	
Date / *Date* / Fecha	Total [1]	Agriculture, forestry, fishing / *Agriculture, sylviculture, pêche* / Agricultura, silvicultura, pesca	Manufacturing / *Industries manufacturières* / Industrias manufactureras	Electricity, gas. water / *Electricité, gaz, eau* / Electricidad, gas, agua	Construction / *Construction* / Construcción	Trade [2] / *Commerce [2]* / Comercio [2]	Transport, storage, communication / *Transports, entrepôts, communications* / Transportes, almacenaje, comunicaciones	Financing, insur., real est., business serv. / *Banques, assur., aff. inm., serv. aux entreprises* / Bancos, seguros, bienes inm., serv. para empresas	Community, social and pers. services [3] / *Services à collectivité, services sociaux et pers. [3]* / Servicios comunales, sociales y personales [3]	Persons seeking work for the first time / *Personnes en quête d'emploi pour la première fois* / Personas en busca de trabajo por primera vez
1972	125 900	5 100	29 500		10 500	24 100	5 400	5 900	22 200	21 700
1973	107 700	4 600	23 200		8 200	20 700	5 000	5 200	20 800	18 400
1974	133 200	6 600	31 600		12 300	24 800	5 600	6 900	24 200	19 600

[1] Incl. mining and quarrying (not shown separately in the table). [2] Excl. restaurants and hotels. [3] Incl. restaurants and hotels.

[1] *Y compris les industries extractives (pas indiquées séparément dans le tableau).* [2] *Non compris les restaurants et les hôtels.* [3] *Y compris les restaurants et les hôtels.*

[1] Incl. las minas y canteras (no indicadas separadamente en el cuadro). [2] Excl. los restaurantes y los hoteles. [3] Incl. los restaurantes y los hoteles.

B — Occupational groups *(Labour force sample surveys)*
Groupes de professions *(Enquêtes par sondage sur la main-d'œuvre)*
Grupos de ocupaciones *(Encuestas por muestra sobre la fuerza trabajadora)*

(ISCO — CITP — CIUO 1958)

Date / *Date* / Fecha	Total	Professional, technical and related workers / *Professions libérales, techniciens et assimilés* / Profesiones liberales, técnicos y asimilados	Administrative, executive, managerial workers / *Directeurs, cadres administratifs supérieurs* / Administradores, gerentes, directores	Clerical workers / *Employés de bureau* / Empleados de oficina	Sales workers / *Vendeurs* / Vendedores	Farmers, fishermen and related workers / *Agriculteurs, pêcheurs et assimilés* / Agricultores, pescadores y asimilados	Workers in transport and communication occupations / *Travailleurs dans les professions des transports et des communications* / Trabajadores de los transportes y comunicaciones	Miners, quarrymen and related workers / *Mineurs, carriers et assimilés* / Mineros, canteros y asimilados	Craftsmen, prod. process workers, labourers not elsewhere classified / *Artisans, ouvriers de métier et à la production, manœuvres non classés ailleurs* / Artesanos, trabaj. ocupados en los div. procesos de prod., peones no clasif. bajo otros epígr.	Service workers / *Travailleurs spécialisés dans les services* / Trabajadores de los servicios	Persons seeking work for the first time / *Personnes en quête d'emploi pour la première fois* / Personas en busca de trabajo por primera vez
		[1]	[1]				[1]				
1965	60 700	—	—	6 400	4 700	5 100	—	18 900		7 800	11 400
1966	71 500	—	—	7 700	6 200	4 300	—	23 700		8 600	13 400
1967	79 100	4 000	—	9 200	6 800	4 700	—	26 000		9 900	13 900
1968	77 800	4 100	—	8 800	7 400	4 600	—	23 300		9 900	15 300
1969	80 000	—	—	10 000	7 800	5 100	—	24 200		10 600	14 100
1970	74 700	—	—	11 100	7 200	4 500	—	23 400		8 100	12 300
1971	87 600	4 700	—	12 000	8 100	5 200	4 000	29 000		10 200	13 300
1972	125 900	6 600	—	14 900	12 000	5 800	5 600	43 600		14 200	21 700
1973	107 700	5 800	—	14 500	10 900	5 100	4 300	33 100		13 400	18 400
1974	133 200	7 600	—	17 300	11 900	7 300	5 200	47 100		15 400	19 600

[1] Figures of less than 4,000 persons are indicated by a dash.

[1] *Les chiffres inférieurs à 4 000 personnes sont indiqués par un tiret.*

[1] Las cifras inferiores a 4 000 personas están indicadas por un guión.

Hours of work

Durée du travail

Horas de trabajo

Hours of work

Tables 12 to 16 generally show the *average number of hours of work per week per wage earner*. In a few cases hours per day or per month have been shown in the absence of hours per week. Some of the series refer to average hours per week for all employees or even for all categories of workers, as indicated in footnotes. Unless otherwise stated, the series relate to workers of both sexes, irrespective of age.

Where possible, the data presented are statistics of average *hours actually worked*; where such data are lacking, statistics of average *hours paid for* are given. In a few cases where absolute data are not available, index numbers of hours of work have been provided.[1] Statistics of hours actually worked generally comprise all hours worked during normal periods of work, overtime, time spent at the place of work waiting or standing by, as well as time corresponding to short rest periods at the workplace, including tea and coffee breaks. In addition to hours actually worked, statistics of hours paid for include hours paid for but not worked, such as paid annual vacation, paid public holidays, paid sick leave and other paid leave.

Statistics of average hours of work are mostly obtained from payrolls data supplied by a sample of establishments often furnishing at the same time data on wages and on employment. Average hours worked or paid for per week or per month are usually compiled by dividing the total number of man-hours actually worked or paid for during a week or a month by the average number of workers on the payrolls during the same period. Average hours actually worked or paid for per day are generally compiled by dividing the total number of man-hours actually worked or paid for during a week, fortnight or month by the total number of man-days actually worked or paid for during the same period.

In a few cases, statistics on hours worked are obtained from household *sample surveys*. The information is collected from individuals and the data obtained are therefore not fully comparable with the data obtained from establishments.

In making comparisons of data on hours of work, it should be borne in mind that the data are influenced by the number of days normally worked per week, regulations and customs regarding Saturday and overtime work, the extent of absenteeism, labour turnover, etc. Differences in national definitions of hours worked, the coverage of the series and the methods of compilation must also be taken into account.[2]

As of the 1974 issue of the *Year Book*, changes have been made in the presentation of the data shown in certain tables owing to the introduction of the revised 1968 edition of the International Standard Industrial Classification of All Economic Activities (ISIC); see " Preface ".

Table 12

Hours of work in non-agricultural sectors

Unless otherwise indicated in footnotes, the data shown in this table cover the following divisions of economic activity: Mining and quarrying; Manufacturing; Electricity, gas and water; Construction; Wholesale and retail trade, restaurants and hotels; Transport, storage and communication; Financing, insurance, real estate and business services; Community, social and personal services. In some cases, however, these divisions are only represented by certain of the groups composing them.

---

[1] For the descriptions of the various national series, their scope, methods of compilation used, etc., see ILO: *Technical Guide 1976* (description of general series published in the *Bulletin* and the *Year Book of Labour Statistics*), Vol. II, " Employment—Unemployment—Hours of Work—Wages " (Geneva, 1976).

[2] For a review of the problems concerning definitions, methods of collection and tabulation of data on hours of work, see ILO: *Statistics of Hours of Work*, Tenth International Conference of Labour Statisticians, Report III: (Geneva, 1962). See also the resolution concerning statistics of hours of work adopted by the Tenth International Conference of Labour Statisticians in 1962 and published in *Official Bulletin* (Geneva, ILO), Vol. XLVI, No. 1, Jan. 1963.

Table 13

Hours of work in manufacturing

Part A of table 13 generally shows hours of work per worker in manufacturing industries as a whole; where in a few cases other industries are also included in the series, this is indicated in footnotes.

Part B of table 13 shows hours of work in specified manufacturing industries for most of the countries represented in Part A. So far as possible, the different manufacturing industries have been arranged according to the International Standard Classification of All Economic Activities (see Appendix) with the corresponding code number of the different industrial major groups.

Part C of table 13 shows the percentage distribution of workers in manufacturing according to the number of hours actually worked or paid for per week. So far as the data permit, groups working less than 40 hours per week are distinguished from those working 40 hours or more. These data are in some cases based on the hours of work reported for individual workers and in others on estimates of the time worked by establishments or groups of workers.

Tables 14 to 16

Hours of work in mining and quarrying; construction; transport, storage and communication

Tables 14 to 16 show statistics of average hours of work per week in three major divisions of economic activity as follows: Table 14. Mining and quarrying; table 15. Construction; and table 16. Transport, storage and communication (excl. sea transport).

The statistics of hours of work in mining often exclude coal mining owing to the particular conditions regulating work in that industry in the different countries (especially the widespread application of systems of payment by results and of payment for travelling time). The statistics of hours of work in construction refer in many cases to building or to certain categories of building workers.

Durée du travail

Les tableaux 12 à 16 donnent généralement la *durée moyenne du travail par semaine, par ouvrier*. Dans quelques cas, c'est la durée du travail par jour ou par mois qui est indiquée, en l'absence de la durée hebdomadaire. Certaines des séries se rapportent à la durée hebdomadaire moyenne pour tous les travailleurs salariés ou même pour toutes les catégories de travailleurs, selon ce qu'indiquent les notes de bas de page. Sauf indication contraire, les séries couvrent les travailleurs des deux sexes, sans considération d'âge.

Dans la mesure du possible, les données présentées sont des statistiques du nombre moyen d'*heures réellement effectuées*; lorsque ces données manquent, elles sont remplacées par des statistiques du nombre moyen d'*heures rémunérées*. Dans quelques cas où l'on ne dispose pas de données en chiffres absolus, ce sont les nombres-indices de la durée du travail qui ont été reproduits [1]. Les statistiques du nombre d'heures de travail réellement effectuées englobent généralement toutes les heures de travail effectuées au cours des périodes normales de travail, les heures supplémentaires, les heures passées sur le lieu de travail à attendre ou à rester à la disposition, ainsi que le temps correspondant à de courtes périodes de repos passées sur le lieu de travail, y compris les pauses pour le thé et le café. Outre les heures de travail réellement effectuées, les statistiques des heures rémunérées comprennent les heures de travail payées mais non effectuées, telles que congés annuels, jours fériés, congés de maladie et autres congés payés.

Les statistiques de la durée moyenne du travail sont tirées le plus souvent des bordereaux de salaires remis par un échantillon d'établissements, qui fournissent fréquemment en même temps des données sur les salaires et sur l'emploi. Le nombre moyen d'heures de travail réellement effectuées ou rémunérées par semaine ou par mois est géné-ralement obtenu en divisant le nombre total des heures-homme réellement effectuées ou rémunérées pendant une semaine ou un mois par le nombre moyen des travailleurs figurant sur les bordereaux de salaires pendant la même période. La durée moyenne de la journée de travail effectuée ou rémunérée est généralement obtenue en divisant le nombre total d'heures-homme réellement effectuées ou rémunérées pendant une semaine, une quinzaine ou un mois par le nombre total des journées-homme réellement effectuées ou rémunérées pendant la même période.

Dans quelques cas peu nombreux, les statistiques de la durée du travail ont été obtenues à partir d'*enquêtes par sondage* dans les ménages. Les renseignements sont recueillis auprès des particuliers; les données obtenues ne sont donc pas entièrement comparables avec celles que fournissent les établissements.

En comparant les données relatives à la durée du travail, il ne faut pas perdre de vue que ces données sont influencées par le nombre de journées normalement effectuées par semaine, par les règlements et les usages concernant le travail du samedi et les heures supplémentaires, par le degré d'absentéisme, le mouvement de la main-d'œuvre, etc. Il faut également tenir compte des différences dans les définitions nationales du travail effectif, la portée des séries et les méthodes d'établissement de ces séries [2].

Dès l'édition de 1974 de l'*Annuaire* des modifications ont été apportées à la présentation des données de certains tableaux en raison de l'introduction de la version révisée 1968 de la Classification internationale type par industrie de toutes les branches d'activité économique (CITI); voir « Préface ».

---

[1] Pour les descriptions des diverses séries nationales, de leur portée, des méthode utilisées, etc., voir BIT: *Guide technique 1976* (descriptions des séries générales publiées dans le *Bulletin* et l'*Annuaire des statistiques du travail*), vol. II, « Emploi — Chômage — Durée du travail — Salaires » (Genève, 1976).

[2] Pour une étude des problèmes relatifs aux définitions, aux méthodes d'établissement des séries et à la tabulation des données concernant la durée du travail, voir BIT, dixième Conférence internationale des statisticiens du travail, rapport III: *Statistiques de la durée du travail* (Genève, 1962). Voir également la résolution concernant les statistiques des heures de travail, adoptée par la dixième Conférence internationale des statisticiens du travail en 1962 et publiée dans *Bulletin officiel* (Genève, BIT), vol. XLVI, n° 1, janv. 1963.

Tableau 12

Durée du travail dans les secteurs non agricoles

Sauf indication contraire figurant en notes de bas de page, les données présentées dans ce tableau couvrent les branches d'activité économique ci-après: industries extractives; industries manufacturières; électricité, gaz et eau; construction; commerce de gros et de détail, restaurants et hôtels; transports, entrepôts et communications; banque, assurances, affaires immobilières et services fournis aux entreprises; services fournis à la collectivité, services sociaux et services personnels. Dans certains cas, toutefois, ces branches d'activité ne sont représentées que par une partie seulement des classes qui les composent.

Tableau 13

Durée du travail dans les industries manufacturières

La partie A du tableau 13 indique généralement la durée du travail par travailleur dans l'ensemble des industries manufacturières; dans les quelques cas où d'autres branches d'activité sont également comprises dans la série, une indication est donnée à ce sujet en notes de bas de page.

La partie B du tableau 13 indique la durée du travail dans des industries manufacturières spécifiées, pour la plupart des pays représentés dans la partie A. Dans la mesure du possible, les différentes industries manufacturières ont été ordonnées conformément à la Classification internationale type, par industrie, de toutes les branches d'activité économique (voir annexe), avec indication du numéro de code correspondant aux différentes classes d'industries.

La partie C du tableau 13 fournit des données (exprimées en pourcentages) sur la répartition des travailleurs dans les industries manufacturières selon le nombre d'heures de travail réellement effectuées ou rémunérées par semaine. Dans la mesure où les données le permettent, les groupes qui travaillent moins de quarante heures par semaine sont séparés de ceux qui travaillent quarante heures ou plus. Ces données reposent dans certains cas sur la durée du travail enregistrée pour des travailleurs individuels, dans d'autres cas, sur l'évaluation du nombre d'heures de travail effectuées par établissement ou par groupe de travailleurs.

Tableaux 14 à 16

Durée du travail dans les industries extractives; la construction; les transports, entrepôts et communications

Les tableaux 14 à 16 contiennent des statistiques de la durée moyenne du travail par semaine dans trois branches d'activité économique particulièrement importantes, à savoir: tableau 14, industries extractives; tableau 15, construction; tableau 16, transports, entrepôts et communications (non compris les transports par mer).

Les statistiques de la durée du travail dans les industries extractives font fréquemment exclusion des mines de charbon, en raison des conditions particulières régissant le travail dans cette branche d'activité dans les différents pays (notamment l'application très étendue de systèmes de rémunération au rendement et de rémunération du temps nécessaire aux trajets). Les statistiques de la durée du travail dans la construction concernent très souvent l'industrie du bâtiment ou certaines catégories de travailleurs du bâtiment.

Horas de trabajo

Los cuadros 12 a 16 representan generalmente el *promedio de horas de trabajo por semana y por obrero*. En ciertos casos, cuando no existen horas de trabajo por semana, se presentan las horas de trabajo por día o por mes. Tal como se indica en las notas de pie de página, algunas de las series se refieren al promedio de las horas semanales para todas las personas empleadas e inclusive para todas las categorías de trabajadores. Salvo indicación contraria, las series abarcan los trabajadores de ambos sexos, sin distinción de edad.

Cada vez que es posible, los datos que se presentan son estadísticas de promedios de *horas efectivamente trabajadas*; cuando faltan dichos datos, se dan estadísticas de promedios de *horas pagadas*. En ciertos casos, cuando no se dispone de cifras absolutas, se presentan índices de horas de trabajo [1]. Las estadísticas de las horas efectivamente trabajadas comprenden generalmente todas las horas trabajadas durante el tiempo normal de trabajo, las horas extraordinarias, el tiempo empleado en el lugar de trabajo esperando o permaneciendo disponible, así como los cortos períodos de descanso en el lugar de trabajo, incluidas las pausas para tomar el café o el té. Las estadísticas de horas pagadas incluyen, además de las horas efectivamente trabajadas, las horas remuneradas pero no trabajadas, tales como las vacaciones anuales, días feriados, ausencias por motivo de enfermedad y otros permisos pagados.

Las estadísticas de promedios de horas de trabajo se obtienen generalmente de los datos de las nóminas de salarios proporcionados por una muestra de establecimientos que presentan también datos sobre los salarios y el empleo. El promedio de las horas efectivamente trabajadas o pagadas por semana o por mes se obtiene generalmente dividiendo el número total de horas-hombre efectivamente trabajadas o pagadas durante una semana o un mes por el promedio de trabajadores que figuren en las nóminas de salarios durante el mismo período. El promedio de las horas efectivamente trabajadas o pagadas por día se obtiene generalmente dividiendo el número total de horas-hombre efectivamente trabajadas o pagadas durante una semana, una quincena o un mes por el número total de días-hombre efectivamente trabajados o pagados durante el mismo período.

En ciertos casos, las estadísticas de horas efectivamente trabajadas se obtienen mediante *encuestas por muestras* sobre las familias. La información se obtiene de los individuos y, por lo tanto, los datos pueden no ser enteramente comparables con aquellos que se obtienen de los establecimientos.

Al hacer comparaciones sobre los datos de horas de trabajo debe tenerse presente que los mismos están influidos por el número normal de días de trabajo por semana, por las disposiciones reglamentarias y costumbres respecto al trabajo durante el sábado y a las horas extraordinarias, la frecuencia del absentismo, la rotación de la mano de obra, etc. Deben tenerse presentes también las diferencias en las definiciones de cada país sobre las horas efectivamente trabajadas, el alcance de las series y los métodos de compilación [2].

A partir de la edición de 1974 del *Anuario* se ha modificado la presentación de los datos de ciertos cuadros debido a la introducción de la edición revisada 1968 de la Clasificación industrial internacional uniforme de todas las actividades económicas (CIIU); véase « Prefacio ».

---

[1] Para las descripciones de las diversas series nacionales, su alcance, métodos de compilación utilizados, etc., véase OIT: *Guía Técnica 1976* (descripciones generales de las series publicadas en el *Boletín* y el *Anuario de Estadísticas del Trabajo*), vol. II, « Empleo — Desempleo — Horas de trabajo — Salarios » (Ginebra, 1976).

[2] Como revisión de los problemas relativos a las definiciones, métodos de obtención y tabulación de los datos sobre las horas de trabajo, véase OIT: *Estadísticas de la duración del trabajo*, décima Conferencia Internacional de Estadígrafos del Trabajo, Informe III (Ginebra, 1962). Véase también la resolución sobre las estadísticas de las horas de trabajo, adoptada por la décima Conferencia Internacional de Estadígrafos del Trabajo en 1962 y publicada en *Boletín Oficial* (Ginebra, OIT), vol. XLVI, núm. 1, enero de 1963.

Cuadro 12

Horas de trabajo en los sectores no agrícolas

Salvo indicación contraria en notas de pie de página, los datos que se presentan en este cuadro incluyen las siguientes divisiones de la actividad económica: minas y canteras; industrias manufactureras; electricidad, gas y agua; construcción; comercio al por mayor y al por menor y restaurantes y hoteles; transportes, almacenaje y comunicaciones; establecimientos financieros, seguros, bienes inmuebles y servicios prestados a las empresas; servicios comunales, sociales y personales. En algunos casos, estas divisiones sólo están representadas por una parte de los grupos que las componen.

Cuadro 13

Horas de trabajo en las industrias manufactureras

La parte A del cuadro 13 indica generalmente las horas de trabajo por obrero en todas las industrias manufactureras; cuando en ciertos casos se incluyen otras industrias, así se indica en notas de pie de página.

La parte B del cuadro 13 presenta las horas de trabajo en industrias manufactureras especificadas para la mayoría de los países que figuran en la parte A. En la medida de lo posible, las diferentes industrias manufactureras han sido ordenadas según la Clasificación industrial internacional uniforme de todas las actividades económicas (véase apéndice) con indicación del correspondiente número de código de los diferentes grupos de industrias.

La parte C del cuadro 13 indica la repartición en porcentajes de los trabajadores en las industrias manufactureras según el número de horas efectivamente trabajadas o pagadas por semana. En cuanto lo han permitido los datos, se indican los grupos que trabajan menos de 40 horas por semana y aquellos que trabajan 40 horas o más. En algunos casos, estos datos se basan en las horas de trabajo efectivamente trabajadas por

trabajadores individuales, y en otros, en evaluaciones del tiempo trabajado por los establecimientos o grupos de trabajadores.

Cuadros 14 a 16

Horas de trabajo en minas y canteras; construcción; transportes, almacenaje y comunicaciones

Los cuadros 14 a 16 presentan las estadísticas del promedio de horas de trabajo por semana en tres divisiones principales de actividad económica, a saber: cuadro 14: minas y canteras; cuadro 15: construcción; cuadro 16: transportes, almacenaje y comunicaciones (excl. el transporte marítimo).

Las estadísticas sobre horas de trabajo en las minas excluyen frecuentemente la minería del carbón, a causa de las condiciones particulares que regulan el trabajo en esa industria en los distintos países (especialmente debido a la extensa aplicación de los sistemas de pago por rendimiento y al pago por el tiempo empleado en ir al trabajo). Las estadísticas de horas de trabajo en la construcción se refieren, en muchos casos, solamente a la edificación o a ciertas categorías de trabajadores de esta rama.

12 Hours of work in non-agricultural sectors
Durée du travail dans les secteurs non agricoles
Horas de trabajo en los sectores no agrícolas

Hours of work per week   Durée du travail par semaine   Horas de trabajo por semana

Country — Pays — País	Code Code Clave	1965	1966	1967	1968	1969	1970	1971	1972	1973	1974	1975 (VI)
AFRICA — AFRIQUE AFRICA												
Algérie [1]	(a)	.	.	.	43.2	43.5	43.2	42.5	42.8	42.8	...	.
Egypt [2]	(b)	53	59	50	51	51	56	...	...	...	...	.
Mali [3]	(a)	.	.	.	.	.	.	42.3	43.3	44.2	44.6	.
Sierra Leone [4]	(a)	.	43.6	44.0	46.0	49.8	48.3	48.0	49.4	54.3	47.9	.
AMERICA — AMÉRIQUE AMÉRICA												
Guyana [5]	(b)	.	45.2	45.8	46.4	46.1	48.7	48.2	...	...	...	...
Perú (Lima-Callao) [6,7]	(a)	48.9	47.3	47.7	47.4	.	.	.	.	48.5	48.6	...
Puerto Rico [8]	(a)	38.1	38.2	38.5	37.9	38.3	37.8	37.8	37.7	37.9	36.8	37.3 [24]
United States	(b)	38.8	38.6	38.0	37.8	37.7	37.1	37.0	37.1	37.1	36.6	36.3
Venezuela [9]	(a)	.	.	.	.	.	42.9	42.6	42.8	43.1	42.9 *	...
ASIA — ASIE ASIA												
Cyprus [10,11]	(a)	44	44	44	44	44	44	44	44	44	43 *	.
Israel [8,12]	(a)	39.7	39.4	❘ 37.6 [13]	39.5	40.0	❘ 39.6 [14]	39.5	40.1	37.3	37.6	38.6 [25]
Japan [8]	(a)	44.5	44.6	❘ 44.6 [13]	44.5	43.9	❘ 43.1 [13]	42.7	42.4	❘ 42.0 [13]	40.5	40.9
Korea, Rep. of [8]	(a)	57.0	57.2	56.8	58.5	57.2	❘ 51.7 [15]	51.9	50.8	50.5	49.7	.
Philippines [8,16]	(a)	45.5	49.6	50.2	49.4	48.1	...	45.8	44.9	45.0	44.8	.
Singapore [17]	(a)	47.8	47.3	47.6	47.1	48.0	47.8	48.4	48.6	48.4	47.5	.
Sri Lanka [18]	(b) [19]	8.7	8.8	8.9	9.2	9.0	9.1	9.1	9.1	9.1	9.4	.
Thailand (Bangkok) [6,20]	(b) [8]	46.4	46.9	47.6	45.8	47.9	48.7	46.4	...	...	...	.
EUROPE — EUROPE EUROPA												
España [8,21]	(a)	44.6	44.4	44.0	44.0	44.1	43.9	43.6	44.6	44.0	43.7	...
France [22]	(a)	46.4	46.6	46.1	46.0	45.9	45.5	45.1	❘ 44.6 [23]	44.4	43.7	42.8

EXPLANATORY NOTES: See p. 483.   NOTES EXPLICATIVES: Voir p. 485.   NOTAS EXPLICATIVAS: Véase pág. 487.

(a) : Hours actually worked — *Heures réellement effectuées* — Horas efectivamente trabajadas.
(b) : Hours paid for — *Heures rémunérées* — Horas pagadas.

[1] April of each year. [2] Oct. of each year. [3] Dec. of each year. [4] Excl. commerce and services. Adults only. May and Nov. of each year. [5] Excl. commerce. [6] Excl. mining and quarrying. [7] June of each year. [8] Incl. salaried employees. [9] Excl. construction and transport. [10] Adults only. [11] Oct. of each year, except for 1969: Sep. [12] Incl. agriculture, forestry and fishing. [13] Sampling design revised. [14] Industrial classification revised. [15] Series replacing former series. [16] May of each year. [17] Incl. agriculture. July of each year. Beginning 1969: adults only. [18] Excl. services. March and Sep. of each year. [19] Per day. [20] Sep. of each year, except for 1965: June; 1967: July and 1969: Oct. [21] Excl. communication and services. [22] Excl. communication, Government and private domestic services. [23] Beginning Dec. 1972: revised series. [24] March. [25] First quarter.

[1] *Avril de chaque année.* [2] *Oct. de chaque année.* [3] *Déc. de chaque année.* [4] *Non compris le commerce et les services. Adultes seulement. Mai et nov. de chaque année.* [5] *Non compris le commerce.* [6] *Non compris les industries extractives.* [7] *Juin de chaque année.* [8] *Y compris les employés.* [9] *Non compris la construction et les transports.* [10] *Adultes seulement.* [11] *Oct. de chaque année, sauf pour 1969 : sept.* [12] *Y compris l'agriculture, la sylviculture et la pêche.* [13] *Plan d'échantillonnage révisé.* [14] *Classification industrielle révisée.* [15] *Série remplaçant la précédente.* [16] *Mai de chaque année.* [17] *Y compris l'agriculture. Juillet de chaque année. A partir de 1969 : adultes seulement.* [18] *Non compris les services. Mars et sept. de chaque année.* [19] *Par jour.* [20] *Sept. de chaque année, sauf pour 1965 : juin ; 1967 : juillet, et 1969 : oct.* [21] *Non compris les transports et les services.* [22] *Non compris les communications, les services gouvernementaux et les services domestiques privés.* [23] *A partir de déc. 1972 : série révisée.* [24] *Mars.* [25] *Premier trimestre.*

[1] Abril de cada año. [2] Oct. de cada año. [3] Dic. de cada año. [4] Excl. el comercio y los servicios. Adultos solamente. Mayo y nov. de cada año. [5] Excl. el comercio. [6] Excl. las minas y canteras. [7] Junio de cada año. [8] Incl. los empleados. [9] Excl. la construcción y los transportes. [10] Adultos solamente. [11] Oct. de cada año, salvo 1969: sept. [12] Incl. la agricultura, la silvicultura y la pesca. [13] Diseño de la muestra revisado. [14] Clasificación industrial revisada. [15] Serie que substituye a la anterior. [16] Mayo de cada año. [17] Incl. la agricultura. Julio de cada año. A partir de 1969: adultos solamente. [18] Excl. los servicios. Marzo y sept. de cada año. [19] Por día. [20] Sept. de cada año, salvo para 1965: junio; 1967: julio, y 1969: oct. [21] Excl. los transportes y los servicios. [22] Excl. las comunicaciones, los servicios gubernamentales y los servicios domésticos privados. [23] A partir de dic. de 1972: serie revisada. [24] Marzo. [25] Primer trimestre.

HOURS

12 **Hours of work in non-agricultural sectors**
Durée du travail dans les secteurs non agricoles
Horas de trabajo en los sectores no agrícolas

Hours of work per week — Durée du travail par semaine — Horas de trabajo por semana

Country — Pays — País	Code Code Clave	1965	1966	1967	1968	1969	1970	1971	1972	1973	1974	1975 (VI)
Germany, Fed. Rep. of △[1]	(b)	44.3	43.9	42.3	43.3	44.0	44.0	43.2	42.8	|42.8[2]	41.9	40.7[22]
Gibraltar [3,4]	(b)	.	.	.	.	.	48.1	47.6	47.7	49.4	47.4	.
Ireland [5,6]	(a)	43.9	|43.9[7]	43.4	43.3	|43.1[8]	42.8	42.4	42.5	...	...	.
Italie [9]	(a)[10]	7.72	7.85	7.88	7.88	7.82	7.80	7.83	7.80	7.70	7.70*	...
Luxembourg [11,12]	(a)	.	.	45.7	45.3	45.6	45.0	44.7	|43.9[13]	43.7	43.6	.
Malta [14,15]	(b)	46.5	45.8	46.0	45.4	44.4	43.2	43.1	42.5	...		.
Pays-Bas [11]	(a)	46.4	46.2	45.7	45.4	45.2	44.4	44.0	43.6	43.1	...	.
United Kingdom [11,16]												
Males[15] — Hommes[15] — Hombres[15]	(a)	47.0	46.0	46.2	46.4	46.5	|45.7[13]	44.7	45.0	45.6	45.1	.
Females[15] — Femmes[15] — Mujeres[15]	(a)	38.7	38.1	38.2	38.3	38.1	|37.9[13]	37.7	37.9	37.7	37.4	.
Yugoslavia [14,17]	(b)[18]	202	199	191	187	185	183	182	182	182	182 *	.
OCEANIA — OCÉANIE OCEANÍA												
Australia [11,19]												
Males[15] — Hommes[15] — Hombres[15]	(b)[14]	.	43.0	43.1	43.3	43.6	43.5	43.2	|42.0[20]	42.3	41.3 *	.
Females[15] — Femmes[15] — Mujeres[15]	(b)[14]	.	39.2	39.2	39.1	39.4	39.4	39.3	|38.9[20]	39.0	38.5 *	.
New Zealand [14,21]	(a)	39.1	38.9	38.6	38.4	38.5	38.3	37.7	37.6	37.7	37.6	37.4[22]

EXPLANATORY NOTES: See p. 483. NOTES EXPLICATIVES: Voir p. 485. NOTAS EXPLICATIVAS: Véase pág. 487.

(a): Hours actually worked — Heures réellement effectuées — Horas efectivamente trabajadas.
(b): Hours paid for — Heures rémunérées — Horas pagadas.

[1] Excl. commerce, transport, financing, insurance, real estate, etc., and services. [2] Sampling design revised. [3] Excl. mining and quarrying. [4] April and Oct. of each year, except for 1973: Oct., and 1974: April. [5] Excl. commerce and transport. [6] Sep. of each year, except for 1965-68: Oct. [7] Scope of series revised. [8] Series replacing former series. [9] Excl. commerce, transport and services. [10] Per day. [11] Oct. of each year. [12] Excl. electricity, gas and water, commerce, transport, financing, insurance, real estate, etc., and services. [13] New industrial classification. [14] Incl. salaried employees. [15] Adult only. [16] Excl. coal mines, commerce, railways, financing, insurance, real estate, etc. [17] Socialised sector. [18] Per month. [19] Incl. forestry. [20] Scope of series enlarged. [21] Incl. forestry and logging. April and Oct. of each year. [22] April.

[1] Non compris le commerce, les transports, les banques, les assurances, les affaires immobilières, etc., et les services. [2] Plan d'échantillonnage révisé. [3] Non compris les industries extractives. [4] Avril et oct. de chaque année, sauf pour 1973 : oct., et 1974 : avril. [5] Non compris le commerce et les transports. [6] Sept. de chaque année, sauf pour 1965-1968 : oct. [7] Portée de la série révisée. [8] Série remplaçant la précédente. [9] Non compris le commerce, les transports et les services. [10] Par jour. [11] Oct. de chaque année. [12] Non compris l'électricité, le gaz et l'eau, le commerce, les transports, les banques, les assurances, les affaires immobilières, etc., et les services. [13] Nouvelle classification industrielle. [14] Y compris les employés. [15] Adultes seulement. [16] Non compris les mines de charbon, le commerce, les chemins de fer, les banques, les assurances, les affaires immobilières, etc. [17] Secteur socialisé. [18] Par mois. [19] Y compris la sylviculture. [20] Portée de la série élargie. [21] Y compris la sylviculture et l'exploitation forestière. Avril et oct. de chaque année. [22] Avril.

[1] Excl. el comercio, los transportes, los establecimientos financieros, los seguros, los bienes inmuebles, etc., y los servicios. [2] Diseño de la muestra revisado. [3] Excl. las minas y canteras. [4] Abril y oct. de cada año, salvo 1973: oct., y 1974: abril. [5] Excl. el comercio y los transportes. [6] Sept. de cada año, salvo para 1965-1968: oct. [7] Alcance de la serie revisado. [8] Serie que substituye a la anterior. [9] Excl. el comercio, los transportes y los servicios. [10] Por día. [11] Oct. de cada año. [12] Excl. la electricidad, el gas y el agua, el comercio, los transportes, los establecimientos financieros, los seguros, los bienes inmuebles, etc., y los servicios. [13] Nueva clasificación industrial. [14] Incl. los empleados. [15] Adultos solamente. [16] Excl. las minas de carbón, el comercio, los ferrocarriles, los establecimientos financieros, los seguros, los bienes inmuebles, etc. [17] Sector socializado. [18] Por mes. [19] Incl. la silvicultura. [20] El alcance de la serie es mayor. [21] Incl. la silvicultura y la explotación de la madera. Abril y oct. de cada año. [22] Abril.

13 Hours of work in manufacturing
Durée du travail dans les industries manufacturières
Horas de trabajo en las industrias manufactureras

A All industries
Ensemble des industries
Todas las industrias

Hours of work per week — Durée du travail par semaine — Horas de trabajo por semana

Country — Pays — País	Code Code Clave	1965	1966	1967	1968	1969	1970	1971	1972	1973	1974	1975 (VI)
AFRICA — AFRIQUE AFRICA												
Algérie [1]	(a)	.	.	.	42.7	42.2	42.4	41.1	40.7	40.8	...	.
Egypt [2]	(b)	53	62	49	50	49	55	...	...	...	...	.
Mali [3]	(a)	.	.	.	.	.	.	42.3	43.3	44.2	44.6	.
Sierra Leone [4],[5]	(a)	.	41.1	42.2	44.2	42.4	45.1	41.5	42.8	49.6	46.6	.
South Africa, Rep. of [6]	(a) [7]	46.1	46.4	45.9	46.1	47.0	47.1	47.1	46.5	47.5	48.5	
AMERICA — AMÉRIQUE AMÉRICA												
Barbados	(a)	42	41	42	41	41	41	39	40 [8]	36	...	.
Canada	(b)	41.1	40.8	40.3	40.3	40.0	39.7	39.7	40.0	39.6	38.9	38.4 *
Colombia	(b)	50	50	50	50	50	50 [9]	...	...	...	...	...
Ecuador	(a)	44	44	45	45	49	48	48	48	49	...	...
El Salvador (San Salvador) [10]												
Males — Hommes — Hombres	(b)	45.6	47.3	47.7	48.4	47.7	48.0	47.5	46.4	47.0	...	...
Females — Femmes — Mujeres	(b)	44.3	44.8	45.8	45.7	44.2	45.2	46.0	45.3	46.2	...	...
Guatemala (Guatemala)	(a)	46.1	46.0	46.2	46.0	46.2	45.9	46.3	46.6	47.6	48.6 *	...
Guyana	(b)	.	42.6	42.6	45.5	46.6	46.3	46.9	...	...	...	...
México [2]	(a)	45.5	46.1	43.5	❘ 45.6 [11]	45.6	45.1	44.7 *	...	...	...	...
Panamá	(a)	43.0	42.7	41.8	42.8	43.4	42.3	44.7	43.8	43.1 *	...	...
Perú (Lima-Callao) [12]	(a)	48.4	46.5	47.4	47.1	.	.	.	.	...	47.2	...
Puerto Rico	(b)	36.9	37.3	37.3	37.2	37.0	36.6	37.2	37.2	37.0	36.9	36.7
United States	(b)	41.2	41.4	40.6	40.7	40.6	39.8	39.9	40.6	40.7	40.0	39.4
Venezuela	(a)	.	.	.	.	.	44.4	43.3	43.6	43.8	45.2 *	...
ASIA — ASIE ASIA												
Burma [13]	(a) [14]	7.5	7.6	7.4	7.6	7.6	7.7	7.6	7.5 [15]	7.7 [8]	...	.
Cyprus [4],[16]	(a)	46	44	46	46	45	45	45	44	44	43	

EXPLANATORY NOTES: See p. 483.   NOTES EXPLICATIVES: Voir p. 485.   NOTAS EXPLICATIVAS: Véase pág. 487.

(a) : Hours actually worked — *Heures réellement effectuées* — Horas efectivamente trabajadas.
(b) : Hours paid for — *Heures rémunérées* — Horas pagadas.

[1] April of each year. [2] Oct. of each year. [3] Dec. of each year. [4] Adults only. [5] May and Nov. of each year. [6] White manual workers. [7] 1965: Jan.; 1966: Feb.-Aug. and Nov.-Dec. [8] March and Sep. [9] Jan.-June. [10] Metropolitan area. [11] Scope of series revised. [12] June of each year. [13] Workers engaged for less than 30 days (excl. casual workers). [14] Per day. [15] April and Sep. [16] Oct. of each year, except for 1969: Sep.

[1] *Avril de chaque année.* [2] *Oct. de chaque année.* [3] *Déc. de chaque année.* [4] *Adultes seulement.* [5] *Mai et nov. de chaque année.* [6] *Travailleurs manuels (population blanche).* [7] *1965: janv.; 1966: fév.-août et nov.-déc.* [8] *Mars et sept.* [9] *Janv.-juin.* [10] *Région métropolitaine.* [11] *Portée de la série révisée.* [12] *Juin de chaque année.* [13] *Travailleurs engagés pour moins de 30 jours (non compris les travailleurs occasionnels).* [14] *Par jour.* [15] *Avril et sept.* [16] *Oct. de chaque année, sauf pour 1969 : sept.*

[1] Abril de cada año. [2] Oct. de cada año. [3] Dic. de cada año. [4] Adultos solamente. [5] Mayo y nov. de cada año. [6] Trabajadores manuales (población blanca). [7] 1965: enero; 1966: febr.-agosto y nov.-dic. [8] Marzo y sept. [9] Enero-junio. [10] Area metropolitana. [11] Alcance de la serie revisado. [12] Junio de cada año. [13] Trabajadores ocupados durante menos de 30 días (excl. los trabajadores ocasionales). [14] Por día. [15] Abril y sept. [16] Oct. de cada año, salvo 1969: sept.

13 Hours of work in manufacturing
Durée du travail dans les industries manufacturières
Horas de trabajo en las industrias manufactureras

A All industries
Ensemble des industries
Todas las industrias

Hours of work per week — Durée du travail par semaine — Horas de trabajo por semana

Country — Pays — País	Code Code Clave	1965	1966	1967	1968	1969	1970	1971	1972	1973	1974	1975 (VI)
Israel [1,2]	(a)	41.9	41.7	❘39.9 [3]	41.7	42.5	❘42.1 [4]	41.7	42.8	39.2	39.7	41.0 [24]
Japan [2]	(a)	44.3	44.6	❘44.8 [3]	44.6	43.9	❘43.3 [3]	42.6	42.3	❘42.0 [3]	40.0	40.2
Korea, Rep. of [2]	(a)	57.0	57.4	53.8	57.6	56.3	❘52.3 [5]	51.9	51.6	51.3	50.0	.
Philippines [2,6]	(a)	45.6	46.7	46.7	42.1	42.0	...	44.8	43.4	43.6	43.8	
Singapore [7]	(a)	47.2	47.4	47.4	48.3	49.2	48.7	49.4	49.5	48.8	47.9	.
Sri Lanka [8]	(b) [9]	8.8	8.8	8.8	9.4	9.2	9.2	9.1	9.3	9.3	9.8	.
République arabe syrienne [10]	(a)	.	.	44.6	47.0	48.6	48.0	44.9	47.1	46.3 [11]	44.5 [11]	
Thailand (Bangkok) [2,12] . .	(b)	50.5	46.2	51.3	47.6	47.5	47.7	48.1	...	...	...	

EUROPE — EUROPE
EUROPA

Country — Pays — País	Code Code Clave	1965	1966	1967	1968	1969	1970	1971	1972	1973	1974	1975 (VI)
Austria [1]	(a)	38.7	38.7	38.4	38.6	38.6	37.4	❘37.1 [13]	36.4	36.0	35.9	34.0 [25]
Belgique [14,15]	(a)	.	42.3	41.5	41.4	41.0	39.9	39.7	❘38.7 [16]	37.6	36.6	.
Czechoslovakia [17]	(a)	47.7	46.5	45.3	44.6	43.9	43.8	43.8	43.7	43.6	43.6	43.4 [25]
Denmark [1]	(a)	39.7	39.0	38.9	37.8	37.5	36.2	35.8	35.4	33.4	34.2 *	34.8*[26]
España [2]	(a)	44.4	44.4	44.1	44.1	44.1	44.1	43.9	44.9	44.2	43.8	.
Finland [1]	(a)	44.0	42.1	39.8	39.1	38.8	38.3	38.5	38.2	38.0	38.4	.
France	(a)	45.6	45.9	45.4	45.3	45.4	44.8	44.5	❘44.0 [18]	43.6	42.9	41.8
Germany, Fed. Rep. of Δ	(b)	44.1	43.7	42.0	43.0	43.8	43.8	43.0	42.7	❘42.8 [3]	41.9	40.4 [27]
Gibraltar [19]	(b)	.	.	.	.	.	49.5	53.5	52.4	51.2	48.0	.
Grèce	(b)	43.8	43.3	43.6	43.7	43.8	44.6	44.1	44.6	43.4	43.8	41.2 [11]
Hongrie [17]	(a) [20]	178.6	179.3	178.4	173.3	164.5	❘165.0 [21]	165.4	163.8	162.3	161.4 *	157.2 *
Ireland [22]	(a)	44.0	43.8	43.3	43.3	❘42.9 [5]	42.7	42.3	42.3	42.2	41.5	40.4 [26]
Italie	(a) [9]	7.87	7.88	7.92	7.92	7.83	7.80	7.73	7.78	7.67	7.65 *	
Luxembourg [14]	(a)	.	44.8	43.9	44.6	45.0	44.0	43.6	❘42.4 [16]	42.3	42.4	.
Malta [2,23]	(b)	46.8	46.2	46.2	46.2	45.3	44.2	43.4	42.4	...	...	
Norway												
Males [1] — Hommes [1] — Hombres [1]	(a)	38.3	38.1	37.8	36.7	35.6	35.3	34.8	34.4	34.0	33.6	.
Females — Femmes — Mujeres	(a)	34.0	33.9	33.1	32.3	31.6	30.9	30.0	29.9	29.3	28.7	.
Pays-Bas [14]	(a)	46.1	46.1	45.3	45.3	45.1	44.2	43.8	43.4	43.0	...	

EXPLANATORY NOTES: See p. 483. NOTES EXPLICATIVES: Voir p. 485. NOTAS EXPLICATIVAS: Véase pág. 487.

(a) : Hours actually worked — *Heures réellement effectuées* — Horas efectivamente trabajadas.
(b) : Hours paid for — *Heures rémunérées* — Horas pagadas.

[1] Incl. mining and quarrying. [2] Incl. salaried employees. [3] Sampling design revised. [4] Industrial classification revised. [5] Series replacing former series. [6] May of each year. [7] July of each year. Beginning 1969: adults only. [8] March and Sep. of each year. [9] Per day. [10] Nov. of each year. [11] May. [12] Sep. of each year, except for 1965: June; 1967: July and 1969: Oct. [13] Scope of series enlarged. [14] Oct. of each year. [15] 1966-1971: excl. primary iron and steel. [16] New industrial classification. [17] State industry. [18] Beginning Dec. 1972: revised series. [19] April and Oct. of each year, except for 1973: Oct. and 1974: April. [20] Per month. [21] Revised series. [22] Sep. of each year, except for 1965-68: Oct. [23] Adult only. [24] First quarter. [25] Second quarter. [26] March. [27] April.

[1] *Y compris les industries extractives.* [2] *Y compris les employés.* [3] *Plan d'échantillonnage révisé.* [4] *Classification industrielle révisée.* [5] *Série remplaçant la précédente.* [6] *Mai de chaque année.* [7] *Juillet de chaque année. A partir de 1969: adultes seulement.* [8] *Mars et sept. de chaque année.* [9] *Par jour.* [10] *Nov. de chaque année.* [11] *Mai.* [12] *Sept. de chaque année, sauf pour 1965: juin; 1967: juillet, et 1969: oct.* [13] *Portée de la série élargie.* [14] *Oct. de chaque année.* [15] *1966-1971: non compris la sidérurgie.* [16] *Nouvelle classification industrielle.* [17] *Industrie d'Etat.* [18] *A partir de déc. 1972: série révisée.* [19] *Avril et oct. de chaque année, sauf pour 1973: oct., et 1974: avril.* [20] *Par mois.* [21] *Série révisée.* [22] *Sept. de chaque année, sauf pour 1965-1968: oct.* [23] *Adultes seulement.* [24] *Premier trimestre.* [25] *Deuxième trimestre.* [26] *Mars.* [27] *Avril.*

[1] Incl. las minas y canteras. [2] Incl. los empleados. [3] Diseño de la muestra revisado. [4] Clasificación industrial revisada. [5] Serie que substituye a la anterior. [6] Mayo de cada año. [7] Julio de cada año. A partir de 1969: adultos solamente. [8] Marzo y sept. de cada año. [9] Por día. [10] Nov. de cada año. [11] Mayo. [12] Sept. de cada año, salvo para 1965: junio; 1967: julio, y 1969: oct. [13] El alcance de la serie es mayor. [14] Oct. de cada año. [15] 1966-1971: excl. la siderurgia. [16] Nueva clasificación industrial. [17] Industria de Estado. [18] A partir de dic. de 1972: serie revisada. [19] Abril y oct. de cada año, salvo para 1973: oct., y 1974: abril. [20] Por mes. [21] Serie revisada. [22] Sept. de cada año, salvo para 1965-1968: oct. [23] Adultos solamente. [24] Primer trimestre. [25] Segundo trimestre. [26] Marzo. [27] Abril.

13 Hours of work in manufacturing
Durée du travail dans les industries manufacturières
Horas de trabajo en las industrias manufactureras

A All industries
Ensemble des industries
Todas las industrias

Hours of work per week   **Durée du travail par semaine**   **Horas de trabajo por semana**

Country — *Pays* — País	Code *Code* Clave	1965	1966	1967	1968	1969	1970	1971	1972	1973	1974	1975 (VI)
Pologne [1]	*(a)* [2]	*177*	*177*	*175*	*175*	*173*	*172*	*171*	*169*	*168*	*166*	...
Portugal	*(a)*	44.8	44.5	45.4	44.7	44.3	44.8	...	...	...	...	.
Suisse	*(b)*	44.9	44.8	44.7	44.6	44.7	44.7	44.6	44.4	44.3	44.1	43.1
Sweden [3]	*(a)* [2]	*161*	*161*	*158*	| *155*	*152*	*151*	*148*	*143*	*140 **	...	
United Kingdom [4]												
Males [5] — *Hommes* [5] — *Hombres* [5]	*(a)*	46.1	45.0	45.3	45.8	45.7	| 44.9 [6]	43.6	44.1	44.7	44.0	.
Females [5] — *Femmes* [5] — *Mujeres* [5]	*(a)*	38.6	38.0	38.0	38.2	37.9	| 37.7 [6]	37.5	37.7	37.5	37.2	.
Yugoslavia [7, 8]	*(b)* [2]	*201*	*196*	*189*	*188*	*188*	*184*	*182*	*181*	*181*	*181 **	
OCEANIA — OCÉANIE OCEANÍA												
Australia [4, 8]												
Males [5] — *Hommes* [5] — *Hombres* [5]	*(b)*	.	43.5	43.7	43.7	44.1	44.0	43.5	| 43.1 [9]	43.6	42.2 *	.
Females [5] — *Femmes* [5] — *Mujeres* [5] . . .	*(b)*	.	39.4	39.3	39.3	39.8	39.7	39.6	| 39.6 [9]	39.8	38.9 *	.
Fiji	*(a)*	.	.	.	.	.	44.6	45.0	44.9	45.1	...	
New Zealand [8, 10]	*(a)*	40.7	40.6	40.2	40.2	40.5	40.4	| 39.8 [3]	39.8	40.1	39.8	*39.4* [13]
URSS [11,12]	*(a)* [8]	40.2	40.4	40.2	40.4	40.5	40.6	40.5	40.7	40.9	40.6	.
RSS de Biélorussie [11,8]	*(a)*	40.6	.	40.7	39.6	39.3	39.2	39 1	40.4	40.3	40.4 *	

EXPLANATORY NOTES: See p. 483.   NOTES EXPLICATIVES: Voir p. 485.   NOTAS EXPLICATIVAS: Véase pág. 487.

(a) : Hours actually worked — *Heures réellement effectuées* — Horas efectivamente trabajadas.
(b) : Hours paid for — *Heures rémunérées* — Horas pagadas.

[1] Socialised sector. Incl. mining and quarrying. [2] Per month. [3] 1965-67: incl. mining and quarrying. [4] Oct. of each year. [5] Adults only. [6] New industrial classification. [7] Socialised sector. Incl. mining, quarrying and electricity. [8] Incl. salaried employees. [9] Scope of series enlarged. [10] April and Oct. of each year. [11] Socialised sector. [12] Incl. Byelorussian SSR, shown separately in this table. [13] April.

[1] *Secteur socialisé. Y compris les industries extractives.* [2] *Par mois.* [3] *1965-1967 : y compris les industries extractives.* [4] *Oct. de chaque année.* [5] *Adultes seulement.* [6] *Nouvelle classification industrielle.* [7] *Secteur socialisé. Y compris les industries extractives et l'électricité.* [8] *Y compris les employés.* [9] *Portée de la série élargie.* [10] *Avril et oct. de chaque année.* [11] *Secteur socialisé.* [12] *Y compris la RSS de Biélorussie, figurant séparément dans ce tableau.* [13] *Avril.*

[1] Sector socializado. Incl. las minas y canteras. [2] Por mes. [3] 1965-1967: incl. las minas y canteras. [4] Oct. de cada año. [5] Adultos solamente. [6] Nueva clasificación industrial. [7] Sector socializado. Incl. las minas y canteras y la electricidad. [8] Incl. los empleados. [9] El alcance de la serie es mayor. [10] Abril y oct. de cada año. [11] Sector socializado. [12] Incl. la RSS de Bielorrusia, que figura separadamente en este cuadro. [13] Abril.

13 Hours of work in manufacturing
Durée du travail dans les industries manufacturières
Horas de trabajo en las industrias manufactureras

B By industry
Par industrie
Por industria

AFRICA — AFRIQUE — AFRICA

Algérie

Hours actually worked per week
Heures réellement effectuées par semaine
Horas efectivamente trabajadas por semana

	311-313	321-322	323-324	33	34
Date [1] *Date [1]* Fecha [1]	Food, beverages *Aliments, boissons* Alimentos, bebidas	Textiles, clothing *Textiles, habillement* Textiles, vestidos	Leather, leather products, footwear *Cuir, articles en cuir, chaussures* Cuero, artículos de cuero, calzado	Wood, furniture *Bois, ameublement* Madera, mobiliario	Paper, printing, publishing *Papier, imprimerie, édition* Papel, imprentas, editoriales
1968	42.5	41.5	40.0	41.8	40.5
1969	41.8	44.2	40.0	40.2	43.0
1970	43.0	41.5	41.5	41.2	43.0
1971	40.5	38.8	41.8	41.0	42.8
1972	41.2	38.2	41.2	41.2	42.2
1973	41.2	39.2	41.5	40.8	41.0

	351-352; 355	369 ×	37	381-383	390
Date [1] *Date [1]* Fecha [1]	Chemicals, rubber products *Industrie chimique, caoutchouc* Productos químicos, caucho	Building material *Matériaux de construction* Materiales de construcción	Basic metal industries *Industrie métallurgique de base* Industrias metalúrgicas básicas	Metal products, machinery, etc. *Produits métalliques, machines, etc.* Productos metálicos, maquinaria, etc.	Other manufacturing industries *Autres industries manufacturières* Otras industrias manufactureras
1968	42.2	42.5	40.8	42.5	40.5
1969	41.2	44.5	40.8	41.8	39.5
1970	41.8	44.8	41.5	43.2	43.0
1971	42.0	44.2	41.2	42.8	41.2
1972	41.8	42.8	41.5	41.2	39.8
1973	43.0	41.8	40.0	41.0	44.2

[1] April of each year.   [1] *Avril de chaque année.*   [1] Abril de cada año.

13 **Hours of work in manufacturing**
     Durée du travail dans les industries manufacturières
     Horas de trabajo en las industrias manufactureras

B   By industry
     Par industrie
     Por industria

Egypt

Hours paid for per week
Heures rémunérées par semaine
Horas pagadas por semana

Date [1] *Date* [1] Fecha [1]	Food *Aliments* Alimentos	Tobacco *Tabac* Tabaco	Textiles	Clothing *Habillement* Vestido	Wood *Bois* Madera	Paper, paper products *Papier, articles en papier* Papel, artículos de papel
1965	54	55	54	49	48	48
1966	55	50	54	50	49	42
1967	52	47	49	49	50	49
1968	53	47	50	46	51	49
1969	55	62	48	47	47	49
1970	56	54	54	52	54	51

Date [1] *Date* [1] Fecha [1]	Printing, publishing *Imprimerie, édition* Imprentas, editoriales	Chemicals *Industrie chimique* Productos químicos	Non-metallic mineral products *Produits minéraux non métalliques* Productos minerales no metálicos	Metal products *Produits métalliques* Productos metálicos	Transport equipment *Matériel de transport* Material de transporte
1965	47	52	44	47	58
1966	50	51	49	47	47
1967	50	51	48	50	47
1968	50	54	47	48	53
1969	49	52	49	49	54
1970	50	53	55	54	61

[1] Oct. of each year.   [1] *Oct. de chaque année.*   [1] Oct. de cada año.

13 B

Hours of work in manufacturing
Durée du travail dans les industries manufacturières
Horas de trabajo en las industrias manufactureras

By industry
Par industrie
Por industria

South Africa, Rep. of

Hours actually worked per week [1]
Heures réellement effectuées par semaine [1]
Horas efectivamente trabajadas por semana [1]

Date [2] / Date [2] / Fecha [2]	Food / Aliments / Alimentos	Beverages / Boissons / Bebidas	Tobacco / Tabac / Tabaco	Textiles	Clothing / Habillement / Vestido	Footwear / Chaussures / Calzado	Wood / Bois / Madera	Furniture / Ameublement / Mobiliario	Paper, paper products / Papier, articles en papier / Papel, artículos de papel	Printing, publishing / Imprimerie, édition / Imprentas, editoriales
1965	48.0	44.8	42.1	47.4	41.0		49.4	45.7	46.0	41.6
1966 [3]	48.2	46.0	43.3	47.8	42.0		48.5	44.1	44.8	41.4
1967 [4]	49.4	47.5	44.6	47.4	42.4	42.4	47.2	44.0	46.6	41.3
1968	47.4	46.2	41.8	46.2	40.2	42.1	44.8	44.4	46.3	37.0
1969	47.6	46.5	44.2	47.5	40.3	41.0	45.7	45.2	45.5	42.2
1970	47.8	48.4	42.2	46.9	41.5	40.6	46.8	44.5	47.9	42.5
1971	48.0	48.0	44.2	46.0	41.7	40.3	47.0	44.2	48.5	42.4
1972	47.6	47.4	41.6	47.5	41.1	41.5	45.7	43.0	47.6	40.9
1973	48.1	47.4	42.5	47.7	42.2	42.7	46.0	44.1	48.1	41.3
1974	47.9	47.3	42.5	46.0	42.3	41.7	45.5	44.4	47.6	43.5

Date [2] / Date [2] / Fecha [2]	Leather, leather products / Cuir, articles en cuir / Cuero, artículos de cuero	Rubber products / Industrie du caoutchouc / Productos de caucho	Chemicals / Industrie chimique / Productos químicos	Non-metallic mineral products / Produits minéraux non métalliques / Productos minerales no metálicos	Basic metal industries / Industrie métallurgique de base / Industrias metalúrgicas básicas	Metal products / Produits métalliques / Productos metálicos	Machinery (non-electrical) / Machines (non électriques) / Maquinaria (no eléctrica)	Electrical machinery / Machines électriques / Maquinaria eléctrica	Transport equipment / Matériel de transport / Material de transporte	Miscellaneous manufacturing / Industries manufacturières diverses / Industrias manufactureras diversas
1965	44.1	48.9	44.7	46.7	46.9	48.6	46.3	43.9	46.7	45.4
1966 [3]	44.1	47.6	44.6	48.4	47.8	50.3	48.4	46.1	45.8	42.3
1967 [4]	43.2	48.2	44.5	48.3	48.5	49.2	49.1	45.2	44.7	46.4
1968	41.2	48.9	44.9	48.3	48.2	47.9	48.7	45.4	46.2	46.6
1969	42.5	47.9	44.9	48.7	49.4	48.5	48.3	45.5	47.8	43.9
1970	42.9	47.5	45.4	48.2	49.2	49.7	47.1	46.9	45.8	45.1
1971	43.1	46.9	45.2	49.0	49.9	48.7	47.7	46.7	46.3	46.4
1972	42.4	46.6	44.2	46.8	50.0	47.4	45.7	46.1	45.3	43.0
1973	42.5	48.2	44.2	49.1	49.3	49.6	47.8	48.5	48.4	46.2
1974	46.1	48.1	48.0	49.4	53.3	49.8	47.1	47.9	47.8	43.8

[1] White manual workers. [2] Sep. of each year. [3] Jan. [4] Aug.

[1] Travailleurs manuels (population blanche). [2] Sept. de chaque année. [3] Janv. [4] Août.

[1] Trabajadores manuales (población blanca). [2] Sept. de cada año. [3] Enero. [4] Agosto.

13 Hours of work in manufacturing
Durée du travail dans les industries manufacturières
Horas de trabajo en las industrias manufactureras

B By industry
Par industrie
Por industria

AMERICA — AMÉRIQUE — AMERICA

Canada (1)

Hours paid for per week
Heures rémunérées par semaine
Horas pagadas por semana

	311-312	313	314	321 ×	322	323; 324	324	331
Date	Food	Beverages	Tobacco		Clothing	Leather, leather products, footwear	Footwear	Wood
Date	*Aliments*	*Boissons*	*Tabac*	Textiles [1]	*Habillement*	*Cuir, articles en cuir, chaussures*	*Chaussures*	*Bois*
Fecha	Alimentos	Bebidas	Tabaco		Vestido	Cuero, artículos de cuero, calzado	Calzado	Madera
1965	40.5	41.5	37.6	41.9	37.2	.	.	40.8
1966	40.3	41.5	37.7	41.6	37.1	.	.	40.1
1967	39.8	40.9	37.6	41.2	36.5	38.9	38.8	40.1
1968	39.6	40.5	37.6	41.1	36.7	39.3	39.4	40.1
1969	39.2	40.4	37.0	40.8	36.5	38.4	38.5	39.3
1970	39.3	40.1	37.5	40.4	36.0	38.2	38.1	38.7
1971	38.8	40.2	36.8	40.5	36.3	38.5	38.5	39.1
1972	39.0	40.1	36.7	40.8	36.4	38.5	38.3	39.6
1973	38.5	39.8	36.6	40.4	36.0	37.9	38.0	39.2
1974	37.8	39.2	36.8	39.3	35.7	37.3	37.4	37.9

	332	341	342	351-352	353	354	355	356
Date	Furniture	Paper, paper products	Printing, publishing	Chemicals	Petroleum refineries	Products of petroleum and coal	Rubber products	Plastic products
Date	*Ameublement*	*Papier, articles en papier*	*Imprimerie, édition*	*Industrie chimique*	*Raffineries de pétrole*	*Dérivés du pétrole et du charbon*	*Produits en caoutchouc*	*Articles en matière plastique*
Fecha	Mobiliario	Papel, artículos de papel	Imprentas, editoriales	Productos químicos	Refinerías de petróleo	Derivados del petróleo y del carbón	Productos de caucho	Productos plásticos
1965	42.7	41.8	39.1	41.1	.	.	41.8	.
1966	42.1	41.8	38.9	41.2	.	.	41.5	.
1967	41.8	41.3	38.6	40.8	42.6	42.5	41.2	40.8
1968	41.5	41.2	38.1	40.7	43.1	43.0	41.0	40.5
1969	41.5	41.1	37.9	40.7	43.0	42.9	41.1	40.1
1970	40.5	40.9	37.2	40.6	42.3	42.2	40.7	40.0
1971	41.3	40.4	37.2	40.2	42.0	41.9	40.6	40.6
1972	41.7	40.8	37.7	40.8	42.6	42.5	40.9	40.1
1973	40.6	40.4	37.2	40.8	43.4	43.2	41.0	39.0
1974	39.8	40.0	36.1	40.0	42.0	41.6	40.0	38.1

[1] Excl. knitting mills.　　　　[1] *Non compris les fabriques de bonneterie et de tricot.*　　　　[1] Excl. las fábricas de tejidos de punto.

13 Hours of work in manufacturing
Durée du travail dans les industries manufacturières
Horas de trabajo en las industrias manufactureras

B By industry
Par industrie
Por industria

Canada (2)

Hours paid for per week
Heures rémunérées par semaine
Horas pagadas por semana

Date / Date / Fecha	36 Non-metallic mineral products / Produits minéraux non métalliques / Productos minerales no metálicos	Basic metal industries / Industrie métallurgique de base / Industrias metalúrgicas básicas		381 Metal products / Produits métalliques / Productos metálicos	382 Machinery (non-electrical) / Machines (non électriques) / Maquinaria (no eléctrica)	383 Electrical machinery and apparatus / Machines et appareils électriques / Maquinaria y aparatos eléctricos	384 Transport equipment / Matériel de transport / Material de transporte	385 Scientific, measuring, optical, etc., equipment / Matériel scientifique, de précision, d'optique, etc. / Equipo científico, de medida, de óptica, etc.	390 Other manufacturing industries / Autres industries manufacturières / Otras industrias manufactureras
		371 Iron and steel / Sidérurgie / Hierro y acero	372 Non-ferrous metal / Métaux non ferreux / Metales no ferrosos						
1965	43.4	.	.	42.0	42.1	40.9	41.9	.	41.1
1966	43.3	.	.	41.8	42.1	40.8	41.2	.	40.9
1967	42.7	39.9	41.4	41.1	41.1	39.9	40.8	40.0	40.4
1968	42.7	40.3	41.6	41.0	41.1	40.1	40.9	39.7	40.2
1969	42.4	40.1	41.5	40.8	40.9	40.1	40.6	39.6	40.0
1970	41.7	40.2	40.8	40.5	40.7	39.3	40.3	39.1	39.8
1971	42.0	39.9	41.7	40.4	40.4	39.3	39.9	41.5	41.0
1972	42.2	40.2	41.7	40.8	40.5	39.7	40.8	40.6	40.5
1973	41.6	39.8	41.3	40.4	40.7	39.5	40.6	40.5	39.4
1974	40.7	39.9	40.5	39.4	39.7	39.0	39.8	39.3	38.3

13 B

Hours of work in manufacturing
Durée du travail dans les industries manufacturières
Horas de trabajo en las industrias manufactureras

By industry
Par industrie
Por industria

Colombia

Hours paid for per week
Heures rémunérées par semaine
Horas pagadas por semana

Date / Date / Fecha	Food / Aliments / Alimentos	Beverages / Boissons / Bebidas	Tobacco / Tabac / Tabaco	Textiles	Clothing / Habillement / Vestido	Wood / Bois / Madera	Furniture / Ameublement / Mobiliario	Paper, paper products / Papier, articles en papier / Papel, artículos de papel	Printing, publishing / Imprimerie, édition / Imprentas, editoriales	Leather, leather products / Cuir, articles en cuir / Cuero, artículos de cuero
1965	52	52	50	49	48	50	48	50	50	49
1966	52	52	49	49	48	50	49	50	49	48
1967	52	52	49	49	47	50	48	50	49	48
1968	52	54	49	49	48	50	49	51	50	49
1969	51	54	49	49	48	50	48	51	49	49
1970[1]	52	55	51	49	47	50	49	50	50	49

Date / Date / Fecha	Rubber products / Industrie du caoutchouc / Productos de caucho	Chemicals / Industrie chimique / Productos químicos	Products of petroleum and coal / Dérivés du pétrole et du charbon / Derivados del petróleo y del carbón	Non-metallic mineral products / Produits minéraux non métalliques / Productos minerales no metálicos	Basic metal industries / Industrie métallurgique de base / Industrias metalúrgicas básicas	Metal products / Produits métalliques / Productos metálicos	Machinery (non-electrical) / Machines (non électriques) / Maquinaria (no eléctrica)	Electrical machinery / Machines électriques / Maquinaria eléctrica	Transport equipment / Matériel de transport / Material de transporte	Miscellaneous manufacturing / Industries manufacturières diverses / Industrias manufactureras diversas
1965	48	50	56	51	51	50	49	50	52	50
1966	48	51	58	51	51	49	49	49	51	50
1967	48	50	63	50	52	49	49	49	51	50
1968	48	50	57	50	51	50	49	49	52	50
1969	48	51	54	50	51	49	50	50	51	50
1970[1]	48	51	56	50	52	49	49	50	50	48

[1] Jan.-June.   [1] *Janv.-juin.*   Enero-junio.

13 Hours of work in manufacturing
Durée du travail dans les industries manufacturières
Horas de trabajo en las industrias manufactureras

B By industry
Par industrie
Por industria

Ecuador

Hours actually worked per week
Heures réellement effectuées par semaine
Horas efectivamente trabajadas por semana

Date / Date / Fecha	311-312 Food / Aliments / Alimentos	313 Beverages / Boissons / Bebidas	314 Tobacco / Tabac / Tabaco	321 Textiles	322; 324 Clothing, footwear / Habillement, chaussures / Vestido, calzado	323 Leather, leather products / Cuir, articles en cuir / Cuero, artículos de cuero	331 Wood / Bois / Madera	341 Paper, paper products / Papier, articles en papier / Papel, artículos de papel
1965	48	50	40	44	43	43	51	45
1966	48	49	39	45	42	43	56	45
1967	48	46	40	46	43	44	61	46
1968	50	47	41	46	43	44	63	47
1969	52	54	44	45	43	48	53	52
1970	49	56	45	45	43	45	51	49
1971	51	55	46	45	43	46	51	48
1972	52	53	44	45	41	42	54	48
1973	54	52	45	45	42	44	56	49

Date / Date / Fecha	342 Printing, publishing / Imprimerie, édition / Imprentas, editoriales	351 Industrial chemicals / Chimie industrielle / Química industrial	355 Rubber products / Produits en caoutchouc / Productos de caucho	369 Non-metallic mineral products [1] / Produits minéraux non métalliques [1] / Productos minerales no metálicos [1]	381 Metal products / Produits métalliques / Productos metálicos	382 Machinery (non-electrical) / Machines (non électriques) / Maquinaria (no eléctrica)	383 Electrical machinery and apparatus / Machines et appareils électriques / Maquinaria y aparatos eléctricos	384 Transport equipment / Matériel de transport / Material de transporte	390 Other manufacturing industries / Autres industries manufacturières / Otras industrias manufactureras
1965	46	45	42	44	44	43	40	48	43
1966	48	47	42	46	42	44	42	49	43
1967	48	50	41	46	44	43	42	50	43
1968	48	44	41	48	45	44	42	53	43
1969	52	48	42	47	46	43	41	53	47
1970	50	46	48	49	46	41	41	52	47
1971	47	48	44	46	45	42	40	50	47
1972	47	46	41	52	47	43	37	45	49
1973	47	46	44	53	46	46	35	46	48

[1] Excl. pottery, china, earthenware and glass.

[1] *Non compris le grès, les porcelaines, les faïences et le verre.*

[1] Excl. el barro, la loza, la porcelana y el vidrio.

13 B

Hours of work in manufacturing
Durée du travail dans les industries manufacturières
Horas de trabajo en las industrias manufactureras

By industry
Par industrie
Por industria

El Salvador (San Salvador) [1]

Hours paid for per week
Heures rémunérées par semaine
Horas pagadas por semana

Date / Date / Fecha	311-312	313	321	322; 324	332	34	36	371	384	390
	Food	Beverages		Clothing, footwear	Furniture	Paper, printing, publishing	Non-metallic mineral products	Iron and steel basic industries	Transport equipment	Other manufacturing industries
	Aliments	Boissons	Textiles	Habillement, chaussures	Ameublement	Papier, imprimerie, édition	Produits minéraux non métalliques	Sidérurgie	Matériel de transport	Autres industries manufacturières
	Alimentos	Bebidas		Vestido, calzado	Mobiliario	Papel, imprentas, editoriales	Productos minerales no metálicos	Industrias básicas de hierro y acero	Material de transporte	Otras industrias manufactureras
Males — Hommes — Hombres										
1966	50.0	55.6	43.8	45.2	46.9	48.8	51.2	46.1	45.3	45.9
1967	51.3	52.4	44.4	46.3	43.4	52.6	47.3	47.5	46.1	48.4
1968	51.1	52.9	43.9	45.4	46.1	55.3	48.1	44.7	48.4	47.8
1969	49.9	58.6	44.1	45.0	46.1	50.8	54.6	45.3	44.3	46.0
1970	51.6	57.9	44.3	44.1	46.1	46.3	53.7	45.8	50.7	48.0
1971	52.9	56.7	42.6	45.5	47.7	47.7	51.1	46.1	43.7	48.8
1972	48.5	57.8	41.5	44.4	45.1	49.6	47.4	46.0	42.7	48.4
1973	48.1	59.3	45.0	44.2	43.9	46.8	49.7	45.8	45.2	47.8

Date / Date / Fecha	311-312	313	321	322; 324	34	390
	Food	Beverages		Clothing, footwear	Paper, printing, publishing	Other manufacturing industries
	Aliments	Boissons	Textiles	Habillement, chaussures	Papier, imprimerie, édition	Autres industries manufacturières
	Alimentos	Bebidas		Vestido, calzado	Papel, imprentas, editoriales	Otras industrias manufactureras
Females — Femmes — Mujeres						
1966	45.9	51.2	43.9	44.8	44.7	45.5
1967	46.1	49.9	44.1	48.1	44.9	49.3
1968	46.9	52.7	44.3	46.2	47.2	49.1
1969	47.0	50.8	44.2	43.2	46.7	45.6
1970	47.2	51.4	44.1	43.8	45.4	46.4
1971	50.8	51.4	43.1	45.0	48.8	46.6
1972	50.6	53.2	40.5	46.2	53.6	46.7
1973	50.9	47.5	44.4	44.1	45.8	47.5

[1] Metropolitan area.   [1] Région métropolitaine.   [1] Area metropolitana.

13 Hours of work in manufacturing
Durée du travail dans les industries manufacturières
Horas de trabajo en las industrias manufactureras

B By industry
Par industrie
Por industria

Guatemala (Guatemala)

Hours actually worked per week
Heures réellement effectuées par semaine
Horas efectivamente trabajadas por semana

Date / Date / Fecha	311-312 Food / Aliments / Alimentos	313 Beverages / Boissons / Bebidas	314 Tobacco / Tabac / Tabaco	321 Textiles	322; 324 Clothing, footwear / Habillement, chaussures / Vestido, calzado	323 Leather, leather products / Cuir, articles en cuir / Cuero, artículos de cuero	331 Wood / Bois / Madera
1965	44.5	50.3	44.6	45.7	44.5	46.2	45.4
1966	45.1	50.5	44.2	44.9	44.3	47.2	45.9
1967	46.0	49.5	44.3	45.6	44.6	46.3	46.8
1968	46.2	48.8	44.6	44.7	44.6	41.6	43.3
1969	45.8	49.7	45.1	44.4	44.9	44.2	46.3
1970	45.5	48.9	45.0	44.5	44.9	46.9	46.2
1971	45.0	47.9	45.2	44.4	45.5	46.9	46.1
1972	46.8	49.3	45.5	45.0	45.4	48.8	46.7
1973	46.5	50.7	44.9	46.4	45.4	47.8	48.0
1974 *	46.2	51.9	44.3	47.8	45.4	46.8	49.3

Date / Date / Fecha	332 Furniture / Ameublement / Mobiliario	34 Paper, printing, publishing / Papier, imprimerie, édition / Papel, imprentas, editoriales	351-352; 355 Chemicals, rubber products / Industrie chimique, produits en caoutchouc / Productos químicos y de caucho	36 Non-metallic mineral products / Produits minéraux non métalliques / Productos minerales no metálicos	37 Basic metal industries / Industrie métallurgique de base / Industrias metalúrgicas basicas	383 Electrical machinery and apparatus / Machines et appareils électriques / Maquinaria y aparatos eléctricos	384 Transport equipment / Matériel de transport / Material de transporte
1965	45.2	47.3	46.4	47.4	45.2	46.3	43.6
1966	45.0	48.1	45.9	46.9	46.0	46.4	43.9
1967	43.6	49.9	46.5	47.4	45.9	44.8	44.3
1968	43.8	50.6	45.1	46.1	44.7	45.0	45.3
1969	45.8	50.3	45.0	47.1	44.7	44.8	45.1
1970	45.4	48.6	46.2	47.3	45.6	44.6	45.1
1971	46.5	46.8	48.2	46.7	46.0	44.5	45.6
1972	46.4	48.0	48.2	46.7	46.6	44.9	46.0
1973	45.5	47.9	50.3	48.2	48.4	45.0	48.0
1974 *	44.6	47.8	52.5	51.8	50.3	45.1	50.1

13 B

Hours of work in manufacturing
Durée du travail dans les industries manufacturières
Horas de trabajo en las industrias manufactureras

By industry
Par industrie
Por industria

México

Hours actually worked per week
Heures réellement effectuées par semaine
Horas efectivamente trabajadas por semana

Date [1] / Date [1] / Fecha [1]	Food / Aliments / Alimentos	Beverages / Boissons / Bebidas	Tobacco / Tabac / Tabaco	Textiles	Clothing / Habillement / Vestido	Wood, furniture / Bois, ameublement / Madera, mobiliario
1965	46.4	40.8	43.9	45.1	46.5	45.3
1966	47.5	44.7	46.4	44.6	46.2	45.7
1967	45.1	43.3	39.1	44.1	46.6	45.0
1968 [2]	45.6	44.1	40.9	42.5	45.7	45.6
1969	43.8	43.9	44.0	45.1	46.1	47.3
1970	43.4	41.9	40.5	41.2	46.5	46.5
1971	45.1	39.6	42.4	43.7	46.5	45.6

Date [1] / Date [1] / Fecha [1]	Paper, paper products / Papier, articles en papier / Papel, artículos de papel	Printing, publishing / Imprimerie, édition / Imprentas, editoriales	Leather, leather products / Cuir, articles en cuir / Cuero, artículos de cuero	Rubber products / Industrie du caoutchouc / Productos de caucho	Chemicals / Industrie chimique / Productos químicos	Miscellaneous manufacturing / Industries manufacturières diverses / Industrias manufactureras diversas
1965	45.7	48.3	46.5	46.3	45.1	46.4
1966	48.4	45.3	45.0	44.7	46.6	46.0
1967	47.6	46.1	46.2	45.4	46.8	45.6
1968 [2]	47.1	45.6	46.8	47.1	46.0	46.1
1969	47.4	45.8	46.8	46.7	45.8	49.0
1970	47.6	45.9	47.4	46.8	45.3	45.6
1971	46.5	45.2	45.5	44.9	46.1	45.0

[1] Oct. of each year. [2] Scope of series revised.   [1] *Oct. de chaque année.* [2] *Portée de la série révisée.*   [1] Oct. de cada año. [2] Alcance de la serie revisado.

13 B

Hours of work in manufacturing
Durée du travail dans les industries manufacturières
Horas de trabajo en las industrias manufactureras

By industry
Par industrie
Por industria

Panamá (1)

Hours actually worked per week
Heures réellement effectuées par semaine
Horas efectivamente trabajadas por semana

	311-312	313	314	321	322	323	324	331	332
Date / Date / Fecha	Food / Aliments / Alimentos	Beverages / Boissons / Bebidas	Tobacco / Tabac / Tabaco	Textiles	Clothing / Habillement / Vestido	Leather, leather products / Cuir, articles en cuir / Cuero, artículos de cuero	Footwear / Chaussures / Calzado	Wood / Bois / Madera	Furniture / Ameublement / Mobiliario
1965	47.1	47.1	37.2	.	37.2	40.9	42.6	46.2	43.3
1966	44.5	46.5	36.2	39.0	37.4	40.6	43.3	42.3	40.7
1967	44.5	46.4	35.4	25.1	37.3	40.4	40.6	42.1	40.6
1968	45.3	41.8	37.7	38.7	38.1	43.1	40.7	42.9	42.8
1969	45.2	49.8	34.6	42.6	38.5	42.7	41.0	44.1	44.0
1970	43.5	46.3	35.6	41.9	37.1	44.0	40.8	42.6	42.5
1971	46.9	45.2	38.3	45.9	38.6	46.7	41.8	46.4	45.4
1972	45.6	47.4	40.6	42.5	40.0	44.7	44.8	45.0	46.4
1973 *	40.1	48.0	36.1	47.3	41.0	45.3	45.2	47.1	44.7

	341	342	351	352	355	356	361	362	369
Date / Date / Fecha	Paper, paper products / Papier, articles en papier / Papel, artículos de papel	Printing, publishing / Imprimerie, édition / Imprentas, editoriales	Industrial chemicals / Chimie industrielle / Química industrial	Other chemical products / Autres produits chimiques / Otros productos químicos	Rubber products / Produits en caoutchouc / Productos de caucho	Plastic products / Articles en matière plastique / Productos plásticos	Pottery, china, earthenware / Grès, porcelaines, faïences / Barro, loza, porcelana	Glass / Verre / Vidrio	Other non-metallic mineral products / Autres produits minéraux non métalliques / Otros productos minerales no metálicos
1965	39.1	42.9	.	41.2	40.8	39.7	41.0	.	40.1
1966	44.1	43.1	.	43.8	41.0	41.1	41.5	.	41.5
1967	40.2	42.8	.	42.0	39.5	33.7	42.3	47.0	42.7
1968	45.6	43.0	.	47.4	44.3	36.8	31.0	48.0	45.0
1969	43.2	43.2	44.6	48.9	39.3	41.6	43.6	45.3	43.0
1970	42.6	44.8	45.2	47.5	41.7	42.9	44.3	43.3	43.8
1971	43.5	47.3	49.4	46.1	43.6	43.9	.	45.4	47.3
1972	46.1	50.8	45.1	46.6	46.3	44.3	.	46.8	49.4
1973 *	42.9	48.2	47.1	39.7	46.5	43.4	.	44.0	47.1

13 Hours of work in manufacturing
Durée du travail dans les industries manufacturières
Horas de trabajo en las industrias manufactureras

B By industry
Par industrie
Por industria

Panamá (2)

Hours actually worked per week
Heures réellement effectuées par semaine
Horas efectivamente trabajadas por semana

Date Date Fecha	371 Iron and steel basic industries Sidérurgie Industrias básicas de hierro y acero	381 Metal products Produits métalliques Productos metálicos	382 Machinery (non-electrical) Machines (non électriques) Maquinaria (no eléctrica)	383 Electrical machinery and apparatus Machines et appareils électriques Maquinaria y aparatos eléctricos	384 Transport equipment Matériel de transport Material de transporte	385 Scientific, measuring, optical, etc., equipment Matériel scientifique, de précision, d'optique, etc. Equipo científico, de medida, de óptica, etc.	353-354; 372; 390 Miscellaneous manufacturing Industries manufacturières diverses Industrias manufactureras diversas
1965	.	41.8	38.5	45.6	42.0	.	47.3
1966	.	42.0	40.5	42.3	40.9	.	48.2
1967	39.2	44.1	42.2	42.4	41.6	.	41.1
1968	48.3	43.9	41.2	42.3	41.4	.	43.2
1969	48.3	44.7	45.2	41.6	43.6	.	37.5
1970	43.3	41.9	42.0	39.8	40.9	42.5	35.6
1971	48.8	43.5	47.2	42.8	43.1	46.0	43.8
1972	47.9	42.8	47.4	43.8	46.7	43.2	45.6
1973 *	42.5	42.6	46.4	43.8	48.2	42.8	53.6

Puerto Rico (1)

Hours paid for per week
Heures rémunérées par semaine
Horas pagadas por semana

Date [1] Date [1] Fecha [1]	311-313 Food, beverages Aliments, boissons Alimentos, bebidas	314 Tobacco Tabac Tabaco	321 Textiles	322 Clothing Habillement Vestido	323 Leather, leather products Cuir, articles en cuir Cuero, artículos de cuero	324 Footwear Chaussures Calzado	33 Wood, furniture Bois, ameublement Madera, mobiliario
1968	37.7	37.1	40.3	36.2	36.5	34.8	40.0
1969	36.6	39.6	36.9	35.0	36.1	32.8	36.5
1970	39.0	37.6	38.1	34.8	38.1	36.5	39.2
1971	36.4	37.4	37.7	35.2	37.3	34.0	35.2
1972	37.3	38.2	37.8	35.1	38.9	36.1	37.0
1973	39.9	37.9	36.5	34.5	37.1	37.2	36.6
1974	37.6	38.5	36.7	34.5	36.8	36.2	37.3

[1] Oct. of each year.　　　　[1] Oct. de chaque année.　　　　[1] Oct. de cada año.

13 Hours of work in manufacturing / Durée du travail dans les industries manufacturières / Horas de trabajo en las industrias manufactureras

B By industry / Par industrie / Por industria

Puerto Rico (2)

Hours paid for per week
Heures rémunérées par semaine
Horas pagadas por semana

Date [1] / Date [1] Fecha [1]	341 Paper, paper products / Papier, articles en papier / Papel, artículos de papel	342 Printing, publishing / Imprimerie, édition / Imprentas, editoriales	351-352 Chemicals / Industrie chimique / Productos químicos	353-354 Refineries and products of petroleum and coal / Raffineries et dérivés du pétrole et du charbon / Refinerías y derivados del petróleo y del carbón	355-356 Rubber and plastic products / Produits en caoutchouc et en plastique / Productos de caucho, de plástico	361 Pottery, china, earthenware / Grès, porcelaines, faïences / Barro, loza, porcelana	362 Glass / Verre / Vidrio
1968	40.8	40.0	39.7	41.9	37.6	42.9	40.0
1969	39.3	39.1	39.4	42.2	37.7	41.9	39.4
1970	37.1	39.2	40.1	40.9	36.6	41.6	37.6
1971	38.7	39.0	40.5	38.5	36.8	42.6	38.2
1972	39.5	40.1	40.8	42.5	36.4	43.4	38.7
1973	39.6	40.9	39.9	41.9	38.4	42.1	41.1
1974	40.4	38.8	40.8	38.8	38.2	46.1	40.9

Date [1] / Date [1] Fecha [1]	369 Other non-metallic mineral products / Autres produits minéraux non métalliques / Otros productos minerales no metálicos	381 Metal products / Produits métalliques / Productos metálicos	382 Machinery (non-electrical) / Machines (non électriques) / Maquinaria (no eléctrica)	383 Electrical machinery and apparatus / Machines et appareils électriques / Maquinaria y aparatos eléctricos	384 Transport equipment / Matériel de transport / Material de transporte	385 Scientific, measuring, optical, etc., equipment / Matériel scientifique, de précision, d'optique, etc. / Equipo científico, de medida, de óptica, etc.	390 Other manufacturing industries / Autres industries manufacturières / Otras industrias manufactureras
1968	38.5	40.5	42.1	37.8	35.9	40.2	37.8
1969	37.7	39.1	42.8	40.1	37.3	40.4	35.9
1970	38.6	39.5	41.9	39.3	38.4	40.3	34.7
1971	37.7	38.6	39.4	39.1	33.9	39.0	36.9
1972	38.5	38.8	42.0	40.2	36.8	39.0	36.3
1973	37.8	38.6	41.3	39.7	40.4	39.0	37.4
1974	38.7	38.3	39.5	38.5	38.6	38.7	36.5

[1] Oct. of each year.   [1] Oct. de chaque année.   [1] Oct. de cada año.

13 Hours of work in manufacturing
Durée du travail dans les industries manufacturières
Horas de trabajo en las industrias manufactureras

B By industry
Par industrie
Por industria

United States (1)

Hours paid for per week
Heures rémunérées par semaine
Horas pagadas por semana

	311-313	314	321	322	323-324	331	332
Date *Date* Fecha	Food, beverages *Aliments, boissons* Alimentos, bebidas	Tobacco *Tabac* Tabaco	Textiles	Clothing *Habillement* Vestido	Leather, leather products footwear *Cuir, articles en cuir, chaussures* Cuero, artículos de cuero, calzado	Wood *Bois* Madera	Furniture *Ameublement* Mobiliario
1965	41.1	37.9	41.8	36.4	38.2	40.9	41.6
1966	41.2	38.9	41.9	36.4	38.6	40.8	41.5
1967	40.9	38.6	40.9	36.0	38.1	40.2	40.4
1968	40.8	37.9	41.2	36.1	38.3	40.6	40.6
1969	40.8	37.4	40.8	35.9	37.2	40.2	40.4
1970	40.5	37.8	39.9	35.3	37.2	39.7	39.2
1971	40.3	37.8	40.6	35.6	37.7	40.3	39.8
1972	40.4	37.5	41.4	36.0	38.3	41.0	40.5
1973	40.4	38.5	40.9	35.8	37.9	40.6	39.9
1974	40.4	38.0	39.4	35.1	37.2	39.7	39.0

	341	342	351	352	353-354	355-356	36
Date *Date* Fecha	Paper, paper products *Papier, articles en papier* Papel, artículos de papel	Printing, publishing *Imprimerie, édition* Imprentas, editoriales	Industrial chemicals *Chimie industrielle* Química industrial	Other chemical products *Autres produits chimiques* Otros productos químicos	Refineries and products of petroleum and coal *Raffineries et dérivés du pétrole et du charbon* Refinerías y derivados del petróleo y del carbón	Rubber and plastic products *Produits en caoutchouc et en plastique* Productos de caucho, de plástico	Non-metallic mineral products *Produits minéraux non métalliques* Productos minerales no metálicos
1965	43.1	38.6	42.0	41.9	42.2	42.0	42.0
1966	43.4	38.8	42.3	41.9	42.4	42.0	42.0
1967	42.8	38.4	41.9	41.3	42.7	41.4	41.6
1968	42.9	38.3	42.2	41.3	42.5	41.5	41.8
1969	43.0	38.4	42.4	41.2	42.6	41.1	42.0
1970	41.9	37.7	42.3	41.3	42.7	40.3	41.2
1971	42.1	37.5	42.0	41.4	42.5	40.3	41.6
1972	42.8	37.9	42.3	41.4	42.3	41.2	41.9
1973	42.7	37.9	42.7	41.7	42.3	41.1	42.1
1974	42.1	37.6	42.7	41.3	42.4	40.1	41.4

HOURS

13 Hours of work in manufacturing
Durée du travail dans les industries manufacturières
Horas de trabajo en las industrias manufactureras

B By industry
Par industrie
Por industria

United States (2)

Hours paid for per week
Heures rémunérées par semaine
Horas pagadas por semana

Date / Date / Fecha	37 Basic metal industries / Industrie métallurgique de base / Industrias metalúrgicas básicas	381 Metal products / Produits métalliques / Productos metálicos	382 Machinery (non-electrical) / Machines (non électriques) / Maquinaria (no eléctrica)	383 Electrical machinery and apparatus / Machines et appareils électriques / Maquinaria y aparatos eléctricos	384 Transport equipment / Matériel de transport / Material de transporte	385 Scientific, measuring, optical, etc., equipment / Matériel scientifique, de précision, d'optique, etc. / Equipo científico, de medida, de óptica, etc.	390 Other manufacturing industries / Autres industries manufacturières / Otras industrias manufactureras
1965	42.1	42.1	43.1	41.0	42.9	41.4	39.9
1966	42.1	42.4	43.8	41.2	42.6	42.1	40.0
1967	41.1	41.5	42.6	40.2	41.4	41.3	39.4
1968	41.6	41.7	42.1	40.3	42.2	40.5	39.4
1969	41.8	41.6	42.5	40.4	41.5	40.7	39.0
1970	40.5	40.7	41.1	39.8	40.3	40.1	38.7
1971	40.4	40.4	40.6	39.9	40.7	39.8	38.9
1972	41.6	41.2	42.0	40.5	41.8	40.6	39.3
1973	42.4	41.6	42.6	40.4	41.9	40.8	38.9
1974	41.7	40.8	42.2	39.7	40.1	40.2	38.5

508

13 B

Hours of work in manufacturing
Durée du travail dans les industries manufacturières
Horas de trabajo en las industrias manufactureras

By industry
Par industrie
Por industria

Venezuela

Hours actually worked per week
Heures réellement effectuées par semaine
Horas efectivamente trabajadas por semana

Date / Date / Fecha	311-312 Food / Aliments / Alimentos	313 Beverages / Boissons / Bebidas	314 Tobacco / Tabac / Tabaco	321-322 Textiles, clothing / Textiles, habillement / Textiles, vestido	324 Footwear / Chaussures / Calzado	331 Wood / Bois / Madera	341 Paper, paper products / Papier, articles en papier / Papel, artículos de papel
1970	44.3	44.4	44.8	46.4	43.3	45.8	44.5
1971	43.0	43.2	42.6	45.7	43.1	43.7	43.9
1972	...	...	...	...	...	...	...
1973	41.2	44.2	41.4	43.6	44.9	44.3	46.4
1974 *	43.6	44.7	44.5	44.9	43.8	45.7	47.1

Date / Date / Fecha	342 Printing, publishing / Imprimerie, édition / Imprentas, editoriales	351-352 Chemicals / Industrie chimique / Productos químicos	355 Rubber products / Produits en caoutchouc / Productos de caucho	371 Iron and steel basic industries / Sidérurgie / Industrias básicas de hierro y acero	381 Metal products / Produits métalliques / Productos metálicos	384 Transport equipment / Matériel de transport / Material de transporte
1970	42.9	42.1	43.3	45.7	45.4	40.3
1971	42.0	40.8	42.1	44.5	44.5	40.3
1972	...	...	...	...	...	...
1973	43.6	44.1	44.3	43.7	44.0	41.0
1974 *	44.3	45.9	45.5	44.4	45.3	43.5

HOURS

13 B

Hours of work in manufacturing
Durée du travail dans les industries manufacturières
Horas de trabajo en las industrias manufactureras

By industry
Par industrie
Por industria

ASIA — ASIE — ASIA

Burma

Hours actually worked per day [1]
Heures réellement effectuées par jour [1]
Horas efectivamente trabajadas por día [1]

	311-312	313	314	321	322; 324	323	331
Date	Food	Beverages	Tobacco		Clothing, footwear	Leather, leather products	Wood
Date	*Aliments*	*Boissons*	*Tabac*	Textiles	*Habillement, chaussures*	*Cuir, articles en cuir*	*Bois*
Fecha	Alimentos	Bebidas	Tabaco		Vestido, calzado	Cuero, artículos de cuero	Madera
1965	7.6	7.8	7.5	7.4	7.3	7.4	7.7
1966	7.6	7.7	7.6	7.5	7.7	7.8	7.5
1967	7.4	7.1	7.6	7.4	7.5	7.6	7.4
1968	7.8	7.4	7.8	7.5	6.9	7.2	7.5
1969	7.8	7.3	7.7	7.1	7.8	7.4	7.4
1970	7.7	7.3	7.7	7.5	7.6	7.0	7.5
1971	7.8	7.1	7.6	7.5	7.4	7.3	7.5
1972 [2]	7.6	7.7	7.4	7.2	7.3	7.4	7.5
1973 [3]	7.8	7.7	7.6	7.6	7.9	7.0	7.5

	342	352	355	362	369	381	384
Date	Printing, publishing	Chemical products	Rubber products	Glass	Other non-metallic mineral products [4]	Metal products	Transport equipment
Date	*Imprimerie édition*	*Produits chimiques*	*Produits en caoutchouc*	*Verre*	*Autres produits minéraux non métalliques* [4]	*Produits métalliques*	*Matériel de transport*
Fecha	Imprentas, editoriales	Productos químicos	Productos de caucho	Vidrio	Otros productos minerales no metálicos [4]	Productos metálicos	Material de transporte
1965	7.4	7.5	7.5	8.0		7.5	.
1966	7.3	7.7	7.3	8.0		7.4	7.1
1967	7.3	7.4	7.2	8.0		7.3	7.2
1968	7.3	7.3	7.3	8.0		7.4	7.5
1969	7.3	7.7	7.5	.		7.6	7.4
1970	7.4	7.4	7.4	.		7.7	7.9
1971	7.4	7.5	7.4	.		7.7	7.9
1972 [2]	7.8	7.7	7.7	7.8	8.0	7.1	7.9
1973 [3]	7.7	6.6	7.4	7.5	8.0	7.1	7.5

[1] Workers engaged for less than 30 days (excl. casual workers). [2] April and Sep. [3] March and Sep. [4] Excl. pottery, china, earthenware and glass.

[1] *Travailleurs engagés pour moins de 30 jours (non compris les travailleurs occasionnels).* [2] *Avril et sept.* [3] *Mars et sept.* [4] *Non compris le grès, les porcelaines et les faïences.*

[1] Trabajadores ocupados durante menos de 30 días (excl. los trabajadores ocasionales). [2] Abril y sept. [3] Marzo y sept. [4] Excl. el barro, la loza, la porcelana y el vidrio.

13 Hours of work in manufacturing
Durée du travail dans les industries manufacturières
Horas de trabajo en las industrias manufactureras

B By industry
Par industrie
Por industria

Cyprus

Hours actually worked per week [1]
Heures réellement effectuées par semaine [1]
Horas efectivamente trabajadas por semana [1]

Date [2] Date [2] Fecha [2]	311-312 Food Aliments Alimentos	313 Beverages Boissons Bebidas	314 Tobacco Tabac Tabaco	321 Textiles	322 Clothing Habillement Vestido	323 Leather, leather products Cuir, articles en cuir Cuero, artículos de cuero	324 Footwear Chaussures Calzado	331 Wood Bois Madera	332 Furniture Ameublement Mobiliario
1965	53	51	43	52	42	44	43	44	45
1966	41	49	43	45	44	43	45	44	43
1967	48	51	44	46	45	44	46	44	44
1968	45	51	44	45	45	44	46	45	44
1969	44	44	44	44	44	43	44	45	44
1970	44	46	44	44	43	44	44	46	44
1971	48	49	42	45	43	44	42	43	44
1972	43	48	42	44	42	44	41	43	44
1973	43	46	35	43	43	43	41	41	44
1974	44	45	41	42	41	41	40	46	40

Date [2] Date [2] Fecha [2]	341 Paper, paper products Papier, articles en papier Papel, artículos de papel	342 Printing, publishing Imprimerie, édition Imprentas, editoriales	351 Industrial chemicals Chimie industrielle Química industrial	355 Rubber products Produits en caoutchouc Productos de caucho	369 Non-metallic mineral products [3] Produits minéraux non métalliques [3] Productos minerales no metálicos [3]	381 Metal products Produits métalliques Productos metálicos	382 Machinery (non-electrical) Machines (non électriques) Maquinaria (no eléctrica)	383 Electrical machinery and apparatus Machines et appareils électriques Maquinaria y aparatos eléctricos	384 Transport equipment Matériel de transport Material de transporte	390 Other manufacturing industries Autres industries manufacturières Otras industrias manufactureras
1965	44	47	51	44	44	47	46	44	44	44
1966	44	48	54	44	45	44	45	41	44	43
1967	44	46	48	44	47	44	44	44	44	43
1968	44	47	48	44	47	46	45	44	44	48
1969	44	46	44	44	47	45	45	44	47	47
1970	44	47	44	44	47	45	44	44	45	44
1971	44	48	48	46	46	44	43	50	44	45
1972	47	46	44	43	45	44	47	50	45	46
1973	47	45	44	45	49	43	43	43	44	45
1974	32	42	45	41	43	41	40	43	46	44

[1] Adults only. [2] Oct. of each year, except for 1969: Sep. [3] Excl. pottery, china, earthenware and glass.

[1] *Adultes seulement.* [2] *Oct. de chaque année, sauf pour 1969 : sept.* [3] *Non compris le grès, les porcelaines, les faïences et le verre.*

[1] Adultos solamente. [2] Oct. de cada año, salvo 1969: sept. [3] Excl. el barro, la loza, la porcelana y el vidrio.

13 Hours of work in manufacturing
Durée du travail dans les industries manufacturières
Horas de trabajo en las industrias manufactureras

B By industry
Par industrie
Por industria

Israel

Hours actually worked per week [1]
Heures réellement effectuées par semaine [1]
Horas efectivamente trabajadas por semana [1]

Date / Date / Fecha	31 Food, beverages, tobacco / Aliments, boissons, tabac / Alimentos, bebidas, tabaco	321 Textiles	322 Clothing / Habillement / Vestido	323-324 Leather, leather products, footwear / Cuir, articles en cuir, chaussures / Cuero, artículos de cuero, calzado	33 Wood, furniture / Bois, ameublement / Madera, mobiliario	341 Paper, paper products / Papier, articles en papier / Papel, artículos de papel
1972	42.2	43.6	41.9	42.7	43.1	43.9
1973	39.0	40.1	40.0	36.3	38.2	41.5
1974	38.1	40.2	39.2	38.0	39.1	41.3

Date / Date / Fecha	342 Printing, publishing / Imprimerie, édition / Imprentas, editoriales	351-354 Chemicals, petroleum, refineries [2] / Industrie chimique, raffineries de pétrole [2] / Productos químicos, refinerías de petróleo [2]	355-356 Rubber and plastic products / Produits en caoutchouc et en plastique / Productos de caucho, de plástico	36 Non-metallic mineral products / Produits minéraux non métalliques / Productos minerales no metálicos	37 Basic metal industries / Industrie métallurgique de base / Industrias metalúrgicas básicas	381 Metal products / Produits métalliques / Productos metálicos
1972	39.6	43.2	41.7	44.0	44.8	42.7
1973	38.4	38.6	38.3	40.4	39.4	39.4
1974	40.1	39.4	38.2	39.6	39.0	39.8

Date / Date / Fecha	382 Machinery (non-electrical) / Machines (non électriques) / Maquinaria (no eléctrica)	383 Electrical machinery and apparatus / Machines et appareils électriques / Maquinaria y aparatos eléctricos	384 Transport equipment / Matériel de transport / Material de transporte	390 Diamonds / Diamants / Diamantes	390 Other manufacturing industries / Autres industries manufacturières / Otras industrias manufactureras
1972	44.3	43.2	43.6	43.0	40.9
1973	39.9	38.8	40.7	38.4	37.8
1974	40.2	39.9	41.8	38.9	39.4

[1] Incl. salaried employees. [2] Incl. products of petroleum and coal.
[1] Y compris les employés. [2] Y compris les dérivés du pétrole et du charbon.
[1] Incl. los empleados. [2] Incl. los derivados del petróleo y del carbón.

13 Hours of work in manufacturing
Durée du travail dans les industries manufacturières
Horas de trabajo en las industrias manufactureras

B By industry
Par industrie
Por industria

Japan (1)

Hours actually worked per week [1]
Heures réellement effectuées par semaine [1]
Horas efectivamente trabajadas por semana [1]

	311-313	314	321	322	323-324	331	332
Date / Date / Fecha	Food, beverages / *Aliments, boissons* / Alimentos, bebidas	Tobacco / *Tabac* / Tabaco	Textiles	Clothing / *Habillement* / Vestido	Leather, leather products, footwear / *Cuir, articles en cuir, chaussures* / Cuero, artículos de cuero, calzado	Wood / *Bois* / Madera	Furniture / *Ameublement* / Mobiliario
1965	44.7	38.0	44.7	44.3	44.8	45.2	45.2
1966	44.3	36.7	44.8	44.2	44.2	45.4	45.6
1967 [2]	44.6	36.5	44.5	43.8	44.3	45.5	45.2
1968	43.9		44.2	43.6	43.9	45.3	44.9
1969	43.2		43.8	43.0	43.7	44.9	44.4
1970 [2]	42.4		43.5	42.3	43.3	44.1	44.2
1971	42.2		43.4	42.2	42.5	43.8	43.9
1972	41.9		43.2	41.8	42.4	44.2	44.0
1973 [2]	41.4		42.4	41.2	42.8	43.9	43.1
1974	40.4		40.1	39.7	41.0	41.9	40.9

	341	342	351-352	353-354	355	36	371
Date / Date / Fecha	Paper, paper products / *Papier, articles en papier* / Papel, artículos de papel	Printing, publishing / *Imprimerie, édition* / Imprentas, editoriales	Chemicals / *Industrie chimique* / Productos químicos	Refineries and products of petroleum and coal / *Raffineries et dérivés du pétrole et du charbon* / Refinerías y derivados del petróleo y del carbón	Rubber products / *Produits en caoutchouc* / Productos de caucho	Non-metallic mineral products / *Produits minéraux non métalliques* / Productos minerales no metálicos	Iron and steel basic industries / *Sidérurgie* / Industrias básicas de hierro y acero
1965	44.7	47.1	41.7	43.0	43.4	44.1	44.8
1966	44.7	46.9	41.7	42.9	43.9	44.1	45.1
1967 [2]	44.6	47.0	41.5	42.5	43.8	44.5	46.3
1968	44.4	47.0	41.7	42.7	43.4	44.3	46.1
1969	44.0	46.4	41.2	42.4	42.3	43.7	45.3
1970 [2]	43.5	45.0	40.9	42.6	41.7	43.8	44.4
1971	42.7	44.8	40.4	42.5	41.1	43.1	42.7
1972	42.1	44.4	39.7	41.4	40.8	43.0	42.2
1973 [2]	41.8	43.6	39.1	41.2	40.8	43.1	42.6
1974	39.5	41.7	37.9	40.6	38.5	41.1	41.0

[1] Incl. salaried employees. [2] Sampling design revised.   [1] *Y compris les employés.* [2] *Plan d'échantillonnage révisé.*   [1] Incl. los empleados. [2] Diseño de la muestra revisado.

13 Hours of work in manufacturing
Durée du travail dans les industries manufacturières
Horas de trabajo en las industrias manufactureras

B By industry
Par industrie
Por industria

Japan (2)

Hours actually worked per week [1]
Heures réellement effectuées par semaine [1]
Horas efectivamente trabajadas por semana [1]

Date / Date / Fecha	372 Non-ferrous metal basic industries / Métaux non ferreux (industrie de base) / Industrias básicas de metales no ferrosos	381 Metal products / Produits métalliques / Productos metálicos	382 Machinery (non-electrical) / Machines (non électriques) / Maquinaria (no eléctrica)	383 Electrical machinery and apparatus / Machines et appareils électriques / Maquinaria y aparatos eléctricos	384 Transport equipment / Matériel de transport / Material de transporte	385 Scientific, measuring, optical, etc., equipment / Matériel scientifique, de précision, d'optique, etc. / Equipo científico, de medida, de óptica, etc.	390 Other manufacturing industries / Autres industries manufacturières / Otras industrias manufactureras
1965	.	45.6	44.8	42.6	45.1	43.3	44.4
1966	45.0	46.1	45.7	43.3	45.8	43.4	44.8
1967 [2]	45.2	46.4	46.2	43.5	46.3	42.7	44.3
1968	45.3	45.9	46.0	43.4	45.8	42.6	44.0
1969	44.9	45.7	45.1	42.7	44.8	41.8	43.7
1970 [2]	44.4	44.6	44.9	41.6	44.5	41.6	43.2
1971	43.3	44.1	43.2	40.6	43.6	41.0	42.9
1972	43.0	43.7	42.8	41.0	43.3	40.5	42.7
1973 [2]	42.8	43.2	43.0	40.8	43.5	40.1	41.8
1974	39.7	40.5	40.7	38.3	40.9	38.7	39.6

[1] Incl. salaried employees. [2] Sampling design revised.   [1] *Y compris les employés.* [2] *Plan d'échantillonnage révisé.*   [1] Incl. los empleados. [2] Diseño de la muestra revisado.

13 Hours of work in manufacturing
Durée du travail dans les industries manufacturières
Horas de trabajo en las industrias manufactureras

B By industry
Par industrie
Por industria

Korea, Rep. of (1)

Hours actually worked per week [1]
Heures réellement effectuées par semaine [1]
Horas efectivamente trabajadas por semana [1]

Date / Date / Fecha	311-312 Food / Aliments / Alimentos	313 Beverages / Boissons / Bebidas	321 Textiles	322; 324 Clothing, footwear / Habillement, chaussure / Vestido, calzado	323 Leather, leather products / Cuir, articles en cuir / Cuero, artículos de cuero	331 Wood / Bois / Madera	332 Furniture / Ameublement / Mobiliario	341 Paper, paper products / Papier, articles en papier / Papel, artículos de papel	342 Printing, publishing / Imprimerie, édition / Imprentas, editoriales
1970	53.4	52.0	53.1	53.9	49.5	58.1	51.0	52.8	52.2
1971	52.3	51.5	52.0	54.3	50.2	58.8	51.6	51.2	52.6
1972	51.3	50.1	51.7	55.3	52.7	55.0	51.0	52.6	49.9
1973	51.6	51.1	53.0	54.6	49.9	59.3	50.1	51.8	48.4
1974	48.2	50.5	49.8	49.8	49.1	53.6	50.0	48.7	49.0

Date / Date / Fecha	351 Industrial chemicals / Chimie industrielle / Química industrial	352 Other chemical products / Autres produits chimiques / Otros productos químicos	353 Petroleum refineries / Raffineries de pétrole / Refinerías de petróleo	354 Products of petroleum and coal / Dérivés du pétrole et du charbon / Derivados del petróleo y del carbón	355 Rubber products / Produits en caoutchouc / Productos de caucho	356 Plastic products / Articles en matière plastique / Productos plásticos	361 Pottery, china, earthenware / Grès, porcelaines, faïences / Barro, loza, porcelana	362 Glass, and glass products / Verre / Vidrio	369 Other non-metallic mineral products / Autres produits minéraux / Otros productos minerales
1970	.	.	.	.	53.0	. .		44.9	
1971	.	.	.	.	53.9	.		52.0	
1972	.	.	.	.	52.7	.		52.0	
1973	50.0	48.8	46.7	46.9	52.8	53.0	50.3	51.3	50.9
1974	49.5	48.6	45.6	49.0	51.6	50.7	47.8	50.6	49.6

[1] Incl. salaried employees.   [1] *Y compris les employés.*   [1] Incl. los empleados.

13   B

Hours of work in manufacturing
Durée du travail dans les industries manufacturières
Horas de trabajo en las industrias manufactureras

By industry
Par industrie
Por industria

Korea, Rep. of (2)

Hours actually worked per week [1]
Heures réellement effectuées par semaine [1]
Horas efectivamente trabajadas por semana [1]

	371	372	381	382	383	384	385	390
Date *Date* Fecha	Basic metal industries *Industrie métallurgique de base* Industrias metalúrgicas básicas		Metal products *Produits métalliques* Productos metálicos	Machinery (non-electrical) *Machines (non électriques)* Maquinaria (no eléctrica)	Electrical machinery and apparatus *Machines et appareils électriques* Maquinaria y aparatos eléctricos	Transport equipment *Matériel de transport* Material de transporte	Scientific, measuring, optical, etc., equipment *Matériel scientifique, de précision, d'optique, etc.* Equipo científico, de medida, de óptica, etc.	Other manufacturing industries *Autres industries manufacturières* Otras industrias manufactureras
	Iron and steel *Sidérurgie* Hierro y acero	Non-ferrous metal *Métaux non ferreux* Metales no ferrosos						
1970	55.3		53.8	53.3	49.7	50.5	.	48.9
1971	52.9		52.7	51.9	51.0	51.4	.	49.1
1972	52.0		50.8	49.8	49.4	52.5	.	48.7
1973	54.4	53.4	52.2	51.7	49.4	49.2	48.9	49.9
1974	51.8	48.0	51.7	50.7	47.6	50.3	47.7	49.5

[1] Incl. salaried employees.   [1] *Y compris les employés.*   [1] Incl. los empleados.

Singapore (1)

Hours actually worked per week
Heures réellement effectuées par semaine
Horas efectivamente trabajadas por semana

	311-312	313	314	321	322	323	324	331	332
Date [1] *Date* [1] Fecha [1]	Food *Aliments* Alimentos	Beverages *Boissons* Bebidas	Tobacco *Tabac* Tabaco	Textiles	Clothing *Habillement* Vestido	Leather, leather products *Cuir, articles en cuir* Cuero, artículos de cuero	Footwear *Chaussures* Calzado	Wood *Bois* Madera	Furniture *Ameublement* Mobiliario
1971	47.4	47.4	43.9	49.7	47.6	46.6	46.6	50.4	46.7
1972	46.8	48.0	43.0	49.0	45.6	42.7	46.1	51.0	47.3
1973 [2]	47.1	48.0	44.4	47.9	47.5	45.6	44.7	51.0	47.7

[1] July of each year.   [1] *Juillet de chaque année.*   [1] Julio de cada año.

13 Hours of work in manufacturing / Durée du travail dans les industries manufacturières / Horas de trabajo en las industrias manufactureras

B By industry / Par industrie / Por industria

Singapore (2)

Hours actually worked per week
Heures réellement effectuées par semaine
Horas efectivamente trabajadas por semana

Date [1] / Date [1] / Fecha [1]	341 Paper, paper products / Papier, articles en papier / Papel, artículos de papel	342 Printing, publishing / Imprimerie, édition / Imprentas, editoriales	351 Industrial chemicals / Chimie industrielle / Química industrial	352 Other chemical products / Autres produits chimiques / Otros productos químicos	353 Petroleum refineries / Raffineries de pétrole / Refinerías de petróleo	355 Rubber products / Produits en caoutchouc / Productos de caucho	356 Plastic products / Articles en matière plastique / Productos plásticos	361-362 Pottery, china, earthenware and glass / Grès, porcelaine, faïences et verre / Barro, loza, porcelana y vidrio	369 Other non-metallic mineral products / Autres produits minéraux non métalliques / Otros productos minerales no metálicos
1971	49.6	47.7	49.8	46.6	45.6	45.5	47.7	47.6	48.7
1972	51.1	48.9	53.5	46.4	46.6	45.4	48.6	48.3	49.6
1973	49.7	51.2	53.6	46.7	48.8	46.0	48.1	45.7	50.0

Date [1] / Date [1] / Fecha [1]	371 Iron and steel / Sidérurgie / Hierro y acero	372 Non-ferrous metal / Métaux non ferreux / Metales no ferrosos	381 Metal products / Produits métalliques / Productos metálicos	382 Machinery (non-electrical) / Machines (non électriques) / Maquinaria (no eléctrica)	383 Electrical machinery and apparatus / Machines et appareils électriques / Maquinaria y aparatos eléctricos	384 Transport equipment / Matériel de transport / Material de transporte	385 Scientific, measuring, optical, etc., equipment / Matériel scientifique, de précision, d'optique, etc. / Equipo científico, de medida, de óptica, etc.	390 Other manufacturing industries / Autres industries manufacturières / Otras industrias manufactureras
1971	52.1	49.0	49.5	51.2	46.2	57.6	47.2	49.9
1972	49.1	48.1	49.3	50.5	48.5	57.7	46.5	46.3
1973	48.8	42.6	49.4	50.4	45.9	57.3	46.2	45.1

Columns 371-372 header span: Basic metal industries / Industrie métallurgique de base / Industrias metalúrgicas básicas

[1] July of each year.

[1] *Juillet de chaque année.*

[1] Julio de cada año.

13 B

Hours of work in manufacturing
Durée du travail dans les industries manufacturières
Horas de trabajo en las industrias manufactureras

By industry
Par industrie
Por industria

République arabe syrienne (1)

Hours actually worked per week
Heures réellement effectuées par semaine
Horas efectivamente trabajadas por semana

Date [1] Date [1] Fecha [1]	311-312 Food Aliments Alimentos	313 Beverages Boissons Bebidas	314 Tobacco Tabac Tabaco	321 Textiles	322; 324 Clothing, footwear Habillement, chaussures Vestido, calzado	323 Leather, leather products Cuir, articles en cuir Cuero, artículos de cuero	331 Wood Bois Madera
1967	47.8	49.5	42.4	.	47.2	45.2	45.7
1968	50.1	47.0	40.1	.	47.9	43.8	46.3
1969	51.1	54.3	42.5	.	51.2	44.5	48.1
1970	50.6	55.8	36.7	.	50.3	45.9	50.3
1971	49.4	48.8	36.8	43.2	49.0	41.2	43.5
1972	52.5	53.1	39.1	46.7	44.2	42.7	41.0
1973 [2]	49.2	73.5	39.9	48.7	45.2	42.2	42.0
1974 [2]	45.1	59.3	41.6	44.0	50.3	41.9	54.0

Date [1] Date [1] Fecha [1]	341 Paper, paper products Papier, articles en papier Papel, artículos de papel	342 Printing, publishing Imprimerie, édition Imprentas, editoriales	351 Industrial chemicals Chimie industrielle Química industrial	352 Other chemical products Autres produits chimiques Otros productos químicos	353 Petroleum refineries Raffineries de pétrole Refinerías de petróleo	354 Products of petroleum and coal Dérivés du pétrole et du charbon Derivados del petróleo y del carbón	355 Rubber products Produits en caoutchouc Productos de caucho
1967	46.2	46.0	49.7		.	.	44.6
1968	46.3	47.4	47.3		.	.	46.9
1969	45.7	40.9	46.0		.	.	51.6
1970	49.0	35.2	42.7		.	.	48.2
1971	47.4	40.2	49.6		41.1	37.5	45.8
1972	45.6	46.7	49.1		40.1	40.1	45.7
1973 [2]	44.4	41.2	48.9	51.0	39.1	43.9	53.7
1974 [2]	47.7	50.2	47.8	48.2	44.6	44.0	50.8

[1] Nov. of each year. [2] May.   [1] Nov. de chaque année. [2] Mai.   [1] Nov. de cada año. [2] Mayo.

13 B

Hours of work in manufacturing
Durée du travail dans les industries manufacturières
Horas de trabajo en las industrias manufactureras

By industry
Par industrie
Por industria

République arabe syrienne (2)

Hours actually worked per week
Heures réellement effectuées par semaine
Horas efectivamente trabajadas por semana

Date [1] Date [1] Fecha [1]	356 Plastic products Articles en matière plastique Productos plásticos	361 Pottery, china, earthenware Grès, porcelaines, faïences Barro, loza, porcelana	362 Glass Verre Vidrio	369 Other non-metallic mineral products Autres produits minéraux non métalliques Otros productos minerales no metálicos	371 Iron and steel basic industries Sidérurgie Industrias básicas de hierro y acero	381 Metal products Produits métalliques Productos metálicos	382 Machinery (non-electrical) Machines (non électriques) Maquinaria (no eléctrica)	383 Electrical machinery and apparatus Machines et appareils électriques Maquinaria y aparatos eléctricos
1967	.	.	.	.	46.8	48.0	47.6	42.2
1968	.	.	.	.	45.8	47.3	45.5	44.5
1969	.	.	.	.	60.8	.	.	45.0
1970	.	.	.	.	45.7	.	.	43.9
1971	42.2	46.7	42.5	47.4	43.0	44.2	38.7	36.5
1972	47.5	44.4	42.5	49.2	46.3	48.7	43.6	40.6
1973 [2]	48.8	42.3	38.7	47.1	46.5	44.1	45.0	40.5
1974 [2]	44.1	42.0	39.8	48.0	48.0	43.9	45.0	45.3

[1] Nov. of each year. [2] May.   [1] Nov. de chaque année. [2] Mai.   [1] Nov. de cada año. [2] Mayo.

13 Hours of work in manufacturing
Durée du travail dans les industries manufacturières
Horas de trabajo en las industrias manufactureras

B By industry
Par industrie
Por industria

EUROPE — EUROPE — EUROPA

Austria (1)

Hours actually worked per week
Heures réellement effectuées par semaine
Horas efectivamente trabajadas por semana

Date / Date / Fecha	31 — Food, beverages, tobacco / Aliments, boissons, tabac / Alimentos, bebidas, tabaco	321 — Textiles	322 — Clothing / Habillement / Vestido	323 × — Leather / Cuir / Cuero	323 ×-324 — Leather products, footwear / Articles en cuir, chaussures / Artículos de cuero, calzado	33 — Wood, furniture / Bois, ameublement / Madera, mobiliario
1965	39.9	37.5	37.5	39.5	37.4	40.2
1966	40.3	37.5	37.3	39.5	37.7	40.4
1967	40.2	37.2	36.8	38.9	36.4	40.0
1968	40.1	37.6	37.3	39.6	36.7	40.1
1969	39.6	37.7	37.2	39.8	38.0	39.9
1970	38.5	36.6	35.7	38.3	36.7	38.4
1971 [1]	38.2	36.2	35.9	39.0	39.1	38.7
1972	38.0	35.6	34.4	38.1	35.8	38.0
1973	37.9	35.1	34.0	37.4	35.1	37.5
1974	38.1	35.2	34.2	37.4	34.2	37.4

Date / Date / Fecha	341 — Paper / Papier / Papel	341 — Paper products / Articles en papier / Artículos de papel	35 × — Chemicals, products of petroleum and coal, rubber, plastics [2] / Industrie chimique, dérivés du pétrole et du charbon, caoutchouc, plastique [2] / Productos químicos, derivados del petróleo y del carbón, caucho, plástico [2]	353 — Petroleum refineries [3] / Raffineries de pétrole [3] / Refinerías de petróleo [3]	36 × — Non-metallic mineral products [4] / Produits minéraux non métalliques [4] / Productos minerales no metálicos [4]	362 — Glass / Verre / Vidrio
1965	41.2	39.0	37.3	.	41.5	38.2
1966	40.9	38.1	36.5	37.2	41.6	38.8
1967	41.1	38.5	37.2	36.7	41.1	38.2
1968	41.0	39.2	37.2	36.9	41.4	38.4
1969	39.8	38.8	36.9	36.9	40.8	38.1
1970	37.9	37.9	35.6	36.7	39.8	36.9
1971 [1]	37.5	38.0	36.2	36.8	40.0	37.3
1972	37.8	36.8	35.5	35.7	39.3	36.5
1973	38.1	36.1	35.2	35.3	38.8	35.9
1974	37.3	36.5	35.2	35.1	38.9	36.7

[1] Scope of series enlarged. [2] Excl. petroleum refineries. [3] Incl. crude petroleum and natural gas production. [4] Excl. glass.

[1] *Portée de la série élargie.* [2] *Non compris les raffineries de pétrole.* [3] *Y compris la production de pétrole brut et de gaz naturel.* [4] *Non compris le verre.*

[1] El alcance de la serie es mayor. [2] Excl. las refinerías de petróleo. [3] Incl. la producción de petróleo crudo y gas natural. [4] Excl. el vidrio.

13 Hours of work in manufacturing
Durée du travail dans les industries manufacturières
Horas de trabajo en las industrias manufactureras

B By industry
Par industrie
Por industria

Austria (2)

Hours actually worked per week
Heures réellement effectuées par semaine
Horas efectivamente trabajadas por semana

Date / Date / Fecha	371			381; 385	382; 384 ×	383	384 ×
	Basic metal industries / Industrie métallurgique de base / Industrias metalúrgicas básicas			Metal products [2]	Machinery (non-electrical), transport equipment [3]	Electrical machinery and apparatus	Motor vehicles
		372		Produits métalliques [2]	Machines (non électriques), matériel de transport [3]	Machines et appareils électriques	Véhicules automobiles
	Iron and steel	Foundries	Non-ferrous metal				
	Sidérurgie	Fonderie	Métaux non ferreux	Productos metálicos [2]	Maquinaria (no eléctrica), material de transporte [3]	Maquinaria y aparatos eléctricos	Vehículos automóviles
	Hierro y acero	Fundición	Metales no ferrosos				
1965	.	39.9	39.3	38.5	39.4	38.0	37.7
1966	39.1	39.7	39.3	38.3	39.5	37.7	37.8
1967	38.5	39.0	38.9	37.9	39.3	37.2	37.2
1968	38.9	39.5	39.6	38.4	39.5	37.8	36.9
1969	39.8	39.7	39.5	38.4	39.6	37.1	37.3
1970	38.9	38.3	37.8	37.3	38.5	36.1	36.7
1971 [1]	36.6	37.9	37.1	36.8	38.1	36.0	35.6
1972	36.0	36.5	36.6	36.1	37.1	35.2	34.8
1973	36.2	36.5	35.0	36.0	36.8	34.8	34.7
1974	36.1	36.4	36.5	35.7	36.4	34.9	34.4

[1] Scope of series enlarged. [2] Incl. scientific, measuring, optical, etc., equipment. [3] Excl. motor vehicles.

[1] *Portée de la série élargie.* [2] *Y compris le matériel scientifique, de précision, d'optique, etc.* [3] *Non compris les véhicules automobiles.*

[1] El alcance de la serie es mayor. [2] Incl. el equipo científico, de medida, de óptica, etc. [3] Excl. los vehículos automóviles.

Belgique (1)

Hours actually worked per week
Heures réellement effectuées par semaine
Horas efectivamente trabajadas por semana

Date [1] / Date [1] / Fecha [1]	311 ×-312	313	314	321	322 ×	323	324	331	332
	Food	Beverages	Tobacco		Clothing	Leather, leather products	Footwear	Wood	Furniture
	Aliments	Boissons	Tabac	Textiles	Habillement	Cuir, articles en cuir	Chaussures	Bois	Ameublement
	Alimentos	Bebidas	Tabaco		Vestido	Cuero, artículos de cuero	Calzado	Madera	Mobiliario
1966	42.6	42.7	42.0	42.2	42.5	43.8	42.2	43.3	43.7
1967	42.3	41.9	41.2	40.7	40.7	42.2	39.7	43.4	43.3
1968	41.7	41.2	40.1	41.5	40.7	42.5	39.8	42.9	43.7
1969	41.3	41.2	40.5	40.6	40.2	41.0	38.1	42.8	42.4
1970	40.9	40.0	39.9	39.5	38.7	40.6	38.7	41.4	40.9
1971	40.3	40.5	38.7	39.3	39.6	39.8	38.5	42.1	40.5
1972 [2]	39.2	38.9	37.5	38.0	38.3	38.6	36.2	40.7	40.4
1973	38.7	39.1	37.0	36.2	36.1	37.4	35.8	39.9	39.8
1974	36.8	36.9	37.3	34.3	35.6	36.5	32.4	36.9	38.4

[1] Oct. of each year. [2] New industrial classification.

[1] *Oct. de chaque année.* [2] *Nouvelle classification industrielle.*

[1] Oct. de cada año. [2] Nueva clasificación industrial.

13 B

Hours of work in manufacturing
Durée du travail dans les industries manufacturières
Horas de trabajo en las industrias manufactureras

By industry
Par industrie
Por industria

Belgique (2)

Hours actually worked per week
Heures réellement effectuées par semaine
Horas efectivamente trabajadas por semana

	341	342	351			353	355	361	362
Date [1]	Paper, paper products	Printing, publishing	Basic industrial chemicals	Fertilizers and pesticides [2]	Synthetic and man-made fibres	Petroleum refineries	Rubber products	Pottery, china, earthenware	Glass
Date [1]	Papier, articles en papier	Imprimerie, édition	Industrie chimique de base	Engrais et pesticides [2]	Fibres synthétiques et artificielles	Raffineries de pétrole	Produits en caoutchouc	Grès, porcelaines, faïences	Verre
Fecha [1]	Papel, artículos de papel	Imprentas, editoriales	Química industrial básica	Abonos y plaguicidas [2]	Fibras sintéticas y artificiales	Refinerías de petróleo	Productos de caucho	Barro, loza, porcelana	Vidrio
1966	43.0	41.6	.	.	37.7	38.2	41.8	40.9	41.7
1967	42.8	40.5	40.8	42.4	39.3	38.2	42.0	42.4	42.0
1968	42.1	39.8	40.7	42.4	39.6	38.3	42.0	41.9	42.1
1969	41.9	39.7	40.5	40.7	39.7	38.5	41.2	41.1	41.4
1970	41.2	39.7	39.0	40.4	37.4	37.6	39.7	35.0	39.1
1971	40.2	39.7	38.9	39.0	38.5	38.9	40.9	40.5	38.3
1972 [3]	38.9	38.7	37.9	37.6	37.2	36.4	39.3	39.4	39.6
1973	38.3	38.0	36.7	37.5	36.3	38.7	38.4	38.3	38.7
1974	37.1	37.5	35.5	36.3	33.7	38.8	37.7	37.7	36.3

	369 ×	372	381	382	383	384	385	390
Date [1]	Cement	Non-ferrous metal basic industries	Metal products	Machinery (non-electrical)	Electrical machinery and apparatus	Transport equipment	Scientific, measuring optical, etc., equipment	Other manufacturing industries
Date [1]	Ciment	Métaux non ferreux (industrie de base)	Produits métalliques	Machines (non électriques)	Machines et appareils électriques	Matériel de transport	Matériel scientifique, de précision, d'optique, etc.	Autres industries manufacturières
Fecha [1]	Cemento	Industrias básicas de metales no ferrosos	Productos metálicos	Maquinaria (no eléctrica)	Maquinaria y aparatos eléctricos	Material de transporte	Equipo científico, de medida, de óptica, etc.	Otras industrias manufactureras
1966	41.8	41.8	42.2	41.9	43.8	42.2	.	.
1967	42.9	42.3	41.8	41.4	41.1	41.6	.	.
1968	42.2	41.9	40.8	41.6	42.4	41.3	.	.
1969	41.8	41.1	40.8	42.1	41.5	40.7	.	.
1970	40.1	40.2	38.9	40.4	40.1	40.4	.	.
1971	39.9	40.4	39.6	40.2	38.8	39.4	.	.
1972 [3]	37.6	38.9	38.3	38.6	38.9	38.6	38.6	39.3
1973	36.3	38.4	36.7	38.1	36.6	38.3	37.2	38.4
1974	35.8	37.4	37.3	37.5	36.3	37.5	38.0	37.4

[1] Oct. of each year. [2] Incl. drugs and medicines. [3] New industrial classification.

[1] Oct. de chaque année. [2] Y compris les produits pharmaceutiques. [3] Nouvelle classification industrielle.

[1] Oct. de cada año. [2] Incl. los productos farmacéuticos y medicamentos. [3] Nueva clasificación industrial.

13 B

Hours of work in manufacturing
Durée du travail dans les industries manufacturières
Horas de trabajo en las industrias manufactureras

By industry
Par industrie
Por industria

Czechoslovakia (1)[1]

Hours actually worked per week
Heures réellement effectuées par semaine
Horas efectivamente trabajadas por semana

Date / Date / Fecha	311-312 Food / Aliments / Alimentos	313 Beverages / Boissons / Bebidas	314 Tobacco / Tabac / Tabaco	321 Textiles	322 Clothing / Habillement / Vestido	323 Leather, leather products / Cuir, articles en cuir / Cuero, artículos de cuero	324 Footwear / Chaussures / Calzado	331 Wood / Bois / Madera	332 Furniture / Ameublement / Mobiliario
1966	49.2	.	.	44.4	43.4	45.0	44.1	46.5	45.9
1967	48.0	.	.	43.5	42.0	45.7	42.7	45.4	44.8
1968	47.4	.	.	42.7	41.3	44.9	42.0	44.6	44.0
1969	46.3	.	.	42.0	40.9	42.3	41.6	43.8	43.2
1970	46.1	.	.	41.9	40.9	41.9	41.6	43.8	43.2
1971	46.1	45.6	43.2	41.9	40.8	42.2	41.5	43.8	43.2
1972	46.3	45.6	42.8	41.7	40.7	42.0	41.5	43.8	43.4
1973	46.1	45.4	43.0	41.7	40.6	42.0	41.5	43.6	43.0
1974	46.5	45.2	43.2	41.6	40.9	41.9	41.9	43.6	43.0

Date / Date / Fecha	341 Paper, paper products / Papier, articles en papier / Papel, artículos de papel	342 Printing, publishing / Imprimerie, édition / Imprentas, editoriales	351 Industrial chemicals / Chimie industrielle / Química industrial	352 Other chemical products / Autres produits chimiques / Otros productos químicos	353 Petroleum refineries / Raffineries de pétrole / Refinerías de petróleo	354 Products of petroleum and coal / Dérivés du pétrole et du charbon / Derivados del petróleo y del carbón	355 Rubber products / Produits en caoutchouc / Productos de caucho	361 Pottery, china, earthenware / Grès, porcelaines, faïences / Barro, loza, porcelana	362 Glass / Verre / Vidrio
1966	46.2	45.9	46.3	45.9	45.2	45.8	45.1	.	.
1967	44.8	45.3	44.1	43.7	44.2	44.8	43.6	.	.
1968	44.4	44.5	43.7	43.3	43.8	44.4	43.2	.	.
1969	44.2	43.5	42.9	42.5	42.6	43.2	42.8	.	.
1970	44.2	43.3	43.3	42.9	42.7	43.3	42.6	.	.
1971	44.2	43.2	43.3	42.9	43.1	43.7	42.7	43.1	42.7
1972	44.2	43.1	43.2	43.0	42.8	43.8	42.8	42.7	42.7
1973	43.9	43.4	43.0	42.7	42.8	43.5	42.6	42.2	42.5
1974	43.9	43.2	42.9	42.7	42.7	43.6	42.5	42.1	42.3

[1] State industry.   [1] *Industrie d'Etat.*   [1] Industria de Estado.

13 Hours of work in manufacturing
Durée du travail dans les industries manufacturières
Horas de trabajo en las industrias manufactureras

B By industry
Par industrie
Por industria

Czechoslovakia (2) [1]

Hours actually worked per week
Heures réellement effectuées par semaine
Horas efectivamente trabajadas por semana

Date / Date / Fecha	369 Other non-metallic mineral products / Autres produits minéraux non métalliques / Otros productos minerales no metálicos	371 Basic metal industries — Iron and steel / Sidérurgie / Hierro y acero	372 Non-ferrous metal / Métaux non ferreux / Metales no ferrosos	381 Metal products / Produits métalliques / Productos metálicos	382 Machinery (non-electrical) / Machines (non électriques) / Maquinaria (no eléctrica)	383 Electrical machinery and apparatus / Machines et appareils électriques / Maquinaria y aparatos eléctricos	384 Transport equipment / Matériel de transport / Material de transporte	385 Scientific, measuring, optical, etc., equipment / Matériel scientifique, de précision, d'optique, etc. / Equipo científico, de medida, de óptica, etc.	390 Other manufacturing industries / Autres industries manufacturières / Otras industrias manufactureras
1966	.	46.1	46.4	.	.	.	.	.	46.2
1967	.	44.3	44.6	.	.	.	.	.	45.9
1968	.	43.9	44.2	.	.	.	.	.	44.2
1969	.	43.1	43.4	.	.	.	.	.	43.3
1970	.	43.3	43.6	.	.	.	.	.	43.2
1971	45.2	43.4	43.7	43.3	45.4	42.8	44.1	43.8	43.3
1972	45.3	43.3	44.0	43.5	45.3	42.9	44.0	43.9	43.3
1973	45.0	43.0	43.7	43.2	45.2	42.9	43.9	43.8	43.2
1974	44.7	42.8	43.7	43.2	45.2	42.8	44.0	43.8	43.2

[1] State industry.   [1] *Industrie d'Etat.*   [1] Industria de Estado.

13 Hours of work in manufacturing
Durée du travail dans les industries manufacturières
Horas de trabajo en las industrias manufactureras

B By industry
Par industrie
Por industria

Denmark

Hours actually worked per week
Heures réellement effectuées par semaine
Horas efectivamente trabajadas por semana

	311-312	313	314	321	322	323	324	331	332
Date / Date / Fecha	Food / Aliments / Alimentos	Beverages / Boissons / Bebidas	Tobacco / Tabac / Tabaco	Textiles	Clothing / Habillement / Vestido	Leather, leather products / Cuir, articles en cuir / Cuero, artículos de cuero	Footwear / Chaussures / Calzado	Wood / Bois / Madera	Furniture / Ameublement / Mobiliario
1971	36.3	35.1	34.2	34.4	32.2	35.4	34.0	36.9	36.0
1972	35.8	34.8	34.2	33.8	32.0	35.0	34.7	37.2	36.3
1973	34.6	33.2	30.6	31.9	30.9	33.4	32.7	35.2	34.5
1974 *	34.4	33.1	32.1	32.0	29.8	34.2	34.2	35.5	34.7

	341	342	351	352	353	354	355	356	361
Date / Date / Fecha	Paper, paper products / Papier, articles en papier / Papel, artículos de papel	Printing, publishing / Imprimerie, édition / Imprentas, editoriales	Industrial chemicals / Chimie industrielle / Química industrial	Other chemical products / Autres produits chimiques / Otros productos químicos	Petroleum refineries / Raffineries de pétrole / Refinerías de petróleo	Products of petroleum and coal / Dérivés du pétrole et du charbon / Derivados del petróleo y del carbón	Rubber products / Produits en caoutchouc / Productos de caucho	Plastic products / Articles en matière plastique / Productos plásticos	Pottery, china, earthenware / Grès, porcelaines, faïences / Barro, loza, porcelana
1971	36.4	36.5	37.1	34.7	39.4	41.9	36.6	35.6	33.9
1972	36.2	36.2	37.1	34.4	36.4	40.3	35.6	35.0	32.5
1973	33.6	34.9	35.4	33.1	34.6	38.7	33.1	33.8	29.6
1974 *	34.5	34.9	35.1	33.7	35.8	40.0	35.2	33.9	31.2

	362	369	371	372	381	382	383	384	385	390
			Basic metal industries / Industrie métallurgique de base / Industrias metalúrgicas básicas							
Date / Date / Fecha	Glass / Verre / Vidrio	Other non-metallic mineral products / Autres produits minéraux non métalliques / Otros productos minerales no metálicos	Iron and steel / Sidérurgie / Hierro y acero	Non-ferrous metal / Métaux non ferreux / Metales no ferrosos	Metal products / Produits métalliques / Productos metálicos	Machinery (non-electrical) / Machines (non électriques) / Maquinaria (no eléctrica)	Electrical machinery and apparatus / Machines et appareils électriques / Maquinaria y aparatos eléctricos	Transport equipment / Matériel de transport / Material de transporte	Scientific, measuring, optical, etc., equipment / Matériel scientifique, de précision, d'optique, etc. / Equipo científico, de medida, de óptica, etc.	Other manufacturing industries / Autres industries manufacturières / Otras industrias manufactureras
1971	36.5	38.4	36.7	35.5	35.6	36.9	34.6	35.9	34.5	35.3
1972	35.6	38.2	36.3	35.1	35.4	36.3	34.5	35.5	34.7	34.5
1973	34.4	35.6	33.9	32.1	33.9	33.9	32.0	33.3	32.4	32.3
1974 *	36.2	37.3	35.9	34.0	34.6	35.1	33.2	33.4	33.6	33.7

13 Hours of work in manufacturing / Durée du travail dans les industries manufacturières / Horas de trabajo en las industrias manufactureras

B By industry / Par industrie / Por industria

España

Hours actually worked per week [1]
Heures réellement effectuées par semaine [1]
Horas efectivamente trabajadas por semana [1]

Date / Date / Fecha	31 Food, beverages, tobacco / Aliments, boissons, tabac / Alimentos, bebidas, tabaco	321 Textiles	322-324 Clothing, leather, leather products, footwear / Habillement, cuir, articles en cuir, chaussures / Vestido, cuero, artículos de cuero, calzado	33 Wood, furniture / Bois, ameublement / Madera, mobiliario	341 Paper, paper products / Papier, articles en papier / Papel, artículos de papel
1965	42.9	42.1	44.8	45.2	45.7
1966	43.3	42.2	44.9	45.1	46.1
1967	42.7	42.1	44.4	44.0	45.2
1968	42.6	41.8	44.9	44.0	45.4
1969	42.3	42.0	44.9	44.1	45.6
1970	42.2	42.2	44.7	44.3	45.2
1971	42.8	41.9	44.5	44.3	45.6
1972	44.0	42.8	45.9	46.1	47.0
1973	44.1	41.8	45.0	44.6	44.0
1974	44.5	41.9	44.2	45.4	47.0

Date / Date / Fecha	342 Printing, publishing / Imprimerie, édition / Imprentas, editoriales	351-352 Chemicals / Industrie chimique / Productos químicos	353-354 Refineries and products of petroleum and coal / Raffineries et dérivés du pétrole et du charbon / Refinerías y derivados del petróleo y del carbón	355 Rubber products / Produits en caoutchouc / Productos de caucho	37-38 × Metal industries, machinery, etc. [2] / Industrie métallurgique, machines, etc. [2] / Industrias metalúrgicas, maquinaria, etc. [2]
1965	41.8	46.0	45.6	43.3	45.4
1966	41.6	46.2	45.8	43.1	45.3
1967	41.7	46.3	46.1	44.6	44.8
1968	41.1	45.9	46.0	43.9	45.1
1969	41.2	45.7	45.5	44.1	45.2
1970	41.2	45.8	45.4	43.5	45.0
1971	41.5	45.6	45.1	41.9	44.7
1972	42.1	46.3	46.6	43.3	45.5
1973	43.2	44.1	45.6	49.6	44.7
1974	41.8	44.7	44.8	41.6	44.0

[1] Incl. salaried employees. [2] Excl. scientific, measuring, optical, etc., equipment.

[1] Y compris les employés. [2] Non compris le matériel scientifique, de précision, d'optique, etc.

[1] Incl. los empleados. [2] Excl. el equipo científico, de medida, de óptica, etc.

13 Hours of work in manufacturing
Durée du travail dans les industries manufacturières
Horas de trabajo en las industrias manufactureras

B By industry
Par industrie
Por industria

Finland

Hours actually worked per week
Heures réellement effectuées par semaine
Horas efectivamente trabajadas por semana

Date / Date / Fecha	Food / Aliments / Alimentos	Textiles	Sawmills / Scieries / Aserraderos	Paper, paper products / Papier, articles en papier / Papel, artículos de papel	Leather, leather products / Cuir, articles en cuir / Cuero, artículos de cuero	Chemicals / Industrie chimique / Productos químicos	Non-metallic mineral products / Produits minéraux non métalliques / Productos minerales no metálicos	Metal industries, machinery (non-electrical) / Industrie métallurgique, machines (non électriques) / Industrias metalúrgicas, maquinaria (no eléctrica)
1965	45.5	43.1	43.9	43.8	42.6	43.9	43.3	44.9
1966	43.4	41.8	41.3	42.0	41.3	42.1	41.9	42.5
1967	41.0	39.0	39.8	40.0	39.4	40.2	39.8	39.6
1968	40.3	39.7	39.1	39.4	39.1	39.5	39.1	39.0
1969	39.7	39.1	39.0	40.0	39.0	39.4	38.3	39.1
1970	40.5	38.8	40.1	40.9	38.3	40.3	39.6	40.3
1971	38.8	37.6	38.3	39.0	37.5	38.8	38.3	38.8
1972	39.1	37.9	38.2	38.4	37.3	39.0	38.5	38.3
1973	40.4	37.2	38.7	38.5	37.4	39.4	38.4	38.4
1974	39.1	37.6	37.8	38.5	34.4	39.8	38.5	38.1

France

Hours actually worked per week
Heures réellement effectuées par semaine
Horas efectivamente trabajadas por semana

Date / Date / Fecha	Food, beverages / Aliments, boissons / Alimentos, bebidas	Textiles	Clothing [1] / Habillement [1] / Vestido [1]	Wood, furniture / Bois, ameublement / Madera, mobiliario	Paper, paper products / Papier, articles en papier / Papel, artículos de papel	Printing, publishing / Imprimerie, édition / Imprentas, editoriales	Leather, leather products, footwear / Cuir, articles en cuir, chaussure / Cuero, artículos de cuero, calzado	Rubber products, chemicals [2] / Caoutchouc, industrie chimique [2] / Caucho, productos químicos [2]	Non-metallic mineral products / Produits minéraux non métalliques / Productos minerales no metálicos	Basic metal industries / Industrie métallurgique de base / Industrias metalúrgicas básicas	Metal products, machinery, etc. / Produits métalliques, machines, etc. / Productos metálicos, maquinaria, etc.
1965	47.5	42.2	41.3	48.1	46.4	44.0	43.7	45.7	47.6	47.8	47.1
1966	47.4	43.7	42.2	48.2	46.6	44.2	44.5	45.6	47.2	47.5	47.1
1967	47.3	42.2	41.5	48.0	46.2	44.2	43.9	45.3	46.8	47.4	46.9
1968	47.1	42.9	41.6	47.3	46.0	43.7	43.8	45.0	46.5	47.2	46.6
1969	46.9	43.9	42.2	47.2	46.0	43.7	44.2	44.8	46.2	46.5	46.4
1970	46.6	42.9	41.2	46.7	45.5	43.2	43.4	44.2	45.6	45.7	45.9
1971	46.4	43.1	41.7	46.7	44.9	43.3	43.9	43.4	44.6	45.0	45.3
1972 [3]	45.7	43.1	41.8	46.5	44.2	43.4	43.5	42.9	44.0	44.2	44.4
1973	45.4	42.8	41.1	46.2	43.9	43.5	42.8	42.0	43.9	43.4	43.8
1974	44.7	41.9	40.9	45.2	42.6	43.0	42.5	41.2	43.4	42.6	43.1

[1] Excl. footwear. [2] Incl. products of petroleum and coal. [3] Beginning Dec. 1972: revised series.

[1] Non compris la chaussure. [2] Y compris les dérivés du pétrole et du charbon. [3] A partir de déc. 1972 : série révisée.

[1] Excl. el calzado. [2] Incl. los derivados del pétróleo y del carbón. [3] A partir de dic. de 1972: serie revisada.

13 Hours of work in manufacturing
Durée du travail dans les industries manufacturières
Horas de trabajo en las industrias manufactureras

B By industry
Par industrie
Por industria

Germany, Fed. Rep. of △ (1)

Hours paid for per week
Heures rémunérées par semaine
Horas pagadas por semana

Date / Date / Fecha	31 Food, beverages, tobacco / Aliments, boissons, tabac / Alimentos, bebidas, tabaco	314 Tobacco / Tabac / Tabaco	321 Textiles	322 Clothing / Habillement / Vestido	323 × Leather, leather products [2] / Cuir, articles en cuir [2] / Cuero, artículos de cuero [2]	324 Footwear / Chaussures / Calzado	331 Wood / Bois / Madera	332 Furniture / Ameublement / Mobiliario	341 Paper, paper products / Papier, articles en papier / Papel, artículos de papel	342 Printing, publishing / Imprimerie, édition / Imprentas, editoriales
1967	44.9	40.2	41.2	39.5	40.2	38.5	44.5	42.1	46.6	42.3
1968	44.7	40.5	42.4	40.7	41.3	40.9	44.7	43.0	46.5	42.9
1969	45.2	40.8	42.8	41.0	41.8	41.1	45.2	42.9	46.7	43.5
1970	45.1	40.7	42.6	40.7	41.5	40.7	45.6	43.0	46.2	43.3
1971	44.8	40.9	42.3	40.4	41.3	40.5	45.1	43.0	45.7	43.0
1972	44.4	40.7	42.2	40.2	41.0	39.8	44.7	42.9	45.7	43.0
1973 [1]	44.5	40.5	41.9	39.6	41.1	39.3	44.5	42.5	45.3	42.7
1974	43.8	40.1	40.9	39.2	40.3	39.3	43.7	41.3	44.5	41.8

Date / Date / Fecha	351 Industrial chemicals [3] / Chimie industrielle [3] / Química industrial	352 Synthetic fibres / Fibres synthétiques / Fibras sintéticas	353 Other chemical products / Autres produits chimiques / Otros productos químicos	355 Petroleum refineries / Raffineries de pétrole / Refinerías de petróleo	356 Rubber products / Produits en caoutchouc / Productos de caucho	361 Plastic products / Articles en matière plastique / Productos plásticos	362 Pottery, china, earthenware / Grès, porcelaines, faïences / Barro, loza, porcelana	369 Glass, and glass products / Verre / Vidrio	369 Other non-metallic mineral products / Autres produits minéraux non métalliques / Otros productos minerales no metálicos
1967	44.0	43.0	42.9	44.0	...	42.8	...	42.6	47.0
1968	43.5	42.8	43.0	42.9	...	43.7	...	42.5	47.3
1969	44.0	42.8	43.3	43.0	...	43.9	...	43.0	48.2
1970	43.2	42.0	42.2	42.7	...	43.4	...	43.3	48.7
1971	42.6	42.0	41.9	42.0	...	43.0	...	43.1	48.3
1972	42.3	41.6	42.1	41.3	...	42.7	...	43.1	47.8
1973 [1]	43.1	41.5	42.3	41.7	42.1	42.7	42.1	42.8	46.7
1974	42.6	41.0	41.8	41.4	40.5	41.5	41.4	41.4	45.2

[1] Sampling design revised. [2] Excl. tanneries and leather finishing, fur dressing and dyeing industries. [3] Excl. synthetic fibres.

[1] *Plan d'échantillonnage révisé.* [2] *Non compris la tannerie-mégisserie, la préparation et teinture des fourrures.* [3] *Non compris les fibres synthétiques.*

[1] Diseño de la muestra revisado. [2] Excl. la curtiduría y talleres de acabado y la industria de la preparación y teñido de pieles. [3] Excl. las fibras sintéticas.

13 Hours of work in manufacturing
Durée du travail dans les industries manufacturières
Horas de trabajo en las industrias manufactureras

B By industry
Par industrie
Por industria

Germany, Fed. Rep. of △ (2)

Hours paid for per week
Heures rémunérées par semaine
Horas pagadas por semana

Date / Date / Fecha	371 Basic metal industries / Industrie métallurgique de base / Industrias metalúrgicas básicas — Iron and steel / Sidérurgie / Hierro y acero	372 Non-ferrous metal / Métaux non ferreux / Metales no ferrosos	381 Metal products / Produits métalliques / Productos metálicos	382 Machinery (non-electrical) / Machines (non électriques) / Maquinaria (no eléctrica)	383 Electrical machinery and apparatus / Machines et appareils électriques / Maquinaria y aparatos eléctricos	384 × Motor vehicles [2] / Véhicules à moteur [2] / Vehículos de motor [2]	Ship building / Construction navale / Construcciones navales	Manufacture of aircraft / Construction aéronautique / Fabricación de aeronaves	385 Scientific, measuring, optical, etc., equipment / Matériel scientifique, de précision, d'optique, etc. / Equipo científico, de medida, de óptica, etc.	390 Other manufacturing industries / Autres industries manufacturières / Otras industrias manufactureras
1967	42.2	42.7	41.5	42.2	40.8	39.7	45.9	42.6	40.7	41.2
1968	43.5	43.9	43.3	43.7	41.7	42.8	47.0	42.3	41.3	41.3
1969	44.6	44.8	44.4	45.1	42.4	43.7	48.2	42.7	41.8	42.6
1970	44.8	44.4	44.6	45.3	42.5	44.0	48.3	43.1	41.8	42.2
1971	43.1	43.4	43.6	43.9	41.5	42.8	47.7	42.8	40.8	41.3
1972	42.9	43.6	43.3	43.3	41.7	41.6	46.9	42.1	40.9	41.3
1973 [1]	43.6	44.0	43.5	43.6	41.5	42.1	46.9	42.4	41.3	41.5
1974	43.1	43.0	42.4	43.2	40.8	39.2	46.9	42.6	40.6	40.8

[1] Sampling design revised. [2] Incl. bicycles and miscellaneous transport equipment.

[1] *Plan d'échantillonnage révisé.* [2] *Y compris les cycles et matériel de transport divers.*

[1] Diseño de la muestra revisado. [2] Incl. las bicicletas y material de transporte diverso.

13 B

Hours of work in manufacturing
Durée du travail dans les industries manufacturières
Horas de trabajo en las industrias manufactureras

By industry
Par industrie
Por industria

Grèce

Hours paid for per week
Heures rémunérées par semaine
Horas pagadas por semana

Date [1] / Date [1] / Fecha [1]	Food / Aliments / Alimentos	Beverages / Boissons / Bebidas	Tobacco / Tabac / Tabaco	Textiles	Clothing / Habillement / Vestido	Wood / Bois / Madera	Furniture / Ameublement / Mobiliario	Paper, paper products / Papier, articles en papier / Papel, artículos de papel	Printing, publishing / Imprimerie, édition / Imprentas, editoriales	Leather, leather products / Cuir, articles en cuir / Cuero, artículos de cuero
1965	41.5	46.1	43.2	44.9	41.4	41.1	39.7	49.4	45.2	42.1
1966	41.2	46.7	42.8	44.2	41.5	39.4	42.4	44.5	45.5	44.9
1967	40.7	43.9	44.6	45.8	43.5	42.1	40.8	49.8	43.1	42 5
1968	41.5	43.9	42.5	44.7	42.6	41.1	39.4	47.1	44.5	45.7
1969	41.9	44.1	43.6	44.8	42.1	42.9	41.4	45.3	46.7	43.6
1970	42.3	45.0	39.2	45.8	42.1	42.1	42.1	44.6	45.8	44.5
1971	41.4	45.5	44.7	44.5	43.3	41.8	41.2	47.2	45.4	46.3
1972	41.8	44.5	45.6	44.5	42.9	40.7	40.8	46.6	46.0	45.3
1973	42.6	41.8	42.7	43.7	41.5	41.9	42.6	44.8	45.3	45.0
1974	40.9	43.4	43.2	44.2	44.3	42.8	43.8	45.3	46.5	46.1

Date [1] / Date [1] / Fecha [1]	Rubber products / Industrie du caoutchouc / Productos de caucho	Chemicals / Industrie chimique / Productos químicos	Products of petroleum and coal / Dérivés du pétrole et du charbon / Derivados del petróleo y del carbón	Non-metallic mineral products / Produits minéraux non métalliques / Productos minerales no metálicos	Basic metal industries / Industrie métallur-gique de base / Industrias metalúrgicas básicas	Metal products / Produits métalliques / Productos metálicos	Machinery (non-electrical) / Machines (non élec-triques) / Maquinaria (no eléctrica)	Electrical machinery / Machines électriques / Maquinaria eléctrica	Transport equipment / Matériel de transport / Material de transporte	Miscellaneous manufactur-ing / Industries manufactu-rières diverses / Industrias manufactu-reras diversas
1965	43.1	45.5	48.8	43.6	52.2	45.0	44.8	44.0	46.4	42.8
1966	43.6	45.6	46.5	44.2	45.6	43.8	44.5	44.2	46.3	42.6
1967	43.9	46.1	47.2	44.5	48.0	44.1	44.1	44.6	49.0	42.3
1968	43.3	45.8	44.5	44.6	49.5	43.8	45.1	43.8	46.9	41.9
1969	44.6	46.3	47.2	45.2	51.8	45.1	43.8	44.6	46.3	44.0
1970	44.7	45.4	46.2	46.4	50.6	44.5	44.4	44.4	47.7	43.7
1971	43.4	46.3	46.3	45.4	50.6	44.3	46.0	44.2	44.8	42.6
1972	45.4	46.1	45.5	45.5	57.1	44.3	46.6	43.4	46.3	43.8
1973	42.2	44.7	46.9	42.9	51.8	44.8	45.3	40.9	42.6	43.5
1974	43.3	44.7	47.7	43.6	50.4	43.9	43.4	43.6	43.6	41.1

[1] Nov. of each year.   [1] *Nov. de chaque année.*   [1] Nov. de cada año.

13 B

**Hours of work in manufacturing
Durée du travail dans les industries manufacturières
Horas de trabajo en las industrias manufactureras**

**By industry
Par industrie
Por industria**

Hongrie (1) [1]

Hours actually worked per month
Heures réellement effectuées par mois
Horas efectivamente trabajadas por mes

Date / Date / Fecha	311-312 Food / Aliments / Alimentos	313 Beverages / Boissons / Bebidas	314 Tobacco / Tabac / Tabaco	321 Textiles	322 Clothing / Habillement / Vestido	323 Leather, leather products / Cuir, articles en cuir / Cuero, artículos de cuero	324 Footwear / Chaussures / Calzado	331 Wood / Bois / Madera	332 Furniture / Ameublement / Mobiliario
1965	189	185	183	174	.	.	.	180	181
1966	190	186	182	175	.	.	.	181	182
1967	188	185	184	175	.	.	.	182	181
1968	183	180	174	171	173	171	173	178	177
1969	173	170	166	163	166	161	166	168	168
1970 [2]	171	171	164	164	164	162	166	167	166
1971	172	171	166	164	165	161	166	167	167
1972	170	169	164	163	163	162	166	166	165
1973	168	169	161	161	162	156	164	165	165
1974 *	168	169	159	159	160	154	162	164	164

Date / Date / Fecha	341 Paper, paper products / Papier, articles en papier / Papel, artículos de papel	342 Printing, publishing / Imprimerie, édition / Imprentas, editoriales	351 Industrial chemicals / Chimie industrielle / Química industrial	352 Other chemical products / Autres produits chimiques / Otros productos químicos	353 Petroleum refineries / Raffineries de pétrole / Refinerías de petróleo	354 Products of petroleum and coal / Dérivés du pétrole et du charbon / Derivados del petróleo y del carbón	355 Rubber products / Produits en caoutchouc / Productos de caucho	356 Plastic products / Articles en matière plastique / Productos plásticos	361 Pottery, china, earthenware / Grès, porcelaines, faïences / Barro, loza, porcelana
1965	169	169	.	.	.	.	.	.	.
1966	171	169	.	.	.	.	.	.	.
1967	170	170	.	.	.	.	.	.	.
1968	165	165	163	161	166	163	165	171	161
1969	161	156	158	156	161	155	162	164	159
1970 [2]	161	157	160	157	162	...	163	166	159
1971	160	158	161	158	163	...	165	167	161
1972	160	157	160	156	161	...	163	165	159
1973	159	156	158	155	160	...	161	164	159
1974 *	158	155	157	154	158	...	162	165	157

[1] State industry. [2] Revised series.   [1] Industrie d'Etat. [2] Série révisée.   [1] Industria de Estado. [2] Serie revisada.

13 Hours of work in manufacturing
Durée du travail dans les industries manufacturières
Horas de trabajo en las industrias manufactureras

B By industry
Par industrie
Por industria

Hongrie (2) [1]

Hours actually worked per month
Heures réellement effectuées par mois
Horas efectivamente trabajadas por mes

	362	369	371	372	381	382	383	384	385	390
	Glass	Other non-metallic mineral products	Basic metal industries *Industrie métallurgique de base* Industrias metalúrgicas básicas		Metal products	Machinery (non-electrical)	Electrical machinery and apparatus	Transport equipment	Scientific, measuring, optical, etc., equipment	Other manufac- turing industries
Date *Date* Fecha	*Verre* Vidrio	*Autres produits minéraux non métalliques* Otros productos minerales no metálicos	Iron and steel *Sidérurgie* Hierro y acero	Non-ferrous metal *Métaux non ferreux* Metales no ferrosos	*Produits métalliques* Productos metálicos	*Machines (non électriques)* Maquinaria (no eléctrica)	*Machines et appareils électriques* Maquinaria y aparatos eléctricos	*Matériel de transport* Material de transporte	*Matériel scientifique, de précision, d'optique, etc.* Equipo científico, de medida, de óptica, etc.	*Autres industries manufac- turières* Otras industrias manufac- tureras
1965	.	.	.	.	.	183	180	181	.	.
1966	.	.	.	.	.	183	180	181	.	.
1967	.	.	.	.	.	181	180	180	.	.
1968	164	174	169	172	173	177	176	173	172	174
1969	158	165	162	163	163	166	165	163	164	164
1970 [2]	159	171	162	163	163	167	166	166	163	163
1971	160	168	162	161	164	167	167	167	166	164
1972	160	163	160	162	162	165	166	164	164	162
1973	159	162	161	161	162	164	164	162	163	160
1974 *	157	160	159	159	161	163	164	162	161	159

[1] State industry. [2] Revised series.   [1] *Industrie d'Etat.* [2] *Série révisée.*   [1] Industria de Estado. [2] Serie revisada.

13 Hours of work in manufacturing
Durée du travail dans les industries manufacturières
Horas de trabajo en las industrias manufactureras

B By industry
Par industrie
Por industria

Ireland

Hours actually worked per week
Heures réellement effectuées par semaine
Horas efectivamente trabajadas por semana

Date [1] / Date [1] / Fecha [1]	Food / Aliments / Alimentos	Beverages / Boissons / Bebidas	Tobacco / Tabac / Tabaco	Textiles	Clothing / Habillement / Vestido	Wood, furniture / Bois, ameublement / Madera, mobiliario	Paper, printing, publishing / Papier, imprimerie, édition / Papel, imprentas, editoriales	Rubber, leather, leather products / Caoutchouc, cuir, articles en cuir / Caucho, cuero, artículos de cuero	Chemicals / Industrie chimique / Productos químicos	Non-metallic mineral products / Produits minéraux non métalliques / Productos minerales no metálicos	Metal products, machinery, etc. / Produits métalliques, machines, etc. / Productos metálicos, maquinaria, etc.
Males [2] — Hommes [2] — Hombres [2]											
1965	47.6	46.3	45.9	44.5	42.6	45.2	47.9	45.0	45.7	45.4	44.8
1966	47.9	45.9	43.3	43.9	41.7	44.4	47.8	44.7	45.0	45.1	45.1
1967	47.6	44.6	44.1	43.6	42.6	43.1	46.6	44.5	46.4	45.6	43.5
1968	47.4	44.6	46.9	44.2	43.1	42.7	45.2	43.6	47.3	45.3	43.9
1969 [3]	47.9	45.3	43.2	44.1	43.2	43.7	45.7	43.6	44.3	46.1	43.9
1970	47.8	45.6	46.4	43.8	41.8	42.8	45.0	44.9	44.3	46.2	44.1
1971	47.7	45.4	44.9	42.5	41.7	42.2	43.3	44.1	45.6	44.7	43.6
1972	47.6	47.6	44.8	43.7	40.9	43.0	44.2	42.9	46.1	43.8	43.5
1973	47.0	47.0	46.5	42.8	41.4	42.5	44.6	40.1	45.8	45.3	43.6
1974	46.9	47.1	45.5	42.5	39.8	41.6	43.8	41.9	45.5	43.0	41.6
Females [2] — Femmes [2] — Mujeres [2]											
1965	40.4	31.4	42.0	42.6	40.5	41.1	42.1	40.2	40.9	44.0	41.7
1966	40.6	31.1	38.9	41.2	40.2	40.7	41.1	40.2	40.6	42.7	42.7
1967	40.8	28.9	39.7	41.2	40.4	40.5	40.2	41.6	39.9	41.8	42.1
1968	40.0	28.7	42.3	41.1	40.1	40.8	40.5	41.7	39.8	41.1	40.4
1969 [3]	37.8	30.5	39.2	40.6	39.8	39.0	41.0	40.2	38.0	40.4	39.4
1970	37.5	29.3	41.5	39.3	38.8	38.4	40.1	39.4	38.4	39.6	38.7
1971	37.4	29.3	40.7	38.4	38.1	40.0	40.2	39.2	38.6	40.2	38.5
1972	36.3	30.6	40.8	39.3	38.1	36.7	38.6	38.9	38.3	37.0	39.5
1973	36.7	28.9	42.5	37.8	38.0	38.0	39.9	35.5	38.2	38.2	38.4
1974	35.6	28.5	41.0	38.1	37.4	36.7	37.9	36.8	37.2	37.5	37.1

[1] Sep. of each year, except for 1965-68: Oct.   [2] 1965-68: adults only. Beginning 1969: workers on adult rates of pay.   [3] Series replacing former series.

[1] Sept. de chaque année, sauf pour 1965-1968 : oct.   [2] 1965-1968 : adultes seulement. A partir de 1969 : travailleurs rémunérés sur la base de taux de salaire pour adultes.   [3] Série remplaçant la précédente.

[1] Sept. de cada año, salvo 1965-1968: oct.   [2] 1965-1968: adultos solamente. A partir de 1969: trabajadores pagados sobre la base de tarifas de salarios para adultos.   [3] Serie que substituye a la anterior.

13 Hours of work in manufacturing
Durée du travail dans les industries manufacturières
Horas de trabajo en las industrias manufactureras

B By industry
Par industrie
Por industria

Italie

Hours actually worked per month
Heures réellement effectuées par mois
Horas efectivamente trabajadas por mes

Date / Date / Fecha	Food / Aliments / Alimentos	Beverages / Boissons / Bebidas	Tobacco / Tabac / Tabaco	Textiles	Clothing / Habillement / Vestido	Wood / Bois / Madera	Furniture / Ameublement / Mobiliario	Paper, paper products / Papier, articles en papier / Papel, artículos de papel	Printing, publishing / Imprimerie, édition / Imprentas, editoriales	Leather, leather products / Cuir, articles en cuir / Cuero, artículos de cuero
1965	160	168	124	135	132	148	153	160	161	144
1966	159	168	127	149	141	152	157	164	163	149
1967	157	167	131	144	139	151	154	164	161	151
1968	160	166	127	145	140	153	156	163	168	151
1969	158	163	120	144	139	150	152	160	156	149
1970	155	160	122	137	136	150	152	156	156	145
1971	151	157	112	133	134	146	149	148	149	142
1972	147	150	120	134	130	143	147	149	148	139
1973	144	150	122	130	125	140	143	145	141	135
1974 *[1]	135	145	110	113	113	128	130	127	126	117

Date / Date / Fecha	Rubber products / Industrie du caoutchouc / Productos de caucho	Chemicals / Industrie chimique / Productos químicos	Products of petroleum and coal / Dérivés du pétrole et du charbon / Derivados del petróleo y del carbón	Non-metallic mineral products / Produits minéraux non métalliques / Productos minerales no metálicos	Basic metal industries / Industrie métallurgique de base / Industrias metalúrgicas básicas	Metal products / Produits métalliques / Productos metálicos	Machinery (non-electrical) / Machines (non électriques) / Maquinaria (no eléctrica)	Electrical machinery / Machines électriques / Maquinaria eléctrica	Transport equipment / Matériel de transport / Material de transporte	Miscellaneous manufacturing / Industries manufacturières diverses / Industrias manufactureras diversas
1965	155	163	171	151	164	154	154	151	159	154
1966	162	165	169	155	162	159	158	155	161	157
1967	161	164	169	158	166	163	163	159	166	158
1968	156	164	170	159	165	162	162	159	165	156
1969	152	157	166	156	152	150	151	146	149	152
1970	149	156	164	155	154	155	155	150	152	150
1971	144	149	157	147	146	146	149	139	146	145
1972	142	140	151	143	142	140	142	133	138	142
1973	132	140	151	143	136	136	136	126	131	137
1974 *[1]	120	125	138	134	130	127	127	113	121	120

[1] Third quarter.

[1] Troisième trimestre.

[1] Tercer trimestre.

13 B

Hours of work in manufacturing
Durée du travail dans les industries manufacturières
Horas de trabajo en las industrias manufactureras

By industry
Par industrie
Por industria

Luxembourg

Hours actually worked per week
Heures réellement effectuées par semaine
Horas efectivamente trabajadas por semana

	11-312	313	314	322; 324	331	332	34	351	352
Date [1]	Food	Beverages	Tobacco	Clothing, footwear	Wood	Furniture	Paper, printing, publishing	Industrial chemicals	Other chemical products
Date [1]	*Aliments*	*Boissons*	*Tabac*	*Habillement, chaussures*	*Bois*	*Ameublement*	*Papier, imprimerie, édition*	*Chimie industrielle*	*Autres produits chimiques*
Fecha [1]	Alimentos	Bebidas	Tabaco	Vestido, calzado	Madera	Mobiliario	Papel, imprentas, editoriales	Química industrial	Otros productos químicos
1966	50.5	49.9	45.7	.	47.8	51.2	43.8	47.3	.
1967	49.7	48.5	46.3	42.3	49.4	48.7	44.0	47.4	.
1968	48.2	48.1	45.1	46.4	46.6	49.6	44.1	47.7	.
1969	48.8	47.7	45.6	43.3	49.5	50.3	44.7	47.4	.
1970	47.0	50.3	44.7	43.9	47.1	48.6	44.1	46.1	.
1971	45.9	46.1	44.5	42.7	44.8	47.4	44.1	46.0	.
1972 [2]	46.5	46.9	44.6	45.2	44.5	46.9	42.9	42.3	39.8
1973	45.2	48.0	42.3	41.1	44.3	46.1	43.6	43.6	39.6
1974	46.0	46.7	41.2	41.3	43.8	46.7	42.0	43.0	41.4

	355	356	36	371	372	381	382	383	384
				Basic metal industries					
Date [1]	Rubber products	Plastic products	Non-metallic mineral products	*Industrie métallurgique de base*		Metal products	Machinery (non-electrical)	Electrical machinery and apparatus	Transport equipment
				Industrias metalúrgicas básicas					
Date [1]	*Produits en caoutchouc*	*Articles en matière plastique*	*Produits minéraux non métalliques*	Iron and steel	Non-ferrous metal	*Produits métalliques*	*Machines (non électriques)*	*Machines et appareils électriques*	*Matériel de transport*
Fecha [1]	Productos de caucho	Productos plásticos	Productos minerales no metálicos	*Sidérurgie*	*Métaux non ferreux*	Productos metálicos	Maquinaria (no eléctrica)	Maquinaria y aparatos eléctricos	Material de transporte
				Hierro y acero	Metales no ferrosos				
1966	.	.	47.6	.	.	49.5	46.8	48.8	46.0
1967	.	47.4	46.4	.	.	49.1	46.2	51.3	46.1
1968	.	47.3	46.9	.	.	49.3	46.5	46.3	43.9
1969	.	45.7	46.6	.	.	49.1	48.9	46.5	44.5
1970	.	45.6	47.8	.	.	50.8	47.3	46.4	45.4
1971	.	44.0	47.0	.	.	48.7	48.2	44.7	43.8
1972 [2]	44.9	44.8	45.2	40.8	48.0	46.0	46.6	45.8	42.4
1973	45.0	42.5	44.8	40.9	...	46.1	43.4	46.5	46.7
1974	42.0	42.5	43.9	41.2	...	44.9	44.9	44.0	43.4

[1] Oct. of each year. [2] New industrial classification. [1] *Oct. de chaque année.* [2] *Nouvelle classification industrielle.* [1] Oct. de cada año. [2] Nueva clasificación industrial.

13 Hours of work in manufacturing
Durée du travail dans les industries manufacturières
Horas de trabajo en las industrias manufactureras

B By industry
Par industrie
Por industria

Malta

Hours paid for per week [1]
Heures rémunérées par semaine [1]
Horas pagadas por semana [1]

Date / Date / Fecha	Food / Aliments / Alimentos	Beverages / Boissons / Bebidas	Tobacco / Tabac / Tabaco	Textiles	Clothing / Habillement / Vestido	Wood, cork / Bois, liège / Madera, corcho	Furniture / Ameublement / Mobiliario	Printing, publishing / Imprimerie, édition / Imprentas, editoriales
1965	48.8	48.0	44.0	47.0	48.2	47.0	47.7	44.0
1966	47.0	47.7	45.1	45.0	47.2	46.2	47.5	43.7
1967	47.2	47.8	46.6	45.1	46.0	48.1	47.4	44.0
1968	46.6	46.2	45.5	45.1	47.3	47.1	47.6	43.7
1969	46.5	44.5	43.7	45.1	46.1	45.5	47.5	43.3
1970	46.4	43.6	41.8	42.6	46.0	46.7	45.9	43.9
1971	44.8	43.1	42.1	42.2	43.4	46.5	44.7	41.5
1972	44.8	43.6	40.5	41.1	41.7	46.5	43.1	41.3

Date / Date / Fecha	Chemicals / Industrie chimique / Productos químicos	Products of petroleum and coal / Dérivés du pétrole et du charbon / Derivados del petróleo y del carbón	Non-metallic mineral products / Produits minéraux non métalliques / Productos minerales no metálicos	Metal products / Produits métalliques / Productos metálicos	Machinery (non-electrical) / Machines (non électriques) / Maquinaria (no eléctrica)	Electrical machinery / Machines électriques / Maquinaria eléctrica	Transport equipment / Matériel de transport / Material de transporte	Miscellaneous manufacturing / Industries manufacturières diverses / Industrias manufactureras diversas
1965	48.0	48.0	46.8	46.2	47.0	46.3	44.2	46.0
1966	45.8	48.0	45.5	47.1	47.2	45.7	44.1	47.1
1967	45.2	49.8	46.5	46.7	47.5	46.4	44.2	46.4
1968	45.9	50.2	45.7	47.1	47.1	46.4	42.7	45.5
1969	45.0	48.0	45.8	47.1	45.6	44.3	40.9	45.4
1970	42.3	48.2	45.4	44.7	44.2	43.9	38.5	43.7
1971	44.2	48.1	45.5	43.0	42.6	42.3	38.5	42.2
1972	43.3	45.1	44.7	40.4	40.8	41.0	38.6	41.3

[1] Incl. salaried employees; adults only.   [1] Y compris les employés ; adultes seulement.   [1] Incl. los empleados; adultos solamente.

13 B

Hours of work in manufacturing
Durée du travail dans les industries manufacturières
Horas de trabajo en las industrias manufactureras

By industry
Par industrie
Por industria

Norway (1)

Hours actually worked per week
Heures réellement effectuées par semaine
Horas efectivamente trabajadas por semana

Date / Date / Fecha	Food / Aliments / Alimentos	Beverages / Boissons / Bebidas	Tobacco / Tabac / Tabaco	Textiles	Clothing [1] / Habillement [1] / Vestido [1]	Wood products [2] / Ouvrages en bois [2] / Productos de madera [2]	Furniture / Ameublement / Mobiliario
Males — *Hommes* — Hombres							
1965	39.7	39.0	37.6	38.5	38.3	38.5	38.6
1966	40.0	39.5	37.5	38.3	38.1	38.5	38.2
1967	39.6	39.1	37.7	38.3	38.1	38.3	38.1
1968	38.4	38.0	36.2	37.0	36.3	37.0	37.0
1969	37.2	37.0	36.3	35.7	36.1	36.0	36.6
1970	36.9	37.2	36.1	35.2	35.9	35.5	36.1
1971	36.8	36.9	36.7	34.4	35.0	35.2	35.8
1972	36.3	36.7	36.0	34.5	35.1	35.0	35.5
1973	35.3	35.4	35.3	34.5	34.6	34.7	35.0
1974	34.3	35.7	31.3	33.9	34.1	34.1	33.8
Females — *Femmes* — Mujeres							
1965	33.1	34.9	33.3	33.4	34.3	.	34.6
1966	33.6	34.7	32.8	33.2	34.2	.	35.4
1967	33.0	36.1	32.9	32.1	33.2	.	34.4
1968	31.6	34.0	32.9	31.9	32.6	.	33.3
1969	31.8	32.8	30.8	31.1	32.0	.	32.4
1970	31.2	31.7	29.8	30.0	31.4	.	31.9
1971	29.6	31.9	30.0	29.5	30.6	.	31.8
1972	29.2	31.9	30.9	30.3	30.7	.	31.5
1973	28.7	32.0	30.6	29.5	30.2	.	30.9
1974	28.2	30.2	27.7	28.7	29.7	.	30.9

[1] Excl. footwear. [2] For building only.

[1] *Non compris la chaussure.* [2] *Pour le bâtiment seulement.*

[1] Excl. el calzado. [2] Para la edificación solamente.

13 Hours of work in manufacturing / Durée du travail dans les industries manufacturières / Horas de trabajo en las industrias manufactureras — B By industry / Par industrie / Por industria

Norway (2)

Hours actually worked per week
Heures réellement effectuées par semaine
Horas efectivamente trabajadas por semana

Date / Date / Fecha	Paper, paper products / Papier, articles en papier / Papel, artículos de papel	Printing, publishing / Imprimerie, édition / Imprentas, editoriales	Leather, leather products / Cuir, articles en cuir / Cuero, artículos de cuero	Rubber products, chemicals / Caoutchouc, industrie chimique / Caucho, productos químicos	Non-metallic mineral products / Produits minéraux non métalliques / Productos minerales no metálicos	Metal industries, machinery, etc. / Industrie métallurgique, machines, etc. / Industrias metalúrgicas, maquinaria, etc.
Males (concl.) — Hommes (fin) — Hombres (fin)						
1965	38.1	39.3	38.1	38.4	38.3	38.1
1966	38.0	39.0	37.9	38.4	38.2	37.5
1967	37.4	38.8	37.4	37.6	37.6	37.5
1968	36.5	38.0	36.4	36.5	36.8	36.4
1969	35.6	37.5	35.0	35.5	35.9	35.0
1970	35.9	37.1	35.2	34.9	35.8	34.7
1971	34.5	37.6	34.3	34.7	35.3	34.3
1972	34.4	37.4	34.6	34.4	34.9	33.6
1973	34.3	36.8	34.5	34.4	34.3	33.0
1974	34.1	36.2	34.2	33.8	34.3	32.8
Females (concl.) — Femmes (fin) — Mujeres (fin)						
1965	33.7	36.2	32.8	34.2	33.0	34.6
1966	33.0	36.1	33.6	33.9	33.6	35.0
1967	32.0	35.2	33.7	33.0	33.1	34.3
1968	31.3	34.9	31.8	31.5	32.7	33.3
1969	30.6	33.5	31.2	30.8	31.9	31.6
1970	29.3	33.2	29.0	29.8	32.6	30.7
1971	28.0	33.0	28.4	29.1	31.3	30.3
1972	29.0	32.9	29.7	28.8	31.2	29.3
1973	28.9	32.4	31.0	28.7	30.3	28.4
1974	28.2	32.0	28.6	28.9	28.8	27.8

13 B

Hours of work in manufacturing
Durée du travail dans les industries manufacturières
Horas de trabajo en las industrias manufactureras

By industry
Par industrie
Por industria

Pays-Bas (1)

Hours actually worked per week [1]
Heures réellement effectuées par semaine [1]
Horas efectivamente trabajadas por semana [1]

	311-312	313	314	321	322	323	324
Date [2]	Food	Beverages	Tobacco		Clothing	Leather, leather products	Footwear
Date [2]	Aliments	Boissons	Tabac	Textiles	Habillement	Cuir, articles en cuir	Chaussures
Fecha [2]	Alimentos	Bebidas	Tabaco		Vestido	Cuero, artículos de cuero	Calzado
1965	49.1	48.0	46.2	45.1	46.0	47.1	46.3
1966	48.0	46.5	46.0	45.0	46.2	47.0	46.0
1967	48.1	46.1	46.0	44.4	44.7	48.0	45.8
1968	47.5	45.5	46.2	44.1	45.2	48.6	45.9
1969	47.0	45.4	45.6	43.8	44.8	47.8	45.3
1970	46.3	44.4	44.3	44.1	43.8	46.5	44.3
1971	46.0	43.2	43.8	43.5	43.5	45.0	43.7
1972	45.2	42.3	43.1	43.4	43.8	45.8	42.8
1973	44.3	41.9	42.8	43.3	43.4	42.3	42.4

	331	332	341	342	351	352	353-354
Date [2]	Wood	Furniture	Paper, paper products	Printing, publishing	Industrial chemicals	Other chemical products	Refineries and products of petroleum and coal
Date [2]	Bois	Ameublement	Papier, articles en papier	Imprimerie, édition	Chimie industrielle	Autres produits chimiques	Raffineries et dérivés du pétrole et du charbon
Fecha [2]	Madera	Mobiliario	Papel, artículos de papel	Imprentas, editoriales	Química industrial	Otros productos químicos	Refinerías y derivados del petróleo y del carbón
1965	46.7	46.7	46.5	46.1	.	.	.
1966	46.7	46.2	46.4	46.5	44.7	46.4	43.7
1967	46.6	46.4	45.8	45.6	43.9	46.0	43.7
1968	46.0	45.4	45.8	45.6	43.8	45.2	43.6
1969	46.0	45.2	45.4	45.4	43.6	44.7	43.7
1970	44.9	44.3	43.9	44.2	42.6	44.0	43.3
1971	44.7	43.6	43.7	43.7	42.6	43.7	43.1
1972	44.6	43.7	43.4	43.3	41.7	42.7	43.6
1973	43.9	42.6	42.5	43.0	41.0	41.9	40.4

[1] Adult males. [2] Oct. of each year.   [1] Hommes adultes. [2] Oct. de chaque année.   [1] Hombres adultos. [2] Oct. de cada año.

13 B Hours of work in manufacturing / Durée du travail dans les industries manufacturières / Horas de trabajo en las industrias manufactureras — By industry / Par industrie / Por industria

Pays-Bas (2)

Hours actually worked per week [1]
Heures réellement effectuées par semaine [1]
Horas efectivamente trabajadas por semana [1]

Date [2] / Date [2] Fecha [2]	355-356	36	37	381	382	383	384	385;390
	Rubber and plastic products	Non-metallic mineral products	Basic metal industries	Metal products	Machinery (non-electrical)	Electrical machinery and apparatus	Transport equipment	Other manufacturing industries [3]
	Produits en caoutchouc et en plastique	Produits minéraux non métalliques	Industrie métallurgique de base	Produits métalliques	Machines (non électriques)	Machines et appareils électriques	Matériel de transport	Autres industries manufacturières [3]
	Productos de caucho, de plástico	Productos minerales no metálicos	Industrias metalúrgicas básicas	Productos metálicos	Maquinaria (no eléctrica)	Maquinaria y aparatos eléctricos	Material de transporte	Otras industrias manufactureras [3]
1965	46.7	47.3	.	.	.	.	.	.
1966	45.9	47.3	45.8	46.8	46.6	45.4	46.3	46.0
1967	45.8	47.2	45.2	45.5	44.9	43.7	44.9	44.6
1968	45.7	46.9	45.6	45.9	45.1	43.9	45.3	44.3
1969	45.2	46.9	45.4	45.9	45.7	43.6	45.4	44.4
1970	43.8	46.0	44.9	45.2	44.5	43 0	44.1	43.3
1971	43.4	45.6	43.9	44.6	44.2	42.6	43.9	42.6
1972	42.8	45.1	43.5	44.0	43.6	41.6	43.6	42.7
1973	42.5	45.0	44.0	44.5	43.8	41.5	43.8	42.3

[1] Adult males. [2] Oct. of each year. [3] Incl. scientific, measuring, optical, etc., equipment.

[1] Hommes adultes. [2] Oct. de chaque année. [3] Y compris le matériel scientifique, de précision, d'optique, etc.

[1] Hombres adultos. [2] Oct. de cada año. [3] Incl. el equipo científico, de medida, de óptica, etc.

13 Hours of work in manufacturing / Durée du travail dans les industries manufacturières / Horas de trabajo en las industrias manufactureras

B By industry / Par industrie / Por industria

Portugal

Hours actually worked per week
Heures réellement effectuées par semaine
Horas efectivamente trabajadas por semana

Date / Date / Fecha	Food / Aliments / Alimentos	Beer / Bière / Cerveza	Tobacco / Tabac / Tabaco	Textiles	Cork / Liège / Corcho	Paper, paper products / Papier, articles en papier / Papel, artículos de papel	Leather, leather products / Cuir, articles en cuir / Cuero, artículos de cuero
1965	42.6	45.9	47.4	45.7	40.6	45.1	44.5
1966	41.3	46.1	48.7	44.9	40.5	44.9	44.2
1967	45.8	46.9	48.8	44.6	42.8	46.2	43.8
1968	38.3	51.3	45.6	45.1	44.4	46.6	44.8
1969	37.3	48.7	43.3	44.9	43.5	46.9	44.8
1970	41.3	49.8	45.8	45.1	44.6	46.3	42.4

Date / Date / Fecha	Rubber products / Industrie du caoutchouc / Productos de caucho	Chemicals / Industrie chimique / Productos químicos	Products of petroleum and coal / Dérivés du pétrole et du charbon / Derivados del petróleo y del carbón	Non-metallic mineral products / Produits minéraux non métalliques / Productos minerales no metálicos	Metal products / Produits métalliques / Productos metálicos	Electrical machinery / Machines électriques / Maquinaria eléctrica	Transport equipment / Matériel de transport / Material de transporte	Miscellaneous manufacturing / Industries manufacturières diverses / Industrias manufactureras diversas
1965	47.1	46.1	39.5	45.3	44.3	46.6	49.8	44.0
1966	48.4	46.6	40.0	45.6	42.8	49.1	52.0	44.6
1967	46.2	44.3	41.8	45.1	45.6	49.8	53.2	44.2
1968	45.8	45.8	38.3	46.0	44.7	48.4	53.4	42.2
1969	43.8	45.1	30.2	46.1	45.0	46.4	53.7	45.3
1970	44.6	44.2	35.9	46.7	42.9	37.7	50.9	43.3

13 **Hours of work in manufacturing**
Durée du travail dans les industries manufacturières
Horas de trabajo en las industrias manufactureras

B **By industry**
Par industrie
Por industria

Suisse

Hours paid for per week
Heures rémunérées par semaine
Horas pagadas por semana

Date / Date / Fecha	Food / Aliments / Alimentos	Beverages / Boissons / Bebidas	Tobacco / Tabac / Tabaco	Textiles	Clothing / Habillement / Vestido	Wood, furniture / Bois, ameublement / Madera, mobiliario	Paper, paper products / Papier, articles en papier / Papel, artículos de papel	Printing, publishing / Imprimerie, édition / Imprentas, editoriales
1966	45.0	45.2	44.7	45.2	44.8	45.9	45.3	43.8
1967	44.8	45.0	44.7	45.0	44.8	45.8	45.2	43.8
1968	44.7	45.1	44.6	45.0	44.7	45.6	45.1	43.7
1969	44.7	45.0	44.7	44.9	44.8	45.6	45.1	43.8
1970	44.8	45.1	44.4	44.9	44.7	45.6	44.9	43.7
1971	44.7	45.1	44.2	44.7	44.6	45.4	44.9	43.5
1972	44.4	44.4	43.8	44.6	44.2	45.3	44.7	43.0
1973	44.2	44.7	43.8	44.4	44.0	45.3	44.5	42.4
1974	44.1	44.5	43.5	44.3	43.9	45.2	44.4	42.2

Date / Date / Fecha	Leather, leather products / Cuir, articles en cuir / Cuero, artículos de cuero	Rubber / Caoutchouc / Caucho	Chemicals / Industrie chimique / Productos químicos	Non-metallic mineral products / Produits minéraux non métalliques / Productos minerales no metálicos	Metal industries, machinery, etc. / Industrie métallurgique, machines, etc. / Industrias metalúrgicas, maquinaria, etc.	Watchmaking / Horlogerie / Relojería	Jewellery / Bijouterie / Joyería
1966	45.3	44.7	43.6	46.2	44.8	43.8	44.1
1967	45.3	44.7	43.3	45.8	44.7	43.6	43.9
1968	45.2	44.6	43.3	45.6	44.8	43.7	43.9
1969	45.2	44.6	43.2	45.6	44.9	43.6	44.0
1970	44.9	44.4	43.1	45.6	45.0	43.6	43.9
1971	44.5	44.2	42.9	45.6	44.9	43.6	43.7
1972	44.2	44.4	42.8	45.5	44.7	43.6	43.5
1973	44.1	44.3	42.7	45.4	44.7	43.5	43.4
1974	43.6	44.0	42.6	45.1	44.6	43.4	43.4

13 B

Hours of work in manufacturing
Durée du travail dans les industries manufacturières
Horas de trabajo en las industrias manufactureras

By industry
Par industrie
Por industria

Sweden (1)

Hours actually worked per month
Heures réellement effectuées par mois
Horas efectivamente trabajadas por mes

Date / Date / Fecha	311-312 Food / Aliments / Alimentos	313 Beverages / Boissons / Bebidas	314 Tobacco / Tabac / Tabaco	321 Textiles	322 Clothing / Habillement / Vestido	323 Leather, leather products / Cuir, articles en cuir / Cuero, artículos de cuero	324 Footwear / Chaussures / Calzado	331 Wood / Bois / Madera	332 Furniture / Ameublement / Mobiliario
1967	160	167	148	155	149	154	149	161	158
1968	155	166	144	152	147	147	148	157	154
1969	152	164	134	150	145	...	144	154	153
1970	150	158	142	149	139	144	145	153	149
1971	148	159	132	145	140	144	138	151	146
1972	143	157	137	144	138	141	140	147	143
1973 *	138	155	126	138	134	136	135	146	142

Date / Date / Fecha	341 Paper, paper products / Papier, articles en papier / Papel, artículos de papel	342 Printing, publishing / Imprimerie, édition / Imprentas, editoriales	351 Industrial chemicals / Chimie industrielle / Química industrial	352 Other chemical products / Autres produits chimiques / Otros productos químicos	353 Petroleum refineries / Raffineries de pétrole / Refinerías de petróleo	354 Products of petroleum and coal / Dérivés du pétrole et du charbon / Derivados del petróleo y del carbón	355 Rubber products / Produits en caoutchouc / Productos de caucho	356 Plastic products / Articles en matière plastique / Productos plásticos	361 Pottery, china, earthenware / Grès, porcelaines, faïences / Barro, loza, porcelana
1967	160	158	163	155	169	165	156	154	145
1968	157	156	161	152	171	149	154	151	142
1969	154	153	156	147	173	157	150	144	149
1970	154	152	155	147	167	155	147	147	145
1971	153	150	153	143	162	153	145	147	148
1972	145	145	145	138	144	148	138	138	132
1973 *	144	143	145	131	147	141	138	136	124

13 B Hours of work in manufacturing
Durée du travail dans les industries manufacturières
Horas de trabajo en las industrias manufactureras

By industry
Par industrie
Por industria

Sweden (2)

Hours actually worked per month
Heures réellement effectuées par mois
Horas efectivamente trabajadas por mes

Date / Date / Fecha	362	369	371	372	381	382	383	384	385	390
	Glass, and glass products	Other non-metallic mineral products	Basic metal industries — Industrie métallurgique de base — Industrias metalúrgicas básicas		Metal products	Machinery (non-electrical)	Electrical machinery and apparatus	Transport equipment	Scientific, measuring, optical, etc., equipment	Other manufacturing industries
	Verre	Autres produits minéraux non métalliques	Iron and steel — Sidérurgie — Hierro y acero	Non-ferrous metal — Métaux non ferreux — Metales no ferrosos	Produits métalliques	Machines (non électriques)	Machines et appareils électriques	Matériel de transport	Matériel scientifique, de précision, d'optique, etc.	Autres industries manufacturières
	Vidrio	Otros productos minerales no metálicos			Productos metálicos	Maquinaria (no eléctrica)	Maquinaria y aparatos eléctricos	Material de transporte	Equipo científico, de medida, de óptica, etc.	Otras industrias manufactureras
1967	155	160	163	162	159	160	157	159	154	158
1968	151	155	159	157	154	157	151	155	148	149
1969	147	152	153	155	152	154	144	152	149	142
1970	149	151	157	152	151	152	146	152	145	144
1971	147	149	153	151	148	148	143	147	147	141
1972	142	144	146	145	144	145	140	142	143	137
1973	138	145	144	141	140	140	136	140	136	132

13 **Hours of work in manufacturing**
Durée du travail dans les industries manufacturières
Horas de trabajo en las industrias manufactureras

B **By industry**
Par industrie
Por industria

United Kingdom (1)

Hours actually worked per week
Heures réellement effectuées par semaine
Horas efectivamente trabajadas por semana

	31	321	322	323	324	33	34	351-352
Date [1] Date [1] Fecha [1]	Food, beverages, tobacco Aliments, boissons, tabac Alimentos, bebidas, tabaco	Textiles	Clothing Habillement Vestido	Leather, leather products Cuir, articles en cuir Cuero, artículos de cuero	Footwear Chaussures Calzado	Wood, furniture Bois, ameublement Madera, mobiliario	Paper, printing, publishing Papier, imprimerie, édition Papel, imprentas, editoriales	Chemicals Industrie chimique Productos químicos
	Adult males — *Hommes adultes* — Hombres adultos							
1969	47.6	45.8	42.5	44.9	41.0	45.8	46.1	46.1
1970	46.8	44.7	41.9	44.8	40.7	45.6	45.3	44.9
1971	46.4	44.1	41.6	44.5	40.6	44.7	44.4	44.0
1972	46.4	44.7	42.1	44.1	40.5	45.0	44.7	44.2
1973	47.1	44.9	42.4	44.3	41.5	45.1	45.1	44.6
1974	46.6	44.0	42.2	43.9	39.4	43.8	43.9	43.7
	Adult females — *Femmes adultes* — Mujeres adultas							
1969	38.6	37.7	37.1	36.8	36.9	37.5	39.3	38.9
1970	38.5	37.3	37.3	37.1	36.9	37.4	38.9	38.7
1971	38.2	37.3	36.8	37.0	36.9	37.7	38.7	38.4
1972	38.2	37.6	36.8	37.3	36.6	38.1	38.9	38.7
1973	38.6	37.3	36.4	36.7	36.6	37.5	38.6	38.5
1974	38.0	37.2	36.2	36.0	35.3	37.7	38.7	38.3

[1] Oct. of each year.   [1] *Oct. de chaque année.*   ˙ Oct. de cada año.

13 Hours of work in manufacturing / Durée du travail dans les industries manufacturières / Horas de trabajo en las industrias manufactureras

B By industry / Par industrie / Por industria

United Kingdom (2)

Hours actually worked per week
Heures réellement effectuées par semaine
Horas efectivamente trabajadas por semana

	353-354	355	356	361	362	369	371
Date [1] / Date [1] / Fecha [1]	Refineries and products of petroleum and coal \ / *Raffineries et dérivés du pétrole et du charbon* / Refinerías y derivados del petróleo y del carbón	Rubber products / *Produits en caoutchouc* / Productos de caucho	Plastic products / *Articles en matière plastique* / Productos plásticos	Pottery, china, earthenware / *Grès, porcelaines, faïences* / Barro, loza, porcelana	Glass / *Verre* / Vidrio	Other non-metallic mineral products / *Autres produits minéraux non métalliques* / Otros productos minerales no metálicos	Iron and steel basic industries / *Sidérurgie* . / Industrias básicas de hierro y acero
Adult males *(cont.)* — *Hommes adultes* (suite) — Hombres adultos *(cont.)*							
1969	44.3	45.5	46.5	45.7	46.5	48.5	46.0
1970	44.0	44.7	45.9	45.0	45.7	47.6	45.3
1971	43.6	42.7	44.9	43.8	44.3	50.4	43.2
1972	42.9	43.2	45.3	44.1	45.2	47.4	44.7
1973	42.3	43.9	46.0	44.7	44.8	48.3	45.2
1974	43.8	43.0	44.6	44.5	43.8	47.2	45.0
Adult females *(cont.)* — *Femmes adultes* (suite) — Mujeres adultas *(cont.)*							
1969	39.9	38.7	38.5	36.4	38.3	38.2	38.0
1970	39.2	38.3	38.1	35.8	38.8	38.1	37.3
1971	39.3	37.9	37.5	35.9	37.9	36.5	37.5
1972	38.6	38.0	38.0	36.0	39.2	36.3	38.4
1973	38.6	37.4	38.0	35.5	37.7	37.7	37.3
1974	38.8	38.1	37.3	35.6	37.5	36.7	37.1

[1] Oct. of each year.　　　　[1] *Oct. de chaque année.*　　　　[1] Oct. de cada año.

13 Hours of work in manufacturing
Durée du travail dans les industries manufacturières
Horas de trabajo en las industrias manufactureras

B By industry
Par industrie
Por industria

United Kingdom (3)

Hours actually worked per week
Heures réellement effectuées par semaine
Horas efectivamente trabajadas por semana

Date [1] Date [1] Fecha [1]	372 Non-ferrous metal basic industries *Métaux non ferreux (industrie de base)* Industrias básicas de metales no ferrosos	381 Metal products *Produits métalliques* Productos metálicos	382 Machinery (non-electrical) *Machines (non électriques)* Maquinaria (no eléctrica)	383 Electrical machinery and apparatus *Machines et appareils électriques* Maquinaria y aparatos eléctricos	384 Transport equipment *Matériel de transport* Material de transporte	385 Scientific, measuring, optical, etc., equipment *Matériel scientifique, de précision, d'optique, etc.* Equipo científico, de medida, de óptica, etc.	390 Other manufacturing industries *Autres industries manufacturières* Otras industrias manufactureras
Adult males *(concl.)* — *Hommes adultes* (fin) — Hombres adultos *(fin)*							
1969	45.1	46.0	45.9	45.2	44.0	44.1	47.1
1970	44.2	45.2	44.9	44.4	43.1	44.1	46.7
1971	43.4	43.2	43.0	43.4	41.8	42.8	46.0
1972	44.4	43.9	43.5	43.4	42.6	43.4	45.1
1973	44.6	44.7	44.6	44.0	43.2	43.9	45.1
1974	44.3	43.7	44.2	43.4	42.5	43.7	44.6
Adult females *(concl.)* — *Femmes adultes* (fin) — Mujeres adultas *(fin)*							
1969	47.9	47.6	38.4	38.0	38.0	37.9	37.9
1970	37.5	37.4	38.1	37.7	37.9	38.2	37.4
1971	37.0	37.1	37.9	37.7	37.7	38.2	37.5
1972	38.2	37.7	38.4	37.8	38.2	38.2	37.7
1973	37.9	37.3	38.1	37.4	37.9	38.2	37.5
1974	37.9	37.1	38.0	37.2	37.8	37.9	37.3

[1] Oct. of each year.　　　　　　[1] *Oct. de chaque année.*　　　　　　[1] Oct. de cada año.

HOURS

13 Hours of work in manufacturing
Durée du travail dans les industries manufacturières
Horas de trabajo en las industrias manufactureras

B By industry
Par industrie
Por industria

Yugoslavia [1] (1)

Hours paid for per month
Heures rémunérées par mois
Horas pagadas por mes

Date / Date / Fecha	311-312 Food / Aliments / Alimentos	313 Beverages / Boissons / Bebidas	314 Tobacco / Tabac / Tabaco	321 Textiles	322 Clothing / Habillement / Vestido	323 Leather, leather products / Cuir, articles en cuir / Cuero, artículos de cuero	324 Footwear / Chaussures / Calzado	331 Wood / Bois / Madera	332 Furniture / Ameublement / Mobiliario
1967	190	186	183	186	189	192	186	190	189
1968	189	187	181	184	187	194	188	191	188
1969	187	184	180	183	186	192	186	190	188
1970	184	181	177	176	179	186	180	185	183
1971	183	181	177	176	179	183	178	180	177
1972	181	182	177	175	178	180	174	179	176
1973	181	182	177	175	178	180	174	179	176
1974 *	181	182	177	175	178	180	174	179	176

Date / Date / Fecha	341 Paper, paper products / Papier, articles en papier / Papel, artículos de papel	342 Printing, publishing / Imprimerie, édition / Imprentas, editoriales	351; 356 Industrial chemicals [2] / Chimie industrielle [2] / Química industrial [2]	352 Other chemical products / Autres produits chimiques / Otros productos químicos	353 Petroleum refineries / Raffineries de pétrole / Refinerías de petróleo	354 Products of petroleum and coal / Dérivés du pétrole et du charbon / Derivados del petróleo y del carbón	355 Rubber products / Produits en caoutchouc / Productos de caucho	361 Pottery, china, earthenware / Grès, porcelaines, faïences / Barro, loza, porcelana	362 Glass, and glass products / Verre / Vidrio
1967	188	186	187	181	180	184	183	188	189
1968	189	186	185	179	181	182	180	183	184
1969	188	190	189	183	182	187	179	185	186
1970	187	182	187	181	183	178	180	181	182
1971	184	182	186	180	183	178	178	180	181
1972	182	182	184	178	182	177	175	180	181
1973	182	182	184	178	182	177	175	180	181
1974 *	182	182	184	178	182	177	175	180	181

[1] Socialised sector; incl. salaried employees. [2] Incl. plastic products.

[1] Secteur socialisé; y compris les employés. [2] Y compris les articles en matière plastique.

[1] Sector socializado; incl. los empleados. [2] Incl. productos plásticos.

13 Hours of work in manufacturing
Durée du travail dans les industries manufacturières
Horas de trabajo en las industrias manufactureras

B By industry
Par industrie
Por industria

Yugoslavia [1] (2)

Hours paid for per month
Heures rémunérées par mois
Horas pagadas por mes

Date / Date / Fecha	369 Other non-metallic mineral products / Autres produits minéraux non métalliques / Otros productos minerales no metálicos	371 Basic metal industries [2] / Industrie métallurgique de base [2] / Industrias metalúrgicas básicas [2] — Iron and steel / Sidérurgie / Hierro y acero	372 Non-ferrous metal / Métaux non ferreux / Metales no ferrosos	381 Metal products / Produits métalliques / Productos metálicos	382 Machinery (non-electrical) / Machines (non électriques) / Maquinaria (no eléctrica)	383 Electrical machinery and apparatus / Machines et appareils électriques / Maquinaria y aparatos eléctricos	384 Transport equipment / Matériel de transport / Material de transporte	385 Scientific, measuring, optical, etc., equipment / Matériel scientifique, de précision, d'optique, etc. / Equipo científico, de medida, de óptica, etc.	390 Other manufacturing industries / Autres industries manufacturières / Otras industrias manufactureras
1967	193	189	186	186	187	183	182	191	178
1968	192	189	187	187	188	185	183	182	178
1969	190	192	185	190	191	184	187	185	180
1970	185	188	181	187	188	174	183	182	181
1971	186	186	180	185	186	176	182	180	180
1972	184	184	178	182	183	180	180	177	176
1973	184	184	178	182	183	180	180	177	176
1974 *	184	184	178	182	183	180	180	177	176

[1] Socialized sector; incl. salaried employees. [2] Incl. ores extraction.

[1] *Secteur socialisé ; y compris les employés.* [2] *Y compris l'extraction des minerais.*

[1] Sector socializado; incl. los empleados. [2] Incl. la extracción de minerales.

13 Hours of work in manufacturing
Durée du travail dans les industries manufacturières
Horas de trabajo en las industrias manufactureras

B By industry
Par industrie
Por industria

OCEANIA — OCÉANIE — OCEANIA

Australia

Hours paid for per week [1]
Heures payées par semaine [1]
Horas pagadas por semana [1]

	31	321-322; 324	34	351-353	37	381-383	384	.
Date [2]	Food, beverages, tobacco	Textiles, clothing, footwear	Paper, printing, publishing	Chemicals, petroleum refineries	Basic metal industries	Metal products, machinery, etc.	Transport equipment	Other manufac- turing industries
Date [2] / Fecha [2]	*Aliments, boissons, tabac*	*Textiles, habillement, chaussures*	*Papier, imprimerie, édition*	*Industrie chimique, raffineries de pétrole*	*Industrie métallurgique de base*	*Produits métalliques, machines, etc.*	*Matériel de transport*	*Autres industries manufacturières*
	Alimentos, bebidas, tabaco	Textiles, vestido, calzado	Papel, imprentas, editoriales	Productos químicos, refinerías de petróleo	Industrias metalúrgicas básicas	Productos metálicos, maquinaria, etc.	Material de transporte	Otras industrias manufactureras
Adult males — *Hommes adultes* — Hombres adultos								
1966	43.5	42.9	42.3	42.3	44.3	44.2	42.6	43.5
1967	44.1	42.8	42.3	42.5	44.5	44.2	43.1	44.0
1968	43.6	43.2	42.1	43.5	44.8	44.8	41.9	43.8
1969	43.7	43.8	42.7	43.0	45.5	44.7	43.2	44.3
1970	43.6	43.6	42.7	42.9	45.0	44.8	43.0	44.2
1971	43.6	43.7	42.3	42.5	43.8	44.1	42.6	43.8
1972 [3]	43.4	43.4	42.5	42.5	44.0	43.2	41.9	43.9
1973	43.6	44.1	42.8	42.1	44.8	43.9	42.7	44.2
1974	42.7	41.3	41.3	41.6	43.9	42.4	40.6	42.4
Adult females — *Femmes adultes* — Mujeres adultas								
1966	39.5	39.3	39.7	39.0	39.8	39.7	39.2	39.4
1967	39.9	39.1	39.8	39.2	39.9	39.0	39.5	39.8
1968	39.7	39.1	39.2	39.2	40.0	39.4	38.9	39.6
1969	39.6	39.7	39.4	39.3	40.6	40.3	39.8	39.8
1970	39.1	39.5	39.5	39.6	40.5	40.5	39.5	39.8
1971	39.3	39.2	39.6	39.2	39.7	40.2	39.9	39.8
1972 [3]	39.8	39.3	39.7	38.6	40.0	39.9	3.99	39.7
1973	40.4	39.3	40.2	39.5	40.1	40.0	40.3	39.9
1974	39.4	38.3	38.9	38.7	39.3	39.3	38.6	39.1

[1] Incl. salaried employees. [2] Oct. of each year. [3] Scope of the series enlarged.

[1] *Y compris les employés.* [2] *Oct. de chaque année.* [3] *Portée de la série élargie.*

[1] Incl. los empleados. [2] Oct. de cada año. [3] El alcance de la serie es mayor.

HEURES
HORAS

13 Hours of work in manufacturing
Durée du travail dans les industries manufacturières
Horas de trabajo en las industrias manufactureras

B By industry
Par industrie
Por industria

New Zealand

Hours actually worked per week [1]
Heures réellement effectuées par semaine [1]
Horas efectivamente trabajadas por semana [1]

Date [2] / Date [2] / Fecha [2]	311-312 Food / Aliments / Alimentos	313 Beverages / Boissons / Bebidas	314 Tobacco / Tabac / Tabaco	321 Textiles	322 Clothing / Habillement / Vestido	323 Leather, leather products / Cuir, articles en cuir / Cuero, artículos de cuero	324 Footwear / Chaussures / Calzado	331 Wood / Bois / Madera	332 Furniture / Ameublement / Mobiliario
1971	40.5	42.4	39.7	38.4	34.6	37.9	36.6	41.0	39.4
1972	40.2	42.4	41.8	38.6	34.3	37.3	37.1	40.9	39.5
1973	40.2	42.0	41.2	39.0	34.1	36.8	36.9	41.5	40.1
1974	40.0	41.0	39.8	38.3	33.8	36.7	36.4	41.5	39.3

Date [2] / Date [2] / Fecha [2]	341 Paper, paper products / Papier, articles en papier / Papel, artículos de papel	342 Printing, publishing / Imprimerie, édition / Imprentas, editoriales	351 Industrial chemicals / Chimie industrielle / Química industrial	352 Other chemical products / Autres produits chimiques / Otros productos químicos	354 Products of petroleum and coal / Dérivés du pétrole et du charbon / Derivados del petróleo y del carbón	355 Rubber products / Produits en caoutchouc / Productos de caucho	356 Plastic products / Articles en matière plastique / Productos plásticos	361 Pottery, china, earthenware / Grès, porcelaines, faïences / Barro, loza, porcelana	362 Glass / Verre / Vidrio
1971	41.6	38.4	42.3	38.2	41.8	40.5	41.2	37.8	43.0
1972	41.5	38.3	43.1	38.1	42.7	40.7	41.2	41.3	43.5
1973	42.4	38.4	43.3	38.0	44.1	41.1	41.9	35.7	42.4
1974	47.7	38.3	43.2	38.0	44.1	39.8	41.0	33.5	39.2

Date [2] / Date [2] / Fecha [2]	369 Other non-metallic mineral products / Autres produits minéraux non métalliques / Otros productos minerales no metálicos	371 Iron and steel / Sidérurgie / Hierro y acero	372 Non-ferrous metal / Métaux non ferreux / Metales no ferrosos	381 Metal products / Produits métalliques / Productos metálicos	382 Machinery (non-electrical) / Machines (non électriques) / Maquinaria (no eléctrica)	383 Electrical machinery and apparatus / Machines et appareils électriques / Maquinaria y aparatos eléctricos	384 Transport equipment / Matériel de transport / Material de transporte	385 Scientific, measuring, optical, etc., equipment / Matériel scientifique, de précision, d'optique, etc. / Equipo científico, de medida, de óptica, etc.	390 Other manufacturing industries / Autres industries manufacturières / Otras industrias manufactureras
1971	42.8	44.0	42.8	41.4	41.6	39.0	41.1	37.6	36.4
1972	43.3	43.5	43.3	41.5	41.6	39.2	40.8	37.6	36.9
1973	44.2	45.8	43.8	41.9	42.0	39.5	41.5	38.1	36.8
1974	42.9	45.1	43.2	41.4	41.6	38.8	42.3	37.7	36.0

[371-372: Basic metal industries / Industrie métallurgique de base / Industrias metalúrgicas básicas]

[1] Incl. salaried employees. [2] April and October of each year. — [1] Y compris les employés. [2] Avril et oct. de chaque année. — [1] Incl. los empleados. [2] Abril y oct. de cada año.

551

HOURS

13 Hours of work in manufacturing / Durée du travail dans les industries manufacturières / Horas de trabajo en las industrias manufactureras — B By industry / Par industrie / Por industria

URSS [1]

Hours actually worked per week
Heures réellement effectuées par semaine
Horas efectivamente trabajadas por semana

Date / Date / Fecha	31 Food, beverages, tobacco / Aliments, boissons, tabac / Alimentos, bebidas, tabaco — Total	31 — Tobacco / Tabac / Tabaco	321 Textiles	322 Clothing / Habillement / Vestido	323-324 Leather, leather products, footwear / Cuir, articles en cuir, chaussures / Cuero, artículos de cuero, calzado	33 Wood, furniture / Bois, ameublement / Madera, mobiliario — Total	33 — Furniture / Ameublement / Mobiliario
1965	40.7	40.8	40.4	40.2	40.9	41.0	40.9
1966	40.8	40.3	40.4	40.6	40.4	41.0	41.0
1967	41.0	41.0	40.0	40.3	40.3	40.6	40.8
1968	41.0	40.8	40.6	40.4	40.3	40.8	40.5
1969	41.0	40.8	41.0	40.0	40.4	40.9	40.5
1970	41.0	40.8	40.4	40.4	40.4	40.8	40.5
1971	41.0	40.8	40.6	40.2	40.2	40.7	40.6
1972	41.0	40.8	40.7	40.3	40.5	40.8	40.7
1973	41.0	40.8	40.6	40.3	40.4	40.9	40.7
1974 *	41.0	41.0	40.7	40.3	40.3	40.7	40.8

Date / Date / Fecha	341 Paper, paper products / Papier, articles en papier / Papel, artículos de papel	35 Chemicals / Industrie chimique / Productos químicos — Total	35 — Petroleum refineries / Raffineries de pétrole / Refinerías de petróleo	35 — Rubber products / Produits en caoutchouc / Productos de caucho	371 Iron and steel basic industries / Sidérurgie / Industrias básicas de hierro y acero	38 Metal products, machinery, etc. / Produits métalliques, machines, etc. / Productos metálicos, maquinaria, etc. — Total	38 — Electrical machinery / Machines électriques / Maquinaria eléctrica
1965	40.9	39.7	39.8	40.1	40.6	39.8	40.2
1966	40.8	39.4	40.0	40.0	40.7	40.4	40.4
1967	41.0	39.5	39.9	40.7	40.6	40.4	39.8
1968	41.0	39.5	40.4	40.5	40.7	40.5	40.2
1969	41.0	39.7	40.2	40.1	40.6	40.7	40.0
1970	41.0	39.9	40.3	40.4	40.6	40.5	40.1
1971	40.9	39.7	40.0	40.6	40.6	40.4	40.0
1972	41.0	39.8	40.2	40.5	40.9	40.6	40.0
1973	41.0	39.7	40.1	40.2	40.8	40.6	40.1
1974 *	41.0	39.8	40.3	40.3	40.9	40.6	40.4

[1] Socialised sector. Incl. salaried employees. Incl. Byelorussian SSR, shown separately in this table.

[1] Secteur socialisé. Y compris les employés. Y compris la RSS de Biélorussie, figurant séparément dans ce tableau.

[1] Sector socializado. Incl. los empleados. Incl. la RSS de Bielorrusia, que figura separadamente en este cuadro.

13 Hours of work in manufacturing
Durée du travail dans les industries manufacturières
Horas de trabajo en las industrias manufactureras

B By industry
Par industrie
Por industria

RSS de Biélorussie [1]

Hours actually worked per week
Heures réellement effectuées par semaine
Horas efectivamente trabajadas por semana

Date / Date / Fecha	31 Food. beverages, tobacco / Aliments, boissons, tabac / Alimentos, bebidas, tabaco		321 Textiles	322 Clothing / Habillement / Vestido	323-324 Leather and fur products footwear / Articles en cuir et en fourrure, chaussure / Productos de cuero y piel, calzado
	Total	Tobacco / Tabac / Tabaco			
1967	41.3	40.7	40.5	40.3	40.2
1968	39.8	39.7	40.0	40.1	39.9
1969	39.7	39.9	39.5	39.8	39.7
1970	39.4	39.9	39.3	39.7	39.6
1971	39.3	40.2	39.2	39.8	39.7
1972	41.0	40.2	40.3	40.2	40.6
1973	40.9	...	40.1	40.0	39.4
1974 *	40.9	...	40.3	40.1	40.4

Date / Date / Fecha	33 Wood, furniture / Bois, ameublement / Madera, mobiliario		341 Paper, paper products / Papier, articles en papier / Papel, artículos de papel	38 Metal products, machinery, etc. / Produits métalliques, machines, etc. / Productos metálicos, maquinaria, etc.	
	Total	Furniture / Ameublement / Mobiliario		Total	Electrical machinery / Machines électriques / Maquinaria eléctrica
1967	40.6	40.5	41.8	40.4	39.8
1968	39.5	40.6	39.5	39.5	39.2
1969	39.2	40.0	39.2	39.2	39.2
1970	39.2	39.7	39.2	39.1	39.0
1971	39.4	39.5	39.2	39.1	39.1
1972	40.8	39.1	40.9	40.2	39.3
1973	40.7	...	41.0	40.3	...
1974 *	40.7	...	40.9	40.4	...

[1] Socialised sector. Incl. salaried employees.   [1] *Secteur socialisé. Y compris les employés.*   [1] Sector socializado. Incl. los empleados.

13 Hours of work in manufacturing / Durée du travail dans les industries manufacturières / Horas de trabajo en las industrias manufactureras

C Distribution (%) of workers according to hours of work per week / Répartition (%) des travailleurs selon les heures de travail par semaine / Repartición (%) de los trabajadores según las horas de trabajo por semana

Country — Pays — País	Code Code Clave	1965	1966	1967	1968	1969	1970	1971	1972	1973	1974
AMERICA — AMÉRIQUE AMÉRICA											
México [1]	(a)										
→ 40		7.0	4.1	7.2	0.9 [2]	5.1	14.5	5.2	...	...	...
40-44		24.0	31.0	15.0	26.9 [2]	24.3	26.6	43.0	...	...	...
45-47		58.3	54.4	71.5	64.4 [2]	58.6	53.4	50.3	...	...	...
48 →		10 7	10.5	6.3	7.8 [2]	12.0	5.5	1.5	...	...	...
Puerto Rico	(a) [3]										
→ 34		27.4	22.7	20.0	22.4	18.5	21.2	19.9	19.4	18.1	24.5
35-39		6.2	6.1	6.8	6.7	7.4	7.1	7.8	9.7	9.5	9.3
40		40.8	46.9	49.7	51.2	55.2	55.7	58.6	58.6	60.5	56.9
41-48		22.8	22.0	21.2	17.8	17.1	14.5	12.0	10.3	10.0	7.8
49 →		2.8	2.3	2.3	1.9	1.8	1.5	1.7	2.0	1.9	1.5
United States [1]	(a) [3]										
→ 34		19.5	19.6	22.1	20.1	22.7	25.2	28.9	27.8	28.1	22.4
35-39		6.1	6.0	6.2	6.7	6.7	6.6	6.3	6.5	6.5	7.3
40		43.4	43.5	42.2	43.3	42.7	42.9	40.5	40.0	37.7	42.9
41-47		8.7	8.6	} 14.2	14.2	13.1	12.0	11.3	11.7	11.4	11.6
48		6.8	6.5								
49 →		15.6	15.6	15.2	15.7	14.8	13.3	13.0	14.0	16.3	15.8
Uruguay (Montevideo)	(a) [4]										
→ 30		.	.	.	.	11.9	12.4	13.2	11.9 [5]	15.8 [6]	...
31-47		.	.	.	.	36.4	41.4	41.9	47.9 [5]	33.2 [6]	...
48 →		.	.	.	.	51.7	46.2	44.9	40.2 [5]	51.0 [6]	...
ASIA — ASIE ASIA											
Cyprus [1,7]	(a) [8]										
→ 43		24.2	15.4	11.2	7.0	1.4 [9]	5.0	19.4	40.0	59.3	73.1
44		54.9	69.4	55.9	40.5	54.6 [9]	35.1	35.0	22.4	22.8	7.0
45-47		6.7	3.2	9.8	29.9	43.0 [9]	58.5	28.7	30.3	17.9	18.8
48 →		14.2	12.0	23.1	22.6	1.0 [9]	1.4	16.9	7.3	.	1.1
Israel [10]	(a) [4]										
→ 34		9.7	10.3	13.3 [11]	10.3	7.3	4.9 [12]	5.1	7.7	11.3	10.0
35-49		86.2	85.8	82.7 [11]	85.8	88.5	89.9 [12]	88.5	85.3	79.4	79.4
50 →		4.1	3.9	4.0 [11]	3.9	4.2	5.2 [12]	6.4	7.0	9.3	10.6

EXPLANATORY NOTES: See p. 483.　　　NOTES EXPLICATIVES: Voir p. 485.　　　NOTAS EXPLICATIVAS: Véase pág. 487.

(a): Hours actually worked — *Heures réellement effectuées* — Horas efectivamente trabajadas.
(b): Hours paid for — *Heures rémunérées* — Horas pagadas.

[1] Oct. of each year. [2] Scope of series revised. [3] Non-agricultural workers. Incl. salaried employees. [4] Incl. salaried employees. [5] Jan.-May. [6] Feb.-June. [7] Adults only. [8] 1965-66: until 43 hours, 44 to 47 hours, 48 hours, 49 hours and over. [9] Sep. [10] Incl. mining and quarrying. [11] Sampling design revised. [12] Industrial classification revised.

[1] *Oct. de chaque année.* [2] *Portée de la série révisée.* [3] *Travailleurs non agricoles. Y compris les employés.* [4] *Y compris les employés.* [5] *Janv-mai.* [6] *Fév.-juin.* [7] *Adultes seulement.* [8] *1965-1966 : jusqu'à 43 heures, 44 à 47 heures, 48 heures, 49 heures et plus.* [9] *Sept.* [10] *Y compris les industries extractives.* [11] *Plan d'échantillonnage révisé.* [12] *Classification industrielle révisée.*

[1] Oct. de cada año. [2] Alcance de la serie revisado. [3] Trabajadores no agrícolas. Incl. los empleados. [4] Incl. los empleados. [5] Enero-mayo. [6] Febr.-junio. [7] Adultos solamente. [8] 1965-1966: hasta 43 horas, 44 a 47 horas, 48 horas, 49 horas y más. [9] Sept. [10] Incl. las minas y canteras. [11] Diseño de la muestra revisado. [12] Clasificación industrial revisada.

13 Hours of work in manufacturing
Durée du travail dans les industries manufacturières
Horas de trabajo en las industrias manufactureras

C

Distribution (%) of workers
according to hours of work per week

Répartition (%) des travailleurs
selon les heures de travail par semaine

Repartición (%) de los trabajadores
según las horas de trabajo por semana

Country — Pays — País	Code Code Clave	1965	1966	1967	1968	1969	1970	1971	1972	1973	1974
Korea, Rep. of [1]	(a)[2]										
→ 35		8.0	7.8	7.0	4.2	5.9[3]	6.6	8.4	5.6	8.2	4.6 *
36-44		8.3	7.0	7.0	6.6	11.5[3]	16.5	13.8	12.2	9.9	9.2 *
45-53		18.2	18.2	21.0	22.6	26.7[3]	27.4	23.0	20.2	16.2	16.9 *
54 →		65.5	67.0	65.0	66.6	55.9[3]	49.5	54.8	62.0	65.7	69.3 *
Philippines [4]	(a)[2]										
→ 39		17.8	17.3	16.6	...	31.8	...	24.0	26.8	24.6	...
40-48		56.0	50.1	50.4	...	45.0	...	38.4	39.3	42.2	...
49 →		26.3	32.6	33.0	...	23.2	...	37.6	33.9	33.2	...
République arabe syrienne [5]	(a)										
→ 40		.	.	.	.	.	12.4	15.7	14.6	19.5[6]	2.2[6]
40-44		.	.	.	11.9	17.8	12.2	47.9	12.2	7.9[6]	64.3[6]
45-48		.	.	.	58.2	5.8	4.3	7.0	42.1	16.8[6]	28.4[6]
48 →		.	.	.	29.9	76.4	71.1	29.4	31.1	55.8[6]	5.1[6]
EUROPE — EUROPE EUROPA											
Austria [7,8]	(a)										
→ 40		2.1	2.3	1.9	1.9	1.9	5.8	9.8[9]	10.8	10.8	12.4
41-47		87.2	87.4	89.0	88.9	88.7	87.1	82.7[9]	81.4	81.2	78.6
48-49		2.8	2.6	2.4	2.3	2.1	2.9	2.6[9]	2.5	2.6	2.2
50 →		7.9	7.7	6.7	6.9	7.3	4.2	5.2[9]	5.3	5.4	6.8
Czechoslovakia [10]	(a)										
→ 35		.	1.5	1.5	2.2	2.4	2.8	3.0	3.2	3.5	3.6
35-39		.	0.5	0.5	0.4	0.6	0.7	0.7	0.6	0.6	0.5
40		.	3.3	3.5	5.7	19.7	19.9	19.3	19.4	19.8	19.0
40-44		.	93.7	93.8	91.6	77.3	76.7	77.0	76.8	76.1	76.9
45-48		.	1.0	0.7	0.1	—	—	—	—	—	—
France	(a)										
→ 39		3.5	.	3.2	2.4	1.0	2.0	1.5	1.4[11]	0.7	1.4
40		16.2	.	15.6	15.3	12.2	15.6	15.8	16.2[11]	15.8	23.4
41-48		64.5	.	67.3	69.7	75.5	73.4	74.9	76.4[11]	79.0	71.9
49 →		15.8	.	13.9	12.6	11.3	9.0	7.8	6.0[11]	4.5	3.3

EXPLANATORY NOTES: See p. 483.   NOTES EXPLICATIVES: Voir p. 485.   NOTAS EXPLICATIVAS: Véase pág. 487.

(a) : Hours actually worked — *Heures réellement effectuées* — Horas efectivamente trabajadas.
(b) : Hours paid for — *Heures rémunérées* — Horas pagadas.

[1] 1965-68: until 29 hours, 30 to 39 hours, 40 to 49 hours, 50 hours and over. [2] Incl. salaried employees. [3] Series replacing former series. [4] May of each year. [5] Nov. of each year. [6] May. [7] Incl. mining, construction, gas and electricity. [8] 1965-69: until 39 hours, 40-47 hours, 48 hours, 49 hours and over. [9] Scope of series enlarged. [10] State industry. [11] Beginning Dec. 1972: revised series.

[1] *1965-1968 : jusqu'à 29 heures, 30 à 39 heures, 40 à 49 heures, 50 heures et plus.* [2] *Y compris les employés.* [3] *Série remplaçant la précédente.* [4] *Mai de chaque année.* [5] *Nov. de chaque année.* [6] *Mai.* [7] *Y compris les mines, la construction, le gaz et l'électricité.* [8] *1965-1969 : jusqu'à 39 heures, 40-47 heures, 48 heures, 49 heures et plus.* [9] *Portée de la série élargie.* [10] *Industrie d'Etat.* [11] *A partir de déc. 1972 : série révisée.*

[1] 1965-1968: hasta 29 horas, 30 a 39 horas, 40 a 49 horas, 50 horas y más. [2] Incl. los empleados. [3] Serie que substituye a la anterior. [4] Mayo de cada año. [5] Nov. de cada año. [6] Mayo. [7] Incl. las minas, la construcción, el gas y la electricidad. [8] 1965-1969: hasta 39 horas, 40-47 horas, 48 horas, 49 horas y más. [9] El alcance de la serie es mayor. [10] Industria de Estado. [11] A partir de dic. de 1972: serie revisada.

13 Hours of work in manufacturing
Durée du travail dans les industries manufacturières
Horas de trabajo en las industrias manufactureras

C Distribution (%) of workers according to hours of work per week
Répartition (%) des travailleurs selon les heures de travail par semaine
Repartición (%) de los trabajadores según las horas de trabajo por semana

Country — Pays — País	Code Code Clave	1965	1966	1967	1968	1969	1970	1971	1972	1973	1974
Hongrie [1]	(a)										
→ 43		.	.	} 19.6	55.4	94.2	} 97.5 [2] {	21.6	22.1	22.6	22.5
44		.	.					75.1	75.6	75.4	75.6
45-47		.	.					0.5	0.3	0.2	0.3
48		.	.	78.7	43.4	5.8	2.4 [2]	2.7	1.9	1.7	1.5
48 →		.	.	1.7	1.2	—	0.1 [2]	0.1	0.1	0.1	0.1
Italie	(a)										
→ 32		.	.	3.3	2.9	2.7	2.9	4.8	3.3	2.7	...
33-40		.	.	3.5	3.6	4.0	4.5	5.8	10.4	15.0	...
41-44		.	.	34.9	37.6	45.2	67.1	73.8	74.8	73.1	...
45 →		.	.	58.3	55.9	48.1	25.5	15.6	11.5	9.2	...
Suisse	(b)										
→ 39		1.8	1.9	2.1	2.1	2.3	2.5	2.9	3.4	3.7	4.1
40-45		71.3	71.3	73.5	73.6	72.6	72.7	72.6	75.4	76.1	77.7
46		12.8	14.2	14.4	13.9	14.1	13.6	13.5	11.3	10.8	9.6
47 →		14.1	12.6	10.0	10.4	11.0	11.2	11.0	9.9	9.4	8.6
Yugoslavia [3]	(b)										
→ 36		1.1	1.1	1.0	—	—	—	—	—	—	—
37-42 [4]		21.5	36.1	56.4	70.2	74.6	86.1	100.0	100.0	100.0	100.0
43-48		75.7	61.5	42.6	29.8	25.4	13.9	—	—	—	—
49 →		1.7	1.3	—	—	—	—	—	—	—	—
OCEANIA — OCÉANIE OCEANÍA											
Australia [5]	(a)										
→ 34		.	.	14.4	13.0	15.6	14.2	13.5	15.2	17.3	16.0
35-39		.	.	6.2	6.3	6.6	7.5	6.9	6.8	7.1	8.0
40		.	.	55.7	56.4	52.0	50.2	52.6	53.8	48.0	48.6
41-47		.	.	9.5	9.5	9.5	10.3	10.1	9.4	10.1	10.3
48 →		.	.	14.2	14.8	16.3	17.8	16.9	14.8	17.5	17.1

EXPLANATORY NOTES: See p. 483.   NOTES EXPLICATIVES: Voir p. 485.   NOTAS EXPLICATIVAS: Véase pág. 487.

(a): Hours actually worked — *Heures réellement effectuées* — Horas efectivamente trabajadas.
(b): Hours paid for — *Heures rémunérées* — Horas pagadas.

[1] State industry. [2] Revised series. [3] Socialised sector. Incl. mining and quarrying. Incl. salaried employees. 1967 and 1970: March and 1968-69: Dec. [4] Beginning 1971: 42 hours per week. [5] Civilian labour force employed.

[1] *Industrie d'Etat.* [2] *Série révisée.* [3] *Secteur socialisé. Y compris les industries extractives. Y compris les employés. 1967 et 1970: mars, et 1968-69: déc.* [4] *A partir de 1971: 42 heures par semaine.* [5] *Main d'œuvre civile occupée.*

[1] Industria de Estado. [2] Serie revisada. [3] Sector socializado. Incl. las minas y canteras. Incl. los empleados. 1967 y 1970: marzo, y 1968-69: dic. [4] A partir de 1971: 42 horas por semana. [5] Fuerza trabajadora civil ocupada.

14 Hours of work in mining and quarrying
Durée du travail dans les industries extractives
Horas de trabajo en las minas y canteras

Hours of work per week — Durée du travail par semaine — Horas de trabajo por semana

| | AFRICA — AFRIQUE — AFRICA | | | AMERICA — AMÉRIQUE — AMÉRICA | | | | |
| | | | | Canada | | | Colombia | |
Date / Date / Fecha	Algérie [1]	Egypt [2]	Sierra Leone [3]	Coal mining / Mines de charbon / Minas de carbón	Metal mining / Mines métallifères / Minas metalíferas	All mining and quarrying / Ensemble des industries extractives / Todas las minas y canteras	Petroleum extraction / Extraction du pétrole / Extracción de petróleo	Ecuador
	(a)	(b)	(a)	(b)	(b)	(b)	(a) [4]	(a)
1965	.	49	.	41.3	41.9	42.4	197	51
1966	.	46	45.8	42.5	41.5	42.2	206	56
1967	.	52	45.1	42.6	41.3	41.9	207	52
1968	43.7	48	50.1	41.8	41.2	41.8	211	50
1969	44.2	53	52.3	41.9	40.7	41.4	205	57
1970	41.4	49	47.5	42.1	40.3	41.0	210	57
1971	42.6	...	47.1	41.1	39.3	40.4	224	55
1972	40.2	...	49.8	40.4	39.0	40.3	216 [5]	53
1973	40.5	...	55.8	40.7	39.6	40.9	...	51
1974	...	...	48.3	39.8 *	39.4 *	40.4 *	...	...

| | AMERICA — AMÉRIQUE — AMÉRICA | | | | | | ASIA — ASIE / ASIA |
| | | | | | Venezuela | | Burma [6] |
Date / Date / Fecha	Guyana	México [2]	Puerto Rico	United States	Petroleum extraction / Extraction du pétrole / Extracción de petróleo	Iron ore mining / Extraction du minerai de fer / Extracción de mineral de hierro	Metal mining / Mines métallifères / Minas metalíferas
	(b)	(a)	(b)	(b)	(a)	(a)	(a) [7]
1965	.	48.0	37.6	42.3	.	.	7.9
1966	44.4	48.0	38.1	42.7	.	.	7.8
1967	46.8	48.0	38.7	42.6	.	.	7.9
1968	45.3	48.0	37.8	42.6	.	.	7.9
1969	44.4	48.0	38.2	43.0	.	.	7.7
1970	43.1	48.0	37.5	42.7	36.1	40.2	7.9
1971	45.7	48.0 *	39.8	42.3	36.4	39.9	8.0
1972	40.1	44.0 *	39.3	42.5	37.3	36.9	7.7 [8]
1973	40.1	...	39.1	42.5	36.8	37.3	7.6 [9]
1974	...	...	37.6	42.4	39.3	40.2	...

EXPLANATORY NOTES: See p. 483. — NOTES EXPLICATIVES: Voir p. 485. — NOTAS EXPLICATIVAS: Véase pág. 487.

(a): Hours actually worked — Heures réellement effectuées — Horas efectivamente trabajadas.
(b): Hours paid for — Heures rémunérées — Horas pagadas.

[1] April of each year. [2] Oct. of each year. [3] Adults only. May and Nov. of each year. [4] Per month. [5] Jan-Sep. [6] Workers engaged for less than 30 days (excl. casual workers). [7] Per day. [8] April and Sep. [9] March and Sep.

[1] Avril de chaque année. [2] Oct. de chaque année. [3] Adultes seulement. Mai et nov. de chaque année. [4] Par mois. [5] Janv.-sept. [6] Travailleurs engagés pour moins de 30 jours (non compris les travailleurs occasionnels). [7] Par jour. [8] Avril et sept. [9] Mars et sept.

[1] Abril de cada año. [2] Oct. de cada año. [3] Adultos solamente. Mayo y nov. de cada año. [4] Por mes. [5] Enero-sept. [6] Trabajadores ocupados durante menos de 30 días (excl. los trabajadores ocasionales). [7] Por día. [8] Abril y sept. [9] Marzo y sept.

HOURS

14 Hours of work in mining and quarrying
Durée du travail dans les industries extractives
Horas de trabajo en las minas y canteras

Hours of work per week — Durée du travail par semaine — Horas de trabajo por semana

Date / Date / Fecha	Cyprus [1,2]	India Coal mining — Mines de charbon — Minas de carbón	India Metal mining — Mines métallifères — Minas metalíferas	Japan	Korea, Rep. of	Philippines [7]	Singapore [8]	Sri Lanka [10] Plumbago mining — Mines de plombagine — Minas de plombagina
	(a)	(a)	(a)	(a) [4]	(a) [4]	(a) [4]	(a) [9]	(b) [11]
1965	43	48.00	47.8	45.0	55.2	47.2	43.7	7.4
1966	44	48.00	46.1	45.6	53.8	50.4	44.8	7.5
1967	44	47.80	47.2	45.1 [5]	54.9	55.2	44.7	7.3
1968	42	47.71	47.0	44.8	54.0	51.3	44.3	7.9
1969	42 [3]	47.70	47.2	44.7	53.6	45.7	45.6	8.6
1970	42	47.74	47.3	44.6 [5]	45.1 [6]	...	47.3	8.8
1971	44	47.87	47.2	43.9	45.4	49.8	48.2	9.1
1972	46	47.92	47.5	43.8	42.7	47.6	50.4	8.4
1973	44	47.83	47.4	44.3 [5]	43.7	47.0	51.3	8.7
1974	44	47.83 *	...	44.1	...	...	47.8	8.2

Date / Date / Fecha	ASIA — ASIE — ASIA Rép. arabe syrienne [12] Phosphate mining — Mines de phosphate — Minas de fosfato	Belgique [1,15]	Czechoslovakia [17]	Denmark	España	Finland	France	Germany, Fed. Rep. of △ [19]
	(a) [13]	(a)	(a)	(a)	(a) [4]	(a)	(a)	(b) [13]
1965	.	.	.	45.9	41.3	44.2	44.3	43.4
1966	.	44.2	46.0	44.9	39.8	43.4	44.8	41.8
1967	.	43.2	44.8	47.1	39.2	41.4	44.3	40.7
1968	.	43.8	44.0	44.4	38.9	40.6	43.3	42.3
1969	.	43.2	43.4	43.2	37.8	40.0	43.6	43.0
1970	35.2	42.5	43.3	41.1	37.3	40.5	43.4	42.7
1971	47.8	42.9	43.5	40.7	36.9	39.6	42.6	41.7
1972	49.0	40.5 [16]	43.0	41.5	38.2	40.8	42.1 [18]	40.6
1973	51.0 [14]	39.1	43.0	39.4 *	34.9	40.8	41.6	41.8 [5]
1974	42.4 * [14]	38.9	43.0	...	36.4	40.4	41.2	41.7

EXPLANATORY NOTES: See p. 483. — NOTES EXPLICATIVES: Voir p. 485. — NOTAS EXPLICATIVAS: Véase pág. 487.

(a) : Hours actually worked — *Heures réellement effectuées* — Horas efectivamente trabajadas.
(b) : Hours paid for — *Heures rémunérées* — Horas pagadas.

[1] Oct. of each year. [2] Adults only. [3] Sep. [4] Incl. salaried employees. [5] Sampling design revised. [6] Series replacing former series. [7] May of each year. [8] July of each year. [9] Beginning 1969: adults only. [10] March and Sep. of each year. [11] Per day. [12] Nov. of each year. [13] Adult males. [14] May. [15] Excl. coal mining. [16] New industrial classification. [17] State industry. [18] Beginning Dec. 1972: revised series. [19] Excl. quarrying.

[1] *Oct. de chaque année.* [2] *Adultes seulement.* [3] *Sept.* [4] *Y compris les employés.* [5] *Plan d'échantillonnage révisé.* [6] *Série remplaçant la précédente.* [7] *Mai de chaque année.* [8] *Juillet de chaque année.* [9] *A partir de 1969: adultes seulement.* [10] *Mars et sept. de chaque année.* [11] *Par jour.* [12] *Nov. de chaque année.* [13] *Hommes adultes.* [14] *Mai.* [15] *Non compris les mines de charbon.* [16] *Nouvelle classification industrielle.* [17] *Industrie d'Etat.* [18] *A partir de déc. 1972: série révisée.* [19] *Non compris les carrières.*

[1] Oct. de cada año. [2] Adultos solamente. [3] Sept. [4] Incl. los empleados. [5] Diseño de la muestra revisado. [6] Serie que substituye a la anterior. [7] Mayo de cada año. [8] Julio de cada año. [9] A partir de 1969: adultos solamente. [10] Marzo y sept. de cada año. [11] Por día. [12] Nov. de cada año. [13] Hombres adultos. [14] Mayo. [15] Excl. las minas de carbón. [16] Nueva clasificación industrial. [17] Industria de Estado. [18] A partir de dic. de 1972: serie revisada. [19] Excl. las canteras.

14 Hours of work in mining and quarrying
Durée du travail dans les industries extractives
Horas de trabajo en las minas y canteras

Hours of work per week   Durée du travail par semaine   Horas de trabajo por semana

				EUROPE — EUROPE — EUROPA					
				Luxembourg [7]		Malta		Pays-Bas [7]	
Date *Date* Fecha	Hongrie [1]	Ireland [4]	Italie	Mining and quarrying *Industries extractives* Minas y canteras	Iron ore mining *Extraction du minerai de fer* Extracción de mineral de hierro	Stone quarrying and clay pits *Carrières de pierre et argile* Canteras de piedra y arcilla	Norway	Coal mining *Mines de charbon* Minas de carbón	
	(a) [2]	*(a)*	*(a)* [6]	*(a)*		*(b)* [9,10]	*(a)* [9]	*(a)*	
1965	178.6	45.7	7.92 [7]	.	.	47.0	36.7	42.4	
1966	177.4	46.1	7.92	45.7	41.1	47.0	36.1	42.2	
1967	173.4	45.5	7.92	42.6	40.6	46.2	36.1	41.9	
1968	165.0	44.7	7.92	43.7	41.5	46.5	35.9	42.1	
1969	161.9	47.6 [5]	7.90	43.8	41.8	46.4	34.8	42.2	
1970	165.7 [3]	47.2	7.87	43.1	41.1	43.8	34.5	42.3	
1971	164.4	48.2	7.91	41.9	39.8	44.3	34.2	42.1	
1972	160.9	47.8	7.55	42.2 [8]	40.4 [8]	44.7	33.8	42.0	
1973	160.2	48.0	7.56	43.1	40.8	...	33.5	41.9	
1974	159.8 *	44.4	7.59 *	...	42.6	...	33.5	...	

			EUROPE — EUROPE — EUROPA			OCEANIA — OCÉANIE — OCEANÍA			
			United Kingdom [7]	Yugoslavia [12]			New Zealand [14]		
Date *Date* Fecha	Portugal [11]	Sweden	Miscellaneous minerals, excl. coal *Minerais divers, non compris le charbon* Minerales varios, excl. el carbón	Coal mining *Mines de charbon* Minas de carbón	Australia [7]	Fiji	Coal mining *Mines de charbon* Minas de carbón	Other mining and quarrying *Autres industries extractives* Otras minas y canteras	URSS [12]
	(a)	*(a)* [2]	*(a)* [9]	*(b)* [2,10]	*(b)* [9,10]	*(a)*	*(a)* [10]		*(a)* [10]
1965	40.8	.	50.8	205	.	.	35.6	47.5	38.9
1966	40.4	.	50.8	197	42.9	.	35.7	46.7	38.9
1967	39.6	.	50.9	192	43.8	.	35.4	36.2	38.9
1968	40.6	149	51.1	190	43.4	.	34.6	45.7	38.9
1969	38.8	144	51.9	180	44.8	.	35.4	47.0	39.0
1970	38.1	143	51.8 [8]	187	44.8	45.5	34.8	47.4	38.6
1971	...	146	49.3	185	44.0	45.4	35.5	45.1	38.8
1972	...	140	49.0	184	43.6 [13]	44.9	36.9	45.5	38.5
1973	...	138	48.8	185	43.9	45.0	37.5	47.4	38.5
1974	...	...	48.0	184 *	42.2 *	...	38.0	47.0	38.7

EXPLANATORY NOTES: See p. 483.   NOTES EXPLICATIVES: Voir p. 485.   NOTAS EXPLICATIVAS: Véase pág. 487.

(a) : Hours actually worked — *Heures réellement effectuées* — Horas efectivamente trabajadas.
(b) : Hours paid for — *Heures rémunérées* — Horas pagadas.

[1] State industry. [2] Per month. [3] Revised series. [4] Sep. of each year, except for 1965-68: Oct. [5] Series replacing former series. [6] Per day. [7] Oct. of each year. [8] New industrial classification. [9] Adult males. [10] Incl. salaried employees. [11] Official estimates. [12] Socialised sector. [13] Scope of series enlarged. [14] April and Oct. of each year.

[1] *Industries d'Etat.* [2] *Par mois.* [3] *Série révisée.* [4] *Sept. de chaque année, sauf pour 1965-1968 : oct.* [5] *Série remplaçant la précédente.* [6] *Par jour.* [7] *Oct. de chaque année.* [8] *Nouvelle classification industrielle.* [9] *Hommes adultes.* [10] *Y compris les employés.* [11] *Evaluations officielles.* [12] *Secteur socialisé.* [13] *Portée de la série élargie.* [14] *Avril et oct. de chaque année.*

[1] Industria de Estado. [2] Por mes. [3] Serie revisada. [4] Sept. de cada año, salvo 1965-1968: oct. [5] Serie que substituye a la anterior. [6] Por día. [7] Oct. de cada año. [8] Nueva clasificación industrial. [9] Hombres adultos. [10] Incl. los empleados. [11] Estimaciones oficiales. [12] Sector socializado. [13] El alcance de la serie es mayor. [14] Abril y oct. de cada año.

15   Hours of work in construction
Durée du travail dans la construction
Horas de trabajo en la construcción

Hours of work per week   Durée du travail par semaine   Horas de trabajo por semana

Date / Date / Fecha	AFRICA — AFRIQUE — AFRICA					AMERICA — AMÉRIQUE — AMÉRICA	
	Algérie [1]	Egypt [2]	Mali	Sierra Leone [4]	South Africa, Rep. of [5]	Barbados	Canada
	(a)	(b)	(a) [3]	(a)	(a) [6]	(a)	(b)
1965	.	53	.	.	47.0	40	41.4
1966	.	50	.	43.0	48.4	42	42.2
1967	.	47	.	43.5	46.8	41	41:3
1968	46.0	52	.	41.6	45.3	44	40.5
1969	45.0	53	.	45.0	46.7	46	39.8
1970	45.0	57	.	55.3	47.6	42	39.2
1971	46.2	...	42.0	47.1	46.1	47	39.2
1972	47.2	...	42.9	50.3	45.5	...	40.1
1973	45.8	...	44.4	42.2	46.7	40	39.5
1974	...	...	45.3	48.6	47.4	...	39.1 *

Date / Date / Fecha	AMERICA — AMÉRIQUE — AMÉRICA					ASIA — ASIE — ASIA	
	El Salvador (San Salvador) [7]	Guyana	México [2]	Perú [8] (Lima-Callao)	United States	Cyprus [2], [9]	Israel
	(b)	(b)	(a)	(a)	(b)	(a)	(a) [11]
1965	43.9	.	53.2	48.2	37.4	43	40.8
1966	43.9	40.5	48.0	47.8	37.6	43	40.5
1967	42.2	41.6	51.2	47.7	37.7	44	38.6 [12]
1968	42.8	43.2	52.4	45.4	37.4	44	41.3
1969	44.3	45.5	50.9	.	37.9	40 [10]	42.0
1970	44.7	49.4	49.7	.	37.4	44	42.2 [13]
1971	44.8	52.6	48.0 *	.	37.3	44	41.9
1972	44.5	50.5	46.0 *	.	36.9	43	42.9
1973	43.2	45.7	...	...	37.1	44	39.2
1974	...	...	...	46.0	36.9	42	39.2

EXPLANATORY NOTES: See p. 483.   NOTES EXPLICATIVES: Voir p. 485.   NOTAS EXPLICATIVAS: Véase pág. 487.

(a) : Hours actually worked — *Heures réellement effectuées* — Horas efectivamente trabajadas.
(b) : Hours paid for — *Heures rémunérées* — Horas pagadas.

[1] April of each year. [2] Oct. of each year. [3] Dec. of each year. [4] Adults only. [5] White manual workers. [6] 1965: Jan.; 1966: Nov.-Dec. [7] Metropolitan area. Males only. [8] June of each year. [9] Adults only. [10] Sep. [11] Incl. salaried employees. [12] Sampling design revised. [13] Industrial classification revised.

[1] *Avril de chaque année.* [2] *Oct. de chaque année.* [3] *Déc. de chaque année.* [4] *Adultes seulement. Mai et nov. de chaque année.* [5] *Travailleurs manuels (population blanche).* [6] *1965 : janv. ; 1966 : nov.-déc.* [7] *Région métropolitaine. Hommes seulement.* [8] *Juin de chaque année.* [9] *Adultes seulement.* [10] *Sept.* [11] *Y compris les employés.* [12] *Plan d'échantillonnage révisé.* [13] *Classification industrielle révisée.*

[1] Abril de cada año. Oct. de cada año. [3] Dic. de cada año. [4] Adultos solamente. Mayo y nov. de cada año. [5] Trabajadores manuales (población blanca). [6] 1965: enero; 1966: nov.-dic. [7] Area metropolitana. Hombres solamente. [8] Junio de cada año. [9] Adultos solamente. [10] Sept. [11] Incl. los empleados. [12] Diseño de la muestra revisado. [13] Clasificación industrial revisada.

15 Hours of work in construction
Durée du travail dans la construction
Horas de trabajo en la construcción

Hours of work per week | Durée du travail par semaine | Horas de trabajo por semana

Date / Date / Fecha	ASIA — ASIE — ASIA					
	Japan	Korea, Rep. of	Philippines 4	Singapore 5	Sri Lanka 7	Thailand (Bangkok)
	(a) 1	(a) 1	(a) 1	(a) 6	(b) 8	(b) 1, 9
1965	47.3	49.6	44.9	48.8	8.1	.
1966	46.9	51.8	47.5	47.2	7.9	43.9
1967	46.6 2	53.5	49.2	50.7	8.1	48.5
1968	46.8	54.6	47.3	43.5	7.9	46.4
1969	46.2	53.3	46.7	49.3	8.0	45.8
1970	46.0 2	47.3 3	...	48.5	8.0	48.4
1971	46.1	51.2	46.5	50.6	8.0	46.0
1972	46.1	48.8	46.5	49.9	8.0	...
1973	45.5 2	47.8	45.1	53.2	7.5	...
1974	44.3	...	...	48.7	8.5	...

Date / Date / Fecha	EUROPE — EUROPE — EUROPA					
	Austria	Belgique 10	España	France	Germany, Fed. Rep. of △ 13	Gibraltar 15
	(b)	(a)	(a) 1	(a)	(b) 14	(b)
1965	.	.	46.3	49.9	44.8	.
1966	.	43.2	44.3	49.8	44.6	.
1967	.	43.1	45.4	49.3	43.6	.
1968	.	43.0	45.9	49.0	44.1	.
1969	.	43.0	46.5	49.1	44.6	.
1970	38.6	41.3	45.7	49.0	44.7	53.8
1971	38.1	41.3	45.0	48.6	44.1	54.4
1972	37.9	41.3 11	45.9	48.1 12	43.6	52.0
1973	37.4	39.8	46.1	47.9	43.1 2	54.4
1974	37.1	37.3	46.0	47.2	42.0	52.2

EXPLANATORY NOTES: See p. 483.   NOTES EXPLICATIVES: Voir p. 485.   NOTAS EXPLICATIVAS: Véase pág. 487.

(a) : Hours actually worked — *Heures réellement effectuées* — Horas efectivamente trabajadas.
(b) : Hours paid for — *Heures rémunérées* — Horas pagadas.

1 Incl. salaried employees. 2 Sampling design revised. 3 Series replacing former series. 4 May of each year. 5 July of each year. 6 Beginning 1969: adults only. 7 Building only. March and Sep. of each year. 8 Per day. 9 Sep. of each year, except for 1967: July, and 1969: Oct. 10 Oct. of each year. 11 New industrial classification. 12 Beginning Dec. 1972: revised series. 13 Building only. 14 Males only. 15 April and Oct. of each year, except for 1973: Oct., and 1974: April.

1 *Y compris les employés.* 2 *Plan d'échantillonnage révisé.* 3 *Série remplaçant la précédente.* 4 *Mai de chaque année.* 5 *Juillet de chaque année.* 6 *A partir de 1969: adultes seulement.* 7 *Bâtiment seulement. Mars et sept. de chaque année.* 8 *Par jour.* 9 *Sept. de chaque année, sauf pour 1967: juillet, et 1969: oct.* 10 *Oct. de chaque année.* 11 *Nouvelle classification industrielle.* 12 *A partir de déc. 1972: série révisée.* 13 *Bâtiment seulement.* 14 *Hommes seulement.* 15 *Avril et oct. de chaque année, sauf pour 1973: oct., et 1974: avril.*

1 Incl. los empleados. 2 Diseño de la muestra revisado. 3 Serie que substituye a la anterior. 4 Mayo de cada año. 5 Julio de cada año. 6 A partir de 1969: adultos solamente. 7 Edificación solamente. Marzo y sept. de cada año, salvo 1967: julio, y 1969: oct. 10 Oct. de cada año. 11 Nueva clasificación industrial. 12 A partir de dic. de 1972: serie revisada. 13 Edificación solamente. 14 Hombres solamente. 15 Abril y oct. de cada año, salvo 1973: oct., y 1974: abril.

15 Hours of work in construction
Durée du travail dans la construction
Horas de trabajo en la construcción

Hours of work per week | Durée du travail par semaine | Horas de trabajo por semana

Date / Date / Fecha	EUROPE — EUROPE — EUROPA						
	Hongrie [1]	Ireland [4]		Italie	Luxembourg [8]	Malta	Pays-Bas [8]
	(a) [2]	(a) [5]	(a) [6]	(a) [7]	(a)	(b) [10, 11]	(a)
1965	186.0	.	.	6.87	.	47.0	46.3
1966	186.9	.	.	7.60	52.6	47.5	46.1
1967	185.9	.	.	7.47	52.3	47.2	46.2
1968	179.5	.	.	7.62	49 6	46.8	45.3
1969	168.4	48.6	47.9	7.62	49.0	46.4	45.4
1970	170.3 [3]	46.6	46.6	7.68	50.4	45.9	44.3
1971	168.9	47.6	47.7	7.78	50.6	45.8	44.1
1972	166.0	46.7	46.3	7.50	50.7 [9]	44.5	43.8
1973	164.7	47.1	46.5	7.52	51.4	...	42.7
1974	164.4 *	45.7	45.5	7.54 *	48.4	...	...

Date / Date / Fecha	EUROPE — EUROPE — EUROPA			OCEANIA — OCÉANIE — OCEANÍA			URSS [12]
	Suisse	United Kingdom [8]	Yugoslavia [12]	Australia [8]	Fiji	New Zealand [14]	
	(b)	(a) [11]	(b) [2, 10]	(b) [10, 11]	(a)	(a) [10]	(a) [10]
1965	47.1	49.8	200	.	.	44.5	40.9
1966	47.1	48.5	199	44.5	.	44.5	41.0
1967	46.6	48.3	194	43.6	.	43.7	40.9
1968	46.5	47.8	192	45 2	.	43.0	40.6
1969	46.6	48.2	190	44.6	.	44.3	40.7
1970	46.3	47.5 [9]	187	44.8	44.2	44.1	40.9
1971	46.4	47.2	182	45.6	44.4	43.6	40.8
1972	46.7	47.0	184	42.9 [13]	44.0	43.4	40.9
1973	46.6	47.2	184	42.4	44.2	44.3	40.9
1974	46.1	46.8	184 *	41.8 *	...	44.1	40.7

EXPLANATORY NOTES: See p. 483. | NOTES EXPLICATIVES: Voir p. 485. | NOTAS EXPLICATIVAS: Véase pág. 487.

(a) : Hours actually worked — *Heures réellement effectuées* — Horas efectivamente trabajadas.
(b) : Hours paid for — *Heures rémunérées* — Horas pagadas.

[1] State industry. [2] Per month. [3] Revised series. [4] Sep. of each year. Private sector only. [5] Skilled workers. [6] Semi-skilled and unskilled workers. [7] Per day. [8] Oct. of each year. [9] New industrial classification. [10] Incl. salaried employees. [11] Adult males. [12] Socialised sector. [13] Scope of series enlarged [14] April and Oct. of each year.

[1] *Industrie d'Etat.* [2] *Par mois.* [3] *Série révisée.* [4] *Sept. de chaque année. Secteur privé seulement.* [5] *Ouvriers qualifiés.* [6] *Ouvriers semi-qualifiés et non qualifiés.* [7] *Par jour.* [8] *Oct. de chaque année.* [9] *Nouvelle classification industrielle.* [10] *Y compris les employés.* [11] *Hommes adultes.* [12] *Secteur socialisé.* [13] *Portée de la série élargie.* [14] *Avril et oct. de chaque année.*

[1] Industria de Estado. [2] Por mes. [3] Serie revisada. [4] Sept. de cada año. Sector privado solamente. [5] Obreros calificados. [6] Obreros semicalificados y no calificados. [7] Por día. [8] Oct. de cada año. [9] Nueva clasificación industrial. [10] Incl. los empleados. [11] Hombres adultos. [12] Sector socializado. [13] El alcance de la serie es mayor. [14] Abril y oct. de cada año.

16 Hours of work in transport, storage and communication (Excl. sea transport)
Durée du travail dans les transports, entrepôts et communications (Non compris les transports par mer)
Horas de trabajo en los transportes, almacenaje y comunicaciones (Excl. el transporte marítimo)

Hours of work per week Durée du travail par semaine Horas de trabajo por semana

Date / Date / Fecha	AFRICA — AFRIQUE — AFRICA				AMERICA — AMÉRIQUE — AMÉRICA			
	Algérie [1]	Egypt [2]	Mali	Sierra Leone [4]	Barbados	Canada — Local transport / Transports locaux / Transportes locales	Guyana	México [2] — Transport / Transports / Transportes
	(a)	(b)	(a) [3]	(a)	(a)	(b)	(b)	(a)
1965	.	59	.	.	42	42.8	.	...
1966	.	58	.	45.8	41	42.9	49.3	...
1967	.	51	.	45.7	43	42.8	45.6	...
1968	44.0	54	.	42.8	42	41.5	47.1	...
1969	47.5	56	.	52.0	42	41.7	43.7	48
1970	44.8	59	.	46.6	43	42.0	49.5	48
1971	45.0	...	42.3	58.6	42	41.9	48.6	48 *
1972	47.5	...	40.0	49.5	...	42.1	48.5	50 *
1973	43.8	...	...	55.9	41	41.9	47.7	...
1974	...	...	42.4	45.3	...	41.6 *	...	...

Date / Date / Fecha	AMERICA — AMÉRIQUE — AMÉRICA			ASIA — ASIE — ASIA			
	Perú (Lima-Callao) [5] — Transport / Transports / Transportes	United States — Principal railways / Grandes lignes de chemin de fer / Líneas principales de ferrocarriles	United States — Local railways and buses [6] / Chemins de fer et autobus locaux [6] / Ferrocarriles y autobuses locales [6]	Burma [7] — Transport / Transports / Transportes	Cyprus [2,11] — Transport / Transports / Transportes	Israel	Japan
	(a)	(b)	(b)	(a) [8]	(a)	(a) [13]	(a) [13]
1965	62.9	43 6	42.1	8.0	62	41.9	45.6
1966	52.2	43.9	42.4	8.0	57	42.2	45.4
1967	51.1	43.2	42.2	8.0	59	39.6 [14]	45.3 [14]
1968	47.3	43.9	42.0	8.0	60	41.4	45.3
1969	.	44.2	42.2	7.9	61 [12]	42.0	44.6
1970	.	44.2	42.1	7.6	50	42.8 [15]	44.2 [14]
1971	.	43.2	41.8	7.7	50	42.7	43.7
1972	.	43.9	41.5	7.9 [9]	47	42.8	43.6
1973	.	44.5	41.4	7.9 [10]	47	39.0	43.9 [14]
1974	47.0	44.0	40.7	...	45	39.7	42.7

EXPLANATORY NOTES: See p. 483. NOTES EXPLICATIVES: Voir p. 485. NOTAS EXPLICATIVAS: Véase pág. 487.

(a): Hours actually worked — Heures réellement effectuées — Horas efectivamente trabajadas.
(b): Hours paid for — Heures rémunérées — Horas pagadas.

[1] April of each year. [2] Oct. of each year. [3] Dec. of each year. [4] Incl. sea transport. Adults only. May and Nov. of each year. [5] June of each year. [6] Excl. government-operated transport. [7] Incl. sea transport. Workers engaged for less than 30 days (excl. casual workers). [8] Per day. [9] April and Sep. [10] March and Sep. [11] Adults only. [12] Sep. [13] Incl. salaried employees. [14] Sampling design revised. [15] Industrial classification revised.

[1] Avril de chaque année. [2] Oct. de chaque année. [3] Déc. de chaque année. [4] Y compris les transports par mer. Adultes seulement. Mai et nov. de chaque année. [5] Juin de chaque année. [6] Non compris les transports gérés par le gouvernement. [7] Y compris les transports par mer. Travailleurs engagés pour moins de 30 jours (non compris les travailleurs occasionnels). [8] Par jour. [9] Avril et sept. [10] Mars et sept. [11] Adultes seulement. [12] Sept. [13] Y compris les employés. [14] Plan d'échantillonnage révisé. [15] Classification industrielle révisée.

[1] Abril de cada año. [2] Oct. de cada año. [3] Dic. de cada año. [4] Incl. el transporte marítimo. Adultos solamente. Mayo y nov. de cada año. [5] Junio de cada año. [6] Excl. los transportes administrados por el Gobierno. [7] Incl. el transporte marítimo. Trabajadores ocupados durante menos de 30 días (excl. los trabajadores ocasionales). [8] Por día. [9] Abril y sept. [10] Marzo y sept. [11] Adultos solamente. [12] Sept. [13] Incl. los empleados. [14] Diseño de la muestra revisado. [15] Clasificación industrial revisada.

16 Hours of work in transport, storage and communication (Excl. sea transport)
Durée du travail dans les transports, entrepôts et communications (Non compris les transports par mer)
Horas de trabajo en los transportes, almacenaje y comunicaciones (Excl. el transporte marítimo)

Hours of work per week · Durée du travail par semaine · Horas de trabajo por semana

Date / Date / Fecha	ASIA — ASIE — ASIA						EUROPE — EUROPE — EUROPA	
	Korea, Rep. of	Malaysia [3] / West Malaysia / Road haulage / Camionnage / Camionaje	Philippines [5] / Transport and communication [6] / Transports et communications [6] / Transportes y comunicaciones [6]	Singapore [3,6]	Sri Lanka [8] / Transport / Transports / Transportes	Thailand [10] (Bangkok)	France [11]	Gibraltar [13]
	(a) [1]	(a) [4]	(a) [1]	(a) [7]	(b) [9]	(b) [1]	(a)	(b)
1965	63.4	208	49.2	49.1	9.1	.	47.7	.
1966	63.8	208	52.9	46.4	9.1	51.1	47.7	.
1967	63.9	.	53.8	47.9	9.6	44.6	47.6	.
1968	64.6	.	53.1	48.1	9.3	43.1	47.1	.
1969	61.5	.	51.2	47.8	9.0	49.3	46.5	.
1970	53.7 [2]	.	...	47.7	9.0	45.4	45.8	48.6
1971	55.5	215	52.6	48.4	9.5	44.6	45.2 [12]	49.2
1972	50.8	213	50.0	43.2	9.2	...	44.1	48.8
1973	51.3	213	48.3	45.8	9.0	...	43.5	50.0 [14]
1974	...	213	...	47.5	8.9	...	42.8	46.8 [15]

Date / Date / Fecha	EUROPE — EUROPE — EUROPA				OCEANIA — OCÉANIE — OCEANÍA		
	Malta / Transport / Transports / Transportes	Pays-Bas [17] / Transport / Transports / Transportes	United Kingdom [17,18]	Yugoslavia [6,20]	Australia [6,17]	Fiji	New Zealand [13] / Transport and communication / Transports et communications / Transportes y comunicaciones
	(b) [1,16]	(a)	(a) [16]	(b) [1,4]	(b) [1,16]	(a)	(a) [1]
1965	52.5	48.2	.	212	.	.	42.7
1966	50.0	48.0	50.3	208	46.4	.	43.0
1967	51.2	47.5	50.0	199	46.6	.	41.7
1968	48.0	46.9	50.4	188	45.8	.	41.2
1969	45.8	46.4	50.7	188	46.6	.	41.5
1970	45.4	45.6	49.2 [19]	189	46.1	43.8	41.5
1971	46.1	45.0	48.0	187	44.9	44.4	41.0
1972	47.7	44.9	48.5	188	42.5 [21]	44.3	40.9
1973	...	44.4	49.6	188	43.3	44.8	41.7
1974	...	...	49.5	188 *	42.0 *	...	42.1

EXPLANATORY NOTES: See p. 483. · NOTES EXPLICATIVES: Voir p. 485. · NOTAS EXPLICATIVAS: Véase pág. 487.

(a) : Hours actually worked — *Heures réellement effectuées* — Horas efectivamente trabajadas.
(b) : Hours paid for — *Heures rémunérées* — Horas pagadas.

[1] Incl. salaried employees. [2] Series replacing former series. [3] July of each year. [4] Per month. [5] May of each year. [6] Incl. sea transport. [7] Beginning 1969: adults only. [8] March and Sep. of each year. [9] Per day. [10] Sep. of each year, except for 1967: July and 1969: Oct. [11] Excl. communication. [12] Beginning Dec. 1972: revised series. [13] April and Oct. of each year. [14] Oct. [15] April. [16] Adult males. [17] Oct. of each year. [18] Excl. railways. Excl. London Transport. [19] New industrial classification. [20] Socialised sector. [21] Scope of series enlarged. 1966-71: excl. communication.

[1] *Y compris les employés.* [2] *Série remplaçant la précédente.* [3] *Juillet de chaque année.* [4] *Par mois.* [5] *Mai de chaque année.* [6] *Y compris les transports par mer.* [7] *A partir de 1969: adultes seulement.* [8] *Mars et sept. de chaque année.* [9] *Par jour.* [10] *Sept. de chaque année, sauf pour 1967: juillet, et 1969: oct.* [11] *Non compris les communications.* [12] *A partir de déc. 1972: série révisée.* [13] *Avril et oct. de chaque année.* [14] *Oct.* [15] *Avril.* [16] *Hommes adultes.* [17] *Oct. de chaque année.* [18] *Non compris les chemins de fer. Non compris les services de transports londoniens.* [19] *Nouvelle classification industrielle.* [20] *Secteur socialisé.* [21] *Portée de la série élargie. 1966-1971: non compris les communications.*

[1] Incl. los empleados. [2] Serie que substituye a la anterior. [3] Julio de cada año. [4] Por mes. [5] Mayo de cada año. [6] Incl. el transporte marítimo. [7] A partir de 1969: adultos solamente. [8] Marzo y sept. de cada año. [9] Por día. [10] Sept. de cada año, salvo 1967: julio, y 1969: oct. [11] Excl. las comunicaciones. [12] A partir de dic. de 1972: serie revisada. [13] Abril y oct. de cada año. [14] Oct. [15] Abril. [16] Hombres adultos. [17] Oct. de cada año. [18] Excl. los ferrocarriles. Excl. los transportes londinenses. [19] Nueva clasificación industrial. [20] Sector socializado. [21] El alcance de la serie es mayor. 1966-1971: excl. las comunicaciones.

Labour productivity
Productivité du travail
Productividad del trabajo

Labour productivity

Tables 17 A, 17 B and 17 C show indices on labour productivity, defined as the ratio of output to the corresponding input of labour. Labour productivity indices reflect changes in this ratio over time for the whole of the economic unit concerned.

Labour productivity data are obtained indirectly by relating output statistics to statistics on labour input; when making international comparisons of labour productivity indices allowance should therefore be made for the influence of differences from one country to another in the methods of measuring output and labour input.[1]

It should also be borne in mind when interpreting these figures that labour input is but one of a number of factors contributing to production, and that variations in the output-labour input ratio are due to the influence of all production factors; thus any change in techniques, in the industrial structure, in social conditions or in the general economic situation may affect labour productivity. For instance, a change in the relative importance of the industries making up an economic sector may lead to a rise or fall in the labour productivity for that sector, even though labour productivity has not varied in any one of the industries concerned.

product, and national income. The computations may be based on market prices or factor costs.[2] Obviously, the results of the computations of national output measured in accordance with these different concepts may vary considerably; nevertheless, the effect of these differences is appreciably attenuated when, as in the present case, *variations over time* in the level of national output are concerned.

Labour input is measured in terms either of the number of persons employed or of the number of hours worked by the economically active population. These data are calculated from statistics, which are more or less complete, obtained from different sources: population censuses, labour force sample surveys, social security schemes, labour registration. Labour productivity indices based on one and the same measure of labour input (number of persons employed or number of hours of work) are relatively suitable for comparison, even though the definition of the total number of persons employed may or may not, depending on the country, cover domestic servants, casual workers, part-time workers, homeworkers or the armed forces, and evaluations based on hours of work may refer either to hours actually worked or to hours paid for.

Table 17 A

Indices of labour productivity—National economy

Labour productivity indices for the whole of the national economy are shown in table 17 A. The volume of national production, used as the numerator in these series, is calculated on the basis of data derived from national accounts. The most frequently used concepts are gross or net domestic product, gross or net national

Tables 17 B and 17 C

Indices of labour productivity—Industrial sector and manufacturing

Except where otherwise indicated in a footnote, the indices shown in table 17 B relate to labour productivity for the whole industrial sector, i.e. mining and quarrying, manufacturing, electricity, gas and steam and water supply. Labour productivity indices for manufacturing are shown separately in table 17 C.

---

[1] For a study of the problems of definition, computation methods, etc., see ILO: *Measuring Labour Productivity*, Studies and Reports, New Series, No. 75 (Geneva, 1969).

[2] For definitions of the various concepts and methods of measurement see United Nations: *A System of National Accounts*, Studies in Methods, Series F, No. 2, Rev. 3 (New York, 1968).

The production indices used in compiling these data are generally derived from statistics of industrial production. The majority of countries measure the variation in *net* production, taking account only of the value added by each industry. Series covering production in individual industries, based on quantities produced or other indicators (value of output, turnover, quantity of raw materials used), are weighted by the value added for that industry or by the number of hours worked. Some countries, however, measure the variation in *gross* production, generally obtained by aggregating the value (adjusted to take account of price changes) of finished and semi-finished products and services of an industrial nature furnished by all the undertakings covered by the surveys. Labour productivity indices based on gross production cannot be compared with those based on net production.

Labour input is generally measured in terms of employment or hours of work statistics derived from the same sources as the output data. Although the number of persons may refer to persons employed, to employees, to wage earners or to production workers, and the number of hours may refer to hours worked by wage earners or by all employees, or to hours paid for, labour productivity indices based on one and the same measure of labour input (number of persons employed or number of hours of work) are relatively suitable for comparison.

Productivité du travail

Les tableaux 17 A, 17 B et 17 C présentent des indices de la productivité du travail, définie comme le rapport de la production à la quantité de travail dépensée pour obtenir cette production. Les indices de la productivité du travail mesurent l'évolution de ce rapport au cours du temps pour un ensemble économique donné.

Les données relatives à la productivité du travail sont obtenues de manière indirecte, en rapportant des statistiques relatives à la production à des statistiques relatives au travail, et, lors des comparaisons internationales des indices de la productivité du travail, il y a lieu de tenir compte de l'influence sur les données des différences d'un pays à un autre dans les méthodes de mesure de la production et du travail [1].

Il faut d'autre part se souvenir, dans l'interprétation de ces chiffres, que le travail n'est qu'un des facteurs qui contribuent à la production, et que la variation du rapport de la production au travail est due aux influences de l'ensemble des facteurs de production: ainsi, toute modification des moyens techniques, de la structure industrielle, des conditions sociales ou de la situation économique en général peut exercer une influence sur la productivité du travail. Par exemple, une modification dans l'importance relative des industries composant un secteur économique peut entraîner un accroissement ou une diminution de la productivité du travail de ce secteur, même si la productivité du travail n'a varié dans aucune des industries considérées.

Tableau 17 A

Indices de la productivité du travail: Economie nationale

Les indices de la productivité du travail relatifs à l'ensemble de l'économie nationale sont présentés dans le tableau 17 A. Le volume de la production nationale, utilisé comme numéra-teur dans ces séries, est évalué à partir des données fournies par la comptabilité nationale. Les concepts le plus souvent utilisés sont le produit intérieur brut ou net, le produit national brut ou net, et le revenu national. Les évaluations peuvent être faites aux prix du marché ou au coût des facteurs [2]. Les mesures de la production nationale qui résultent de l'application de ces divers concepts sont évidemment différentes; néanmoins, l'influence de ces différences s'atténue sensiblement lorsqu'il s'agit, comme c'est ici le cas, de mesurer les *variations* dans le temps du niveau de la production nationale.

Le travail fourni est mesuré soit par le nombre de personnes employées, soit par le nombre d'heures de travail effectuées par l'ensemble de la population active. Ces données sont évaluées sur la base de statistiques plus ou moins complètes, fondées sur des sources diverses: recensements de la population, enquêtes par sondage sur la main-d'œuvre, systèmes de sécurité sociale, enregistrements de la main-d'œuvre. Les indices de la productivité du travail fondés sur une même mesure du travail (nombre de personnes, d'une part, ou nombre d'heures de travail, d'autre part) sont relativement comparables, bien que la définition du nombre total de personnes employées couvre ou ne comprenne pas, suivant les pays, le personnel domestique, les travailleurs occasionnels, les travailleurs à temps partiel, les travailleurs à domicile ou les forces armées, et que, dans les évaluations relatives aux heures de travail, il puisse s'agir soit des heures effectuées, soit des heures payées.

Tableaux 17 B et 17 C

Indices de la productivité du travail: Secteur industriel et industries manufacturières

Les indices présentés dans le tableau 17 B se rapportent, sauf exception indiquée en bas de

---

[1] Pour l'étude des problèmes relatifs aux définitions, aux méthodes de calcul, etc., voir BIT: *La mesure de la productivité du travail*, Etudes et documents, nouvelle série, n° 75 (Genève, 1969).

[2] Voir les définitions des divers concepts et des méthodes de mesure dans Nations Unies: *Système de comptabilité nationale*, Etudes méthodologiques, série F, n° 2, rev. 3 (New York, 1970).

page, à la productivité du travail de l'ensemble du secteur industriel, c'est-à-dire des industries extractives, des industries manufacturières, de l'électricité, de la production et de la distribution du gaz et de la vapeur et de la distribution publique de l'eau. Les indices de la productivité du travail dans l'ensemble des industries manufacturières sont présentés séparément dans le tableau 17 C.

Les indices de la production utilisés pour établir ces données sont généralement tirés des statistiques de la production industrielle. La plupart des pays mesurent la variation de la production *nette*, en tenant compte seulement de la valeur ajoutée par chaque industrie. Les séries relatives à la production de chaque industrie, fondées sur les quantités physiques produites ou sur d'autres indicateurs (valeur de la production, chiffre d'affaires, quantité de matières premières utilisées), sont pondérées par la valeur ajoutée correspondant à cette industrie ou par le nombre d'heures de travail effectuées. Certains pays mesurent cependant la variation de la production *brute*, obtenue en général en additionnant la valeur (corrigée pour tenir compte des variations des prix) des produits finis, des produits semi-finis et des services à caractère industriel de toutes les entreprises couvertes par les enquêtes. Les indices de la productivité du travail fondés sur la production brute ne sont pas comparables à ceux qui sont fondés sur la production nette.

Le travail est en général mesuré à l'aide de statistiques de l'emploi ou de la durée du travail dérivées des mêmes sources que les données sur la production. Bien que le nombre de personnes puisse correspondre aux personnes occupées, aux salariés, aux ouvriers, ou aux ouvriers affectés à la production, et que le nombre d'heures de travail puisse correspondre aux heures effectuées par les ouvriers ou par l'ensemble des salariés, ou aux heures payées, les indices de la productivité du travail fondés sur une même mesure du travail (nombre de personnes, d'une part, ou nombre d'heures de travail, d'autre part) sont relativement comparables.

Productividad del trabajo

Los cuadros 17 A, 17 B y 17 C presentan los índices de la productividad del trabajo, definida ésta como la razón entre la producción y la cantidad de trabajo empleada para obtener dicha producción. Los índices de la productividad del trabajo miden la evolución de esta razón a través del tiempo en un conjunto económico determinado.

Los datos relativos a la productividad del trabajo se obtienen en forma indirecta, relacionando las estadísticas sobre la producción con las estadísticas relativas al trabajo, y al efectuar comparaciones internacionales de los índices de la productividad del trabajo hay que considerar la influencia que pueden tener sobre las cifras las diferencias de un país a otro en los métodos de medición de la producción y del trabajo [1].

Por otra parte, hay que recordar, al interpretar estas cifras, que el trabajo es tan sólo uno de los factores que contribuyen a la producción, y que la variación de la razón entre la producción y el trabajo puede deberse a las influencias de los demás factores de producción; así, toda modificación de los medios técnicos, de la estructura industrial, de las condiciones sociales y de la situación económica en general puede tener influencia sobre la productividad del trabajo. Por ejemplo, la modificación de la importancia relativa de las industrias que componen un sector económico puede ocasionar un aumento o una disminución de la productividad del trabajo en dicho sector, aunque no haya variado la productividad del trabajo en ninguna de las industrias consideradas.

Cuadro 17 A

Indices de la productividad del trabajo: Economía nacional

En el cuadro 17 A se presentan los índices de la productividad del trabajo relativos al conjunto de la economía nacional. El volumen de la producción nacional, que se utiliza como numerador en estas series, es evaluado a partir de los datos proporcionados por la contabilidad nacional. Los conceptos que se utilizan con más frecuencia son el producto interior bruto o neto, el producto nacional bruto o neto y la renta nacional. Las evaluaciones pueden hacerse sea a precios del mercado o según el costo de los factores [2]. Las medidas de la producción nacional que provienen de la aplicación de estos diversos conceptos son evidentemente diferentes; sin embargo, el efecto de tales diferencias se ve considerablemente disminuido cuando se trata, como ocurre en este caso, de medir las *variaciones* a través del tiempo del nivel de la producción nacional.

El trabajo proporcionado se mide ya sea por el número de personas empleadas o por el número de horas de trabajo efectuadas por el conjunto de la población activa. Estos datos se evalúan a base de estadísticas más o menos completas que provienen de diversas fuentes: censos de población, encuestas por muestreo de la mano de obra, sistemas de seguro social, registros de la mano de obra. Los índices de la productividad del trabajo que se basan sobre una misma medida del trabajo (ya sea número de personas o número de horas de trabajo) son relativamente comparables, a pesar de que la definición del número total de personas empleadas pueda comprender o no, según los países, el personal de servicio doméstico, los trabajadores ocasionales, los trabajadores a tiempo parcial, los trabajadores a domicilio o las fuerzas armadas, y que las evaluaciones respecto a las horas de trabajo pueden referirse a las horas efectuadas o a las horas pagadas.

---

[1] Para el estudio de los problemas relativos a las definiciones, métodos de cálculo, etc., véase OIT:

Métodos para las estadísticas de la productividad del trabajo, Estudios y documentos, nueva serie, núm. 18 (Ginebra, 1951), y *La mesure de la productivité du travail*, Etudes et documents, nouvelle série, n° 75 (Ginebra, 1969; en inglés y francés solamente).

[2] Véanse las definiciones de los diversos conceptos y métodos de medición en Naciones Unidas: *Un sistema de cuentas nacionales*, Estudios de métodos, serie F, núm. 2, rev. 3 (Nueva York, 1970).

Cuadros 17 B y 17 C

Indices de la productividad del trabajo: Sector industrial e industrias manufactureras

Salvo las excepciones indicadas en notas al pie de página, los índices que se presentan en el cuadro 17 B se refieren a la productividad del trabajo del conjunto del sector industrial, es decir, las industrias extractivas, las industrias manufactureras, las industrias de la electricidad, de producción y de distribución de gas y de vapor y de la distribución pública de agua. Los índices de la productividad del trabajo del conjunto de las industrias manufactureras se presentan por separado en el cuadro 17 C.

Los índices de la producción que se utilizan para establecer estos datos se han obtenido generalmente de las estadísticas de la producción industrial. La mayoría de los países calculan la variación de la producción *neta* teniendo en cuenta tan sólo el valor añadido para cada industria. Las series relativas a la producción de cada industria, que se basan sobre cantidades físicas producidas o sobre otros índices (valor de la producción, monto de los negocios, cantidad de materias primas utilizadas), son ponderadas por el valor añadido que corresponde a cada industria o por el número de horas de trabajo efectuadas. Sin embargo, algunos países miden la variación de la producción *bruta* obtenida, por lo general, añadiendo el valor (que se halla corregido para tener cuenta de las variaciones de precios) de los productos terminados, de los productos semiterminados y de los servicios de carácter industrial de todas las empresas comprendidas en las encuestas. Los índices de la productividad del trabajo que se basan en la producción bruta no pueden compararse con aquellos establecidos a partir de la producción neta.

El trabajo es calculado por lo general a partir de estadísticas del empleo o de la duración del trabajo obtenidas de las mismas fuentes que los datos sobre la producción. Aunque el número de personas pueda corresponder a las personas ocupadas, a los asalariados, a los obreros o a los obreros destinados a la producción, y aunque el número de horas de trabajo pueda referirse a las horas efectuadas por los obreros o por el conjunto de los asalariados, o a las horas pagadas, son relativamente comparables los índices de la productividad del trabajo que se basan sobre una misma medida del trabajo (número de personas, por una parte, y número de horas de trabajo, por otra).

17 A

Indices of labour productivity
Indices de la productivité du travail
Indices de la productividad del trabajo

National economy
Economie nationale
Economía nacional

(1970 = 100)

Country — Pays — País	Code Code Clave	1965	1966	1967	1968	1969	1970	1971	1972	1973	1974
AFRICA — AFRIQUE AFRICA											
Zambia	A/2	.	95	97	97	97	**100**	93	101	97	...
AMERICA — AMÉRIQUE AMÉRICA											
Bolivia	A/1 [1]	83	87	90	95	97	**100**	101	104	108	111
»	B/1 [1]	82	86	88	94	96	**100**	103	106	...	...
Canada	A/1 [2]	86	89	90	95	98	**100**	105	108	111	...
»	A/5 [2]	81	86	87	93	97	**100**	105	109	112	...
Chile	A/1	95	99	97	98	99	**100**	...	...	...	...
»	B/1	93	98	97	97	99	**100**	...	...	...	...
Ecuador	A/. [3]	91	92	95	97	98	**100**	98 *	104 *	117 *	...
México	A/. [3]	76	81	84	90	94	**100**	...	...	...	...
Panamá	.[4]/1	86	87	91	92	97	**100**	107	110	114	113 *
»	.[5]/1	86	87	91	93	97	**100**	107	110	115	115 *
United States [6]	A/1	92	96	97	100	101	**100**	103	107	109	105
» » [6]	A/5 [7]	88	92	94	98	99	**100**	104	107	110	105
» » [6]	A/5 [8]	90	94	96	99	99	**100**	104	108	110	107
ASIA — ASIE ASIA											
Israel	A/1	75	77	.	86	94	**100**	106	114	122	126
»	A/5	76	77	.	86	94	**100**	107	113	123	127
Japan	A/1	62	67	74	83	91	**100**	107	116	125	124
Philippines	B/1	.	.	81	84	98	**100**	94	92	99	95 *
Singapore	A/1	70	75	80	87	94	**100**	106	115	118	123 *

EXPLANATORY NOTES: See p. 567.   NOTES EXPLICATIVES: Voir p. 569.   NOTAS EXPLICATIVAS: Véase pág. 571.

A: Gross national or domestic product
Produit national ou intérieur brut
Producto nacional o interno bruto

B: Net national or domestic product
Produit national ou intérieur net
Producto nacional o interno neto

C: Gross production
Production brute
Producción bruta

D: Net production
Production nette
Producción neta

Per
Par
Por

1: Employed person — *Personne employée* — Persona ocupada.
2: Worker or employee — *Travailleur ou salarié* — Trabajador o asalariado.
3: Wage earner — *Ouvrier* — Obrero.
4: Man-day — *Jour-homme* — Día-hombre.
5: Man-hour — *Heure-homme* — Hora-hombre.

[1] Official estimates. [2] Excl. public administration. [3] Per economically active person. [4] Gross national product. [5] Gross domestic product. [6] Private economy and certain governmental sectors. [7] Based on estimated number of hours worked. [8] Based on estimated number of hours paid for.

[1] *Evaluations officielles.* [2] *Non compris l'administration publique.* [3] *Par personne économiquement active.* [4] *Produit national brut.* [5] *Produit intérieur brut.* [6] *Economie privée et certains secteurs gouvernementaux.* [7] *Fondés sur le nombre estimé des heures de travail effectuées.* [8] *Fondés sur le nombre estimé des heures de travail rémunérées.*

[1] Estimaciones oficiales. [2] Excl. la administración pública. [3] Por persona económicamente activa. [4] Producto nacional bruto. [5] Producto interno bruto. [6] Economía privada y ciertos sectores gubernamentales. [7] Basados en una estimación del número de horas de trabajo efectuadas. [8] Basados en una estimación del número de horas de trabajo remuneradas.

17 Indices of labour productivity
Indices de la productivité du travail
Indices de la productividad del trabajo

A National economy
Economie nationale
Economía nacional

(1970 = 100)

Country — Pays — País	Code Code Clave	1965	1966	1967	1968	1969	1970	1971	1972	1973	1974
EUROPE — EUROPE EUROPA											
Austria	A/1	75	80	82	87	93	**100**	105	111	116	120
Belgique	A/1	81	83	86	90	95	**100**	102	108	...	...
Czechoslovakia	.¹/2	78	84	88	92	97	**100**	104	109	113	...
Denmark	A/1	84	85	88	92	98	**100**	103	108	111	113
»	B/1	85	86	88	93	99	**100**	103	108	110	111
Finland	A/1	82	83	86	89	95	**100**	104	110	114 *	117 *
France	.²/5	77	80	84	90	95	**100**	105	113 *	120 *	124 *
Germany, Fed. Rep. of △	A/1	79	81	84	90	96	**100**	103	106 *	112 *	114 *
» » » △	B/1	80	82	84	90	96	**100**	102	105 *	110 *	112 *
Ireland	A/1	81	82	87	93	96	**100**	106	111	118	...
Italie	A/1	75	81	85	91	96	**100**	102	106	112	115
»	B/1	75	81	85	91	96	**100**	102	106	113	115
Luxembourg	A/1	85	86	87	92	99	**100**	98	100 *	105 *	108 *
Malta	A/1	71	76	79	85	92	**100**	99 *	...	...	...
Norway	A/1	83	87	91	94	98	**100**	104	108	112	116
»	B/1	83	86	90	94	98	**100**	104	108	112	115

EXPLANATORY NOTES: See p. 567.   NOTES EXPLICATIVES: Voir p. 569.   NOTAS EXPLICATIVAS: Véase pág. 571.

A: Gross national or domestic product
Produit national ou intérieur brut
Producto nacional o interno bruto

B: Net national or domestic product
Produit national ou intérieur net
Producto nacional o interno neto

C: Gross production
Production brute
Producción bruta

D: Net production
Production nette
Producción neta

Per
Par
Por

1: Employed person — *Personne employée* — Persona ocupada.
2: Worker or employee — *Travailleur ou salarié* — Trabajador o asalariado.
3: Wage earner — *Ouvrier* — Obrero.
4: Man-day — *Jour-homme* — Día-hombre.
5: Man-hour — *Heure-homme* — Hora-hombre.

¹ Net national income. ² Final gross production.   ¹ *Revenu national net.* ² *Production finale brute.*   ¹ Renta nacional neta. ² Producción final bruta.

17 | Indices of labour productivity
Indices de la productivité du travail
Indices de la productividad del trabajo

A | National economy
Economie nationale
Economía nacional

(1970 = 100)

Country — *Pays* — País	Code *Code* Clave	1965	1966	1967	1968	1969	1970	1971	1972	1973	1974
Pays-Bas	A/1	79	81	86	90	95	**100**	103 *	109 *	...	...
Pologne	A/1	81	85	88	94	95	**100**	106	114	123 *	...
»	B/1	82	86	89	95	96	**100**	107	115	124 *	...
Roumanie	A/1	68	74	80	86	92	**100**	113	124	136	152
»	B/1	69	75	81	86	93	**100**	113	124	137	153
Sweden	A/1	86	88	92	95	97	**100**	101	103	106	108
»	A/5	81	83	89	93	97	**100**	102	108	112	115
Turquie	A/1	77	83	84	91	93	**100**	105	110	114	...
United Kingdom	A/1	88	89	92	96	98	**100**	104	106	109	...
OCEANIA — OCÉANIE OCEANÍA											
New Zealand [1]	.[2]/1	94	95	94	96	99	**100**	102 *	106 *	...	...
URSS	.[3]/1	73	78	84	89	93	**100**	104	107	115	120

EXPLANATORY NOTES: See p. 567.

Codes and abbreviations: See p. 574.

[1] Year ending in March of the following year.   [2] Volume of production.   [3] Gross material product.

NOTES EXPLICATIVES: Voir p. 569.

Codes et abréviations: Voir p. 574.

[1] *Année se terminant en mars de l'année suivante.*
[2] *Volume de la production.*   [3] *Produit matériel brut.*

NOTAS EXPLICATIVAS: Véase pág. 571.

Claves y abreviaturas: Véase pág. 574.

[1] Año que termina en marzo del año siguiente.   [2] Volumen de la producción.   [3] Producto material bruto.

17 Indices of labour productivity / Indices de la productivité du travail / Indices de la productividad del trabajo — B Industrial sector / Secteur industriel / Sector industrial

(1970 = 100)

Country — Pays — País	Code / Code / Clave	1965	1966	1967	1968	1969	1970	1971	1972	1973	1974
AFRICA — AFRIQUE / AFRICA											
Ghana	C/1	85	90	97	98	94	**100**	...	...	...	...
»	D/1	99	110	114	106	94	**100**	...	...	...	...
Tunisie	C/1	78	80	90	94	98	**100**	103	...	...	...
Zambia	C/2	.	96	99	101	102	**100**	93	103	100	...
AMERICA — AMÉRIQUE / AMÉRICA											
Bolivia	C/1 [1]	87	92	103	103	100	**100**	98	106	111	...
»	D/1	76	85	93	95	99	**100**	101	98	105	...
Chile	C/1	91	97	99	100	102	**100**	...	...	...	...
»	D/1	91	96	98	98	102	**100**	...	...	...	...
Ecuador	C/1	78	91	90	94	98	**100**	105 *	102 *	...	...
México	C/. [2]	76	80	84	90	92	**100**	...	...	...	...
United States	C/1	95	98	99	101	101	**100**	103	107	110	106
» »	C/2	97	99	99	101	101	**100**	103	107	110	106
» »	C/5 [3]	92	95	97	100	99	**100**	104	108	110	107
ASIA — ASIE / ASIA											
Israel [1]	D/2	*95*	*98*	*100*	*92* [4]	*96*	**100**	106	112	117	118
» [1]	D/4 [5]	*90*	*95*	*100*	*91* [4]	*95*	**100**	104	110	120	124
Japan	D/4 [6]	54	60	70	80	91	**100**	105	116	139	140
Korea, Rep. of	C/4 [5]	50	52	61	72	88	**100** [4]	109	118	127	140
EUROPE — EUROPE / EUROPA											
Austria [7]	D/2	73	77	80	88	95	**100**	105	111	114	119 *
» [7]	D/5 [5]	69	74	78	85	92	**100**	107	116	121	129 *
Belgique	8/1	70	75	78	85	92	**100**	103	111	...	...

EXPLANATORY NOTES: See p. 567.   NOTES EXPLICATIVES: Voir p. 569.   NOTAS EXPLICATIVAS: Véase pág. 571.

A: Gross national or domestic product
Produit national ou intérieur brut
Producto nacional o interno bruto

B: Net national or domestic product
Produit national ou intérieur net
Producto nacional o interno neto

C: Gross production
Production brute
Producción bruta

D: Net production
Production nette
Producción neta

Per / Par / Por

1: Employed person — *Personne employée* — Persona ocupada.
2: Worker or employee — *Travailleur ou salarié* — Trabajador o asalariado.
3: Wage earner — *Ouvrier* — Obrero.
4: Man-day — *Jour-homme* — Día-hombre.
5: Man-hour — *Heure-homme* — Hora-hombre.

[1] Excl. electricity, gas and water. [2] Per economically active person. [3] Based on estimated number of hours paid for. [4] Series replacing former series. [5] Wage earners only. [6] Excl. water. [7] Excl. electricity. [8] Contribution to the gross domestic product.

[1] *Non compris l'électricité, le gaz et l'eau.* [2] *Par personne économiquement active.* [3] *Fondés sur le nombre estimé d'heures de travail rémunérées.* [4] *Série remplaçant la précédente.* [5] *Ouvriers seulement.* [6] *Non compris l'eau.* [7] *Non compris l'électricité.* [8] *Contribution au produit intérieur brut.*

[1] Excl. la electricidad, el gas y el agua. [2] Por persona económicamente activa. [3] Basados en una estimación del número de horas de trabajo remuneradas. [4] Serie que substituye a la anterior. [5] Obreros solamente. [6] Excl. el agua. [7] Excl. la electricidad. [8] Contribución al producto interno bruto.

17 B

Indices of labour productivity
Indices de la productivité du travail
Indices de la productividad del trabajo

Industrial sector
Secteur industriel
Sector industrial

(1970 = 100)

Country — Pays — País	Code Code Clave	1965	1966	1967	1968	1969	1970	1971	1972	1973	1974
Bulgarie	C/2 [1]	72	74	79	88	94	**100**	107	113	121	130 *
»	C/3 [1]	71	74	80	87	93	**100**	107	115	122	130 *
Czechoslovakia	C/2	77	81	85	89	93	**100**	106	113	119	125
»	C/3	76	79	84	88	93	**100**	106	113	120	127
»	C/4 [2]	65	71	79	85	95	**100**	105	112	119	127
»	C/5 [2]	69	74	82	87	95	**100**	105	112	120	128
España	D/1	65	74	78	84	94	**100**	104	...	...	...
»	D/5 [2]	65	74	79	85	96	**100**	104	...	...	...
Finland	D/1	80	83	85	89	96	**100**	102	110 *	114	119 *
France	D/5	71	76	80	89	94	**100**	106	114 *	121 *	125 *
German Democratic Republic △ . .	C/2	75	80	84	88	94	**100**	105	110	116	123
» » » △ . .	C/3 [3]	71	75	83	86	93	**100**	107	112	118	125
» » » △[1] . .	C/5 [2]	70	75	81	87	94	**100**	105	109	115	123
Germany, Fed. Rep. of △[4]	D/1	79	81	84	91	98	**100**	102	108	115	116
» » » △[4]	D/3	77	79	83	91	97	**100**	103	111	118	121
» » » △[4]	D/5	78	81	86	91	97	**100**	105	112	119	123
» » » △[4]	D/5 [2]	76	79	85	90	97	**100**	106	115	123	128
Hongrie	C/1	83	88	92	93	93	**100**	107	114	120	129 *
»	D/1	86	89	93	94	94	**100**	105	110	116	123 *
Ireland	D/3 [4]	78	81	86	92	94	**100**	105	109	118 *	120 *
Italie	.[5]/1	72	79	84	91	95	**|100 [6]**	101	106	115	117
Luxembourg	C/1	83	83	84	90	99	**100**	96	97 *	103 *	105 *
Malta	C/1	89	97	93	94	97	**100**	...	...	...	...
Norway [4]	.[7]/1	84	87	90	93	99	**100**	103	108	113	117
» [4]	.[7]/5 [2]	74	77	80	86	94	**100**	105	112	116	...

EXPLANATORY NOTES: See p. 567.

Codes and abbreviations: See p. 576.

[1] Socialised sector. [2] Wage earners only. [3] Production workers, incl. home workers. [4] Excl. electricity, gas and water. [5] Contribution to the gross domestic product. 1965-69: net production per employed person. [6] Series replacing former series. [7] Contribution to the gross domestic product.

NOTES EXPLICATIVES: Voir p. 569.

Codes et abréviations: Voir p. 576.

[1] Secteur socialisé. [2] Ouvriers seulement. [3] Ouvriers affectés à la production, y compris les travailleurs à domicile. [4] Non compris l'électricité, le gaz et l'eau. [5] Contribution au produit intérieur brut. 1965-1969: production nette par personne employée. [6] Série remplaçant la précédente. [7] Contribution au produit intérieur brut.

NOTAS EXPLICATIVAS: Véase pág. 571.

Claves y abreviaturas: Véase pág. 576.

[1] Sector socializado. [2] Obreros solamente. [3] Obreros de la producción, incl. los trabajadores a domicilio. [4] Excl. la electricidad, el gas y el agua. [5] Contribución al producto interno bruto. 1965-1969: producción neta por persona ocupada. [6] Serie que substituye a la anterior. [7] Contribución al producto interno bruto.

17 Indices of labour productivity
Indices de la productivité du travail
Indices de la productividad del trabajo

B Industrial sector
Secteur industriel
Sector industrial

(1970 = 100)

Country — Pays — País	Code Code Clave	1965	1966	1967	1968	1969	1970	1971	1972	1973	1974
Pays-Bas	D/1	63	67	73	83	92	100 [1]	107	116	126	132
Pologne	C/1 [2]	79	82	85	89	94	100	105	112	121	132 *
Portugal	D/1	77	81	86	90	95	100	105	…	…	…
Roumanie	D/2	70	76	83	89	93	100	104	110	119	127
Sweden	C/1	76	79	84	90	95	100	103	109	114	117
»	C/5	71	75	81	89	95	100	105	113	121	125
»	D/1	75	77	83	90	96	100	103	108	114	117
»	D/5	70	73	80	88	95	100	105	112	120	125
Turquie	D/1	84	91	91	96	101	100	103	119	125 *	…
United Kingdom	D/1 [3]	84	86	89	96	98	100	104	108	115	112
Yugoslavia	D/2	78	81	83	88	95	100	105	109	111	118
URSS [4]	C/1	76	79	85	89	93	100	106	112	119	126
» [4]	C/3	75	79	85	89	94	100	106	111	118	126
RSS de Biélorussie	C/1	72	77	82	87	92	100	108	114	123	132
» » »	C/3	70	76	81	87	93	100	107	114	123	133
RSS d'Ukraine	C/1	79	81	86	90	94	100	105	110	116	123

EXPLANATORY NOTES: See p. 567.　　　NOTES EXPLICATIVES: Voir p. 569.　　　NOTAS EXPLICATIVAS: Véase pág. 571.

A: Gross national or domestic product
Produit national ou intérieur brut
Producto nacional o interno bruto

B: Net national or domestic product
Produit national ou intérieur net
Producto nacional o interno neto

C: Gross production
Production brute
Producción bruta

D: Net production
Production nette
Producción neta

Per
Par
Por

1: Employed person — *Personne employée* — Persona ocupada.

2: Worker or employee — *Travailleur ou salarié* — Trabajador o asalariado.

3: Wage earner — *Ouvrier* — Obrero.

4: Man-day — *Jour-homme* — Día-hombre.

5: Man-hour — *Heure-homme* — Hora-hombre.

[1] Series replacing former series.　[2] Socialised sector. Excl. water.　[3] Incl. construction.　[4] Incl. Byelorussian SSR and Ukrainian SSR, shown separately in this table.

[1] *Série remplaçant la précédente.*　[2] *Secteur socialisé. Non compris l'eau.*　[3] *Y compris la construction.*　[4] *Y compris les RSS de Biélorussie et d'Ukraine, figurant séparément dans ce tableau.*

[1] Serie que substituye a la anterior.　[2] Sector socializado. Excl. el agua.　[3] Incl. la construcción.　[4] Incl. las RSS de Bielorrusia y de Ucrania, que figuran separadamente en este cuadro.

17 Indices of labour productivity
Indices de la productivité du travail
Indices de la productividad del trabajo

C Manufacturing
Industries manufacturières
Industrias manufactureras

(1970 = 100)

Country — Pays — País	Code Code Clave	1965	1966	1967	1968	1969	1970	1971	1972	1973	1974
AFRICA — AFRIQUE AFRICA											
Ghana	C/1	*78*	*83*	*92*	*97*	**100**	...	...	...	...	...
»	D/1	*87*	*96*	*100*	*95*	**100**	...	...	...	...	...
Zambia	C/2	84	88	97	104	101	**100**	96	111	118	...
AMERICA — AMÉRIQUE AMÉRICA											
Bolivia	C/1	97	105	108	104	100	**100**	99	101	102	...
»	D/1	85	94	96	96	100	**100**	99	101	109	...
Brésil	C/1	74	80	78	82	89	**100**	...	118	...	...
»	C/3	78	85	83	86	95	**100**	...	125	...	...
»	D/1	79	91	86	90	96	**100**	...	116	...	...
»	D/3	83	96	92	94	102	**100**	...	123	...	...
Canada	D/1	84	86	88	94	99	**100**	107	111	113	...
»	D/5	82	84	87	93	98	**100**	107	110	113	...
Colombia	C/1	*88*	*91*	*95*	*101*	**100**	...	...	...	...	...
»	C/2	*90*	*92*	*96*	*102*	**100**	...	...	...	...	...
»	C/3	*88*	*91*	*95*	*102*	**100**	...	...	...	...	...
Chile	C/1	92	98	100	101	102	**100**	...	...	...	...
»	D/1	95	99	100	101	102	**100**	...	...	...	...
Ecuador	C/1	86	86	88	93	97	**100**	103 *	109 *	118 *	...
México	C/. [1]	77	82	85	90	95	**100**	...	...	...	...
United States	C/1	94	95	94	99	101	**100**	107	114	121	120
» »	C/2	94	95	94	99	101	**100**	107	114	121	120
	C/5 [2]	91	93	93	97	100	**100**	107	113	119	120
ASIA — ASIE ASIA											
Cyprus	D/1	79	82	85	86	91	**100**	102	117	120	...
Japan	D/4	53	60	70	80	91	**100**	104	116	139	140
Korea, Rep. of	C/4 [3]	48	50	59	70	89	**100** [4]	110	120	130	144
Philippines	.5/1	*92*	*97*	*100*	*91* [4]	*96*	**100**	94	104	119	116

EXPLANATORY NOTES: See p. 567.

Codes and abbreviations: See p. 578.

[1] Per economically active person. [2] Based on estimated numbers of hours paid for. [3] Wage earners only. [4] Series replacing former series. [5] Contribution to the net domestic product.

NOTES EXPLICATIVES: Voir p. 569.

Codes et abréviations: Voir p. 578.

[1] *Par personne économiquement active.* [2] *Fondés sur le nombre estimé des heures de travail rémunérées.* [3] *Ouvriers seulement.* [4] *Série remplaçant la précédente.* [5] *Contribution au produit intérieur net.*

NOTAS EXPLICATIVAS: Véase pág. 571.

Claves y abreviaturas: Véase pág. 578.

[1] Por persona económicamente activa. [2] Basados en una estimación del número de horas de trabajo remuneradas. [3] Obreros solamente. [4] Serie que substituye a la anterior. [5] Contribución al producto interno neto.

PRODUCTIVITY

17 Indices of labour productivity / Indices de la productivité du travail / Indices de la productividad del trabajo
C Manufacturing / Industries manufacturières / Industrias manufactureras

(1970 = 100)

Country — Pays — País	Code / Code / Clave	1965	1966	1967	1968	1969	1970	1971	1972	1973	1974
EUROPE — EUROPE EUROPA											
Belgique	.[1]/1	72	76	79	86	93	**100**	102	109	...	...
Czechoslovakia	C/2	78	81	86	89	93	**100**	107	113	120	127
»	C/3	77	80	85	88	92	**100**	106	113	121	128
»	C/4 [2]	65	72	79	85	95	**100**	105	112	120	129
»	C/5 [2]	70	75	82	87	95	**100**	105	112	120	128
Denmark	D/5 [3]	.	73	81	89	97	**100**	108	120	...	...
España	D/1	66	74	78	83	94	**100**	103	...	...	...
»	D/5 [2]	66	75	79	85	96	**100**	103	...	...	...
Finland	D/1	80	83	86	90	95	**100**	102	111	114 *	118 *
Germany, Fed. Rep. of △[4]	D/1	80	81	84	91	98	**100**	102	108	115	116
» » » △[4]	D/3	78	80	84	91	98	**100**	103	111	119	121
» » » △[4]	D/5	79	82	86	91	97	**100**	105	112	120	124
» » » △[4]	D/5 [2]	77	80	86	91	97	**100**	106	115	123	129
Hongrie	C/1 [5]	84	89	93	93	93	**100**	107	113	119	127 *
»	D/1 [5]	85	89	93	94	94	**100**	106	110	116	123 *
Ireland	D/3	82	84	89	95	97	**100**	105	110	118 *	121 *
Italie	.[6]/1	72	79	85	91	95	**| 100 [7]**	100	106	114	118
Malta	C/1	94	100	94	95	97	**100**	...	...	...	...
Norway	D/1	84	88	90	94	99	**100**	103	106	112	116
»	D/5 [2]	74	77	81	86	94	**100**	104	109	114	...
Pays-Bas	D/1	69	73	78	86	94	**| 100 [7]**	105	112	121	124
Pologne	C/1 [8]	80	83	85	89	94	**100**	105	112	121	132 *

EXPLANATORY NOTES: See p. 567. NOTES EXPLICATIVES: Voir p. 569. NOTAS EXPLICATIVAS: Véase pág. 571.

A: Gross national or domestic product
Produit national ou intérieur brut
Producto nacional o interno bruto

B: Net national or domestic product
Produit national ou intérieur net
Producto nacional o interno neto

C: Gross production
Production brute
Producción bruta

D: Net production
Production nette
Producción neta

Per / Par / Por

1: Employed person — *Personne employée* — Persona ocupada.

2: Worker or employee — *Travailleur ou salarié* — Trabajador o asalariado.

3: Wage earner — *Ouvrier* — Obrero.

4: Man-day — *Jour-homme* — Día-hombre.

5: Man-hour — *Heure-homme* — Hora-hombre.

[1] Contribution to the gross domestic product. [2] Wage earners only. [3] Incl. mining and quarrying. [4] Excl. manufacture of aircraft. [5] State industry. [6] Contribution to the gross domestic product. 1965-69: net production per employed person. [7] Series replacing former series. [8] Socialised sector.

[1] Contribution au produit intérieur brut. [2] Ouvriers seulement. [3] Y compris les industries extractives. [4] Non compris la construction d'avions. [5] Industrie d'Etat. [6] Contribution au produit intérieur brut. 1965-1969: production nette par personne employée. [7] Série remplaçant la précédente. [8] Secteur socialisé.

[1] Contribución al producto interno bruto. [2] Obreros solamente. [3] Incl. las minas y canteras. [4] Excl. la construcción de aviones. [5] Industria de Estado. [6] Contribución al producto interno bruto. 1965-1969: producción neta por persona ocupada. [7] Serie que substituye a la anterior. [8] Sector socializado.

17 Indices of labour productivity
Indices de la productivité du travail
Indices de la productividad del trabajo

C Manufacturing
Industries manufacturières
Industrias manufactureras

(1970 = 100)

Country — Pays — País	Code Code Clave	1965	1966	1967	1968	1969	1970	1971	1972	1973	1974
Sweden	C/1	76	79	85	90	95	**100**	103	108	114	117
»	C/5	72	75	81	91	98	**100**	105	113	121	125
»	D/1	75	78	83	90	95	**100**	103	107	113	116
»	D/5	70	74	80	88	95	**100**	104	111	119	124
United Kingdom	D/1	85	87	90	97	99	**100**	103	109	118	115
OCEANIA — OCÉANIE OCEANÍA											
New Zealand [1]	D/1	89	92	92	93	99	**100**	103	108	...	...
URSS [2]	C/1	76	80	85	89	94	**100**	106	111	118	126
RSS de Biélorussie	C/1	73	78	83	87	93	**100**	107	114	122	131
» » »	C/3	71	77	82	87	93	**100**	107	113	122	132
RSS d'Ukraine	C/1	80	82	87	91	95	**100**	105	109	116	123

EXPLANATORY NOTES: See p. 567.

Codes and abbreviations: See p. 580.

[1] Year ending in March of the following year. [2] Incl. Byelorussian SSR and Ukrainian SSR shown separately in this table.

NOTES EXPLICATIVES: Voir p. 569.

Codes et abréviations: Voir p. 580.

[1] Année se terminant en mars de l'année suivante.
[2] Y compris les RSS de Biélorussie et d'Ukraine, figurant séparément dans ce tableau.

NOTAS EXPLICATIVAS: Véase pág. 571.

Claves y abreviaturas: Véase pág. 580.

[1] Año que termina en marzo del año siguiente. [2] Incl. las RSS de Bielorrusia y de Ucrania, que figuran separadamente en este cuadro.

VI

CHAPTER

CHAPITRE

CAPITULO

Wages

Salaires

Salarios

Wages

Tables 18 to 23 generally present *average gross money wages* per wage earner (i.e. wages before deduction of income taxes and social security contributions payable by the worker). Where in some cases the series also cover salaried employees, this is indicated in a footnote.

The statistics shown are, in general, *average earnings*; only where such data are lacking are *wage rates* given. Occasionally wage indices are given in the absence of absolute wage data. Wages per hour and per week are shown for each country whenever available; in the absence of such data, wages per day or per month have been given, especially in table 23 on wages in agriculture. Data are shown, as far as possible, for both sexes combined and for each sex separately. Where not otherwise stated, the series relate to workers of both sexes, irrespective of age.

Statistics of average earnings are usually derived from payroll data supplied by a sample of establishments often furnishing at the same time data on hours of work and on employment.[1] Average earnings per hour (or day) are normally compiled by dividing the total wages paid in a given period by total man-hours (or man-days) actually worked or paid for in that period, and earnings per week (or month) by dividing the total wages paid in a given week (or month) by the average number of workers employed in the same period. The data usually cover cash payments received from employers, i.e. remuneration for normal working hours, overtime pay, incentive pay, earnings of piece workers; remuneration for time not worked (annual vacation, public holidays, sick leave and other paid leave); bonuses and gratuities, cost-of-living allowances and special premiums (such as end-of-year bonuses). They frequently also include the value of payments in kind, while family allowances are mostly excluded from statistics of earnings. In a few cases average earnings are compiled on the basis of *social insurance records*. Social insurance statistics usually yield lower averages than payroll data because overtime pay, incentive pay and the like may be excluded as well as wages exceeding a certain upper limit. Moreover, the insurance scheme may be restricted to lower-paid workers only, or higher-paid workers may be under-represented in the compilation of average earnings.

Statistics of wage rates are in most cases based on collective agreements, arbitration awards or other wage-setting decisions, which generally specify minimum rates for particular occupations or groups of workers. In some countries rates actually paid correspond closely to these minima. In countries where the fixing of wage rates is widespread, series of average wage rates in particular industries or groups of industries are calculated, using as weights the numerical importance in a given year of the different occupations for which rates are available in the industries covered. Data on wage rates usually refer only to rates for adults working normal hours, and therefore payments for overtime premiums and other supplementary wage elements are not taken into account; cost-of-living allowances, however, are often included, and other allowances fixed in the wage-setting process, such as housing allowances, are sometimes included. Some countries obtain average *rates actually paid* (straight-time earnings) from establishment payrolls in a similar way as average earnings are obtained. Rates actually paid usually cover the remuneration on the basis of normal time worked, both for normal and overtime hours, but excludes incentive pay and other bonuses as well as the premium part of overtime pay. Rates actually paid are sometimes also gathered by labour inspectors.

In making comparisons between wage series account must be taken of differences in concepts, scope, methods of compilation and of presentation of the data.[2] Earnings data show fluctua-

---

[1] For a detailed discussion of wage statistical methods, see ILO: *Wages and Payrolls Statistics*, Studies and Reports, New Series, No. 16 (Geneva, 1949).

[2] For the descriptions of the various national series, their scope, methods of compilation used, etc., see ILO: *Technical Guide 1976* (descriptions of general series published in the *Bulletin* and the *Year Book of Labour Statistics*), Vol. II. " Employment—Unemployment—Hours of Work—Wages " (Geneva, 1976).

tions which reflect the influence both of changes in wage rates and supplementary wage payments. Weekly, daily and monthly earnings are in addition much dependent on variations in average hours of work. Statistics of wage rates do not reflect the influence of changes in wage supplements nor the influence of variations in hours of work. The fluctuations of average earnings obtained from global payrolls are also influenced by changes in the employment structure, i.e. the relative importance of males, females, unskilled and skilled labour, etc., while average wage rates are normally compiled using the employment structure of a given year as weights. Average hourly earnings are generally higher than hourly rates because the former include overtime payments, premiums, bonuses and allowances which do not enter into statistics of wage rates. Average weekly or monthly earnings should also be higher than the corresponding rates, but may sometimes fall short of wage rates because of loss of working time through sickness, absenteeism or part-time work.

Time comparisons are less affected by differences in concepts, definitions and methods of compilation of the data than comparisons of wage levels at a given date.

The assessment of international differences in the *real wage income* of workers involves a conversion of the data into a common reference currency by means of particular conversion factors reflecting the relative purchasing power (with regard to consumer goods and services) of the currencies concerned. Satisfactory comparisons of this kind can only be made for countries with similar characteristics and are preferably based on special uniform inquiries which normally use the concept of net earnings and include family allowances.[1] Crude indicators of trends of real wages are usually obtained in an easier way by dividing average gross earnings (or indices of gross earnings) by an index of consumer prices.

Comparisons of *total labour cost* between different industries of one country or between different countries cannot be based on wage statistics alone. Although gross earnings obviously represent the most important component of labour cost, wage supplements such as family allowances, certain bonuses and gratuities or contributions paid by the employer to social security funds or in respect of welfare services furnished by the establishment to its workers, form an important element of total labour cost in certain industries and countries which are not usually included in statistics of earnings. Statistics of total labour cost are therefore mostly the subject of special studies.[2]

As of the 1974 issue of the *Year Book*, changes have been made in the presentation of the data shown in certain tables owing to the introduction of the revised 1968 edition of the International Standard Industrial Classification of All Economic Activities (ISIC); see "Preface".

Table 18

Wages in non-agricultural sectors

Unless otherwise indicated in footnotes, the wage series shown in this table cover the following divisions of economic activity: Mining and quarrying; Manufacturing; Electricity, gas and water; Construction; Wholesale and retail trade, restaurants and hotels; Transports, storage and communication; Financing, insurance, real estate and business services; Community, social and personal services. In some cases, however, these divisions are only represented by certain of the groups composing them.

Table 19

Wages in manufacturing

Part A of table 19 shows wages in manufacturing industries as a whole; where in a few cases other industries are also included in the series, this is indicated in a footnote.

---

[1] See, e.g. Statistical Office of the European Communities: *Salaires CEE, 1964*, Statistiques sociales, 1966, No. 5 (in French only).

[2] See, e.g. ILO: *Labour Costs in European Industry*, Studies and Reports, New Series, No. 52 (Geneva, 1959).

Part B of table 19 shows wages in specified manufacturing industries. The data are presented separately for each country.

So far as possible, the different manufacturing industries have been arranged according to the International Standard Industrial Classification of All Economic Activities (see Appendix) with the corresponding code number of the different industrial major groups.

Tables 20 to 22

Wages in mining and quarrying; construction; and transport, storage and communication

Tables 20 to 22 show statistics of wages in three major divisions of economic activity as follows: table 20, Mining and quarrying; table 21, Construction; and table 22, Transport, storage and communication (excl. sea transport).

Table 23

Wages in agriculture

The statistics of agricultural wages presented in table 23 refer in most cases to general farm labourers. A distinction is made between *permanent* workers, *seasonal* workers and *day* workers; in the last-mentioned group, *regular* day labourers and *casual* day labourers are distinguished.

The methods of payment and the types of labour contracts and arrangements in agriculture are often quite different from those in other activities. To indicate the nature of the wage statistics given in each column a special notation has been adopted: the sign I at the top of the column indicates that the statistics refer to total wages which are paid entirely in cash; the sign II standing alone indicates that the figures refer to the money part of the wages only, although the workers receive payments in kind in addition; where the sign *a* is added, it indicates that the value of meals furnished is included in the amounts of wages shown and, similarly,

b indicates that the value of lodging furnished is included. Although the figures are identified in some cases as representing rates of pay or earnings, it should be noted that in most countries there is little or no difference between the nominal rates of remuneration and the actual earnings of agricultural workers.

International comparisons of wages are subject to greater reservations with respect to agriculture than for other activities. The nature of the work carried out by the different categories of farm workers and the length of the working day and week also show considerable variation from one country to another. Seasonal fluctuations in agricultural wages are more important in some countries than in others.

In general, series marked I, representing the complete wage of workers who are remunerated entirely in cash, are more comparable internationally than series marked either II + a + b or II alone. Comparisons between series marked II alone, in which the figures do not include the value of board and lodging provided by the employer, are subject to special reservations owing to differences in each case in the relative importance of these payments in kind.

A major drawback for international comparisons of series marked II + a + b lies in the lack of uniformity in the methods followed in the different countries for estimating the money value of the payments in kind included. Where the data relate to similar occupations and units of time (day, week or month), these series may nevertheless be considered to be roughly comparable with one another and with series marked I, which also refer to the complete wage of the workers covered.

Table 24

Compensation of employees and national income

The figures for this table have been furnished by the Statistical Office of the United Nations.

The figures shown under *compensation of employees* generally comprise all payments by resident producers of (i) wages and salaries (in cash and in kind) to their employees, and (ii) contributions (payed or imputed) in respect of their employees to social security schemes, private pension, family allowances, health and other casualty insurance, life insurance and similar schemes.

Since statistics of total compensation generally take the form of global estimates and include certain non-wage elements of remuneration, they should not be identified with " total wages and salaries paid ".

National income at market prices is here defined as the sum of (i) compensation of resident employees, (ii) the excess of the property and entrepreneurial income receivable by resident economic agents over the property and entrepreneurial income payable by them, and (iii) indirect taxes *reduced* by subsidies.

The percentage which *compensation of employees* constitutes of *national income* is not strictly comparable between countries at any given date on account of the varying methods of estimation used.

Data shown in *italics* are based on the present (new) System of National Accounts (SNA); the other data are based on the former SNA.

For further definitions of accounting concepts and for more detailed statistics, the reader is referred to the publications of the United Nations Statistical Office. [1]

[1] See, in particular, United Nations, Statistical Office: *A System of National Accounts*, Studies in Methods, Series F, No. 2, Rev. 3 (New York, 1968), *Yearbook of National Accounts Statistics, 1973* (New York, 1975), and *Monthly Bulletin of Statistics*.

Salaires

Les tableaux 18 à 23 indiquent généralement les *salaires nominaux bruts moyens* par ouvrier (autrement dit, les salaires avant déduction de l'impôt sur le revenu et des cotisations de sécurité sociale à la charge du travailleur). Quand les employés sont également compris dans une série, ce fait est indiqué en note de bas de page.

Les statistiques fournies sont en général celles des *gains moyens*; les *taux de salaire* ne sont donnés que lorsque les gains moyens ne sont pas disponibles. Exceptionnellement, ce sont les indices des salaires qui sont reproduits, à défaut de données absolues sur les salaires. Les salaires horaires et hebdomadaires ont été fournis pour chaque pays lorsqu'ils étaient disponibles; en l'absence de ces données, ce sont les salaires journaliers ou mensuels qui ont été indiqués, notamment au tableau 23, qui concerne les salaires payés dans l'agriculture. Les données sont présentées, dans la mesure du possible, pour l'ensemble des deux sexes et aussi pour chaque sexe séparément. Sauf indication contraire, les séries couvrent les travailleurs des deux sexes, sans considération d'âge.

Les *statistiques des gains moyens* sont généralement tirées des bordereaux de salaires remis par un échantillon d'établissements, qui fournissent fréquemment en même temps des données sur la durée du travail et sur l'emploi[1]. Les gains moyens horaires (ou journaliers) sont généralement obtenus en divisant le total des salaires payés au cours d'une période déterminée par le nombre total d'heures-homme (ou de journées-homme) réellement effectuées ou rémunérées pendant cette période, et les gains hebdomadaires (ou mensuels) en divisant le total des salaires payés au cours d'une semaine donnée (ou d'un mois donné) par le nombre moyen de travailleurs employés pendant la même période. Les données comprennent généralement les paiements en espèces reçus de l'employeur, c'est-à-dire la rémunération pour les heures normales de travail, le paiement des heures supplémentaires, les primes de stimulation, les

gains des travailleurs aux pièces; la rémunération pour les heures de travail payées, mais non effectuées (congés annuels, jours fériés, congés de maladie et autres congés payés); les primes et gratifications, les allocations de cherté de vie et les versements spéciaux (par exemple, les gratifications de fin d'année). Elles englobent souvent la valeur des paiements en nature; par contre les allocations familiales sont généralement exclues des statistiques des gains. Dans quelques cas, les gains moyens sont calculés à partir de *registres d'assurances sociales*. Les données sur les gains tirées des statistiques d'assurances sociales fournissent généralement des moyennes inférieures à celles qui sont obtenues à partir des bordereaux de salaires, les heures supplémentaires, les primes de stimulation, etc., pouvant en être exclues, de même que les salaires qui dépassent un certain niveau. De plus, le régime d'assurance peut ne couvrir que les travailleurs à salaires modestes ou, si les travailleurs à salaires élevés sont inclus, ils peuvent ne pas être représentés entièrement pour le calcul des gains moyens.

Les *statistiques des taux de salaire* se fondent le plus souvent sur les conventions collectives, les décisions d'arbitrage ou les décisions d'autorités réglementant les salaires, qui spécifient généralement des taux minima pour des professions particulières ou des catégories de travailleurs déterminées. Dans quelques pays, les taux effectivement payés sont très proches de ces minima. Dans d'autres, où il est d'usage de fixer des taux de salaire, on calcule les séries des taux de salaire moyens dans des branches d'activité économique particulières ou dans des groupes de branches d'activité, en pondérant ces taux suivant l'importance numérique que revêtent, au cours d'une année donnée, les différentes professions pour lesquelles on connaît les taux appliqués dans les branches d'activité couvertes par ces statistiques. Les données relatives aux taux de salaire ne concernent généralement que les taux de rémunération des adultes travaillant pendant l'horaire normal. Par conséquent, il n'est pas tenu compte de la rémunération des heures supplémentaires et des autres éléments qui s'ajoutent au salaire; cependant, les

---

[1] On trouvera une étude plus détaillée des méthodes statistiques d'enregistrement des salaires dans BIT: *Statistiques des bordereaux de salaires et des gains*, Etudes et documents, nouvelle série, n° 16 (Genève, 1949).

allocations de cherté de vie sont souvent comprises dans les calculs, de même que d'autres allocations déterminées par la procédure de fixation des salaires, par exemple l'indemnité de logement. Dans quelques pays, on obtient les *taux moyens effectivement payés* (rémunération au temps exclusivement) en utilisant les bordereaux de salaires des établissements, de la même façon que pour les gains moyens. En général, les taux effectivement payés comprennent la rémunération calculée sur la base de la durée normale du travail, aussi bien pour les heures supplémentaires que pour la durée normale du travail, mais ils ne tiennent pas compte des primes de stimulation et d'autres versements spéciaux, pas plus que de la part de la rémunération des heures supplémentaires correspondant aux primes. Parfois, ce sont les inspecteurs du travail qui prennent note des taux effectivement payés.

Lorsqu'on fait une comparaison entre des séries concernant les salaires, il y a lieu de tenir compte des différences que peuvent présenter les notions, la portée économique, les méthodes d'établissement des séries et la présentation des données[1]. Les données concernant les gains sont sujettes à des fluctuations qui traduisent des changements survenus aussi bien dans les taux de salaire que dans les paiements supplémentaires. En outre, les gains hebdomadaires, journaliers et mensuels dépendent très fortement des variations de la durée moyenne du travail. Par contre, les statistiques des taux de salaire ne subissent pas l'influence des changements affectant les suppléments de salaire, ni celle des variations de la durée du travail. Les fluctuations des gains moyens obtenus à partir de l'ensemble des bordereaux de salaires sont également influencées par les changements survenus dans la structure de l'emploi, c'est-à-dire par l'importance relative des travailleurs, des travailleuses, de la main-d'œuvre non qualifiée et de la main-d'œuvre qualifiée, etc., tandis que les taux de

salaire moyens sont calculés le plus souvent en prenant la structure de l'emploi d'une année donnée comme coefficient de pondération. Les gains horaires moyens sont généralement plus élevés que les taux de salaire horaires, les premiers comprenant la rémunération des heures supplémentaires, les gratifications, les primes et les allocations, qui n'entrent pas dans les statistiques des taux de salaire. Les gains hebdomadaires ou mensuels moyens devraient aussi être plus élevés que les taux de salaire correspondants, mais il arrive qu'ils leur soient inférieurs en raison des heures de travail perdues du fait de la maladie, de l'absentéisme ou du travail à temps partiel.

Les comparaisons dans le temps se ressentent moins des différences de notions, de définitions et de méthodes de calcul que les comparaisons des niveaux de salaire à une date donnée.

Pour évaluer les différences internationales du *revenu réel provenant des salaires* il faut convertir les données en prenant une devise commune de référence, au moyen de facteurs de conversion particuliers traduisant le pouvoir d'achat relatif (en ce qui concerne les biens de consommation et les services) des devises entrant en considération. On ne peut faire des comparaisons de ce genre avec des résultats satisfaisants que pour des pays ayant des caractéristiques analogues; ces comparaisons se fonderont de préférence sur des enquêtes spéciales uniformes, utilisant habituellement la notion de gain net et englobant les allocations familiales [2]. On obtient généralement avec plus de facilité des indicateurs approximatifs des tendances des salaires réels en divisant les gains bruts moyens (ou les indices des gains bruts) par un indice des prix à la consommation.

Une comparaison du *coût total de la main-d'œuvre* entre différentes branches d'activité d'un même pays ou entre différents pays ne peut pas se fonder sur les seules statistiques des salaires. Bien que les gains bruts représentent incontestablement l'élément le plus important

---

[1] Pour les descriptions des diverses séries nationales, de leur portée, des méthodes de calcul utilisées, etc., voir BIT: *Guide technique 1976* (description des séries générales publiées dans le *Bulletin* et l'*Annuaire des statistiques du travail*), vol. II, « Emploi — Chômage — Durée du travail — Salaires » (Genève, 1976).

[2] Voir notamment Office statistique des Communautés européennes: *Salaires CEE, 1964*, Statistiques sociales, 1966, nᵒ 5.

du coût de la main-d'œuvre, les suppléments de rémunération tels que les allocations familiales, certaines primes et gratifications, les cotisations payées par l'employeur à des caisses de sécurité sociale ou les versements qu'il fait au titre de services sociaux fournis par l'établissement à son personnel, constituent un élément important du coût total de la main-d'œuvre dans certaines branches d'activité et dans certains pays; toutefois, ces prestations ne sont généralement pas comprises dans les statistiques des gains. C'est pourquoi les statistiques concernant le coût total de la main-d'œuvre font le plus souvent l'objet d'études spéciales [1].

Dès l'édition de 1974 de l'*Annuaire*, des modifications ont été apportées à la présentation des données de certains tableaux en raison de l'introduction de l'édition révisée 1968 de la Classification internationale type par industrie de toutes les branches d'activité économique (CITI); voir « Préface ».

Tableau 18

Salaires dans les secteurs non agricoles

Sauf indication contraire figurant en notes de bas de page, les séries présentées dans ce tableau couvrent les branches d'activité économique ci-après: industries extractives; industries manufacturières; électricité, gaz et eau; construction; commerce de gros et de détail, restaurants et hôtels; transports, entrepôts et communications; banque, assurances, affaires immobilières et services fournis aux entreprises; services fournis à la collectivité, services sociaux et services personnels. Dans quelques cas, toutefois, ces branches d'activité ne sont représentées que par une partie seulement des classes qui les composent.

---

[1] Voir notamment BIT: *Coût de la main-d'œuvre dans l'industrie européenne*, Etudes et documents, nouvelle série, n° 52 (Genève, 1959).

Tableau 19

Salaires dans les industries manufacturières

La partie A du tableau 19 indique les salaires dans l'ensemble des industries manufacturières; dans les quelques cas où d'autres branches d'activité sont également comprises dans la série, une indication est donnée à ce sujet en note de bas de page.

La partie B du tableau 19 concerne les salaires dans les industries manufacturières spécifiées. Les données sont présentées séparément pour chaque pays.

Dans toute la mesure possible, les différentes industries manufacturières ont été ordonnées conformément à la Classification internationale type, par industrie, de toutes les branches d'activité économique (voir annexe), avec indication du numéro de code correspondant aux différentes classes d'industries.

Tableaux 20 à 22

Salaires dans les industries extractives, dans la construction, ainsi que dans les transports, entrepôts et communications

Les tableaux 20 à 22 contiennent les statistiques des salaires dans trois branches d'activité économique principales, à savoir: tableau 20, industries extractives; tableau 21, construction; tableau 22, transports, entrepôts et communications (non compris les transports par mer).

Tableau 23

Salaires dans l'agriculture

Les statistiques des salaires dans l'agriculture présentées au tableau 23 se rapportent, dans la plupart des cas, aux travailleurs agricoles non spécialisés. Une distinction est faite entre les travailleurs *permanents*, les travailleurs *saisonniers* et les travailleurs *journaliers*; dans ce dernier groupe, on distingue les travailleurs journaliers *réguliers* et les travailleurs journaliers *occasionnels*.

Les modes de rémunération, les types de contrats de travail et les dispositions prises dans l'agriculture sont souvent très différents de ceux qui prévalent dans les autres branches d'activité. Pour indiquer le genre de statistiques des salaires présentées dans chaque colonne, on a adopté une notation spéciale: le symbole I placé en haut de la colonne indique que les statistiques se rapportent aux salaires totaux payés entièrement en espèces; le symbole II représenté seul indique que les chiffres se rapportent seulement à la partie du salaire payée en espèces, bien que les travailleurs reçoivent en outre des prestations en nature; l'adjonction du symbole *a* indique que la valeur des repas fournis est comprise dans le montant des salaires, tandis que le symbole *b* indique que le montant des salaires englobe la valeur du logement fourni. Bien qu'il soit précisé dans certains cas que les chiffres représentent des taux de salaire ou des gains, il y a lieu de relever que, dans la plupart des pays, on ne note que peu ou pas de différence entre les taux nominaux de rémunération et les gains effectifs des travailleurs agricoles.

Les comparaisons internationales des salaires sont sujettes à de plus grandes réserves pour l'agriculture que pour les autres branches d'activité. La nature du travail effectué par les différentes catégories de travailleurs agricoles et la durée de la journée de travail ou de la semaine de travail présentent également des différences considérables d'un pays à un autre. Les fluctuations saisonnières des salaires agricoles sont plus accusées dans certains pays que dans d'autres.

En général, les séries marquées I, qui représentent le salaire complet des travailleurs rémunérés entièrement en espèces, se prêtent mieux à une comparaison internationale que les séries marquées II + *a* + *b* ou simplement II. Les comparaisons entre les séries marquées II, dans lesquelles les chiffres ne comprennent pas la valeur des repas et du logement fournis par l'employeur, doivent faire l'objet de réserves spéciales car l'importance relative de ces paiements en nature diffère dans chaque cas.

Une réserve importante concernant les comparaisons internationales des séries marquées II + *a* + *b* réside dans le manque d'uniformité des méthodes suivies dans les différents pays pour estimer la valeur nominale des paiements en nature. Quand les données se rapportent aux mêmes professions et unités de temps (journée, semaine ou mois), ces séries peuvent néanmoins être considérées comme approximativement comparables entre elles ainsi qu'avec les séries marquées I, qui se rapportent également aux salaires complets des travailleurs couverts par ces séries.

Tableau 24

Rémunération des salariés et revenu national

Les chiffres de ce tableau ont été fournis par le Bureau de statistique des Nations Unies.

Les chiffres figurant sous la rubrique *rémunération des salariés* comprennent, en général, tous les paiements effectués par les producteurs-résidents à leur personnel, ou au bénéfice de ce dernier, sous forme: i) de salaires et traitements (en espèces ou en nature); ii) de cotisations (effectives ou imputées) à des régimes de sécurité sociale, des régimes privés de retraite, d'allocations familiales, d'assurance-maladie, d'assurance-accidents, d'assurance-vie ou autres systèmes analogues.

Etant donné que les statistiques de la rémunération totale prennent généralement la forme d'estimations globales et comprennent certains éléments de rémunération autres que le salaire, la rémunération totale ne doit pas être assimilée au « total des salaires et traitements payés ».

Le *revenu national* aux prix du marché est constitué, au sens du présent texte, par la somme: i) de la rémunération des salariés-résidents; ii) de l'excédent du revenu de la propriété et de l'entreprise que les agents-résidents économiques doivent recevoir sur le revenu de la propriété et de l'entreprise qu'ils doivent payer; iii) des impôts indirects *diminués* des subventions d'exploitation.

Les pourcentages du *revenu national* qui sont indiqués sous *rémunération des salariés* ne sont pas strictement comparables de pays à pays à une date donnée, en raison de la diversité des méthodes utilisées pour les évaluations.

Les données en *italique* sont fondées sur le nouveau Système de comptabilité nationale (SCN); les autres données sont fondées sur l'ancien SCN.

Pour les définitions des termes comptables et pour des statistiques plus détaillées, le lecteur voudra bien se reporter aux publications du Bureau de statistique des Nations Unies [1].

[1] Voir en particulier Nations Unies, Bureau de statistique: *Système de comptabilité nationale*, Etudes méthodologiques, série F, n⁰ 2, rev. 3 (New York, 1970), *Yearbook of National Accounts Statistics, 1973* (New York, 1975; en anglais seulement), et *Bulletin mensuel de statistique*.

Salarios

Los cuadros 18 a 23 presentan generalmente el *promedio de los salarios nominales brutos* por obrero (es decir, antes de la deducción de los impuestos a la renta y las cotizaciones del seguro social a cargo del trabajador). Cuando en ciertos casos los empleados han sido incluidos, así se indica en una nota de pie de página.

Las estadísticas presentadas se refieren generalmente a las *ganancias medias*; sólo cuando faltan datos de éstas se las reemplaza por estadísticas de *tarifas de salarios*. Cuando faltan cifras absolutas, se ofrecen índices de salarios. Los salarios por hora y por semana se presentan por países; a falta de tales datos, se dan los salarios por día o por mes, especialmente en el cuadro 23, relativo a los salarios en la agricultura. Los datos se refieren, en la medida de lo posible, a uno y otro sexo o bien a cada sexo por separado. Salvo indicación contraria, las series abarcan los trabajadores de uno y otro sexo, sin distinción de edades.

Las estadísticas de ganancias medias se obtienen por lo general de los datos de las nóminas de salarios proporcionados por una muestra de establecimientos, los que suelen dar al mismo tiempo indicaciones concernientes a las horas de trabajo y al empleo [1]. Por regla general, las ganancias medias por hora (o por día) se obtienen dividiendo el total de los salarios pagados en un período dado por el número de horas-hombre (o días-hombre) efectivamente trabajadas o pagadas durante ese mismo período; las ganancias por semana (o por mes) se calculan dividiendo el total de los salarios pagados en una semana dada (o mes) por el promedio de trabajadores empleados durante el período. Generalmente, los datos comprenden los pagos en dinero recibidos de los empleadores, es decir, la remuneración por las horas normales de trabajo, pagos por horas extraordinarias, las primas de estímulo, las ganancias de los trabajadores a destajo; la remuneración por horas de trabajo pagadas pero no efectuadas (vacaciones anuales, días feriados, ausencias por motivo de enfermedad y otros permisos pagados); las primas y gratificaciones, las asignaciones por carestía de vida y primas especiales (tales como la bonificación de fin de año). Con frecuencia incluyen también el valor de los pagos en especie; las asignaciones familiares se excluyen en la mayoría de los casos de las estadísticas de ganancias. En ciertos casos, las ganancias medias se obtienen de los *registros del seguro social*. Las estadísticas del seguro social arrojan, generalmente, promedios más bajos que los que se obtienen de las planillas de pago, pues aquéllos pueden excluir los pagos por horas extraordinarias, las primas de estímulo, etc., y además pueden no comprender los salarios de un valor superior a cierto límite. Más aún: el sistema de seguro puede limitarse solamente a los trabajadores de salarios bajos, o, si incluye a los de salarios altos, éstos pueden estar representados de manera incompleta en la compilación de las ganancias medias.

Las estadísticas de tarifas de salarios se basan de ordinario en los contratos colectivos, en las decisiones arbitrales o en otros procedimientos de fijación de salarios, donde generalmente se especifican las tarifas mínimas en determinadas ocupaciones o para grupos particulares de trabajadores. En algunos países las tarifas realmente pagadas se aproximan mucho a esos mínimos. En países donde está muy generalizada la práctica de fijar las tarifas de salarios, se calculan las series de las tarifas medias de salarios en determinadas industrias o grupos de industrias utilizando como ponderaciones las cifras correspondientes a la importancia numérica en un año dado de las diferentes ocupaciones sobre las cuales se dispone de tarifas en las industrias comprendidas en las estadísticas. Las estadísticas de tarifas de salarios se refieren generalmente sólo a las tarifas para los adultos que trabajan las horas normales, y por lo mismo no se incluyen los pagos por horas extraordinarias y por suplementos de salarios. En cambio, con frecuencia se incluyen en las estadísticas tanto las asignaciones por carestía de vida como otras asignaciones determinadas por el sistema de fijación de salarios (por ejemplo, los subsidios de vivienda). Algunos países establecen promedios de *tarifas efectivamente pagadas* (ganancias de tiempo seguido) sir-

---

[1] Para un estudio detallado de los métodos estadísticos de salarios, véase *Estadísticas de nóminas de salarios y de ganancias*, Estudios y documentos, nueva serie, núm. 16 (Ginebra, 1949).

viéndose de las nóminas de pagos de establecimientos y utilizando el mismo método que para las ganancias medias. Las tarifas efectivamente pagadas comprenden en general la remuneración del tiempo normalmente trabajado, es decir, las horas ordinarias y las extraordinarias, pero excluyen las primas de estímulo y otras gratificaciones, como también la porción correspondiente a las primas en la remuneración por horas extraordinarias. Las tarifas efectivamente pagadas son compiladas a veces por los inspectores del trabajo.

Al hacer comparaciones entre las series de salarios se deben tener presentes las diferencias de conceptos, alcance, métodos de compilación y de presentación de las estadísticas [1]. Los datos sobre las ganancias presentan fluctuaciones que reflejan la influencia tanto de los cambios en las tarifas de salarios como en los demás suplementos de los salarios. Además, las ganancias diarias, semanales o mensuales dependen en gran parte de las variaciones en el promedio de horas de trabajo. Las estadísticas de las tarifas de salarios no revelan la influencia de las modificaciones de los suplementos de los salarios ni la influencia de las variaciones de las horas de trabajo. Las fluctuaciones de las ganancias medias que se obtienen de las nóminas de salarios globales dependen también de los cambios en la estructura del empleo, es decir, la mayor o menor importancia relativa que tengan los hombres, las mujeres, los trabajadores no calificados y los trabajadores calificados, etc.; las tarifas medias de salarios se calculan ordinariamente utilizando como ponderación la estructura del empleo en un año determinado. Las ganancias medias por hora son ordinariamente mayores que las tarifas por hora, ya que las primeras incluyen el pago de las horas extraordinarias, las primas, las bonificaciones y otras gratificaciones que no se incluyen en las estadísticas de tarifas de salarios. Las ganancias medias por semana o por mes son

más elevadas que sus correspondientes tarifas, pero a veces pueden no existir dichas tarifas de salarios por razón de la pérdida de tiempo laborable a causa de enfermedad, absentismo o trabajo a media jornada.

Las comparaciones en el tiempo se ven menos afectadas por las diferencias de conceptos, definiciones y métodos de compilación de los datos que las comparaciones de los niveles de salarios en una fecha determinada.

La determinación de las diferencias internacionales en el *ingreso real en salario* de los trabajadores requiere la conversión de los datos a una moneda común de referencia mediante el empleo de factores particulares que indiquen el poder de compra de las monedas en cuestión respecto de los bienes de consumo y los servicios. Sólo pueden hacerse comparaciones satisfactorias de este género entre países de características similares, y ellas deben basarse de preferencia en encuestas uniformes especiales que utilicen ordinariamente el concepto de ganancias netas e incluyan las asignaciones familiares [2]. En general, pueden obtenerse más fácilmente indicaciones aproximadas de las tendencias de los salarios reales dividiendo las ganancias brutas medias (o los índices de ganancias brutas) por el índice de precios del consumo.

Las comparaciones del *costo total de la mano de obra* entre diferentes industrias de un país o entre diversos países no pueden efectuarse utilizando sólo las estadísticas de salarios. Aunque las ganancias brutas constituyen evidentemente la parte más importante del costo de la mano de obra, los suplementos de los salarios tales como las asignaciones familiares, ciertas bonificaciones y gratificaciones o las contribuciones pagadas por el empleador a las cajas del seguro social o los servicios de bienestar proporcionados a los trabajadores por los establecimientos constituyen una porción considerable del costo total de la mano de obra en determinadas industrias y en ciertos países que no figuran normalmente en las estadísticas de ganancias. Las estadísticas del costo total de la mano de obra son, por lo

---

[1] Para las descripciones de las diversas series nacionales, su alcance, métodos de compilación utilizados, etc., véase OIT: *Guía Técnica 1976* (descripciones de las series generales publicadas en el *Boletín* y el *Anuario de Estadísticas del Trabajo*), vol. II, « Empleo — Desempleo — Horas de trabajo — Salarios » (Ginebra, 1976).

[2] Véase, por ejemplo, Office statistique des Communautés européennes: *Salaires CEE, 1964*, Statistiques sociales, 1966, nº 5 (en francés solamente).

tanto, en la mayoría de los casos, objeto de estudios especiales [1].

A partir de la edición de 1974 del *Anuario*, **se ha modificado la presentación de los datos de ciertos cuadros, debido a la introducción de la edición revisada 1968 de la Clasificación industrial internacional uniforme de todas las actividades económicas (CIIU); véase « Prefacio ».**

Cuadro 18

Salarios en los sectores no agrícolas

Salvo indicación contraria en notas de pie de página, las series de salarios de este cuadro incluyen las siguientes divisiones de la actividad económica: minas y canteras; industrias manufactureras; electricidad, gas y agua; construcción; comercio al por mayor y al por menor y restaurantes y hoteles; transportes, almacenaje y comunicaciones; establecimientos financieros, seguros, bienes inmuebles y servicios prestados a las empresas; servicios comunales, sociales y personales. En algunos casos, estas divisiones sólo están representadas por una parte de los grupos que las componen.

Cuadro 19

Salarios en las industrias manufactureras

La parte A del cuadro 19 indica las estadísticas de salarios en todas las industrias manufactureras; cuando en ciertos casos se incluyen otras industrias, así se indica en notas de pie de página.

La parte B del cuadro 19 presenta las estadísticas de salarios en industrias manufactureras especificadas. Se presentan los datos de cada país por separado.

En la medida de lo posible, las diferentes industrias manufactureras han sido ordenadas según la Clasificación industrial internacional uniforme de todas las actividades económicas

---

[1] Véase, por ejemplo, OIT: *Coût de la main-d'œuvre dans l'industrie européenne*, Etudes et documents, nouvelle série, n° 52 (Ginebra, 1959; en inglés y francés solamente).

(véase apéndice), con indicación del correspondiente número de código de los diferentes grupos de industrias.

Cuadros 20 a 22

Salarios en minas y canteras; construcción; transportes, almacenaje y comunicaciones

Los cuadros 20 a 22 presentan las estadísticas de salarios en tres divisiones principales de actividad económica, a saber: cuadro 20: minas y canteras; cuadro 21: construcción; cuadro 22: transportes, almacenaje y comunicaciones (excl. el transporte marítimo).

Cuadro 23

Salarios en la agricultura

Las estadísticas de los salarios en la agricultura presentadas en el cuadro 23 se refieren ordinariamente a los trabajadores agrícolas en general. Se distingue entre trabajadores *permanentes*, trabajadores *de temporada* y *jornaleros*; este último grupo se subdivide en jornaleros *regulares* y jornaleros *ocasionales*.

Los sistemas de remuneración y los tipos de contratos y de acuerdos en la agricultura son a menudo muy diferentes de los que rigen en otras actividades. Para indicar el género de las estadísticas de salarios presentadas en cada columna se ha adoptado una notación especial: el símbolo I en la parte superior de la columna indica que las cifras se refieren a salarios totales pagados por entero en dinero. El símbolo II, a solas, indica que las cifras se refieren únicamente a la porción en dinero de los salarios, aun cuando los trabajadores reciban pagos en especie; cuando se ha agregado el símbolo *a*, las cifras incluyen, como parte del salario, las comidas suministradas, y, del mismo modo, el símbolo *b* indica que se incluye el valor del alojamiento proporcionado. Aunque se indica en ciertos casos que las cifras representan tarifas de salarios o ganancias, es característico de la agricultura que en la mayoría de los países haya poca o ninguna diferencia entre las tarifas nominales de salarios y las ganancias efectivas de los agricultores.

Las comparaciones internacionales de salarios en la agricultura se hallan sujetas a reservas aún mayores que las de otras actividades. La naturaleza del trabajo que efectúan las diferentes categorías de trabajadores agrícolas y la duración de la jornada o de la semana de trabajo varían considerablemente de un país a otro. En ciertos países, los salarios agrícolas sufren variaciones estacionales más importantes que en otros.

En general, las series marcadas con el símbolo I, que representan el salario total de aquellos trabajadores cuya remuneración se paga enteramente en efectivo, se prestan mejor a la comparación internacional que las series marcadas ya sea con II + a + b o simplemente con II. Las comparaciones entre las series marcadas solamente II, en las que las cifras no incluyen el valor de la alimentación ni el del alojamiento proporcionados por el empleador, deben ser objeto de especiales reservas, dadas las diferencias en la importancia relativa de estos pagos en especie.

Un inconveniente importante en las comparaciones internacionales de las series marcadas II + a + b es la falta de uniformidad de los métodos utilizados en los diferentes países para estimar el valor en dinero de los pagos en especie incluidos en los datos. Cuando las informaciones se refieren a las mismas ocupaciones y unidades de tiempo (día, semana o mes), estas series pueden considerarse como aproximadamente comparables, tanto entre sí como con las series marcadas I, que corresponden también a los salarios totales de los trabajadores comprendidos.

Las cifras que indican la *remuneración de los asalariados* comprenden generalmente todos los pagos efectuados por los productores residentes a sus empleados o en beneficio de éstos, en forma de: i) sueldos y salarios (en dinero y en especie), y ii) contribuciones (efectivas o imputadas) a la seguridad social, cajas privadas de pensiones, subsidios familiares, seguros de enfermedad y accidentes, seguros de vida y otros regímenes análogos.

Como las estadísticas de las remuneraciones totales son generalmente estimaciones globales que incluyen elementos de remuneración que no forman parte de los sueldos y salarios, no deben identificarse con el « total de salarios y sueldos pagados ».

La *renta nacional* a precios de mercado se define aquí como la suma de: i) la remuneración de los empleados residentes; ii) la diferencia entre la renta de la propiedad y de la empresa a recibir por los agentes económicos residentes y la renta de la propiedad y de la empresa a pagar por ellos, y iii) los impuestos indirectos *netos* de subvenciones.

En razón de los diversos métodos empleados en las evaluaciones, los porcentajes de la *remuneración de los asalariados* con respecto a la *renta nacional* no son estrictamente comparables entre países, en una fecha dada.

Los datos en *itálicas* están basados sobre el nuevo Sistema de cuentas nacionales (SCN); los otros datos están basados sobre el antiguo SCN.

Respecto a definiciones más completas de los conceptos de contabilidad nacional y a estadísticas más detalladas, se recomienda la consulta de las publicaciones de la Oficina de Estadística de las Naciones Unidas [1].

Cuadro 24

Remuneración de asalariados y renta nacional

Las cifras de este cuadro han sido proporcionadas por la Oficina de Estadística de las Naciones Unidas.

---

[1] Véanse, en particular, Naciones Unidas, Oficina de Estadística: *Un sistema de cuentas nacionales*, Estudios de métodos, serie F, núm. 2, rev. 3 (Nueva York, 1970); *Yearbook of National Accounts Statistics, 1973* (Nueva York, 1975), y *Bulletin mensuel de statistique* (en inglés y francés solamente).

WAGES

18 Wages in non-agricultural sectors
Salaires dans les secteurs non agricoles
Salarios en los sectores no agrícolas

Earnings *(E.G.)* or rates *(R.T.)* per hour, day, week or month

Gains *(E.G.)* ou taux *(R.T.)* par heure, jour, semaine ou mois

Ganancias *(E.G.)* o tarifas *(R.T.)* por hora día, semana o mes

Date / *Date* / Fecha	AFRICA — AFRIQUE — AFRICA					
	Algérie	Egypt			Ghana	Malawi
	Hour / *Heure* / Hora	Week [2] — *Semaine* [2] — Semana [2]			Month / *Mois* / Mes	Month / *Mois* / Mes
		Males / *Hommes* / Hombres	Females / *Femmes* / Mujeres	M. + F. / H. + F. / H. + M.		
	(E.G.) [1]	*(E.G.)*			*(E.G.)* [3]	*(E.G.)* [3]
	Dinars	Piastres	Piastres	Piastres	Cedis	Kwacha
1965	.	329	211	323	47.04	.
1966	.	349	250	343	50.99	.
1967	.	337	230	331	54.90	.
1968	2.24	373	253	366	62.80	33.42
1969	2.07	409	289	402	65.91	36.27
1970	2.80	410	252	401	72.91	37.13
1971	2.63	...	...	...	77.38	37.06
1972	2.88	...	...	...	81.11 * [4]	36.84
1973	2.94	...	...	...	...	37.71
1974	...	...	...	...	...	40.99
1975: VI	.		.	.	...	44.27 [13]

Date / *Date* / Fecha	AFRICA — AFRIQUE — AFRICA					
	Mali	Mauritius	Sierra Leone [7]	Tanzania (Tanganyika)	Zambia	
	Hour / *Heure* / Hora	Day [6] / *Jour* [6] / Día [6]	Week [8] / *Semaine* [8] / Semana [8]	Month [9] / *Mois* [9] / Mes [9]	Month — *Mois* — Mes	
					Zambians / *Zambiens* / Zambianos	Others / *Autres* / Otros
	(E.G.) [5]	*(E.G.)*	*(E.G.)*	*(E.G.)* [10]	*(E.G.)* [3, 11]	
	Francs	Rupees	Leones	Shillings	Kwacha	Kwacha
1965	.	.	.	286	38.6	293.4
1966	.	5.86	7.06	315	46.4	346.2
1967	.	5.71	7.29	336	64.8	384.8
1968	.	5.67	6.78	350	68.0	353.0
1969	.	5.62	7.98	413	72.0	429.0
1970	.	5.94	8.36	400	77.4	420.9
1971	73.00	6.58	8.48	...	86.5	470.0
1972	73.96	7.58	8.89	...	85.1	397.8
1973	...	7.64	8.77	...	85.3 [12]	401.5 [12]
1974	109.88	9.69	9.35	...	93.6 [12]	422.9 [12]
1975: VI	.	.	.	.	.	.

EXPLANATORY NOTES: See p. 585.

[1] April of each year. [2] Oct. of each year. [3] Incl. salaried employees. [4] Average of March, June and Sep. [5] Dec. of each year. [6] March and Sep. of each year. [7] Excl. commerce and services. Adults only. [8] May and Nov. of each year. [9] June of each year. [10] Adult males. [11] 1965-69: incl. the value of payments in kind. Beginning 1967: fourth quarter of each year. [12] June. [13] First quarter.

NOTES EXPLICATIVES: Voir p. 589.

[1] *Avril de chaque année.* [2] *Oct. de chaque année.* [3] *Y compris les employés.* [4] *Moyenne de mars, juin et sept.* [5] *Déc. de chaque année.* [6] *Mars et sept. de chaque année.* [7] *Non compris le commerce et les services. Adultes seulement.* [8] *Mai et nov. de chaque année.* [9] *Juin de chaque année.* [10] *Hommes adultes.* [11] *1965-1969: y compris la valeur des paiements en nature. A partir de 1967: quatrième trimestre de chaque année.* [12] *Juin.* [13] *Premier trimestre.*

NOTAS EXPLICATIVAS: Véase pág. 594.

[1] Abril de cada año. [2] Oct. de cada año. [3] Incl. los empleados. [4] Promedio de marzo, junio y sept. [5] Dic. de cada año. [6] Marzo y sept de cada año. [7] Excl. el comercio y los servicios. Adultos solamente. [8] Mayo y nov. de cada año. [9] Junio de cada año. [10] Hombres adultos. [11] 1965-1969: incl. el valor de los pagos en especie. A partir de 1967: cuarto trimestre de cada año. [12] Junio. [13] Primer trimestre.

18 Wages in non-agricultural sectors
Salaires dans les secteurs non agricoles
Salarios en los sectores no agrícolas

Earnings *(E.G.)* or rates *(R.T.)* per hour, day, week or month

Gains *(E.G.)* ou taux *(R.T.)* par heure, jour, semaine ou mois

Ganancias *(E.G.)* o tarifas *(R.T.)* por hora, día, semana o mes

Date / Date / Fecha	AMERICA — AMÉRIQUE — AMÉRICA							
	Antilles néerlandaises [1]	Barbados [2]	Bolivia	Canada [6]		Guyana [9]	Perú [2] (Lima-Callao)	Trinidad and Tobago
	Hour / Heure / Hora	Week / Semaine / Semana	Month / Mois / Mes	Week / Semaine / Semana	Hour [8] / Heure [8] / Hora [8]	Week / Semaine / Semana	Day / Jour / Día	Day [11] / Jour [11] / Día [11]
	(E.G.)	(E.G.) [3]	(E.G.) [7]	(E.G.) [7]	(R.T.)	(E.G.)	(E.G.) [10]	(R.T.) [12]
	Guilders	Dollars	Pesos	Dollars	(1970 = 100)	Dollars	Soles	(1970 = 100)
1965	.	30.59	.	91.01	69.4	.	72.60	82.2
1966	2.45	31.58	.	96.34	73.9	33.26	71.96	85.0
1967	2.55	29.69 [4]	.	102.83	79.5	38.27	77.74	86.9
1968	2.75	36.72	.	109.88	85.7	45.79	95.84	90.5
1969	2.83	38.38	.	117.64	92.4	49.95	107.32	95.3
1970	...	44.23	1 015.05	126.82	**100.0**	50.96	115.12	**100.0**
1971	...	52.14	1 095.45	137.64	108.6	55.28	123.52	106.5
1972	...	48.40 [4]	1 129.20	149.22	117.6	...	154.32	120.3
1973	...	58.58	1 260.03	160.46	...	...	189.17	132.8
1974	...	63.31 [5]	1 750.45	178.08	...	...	218.22	148.6
1975: VI	.	...	...	202.80 *	.	.	...	.

Date / Date / Fecha	AMERICA — AMÉRIQUE — AMÉRICA			ASIA — ASIE — ASIA		
	United States		Uruguay [2, 13]	Venezuela [15]	Cyprus [16]	Israel	Japan
	Hour / Heure / Hora	Week / Semaine / Semana	Month / Mois / Mes	Month / Mois / Mes	Hour / Heure / Hora	Month / Mois / Mes	Month / Mois / Mes
	(E.G.)		(R.T.) [14]	(E.G.)	(R.T.) [8]	(E.G.) [7]	(E.G.) [7, 18]
	.	.	(1970 = 100)	Bolívares	(1970 = 100)	Pounds	Yen
1965	2.45	95.06	.	.	69	490	39 360
1966	2.56	98.82	.	.	72	583	43 925
1967	2.68	101.84	33.0	.	75	585	48 714 [19]
1968	2.85	107.73	66.4	.	80	610 [17]	55 405
1969	3.04	114.61	87.1	1 098	91	638	64 333
1970	3.22	119.46	**100.0**	1 201	**100**	692	75 670 [19]
1971	3.44	127.28	127.9	1 254	112	797	86 834
1972	3.67	136.16	187.6	1 316	129	904	100 586
1973	3.92	145.43	362.0	1 356	151	1 147	122 545 [19]
1974	4.22	154.45	629.8	1 530 *	...	1 561	154 967
1975: VI	4.50	163.35	918.9 [20]	...	.	1 969 [21]	212 243

EXPLANATORY NOTES: See p. 585.

[1] Excl. commerce. Males only. [2] Excl. mining and quarrying. [3] Adult males. [4] March and Sep. [5] Average of March, June and Sep. [6] Incl. forestry and logging. [7] Incl. salaried employees. [8] Oct. of each year. [9] Excl. commerce. [10] June of each year. [11] May and Nov. of each year. [12] Minimum rates. Adults only. [13] Montevideo; private sector only. Incl. salaried employees. [14] Minimum rates; incl. social benefits. [15] Excl. construction and transport. [16] Incl. agriculture. [17] Series replacing former series. [18] Incl. family allowances, mid- and end-of-year bonuses. [19] Sampling design revised. [20] March. [21] April.

NOTES EXPLICATIVES: Voir p. 589.

[1] *Non compris le commerce. Hommes seulement.* [2] *Non compris les industries extractives.* [3] *Hommes adultes.* [4] *Mars et sept.* [5] *Moyenne de mars, juin et sept.* [6] *Y compris la sylviculture et l'exploitation forestière.* [7] *Y compris les employés.* [8] *Oct. de chaque année.* [9] *Non compris le commerce.* [10] *Juin de chaque année.* [11] *Mai et nov. de chaque année.* [12] *Taux minima. Adultes seulement.* [13] *Montevideo; secteur privé seulement. Y compris les employés.* [14] *Taux minima; y compris les prestations sociales.* [15] *Non compris la construction et les transports.* [16] *Y compris l'agriculture.* [17] *Série remplaçant la précédente.* [18] *Y compris les allocations familiales et les primes de mi- et de fin d'année.* [19] *Plan d'échantillonnage révisé.* [20] *Mars.* [21] *Avril.*

NOTAS EXPLICATIVAS: Véase pág. 594.

[1] Excl. el comercio. Hombres solamente. [2] Excl. las minas y canteras. [3] Hombres adultos. [4] Marzo y sept. [5] Promedio de marzo, junio y sept. [6] Incl. la silvicultura y la explotación de la madera. [7] Incl. los empleados. [8] Oct. de cada año. [9] Excl. el comercio. [10] Junio de cada año. [11] Mayo y nov. de cada año. [12] Tarifas mínimas. Adultos solamente. [13] Montevideo; sector privado solamente. Incl. los empleados. [14] Tarifas mínimas; incl. las prestaciones sociales. [15] Excl. la construcción y los transportes. [16] Incl. la agricultura. [17] Serie que substituye a la anterior. [18] Incl. las asignaciones familiares y las primas de mitad y de fin de año. [19] Diseño de la muestra revisado. [20] Marzo. [21] Abril.

WAGES

18 Wages in non-agricultural sectors
Salaires dans les secteurs non agricoles
Salarios en los sectores no agrícolas

Earnings *(E.G.)* or rates *(R.T.)* per hour, day, week or month

Gains *(E.G.)* ou taux *(R.T.)* par heure, jour, semaine ou mois

Ganancias *(E.G.)* o tarifas *(R.T.)* por hora, día, semana o mes

Date / Date / Fecha	Korea, Rep. of [1] Month / Mois / Mes (E.G.) [2,3]	Philippines [4,5] Month / Mois / Mes (E.G.)	Day[6] — Jour[6] — Día[6] Skilled workers / Ouvriers qualifiés / Obreros calificados (R.T.)	Unskilled workers / Ouvriers non qualifiés / Obreros no calificados (R.T.)	Singapore [8] Hour[9] / Heure[9] / Hora[9] (E.G.) [10]	Sri Lanka Hour[11] / Heure[11] / Hora[11] (E.G.) [12]	Day[11] / Jour[11] / Día[11]
	Won	Pesos	Pesos	Pesos	Cents	Cents	Rupees
1965	.	192	8.51	6.34	93	79.77	7.05
1966	.	211	8.94	6.81	92	80.90	7.29
1967	.	224	9.35	7.13	97	82.48	7.41
1968	.	225	10.11	7.93	96	87.28	7.99
1969	11 610	234	10.64	8.30	96	91.90	8.28
1970	17 363	252	11.30	9.21	96	98.97	8.94
1971	20 988	272	11.89	9.84	99	104.25	9.29
1972	23 146	301	12.48	10.42	104	114.80	10.35
1973	26 954	337	13.14	10.69	119	109.18	9.97
1974	35 542	337 [7]	14.29 [7]	11.41 [7]	136	134.10	12.48
1975: VI	...	...	...	...	.	.	.

ASIA — ASIE — ASIA

Date / Date / Fecha	Sri Lanka Day[5] / Jour[5] / Día[5] (R.T.) [13,14]	Sud Viet-Nam, Rép. du [15] (Saigon-Cholon) — Day — Jour — Día Skilled workers / Ouvriers qualifiés[14] / Obreros calificados[14] M.+F. / H.+F. / H.+M. (E.G.) [3]	Labourers / Manœuvres[14] / Obreros no calificados[14] Males / Hommes / Hombres	Females / Femmes / Mujeres	M.+F. / H.+F. / H.+M.	République arabe syrienne Month[14] / Mois[14] / Mes[14] (R.T.) [1,13]	Thailand (Bangkok) Hour[17] / Heure[17] / Hora[17] (E.G.) [1]
	Rupees	Piastres	Piastres	Piastres	Piastres	Pounds	Baht
1965	3.88	126.86	97.53	77.81	89.12	170	.
1966	3.89	198.89	155.30	122.10	140.38	171	4.39
1967	4.05	307.36	221.21	202.26	212.97	172	5.30
1968	4.72	376.22	267.66	238.50	253.27	175	4.72
1969	4.72	451.35	338.08	290.64	315.46	175	4.60
1970	4.85	551.08	441.53	404.04	423.38	177	5.25
1971	5.15	669.36	557.44	482.37	523.05	182	5.94
1972	5.30	766.29	658.75	566.45	618.22	184	...
1973	5.83	968.50 [16]	842.60 [16]	662.20 [16]	759.40 [16]	184	...
1974	6.88	...	...	...	...	...	...
1975: VI	8.22	...	...	...	...	...	...

EXPLANATORY NOTES: See p. 585.

[1] Incl. salaried employees. [2] Incl. family allowances. [3] Incl. the value of payments in kind. [4] Earnings per month: excl. construction. [5] Rates per day: excl. mining, quarrying and services. [6] Manila. [7] Jan.-Sep. [8] Incl. agriculture. [9] July of each year. [10] Beginning 1969: adults only. [11] March and Sep. of each year. [12] Excl. services. [13] Minimum rates. [14] Adults only. [15] Excl. mining and quarrying. [16] June. [17] Sep. of each year, except for 1967: July, and 1969: Oct.

NOTES EXPLICATIVES: Voir p. 589.

[1] *Y compris les employés.* [2] *Y compris les allocations familiales.* [3] *Y compris la valeur des paiements en nature.* [4] *Gains par mois : non compris la construction.* [5] *Taux par jour : non compris les industries extractives et les services.* [6] *Manille.* [7] *Janv.-sept.* [8] *Y compris l'agriculture.* [9] *Juillet de chaque année.* [10] *A partir de 1969 : adultes seulement.* [11] *Mars et sept. de chaque année.* [12] *Non compris les services.* [13] *Taux minima.* [14] *Adultes seulement.* [15] *Non compris les industries extractives.* [16] *Juin.* [17] *Sept. de chaque année, sauf pour 1967 : juillet, et 1969 : oct.*

NOTAS EXPLICATIVAS: Véase pág. 594.

[1] Incl. los empleados. [2] Incl. las asignaciones familiares. [3] Incl. el valor de los pagos en especie. [4] Ganancias por mes: excl. la construcción. [5] Tarifas por día: excl. las minas, las canteras y los servicios. [6] Manila. [7] Enero-sept. [8] Incl. la agricultura. [9] Julio de cada año. [10] A partir de 1969: adultos solamente. [11] Marzo y sept. de cada año. [12] Excl. los servicios. [13] Tarifas mínimas. [14] Adultos solamente. [15] Excl. las minas y canteras. [16] Junio. [17] Sept. de cada año, salvo 1967: julio, y 1969: oct.

18 Wages in non-agricultural sectors
Salaires dans les secteurs non agricoles
Salarios en los sectores no agrícolas

Earnings *(E.G.)* or rates *(R.T.)* per hour, day, week or month

Gains *(E.G.)* ou taux *(R.T.)* par heure, jour, semaine ou mois

Ganancias *(E.G.)* o tarifas *(R.T.)* por hora, día, semana o mes

Date / *Date* / Fecha	Austria [1]	Belgique [2]	Bulgarie [3]	Czechoslovakia [3]	Denmark [7] Hour — *Heure* — Hora		
	Month / *Mois* / Mes	Hour / *Heure* / Hora	Month / *Mois* / Mes	Month / *Mois* / Mes	Males [8] / *Hommes* [8] / Hombres [8]	Females [8] / *Femmes* [8] / Mujeres [8]	M. + F. [8] / *H. + F.* [8] / H. + M. [8]
	(E.G.)	*(E.G.)*	*(E.G.)* [4, 5]	*(E.G.)* [5, 6]	*(E.G.)*		
	Schilling	(1970 = 100)	Leva	Korunas	Öre	Öre	Öre
1965	3 010	67	92.4	1 493	1 040	742	985
1966	3 333	74	96.4	1 534	1 162	839	1 104
1967	3 620	79	107.0	1 618	1 268	926	1 206
1968	4 130	83	113.8	1 750	1 415	1 043	1 347
1969	4 230	89	117.2	1 905	1 586	1 165	1 510
1970	4 590	**100**	123.8	1 938	1 753	1 290	1 670
1971	5 270	112	126.5	2 009	2 008	1 505	1 917
1972	5 820	128	130.9	2 091	2 245	1 714	2 149
1973	6 570	149	139.2	2 161	2 585	2 040	2 486
1974	7 500	180	143.2 *	2 232	3 071	2 497	2 967
1975: VI	.	211 *	.	2 292 [15]	3 420 [16]	2 838 [16]	3 315 [16]

Date / *Date* / Fecha	España [9]	France			
	Hour / *Heure* / Hora	Hour [10] / *Heure* [10] / Hora [10]	Hour — *Heure* — Hora		
			Males [8] / *Hommes* [8] / Hombres [8]	Females [8] / *Femmes* [8] / Mujeres [8]	M. + F. [8] / *H. + F.* [8] / H. + M. [8]
	(E.G.) [5]	*(E.G.)* [11]	*(R.T.)* [11]		
	Pesetas	Francs	Francs	Francs	Francs
1965	21.30	3.70	3.19	2.65	3.06
1966	24.92	3.91	3.38	2.81	3.24
1967	28.82	4.18	3.57	2.98	3.43
1968	31.44	4.76	3.97	3.40	3.83
1969	35.12	5.23	4.38	3.80	4.24
1970	40.09	5.84	4.82	4.19	4.66
1971	45.73	6.55	5.34	4.66	5.17
1972	53.55	7.46 [12]	5.97 [14]	5.24 [14]	5.80 [14]
1973	64.10	8.57	7.16	6.12	6.93
1974	81.30	9.48 [13]	8.50	7.33	8.24
1975: VI	.	.	9.58 [17]	8.27 [17]	9.28 [17]

EXPLANATORY NOTES: See p. 585.

[1] Excl. commerce. [2] Excl. commerce, transport, financing, insurance, real estate, etc., and services. [3] Socialised sector. [4] Incl. state agricultural undertakings. [5] Incl. salaried employees. [6] Incl. agriculture (except agricultural cooperatives), machine-tractor stations and state farms. [7] Excl. mining and quarrying, commerce, transport, financing, insurance, real estate, etc. [8] Adults only. [9] Excl. transport and services. [10] Oct. of each year, except for 1965-1966: Sep. and 1967: March. [11] Excl. mining and quarrying, state-operated transport (SNCF and RATP), communication, government and private domestic services. [12] Series replacing former series. [13] April. [14] Beginning Dec. 1972: revised series. [15] Second quarter. [16] First quarter. [17] March.

NOTES EXPLICATIVES: Voir p. 589.

[1] *Non compris le commerce.* [2] *Non compris le commerce, les transports, les banques, les assurances, les affaires immobilières etc., et les services.* [3] *Secteur socialisé.* [4] *Y compris les entreprises agricoles d'Etat.* [5] *Y compris les employés.* [6] *Y compris l'agriculture (à l'exclusion des coopératives agricoles), les stations de machines agricoles et de tracteurs et les fermes de l'Etat.* [7] *Non compris les industries extractives, le commerce, les transports, les banques, les assurances, les affaires immobilières, etc.* [8] *Adultes seulement.* [9] *Non compris les transports et les services.* [10] *Oct. de chaque année, sauf pour 1965-1966 : sept., et 1967 : mars.* [11] *Non compris les industries extractives, les transports gérés par l'Etat (SNCF et RATP), les communications, les services gouvernementaux et les services domestiques privés.* [12] *Série remplaçant la précédente.* [13] *Avril.* [14] *A partir de déc. 1972 : série révisée.* [15] *Deuxième trimestre.* [16] *Premier trimestre.* [17] *Mars.*

NOTAS EXPLICATIVAS: Véase pág. 594.

[1] Excl. el comercio. [2] Excl. el comercio, los transportes, los establecimientos financieros, los seguros, los bienes inmuebles, etc., y los servicios. [3] Sector socializado. [4] Incl. las empresas agrícolas del Estado. [5] Incl. los empleados. [6] Incl. la agricultura (pero excl. las cooperativas agrícolas), las estaciones de máquinas agrícolas y de tractores y las granjas del Estado. [7] Excl. las minas y las canteras, el comercio, los transportes, los establecimientos financieros, los seguros, los bienes inmuebles, etc. [8] Adultos solamente. [9] Excl. los transportes y los servicios. [10] Oct. de cada año, salvo 1965-1966: sept., y 1967: marzo. [11] Excl. las minas, las canteras, los transportes administrados por el Estado (SNCF y RATP), las comunicaciones, los servicios gubernamentales y los servicios domésticos privados. [12] Serie que substituye a la anterior. [13] Abril. [14] A partir de dic. de 1972: serie revisada. [15] Segundo trimestre. [16] Primer trimestre. [17] Marzo.

18 Wages in non-agricultural sectors
Salaires dans les secteurs non agricoles
Salarios en los sectores no agrícolas

Earnings *(E.G.)* or rates *(R.T.)* per hour, day, week or month

Gains *(E.G.)* ou taux *(R.T.)* par heure, jour, semaine ou mois

Ganancias *(E.G.)* o tarifas *(R.T.)* por hora, día, semana o mes

Date / Date / Fecha	German Democratic Republic △ [1,2] Month Mois Mes (E.G.) [3,4]	Germany, Fed. Rep. of △ [5] Hour — Heure — Hora Males Hommes Hombres (E.G.) [6]	Germany, Fed. Rep. of △ [5] Females Femmes Mujeres	Germany, Fed. Rep. of △ [5] M. + F. H. + F. H. + M.	Germany, Fed. Rep. of △ [5] Week Semaine Semana M. + F. H. + F. H. + M.	Gibraltar [8] Week [9] Semaine [9] Semana [9] (E.G.)	Hongrie [1,2] Month Mois Mes (E.G.) [3,10]
	Mark	Mark	Mark	Mark	Mark	£	Forints
1965	640	4.54	3.09	4.26	189.00	.	1 772
1966	653	4.84	3.33	4.55	200.00	.	1 862
1967	669	4.99	3.46	4.69	199.00	.	1 921
1968	700	5.18	3.60	4.88	211.00	.	1 928
1969	730	5.71	3.97	5.37	237.00	.	2 012
1970	762	6.49	4.49	6.09	268.00	13.72	2 139 [11]
1971	792	7.25	5.05	6.82	295.00	16.06	2 239
1972	818	7.89	5.53	7.42	319.00	17.60	2 342
1973	843	8.76 [7]	6.16 [7]	8.23 [7]	353.00 [7]	23.40	2 512
1974	867 *	9.68	6.90	9.13	382.00	24.44	2 682 *
1975: VI	.	10.33 [19]	7.46 [19]	9.77 [19]	397.00 [19]	.	2 803 * [20]

EUROPE — EUROPE — EUROPA

Date / Date / Fecha	Iceland [12] (Reykjavik) Hour — Heure — Hora Males — Hommes — Hombres Skilled Qualifiés Calificados (E.G.)	Iceland [12] Males — Hommes — Hombres Unskilled Non qualifiés No calificados	Iceland [12] Females Femmes Mujeres	Iceland [12] Total	Ireland (1) [13] Hour — Heure — Hora [14] Males [15] Hommes [15] Hombres [15] (E.G.)	Ireland (1) [13] Females [15] Femmes [15] Mujeres [15]	Ireland (1) [13] M. + F. [18] H. + F. [18] H. + M. [18]
	Kronur	Kronur	Kronur	Kronur	Pence	Pence	Pence
1965	79.63	61.92	42.15	60.70	29.5	17.2	25.3
1966	97.18	75.11	55.52	79.90	32.6 [16]	19.2 [16]	27.7 [16]
1967	101.25	79.00	60.48	84.01	34.7	20.0	29.4
1968	105.80	83.76	64.52	88.59	38.5	22.3	32.6
1969	117.54	95.13	75.11	99.97	44.8 [17]	24.7 [17]	37.3 [17]
1970	146.82	116.41	90.89	123.23	51.8	29.8	43.4
1971	174.77	133.16	105.14	143.52	59.2	34.3	50.2
1972	225.20	177.12	139.64	188.25	...	...	57.4 *
1973	289.89	224.44	169.76	239.15	...	...	...
1974	469.70	346.90	258.37	...	...	...	...
1975: VI	...	...	...	...	.	.	.

EXPLANATORY NOTES: See p. 585.

[1] State sector. [2] Incl. agriculture. [3] Incl. salaried employees. [4] Incl. family allowances. [5] Excl. commerce, transport, financing, insurance, real estate, etc., and services. [6] Incl. family allowances paid directly by the employers. [7] Sampling design revised. [8] Excl. mining and quarrying. [9] April and Oct. of each year, except for 1973: Oct., and 1974: April. [10] Incl. the value of payments in kind. Incl. loyalty money. [11] Revised series. [12] Excl. mining, quarrying and services. [13] Excl. commerce and transport. [14] Sep. of each year, except for 1965-68: Oct. [15] 1965-68: adults only. Beginning 1969: wages-earners (incl. juveniles) on adult rates of pay. [16] Scope of series revised. [17] Series replacing former series. [18] Incl. juveniles. [19] April. [20] Second quarter.

NOTES EXPLICATIVES: Voir p. 589.

[1] *Secteur d'Etat.* [2] *Y compris l'agriculture.* [3] *Y compris les employés.* [4] *Y compris les allocations familiales.* [5] *Non compris le commerce, les transports, les banques, les assurances, les affaires immobilières, etc., et les services.* [6] *Y compris les allocations familiales payées directement par les employeurs.* [7] *Plan d'échantillonnage révisé.* [8] *Non compris les industries extractives.* [9] *Avril et oct. de chaque année, sauf pour 1973 : oct., et 1974 : avril.* [10] *Y compris la valeur des paiements en nature. Y compris les primes d'assiduité.* [11] *Série révisée.* [12] *Non compris les mines, les carrières et les services.* [13] *Non compris le commerce et les transports.* [14] *Sept. de chaque année, sauf pour 1965-1968 : oct.* [15] *1965-1968 : adultes seulement. A partir de 1969 : ouvriers (y compris les jeunes gens) rémunérés sur la base de taux de salaire pour adultes.* [16] *Portée de la série révisée.* [17] *Série remplaçant la précédente.* [18] *Y compris les jeunes gens.* [19] *Avril.* [20] *Deuxième trimestre.*

NOTAS EXPLICATIVAS: Véase pág. 594.

[1] Sector de Estado. [2] Incl. la agricultura. [3] Incl. los empleados. [4] Incl. las asignaciones familiares. [5] Excl. el comercio, los transportes, los establecimientos financieros, los seguros, los bienes inmuebles, etc., y los servicios. [6] Incl. las asignaciones familiares pagadas directamente por los empleadores. [7] Diseño de la muestra revisado. [8] Excl. las minas y canteras. [9] Abril y oct. de cada año, salvo 1973: oct., y 1974: abril. [10] Incl. el valor de los pagos en especie. Incl. las primas de asiduidad. [11] Serie revisada. [12] Excl. las minas, las canteras y los servicios. [13] Excl. el comercio y los transportes. [14] Sept. de cada año, salvo 1965-1968: oct. [15] 1965-1968: adultos solamente. A partir de 1969: obreros (incl. los jóvenes) pagados sobre la base de tarifas de salarios para adultos. [16] Alcance de la serie revisado. [17] Serie que substituye a la anterior. [18] Incl. los jóvenes. [19] Abril. [20] Segundo trimestre.

18 Wages in non-agricultural sectors
Salaires dans les secteurs non agricoles
Salarios en los sectores no agrícolas

Earnings *(E.G.)* or rates *(R.T.)* per hour, day, week or month

Gains *(E.G.)* ou taux *(R.T.)* par heure, jour, semaine ou mois

Ganancias *(E.G.)* o tarifas *(R.T.)* por hora, día, semana o mes

	EUROPE — EUROPE — EUROPA						
Date *Date* Fecha	Ireland (2) [1]			Italie [7]		Luxembourg	Pays-Bas
	Week [2] — *Semaine* [2] — Semana [2]			Hour *Heure* Hora		Hour *Heure* Hora	Day *Jour* Día
	Males [3] *Hommes* [3] Hombres [3]	Females [3] *Femmes* [3] Mujeres [3]	M. + F. [6] H. + F. [6] H. + M. [6]				
	(E.G.)			*(E.G.)* [8]	*(R.T.)*	*(E.G.)* [9]	*(E.G.)* [11, 12]
	Pounds	Pounds	Pounds	Lire	(1970 = 100)	Francs	Guilders
1965	13.36	7.05	11.18	400	.	61.06	21.06
1966	14.74 [4]	7.82 [4]	12.15 [4]	415	.	64.42	23.22
1967	15.48	8.13	12.77	439	74.4	64.94	.
1968	17.15	8.97	14.12	459	77.2	71.51	39.36 [5]
1969	20.14 [5]	9.71 [5]	16.07 [5]	502	82.9	76.16	44.63
1970	23.14	11.47	18.58	617	**100.0**	86.48	48.89
1971	26.17	13.07	21.26	712	111.9	92.61	55.96
1972	30.05	15.01	24.38	797	122.2	101.86 [10]	...
1973	...	...	...	974	150.4	116.34	...
1974	...	...	...	1 217 *	180.6	144.85	...
1975: VI	.	.	.		231.8	.	.

	EUROPE — EUROPE — EUROPA						
Date *Date* Fecha	Pologne [13]	Roumanie [14]	Suisse [15]				Turquie
	Month *Mois* Mes	Month *Mois* Mes	Hour — *Heure* — Hora				Day *Jour* Día
			Males [16] — *Hommes* [16] — Hombres [16]			Females [16] *Femmes* [16] Mujeres [16]	
			Skilled and semi-skilled *Qualifiés et semi-qualifiés* Calificados y semicalificados	Unskilled *Non qualifiés* No calificados	Total		
	(E.G.) [8, 11]	*(E.G.)* [11]	*(E.G.)* [12]				*(E.G.)* [11]
	Zlotys	Lei	Francs	Francs	Francs	Francs	Liras
1965	1 895	.	5.28	4.51	5.01	3.10	21.62
1966	...		5.63	4.85	5.37	3.36	23.53
1967	...	1 211	6.16	5.21	5.84	3.57	25.83
1968	...	1 248	6.53	5.53	6.20	3.83	28.22
1969	...	1 299	6.86	5.81	6.51	4.04	32.13
1970	2 277	1 434	7.38	6.31	6.99	4.39	35.32
1971	2 399	1 471	8.25	7.12	7.85	5.01	39.32
1972	2 542	1 498	9.16	7.95	8.75	5.54	43.88
1973	2 830	1 563	10.44 [5]	8.87 [5]	9.29 [5]	6.18 [5]	54.41
1974	3 211 *	1 663	11.96	10.11	10.57	7.06	68.26
1975: VI	3 386 * [17]	.	.	.	.	.	.

EXPLANATORY NOTES: See p. 585.

[1] Excl. commerce and transport. [2] Sep. of each year, except for 1965-68: Oct. [3] 1965-68: adults only. Beginning 1969: workers (incl. juveniles) on adults rates of pay. [4] Scope of series revised. [5] Series replacing former series. [6] Incl. juveniles. [7] Excl. commerce, transport and services. [8] Incl. the value of payments in kind. [9] Oct. of each year. Excl. electricity, gas, water, commerce, transport, financing, insurance, real estate, etc., and services. [10] New industrial classification. [11] Incl. salaried employees. [12] Accident insurance statistics. [13] Socialised sector. Incl. sea fishing. [14] Socialised sector. Incl. agriculture and forestry. [15] Incl. forestry but excl. services. [16] Adults only. [17] First quarter.

NOTES EXPLICATIVES: Voir p. 589.

[1] *Non compris le commerce et les transports.* [2] *Sept. de chaque année, sauf pour 1965-1968 : oct.* [3] *1965-1968 : adultes seulement. A partir de 1969 : travailleurs (y compris les jeunes gens) rémunérés sur la base de taux de salaire pour adultes.* [4] *Portée de la série révisée.* [5] *Série remplaçant la précédente.* [6] *Y compris les jeunes gens.* [7] *Non compris le commerce, les transports et les services.* [8] *Y compris la valeur des paiements en nature.* [9] *Oct. de chaque année. Non compris l'électricité, le gaz, l'eau, le commerce, les transports, les banques, les assurances, les affaires immobilières, etc., et les services.* [10] *Nouvelle classification industrielle.* [11] *Y compris les employés.* [12] *Statistiques d'assurance-accidents.* [13] *Secteur socialisé. Y compris la pêche maritime.* [14] *Secteur socialisé. Y compris l'agriculture et la sylviculture.* [15] *Y compris la sylviculture, mais non compris les services.* [16] *Adultes seulement.* [17] *Premier trimestre.*

NOTAS EXPLICATIVAS: Véase pág. 594.

[1] Excl. el comercio y los transportes. [2] Sept. de cada año, salvo 1965-1968: oct. [3] 1965-1968: adultos solamente. A partir de 1969: trabajadores (incl. los jóvenes) pagados sobre la base de tarifas de salarios para adultos. [4] Alcance de la serie revisado. [5] Serie que substituye a la anterior. [6] Incl. los jóvenes. [7] Excl. el comercio, los transportes y los servicios. [8] Incl. el valor de los pagos en especie. [9] Oct. de cada año. Excl. la electricidad, el gas, el agua, el comercio, los transportes, los establecimientos financieros, los seguros, los bienes inmuebles, etc., y los servicios. [10] Nueva clasificación industrial. [11] Incl. los empleados. [12] Estadísticas del seguro de accidentes. [13] Sector socializado. Incl. la pesca marítima. [14] Sector socializado. Incl. la agricultura y la silvicultura. [15] Incl. la silvicultura pero excl. los servicios. [16] Adultos solamente. [17] Primer trimestre.

WAGES

18 Wages in non-agricultural sectors
Salaires dans les secteurs non agricoles
Salarios en los sectores no agrícolas

Earnings *(E.G.)* or rates *(R.T.)* per hour, day, week or month

Gains *(E.G.)* ou taux *(R.T.)* par heure, jour, semaine ou mois

Ganancias *(E.G.)* o tarifas *(R.T.)* por hora, día, semana o mes

	EUROPE — EUROPE — EUROPA					OCEANIA — OCÉANIE — OCEANÍA	
	United Kingdom [1]				Yugoslavia [5]	Australia	
Date	Hour [2] — *Heure* [2] — Hora [2]		Week [2] — *Semaine* [2] — Semana [2]		Month	Hour — *Heure* — Hora	
Date	Males [3]	Females [3]	Males [3]	Females [3]	*Mois*	Males [3]	Females [3]
Fecha	*Hommes* [3]	*Femmes* [3]	*Hommes* [3]	*Femmes* [3]	*Mes*	*Hommes* [3]	*Femmes* [3]
	Hombres [3]	Mujeres [3]	Hombres [3]	Mujeres [3]		Hombres [3]	Mujeres [3]
	(E.G.)				*(E.G.)* [6]	*(R.T.)* [7]	
	Pence	Pence	£	£	Dinars	Cents	Cents
1965	41.7	24.8	19.59	9.60	.	100.9	72.5
1966	44.1	26.4	20.30	10.07	705	105.0	75.4
1967	46.3	27.6	21.38	10.56	798	111.0	80.4
1968	49.6	29.5	23.00	11.30	877	117.4	84.0
1969	53.4 [4]	31.8 [4]	24.83 [4]	12.11 [4]	1 006	124.5	90.6
1970	61.4	36.9	28.05	13.99	1 189	131.6	97.3
1971	69.2	41.9	30.93	15.80	1 446	148.2	111.7
1972	79.6	48.3	35.82	18.30	1 690	161.4	125.9
1973	89.7	56.1	40.92	21.16	1 949	182.8	147.0
1974	107.8	72.2	48.63	27.01	2 486	231.8 *	200.6 *
1975: VI	.	.	.	.	3 020	226.8 * [14]	242.1 * [14]

	OCEANIA — OCÉANIE — OCEANÍA				URSS [5, 13]	RSS de Biélorussie [5]	RSS d'Ukraine [5]
	Australia [8, 9]	Fiji [8]	New Zealand [11]				
Date	Week *Semaine* Semana	Day [10]	Hour [12]	Week *Semaine* Semana	Month	Month	Month
Date	Males	*Jour* [10]	*Heure* [12]	Males [3]	*Mois*	*Mois*	*Mois*
Fecha	*Hommes*	Día [10]	Hora [12]	*Hommes* [3]	Mes	Mes	Mes
	Hombres			Hombres [3]			
	(E.G.) [6]	*(R.T.)*	*(E.G.)* [6, 9]	*(R.T.)* [7]	*(E.G.)* [6]	*(E.G.)* [6]	*(E.G.)* [6]
	Dollars	Dollars	Dollars	Dollars	Roubles	Roubles	Roubles
1965	56.90	1.83	0.95	.	99.4	.	96.0
1966	59.80	1.96	0.99	33.97	102.9	.	98.7
1967	63.70	2.01	1.04	35.81	107.3	.	102.0
1968	67.70	2.20	1.10	37.16	115.2	.	108.9
1969	73.60	2.32	1.16	39.19	119.7	.	112.4
1970	79.80	2.47	1.29	43.84	124.9	.	116.8
1971	89.50	2.72	1.54	55.01	128.3	114.9	120.1
1972	96.70	3.06	1.72	59.74	132.5	118.6	123.4
1973	108.80	3.96	1.94	66.46	137.1	123.5	126.5
1974	133.50	...	2.26	75.47	143.1 *	126.7 *	129.6 *
1975: VI	155.90 [15]	...	2.52 [14]	...	.	.	.

EXPLANATORY NOTES: See p. 585.

[1] Excl. coal mining, commerce, railways, financing, insurance, real estate, etc. [2] Oct. of each year. [3] Adults only. [4] New industrial classification. [5] Socialised sector. [6] Incl. salaried employees. [7] Minimum rates. [8] Incl. agriculture. [9] Incl. the value of payments in kind. [10] June of each year. [11] Earnings per hour: incl. forestry and logging. Rates per week: excl. commerce. [12] April and Oct. of each year. [13] Incl. Byelorussian SSR and Ukrainian SSR, shown separately in this table. [14] April. [15] Second quarter.

NOTES EXPLICATIVES: Voir p. 589.

[1] *Non compris les mines de charbon, le commerce, les chemins de fer, les banques, les assurances, les affaires immobilières, etc.* [2] *Oct. de chaque année.* [3] *Adultes seulement.* [4] *Nouvelle classification industrielle.* [5] *Secteur socialisé.* [6] *Y compris les employés.* [7] *Taux minima.* [8] *Y compris l'agriculture.* [9] *Y compris la valeur des paiements en nature.* [10] *Juin de chaque année.* [11] *Gains par heure : y compris la sylviculture et l'exploitation forestière. Taux par semaine : non compris le commerce.* [12] *Avril et oct. de chaque année.* [13] *Y compris les RSS de Biélorussie et d'Ukraine, figurant séparément dans ce tableau.* [14] *Avril.* [15] *Deuxième trimestre.*

NOTAS EXPLICATIVAS: Véase pág. 594.

[1] Excl. las minas de carbón, el comercio, los ferrocarriles, los establecimientos financieros, los seguros, los bienes inmuebles, etc. [2] Oct. de cada año. [3] Adultos solamente. [4] Nueva clasificación industrial. [5] Sector socializado. [6] Incl. los empleados. [7] Tarifas mínimas. [8] Incl. la agricultura. [9] Incl. el valor de los pagos en especie. [10] Junio de cada año. [11] Ganancias por hora: incl. la silvicultura y la explotación de la madera. Tarifas por semana: excl. el comercio. [12] Abril y oct. de cada año. [13] Incl. las RSS de Bielorrusia y de Ucrania, que figuran separadamente en este cuadro. [14] Abril. [15] Segundo trimestre.

19 Wages in manufacturing
Salaires dans les industries manufacturières
Salarios en las industrias manufactureras

A All industries
Ensemble des industries
Todas las industrias

Earnings *(E.G.)* or rates *(R.T.)* per hour, day, week or month

Gains *(E.G.)* ou taux *(R.T.)* par heure, jour, semaine ou mois

Ganancias *(E.G.)* o tarifas *(R.T.)* por hora, día, semana o mes

Date *Date* Fecha	AFRICA — AFRIQUE — AFRICA					
	Algérie	Egypt			Ghana	Haute-Volta
	Hour *Heure* Hora	Week [2] — *Semaine* [2] — Semana [2]			Month *Mois* Mes	Month *Mois* Mes
		Males *Hommes* Hombres	Females *Femmes* Mujeres	M. + F. *H. + F.* H. + M.		
	(E.G.) [1]	*(E.G.)*			*(E.G.)* [3]	*(E.G.)*
	Dinars	Piastres	Piastres	Piastres	Cedis	Francs (CFA)
1965	.	305	235	301	47.63	.
1966	.	336	247	334	52.77	.
1967	.	324	229	318	54.47	.
1968	.	363	246	356	61.14	.
1969	2.36	410	298	403	64.81	13 396
1970	2.56	406	258	397	76.35	13 301
1971	2.63	...	...	...	77.59	22 317
1972	2.85	...	...	...	77.50 * [4]	...
1973	3.38	...	...	...	...	...
1974	...	...	...	...	...	...
1975: VI	.	.	.	.	...	.

Date *Date* Fecha	AFRICA — AFRIQUE — AFRICA					
	Malawi	Mali	Maroc (Casablanca)	Mauritius	Sierra Leone	South Africa, Rep. of
	Month *Mois* Mes	Hour [5] *Heure* [5] Hora [5]	Hour *Heure* Hora	Day [7] *Jour* [7] Día [7]	Week [8] *Semaine* [8] Semana [8]	Week *Semaine* Semana
	(E.G.) [3]	*(E.G.)*	*(R.T.)* [6]	*(E.G.)*	*(E.G.)* [9]	*(R.T.)* [10]
	Kwacha	Francs	Dirhams	Rupees	Leones	(1969 = 100)
1965	.	.	0.85	.	.	90.0
1966	.	.	0.85	5.79	7.26	92.1
1967	.	.	0.85	5.66	7.57	95.2
1968	24.46	.	0.85	5.68	7.05	96.5
1969	27.61	.	0.85	5.95	7.88	**100.0**
1970	28.16	.	0.85	6.30	8.28	...
1971	29.56	78.00	0.96	6.02	8.35	...
1972	32.59	72.31	0.96	6.30	8.15	...
1973	32.26	85.33	1.15	5.86	12.23	...
1974	37.78	111.24	2.21	7.18	10.13 *	...
1975: VI	37.42 [11]	.	.	.	.	.

EXPLANATORY NOTES: See p. 585.

[1] April of each year. [2] Oct. of each year. [3] Incl. salaried employees. [4] Average of March, June and Sep. [5] Dec. of each year. [6] Minimum rates. Adult males. Dec. of each year. [7] March and Sep. of each year. [8] May and Nov. of each year. [9] Adults only. [10] Minimum rates. White adult males. Sep. of each year. [11] First quarter.

NOTES EXPLICATIVES: Voir p. 589.

[1] *Avril de chaque année.* [2] *Oct. de chaque année.* [3] *Y compris les employés.* [4] *Moyenne de mars, juin et sept.* [5] *Déc. de chaque année.* [6] *Taux minima. Hommes adultes. Déc. de chaque année.* [7] *Mars et sept. de chaque année.* [8] *Mai et nov. de chaque année.* [9] *Adultes seulement.* [10] *Taux minima. Hommes adultes (population blanche). Sept. de chaque année.* [11] *Premier trimestre.*

NOTAS EXPLICATIVAS: Véase pág. 594.

[1] Abril de cada año. [2] Oct. de cada año. [3] Incl. los empleados. [4] Promedio de marzo, junio y sept. [5] Dic. de cada año. [6] Tarifas mínimas. Hombres adultos. Dic. de cada año. [7] Marzo y sept. de cada año. [8] Mayo y nov. de cada año. [9] Adultos solamente. [10] Tarifas mínimas. Hombres adultos (población blanca). Sept. de cada año. [11] Primer trimestre.

WAGES

19 | Wages in manufacturing / Salaires dans les industries manufacturières / Salarios en las industrias manufactureras | A | All industries / Ensemble des industries / Todas las industrias

Earnings *(E.G.)* or rates *(R.T.)* per hour, day, week or month

Gains *(E.G.)* ou taux *(R.T.)* par heure, jour, semaine ou mois

Ganancias *(E.G.)* o tarifas *(R.T.)* por hora, día, semana o mes

	AFRICA — AFRIQUE — AFRICA			AMERICA — AMÉRIQUE — AMÉRICA		
	Tanzania (Tanganyika)	Zambia		Argentina	Barbados	Bolivia
Date		Month — *Mois* — Mes				
Date	Month [1]	Zambians	Others	Hour	Week	Month
Fecha	*Mois* [1]	*Zambiens*	*Autres*	*Heure*	*Semaine*	*Mois*
	Mes [1]	Zambianos	Otros	Hora	Semana	Mes
	(E.G.) [2]	*(E.G.)* [3, 4]		*(E.G.)* [6]	*(E.G.)* [2]	*(E.G.)* [3]
	Shillings	Kwacha	Kwacha	Pesos	Dollars	Pesos
1965	258	40.5	260.7	69.30	30.10	.
1966	293	40.3	302.7	94.47	31.52	.
1967	328	56.3	381.8	122.33	29.88 [8]	.
1968	331	52.9	415.9	127.09	34.10	.
1969	351	62.0	429.5	139.75	37.38	.
1970	372	65.0	436.5	1.65 [7]	44.21	902.22
1971	...	72.6	476.2	2.27	47.84	1 054.44
1972	...	75.3	408.7	3.31	49.57 [8]	1 088.19
1973	...	73.7 [5]	462.0 [5]	5.82	60.63	1 219.44
1974	...	86.4 [5]	459.3 [5]	...	66.99 [9]	1 709.44
1975: VI	...	.	.	.	...	...

	AMERICA — AMÉRIQUE — AMÉRICA				
	Brésil	Canada		Colombia	Chile
Date	Month	Hour	Week	Hour	Month [10]
Date	*Mois*	*Heure*	*Semaine*	*Heure*	*Mois* [10]
Fecha	Mes	Hora	Semana	Hora	Mes [10]
	(E.G.) [3]	*(E.G.)*		*(E.G.)*	*(E.G.)*
	Cruzeiros	Dollars	Dollars	Pesos	Escudos
1965	.	2.12	86.89	3.65	212.14
1966	171.12	2.25	91.65	4.15	307.18
1967	224.25	2.40	96.84	4.58	391.50
1968	292.98	2.58	104.00	5.05	525.16
1969	371.53	2.79	111.72	5.53	722.39
1970	442.36	3.01	119.69	6.47	1 041.63
1971	...	3.28	130.16	7.39	1 480.69
1972	750.78	3.54	141.47	8.04	2 408.20
1973	...	3.85	152.46	9.21 *	7 265.56
1974	...	4.37	169.96	...	...
1975: VI	.	5.07 *	212.38 *	...	.

EXPLANATORY NOTES: See p. 585.

[1] June of each year. [2] Adult males. [3] Incl. salaried employees. [4] 1965-69: incl. the value of payments in kind. Beginning 1967: fourth quarter of each year. [5] June. [6] Minimum earnings; unskilled workers. [7] New currency introduced in Jan. 1970: 1 new peso = 100 old pesos. [8] March and Sep. [9] Average of March, June and Sep. [10] April of each year. Incl. the value of payments in kind.

NOTES EXPLICATIVES: Voir p. 589.

[1] *Juin de chaque année.* [2] *Hommes adultes.* [3] *Y compris les employés.* [4] *1965-1969 : y compris la valeur des paiements en nature. A partir de 1967 : quatrième trimestre de chaque année.* [5] *Juin.* [6] *Gains minima ; ouvriers non qualifiés.* [7] *Nouvelle monnaie introduite en janv. 1970 : 1 nouveau peso = 100 anciens pesos.* [8] *Mars et sept.* [9] *Moyenne de mars, juin et sept.* [10] *Avril de chaque année. Y compris la valeur des paiements en nature.*

NOTAS EXPLICATIVAS: Véase pág. 594.

[1] Junio de cada año. [2] Hombres adultos. [3] Incl. los empleados. [4] 1965-1969: incl. el valor de los pagos en especie. A partir de 1967: cuarto trimestre de cada año. [5] Junio. [6] Ganancias mínimas; obreros no calificados. [7] Nueva moneda adoptada en enero de 1970: 1 nuevo peso = 100 antiguos. [8] Marzo y sept. [9] Promedio de marzo, junio y sept. [10] Abril de cada año. Incl. el valor de los pagos en especie.

19

Wages in manufacturing
Salaires dans les industries manufacturières
Salarios en las industrias manufactureras

A

All industries
Ensemble des industries
Todas las industrias

Earnings *(E.G.)* or rates *(R.T.)* per hour, day, week or month

Gains *(E.G.)* ou taux *(R.T.)* par heure, jour, semaine ou mois

Ganancias *(E.G.)* o tarifas *(R.T.)* por hora, día, semana o mes

Date / *Date* / Fecha	República Dominicana	Ecuador		El Salvador (San Salvador) [2]			
	Month / *Mois* / Mes	Hour / *Heure* / Hora	Week / *Semaine* / Semana	Hour — *Heure* — Hora		Week — *Semaine* — Semana	
				Males / *Hommes* / Hombres	Females / *Femmes* / Mujeres	Males / *Hommes* / Hombres	Females / *Femmes* / Mujeres
	(E.G.) [1]	*(E.G.)*		*(E.G.)*			
	Pesos	Sucres	Sucres	Colones	Colones	Colones	Colones
1965	76.59	3.22	184	0.81	0.57	37.02	25.51
1966	71.73	3.40	193	0.83	0.61	39.45	27.28
1967	57.85	3.57	206	0.86	0.61	40.84	27.98
1968	64.48	3.91	226	0.89	0.72	43.13	32.89
1969	74.40	5.60	274	0.92	0.75	43.68	32.51
1970	72.06	6.10	293	0.94	0.77	45.08	34.80
1971	73.14	6.80	331	0.96	0.75	45.73	34.33
1972	78.15	8.10	391	0.99	0.77	45.70	35.19
1973	74.42	8.90	440	1.03	0.85	48.63	39.06
1974	...	...	...	1.13	0.94	53.61	44.75
1975: VI	.	...	...	...	...	...	...

Date / *Date* / Fecha	Guatemala (Guatemala)	Guyana	México	Nicaragua	Panamá	Perú (Lima-Callao)
	Hour / *Heure* / Hora	Week / *Semaine* / Semana	Month / *Mois* / Mes	Hour / *Heure* / Hora	Hour / *Heure* / Hora	Day / *Jour* / Día
	(E.G.)	*(E.G.)*	*(E.G.)*	*(E.G.)*	*(E.G.)*	*(E.G.)* [4]
	Centavos	Dollars	Pesos	Córdobas	Balboas	Soles
1965	37.3	.	1 324	2.08	0.65	75.54
1966	38.8	22.22	1 385	3.33	0.67	81.96
1967	40.1	26.26	1 468	3.54	0.70	...
1968	41.4	30.54	1 544 [3]	3.79	0.73	100.57
1969	43.3	33.88	1 621	...	0.74	112.52
1970	43.3	36.14	1 703	...	0.80	120.50
1971	43.5	35.90	1 851	...	0.81	128.65
1972	43.6	...	1 956	...	0.78	159.39
1973	43.6	...	2 202	...	...	195.50
1974	43.6 *	...	2 815	...	...	242.06
1975: VI	...	.	3 237 [5]	.	.	...

EXPLANATORY NOTES: See p. 585.

NOTES EXPLICATIVES: Voir p. 589.

NOTAS EXPLICATIVAS: Véase pág. 594.

[1] Incl. salaried employees. [2] Metropolitan area. [3] Beginning 1968: scope of series revised each year. [4] June of each year. [5] March.

[1] *Y compris les employés.* [2] *Région métropolitaine.* [3] *A partir de 1968 : portée de la série révisée chaque année.* [4] *Juin de chaque année.* [5] *Mars.*

[1] Incl. los empleados. [2] Area metropolitana. [3] A partir de 1968: alcance de la serie revisado cada año. [4] Junio de cada año. [5] Marzo.

WAGES

19 A

19 Wages in manufacturing
Salaires dans les industries manufacturières
Salarios en las industrias manufactureras

A All industries
Ensemble des industries
Todas las industrias

Earnings *(E.G.)* or rates *(R.T.)* per hour, day, week or month

Gains *(E.G.)* ou taux *(R.T.)* par heure, jour, semaine ou mois

Ganancias *(E.G.)* o tarifas *(R.T.)* por hora, día, semana o mes

AMERICA — AMÉRIQUE — AMÉRICA

Date / Date / Fecha	Puerto Rico		Surinam	United States		Uruguay [1]	Venezuela
	Hour / Heure / Hora	Week / Semaine / Semana	Month / Mois / Mes	Hour / Heure / Hora	Week / Semaine / Semana	Month / Mois / Mes	Month / Mois / Mes
	(E.G.)		(E.G.)	(E.G.)		(R.T.) [2, 3]	(E.G.)
	Cents	$	Guilders	$	$	(1970 = 100)	Bolívares
1965	123.5	45.57	.	2.61	107.53	.	793.0
1966	129.5	48.30	.	2.72	112.34	.	806.5
1967	139.4	52.00	.	2.83	114.90	33.8	845.1
1968	154.7	57.74	.	3.01	122.51	70.3	914.3
1969	165.4	61.20	.	3.19	129.51	90.4	889.1
1970	176.0	64.59	.	3.36	133.73	**100.0**	959.9
1971	187.0	69.56	126	3.57	142.44	128.3	1 021.3
1972	200.0	74.40	132	3.81	154.69	190.4	1 093.8
1973	213.0	78.81	138	4.07	165.65	362.4	1 092.6
1974	232.0	85.61	...	4.40	176.00	637.4	1 283.0 *
1975: VI	255.0 [13]	91.87 [14]	.	4.76	187.54	925.9 [14]	...

ASIA — ASIE — ASIA

Date / Date / Fecha	Burma		Cyprus	Hong Kong	India [10]	Israel [11]
	Month — Mois — Mes		Week [6] / Semaine [6] / Semana [6]	Day [8] / Jour [8] / Día [8]	Month / Mois / Mes	Day / Jour / Día
	Males [2] / Hommes [2] / Hombres [2]	Females [2] / Femmes [2] / Mujeres [2]				
	(E.G.)		(E.G.) [7]	(R.T.)	(E.G.)	(E.G.) [2]
	Kyats	Kyats	Pounds	Dollars	Rupees	Pounds
1965	158.20	133.60	5.64	9.54 [9]	162.9	17.6
1966	154.24	136.31	6.46	10.16	176.0	20.4
1967	160.53	140.27	6.34	10.87	189.2	21.4
1968	155.97	130.45	6.72	11.43	204.1	22.6 [12]
1969	155.48	133.16	7.48	12.67	215.9	23.4
1970	162.57	136.25	8.12	14.78	227.2	26.2
1971	163.28	136.57	8.78	17.31	235.2	29.0
1972	139.90 [4]	132.12 [4]	10.16	19.14	250.9 *	33.0
1973	172.49 [5]	152.91 [5]	11.66	21.37	...	40.8
1974	...	...	13.71	22.49	...	56.0
1975: VI	.	.	.	.	.	76.6

EXPLANATORY NOTES: See p. 585.

[1] Montevideo; private sector only. [2] Incl. salaried employees. [3] Minimum rates; incl. social benefits. [4] April and Sep. [5] March and Sep. [6] Oct. of each year, except for 1969: Sep. [7] Adults only. [8] March and Sep. of each year. [9] March and August. [10] The number of states covered by the series varies according to the years. Incl. services, electricity, gas and water. [11] Beginning 1968: incl. mining and quarrying. [12] Scope of series enlarged. [13] May. [14] March.

NOTES EXPLICATIVES: Voir p. 589.

[1] *Montevideo ; secteur privé seulement.* [2] *Y compris les employés.* [3] *Taux minima ; y compris les prestations sociales.* [4] *Avril et sept.* [5] *Mars et sept.* [6] *Oct. de chaque année, sauf pour 1969 : sept.* [7] *Adultes seulement.* [8] *Mars et sept. de chaque année.* [9] *Mars et août.* [10] *Le nombre d'Etats couverts par la série varie selon les années. Y compris les services, l'électricité, le gaz et l'eau.* [11] *A partir de 1968 : y compris les industries extractives.* [12] *Portée de la série élargie.* [13] *Mai.* [14] *Mars.*

NOTAS EXPLICATIVAS: Véase pág. 594.

[1] Montevideo; sector privado solamente. [2] Incl. los empleados. [3] Tarifas mínimas; incl. las prestaciones sociales. [4] Abril y sept. [5] Marzo y sept. [6] Oct. de cada año, salvo 1969: sept. [7] Adultos solamente. [8] Marzo y sept. de cada año. [9] Marzo y agosto. [10] El número de Estados cubiertos por la serie varía según los años. Incl. los servicios, la electricidad, el gas y el agua. [11] A partir de 1968: incl. las minas y canteras. [12] El alcance de la serie es mayor. [13] Mayo. [14] Marzo.

19 Wages in manufacturing
Salaires dans les industries manufacturières
Salarios en las industrias manufactureras

A All industries
Ensemble des industries
Todas las industrias

Earnings *(E.G.)* or rates *(R.T.)* per hour, day, week or month

Gains *(E.G.)* ou taux *(R.T.)* par heure, jour, semaine ou mois

Ganancias *(E.G.)* o tarifas *(R.T.)* por hora, día, semana o mes

Date / Date / Fecha	ASIA — ASIE — ASIA						
	Japan	Korea, Rep. of	Pakistan	Philippines	Singapore	Sri Lanka	
	Month	Month	Month	Month	Hour [7]	Hour [9]	Day [9]
	Mois	*Mois*	*Mois*	*Mois*	*Heure* [7]	*Heure* [9]	*Jour* [9]
	Mes	Mes	Mes	Mes	Hora [7]	Hora [9]	Día [9]
	(E.G.) [1, 2]	*(E.G.)* [1, 4]	*(E.G.)*	*(E.G.)*	*(E.G.)* [8]	*(E.G.)*	
	Yen	Won	Rupees	Pesos	Cents	Cents	Rupees
1965	36 106	4 600	116.2	158	94	75.27	6.69
1966	40 510	5 420	127.8	171	91	74.69	6.82
1967	45 568 [3]	6 640	117.9	180	97	76.03	6.89
1968	52 699	8 400	129.6	182	96	81.15	7.53
1969	61 755	11 270 [5]	155.6	190	92	83.88	7.65
1970	71 447 [3]	14 150	152.7	215	90	90.52	8.28
1971	81 010	17 349	150.6	245	92	93.39	8.24
1972	93 627	20 104	193.0 *	275	98	109.27	9.89
1973	116 271 [3]	22 330	...	301	108	104.67	9.75
1974	146 464	30 209	...	314 [6]	126	127.21	12.30
1975: VI	188 981	35 094 [17]	.	...	.	.	.

Date / Date / Fecha	ASIA — ASIE — ASIA		EUROPE — EUROPE — EUROPA			
	République arabe syrienne [1]	Thailand (Bangkok)	Austria [12]	Belgique	Bulgarie [12, 15]	Czechoslovakia [16]
	Month	Hour [11]	Month	Hour [13]	Month	Month
	Mois	*Heure* [11]	*Mois*	*Heure* [13]	*Mois*	*Mois*
	Mes	Hora [11]	Mes	Hora [13]	Mes	Mes
	(R.T.) [10]	*(E.G.)* [1]	*(E.G.)*	*(E.G.)*	*(E.G.)* [1]	*(E.G.)*
	Pounds	Baht	Schilling	Francs	Leva	Korunas
1965	133	3.75	3 141	44.03	95	1 459
1966	135	3.27	3 514	48.58	98	1 486
1967	136	3.42	3 781	51.36	106	1 550
1968	140	3.58	4 018	54.22	113	1 653
1969	144	3.72	4 263	59.54	117	1 757
1970	148	3.66	4 662	66.16	124	1 841
1971	148	4.47	5 297 [5]	75.14	127	1 904
1972	148	...	5 912	87.58 [14]	132	1 979
1973	148	...	6 665	99.83	141	2 038
1974	...	...	7 710	125.28	144 *	2 144 *
1975: VI	.	.	9 695	.	.	2 218 * [18]

EXPLANATORY NOTES: See p. 585.

[1] Incl. salaried employees. [2] Incl. family allowances, mid- and end-of-year bonuses. [3] Sampling design revised. [4] Incl. family allowances. [5] Scope of series en larged. [6] Jan.-Sep. [7] July of each year. [8] Beginning 1969: adults only. [9] March and Sep. of each year. [10] Minimum rates. Adults only. [11] Sep. of each year except for 1965: June, 1967: July and 1969: Oct. [12] Incl. mining and quarrying. [13] Oct. of each year. [14] New industrial classification. [15] Socialised sector. [16] State industry. [17] May. [18] Second quarter.

NOTES EXPLICATIVES: Voir p. 589.

[1] *Y compris les employés.* [2] *Y compris les allocations familiales et les primes de mi- et de fin d'année.* [3] *Plan d'échantillonnage révisé.* [4] *Y compris les allocations familiales.* [5] *Portée de la série élargie.* [6] *Janv.-sept.* [7] *Juillet de chaque année.* [8] *A partir de 1969: adultes seulement.* [9] *Mars et sept. de chaque année.* [10] *Taux minima. Adultes seulement.* [11] *Sept. de chaque année sauf pour 1965: juin, 1967: juillet et 1969: oct.* [12] *Y compris les industries extractives.* [13] *Oct. de chaque année.* [14] *Nouvelle classification industrielle.* [15] *Secteur socialisé.* [16] *Industrie d'Etat.* [17] *Mai.* [18] *Deuxième trimestre.*

NOTAS EXPLICATIVAS: Véase pág. 594.

[1] Incl. los empleados. [2] Incl. las asignaciones familiares y las primas de mitad y de fin de año. [3] Diseño de la muestra revisado. [4] Incl. las asignaciones familiares. [5] El alcance de la serie es mayor. [6] Enero-sept. [7] Julio de cada año. [8] A partir de 1969: adultos solamente. [9] Marzo y sept. de cada año. [10] Tarifas mínimas. Adultos solamente. [11] Sept. de cada año, salvo para 1965: junio, 1967: julio, y 1969: oct. [12] Incl. las minas y canteras. [13] Oct. de cada año. [14] Nueva clasificación industrial. [15] Sector socializado. [16] Industria de Estado. [17] Mayo. [18] Segundo trimestre.

WAGES

19 A

Wages in manufacturing
Salaires dans les industries manufacturières
Salarios en las industrias manufactureras

All industries
Ensemble des industries
Todas las industrias

Earnings *(E.G.)* or rates *(R.T.)* per hour,
day, week or month

Gains *(E.G.)* ou taux *(R.T.)* par heure,
jour, semaine ou mois

Ganancias *(E.G.)* o tarifas *(R.T.)* por hora,
día, semana o mes

Date / *Date* / Fecha	Denmark Hour[1] — *Heure*[1] — Hora[1]			España Hour *Heure* Hora	Finland[5] Hour — *Heure* — Hora			France Hour *Heure* Hora
	Males[2] *Hommes*[2] Hombres[2]	Females[2] *Femmes*[2] Mujeres[2]	M. + F.[2] *H. + F.*[2] H. + M.[2]		Males *Hommes* Hombres	Females *Femmes* Mujeres	M. + F. *H. + F.* H. + M.	
	(E.G.)[3]			*(E.G.)*[4]	*(E.G.)*[6]			*(R.T.)*[2]
	Öre	Öre	Öre	Pesetas	Markkaa	Markkaa	Markkaa	Francs
1965	985	705	923	21.57	3.60	2.45	3.19	3.00
1966	1 107	794	1 040	25.13	3.89	2.68	3.45	3.18
1967	1 195	869	1 128	28.81	4.21	2.91	3.74	3.37
1968	1 355	1 003	1 283	31.16	4.69	3.25	4.18	3.79
1969	1 488	1 105	1 407	34.69	5.10	3.56	4.56	4.21
1970	1 654	1 231	1 568	39.47	5.64	3.97	5.06	4.66
1971	1 871	1 434	1 789	44.81	6.51	4.61	5.85	5.18
1972	2 080	1 621	1 993	52.20	7.43	5.30	6.69	5.82[7]
1973	2 421	1 992	2 337	62.48	8.68	6.22	7.78	7.05
1974	2 899	2 430	2 813	78.82	10.60	7.67	9.54	8.39
1975: VI	.	.	.	.	11.93[12]	8.50[12]	10.73[12]	9.44[13]

EUROPE — EUROPE — EUROPA

Date / *Date* / Fecha	German Dem. Rep. △[5,8] Month *Mois* Mes	Germany, Fed. Rep. of △ Hour — *Heure* — Hora			Week *Semaine* Semana	Grèce Hour — *Heure* — Hora		
		Males *Hommes* Hombres	Females *Femmes* Mujeres	M. + F. *H. + F.* H. + M.	M. + F. *H. + F.* H. + M.	Males *Hommes* Hombres	Females *Femmes* Mujeres	M. + F. *H. + F.* H. + M.
	(E.G.)[9]	*(E.G.)*[10]				*(E.G.)*		
	Mark	Mark	Mark	Mark	Mark	Drachmas	Drachmas	Drachmas
1965	640	4.49	3.09	4.12	182.00	11.77	7.31	10.13
1966	653	4.80	3.33	4.42	193.00	13.25	8.33	11.40
1967	663	4.99	3.45	4.60	194.00	14.50	9.74	12.74
1968	691	5.19	3.60	4.79	206.00	15.43	10.56	13.67
1969	713	5.72	3.97	5.28	232.00	16.88	11.68	15.06
1970	748	6.45	4.49	5.96	261.00	17.93	12.19	15.95
1971	777	7.20	5.05	6.66	287.00	19.70	13.04	17.35
1972	799	7.82	5.53	7.24	309.00	21.42	14.39	18.94
1973	828	8.69[11]	6.16[11]	8.03[11]	353.00[11]	25.12	16.46	22.04
1974	838 *	9.64	6.90	8.94	373.00	31.84	21.30	27.87
1975: VI	.	10.40[14]	7.45[14]	9.68[14]	391.00[14]	37.9[15]	26.4[15]	33.6[15]

EXPLANATORY NOTES: See p. 585.

[1] July-Sep. of each year. [2] Adults only. [3] Excl. vacation pay. [4] Incl. salaried employees. [5] Incl. mining and quarrying. [6] Incl. the value of payments in kind. [7] Beginning Dec. 1972: revised series. [8] State sector. [9] Incl. family allowances. [10] Incl. family allowances paid directly by the employers. [11] Sampling design revised. [12] First quarter. [13] March. [14] April. [15] May.

NOTES EXPLICATIVES: Voir p. 589.

[1] *Juillet-sept. de chaque année.* [2] *Adultes seulement.* [3] *Non compris les versements pour congés payés.* [4] *Y compris les employés.* [5] *Y compris les industries extractives.* [6] *Y compris la valeur des paiements en nature.* [7] *A partir de déc. 1972: série révisée.* [8] *Secteur d'Etat.* [9] *Y compris les allocations familiales.* [10] *Y compris les allocations familiales payées directement par les employeurs.* [11] *Plan d'échantillonnage révisé.* [12] *Premier trimestre.* [13] *Mars.* [14] *Avril.* [15] *Mai.*

NOTAS EXPLICATIVAS: Véase pág. 594.

[1] Julio-sept. de cada año. [2] Adultos solamente. [3] Excl. los pagos por vacaciones. [4] Incl. los empleados. [5] Incl. las minas y canteras. [6] Incl. el valor de los pagos en especie. [7] A partir de dic. de 1972: serie revisada. [8] Sector de Estado. [9] Incl. las asignaciones familiares. [10] Incl. las asignaciones familiares pagadas directamente por los empleadores. [11] Diseño de la muestra revisado. [12] Primer trimestre. [13] Mars. [14] Avril. [15] Mayo.

19 A

Wages in manufacturing
Salaires dans les industries manufacturières
Salarios en las industrias manufactureras

All industries
Ensemble des industries
Todas las industrias

Earnings *(E.G.)* or rates *(R.T.)* per hour, day, week or month

Gains *(E.G.)* ou taux *(R.T.)* par heure, jour, semaine ou mois

Ganancias *(E.G.)* o tarifas *(R.T.)* por hora, día, semana o mes

Date / *Date* / Fecha	Hongrie [1]	Ireland					Italie	
	Month / *Mois* / Mes	Hour [4] — *Heure* [4] — Hora [4]			Week [4] — *Semaine* [4] Semana [4]		Hour / *Heure* / Hora	
		Males [5] / *Hommes* [5] / Hombres [5]	Females [5] / *Femmes* [5] / Mujeres [5]	M. + F. [7] / H. + F. [7] / H. + M. [7]	M. + F. [7] / H. + F. [7] / H. + M. [7]			
	(E.G.) [2]	(E.G.)					(E.G.) [8]	(R.T.)
	Forints	Pence	Pence	Pence	Pounds		Lire	(1970 = 100)
1965	1 707	30.5	17.3	24.4	10.75		386	.
1966	1 786	33.8	19.3	27.3	11.95		401	.
1967	1 825	35.7	20.1	28.8	12.50		426	73.8
1968	1 869	39.5	22.4	31.9	13.81		445	76.5
1969	1 936	45.7 [6]	24.8 [6]	36.0 [6]	15.46 [6]		489	82.2
1970	2 039 [3]	53.0	29.8	42.4	18.10		606	**100.0**
1971	2 114	60.7	34.3	49.1	20.74		703	113.5
1972	2 210	69.2	39.6	55.9	23.64		788	125.4
1973	2 449	82.9	49.4	68.7	28.99		966	155.8
1974	2 626 *	99.6	59.3	83.0	34.46		1 213 *	190.7
1975: VI	2 682 *	…	…	…	…		.	242.5

EUROPE — EUROPE — EUROPA

Date / *Date* / Fecha	Luxembourg	Norway		Pays-Bas (1)			
	Hour [9] / *Heure* [9] / Hora [9]	Hour — *Heure* — Hora		Hour [9] — *Heure* [9] — Hora [9]			Week [9] — *Semaine* [9] Semana [9]
		Males [11] / *Hommes* [11] / Hombres [11]	Females [11] / *Femmes* [11] / Mujeres [11]	Males [11] / *Hommes* [11] / Hombres [11]	Females [11] / *Femmes* [11] / Mujeres [11]	M. + F. [7] / H. + F. [7] / H. + M. [7]	M. + F. [7] / H. + F. [7] / H. + M. [7]
	(E.G.)	(E.G.) [8]		(E.G.)			
	Francs	Kroner	Kroner	Cents	Cents	Cents	Guilders
1965	63.85	9.00	6.48	341	228	298	139.20
1966	66.73	9.64	7.04	374	260	328	152.75
1967	67.66	10.37	7.70	403	282	353	161.76
1968	73.22	11.21	8.38	436	313	383	175.05
1969	77.84	12.28	9.19	481	343	423	192.77
1970	88.51	13.75	10.32	548	392	482	215.68
1971	95.18	15.45	11.65	628	453	553	244.71
1972	108.91 [10]	16.82	12.82	698	508	616	270.06
1973	121.18 [10]	18.61	14.18	797	588	705	306.11
1974	151.94	21.83	16.75	…	…	…	…
1975: VI	.	24.69 [12]	19.12 [12]	.	.	.	.

EXPLANATORY NOTES: See p. 585.

[1] State industry. Incl. mining and quarrying. [2] Incl. the value of payments in kind. Incl. loyalty money. [3] Revised series. [4] Sep. of each year, except for 1965-68: Oct. [5] 1965-68: adults only. Beginning 1969: wage-earners (incl. juveniles) on adult rates of pay. [6] Series replacing former series. [7] Incl. juveniles. [8] Incl. the value of payments in kind. [9] Oct. of each year. [10] New industrial classification. [11] Adults only. [12] First quarter.

NOTES EXPLICATIVES: Voir p. 589.

[1] *Industrie d'Etat. Y compris les industries extractives.* [2] *Y compris la valeur des paiements en nature. Y compris les primes d'assiduité.* [3] *Série révisée.* [4] *Sept. de chaque année, sauf pour 1965-1968 : oct.* [5] *1965-1968 : adultes seulement. A partir de 1969 : ouvriers (y compris les jeunes gens) rémunérés sur la base de taux de salaire pour adultes.* [6] *Série remplaçant la précédente.* [7] *Y compris les jeunes gens.* [8] *Y compris la valeur des paiements en nature.* [9] *Oct. de chaque année.* [10] *Nouvelle classification industrielle.* [11] *Adultes seulement.* [12] *Premier trimestre.*

NOTAS EXPLICATIVAS: Véase pág. 594.

[1] Industria de Estado. Incl. las minas y canteras. [2] Incl. el valor de los pagos en especie. Incl. las primas de asiduidad. [3] Serie revisada. [4] Sept. de cada año, salvo 1965-1968: oct. [5] 1965-1968: adultos solamente. A partir de 1969: obreros (incl. los jóvenes) pagados sobre la base de tarifas de salarios para adultos. [6] Serie que substituye a la anterior. [7] Incl. los jóvenes. [8] Incl. el valor de los pagos en especie. [9] Oct. de cada año. [10] Nueva clasificación industrial. [11] Adultos solamente. [12] Primer trimestre.

19 — A

Wages in manufacturing
Salaires dans les industries manufacturières
Salarios en las industrias manufactureras

All industries
Ensemble des industries
Todas las industrias

Earnings *(E.G.)* or rates *(R.T.)* per hour, day, week or month

Gains *(E.G.)* ou taux *(R.T.)* par heure, jour, semaine ou mois

Ganancias *(E.G.)* o tarifas *(R.T.)* por hora, día, semana o mes

Date / Date / Fecha	Pays-Bas (2) Hour *Heure* Hora (R.T.)[1]	Pologne[2,3] Month *Mois* Mes (E.G.)[4,5]	Roumanie[3,6] Month *Mois* Mes (E.G.)[4]	Suisse Hour — Heure — Hora Males[1] — Hommes[1] — Hombres[1] Skilled and semi-skilled / Qualifiés et semi-qualifiés / Calificados y semicalificados (E.G.)[7]	Suisse Unskilled / Non qualifiés / No calificados (E.G.)[7]	Suisse Total (E.G.)[7]	Suisse Females[1] *Femmes*[1] Mujeres[1] (E.G.)[7]
	(1970 = 100)	Zlotys	Lei	Francs	Francs	Francs	Francs
1965	63	2 013	.	5.23	4.42	4.93	3.10
1966	71	2 072	.	5.58	4.76	5.29	3.36
1967	76	2 143	1 222	6.09	5.09	5.76	3.57
1968	83	2 230	1 254	6.45	5.42	6.11	3.82
1969	91	2 317	1 313	6.78	5.73	6.44	4.04
1970	**100**	2 382	1 432	7.30	6.25	6.96	4.39
1971	113	2 508	1 461	8.15	7.06	7.82	5.01
1972	128	2 627	1 482	9.06	7.87	8.72	5.54
1973	146	2 866	1 549	9.76[8]	8.26[8]	9.07[8]	6.14[8]
1974	173	3 275 *	1 660	11.07	9.35	10.23	7.02
1975: VI	193	3 697 *	.	.	.	.	.

EUROPE — EUROPE — EUROPA

Date / Date / Fecha	Suisse Hour[9] — Heure[9] — Hora[9] Males[1] — Hommes[1] — Hombres[1] Skilled / Qualifiés / Calificados (E.G.)[10]	Suisse Semi-skilled and unskilled / Semi-qualifiés et non qualifiés / Semicalificados y no calificados (E.G.)[10]	Suisse Total (E.G.)[10]	Suisse Females[1] *Femmes*[1] Mujeres[1] (E.G.)[10]	Sweden[12] Hour — Heure — Hora Males[13] *Hommes*[13] Hombres[13] (E.G.)[14]	Sweden[12] Females[13] *Femmes*[13] Mujeres[13] (E.G.)[14]	Sweden[12] M. + F. / H. + F. / H. + M. (E.G.)[14]	Turquie Day *Jour* Día (E.G.)[4]
	Francs	Francs	Francs	Francs	Kronor	Kronor	Kronor	Liras
1965	5.77	4.80	5.20	3.26	9.45	7.08	8.78	20.66
1966	6.17	5.16	5.58	3.52	10.26	7.85	9.60	22.66
1967	6.53	5.50	5.94	3.76	11.10	8.61	10.44	24.75
1968	6.89[11]	5.77[11]	6.24[11]	3.94[11]	11.83[15]	9.25[15]	11.17[15]	27.06
1969	7.30	6.17	6.64	4.23	12.85	10.16	12.15	31.80
1970	8.01	6.85	7.33	4.74	14.28	11.43	13.52	35.72
1971	8.97	7.78	8.27	5.37	15.64[11]	12.88[11]	14.91[11]	40.74
1972	10.07	8.66	9.24	5.98	17.49	14.65	16.76	45.21
1973	11.31	9.75	10.40	6.80	19.00	15.97	18.19	57.28
1974	12.71	11.03	11.73	7.71	19.05 *[15]	16.04 *[15]	17.81 *[15]	70.92
1975: VI	.	.	.	.	20.31[16]	17.07[16]	19.50[16]	.

EXPLANATORY NOTES: See p. 585.

[1] Adults only. [2] Socialised sector. Incl. sea fishing. [3] Incl. mining and quarrying. [4] Incl. salaried employees. [5] Incl. the value of payments in kind. [6] Socialised sector. [7] Accident insurance statistics. [8] Series replacing former series. [9] Oct. of each year. [10] Statistics of establishments. Incl. family allowances. [11] New industrial classification. [12] 1965-70: incl. mining and quarrying. [13] Adults only (both sexes together: incl. juveniles). [14] Incl. holiday and sick-leave payments and the value of payments in kind (except for 1974). [15] Sampling design revised. [16] May.

NOTES EXPLICATIVES: Voir p. 589.

[1] *Adultes seulement.* [2] *Secteur socialisé. Y compris la pêche maritime.* [3] *Y compris les industries extractives.* [4] *Y compris les employés.* [5] *Y compris la valeur des paiements en nature.* [6] *Secteur socialisé.* [7] *Statistiques d'assurance-accidents.* [8] *Série remplaçant la précédente.* [9] *Oct. de chaque année.* [10] *Statistiques d'établissements. Y compris les allocations familiales.* [11] *Nouvelle classification industrielle.* [12] *1965-1970 : y compris les industries extractives.* [13] *Adultes seulement (ensemble des deux sexes : y compris les jeunes gens).* [14] *Y compris les versements au titre des vacances et congés de maladie et la valeur des paiements en nature (sauf pour 1974).* [15] *Plan d'échantillonnage révisé.* [16] *Mai.*

NOTAS EXPLICATIVAS: Véase pág. 594.

[1] Adultos solamente. [2] Sector socializado. Incl. la pesca marítima. [3] Incl. las minas y canteras. [4] Incl. los empleados. [5] Incl. el valor de los pagos en especie. [6] Sector socializado. [7] Estadísticas del seguro de accidentes. [8] Serie que substituye a la anterior. [9] Oct. de cada año. [10] Estadísticas de establecimientos. Incl. las asignaciones familiares. [11] Nueva clasificación industrial. [12] 1965-1970: incl. las minas y canteras. [13] Adultos solamente (ambos sexos: incl. los jóvenes). [14] Incl. los pagos por vacaciones y licencias de enfermedad y el valor de los pagos en especie (salvo 1974). [15] Diseño de la muestra revisado. [16] Mayo.

19 A

Wages in manufacturing — All industries
Salaires dans les industries manufacturières — Ensemble des industries
Salarios en las industrias manufactureras — Todas las industrias

Earnings *(E.G.)* or rates *(R.T.)* per hour, day week or month

Gains *(E.G.)* ou taux *(R.T.)* par heure, jour, semaine ou mois

Ganancias *(E.G.)* o tarifas *(R.T.)* por hora, día, semana o mes

Date / Date / Fecha	EUROPE — EUROPE — EUROPA				Yugoslavia [4]	OCEANIA — OCÉANIE — OCEANÍA		
	United Kingdom					Australia		
	Hour [1] — *Heure* [1] — Hora [1]		Week [1] — *Semaine* [1] — Semana [1]		Month / *Mois* / Mes	Week [1] — *Semaine* [1] — Semana [1]		Hour — *Heure* Hora
	Males [2] *Hommes* [2] Hombres [2]	Females [2] *Femmes* [2] Mujeres [2]	Males [2] *Hommes* [2] Hombres [2]	Females [2] *Femmes* [2] Mujeres [2]		Males [2] *Hommes* [2] Hombres [2]	Females [2] *Femmes* [2] Mujeres [2]	Males [2] *Hommes* [2] Hombres [2]
	(E.G.)				*(E.G.)* [5]	*(E.G.)* [5]		*(R.T.)* [7]
	Pence	Pence	£	£	Dinars	Dollars	Dollars	Cents
1965	43.8	24.9	20.16	9.60	.	.	.	98.8
1966	46.2	26.5	20.78	10.06	686	60.7	34.3	102.6
1967	48.3	27.7	21.89	10.54	755	64.5	36.3	108.4
1968	51.6	29.6	23.62	11.31	830	68.6	37.6	115.5
1969	55.9 [3]	32.0 [3]	25.54 [3]	12.11 [3]	959	73.3	41.2	122.0
1970	64.4	37.1	28.91	13.98	1 120	78.7	45.2	128.1
1971	72.0	42.1	31.37	15.80	1 364	88.9	53.0	143.6
1972	82.1	48.7	36.20	18.34	1 592	95.1 [6]	59.0 [6]	156.4
1973	92.9	56.4	41.52	21.15	1 874	112.7	71.4	176.3
1974	111.6	72.7	49.12	27.05	2 420	144.9 *	99.4 *	222.5 *
1975: VI	.	.	.	.	2 851	.	.	254.9 * [15]

Date / Date / Fecha	OCEANIA — OCÉANIE — OCEANÍA					URSS [13, 14]	RSS de Biélorussie [13]	RSS d'Ukraine [13]
	Australia	Fiji	New Zealand		Nouvelle-Calédonie			
	Hour — *Heure* Hora	Day [8] *Jour* [8] Día [8]	Hour *Heure* Hora	Week — *Semaine* Semana	Hour — *Heure* Hora	Month *Mois* Mes	Month *Mois* Mes	Month *Mois* Mes
	Females [2] *Femmes* [2] Mujeres [2]			Males [2] *Hommes* [2] Hombres [2]	Labourers [10] *Manœuvres* [10] Obreros no calificados [10]			
	(R.T.) [7]	*(R.T.)*	*(E.G.)* [5, 9]	*(R.T.)* [7]	*(R.T.)* [11]	*(E.G.)* [5]	*(E.G.)* [5]	*(E.G.)* [5]
	Cents	Dollars	Dollars	Dollars	Francs (CFP)	Roubles	Roubles	Roubles
1965	69.2	1.98	0.93	.	76.74	97.7	.	93.9
1966	71.7	2.13	0.98	34.60	78.07	101.5	.	97.1
1967	76.5	2.20	1.03	36.34	82.22	107.3	.	101.8
1968	79.7	2.28	1.08	37.62	87.35	115.9	.	110.1
1969	85.5	2.44	1.14	39.66	92.55	122.0	.	115.3
1970	91.8	2.55	1.28	44.57	105.05	127.5	.	120.0
1971	105.0	2.69	1.54 [3]	56.96	113.70	131.7	.	123.9
1972	118.9	3.21	1.68	61.48	108.20 [12]	136.4	125.4	127.7
1973	137.0	3.78	1.92	68.20	112.73 *	141.3	129.6	131.5
1974	188.6 *	...	2.22	77.46	127.13 *	149.8 *	134.1 *	135.7 *
1975: VI	231.5 * [15]	...	2.49 [15]	.	.	.	.	.

EXPLANATORY NOTES: See p. 585.

[1] Oct. of each year. [2] Adults only. [3] New industrial classification. [4] Socialised sector. Incl. mining and quarrying. [5] Incl. salaried employees. [6] Scope of series enlarged. [7] Minimum rates. [8] June of each year. [9] Incl. the value of payments in kind. April and Oct. of each year. [10] First category. [11] Beginning Sep. 1972: excl. production bonuses. [12] Sep.-Dec. [13] Socialised sector. [14] Incl. Byellorussian SSR and Ukrainien SSR, shown separately in this table. [15] April.

NOTES EXPLICATIVES: Voir p. 589.

[1] *Oct. de chaque année.* [2] *Adultes seulement.* [3] *Nouvelle classification industrielle.* [4] *Secteur socialisé. Y compris les industries extractives.* [5] *Y compris les employés.* [6] *Portée de la série élargie.* [7] *Taux minima.* [8] *Juin de chaque année.* [9] *Y compris la valeur des paiements en nature. Avril et oct. de chaque année.* [10] *Première catégorie.* [11] *A partir de sept. 1972: non compris les primes de productivité.* [12] *Sept.-déc.* [13] *Secteur socialisé.* [14] *Y compris les RSS de Biélorussie et d'Ukraine, figurant séparément dans ce tableau.* [15] *Avril.*

NOTAS EXPLICATIVAS: Véase pág. 594.

[1] Oct. de cada año. [2] Adultos solamente. [3] Nueva clasificación industrial. [4] Sector socializado. Incl. las minas y canteras. [5] Incl. los empleados. [6] El alcance de la serie es mayor. [7] Tarifas mínimas. [8] Junio de cada año. [9] Incl. el valor de los pagos en especie. Abril y oct. de cada año. [10] Primera categoría. [11] A partir de sept. 1972: excl. las primas de producción. [12] Sept.-dic. [13] Sector socializado. [14] Incl. las RSS de Bielorrusia y de Ucrania, que figuran separadamente en este cuadro. [15] Abril.

19 Wages in manufacturing / Salaires dans les industries manufacturières / Salarios en las industrias manufactureras — B By industry / Par industrie / Por industria

AFRICA — AFRIQUE — AFRICA

Algérie

Average hourly earnings *(dinars)*
Gains horaires moyens *(dinars)*
Promedio de ganancias por hora *(dinars)*

Date [1] / Date [1] / Fecha [1]	311-313 Food, beverages / Aliments, boissons / Alimentos, bebidas	321-322 Textiles, clothing / Textiles, habillement / Textiles, vestidos	323-324 Leather, leather products, footwear / Cuir, articles en cuir, chaussures / Cuero, artículos de cuero, calzado	33 Wood, furniture / Bois, ameublement / Madera, mobiliario	34 Paper, printing, publishing / Papier, imprimerie, édition / Papel, imprentas, editoriales
1969	2.38	2.19	2.60	2.03	2.79
1970	2.30	2.30	2.25	2.90	2.55
1971	2.59	2.38	2.64	2.42	2.81
1972	2.49	2.52	2.91	2.82	2.84
1973	2.94	3.42	3.03	2.99	3.18

Date [1] / Date [1] / Fecha [1]	351-352; 355 Chemicals, rubber products / Industrie chimique, caoutchouc / Productos químicos, caucho	369 × Building material / Matériaux de construction / Materiales de construcción	37 Basic metal industries / Industrie métallurgique de base / Industrias metalúrgicas básicas	381-383 Metal products, machinery, etc. / Produits métalliques, machines, etc. / Productos metálicos, maquinaria, etc.	390 Other manufacturing industries / Autres industries manufacturières / Otras industrias manufactureras
1969	2.55	1.92	2.40	2.78	1.59
1970	2.40	2.15	3.05	2.95	2.85
1971	3.28	1.84	3.44	3.18	2.14
1972	3.48	2.58	3.99	3.46	1.73
1973	3.59	3.44	3.94	3.61	3.48

[1] April of each year.   [1] *Avril de chaque année.*   [1] Abril de cada año.

19 Wages in manufacturing
Salaires dans les industries manufacturières
Salarios en las industrias manufactureras

B By industry
Par industrie
Por industria

Egypt

Average weekly earnings *(piastres)*
Gains hebdomadaires moyens *(piastres)*
Promedio de ganancias por semana *(piastres)*

Date [1] / *Date* [1] / Fecha [1]	Food / *Aliments* / Alimentos	Tobacco / *Tabac* / Tabaco	Textiles	Clothing / *Habillement* / Vestido	Wood / *Bois* / Madera
1965	258	405	303	243	227
1966	253	432	310	239	237
1967	268	391	300	259	243
1968	289	518	346	255	248
1969	376	551	404	305	283
1970	335	483	382	273	294

Date [1] / *Date* [1] / Fecha [1]	Paper, paper products / *Papier, articles en papier* / Papel, artículos de papel	Printing, publishing / *Imprimerie, édition* / Imprentas, editoriales	Chemicals / *Industrie chimique* / Productos químicos	Non-metallic mineral products / *Produits minéraux non métalliques* / Productos minerales no metálicos	Metal products, machinery (non-electrical) / *Produits métalliques, machines (non électriques)* / Productos metálicos, maquinaria (no eléctrica)	Transport equipment / *Matériel de transport* / Material de transporte
1965	236	318	316	300	309	366
1966	266	343	314	361	341	380
1967	260	354	319	317	344	418
1968	316	431	336	352	493	465
1969	314	414	361	372	368	474
1970	307	413	414	413	445	586

[1] Oct. of each year.   [1] *Oct. de chaque année.*   [1] Oct. de cada año.

19 Wages in manufacturing
Salaires dans les industries manufacturières
Salarios en las industrias manufactureras

B By industry
Par industrie
Por industria

Ghana

Average monthly earnings [1] *(cedis)*
Gains mensuels moyens [1] *(cedis)*
Promedio de ganancias por mes [1] *(cedis)*

Date [2] / Date [2] / Fecha [2]	Food / Aliments / Alimentos	Beverages / Boissons / Bebidas	Tobacco / Tabac / Tabaco	Clothing / Habillement / Vestido	Wood / Bois / Madera	Furniture / Ameublement / Mobiliario	Printing, publishing / Imprimerie, édition / Imprentas, editoriales	Leather, leather products / Cuir, articles en cuir / Cuero, artículos de cuero
1965	37.52	41.01	103.45	46.30	40.10	43.45	51.59	43.74
1966	42.77	73.21	114.38	47.74	47.39	57.66	61.50	73.79
1967	36.96	64.88	98.35	42.14	45.78	42.29	52.14	58.81
1968	37.57	71.14	125.61	49.88	44.07	45.43	63.91	62.58
1969	41.92	73.91	149.77	49.20	44.99	43.31	58.24	53.86
1970	51.55	109.32	152.65	59.66	50.13	41.65	75.79	48.14
1971	51.57	103.25	167.49	61.18	56.17	50.62	72.31	46.81
1972 [3] *	61.92	93.97	...	46.64	55.90	54.91	60.19	41.52

Date [2] / Date [2] / Fecha [2]	Rubber products / Industrie du caoutchouc / Productos de caucho	Chemicals / Industrie chimique / Productos químicos	Non-metallic mineral products / Produits minéraux non métalliques / Productos minerales no metálicos	Metal products / Produits métalliques / Productos metálicos	Machinery (non-electrical) / Machines (non électriques) / Maquinaria (no eléctrica)	Electrical machinery / Machines électriques / Maquinaria eléctrica	Transport equipment / Matériel de transport / Material de transporte	Miscellaneous manufacturing / Industries manufacturières diverses / Industrias manufactureras diversas
1965	33.98	63.42	37.03	71.86	74.00	55.18	54.43	33.76
1966	53.62	84.42	60.18	77.21	126.14	65.64	71.32	40.74
1967	49.57	73.65	39.16	90.18	162.97	106.79	73.35	39.82
1968	68.08	87.75	70.44	97.84	96.39	88.72	76.26	47.04
1969	82.83	84.65	65.14	81.36	114.41	106.80	83.77	43.71
1970	106.80	100.75	67.87	105.11	128.64	155.16	147.22	73.02
1971	56.07	104.35	210.96	157.44	156.73	102.48	112.20	65.76
1972 [3] *	78.41	96.65	187.53	78.38	120.58	205.68	87.59	84.90

[1] Incl. salaried employees. [2] Dec. of each year. [3] Sep.

[1] *Y compris les employés.* [2] *Déc. de chaque année.* [3] *Sept.*

[1] Incl. los empleados. [2] Dic. de cada año. [3] Sept.

19 Wages in manufacturing
Salaires dans les industries manufacturières
Salarios en las industrias manufactureras

B By industry
Par industrie
Por industria

Malawi

Average monthly earnings [1] *(kwacha)*
Gains mensuels moyens [1] *(kwacha)*
Promedio de ganancias por mes [1] *(kwacha)*

Date / Date / Fecha	311-312 Food / Aliments / Alimentos	313 Beverages / Boissons / Bebidas	314 Tobacco / Tabac / Tabaco	321 Textiles	322 Clothing / Habillement / Vestido	323 Leather, leather products / Cuir, articles en cuir / Cuero, artículos de cuero	324 Footwear / Chaussures / Calzado
1970	34.40	23.00	28.20	24.40	19.60 [2]	20.20	.
1971	.	.	.	29.41	.	19.34	26.70
1972	30.88	24.12	23.82	29.41	23.22	19.34	26.70
1973	34.20	28.00	25.14	29.94	26.26	16.74	39.24
1974	41.40	32.29	33.21	33.27	29.72	20.36	37.89

Date / Date / Fecha	331 Wood / Bois / Madera	332 Furniture / Ameublement / Mobiliario	341 Paper, paper products / Papier, articles en papier / Papel, artículos de papel	342 Printing, publishing / Imprimerie, édition / Imprentas, editoriales	351 Industrial chemicals / Chimie industrielle / Química industrial	352 Other chemical products / Autres produits chimiques / Otros productos químicos	355 Rubber products / Produits en caoutchouc / Productos de caucho
1970	.	24.40	52.80	.	56.00	.	55.00
1971	.	.	.	.	.	.	.
1972	23.96	23.22	65.38	41.74	78.58	73.13	58.80
1973	20.38	22.04	36.20	90.91	93.69	74.10	60.10
1974	20.54	34.83	35.78	46.35	92.71	90.10	65.01

Date / Date / Fecha	356 Plastic products / Articles en matière plastique / Productos plásticos	369 Non-metallic mineral products [3] / Produits minéraux non métalliques [3] / Productos minerales no metálicos [3]	381 Metal products / Produits métalliques / Productos metálicos	382 Machinery (non-electrical) / Machines (non électriques) / Maquinaria (no eléctrica)	383 Electrical machinery and apparatus / Machines et appareils électriques / Maquinaria y aparatos eléctricos	384 Transport equipment / Matériel de transport / Material de transporte	390 Other manufacturing industries / Autres industries manufacturières / Otras industrias manufactureras
1970	.	38.20	47.40	.	.	104.00	48.40
1971	.	.	.	.	.	.	.
1972	24.71	38.05	41.49	48.37	47.35	97.26	51.55
1973	44.42	31.40	48.99	60.97	59.08	108.96	...
1974	67.68	41.30	46.57	54.87	57.24	116.50	142.57

[1] Incl. salaried employees. [2] Incl. footwear. [3] Excl. pottery, china, earthenware and glass.

[1] *Y compris les employés.* [2] *Y compris la chaussure.* [3] *Non compris le grès, les porcelaines, les faïences et le verre.*

[1] Incl. los empleados. [2] Incl. el calzado. [3] Excl. el barro, la loza, la porcelana y el vidrio.

19 Wages in manufacturing
Salaires dans les industries manufacturières
Salarios en las industrias manufactureras

B By industry
Par industrie
Por industria

Mauritius

Average daily earnings *(rupees)*
Gains journaliers moyens *(rupees)*
Promedio de ganancias por día *(rupees)*

	311-312	313	314	321	322	323; 355	324	33
Date [1] Date [1] Fecha [1]	Food *Aliments* Alimentos	Beverages *Boissons* Bebidas	Tobacco *Tabac* Tabaco	Textiles	Clothing *Habillement* Vestido	Leather, leather products, rubber *Cuir, articles en cuir, caoutchouc* Cuero, artículos de cuero, caucho	Footwear *Chaussures* Calzado	Wood, furniture *Bois, ameublement* Madera, mobiliario
1966	5.51	4.15	6.30	4.44	...	5.50	...	6.49
1967	6.09	4.23	6.15	4.43	...	6.03	...	7.05
1968	5.83	4.00	6.05	4.45	...	6.83	...	7.73
1969	5.93	4.22	6.43	5.21	...	5.34	...	7.94
1970	6.35	4.52	6.81	5.02	...	4.92	...	7.67
1971	6.30	4.54	6.51	5.22	...	4.10	...	7.33
1972	6.22	5.25	6.67	5.54	3.24	5.19	6.74	7.32
1973	5.82	5.79	7.78	5.81	3.23	4.17	7.15	8.75
1974	8.08	6.41	7.93	6.89	4.26	5.17	8.31	9.73

	342	351-352	381	382	383	384	390
Date [1] Date [1] Fecha [1]	Printing, publishing *Imprimerie, édition* Imprentas, eidtoriales	Chemicals *Industrie chimique* Productos químicos	Metal products *Produits métalliques* Productos metálicos	Machinery (non-electrical) *Machines (non électriques)* Maquinaria (no eléctrica)	Electrical machinery and apparatus *Machines et appareils électriques* Maquinaria y aparatos eléctricos	Transport equipment *Matériel de transport* Material de transporte	Other manufacturing industries *Autres industries manufacturières* Otras industrias manufactureras
1966	7.43	3.91	6.28	6.60	6.50	7.48	3.74
1967	6.51	3.61	5.73	6.75	5.65	6.23	5.14
1968	6.78	4.38	5.08	6.53	6.34	6.37	5.53
1969	7.03	4.38	5.67	6.80	5.46	6.78	6.35
1970	8.05	4.50	6.35	7.35	5.02	7.32	6.55
1971	7.58	4.49	6.01	7.02	6.03	8.42	3.63
1972	8.44	4.78	6.62	8.52	6.96	12.93	3.95
1973	8.30	5.15	6.72	8.31	5.18	9.14	4.08
1974	10.76	5.94	9.56	12.33	4.86	19.69	5.91

[1] March and Sep. of each. year.   [1] *Mars et sept. de chaque année.*   [1] Marzo y sept. de cada año.

19 Wages in manufacturing
Salaires dans les industries manufacturières
Salarios en las industrias manufactureras

B By industry
Par industrie
Por industria

Zambia (1)

Average monthly earnings [1] *(kwacha)*
Gains mensuels moyens [1] *(kwacha)*
Promedio de ganancias por mes [1] *(kwacha)*

Date [2] / Date [2] / Fecha [2]	311-312	313-314	321	322	323-324	331	332
	Food	Beverages, tobacco		Clothing	Leather, leather products, footwear	Wood	Furniture
	Aliments	*Boissons, tabac*	Textiles	*Habillement*	*Cuir, articles en cuir, chaussures*	*Bois*	*Ameublement*
	Alimentos	Bebidas, tabaco		Vestido	Cuero, artículos de cuero, calzado	Madera	Mobiliario
1969	77	122	67	60	60	47	75
1970	85	128	66	67	57	51	78
1971	80	135	73	78	57	50	82
1972	94	107	76	77	58	43	81
1973 [3]	86	111	76	70	58	47	93
1974 [3]	87	120	87	79	65	61	104

Date [2] / Date [2] / Fecha [2]	341	342	351	352-354	355	356	361
	Paper, paper products	Printing, publishing	Industrial chemicals	Other chemical products, petroleum refineries [4]	Rubber products	Plastic products	Pottery, china, earthenware
	Papier, articles en papier	*Imprimerie, édition*	*Chimie industrielle*	*Autres produits chimiques, raffineries de pétrole* [4]	*Produits en caoutchouc*	*Articles en matière plastique*	*Grès, porcelaines faïences*
	Papel, artículos de papel	Imprentas, editoriales	Química industrial	Otros productos químicos, refinerías de petróleo [4]	Productos de caucho	Productos plásticos	Barro, loza, porcelana
1969	107	121	119	97	117	105	75
1970	106	133	130	106	132	132	83
1971	112	133	152	125	121	122	89
1972	121	113	169	142	101	124	59
1973 [3]	128	149	165	143	181	123	50
1974 [3]	144	152	212	156	202	141	85

[1] Incl. salaried employees. [2] Fourth quarter of each year. [3] June. [4] Incl. products of petroleum and coal.

[1] *Y compris les employés.* [2] *Quatrième trimestre de chaque année.* [3] *Juin.* [4] *Y compris les dérivés du pétrole et du charbon.*

[1] Incl. los empleados. [2] Cuarto trimestre de cada año. [3] Junio. [4] Incl. los derivados del petróleo y del carbón.

19 Wages in manufacturing
Salaires dans les industries manufacturières
Salarios en las industrias manufactureras

B By industry
Par industrie
Por industria

Zambia (2)

Average monthly earnings [1] *(kwacha)*
Gains mensuels moyens [1] *(kwacha)*
Promedio de ganancias por mes [1] *(kwacha)*

	369	37	381	382	383	384	385; 390
Date [2] Date [2] Fecha [2]	Other non-metallic mineral products [4] *Autres produits minéraux non métalliques* [4] Otros productos minerales no metálicos [4]	Basic metal industries *Industrie métallurgique de base* Industrias metalúrgicas básicas	Metal products *Produits métalliques* Productos metálicos	Machinery (non-electrical) *Machines (non électriques)* Maquinaria (no eléctrica)	Electrical machinery and apparatus *Machines et appareils électriques* Maquinaria y aparatos eléctricos	Transport equipment *Matériel de transport* Material de transporte	Other manufacturing industries [5] *Autres industries manufacturières* [5] Otras industrias manufactureras [5]
1969	79	93	91	121	101	99	88
1970	86	95	102	120	130	112	97
1971	89	103	108	177	150	124	133
1972	107	115	121	131	167	99	107
1973 [3]	107	130	114	152	216	118	95
1974 [3]	121	123	125	196	173	144	86

[1] Incl. salaried employees. [2] Fourth quarter of each year. [3] June. [4] Excl. glass. [5] Incl. scientific, measuring, optical, etc., equipment.

[1] *Y compris les employés.* [2] *Quatrième trimestre de chaque année.* [3] *Juin.* [4] *Non compris le verre.* [5] *Y compris le matériel scientifique, de précision, d'optique, etc.*

[1] Incl. los empleados. [2] Cuarto trimestre de cada año. [3] Junio. [4] Excl. el vidrio. [5] Incl. el equipo científico, de medida, de óptica, etc.

19 Wages in manufacturing
Salaires dans les industries manufacturières
Salarios en las industrias manufactureras

B By industry
Par industrie
Por industria

AMERICA — AMÉRIQUE — AMERICA

Argentina

Average hourly earnings[1] *(pesos)*
Gains horaires moyens[1] *(pesos)*
Promedio de ganancias por hora[1] *(pesos)*

Date / Date / Fecha	Food / Aliments / Alimentos	Dairy products / Produits laitiers / Productos lácteos	Beverages / Boissons / Bebidas	Tobacco / Tabac / Tabaco	Cotton / Coton / Algodón	Wool / Laine / Lana	Clothing / Habillement / Vestido	Footwear / Chaussure / Calzado	Wood / Bois / Madera
1965	65.56	72.89	64.64	65.78	65.27	68.71	62.94	58.49	71.39
1966	87.49	97.58	84.94	90.05	92.00	96.87	86.77	79.03	96.27
1967	115.53	127.65	106.72	119.57	116.12	122.26	113.00	96.86	122.27
1968	119.60	132.38	112.15	122.60	121.60	128.03	113.00	101.79	128.04
1969	131.67	145.47	123.62	134.91	133.83	140.77	124.54	112.43	140.78
1970 [2]	1.56	1.71	1.48	1.59	1.58	1.66	1.48	1.36	1.66
1971	2.16	2.29	2.14	2.17	2.21	2.29	2.02	1.94	2.30
1972	3.18	3.33	3.18	3.17	3.25	3.36	2.96	2.83	3.36
1973	5.60	5.81	5.73	5.43	5.75	5.85	5.19	5.22	5.65

Date / Date / Fecha	Paper, paper products / Papier, articles en papier / Papel, artículos de papel	Printing, publishing / Imprimerie, édition / Imprentas, editoriales	Leather, leather products / Cuir, articles en cuir / Cuero, artículos de cuero	Rubber products / Industrie du caoutchouc / Productos de caucho	Chemicals / Industrie chimique / Productos químicos	Ceramics / Céramique / Cerámica	Glass / Verre / Vidrio	Basic metal industries / Industrie métallurgique de base / Industrias metalúrgicas básicas	Transport equipment / Matériel de transport / Material de transporte
1965	77.47	65.32	72.17	67.23	90.88	67.57	72.56	77.87	78.75
1966	105.17	82.93	98.50	90.73	132.58	91.57	95.53	101.72	107.50
1967	135.54	115.73	132.72	118.47	166.87	118.00	123.80	129.41	149.47
1968	140.56	115.73	136.08	122.86	175.36	120.99	129.64	136.00	157.95
1969	154.30	127.49	149.47	135.19	191.89	133.17	142.51	149.38	173.09
1970 [2]	1.80	1.52	1.75	1.60	2.20	1.58	1.68	1.75	2.00
1971	2.46	2.08	2.38	2.20	2.94	2.16	2.21	2.43	2.68
1972	3.58	3.06	3.47	3.23	4.23	3.17	3.21	3.55	3.97
1973	6.20	5.41	5.97	5.76	6.54	5.71	5.65	6.40	7.00

[1] Minimum earnings; unskilled workers. [2] New currency introduced in Jan. 1970: 1 new peso = 100 old pesos.

[1] *Gains minima; ouvriers non qualifiés.* [2] *Nouvelle monnaie introduite en janv. 1970: 1 nouveau peso = 100 anciens pesos.*

[1] Ganancias mínimas; obreros no calificados. [2] Nueva moneda adoptada en enero de 1970: 1 nuevo peso = 100 antiguos.

19 Wages in manufacturing
Salaires dans les industries manufacturières
Salarios en las industrias manufactureras

B By industry
Par industrie
Por industria

Bolivia (1)

Average monthly earnings [1] *(pesos)*
Gains mensuels moyens [1] *(pesos)*
Promedio de ganancias por mes [1] *(pesos)*

	311-312	313	314	321	322; 324	323
Date *Date* Fecha	Food *Aliments* Alimentos	Beverages *Boissons* Bebidas	Tobacco *Tabac* Tabaco	Textiles	Clothing, footwear *Habillement,* *chaussures* Vestido, calzado	Leather, leather products *Cuir,* *articles en cuir* Cuero, artículos de cuero
1971	1 131	1 792	1 155	987	1 017	778
1972	1 266	1 927	1 290	1 122	1 152	913
1973	1 386	2 047	1 410	1 242	1 272	1 033
1974	1 786	2 447	1 810	1 642	1 672	1 433

	331	332	341	342	351-352	355
Date *Date* Fecha	Wood *Bois* Madera	Furniture *Ameublement* Mobiliario	Paper, paper products *Papier,* *articles en papier* Papel, artículos de papel	Printing, publishing *Imprimerie,* *édition* Imprentas, editoriales	Chemicals *Industrie* *chimique* Productos químicos	Rubber products *Produits* *en caoutchouc* Productos de caucho
1971	607	676	905	1 050	1 125	899
1972	742	811	1 040	1 185	1 260	1 034
1973	862	931	1 160	1 305	1 380	1 154
1974	1 262	1 331	1 560	1 705	1 780	1 554

[1] Incl. salaried employees.   [1] *Y compris les employés.*   [1] Incl. los empleados.

19 Wages in manufacturing / Salaires dans les industries manufacturières / Salarios en las industrias manufactureras

B By industry / Par industrie / Por industria

Bolivia (2)

Average monthly earnings [1] *(pesos)*
Gains mensuels moyens [1] *(pesos)*
Promedio de ganancias por mes [1] *(pesos)*

Date / Date / Fecha	369 Other non-metallic mineral products / Autres produits minéraux non métalliques / Otros productos minerales no metálicos	37 Basic metal industries / Industrie métallurgique de base / Industrias metalúrgicas básicas	381 Metal products / Produits métalliques / Productos metálicos	382 Machinery (non-electrical) / Machines (non électriques) / Maquinaria (no eléctrica)	383 Electrical machinery and apparatus / Machines et appareils électriques / Maquinaria y aparatos eléctricos	384 Transport equipment / Matériel de transport / Material de transporte	390 Other manufacturing industries / Autres industries manufacturières / Otras industrias manufactureras
1971	1 121	1 452	692	898	634	796	780
1972	1 256	1 587	827	1 033	769	931	915
1973	1 376	1 707	947	1 153	889	1 051	1 035
1974	1 776	2 107	1 347	1 553	1 289	1 451	1 435

[1] Incl. salaried employees.   [1] *Y compris les employés.*   [1] Incl. los empleados.

Brésil (1)

Average monthly earnings [1] *(cruzeiros)*
Gains mensuels moyens [1] *(cruzeiros)*
Promedio de ganancias por mes [1] *(cruzeiros)*

Date / Date / Fecha	311-312 Food / Aliments / Alimentos	313 Beverages / Boissons / Bebidas	314 Tobacco / Tabac / Tabaco	321 Textiles	322; 324 Clothing, footwear / Habillement, chaussures / Vestido, calzado	323 Leather, leather products / Cuir, articles en cuir / Cuero, artículos de cuero
1966	157.82	161.76	144.49	120.37	118.19	129.55
1967	168.57	214.63	185.42	161.36	158.23	179.35
1968	212.58	288.73	253.98	214.77	197.68	223.85
1969	262.83	357.50	325.35	265.69	244.55	272.05
1970	299.10	441.65	440.62	329.00	279.16	312.29
1971	...	...	...	...	...	...
1972	528.40	747.97	618.85	550.26	459.06	555.19

[1] Incl. salaried employees.   [1] *Y compris les employés.*   [1] Incl. los empleados.

19 Wages in manufacturing
Salaires dans les industries manufacturières
Salarios en las industrias manufactureras

B By industry
Par industrie
Por industria

Brésil (2)

Average monthly earnings [1] *(cruzeiros)*
Gains mensuels moyens [1] *(cruzeiros)*
Promedio de ganancias por mes [1] *(cruzeiros)*

	331	332	341	342	351-354	355
Date	Wood	Furniture	Paper, paper products	Printing, publishing	Chemicals, petroleum refineries [2]	Rubber products
Date	*Bois*	*Ameublement*	*Papier, articles en papier*	*Imprimerie, édition*	*Industrie chimique, raffineries de pétrole* [2]	*Produits en caoutchouc*
Fecha	Madera	Mobiliario	Papel, artículos de papel	Imprentas, editoriales	Productos químicos, refinerías de petróleo [2]	Productos de caucho
1966	108.65	139.02	163.04	192.67	244.08	204.50
1967	136.75	178.42	225.77	264.87	331.43	277.67
1968	171.90	231.91	290.45	358.77	426.07	347.13
1969	219.05	294.29	368.40	465.81	556.87	418.73
1970	250.85	333.09	456.50	589.54	668.31	490.25
1971	...	...	...	...	...	...
1972	430.44	584.35	767.08	967.52	1 385.06	857.87

	356	36	37; 381	382	383	384	385-390
Date	Plastic products	Non-metallic mineral products	Metal industries	Machinery (non-electrical)	Electrical machinery and apparatus	Transport equipment	Other manufacturing industries [3]
Date	*Articles en matière plastique*	*Produits minéraux non métalliques*	*Industrie métallurgique*	*Machines (non électriques)*	*Machines et appareils électriques*	*Matériel de transport*	*Autres industries manufacturières* [3]
Fecha	Productos plásticos	Productos minerales no metálicos	Industrias metalúrgicas	Maquinaria (no eléctrica)	Maquinaria y aparatos eléctricos	Material de transporte	Otras industrias manufactureras [3]
1966	175.33	132.78	195.45	209.96	207.74	263.45	161.00
1967	275.78	170.41	258.15	285.15	286.58	347.75	203.40
1968	271.05	231.72	331.61	390.21	377.73	455.00	266.30
1969	388.11	368.95	421.88	502.16	467.72	575.96	345.85
1970	425.86	318.15	487.74	614.40	551.54	653.15	423.61
1971	...	...	...	...	...	...	...
1972	762.56	574.68	829.18	992.79	921.71	1 175.09	657.29

[1] Incl. salaried employees. [2] Incl. products of petroleum and coal. [3] Incl. scientific, measuring, optical, etc., equipment.

[1] *Y compris les employés.* [2] *Y compris les dérivés du pétrole et du charbon.* [3] *Y compris le matériel scientifique, de précision, d'optique, etc.*

[1] Incl. los empleados. [2] Incl. los derivados del petróleo y del carbón. [3] Incl. el equipo científico, de medida, de óptica, etc.

19 Wages in manufacturing
Salaires dans les industries manufacturières
Salarios en las industrias manufactureras

B By industry
Par industrie
Por industria

Canada (1)

Average hourly earnings *(dollars)*
Gains horaires moyens *(dollars)*
Promedio de ganancias por hora *(dollars)*

	311-312	313	314	321 ×	322	323-324	324	331
Date *Date* Fecha	Food *Aliments* Alimentos	Beverages *Boissons* Bebidas	Tobacco *Tabac* Tabaco	Textiles	Clothing *Habillement* Vestido	Leather, leather products *Cuir, articles en cuir* Cuero, artículos de cuero	Footwear *Chaussures* Calzado	Wood *Bois* Madera
1965	1.79	2.28	2.22	1.64	1.40	1.45	.	1.95
1966	1.88	2.41	2.40	1.75	1.49	1.54	.	2.09
1967	2.06	2.59	2.54	1.89	1.60	1.65	1.61	2.27
1968	2.22	2.76	2.78	2.04	1.73	1.76	1.70	2.47
1969	2.39	3.08	3.06	2.21	1.87	1.90	1.84	2.68
1970	2.60	3.37	3.41	2.37	2.00	2.03	1.97	2.89
1971	2.85	3.66	3.84	2.57	2.18	2.21	2.12	3.22
1972	3.36	4.44	4.09	2.76	2.35	2.35	2.25	3.51
1973	3.38	4.38	4.52	2.97	2.54	2.57	2.47	3.92
1974	3.90	4.94	5.06	3.39	2.89	2.95	2.86	4.50

	332	341	342	351-352	353	354	355	356
Date *Date* Fecha	Furniture *Ameublement* Mobiliario	Paper, paper products *Papier, articles en papier* Papel, artículos de papel	Printing, publishing *Imprimerie, édition* Imprentas, editoriales	Chemicals *Industrie chimique* Productos químicos	Petroleum refineries *Raffineries de pétrole* Refinerías de petróleo	Products of petroleum and coal *Dérivés du pétrole et du charbon* Derivados del petróleo y del carbón	Rubber products *Produits en caoutchouc* Productos de caucho	Plastic products *Articles en matière plastique* Productos plásticos
1965	1.68	2.45	2.59	2.32	.	.	2.17	.
1966	1.79	2.67	2.72	2.42	.	.	2.32	.
1967	1.91	2.85	2.87	2.60	3.42	3.38	2.46	1.93
1968	2.05	3.03	3.06	2.77	3.67	3.63	2.60	2.05
1969	2.22	3.28	3.31	2.98	3.84	3.81	2.91	2.20
1970	2.40	3.49	3.56	3.22	4.25	4.21	3.13	2.39
1971	2.37	3.88	3.86	3.48	4.54	4.48	3.33	2.59
1972	2.74	4.17	4.20	3.74	4.96	4.92	3.67	2.76
1973	3.00	4.47	4.56	4.01	5.19	5.19	3.90	2.98
1974	3.41	5.18	5.00	4.49	6.01	5.95	4.25	3.35

1 Excl. knitting mills.   1 *Non compris les fabriques de bonneterie et de tricot.*   1 Excl. las fábricas de tejidos de punto.

19 Wages in manufacturing
Salaires dans les industries manufacturières
Salarios en las industrias manufactureras

B By industry
Par industrie
Por industria

Canada (2)

Average hourly earnings *(dollars)*
Gains horaires moyens *(dollars)*
Promedio de ganancias por hora *(dollars)*

	36	371	372	381	382	383	384	385	390
	Non-metallic mineral products	Basic metal industries		Metal products	Machinery (non-electrical)	Electrical machinery and apparatus	Transport equipment	Scientific, measuring, optical, etc., equipment	Other manufac-turing industries
Date		*Industrie métallurgique de base*							
Date		Industrias metalúrgicas básicas							
	Produits minéraux non métalliques			*Produits métalliques*	*Machines (non électriques)*	*Machines et appareils électriques*	*Matériel de transport*	*Matériel scientifique, de précision, d'optique, etc.*	*Autres industries manufac-turières*
Fecha		Iron and steel	Non-ferrous metal						
	Productos minerales no metálicos	*Sidérurgie* Hierro y acero	*Métaux non ferreux* Metales no ferrosos	Productos metálicos	Maquinaria (no eléctrica)	Maquinaria y aparatos eléctricos	Material de transporte	Equipo científico, de medida, de óptica, etc	Otras industrias manufac-tureras
1965	2.18	.	.	2.24	2.39	2.11	2.59	.	1.71
1966	2.33	.	.	2.39	2.54	2.22	2.67	.	1.81
1967	2.49	3.11	2.55	2.54	2.71	2.33	2.81	2.19	1.95
1968	2.69	3 28	2.76	2.74	2.89	2.51	3.08	2.35	2.09
1969	2.95	3.49	2.90	2.97	3.17	2.70	3.31	2.52	2.25
1970	3.18	3.86	3.12	3.25	3.41	2.91	3.55	2.74	2.42
1971	3.53	4.18	3.38	3.52	3.74	3.12	3.93	3.00	2.62
1972	3.85	4.55	3.66	3.75	4.00	3.30	4.26	3.21	2.80
1973	4.24	4.98	4.02	4.08	4.36	3.53	4.64	3.49	3.03
1974	4.75	5.41	4.54	4.61	4.88	4.04	5.18	3.82	3.41

Colombia (1)

Average hourly earnings *(pesos)*
Gains horaires moyens *(pesos)*
Promedio de ganancias por hora *(pesos)*

	Food	Beverages	Tobacco		Clothing	Wood	Furniture	Paper, paper products	Printing, publishing	Leather, leather products
Date										
Date	*Aliments*	*Boissons*	*Tabac*	Textiles	*Habillement*	*Bois*	*Ameublement*	*Papier, articles en papier*	*Imprimerie, édition*	*Cuir, articles en cuir*
Fecha	Alimentos	Bebidas	Tabaco		Vestido	Madera	Mobiliario	Papel, artículos de papel	Imprentas, editoriales	Cuero, artículos de cuero
1964	2.74	4.31	3.21	3.46	2.48	2.66	2.83	3.54	3.34	2.71
1965	3.17	4.72	3.36	3.84	2.65	2.91	3.13	3.97	3.78	3.01
1966	3.61	5.43	3.42	4.41	2.94	3.24	3.51	4.71	4.51	3.41
1967	3.98	5.63	3.55	4.93	3.16	3.50	3.82	5.41	5.26	3.88
1968	4.37	5.80	3.89	5.59	3.37	3.70	4.13	6.09	5.72	4.29
1969	4.75	6.28	4.35	6.27	3.65	4.00	4.40	6.93	6.30	4.72
1970 [1]	5.03	6.61	4.80	6.70	3.89	4.34	4.58	7.48	6.56	4.90

[1] Jan.-June. 　　　　　　[1] *Janv.-juin.* 　　　　　　[1] Enero-junio.

19 B

**Wages in manufacturing
Salaires dans les industries manufacturières
Salarios en las industrias manufactureras**

**By industry
Par industrie
Por industria**

Colombia (2)

Average hourly earnings *(pesos)*
Gains horaires moyens *(pesos)*
Promedio de ganancias por hora *(pesos)*

Date / Date / Fecha	Rubber products / Industrie du caoutchouc / Productos de caucho	Chemicals / Industrie chimique / Productos químicos	Products of petroleum and coal / Dérivés du pétrole et du charbon / Derivados del petróleo y del carbón	Non-metallic mineral products / Produits minéraux non métalliques / Productos minerales no metálicos	Basic metal industries / Industrie métallurgique de base / Industrias metalúrgicas básicas	Metal products / Produits métalliques / Productos metálicos	Machinery (non-electrical) / Machines (non électriques) / Maquinaria (no eléctrica)	Electrical machinery / Machines électriques / Maquinaria eléctrica	Transport equipment / Matériel de transport / Material de transporte	Miscellaneous manufacturing / Industries manufacturières diverses / Industrias manufactureras diversas
1965	4.40	3.05	6.89	3.67	3.75	2.28	3.27	3.57	3.52	2.99
1966	5.15	3.58	7.80	4.09	4.45	3.76	3.85	4.02	3.84	3.24
1967	5.58	4.11	8.34	4.69	4.86	4.22	4.35	4.60	4.24	3.48
1968	6.52	4.46	9.70	5.14	5.32	4.58	4.89	5.16	4.61	3.71
1969	7.19	4.89	10.19	5.58	6.01	4.90	5.41	5.48	5.23	3.99
1970 [1]	7.55	5.22	11.02	6.07	6.46	5.15	5.79	5.78	5.69	4.32

[1] Jan.-June.   [1] *Janv.-juin.*   [1] Enero-junio.

Chile

Average monthly earnings[1] *(escudos)*
Gains mensuels moyens[1] *(escudos)*
Promedio de ganancias por mes[1] *(escudos)*

Date [2] / Date [2] / Fecha [2]	Food / Aliments / Alimentos	Beverages / Boissons / Bebidas	Tobacco / Tabac / Tabaco	Textiles	Clothing / Habillement / Vestido	Paper, paper products / Papier, articles en papier / Papel, artículos de papel	Chemicals / Industrie chimique / Productos químicos	Non-metallic mineral products / Produits minéraux non métalliques / Productos minerales no metálicos
1965	185.87	221.09	386.69	193.11	161.55	387.58	198.46	261.00
1966	276.99	324.65	430.46	288.04	246.98	588.41	288.44	377.67
1967	340.50	440.16	481.43	370.81	355.72	596.35	384.90	442.68
1968	480.00	531.77	583.78	524.67	458.39	817.15	529.34	606.80
1969	651.77	771.65	976.75	667.10	654.10	1 154.63	744.41	755.66
1970	902.83	924.13	1 423.96	933.98	913.87	2 288.76	1 068.58	1 262.00
1971	1 228.79	1 779.74	1 737.38	1 323.57	1 516.36	2 531.22	1 460.69	1 921.04
1972	1 950.75	2 239.71	2 893.75	2 467.16	2 246.23	5 706.74	2 288.36	2 686.97
1973	6 373.86	6 942.34	9 295.42	6 707.40	6 123.40	16 018.10	5 832.25	8 446.25

[1] Incl. the value of payments in kind. [2] April of each year.

[1] *Y compris la valeur des paiements en nature.* [2] *Avril de chaque année.*

[1] Incl. el valor de los pagos en especie. [2] Abril de cada año.

19 Wages in manufacturing
Salaires dans les industries manufacturières
Salarios en las industrias manufactureras

B By industry
Par industrie
Por industria

República Dominicana (1)

Average monthly earnings [1] *(pesos)*
Gains mensuels moyens [1] *(pesos)*
Promedio de ganancias por mes [1] *(pesos)*

Date / Date / Fecha	311-312 Food / Aliments / Alimentos	313 Beverages / Boissons / Bebidas	314 Tobacco / Tabac / Tabaco	321 Textiles	322 Clothing / Habillement / Vestido	323 Leather, leather products / Cuir, articles en cuir / Cuero, artículos de cuero	324 Footwear / Chaussures / Calzado	331 Wood / Bois / Madera
1965	69.65	158.36	92.78	93.12	.	105.67	55.18	52.95
1966	62.75	154.26	82.10	124.68	.	112.70	74.78	59.98
1967	47.70	162.10	119.97	113.97	.	106.88	74.20	65.64
1968	53.68	174.70	122.58	114.23	.	116.28	68.97	129.46
1969	61.68	182.73	134.79	128.40	114.27	113.32	114.28	102.80
1970	59.64	179.94	102.16	134.59	72.54	130.85	105.81	105.04
1971	59.54	187.45	116.75	135.61	70.56	137.57	89.91	94.52
1972	63.24	201.84	144.40	133.36	75.92	112.10	112.89	86.44
1973	57.17	225.66	183.79	93.92	77.61	124.37	127.28	80.93

Date / Date / Fecha	332 Furniture / Ameublement / Mobiliario	341 Paper, paper products / Papier, articles en papier / Papel, artículos de papel	342 Printing, publishing / Imprimerie, édition / Imprentas, editoriales	351 Industrial chemicals / Chimie industrielle / Química industrial	352 Other chemical products / Autres produits chimiques / Otros productos químicos	355 Rubber products / Produits en caoutchoue / Productos de caucho	356 Plastic products / Articles en matière plastique / Productos plásticos	36 Non-metallic mineral products / Produits minéraux non métalliques / Productos minerales no metálicos
1965	87.12	151.82	110.35	135.54	.	127.29	.	157.24
1966	100.83	164.79	157.52	154.14	.	145.56	.	172.59
1967	88.23	173.12	138.48	164.69	.	138.53	.	152.83
1968	91.78	166.82	143.08	160.39	.	133.64	.	151.19
1969	72.64	170.22	148.22	194.21	149.42	146.07	106.54	148.60
1970	94.30	179.48	159.22	205.42	155.12	139.62	113.54	176.81
1971	109.35	201.39	167.77	221.15	158.30	159.99	113.19	194.71
1972	108.58	196.37	156.31	148.91	148.91	148.73	127.02	169.42
1973	99.60	179.00	166.52	198.11	167.15	139.99	125.00	168.05

[1] Incl. salaried employees.   [1] *Y compris les employés.*   [1] Incl. los empleados.

19 Wages in manufacturing
Salaires dans les industries manufacturières
Salarios en las industrias manufactureras

B By industry
Par industrie
Por industria

República Dominicana (2)

Average monthly earnings [1] *(pesos)*
Gains mensuels moyens [1] *(pesos)*
Promedio de ganancias por mes [1] *(pesos)*

	371	372	381	382	383	384	385	390
Date / *Date* / Fecha	Basic metal industries / *Industrie métallurgique de base* / Industrias metalúrgicas básicas		Metal products / *Produits métallurgiques* / Productos metálicos	Machinery (non-electrical) / *Machines (non électriques)* / Maquinaria (no eléctrica)	Electrical machinery and apparatus / *Machines et appareils électriques* / Maquinaria y aparatos eléctricos	Transport equipment / *Matériel de transport* / Material de transporte	Scientific, measuring, optical, etc. equipment / *Matériel scientifique, de précision, d'optique, etc.* / Equipo científico, de medida, de óptica, etc.	Other manufacturing industries / *Autres industries manufacturières* / Otras industrias manufactureras
	Iron and steel / *Sidérurgie* / Hierro y acero	Non-ferrous metal / *Métaux non ferreux* / Metales no ferrosos						
1965	104.61	.	103.48	.	128.69	100.22	.	133.56
1966	73.51	.	142.19	38.96	138.39	95.17	.	114.42
1967	107.40	.	137.34	113.65	158.84	85.95	.	108.86
1968	168.69	.	139.93	.	137.65	86.44	.	127.79
1969	86.03	142.50	147.04	149.21	157.96	135.67	71.60	94.38
1970	178.99	133.33	158.19	182.91	182.80	129.33	90.76	100.69
1971	195.32	146.67	160.65	192.93	156.33	141.56	136.02	104.98
1972	142.86	142.86	160.57	211.98	220.05	144.36	122.11	112.36
1973	278.35	143.74	160.04	200.49	241.33	145.39	137.36	87.53

[1] Incl. salaried employees.   [1] *Y compris les employés.*   [1] Incl. los empleados.

19 Wages in manufacturing / Salaires dans les industries manufacturières / Salarios en las industrias manufactureras

B By industry / Par industrie / Por industria

Ecuador

Average hourly earnings *(sucres)*
Gains horaires moyens *(sucres)*
Promedio de ganancias por hora *(sucres)*

Date / Date / Fecha	311-312 Food / Aliments / Alimentos	313 Beverages / Boissons / Bebidas	314 Tobacco / Tabac / Tabaco	321 Textiles	322; 324 Clothing, footwear / Habillement, chaussures / Vestido, calzado	323 Leather, leather products / Cuir, articles en cuir / Cuero, artículos de cuero	331 Wood / Bois / Madera	341 Paper, paper products / Papier, articles en papier / Papel, artículos de papel	342 Printing, publishing / Imprimerie, édition / Imprentas, editoriales
1965	3.36	4.88	4.74	3.51	2.76	3.33	3.89	2.96	4.76
1966	3.26	5.31	4.99	3.69	2.96	3.49	4.23	3 07	5.06
1967	3.34	5.49	5.57	3.73	2.98	3.38	4.49	3.41	5.36
1968	3.66	5.76	6.35	4.02	3.23	3.53	4.87	3.66	5.72
1969	4.80	7.10	8.20	5.40	3.90	4.60	5.00	8.60	7.10
1970	5.40	8.60	9.20	5.60	4.20	5.60	5.10	8.60	7.20
1971	5.70	9.00	11.90	6.60	5.10	6.20	6.10	9.00	8.60
1972	6.80	10.40	11.60	7.60	5.50	7.20	7.80	13.40	9.60
1973	7.50	11.40	13.40	8.50	6.20	7.30	8.70	14.90	11.00

Date / Date / Fecha	351 Industrial chemicals / Chimie industrielle / Química industrial	355 Rubber products / Produits en caoutchouc / Productos de caucho	369 Non-metallic mineral products [1] / Produits minéraux non métalliques [1] / Productos minerales no metálicos [1]	381 Metal products / Produits métalliques / Productos metálicos	382 Machinery (non-electrical) / Machines (non électriques) / Maquinaria (no eléctrica)	383 Electrical machinery and apparatus / Machines et appareils électriques / Maquinaria y aparatos eléctricos	384 Transport equipment / Matériel de transport / Material de transporte	390 Other manufacturing industries / Autres industries manufacturières / Otras industrias manufactureras
1965	4.57	3.63	3.97	2.66	4.17	2.80	3.61	4.87
1966	4.66	4.08	4.08	3.13	4.47	2.87	3.71	5.19
1967	4.75	4.20	4.46	3.47	4.52	3.20	3.82	4.28
1968	4.67	3.73	4.86	3.54	4.83	3.61	4.11	6.74
1969	6.60	13.60	7.30	5.10	5.00	6.90	5.30	5.30
1970	7.50	15.30	7.80	6.20	8.10	7.90	6.00	5.60
1971	8.40	19.30	9.80	6.60	8.80	9.40	7.00	6.40
1972	10.50	23.70	9.90	7.50	9.50	12.30	8.00	6.90
1973	12.30	23.70	11.00	9.00	9.20	14.50	8.90	7.70

[1] Excl. pottery, china, earthenware and glass.

[1] *Non compris le grès, les porcelaines, les faïences et le verre.*

[1] Excl. el barro, la loza, la porcelana y el vidrio.

19 **Wages in manufacturing**
Salaires dans les industries manufacturières
Salarios en las industrias manufactureras

B **By industry**
Par industrie
Por industria

El Salvador (San Salvador) [1]

Average hourly earnings *(colones)*
Gains horaires moyens *(colones)*
Promedio de ganancias por hora *(colones)*

	311-312	313	321	322; 324	332	34	36	371	384	390
Date *Date* Fecha	Food *Aliments* Alimentos	Beverages *Boissons* Bebidas	Textiles	Clothing, footwear *Habillement, chaussures* Vestido, calzado	Furniture *Ameublement* Mobiliario	Paper printing, publishing *Papier, imprimerie, édition* Papel, imprentas, editoriales	Non-metallic mineral products *Produits minéraux non métalliques* Productos minerales no metálicos	Iron and steel basic industries *Sidérurgie* Industrias básicas de hierro y acero	Transport equipment *Matériel de transport* Material de transporte	Other manufacturing industries *Autres industries manufacturières* Otras industrias manufactureras
	Males — *Hommes* — Hombres									
1968	0.95	1.08	0.97	0.83	0.80	0.88	0.66	0.86	0.71	0.96
1969	1.02	1.14	0.93	0.88	0.79	0.94	0.68	0.93	0.75	0.94
1970	1.01	1.15	0.96	0.94	0.86	0.96	0.68	0.99	0.82	0.97
1971	1.08	1.15	0.97	0.99	0.85	0.96	0.72	0.99	0.79	0.93
1972	1.05	1.19	1.01	1.01	0.80	1.04	0.74	0.95	0.84	1.01
1973	1.12	1.23	1.07	1.06	0.80	1.05	0.81	0.98	0.93	1.08

	311-312	313	321	322; 324	34	390
Date *Date* Fecha	Food *Aliments* Alimentos	Beverages *Boissons* Bebidas	Textiles	Clothing, footwear *Habillement, chaussures* Vestido, calzado	Paper, printing, publishing *Papier, imprimerie, édition* Papel, imprentas, editoriales	Other manufacturing industries *Autres industries manufacturières* Otras industrias manufactureras
	Females — *Femmes* — Mujeres					
1968	0.58	0.55	0.83	0.60	0.75	0.69
1969	0.59	0.57	0.83	0.65	0.73	0.72
1970	0.62	0.68	0.87	0.70	0.83	0.76
1971	0.59	0.64	0.85	0.76	0.88	0.72
1972	0.61	0.62	0.90	0.79	0.82	0.78
1973	0.68	0.68	0.98	0.84	0.78	0.83

[1] Metropolitan area.   [1] *Région métropolitaine.*   [1] Area metropolitana.

19 Wages in manufacturing
Salaires dans les industries manufacturières
Salarios en las industrias manufactureras

B By industry
Par industrie
Por industria

Guatemala (Guatemala)

Average hourly earnings *(centavos)*
Gains horaires moyens *(centavos)*
Promedio de ganancias por hora *(centavos)*

	311-312	313	314	321	322; 324	323	331
Date *Date* Fecha	Food *Aliments* Alimentos	Beverages *Boissons* Bebidas	Tobacco *Tabac* Tabaco	Textiles	Clothing, footwear *Habillement, chaussures* Vestido, calzado	Leather, leather products *Cuir, articles en cuir* Cuero, artículos de cuero	Wood *Bois* Madera
1965	29.3	36.5	62.5	30.7	27.0	24.6	23.0
1966	29.4	39.6	62.5	35.9	28.2	24.7	23.8
1967	31.4	40.5	61.6	34.5	28.3	27 1	24.9
1968	33.2	43.6	66.2	33.9	30.1	24.0	25.5
1969	24.9	47.9	70.4	36.5	30.9	23.8	26.1
1970	34.5	47.2	69.3	35.4	30.9	26.7	27.3
1971	35.3	46.1	72.9	37.5	30.9	23.8	28.8
1972	35.2	46.5	71.1	37.7	30.9	23.8	28.9
1973	35.9	46.8	73.6	39.7	29.8	25.9	29.5
1974 *	41.0	44.5	73.3	42.7	29.8	24.5	29.8

	332	34	351-352; 355	36	37	383	384
Date *Date* Fecha	Furniture *Ameublement* Mobiliario	Paper, printing, publishing *Papier, imprimerie, édition* Papel, imprentas, editoriales	Chemicals, rubber products *Industrie chimique, produits en caoutchouc* Productos químicos y de caucho	Non-metallic mineral products *Produits minéraux non métalliques* Productos minerales no metálicos	Basic metal industries *Industrie métallurgique de base* Industrias metalúrgicas básicas	Electrical machinery and apparatus *Machines et appareils électriques* Maquinaria y aparatos eléctricos	Transport equipment *Matériel de transport* Material de transporte
1965	31.7	46.2	30.6	44.9	29.0	36.8	36.7
1966	32.0	46.0	32.5	47.3	30.7	34.5	35.4
1967	30.9	49.7	33.9	48.3	32.6	34.8	35.7
1968	31.3	52.2	35.1	49.7	33.2	36.8	45.1
1969	33.3	54.6	39.5	53.8	33.3	36.1	46.8
1970	33.1	50.4	39.3	56.1	33.6	37.9	48.3
1971	31.2	51.5	36.4	57.4	35.9	38.3	51.3
1972	31.8	52.6	36.7	57.7	35.9	38.1	53.0
1973	30.1	51.8	35.9	50.4	38.5	39.8	54.5
1974 *	28.8	51.6	35.2	43.2	44.0	40.4	56.0

19 Wages in manufacturing
Salaires dans les industries manufacturières
Salarios en las industrias manufactureras

B By industry
Par industrie
Por industria

México [1]

Average monthly earnings *(pesos)*
Gains mensuels moyens *(pesos)*
Promedio de ganancias por mes *(pesos)*

Date *Date* Fecha	Milling (wheat) *Minoterie (blé)* Molinos (trigo)	Canning *Conserves* Conservas	Beer *Bière* Cerveza	Cigars *Cigares* Cigarros	Silk, artificial silk *Soie, soie artificielle* Seda, seda artificial	Paper, paper products *Papier, articles en papier* Papel, artículos de papel
1965	.	724	1 526	1 067	1 253	1 381
1966	.	763	1 454	1 196	1 343	1 496
1967	.	830	1 467	1 365	1 388	1 526
1968	1 135	880	1 756	1 447	1 537	1 681
1969	1 153	953	1 762	1 605	1 595	1 722
1970	1 239	998	1 975	1 699	1 499	1 946
1971	1 294	1 123	1 997	1 867	1 848	2 084
1972	1 431	1 190	1 832	2 138	1 947	2 260
1973	1 572	1 296	2 277	2 324	2 814	2 583

Date *Date* Fecha	Rubber products *Industrie du caoutchouc* Productos de caucho	Vegetable oils *Huiles végétales* Aceites vegetales	Matches *Allumettes* Cerillas	Soap *Savon* Jabón	Glass *Verre* Vidrio	Cement *Ciment* Cemento	Iron and steel foundries *Fonderies de fer et d'acier* Fundición de hierro y acero
1965	2 213	1 078	1 000	.	1 512	1 422	1 454
1966	2 363	1 173	1 142	.	1 262	1 598	1 599
1967	2 815	1 137	1 097	.	1 327	1 685	1 725
1968	2 803	1 253	1 198	1 483	1 472	1 840	1 826
1969	3 502	1 325	1 224	1 504	1 559	1 883	1 981
1970	3 680	1 403	1 294	1 621	1 726	1 984	2 011
1971	4 073	1 469	1 384	1 778	1 876	2 257	2 159
1972	4 462	1 560	1 540	1 952	1 960	2 808	2 309
1973	5 257	1 715	1 783	2 194	2 211	3 126	2 594

[1] Beginning 1968: scope of series revised each year.   [1] *A partir de 1968 : portée de la série révisée chaque année.*   [1] A partir de 1968: alcance de la serie revisado cada año.

19 Wages in manufacturing / Salaires dans les industries manufacturières / Salarios en las industrias manufactureras — B By industry / Par industrie / Por industria

Panamá (1)

Average hourly earnings *(balboas)*
Gains horaires moyens *(balboas)*
Promedio de ganancias por hora *(balboas)*

Date / Date / Fecha	311-312 Food / Aliments / Alimentos	313 Beverages / Boissons / Bebidas	314 Tobacco / Tabac / Tabaco	321 Textiles	322 Clothing / Habillement / Vestido	323 Leather, leather products / Cuir, articles en cuir / Cuero, artículos de cuero	324 Footwear / Chaussures / Calzado	331 Wood / Bois / Madera	332 Furniture / Ameublement / Mobiliario
1965	0.60	0.63	0.68	.	0.52	0.56	0.58	0.45	0.64
1966	0.57	0.63	0.71	0.54	0.55	0.59	0.61	0.53	0.69
1967	0.59	0.64	0.74	0.66	0.62	0.61	0.68	0.58	0.74
1968	0.60	0.66	0.78	0.68	0.64	0.61	0.72	0.61	0.70
1969	0.62	0.65	0.83	0.50	0.65	0.75	0.74	0.63	0.72
1970	0.67	0.70	0.76	0.57	0.67	0.71	0.72	0.65	0.73
1971	0.68	0.82	0.89	0.61	0.71	0.73	0.83	0.66	0.76
1972	0.67	0.79	0.88	0.83	0.71	0.69	0.79	0.66	0.85
1973 *	0.84	1.01	1.04	0.80	0.69	0.70	0.79	0.68	0.92

Date / Date / Fecha	341 Paper, paper products / Papier, articles en papier / Papel, artículos de papel	342 Printing, publishing / Imprimerie, édition / Imprentas, editoriales	351 Industrial chemicals / Chimie industrielle / Química industrial	352 Industrial chemical products / Autres produits chimiques / Otros productos químicos	355 Other products / Produits en caoutchouc / Productos de caucho	356 Rubber products / Articles en matière plastique / Productos plásticos	361 Pottery, china, earthenware / Grès, porcelaines, faïences / Barro, loza, porcelana	362 Glass / Verre / Vidrio	369 Other non-metallic mineral products / Autres produits minéraux non métalliques / Otros productos minerales no metálicos
1965	0.67	0.81	.	0.68	0.83	0.86	0.59	.	0.70
1966	0.67	0.80	.	0.65	0.98	0.78	0.82	.	0.66
1967	0.83	0.83	.	0.65	0.95	0.80	0.80	0.73	0.71
1968	0.77	0.85	.	0.61	0.96	0.70	0.85	0.75	0.69
1969	0.83	0.83	1.02	0.65	0.93	0.75	0.67	0.87	0.76
1970	0.89	0.91	0.84	0.69	1.11	0.80	0.68	0.92	0.77
1971	0.96	0.95	1.06	0.80	0.95	0.81	.	0.76	0.78
1972	0.87	0.97	0.91	0.81	1.04	0.89	.	0.72	0.76
1973 *	1.05	1.12	0.99	0.93	1.10	0.91	.	0.73	0.95

19 Wages in manufacturing
Salaires dans les industries manufacturières
Salarios en las industrias manufactureras

B By industry
Par industrie
Por industria

Panamá (2)

Average hourly earnings *(balboas)*
Gains horaires moyens *(balboas)*
Promedio de ganancias por hora *(balboas)*

	371	381	382	383	384	385	353-354; 372; 390
Date *Date* Fecha	Iron and steel basic industries *Sidérurgie* Industrias básicas de hierro y acero	Metal products *Produits métalliques* Productos metálicos	Machinery (non-electrical) *Machines (non électriques)* Maquinaria (no eléctrica)	Electrical machinery and apparatus *Machines et appareils électriques* Maquinaria y aparatos eléctricos	Transport equipment *Matériel de transport* Material de transporte	Scientific, measuring, optical, etc., equipment *Matériel scientifique, de précision, d'optique, etc.* Equipo científico, de medida, de óptica, etc.	Miscellaneous manufacturing *Industries manufacturières diverses* Industrias manufactureras diversas
1965	.	0.71	1.16	0.68	0.71	•	1.19
1966	.	0.70	0.99	0.72	0.74	.	1.25
1967	0.66	0.71	1.09	0.88	0.77	.	1.73
1968	0.67	0.74	0.97	0.87	0.70	•	1.59
1969	0.73	0.84	0.96	0.77	0.77	.	1.95
1970	0.86	0.95	0.99	0.90	1.27	0.89	2.66
1971	0.78	0.86	0.89	0.89	1.04	1.03	1.93
1972	0.81	0.83	1.08	0.77	1.29	1.11	2.17
1973 *	0.81	0.91	1.11	0.86	0.88	0.92	1.71

Puerto Rico (1)

Average hourly earnings *(dollars)*
Gains horaires moyens *(dollars)*
Promedio de ganancias por hora *(dollars)*

	311-313	314	321	322	323	324	33
Date [1] *Date [1]* Fecha [1]	Food, beverages *Aliments, boissons* Alimentos, bebidas	Tobacco *Tabac* Tabaco	Textiles	Clothing *Habillement* Vestido	Leather, leather products *Cuir, articles en cuir* Cuero, artículos de cuero	Footwear *Chaussures* Calzado	Wood, furniture *Bois, ameublement* Madera, mobiliario
1968	1.63	1.34	1.50	1.47	1.30	1.32	1.41
1969	1.73	1.47	1.56	1.58	1.43	1.56	1.57
1970	1.82	1.49	1.61	1.60	1.47	1.62	1.67
1971	1.94	1.56	1.73	1.70	1.56	1.65	1.73
1972	2.07	1.63	1.79	1.76	1.58	1.66	1.82
1973	2.24	1.79	1.96	1.84	1.68	1.71	1.92
1974	2.42	1.96	2.10	1.97	1.83	1.84	2.11

[1] Oct. of each year.   [1] *Oct. de chaque année.*   [1] Oct. de cada año.

19 Wages in manufacturing
Salaires dans les industries manufacturières
Salarios en las industrias manufactureras

B By industry
Par industrie
Por industria

Puerto Rico (2)

Average hourly earnings *(dollars)*
Gains horaires moyens *(dollars)*
Promedio de ganancias por hora *(dollars)*

	341	342	351-352	353-354	355-356	361	362
Date [1] Date [1] Fecha [1]	Paper, paper products *Papier, articles en papier* Papel, artículos de papel	Printing, publishing *Imprimerie, édition* Imprentas, editoriales	Chemicals *Industrie chimique* Productos químicos	Refineries and products of petroleum and coal *Raffineries et dérivés du pétrole et du charbon* Refinerías y derivados del petróleo y del carbón	Rubber and plastic products *Produits en caoutchouc et en plastique* Productos de caucho y de plástico	Pottery, china, earthenware, *Grès, porcelaines, faïences* Barro, loza, porcelana	Glass *Verre* Vidrio
1968	1.85	2.07	1.98	3.06	1.44	2.37	2.12
1969	1.99	2.19	2.08	3.34	1.60	2.52	2.22
1970	2.05	2.30	2.26	3.20	1.71	2.52	2.22
1971	2.21	2.38	2.36	3.55	1.78	2.84	2.47
1972	2.36	2.70	2.64	4.00	1.87	3.31	2.54
1973	2.52	2.99	2.99	4.58	2.00	3.48	2.54
1974	2.72	3.10	3.22	4.52	2.20	3.91	2.83

	369	381	382	383	384	385	390
Date [1] Date [1] Fecha [1]	Other non-metallic mineral products *Autres produits minéraux non métalliques* Otros productos minerales no metálicos	Metal products *Produits métalliques* Productos metálicos	Machinery (non-electrical) *Machines (non électriques)* Maquinaria (no eléctrica)	Electrical machinery and apparatus *Machines et appareils électriques* Maquinaria y aparatos eléctricos	Transport equipment *Matériel de transport* Material de transporte	Scientific, measuring, optical, etc., equipment *Matériel scientifique, de précision, d'optique, etc.* Equipo científico, de medida, de óptica, etc.	Other manufacturing industries *Autres industries manufacturières* Otras industrias manufactureras
1968	1.68	1.92	2.10	1.78	1.94	1.73	1.46
1969	1.78	1.99	2.38	1.84	2.12	1.79	1.57
1970	1.94	2.03	2.25	1.91	2.22	1.92	1.66
1971	2.00	2.17	2.62	2.00	2.21	2.06	1.78
1972	2.19	2.23	2.96	2.16	2.35	2.16	1.91
1973	2.41	2.55	2.70	2.27	2.59	2.35	2.03
1974	2.59	2.79	2.91	2.55	2.87	2.57	2.40

[1] Oct. of each year.   [1] *Oct. de chaque année.*   [1] Oct. de cada año.

19 **Wages in manufacturing**
Salaires dans les industries manufacturières
Salarios en las industrias manufactureras

B **By industry**
Par industrie
Por industria

United States (1)

Average hourly earnings *(dollars)*
Gains horaires moyens *(dollars)*
Promedio de ganancias por hora *(dollars)*

Date / Date / Fecha	311-313 Food, beverages / Aliments, boissons / Alimentos, bebidas	314 Tobacco / Tabac / Tabaco	321 Textiles	322 Clothing / Habillement / Vestido	323-324 Leather, leather products, footwear / Cuir, articles en cuir, chaussures / Cuero, artículos de cuero, calzado	331 Wood / Bois / Madera	332 Furniture / Ameublement / Mobiliario
1965	2.43	2.09	1.87	1.83	1.88	2.17	2.12
1966	2.52	2.19	1.96	1.89	1.94	2.25	2.21
1967	2.64	2.27	2.06	2.03	2.07	2.37	2.33
1968	2.80	2.48	2.21	2.21	2.23	2.57	2.47
1969	2.96	2.62	2.34	2.31	2.36	2.74	2.62
1970	3.16	2.91	2.45	2.39	2.49	2.96	2.77
1971	3.38	3.16	2.57	2.49	2.60	3.17	2.90
1972	3.59	3.47	2.74	2.62	2.71	3.36	3.06
1973	3.82	3.76	2.95	2.78	2.81	3.62	3.26
1974	4.15	4.13	3.18	2.99	3.01	3.91	3.49

Date / Date / Fecha	341 Paper, paper products / Papier, articles en papier / Papel, artículos de papel	342 Printing, publishing / Imprimerie, édition / Imprentas, editoriales	351 Industrial chemicals / Chimie industrielle / Química industrial	352 Other chemical products / Autres produits chimiques / Otros productos químicos	353-354 Refineries and products of petroleum and coal / Raffineries et dérivés du pétrole et du charbon / Refinerías y derivados del petróleo y del carbón	355-356 Rubber and plastic products / Produits en caoutchouc et en plastique / Productos de caucho y de plástico	36 Non-metallic mineral products / Produits minéraux non métalliques / Productos minerales no metálicos
1965	2.65	3.06	3.24	2.78	3.28	2.61	2.62
1966	2.75	3.16	3.33	2.88	3.41	2.67	2.72
1967	2.87	3.28	3.45	3.00	3.58	2.74	2.82
1968	3.05	3.48	3.62	3.17	3.75	2.92	2.99
1969	3.24	3.69	3.84	3.33	4.00	3.07	3.19
1970	3.44	3.92	4.08	3.48	4.28	3.20	3.40
1971	3.67	4.20	4.37	3.72	4.57	3.40	3.67
1972	3.94	4.48	4.68	3.99	4.93	3.60	3.94
1973	4.19	4.68	4.97	4.25	5.21	3.80	4.21
1974	4.50	4.96	5.38	4.61	5.63	4.03	4.52

WAGES

19 Wages in manufacturing
Salaires dans les industries manufacturières
Salarios en las industrias manufactureras

B By industry
Par industrie
Por industria

United States (2)

Average hourly earnings *(dollars)*
Gains horaires moyens *(dollars)*
Promedio de ganancias por hora *(dollars)*

Date / Date / Fecha	37	381	382	383	384	385	390
	Basic metal industries	Metal products	Machinery (non-electrical)	Electrical machinery and apparatus	Transport equipment	Scientific, measuring, optical, etc., equipment	Other manufacturing industries
	Industrie métallurgique de base	*Produits métalliques*	*Machines (non électriques)*	*Machines et appareils électriques*	*Matériel de transport*	*Matériel scientifique, de précision, d'optique, etc.*	*Autres industries manufacturières*
	Industrias metalúrgicas básicas	Productos metálicos	Maquinaria (no eléctrica)	Maquinaria y aparatos eléctricos	Material de transporte	Equipo científico, de medida, de óptica, etc.	Otras industrias manufactureras
1965	3.18	2.76	2.96	2.58	3.21	2.62	2.14
1966	3.28	2.88	3.09	2.65	3.33	2.73	2.22
1967	3.34	2.98	3.19	2.77	3.44	2.85	2.35
1968	3.55	3.16	3.36	2.93	3.69	2.98	2.50
1969	3.79	3.34	3.58	3.09	3.89	3.15	2.66
1970	3.93	3.53	3.77	3.28	4.05	3.35	2.83
1971	4.23	3.74	3.99	3.48	4.41	3.53	2.97
1972	4.67	4.00	4.28	3.68	4.73	3.73	3.11
1973	5.04	4.26	4.56	3.88	5.06	3.90	3.27
1974	5.60	4.59	4.92	4.15	5.47	4.19	3.50

19 Wages in manufacturing
Salaires dans les industries manufacturières
Salarios en las industrias manufactureras

B By industry
Par industrie
Por industria

Uruguay [1]

Monthly rates [2] *(Indices)*
Taux mensuels [2] *(Indices)*
Tarifas por mes [2] *(Indices)*

(1970 = 100)

Date / Date / Fecha	311-312 Food / Aliments / Alimentos	313 Beverages / Boissons / Bebidas	314 Tobacco / Tabac / Tabaco	321 Textiles	322 Clothing / Habillement / Vestido	341 Paper, paper products / Papier, articles en papier / Papel, artículos de papel	342 Printing, publishing / Imprimerie, édition / Imprentas, editoriales
1967	32.0	33.4	30.6	32.9	34.4	35.3	38.4
1968	65.4	67.7	80.8	76.6	71.1	74.1	72.5
1969	89.7	90.9	91.6	90.3	90.6	90.7	90.9
1970	**100.0**	**100.0**	**100.0**	**100.0**	**100.0**	**100.0**	**100.0**
1971	125.1	127.0	121.8	127.4	128.4	129.7	109.7
1972	183.0	222.6	183.7	186.4	193.6	195.6	225.4
1973	343.5	451.4	341.5	361.0	380.3	348.8	439.6
1974	399.2	538.3	379.7	418.7	421.7	404.4	529.2

Date / Date / Fecha	351-353 Chemicals, petroleum refineries / Industrie chimique, raffineries de pétrole / Productos químicos, refinerías de petróleo	354 Products of petroleum and coal / Dérivés du pétrole et du charbon / Derivados del petróleo y del carbón	355 Rubber products / Produits en caoutchouc / Productos de caucho	381 Metal products / Produits métalliques / Productos metálicos	382-383; 385 Machinery [3] / Machines [3] / Maquinaria [3]	384 Transport equipment / Matériel de transport / Material de transporte	390 Other manufacturing industries / Autres industries manufacturières / Otras industrias manufactureras
1967	36.7	38.1	34.8	33.8	37.8	34.8	29.4
1968	67.2	79.4	75.1	68.9	79.5	60.7	47.5
1969	88.6	89.9	91.6	91.0	89.8	90.9	90.9
1970	**100.0**	**100.0**	**100.0**	**100.0**	**100.0**	**100.0**	**100.0**
1971	127.1	127.5	125.9	126.8	127.5	97.1	126.8
1972	182.6	201.5	183.8	187.7	183.7	181.7	181.7
1973	357.4	410.0	341.8	407.2	345.0	371.5	339.3
1974	423.3	417.6	380.0	377.2	379.7	377.2	377.2

[1] Montevideo; private sector only. Incl. salaried employees. [2] Minimum rates. Incl. social benefits. [3] Incl. scientific, measuring, optical, etc., equipment.

[1] *Montevideo ; secteur privé seulement. Y compris les employés.* [2] *Taux minima. Y compris les prestations sociales.* [3] *Y compris le matériel scientifique, de précision, d'optique, etc.*

[1] Montevideo; sector privado solamente. Incl. los empleados. [2] Tarifas mínimas. Incl. las prestaciones sociales. [3] Incl. el equipo científico, de medida, de óptica, etc.

19 Wages in manufacturing / Salaires dans les industries manufacturières / Salarios en las industrias manufactureras

B By industry / Par industrie / Por industria

Venezuela

Average monthly earnings *(bolívares)*
Gains mensuels moyens *(bolívares)*
Promedio de ganancias por mes *(bolívares)*

Date / *Date* / Fecha	311-312 Food / *Aliments* / Alimentos	313 Beverages / *Boissons* / Bebidas	314 Tobacco / *Tabac* / Tabaco	321-322 Textiles, clothing / *Textiles, habillement* / Textiles, vestido	324 Footwear / *Chaussures* / Calzado	33 Wood, furniture / *Bois, ameublement* / Madera, mobiliario	341 Paper, paper products / *Papier, articles en papier* / Papel, artículos de papel
1965	544.6	881.4	678.0	725.6	744.4	605.5	806.4
1966	555.7	971.0	689.5	695.4	717.3	615.2	820.0
1967	598.0	948.6	743.5	710.9	750.1	624.2	783.1
1968	585.4	922.6	661.5	713.6	674.9	608.9	766.8
1969	592.1	917.3	675.2	723.4	695.2	615.8	791.0
1970	651.0	1 014.0	833.0	736.0	649.0	635.0	809.0
1971	756.0	1 096.0	919.0	860.0	763.0	655.0	886.0
1972	788.4	1 283.4	1 032.7	895.1	749.3	656.9	984.6
1973	886.0	1 319.0	1 215.0	918.0	829.0	777.0	1 079.0
1974 *	964.0	1 361.0	1 334.0	1 034.0	878.0	823.0	1 231.0

Date / *Date* / Fecha	342 Printing, publishing / *Imprimerie, édition* / Imprentas, editoriales	351-352 Chemicals / *Industrie chimique* / Productos químicos	355 Rubber products / *Produits en caoutchouc* / Productos de caucho	371 Basic metal industries / *Industrie métallurgique de base* / Industrias metalúrgicas básicas: Iron and steel / *Sidérurgie* / Hierro y acero	372 Non-ferrous metal / *Métaux non ferreux* / Metales no ferrosos	384 Transport equipment / *Matériel de transport* / Material de transporte
1965	1 143.7	944.1	980.6	953.4	903.6	1 031.1
1966	1 181.7	921.6	1 021.5	915.3	982.5	1 149.0
1967	1 196.4	938.2	1 112.0	1 024.6	953.6	1 288.4
1968	1 168.3	938.7	1 013.8	1 030.8	937.5	1 342.5
1969	1 183.7	941.6	1 032.4	1 042.3	953.2	1 387.4
1970	1 348.0	899.0	1 136.0	1 096.0	925.0	1 329.0
1971	1 410.0	1 047.0	1 152.0	1 155.0	1 005.0	1 473.0
1972	1 506.3	1 098.4	1 310.0	1 236.3	1 229.8	1 674.7
1973	1 585.0	1 371.0	1 450.0	1 284.0	1 145.0	1 493.0
1974 *	1 758.0	1 523.0	1 648.0	1 367.0	1 300.0	1 721.0

19 Wages in manufacturing / Salaires dans les industries manufacturières / Salarios en las industrias manufactureras

B By industry / Par industrie / Por industria

ASIA — ASIE — ASIA

Bangladesh (Dacca)

Average monthly earnings *(taka)*
Gains mensuels moyens *(taka)*
Promedio de ganancias por mes *(taka)*

Date / Date / Fecha	311-312 Food / Aliments / Alimentos	313 Beverages / Boissons / Bebidas	314 Tobacco / Tabac / Tabaco	321 Textiles	322 Clothing / Habillement / Vestido	323 Leather, leather products / Cuir, articles en cuir / Cuero, artículos de cuero	324 Footwear / Chaussures / Calzado	331 Wood / Bois / Madera	332 Furniture / Ameublement / Mobiliario
1968	90.04	136.75	165.68	109.27	94.45	112.55	103.33	125.92	114.82
1969	84.74	175.54	194.54	118.29	96.31	131.48	103.26	127.38	124.82
1970	112.32	214.05	220.22	156.58	119.93	147.01	131.03	132.89	130.50

Date / Date / Fecha	341 Paper, paper products / Papier, articles en papier / Papel, artículos de papel	342 Printing, publishing / Imprimerie, édition / Imprentas, editoriales	351 Industrial chemicals / Chimie industrielle / Química industrial	352 Other chemical products / Autres produits chimiques / Otros productos químicos	353 Petroleum refineries / Raffineries de pétrole / Refinerías de petróleo	354 Products of petroleum and coal / Dérivés du pétrole et du charbon / Derivados del petróleo y del carbón	355 Rubber products / Produits en caoutchouc / Productos de caucho	356 Plastic products / Articles en matière plastique / Productos plásticos	361 Pottery, china, earthenware / Grès, porcelaines, faïences / Barro, loza, porcelana
1968	166.43	127.70	111.91	101.19	287.04	108.79	115.85	69.44	90.28
1969	200.62	161.46	140.29	95.27	428.69	404.64	99.67	77.55	50.00
1970	211.85	197.51	201.53	156.79	560.61	307.97	94.59	92.66	172.29

Date / Date / Fecha	362 Glass / Verre / Vidrio	369 Other non-metallic mineral products / Autres produits minéraux non métalliques / Otros productos minerales no metálicos	371 Iron and steel / Sidérurgie / Hierro y acero	372 Non-ferrous metal / Métaux non ferreux / Metales no ferrosos	381 Metal products / Produits métalliques / Productos metálicos	382 Machinery (non-electrical) / Machines (non électriques) / Maquinaria (no eléctrica)	383 Electrical machinery and apparatus / Machines et appareils électriques / Maquinaria y aparatos eléctricos	384 Transport equipment / Matériel de transport / Material de transporte	390 Other manufacturing industries / Autres industries manufacturières / Otras industrias manufactureras
1968	96.77	127.15	150.45	83.33	113.73	107.71	137.25	134.05	115.18
1969	88.54	146.64	121.74	97.22	102.81	124.48	136.99	162.49	117.70
1970	115.67	142.22	191.54	.	154.53	149.87	160.03	196.99	95.61

Note: Columns 371 and 372 are grouped under "Basic metal industries / Industrie métallurgique de base / Industrias metalúrgicas básicas".

19 Wages in manufacturing / Salaires dans les industries manufacturières / Salarios en las industrias manufactureras — B By industry / Par industrie / Por industria

Burma

Average hourly earnings [1] *(kyats)*
Gains horaires moyens [1] *(kyats)*
Promedio de ganancias por hora [1] *(kyats)*

	311-312	313	314	321	322; 324	323	331
Date / Date / Fecha	Food / Aliments / Alimentos	Beverages / Boissons / Bebidas	Tobacco / Tabac / Tabaco	Textiles	Clothing, footwear / Habillement, chaussures / Vestido, calzado	Leather, leather products / Cuir, articles en cuir / Cuero, artículos de cuero	Wood / Bois / Madera
1965	0.41	0.47	0.34	0.51	0.68	0.43	0.45
1966	0.39	0.45	0.33	0.61	0.66	0.46	0.47
1967	0.44	0.56	0.33	0.60	0.62	0.41	0.49
1968	0.45	0.62	0.34	0.60	0.59	0.52	0.48
1969	0.49	0.64	0.32	0.66	0.61	0.50	0.49
1970	0.51	0.60	0.32	0.62	0.69	0.54	0.49
1971	0.50	0.63	0.34	0.72	0.87	0.52	0.50
1972 [2]	0.47	0.53	0.33	0.63	0.96	0.67	0.51
1973 [3]	0.59	0.54	0.35	0.75	0.61	0.56	0.56

	342	352	355	362	369	381	384
Date / Date / Fecha	Printing, publishing / Imprimerie, édition / Imprentas, editoriales	Chemical products / Produits chimiques / Productos químicos	Rubber products / Produits en caoutchouc / Productos de caucho	Glass / Verre / Vidrio	Other non-metallic mineral products [4] / Autres produits minéraux non métalliques [4] / Otros productos minerales no metálicos [4]	Metal products / Produits métalliques / Productos metálicos	Transport equipment / Matériel de transport / Material de transporte
1965	0.57	0.70	0.69	0.41		...	.
1966	0.46	0.61	0.74	0.54		...	0.75
1967	0.53	0.65	0.61	0.49		...	0.70
1968	0.51	0.65	0.66	0.39		...	0.83
1969	0.59	0.76	0.63	.		...	0.48
1970	0.63	0.64	0.64	.		...	0.44
1971	0.60	0.63	0.60	.		0.63	0.85
1972 [2]	0.53	0.72	0.45	0.59	0.45	0.52	0.75
1973 [3]	0.66	0.75	0.70	0.88	0.39	0.61	0.88

[1] Workers engaged for less than 30 days (excl. casual workers). [2] April and Sept. [3] March and Sep. [4] Excl. pottery, china and earthenware.

[1] *Travailleurs engagés pour moins de 30 jours (non compris les travailleurs occasionnels).* [2] *Avril et sept.* [3] *Mars et sept.* [4] *Non compris le grès, les porcelaines et les faïences.*

[1] Trabajadores ocupados durante menos de 30 días (excl. los trabajadores ocasionales). [2] Abril y sept. [3] Marzo y sept. [4] Excl. el barro, la loza y la porcelana.

19 B

Wages in manufacturing
Salaires dans les industries manufacturières
Salarios en las industrias manufactureras

By industry
Par industrie
Por industria

Cyprus

Average weekly earnings[1] *(pounds)*
Gains hebdomadaires moyens[1] *(pounds)*
Promedio de ganancias por semana[1] *(pounds)*

Date [2] Date [2] Fecha [2]	311-312 Food Aliments Alimentos	313 Beverages Boissons Bebidas	314 Tobacco Tabac Tabaco	321 Textiles	322 Clothing Habillement Vestido	323 Leather, leather products Cuir, articles en cuir Cuero, artículos de cuero	324 Footwear Chaussures Calzado	331 Wood Bois Madera	332 Furniture Ameublement Mobiliario	341 Paper, paper products Papier, articles en papier Papel, artículos de papel
1965	5.76	7.19	4.85	4.06	4.19	4.20	5.73	7.63	7.73	3.50 [3]
1966	4.86	7.43	4.97	4.12	4.00	4.27	5.92	7.50	7.60	4.05 [3]
1967	5.74	6.94	5.38	4.09	4.19	4.58	6.51	8.13	8.57	4.40 [3]
1968	6.01	7.95	5.37	4.12	4.66	5.64	6.75	8.55	8.77	4.40 [3]
1969	6.01	7.62	6.53	5.20	4.85	5.72	7.22	7.76	9.34	6.53
1970	6.39	8.20	6.90	5.47	4.94	6.32	8.05	8.80	10.05	6.65
1971	7.77	9.98	7.48	5.67	6.08	6.87	9.33	8.90	11.10	7.07
1972	8.52	12.19	6.56	6.69	6.67	8.48	10.74	10.80	11.93	9.60
1973	9.45	13.18	5.87	8.21	7.81	8.68	12.15	11.41	13.96	11.50
1974	11.85	15.75	10.87	8.62	8.49	9.10	14.20	16.11	16.99	9.14

Date [2] Date [2] Fecha [2]	342 Printing, publishing Imprimerie, édition Imprentas, editoriales	351 Industrial chemicals Chimie industrielle Química industrial	355 Rubber products Produits en caoutchouc Productos de caucho	369 Non-metallic mineral products [4] Produits minéraux non métalliques [4] Productos minerales no metálicos [4]	381 Metal products Produits métalliques Productos metálicos	382 Machinery (non- electrical) Machines (non électriques) Maquinaria (no eléctrica)	383 Electrical machinery and apparatus Machines et appareils électriques Maquinaria y aparatos eléctricos	384 Transport equipment Matériel de transport Material de transporte	390 Other manufacturing industries Autres industries manufacturières Otras industrias manufactureras
1965	7.28	5.89	12.05	6.77	7.20	9.28	.	5.06	5.36
1966	7.26	5.93	11.66	7.31	7.58	8.76	.	5.39	5.60
1967	7.25	5.60	11.49	7.96	7.96	8.91	.	6.37	6.32
1968	8.21	7.30	10.78	8.53	8.34	9.43	.	6.54	8.06
1969	9.37	5.96	10.38	9.71	8.51	10.10	7.93	9.87	8.05
1970	10.79	7.10	9.76	10.90	9.31	10.24	8.11	10.00	7.76
1971	11.49	8.45	9.96	11.74	10.50	11.05	10.02	11.35	8.72
1972	13.85	8.50	11.05	13.04	11.57	14.45	12.65	13.17	10.24
1973	16.83	10.03	13.29	16.92	13.76	15.82	13.35	14.57	11.96
1974	16.83	12.86	14.38	20.59	13.90	12.82	14.74	15.60	17.86

[1] Adults only. [2] Oct. of each year, except 1969: Sep. [3] Females only. [4] Excl. pottery, china, earthenware and glass.

[1] *Adultes seulement.* [2] *Oct. de chaque année, sauf pour 1969: sept.* [3] *Femmes seulement.* [4] *Non compris le grès, les porcelaines, les faïences et le verre.*

[1] Adultos solamente. [2] Oct. de cada año, salvo 1969: sept. [3] Mujeres solamente. [4] Excl. el barro, la loza, la porcelana y el vidrio.

19 Wages in manufacturing
Salaires dans les industries manufacturières
Salarios en las industrias manufactureras

B By industry
Par industrie
Por industria

India [1]

Average monthly earnings *(rupees)*
Gains mensuels moyens *(rupees)*
Promedio de ganancias por mes *(rupees)*

Date / Date / Fecha	Textiles	Clothing / Habillement / Vestido	Wood / Bois / Madera	Furniture / Ameublement / Mobiliario	Paper, paper products / Papier, articles en papier / Papel, artículos de papel	Printing, publishing / Imprimerie, édition / Imprentas, editoriales	Leather, leather products / Cuir, articles en cuir / Cuero, artículos de cuero	Rubber products / Industrie du caoutchouc / Productos de caucho	Chemicals / Industrie chimique / Productos químicos
1965	163.6	165.6	102.1	126.9	148.0	155.5	134.8	164.3	176.0
1966	178.8	164.6	112.7	126.9	157.2	166.0	145.8	169.1	192.3
1967	193.8	171.6	114.4	137.0	177.7	187.1	146.9	206.3	202.7
1968	204.3	192.1	125.9	165.0	193.0	210.7	166.4	230.9	216.5
1969	216.8	195.4	126.7	173.5	200.0	216.5	206.0	219.7	226.9
1970	230.3	201.6	131.7	188.3	223.8	226.3	171.2	237.4	232.2
1971	233.7	207.1	146.9	165.3	233.6	242.5	237.7	199.4	241.6
1972 *	257.0	232.7	172.3	169.8	209.8	277.6	239.3	216.2	249.7

Date / Date / Fecha	Products of petroleum and coal / Dérivés du pétrole et du charbon / Derivados del petróleo y del carbón	Non-metallic mineral products / Produits minéraux non métalliques / Productos minerales no metálicos	Basic metal industries / Industrie métallurgique de base / Industrias metalúrgicas básicas	Metal products / Produits métalliques / Productos metálicos	Machinery (non-electrical) / Machines (non électriques) / Maquinaria (no eléctrica)	Electrical machinery / Machines électriques / Maquinaria eléctrica	Transport equipment / Matériel de transport / Material de transporte	Miscellaneous manufacturing / Industries manufacturières diverses / Industrias manufactureras diversas
1965	229.6	104.2	198.2	161.2	148.4	184.1	183.9	165.6
1966	242.4	115.2	212.9	164.8	168.2	189.8	200.4	169.3
1967	247.9	121.4	224.3	186.1	179.4	191.8	209.9	187.3
1968	241.8	132.5	233.8	202.3	189.3	222.1	233.4	214.2
1969	295.1	139.7	247.7	206.8	210.0	229.3	247.0	221.5
1970	314.8	151.1	239.4	203.9	229.0	276.1	254.8	229.7
1971	302.7	156.7	263.8	214.7	232.9	256.3	292.5	250.6
1972 *	293.4	167.1	268.2	210.6	254.8	273.0	310.9	232.2

[1] The number of states covered by the series varies according to the years.

[1] *Le nombre d'Etats couverts par la série varie selon les années.*

[1] El número de Estados cubiertos por la serie varía según los años.

19 Wages in manufacturing / Salaires dans les industries manufacturières / Salarios en las industrias manufactureras

B By industry / Par industrie / Por industria

Israel

Average daily earnings [1] *(pounds)*
Gains journaliers moyens [1] *(pounds)*
Promedio de ganancias por día [1] *(pounds)*

	34	321	322	323-324	33	341	342	351-354
Date / Date / Fecha	Food, beverages, tobacco / Aliments, boissons, tabac / Alimentos, bebidas, tabaco	Textiles	Clothing / Habillement / Vestido	Leather, leather products, footwear / Cuir, articles en cuir, chaussures / Cuero, artículos de cuero, calzado	Wood, furniture / Bois, ameublement / Madera, mobiliario	Paper, paper products / Papier articles en papier / Papel, artículos de papel	Printing, publishing / Imprimerie, édition / Imprentas, editoriales	Chemicals, petroleum refineries [3] / Industrie chimique, raffineries de pétrole [3] / Productos químicos, refinerías de petróleo [3]
1965	17.0	15.7	11.5	15.2	16.2	15.4	19.5	20.5
1966	19.6	18.0	13.4	17.0	18.4	18.1	24.2	24.1
1967	20.6	18.8	13.2	17.7	19.3	19.2	25.4	25.4
1968 [2]	20.2	19.2	14.2	18.0	21.1	20.3	26.0	26.7
1969	20.7	19.4	15.7	21.5	22.6	21.3	28.3	27.8
1970	23.6	21.9	17.9	22.8	25.8	24.5	31.5	31.3
1971	26.2	24.6	19.7	23.9	29.0	25.9	35.0	35.1
1972	29.3	29.3	23.4	27.0	31.4	30.0	38.8	40.9
1973	37.0	38.6	29.0	32.6	37.1	37.6	47.2	52.4
1974	49.0	51.7	38.0	43.8	56.6	46.7	62.5	70.9

	355-356	36	37	381	382	383	384	390	
Date / Date / Fecha	Rubber and plastic products / Produits en caoutchouc et en plastique / Productos de caucho y de plástico	Non-metallic mineral products / Produits minéraux non métalliques / Productos minerales no metálicos	Basic metal industries / Industrie métallurgique de base / Industrias metalúrgicas básicas	Metal products / Produits métallurgiques / Productos metálicos	Machinery (non-electrical) / Machines (non électriques) / Maquinaria (no eléctrica)	Electrical machinery and apparatus / Machines et appareils électriques / Maquinaria y aparatos eléctricos	Transport equipment / Matériel de transport / Material de transporte	Diamonds / Diamants / Diamantes	Other manufacturing industries / Autres industries manufacturières / Otras industrias manufactureras
1965	17.4	20.6	21.7	17.5	18.2	17.0	19.7	19.9	14.2
1966	19.5	24.5	25.6	20.0	20.9	19.3	23.3	23.0	16.1
1967	21.7	25.0	25.7	20.6	22.0	20.5	24.4	23.8	17.5
1968 [2]	22.6	26.7	27.5	21.5	23.8	21.4	25.6	25.3	18.7
1969	23.0	26.6	28.8	23.9	26.5	24.0	29.0	26.5	20.9
1970	25.1	30.4	32.8	26.5	29.7	26.9	32.4	26.9	21.8
1971	28.1	34.3	36.9	29.9	32.5	30.0	34.6	28.9	25.0
1972	30.8	37.8	41.3	33.7	36.6	33.8	38.8	33.2	29.2
1973	37.2	48.5	51.2	42.1	46.0	41.6	51.0	40.1	34.2
1974	51.9	66.8	68.1	57.7	61.7	58.1	72.4	53.5	46.7

[1] Incl. salaried employees.   [2] Sampling design revised.
[3] Incl. products of petroleum and coal.

[1] *Y compris les employés.*   [2] *Plan d'échantillonnage révisé.*   [3] *Y compris les dérivés du pétrole et du charbon.*

[1] Incl. los empleados.   [2] Diseño de la muestra revisado.   [3] Incl. los derivados del petróleo y del carbón.

19 Wages in manufacturing / Salaires dans les industries manufacturières / Salarios en las industrias manufactureras

B By industry / Par industrie / Por industria

Japan (1)

Average monthly earnings [1] *(yen)*
Gains mensuels moyens [1] *(yen)*
Promedio de ganancias por mes [1] *(yen)*

Date / Date / Fecha	311-313 Food, beverages / Aliments, boissons / Alimentos, bebidas	314 Tobacco / Tabac / Tabaco	321 Textiles	322 Clothing / Habillement / Vestido	323-324 Leather, leather products, footwear / Cuir, articles en cuir, chaussures / Cuero, artículos de cuero, calzado	331 Wood / Bois / Madera	332 Furniture / Ameublement / Mobiliario
1965	32 345	49 340	25 068	22 003	32 953	27 102	28 993
1966	35 122	53 751	27 639	24 274	35 472	30 424	32 453
1967 [2]	38 603	58 053	30 693	26 695	38 746	35 248	32 961
1968	46 032		35 580	30 592	44 469	41 105	41 278
1969	53 125		42 071	35 924	52 220	47 970	48 055
1970 [2]	62 801		52 657	40 041	59 400	54 777	55 250
1971	73 643		59 924	45 876	65 919	63 214	63 164
1972	85 366		70 069	53 416	75 398	75 702	73 863
1973 [2]	96 328		89 536	69 948	93 573	98 460	92 050
1974	123 998		103 992	85 686	118 303	118 780	117 021

Date / Date / Fecha	341 Paper, paper products / Papier, articles en papier / Papel, artículos de papel	342 Printing, publishing / Imprimerie, édition / Imprentas, editoriales	351-252 Chemicals / Industrie chimique / Productos químicos	353-354 Refineries and products of petroleum and coal / Raffineries et dérivés du pétrole et du charbon / Refinerías y derivados del petróleo y del carbón	355 Rubber products / Produits en caoutchouc / Productos de caucho	36 Non-metallic mineral products / Produits minéraux non métalliques / Productos minerales no metálicos	371 Iron and steel basic industries / Sidérurgie / Industrias básicas de hierro y acero
1965	37 795	47 639	44 091	52 513	32 085	36 702	49 281
1966	42 346	52 544	49 138	58 009	36 907	40 702	55 345
1967 [2]	47 473	57 924	55 302	67 669	40 703	44 778	64 635
1968	53 968	65 531	62 768	78 639	47 078	51 942	73 596
1969	63 595	74 860	73 751	88 075	55 465	60 915	86 201
1970 [2]	73 159	87 257	86 785	98 028	64 740	70 543	100 710
1971	85 171	100 810	98 657	114 112	75 270	79 395	109 798
1972	97 084	115 881	112 969	127 114	89 652	91 606	122 362
1973 [2]	118 919	140 006	140 429	153 822	113 173	110 784	155 080
1974	157 377	178 142	183 213	200 264	143 607	143 251	200 001

[1] Incl. salaried employees. Incl. family allowances, mid- and end-of-year bonuses. [2] Sampling design revised.

[1] Y compris les employés. Y compris les allocations familiales et les primes de mi- et de fin d'année. [2] Plan d'échantillonnage révisé.

[1] Incl. los empleados. Incl. las asignaciones familiares y las primas de mitad y de fin de año. [2] Diseño de la muestra revisado.

19

Wages in manufacturing
Salaires dans les industries manufacturières
Salarios en las industrias manufactureras

B

By industry
Par industrie
Por industria

Japan (2)

Average monthly earnings [1] *(yen)*
Gains mensuels moyens [1] *(yen)*
Promedio de ganancias por mes [1] *(yen)*

Date / Date / Fecha	372 Non-ferrous metal basic industries / Métaux non ferreux (industrie de base) / Industrias básicas de metales no ferrosos	381 Metal products / Produits métalliques / Productos metálicos	382 Machinery (non-electrical) / Machines (non électriques) / Maquinaria (no eléctrica)	383 Electrical machinery and apparatus / Machines et appareils électriques / Maquinaria y aparatos eléctricos	384 Transport equipment / Matériel de transport / Material de transporte	385 Scientific, measuring, optical, etc., equipment / Matériel scientifique, de précision, d'optique, etc. / Equipo científico, de medida, de óptica, etc.	390 Other manufacturing industries / Autres industries manufacturières / Otras industrias manufactureras
1965	.	35 134	38 564	32 082	43 781	34 834	30 087
1966	47 909	39 704	44 486	37 004	48 954	39 817	34 282
1967 [2]	54 497	45 160	51 248	41 152	54 476	45 240	37 811
1968	62 829	53 366	59 407	48 455	61 508	51 407	44 882
1969	73 246	62 155	70 045	57 173	71 271	61 319	53 669
1970 [2]	85 419	71 353	81 222	63 830	82 769	69 153	60 398
1971	95 818	80 408	88 782	72 841	94 784	76 955	69 713
1972	110 617	92 436	102 513	87 086	106 169	90 637	82 286
1973 [2]	136 760	117 647	131 647	105 419	132 231	111 277	102 047
1974	170 487	148 247	165 863	129 570	163 382	137 227	130 443

[1] Incl. salaried employees. Incl. family allowances, mid- and end-of-year bonuses. [2] Sampling design revised.

[1] *Y compris les employés. Y compris les allocations familiales et les primes de mi- et de fin d'année.* [2] *Plan d'échantillonnage révisé.*

[1] Incl. los empleados. Incl. las asignaciones familiares y las primas de mitad y de fin de año. [2] Diseño de la muestra revisado.

19 B Wages in manufacturing / Salaires dans les industries manufacturières / Salarios en las industrias manufactureras — By industry / Par industrie / Por industria

Korea, Rep. of (1)

Average monthly earnings [1] *(won)*
Gains mensuels moyens [1] *(won)*
Promedio de ganancias por mes [1] *(won)*

Date / Date / Fecha	311-312 Food / Aliments / Alimentos	313 Beverages / Boissons / Bebidas	314 Tobacco / Tabac / Tabaco	321 Textiles	322 Clothing / Habillement / Vestido	323 Leather, leather products / Cuir, articles en cuir / Cuero, artículos de cuero	324 Footwear / Chaussures / Calzado	331 Wood / Bois / Madera	332 Furniture / Ameublement / Mobiliario
1970	15 371	12 884	26 673	11 389	9 904	12 653	14 674	14 841	10 698
1971	18 938	16 465	32 746	13 346	11 765	14 519	15 404	17 154	12 980
1972	21 228	21 173	37 203	16 338	13 351	15 836	18 435	20 345	14 001
1973	23 479	27 560	...	19 143	14 952	19 197		23 623	14 919
1974	30 313	39 519	...	27 571	19 931	24 469	...	30 548	20 398

Date / Date / Fecha	341 Paper, paper products / Papier, articles en papier / Papel, artículos de papel	342 Printing, publishing / Imprimerie, édition / Imprentas, editoriales	351 Industrial chemicals / Chimie industrielle / Química industrial	352 Other chemical products / Autres produits chimiques / Otros productos químicos	353 Petroleum refineries / Raffineries de pétrole / Refinerías de petróleo	354 Products of petroleum and coal / Dérivés du pétrole et du charbon / Derivados del petróleo y del carbón	355 Rubber products / Produits en caoutchouc / Productos de caucho	356 Plastic products / Articles en matière plastique / Productos plásticos	361 Pottery, china, earthenware / Grès, porcelaines, faïences / Barro, loza, porcelana
1970	15 619	19 051	22 851	18 410	39 162	14 094	11 679	14 518	9 480
1971	19 498	22 534	26 877	22 412	53 605	17 456	13 114	15 572	10 755
1972	22 829	26 249	31 008	27 138	58 074	21 543	16 120	17 055	11 665
1973	25 313	29 844	49 143	29 776	61 487	28 473	17 549	24 999	15 571
1974	34 074	38 013	58 711	39 457	92 411	34 420	24 096	33 067	21 652

[1] Incl. salaried employees. Incl. family allowances.

[1] *Y compris les employés. Y compris les allocations familiales.*

[1] Incl. los empleados. Incl. las asignaciones familiares.

19 B

Wages in manufacturing
Salaires dans les industries manufacturières
Salarios en las industrias manufactureras

By industry
Par industrie
Por industria

Korea, Rep. of (2)

Average monthly earnings [1] *(won)*
Gains mensuels moyens [1] *(won)*
Promedio de ganancias por mes [1] *(won)*

Date / Date / Fecha	362 Glass, and glass products / Verre / Vidrio	369 Other non-metallic mineral products / Autres produits minéraux / Otros productos minerales	371 Basic metal industries / Industrie métallurgique de base / Industrias metalúrgicas básicas — Iron and steel / Sidérurgie / Hierro y acero	372 Non-ferrous metal / Métaux non ferreux / Metales no ferrosos	381 Metal products / Produits métallurgiques / Productos metálicos	382 Machinery (non-electrical) / Machines (non électriques) / Maquinaria (no eléctrica)	383 Electrical machinery and apparatus / Machines et appareils électriques / Maquinaria y aparatos eléctricos	384 Transport equipment / Matériel de transport / Material de transporte	385 Scientific, measuring, optical, etc., equipment / Matériel scientifique, de précision, d'optique, etc. / Equipo científico, de medida, de óptica, etc.	390 Other manufacturing industries / Autres industries manufacturières / Otras industrias manufactureras
1970	17 020	17 400	19 118	15 872	13 326	14 992	14 180	21 335	13 130	13 633
1971	21 132	21 132	23 701	16 516	15 928	16 324	17 968	24 526	14 613	13 993
1972	22 418	24 782	28 250	20 345	18 376	19 804	19 294	27 696	17 619	14 791
1973	30 554	27 236	38 707	35 609	20 653	25 697	20 243	26 141	22 520	15 970
1974	36 991	37 050	54 145	45 906	29 352	33 449	27 848	41 141	26 660	22 291

[1] Incl. salaried employees. Incl. family allowances. [1] *Y compris les employés. Y compris les allocations familiales.* [1] Incl. los empleados. Incl. las asignaciones familiares.

Pakistan

Average monthly earnings *(rupees)*
Gains mensuels moyens *(rupees)*
Promedio de ganancias por mes *(rupees)*

Date / Date / Fecha	Textiles	Wood, stone, glass / Bois, pierre, verre / Madera, piedra, vidrio	Paper, printing, publishing / Papier, imprimerie, édition / Papel, imprentas, editoriales	Skins, hides / Peaux, cuirs / Pieles, cuero	Chemicals, dyes / Industrie chimique, teintures / Productos químicos, tinturas	Minerals, metals / Minéraux, métaux / Minerales, metales	Ordnance / Arsenaux / Arsenales	Engineering / Mécanique / Mecánica	Miscellaneous manufacturing / Industries manufacturières diverses / Industrias manufactureras diversas
1965	112.3	98.0	135.7	142.3	105.1	137.1	125.3	124.9	121.5
1966	123.4	115.5	152.1	141.2	138.3	131.9	127.1	135.5	120.4
1967	107.5	133.3	152.4	142.0	137.4	138.5	145.1	132.2	123.5
1968	123.2	138.1	174.1	164.7	153.3	129.4	...	136.6	115.6
1969	156.1	153.2	179.1	156.4	159.6	138.0	160.4	159.3	144.3
1970	143.1	127.1	168.9	161.2	168.5	142.6	...	154.9	140.1
1971	154.5	156.8	105.4	146.2	198.5	155.3	...	133.0	128.6
1972 *	183.2	171.6	108.7	108.8	106.2	174.5	...	194.1	132.8

19 Wages in manufacturing
Salaires dans les industries manufacturières
Salarios en las industrias manufactureras

B By industry
Par industrie
Por industria

Philippines

Average monthly earnings [1] *(pesos)*
Gains mensuels moyens [1] *(pesos)*
Promedio de ganancias por mes [1] *(pesos)*

Date / Date / Fecha	Food / Aliments / Alimentos	Beverages / Boissons / Bebidas	Tobacco / Tabac / Tabaco	Textiles	Clothing / Habillement / Vestido	Wood / Bois / Madera	Furniture / Ameublement / Mobiliario	Paper, paper products / Papier, articles en papier / Papel, artículos de papel	Printing, publishing / Imprimerie, édition / Imprentas, editoriales	Leather, leather products / Cuir, articles en cuir / Cuero, artículos de cuero
1965	150	244	115	143	102	150	139	191	208	104
1966	164	292	125	152	106	165	140	205	214	114
1967	175	281	135	158	107	193	142	221	229	102
1968	188	288	148	158	105	191	142	230	247	105
1969 [2]	191	281	152	177	116	171	153	241	281	153
1970	215	340	152	181	154	210	164	290	305	158
1971	242	403	217	236	140	242	205	335	355	178

Date / Date / Fecha	Rubber products / Industrie du caoutchouc / Productos de caucho	Chemicals / Industrie chimique / Productos químicos	Non-metallic mineral products / Produits minéraux non métalliques / Productos minerales no metálicos	Basic metal industries / Industrie métallurgique de base / Industrias metalúrgicas básicas	Metal products / Produits métalliques / Productos metálicos	Machinery (non-electrical) / Machines (non électriques) / Maquinaria (no eléctrica)	Electrical machinery / Machines électriques / Maquinaria eléctrica	Transport equipment / Matériel de transport / Material de transporte	Miscellaneous manufacturing / Industries manufacturières diverses / Industrias manufactureras diversas
1965	190	222	208	177	148	203	142	183	140
1966	172	235	224	171	149	225	146	175	166
1967	173	238	225	193	156	234	157	166	160
1968	163	238	256	210	151	233	157	170	160
1969 [2]	195	271	245	279	222	200	214	213	162
1970	285	365	245	320	232	220	227	242	200
1971	260	380	306	310	313	243	280	260	222

[1] Production worker. 1965-68 wage earners. [2] Series replacing former series.

[1] *Travailleur à la production. 1965-1968 : ouvriers.*
[2] *Série remplaçant la précédente.*

[1] Trabajadores de la producción. 1965-1968: obreros.
[2] Serie que substituye a la anterior.

19 Wages in manufacturing / Salaires dans les industries manufacturières / Salarios en las industrias manufactureras

B By industry / Par industrie / Por industria

Singapore

Average hourly earnings *(cents)*
Gains horaires moyens *(cents)*
Promedio de ganancias por hora *(cents)*

Date [1] / Date [1] / Fecha [1]	311-312 Food / Aliments / Alimentos	313 Beverages / Boissons / Bebidas	314 Tobacco / Tabac / Tabaco	321 Textiles	322 Clothing / Habillement / Vestido	323 Leather, leather products / Cuir, articles en cuir / Cuero, artículos de cuero	324 Footwear / Chaussures / Calzado	331 Wood / Bois / Madera	332 Furniture / Ameublement / Mobiliario
1971	76	110	116	63	58	65	69	96	100
1972	81	118	119	68	60	61	74	99	103
1973	99	135	146	85	71	77	83	112	106

Date [1] / Date [1] / Fecha [1]	341 Paper, paper products / Papier, articles en papier / Papel, artículos de papel	342 Printing, publishing / Imprimerie, édition / Imprentas, editoriales	351 Industrial chemicals / Chimie industrielle / Química industrial	352 Other chemical products / Autres produits chimiques / Otros productos químicos	353 Petroleum refineries / Raffineries de pétrole / Refinerías de petróleo	355 Rubber products / Produits en caoutchouc / Productos de caucho	356 Plastic products / Articles en matière plastique / Productos plásticos	361-362 Pottery, china, earthenware and glass / Grès, porcelaine, faïences et verre / Barro, loza, porcelana y vidrio	369 Other non-metallic mineral products / Autres produits minéraux non métalliques / Otros productos minerales no metálicos
1971	65	107	118	76	230	81	68	107	111
1972	72	117	117	96	232	86	73	121	112
1973	79	128	126	107	264	97	91	139	115

Date [1] / Date [1] / Fecha [1]	371 Iron and steel / Sidérurgie / Hierro y acero	372 Non-ferrous metal / Métaux non ferreux / Metales no ferrosos	381 Metal products / Produits métalliques / Productos metálicos	382 Machinery (non-electrical) / Machines (non électriques) / Maquinaria (no eléctrica)	383 Electrical machinery and apparatus / Machines et appareils électriques / Maquinaria y aparatos eléctricos	384 Transport equipment / Matériel de transport / Material de transporte	385 Scientific, measuring, optical, etc., equipment / Matériel scientifique, de précision, d'optique, etc. / Equipo científico, de medida, de óptica, etc.	390 Other manufacturing industries / Autres industries manufacturières / Otras industrias manufactureras
1971	110	108	93	109	75	135	68	65
1972	126	115	94	118	81	148	77	66
1973	132	148	108	134	93	157	96	86

Basic metal industries / Industrie métallurgique de base / Industrias metalúrgicas básicas (371-372)

[1] July of each year.   [1] *Juillet de chaque année.*   [1] Julio de cada año.

WAGES

19 B

Wages in manufacturing
Salaires dans les industries manufacturières
Salarios en las industrias manufactureras

By industry
Par industrie
Por industria

République arabe syrienne (1)

Average weekly earnings [1] *(pounds)*
Gains hebdomadaires moyens [1] *(pounds)*
Promedio de ganancias por semana [1] *(pounds)*

	311-312	313	314	321	322; 324	323	331
Date [2]	Food	Beverages	Tobacco		Clothing, footwear	Leather, leather products	Wood
Date [2]	*Aliments*	*Boissons*	*Tabac*	Textiles	*Habillement, chaussures*	*Cuir, articles en cuir*	*Bois*
Fecha [2]	Alimentos	Bebidas	Tabaco		Vestido, calzado	Cuero, artículos de cuero	Madera
1967	37.20	36.65	42.90	.	32.00	39.00	33.30
1968	39.15	36.65	40.20	.	34.00	38.40	37.50
1969	43.67	55.94	45.95	.	38.75	48.29	50.06
1970	47.20	59.90	46.55	.	39.65	51.35	45.10
1971	47.10	53.50	43.05	57.10	42.35	57.10	55.80
1972	55.65	68.15	48.50	65.55	48.55	77.10	54.20
1973 [3]	72.50	91.70	61.65	78.40	58.95	79.05	55.10
1974 [3]	64.20	82.40	59.50	74.50	61.10	73.10	64.80

	341	342	351	352	353	354	355
Date [2]	Paper, paper products	Printing, publishing	Industrial chemicals	Other chemical products	Petroleum refineries	Products of petroleum and coal	Rubber products
Date [2]	*Papier, articles en papier*	*Imprimerie, édition*	*Chimie industrielle*	*Autres produits chimiques*	*Raffineries de pétrole*	*Dérivés du pétrole et du charbon*	*Produits en caoutchouc*
Fecha [2]	Papel, artículos de papel	Imprentas, editoriales	Química industrial	Otros productos químicos	Refinerías de petróleo	Derivados del petróleo y del carbón	Productos de caucho
1967	31.95	43.25	.	41.35	.	.	37.65
1968	35.95	45.80	.	41.35	.	.	37.75
1969	39.28	53.87	.	45.36	.	.	43.32
1970	50.80	56.25	.	46.40	.	.	47.75
1971	42.00	59.90	.	53.90	75.85	45.70	51.60
1972	50.35	66.00	.	69.35	80.70	45.75	63.45
1973 [3]	62.55	78.25	102.10	78.30	91.15	54.00	76.60
1974 [3]	64.10	84.70	101.25	78.95	94.40	53.25	80.40

[1] Adults only. [2] Nov. of each year. [3] May.   [1] *Adultes seulement.* [2] *Nov. de chaque année.* [3] *Mai.*   [1] Adultos solamente. [2] Nov. de cada año. [3] Mayo.

19 Wages in manufacturing
Salaires dans les industries manufacturières
Salarios en las industrias manufactureras

B By industry
Par industrie
Por industria

République arabe syrienne (2)

Average weekly earnings [1] *(pounds)*
Gains hebdomadaires moyens [1] *(pounds)*
Promedio de ganancias por semana [1] *(pounds)*

Date [2] Date [2] Fecha [2]	356 Plastic products *Articles en matière plastique* Productos plásticos	361 Pottery, china, earthenware *Grès, porcelaines, faïences* Barro, loza, porcelana	362 Glass *Verre* Vidrio	369 Other non-metallic mineral products *Autres produits minéraux non métalliques* Otros productos minerales no metálicos	371 Iron and steel basic industries *Sidérurgie* Industrias básicas de hierro y acero	381 Metal products *Produits métalliques* Productos metálicos	382 Machinery (non- electrical) *Machines (non électriques)* Maquinaria (no eléctrica)	383 Electrical machinery and apparatus *Machines et appareils électriques* Maquinaria y aparatos eléctricos
1967	.	.	.	.	31.50	27.35	30.00	37.90
1968	.	.	.	.	32.95	30.55	30.45	39.95
1969	.	.	.	.	59.39	...	...	54.31
1970	.	.	.	.	53.55	...	...	49.30
1971	39.20	43.90	49.65	57.80	43.80	50.10	56.50	51.35
1972	55.30	47.55	67.30	81.15	54.45	63.50	56.60	64.05
1973 [3]	52.25	57.65	75.70	97.55	67.05	68.10	69.75	69 00
1974 [3]	51.45	64.10	84.15	89.90	68.05	66.55	73.60	74.50

[1] Adults only. [2] Nov. of each year. [3] May.   [1] *Adultes seulement.* [2] *Nov. de chaque année.* [3] *Mai.*   [1] Adultos solamente. [2] Nov. de cada año. [3] Mayo.

19 Wages in manufacturing / Salaires dans les industries manufacturières / Salarios en las industrias manufactureras

B By industry / Par industrie / Por industria

EUROPE — EUROPE — EUROPA

Austria

Average monthly earnings *(schilling)*
Gains mensuels moyens *(schilling)*
Promedio de ganancias por mes *(schilling)*

Date / Date / Fecha	Food, beverages, tobacco / Aliments, boissons, tabac / Alimentos, bebidas, tabaco	Textiles	Clothing [2] / Habillement [2] / Vestido [2]	Wood [3], furniture / Bois [3], ameublement / Madera [3], mobiliario	Paper / Papier / Papel	Paper products / Articles en papier / Artículos de papel	Leather / Cuir / Cuero	Leather products, footwear / Articles en cuir, chaussures / Artículos de cuero, calzado
1965	3 302	2 393	2 103	2 942	3 783	2 661	2 606	2 343
1966	3 638	2 678	2 356	3 273	4 241	2 951	2 883	2 623
1967	3 953	2 830	2 529	3 608	4 783	3 267	3 059	2 863
1968	4 181	2 994	2 685	3 798	5 352	3 451	3 152	2 986
1969	4 400	3 233	2 819	3 970	5 849	3 769	3 320	3 176
1970	4 807	3 474	3 047	4 361	6 262	4 233	3 804	3 349
1971 [1]	5 372	3 925	3 344	4 950	6 820	4 588	4 206	3 861
1972	6 139	4 387	3 718	5 655	7 483	5 081	4 665	4 462
1973	6 627	4 964	4 104	6 322	8 400	5 614	5 061	4 853
1974	7 864	5 606	4 588	7 264	9 668	6 655	5 705	5 437

Date / Date / Fecha	Rubber products, chemicals / Caoutchouc, industrie chimique / Caucho, productos químicos	Non-metallic mineral products / Produits minéraux non métalliques / Productos minerales no metálicos	Glass / Verre / Vidrio	Non-ferrous metals / Métaux non ferreux / Metales no ferrosos	Primary iron and steel / Sidérurgie / Siderurgia	Metal products, miscellaneous manufacturing / Produits métalliques, industries manufacturières diverses / Productos metálicos, industrias manufactureras diversas	Machinery (non-electrical) / Machines (non électriques) / Maquinaria (no eléctrica)	Electrical machinery / Machines électriques / Maquinaria eléctrica	Transport equipment / Matériel de transport / Material de transporte
1965	3 369	3 531	3 290	3 488	3 699	2 987	3 535	2 903	3 042
1966	3 751	3 981	3 465	3 944	4 047	3 356	3 968	3 269	3 484
1967	3 985	4 270	3 873	4 173	4 299	3 610	4 239	3 524	3 873
1968	4 321	4 534	4 074	4 581	4 566	3 860	4 502	3 810	3 944
1969	4 493	4 831	4 306	4 844	4 791	4 129	4 787	3 971	4 258
1970	4 902	5 267	4 648	5 466	5 238	4 428	5 258	4 278	4 621
1971 [1]	5 614	5 916	5 442	6 030	6 271	5 101	6 099	4 839	5 541
1972	6 251	6 856	6 104	6 819	6 805	5 707	6 792	5 367	6 140
1973	6 997	7 540	6 947	7 749	7 678	6 453	7 698	6 049	6 908
1974	8 203	8 619	8 047	8 992	9 008	7 447	8 833	6 881	7 949

[1] Scope of series enlarged. [2] Excl. footwear. [3] Excl. sawmills.

[1] *Portée de la série élargie.* [2] *Non compris la chaussure.* [3] *Non compris les scieries.*

[1] El alcance de la serie es mayor. [2] Excl. el calzado. [3] Excl. los aserraderos.

19 Wages in manufacturing
Salaires dans les industries manufacturières
Salarios en las industrias manufactureras

B By industry
Par industrie
Por industria

Belgique (1)

Average hourly earnings *(francs)*
Gains horaires moyens *(francs)*
Promedio de ganancias por hora *(francs)*

	311-312	313	314	321	322 ×	323	324	331	332
Date [1]	Food	Beverages	Tobacco		Clothing	Leather, leather products	Footwear	Wood	Furniture
Date [1]	*Aliments*	*Boissons*	*Tabac*	Textiles	*Habillement*	*Cuir, articles en cuir*	*Chaussures*	*Bois*	*Ameublement*
Fecha [1]	Alimentos	Bebidas	Tabaco		Vestido	Cuero, artículos de cuero	Calzado	Madera	Mobiliario
1966	43.47	47.77	41.06	41.83	33.28	40.77	43.47	44.71	46.75
1967	45.59	50.56	43.60	44.32	35.16	43.38	45.14	48.00	49.18
1968	48.74	54.13	47.00	46.55	37.38	46.62	47 39	50.69	53.16
1969	53.30	59.15	51.93	51.52	40.86	50.91	51.85	55.62	58.19
1970	58.40	63.90	57.40	56.05	46.13	55.01	57.50	62.88	65.14
1971	67.95	72.77	66.30	63.67	50.61	62.12	63.86	70.22	70.48
1972 [2]	77.44	83.71	81.67	74.68	58.46	72.66	72.76	81.03	80.00
1973	88.21	94.61	92.45	85.20	65.59	82.04	84.23	90.14	87.57
1974	111.34	119.51	113.33	107.06	82.09	98.11	102.70	116.03	114.54

	341	342	351			353	355	361	362
Date [1]	Paper, paper products	Printing, publishing	Basic industrial chemicals	Fertilizers and pesticides [3]	Synthetic and man-made fibres	Petroleum refineries	Rubber products	Pottery, china, earthenware	Glass
Date [1]	*Papier, articles en papier*	*Imprimerie, édition*	*Industrie chimique de base*	*Engrais et pesticides [3]*	*Fibres synthétiques et artificielles*	*Raffineries de pétrole*	*Produits en caoutchouc*	*Grès, porcelaines, faïences*	*Verre*
Fecha [1]	Papel, artículos de papel	Imprentas, editoriales	Química industrial básica	Abonos y plaguicidas [3]	Fibras sintéticas y artificiales	Refinerías de petróleo	Productos de caucho	Barro, loza, porcelana	Vidrio
1966	47.88	52.17	58.40	51.82	54.04	78.36	50.26	43.95	48.17
1967	50.88	56.79	63.40	55.56	59.78	85.10	53.14	45.52	49.98
1968	53.17	61.45	66.67	57.30	60.50	88.22	55.29	47.86	52.98
1969	59.82	65.12	73.52	63.46	67.44	94.01	61.67	52.98	59.13
1970	65.91	72.40	81.38	70.40	73.08	105.03	69.11	59.78	66.28
1971	74.88	85.15	94.35	81.72	84.37	123.38	78.02	67.88	75.03
1972 [2]	85.41	93.32	115.24	95.96	100.27	143.02	93.00	79.14	88.51
1973	96.52	108.96	126.62	107.60	114.18	158.29	104.50	90.83	102.29
1974	119.92	142.21	157.25	137.19	141.15	190.20	132.76	112.61	128.39

[1] Oct. of each year. [2] New industrial classification. [3] Incl. drugs and medicines.

[1] *Oct. de chaque année.* [2] *Nouvelle classification industrielle.* [3] *Y compris les produits pharmaceutiques et les médicaments.*

[1] Oct. de cada año. [2] Nueva clasificación industrial. [3] Incl. los productos farmacéuticos y medicamentos.

19 Wages in manufacturing
Salaires dans les industries manufacturières
Salarios en las industrias manufactureras

B By industry
Par industrie
Por industria

Belgique (2)

Average hourly earnings *(francs)*
Gains horaires moyens *(francs)*
Promedio de ganancias por hora *(francs)*

	369 ×	371	372	381	382	383	384	385	390
Date [1] *Date [1]* Fecha [1]	Cement *Ciment* Cemento	Basic metal industries *Industrie métallurgique de base* Industrias metalúrgicas básicas		Metal products *Produits métalliques* Productos metálicos	Machinery (non-electrical) *Machines (non électriques)* Maquinaria (no eléctrica)	Electrical machinery and apparatus *Machines et appareils électriques* Maquinaria y aparatos eléctricos	Transport equipment *Matériel de transport* Material de transporte	Scientific, measuring, optical, etc., equipment *Matériel scientifique, de précision, d'optique, etc.* Equipo científico, de medida, de óptica, etc.	Other manufacturing industries *Autres industries manufacturières* Otras industrias manufactureras
		Iron and steel *Sidérurgie* Hierro y acero	Non-ferrous metal *Métaux non ferreux* Metales no ferrosos						
1966	62.12	65.39	56.69	49.44	52.22	48.80	56.34	.	.
1967	65.35	69.54	60.54	52.12	56.20	51.19	59.53	.	.
1968	72.23	73.59	62.00	54.88	59.18	54.46	63.21	.	.
1969	77.14	81.23	68.86	60.08	63.93	60.11	69.93	.	.
1970	84.43	88.67	76.30	67.65	71.66	67.59	79.46	.	.
1971	93.34	103.50	88.37	75.62	81.42	76.89	88.52	.	.
1972 [2]	111.31	119.49	104.41	88.99	94.23	86.96	102.11	79.03	65.93
1973	123.78	134.89	120.57	102.41	107.99	100.59	115.78	91.43	75.23
1974	151.93	171.89	151.86	128.28	133.94	126.83	144.76	117.18	90.01

[1] Oct. of each year. [2] New industrial classification.

[1] *Oct. de chaque année.* [2] *Nouvelle classification industrielle.*

[1] Oct. de cada año. [2] Nueva clasificación industrial.

19 B

Wages in manufacturing
Salaires dans les industries manufacturières
Salarios en las industrias manufactureras

By industry
Par industrie
Por industria

Bulgarie [1]

Average monthly earnings [2] *(leva)*
Gains mensuels moyens [2] *(leva)*
Promedio de ganancias por mes [2] *(leva)*

	31	321	322	323-324	33	341	342
Date	Food, beverage, tobacco		Clothing	Leather, leather products, footwear	Wood, furniture [3]	Paper, paper products	Printing, publishing
Date	*Aliments, boissons, tabac*	Textiles	*Habillement*	*Cuir, articles en cuir, chaussures*	*Bois, ameublement [3]*	*Papier, articles en papier*	*Imprimerie, édition*
Fecha	Alimentos, bebidas, tabaco		Vestido	Cuero, artículos de cuero, calzado	Madera, mobiliario [3]	Papel, artículos de papel	Imprentas, editoriales
1966	89.6	85.0	83.3	96.6	102.0	91.0	86.5
1967	97.3	91.3	88.6	96.6	110.5	100.0	99.5
1968	104.8	97.6	97.3	101.9	118.9	106.7	107.5
1969	109.3	100.0	93.3	102.3	121.3	114.7	115.8
1970	115.2	106.2	99.5	109.0	127.3	118.2	122.2
1971	118.8	109.7	99.7	114.4	131.3	117.4	121.8
1972	123.1	114.6	104.2	119.7	136.4	119.3	128.3
1973	132.0	123.7	112.1	125.1	143.2	124.5	136.4
1974 *	134.5	126.9	113.4	130.2	149.2	128.8	130.2

	351-352; 355	354	361 ×-362	369 ×	371	381-382	390
Date	Chemicals, rubber products [4]	Products of petroleum and coal	China, earthenware, glass	Building material	Iron and steel basic industries [5]	Metal products, machinery (non-electrical)	Other manufacturing industries
Date	*Industrie chimique, caoutchouc [4]*	*Dérivés du pétrole et du charbon*	*Porcelaines, faïences, verre*	*Matériaux de construction*	*Sidérurgie [5]*	*Produits métalliques, machines (non électriques)*	*Autres industries manufacturières*
Fecha	Productos químicos, caucho [4]	Derivados del petróleo y del carbón	Loza, porcelana, vidrio	Materiales de construcción	Industrias básicas de hierro y acero [5]	Productos metálicos, maquinaria (no eléctrica)	Otras industrias manufactureras
1966	98.8	126.1	97.8	103.7	118.7	103.9	86.8
1967	108.5	139.3	101.3	115.1	131.7	111.9	94.3
1968	113.6	148.1	107.4	123.5	141.5	117.3	102.2
1969	121.3	155.2	111.8	127.3	142.6	123.3	103.4
1970	127.8	165.8	117.7	132.5	148.2	129.8	108.9
1971	129.5	167.4	127.4	137.7	157.2	133.3	110.2
1972	133.7	174.0	132.7	141.2	171.8	138.5	114.5
1973	143.4	186.2	137.4	148.5	176.7	146.9	120.3
1974 *	147.1	192.1	137.7	154.6	182.7	148.7	. . .

[1] State industry. [2] Incl. salaried employees. [3] Incl. logging. [4] Incl. salt mining. [5] Incl. ore mining.

[1] *Industrie d'Etat.* [2] *Y compris les employés.* [3] *Y compris l'exploitation forestière.* [4] *Y compris l'extraction du sel.* [5] *Y compris l'extraction des minerais.*

[1] Industria de Estado. [2] Incl. los empleados. [3] Incl. la explotación de la madera. [4] Incl. la explotación de minas de sal. [5] Incl. la extracción de minerales.

WAGES

19 Wages in manufacturing / Salaires dans les industries manufacturières / Salarios en las industrias manufactureras

B By industry / Par industrie / Por industria

Czechoslovakia [1] (1)

Average monthly earnings *(korunas)*
Gains mensuels moyens *(korunas)*
Promedio de ganancias por mes *(korunas)*

Date / Date / Fecha	311-312 Food / Aliments / Alimentos	313 Beverages / Boissons / Bebidas	314 Tobacco / Tabac / Tabaco	321 Textiles	322 Clothing / Habillement / Vestido	323 Leather, leather products / Cuir, articles en cuir / Cuero, artículos de cuero	324 Footwear / Chaussures / Calzado	331 Wood / Bois / Madera	332 Furniture / Ameublement / Mobiliario
1966	1 388	1 368	1 187	1 180	1 141	1 276	1352	1 368	1 389
1967	1 458	1 426	1 249	1 231	1 169	1 281	1 421	1 457	1 438
1968	1 658	1 575	1 340	1 335	1 271	1 407	1 522	1 577	1 545
1969	1 770	1 702	1 437	1 431	1 393	1 540	1 656	1 721	1 656
1970	1 832	1 791	1 502	1 485	1 431	1 585	1 739	1 775	1 717
1971	1 881	1 880	1 597	1 536	1 459	1 641	1 797	1 842	1 770
1972	1 959	1 962	1 661	1 592	1 523	1 734	1 853	1 907	1 858
1973	2 017	2 014	1 733	1 644	1 572	1 787	1 885	1 955	1 919
1974	2 087	2 086	1 825	1 713	1 645	1 852	1 978	2 027	1 976

Date / Date / Fecha	341 Paper, paper products / Papier, articles en papier / Papel, artículos de papel	342 Printing, publishing / Imprimerie, édition / Imprentas, editoriales	351 Industrial chemicals / Chimie industrielle / Química industrial	352 Other chemical products / Autres produits chimiques / Otros productos químicos	353 Petroleum refineries / Raffineries de pétrole / Refinerías de petróleo	354 Products of petroleum and coal / Dérivés du pétrole et du charbon / Derivados del petróleo y del carbón	355 Rubber products / Produits, en caoutchouc / Productos de caucho	361 Pottery, china, earthenware / Grès, porcelaines, faïences / Barro, loza, porcelana	362 Glass / Verre / Vidrio
1966	1 426	1 420	1 648	1 258	1 727	1 881	1 501	1 316	1 328
1967	1 466	1 426	1 705	1 372	1 803	1 955	1 542	1 372	1 383
1968	1 564	1 581	1 791	1 475	1 938	2 089	1 626	1 463	1 504
1969	1 671	1 699	1 870	1 598	2 037	2 244	1 737	1 557	1 615
1970	1 742	1 900	1 967	1 676	2 130	2 322	1 835	1 649	1 662
1971	1 808	1 929	2 045	1 716	2 208	2 388	1 978	1 681	1 710
1972	1 872	1 997	2 123	1 777	2 281	2 444	2 059	1 729	1 790
1973	1 938	2 025	2 172	1 834	2 341	2 479	2 111	1 769	1 841
1974	2 008	2 076	2 241	1 906	2 430	2 586	2 189	1 818	1 932

[1] State industry.   [1] *Industrie d'État.*   [1] Industria de Estado.

19 Wages in manufacturing
Salaires dans les industries manufacturières
Salarios en las industrias manufactureras

B By industry
Par industrie
Por industria

Czechoslovakia [1] (2)

Average monthly earnings *(korunas)*
Gains mensuels moyens *(korunas)*
Promedio de ganancias por mes *(korunas)*

	369	371	372	381	382	383	384	385	390
		Basic metal industries *Industrie métallurgique de base* Industrias metalúrgicas básicas							
Date *Date* Fecha	Other non-metallic mineral products *Autres produits minéraux non métalliques* Otros productos minerales no metálicos	Iron and steel *Sidérurgie* Hierro y acero	Non-ferrous metal *Métaux non ferreux* Metales no ferrosos	Metal products *Produits métalliques* Productos metálicos	Machinery (non-electrical) *Machines (non électriques)* Maquinaria (no eléctrica)	Electrical machinery and apparatus *Machines et appareils électriques* Maquinaria y aparatos eléctricos	Transport equipment *Matériel de transport* Material de transporte	Scientific, measuring, optical, etc., equipment *Matériel scientifique, de précision, d'optique, etc.* Equipo científico, de medida, de óptica, etc.	Other manufacturing industries *Autres industries manufacturières* Otras industrias manufactureras
1966	1 623	1 890	1 636	1 401	1 688	1 381	1 606	1 493	1 404
1967	1 689	1 960	1 703	1 466	1 766	1 432	1 674	1 561	1 480
1968	1 790	2 049	1 786	1 549	1 850	1 506	1 774	1 620	1 565
1969	1 936	2 149	1 912	1 648	1 971	1 574	1 883	1 717	1 645
1970	2 027	2 253	1 986	1 749	2 088	1 664	1 986	1 819	1 624
1971	2 102	2 345	2 053	1 817	2 168	1 711	2 071	1 879	1 682
1972	2 174	2 446	2 157	1 880	2 262	1 771	2 148	1 945	1 726
1973	2 230	2 534	2 204	1 940	2 324	1 835	2 205	2 005	1 781
1974	2 317	2 630	2 278	2 006	2 409	1 896	2 272	2 080	1 853

[1] State industry.

[1] *Industrie d'Etat.*

[1] Industria de Estado.

WAGES

19 B

Wages in manufacturing
Salaires dans les industries manufacturières
Salarios en las industrias manufactureras

By industry
Par industrie
Por industria

Denmark

Average hourly earnings [1] *(öre)*
Gains horaires moyens [1] *(öre)*
Promedio de ganancias por hora [1] *(öre)*

	311-312	313	314	321	322; 324	323
Date [2]	Food	Beverages	Tobacco		Clothing, footwear	Leather, leather products
Date [2]	*Aliments*	*Boissons*	*Tabac*	Textiles	*Habillement, chaussures*	*Cuir, articles en cuir*
Fecha [2]	Alimentos	Bebidas	Tabaco		Vestido, calzado	Cuero, artículos de cuero
1972	1 779	2 461	1 625	1 704	1 645	1 696
1973	2 092	3 053	1 936	2 050	1 917	1 991
1974	2 472	3 554	2 411	2 475	2 315	2 423

	331	332; 381 ×	341	342	351-352	353-354
Date [2]	Wood	Furniture [3]	Paper, paper products	Printing, publishing	Chemicals	Refineries and products of petroleum and coal
Date [2]	*Bois*	*Ameublement* [3]	*Papier, articles en papier*	*Imprimerie, édition*	*Industrie chimique*	*Raffineries et dérivés du pétrole et du charbon*
Fecha [2]	Madera	Mobiliario [3]	Papel, artículos de papel	Imprentas, editoriales	Productos químicos	Refinerías y derivados del petróleo y del carbón
1972	1 933	1 867	2 005	2 346	1 844	2 020
1973	2 228	2 176	2 346	2 704	2 201	2 375
1974	2 578	2 560	2 874	3 273	2 668	2 746

	355	36	381 ×	382-383	384	356; 385; 390
Date [2]	Rubber products	Non-metallic mineral products	Metal products	Machinery	Transport equipment	Miscellaneous manufacturing
Date [2]	*Produits en caoutchouc*	*Produits minéraux non métalliques*	*Produits métalliques*	*Machines*	*Matériel de transport*	*Industries manufacturières diverses*
Fecha [2]	Productos de caucho	Productos minerales no metálicos	Productos metálicos	Maquinaria	Material de transporte	Industrias manufactureras diversas
1972	1 786	1 967	1 986	1 956	2 174	1 761
1973	2 091	2 316	2 330	2 292	2 475	2 061
1974	2 489	2 655	2 805	2 792	2 988	2 471

[1] Excl. vacation pay. [2] July-Sept. of each year.
[3] Incl. metal furniture.

[1] *Non compris les versements pour congés payés.*
[2] *Juillet-sept. de chaque année.* [3] *Y compris les meubles en métal.*

[1] Excl. los pagos por vacaciones. [2] Julio-sept. de cada año. [3] Incl. los muebles metálicos.

19 Wages in manufacturing
Salaires dans les industries manufacturières
Salarios en las industrias manufactureras

B By industry
Par industrie
Por industria

España

Average hourly earnings [1] *(pesetas)*
Gains horaires moyens [1] *(pesetas)*
Promedio de ganancias por hora [1] *(pesetas)*

Date / Date / Fecha	31 Food, beverages, tobacco / Aliments, boissons, tabac / Alimentos, bebidas, tabaco	321 Textiles	322-324 Clothing, leather, leather products, footwear / Habillement, cuir, articles en cuir, chaussures / Vestido, cuero, artículos de cuero, calzado	33 Wood, furniture / Bois, ameublement / Madera, mobiliario	341 Paper, paper products / Papier, articles en papier / Papel, artículos de papel
1965	18.86	19.42	15.33	16.92	22.12
1966	21.55	22.52	18.00	18.33	26.13
1967	25.59	27.05	19.62	21.02	30.31
1968	28.39	28.57	21.04	23.21	32.38
1969	31.34	30.73	23.95	24.84	35.36
1970	35.26	33.77	26.70	27.00	39.75
1971	39.66	37.92	29.55	30.27	48.45
1972	44.88	43.68	33.86	34.50	57.35
1973	51.71	51.01	39.75	40.74	68.69
1974	61.86	62.99	49.67	49.58	87.27

Date / Date / Fecha	342 Printing, publishing / Imprimerie, édition / Imprentas, editoriales	351-352 Chemicals / Industrie chimique / Productos químicos	353-354 Refinerie and products of petroleum and coal / Raffineries et dérivés du pétrole et du charbon / Refinerías y derivados del petróleo y del carbón	355 Rubber products / Produits en caoutchouc / Productos de caucho	37-38 × Metal industries, machinery, etc. [2] / Industrie métallurgique, machines, etc. [2] / Industrias metalúrgicas, maquinaria, etc. [2]
1965	24.08	24.37	18.66	31.47	24.11
1966	28.00	27.74	21.88	36.12	28.35
1967	32.47	31.29	25.94	38.74	31.86
1968	34.87	34.61	27.95	43.02	34.39
1969	39.61	38.13	31.04	46.71	38.86
1970	43.10	43.05	35.38	57.19	45.04
1971	49.51	49.14	41.38	65.56	51.20
1972	57.59	56.11	47.36	71.41	60.82
1973	68.37	69.03	58.58	86.70	73.56
1974	83.22	87.63	87.40	114.69	93.45

[1] Incl. salaried employees. [2] Excl. scientific, measuring, optical, etc., equipment.

[1] *Y compris les employés.* [2] *Non compris le matériel scientifique, de précision, d'optique, etc.*

[1] Incl. los empleados. [2] Excl. el equipo científico, de medida, de óptica, etc.

19 Wages in manufacturing / Salaires dans les industries manufacturières / Salarios en las industrias manufactureras

B By industry / Par industrie / Por industria

Finland

Average hourly earnings [1] *(markkaa)*
Gains horaires moyens [1] *(markkaa)*
Promedio de ganancias por hora [1] *(markkaa)*

Date / Date / Fecha	Cotton / Coton / Algodón	Sawmills / Scieries / Aserraderos	Wood products / Ouvrages en bois / Artículos de madera	Cellulose / Cellulose / Celulosa	All pulps / Toutes pâtes à papier / Pulpas de madera de toda clase	Paper / Papier / Papel	Printing, publishing / Imprimerie, édition / Imprentas, editoriales	Rubber, leather, leather products [2] / Caoutchouc, cuir, articles en cuir [2] / Caucho, cuero, artículos de cuero [2]	Primary iron and steel / Sidérurgie / Siderurgia	Metal products, machinery, etc. / Produits métalliques, machines, etc. / Productos metálicos, maquinaria, etc.
Adult males — *Hommes adultes* — Hombres adultos										
1965	3.06	3.45	3.12	3.86	3.74	3.88	4.16	3.09	3.66	3.70
1966	3.36	3.70	3.61	4.12	4.08	4.16	4.52	3.45	3.92	3.89
1967	3.65	4.08	3.75	4.40	4.30	4.48	4.97	3.66	4.14	4.25
1968	4.04	4.52	4.15	4.85	4.79	4.94	6.09	4.16	4.81	4.73
1969	4.37	4.88	4.45	5.25	5.19	5.37	6.37	4.51	5.35	5.18
1970	4.86	5.36	4.96	5.65	5.72	5.85	6.81	4.99	5.93	5.86
1971	5.57	6 19	5.74	6.84	6.87	7.06	7.37	5.74	6.69	6.64
1972	6.42	6.96	6.39	7.72	7.85	8.13	8.32	6.47	7.86	7.70
1973	7.73	8.05	7.66	9.08	9.30	9.61	9.60	7.56	9.08	9.13
1974	9.77	9.77	9.48	11.14	11.22	11.69	11.36	9.14	10.94	11.05

Date / Date / Fecha	Cotton / Coton / Algodón	Knitting / Tricot / Tejidos de punto	Wool / Laine / Lana	Plywood / Contre-plaqué / Madera terciada	Wood, wood products / Bois, produits en bois / Madera, productos de madera	All pulps / Toutes pâtes à papier / Pulpas de madera de toda clase	Paper / Papier / Papel	Printing, publishing / Imprimerie, édition / Imprentas, editoriales	Rubber, leather, leather products [2] / Caoutchouc, cuir, articles en cuir [2] / Caucho, cuero, artículos de cuero [2]	Porcelain, earthenware / Porcelaine, faïence / Porcelana, loza	Metal products, machinery, etc. / Produits métalliques, machines, etc. / Productos metálicos, maquinaria, etc.
Adult females — *Femmes adultes* — Mujeres adultas											
1965	2.16	2.38	2.24	2.48	2.30	2.75	2.87	2.80	2.32	2.77	2.39
1966	2.34	2.63	2.48	2.68	2.64	2.92	3.09	3.03	2.58	2.99	2.74
1967	2.52	2.84	2.66	2.93	2.84	3.09	3.37	3.37	2.72	3.28	2.97
1968	2.78	3.13	2.97	3.21	3.13	3.54	3.69	4.11	3.16	3.80	3.27
1969	3.04	3.45	3.23	3.58	3.51	3.89	4.06	4.37	3.46	4.15	3.62
1970	3.43	3.81	3.62	3.95	3.90	4.37	4.54	4.75	3.88	4.54	4.13
1971	3.97	4.36	4.22	4.56	4.65	5.27	5.53	5.27	4.52	5.14	4.81
1972	4.65	4.96	4.87	5.19	5.27	6.16	6.33	6.14	5.14	5.80	5.67
1973	5.64	5.75	5.72	6.15	6.19	7.35	7.48	7.26	5.96	6.73	6.70
1974	7.23	7.14	7.51	7.27	7.71	8.88	9.19	8.90	7.15	8.11	8.27

[1] Incl. the value of payments in kind. [2] Incl. footwear.

[1] *Y compris la valeur des paiements en nature.* [2] *Y compris la chaussure.*

[1] Incl. el valor de los pagos en especie. [2] Incl. el calzado.

19 Wages in manufacturing
Salaires dans les industries manufacturières
Salarios en las industrias manufactureras

B By industry
Par industrie
Por industria

France

Average hourly earnings *(francs)*
Gains horaires moyens *(francs)*
Promedio de ganancias por hora *(francs)*

Date [1] *Date* [1] Fecha [1]	Food, beverages *Aliments, boissons* Alimentos, bebidas	Textiles	Clothing *Habillement* Vestido	Wood, furniture *Bois, ameublement* Madera, mobiliario	Paper, paper products *Papier, articles en papier* Papel, artículos de papel	Printing, publishing *Imprimerie, édition* Imprentas, editoriales
1965	3.40	3.04	3.02	3.31	3.62	5.31
1966	3.62	3.21	3.20	3.55	3.85	5.61
1967	3.87	3.46	3.36	3.71	4.13	6.06
1968	4.45	4.01	4.00	4.35	4.77	6.91
1969	4.86	4.38	4.26	4.74	5.34	7.85
1970	5.49	4.97	4.73	5.25	6.08	8.57
1971	6.22	5.63	5.34	5.83	6.67	9.43
1972 [2]	7.04	6.57	5.80	6.27	7 66	9.65
1973	8.11	7.61	6.70	7.48	8.88	11.01

Date [1] *Date* [1] Fecha [1]	Leather, leather products *Cuir, articles en cuir* Cuero, artículos de cuero	Rubber products, chemicals *Industrie du caoutchouc, industrie chimique* Productos de caucho, productos químicos	Glass, ceramics, building materials *Verre, céramique, matériaux de construction* Vidrio, cerámica, material de construcción	Basic metal industries *Industrie métallurgique de base* Industrias metalúrgicas básicas	Machinery *Machines* Maquinaria
1965	3.13	4.12	3.84	4.00	4.03
1966	3.29	4.33	4.02	4.18	4.28
1967	3.53	4.71	4.29	4.41	4.57
1968	4.05	5.33	5.04	5.09	5.16
1969	4.45	5.89	5.54	5.66	5.70
1970	4.96	6.67	6.29	6.35	6.38
1971	5.70	7.52	7.22	7.41	7.16
1972 [2]	5.97	8.14	7.78	8.05	7.81
1973	6.91	9.50	9.09	9.25	8.88

[1] Oct. of each year, except for 1965-1971: Sep. [2] Series replacing former series.

[1] *Oct. de chaque année, sauf pour 1965-1971: sept.* [2] *Série remplaçant la précédente.*

[1] Oct. de cada año, salvo 1965-1971: sept. [2] Serie que substituye a la anterior.

WAGES

19 B

Wages in manufacturing
Salaires dans les industries manufacturières
Salarios en las industrias manufactureras

By industry
Par industrie
Por industria

Germany, Fed. Rep. of △ (1)

Average hourly earnings [1] *(mark)*
Gains horaires moyens [1] *(mark)*
Promedio de ganancias por hora [1] *(mark)*

Date / Date / Fecha	31	314	321	322	323 ×	324	331	332	341	342
	Food, beverages, tobacco / Aliments, boissons, tabac / Alimentos, bebidas, tabaco	Tobacco / Tabac / Tabaco	Textiles	Clothing / Habillement / Vestido	Leather, leather products [3] / Cuir, articles en cuir [3] / Cuero, artículos de cuero [3]	Footwear / Chaussures / Calzado	Wood / Bois / Madera	Furniture / Ameublement / Mobiliario	Paper, paper products / Papier, articles en papier / Papel, artículos de papel	Printing, publishing / Imprimerie, édition / Imprentas, editoriales
1967	4.16	3.75	3.89	3.52	3.68	3.82	4.20	4.70	4.72	5.38
1968	4.31	3.94	4.08	3.66	3.79	3.97	4.35	4.86	4.88	5.62
1969	4.70	4.32	4.43	4.02	4.09	4.28	4.78	5.30	5.34	6.18
1970	5.28	4.88	5.08	4.53	4.50	4.75	5.41	5.97	6.19	6.94
1971	5.95	5.53	5.56	5.06	4.95	5.31	6.11	6.68	6.94	7.71
1972	6.55	6 24	6.07	5.55	5.40	5.78	6.76	7.38	7.52	8.41
1973 [2]	7.29	6.73	6.83	6.19	6.02	6.40	7.50	8.17	8.31	9.34
1974	8.16	7.60	7.59	6.78	6.58	7.00	8.32	9.04	9.38	10.33

Date / Date / Fecha	351	352	353	355	356	361	362	369
	Industrial chemicals [4] / Chimie industrielle [4] / Química industrial [4]	Synthetic fibres / Fibres synthétiques / Fibras sintéticas	Other chemical products / Autres produits chimiques / Otros productos químicos	Petroleum refineries / Raffineries de pétrole / Refinerías de petróleo	Rubber products / Produits en caoutchouc / Productos de caucho	Plastic products / Articles en matière plastique / Productos plásticos	Pottery, china, earthenware / Grès, porcelaines, faïences / Barro, loza, porcelana	Glass, and glass products / Verre / Vidrio

Date / Date / Fecha	351	352	353	355	356	361	362	369
	Industrial chemicals [4]	Synthetic fibres	Other chemical products	Petroleum refineries	Rubber products	Plastic products	Pottery, china, earthenware	Glass, and glass products	Other non-metallic mineral products / Autres produits minéraux / Otros productos minerales
1967	5.28	5.00	4.31	5.49	...	4.11	...	4.63	4.83
1968	5.58	5.28	4.53	5.82	...	4.27	...	4.94	5.02
1969	6 08	5.76	4.94	6.37	...	4.62	...	5.33	5.47
1970	7 06	6.65	5.76	7.34	...	5.34	...	6.01	6.36
1971	7.84	7.40	6.41	8.35	...	5.97	...	6.79	7.12
1972	8.49	8.07	6.97	9.27	...	6.54	...	7.41	7.82
1973 [2]	9.27	9.00	7.74	10.29	8.27	7.21	6 95	8.11	8.62
1974	10.55	10.18	8.71	11.73	9.20	8.01	7.79	8.89	9.52

[1] Incl. family allowances paid directly by the employers. [2] Sampling design revised. [3] Excl. tanneries and leather finishing, fur dressing and dyeing industries. [4] Excl. synthetic fibres.

[1] *Y compris les allocations familiales payées directement par les employeurs.* [2] *Plan d'échantillonnage révisé.* [3] *Non compris la tannerie-mégisserie, la préparation et teinture des fourrures.* [4] *Non compris les fibres synthétiques.*

[1] Incl. las asignaciones familiares pagadas directamente por los empleadores. [2] Diseño de la muestra revisado. [3] Excl. la curtiduría y talleres de acabado y la industria de la preparación y teñido de pieles. [4] Excl. las fibras sintéticas.

19 Wages in manufacturing
Salaires dans les industries manufacturières
Salarios en las industrias manufactureras

B By industry
Par industrie
Por industria

Germany, Fed. Rep. of △ (2)

Average hourly earnings [1] *(mark)*
Gains horaires moyens [1] *(mark)*
Promedio de ganancias por hora [1] *(mark)*

Date / Date / Fecha	371		372	381	382	383	384 ×			385	390
	Basic metal industries / *Industrie métallurgique de base* / Industrias metalúrgicas básicas			Metal products / *Produits métallurgiques* / Productos metálicos	Machinery (non-electrical) / *Machines (non électriques)* / Maquinaria (no eléctrica)	Electrical machinery and apparatus / *Machines et appareils électriques* / Maquinaria y aparatos eléctricos	Motor vehicles [3] / *Véhicules à moteur* [3] / Vehículos de motor [3]	Ship building / *Construction navale* / Construcciones navales	Manufacture of aircraft / *Construction aéronautique* / Fabricación de aeronaves	Scientific, measuring, optical, etc. equipment / *Matériel scientifique, de précision, d'optique, etc.* / Equipo científico, de medida, de óptica, etc.	Other manufacturing industries / *Autres industries manufacturières* / Otras industrias manufactureras
	Iron and steel / *Sidérurgie* / Hierro y acero		Non-ferrous metal / *Métaux non ferreux* / Metales no ferrosos								
1967	5.19		4.83	4.56	4.99	4.29	5.30	5.25	4.89	4.30	3.96
1968	5.41		5.07	4.75	5.18	4.45	5.51	5.38	5.01	4.45	4.11
1969	6.01		5.59	5.25	5.76	4.90	6.09	5.93	5.60	4.91	4.51
1970	6.83		6.22	5.84	6.41	5.43	6.83	6.58	6.26	5.41	4.99
1971	7.38		6.93	6.50	7.19	6.17	7.74	7.34	7.06	6.09	5.62
1972	7.90		7.53	7.05	7.82	6.74	8.33	7.97	7.68	6.63	6.20
1973 [2]	8.83		8.38	7.79	8.68	7.44	9.21	8.88	8.64	7.32	6.85
1974	9.84		9.30	8.56	9.58	8.26	10.23	9.95	9.68	8.12	7.66

[1] Incl. family allowances paid directly by the employers. [2] Sampling design revised. [3] Incl. bicycles and miscellaneous transport equipment.

[1] *Y compris les allocations familiales payées directement par les employeurs.* [2] *Plan d'échantillonnage révisé.* [3] *Y compris les cycles et matériel de transport divers.*

[1] Incl. las asignaciones familiares pagadas directamente por los empleadores. [2] Diseño de la muestra revisado. [3] Incl. las bicicletas y material de transporte diverso.

19 Wages in manufacturing
Salaires dans les industries manufacturières
Salarios en las industrias manufactureras

B By industry
Par industrie
Por industria

Grèce

Average hourly earnings *(drachmas)*
Gains horaires moyens *(drachmas)*
Promedio de ganancias por hora *(drachmas)*

Date [1] Date [1] Fecha [1]	Food *Aliments* Alimentos	Beverages *Boissons* Bebidas	Tobacco *Tabac* Tabaco	Textiles	Clothing *Habillement* Vestido	Wood *Bois* Madera	Furniture *Ameublement* Mobiliario	Paper, paper products *Papier, articles en papier* Papel, artículos de papel	Printing, publishing *Imprimerie, édition* Imprentas, editoriales	Leather, leather products *Cuir, articles en cuir* Cuero, artículos de cuero
1965	9.91	10.13	9.30	8.84	9.11	8.87	10.23	9.13	15.38	10.36
1966	11.20	12.01	11.42	10.63	10.37	10.50	11.81	10.59	16.74	11.83
1967	12.78	13.10	11.67	12.14	12.06	11.93	12.24	11.64	16.45	14.30
1968	13.56	13.74	12.99	12.94	12.66	13.31	13.85	13.48	18.60	15.15
1969	14.69	14.65	13.73	14.39	14.49	14.05	15.52	14.83	19.20	15.91
1970	16.02	15.12	14.29	15.12	14.89	14.60	16.45	16.38	20.92	17.46
1971	16.23	16.08	15.62	16.45	16.89	15.92	18.28	17.18	22.75	18.34
1972	17.02	17.14	15.72	17.83	17.73	16.75	19.62	18.69	23.61	19.34
1973	19.29	22.16	18.89	20.26	17.26	20.73	21.31	19.86	29.34	21.65
1974	26.69	29.36	24.57	28.59	23.96	27.25	27.47	29.37	37.48	29.71

Date [1] Date [1] Fecha [1]	Rubber products *Industrie du caoutchouc* Productos de caucho	Chemicals *Industrie chimique* Productos químicos	Products of petroleum and coal *Dérivés du pétrole et du charbon* Derivados del petróleo y del carbón	Non-metallic mineral products *Produits minéraux non métalliques* Productos minerales no metálicos	Basic metal industries *Industrie métallur- gique de base* Industrias metalúrgicas básicas	Metal products *Produits métalliques* Productos metálicos	Machinery (non- electrical) *Machines (non électriques)* Maquinaria (no eléctrica)	Electrical machinery *Machines électriques* Maquinaria eléctrica	Transport equipment *Matériel de transport* Material de transporte	Miscellaneous manu- facturing *Industries manu- facturières diverses* Industrias manu- factureras diversas
1965	9.46	11.13	15.03	12.06	17.50	10.43	10.58	10.28	12.91	10.74
1966	11.42	12.32	15.91	13.98	20.17	11.85	12.39	11.55	13.86	12.29
1967	13.14	13.55	17.48	15.01	19.30	13.47	13.37	13.48	14.34	13.59
1968	14.44	14.41	17.26	15.72	21.19	14.26	14.20	14.54	15.21	13 41
1969	15.69	15.25	18.38	17.30	24.01	15.43	15.17	14.79	16.39	14.55
1970	16.92	16.17	19.42	18.04	26.14	17.21	16.52	16.51	18.79	14.06
1971	17.67	16.86	21.42	19.05	29.23	18.59	18.13	17.37	20.21	15.19
1972	19.68	18.54	22.28	20.08	29.88	19.56	19.09	18.88	21.45	15.82
1973	23.83	23.58	27.38	22.35	34.64	23.16	23.83	21.18	28.92	19.51
1974	29.25	28.97	35.10	30.24	43.15	29.89	31.83	28.69	37.53	28.28

[1] Nov. of each year.   [1] *Nov. de chaque année.*   [1] Nov. de cada año.

19 Wages in manufacturing
Salaires dans les industries manufacturières
Salarios en las industrias manufactureras

B By industry
Par industrie
Por industria

Hongrie [1] (1)

Average monthly earnings [2] *(forints)*
Gains mensuels moyens [2] *(forints)*
Promedio de ganancias por mes [2] *(forints)*

Date / Date / Fecha	311-312 Food / Aliments / Alimentos	313 Beverages / Boissons / Bebidas	314 Tobacco / Tabac / Tabaco	321 Textiles	322 Clothing / Habillement / Vestido	323 Leather, leather products / Cuir, articles en cuir / Cuero, artículos de cuero	324 Footwear / Chaussures / Calzado	331 Wood / Bois / Madera	332 Furniture / Ameublement / Mobiliario
1968	1 704	1 592	1 621	1 610	1 496	1 771	1 599	1 698	1 728
1969	1 767	1 680	1 663	1 659	1 542	1 862	1 644	1 767	1 770
1970 [3]	1 859	1 753	1 688	1 763	1 596	1 961	1 750	1 916	1 835
1971	1 960	1 843	1 757	1 814	1 640	2 031	1 741	2 011	1 884
1972	2 081	1 934	1 872	1 909	1 734	2 163	1 828	2 110	1 957
1973	2 320	2 148	2 036	2 124	1 971	2 350	2 035	2 315	2 159
1974 *	2 498	2 296	2 183	2 272	2 072	2 513	2 170	2 467	2 303

Date / Date / Fecha	341 Paper, paper products / Papier, articles en papier / Papel, artículos de papel	342 Printing, publishing / Imprimerie, édition / Imprentas, editoriales	351 Industrial chemicals / Chimie industrielle / Química industrial	352 Other chemical products / Autres produits chimiques / Otros productos químicos	353 Petroleum refineries / Raffineries de pétrole / Refinerías de petróleo	354 Products of petroleum and coal / Dérivés du pétrole et du charbon / Derivados del petróleo y del carbón	355 Rubber products / Produits en caoutchouc / Productos de caucho	356 Plastic products / Articles en matière plastique / Productos plásticos	361 Pottery, china, earthenware / Grès, porcelaines, faïences / Barro, loza, porcelana
1968	1 777	1 782	1 807	1 706	1 804	1 972	1 795	1 603	1 697
1969	1 847	1 846	1 859	1 793	1 918	2 043	1 867	1 651	1 745
1970 [3]	1 942	1 959	1 956	1 879	1 999	...	1 995	1 732	1 799
1971	2 040	2 091	2 027	1 987	2 142	...	2 152	1 817	1 931
1972	2 378	2 224	2 149	2 084	2 227	...	2 217	1 909	2 010
1973	2 378	2 450	2 422	2 308	2 517	...	2 409	2 122	2 265
1974 *	2 602	2 638	2 624	2 512	2 746	...	2 583	2 290	2 431

[1] State industry. [2] Incl. the value of payments in kind. [3] Revised series.

[1] *Industrie d'Etat.* [2] *Y compris la valeur des paiements en nature.* [3] *Série révisée.*

[1] Industria de Estado. [2] Incl. el valor de los pagos en especie. [3] Serie revisada.

19 Wages in manufacturing
Salaires dans les industries manufacturières
Salarios en las industrias manufactureras

B By industry
Par industrie
Por industria

Hongrie [1] (2)

Average monthly earnings [2] *(forints)*
Gains mensuels moyens [2] *(forints)*
Promedio de ganancias por mes [2] *(forints)*

Date / Date / Fecha	362 Glass / Verre / Vidrio	369 Other non-metallic mineral products / Autres produits minéraux non métalliques / Otros productos minerales no metálicos	371 Iron and steel / Sidérurgie / Hierro y acero	372 Non-ferrous metal / Métaux non ferreux / Metales no ferrosos	381 Metal products / Produits métalliques / Productos metálicos	382 Machinery (non-electrical) / Machines (non electriques) / Maquinaria (no eléctrica)	383 Electrical machinery and apparatus / Machines et appareils électriques / Maquinaria y aparatos eléctricos	384 Transport equipment / Matériel de transport / Material de transporte	385 Scientific, measuring, optical, etc., equipment / Matériel scientifique, de précision, d'optique, etc. / Equipo científico, de medida, de óptica, etc.	390 Other manufacturing industries / Autres industries manufacturières / Otras industrias manufactureras
			Basic metal industries / Industrie métallurgique de base / Industrias metalúrgicas básicas							
1968	1 718	1 829	2 020	1 940	1 741	1 886	1 728	1 898	1 818	1 661
1969	1 784	1 878	2 103	2 005	1 798	1 963	1 793	1 985	1 906	1 722
1970 [3]	1 871	2 112	2 196	2 148	1 885	2 061	1 873	2 094	1 949	1 807
1971	1 947	2 183	2 288	2 256	1 964	2 139	1 935	2 185	2 057	1 879
1972	2 080	2 239	2 401	2 355	2 047	2 226	2 041	2 294	2 145	1 988
1973	2 310	2 443	2 701	2 624	2 265	2 465	2 257	2 542	2 366	2 124
1974 *	2 445	2 599	2 937	2 965	2 409	2 629	2 441	2 739	2 513	2 265

[1] State industry. [2] Incl. the value of payments in kind. [3] Revised series.

[1] *Industrie d'Etat.* [2] *Y compris la valeur des paiements en nature.* [3] *Série révisée.*

[1] Industria de Estado. [2] Incl. el valor de los pagos en especie. [3] Serie revisada.

19 Wages in manufacturing / Salaires dans les industries manufacturières / Salarios en las industrias manufactureras

B By industry / Par industrie / Por industria

Ireland

Average hourly earnings *(pence)*
Gains horaires moyens *(pence)*
Promedio de ganancias por hora *(pence)*

Date [1] / Date [1] / Fecha [1]	Food / Aliments / Alimentos	Beverages / Boissons / Bebidas	Tobacco / Tabac / Tabaco	Textiles	Clothing / Habillement / Vestido	Wood, furniture / Bois, ameublement / Madera, mobiliario	Paper, printing, publishing / Papier, imprimerie, édition / Papel, imprentas, editoriales	Rubber, leather, leather products / Caoutchouc, cuir, articles en cuir / Caucho, cuero, artículos de cuero	Chemicals / Industrie chimique / Productos químicos	Non-metallic mineral products / Produits minéraux non métalliques / Productos minerales no metálicos	Metal products, machinery, etc. / Produits métalliques, machines, etc. / Productos metálicos, maquinaria, etc.
Males [2] — Hommes [2] — Hombres [2]											
1965	27.6	33.9	40.6	27.7	31.7	26.4	35.8	34.8	30.9	30.3	31.5
1966	30.5	37.1	44.3	31.0	34.1	29.2	40.1	38.5	34.2	34.0	35.4
1967	32.4	40.9	46.4	32.0	36.3	30.6	41.9	38.5	36.3	35.6	38.2
1968	35.8	47.0	49.3	36.8	39.3	34.3	46.1	44.0	43.9	40.2	40.0
1969 [3]	41.5	52.7	55.3	42.1	43.1	38.6	53.1	49.0	49.8	46.3	48.2
1970	49.4	63.4	65.6	47.2	51.7	45.5	62.6	56.3	57 2	53.5	53.9
1971	55.4	71.0	70.7	55.7	57.6	52.7	69.4	68.0	65.7	62.8	62.9
1972	62.1	79.5	84.0	63.0	62.5	60.7	80.5	75.3	74.9	74.4	71.3
1973	76.1	100.3	96.5	77.6	76.1	71.5	94.4	94.0	91.8	89.9	82.5
1974	92.6	117.8	114.4	92.6	86.8	84.3	113.8	109.4	112.0	104.4	100.5
Females [2] — Femmes [2] — Mujeres [2]											
1965	16.2	19.2	23.5	16.4	18.3	16.6	19.3	18.3	16.9	15.5	16.2
1966	18.2	20.3	25.9	19.2	20.0	18.2	21.6	20.3	18.6	17.4	18.0
1967	18.9	22.3	26.8	19.8	20.9	19.8	22.0	19.7	20.4	20.0	19.2
1968	21.7	24.7	29.1	21.9	22.9	22.4	24.2	20.5	22.1	22.6	22.0
1969 [3]	25.4	27.9	31.0	23.7	24.7	24.3	26.2	25.4	24.3	25.3	24.3
1970	30.8	39.1	39.5	27.4	31.0	29.9	31.6	31.1	28.9	28.4	27.8
1971	34.7	44.5	44.9	32.7	34.8	36.3	36.2	35.3	33.0	32.8	32.4
1972	40.4	49.9	54.4	38.1	38.5	42.0	41.1	38.2	39.8	39.4	38.9
1973	51.4	61.3	61.4	48.6	47.7	48.7	50.1	48.9	48.1	50.5	48.4
1974	60.8	78.2	80.7	57.2	56.1	56.3	59.0	57.1	57.5	62.3	61.7

[1] Sep. of each year, except for 1965-68: Oct. [2] 1965-68: adults only. Beginning 1969: workers on adult rates of pay. [3] Series replacing former series.

[1] *Sept. de chaque année, sauf pour 1965-1968: oct.* [2] *1965-1968: adultes seulement. A partir de 1969: travailleurs rémunérés sur la base de taux de salaire pour adultes.* [3] *Série remplaçant la précédente.*

[1] Sept. de cada año, salvo 1965-1968: oct. [2] 1965-1968: adultos solamente. A partir de 1969: trabajadores pagados sobre la base de tarifas de salarios para adultos. [3] Serie que substituye a la anterior.

19 Wages in manufacturing / Salaires dans les industries manufacturières / Salarios en las industrias manufactureras

B By industry / Par industrie / Por industria

Italie

Average hourly earnings [1] *(lire)*
Gains horaires moyens [1] *(lire)*
Promedio de ganancias por hora [1] *(lire)*

Date / Date / Fecha	Food / Aliments / Alimentos	Beverages / Boissons / Bebidas	Tobacco / Tabac / Tabaco	Textiles	Clothing / Habillement / Vestido	Wood / Bois / Madera	Furniture / Ameublement / Mobiliario	Paper, paper products / Papier, articles en papier / Papel, artículos de papel	Printing, publishing / Imprimerie, édition / Imprentas, editoriales	Leather, leather products / Cuir, articles en cuir / Cuero, artículos de cuero
1965	369	406	338	320	266	287	290	392	542	306
1966	388	426	461	332	357	323	307	416	561	319
1967	411	449	550	330	344	326	323	444	612	332
1968	428	474	579	372	312	354	352	472	640	356
1969	486	523	665	410	339	387	387	542	718	385
1970	572	610	737	503	382	445	441	625	784	459
1971	651	688	831	593	510	555	554	731	943	571
1972	792	785	873	659	572	612	610	851	1 025	640
1973	930	973	913	762	701	769	782	1 033	1 269	789
1974 * [2]	1 200	1 342	1 372	1 099	862	1 018	1 019	1 338	1 418	1 025

Date / Date / Fecha	Rubber products / Industrie du caoutchouc / Productos de caucho	Chemicals / Industrie chimique / Productos químicos	Products of petroleum and coal / Dérivés du pétrole et du charbon / Derivados del petróleo y del carbón	Non-metallic mineral products / Produits minéraux non métalliques / Productos minerales no metálicos	Basic metal industries / Industrie métallurgique de base / Industrias metalúrgicas básicas	Metal products / Produits métalliques / Productos metálicos	Machinery (non-electrical) / Machines (non électriques) / Maquinaria (no eléctrica)	Electrical machinery / Machines électriques / Maquinaria eléctrica	Transport equipment / Matériel de transport / Material de transporte	Miscellaneous manufacturing / Industries manufacturières diverses / Industrias manufactureras diversas
1965	453	418	579	359	482	434	391	404	493	349
1966	473	441	612	370	502	450	406	414	508	368
1967	486	472	641	389	530	476	431	439	541	383
1968	513	489	684	415	548	495	495	454	564	401
1969	579	542	772	459	611	545	491	499	615	443
1970	669	727	961	563	795	690	625	643	772	526
1971	851	840	9 128	668	897	759	694	714	854	656
1972	960	948	1 295	753	983	837	777	788	943	752
1973	1 083	1 180	1 487	942	1 213	1 043	973	984	1 117	891
1974 * [2]	1 516	1 538	1 876	1 256	1 520	1 327	1 255	1 230	1 389	1 222

[1] Incl. the value of payments in kind. [2] Third quarter.   [1] *Y compris la valeur des paiements en nature.* [2] *Troisième trimestre.*   [1] Incl. el valor de los pagos en especie. [2] Tercer trimestre.

19 Wages in manufacturing / Salaires dans les industries manufacturières / Salarios en las industrias manufactureras

B By industry / Par industrie / Por industria

Luxembourg

Average hourly earnings *(francs)*
Gains horaires moyens *(francs)*
Promedio de ganancias por hora *(francs)*

Date [1] / Date [1] / Fecha [1]	311-312	313	314	322; 324	331	332	34	351	352
	Food / Aliments / Alimentos	Beverages / Boissons / Bebidas	Tobacco / Tabac / Tabaco	Clothing, footwear / Habillement, chaussure / Vestido, calzado	Wood / Bois / Madera	Furniture / Ameublement / Mobiliario	Paper, printing, publishing / Papier, imprimerie, édition / Papel, imprentas, editoriales	Industrial chemicals / Chimie industrielle / Química industrial	Other chemical products / Autres produits chimiques / Otros productos químicos
1965	.	49.89	42.58	27.76	42.42	45.88	55.56	45.31	.
1966	.	51.92	45.82	29.31	43.91	51.22	56.83	48.71	.
1967	.	53.83	46.97	32.09	43.68	56.27	59.77	50.70	.
1968	.	56.86	52.49	32.48	49.41	57.11	66.85	52.45	.
1969	.	58.62	52.54	34.19	48.20	61.37	72.08	54.75	.
1970	.	65.74	61.35	39.53	54.27	66.52	81.50	62.23	.
1971	.	75.51	65.19	46.77	60.64	81.80	94.35	70.64	.
1972 [2]	78.54	84.64	72.48	54.87	72.55	89.69	99.94	69.18	122.78
1973	87.10	95.71	82.40	60.48	83.35	101.73	117.39	87.70	127.25
1974	100.62	114.84	97.16	68.64	103.43	122.18	135.02	110.44	154.90

Date [1] / Date [1] / Fecha [1]	355	356	36	371	372	381	382	383	384
				Basic metal industries / Industrie métallurgique de base / Industrias metalúrgicas básicas					
	Rubber products / Produits en caoutchouc / Productos de caucho	Plastic products / Articles en matière plastique / Productos plásticos	Non-metallic mineral products / Produits minéraux non métalliques / Productos minerales no metálicos	Iron and steel / Sidérurgie / Hierro y acero	Non-ferrous metal / Métaux non ferreux / Metales no ferrosos	Metal products / Produits métalliques / Productos metálicos	Machinery (non-electrical) / Machines (non électriques) / Maquinaria (no eléctrica)	Electrical machinery and apparatus / Machines et appareils électriques / Maquinaria y aparatos eléctricos	Transport equipment / Matériel de transport / Material de transporte
1965	.	.	.	.	.	.	.	.	.
1966	.	58.29	.	73.36	.	.	.	.	.
1967	.	58.31	.	74.30	.	.	.	.	.
1968	.	59.61	.	81.83	.	.	.	.	.
1969	.	63.05	.	86.01	.	.	.	.	.
1970	.	68.39	.	98.48	.	.	.	.	.
1971	.	82.57	.	104.68	.	.	.	.	.
1972 [2]	105.50	96.42	89.30	121.02	90.58	87.24	91.11	85.44	75.23
1973	119.86	109.92	100.75	136.75	97.95	98.25	100.67	98.12	88.47
1974	156.26	128.30	120.97	174.26	128.27	121.38	126.69	115.33	112.82

[1] Oct. of each year. [2] New industrial classification.   [1] *Oct. de chaque année.* [2] *Nouvelle classification industrielle.*   [1] Oct. de cada año. [2] Nueva clasificación industrial.

19 Wages in manufacturing
Salaires dans les industries manufacturières
Salarios en las industrias manufactureras

B By industry
Par industrie
Por industria

Malta (1)

Average hourly earnings[1] *(cents)*
Gains horaires moyens[1] *(cents)*
Promedio de ganancias por hora[1] *(cents)*

Date / Date / Fecha	Food / Aliments / Alimentos	Beverages / Boissons / Bebidas	Tobacco / Tabac / Tabaco	Textiles	Clothing / Habillement / Vestido	Wood / Bois / Madera	Furniture / Ameublement / Mobiliario	Printing, publishing / Imprimerie, édition / Imprentas, editoriales
Adult males — *Hommes adultes* — Hombres adultos							
1965	13.7	14.4	18.2	14.8	13.0	13.5	14.3	17.2
1966	15.0	14.7	18.1	15.1	14.5	15.1	14.5	17.5
1967	15.1	14.7	18.6	15.7	15.4	15.1	15.2	17.7
1968	16.3	17.0	20.0	17.1	16.3	16.1	15.8	18.8
1969	17.3	18.6	24.2	18.8	16.7	17.4	17.4	21.9
1970	18.8	21.5	27.6	21.8	18.7	18.2	19.6	22.7
1971	20.1	21.5	28.8	22.4	20.7	19.5	21.6	25.9
1972	21.4	23.8	32.4	26.2	22.1	19.3	24.0	27.9

Date / Date / Fecha	Chemicals / Industrie chimique / Productos químicos	Products of petroleum and coal / Dérivés du pétrole et du charbon / Derivados del petróleo y del carbón	Non-metallic mineral products / Produits minéraux non métalliques / Productos minerales no metálicos	Metal products / Produits métalliques / Productos metálicos	Machinery (non-electrical) / Machines (non électriques) / Maquinaria (no eléctrica)	Electrical machinery / Machines électriques / Maquinaria eléctrica	Transport equipment / Matériel de transport / Material de transporte	Miscellaneous manufacturing / Industries manufacturières diverses / Industrias manufactureras diversas
Adult males (concl.) — *Hommes adultes* (fin) — Hombres adultos *(fin)*							
1965	14.0	13.2	14.6	14.6	13.8	15.9	18.2	14.4
1966	14.2	13.2	15.1	15.1	14.7	16.1	19.6	14.9
1967	14.6	13.4	15.0	15.8	14.7	16.6	19.9	15.4
1968	15.4	14.2	16.4	16.3	16.5	18.6	22.8	16.3
1969	17.5	14.8	17.8	17.8	18.8	19.7	26.1	17.9
1970	20.3	16.7	20.6	21.0	22.5	21.8	29.4	20.5
1971	22.0	16.7	21.9	23.6	24.2	25.6	30.6	23.5
1972	22.8	21.1	24.2	27.0	29.4	27.0	32.3	25.5

[1] Incl. salaried employees.   [1] *Y compris les employés.*   [1] Incl. los empleados.

19 Wages in manufacturing
Salaires dans les industries manufacturières
Salarios en las industrias manufactureras

B By industry
Par industrie
Por industria

Malta (2)

Average hourly earnings [1] *(cents)*
Gains horaires moyens [1] *(cents)*
Promedio de ganancias por hora [1] *(cents)*

Date / Date / Fecha	Food / Aliments / Alimentos	Beverages / Boissons / Bebidas	Tobacco / Tabac / Tabaco	Textiles	Clothing / Habillement / Vestido	Printing, publishing / Imprimerie, édition / Imprentas, editoriales	Chemicals / Industrie chimique / Productos químicos	Miscellaneous manufacturing / Industries manufacturières diverses / Industrias manufactureras diversas
			Adult females — *Femmes adultes* — Mujeres adultas					
1965	6.1	7.9	7.6	9.0	8.5	8.5	4.0	6.7
1966	6.3	8.8	8.3	9.2	9.2	8.4	4.9	7.1
1967	7.6	8.6	8.9	9.6	9.7	9.0	6.9	8.4
1968	9.4	9.8	9.3	10.8	10.2	9.9	6.9	9.4
1969	10.1	11.1	12.0	11.7	11.1	11.9	8.2	10.5
1970	11.1	12.9	14.4	13.0	11.7	13.2	13.0	13.2
1971	12.3	13.3	14.4	14.5	13.5	14.6	13.4	14.7
1972	13.5	14.5	16.3	16.3	15.3	15.4	15.5	15.8

[1] Incl. salaried employees.   [1] *Y compris les employés.*   [1] Incl. los empleados.

673

19 Wages in manufacturing
Salaires dans les industries manufacturières
Salarios en las industrias manufactureras

B By industry
Par industrie
Por industria

Norway (1)

Average hourly earnings [1] *(kroner)*
Gains horaires moyens [1] *(kroner)*
Promedio de ganancias por hora [1] *(kroner)*

	311-312	313	314	321	322	323	324	331	332
Date [2] *Date* [2] Fecha [2]	Food *Aliments* Alimentos	Beverages *Boissons* Bebidas	Tobacco *Tabac* Tabaco	Textiles	Clothing *Habillement* Vestido	Leather, leather products *Cuir, articles en cuir* Cuero, artículos de cuero	Footwear *Chaussures* Calzado	Wood *Bois* Madera	Furniture *Ameublement* Mobiliario
Adult males — *Hommes adultes* — Hombres adultos									
1972	15.53	15.73	15.03	14.70	14.73	15.39	14.77	15.45	15.90
1973	17.08	18.32	16.51	16.02	16.05	16.64	16.64	16.94	17.16
1974	20.34	21.50	19.54	19.58	19.34	19.44	18.92	20.80	20.48
Adult females — *Femmes adultes* — Mujeres adultas									
1972	12.46	13.40	13.23	12.20	12.34	12.00	12.00	13.56	14.12
1973	13.76	14.99	14.36	13.27	13.36	13.43	13.33	14.81	15.52
1974	16.57	18.25	17.51	16.49	15.77	15.59	15.65	17.74	18.52

[1] Incl. the value of payments in kind. [2] Third quarter of each year.

[1] *Y compris la valeur des paiements en nature.* [2] *Troisième trimestre de chaque année.*

[1] Incl. el valor de los pagos en especie. [2] Tercer trimestre de cada año.

19 Wages in manufacturing
Salaires dans les industries manufacturières
Salarios en las industrias manufactureras

B By industry
Par industrie
Por industria

Norway (2)

Average hourly earnings [1] *(kroner)*
Gains horaires moyens [1] *(kroner)*
Promedio de ganancias por hora [1] *(kroner)*

	341	342	351	352	354	355	356	361	362
Date [2] *Date [2]* Fecha [2]	Paper, paper products *Papier, articles en papier* Papel, artículos de papel	Printing, publishing *Imprimerie, édition* Imprentas, editoriales	Industrial chemicals *Chimie industrielle* Química industrial	Other chemical products *Autres produits chimiques* Otros productos químicos	Products of petroleum and coal *Dérivés du pétrole et du charbon* Derivados del petróleo y del carbón	Rubber products *Produits en caoutchouc* Productos de caucho	Plastic products *Articles en matière plastique* Productos plásticos	Pottery, china, earthenware *Grès, porcelaines, faïences* Barro, loza, porcelana	Glass *Verre* Vidrio
Adult males *(cont.)* — *Hommes adultes* (suite) — Hombres adultos *(cont.)*									
1972	16.61	19.76	17.13	16.58	17.10	16.05	16.29	16.04	16.25
1973	18.24	21.67	18.83	18.70	18.24	17.52	17.93	17.94	18.04
1974	22.53	24.99	24.55	21.59	22.87	20.44	21.54	21.85	21.10
Adult females *(cont.)* — *Femmes adultes* (suite) — Mujeres adultas *(cont.)*									
1972	13.34	15.12	.	13.29	.	12.88	13.04	11.33	14.17
1973	14.73	16.74	.	15.12	.	14.79	14.42	12.84	15.84
1974	18.18	19.57	.	17.45	.	17.72	18.32	16.50	18.66

[1] Incl. the value of payments in kind.　[2] Third quarter of each year.

[1] *Y compris la valeur des paiements en nature.*　[2] *Troisième trimestre de chaque année.*

[1] Incl. el valor de los pagos en especie.　[2] Tercer trimestre de cada año.

19 Wages in manufacturing / Salaires dans les industries manufacturières / Salarios en las industrias manufactureras

B By industry / Par industrie / Por industria

Norway (3)

Average hourly earnings [1] *(kroner)*
Gains horaires moyens [1] *(kroner)*
Promedio de ganancias por hora [1] *(kroner)*

	369	371	372	381	382	383	384	385	390
Date [2] / Date [2] / Fecha [2]	Other non-metallic mineral products / *Autres produits minéraux non métalliques* / Otros productos minerales no metálicos	Basic metal industries / *Industrie métallurgique de base* / Industrias metalúrgicas básicas		Metal products / *Produits métalliques* / Productos metálicos	Machinery (non-electrical) / *Machines (non électriques)* / Maquinaria (no eléctrica)	Electrical machinery and apparatus / *Machines et appareils électriques* / Maquinaria y aparatos eléctricos	Transport equipment / *Matériel de transport* / Material de transporte	Scientific, measuring, optical, etc., equipment / *Matériel scientifique, de précision, d'optique, etc.* / Equipo científico, de medida, de óptica, etc.	Other manufacturing industries / *Autres industries manufacturières* / Otras industrias manufactureras
		Iron and steel / *Sidérurgie* / Hierro y acero	Non-ferrous metal / *Métaux non ferreux* / Metales no ferrosos						
Adult males (concl.) — Hommes adultes (fin) — Hombres adultos (fin)									
1972	17.38	17.93	17.38	16.78	18.08	17.81	18.04	15.44	16.63
1973	18.83	19.80	18.68	18.85	19.90	19.93	20.04	16.75	18.15
1974	23.14	23.80	23.25	22.97	23.25	22.98	23.81	21.54	21.58
Adult females (concl.) — Femmes adultes (fin) — Mujeres adultas (fin)									
1972	.	.	13.92	14.00	15.73	15.05	.	.	13.43
1973	.	.	...	15.82	17.67	16.60	.	.	15.09
1974	.	.	...	18.69	19.84	19.71	.	.	18.13

[1] Incl. the value of payments in kind. [2] Third quarter of each year.   [1] *Y compris la valeur des paiements en nature.* [2] *Troisième trimestre de chaque année.*   [1] Incl. el valor de los pagos en especie. [2] Tercer trimestre de cada año.

19 Wages in manufacturing
Salaires dans les industries manufacturières
Salarios en las industrias manufactureras

B By industry
Par industrie
Por industria

Pays-Bas (1)

Average hourly earnings [1] *(cents)*
Gains horaires moyens [1] *(cents)*
Promedio de ganancias por hora [1] *(cents)*

	311-312	313	314	321	322	323	324
Date [2] Date [2] Fecha [2]	Food *Aliments* Alimentos	Beverages *Boissons* Bebidas	Tobacco *Tabac* Tabaco	Textiles	Clothing *Habillement* Vestido	Leather, leather products *Cuir, articles en cuir* Cuero, artículos de cuero	Footwear *Chaussures* Calzado
1965	334	328	324	28	316	314	304
1966	366	352	342	362	349	336	335
1967	388	380	358	389	377	351	352
1968	420	405	383	431	408	384	382
1969	468	456	426	470	441	427	421
1970	543	526	487	516	488	495	480
1971	626	615	574	592	544	572	558
1972	696	701	622	656	606	637	630
1973	806	821	732	754	688	726	728

	331	332	341	342	352	351	353-354
Date [2] Date [2] Fecha [2]	Wood *Bois* Madera	Furniture *Ameublement* Mobiliario	Paper, paper products *Papier, articles en papier* Papel, artículos de papel	Printing, publishing *Imprimerie, édition* Imprentas, editoriales	Industrial chemicals *Chimie industrielle* Química industrial	Other chemical products *Autres produits chimiques* Otros productos químicos	Refineries and products of petroleum and coal *Raffineries et dérivés du pétrole et du charbon* Refinerías, y derivados del petróleo y del carbón
1965	322	330	359	357	.	.	.
1966	353	361	393	392	413	370	510
1967	377	379	421	419	442	400	553
1968	407	419	455	460	488	432	585
1969	447	459	503	506	539	480	632
1970	511	527	586	584	609	554	744
1971	592	614	672	686	694	634	849
1972	663	660	747	793	783	706	884
1973	749	761	864	889	893	823	1 036

[1] Adult males.   [2] Oct. of each year.   [1] *Hommes adultes.*   [2] *Oct. de chaque année.*   [1] Hombres adultos.   [2] Oct. de cada año.

19 Wages in manufacturing / Salaires dans les industries manufacturières / Salarios en las industrias manufactureras — B By industry / Par industrie / Por industria

Pays-Bas (2)

Average hourly earnings [1] *(cents)*
Gains horaires moyens [1] *(cents)*
Promedio de ganancias por hora [1] *(cents)*

	355-356	36	37	381	382	383	384	385; 390
Date [2] / Date [2] / Fecha [2]	Rubber and plastic products / Produits en caoutchouc et en plastique / Productos de caucho, de plástico	Non-metallic mineral products / Produits minéraux non métalliques / Productos minerales no metálicos	Basic metal industries / Industrie métallurgique de base / Industrias metalúrgicas básicas	Metal products / Produits métalliques / Productos metálicos	Machinery (non-electrical) / Machines (non électriques) / Maquinaria (no eléctrica)	Electrical machinery and apparatus / Machines et appareils électriques / Maquinaria y aparatos eléctricos	Transport equipment / Matériel de transport / Material de transporte	Other manufacturing industries [3] / Autres industries manufacturières [3] / Otras industrias manufactureras [3]
1965	358	338	.	.	.	.	.	.
1966	381	371	423	366	376	362	378	365
1967	408	393	449	400	410	395	416	389
1968	434	422	485	430	438	428	443	410
1969	482	476	527	475	488	467	488	453
1970	553	545	591	540	559	517	557	512
1971	651	630	659	616	638	587	637	576
1972	735	705	737	689	696	651	702	639
1973	847	801	846	776	800	745	787	726

[1] Adult males. [2] Oct. of each year. [3] Incl. scientific measuring, optical, etc., equipment.

[1] *Hommes adultes.* [2] *Oct. de chaque année.* [3] *Y compris le matériel scientifique, de précision, d'optique, etc.*

[1] Hombres adultos. [2] Oct. de cada año. [3] Incl. el equipo científico, de medida, de óptica, etc.

Pologne [1] (1)

Average monthly earnings [2] *(zlotys)*
Gains mensuels moyens [2] *(zlotys)*
Promedio de ganancias por mes [2] *(zlotys)*

	311-312	313	314	321	322	323	324	331	332
Date / Date / Fecha	Food / Aliments / Alimentos	Beverages / Boissons / Bebidas	Tobacco / Tabac / Tabaco	Textiles	Clothing / Habillement / Vestido	Leather, leather products / Cuir, articles en cuir / Cuero, artículos de cuero	Footwear / Chaussures / Calzado	Wood / Bois / Madera	Furniture / Ameublement / Mobiliario
1970	2 063	1 857	1 770	2 006	1 864	2 106	1 952	1 951	2 068
1971	2 191	1 982	1 881	2 113	1 963	2 206	2 049	2 053	2 171
1972	2 359	2 114	1 941	2 188	2 038	2 264	2 117	2 163	2 272
1973	2 566	2 356	2 154	2 429	2 185	2 414	2 302	2 346	2 474
1974	2 916	2 676	2 623	2 703	2 469	2 748	2 601	2 666	2 805

[1] Socialised sector. [2] Incl. salaried employees.

[1] *Secteur socialisé.* [2] *Y compris les employés.*

[1] Sector socializado. [2] Incl. los empleados.

19 Wages in manufacturing
Salaires dans les industries manufacturières
Salarios en las industrias manufactureras

B By industry
Par industrie
Por industria

Pologne [1] (2)

Average monthly earnings [2] *(zlotys)*
Gains mensuels moyens [2] *(zlotys)*
Promedio de ganancias por mes [2] *(zlotys)*

Date / Date / Fecha	341 Paper, paper products / *Papier, articles en papier* / Papel, artículos de papel	342 Printing, publishing / *Imprimerie, édition* / Imprentas, editoriales	351 Industrial chemicals / *Chimie industrielle* / Química industrial	352 Other chemical products / *Autres produits chimiques* / Otros productos químicos	353 Petroleum refineries / *Raffineries de pétrole* / Refinerías de petróleo	354 Products of petroleum and coal / *Dérivés du pétrole et du charbon* / Derivados del petróleo y del carbón	355 Rubber products / *Produits en caoutchouc* / Productos de caucho	356 Plastic products / *Articles en matière plastique* / Productos plásticos	361 Pottery, china, earthenware / *Grès, porcelaines, faïences* / Barro, loza, porcelana
1970	1 959	2 191	2 387	2 159	2 427	2 746	2 131	2 053	1 970
1971	2 065	2 306	2 522	3 248	2 504	2 951	2 219	2 143	2 101
1972	2 154	2 375	2 661	2 357	2 641	3 051	2 314	2 244	2 262
1973	2 285	2 593	2 951	2 652	2 954	3 051	2 314	2 244	2 262
1974	2 644	2 964	3 415	2 977	3 431	3 857	2 877	2 643	2 911

Date / Date / Fecha	362 Glass, and glass products / *Verre* / Vidrio	369 Other non-metallic mineral products / *Autres produits minéraux* / Otros productos minerales	371 Iron and steel / *Sidérurgie* / Hierro y acero	372 Non-ferrous metal / *Métaux non ferreux* / Metales no ferrosos	381 Metal products / *Produits métalliques* / Productos metálicos	382 Machinery (non-electrical) / *Machines (non électriques)* / Maquinaria (no eléctrica)	383 Electrical machinery and apparatus / *Machines et appareils électriques* / Maquinaria y aparatos eléctricos	384 Transport equipment / *Matériel de transport* / Material de transporte	385 Scientific, measuring, optical, etc., equipment / *Matériel scientifique, de précision, d'optique, etc.* / Equipo científico, de medida, de óptica, etc.	390 Other manufacturing industries / *Autres industries manufacturières* / Otras industrias manufactureras
1970	2 062	2 189	2 939	2 814	2 226	2 463	2 243	2 489	2 371	2 040
1971	2 149	2 323	3 093	3 000	2 327	2 582	2 350	2 664	2 477	2 160
1972	2 347	2 476	3 234	3 101	2 432	2 704	2 442	2 787	2 590	2 236
1973	2 676	2 700	3 502	3 350	2 655	2 974	2 654	3 048	2 795	2 387
1974	3 002	3 159	4 101	3 967	2 966	3 341	2 979	3 428	3 117	2 671

[1] Socialised sector. [2] Incl. salaried employees.
[1] *Secteur socialisé.* [2] *Y compris les employés.*
[1] Sector socializado. [2] Incl. los empleados.

WAGES

19 Wages in manufacturing
Salaires dans les industries manufacturières
Salarios en las industrias manufactureras

B By industry
Par industrie
Por industria

Portugal

Average daily earnings *(escudos)*
Gains journaliers moyens *(escudos)*
Promedio de ganancias por día *(escudos)*

Date / Date / Fecha	Food / Aliments / Alimentos	Beer / Bière / Cerveza	Tobacco / Tabac / Tabaco	Textiles	Cork / Liège / Corcho	Paper, paper products / Papier, articles en papier / Papel, artículos de papel	Leather, leather products / Cuir, articles en cuir / Cuero, artículos de cuero
1965	35.00	69.60	65.40	39.10	36.90	43.10	45.60
1966	38.30	76.40	63.80	40.90	41.20	48.50	48.90
1967	41.90	83.90	74.60	44.00	43.20	53.20	51.80
1968	45.90	114.00	77.40	45.10	45.70	57.30	55.40
1969	49.40	136.10	94.00	48.60	51.20	64.60	62.90
1970	54.10	142.90	103.50	54.70	59.40	80.50	73.80

Date / Date / Fecha	Rubber products / Industrie du caoutchouc / Productos de caucho	Chemicals / Industrie chimique / Productos químicos	Products of petroleum and coal / Dérivés du pétrole et du charbon / Derivados del petróleo y del carbón	Non-metallic mineral products / Produits minéraux non métalliques / Productos minerales no metálicos	Metal products / Produits métalliques / Productos metálicos	Electrical machinery / Machines électriques / Maquinaria eléctrica	Transport equipment / Matériel de transport / Material de transporte	Miscellaneous manufacturing / Industries manufacturières diverses / Industrias manufactureras diversas
1965	46.50	62.10	118.40	55.50	30.20	56.50	72.20	34.60
1966	51.00	67.70	114.70	60.60	27.00	62.70	82.90	39.30
1967	54.60	74.20	113.60	65.40	31.00	70.20	86.10	44.20
1968	58.90	74.40	129.70	70.80	37.00	77.20	91.50	49.40
1969	67.70	81.70	187.40	80.00	42.20	90.80	100.70	55.00
1970	82.70	99.90	242.00	91.80	44.10	110.30	129.20	66.50

19

Wages in manufacturing
Salaires dans les industries manufacturières
Salarios en las industrias manufactureras

B

By industry
Par industrie
Por industria

Roumanie [1]

Average monthly earnings [2] *(lei)*
Gains mensuels moyens [2] *(lei)*
Promedio de ganancias por mes [2] *(lei)*

Date / Date / Fecha	Food / Aliments / Alimentos	Textiles	Clothing [3] / Habillement [3] / Vestido [3]	Leather, fur, footwear / Cuir, fourrure, chaussures / Cuero, piel, calzado	Wood [4] / Bois [4] / Madera [4]	Cellulose, paper / Cellulose, papier / Celulosa, papel
1965	1 031	1 001	970	1 067	1 136	1 117
1966	1 055	1 008	1 011	1 099	1 139	1 190
1967	1 086	1 013	1 012	1 100	1 155	1 198
1968	1 126	1 037	1 032	1 132	1 191	1 223
1969	1 230	1 138	1 099	1 214	1 238	1 248
1970	1 287	1 202	1 170	1 267	1 362	1 409
1971	1 329	1 212	1 195	1 285	1 391	1 437
1972	1 352	1 224	1 232	1 292	1 424	1 460
1973	1 413	1 327	1 303	1 421	1 483	1 496
1974	1 444	1 453	1 366	1 536	1 582	1 558

Date / Date / Fecha	Printing, publishing / Imprimerie, édition / Imprentas, editoriales	Chemicals / Industrie chimique / Productos químicos	Non-ferrous mineral products [5] / Produits minéraux non ferreux [5] / Productos minerales no ferrosos [5]	Glass, china, earthenware / Verre, porcelaine, faïence / Vidrio, porcelana, loza	Building material / Matériaux de construction / Materiales de construcción	Primary iron and steel [5] / Sidérurgie [5] / Siderurgia [5]	Metal products, machinery, etc. / Produits métalliques, machines, etc. / Productos metálicos, maquinaria, etc.
1965	1 124	1 152	1 339	1 168	1 071	1 343	1 285
1966	1 205	1 235	1 462	1 193	1 128	1 443	1 315
1967	1 203	1 249	1 498	1 205	1 157	1 500	1 341
1968	1 219	1 288	1 552	1 241	1 191	1 536	1 371
1969	1 307	1 331	1 594	1 330	1 270	1 583	1 393
1970	1 398	1 491	1 829	1 398	1 369	1 725	1 544
1971	1 431	1 512	1 885	1 425	1 407	1 775	1 577
1972	1 458	1 527	1 914	1 443	1 444	1 800	1 598
1973	1 473	1 571	1 967	1 557	1 525	1 866	1 651
1974	1 525	1 676	2 053	1 720	1 606	2 020	1 794

[1] Socialised sector. [2] Incl. salaried employees.
[3] Excl. footwear. [4] Incl. exploitation. [5] Incl. ore mining.

[1] *Secteur socialisé.* [2] *Y compris les employés.* [3] *Non compris la chaussure.* [4] *Y compris l'exploitation.* [5] *Y compris l'extraction des minerais.*

[1] Sector socializado. [2] Incl. los empleados. [3] Excl. el calzado. [4] Incl. la explotación. [5] Incl. la extracción de minerales.

19 Wages in manufacturing / Salaires dans les industries manufacturières / Salarios en las industrias manufactureras

B By industry / Par industrie / Por industria

Suisse (1)

Average hourly earnings *(francs)*
Gains horaires moyens *(francs)*
Promedio de ganancias por hora *(francs)*

Date [1] / Date [1] / Fecha [1]	Food / Aliments / Alimentos	Beverages / Boissons / Bebidas	Tobacco / Tabac / Tabaco	Textiles	Clothing / Habillement / Vestido	Wood / Bois / Madera
Adult males (skilled workers) — *Hommes adultes (ouvriers qualifiés)* — Hombres adultos (obreros calificados)						
1965		5.57		5.48	5.15	5.41
1966		6.02		6.09	5.60	5.79
1967		6.36		6.27	5.93	6.13
1968 [2]	6.23	6.96	7.42	6.61	6.12	6.52
1969	6.61	7.16	8.00	7.14	6.31	6.90
1970	7.32	7.97	8.48	7.70	7.24	7.62
1971	8.09	9.02	9.47	8.85	8.04	8.55
1972	9.26	9.84	10.63	9.77	9.08	9.63
1973	10.56	10.88	11.39	10.96	10.26	10.80
1974	11.78	12.39	13.27	12.25	11.40	12.07
Adult males (cont.) (semi-skilled and unskilled workers) — *Hommes adultes (suite) (ouvriers semi-qualifiés et non qualifiés)* — Hombres adultos (cont.) (obreros semicalificados y no calificados)						
1965		4.68		4.41	4.55	4.54
1966		5.04		4.79	4.89	4.86
1967		5.36		5.05	5.19	5.16
1968 [2]	5.42	5.75	5.65	5.29	5.46	5.47
1969	5.77	6.07	6.29	5.73	5.89	5.84
1970	6.52	6.75	6.50	6.46	6.67	6.47
1971	7.33	7.60	7.39	7.62	7.63	7.33
1972	8.26	8.56	7.99	8.50	8.43	8.24
1973	9.25	9.24	8.77	9.61	9.44	9.30
1974	10.41	10.45	10.14	10.91	10.57	10.42
Adult females — *Femmes adultes* — Mujeres adultas						
1965		3.06		3.04	3.15	3.25
1966		3.30		3.27	3.40	3.53
1967		3.49		3.48	3.59	3.77
1968 [2]	3.70	3.87	3.67	3.65	3.81	4.01
1969	3.93	4.10	3.93	3.98	4.11	4.31
1970	4.50	4.58	4.46	4.53	4.65	4.73
1971	5.14	5.27	5.06	5.26	5.31	5.39
1972	5.74	5.74	5.61	5.82	5.90	6.06
1973	6.52	6.54	6.37	6.69	6.62	6.99
1974	7.29	7.36	7.13	7.56	7.36	7.78

[1] Oct. of each year.　[2] New industrial classification.　　　[1] *Oct. de chaque année.*　[2] *Nouvelle classification industrielle.*　　　[1] Oct. de cada año.　[2] Nueva clasificación industrial.

19 Wages in manufacturing
Salaires dans les industries manufacturières
Salarios en las industrias manufactureras

B By industry
Par industrie
Por industria

Suisse (2)

Average hourly earnings *(francs)*
Gains horaires moyens *(francs)*
Promedio de ganancias por hora *(francs)*

Date [1] Date [1] Fecha [1]	Paper, paper products *Papier, articles en papier* Papel, artículos de papel	Leather, leather products *Cuir, articles en cuir* Cuero, artículos de cuero	Printing, publishing *Imprimerie, édition* Imprentas, editoriales	Chemicals *Industrie chimique* Productos químicos	Stone, clay *Pierre, terre cuite* Piedra, arcilla	Metal industries, machinery, etc. *Industrie métallurgique, machines, etc.* Industrias metalúrgicas, maquinaria, etc.	Watchmaking *Horlogerie* Relojería	Jewellery *Bijouterie* Joyería
Adult males *(cont.)* — *Hommes adultes* (suite) — Hombres adultos *(cont.)* (skilled workers) *(ouvriers qualifiés)* (obreros calificados)								
1965	6.04		6.65	6.36	5.71	5.78	6.00	
1966	6.49		6.97	6.93	6.12	6.18	6.37	
1967	6.96		7.42	7.38	6.53	6.54	6.81	
1968 [2]	7.45	6.59	8.01	7.72	6.87	6.91	6.95	7.50
1969	7.66	7.01	8.19	8.33	7.23	7.36	7.54	8.03
1970	8.26	7.66	8.73	9.04	7.96	8.10	8.03	8.41
1971	9.21	8.29	9.65	10.13	9.03	9.12	8.75	9.15
1972	10.38	9.11	11.93	11.40	10.10	10.10	9.47	10.29
1973	11.79	10.25	13.29	12.86	11.38	11.35	10.60	11.69
1974	13.36	11.59	14.94	14.71	12.87	12.74	12.21	12.87
Adult males *(concl.)* — *Hommes adultes* (fin) — Hombres adultos *(fin)* (semi-skilled and unskilled workers) *(ouvriers semi-qualifiés et non qualifiés)* (obreros semicalificados y no calificados)								
1965	5.08		4.78	5.56	4.81	4.85	4.97	
1966	5.46		5.02	6.08	5.14	5.20	5.32	
1967	5.81		5.42	6.54	5.53	5.52	5.70	
1968 [2]	6.25	5.46	5.66	6.72	5.79	5.77	5.77	5.91
1969	6.48	5.89	6.00	7.31	6.12	6.18	6.15	6.26
1970	7.16	6.59	6.44	7.98	6.89	6.88	6.56	6.71
1971	8.18	7.37	7.32	8.99	7.89	7.81	7.26	7.38
1972	9.03	8.10	9.01	10.08	8.86	8.62	7.89	7.90
1973	10.20	9.20	10.18	11.43	9.95	9.73	8.90	8.74
1974	11.43	10.53	11.58	13.28	11.23	10.97	10.26	9.73
Adult females *(concl.)* — *Femmes adultes* (fin) — Mujeres adultas *(fin)*								
1965	3.16		3.22	3.46	3.32	3.39	3.70	
1966	3.41		3.43	3.84	3.56	3.64	4.00	
1967	3.63		3.75	4.19	3.83	3.87	4.32	
1968 [2]	3.84	3.77	4.07	4.42	4.10	4.06	4.37	4.22
1969	4.07	4.06	4.23	4.83	4.36	4.40	4.63	4.57
1970	4.55	4.55	4.73	5.35	4.87	4.96	4.93	5.06
1971	5.25	5.14	5.40	6.07	5.52	5.61	5.35	5.62
1972	5.97	5.73	6.18	6.96	6.29	6.16	5.94	6.23
1973	6.71	6.42	7.24	7.98	7.08	7.00	6.64	6.88
1974	7.66	7.11	8.34	9.16	8.00	7.93	7.87	7.93

[1] Oct. of each year. [2] New industrial classification.   [1] *Oct. de chaque année.* [2] *Nouvelle classification industrielle.*   [1] Oct. de cada año. [2] Nueva clasificación industrial.

19 **Wages in manufacturing**
Salaires dans les industries manufacturières
Salarios en las industrias manufactureras

B By industry
Par industrie
Por industria

Sweden (1)

Average hourly earnings [1] *(kronor)*
Gains horaires moyens [1] *(kronor)*
Promedio de ganancias por hora [1] *(kronor)*

Date / Date / Fecha	311-312 Food / Aliments / Alimentos	313 Beverages / Boissons / Bebidas	314 Tobacco / Tabac / Tabaco	321 Textiles	322 Clothing / Habillement / Vestido	323 Leather, leather products / Cuir, articles en cuir / Cuero, artículos de cuero	324 Footwear / Chaussures / Calzado	331 Wood / Bois / Madera	332 Furniture / Ameublement / Mobiliario
Adult males — *Hommes adultes* — Hombres adultos									
1971	15.18	14.88	16.37	13.98	13.27	14.54	14.20	14.30	14.32
1972	17.24	17.58	18.98	15.89	14.98	16.36	16.05	16.18	15.78
1973	18.53	18.88	20.25	17.24	16.41	17.58	17.21	17.61	17.32
Adult females — *Femmes adultes* — Mujeres adultas									
1971	12.66	13.45	13.49	11.94	11.57	12.19	11.81	12.90	12.85
1972	14.61	15.95	16.30	13.70	13.16	13.89	13.70	14.58	14.29
1973	15.70	17.16	17.49	14.88	14.49	14.95	14.79	15.99	15.70

Date / Date / Fecha	341 Paper, paper products / Papier, articles en papier / Papel, artículos de papel	342 Printing, publishing / Imprimerie, édition / Imprentas, editoriales	351 Industrial chemicals / Chimie industrielle / Química industrial	352 Other chemical products / Autres produits chimiques / Otros productos químicos	353-354 Refineries and products of petroleum and coal / Raffineries et dérivés du pétrole et du charbon / Refinerías y derivados del petróleo y del carbón	355 Rubber products / Produits en caoutchouc / Productos de caucho	356 Plastic products / Articles en matière plastique / Productos plásticos	361 Pottery, china, earthenware / Grès, porcelaines, faïences / Barro, loza, porcelana	362 Glass / Verre / Vidrio
Adult males *(cont.)* — *Hommes adultes* (suite) — Hombres adultos *(cont.)*									
1971	15.55	18.35	14.96	14.98	15.74	15.02	14.57	14.63	15.37
1972	17.83	20.67	16.92	16.65	18.08	16.69	16.35	16.54	17.43
1973	19.30	22.29	18.28	18.00	19.54	17.83	17.49	17.80	19.01
Adult females *(cont.)* — *Femmes adultes* (suite) — Mujeres adultas *(cont.)*									
1971	12.70	13.67	12.67	12.74	—	12.82	12.44	12.40	12.65
1972	14.75	15.66	14.63	14.39	—	14.64	14.03	14.31	14.54
1973	15.93	17.21	15.93	15.66	—	15.90	15.25	15.63	15.94

[1] Incl. holiday and sick-leave payments and the value of payments in kind.

[1] *Y compris les versements au titre des vacances et congés de maladie et la valeur des paiements en nature.*

[1] Incl. los pagos por vacaciones y licencias de enfermedad y el valor de los pagos en especie.

19 **Wages in manufacturing**
Salaires dans les industries manufacturières
Salarios en las industrias manufactureras

B **By industry**
Par industrie
Por industria

Sweden (2)

Average hourly earnings [1] *(kronor)*
Gains horaires moyens [1] *(kronor)*
Promedio de ganancias por hora [1] *(kronor)*

Date / Date / Fecha	369	371	372	381	382	383	384	385	390
	Other non-metallic mineral products / *Autres produits minéraux non métalliques* / Otros productos minerales no metálicos	Basic metal industries / *Industrie métallurgique de base* / Industrias metalúrgicas básicas — Iron and steel / *Sidérurgie* / Hierro y acero	Non-ferrous metal / *Métaux non ferreux* / Metales no ferrosos	Metal products / *Produits métalliques* / Productos metálicos	Machinery (non-electrical) / *Machines (non électriques)* / Maquinaria (no eléctrica)	Electrical machinery and apparatus / *Machines et appareils électriques* / Maquinaria y aparatos eléctricos	Transport equipment / *Matériel de transport* / Material de transporte	Scientific, measuring, optical, etc., equipment / *Matériel scientifique, de précision, d'optique, etc.* / Equipo científico, de medida, de óptica, etc.	Other manufacturing industries / *Autres industries manufacturières* / Otras industrias manufactureras
Adult males (concl.) — Hommes adultes (fin) — Hombres adultos (fin)									
1971	15.16	16.44	15.64	15.78	15.88	15.57	16.43	15.60	14.72
1972	17.19	18.52	17.46	17.23	17.43	17.15	18.46	17.07	16.11
1973	18.40	20.28	18.96	18.77	18.84	18.64	20.22	18.49	17.38
Adult females (concl.) — Femmes adultes (fin) — Mujeres adultas (fin)									
1971	12.76	14.71	13.87	13.23	14.08	13.27	14.98	13.50	12.49
1972	14.77	17.08	15.43	14.71	15.78	14.89	16.84	15.11	13.79
1973	16.02	18.67	16.90	16.07	16.91	16.19	18.65	16.10	15.22

[1] Incl. holiday and sick-leave payments and the value of payments in kind.

[1] *Y compris les versements au titre des vacances et congés de maladie et la valeur des paiements en nature.*

[1] Incl. los pagos por vacaciones y licencias de enfermedad y el valor de los pagos en especie.

19 Wages in manufacturing
Salaires dans les industries manufacturières
Salarios en las industrias manufactureras

B By industry
Par industrie
Por industria

Turquie

Average daily earnings [1] *(liras)*
Gains journaliers moyens [1] *(liras)*
Promedio de ganancias por día [1] *(liras)*

Date / Date / Fecha	Food / Aliments / Alimentos	Beverages / Boissons / Bebidas	Tobacco / Tabac / Tabaco	Textiles	Clothing / Habillement / Vestido	Wood / Bois / Madera	Furniture / Ameublement / Mobiliario	Paper, paper products / Papier, articles en papier / Papel, artículos de papel	Printing, publishing / Imprimerie, édition / Imprentas, editoriales	Leather, leather products / Cuir, articles en cuir / Cuero, artículos de cuero
1965	18.91	25.03	17.54	18.18	18.87	16.07	17.14	25.18	28.90	20.89
1966	20.50	28.07	20.53	19.48	19.05	16.56	17.44	28.13	30.23	21.72
1967	21.73	29.17	21.92	21.39	19.57	18.16	18.61	31.58	31.87	22.38
1968	24.16	33.73	26.35	22.50	21.38	19.22	19.97	34.25	33.60	23.70
1969	26.78	35.99	27.67	27.26	25.71	36.76	22.81	37.89	36.83	26.21
1970	30.36	50.45	54.68	28.26	28.39	24.54	25.64	39.75	44.79	33.02
1971	33.88	45.76	37.33	34.81	29.27	29.17	27.29	40.07	43.76	33.49
1972	37.26	47.28	35.82	40.76	30.84	30.14	29.08	53.51	50.28	34.04
1973	45.86	58.96	64.34	66.02	38.40	35.16	35.35	76.92	55.91	41.88
1974	70.46	77.51	77.63	57.27	52.92	49.15	50.80	77.40	76.91	54.40

Date / Date / Fecha	Rubber products / Industrie du caoutchouc / Productos de caucho	Chemicals / Industrie chimique / Productos químicos	Products of petroleum and coal / Dérivés du pétrole et du charbon / Derivados del petróleo y del carbón	Non-metallic mineral products / Produits minéraux non métalliques / Productos minerales no metálicos	Basic metal industries / Industrie métallurgique de base / Industrias metalúrgicas básicas	Metal products / Produits métalliques / Productos metálicos	Machinery (non-electrical) / Machines (non électriques) / Maquinaria (no eléctrica)	Electrical machinery / Machines électriques / Maquinaria eléctrica	Transport equipment / Matériel de transport / Material de transporte	Miscellaneous manufacturing / Industries manufacturières diverses / Industrias manufactureras diversas
1965	22.59	26.13	40.99	18.35	28.64	22.67	23.94	23.35	23.98	19.34
1966	23.64	27.34	44.09	21.42	33.32	23.33	24.69	24.96	27.76	20.36
1967	27.74	29.61	53.82	23.44	36.55	25.31	27.20	26.99	31.88	23.57
1968	28.06	31.77	56.54	25.14	40.36	27.12	29.66	29.16	34.04	23.96
1969	30.62	32.26	56.63	29.39	44.82	37.43	33.39	33.78	38.19	36.88
1970	32.97	42.75	54.50	31.14	50.61	34.20	37.89	41.17	39.07	30.92
1971	41.30	47.68	67.97	38.19	56.70	40.15	45.33	48.43	61.52	31.49
1972	48.56	59.40	76.80	40.88	67.94	44.91	48.87	54.85	65.05	36.68
1973	56.88	63.59	96.58	54.44	68.14	52.06	55.48	60.22	70.65	40.84
1974	79.90	83.89	95.11	67.00	98.41	66.39	68.48	73.72	92.00	55.25

[1] Incl. salaried employees.   [1] *Y compris les employés.*   [1] Incl. los empleados.

19 B

Wages in manufacturing
Salaires dans les industries manufacturières
Salarios en las industrias manufactureras

By industry
Par industrie
Por industria

United Kingdom (1)

Average hourly earnings [1] *(pence)*
Gains horaires moyens [1] *(pence)*
Promedio de ganancias por hora [1] *(pence)*

	31	321	322	323	324	33	34	351-352
Date [2]	Food, beverages, tobacco		Clothing	Leather, leather products	Footwear	Wood, furniture	Paper, printing, publishing	Chemicals
Date [2]	*Aliments, boissons, tabac*	Textiles	*Habillement*	*Cuir, articles en cuir*	*Chaussures*	*Bois, ameublement*	*Papier, imprimerie, édition*	*Industrie chimique*
Fecha [2]	Alimentos, bebidas, tabaco		Vestido	Cuero, artículos de cuero	Calzado	Madera, mobiliario	Papel, imprentas, editoriales	Productos químicos
Adult males [3] — *Hommes adultes* [3] — Hombres adultos [3]								
1969	50.6	50.1	48.7	47.0	55.6	51.0	63.8	54.8
1970	59.8	56.6	55.5	53.5	62.9	57.2	74.4	65.1
1971	68.1	63.5	59.4	59.0	68.9	65.4	81.2	74.4
1972	77.1	71.7	67.9	67.5	76.9	75.7	92.2	83.2
1973	85.4	81.9	76.2	76.9	87.8	87.3	108.0	92.6
1974	102.9	97.4	92.0	93.1	108.9	104.1	125.2	117.0
Adult females [3] — *Femmes adultes* [3] — Mujeres adultas [3]								
1969	30.8	31.6	30.1	28.8	37.0	34.4	32.1	30.8
1970	37.3	35.9	34.2	32.0	42.3	38.6	39.9	36.9
1971	43.6	40.5	38.2	36.6	46.6	45.3	44.2	42.7
1972	50.8	46.0	43.9	40.6	53.2	51.7	51.1	47.9
1973	58.8	53.3	50.7	48.3	61.5	61.2	59.0	55.8
1974	75.7	68.4	64.8	61.8	78.6	76.6	77.8	75.2

[1] Manual workers. [2] Oct. of each year. [3] Full-time workers only.

[1] *Travailleurs manuels.* [2] *Oct. de chaque année.* [3] *Ouvriers et ouvrières à temps complet seulement.*

[1] Trabajadores manuales. [2] Oct. de cada año. [3] Obreros y obreras de tiempo completo solamente.

19 Wages in manufacturing / Salaires dans les industries manufacturières / Salarios en las industrias manufactureras
B By industry / Par industrie / Por industria

United Kingdom (2)

Average hourly earnings [1] *(pence)*
Gains horaires moyens [1] *(pence)*
Promedio de ganancias por hora [1] *(pence)*

	353-354	355	356	361	362	369	371
Date [2] Date [2] Fecha [2]	Refineries and products of petroleum and coal *Raffineries et dérivés du pétrole et du charbon* Refinerías y derivados del petróleo y del carbón	Rubber products *Produits en caoutchouc* Productos de caucho	Plastic products *Articles en matière plastique* Productos plásticos	Pottery, china, earthenware *Grès, porcelaines, faïences* Barro, loza, porcelana	Glass *Verre* Vidrio	Other non-metallic mineral products *Autres produits minéraux non métalliques* Otros productos minerales no metálicos	Iron and steel basic industries *Sidérurgie* Industrias básicas de hierro y acero
Adult males *(cont.)* [3] — *Hommes adultes* (suite) [3] — Hombres adultos *(cont.)* [3]							
1969	58.0	58.7	52.4	52.2	54.3	51.3	58.4
1970	70.1	68.2	61.1	59.7	65.0	60.3	66.8
1971	78.3	76.4	68.1	67.5	74.6	63.4	73.5
1972	90.6	86.5	77.2	76.4	87.2	88.8	85.6
1973	100.3	95.4	88.2	84.8	97.9	89.0	97.8
1974	130.2	117.0	108.1	100.8	120.1	107.3	116.1
Adult females *(cont.)* [3] — *Femmes adultes* (suite) [3] — Mujeres adultas *(cont.)* [3]							
1969	31.6	32.4	30.4	31.7	32.9	31.9	31.5
1970	39.0	37.7	35.3	36.9	39.6	37.1	35.8
1971	45.3	44.3	40.2	41.7	47.1	41.6	39.6
1972	53.0	51.5	46.1	47.1	57.2	47.6	48.1
1973	66.7	57.4	53.9	54.7	66.2	57.0	54.4
1974	81.0	74.9	71.4	71.2	87.7	73.0	71.5

[1] Manual workers. [2] Oct. of each year. [3] Full-time workers only.

[1] *Travailleurs manuels.* [2] *Oct. de chaque année.* [3] *Ouvriers et ouvrières à temps complet seulement.*

[1] Trabajadores manuales. [2] Oct. de cada año. [3] Obreros y obreras de tiempo completo solamente.

19 B

Wages in manufacturing
Salaires dans les industries manufacturières
Salarios en las industrias manufactureras

By industry
Par industrie
Por industria

United Kingdom (3)

Average hourly earnings [1] *(pence)*
Gains horaires moyens [1] *(pence)*
Promedio de ganancias por hora [1] *(pence)*

	372	381	382	383	384	385	390
Date [2] *Date [2]* Fecha [2]	Non-ferrous metal basic industries *Métaux non ferreux (industrie de base)* Industrias básicas de metales no ferrosos	Metal products *Produits métalliques* Productos metálicos	Machinery (non-electrical) *Machines (non électriques)* Maquinaria (no eléctrica)	Electrical machinery and apparatus *Machines et appareils électriques* Maquinaria y aparatos eléctricos	Transport equipment *Matériel de transport* Material de transporte	Scientific, measuring, optical, etc., equipment *Matériel scientifique, de précision, d'optique, etc.* Equipo científico, de medida, de óptica, etc.	Other manufacturing industries *Autres industries manufacturières* Otras industrias manufactureras
Adult males *(concl.)* [3] — *Hommes adultes* (fin) [3] — Hombres adultos *(fin)* [3]							
1969	56.7	54.1	55.2	54.7	63.9	54.2	49.4
1970	65.7	61.5	63.3	62.4	73.8	60.6	55.4
1971	72.2	67.2	69.4	69.4	83.2	66.5	61.9
1972	83.7	77.5	79.8	79.5	94.3	74.1	69.8
1973	95.5	88.3	90.8	89.0	103.8	84.3	80.2
1974	113.4	107.5	109.7	106.4	122.9	101.4	99.0
Adult females *(concl.)* [3] — *Femmes adultes* (fin) [3] — Mujeres adultas *(fin)* [3]							
1969	32.6	31.5	34.2	33.4	38.3	33.2	30.1
1970	37.2	35.8	40.2	38.6	44.7	38.1	33.9
1971	42.1	40.2	45.3	43.9	51.9	41.4	38.2
1972	50.2	47.6	53.2	51.1	61.5	47.1	42.9
1973	57.9	56.1	61.7	59.8	68.9	56.4	50.3
1974	74.9	72.2	79.0	75.8	87.7	70.9	66.3

[1] Manual workers. [2] Oct. of each year. [3] Full-time workers only.

[1] *Travailleurs manuels.* [2] *Oct. de chaque année.* [3] *Ouvriers et ouvrières à temps complet seulement.*

[1] Trabajadores manuales. [2] Oct. de cada año. [3] Obreros y obreras de tiempo completo solamente.

19 Wages in manufacturing / Salaires dans les industries manufacturières / Salarios en las industrias manufactureras

B By industry / Par industrie / Por industria

Yugoslavia [1] (1)

Average monthly earnings [2] *(dinars)*
Gains mensuels moyens [2] *(dinars)*
Promedio de ganancias por mes [2] *(dinars)*

Date / Date / Fecha	311-312 Food / Aliments / Alimentos	313 Beverages / Boissons / Bebidas	314 Tobacco / Tabac / Tabaco	321 Textiles	322 Clothing / Habillement / Vestido	323 Leather, leather products / Cuir, articles en cuir / Cuero, artículos de cuero	324 Footwear / Chaussures / Calzado	331 Wood / Bois / Madera	332 Furniture / Ameublement / Mobiliario
1966	663	821	585	589	525	687	622	524	543
1967	732	901	655	600	544	723	644	574	584
1968	770	1 075	733	645	647	760	709	621	692
1969	881	1 109	835	750	755	895	799	759	841
1970	1 059	1 282	933	850	849	1 035	887	934	1 035
1971	1 302	1 582	1 219	1 080	1 064	1 263	1 151	1 171	1 258
1972	1 539	1 804	1 529	1 360	1 367	1 542	1 381	1 391	1 474
1973	1 834	2 048	1 822	1 576	1 594	1 789	1 627	1 658	1 700
1974	2 332	2 491	2 229	2 005	1 926	2 147	1 948	2 201	2 184

Date / Date / Fecha	341 Paper, paper products / Papier, articles en papier / Papel, artículos de papel	342 Printing, publishing / Imprimerie, édition / Imprentas, editoriales	351; 356 Industrial chemicals [3] / Chimie industrielle [3] / Química industrial [3]	352 Other chemical products / Autres produits chimiques / Otros productos químicos	353 Petroleum refineries / Raffineries de pétrole / Refinerías de petróleo	354 Products of petroleum and coal / Dérivés du pétrole et du charbon / Derivados del petróleo y del carbón	355 Rubber products / Produits en caoutchouc / Productos de caucho	361 Pottery, china, earthenware / Grès, porcelaines, faïences / Barro, loza, porcelana	362 Glass / Verre / Vidrio
1966	681	824	841	808	1 122	727	707	570	720
1967	739	957	903	863	1 307	789	795	594	694
1968	838	1 059	987	949	1 369	1 013	820	683	739
1969	981	1 214	1 061	1 124	1 399	1 134	968	838	944
1970	1 176	1 434	1 203	1 274	1 770	1 651	1 069	1 010	1 095
1971	1 369	1 674	1 490	1 484	2 184	1 993	1 291	1 228	1 475
1972	1 594	1 887	1 715	1 755	2 392	2 141	1 550	1 478	1 520
1973	1 878	2 132	1 988	2 076	2 942	2 637	1 765	1 752	1 761
1974	2 637	2 748	2 748	2 728	3 834	3 261	2 260	2 139	2 236

[1] Socialised sector. [2] Incl. salaried employees. [3] Incl. plastic products.

[1] *Secteur socialisé.* [2] *Y compris les employés.* [3] *Y compris les articles en matière plastique.*

[1] Sector socializado. [2] Incl. los empleados. [3] Incl. productos plásticos.

19 Wages in manufacturing / Salaires dans les industries manufacturières / Salarios en las industrias manufactureras

B By industry / Par industrie / Por industria

Yugoslavia [1] (2)

Average monthly earnings [2] *(dinars)*
Gains mensuels moyens [2] *(dinars)*
Promedio de ganancias por mes [2] *(dinars)*

Date / Date / Fecha	369 Other non-metallic mineral products [3] / Autres produits minéraux non métalliques [3] / Otros productos minerales no metálicos [3]	371 Basic metal industries [3] / Industrie métallurgique de base [3] / Industrias metalúrgicas básicas [3] — Iron and steel / Sidérurgie / Hierro y acero	372 Non-ferrous metal / Métaux non ferreux / Metales no ferrosos	381 Metal products / Produits métalliques / Productos metálicos	382 Machinery (non-electrical) / Machines (non électriques) / Maquinaria (no eléctrica)	383 Electrical machinery and apparatus / Machines et appareils électriques / Maquinaria y aparatos eléctricos	384 Transport equipment / Matériel de transport / Material de transporte	385 Scientific, measuring, optical, etc., equipment / Matériel scientifique, de précision, d'optique, etc. / Equipo científico, de medida, de óptica, etc.	390 Other manufacturing industries / Autres industries manufacturières / Otras industrias manufactureras
1966	612	830	1 000	713	688	677	774	697	704
1967	707	858	1 010	729	764	755	845	697	822
1968	809	934	1 037	855	852	880	898	825	854
1969	918	1 092	1 110	951	1 003	1 014	1 079	1 118	984
1970	1 110	1 268	1 275	1 113	1 147	1 155	1 239	1 230	1 160
1971	1 209	1 575	1 517	1 340	1 405	1 349	1 478	1 435	1 435
1972	1 597	1 864	1 719	1 579	1 632	1 536	1 698	1 603	1 650
1973	1 842	2 189	2 092	1 752	1 899	1 801	1 938	1 881	1 865
1974	2 332	2 834	2 826	2 330	2 431	2 318	2 490	2 378	2 332

[1] Socialised sector. [2] Incl. salaried employees. [3] Incl. ores extraction.

[1] *Secteur socialisé.* [2] *Y compris les employés.* [3] *Y compris l'extraction des minerais.*

[1] Sector socializado. [2] Incl. los empleados. [3] Incl. la extracción de minerales.

19 Wages in manufacturing
Salaires dans les industries manufacturières
Salarios en las industrias manufactureras

B By industry
Par industrie
Por industria

OCEANIA — OCÉANIE — OCEANIA

Australia

Average weekly earnings [1] *(dollars)*
Gains hebdomadaires moyens [1] *(dollars)*
Promedio de ganancias por semana [1] *(dollars)*

	31	321-322; 324	34	351-353	37	381-383	384	.
Date [2] Date [2] Fecha [2]	Food, beverages, tobacco *Aliments, boissons, tabac* Alimentos, bebidas, tabaco	Textiles, clothing, footwear *Textiles, habillement, chaussures* Textiles, vestido, calzado	Paper, printing, publishing *Papier, imprimerie, édition* Papel, imprentas, editoriales	Chemicals, petroleum refineries *Industrie chimique, raffineries de pétrole* Productos químicos, refinerías de petróleo	Basic metal industries *Industrie métallurgique de base* Industrias metalúrgicas básicas	Metal products, machinery, etc. *Produits métalliques, machines, etc.* Productos metálicos, maquinaria, etc.	Transport equipment *Matériel de transport* Material de transporte	Other manufacturing industries *Autres industries manufacturières* Otras industrias manufacturrras
	Adult males — Hommes adultes — Hombres adultos							
1966	58.00	57.50	66.60	63.00	62.80	61.60	60.50	58.50
1967	62.10	60.00	70.50	65.30	67.30	65.30	65.10	62.60
1968	63.50	63.10	74.50	69.70	73.10	72.00	67.60	65.40
1969	68.50	68.30	79.60	73.90	79.20	75.10	71.90	71.70
1970	73.80	73.40	86.00	79.90	84.90	79.50	78.10	77.00
1971	83.70	82.10	94.20	92.10	92.50	91.30	89.30	86.40
1972 [3]	91.00	89.00	101.60	102.20	103.80	96.20	91.60	93.70
1973	106.60	107.60	119.50	118.70	124.00	112.40	112.30	110.90
1974 *	141.70	123.90	154.10	157.00	163.70	145.20	140.30	137.70
	Adult females — Femmes adultes — Mujeres adultas							
1966	33.90	33.70	36.50	36.30	36.40	34.00	35.90	34.10
1967	36.60	35.70	37.60	38.00	39.60	35.90	37.20	36.10
1968	37.40	36.80	39.50	40.00	42.40	38.10	38.10	36.50
1969	40.40	40.50	41.90	42.70	45.60	42.00	42.40	40.70
1970	43.90	42.60	46.40	47 20	50.40	48.30	48.60	44.90
1971	51.20	49.40	52.90	55.60	59.20	57.40	58.10	52.10
1972 [3]	58.00	53.90	59.40	63.60	65.50	64.20	66.20	58.70
1973	71.00	66.10	71.70	75.70	78.20	74.90	81.10	71.10
1974 *	100.60	88.50	103.40	107.90	111.70	105.90	106.40	95.80

[1] Incl. salaried employees. [2] Oct. of each year.
[3] Scope of series enlarged.

[1] *Y compris les employés.* [2] *Oct. de chaque année.*
[3] *Portée de la série élargie.*

[1] Incl. los empleados. [2] Oct. de cada año. [3] El alcance de la serie es mayor.

19 B
Wages in manufacturing
Salaires dans les industries manufacturières
Salarios en las industrias manufactureras

By industry
Par industrie
Por industria

Fiji

Average weekly earnings *(dollars)*
Gains hebdomadaires moyens *(dollars)*
Promedio de ganancias por semana *(dollars)*

Date / Date / Fecha	311-312 Food / Aliments / Alimentos	313 Beverages / Boissons / Bebidas	322 Clothing / Habillement / Vestido	324 Footwear / Chaussures / Calzado	331 Wood / Bois / Madera	332 Furniture / Ameublement / Mobiliario	341 Paper, paper products / Papier, articles en papier / Papel, artículos de papel	342 Printing, publishing / Imprimerie, édition / Imprentas, editoriales	352 Chemical products / Produits chimiques / Productos químicos
1970	16.98	17.55	11.45	11.00	13.93	14.22	14.26	12.19	13.28
1971	17.49	16.96	10.35	13.27	18.98	14.78	20.93	14.71	14.83
1972	24.46	22.18	13.75	15.31	17.27	17.84	19.14	16.23	17.08
1973	26.03	23.17	13.64	17.38	20.08	19.22	29.06	14.82	19.81

Date / Date / Fecha	355 Rubber products / Produits en caoutchouc / Productos de caucho	356 Plastic products / Articles en matière plastique / Productos plásticos	369 Non-metallic mineral products [1] / Produits minéraux non métalliques [1] / Productos minerales no metálicos [1]	381 Metal products / Produits métalliques / Productos metálicos	382 Machinery (non-electrical) / Machines (non électriques) / Maquinaria (no eléctrica)	383 Electrical machinery and apparatus / Machines et appareils électriques / Maquinaria y aparatos eléctricos	384 Transport equipment / Matériel de transport / Material de transporte	390 Other manufacturing industries / Autres industries manufacturières / Otras industrias manufactureras
1970	14.75	10.50	18.28	20.93	17.27	17.75	12.96	10.50
1971	15.70	17.00	20.07	19.50	16.68	16.39	18.13	12.22
1972	22.49	18.79	21.12	22.18	21.60	18.12	19.20	12.04
1973	19.64	20.90	21.72	28.36	23.36	25.58	22.41	17.62

[1] Excl. pottery, china, earthenware and glass.

[1] *Non compris le grès, les porcelaines, les faïences et le verre.*

[1] Excl. el barro, la loza, la porcelana y el vidrio.

19 Wages in manufacturing
Salaires dans les industries manufacturières
Salarios en las industrias manufactureras

B By industry
Par industrie
Por industria

New Zealand

Average hourly earnings [1] *(dollars)*
Gains horaires moyens [1] *(dollars)*
Promedio de ganancias por hora [1] *(dollars)*

	311-312	313	314	321	322	323	324	331	332
Date [2]	Food	Beverages	Tobacco		Clothing	Leather, leather products	Footwear	Wood	Furniture
Date [2]	*Aliments*	*Boissons*	*Tabac*	Textiles	*Habillement*	*Cuir, articles en cuir*	*Chaussures*	*Bois*	*Ameublement*
Fecha [2]	Alimentos	Bebidas	Tabaco		Vestido	Cuero, artículos de cuero	Calzado	Madera	Mobiliario
1971	1.73	1.54	1.45	1.41	1.03	1.29	1.26	1.53	1.39
1972	1.88	1.63	1.54	1.53	1.15	1.44	1.35	1.65	1.53
1973	2.16	1.98	1.82	1.73	1.37	1.61	1.54	1.87	1.74
1974	2.42	2.19	2.24	2.06	1.62	1.90	1.84	2.15	2.00

	341	342	351	352	354	355	356	361	362
Date [2]	Paper, paper products	Printing, publishing	Industrial chemicals	Other chemical products	Products of petroleum and coal	Rubber products	Plastic products	Pottery, china, earthenware	Glass
Date [2]	*Papier, articles en papier*	*Imprimerie, édition*	*Chimie industrielle*	*Autres produits chimiques*	*Dérivés du pétrole et du charbon*	*Produits en caoutchouc*	*Articles en matière plastique*	*Grès, porcelaines, faïences*	*Verre*
Fecha [2]	Papel, artículos de papel	Imprentas, editoriales	Química industrial	Otros productos químicos	Derivados del petróleo y del carbón	Productos de caucho	Productos plásticos	Barro, loza, porcelana	Vidrio
1971	1.80	1.50	1.75	1.50	1.56	1.77	1.48	1.46	1.62
1972	1.96	1.65	1.90	1.63	1.79	1.94	1.63	1.48	1.79
1973	2.23	1.90	2.18	1.87	2.06	2.26	1.90	1.58	1.87
1974	2.59	2.21	2.55	2.16	2.26	2.66	2.20	1.85	2.36

	369	371	372	381	382	383	384	385	390
		Basic metal industries		Metal products	Machinery (non-electrical)	Electrical machinery and apparatus	Transport equipment	Scientific, measuring, optical, etc., equipment	Other manufacturing industries
Date [2]	Other non-metallic mineral products	*Industrie métallurgique de base*							
Date [2]		Industrias metalúrgicas básicas							
Date [2]	*Autres produits minéraux non métalliques*	Iron and steel	Non-ferrous metal	*Produits métalliques*	*Machines (non électriques)*	*Machines et appareils électriques*	*Matériel de transport*	*Matériel scientifique, de précision, d'optique, etc.*	*Autres industries manufacturières*
Fecha [2]	Otros productos minerales no metálicos	*Sidérurgie* Hierro y acero	*Métaux non ferreux* Metales no ferrosos	Productos metálicos	Maquinaria (no eléctrica)	Maquinaria y aparatos eléctricos	Material de transporte	Equipo científico, de medida, de óptica, etc.	Otras industrias manufactureras
1971	1.55	1.77	1.79	1.55	1.55	1.43	1.61	1.34	1.27
1972	1.68	2.00	1.94	1.67	1.70	1.54	1.76	1.44	1.38
1973	1.91	2.37	2.28	1.89	1.95	1.76	2.01	1.70	1.61
1974	2.24	2.72	2.66	2.18	2.26	2.02	2.33	1.98	1.89

[1] Incl. salaried employees. Incl. the value of payments in kind. [2] April and Oct. of each year.

[1] *Y compris les employés. Y compris la valeur des paiements en nature.* [2] *Avril et oct. de chaque année.*

[1] Incl. los empleados. Incl. el valor de los pagos en especie. [2] Abril y oct. de cada año.

19 Wages in manufacturing / Salaires dans les industries manufacturières / Salarios en las industrias manufactureras

B By industry / Par industrie / Por industria

URSS [1]

Average monthly earnings [2] *(roubles)*
Gains mensuels moyens [2] *(roubles)*
Promedio de ganancias por mes [2] *(roubles)*

Date / Date / Fecha	311-312 Food / Aliments / Alimentos	313 Beverages / Boissons / Bebidas	314 Tobacco / Tabac / Tabaco	321 Textiles	322 Clothing / Habillement / Vestido	323 Leather, leather products / Cuir, articles en cuir / Cuero, artículos de cuero	324 Footwear / Chaussures / Calzado	331 Wood / Bois / Madera	332 Furniture / Ameublement / Mobiliario
1965	85.9	80.2	89.5	81.2	72.8	88.1	81.6	92.1	88.1
1966	89.5	84.3	92.5	85.4	76.8	94.7	86.8	95.3	91.8
1967	95.3	89.9	101.2	92.2	81.3	100.5	94.2	101.6	97.6
1968	104.9	99.8	110.7	101.9	86.9	109.8	105.1	112.4	109.3
1969	110.7	104.3	116.1	105.0	91.2	116.0	107.4	119.5	116.7
1970	115.1	108.2	119.7	108.3	94.8	120.8	110.8	126.4	122.4
1971	118.7	110.3	124.6	112.8	96.6	124.9	112.3	131.4	127.3
1972	122.8	113.0	127.7	115.8	99.4	128.3	113.7	135.4	132.1
1973	127.2	115.4	130.5	120.0	102.8	131.1	118.4	142.1	136.8
1974 *	136.4	122.9	136.3	125.1	109.7	136.0	126.2	150.6	145.1

Date / Date / Fecha	341 Paper, paper products / Papier, articles en papier / Papel, artículos de papel	351 Industrial chemicals / Chimie industrielle / Química industrial	352 Other chemical products / Autres produits chimiques / Otros productos químicos	355 Rubber products / Produits en caoutchouc / Productos de caucho	356 Plastic products / Articles en matière plastique / Productos plásticos	361 Pottery, china, earthenware / Grès, porcelaines, faïences / Barro, loza, porcelana	362 Glass, and glass products / Verre / Vidrio	369 Other non-metallic mineral products / Autres produits minéraux / Otros productos minerales	371 Iron and steel basic industries / Sidérurgie / Industrias básicas de hierro y acero	383 Electrical machinery and apparatus / Machines et appareils électriques / Maquinaria y aparatos eléctricos
1965	101.8	107.9	102.3	107.2	90.7	90.3	98.6	101.5	127.9	101.9
1966	103.7	112.3	106.1	111.0	97.4	93.5	102.0	105.0	131.3	103.3
1967	108.9	119.2	110.8	118.2	102.5	97.6	106.6	110.0	136.0	108.0
1968	116.7	125.0	120.6	128.3	111.9	104.7	114.9	117.6	144.7	116.4
1969	126.0	130.5	126.7	133.9	120.5	112.0	123.2	124.5	148.0	123.0
1970	130.8	136.7	134.0	140.1	125.2	125.2	134.2	137.1	153.2	127.8
1971	135.3	140.5	139.3	146.1	130.9	130.0	139.0	142.2	157.7	132.6
1972	139.0	144.5	143.0	150.9	135.7	133.2	142.4	146.3	161.6	136.9
1973	147.5	149.7	147.0	155.3	137.7	136.8	145.6	151.5	166.1	141.8
1974 *	155.7	158.6	154.6	164.3	142.0	142.4	153.6	158.5	178.4	149.3

[1] Socialised sector. Incl. Byelorussian SSR, shown separately in this table. [2] Incl. salaried employees.

[1] *Secteur socialisé. Y compris la RSS de Biélorussie, figurant séparément dans ce tableau.* [2] *Y compris les employés.*

[1] Sector socializado. Incl. la RSS de Bielorrusia, que figura separadamente en este cuadro. [2] Incl. los empleados.

WAGES

19 B

19
Wages in manufacturing
Salaires dans les industries manufacturières
Salarios en las industrias manufactureras

B
By industry
Par industrie
Por industria

RSS de Biélorussie [1]

Average monthly earnings [2] *(roubles)*
Gains mensuels moyens [2] *(roubles)*
Promedio de ganancias por mes [2] *(roubles)*

Date / Date / Fecha	31			321	322; 324	323	324	331
	Food, beverages, tobacco / *Aliments, boissons, tabac* / Alimentos, bebidas, tabaco			Textiles	Clothing, footwear / *Habillement, chaussures* / Vestido, calzado	Leather, leather products / *Cuir, articles en cuir* / Cuero, artículos de cuero	Footwear / *Chaussures* / Calzado	Wood / *Bois* / Madera
	Total	Beverages / *Boissons* / Bebidas	Tobacco / *Tabac* / Tabaco					
1972	108.1	102.4	129.3	112.1	103.1	129.3	115.3	117.1
1973	111.5	103.9	131.4	115.9	104.2	130.6	116.6	121.5
1974 *	114.2	106.8	135.9	119.5	107.1	134.1	121.8	126.0

Date / Date / Fecha	332	341	355	36	37	38	
	Furniture / *Ameublement* / Mobiliario	Paper, paper products / *Papier, articles en papier* / Papel, artículos de papel	Rubber products / *Industrie du caoutchouc* / Productos de caucho	Non-metallic mineral products / *Produits minéraux non métalliques* / Productos minerales no metálicos	Basic metal industries / *Industrie métallurgique de base* / Industrias metalúrgicas básicas	Metal products, machinery, etc. / *Produits métalliques, machines, etc.* / Productos metálicos, maquinaria, etc.	
						Total	Electrical machinery / *Machines électriques* / Maquinaria eléctrica
1972	121.8	112.9	134.3	132.3	146.7	138.8	127.9
1973	127.2	117.4	139.1	138.2	150.2	143.6	131.3
1974 *	133.9	118.3	151.0	143.7	152.5	148.8	136.4

[1] Socialised sector. [2] Incl. salaried employees.   [1] *Secteur socialisé.* [2] *Y compris les employés.*   [1] Sector socializado. [2] Incl. los empleados.

20 Wages in mining and quarrying
Salaires dans les industries extractives
Salarios en las minas y canteras

Earnings *(E.G.)* or rates *(R.T.)*
per hour *(h.)*, day *(d.j.)*,
week *(w.s.)* or month *(m.)*

Gains *(E.G.)* ou taux *(R.T.)*
par heure *(h.)*, jour *(d.j.)*,
semaine *(w.s.)* ou mois *(m.)*

Ganancias *(E.G.)* o tarifas *(R.T.)*
por hora *(h.)*, día *(d.j.)*,
semana *(w.s.)* o mes *(m.)*

Date / Date / Fecha	AFRICA — AFRIQUE — AFRICA						Maroc — Coal mining / Mines de charbon / Minas de carbón — Underground workers / Ouvriers du fond / Obreros bajo la superficie	Mauritius — Salt mining / Mines de sel / Minas de sal
	Algérie	Egypt	Ghana	Haute-Volta	Malawi	Mali		
	(E.G./h.) [1]	*(E.G./w.s.)* [2]	*(E.G./m.)* [3, 4]	*(E.G./m.)*	*(E.G./m.)* [3]	*(E.G./h.)* [4]	*(E.G./m.)*	*(E.G./d.j.)* [6]
	Dinars	Piastres	Cedis	Francs (CFA)	Kwacha	Francs	Dirhams	Rupees
1965	.	469	44.11	.	.	.	226.42	.
1966	.	529	57.30	.	.	.	205.95	3.13
1967	.	527	54.99	.	.	.	222.01	3.48
1968	.	455	52.09	.	17.37	.	...	3.29
1969	1.81	673	71.18	13 396	20.65	.	366.80	3.64
1970	1.69	502	81.58	13 301	17.53	.	374.00	3.73
1971	2.59	...	94.56	13 401	15.23	72.31	409.47	4.17
1972	3.27	...	80.51 * [5]	...	16.84	72.54	...	4.20
1973	2.68	...	...	...	18.33	85.15	...	4.30
1974	...	...	...	...	24.43	111.22	...	5.06

Date / Date / Fecha	AFRICA — AFRIQUE — AFRICA		Zambia		AMERICA — AMÉRIQUE — AMÉRICA		Belize — Petroleum / Pétrole / Petróleo	
	Sierra Leone	Tanzania (Tanganyika)	Zambians / Zambiens / Zambianos	Others / Autres / Otros	Argentina — Stone quarrying / Carrières de pierre / Canteras de piedra	Barbados		Bolivia
	(E.G./w.s.) [7]	*(E.G./m.)* [8]	*(E.G./m.)* [3, 9]		*(E.G./h.)* [11]	*(R.T./w.s.)*	*(R.T./h.)* [13]	*(E.G./m.)* [3]
	Leones	Shillings	Kwacha	Kwacha	Pesos	Dollars	Cents	Pesos
1965	.	238	68.8	448.2	69.51	24.00	47-50	.
1966	7.24	298	77.9	549.9	92.25	30.00	47-77	.
1967	7.60	325	110.2	634.0	124.77	30.00	47-77	.
1968	6.91	360	104.0	633.7	127.38	33.00	47-77	.
1969	8.77	381	117.7	681.2	140.06	33.00	52-84	.
1970	8.62	446	122.8	583.7	1.65 [12]	47.68	52-84	1 033
1971	8.55	...	129.7	610.8	2.33	57.29	...	1 090
1972	9.06	...	131.3	351.7	3.42	57.50	...	1 225
1973	9.57	...	131.3 [10]	436.7 [10]	5.37	62.09	...	1 345
1974	9.83	...	142.0 [10]	456.4 [10]	...	...	...	1 745

EXPLANATORY NOTES: See p. 585.

[1] April of each year. [2] Oct. of each year. [3] Incl. salaried employees. [4] Dec. of each year. [5] Sep. [6] March and Sep. of each year. [7] Adults only. May and Nov. of each year. [8] Adult males; June of each year. [9] Beginning 1967: fourth quarter of each year. 1965-69: incl. the value of payments in kind. [10] June. [11] Minimum earnings; unskilled workers. [12] New currency introduced in Jan. 1970: 1 new peso = 100 old pesos. [13] Prevailing rates.

NOTES EXPLICATIVES: Voir p. 589.

[1] Avril de chaque année. [2] Oct. de chaque année. [3] Y compris les employés. [4] Déc. de chaque année. [5] Sept. [6] Mars et sept. de chaque année. [7] Adultes seulement. Mai et nov. de chaque année. [8] Hommes adultes; juin de chaque année. [9] A partir de 1967 : quatrième trimestre de chaque année. 1965-1969 : y compris la valeur des paiements en nature. [10] Juin. [11] Gains minima; ouvriers non qualifiés. [12] Nouvelle monnaie introduite en janv. 1970: 1 nouveau peso = 100 anciens pesos. [13] Taux prédominants.

NOTAS EXPLICATIVAS: Véase p. 594.

[1] Abril de cada año. [2] Oct. de cada año. [3] Incl. los empleados. [4] Dic. de cada año. [5] Sept. [6] Marzo y sept. de cada año. [7] Adultos solamente. Mayo y nov. de cada año. [8] Hombres adultos; junio de cada año. [9] A partir de 1967: cuarto trimestre de cada año. 1965-1969: incl. el valor de los pagos en especie. [10] Junio. [11] Ganancias mínimas; obreros no calificados [12] Nueva moneda adoptada en enero de 1970: 1 nuevo peso = 100 antiguos. [13] Tarifas predominantes.

20 Wages in mining and quarrying
Salaires dans les industries extractives
Salarios en las minas y canteras

Earnings *(E.G.)* or rates *(R.T.)*
per hour *(h.)*, day *(d.j.)*,
week *(w.s.)* or month *(m.)*

Gains *(E.G.)* ou taux *(R.T.)*
par heure *(h.)*, jour *(d.j.)*,
semaine *(w.s.)* ou mois *(m.)*

Ganancias *(E.G.)* o tarifas *(R.T.)*
por hora *(h.)*, día *(d.j.)*,
semana *(w.s.)* o mes *(m.)*

		AMERICA — AMÉRIQUE — AMÉRICA						
Date / Date / Fecha	Brésil	Canada				Colombia	Chile	República Dominicana
		All mining and quarrying / Ensemble des industries extractives / Todas las minas y canteras	Metal mining / Mines métallifères / Minas metalíferas	Coal mining / Mines de charbon / Minas de carbón		Petroleum extraction / Extraction du pétrole / Extracción de petróleo	All mining / Ensemble des mines / Todas las minas	
	(E.G./m.) [1]	E.G./h.)	(E.G./w.s.)	(E.G./h.)		(E.G./h.)	(E.G./m.) [2,3]	(E.G./m.) [1]
	Cruzeiros	Dollars	Dollars	Dollars	Dollars	Pesos	Escudos	Pesos
1965	.	2.43	103.30	2.52	1.96	6.22	282.09	159.49
1966	151.72	2.60	109.77	2.70	2.02	6.82	369.30	164.11
1967	210.59	2.84	119.09	2.98	2.13	7.58	650.23	164.76
1968	242.14	3.07	128.28	3.20	2.34	8.55	811.07	163.70
1969	312.83	3.28	135.94	3.38	2.59	9.61	1 222.67	183.80
1970	552.44	3.70	152.10	3.83	3.49	9.96	1 835.31	200.27
1971	...	4.04	163.22	4.17	3.51	9.55	2 796.87	212.54
1972	825.14	4.34	174.90	4.48	3.92	9.99	3 360.48	207.57
1973	...	4.82	197.14	4.94	4.45	...	9 996.88	315.67
1974	...	5.50 *	222.20 *	5.65 *	5.25 *	...	...	...

	AMERICA — AMÉRIQUE — AMÉRICA							
Date / Date / Fecha	Ecuador		Guyana	México	Nicaragua	Puerto Rico	Surinam	Trinidad and Tobago — Mining [6] / Mines [6] / Minas [6]
	(E.G./h.)	(E.G./w.s.)	(E.G./w.s.)	(E.G./h.) [4]	(E.G./h.) [5]	(E.G./h.)	(E.G./m.)	(R.T.) [7]
	Sucres	Sucres	Dollars	Pesos	Córdobas	Cents	Guilders	(1970 = 100)
1965	5.77	396	.	5.01	1.66	135.7	.	76.8
1966	5.84	402	59.49	5.52	1.58	142.5	.	81.7
1967	6.08	401	52.43	5.86	2.85	154.6	.	84.1
1968	6.15	394	73.01	6.41	3.21	173.3	.	86.5
1969	10.50	590	75.23	6.16	2.76	185.6	.	97.0
1970	10.50	594	75.24	6.51	2.98	194.0	.	**100.0**
1971	11.80	622	75.98	7.70	...	207.0	299	103.5
1972	13.20	702	81.30	9.78	...	218.0	313	123.6
1973	15.80	804	87.25	11.64	...	226.0	328	131.8
1974	...	...	...	...	...	238.0	...	151.1

EXPLANATORY NOTES: See p. 585.

NOTES EXPLICATIVES: Voir p. 589.

NOTAS EXPLICATIVAS: Véase pág. 594.

[1] Incl. salaried employees. [2] April of each year. [3] Incl. the value of payments in kind. [4] Oct. of each year. [5] Males only. [6] Incl. asphalt mining and oil refining. [7] Minimum rates. Adults only. May and Nov. of each year.

[1] Y compris les employés. [2] Avril de chaque année. [3] Y compris la valeur des paiements en nature. [4] Oct. de chaque année. [5] Hommes seulement. [6] Y compris les mines d'asphalte et les raffineries de pétrole. [7] Taux minima. Adultes seulement. Mai et nov. de chaque année.

[1] Incl. los empleados. [2] Abril de cada año. [3] Incl. el valor de los pagos en especie. [4] Oct. de cada año. [5] Hombres solamente. [6] Incl. las minas de asfalto y las refinerías de petróleo. [7] Tarifas mínimas. Adultos solamente. Mayo y nov. de cada año.

20 Wages in mining and quarrying
Salaires dans les industries extractives
Salarios en las minas y canteras

Earnings *(E.G.)* or rates *(R.T.)*
per hour *(h.)*, day *(d.j.)*,
week *(w.s.)* or month *(m.)*

Gains *(E.G.)* ou taux *(R.T.)*
par heure *(h.)*, jour *(d.j.)*,
semaine *(w.s.)* ou mois *(m.)*

Ganancias *(E.G.)* o tarifas *(R.T.)*
por hora *(h.)*, día *(d.j.)*,
semana *(w.s.)* o mes *(m.)*

	AMERICA — AMÉRIQUE — AMÉRICA					
	United States					
Date / Date / Fecha	Bituminous coal mining / Mines de charbon bitumineux / Minas de carbón bituminoso	Metal mining / Mines métallifères / Minas metalíferas	Crude petroleum [1] / Pétrole brut [1] / Petróleo crudo [1]	Bituminous coal mining / Mines de charbon bitumineux / Minas de carbón bituminoso	Metal mining / Mines métallifères / Minas metalíferas	Crude petroleum [1] / Pétrole brut [1] / Petróleo crudo [1]
	(E.G./h.)			*(E.G./w.s.)*		
	$	$	$	$	$	$
1965	3.49	3.06	2.74	140.26	127.30	116.18
1966	3.66	3.17	2.87	149.74	133.77	122.26
1967	3.75	3.24	3.03	153.28	136.40	129.38
1968	3.86	3.42	3.22	155.17	148.09	137.82
1969	4.24	3.64	3.43	169.18	156.88	150.23
1970	4.58	3.88	3.57	186.41	165.68	153.51
1971	4.86	4.12	3.75	196.83	171.39	159.75
1972	5.35	4.49	4.00	218.28	186.34	172.00
1973	5.74	4.82	4.29	228.45	203.40	184.90
1974	6.26	5.43	4.82	238.37	226.97	214.97

	AMERICA — AMÉRIQUE — AMÉRICA		ASIA — ASIE — ASIA		
	Venezuela		Burma		
Date / Date / Fecha	Petroleum / Pétrole / Petróleo	Iron / Fer / Hierro	Metal mining / Mines métallifères / Minas metalíferas — Males / Hommes / Hombres	Females / Femmes / Mujeres	Cyprus
	(E.G./m.)		*(E.G./m.)* [2]		*(E.G./w.s.)* [5]
	Bolívares	Bolívares	Kyats	Kyats	Pounds
1965	1 624.0	1 519.0	134.14	160.82	7.99
1966	1 919.5	1 585.3	150.79	161.87	8.76
1967	2 112.3	1 604.8	139.58	143.95	8.51
1968	1 926.3	1 571.4	138.57	125.35	8.60
1969	1 895.4	1 563.6	145.03	131.82	10.22
1970	2 351.0	1 982.0	150.94	114.75	11.43
1971	2 412.0	1 953.0	149.28	116.05	13.37
1972	2 400.0	2 169.0	143.19 [3]	99.48 [3]	16.53
1973	2 310.0	2 189.0	155.78 [4]	128.43 [4]	18.77
1974	2 442.0 *	2 453.0 *	...	...	19.52

EXPLANATORY NOTES: See p. 585.

[1] Incl. natural gas. [2] Incl. salaried employees. [3] April and Sep. [4] March and Sep. [5] Adults only. Oct. of each year, except 1969: Sep.

NOTES EXPLICATIVES: Voir p. 589.

[1] *Y compris le gaz naturel.* [2] *Y compris les employés.* [3] *Avril et sept.* [4] *Mars et sept.* [5] *Adultes seulement. Oct. de chaque année, sauf pour 1969 : sept.*

NOTAS EXPLICATIVAS: Véase pág. 594.

[1] Incl. el gas natural. [2] Incl. los empleados. [3] Abril y sept. [4] Marzo y sept. [5] Adultos solamente. Oct. de cada año, salvo 1969: sept.

WAGES

20 Wages in mining and quarrying
Salaires dans les industries extractives
Salarios en las minas y canteras

Earnings *(E.G.)* or rates *(R.T.)*
per hour *(h.)*, day *(d.j.)*,
week *(w.s.)* or month *(m.)*

Gains *(E.G.)* ou taux *(R.T.)*
par heure *(h.)*, jour *(d.j.)*,
semaine *(w.s.)* ou mois *(m.)*

Ganancias *(E.G.)* o tarifas *(R.T.)*
por hora *(h.)*, día *(d.j.)*,
semana *(w.s.)* o mes *(m.)*

Date / Date / Fecha	ASIA — ASIE — ASIA					
	India		Israel	Japan		
	Coal mining / Mines de charbon / Minas de carbón	Other mining and quarrying / Autres industries extractives / Otras minas y canteras		All mining and quarrying / Ensemble des industries extractives / Todas las minas y canteras	Coal mining / Mines de charbon / Minas de carbón	Metal mining / Mines métallifères / Minas metalíferas
	(E.G./w.s.) [1]	(E.G./d.j.) [1]	(E.G./d.j.) [2]	(E.G./m.) [2,4]		
	Rupees	Rupees	Pounds	Yen	Yen	Yen
1965	31.34	3.22	22.0	41 650	41 223	46 171
1966	34.56	3.67	24.9	46 506	45 503	51 953
1967	46.31	4.36	28.4	49 887 [5]	48 338 [5]	56 995 [5]
1968	49.77	4.72	30.6 [3]	56 318	54 505	64 822
1969	52.31	5.49	32.4	65 884	63 329	75 184
1970	54.19	5.32	35.3	79 209 [5]	74 290 [5]	93 379 [5]
1971	56.27	5.78	43.0	90 887	85 529	106 209
1972	60.17	6.46	50.5	103 679	100 710	117 384
1973	72.66	7.88	58.7	123 249 [5]	122 078 [5]	133 477 [5]
1974	81.59 *	...	86.1	171 810	183 155	183 425

Date / Date / Fecha	ASIA — ASIE — ASIA				
	Korea, Rep. of	Malaysia / West Malaysia / Tin mining / Mines d'étain / Minas de estaño	Philippines	Singapore	République arabe syrienne / Phosphate / Phosphate / Fosfato / Males [11] / Hommes [11] / Hombres [11]
	(E.G./m.) [2,6]	(E.G./m.) [2,8]	(E.G./m.)	(E.G./h.) [8,10]	(E.G./w.s.) [12]
	Won	Dollars	Pesos	Cents	Pounds
1965	7 130	177	177	121	.
1966	8 410	178	192	127	.
1967	10 990	187	220	119	.
1968	12 090	204	226	122	.
1969	15 100 [7]	163	239	126	.
1970	17 921	176	245	130	71.15
1971	21 564	185	276	133	74.55
1972	25 586	175	298	127	80.40
1973	30 415	182	326	137	86.95 [13]
1974	41 068	208	364 [9]	163	77.95 [13]

EXPLANATORY NOTES: See p. 585.

[1] Dec. of each year. [2] Incl. salaried employees. [3] Series replacing former series. [4] Incl. family allowances, mid- and end-of-year bonuses. [5] Sampling design revised. [6] Incl. family allowances. [7] Scope of series enlarged. [8] July of each year. [9] Jan.-Sep. [10] Beginning 1969: adults only. [11] Adults only. [12] Nov. of each year. [13] May.

NOTES EXPLICATIVES: Voir p. 589.

[1] *Déc. de chaque année.* [2] *Y compris les employés.* [3] *Série remplaçant la précédente.* [4] *Y compris les allocations familiales et les primes de mi- et de fin d'année.* [5] *Plan d'échantillonnage révisé.* [6] *Y compris les allocations familiales.* [7] *Portée de la série élargie.* [8] *Juillet de chaque année.* [9] *Janv.-sept.* [10] *A partir de 1969: adultes seulement.* [11] *Adultes seulement.* [12] *Nov. de chaque année.* [13] *Mai.*

NOTAS EXPLICATIVAS: Véase pág. 594.

[1] Dic. de cada año. [2] Incl. los empleados. [3] Serie que substituye a la anterior. [4] Incl. las asignaciones familiares y las primas de la mitad y de fin de año. [5] Diseño de la muestra revisado. [6] Incl. las asignaciones familiares. [7] El alcance de la serie es mayor. [8] Julio de cada año. [9] Enero-sept. [10] A partir de 1969: adultos solamente. [11] Adultos solamente. [12] Nov. de cada año. [13] Mayo.

20 Wages in mining and quarrying
Salaires dans les industries extractives
Salarios en las minas y canteras

Earnings *(E.G.)* or rates *(R.T.)*
per hour *(h.)*, day *(d.j.)*,
week *(w.s.)* or month *(m.)*

Gains *(E.G.)* ou taux *(R.T.)*
par heure *(h.)*, jour *(d.j.)*,
semaine *(w.s.)* ou mois *(m.)*

Ganancias *(E.G.)* o tarifas *(R.T.)*
por hora *(h.)*, día *(d.j.)*,
semana *(w.s.)* o mes *(m.)*

	EUROPE — EUROPE — EUROPA					
	Austria		Belgique	Bulgarie [4]	Czechoslovakia [5]	España
Date / Date / Fecha	All mining — Ensemble des mines — Todas las minas		Males — Hommes — Hombres			
	Hewers underground — Piqueurs du fond — Barreteros bajo la superficie	Other underground workers — Autres ouvriers du fond — Otros obreros bajo la superficie				
	(R.T./h.) [1]		*(E.G./h.)* [2]	*(E.G./m.)*	*(E.G./m.)*	*(E.G./h.)* [6]
	Schilling	Schilling	Francs	Leva	Korunas	Pesetas
1965	12.90	10.30	55.84	120.6	2 158	30.01
1966	14.70	11.50	59.68	126.1	2 165	36.21
1967	14.70	11.50	62.97	139.8	2 237	41.62
1968	15.70	12.30	62.20	148.8	2 394	46.02
1969	17.10	13.40	69.35	154.6	2 594	52.43
1970	17.90	14.00	85.97	165.5	2 637	58.98
1971	21.50	15.60	96.02	171.9	2 803	65.47
1972	24.54	17.34	108.69 [3]	177.5	2 856	76.42
1973	28.00	19.13	123.85	193.5	2 927	89.54
1974	32.00	20.80	150.07	...	3 001	117.17

	EUROPE — EUROPE — EUROPA					
	Finland	France			Germany, Fed. Rep. of △	
Date / Date / Fecha	Metal mining — Mines métallifères — Minas metalíferas	Hard-coal and lignite mining — Mines de houille et de lignite — Minas de hulla y de lignito			Males — Hommes — Hombres	
		All workers — Ensemble des ouvriers — Todos los obreros	Underground workers — Ouvriers du fond — Obreros bajo la superficie	Surface workers — Ouvriers du jour — Obreros de la superficie	All mining — Ensemble des mines — Todas las minas	Coal mining — Mines de charbon — Minas de carbón
	(E.G./h.) [7]	*(E.G./m.)*			*(E.G./h.)*	*(E.G./h.)*
	Markkaa	Francs	Francs	Francs	Mark	Mark
1965	3.76	34.16	36.60	28.73	4.81	4.93
1966	4.10	35.52	37.97	30.01	4.99	5.08
1967	4.42	37.07	39.67	31.47	5.14	5.25
1968	4.92	40.68	43.61	34.91	5.33	5.45
1969	5.31	43.43	46.50	37.55	5.66	5.70
1970	5.95	47.10	50.43	41.03	6.55	6.64
1971	7.00	1 286 [8]	1 358 [8]	1 144 [8]	7.26	7.32
1972	8.04	1 409	1 499	1 244	7.84	7.89
1973	9.26	1 659	1 385	1 558	8.64	8.69
1974	11.15	...	...	...	9.84 [9]	9.92 [9]

EXPLANATORY NOTES: See p. 585.   NOTES EXPLICATIVES: Voir p. 589.   NOTAS EXPLICATIVAS: Véase pág. 594.

[1] Minimum rates. [2] Oct. of each year. [3] New industrial classification. [4] Socialised sector. [5] State industry. [6] Incl. salaried employees. [7] Males only. Incl. the value of payments in kind. [8] Series replacing former series: 1965-70: earnings per day. [9] Sampling design revised.

[1] Taux minima. [2] Oct. de chaque année. [3] Nouvelle classification industrielle. [4] Secteur socialisé. [5] Industrie d'Etat. [6] Y compris les employés. [7] Hommes seulement. Y compris la valeur des paiements en nature. [8] Série remplaçant la précédente : 1965-1970 : gains par jour. [9] Plan d'échantillonnage révisé.

[1] Tarifas mínimas. [2] Oct. de cada año. [3] Nueva clasificación industrial. [4] Sector socializado. [5] Industria de Estado. [6] Incl. los empleados. [7] Hombres solamente. Incl. el valor de los pagos en especie. [8] Serie que substituye a la anterior: 1965-1970: ganancias por día. [9] Diseño de la muestra revisado.

701

20 Wages in mining and quarrying
Salaires dans les industries extractives
Salarios en las minas y canteras

Earnings *(E.G.)* or rates *(R.T.)*
per hour *(h.)*, day *(d.j.)*,
week *(w.s.)* or month *(m.)*

Gains *(E.G.)* ou taux *(R.T.)*
par heure *(h.)*, jour *(d.j.)*,
semaine *(w.s.)* ou mois *(m.)*

Ganancias *(E.G.)* o tarifas *(R.T.)*
por hora *(h.)*, día *(d.j.)*,
semana *(w.s.)* o mes *(m.)*

EUROPE — EUROPE — EUROPA

Date / Date / Fecha	Hongrie [1] — All mining and quarrying / Ensemble des industries extractives / Todas las minas y canteras	Hongrie [1] — Coal mining / Mines de charbon / Minas de carbón	Ireland	Italie	Luxembourg — All mining and quarrying / Ensemble des industries extractives / Todas las minas y canteras	Luxembourg — Iron ore mining / Extraction du minerai de fer / Extracción de mineral de hierro	Malta — Stone quarrying and clay pits / Carrières de pierre et d'argile / Canteras de piedra y arcilla
	(E.G./m.) [2,3]		*(E.G./h.)* [5,6]	*(E.G./h.)* [2]	*(E.G./h.)* [8,9]		*(E.G./h.)* [9,11]
	Forints	Forints	Pence	Lire	Francs	Francs	Cents
1965	2 423	2 532	27.6	442	61.85	77.27	15.0
1966	2 535	2 670	33.0	469	72.80	79.64	15.4
1967	2 600	2 751	37.5	496	72.39	78.60	16.4
1968	2 657	2 826	41.8	521	80.64	89.90	17.7
1969	2 763	2 951	47.5 [7]	559	85.16	94.02	19.8
1970	2 945 [4]	3 157 [4]	51.5	676	98.72	108.39	24.6
1971	3 008	3 220	58.8	783	104.83	113.84	25.8
1972	3 118	3 339	67.7	854	117.15 [10]	128.59 [10]	25.6
1973	3 471	3 724	83.8	1 051	127.94	142.72	...
1974	3 707 *	3 975 *	99.5	1 322 *	159.36	...	...

EUROPE — EUROPE — EUROPA

Date / Date / Fecha	Norway	Pays-Bas — Hard-coal mining / Mines de houille / Minas de hulla — All workers / Ensemble des ouvriers / Todos los obreros	Pays-Bas — Underground workers / Ouvriers du fond / Obreros bajo la superficie	Pays-Bas — Surface workers / Ouvriers du jour / Obreros de la superficie	Pologne [12] — Hard-coal mining / Mines de houille / Minas de hulla	Portugal	Suisse — Males [9] — Hommes [9] — Hombres [9] — Skilled and semi-skilled / Qualifiés et semi-qualifiés / Calificados y semicalificados	Suisse — Unskilled / Non qualifiés / No calificados
	(E.G./h.) [2,9]	*(E.G./h.)*			*(E.G./m.)* [2,11]	*(E.G./h.)* [13]	*(E.G./h.)* [14]	
	Kroner	Guilders	Guilders	Guilders	Zlotys	Escudos	Francs	Francs
1965	9.90	4.09	4.69	3.06	2 915	42.80	5.29	4.63
1966	10.98	4.40	4.98	3.42	3 002	48.50	5.59	4.98
1967	11.68	4.68	5.21	3.77	3 092	53.20	6.13	5.25
1968	12.51	4.99	5.50	4.13	3 274	55.90	5.52	5.63
1969	13.52	5.40	5.92	4.55	3 716	61.30	6.85	5 87
1970	14.92	6.05	6.57	5.35	3 781	73.40	7.46	6.36
1971	16.50	6.45	6.89	5.76	3 968	11.20 [7]	8.33	7.25
1972	17.83	...	...	...	4 146	13.20	8.87	7.78
1973	19.59	...	...	...	4 478	14.90	...	...
1974	22.85	...	...	...	5 480 *	...	...	...

EXPLANATORY NOTES: See p. 585.

NOTES EXPLICATIVES: Voir p. 589.

NOTAS EXPLICATIVAS: Véase pág. 594.

[1] State industry. [2] Incl. the value of payments in kind. [3] Incl. loyalty money. [4] Revised series. [5] Sep. of each year, except for 1965-68: Oct. [6] 1965-68: adult males. Beginning 1969: wage-earners (incl. juveniles) on adult rates of pay. [7] Series replacing former series. [8] Oct. of each year. [9] Adult males. [10] New industrial classification. [11] Incl. salaried employees. [12] Socialised sector. [13] 1965-1970: earnings per day. [14] Accident insurance statistics.

[1] *Industrie d'Etat.* [2] *Y compris la valeur des paiements en nature.* [3] *Y compris les primes d'assiduité.* [4] *Série révisée.* [5] *Sept. de chaque année, sauf pour 1965-1968: oct.* [6] *1965-1968: hommes adultes. A partir de 1969: ouvriers (y compris les jeunes gens) rémunérés sur la base de taux de salaire pour adultes.* [7] *Série remplaçant la précédente.* [8] *Oct. de chaque année.* [9] *Hommes adultes.* [10] *Nouvelle classification industrielle.* [11] *Y compris les employés.* [12] *Secteur socialisé.* [13] *1965-1970: gains par jour.* [14] *Statistiques d'assurance-accidents.*

[1] Industria de Estado. [2] Incl. el valor de los pagos en especie. [3] Incl. las primas de asiduidad. [4] Serie revisada. [5] Sept. de cada año, salvo 1965-1968: oct. [6] 1965-1968: hombres adultos. A partir de 1969: obreros (incl. los jóvenes) pagados sobre la base de tarifas de salarios para adultos. [7] Serie que substituye a la anterior. [8] Oct. de cada año. [9] Hombres adultos. [10] Nueva clasificación industrial. [11] Incl. los empleados. [12] Sector socializado. [13] 1965-1970: ganancias por día. [14] Estadísticas del seguro de accidentes.

20 Wages in mining and quarrying
Salaires dans les industries extractives
Salarios en las minas y canteras

Earnings *(E.G.)* or rates *(R.T.)*
per hour *(h.)*, day *(d.j.)*,
week *(w.s.)* or month *(m.)*

Gains *(E.G.)* ou taux *(R.T.)*
par heure *(h.)*, jour *(d.j.)*,
semaine *(w.s.)* ou mois *(m.)*

Ganancias *(E.G.)* o tarifas *(R.T.)*
por hora *(h.)*, día *(d.j.)*,
semana *(w.s.)* o mes *(m.)*

Date / Date / Fecha	EUROPE — EUROPE — EUROPA						OCEANIA — OCÉANIE — OCEANÍA	
	Sweden		United Kingdom			Yugoslavia [7]		Fiji
	Iron mining / Mines de fer / Minas de hierro	Turquie	Coal mining / Mines de charbon / Minas de carbón	Other mining and quarrying / Autres industries extractives / Otras minas y canteras		Coal mining / Mines de charbon / Minas de carbón	Australia	Mining / Mines / Minas
	(E.G./h.) [1,2]	*(E.G./d.j.)* [4]	*(E.G./w.s.)* [5,6]	*(E.G./h.)* [6]		*(E.G./m.)* [4]	*(E.G./h.)* [4,6]	*(R.T./d.j.)* [9]
	Kronor	Liras	£	Pence		Dinars	Dollars	Dollars
1965	10.95	17.00	21.21	37.5		.	.	1.92
1966	11.78	21.39	22.16	39.4		667	1.77	1.98
1967	12.46	22.33	22.92	41.8		719	1.86	1.99
1968	13.23	27.09	24.12	44.4		824	1.97	2.37
1969	14.32	27.01	25.10	48.0 [3]		926	2.13	2.38
1970	16.26	31.39	28.01	55.7		1 104	2.32	2.63
1971	18.70 [3]	33.09	31.65	63.0		1 452	2.68	2.76
1972	20.83	35.64	38.21	71.7		1 617	2.90 [8]	3.06
1973	22.21	48.31	42.43	81.7		2 106	3.28	3.96
1974	...	59.60	58.21	101.0		2 868	4.43 *	...

Date / Date / Fecha	OCEANIA — OCÉANIE — OCEANÍA				Nouvelle-Calédonie	URSS [7,14]	RSS de Biélorussie [7]	RSS d'Ukraine [7]
	New Zealand							
	Coal mining / Mines de charbon / Minas de carbón	Other mining and quarrying / Autres industries extractives / Otras minas y canteras	Coal mining — Mines de charbon / Minas de carbón		Labourers [12] / Manœuvres [12] / Obreros no calificados [12]	Month / Mois / Mes	Month / Mois / Mes	Month / Mois / Mes
			Truckers / Wagonniers / Vagoneros	Labourers (surface) / Manœuvres (jour) / Obreros no calif. (superficie)				
	(E.G./h.) [4,10]		*(R.T./w.s.)* [1,11]		*(R.T./h.)* [13]	*(E.G.)* [4]	*(E.G.)* [4]	*(E.G.)* [4]
	Dollars	Dollars	Dollars	Dollars	Francs (CFP)	Roubles	Roubles	Roubles
1965	1.37	1.01	.	.	75.69	166.9	.	178.4
1966	1.32	1.03	28.59 [12]	28.13 [12]	77.00	168.7	.	180.0
1967	1.43	1.08	29.72	30.88	81.09	170.2	.	181.4
1968	1.58	1.12	30.75	31.92	83.23	180.4	.	184.6
1969	1.49	1.24	32.26	33.47	102.35	187.0	.	189.4
1970	1.66	1.46	39.14	38.52	110.42	196.6	.	199.2
1971	1.83	1.63	46.97	44.71	120.10	206.5	.	205.4
1972	2.10	1.76	50.40	47.97	...	209.1	139.0	210.5
1973	2.34	2.01	59.47	54.83	...	216.4	141.3	215.2
1974	2.78	2.31	71.38	63.61	...	228.7 *	148.8 *	221.0 *

EXPLANATORY NOTES: See p. 585.

¹ Adult males. ² Incl. holiday and sick-leave payments and the value of payments in kind. ³ New industrial classification. ⁴ Incl. salaried employees. ⁵ Excl. Northern Ireland. ⁶ Adult males; Oct. of each year. ⁷ Socialised sector. ⁸ Scope of series enlarged. ⁹ June of each year. ¹⁰ Incl. the value of payments in kind. April and Oct. of each year. ¹¹ Minimum rates. ¹² First category Dec. of each year. ¹³ Incl. production bonuses. ¹⁴ Incl. Byelorussian SSR and Ukrainian SSR, shown separately in this table.

NOTES EXPLICATIVES: Voir p. 589.

¹ *Hommes adultes.* ² *Y compris les versements au titre des vacances et congés de maladie et la valeur des paiements en nature.* ³ *Nouvelle classification industrielle.* ⁴ *Y compris les employés.* ⁵ *Non compris l'Irlande du Nord.* ⁶ *Hommes adultes; oct. de chaque année.* ⁷ *Secteur socialisé.* ⁸ *Portée de la série élargie.* ⁹ *Juin de chaque année.* ¹⁰ *Y compris la valeur des paiements en nature. Avril et oct. de chaque année.* ¹¹ *Taux minima.* ¹² *Première catégorie. Déc. de chaque année.* ¹³ *Y compris les primes de productivité.* ¹⁴ *Y compris les RSS de Biélorussie et d'Ukraine, figurant séparément dans ce tableau.*

NOTAS EXPLICATIVAS: Véase pág. 594.

¹ Hombres adultos. ² Incl. los pagos por vacaciones y licencias de enfermedad y el valor de los pagos en especie. ³ Nueva clasificación industrial. ⁴ Incl. los empleados. ⁵ Excl. Irlanda del Norte. ⁶ Hombres adultos; oct. de cada año. ⁷ Sector socializado. ⁸ El alcance de la serie es mayor. ⁹ Junio de cada año. ¹⁰ Incl. el valor de los pagos en especie. Abril y oct. de cada año. ¹¹ Tarifas mínimas. ¹² Primera categoría. Dic. de cada año. ¹³ Incl. las primas de producción. ¹⁴ Incl. las RSS de Bielorrusia y de Ucrania, que figuran separadamente en este cuadro.

WAGES

21 Wages in construction / Salaires dans la construction / Salarios en la construcción

Earnings *(E.G.)* or rates *(R.T.)* per hour *(h.)*, day *(d.j.)*, week *(w.s.)* or month *(m.)*

Gains *(E.G.)* ou taux *(R.T.)* par heure *(h.)*, jour *(d.j.)*, semaine *(w.s.)* ou mois *(m.)*

Ganancias *(E.G.)* o tarifas *(R.T.)* por hora *(h.)*, día *(d.j.)*, semana *(w.s.)* o mes *(m.)*

Date / Date / Fecha	Algérie	Cameroun — Skilled workers / Ouvriers qualifiés / Obreros calificados	Egypt	Ghana	Haute-Volta
	(E.G./h.) [1]	(R.T./h.) [2]	(E.G./w.s.) [3]	(E.G./m.) [4],[5]	(E.G./m.)
	Dinars	Francs (CFA)	Piastres	Cedis	Francs (CFA)
1965	.	106	327	31.69	.
1966	.	99-110	311	32.68	.
1967	.	80-131	284	35.58	.
1968	.	84-131	362	34.79	.
1969	2.29	85-103	368	34.69	8 955
1970	2.50	85-162	360	38.53	11 558
1971	2.36	107.39	...	38.41	17 767
1972	2.60	173.20	...	40.47 * [6]	...
1973	2.77	187.30	...	...	...
1974	...	...	...	...	...

Date / Date / Fecha	Malawi	Mali	Mauritius	Sierra Leone	South Africa, Rep. of — Building / Bâtiment / Edificación	Tanzania (Tanganyika)
	(E.G./m.) [5]	(E.G./h.) [4]	(E.G./d.j.) [7]	(E.G./w.s.) [8],[9]	(R.T./w.s.) [10]	(E.G./m.) [11]
	Kwacha	Francs	Rupees	Leones	(1969 = 100)	Shillings
1965	.	.	.	.	86.8	252
1966	.	.	7.16	7 25	90.9	262
1967	.	.	7.37	7.77	92.4	306
1968	20 60	.	7.25	5.31	98.2	343
1969	24.50	.	7.86	5.27	100.0	308
1970	28.27	.	9.02	7.52	...	307
1971	25.47	65.62	8.96	7.34	...	...
1972	25.70	70.95	8.24	7.38	...	...
1973	26.60	88.80	10.00	6.69	...	...
1974	30.30	101.43	11.38	6.87	...	...

EXPLANATORY NOTES: See p. 585.

[1] April of each year. [2] Average rates. [3] Oct. of each year. [4] Dec. of each year. [5] Incl. salaried employees. [6] Sep. [7] March and Sep. of each year. [8] Adults only. [9] May and Nov. of each year. [10] Minimum rates. White adult males. Sep. of each year. [11] Adult males. June of each year.

NOTES EXPLICATIVES: Voir p. 589.

[1] *Avril de chaque année.* [2] *Taux moyens.* [3] *Oct. de chaque année.* [4] *Déc. de chaque année.* [5] *Y compris les employés.* [6] *Sept.* [7] *Mars et sept. de chaque année.* [8] *Adultes seulement.* [9] *Mai et nov. de chaque année.* [10] *Taux minima. Hommes adultes (population blanche). Sept. de chaque année.* [11] *Hommes adultes. Juin de chaque année.*

NOTAS EXPLICATIVAS: Véase pág. 594.

[1] Abril de cada año. [2] Tarifas medias. [3] Oct. de cada año. [4] Dic. de cada año. [5] Incl. los empleados. [6] Sept. [7] Marzo y sept. de cada año. [8] Adultos solamente. [9] Mayo y nov. de cada año. [10] Tarifas mínimas. Hombres adultos (población blanca). Sept. de cada año. [11] Hombres adultos. Junio de cada año.

21 Wages in construction
Salaires dans la construction
Salarios en la construcción

Earnings *(E.G.)* or rates *(R.T.)*
per hour *(h.)*, day *(d.j.)*,
week *(w.s.)* or month *(m.)*

Gains *(E.G.)* ou taux *(R.T.)*
par heure *(h.)*, jour *(d.j.)*,
semaine *(w.s.)* ou mois *(m.)*

Ganancias *(E.G.)* o tarifas *(R.T.)*
por hora *(h.)*, día *(d.j.)*,
semana *(w.s.)* o mes *(m.)*

	AFRICA — AFRIQUE — AFRICA		AMERICA — AMÉRIQUE — AMÉRICA			
	Zambia [1]		Argentina		Belize	
					Building — *Bâtiment* — Edificación	
Date	Zambians	Others	Unskilled workers	Barbados	Semi-skilled workers	Unskilled workers
Date	*Zambiens*	*Autres*	*Ouvriers non qualifiés*		*Ouvriers semi-qualifiés*	*Ouvriers non qualifiés*
Fecha	Zambianos	Otros	Obreros no calificados		Obreros semicalificados	Obreros no calificados
	(E.G./m.) [2,3]		*(E.G./h.)* [5]	*(R.T./h.)* [7]	*(R.T./d.j.)* [8]	
	Kwacha	Kwacha	Pesos	Dollars	Dollars	Dollars
1965	26.8	292.4	76.44	0.60-0.90	3.10	2.88
1966	27.7	325.7	100.26	0.60-0.90	4.20	3.36
1967	41.6	387.5	130.83	0.60-0.95	4.20	3.36
1968	54.1	477.4	139.70	0.60-0.95	4.20	3.36
1969	46.7	474.4	153.38	0.70-1.25	4.84	3.88
1970	46.2	473.0	1.79 [6]	0.70-1.50	4.84	3.88
1971	54.2	530.8	2.44	0.90-1.50	...	...
1972	61.3	403.3	3.55	...	...	...
1973	54.7 [4]	385.7 [4]	6.31	...	...	...
1974	59.9 [4]	370.0 [4]	...	...	...	...

	AMERICA — AMÉRIQUE — AMÉRICA					Grenada (St. George's)	
						Semi-skilled workers	
Date	Bolivia	Canada		El Salvador (San Salvador) [9]		*Ouvriers semi-qualifiés*	Guyana
Date						Obreros semicalificados	
Fecha							
	(E.G./m.) [2]	*(E.G./h.)*	*(E.G./w.s.)*	*(E.G./h.)* [10]	*(E.G./w.s.)* [10]	*(R.T./d.j.)* [11]	*(E.G./w.s.)*
	Pesos	Dollars	Dollars	Colones	Colones	Dollars	Dollars
1965	.	2.54	105.15	0.70	30.97	4.00	.
1966	.	2.80	118.06	0.66	29.20	4.00	25.84
1967	.	3.12	128.76	0.66	27.74	4.00- 4.50	28.53
1968	.	3.33	134.84	0.67	29.54	4.00- 6.00	43.78
1969	.	3.71	147.68	0.62	27.42	5.00- 7.60	45.98
1970	775	4.21	165.04	0.69	30.73	5.00- 7.60	50.92
1971	954	4.75	186.20	0.71	31.98	8.00-10.00	54.95
1972	1 089	5.15	206.52	0.78	34.56	8.00-10.00	53.13
1973	1 209	5.66	223.57	0.89	38.36	8.00-10.00	58.39
1974	1 609	6.43 *	251.41 *	0.93	39.75	8.00-10.00	...

EXPLANATORY NOTES: See p. 585.

[1] Beginning 1967: fourth quarter of each year. [2] Incl. salaried employees. [3] 1965-69: Incl. the value of payments in kind. [4] June. [5] Minimum earnings. [6] New currency introduced in Jan. 1970: 1 new peso = 100 old pesos. [7] Masons, carpenters, roller drivers. [8] Prevailing rates. [9] Metropolitan area. [10] Males only. [11] Minimum rates.

NOTES EXPLICATIVES: Voir p. 589.

[1] *A partir de 1967: quatrième trimestre de chaque année.* [2] *Y compris les employés.* [3] *1965-1969: y compris la valeur des paiements en nature.* [4] *Juin.* [5] *Gains minima.* [6] *Nouvelle monnaie introduite en janv. 1970: 1 nouveau peso = 100 anciens pesos.* [7] *Maçons, charpentiers, conducteurs de rouleaux compresseurs.* [8] *Taux prédominants.* [9] *Région métropolitaine.* [10] *Hommes seulement.* [11] *Taux minima.*

NOTAS EXPLICATIVAS: Véase pág. 594.

[1] A partir de 1967: cuarto trimestre de cada año. [2] Incl. los empleados. [3] 1965-1969: Incl. el valor de los pagos en especie. [4] Junio. [5] Ganancias mínimas. [6] Nueva moneda adoptada en enero de 1970: 1 nuevo peso = 100 antiguos. [7] Albañiles, carpinteros, conductores de apisonadoras. [8] Tarifas predominantes. [9] Area metropolitana. [10] Hombres solamente. [11] Tarifas mínimas.

WAGES

21 Wages in construction
Salaires dans la construction
Salarios en la construcción

Earnings *(E.G.)* or rates *(R.T.)*
per hour *(h.)*, day *(d.j.)*,
week *(w.s.)* or month *(m.)*

Gains *(E.G.)* ou taux *(R.T.)*
par heure *(h.)*, jour *(d.j.)*,
semaine *(w.s.)* ou mois *(m.)*

Ganancias *(E.G.)* o tarifas *(R.?)*
por hora *(h.)*, día *(d.j.)*,
semana *(w.s.)* o mes *(m.)*

Date / Date / Fecha	AMERICA — AMÉRIQUE — AMÉRICA				United States	
	México	Perú (Lima-Callao)	Surinam	Trinidad and Tobago	Building / *Bâtiment* / Edificación	
	(E.G./h.) [1]	*(E.G./d.j.)* [2]	*(E.G./m.)*	*(R.T.)* [3],[4]	*(E.G./h.)*	*(E.G./w.s.)*
	Pesos	Soles	Guilders	(1970 = 100)	$	$
1965	3.40	81.16	.	87.7	3.55	128.16
1966	4.00	88.06	.	89.1	3.76	136.49
1967	4.36	...	.	92.4	3.99	145.64
1968	4.15	115.02	.	92.4	4.26	153.79
1969	4.36	132.31	.	95.7	4.64	169.82
1970	5.31	117.25	.	100.0	5.08	184.40
1971	6.43	135.76	172	105.0	5.49	197.64
1972	...	148.72	180	108.3	5.81	208.00
1973	...	176.00	189	121.5	6.17	222.12
1974	...	200.23	...	175.1	6.54	236.09

Date / Date / Fecha	AMERICA — AMÉRIQUE AMÉRICA	ASIA — ASIE — ASIA				
	Uruguay [5]	Bangladesh (Dacca)		Cyprus	Israel	Japan
		Masons / *Maçons* / Albañiles	Carpenters / *Charpentiers* / Carpinteros			
	(R.T./m.) [6]	*(R.T./d. .)* [7]		*(E.G./w.s.)* [2],[9]	*(E.G./m.)* [6]	*(E.G./m.)* [6],[12]
	(1970 = 100)	Taka	Taka	Pounds	Pounds	Yen
1965	.	.	.	6.82	490	39 439
1966	.	.	.	6.92	559	43 401
1967	36.6	.	.	7.58	558	46 922 [13]
1968	69.0	.	.	8.16	564 [11]	52 163
1969	91.0	.	.	9.97 [10]	588	60 809
1970	100.0	.	.	11.24	637	71 727 [13]
1971	157.8	8.67	6.67	12.97	705	83 348
1972	243.1	9.83	7.83	14.45	807	95 552
1973	497.0	12.69 [8]	10.50 [8]	17.71	986	111 691 [13]
1974	897.1	...	18.00 [8]	19.18	1 354	138 630

EXPLANATORY NOTES: See p. 585.

[1] Oct. of each year. [2] June of each year. [3] Minimum rates. [4] Adults only. May and Nov. of each year. [5] Montevideo; private sector only. Incl. social benefits. Minimum rates. [6] Incl. salaried employees. [7] May of each year. [8] Oct. [9] Adults only. [10] Sep. [11] Series replacing former series. [12] Incl. family allowances, mid- and end-of-year bonuses. [13] Sampling design revised.

NOTES EXPLICATIVES: Voir p. 589.

[1] *Oct. de chaque année.* [2] *Juin de chaque année.* [3] *Taux minima.* [4] *Adultes seulement. Mai et nov. de chaque année.* [5] *Montevideo ; secteur privé seulement. Y compris les prestations sociales. Taux minima.* [6] *Y compris les employés.* [7] *Mai de chaque année.* [8] *Oct.* [9] *Adultes seulement.* [10] *Sept.* [11] *Série remplaçant la précédente.* [12] *Y compris les allocations familiales et les primes de mi- et de fin d'année.* [13] *Plan d'échantillonnage révisé.*

NOTAS EXPLICATIVAS: Véase pág. 594.

[1] Oct. de cada año. [2] Junio de cada año. [3] Tari mínimas. [4] Adultos solamente. Mayo v nov. de c año. [5] Montevideo; sector privado solamente. I las prestaciones sociales. Tarifas mínimas. [6] Incl. empleados. [7] Mayo de cada año. [8] Oct. [9] Adul solamente. [10] Sept. [11] Serie que substituye a anterior. [12] Incl. las asignaciones familiares y primas de mitad y de fin de año. [13] Diseño de muestra revisado.

21 Wages in construction
Salaires dans la construction
Salarios en la construcción

Earnings *(E.G.)* or rates *(R.T.)*
per hour *(h.)*, day *(d.j.)*,
week *(w.s.)* or month *(m.)*

Gains *(E.G.)* ou taux *(R.T.)*
par heure *(h.)*, jour *(d.j.)*,
semaine *(w.s.)* ou mois *(m.)*

Ganancias *(E.G.)* o tarifas *(R.T.)*
por hora *(h.)*, día *(d.j.)*,
semana *(w.s.)* o mes *(m.)*

	ASIA — ASIE — ASIA					
Date / *Date* / Fecha	Korea, Rep. of	Singapore	Sri Lanka		République arabe syrienne [1,5]	Thailand (Bangkok) [1]
			Building / *Bâtiment* / Edificación			
	(E.G./m.) [1,2]	*(E.G./h.)* [3]	*(E.G./h.)* [4]	*(E.G./d.j.)* [4]	*(R.T./m.)* [6]	*(E.G./h.)* [7]
	Won	Cents	Cents	Rupees	Pounds	Baht
1965	·	87	60.18	4.66	180	·
1966	·	90	59.21	4.61	180	6.16
1967	·	99	62.27	4.91	180	8.56
1968	·	97	74.95	5.84	180	5.34
1969	·	102	80.42	6.47	180	6.03
1970	23 174	108	84.75	6.67	180	5.76
1971	26 298	114	85.95	6.73	184	7.56
1972	31 250	124	95 71	7.49	191	...
1973	36 740	135	88.97	6.40	191	...
1974	43 984	158	112.35	9.71	...	...

	EUROPE — EUROPE — EUROPA					
Date / *Date* / Fecha	Austria			Belgique	Bulgarie [11]	Czechoslovakia [12]
	Masons / *Maçons* / Albañiles	Semi-skilled workers / *Ouvriers semi-qualifiés* / Obreros semicalificados	Unskilled workers / *Ouvriers non qualifiés* / Obreros no calificados	Males / *Hommes* / Hombres		
	(R.T./h.) [8]			*(E.G./h.)* [9]	*(E.G./m.)*	*(E.G./m.)*
	Schilling	Schilling	Schilling	Francs	Leva	Korunas
1965	12.30	11.70	10.70	47.30	110.4	1 694
1966	13.30	12.65	11.55	52.82	116.4	1 729
1967	13.95	13.30	12.15	55.71	128.2	1 823
1968	15.00	14.30	13.05	57.89	133.0	1 931
1969	15.96	15.15	13.85	62.22	138.3	2 070
1970	17.89	16.98	15.54	71.90	146.7	2 163
1971	19.19	18.20	16.67	78.11	149.0	2 247
1972	21.70	20.61	18.79	88.73 [10]	153.8	2 344
1973	24.04	22.78	20.80	103.55	161.3	2 401
1974	27.36	25.85	23.63	130.07	166.6 *	...

EXPLANATORY NOTES: See p. 585.

[1] Incl. salaried employees. [2] Incl. family allowances and the value of payments in kind. [3] July of each year. Beginning 1969: adults only. [4] March and Sep. of each year. [5] Adults only. [6] Minimum rates. [7] Sep. of each year, except for 1967: July, and 1969: Oct. [8] Minimum rates. [9] Oct. of each year. [10] New industrial classification. [11] Socialised sector. [12] State industry.

NOTES EXPLICATIVES: Voir p. 589.

[1] *Y compris les employés.* [2] *Y compris les allocations familiales et la valeur des paiements en nature.* [3] *Juillet de chaque année. A partir de 1969: adultes seulement.* [4] *Mars et sept. de chaque année.* [5] *Adultes seulement.* [6] *Taux minima.* [7] *Sept. de chaque année, sauf pour 1967: juillet, et 1969: oct.* [8] *Taux minima.* [9] *Oct. de chaque année.* [10] *Nouvelle classification industrielle.* [11] *Secteur socialisé.* [12] *Industrie d'Etat.*

NOTAS EXPLICATIVAS: Véase pág. 594.

[1] Incl. los empleados. [2] Incl. las asignaciones familiares y el valor de los pagos en especie. [3] Julio de cada año. A partir de 1969: adultos solamente. [4] Marzo y sept. de cada año. [5] Adultos solamente. [6] Tarifas mínimas. [7] Sept. de cada año, salvo 1967: julio, y 1969: oct. [8] Tarifas mínimas. [9] Oct. de cada año. [10] Nueva clasificación industrial. [11] Sector socializado. [12] Industria de Estado.

WAGES

21 Wages in construction
Salaires dans la construction
Salarios en la construcción

Earnings *(E.G.)* or rates *(R.T.)*
per hour *(h.)*, day *(d.j.)*,
week *(w.s.)* or month *(m.)*

Gains *(E.G.)* ou taux *(R.T.)*
par heure *(h.)*, jour *(d.j.)*,
semaine *(w.s.)* ou mois *(m.)*

Ganancias *(E.G.)* o tarifas *(R.T.)*
por hora *(h.)*, día *(d.j.)*,
semana *(w.s.)* o mes *(m.)*

EUROPE — EUROPE — EUROPA

Date / Date / Fecha	Denmark	España	Finland Building / Bâtiment / Edificación	France	German Democratic Republic △ [6]	Germany, Fed. Rep. of △ [8]
	(E.G./h.) [1]	*(E.G./h.)* [2]	*(E.G./h.)* [3]	*(E.G./h.)* [4]	*(E.G./m.)* [7]	*(E.G./h.)* [9]
	Öre	Pesetas	Markkaa	Francs	Mark	Mark
1965	1 050	16.49	4.21	3.78	690	4.66
1966	1 169	18.99	4.63	3.98	704	4.96
1967	1 293	22.45	5.00	4.24	723	4.96
1968	1 453	24.86	5.40	4.74	782	5.16
1969	1 620	27.35	5.89	5.18	798	5.69
1970	1 812.	31.59	6.74	5.72	830	6.67
1971	2 045	36.51	7.82	6.34	843	7.43
1972	2 200	43.06	9.01	7.45 [5]	856	8.12
1973	2 528	51.83	10.63	8.58	871	8.98 [10]
1974	2 917	69.91	13.35	...	908 *	9.68

EUROPE — EUROPE — EUROPA

Date / Date / Fecha	Gibraltar	Hongrie [6]	Ireland [13] Skilled workers / Ouvriers qualifiés / Oberos calificados	Ireland [13] Semi-skilled and unskilled workers / Ouvriers semi-qualifiés et non qualifiés / Obreros semicalificados y no calificados	Italie	Luxembourg Males / Hommes / Hombres
	(E.G./w.s.) [11]	*(E.G./m.)*	*(E.G./h.)*		*(E.G./h.)* [3]	*(E.G./h.)* [14]
	£	Forints	Pence	Pence	Lire	Francs
1965	.	1 756	.	.	414	48.06
1966	.	1 845	.	.	425	50.57
1967	.	1 952	.	.	443	51.23
1968	.	1 990	.	.	462	56.03
1969	.	2 096	49.8	40.6	497	61.09
1970	16.78	2 244 [12]	53.9	44.9	603	69.73
1971	19.06	2 301	62.1	52.8	673	75.34
1972	19.83	2 392	74.5	64.3	735	82.41 [15]
1973	25.50	2 614	81.1	70.6	898	96.40
1974	26.69	2 830 *	97.5	86.4	1 124	117.51

EXPLANATORY NOTES: See p. 585.

[1] Adults only. Excl. vacation pay. July-Sep. of each year. [2] Incl. salaried employees. [3] Incl. the value of payments in kind. [4] Oct. of each year except for 1965-66 and 1968-71: Sep.; 1967: March. [5] Series replacing former series. [6] State sector. [7] Incl. family allowances. [8] Building only. [9] Incl. family allowances paid directly by the employer; males only. [10] Sampling design revised. [11] April and Oct. of each year, except for 1973: Oct. and 1974: April. [12] Revised series. [13] Sep. of each year. Private sector only. [14] Oct. of each year. [15] New industrial classification.

NOTES EXPLICATIVES: Voir p. 589.

[1] *Adultes seulement. Non compris les versements pour congés payés. Juillet-sept. de chaque année.* [2] *Y compris les employés.* [3] *Y compris la valeur des paiements en nature.* [4] *Oct. de chaque année, sauf pour 1965-66 et 1968-1971: sept.; 1967: mars.* [5] *Série remplaçant la précédente.* [6] *Secteur d'Etat.* [7] *Y compris les allocations familiales.* [8] *Bâtiment seulement.* [9] *Y compris les allocations familiales payées directement par les employeurs; hommes seulement.* [10] *Plan d'échantillonnage révisé.* [11] *Avril et oct. de chaque année, sauf pour 1973: oct. et 1974: avril.* [12] *Série révisée.* [13] *Sept. de chaque année. Secteur privé seulement.* [14] *Oct. de chaque année.* [15] *Nouvelle classification industrielle.*

NOTAS EXPLICATIVAS: Véase pág. 594.

[1] Adultos solamente. Excl. los pagos por vacaciones. Julio-sept. de cada año. [2] Incl. los empleados. [3] Incl. el valor de los pagos en especie. [4] Oct. de cada año, salvo 1965-66 y 1968-1971: sept.; 1967: marzo. [5] Serie que substituye a la anterior. [6] Sector de Estado. [7] Incl. las asignaciones familiares. [8] Edificación solamente. [9] Incl. las asignaciones familiares pagadas directamente por los empleadores; hombres solamente. [10] Diseño de la muestra revisado. [11] Abril y oct. de cada año, salvo 1973: oct., y 1974: abril. [12] Serie revisada. [13] Sept. de cada año. Sector privado solamente. [14] Oct. de cada año. [15] Nueva clasificación industrial.

21 Wages in construction
Salaires dans la construction
Salarios en la construcción

Earnings *(E.G.)* or rates *(R.T.)*
per hour *(h.)*, day *(d.j.)*,
week *(w.s.)* or month *(m.)*

Gains *(E.G.)* ou taux *(R.T.)*
par heure *(h.)*, jour *(d.j.)*,
semaine *(w.s.)* ou mois *(m.)*

Ganancias *(E.G.)* o tarifas *(R.T.)*
por hora *(h.)*, día *(d.j.)*,
semana *(w.s.)* o mes *(m.)*

Date / Date / Fecha	EUROPE — EUROPE — EUROPA						
	Malta	Norway	Pays-Bas		Pologne [6]	Portugal	Roumanie [6]
	Males [1] / Hommes [1] / Hombres [1]	Building / Bâtiment / Edificación	Males [1] / Hommes [1] / Hombres [1]				Building / Bâtiment / Edificación
	(E.G./h.) [2]	*(E.G./h.)* [3],[4]	*(E.G./h.)* [5]	*(E.G./w.s.)* [5]	*(E.G./m.)* [2],[3]	*(E.G./h.)*	*(E.G./m.)* [2]
	Cents	Kroner	Guilders	Guilders	Zlotys	Escudos	Lei
1965	15.8	11.89	3.59	166.82	2 178	.	.
1966	15.9	12.93	4.01	185.26	2 262	.	.
1967	17.3	13.82	4.23	196.19	2 385	.	1 325
1968	17.7	14.70	4.63	210.64	2 491	.	1 374
1969	19.9	15.95	5.04	229.54	2 574	.	1 403
1970	21.3	17.55	5.76	256.03	2 675	.	1 555
1971	24.8	19.36	6.83	301.97	2 796	11.60	1 608
1972	25.6	21.04	7.72	340.32	2 992	12.80	1 648
1973	...	22.64	8.94	382.75	3 471	14.80	1 734
1974	...	26.01	...	...	3 876 *	...	1 925

Date / Date / Fecha	EUROPE — EUROPE — EUROPA					
	Suisse [7]		Sweden	Turquie	United Kingdom	
	Males [1] — Hommes [1] — Hombres [1]		Males [1] / Hommes [1] / Hombres [1]		Males [1] / Hommes [1] / Hombres [1]	
	Skilled and semi-skilled / Qualifiés et semi-qualifiés / Calificados y semicalificados	Unskilled / Non qualifiés / No calificados				
	(E.G./h.) [8]		*(E.G./h.)*	*(E.G./d.j.)* [2]	*(E.G./h.)* [5]	*(E.G./w.s.)* [5]
	Francs	Francs	Kronor	Liras	Pence	£
1965	5.43	4.67	12.60	23.52	39.7	19.77
1966	5.78	5 04	13.49	22.82	42.4	20.56
1967	6.34	5.37	14.39	27.09	44.9	21.68
1968	6.71	5.69	15.00	29.03	47.9	22.87
1969	7.03	5.93	16.23	32.15	50.8 [10]	24.46 [10]
1970	7.61	6.43	17.64	33.72	56.5	26.85
1971	8.56	7.27	18.68 [10]	38.25	63.8	30.11
1972	9.57	8.15	20.67	41.71	77.9	36.59
1973	11.02 [9]	9.28 [9]	22.27	48.10	88.7	41.41
1974	12.70	10.69	...	64.51	104.2	48.75

EXPLANATORY NOTES: See p. 585.

[1] Adults only. [2] Incl. salaried employees. [3] Incl. the value of payments in kind. [4] Adult males. [5] Oct. of each year. [6] Socialised sector. [7] Building only. [8] Accident insurance statistics. [9] Series replacing former series. [10] New industrial classification.

NOTES EXPLICATIVES: Voir p. 589.

[1] *Adultes seulement.* [2] *Y compris les employés.* [3] *Y compris la valeur des paiements en nature.* [4] *Hommes adultes.* [5] *Oct. de chaque année.* [6] *Secteur socialisé.* [7] *Bâtiment seulement.* [8] *Statistiques d'assurance-accidents.* [9] *Série remplaçant la précédente.* [10] *Nouvelle classification industrielle.*

NOTAS EXPLICATIVAS: Véase pág. 594.

[1] Adultos solamente. [2] Incl. los empleados. [3] Incl. el valor de los pagos en especie. [4] Hombres adultos. [5] Oct. de cada año. [6] Sector socializado. [7] Edificación solamente. [8] Estadísticas del seguro de accidentes. [9] Serie que substituye a la anterior. [10] Nueva clasificación industrial.

21 Wages in construction
Salaires dans la construction
Salarios en la construcción

Earnings *(E.G.)* or rates *(R.T.)*
per hour *(h.)*, day *(d.j.)*,
week *(w.s.)* or month *(m.)*

Gains *(E.G.)* ou taux *(R.T.)*
par heure *(h.)*, jour *(d.j.)*,
semaine *(w.s.)* ou mois *(m.)*

Ganancias *(E.G.)* o tarifas *(R.T.)*
por hora *(h.)*, dîa *(d.j.)*,
semana *(w.s.)* o mes *(m.)*

Date / Date / Fecha	EUROPE EUROPE EUROPA	OCEANIA — OCÉANIE — OCEANÍA				
		Australia	Fiji	New Zealand (1)		
		Males [3] / Hommes [3] / Hombres [3]		Males [3,7] — Hommes [3,7] — Hombres [3,7]		
	Yugoslavia [1]			Bricklayers / Briqueteurs / Enladrilladores	Carpenters / Charpentiers / Carpinteros	Labourers / Manœuvres / Obreros no calificados
	(E.G./m.) [2]	*(E.G./h.)* [2,4]	*(R.T./d.j.)* [6]	*(R.T./w.s.)* [8]		
	Dinars	Dollars	Dollars	Dollars	Dollars	Dollars
1965	.	.	1.71	.	.	.
1966	632	1.52	2.06	33.51	33.07	29.09
1967	745	1.59	2.14	35.03	34.81	30.51
1968	822	1.72	2.24	37.07	36.17	31.80
1969	926	1.80	2.40	39.06	38.40	33.17
1970	1 127	2.02	2.71	47.23	43.62	36.75
1971	1 364	2.26	2.88	57.55	58.20	46.10
1972	1 636	2.27 [5]	2.98	62.58	63.12	49.92
1973	1 879	2.66	4.11	68.59	68.59	54.88
1974	2 377	3.55 *	...	77.93	77.93	63.34

Date / Date / Fecha	OCEANIA — OCÉANIE — OCEANÍA		URSS [1,12]	RSS de Biélorussie [1]	RSS d'Ukraine [1]
	New Zealand (2)	Nouvelle-Calédonie			
	M. + F. [2] / H. + F. [2] / H. + M. [2]	Labourers [11] / Manœuvres [11] / Obreros no calificados [11]			
	(E.G./h.) [9,10]	*(R.T./h.)*	*(E.G./m.)* [2]	*(E.G./m.)* [2]	*(E.G./m.)* [2]
	Dollars	Francs (CFP)	Roubles	Roubles	Roubles
1965	0.98	66.24	112.4	.	103.3
1966	1.02	67.39	116.7	.	106.2
1967	1.08	71.11	124.2	.	111.2
1968	1.13	72.99	131.2	.	117.1
1969	1.21	81.90	139.9	.	123.3
1970	1.33	100.32	153.0	.	135.0
1971	1.59	109.12	157.4	135.3	139.5
1972	1.75	...	162.3	139.3	143.8
1973	1.96	...	167.2	144.1	146.2
1974	2.25	...	172.5 *	149.1 *	150.5 *

EXPLANATORY NOTES: See p. 585.

NOTES EXPLICATIVES: Voir p. 589.

NOTAS EXPLICATIVAS: Véase pág. 594.

[1] Socialised sector. [2] Incl. salaried employees. [3] Adults only. [4] Oct. of each year. [5] Scope of series enlarged. [6] June of each year. [7] Building only. [8] Minimum rates. [9] Incl. the value of payments in kind. [10] April and Oct. of each year. [11] First category. Dec. of each year. [12] Incl. Byelorussian SSR and Ukrainian SSR, shown separately in this table.

[1] *Secteur socialisé.* [2] *Y compris les employés.* [3] *Adultes seulement.* [4] *Oct. de chaque année.* [5] *Portée de la série élargie.* [6] *Juin de chaque année.* [7] *Bâtiment seulement.* [8] *Taux minima.* [9] *Y compris la valeur des paiements en nature.* [10] *Avril et oct. de chaque année.* [11] *Première catégorie. Déc. de chaque année.* [12] *Y compris les RSS de Biélorussie et d'Ukraine, figurant séparément dans ce tableau.*

[1] Sector socializado. [2] Incl. los empleados. [3] Adultos solamente. [4] Oct. de cada año. [5] El alcance de la serie es mayor. [6] Junio de cada año. [7] Edificación solamente. [8] Tarifas mínimas. [9] Incl. el valor de los pagos en especie. [10] Abril y oct. de cada año. [11] Primera categoría. Dic. de cada año. [12] Incl. las RSS de Bielorrusia y de Ucrania, que figuran separadamente en este cuadro.

22 Wages in transport, storage and communication (Excl. sea transport)
Salaires dans les transports, entrepôts et communications (Non compris les transports par mer)
Salarios en los transportes, almacenaje y comunicaciones (Excl. el transporte marítimo)

rnings *(E.G.)* or rates *(R.T.)*
hour *(h.)*, day *(d.j.)*,
ek *(w.s.)* or month *(m.)*

Gains *(E.G.)* ou taux *(R.T.)*
par heure *(h.)*, jour *(d.j.)*,
semaine *(w.s.)* ou mois *(m.)*

Ganancias *(E.G.)* o tarifas *(R.T.)*
por hora *(h.)*, día *(d.j.)*,
semana *(w.s.)* o mes *(m.)*

		AFRICA — AFRIQUE — AFRICA			
Date / *Date* / Fecha	Algérie	Cameroun — Skilled workers / *Ouvriers qualifiés* / Obreros calificados	Egypt	Ghana	Haute-Volta
	(E.G./h.) [1]	*(R.T./h)* [2]	*(E.G./w.s.)* [3]	*(E.G./m.)* [4, 5]	*(E.G./m.)*
	Dinars	Francs (CFA)	Piastres	Cedis	Francs (CFA)
1965	.	73-115	416	73.83	.
1966	.	99-130	423	58.87	.
1967	.	80-295	413	63.82	.
1968	.	106-295	404	70.13	.
1969	1.63	82-199	430	79.00	16 571
1970	2.10	63-173	440	92.47	19 341
1971	2.91	87-174	...	113.17	20 694
1972	2.43	90-179	...	98.83 * [6]	...
1973	2.01	98-197	...	...	...
1974	...	...	...	...	...

		AFRICA — AFRIQUE — AFRICA			
Date / *Date* / Fecha	Malawi	Mali	Mauritius	Sierra Leone [8, 9]	South Africa, Rep. of — Transport and communication / *Transports et communications* / Transportes y comunicaciones	Tanzania (Tanganyika)
	(E.G./m.) [5]	*(E.G./h.)* [4]	*(E.G./d.j.)* [7]	*(E.G./w.s.)* [10]	*(R.T./w.s.)* [11]	*(E.G./m.)* [12]
	Kwacha	Francs	Rupees	Leones	(1969 = 100)	Shillings
1965	.	.	.	.	*89.1*	384
1966	.	.	10.64	6.60	*89.8*	402
1967	.	.	10.30	6.38	*90.7*	470
1968	43.53	.	10.93	7.92	*98.9*	462
1969	47.06	.	10.70	8.89	**100.0**	538
1970	49.87	.	12.24	7.90	...	469
1971	51.94	82.90	9.11	9.96	...	...
1972	52.91	118.58	12.42	10.63	...	...
1973	56.21	...	12.83	9.51	...	...
1974	58.64	115.64	16.39	9.82	...	...

EXPLANATORY NOTES: See p. 585.

NOTES EXPLICATIVES: Voir p. 589.

NOTAS EXPLICATIVAS: Véase pág. 594.

April of each year. [2] Average rates. [3] Oct. of :h year. [4] Dec. of each year. [5] Incl. salaried ployees. [6] Sep. [7] March and Sep. of each year. dults only. [9] Incl. sea transport. [10] May and Nov. each year. [11] Minimum rates. White adult males. . of each year. [12] Excl. East African Railways. ult males; June of each year.

[1] *Avril de chaque année.* [2] *Taux moyens.* [3] *Oct. de chaque année.* [4] *Déc. de chaque année.* [5] *Y compris les employés.* [6] *Sept.* [7] *Mars et sept. de chaque année.* [8] *Adultes seulement.* [9] *Y compris les transports par mer.* [10] *Mai et nov. de chaque année.* [11] *Taux minima. Hommes adultes (population blanche). Sept. de chaque année.* [12] *Non compris les chemins de fer de l'Est africain. Hommes adultes ; juin de chaque année.*

[1] Abril de cada año. [2] Tarifas medias. [3] Oct. de cada año. [4] Dic. de cada año. [5] Incl. los empleados. [6] Sept. [7] Marzo y sept. de cada año. [8] Adultos solamente. [9] Incl. el transporte marítimo. [10] Mayo y nov. de cada año. [11] Tarifas mínimas. Hombres adultos (población blanca). Sept. de cada año. [12] Excl. los ferrocarriles del Este africano. Hombres adultos; junio de cada año.

22 Wages in transport, storage and communication (Excl. sea transport)
Salaires dans les transports, entrepôts et communications (Non compris les transports par mer)
Salarios en los transportes, almacenaje y comunicaciones (Excl. el transporte marítimo)

Earnings *(E.G.)* or rates *(R.T.)*
per hour *(h.)*, day *(d.j.)*,
week *(w.s.)* or month *(m.)*

Gains *(E.G.)* ou taux *(R.T.)*
par heure *(h.)*, jour *(d.j.)*,
semaine *(w.s.)* ou mois *(m.)*

Ganancias *(E.G.)* o tarifas *(R.)*
por hora *(h.)*, día *(d.j.)*,
semana *(w.s.)* o mes *(m.)*

Date / Date / Fecha	AFRICA — AFRIQUE — AFRICA		AMERICA — AMÉRIQUE — AMERICA				
	Zambia [1]		Argentina	Barbados	Belize	Bermuda	Bolivia
	Zambians / Zambiens / Zambianos	Others / Autres / Otros	Road haulage / Camionnage / Camionaje	Buses / Autobus / Autobuses — Drivers / Conducteurs / Conductores	Transport / Transports / Transportes	Buses / Autobus / Autobuses — Drivers / Conducteurs / Conductores	
	(E.G./m.) [3]		(E.G./h.) [5]	(R.T./w.s.)	(R.T./w.s.) [7]	(R.T./h.)	(E.G./m.) [8]
	Kwacha	Kwacha	Pesos	Dollars	Dollars	Dollars	Pesos
1965	40.4	256.4	58.88	35.00	18.00-25.00	.	.
1966	57.3	371.8	97.00	35.00	25.00-30.00	.	.
1967	77.8	313.8	129.01	40.00	25.00-30.00	.	.
1968	78.9	322.5	129.01	40.00	25.00-30.00	1.84	.
1969	86.2	334.8	141.83	45.00	29.76-37.44	2.16	.
1970	98.7	394.5	1.67 [6]	48.00	29.76-37.44	2.64	982
1971	104.1	445.5	2.27	50.00	...	2.64	1 062
1972	107.3	346.7	3.32	68.00	...	3.13	1 197
1973	111.0 [4]	336.4 [4]	5.75	68.00	...	3.28	1 317
1974	106.3 [4]	348.7 [4]	...	...	...	3.66	1 717

Date / Date / Fecha	AMERICA — AMÉRIQUE — AMÉRICA						
	Canada	Grenada (St. George's)		Guyana [11]	México	Perú (Lima-Callao)	Surinam
		Transport [9] / Transports [9] / Transportes [9]			Transport / Transports / Transportes	Transport / Transports / Transportes	
		Drivers / Conducteurs / Conductores	Conductors / Receveurs / Cobradores				
	(E.G./w.s.) [2]	(R.T./m.) [10]		(E.G./w.s.)	(E.G./h.) [12]	(E.G./d.j.) [14]	(E.G./m.)
	Dollars	Dollars	Dollars	Dollars	Pesos	Soles	Guilders
1965	98.77	60.00	30.00	.	8.00	95.34	.
1966	103.55	60.00	35.00	37.97	5.54	103.44	.
1967	113.20	60.00	35.00	36.06	6.03	...	.
1968	122.70	66.00	48.00	41.82	6.71	108.25	.
1969	131.03	75.00	50.00	43.48	7.99	115.50	.
1970	142.35	75.00	50.00	47.63	8.09	115.76	.
1971	154.14	90.00	60.00	52.51	9.75	130.97	105
1972	167.94	90.00	60.00	...	9.83	159.60	110
1973	181.89	90.00	60.00	...	11.79	222.00	115
1974	204.35 *	90.00	60.00	...	...	183.25 [13]	...

EXPLANATORY NOTES: See p. 585.

NOTES EXPLICATIVES: Voir p. 589.

NOTAS EXPLICATIVAS: Véase pág. 594.

[1] Beginning 1967: fourth quarter of each year. [2] Incl. salaried employees. [3] 1965-69: Incl. the value of payments in kind. [4] June. [5] Minimum earnings: unskilled workers. [6] New currency introduced in Jan. 1970: 1 new peso = 100 old pesos. [7] Prevailing rates. [8] Incl. salaried employees. [9] Public transport. [10] Minimum rates. [11] Excl. storage. [12] Oct. of each year. [13] Incl. storage and communication. [14] June of each year.

[1] A partir de 1967 : quatrième trimestre de chaque année. [2] Y compris les employés. [3] 1965-1969 : y compris la valeur des paiements en nature. [4] Juin. [5] Gains minima ; ouvriers non qualifiés. [6] Nouvelle monnaie introduite en janv. 1970. 1 nouveau peso = 100 anciens pesos. [8] Y compris les employés. [9] Transports publics. [10] Taux minima. [11] Non compris les entrepôts. [12] Oct. de chaque année. [13] Non compris les entrepôts et les communications. [14] Juin de chaque année.

[1] A partir de 1967: cuarto trimestre de cada año. [2] Incl. los empleados. [3] 1965-1969: incl. el valor los pagos en especie. [4] Junio. [5] Ganancias mínima obreros no calificados. [6] Nueva moneda adopta en enero de 1970: 1 nuevo peso = 100 antigu [7] Tarifas predominantes. [8] Incl. los emplead [9] Transportes públicos. [10] Tarifas mínimas. [11] Ex el almacenaje. [12] Oct. de cada año. [13] Incl. el alm cenaje y comunicaciones. [14] Junio de cada año.

22 Wages in transport, storage and communication (Excl. sea transport)
Salaires dans les transports, entrepôts et communications (Non compris les transports par mer)
Salarios en los transportes, almacenaje y comunicaciones (Excl. el transporte marítimo)

Earnings *(E.G.)* or rates *(R.T.)* per hour *(h.)*, day *(d.j.)*, week *(w.s.)* or month *(m.)*

Gains *(E.G.)* ou taux *(R.T.)* par heure *(h.)*, jour *(d.j.)*, semaine *(w.s.)* ou mois *(m.)*

Ganancias *(E.G.)* o tarifas *(R.T.)* por hora *(h.)*, día *(d.j.)*, semana *(w.s.)* o mes *(m.)*

Date / *Date* / Fecha	AMERICA — AMÉRIQUE — AMÉRICA					
	Trinidad and Tobago [1]	United States				Uruguay [4]
		Principal railways / *Grandes lignes de chemin de fer* / Líneas principales de ferrocarriles	Local railways and buses [3] / *Chemins de fer et autobus locaux* [3] / Ferrocarriles y autobuses locales [3]	Principal railways / *Grandes lignes de chemin de fer* / Líneas principales de ferrocarriles	Local railways and buses [3] / *Chemins de fer et autobus locaux* [3] / Ferrocarriles y autobuses locales [3]	
	(R.T.) [2]	*(E.G./h.)*		*(E.G./w.s.)*		*(R.T./m.)* [5,6]
	(1970 = 100)	$	$	$	$	(1970 = 100)
1965	87.8	3.00	2.57	130.80	108.20	.
1966	88.9	3.09	2.65	135.65	112.36	.
1967	89.7	3.24	2.77	139.97	116.89	33.6
1968	90.7	3.44	2.92	151.02	122.64	75.5
1969	93.1	3.68	3.12	162.66	131.66	90.5
1970	**100.0**	3.89	3.38	171.94	142.30	**100.0**
1971	116.9	4.36	3.61	188.35	150.90	127.5
1972	136.5	4.89	3.76	214.67	156.04	187.2
1973	143.7	5.40	3.98	240.30	164.77	363.4
1974	147.8	5.68	4.41	249.42	179.49	618.0

Date / *Date* / Fecha	ASIA — ASIE — ASIA					
	Burma		Cyprus	Israel	Japan	Korea, Rep. of
	Transport [1] / *Transports* [1] / Transportes [1]		Transport / *Transports* / Transportes			
	Males / *Hommes* / Hombres	Females [5] / *Femmes* [5] / Mujeres [5]				
	(E.G./m.)		*(E.G./w.s.)* [9]	*(E.G./m.)* [5]	*(E.G./m.)* [5,12]	*(E.G./m.)* [5,14]
	Kyats	Kyats	Pounds	Pounds	Yen	Won
1965	148.80	215.35	8.44	610	47 164	.
1966	153.02	210.61	8.34	760	52 255	.
1967	149.37	215.13	9.06	762	57 642 [13]	.
1968	152.24	211.70	9.18	823 [11]	64 131	.
1969	145.27	208.55	10.98 [10]	887	72 995	.
1970	147.48	214.61	11.74	994	84 825 [13]	18 551
1971	145.85	212.64	12.65	1 158	97 645	21 080
1972	149.95 [7]	214.58 [7]	14.07	1 302	113 217	26 744
1973	165.58 [8]	217.16 [8]	16.99	1 676	135 732 [13]	28 875
1974	...	...	16.70	2 262	171 363	36 497

EXPLANATORY NOTES: See p. 585.

[1] Incl. sea transport. [2] Minimum rates. Adults only. May and Nov. of each year. [3] Excl. government-operated transport. [4] Montevideo; private sector only. [5] Incl. salaried employees. [6] Minimum rates: incl. social benefits. [7] April and Sep. [8] March and Sep. [9] Oct. of each year. Adults only. [10] Sep. [11] Series replacing former series. [12] Incl. family allowances, mid- and end-of-year bonuses. [13] Sampling design revised. [14] Incl. family allowances and the value of payments in kind.

NOTES EXPLICATIVES: Voir p. 589.

[1] *Y compris les transports par mer.* [2] *Taux minima. Adultes seulement. Mai et nov. de chaque année.* [3] *Non compris les transports gérés par le gouvernement.* [4] *Montevideo; secteur privé seulement.* [5] *Y compris les employés.* [6] *Taux minima; y compris les prestations sociales.* [7] *Avril et sept.* [8] *Mars et sept.* [9] *Oct. de chaque année. Adultes seulement.* [10] *Sept.* [11] *Série remplaçant la précédente.* [12] *Y compris les allocations familiales et les primes de mi- et de fin d'année.* [13] *Plan d'échantillonnage révisé.* [14] *Y compris les allocations familiales et la valeur des paiements en nature.*

NOTAS EXPLICATIVAS: Véase pág. 594.

[1] Incl. el transporte marítimo. [2] Tarifas mínimas. Adultos solamente. Mayo y nov. de cada año. [3] Excl. los transportes administrados por el Gobierno. [4] Montevideo; sector privado solamente. [5] Incl. los empleados. [6] Tarifas mínimas; incl. las prestaciones sociales. [7] Abril y sept. [8] Marzo y sept. [9] Oct. de cada año. Adultos solamente. [10] Sept. [11] Serie que substituye a la anterior. [12] Incl. las asignaciones familiares y las primas de mitad y de fin de año. [13] Diseño de la muestra revisado. [14] Incl. las asignacionse familiares y el valor de los pagos en especie.

22 Wages in transport, storage and communication (Excl. sea transport)
Salaires dans les transports, entrepôts et communications (Non compris les transports par mer)
Salarios en los transportes, almacenaje y comunicaciones (Excl. el transporte marítimo)

Earnings *(E.G.)* or rates *(R.T.)*
per hour *(h.)*, day *(d.j.)*,
week *(w.s.)* or month *(m.)*

Gains *(E.G.)* ou taux *(R.T.)*
par heure *(h.)*, jour *(d.j.)*,
semaine *(w.s.)* ou mois *(m.)*

Ganancias *(E.G.)* o tarifas *(R.T.)*
por hora *(h.)*, día *(d.j.)*,
semana *(w.s.)* o mes *(m.)*

ASIA — ASIE — ASIA

Date / Date / Fecha	Malaysia West Malaysia Road haulage *Camionnage* Camionaje *(E.G./m.)* [1]	Philippines Transport and communication [2] *Transports et communications* [2] Transportes y comunicaciones [2] *(E.G./m.)*	Singapore [2], [3] *(E.G./h.)* [1]	Sri Lanka — Transport / *Transports* / Transportes *(E.G./h.)* [4]	Sri Lanka — Transport *(E.G./d.j.)* [4]	République arabe syrienne [5], [6] *(R.T./m.)* [7]	Thailand (Bangkok) [5] *(E.G./h.)* [8]
	Yen	Dollars	Pesos	Cents	Rupees	Pounds	Baht
1965	210	186	102	106.81	9.65	190	.
1966	210	211	107	109.80	9.81	190	4.00
1967	.	209	108	113.67	10.70	190	5.59
1968	.	215	108	117.39	11.02	190	4.58
1969	.	218	111	125.33	11.44	190	4.29
1970	.	230	113	137.51	12.28	190	5.98
1971	236	239	123	148.27	13.85	190	5.83
1972	242	276	127	144.23	13.31	190	...
1973	280	302	153	125.08	11.32	190	...
1974	320	...	170	158.95	13.91	...	...

EUROPE — EUROPE — EUROPA

Date / Date / Fecha	Austria — Transport and storage / *Transports et entrepôts* / Transportes y almacenaje — Road haulage / *Camionnage* / Camionaje *(R.T./h.)* [7]	Austria — Miscellaneous activities / *Activités diverses* / Actividades diversas *(R.T./h.)* [7]	Belgique — Males [9] / *Hommes* [9] / Hombres [9] *(E.G./d.j.)*	Belgique — Females / *Femmes* / Mujeres *(E.G./d.j.)*	Bulgarie [2], [13] *(E.G./m.)*	Czechoslovakia [14] *(E.G./m.)*	France [16] *(E.G./h.)* [17]
	Schilling	Schilling	Francs	Francs	Leva	Korunas	Francs
1965	13.62	12.38	355.7	239.3	104.5	1 666	4.09
1966	14.98	13.62	382.4	264.7	108.0	1 672	4.22
1967	14.98	13.62	404.1	284.5	118.8	1 761	4.61
1968	16.18	14.71	430.7	298.2	127.1	2 051	5.24
1969	17.62	16.02	467.6	322.9	132.3	2 272	5.75
1970	20.09	18.28	522.3	364.6	141.1	2 288	6.35
1971	20.09	18.28	580.7	408.0	144.5	2 355	7.05
1972	22.62	20.60	659.1	452.4	147.7	2 471	7.71 [15]
1973	24.83	22.62	744.0 [10]	405.4 [10], [12]	160.5	2 356 [15]	8.89
1974	27.20	24.79	1 034.2 [11]	603.3 [11]	164.1 *	2 430	...

EXPLANATORY NOTES: See p. 585.

[1] July of each year. [2] Incl. sea transport. [3] Beginning 1969: adults only. [4] March and Sep. of each year. [5] Incl. salaried employees. [6] Adults only. [7] Minimum rates. [8] Sep. of each year, except for 1967: July, and 1969: Oct. [9] Excl. dockers, boatmen and temporary railroad workers. [10] New industrial classification. [11] Fourth quarter. [12] Second quarter. [13] Socialised sector. [14] State industry. Excl. post, telegraph and telephone. [15] Series replacing former series. [16] Excl. state-operated transport (SNCF and RATP). Excl. communication. [17] Oct. of each year except for 1965-66 and 1968-71: Sep.; 1967: March.

NOTES EXPLICATIVES: Voir p. 589.

[1] *Juillet de chaque année.* [2] *Y compris les transports par mer.* [3] *A partir de 1969: adultes seulement.* [4] *Mars et sept. de chaque année.* [5] *Y compris les employés.* [6] *Adultes seulement.* [7] *Taux minima.* [8] *Sept. de chaque année, sauf pour 1967: juillet, et 1969: oct.* [9] *Non compris les dockers, bateliers et agents temporaires des chemins de fer.* [10] *Nouvelle classification industrielle.* [11] *Quatrième trimestre.* [12] *Deuxième trimestre.* [13] *Secteur socialisé.* [14] *Industrie d'Etat. Non compris les postes, télégraphes et téléphones.* [15] *Série remplaçant la précédente.* [16] *Non compris les transports gérés par l'Etat (SNCF et RATP).* [17] *Oct. de chaque année, sauf pour 1965-66 et 1968-1971: sept.; 1967: mars.*

NOTAS EXPLICATIVAS: Véase pág. 594.

[1] Julio de cada año. [2] Incl. el transporte marítimo. [3] A partir de 1969: adultos solamente. [4] Marzo y sept. de cada año. [5] Incl. los empleados. [6] Adultos solamente. [7] Tarifas mínimas. [8] Sept. de cada año, salvo 1967: julio, y 1969: oct. [9] Excl. los obreros de los muelles, los bateleros y los trabajadores ferroviarios temporeros. [10] Nueva clasificación industrial. [11] Cuarto trimestre. [12] Segundo trimestre. [13] Sector socializado. [14] Industria de Estado. Excl. correos, telégrafos y teléfonos. [15] Serie que substituye a la anterior. [16] Excl. los transportes administrados por el Estado (SNCF y RATP). Excl. las comunicaciones. [17] Oct. de cada año salvo 1965-66 y 1968-1971: sept.; 1967: marzo.

22 Wages in transport, storage and communication (Excl. sea transport)
Salaires dans les transports, entrepôts et communications (Non compris les transports par mer)
Salarios en los transportes, almacenaje y comunicaciones (Excl. el transporte marítimo)

rnings *(E.G.)* or rates *(R.T.)*	Gains *(E.G.)* ou taux *(R.T.)*	Ganancias *(E.G.)* o tarifas *(R.T.)*
hour *(h.),* day *(d. j.),*	par heure *(h.),* jour *(d. j.),*	por hora *(h.),* día *(d. j.),*
ek *(w.s.)* or month *(m.)*	semaine *(w.s.)* ou mois *(m.)*	semana *(w.s.)* o mes *(m.)*

EUROPE — EUROPE — EUROPA

Date / Date / Fecha	German Democratic Republic△[1] Transport *Transports* Transportes (E.G./m.) [2]	Gibraltar (E.G./w.s.) [3]	Hongrie [1] (E.G./m.) [4]	Italie Transport *Transports* Transportes (R.T./h.)	Malta Transport *Transports* Transportes — Males [8] *Hommes* [8] Hombres [8] (E.G./h.) [4]	Malta — Females [8] *Femmes* [8] Mujeres [8] (E.G./h.) [4]	Norway Private land transport *Transports terrestres privés* Transportes terrestres privados — Males [8, 9] *Hommes* [8, 9] Hombres [8, 9] (E.G./h.)
	Mark	£	Forints	(1970 = 100) [6]	Cents	Cents	Kroner
1965	680	.	1 743	*124.5*	14.4	8.5	8.17
1966	696	.	1 809	*127.9*	15.9	9.1	8.69
1967	719	.	1 866	80.9 [7]	17.1	9.2	9.26
1968	747	.	1 946	83.8	20.0	9.2	10.13
1969	787	.	2 057	88.0	22.5	11.1	11.09
1970	816	14.18	2 235 [5]	**100.0**	24.2	15.8	12.25
1971	821	15.39	2 345	111.8	24.1	15.0	13.67
1972	912	17.42	2 457	120.7	23.4	17.6	15.23
1973	909	23.84	2 620	137.0	...	...	17.11
1974	969 *	22.37	2 829 *	173.7	...	...	19.91

EUROPE — EUROPE — EUROPA

Date / Date / Fecha	Pays-Bas Transport and storage *Transports et entrepôts* Transportes y almacenaje (R.T./h.) [10]	Pologne [11] (E.G./m.) [4, 9]	Roumanie [11] Transport *Transports* Transportes (E.G./m.) [4]	Roumanie [11] Communication *Communications* Comunicaciones (E.G./m.) [4]	Suisse [12] Males [8] — *Hommes* [8] — Hombres [8] Skilled and semi-skilled *Qualifiés et semi-qualifiés* Calificados y semicalificados (E.G./h.) [13]	Suisse [12] Unskilled *Non qualifiés* No calificados (E.G./h.) [13]	Sweden [14] Transport *Transports* Transportes Lorry drivers *Conducteurs de camion* Conductores de camión (E.G./h.)	Turquie (E.G./d.j.) [4]
	(1970 = 100)	Zlotys	Lei	Lei	Francs	Francs	Kronor	Liras
1965	65	1 902	.	.	4.97	4.30	8.53	23.79
1966	71	1 928	.	.	5.31	4.62	9.22	28.49
1967	75	2 005	1 287	1 061	5.76	4.93	10.12	31.56
1968	80	2 155	1 325	1 078	6.20	5.28	10.42	33.72
1969	90	2 207	1 357	1 118	6.49	5.67	11.34	38.42
1970	**100**	2 281	1 544	1 239	6.92	6.04	12.70	40.41
1971	115	2 423	1 568	1 250	7.62	6.75	12.89 [15]	46.30
1972	133	2 573	1 599	1 262	8.36	7.54	16.02	52.13
1973	150	2 933	1 626	1 332	9.10 [7]	7.91 [7]	16.55	62.28
1974	173	3 332 *	1 743	1 368	10.51	9.03	18.10	74.17

XPLANATORY NOTES: See p. 585.

State sector. [2] Incl. family allowances. [3] April and of each year, except for 1973: Oct., and 1974: April. cl. salaried employees. [5] Revised series. [6] 1965-indices base 1963 = 100. [7] Series replacing former s. [8] Adults only. [9] Incl. the value of payments in . [10] Incl. vacation pay. [11] Socialised sector. Excl. railways. Beginning 1973: transport only. ccident insurance statistics. [14] Second quarter of year. Adult males. [15] New industrial classification.

NOTES EXPLICATIVES: Voir p. 589.

[1] *Secteur d'Etat.* [2] *Y compris les allocations familiales.* [3] *Avril et oct. de chaque année, sauf pour 1973 : oct., et 1974 : avril.* [4] *Y compris les employés.* [5] *Série révisée.* [6] *1965-66 : indices base 100 en 1963.* [7] *Série remplaçant la précédente.* [8] *Adultes seulement.* [9] *Y compris la valeur des paiements en nature.* [10] *Y compris les versements pour congés payés.* [11] *Secteur socialisé.* [12] *Non compris les chemins de fer. A partir de 1973 : transports seulement.* [13] *Statistiques d'assurance-accidents.* [14] *Deuxième trimestre de chaque année. Hommes adultes.* [15] *Nouvelle classification industrielle.*

NOTAS EXPLICATIVAS: Véase pág. 594.

[1] Sector de Estado. [2] Incl. las asignaciones familiares. [3] Abril y oct. de cada año, salvo 1973: oct., y 1974: abril. [4] Incl. los empleados. [5] Serie revisada. [6] 1965-66: índices base 1963 = 100. [7] Serie que substituye a la anterior. [8] Adultos solamente. [9] Incl. el valor de los pagos en especie. [10] Incl. los pagos por vacaciones. [11] Sector socializado. [12] Excl. los ferrocarriles. A partir de 1973: transportes solamente. [13] Estadísticas del seguro de accidentes. [14] Segundo trimestre de cada año. Hombres adultos. [15] Nueva clasificación industrial.

22 Wages in transport, storage and communication (Excl. sea transport)
Salaires dans les transports, entrepôts et communications (Non compris les transports par mer)
Salarios en los transportes, almacenaje y comunicaciones (Excl. el transporte marítimo)

Earnings *(E.G.)* or rates *(R.T.)*
per hour *(h.)*, day *(d.j.)*,
week *(w.s.)* or month *(m.)*

Gains *(E.G.)* ou taux *(R.T.)*
par heure *(h.)*, jour *(d.j.)*,
semaine *(w.s.)* ou mois *(m.)*

Ganancias *(E.G.)* o tarifas *(R.*
por hora *(h.)*, día *(d.j.)*,
semana *(w.s.)* o mes *(m.)*

Date / Date / Fecha	EUROPE — EUROPE — EUROPA					OCEANIA — OCÉANIE — OCEANÍA		
	United Kingdom				Yugoslavia [6]	Australia		Fiji
	Males [1] / Hommes [1] / Hombres [1]	Females [1,3] / Femmes [1,3] / Mujeres [1,3]	Railways [5] / Chemins de fer [5] / Ferrocarriles [5]			Males [1] / Hommes [1] / Hombres [1]	Communication / Communications / Comunicaciones	Transport / Transports / Transportes
			Males [1] / Hommes [1] / Hombres [1]	Females [1] / Femmes [1] / Mujeres [1]				
	(E.G./h.) [2]		(E.G./w.s.)		(E.G./m.) [7]	(E.G./h.) [7,8]	(R.T./h.) [10,11]	(R.T./d.j.) [12]
	Pence	Pence	£	£	Dinars	Dollars	Cents	Dollars
1965	39.1	30.5	19.05	9.60	.	.	118.8	1.83
1966	41.5	32.6	21.00	10.60	761	1.46	124.4	1.87
1967	43.3	34.0	21.30	11.20	836	1.52	131.9	1.97
1968	48.0	35.7	23.50	12.45	934	1.62	147.1	2.23
1969	50.8 [4]	38.2 [4]	25.95	13.55	1 068	1.75	161.2	2.21
1970	60.3	45.1	29.31	15.92	1 277	1.95	172.6	2.52
1971	70.3	51.6	31.65	18.86	1 556	2.14	193.4	2.86
1972	78.3	58.3	36.15	23.45	1 817	2.49 [9]	217.0	3.38
1973	87.3	67.1	39.49	28.17	2 093	2.89	258.7 *	4.11
1974	105.2	81.6	53.11	32.31	2 618	3.95 *	327.5 *	...

Date / Date / Fecha	OCEANIA — OCÉANIE — OCEANÍA				Nouvelle-Calédonie	URSS [15,16]	RSS de Biélorussie [15]	RSS d'Ukraine [15]
	New Zealand				Labourers [14] / Manœuvres [14] / Obreros no calificados [14]			
	Transport and communication / Transports et communications / Transportes y comunicaciones	Railways / Chemins de fer / Ferrocarriles		Buses / Autobus / Autobuses				
		Engine drivers / Mécaniciens / Maquinistas	Guards / Chefs de train / Jefes de tren	Operators / Conducteurs / Conductores				
	(E.G./h.) [7,13]	(R.T./w.s.) [10]			(R.T./m.) [11]	(E.G./m.) [7]	(E.G./m.) [7]	(E.G./m.) [7]
	Dollars	Dollars	Dollars	Dollars	Francs (CFP)	Roubles	Roubles	Roubles
1965	0.98	.	.	.	11 160	102.1	.	92.8
1966	1.02	47.41	41.19	36.16	11 354	106.1	.	96.0
1967	1.10	49.39	43.06	37.93	12 015	111.7	.	100.3
1968	1.15	52.04	44.55	39.59	12 333	121.1	.	108.9
1969	1.21	57.17	47.35	41.51	14 310	126.0	.	113.1
1970	1.36	65.68	56.13	48.08	16 998	131.0	.	117.0
1971	1.66	75.90	65.07	51.66	18 382	137.5	123.9	122.5
1972	1.87	83.70	71.74	58.13	...	143.8	128.7	127.7
1973	2.06	91.95	79.07	62.83	...	149.6	132.1	130.9
1974	2.40	105.30	90.96	73.75	...	159.3 *	136.5 *	135.3 *

EXPLANATORY NOTES: See p. 585.

NOTES EXPLICATIVES: Voir p. 589.

NOTAS EXPLICATIVAS: Véase pág. 594.

[1] Adults only; Oct. of each year. [2] Manual workers. Excl. railways, London Transport and, for 1965, British Road Services. [3] Full-time workers only. [4] New industrial classification. [5] Excl. Northern Ireland. [6] Socialised sector. Incl. sea transport. [7] Incl. salaried employees. [8] 1966-1972: excl. communication. [9] Scope of series enlarged. [10] Minimum rates; adult males. [11] Dec. of each year. [12] June of each year. [13] Incl. the value of payments in kind. April and Oct. of each year. [14] First category. [15] Socialised sector. [16] Incl. Byelorussian SSR and Ukrainian SSR, shown separately in this table.

[1] *Adultes seulement ; oct. de chaque année.* [2] *Travailleurs manuels. Non compris les chemins de fer, les services de transports londoniens et, pour 1965, les services routiers britanniques.* [3] *Ouvrières à temps complet.* [4] *Nouvelle classification industrielle.* [5] *Non compris l'Irlande du Nord.* [6] *Secteur socialisé. Y compris les transports par mer.* [7] *Y compris les employés.* [8] *1966-1972 : non compris les communications.* [9] *Portée de la série élargie.* [10] *Taux minima ; hommes adultes.* [11] *Déc. de chaque année.* [12] *Juin de chaque année.* [13] *Y compris la valeur des paiements en nature. Avril et oct. de chaque année.* [14] *Première catégorie.* [15] *Secteur socialisé.* [16] *Y compris les RSS de Biélorussie et d'Ukraine, figurant séparément dans ce tableau.*

[1] Adultos solamente; oct. de cada año. [2] Trab[...] dores manuales. Excl. los ferrocarriles, los transp[...] londinenses y 1965: los servicios británicos de carre[...] [3] Obreras de tiempo completo solamente. [4] N[...] clasificación industrial. [5] Excl. Irlanda del N[...] [6] Sector socializado. Incl. el transporte marít[...] [7] Incl. los empleados. [8] 1966-1972: excl. las comu[...] ciones. [9] El alcance de la serie es mayor. [10] Ta[...] mínimas; hombres adultos. [11] Dic. de cada [...] [12] Junio de cada año. [13] Incl. el valor de los pago[...] especie. Abril y oct. de cada año. [14] Primera categ[...] [15] Sector socializado. [16] Incl. las RSS de Bielor[...] y de Ucrania, que figuran separadamente en este cua[...]

23 Wages in agriculture
Salaires dans l'agriculture
Salarios en la agricultura

...rnings *(E.G.)* or rates *(R.T.)*
...hour *(h.)*, day *(d.j.)*,
...k *(w.s.)* or month *(m.)*

Gains *(E.G.)* ou taux *(R.T.)*
par heure *(h.)*, jour *(d.j.)*,
semaine *(w.s.)* ou mois *(m.)*

Ganancias *(E.G.)* o tarifas *(R.T.)*
por hora *(h.)*, día *(d.j.)*,
semana *(w.s.)* o mes *(m.)*

	Cameroun	Ghana		Haute-Volta	Malawi
		AFRICA — AFRIQUE — AFRICA			
	Day labourers	All workers [3]		Permanent labourers	All workers
Date	*Journaliers*	*Ensemble des ouvriers* [3]		*Ouvriers permanents*	*Ensemble des ouvriers*
Date	Jornaleros	Todos los obreros [3]		Obreros permanentes	Todos los obreros
Fecha	M. + F.	Males	Females	M. + F.	M. + F.
	H. + F.	*Hommes*	*Femmes*	*H. + F.*	*H. + F.*
	H. + M.	Hombres	Mujeres	H. + M.	H. + M.
	(R.T./h.) [1,2]	*(E.G./m.)*		*(E.G./m.)*	*(E.G./m.)* [3]
	I	I		I	II
	Francs (CFA)	Cedis	Cedis	Francs (CFA)	Kwacha
1965	26.50	27.28	26.83	.	.
1966	26.50	26.78	24.29	.	.
1967	26.50	26.72	19.72	.	.
1968	28.00	31.67	23.05	.	8.09
1969	29.50	35.19	24.27	11 232	8.15
1970	29.50	34.94	22.80	16 640	8.82
1971	29.50	38.42	23.93	15 876	9.22
1972	29.50	39.64 * [4]	28.69 * [4]	...	9.51
1973	32.50	...	...	...	9.59
1974	37.00	...	...	...	10.90

...XPLANATORY NOTES: See p. 585.　　NOTES EXPLICATIVES: Voir p. 589.　　NOTAS EXPLICATIVAS: Véase pág. 594.

...: Complete wage (workers remunerated wholly in cash).

...: Cash part of remuneration (where received partly in cash and partly in kind). These figures may include the estimated value of payments in kind for:
　　a: board;
　　b: lodging.

I: *Montant total du salaire (cas des travailleurs entièrement rémunérés en espèces)*.

II: *Partie de la rémunération payée en espèces (cas des travailleurs rémunérés partiellement en espèces et partiellement en nature). Ces chiffres peuvent comprendre la valeur estimée des paiements en nature pour:*
　　a: les repas;
　　b: le logement.

I: Salario íntegro (trabajadores remunerados enteramente en dinero).

II: Parte de la remuneración en dinero (en los casos en que ésta consiste en una parte en dinero y otra en especie. Estas cifras pueden incluir el valor estimado de los pagos en especie para:
　　a: los alimentos;
　　b: el alojamiento.

[1] Minimum rates.　[2] Dec. of each year.　[3] Incl. ...ied employees.　[4] Average of March, June and Sep.

[1] *Taux minima.*　[2] *Déc. de chaque année.*　[3] *Y compris les employés.*　[4] *Moyenne de mars, juin et sept.*

[1] Tarifas mínimas.　[2] Dic. de cada año.　[3] Incl. los empleados.　[4] Promedio de marzo, junio y sept.

23 Wages in agriculture
Salaires dans l'agriculture
Salarios en la agricultura

Earnings *(E.G.)* or rates *(R.T.)*
per hour *(h.)*, day *(d.j.)*,
week *(w.s.)* or month *(m.)*

Gains *(E.G.)* ou taux *(R.T.)*
par heure *(h.)*, jour *(d.j.)*,
semaine *(w.s.)* ou mois *(m.)*

Ganancias *(E.G.)* o tarifas *(R.*
por hora *(h.)*, día *(d.j.)*,
semana *(w.s.)* o mes *(m.)*

	AFRICA — AFRIQUE — AFRICA					
	Maroc		Mauritius	Tanzania (Tanganyika)	Tunisie	Zambia	
Date / Date / Fecha	Permanent and seasonal workers [1] / Ouvriers permanents et saisonniers [1] / Obreros permanentes y de temporada [1]		Sugar cane, tea and tobacco plantations / Plantations de canne à sucre, de thé et de tabac / Plantaciones de caña de azúcar, de té y de tabaco	Permanent and seasonal workers / Ouvriers permanents et saisonniers / Obreros permanentes y de temporada	Agricultural workers [1] / Ouvriers agricoles [1] / Obreros agrícolas [1]	Zambians / Zambiens / Zambianos	Others / Autres / Otros
	Males / Hommes / Hombres	Females / Femmes / Mujeres	M. + F. / H. + F. / H. + M.	Males / Hommes / Hombres	Males / Hommes / Hombres	M. + F. / H. + F. / H. + M.	
	(R.T./d.j.) [2,3]		*(E.G./d.j.)* [4]	*(E.G./m.)* [5]	*(E.G./d.j.)* [6]	*(E.G./m.)*	
	I		II + a	II	I [3]	I [7,8]	
	Dirhams	Dirhams	Rupees	Shillings	Millimes	Kwacha	Kwacha
1965	3.89	2.92	.	139	350	14.4	197.0
1966	3.89	2.92	5.44	153	350	16.7	253.3
1967	3.89	2.92	5.61	162	385	20.7	261.8
1968	3.89	2.92	5.49	158	385	29.3	322.7
1969	3.89	2.92	5.74	162	500	30.0	345.3
1970	3.89	2.92	5.88	179	550	23.3	336.3
1971	5.00	4.00	5.69	...	600	28.1	368.4
1972	5.00	4.00	7.54	...	600	33.0	131.3
1973	6.00	4.80	7.64	...	600	34.7 [9]	98.6 [9]
1974	...	...	9.40	...	750	35.5 [9]	110.5 [9]

EXPLANATORY NOTES: See p. 585.   NOTES EXPLICATIVES: Voir p. 589.   NOTAS EXPLICATIVAS: Véase pág. 594.

I: Complete wage (workers remunerated wholly in cash).

II: Cash part of remuneration (where received partly in cash and partly in kind). These figures may include the estimated value of payments in kind for:

   a : board;
   b : lodging.

I: *Montant total du salaire (cas des travailleurs entièrement rémunérés en espèces).*

II: *Partie de la rémunération payée en espèces (cas des travailleurs rémunérés partiellement en espèces et partiellement en nature). Ces chiffres peuvent comprendre la valeur estimée des paiements en nature pour :*

   a : les repas ;
   b : le logement.

I: Salario íntegro (trabajadores remunera enteramente en dinero).

II: Parte de la remuneración en dinero (e casos en que ésta consiste en una par dinero y otra en especie). Estas cifras den incluir el valor estimado de los p en especie para:

   b : los alimentos;
   b : el alojamiento.

[1] Adults only. [2] Minimum rates. [3] Dec. of each year. [4] March and Sep. of each year. [5] June of each year. [6] Minimum daily earnings; excl. wage supplements. [7] All workers. Incl. salaried employees. Beginning 1967: fourth quarter of each year. [8] 1965-69: incl. the value of payment in kind. [9] June.

[1] *Adultes seulement.* [2] *Taux minima.* [3] *Déc. de chaque année.* [4] *Mars et sept. de chaque année.* [5] *Juin de chaque année.* [6] *Gains journaliers minima ; non compris les suppléments de salaire.* [7] *Ensemble des ouvriers. Y compris les employés. A partir de 1967 : quatrième trimestre de chaque année.* [8] *1965-1969 : y compris la valeur des paiements en nature.* [9] *Juin.*

[1] Adultos solamente. [2] Tarifas mínimas. [3] Di cada año. [4] Marzo y sept. de cada año. [5] Jun cada año. [6] Ganancias diarias mínimas; excl. los s mentos al salario. [7] Todos los obreros. Incl. los pleados. A partir de 1967: cuarto trimestre de cada [8] 1965-1969: incl. el valor de los pagos en es [9] Junio.

23 Wages in agriculture
Salaires dans l'agriculture
Salarios en la agricultura

Earnings *(E.G.)* or rates *(R.T.)*
per hour *(h.)*, day *(d.j.)*,
week *(w.s.)* or month *(m.)*

Gains *(E.G.)* ou taux *(R.T.)*
par heure *(h.)*, jour *(d.j.)*,
semaine *(w.s.)* ou mois *(m.)*

Ganancias *(E.G.)* o tarifas *(R.T.)*
por hora *(h.)*, día *(d.j.)*,
semana *(w.s.)* o mes *(m.)*

Date / Date / Fecha	Argentina	Barbados		Belize		Bermuda
		AMERICA — AMÉRIQUE — AMÉRICA				
	Unskilled workers / *Ouvriers non qualifiés* / Obreros no calificados	Day labourers / *Journaliers* / Jornaleros		Casual day labourers / *Journaliers occasionnels* / Jornaleros ocasionales		Agricultural workers / *Ouvriers agricoles* / Obreros agrícolas
		Sugar cane plantations / *Plantations de canne à sucre* / Plantaciones de caña de azúcar		Sugar industry / *Industrie sucrière* / Industria del azúcar	Citrus plantations / *Plantations d'agrumes* / Plantaciones de cítricos	
	Males / *Hommes* / Hombres	Males [4] / *Hommes* [4] / Hombres [4]	Females [4] / *Femmes* [4] / Mujeres [4]	Males / *Hommes* / Hombres		Males / *Hommes* / Hombres
	(E.G./h.) [1]	*(E.G./w.s.)*		*(R.T./d.j.)* [6]		*(R.T./h.)*
	I	I		I		I
	Pesos	Dollars	Dollars	Dollars	Dollars	Dollars
1965	43.99	35.40	24.61	3.50	2.50	.
1966	58.30	21.60	17.53	3.50	2.50	.
1967	76.52	19.47	13.97	3.50	2.50	.
1968	81.59	22.46	15.74	3.50	2.50	1.32
1969	90.92	25.31	18.85	4.00	2.50	1.56
1970	1.14 [2]	26.38	18.56	4.00	2.50	1.91
1971	1.75	31.34	21.67	...	...	1.96
1972	2.50	39.95	25.58	...	...	2.17
1973	3.74 [3]	40.25	23.79	...	...	2.80
1974	...	47.71 [5]	30.36 [5]	...	...	3.14

EXPLANATORY NOTES: See p. 585.

NOTES EXPLICATIVES: Voir p. 589.

NOTAS EXPLICATIVAS: Véase pág. 594.

I: Complete wage (workers remunerated wholly in cash).

II: Cash part of remuneration (where received partly in cash and partly in kind). These figures may include the estimated value of payments in kind for:

  a: board;
  b: lodging.

I: *Montant total du salaire (cas des travailleurs entièrement rémunérés en espèces).*

II: *Partie de la rémunération payée en espèces (cas des travailleurs rémunérés partiellement en espèces et partiellement en nature). Ces chiffres peuvent comprendre la valeur estimée des paiements en nature pour :*

  a: les repas ;
  b: le logement.

I: Salario íntegro (trabajadores remunerados enteramente en dinero).

II: Parte de la remuneración en dinero (en los casos en que ésta consiste en una parte en dinero y otra en especie). Estas cifras pueden incluir el valor estimado de los pagos en especie para:

  a: los alimentos;
  b: el alojamiento.

[1] Minimum earnings. [2] New currency introduced in Jan. 1970: 1 new peso = 100 old pesos. [3] March. [4] Adults only. [5] Average of March, June and Sep. [6] Dec. of each year. Sugar industry: prevailing rates; citrus plantations: minimum rates.

[1] *Gains minima.* [2] *Nouvelle monnaie introduite en janv. 1970 : 1 nouveau peso = 100 anciens pesos.* [3] *Mars.* [4] *Adultes seulement.* [5] *Moyenne de mars, juin et sept.* [6] *Déc. de chaque année. Industrie sucrière : taux prédominants ; plantations d'agrumes : taux minima.*

[1] Ganancias mínimas. [2] Nueva moneda adoptada en enero de 1970: 1 nuevo peso = 100 antiguos. [3] Marzo. [4] Adultos solamente. [5] Promedio de marzo, junio y sept. [6] Dic. de cada año. Industria del azúcar: tarifas predominantes; plantaciones de cítricos: tarifas mínimas.

23 Wages in agriculture
Salaires dans l'agriculture
Salarios en la agricultura

Earnings *(E.G.)* or rates *(R.T.)*
per hour *(h.)*, day *(d.j.)*,
week *(w.s.)* or month *(m.)*

Gains *(E.G.)* ou taux *(R.T.)*
par heure *(h.)*, jour *(d.j.)*,
semaine *(w.s.)* ou mois *(m.)*

Ganancias *(E.G.)* o tarifas *(R.T.)*
por hora *(h.)*, día *(d.j.)*,
semana *(w.s.)* o mes *(m.)*

	AMERICA — AMÉRIQUE — AMÉRICA						
	Canada				Colombia		Costa Rica
Date / Date / Fecha	General farm hands / *Domestiques de ferme* / Peones agrícolas				Agricultural workers [2] / *Ouvriers agricoles* [2] / Obreros agrícolas [2]		General farm hands / *Domestiques de ferme* / Peones agrícolas
							Coffee plantations / *Plantations de caféiers* / Plantaciones de café	Agriculture and livestock production [3] / *Agriculture et élevage* [3] / Agricultura y ganadería [3]
	Males / *Hommes* / Hombres				Males / *Hommes* / Hombres	Females / *Femmes* / Mujeres	M. + F. / H. + F. / H. + M.	
	(R.T./d.j.) [1]		(R.T./m.) [1]		(E.G./d.j.)		(R.T./h.) [4]	
	I	II	I	II	I		II + a + b	
	Dollars	Dollars	Dollars	Dollars	Pesos	Pesos	Colones	Colones
1965	8.90	7.00	196	149	11.95	9.55	1.28	1.15
1966	9.60	7.70	218	168	14.26	10.61	1.28	1.15
1967	10.30	8.10	242	186	14.75	11.35	1.28	1.15
1968	11.00	9.00	262	208	15.55	12.55	1.28	1.15
1969	12.00	10.00	276	228	19.00	14.35	1.34	1.21
1970	12.50	10.10	288	238	19.30	14.75	1.34	1.21
1971	13.10	10.60	300	250	...	...	1.50	1.39
1972	14.03	11.50	323	268	...	...	1.61	1.60
1973	16.00	13.17	371	315	...	...	1.61	1.75
1974	18.57	15.63	433	370	...	...	2.28	2.26

EXPLANATORY NOTES: See p. 585.   NOTES EXPLICATIVES: Voir p. 589.   NOTAS EXPLICATIVAS: Véase pág. 594.

I: Complete wage (workers remunerated wholly in cash).

II: Cash part of remuneration (where received partly in cash and partly in kind). These figures may include the estimated value of payments in kind for:

   a: board;
   b: lodging.

I: *Montant total du salaire (cas des travailleurs entièrement rémunérés en espèces).*

II: *Partie de la rémunération payée en espèces (cas des travailleurs rémunérés partiellement en espèces et partiellement en nature). Ces chiffres peuvent comprendre la valeur estimée des paiements en nature pour :*

   a : les repas ;
   b : le logement.

I: Salario íntegro (trabajadores remunerados enteramente en dinero).

II: Parte de la remuneración en dinero (en los casos en que ésta consiste en una parte en dinero y otra en especie). Estas cifras pueden incluir el valor estimado de los pagos en especie para:

   a : los alimentos;
   b : el alojamiento.

[1] Average of rates on 15 Jan., 15 May and 15 Aug. [2] Adults only. Areas with a hot climate. [3] Excl. plantations. [4] Minimum rates.

[1] *Moyennes des taux au 15 janv., 15 mai et 15 août.* [2] *Adultes seulement. Régions de climat chaud.* [3] *Non compris les plantations.* [4] *Taux minima.*

[1] Promedio de tarifas al 15 de enero, 15 de mayo y 15 de agosto. [2] Adultos solamente. Regiones de clima cálido. [3] Excl. las plantaciones. [4] Tarifas mínimas.

23 Wages in agriculture
Salaires dans l'agriculture
Salarios en la agricultura

Earnings *(E.G.)* or rates *(R.T.)*
per hour *(h.)*, day *(d.j.)*,
week *(w.s.)* or month *(m.)*

Gains *(E.G.)* ou taux *(R.T.)*
par heure *(h.)*, jour *(d.j.)*,
semaine *(w.s.)* ou mois *(m.)*

Ganancias *(E.G.)* o tarifas *(R.T.)*
por hora *(h.)*, día *(d.j.)*,
semana *(w.s.)* o mes *(m.)*

	AMERICA — AMÉRIQUE — AMÉRICA					
	Chile	**Grenada**		**Guyana**		**México**	**Surinam**
Date *Date* Fecha	Permanent and non-permanent workers [1] *Ouvriers permanents et non permanents* [1] Obreros permanentes y no permanentes [1]	Permanent labourers [1] *Ouvriers permanents* [1] Obreros permanentes [1]		Permanent and non-permanent workers *Ouvriers permanents et non permanents* Obreros permanentes y no permanentes — Sugar industry *Industrie sucrière* Industria del azúcar		Regular day labourers *Journaliers stables* Jornaleros estables	Agricultural workers *Ouvriers agricoles* Obreros agrícolas
	Males *Hommes* Hombres	Males *Hommes* Hombres	Females *Femmes* Mujeres	Males *Hommes* Hombres	Females *Femmes* Mujeres	Males *Hommes* Hombres	M. + F. H. + F. H. + M.
	(R.T./d.j.) [2]	*(E.G./w.s.)* [5]		*(E.G./d.j.)*		*(R.T./d.j.)* [2]	*(E.G./m.)*
	I	I		I; II + a + b		II	I
	Escudos	Dollars	Dollars	Dollars	Dollars	Pesos	Guilders
1965	3.26	11.80	10.70	5.59	2.92	13.47	.
1966	4.10	12.10	11.00	5.82	3.09	15.72	.
1967	4.80	8.80	7.60	5.94	3.19	15.72	.
1968	5.58	9.64	8.40	5.92	3.27	18.32	.
1969	7.48	11.60	9.73	6.43	3.58	18.32	.
1970	12.00	12.00	10.00	6.46	3.74	21.20	.
1971	20.00	12.00	9.00	7.68	3.82	21.20	127
1972	30.00 [3]	12.00	9.00	…	…	24.94	133
1973	63.33 [4]	12.00	9.00	…	…	…	139
1974	…	12.00	9.00	…	…	…	…

EXPLANATORY NOTES: See p. 585.

NOTES EXPLICATIVES: Voir p. 589.

NOTAS EXPLICATIVAS: Véase pág. 594.

I: Complete wage (workers remunerated wholly in cash).

II: Cash part of remuneration (where received partly in cash and partly in kind). These figures may include the estimated value of payments in kind for:

    a: board;
    b: lodging.

I: *Montant total du salaire (cas des travailleurs entièrement rémunérés en espèces).*

II: *Partie de la rémunération payée en espèces (cas des travailleurs rémunérés partiellement en espèces et partiellement en nature). Ces chiffres peuvent comprendre la valeur estimée des paiements en nature pour :*

    a: les repas ;
    b: le logement.

I: Salario íntegro (trabajadores remunerados enteramente en dinero).

II: Parte de la remuneración en dinero (en los casos en que ésta consiste en una parte en dinero y otra en especie). Estas cifras pueden incluir el valor estimado de los pagos en especie para:

    a: los alimentos;
    b: el alojamiento.

[1] Adults only. [2] Minimum rates. [3] Jan.-Sep. [4] Beginning October 1972. [5] Excl. end-of-year bonuses ranging from 1 to 10 days' pay.

[1] *Adultes seulement.* [2] *Taux minima.* [3] *Janv.-sept.* [4] *A partir d'octobre 1972.* [5] *Non compris les gratifications de fin d'année allant de 1 à 10 jours de paie.*

[1] Adultos solamente. [2] Tarifas mínimas. [3] Enero-sept. [4] A partir de octubre de 1972. [5] Excl. las bonificaciones de fin de año, que varían entre 1 y 10 días de pago.

23 Wages in agriculture
Salaires dans l'agriculture
Salarios en la agricultura

Earnings *(E.G.)* or rates *(R.T.)*
per hour *(h.)*, day *(d.j.)*,
week *(w.s.)* or month *(m.)*

Gains *(E.G.)* ou taux *(R.T.)*
par heure *(h.)*, jour *(d.j.)*,
semaine *(w.s.)* ou mois *(m.)*

Ganancias *(E.G.)* o tarifas *(R.T.)*
por hora *(h.)*, día *(d.j.)*,
semana *(w.s.)* o mes *(m.)*

Date / *Date* / Fecha	AMERICA — AMÉRIQUE — AMÉRICA							ASIA — ASIE ASIA
	United States [1]					Uruguay		Burma
	All workers / *Ensemble des ouvriers* / Todos los obreros	Day labourers / *Journaliers* / Jornaleros	Permanent and seasonal workers / *Ouvriers permanents et saisonniers* / Obreros permanentes y de temporada			General farm hands / *Domestiques de ferme* / Peones agrícolas		Agricultural workers / *Ouvriers agricoles* / Obreros agrícolas —— Hevea plantations / *Plantations d'hévéas* / Plantaciones de hevea
	Males and females / *Hommes et femmes* / Hombres y mujeres					Males and females / *Hommes et femmes* / Hombres y mujeres		Males / *Hommes* / Hombres
	(R.T./h.) [2],[3]	*(R.T./d.j.)* [2]		*(R.T./m.)* [2]		*(E.G./m.)* [4]		*(E.G./m.)*
	I; II	I	II + a + b	II + b	II + a + b	I	II	I
	$	$	$	$	$	Pesos	Pesos	Kyats
1965	0.951	7.60	7.40	223.00	170.00	920	530	213.19
1966	1.030	8.20	8.00	243.00	185.00	2 150	1 400	244.93
1967	1.120	9.00	8.60	262.00	199.00	4 498	3 140	253.55
1968	1.210	9.90	9.30	283.00	216.00	11 737	8 192	204.59
1969	1.330	10.90	10.10	307.00	234.00	13 850	9 665	211.01
1970	1.420	11.70	10.70	328.00	251.00	17 315	12 070	218.20
1971	1.480	12.20	11.20	340.00	263.00	22 025	15 355	228.55
1972	1.580	13.20	12.00	361.00	280.00	31 715	22 110	230.09
1973	1.730	14.50	13.10	393.00	309.00	56 565	39 500	188.16
1974	1.930 *	16.25 *	14.50 *	427.00 *	336.00 *	120.000	73 080	...

EXPLANATORY NOTES: See p. 585.   NOTES EXPLICATIVES: Voir p. 589.   NOTAS EXPLICATIVAS: Véase pág. 594.

I: Complete wage (workers remunerated wholly in cash).

II: Cash part of remuneration (where received partly in cash and partly in kind). These figures may include the estimated value of payments in kind for:

  a: board;
  b: lodging.

I: *Montant total du salaire (cas des travailleurs entièrement rémunérés en espèces).*

II: *Partie de la rémunération payée en espèces (cas des travailleurs rémunérés partiellement en espèces et partiellement en nature). Ces chiffres peuvent comprendre la valeur estimée des paiements en nature pour :*

  a: les repas ;
  b: le logement.

I: Salario íntegro (trabajadores remunerados enteramente en dinero).

II: Parte de la remuneración en dinero (en los casos en que ésta consiste en una parte en dinero y otra en especie). Estas cifras pueden incluir el valor estimado de los pagos en especie para:

  a: los alimentos;
  b: el alojamiento.

[1] Excl. Alaska and Hawaii. [2] Average of rates on 1 April, 1 July and 1 Oct. of year indicated, and 1 Jan. of following year. [3] Weighted average of all series of agricultural rates, converted to series of rates per hour. [4] Dec. of each year.

[1] *Non compris Alaska et Hawaï.* [2] *Moyenne des taux au 1er avril, 1er juillet et 1er oct. de l'année indiquée et 1er janv. de l'année suivante.* [3] *Moyenne pondérée de toutes les séries de taux dans l'agriculture, converties en séries de taux horaires.* [4] *Déc. de chaque année.*

[1] Excl. Alaska y Hawai. [2] Promedio de tarifas al 1.º de abril, 1.º de julio y 1.º de oct. del año indicado, y 1.º de enero del año siguiente. [3] Promedio ponderado de todas las series de tarifas en la agricultura convertidas en series de tarifas por hora. [4] Dic. de cada año.

23 Wages in agriculture
Salaires dans l'agriculture
Salarios en la agricultura

Earnings *(E.G.)* or rates *(R.T.)*
per hour *(h.)*, day *(d.j.)*,
week *(w.s.)* or month *(m.)*

Gains *(E.G.)* ou taux *(R.T.)*
par heure *(h.)*, jour *(d.j.)*,
semaine *(w.s.)* ou mois *(m.)*

Ganancias *(E.G.)* o tarifas *(R.T.)*
por hora *(h.)*, día *(d.j.)*,
semana *(w.s.)* o mes *(m.)*

	ASIA — ASIE — ASIA							
	Cyprus		India [4]	Israel	Japan [8]		Korea, Rep. of	
Date / Date / Fecha	Agricultural workers [1] / Ouvriers agricoles [1] / Obreros agrícolas [1]		Agricultural workers / Ouvriers agricoles / Obreros agrícolas	Permanent labourers [6] / Ouvriers permanents [6] / Obreros permanentes [6]	Casual day labourers / Journaliers occasionnels / Jornaleros ocasionales		Agricultural workers / Ouvriers agricoles / Obreros agrícolas	
	Males / Hommes / Hombres	Females / Femmes / Mujeres	M. + F. / H. + F. / H. + M.	M. + F. / H. + F. / H. + M.	Males / Hommes / Hombres	Females / Femmes / Mujeres	Males / Hommes / Hombres	Females / Femmes / Mujeres
	(E.G./w.s.) [2]		*(R.T./d.j.)* [5]	*(E.G./m.)*	*(E.G./d.j.)*		*(R.T./d.j.)*	
	II		II	I	II		II [9]	
	Pounds	Pounds	Rupees	Pounds	Yen	Yen	Won	Won
1965	5.85	2.85	1.91	283	838	672	221	141
1966	6.36	2.67	2.20	334	913	743	256	165
1967	7.63 [3]	3.69 [3]	2.47	332	1 011	824	307	207
1968	8.32	4.03	2.52	332 [7]	1 204	1 001	381	260
1969	8.70	4.21	2.63	354	1 333	1 120	463	316
1970	9.85	4.76	2.87	375	1 509	1 226	579	392
1971	10.46	5.06	2.94	446	1 774	1 389	695	472
1972	10.36	5.34	2.90	521	1 964	1 549	803	552
1973	12.52	7.18	2.93	679	2 300	1 818	886	620
1974	15.05	8.41	3.28	970	2 984	2 371	1 167 *	818 *

EXPLANATORY NOTES: See p. 585.

NOTES EXPLICATIVES: Voir p. 589.

NOTAS EXPLICATIVAS: Véase pág. 594.

I: Complete wage (workers remunerated wholly in cash).

II: Cash part of remuneration (where received partly in cash and partly in kind). These figures may include the estimated value of payments in kind for:
  a: board;
  b: lodging.

I: *Montant total du salaire (cas des travailleurs entièrement rémunérés en espèces).*

II: *Partie de la rémunération payée en espèces (cas des travailleurs rémunérés partiellement en espèces et partiellement en nature). Ces chiffres peuvent comprendre la valeur estimée des paiements en nature pour :*
  a: les repas ;
  b: le logement.

I: Salario íntegro (trabajadores remunerados enteramente en dinero).

II: Parte de la remuneración en dinero (en los casos en que ésta consiste en una parte en dinero y otra en especie). Estas cifras pueden incluir el valor estimado de los pagos en especie para:
  a: los alimentos;
  b: el alojamiento.

[1] Adults only. [2] Oct. of each year, except 1969: Sep. [3] Sampling design revised. [4] Maharashtra state. [5] Year beginning in July of year indicated. [6] Incl. salaried employees. [7] Series replacing former series. [8] Excl. Okinawa Prefecture. [9] Incl. the value of allowances in kind.

[1] *Adultes seulement.* [2] *Oct. de chaque année, sauf pour 1969 : sept.* [3] *Plan d'échantillonnage révisé.* [4] *Etat de Maharashtra.* [5] *Année commençant en juillet de l'année indiquée.* [6] *Y compris les employés.* [7] *Série remplaçant la précédente.* [8] *Non compris la préfecture d'Okinawa.* [9] *Y compris la valeur des prestations en nature.*

[1] Adultos solamente. [2] Oct. de cada año, salvo 1969: sept. [3] Diseño de la muestra revisado. [4] Estado de Maharashtra. [5] Año que comienza en julio del año indicado. [6] Incl. los empleados. [7] Serie que substituye a la anterior. [8] Excl. la prefectura de Okinawa. [9] Incl. el valor de las prestaciones en especie.

WAGES

23 Wages in agriculture
Salaires dans l'agriculture
Salarios en la agricultura

Earnings *(E.G.)* or rates *(R.T.)*
per hour *(h.)*, day *(d.j.)*,
week *(w.s.)* or month *(m.)*

Gains *(E.G.)* ou taux *(R.T.)*
par heure *(h.)*, jour *(d.j.)*,
semaine *(w.s.)* ou mois *(m.)*

Ganancias *(E.G.)* o tarifas *(R.T.)*
por hora *(h.)*, día *(d.j.)*,
semana *(w.s.)* o mes *(m.)*

	ASIA — ASIE — ASIA						
	Malaysia		Pakistan	Philippines	Sri Lanka		
	West Malaysia						
Date	Hevea plantations *Plantations d'hévéas* Plantaciones de hevea		General farm hands *Domestiques de ferme* Peones agrícolas	Agricultural workers *Ouvriers agricoles* Obreros agrícolas	Agricultural workers [1] *Ouvriers agricoles* [1] Obreros agrícolas [1]		
Date Fecha	Agricultural workers [1] *Ouvriers agricoles* [1] Obreros agrícolas [1]	Tappers [1] *Saigneurs* [1] Sangradores [1]			Tea plantations *Plantations de thé* Plantaciones de té		
	Males *Hommes* Hombres	Females *Femmes* Mujeres	M. + F. *H. + F.* H. + M.	Males *Hommes* Hombres	M. + F. *H. + F.* H. + M.	Males *Hommes* Hombres	Females *Femmes* Mujeres
	(E.G./m.) [2]		*(E.G./m.)* [2]	*(E.G./d.j.)* [3]	*(E.G./d.j.)*	*(E.G./d.j.)* [4]	
	I		I	I	I + a + b	I	
	Dollars	Dollars	Dollars	Rupees	Pesos	Rupees	Rupees
1965	.	.	.	1.92	.	2.86	2.36
1966	74.54	56.24	93.63	2.17	.	2.84	2.32
1967	74.00	56.00	96.00	2.48	.	2.88	2.41
1968	76.00	58.00	99.00	2.49	.	3.31	2.73
1969	78.00	62.00	116.00	2.48	.	3.31	2.75
1970	78.00	59.00	113.00	3.00	.	3.40	2.74
1971	75.00	59.00	109.00	3.15	3.55	3.47	3.38
1972	76.00	60.00	105.00	3.30	3.72	4.24	3.00
1973	82.00	72.00	143.00	5.75 *	4.40	3.91	3.58
1974	...	...	...	...	...	4.99	3.80

EXPLANATORY NOTES: See p. 585.　　　　NOTES EXPLICATIVES: Voir p. 589.　　　　NOTAS EXPLICATIVAS: Véase pág. 594.

I: Complete wage (workers remunerated wholly in cash).

II: Cash part of remuneration (where received partly in cash and partly in kind). These figures may include the estimated value of payments in kind for:
  a: board;
  b: lodging.

I: *Montant total du salaire (cas des travailleurs entièrement rémunérés en espèces).*

II: *Partie de la rémunération payée en espèces (cas des travailleurs rémunérés partiellement en espèces et partiellement en nature). Ces chiffres peuvent comprendre la valeur estimée des paiements en nature pour:*
  a: les repas;
  b: le logement.

I: Salario íntegro (trabajadores remunerados enteramente en dinero).

II: Parte de la remuneración en dinero (en los casos en que ésta consiste en una parte en dinero y otra en especie). Estas cifras pueden incluir el valor estimado de los pagos en especie para:
  a: los alimentos;
  b: el alojamiento.

[1] Adults only.　[2] July of each year.　[3] Incl. the value of payments in kind.　[4] March and Sep. of each year.

[1] *Adultes seulement.*　[2] *Juillet de chaque année.*　[3] *Y compris la valeur des paiements en nature.*　[4] *Mars et sept. de chaque année.*

[1] Adultos solamente.　[2] Julio de cada año.　[3] Incl. el valor de los pagos en especie.　[4] Marzo y sept. de cada año.

23 Wages in agriculture
Salaires dans l'agriculture
Salarios en la agricultura

Earnings *(E.G.)* or rates *(R.T.)*
per hour *(h.)*, day *(d.j.)*,
week *(w.s.)* or month *(m.)*

Gains *(E.G.)* ou taux *(R.T.)*
par heure *(h.)*, jour *(d.j.)*,
semaine *(w.s.)* ou mois *(m.)*

Ganancias *(E.G.)* o tarifas *(R.T.)*
por hora *(h.)*, día *(d.j.)*,
semana *(w.s.)* o mes *(m.)*

Date / Date / Fecha	ASIA — ASIE — ASIA					EUROPE — EUROPE — EUROPA	
	Sud Viet-Nam, Rép. du			République arabe syrienne		Austria	
	Plantations / Plantations / Plantaciones			Seasonal workers [1] / Ouvriers saisonniers [1] / Obreros de temporada [1]	Permanent labourers [1] / Ouvriers permanents [1] / Obreros permanentes [1]	Agricultural workers [4] / Ouvriers agricoles [4] / Obreros agrícolas [4]	
	Unskilled workers [1] / Ouvriers non qualifiés [1] / Obreros no calificados [1]		Skilled workers [1] / Ouvriers qualifiés [1] / Obreros calificados [1]				
	Males / Hommes / Hombres	Females / Femmes / Mujeres	Males / Hommes / Hombres	M. + F. / H. + F. / H. + M.	M. + F. / H. + F. / H. + M.	Males / Hommes / Hombres	Females / Femmes / Mujeres
	(E.G./d.j.)			(R.T./d.j.) [3]		(R.T./m.)	
	II [2]			I		II + a + b	
	Piastres	Piastres	Piastres	Pounds	Pounds	Schilling	Schilling
1965	55.80	47.90	92.10	.	.	2 106	2 106
1966	74.70	68.40	120.20	.	.	2 203	2 184
1967	97.73	92.60	177.64	.	.	2 445	2 424
1968	119.94	104.20	194.94	.	.	2 617	2 594
1969	143.04	110.41	244.61	4.45	4.13	2 800	2 775
1970	193.01	174.48	388.27	4.45	4.27	2 986	2 960
1971	213.04	227.77	435.35	4.49	4.93	3 255	3 310
1972	371.50	241.80	498.30	4.49	4.93	3 582	3 642
1973	381.60	257.30	543.80	4.61	5.19	4 011	4 078
1974	...	...	...	4.86	5.27	4 648	4 806

EXPLANATORY NOTES: See p. 585.　　　NOTES EXPLICATIVES: Voir p. 589.　　　NOTAS EXPLICATIVAS: Véase pág. 594.

I: Complete wage (workers remunerated wholly in cash).

II: Cash part of remuneration (where received partly in cash and partly in kind). These figures may include the estimated value of payments in kind for:
 a: board;
 b: lodging.

I: *Montant total du salaire (cas des travailleurs entièrement rémunérés en espèces).*

II: *Partie de la rémunération payée en espèces (cas des travailleurs rémunérés partiellement en espèces et partiellement en nature). Ces chiffres peuvent comprendre la valeur estimée des paiements en nature pour :*
 a : les repas ;
 b : le logement.

I: Salario íntegro (trabajadores remunerados enteramente en dinero).

II: Parte de la remuneración en dinero (en los casos en que ésta consiste en una parte en dinero y otra en especie). Estas cifras pueden incluir el valor estimado de los pagos en especie para:
 a : los alimentos;
 b : el alojamiento.

[1] Adults only. [2] Incl. the value of payments in kind. Incl. end-of-year bonuses. Dec. of each year, except for 1973: June. [3] Minimum rates. [4] Permanent workers.

[1] *Adultes seulement.* [2] *Y compris la valeur des paiements en nature. Y compris les primes de fin d'année. Déc. de chaque année, sauf pour 1973 : juin.* [3] *Taux minima.* [4] *Ouvriers permanents.*

[1] Adultos solamente. [2] Incl. el valor de los pagos en especie. Incl. las primas de fin de año. Dic. de cada año, salvo 1973: junio. [3] Tarifas mínimas. [4] Obreros permanentes.

WAGES

23   Wages in agriculture
Salaires dans l'agriculture
Salarios en la agricultura

Earnings *(E.G.)* or rates *(R.T.)*
per hour *(h.)*, day *(d.j.)*,
week *(w.s.)* or month *(m.)*

Gains *(E.G.)* ou taux *(R.T.)*
par heure *(h.)*, jour *(d.j.)*,
semaine *(w.s.)* ou mois *(m.)*

Ganancias *(E.G.)* o tarifas *(R.T.)*
por hora *(h.)*, día *(d.j.)*,
semana *(w.s.)* o mes *(m.)*

	EUROPE — EUROPE — EUROPA						
	Belgique		Bulgarie				Czechoslovakia [4]
	Agricultural workers *Ouvriers agricoles* Obreros agrícolas		State agricultural undertakings *Entreprises agricoles d'Etat* Empresas agrícolas del Estado		Machine-tractor stations *Stations de machines agricoles et de tracteurs* Estaciones de máquinas agrícolas y de tractores		All workers [3] *Ensemble des ouvriers* [3] Todos los obreros [3]
Date *Date* Fecha			Agricultural workers *Ouvriers agricoles* Obreros agrícolas	Total [3]	Workers *Ouvriers* Obreros	Total [3]	
	Males *Hommes* Hombres	Females *Femmes* Mujeres	Males and females *Hommes et femmes* Hombres y mujeres		Males and females *Hommes et femmes* Hombres y mujeres		M. + F. H. + F. H. + M.
	(E.G./d.j.)		*(E.G./m.)*		*(E.G./m.)*		*(E.G./m.)*
	I		II		I		I
	Francs	Francs	Leva	Leva	Leva	Leva	Korunas
1965	.	.	79.5	80.9	83.8	85.0	1 329
1966	276.5	202.8	86.3	87.8	89.3	89.3	1 409 [5]
1967	290.2	218.9	92.9	94.8	102.8	103.3	1 492
1968	305.1	230.4	95.1	97.1	104.4	105.6	1 652
1969	324.0	255.7	96.6	98.5	107.2	108.5	1 790
1970	351.9	272.2	102.4	104.2	113.9	114.6	1 827
1971	392.4	297.6	109.9	110.9	121.1	120.3	1 890
1972	436.7	322.7	117.8	118.9	129.3	127.0	1 978
1973	516.1 [1]	327.1 [1]	128.8	129.4	130.7	136.3	2 090
1974	703.4 [2]	438.0 [2]	131.0	135.0	...	...	2 172

EXPLANATORY NOTES: See p. 585.

NOTES EXPLICATIVES: Voir p. 589.

NOTAS EXPLICATIVAS: Véase pág. 594.

I: Complete wage (workers remunerated wholly in cash).

II: Cash part of remuneration (where received partly in cash and partly in kind). These figures may include the estimated value of payments in kind for:
   a: board;
   b: lodging.

I: *Montant total du salaire (cas des travailleurs entièrement rémunérés en espèces).*

II: *Partie de la rémunération payée en espèces (cas des travailleurs rémunérés partiellement en espèces et partiellement en nature). Ces chiffres peuvent comprendre la valeur estimée des paiements en nature pour:*
   a: les repas;
   b: le logement.

I: Salario íntegro (trabajadores remunerados enteramente en dinero).

II: Parte de la remuneración en dinero (en los casos en que ésta consiste en una parte en dinero y otra en especie). Estas cifras pueden incluir el valor estimado de los pagos en especie para:
   a: los alimentos;
   b: el alojamiento.

[1] New industrial classification. [2] Fourth quarter. [3] Incl. salaried employees. [4] Socialised sector (except agricultural co-operatives); incl. forestry. [5] Scope of series revised.

[1] *Nouvelle classification industrielle.* [2] *Quatrième trimestre.* [3] *Y compris les employés.* [4] *Secteur socialisé (à l'exclusion des coopératives agricoles); y compris la sylviculture.* [5] *Portée de la série révisée.*

[1] Nueva clasificación industrial. [2] Cuarto trimestre. [3] Incl. los empleados. [4] Sector socializado (pero excl. las cooperativas agrícolas); incl. la silvicultura. [5] Alcance de la serie revisado.

23 Wages in agriculture
Salaires dans l'agriculture
Salarios en la agricultura

Earnings *(E.G.)* or rates *(R.T.)*
per hour *(h.)*, day *(d.j.)*,
week *(w.s.)* or month *(m.)*

Gains *(E.G.)* ou taux *(R.T.)*
par heure *(h.)*, jour *(d.j.)*,
semaine *(w.s.)* ou mois *(m.)*

Ganancias *(E.G.)* o tarifas *(R.T.)*
por hora *(h.)*, día *(d.j.)*,
semana *(w.s.)* o mes *(m.)*

	EUROPE — EUROPE — EUROPA						
	Denmark			España	Finland		
	Casual day labourers		General farm hands	Permanent labourers	General farm hands		All workers	
Date	*Journaliers occasionnels*		*Domestiques de ferme*	*Ouvriers permanents*	*Domestiques de ferme*		*Ensemble des ouvriers*	
Date	Jornaleros ocasionales		Peones agrícolas	Obreros permanentes	Peones agrícolas		Todos los obreros	
Fecha	Males [1]	Females [1]	M. + F. [1,4]	Males	Males	Females	Males	Females
	Hommes [1]	*Femmes* [1]	*H. + F.* [1,4]	*Hommes*	*Hommes*	*Femmes*	*Hommes*	*Femmes*
	Hombres [1]	Mujeres [1]	H. + M. [1,4]	Hombres	Hombres	Mujeres	Hombres	Mujeres
	(E.G./h.) [2]		*(E.G./h.)* [5]	*(E.G./d.j.)*	*(E.G./h.)*		*(E.G./h.)*	
	I		II	I	I; II + *a* + *b*			
	Kroner	Kroner	Kroner	Pesetas	Markkaa	Markkaa	Markkaa	Markkaa
1965	5.37	5.56	9 660	98.29	1.88	1.53	2.12	1.58
1966	6.05	6.41	11 011	111.58	1.99	1.62	2.33	1.75
1967	6.54	7.03	12 175	126.43	2.15	1.74	2.52	1.96
1968	7.21	7.86	12 368	137.15	2.37	1.89	2.75	2.11
1969	8.21	9.02	12 712	153.20	2.63	2.19	2.95	2.36
1970	8.66	9.59	14 232	174.37	2.89	2.39	3.27	2.65
1971	13.02	11.55	13 860 [3]	187.64	3.36	2.95	3.71	3.14
1972	14.26	13.09	15 300	214.36	3.95	3.51	4.56	3.73
1973	16.58 [3]		16 500	250.80	5.00	4.56	5.64	4.93
1974	...		...	335.80	6.06	5.82	7.10	6.14

EXPLANATORY NOTES: See p. 585.

NOTES EXPLICATIVES: Voir p. 589.

NOTAS EXPLICATIVAS: Véase pág. 594.

I: Complete wage (workers remunerated wholly in cash).

II: Cash part of remuneration (where received partly in cash and partly in kind). These figures may include the estimated value of payments in kind for:

   a: board;
   b: lodging.

I: *Montant total du salaire (cas des travailleurs entièrement rémunérés en espèces).*

II: *Partie de la rémunération payée en espèces (cas des travailleurs rémunérés partiellement en espèces et partiellement en nature). Ces chiffres peuvent comprendre la valeur estimée des paiements en nature pour :*

   a : les repas ;
   b : le logement.

I: Salario íntegro (trabajadores remunerados enteramente en dinero).

II: Parte de la remuneración en dinero (en los casos en que ésta consiste en una parte en dinero y otra en especie). Estas cifras pueden incluir el valor estimado de los pagos en especie para:

   a : los alimentos;
   b : el alojamiento.

[1] Adults only. [2] April of each year. [3] Series replacing former series. [4] 1965-1970: males only. [5] Per year.

[1] *Adultes seulement.* [2] *Avril de chaque année.* [3] *Série remplaçant la précédente.* [4] *1965-1970 : hommes seulement.* [5] *Par année.*

[1] Adultos solamente. [2] Abril de cada año. [3] Serie que substituye a la anterior. [4] 1965-1970: hombres solamente. [5] Por año.

23 Wages in agriculture
Salaires dans l'agriculture
Salarios en la agricultura

Earnings *(E.G.)* or rates *(R.T.)*
per hour *(h.)*, day *(d.j.)*,
week *(w.s.)* or month *(m.)*

Gains *(E.G.)* ou taux *(R.T.)*
par heure *(h.)*, jour *(d.j.)*,
semaine *(w.s.)* ou mois *(m.)*

Ganancias *(E.G.)* o tarifas *(R.T.)*
por hora *(h.)* día *(d.j.)*,
semana *(w.s.)* o mes *(m.)*

	EUROPE — EUROPE — EUROPA							
	France		German Dem. Rep. △ [2]	Germany, Fed. Rep. of				
Date	General farm hands		Agricultural workers [3]	Skilled day labourers	Day labourers		Farm workers	
Date	*Domestiques de ferme*		*Ouvriers agricoles* [3]	*Journaliers qualifiés*	*Journaliers*		*Ouvriers de ferme*	
	Peones agrícolas		Obreros agrícolas [3]	Jornaleros calificados	Jornaleros		Obreros agrícolas	
Fecha	Males	Females	M. + F.	Males	Males	Females	Males	Females
	Hommes	*Femmes*	*H. + F.*	*Hommes*	*Hommes*	*Femmes*	*Hommes*	*Femmes*
	Hombres	Mujeres	H. + M.	Hombres	Hombres	Mujeres	Hombres	Mujeres
	(E.G./m.) [1]		*(E.G./m.)* [4]	*(R.T./h.)* [5]			*(R.T./m.)* [5]	
	II + a + b		I	II			II	
	Francs	Francs	Mark	Mark	Mark	Mark	Mark	Mark
1965	295.00	227.00	573	2.86	2.70	1.97	343	273
1966	307.80	256.50	603	3.08	2.91	2.13	374	300
1967	334.90	292.80	627	3.08	2.91	2.13	372	298
1968	361.90	282.90	679	3.20	3.02	2.22	392	315
1969	414.00	406.00	686	3.49	3.30	2.42	450	353
1970	480.00	388.00	710	3.80	3.59	2.63	494	390
1971	495.00	465.00	765	4.24	4.01	2.95	564	447
1972	520.00	498.00	795	4.55	4.29	3.16	613	481
1973	610.00	584.00	830	5.02	4.74	3.57	683	540
1974	...	...	859	5.74	5.42	4.14	811	633

EXPLANATORY NOTES: See p. 585.

NOTES EXPLICATIVES: Voir p. 589.

NOTAS EXPLICATIVAS: Véase pág. 594.

I: Complete wage (workers remunerated wholly in cash).

II: Cash part of remuneration (where received partly in cash and partly in kind). These figures may include the estimated value of payments in kind for:

    a: board;
    b: lodging.

I: *Montant total du salaire (cas des travailleurs entièrement rémunérés en espèces).*

II: *Partie de la rémunération payée en espèces (cas des travailleurs rémunérés partiellement en espèces et partiellement en nature). Ces chiffres peuvent comprendre la valeur estimée des paiements en nature pour :*

    a: les repas ;
    b: le logement.

I: Salario íntegro (trabajadores remunerados enteramente en dinero).

II: Parte de la remuneración en dinero (en los casos en que ésta consiste en una parte en dinero y otra en especie. Estas cifras pueden incluir el valor estimado de los pagos en especie para:

    a: los alimentos;
    b: el alojamiento.

[1] April of each year. [2] State sector. [3] Incl. salaried employees. [4] Incl. family allowances. [5] Minimum rates.

[1] *Avril de chaque année.* [2] *Secteur d'Etat.* [3] *Y compris les employés.* [4] *Y compris les allocations familiales.* [5] *Taux minima.*

[1] Abril de cada año. [2] Sector de Estado. [3] Incl. los empleados. [4] Incl. las asignaciones familiares. [5] Tarifas mínimas.

23 Wages in agriculture
Salaires dans l'agriculture
Salarios en la agricultura

Earnings *(E.G.)* or rates *(R.T.)*
per hour *(h.)*, day *(d.j.)*,
week *(w.s.)* or month *(m.)*

Gains *(E.G.)* ou taux *(R.T.)*
par heure *(h.)*, jour *(d.j.)*,
semaine *(w.s.)* ou mois *(m.)*

Ganancias *(E.G.)* o tarifas *(R.T.)*
por hora *(h.)*, día *(d.j.)*,
semana *(w.s.)* o mes *(m.)*

	EUROPE — EUROPE — EUROPA						Ireland	Italie
	Hongrie [1]							
	Workers and employees *Ouvriers et employés* Obreros y empleados					Workers *Ouvriers* Obreros	Permanent labourers [3]	Agricultural workers
Date *Date* Fecha	State farms *Fermes de l'Etat* Granjas del Estado	Specialised agricultural undertakings *Entreprises agricoles spécialisées* Empresas agrícolas especializadas	Forestry *Sylviculture* Silvicultura	Aquiculture *Aquiculture* Acuicultura	Total	Total	*Ouvriers permanents* [3] Obreros permanentes [3]	*Ouvriers agricoles* Obreros agrícolas
	Males and females *Hommes et femmes* Hombres y mujeres				M. + F. H. + F. H. + M.	Males *Hommes* Hombres	M. + F. H. + F. H. + M.	
	(E.G./m.)				*(E.G./m.)*	*(E.G./w.s.)* [4]	*(R.T./h.)*	
	II				II	I	I	
	Forints	Forints	Forints	Forints	Forints	Forints	Pounds	(1970 = 100)
1965	1 551	1 613	1 468	1 610	1 576	1 519	8.04	.
1966	1 631	1 727	1 541	1 699	1 659	1 606	8.68	.
1967	1 698	1 837	1 640	1 767	1 729	1 673	9.02	73.1
1968	1 834	1 906	1 732	1 863	1 825	1 757	9.79	76.8
1969	1 977	2 116	1 888	1 989	1 966	1 900	11.56	85.1
1970	2 121 [2]	2 318 [2]	1 979 [2]	2 270 [2]	2 128 [2]	2 059 [2]	13.07	**100.0**
1971	2 203	2 430	2 086	2 269	2 199	2 128	16.27	113.7
1972	2 290	2 489	2 165	2 350	2 283	2 202	17.77	134.3
1973	2 404	2 552	2 273	2 457	2 391	2 309	19.78	166.5
1974	2 592 *	2 690 *	2 441 *	2 754 *	2 603 *	2 517 *	24.78	219.5

EXPLANATORY NOTES: See p. 585.

NOTES EXPLICATIVES: Voir p. 589.

NOTAS EXPLICATIVAS: Véase pág. 594.

I: Complete wage (workers remunerated wholly in cash).

II: Cash part of remuneration (where received partly in cash and partly in kind). These figures may include the estimated value of payments in kind for:

   a : board;
   b : lodging.

I: *Montant total du salaire (cas des travailleurs entièrement rémunérés en espèces).*

II: *Partie de la rémunération payée en espèces (cas des travailleurs rémunérés partiellement en espèces et partiellement en nature). Ces chiffres peuvent comprendre la valeur estimée des paiements en nature pour :*

   a : les repas ;
   b : le logement.

I: Salario íntegro (trabajadores remunerados enteramente en dinero).

II: Parte de la remuneración en dinero (en los casos en que ésta consiste en una parte en dinero y otra en especie). Estas cifras pueden incluir el valor estimado de los pagos en especie para:

   a : los alimentos;
   b : el alojamiento.

[1] State sector. [2] Revised series. [3] Adults only. [4] Minimum legal wages. July of each year.

[1] *Secteur d'Etat.* [2] *Série révisée.* [3] *Adultes seulement.* [4] *Salaires légaux minima. Juillet de chaque année.*

[1] Sector de Estado. [2] Serie revisada. [3] Adultos solamente. [4] Salarios legales mínimos. Julio de cada año.

23 Wages in agriculture
Salaires dans l'agriculture
Salarios en la agricultura

Earnings *(E.G.)* or rates *(R.T.)* per hour *(h.)*, day *(d.j.)*, week *(w.s.)* or month *(m.)*

Gains *(E.G.)* ou taux *(R.T.)* par heure *(h.)*, jour *(d.j.)*, semaine *(w.s.)* ou mois *(m.)*

Ganancias *(E.G.)* o tarifas *(R.T.)* por hora *(h.)*, día *(d.j.)*, semana *(w.s.)* o mes *(m.)*

Date / Date / Fecha	Norway				Pays-Bas		Pologne [5]	Portugal	
	General farm hands / *Domestiques de ferme* / Peones agrícolas				Agricultural workers / *Ouvriers agricoles* / Obreros agrícolas	All workers [3] / *Ensemble des ouvriers* [3] / Todos los obreros [3]	Agricultural workers [6] / *Ouvriers agricoles* [6] / Obreros agrícolas [6]	Agricultural workers / *Ouvriers agricoles* / Obreros agrícolas	
	Permanent labourers / *Ouvriers permanents* / Obreros permanentes		Casual day labourers / *Journaliers occasionnels* / Jornaleros ocasionales						
	Males / *Hommes* / Hombres	Females / *Femmes* / Mujeres	Males / *Hommes* / Hombres	Females / *Femmes* / Mujeres	Males / *Hommes* / Hombres	Males / *Hommes* / Hombres	M. + F. / H. + F. / H. + M.	Males / *Hommes* / Hombres	Females / *Femmes* / Mujeres
	(E.G./m.) [1]		*(E.G./h.)* [1]		*(E.G./h.)* [2]	*(R.T./h.)* [4]	*(E.G./m.)*	*(E.G./d.j.)*	
	II + a + b		II		II + a + b	I	I	I	
	Kroner	Kroner	Kroner	Kroner	Guilders	(1970 = 100)	Zlotys	Escudos	Escudos
1965	.	.	.	.	2.67	63	1 498	39.42	21.51
1966	.	.	.	.	2.93	70	1 593	42.06	24.70
1967	.	.	.	.	3.26	74	1 675	50.54	27.41
1968	1 403	907	8.36	7.96	3.52	79	1 761	53.60 [7]	31.60 [7]
1969	1 489	932	8.54	8.23	3.76	87	1 828	59.40	34.00
1970	1 684	1 077	10.01	9.54	4.07	**100**	1 867	66.10	37.30
1971	1 878	1 267	10.93	10.71	4.63	112	1 988	74.70	43.10
1972	2 055	1 504	11.94	11.98	5.65	129	2 189	83.90	48.00
1973	2 386	1 479	13.68	12.97	6.39	145	2 457	94.60	55.60
1974	2 772	...	15.67	14.85	...	167	2 806 *	125.70	78.10

EUROPE — EUROPE — EUROPA

EXPLANATORY NOTES: See p. 585. NOTES EXPLICATIVES: Voir p. 589. NOTAS EXPLICATIVAS: Véase pág. 594.

I: Complete wage (workers remunerated wholly in cash).

II: Cash part of remuneration (where received partly in cash and partly in kind). These figures may include the estimated value of payments in kind for:
  a : board;
  b : lodging.

I: *Montant total du salaire (cas des travailleurs entièrement rémunérés en espèces).*

II: *Partie de la rémunération payée en espèces (cas des travailleurs rémunérés partiellement en espèces et partiellement en nature). Ces chiffres peuvent comprendre la valeur estimée des paiements en nature pour :*
  a : les repas ;
  b : le logement.

I: Salario íntegro (trabajadores remunerados enteramente en dinero).

II: Parte de la remuneración en dinero (en los casos en que ésta consiste en una parte en dinero y otra en especie). Estas cifras pueden incluir el valor estimado de los pagos en especie para:
  a : los alimentos;
  b : el alojamiento.

[1] Sep. of each year. [2] Year ending in April of the year indicated. Beginning 1972: Oct. of each year. [3] Adults only. [4] Minimum rates; incl. vacation pay. [5] Socialised sector. [6] Incl. salaried employees. [7] Series replacing former series.

[1] *Sept. de chaque année.* [2] *Année se terminant en avril de l'année indiquée. A partir de 1972: oct. de chaque année.* [3] *Adultes seulement.* [4] *Taux minima; y compris les versements pour congés payés.* [5] *Secteur socialisé.* [6] *Y compris les employés.* [7] *Série remplaçant la précédente.*

[1] Sept. de cada año. [2] Año que termina en abril del año indicado. A partir de 1972: oct. de cada año. [3] Adultos solamente. [4] Tarifas mínimas; incl. los pagos por vacaciones. [5] Sector socializado. [6] Incl. los empleados. [7] Serie que substituye a la anterior.

23 Wages in agriculture
Salaires dans l'agriculture
Salarios en la agricultura

Earnings *(E.G.)* or rates *(R.T.)*
per hour *(h.)*, day *(d.j.)*,
week *(w.s.)* or month *(m.)*

Gains *(E.G.)* ou taux *(R.T.)*
par heure *(h.)*, jour *(d.j.)*,
semaine *(w.s.)* ou mois *(m.)*

Ganancias *(E.G.)* o tarifas *(R.T.)*
por hora *(h.)*, día *(d.j.)*,
semana *(w.s.)* o mes *(m.)*

Date / Date / Fecha	Roumanie [1]	Sweden		Turquie	United Kingdom [6]		Yugoslavia [8]
		All workers [3] / Ensemble des ouvriers [3] / Todos los obreros [3]		Fishermen / Pêcheurs / Pescadores	Regular workers / Ouvriers stables / Obreros estables		Agricultural workers [2] / Ouvriers agricoles [2] / Obreros agricolas [2]
	M. + F. [2] / H. + F. [2] / H. + M. [2]	Males / Hommes / Hombres	Females / Femmes / Mujeres	M. + F. / H. + F. / H. + M.	Males [3] / Hommes [3] / Hombres [3]	Females / Femmes / Mujeres	M. + F. / H. + F. / H. + M.
	(E.G./m.)	*(E.G./h.)*		*(E.G./d.j.)*	*(E.G./w.s.)* [7]		*(E.G./m.)*
	I	I + II [4]		II	I		I
	Lei	Kronor	Kronor	Liras	£	£	Dinars
1965	.	6.56	5.58	16.41	13.80	8.75	.
1966	.	7.97	5.94	21.55	14.55	9.32	587
1967	1 106	8.69	7.39	29.47	15.24	9.55	684
1968	1 132	9.37	6.79	28.34	16.10	10.12	715
1969	1 179	10.16	6.47	36.26	17.54	11.02	822
1970	1 327	11.21	8.99	35.45	19.18	12.45	962
1971	1 372	12.15	10.39	44.11	21.42	14.65	1 267
1972	1 408	13.35 [5]	11.33 [5]	38.74	24.20	15.49	1 505
1973	1 488	14.16	12.92	50.31	29.05	19.28	1 798
1974	1 543	15.95	14.58	53.93	...	...	2 366

EXPLANATORY NOTES: See p. 585.

NOTES EXPLICATIVES: Voir p. 589.

NOTAS EXPLICATIVAS: Véase pág. 594.

I: Complete wage (workers remunerated wholly in cash).

II: Cash part of remuneration (where received partly in cash and partly in kind). These figures may include the estimated value of payments in kind for:

    a : board;
    b : lodging.

I: *Montant total du salaire (cas des travailleurs entièrement rémunérés en espèces).*

II: *Partie de la rémunération payée en espèces (cas des travailleurs rémunérés partiellement en espèces et partiellement en nature). Ces chiffres peuvent comprendre la valeur estimée des paiements en nature pour :*

    a : les repas ;
    b : le logement.

I: Salario íntegro (trabajadores remunerados enteramente en dinero).

II: Parte de la remuneración en dinero (en los casos en que ésta consiste en una parte en dinero y otra en especie). Estas cifras pueden incluir el valor estimado de los pagos en especie para:

    a : los alimentos;
    b : el alojamiento.

[1] State sector. [2] Incl. salaried employees. [3] Adults only. [4] 1965-71: workers remunerated wholly in cash. [5] Beginning 1972: second quarter of each year. [6] Excl. Northern Ireland. [7] Year ending 31 March of following year. [8] Socialised sector.

[1] *Secteur d'Etat.* [2] *Y compris les employés.* [3] *Adultes seulement.* [4] *1965-1971 : travailleurs entièrement rémunérés en espèces.* [5] *A partir de 1972 : deuxième trimestre de chaque année.* [6] *Non compris l'Irlande du Nord.* [7] *Année se terminant le 31 mars de l'année suivante.* [8] *Secteur socialisé.*

[1] Sector de Estado. [2] Incl. los empleados. [3] Adultos solamente. [4] 1965-1971: trabajadores remunerados enteramente en dinero. [5] A partir de 1972: segundo trimestre de cada año. [6] Excl. Irlanda del Norte. [7] Año que termina el 31 de marzo del año siguiente. [8] Sector socializado.

WAGES

23 Wages in agriculture
Salaires dans l'agriculture
Salarios en la agricultura

Earnings *(E.G.)* or rates *(R.T.)*
per hour *(h.)*, day *(d.j.)*,
week *(w.s.)* or month *(m.)*

Gains *(E.G.)* ou taux *(R.T.)*
par heure *(h.)*, jour *(d.j.)*,
semaine *(w.s.)* ou mois *(m.)*

Ganancias *(E.G.)* o tarifas *(R.T.)*
por hora *(h.)*, día *(d.j.)*,
semana *(w.s.)* o mes *(m.)*

Date / Date / Fecha	OCEANIA — OCÉANIE — OCEANÍA				URSS [4], [5]	RSS de Biélorussie [4]	RSS d'Ukraine [4]
	Fiji	New Zealand		Polynésie française			
	Agricultural workers *Ouvriers agricoles* Obreros agrícolas	Farm workers *Ouvriers agricoles* Obreros agrícolas	Dairy farms *Fermes laitières* Granjas lecheras	Workers *Ouvriers* Obreros — Copra harvest and preparation *Ramassage et préparation du coprah* Recogida y preparación de la copra			
	M. + F. *H. + F.* H. + M.	Males *Hommes* Hombres		M. + F. *H. + F.* H. + M.	M. + F. [6] *H. + F.* [6] H. + M. [6]	M. + F. [6] *H. + F.* [6] H. + M. [6]	M. + F. [6] *H. + F.* [6] H. + M. [6]
	(R.T./d.j.) [1]	*(R.T./w.s.)* [2]		*(E.G./h.)* [3]	*(E.G./m.)*	*(E.G./m.)*	*(E.G./m.)*
	I	I		I	I	I	I
	Dollars	Dollars	Dollars	Francs (CFP)	Roubles	Roubles	Roubles
1965	1.48	21.08	23.89	30.25	74.6	.	71.5
1966	1.61	21.67	24.80	36.05	80.0	.	74.5
1967	1.62	22.17	24.80	35.40	84.4	.	76.7
1968	1.58	22.51	24.80	37.85	92.1	.	85.2
1969	1.78	24.03	25.05	37.85	93.2	.	90.0
1970	1.97	26.00	26.00	43.20	100.9	.	95.7
1971	2.13	26.75	26.75	45.00	106.3	79.4	101.5
1972	2.39	27.00	27.00	...	111.8	83.7	104.6
1973	3.12	39.18	39.18	...	117.5	88.8	112.2
1974	...	50.25	50.25	...	124.0 *	91.8 *	115.9 *

EXPLANATORY NOTES: See p. 585.   NOTES EXPLICATIVES: Voir p. 589.   NOTAS EXPLICATIVAS: Véase pág. 594.

I: Complete wage (workers remunerated wholly in cash).

II: Cash part of remuneration (where received partly in cash and partly in kind). These figures may include the estimated value of payments in kind for:

    a: board;
    b: lodging.

I: *Montant total du salaire (cas des travailleurs entièrement rémunérés en espèces).*

II: *Partie de la rémunération payée en espèces (cas des travailleurs rémunérés partiellement en espèces et partiellement en nature). Ces chiffres peuvent comprendre la valeur estimée des paiements en nature pour :*

    a: les repas ;
    b: le logement.

I: Salario íntegro (trabajadores remunerados enteramente en dinero).

II: Parte de la remuneración en dinero (en los casos en que ésta consiste en una parte en dinero y otra en especie). Estas cifras pueden incluir el valor estimado de los pagos en especie para:

    a: los alimentos;
    b: el alojamiento.

[1] June of each year. [2] Minimum rates. [3] Minimum hourly wages. Dec. of each year. [4] State sector. [5] Incl. Byelorussian SSR and Ukrainian SSR, shown separately in this table. [6] Incl. salaried employees.

[1] *Juin de chaque année.* [2] *Taux minima.* [3] *Salaires horaires minima. Déc. de chaque année.* [4] *Secteur d'Etat.* [5] *Y compris les RSS de Biélorussie et d'Ukraine, figurant séparément dans ce tableau.* [6] *Y compris les employés.*

[1] Junio de cada año. [2] Tarifas mínimas. [3] Salarios mínimos por hora. Dic. de cada año. [4] Sector de Estado. [5] Incl. las RSS de Bielorrusia y de Ucrania, que figuran separadamente en este cuadro. [6] Incl. los empleados.

24 Compensation of employees and national income
Rémunération des salariés et revenu national
Remuneración de asalariados y renta nacional

(Millions — *Millions* — Millones)

Country — *Pays* — País	Code *Code* Clave	Currency *Monnaie* Moneda	1965	1966	1967	1968	1969	1970	1971	1972	1973
AFRICA — AFRIQUE AFRICA											
Cameroun [1]	A	Francs (CFA)	...	...	...	243 700	272 700	290 655	...	...	...
	B	»	...	...	...	62 700	70 400	78 296	...	...	...
	%		...	...	...	*(25.7)*	*(25.8)*	*(26.9)*	...	...	...
Dahomey	A [2]	Francs (CFA)	*43 973*	*45 549*	*45 447*	...	...	*57 099*	...	...	...
	B [2]	»	*11 395*	*11 293*	*12 817*	...	...	*16 344*	...	...	...
	%		*(25.9)*	*(24.8)*	*(28.2)*	...	...	*(28.6)*	...	...	...
Egypt [1]	A [3]	Pounds	2 388	2 459	2 510	2 657	2 927	3 086	3 274	...	...
	B	»	979	1 002	1 032	1 106	1 180	1 338	1 415	...	...
	%		*(41.0)*	*(40.7)*	*(41.1)*	*(41.6)*	*(40.3)*	*(43.4)*	*(43.2)*	...	...
Kenya	A [2,3]	Pounds	*347.1*	*404.6*	*426.7*	*468.9*	*511.0*	*563.5*	*632.9*	*703.2*	*789.6*
	B [2]	»	*137.6*	*153.2*	*167.8*	*203.0*	*218.2*	*238.0*	*272.0*	*306.4*	*346.1*
	%		*(39.6)*	*(37.9)*	*(39.3)*	*(43.3)*	*(42.7)*	*(42.2)*	*(43.0)*	*(43.6)*	*(43.8)*
Libyan Arab Rep.	A	Pounds	388.2	501.1	575.0	795.5	955.1	1 004.3	1 316.1	1 413.2	1 749.9
	B	»	111.7	137.6	168.9	219.2	252.9	268.8	415.5	518.2	628.8
	%		*(28.8)*	*(27.5)*	*(29.4)*	*(27.5)*	*(26.5)*	*(26.8)*	*(31.6)*	*(36.7)*	*(35.9)*
Madagascar	A	Francs	...	170 716	183 931	208 700	221 500	245 000	...	...	...
	B	»	...	59 841	63 309	68 500	76 300	80 600	...	...	...
	%		...	*(35.0)*	*(34.4)*	*(32.8)*	*(34.4)*	*(32.9)*	...	...	...
Malawi	A [3]	Kwachas	175.9	198.8	207.7	218.5	240.6	265.9	333.2	369.5	425.8
	B	»	43.0	50.9	55.1	58.8	64.2	69.8	79.3	...	...
	%		*(24.4)*	*(25.6)*	*(26.5)*	*(26.9)*	*(26.7)*	*(26.2)*	*(23.8)*	...	...
Mauritius	A [3]	Rupees	916	911	964	963	1 037	1 055	1 168	1 434	1 868
	B	»	464	470	483	484	498	516	555	656	833
	%		*(50.7)*	*(51.6)*	*(50.1)*	*(50.3)*	*(48.0)*	*(48.9)*	*(47.5)*	*(47.5)*	*(44.6)*
Niger	A [2]	Francs (CFA)	...	*91 900*	*93 300*	*91 000*	*93 100*	...	...	...	...
	B [2]	»	...	*11 000*	*11 700*	*12 300*	*13 800*	...	...	...	...
	%		...	*(12.0)*	*(12.5)*	*(13.5)*	*(14.8)*	...	...	...	...
Sierra Leone [4]	A	Leones	...	242	238	276	315	318	320	...	...
	B	»	...	60	63	67	76	76	78	...	...
	%		...	*(24.8)*	*(26.5)*	*(24.3)*	*(24.1)*	*(23.9)*	*(24.4)*	...	...
South Africa, Rep. of [5]	A [2]	Rand	*6 897*	*7 477*	*8 299*	*8 865*	*9 975*	*10 875*	*12 102*	*13 637*	*16 582*
	B [2]	»	*4 237*	*4 692*	*5 052*	*5 554*	*6 087*	*6 886*	*7 816*	*8 549*	*9 879*
	%		*(61.4)*	*(62.7)*	*(60.9)*	*(62.6)*	*(61.0)*	*(63.3)*	*(64.6)*	*(62.7)*	*(59.6)*
Sudan	A [2]	Pounds	465.8	460.2	497.7	542.5	562.9 [1]	596.3 [1]	701.3 [1]	...	...
	B [2]	»	...	315.2	338.6	366.5	294.3 [1]	307.4 [1]	367.6 [1]	...	...
	%		...	*(68.5)*	*(68.0)*	*(67.6)*	*(52.3)*	*(51.5)*	*(52.4)*	...	...
Swaziland [1]	A	Rand	*38.5*	*43.9*	*40.7*	*44.5*	*58.7*	*62.9*	*81.9*	...	...
	B	»	*21.2*	*22.4*	*26.3*	*26.3*	*30.5*	*33.0*	*43.8*	...	...
	%		*(55.1)*	*(51.0)*	*(64.6)*	*(59.1)*	*(52.0)*	*(52.5)*	*(53.5)*	...	...

EXPLANATORY NOTES: See p. 585.　　　　　　NOTES EXPLICATIVES: Voir p. 589.　　　　　　NOTAS EXPLICATIVAS: Véase pág. 594.

A: National income — *Revenu national* — Renta nacional.
B: Compensation of employees — *Rémunération des salariés* — Remuneración de asalariados.

[1] Twelve months beginning 1 July of year indicated. [2] New SNA. [3] Includes consumption of fixed capital. [4] Twelve months beginning 1 April of year indicated. [5] Estimates prepared by the South African Reserve Bank. Incl. Namibia.

[1] *Douze mois commençant le 1er juillet de l'année indiquée.* [2] *Nouveau SCN.* [3] *Y compris la consommation de capital fixe.* [4] *Douze mois commençant le 1er avril de l'année indiquée.* [5] *Estimations de la South African Reserve Bank. Y compris la Namibie.*

[1] Doce meses que comienzan el 1.º de julio del año indicado. [2] Nuevo SCN. [3] Incluye el consumo de capital fijo. [4] Doce meses que comienzan el 1.º de abril del año indicado. [5] Estimaciones hechas por el South African Reserve Bank. Incl. Namibia.

24 Compensation of employees and national income
Rémunération des salariés et revenu national
Remuneración de asalariados y renta nacional

(Millions — *Millions* — Millones)

Country — *Pays* — País	Code *Code* Clave	Currency *Monnaie* Moneda	1965	1966	1967	1968	1969	1970	1971	1972	1973
Tanzania (Tanganyika) ..	A [1]	Shillings	5 744	6 540	6 837	7 388	7 763	8 636	9 189	10 466	11 751
	B [1]	»	1 784	2 025	2 180	2 362	2 484	2 852	3 156	...	...
	%		(31.1)	(31.0)	(31.9)	(32.0)	(32.0)	(33.0)	(34.3)	...	...
Togo	A	Francs (CFA)	38 674	48 151	51 178	53 651	62 859	68 525	74 292	79 216	...
	B	»	22 866	29 775	29 714	30 967	35 193	...	...	...	...
	%		(59.1)	(61.8)	(58.1)	(57.7)	(56.0)	...	...	...	...
Uganda	A [1]	Shillings	...	...	...	7 286	8 216	9 342	10 209	...	...
	B [1]	»	...	...	...	1 819	1 994	2 136	2 325	...	...
	%		...	...	...	(25.0)	(24.3)	(22.9)	(22.8)	...	...
Zaïre	A [2]	Zaïres	...	250	265	❘ 577	748	1 279	1 123	1 163	...
	B [2]	»	...	205	195	❘ 215	288	448	568	409	...
	%		...	(82.0)	(73.6)	(37.3)	(38.5)	(38.5)	(50.6)	(35.2)	...
Zambia	A [3]	Kwachas	...	684	791	926	1 155	❘ 1 090	968	...	...
	B [3]	»	...	282	350	387	395	❘ 475	563	...	...
	%		...	(41.2)	(44.2)	(41.8)	(34.2)	(43.6)	(58.2)	...	...
AMERICA — AMÉRIQUE AMÉRICA											
Antilles néerlandaises . . .	A	Guilders	415	423	433	462	...	...	...	...	...
	B [4]	»	276	277	...	...	...	...	...	...	...
	%		(66.5)	(65.5)	...	...	...	...	...	...	...
Argentina	A	Pesos	...	44 900	58 700	67 900	79 600	93 800	...	...	...
	B	»	...	18 200	24 200	27 300	31 500	38 500	...	...	...
	%		...	(40.5)	(41.2)	(40.2)	(39.6)	(41.0)	...	...	...
Bolivia	A	Pesos	6 730	7 506	8 299	9 408	10 259	...	...	...	...
	B	»	1 945	2 006	2 180	2 426	2 618	...	...	...	...
	%		(28.9)	(26.7)	(26.3)	(25.8)	(25.5)	...	...	...	...
Canada	A [1]	Dollars	48 159	53 945	58 170	63 756	70 675	74 917	81 912	91 705	105 138
	B [1]	»	28 878	32 629	36 160	39 318	43 949	47 620	52 250	57 955	65 147
	%		(60.0)	(60.5)	(62.2)	(61.7)	(62.2)	(63.6)	(63.8)	(63.2)	(62.0)
Colombia	A	Pesos	54 904	66 080	74 501	86 289	99 264	116 780	137 913	167 056	220 392
	B	»	22 301	26 754	31 049	35 045	41 862	48 746	57 808	68 117	82 885
	%		(40.6)	(40.5)	(41.7)	(40.6)	(42.2)	(41.7)	(41.9)	(40.8)	(37.6)
Costa Rica	A [1]	Colones	3 607	3 939	4 240	4 678	5 195	6 021	6 589	7 459	9 076
	B [1]	»	1 841	2 057	2 214	2 412	2 663	3 057	3 424	3 913	...
	%		(51.0)	(52.2)	(52.2)	(51.6)	(51.3)	(50.8)	(52.0)	(52.5)	...
Chile	A	Escudos	15 708	22 044	28 881	38 968	57 067	83 160	112 366	210 489	...
	B	»	7 332	10 355	13 406	18 707	26 856	40 969	64 927	118 677	...
	%		(46.7)	(47.0)	(46.4)	(48.0)	(47.1)	(49.3)	(57.8)	(56.4)	...
Ecuador	A [1]	Sucres	...	...	...	...	...	30 026	35 476	42 353	58 374
	B [1]	»	...	...	...	...	...	9 972	11 855	13 633	17 851
	%		...	...	...	...	...	(33.2)	(33.4)	(32.2)	(30.6)

EXPLANATORY NOTES: See p. 585.   NOTES EXPLICATIVES: Voir p. 589.   NOTAS EXPLICATIVAS: Véase pág. 594.

A: National income — *Revenu national* — Renta nacional.
B: Compensation of employees — *Rémunération des salariés* — Remuneración de asalariados.

[1] New SNA. [2] Beginning 1968: new SNA. [3] Beginning 1970: new SNA. [4] Includes income from unincorporated enterprises.

[1] *Nouveau SCN.* [2] *A partir de 1968 : nouveau SCN.* [3] *A partir de 1970 : nouveau SCN.* [4] *Y compris le revenu des entreprises non constituées en sociétés.*

[1] Nuevo SCN. [2] A partir de 1968: nuevo SCN. [3] A partir de 1970: nuevo SCN. [4] Incluye el ingreso de las empresas no constituidas en sociedades de capital.

24 Compensation of employees and national income
Rémunération des salariés et revenu national
Remuneración de asalariados y renta nacional

(Millions — *Millions* — Millones)

Country — *Pays* — País	Code *Code* Clave	Currency *Monnaie* Moneda	1965	1966	1967	1968	1969	1970	1971	1972	1973
Guatemala	A [1]	Quetzales	1 153.0	1 210.9	1 253.7	1 343.3	...	...	...	...	...
	B	»	569.5	606.1	...	...	...	...	...	...	...
	%		*(49.4)*	*(50.1)*	...	...	...	...	...	...	...
Guyana	A	Dollars	316.2	335.4	370.1	397.6	428.1	459.3	494.7	544.2	581.8
	B	»	174.4	190.9	207.5	223.9	240.9	262.2	282.9	309.0	355.4
	%		*(55.2)*	*(56.9)*	*(56.1)*	*(56.3)*	*(56.3)*	*(57.1)*	*(57.2)*	*(56.8)*	*(61.1)*
Honduras	A	Lempiras	949	1 028	1 111	1 200	1 251	1 336	1 415	1 527	...
	B	»	402	442	464	510	526	562	619	681	...
	%		*(42.4)*	*(43.0)*	*(41.8)*	*(42.5)*	*(42.0)*	*(42.1)*	*(43.7)*	*(44.6)*	...
Jamaica	A	Dollars	591.6	642.5	692.9	762.7	849.3	933.7	1 034.8	1 141.6	1 372.4
	B	»	325.3	344.7	376.6	417.6	457.2	508.7	566.1	644.1	775.4
	%		*(55.0)*	*(53.6)*	*(54.4)*	*(54.7)*	*(53.8)*	*(54.5)*	*(54.7)*	*(56.4)*	*(56.5)*
México	A	Pesos	230 800	256 400	285 100	...	...	...	...	...	...
	B	»	79 500	90 700	100 400	...	...	...	...	...	...
	%		*(34.4)*	*(35.4)*	*(35.2)*	...	...	...	...	...	...
Nicaragua	A	Córdobas	3 315	3 556	3 889	4 091	4 414	4 945	5 261	5 648	5 980
	B	»	2 156	2 322	2 541	2 671	2 897	3 227	3 447	3 708	4 141
	%		*(65.0)*	*(65.3)*	*(65.3)*	*(65.3)*	*(65.6)*	*(65.3)*	*(65.5)*	*(65.6)*	*(69.7)*
Panamá	A	Balboas	588.2	642.6	709.5	757.4	833.9	924.3	1 019.5	1 145.7	1 290.0
	B	»	428.4	470.9	522.9	573.3	637.3	677.4	732.5	799.3	946.5
	%		*(72.8)*	*(73.3)*	*(73.7)*	*(75.7)*	*(76.4)*	*(73.3)*	*(71.8)*	*(69.8)*	*(73.4)*
Paraguay	A	Guaraníes	51 871	54 038	56 720	59 648	64 149	69 143	77 916	89 868	116 807
	B	»	19 977	21 704	22 905	23 814	25 428	25 770	30 420	35 370	41 320
	%		*(38.5)*	*(40.2)*	*(40.4)*	*(39.9)*	*(39.6)*	*(37.3)*	*(39.0)*	*(39.4)*	*(35.4)*
Perú	A	Soles	106 630	126 170	143 101	168 158	190 100	222 100	244 700	273 300	...
	B	»	46 217	53 850	63 969	74 946	...	93 400	108 700	125 800	...
	%		*(43.3)*	*(42.7)*	*(44.7)*	*(44.6)*	...	*(42.1)*	*(44.4)*	*(46.0)*	...
Puerto Rico [2]	A	$	2 773	3 047	3 359	3 773	4 220	4 698	5 171	5 699	6 201
	B	»	1 601	1 795	2 017	2 308	2 661	3 064	3 414	3 876	4 215
	%		*(57.7)*	*(58.9)*	*(60.0)*	*(61.2)*	*(63.1)*	*(65.2)*	*(66.0)*	*(68.0)*	*(68.0)*
United States	A [3]	$	628 310	689 416	728 886	782 035	838 961	878 650	948 255	*1 040 862*	*1 168 627*
	B [3]	»	395 159	437 023	468 965	516 593	*568 283*	606 624	646 297	710 807	790 220
	%		*(62.9)*	*(63.4)*	*(64.3)*	*(66.1)*	*(67.7)*	*(69.0)*	*(68.2)*	*(68.3)*	*(67.6)*
Uruguay	A	Pesos	50 349	95 053	161 617	356 107	481 542	585 066	703 723	1 195 068	...
	B	»	24 639	42 658	80 120	164 602	234 649	281 119	343 927	566 893	...
	%		*(48.9)*	*(44.9)*	*(49.6)*	*(46.2)*	*(48.7)*	*(48.0)*	*(48.9)*	*(47.4)*	...

EXPLANATORY NOTES: See p. 585.   NOTES EXPLICATIVES: Voir p. 589.   NOTAS EXPLICATIVAS: Véase pág. 594.

A: National income — *Revenu national* — Renta nacional.
B: Compensation of employees — *Rémunération des salariés* — Remuneración de asalariados.

[1] National income at factor cost. [2] Twelve months beginning 1 July of year indicated. [3] Beginning 1968: new SNA.

[1] *Revenu national au coût des facteurs.* [2] *Douze mois commençant le 1er juillet de l'année indiquée.* [3] *A partir de 1968 : nouveau SCN.*

[1] Ingreso nacional al costo de los factores. [2] Doce meses que comienzan el 1.º de julio del año indicado. [3] A partir de 1968: nuevo SCN.

24 Compensation of employees and national income
Rémunération des salariés et revenu national
Remuneración de asalariados y renta nacional

(Millions — *Millions* — Millones)

Country — *Pays* — País	Code *Code* Clave	Currency *Monnaie* Moneda	1965	1966	1967	1968	1969	1970	1971	1972	1973
Venezuela	A [1]	Bolívares	31 222	32 627	34 505	❘ *37 399*	*39 268*	*44 143*	*47 766*	*53 440*	*63 608*
	B [1]	»	16 284	17 452	18 827	❘ *17 981*	*19 084*	*21 015*	*23 199*	*25 716*	*29 205*
	%		*(52.2)*	*(53.5)*	*(54.6)*	*(48.1)*	*(48.6)*	*(47.6)*	*(48.6)*	*(48.1)*	*(45.9)*
ASIA — ASIE ASIA											
Iraq	A	Dinars	730.7	793.6	814.7	911.2	961.3	1 046.6	1 190.2	...	...
	B	»	243.5	261.6	270.8	294.2	320.6	344.0	392.2	...	...
	%		*(33.3)*	*(33.0)*	*(33.2)*	*(32.3)*	*(33.3)*	*(32.9)*	*(32.9)*	...	...
Israel	A	Pounds	9 272	10 164	10 596	12 383	14 291	16 848	20 972	26 285	33 738
	B	»	5 128	5 913	5 988	6 655	7 510	9 074	11 121	13 532	18 228
	%		*(55.3)*	*(58.2)*	*(56.5)*	*(53.7)*	*(52.6)*	*(53.9)*	*(53.0)*	*(51.5)*	*(54.0)*
Japan	A	Yen	27 855 500	31 878 400	37 796 200	44 793 500	51 829 300	61 453 100	69 371 800	79 285 800	96 621 500
	B	»	14 317 100	16 373 900	18 921 100	22 080 500	25 623 300	30 966 100	36 762 000	42 734 100	53 940 500
	%		*(51.4)*	*(51.4)*	*(50.1)*	*(49.3)*	*(49.4)*	*(50.4)*	*(53.0)*	*(53.9)*	*(55.8)*
Jordan	A	Dinars	173.9	178.6	199.2	189.1	225.0	214.2	228.1	243.3	277.5
	B	»	51.7	57.5	66.6	74.0	82.7	82.6	86.6	92.4	...
	%		*(29.7)*	*(32.2)*	*(33.4)*	*(39.1)*	*(36.8)*	*(38.6)*	*(38.0)*	*(38.0)*	...
Korea, Rep. of	A	Won	759 410	973 950	1 194 150	1 496 310	1 953 150	2 429 110	2 959 350	3 583 290	4 519 320
	B	»	212 930	282 040	378 750	486 790	652 010	827 160	1 008 720	1 218 520	1 494 990
	%		*(28.0)*	*(29.0)*	*(31.7)*	*(32.5)*	*(33.4)*	*(34.0)*	*(34.1)*	*(34.0)*	*(33.1)*
Kuwait [2]	A [3]	Dinars	...	642	692	748	790	854	1 091	❘ *1 015*	...
	B [3]	»	...	153	183	195	208	215	259	❘ *277*	...
	%		...	*(23.8)*	*(26.4)*	*(26.1)*	*(26.3)*	*(25.2)*	*(23.7)*	*(27.3)*	...
Malaysia: West Malaysia	A	Dollars	6 985	7 334	...	...	...	...	...	...	...
	B	»	2 882	3 063	...	...	...	...	...	...	...
	%		*(41.3)*	*(41.8)*	...	...	...	...	...	...	...
Sri Lanka	A	Rupees	7 480	7 759	8 484	9 882	10 774	11 932	12 124	13 078	16 021
	B	»	3 498	3 589	3 746	4 343	4 590	5 103	5 303	6 016	7 330
	%		*(46.8)*	*(46.3)*	*(44.1)*	*(43.9)*	*(42.6)*	*(42.8)*	*(43.7)*	*(46.0)*	*(45.7)*
Sud Viet-Nam, Rép. du . .	A	Piastres	140 947	228 919	345 639	372 236	535 300	770 800	934 000	1 055 000	...
	B	»	65 238	123 243	169 208	200 990	261 900	362 800	450 300	...	...
	%		*(46.3)*	*(53.8)*	*(49.0)*	*(54.0)*	*(48.9)*	*(47.1)*	*(48.2)*	...	...
Thailand	A	Baht	80 046	96 180	102 149	109 503	119 912	126 034	133 824	147 062	173 062
	B	»	19 901	22 987	25 869	28 903	31 866	34 054	36 412	38 786	44 326
	%		*(24.9)*	*(23.9)*	*(25.3)*	*(26.4)*	*(26.6)*	*(27.0)*	*(27.2)*	*(26.4)*	*(25.6)*

EXPLANATORY NOTES: See p. 585.　　　　NOTES EXPLICATIVES: Voir p. 589.　　　　NOTAS EXPLICATIVAS: Véase pág. 594.

A: National income — *Revenu national* — Renta nacional.
B: Compensation of employees — *Rémunération des salariés* — Remuneración de asalariados.

[1] Beginning 1968: new SNA. [2] Twelve months beginning 1 April of year indicated. [3] Beginning 1972: new SNA.

[1] *A partir de 1968: nouveau SCN.* [2] *Douze mois commençant le 1er avril de l'année indiquée.* [3] *A partir de 1972: nouveau SCN.*

[1] A partir de 1968: nuevo SCN. [2] Doce meses que comienzan el 1.º de abril del año indicado. [3] A partir de 1972: nuevo SCN.

24 Compensation of employees and national income
Rémunération des salariés et revenu national
Remuneración de asalariados y renta nacional

(Millions — *Millions* — Millones)

Country — *Pays* — País	Code *Code* Clave	Currency *Monnaie* Moneda	1965	1966	1967	1968	1969	1970	1971	1972	1973
EUROPE — **EUROPE** **EUROPA**											
Austria	A	Schilling	220 350	238 370	252 040	270 170	296 500	332 410	369 840	425 100	487 800
	B	»	118 340	130 280	141 550	150 220	163 410	178 550	205 740	233 020	271 200
	%		*(53.7)*	*(54.7)*	*(56.2)*	*(55.6)*	*(55.1)*	*(53.7)*	*(55.6)*	*(54.8)*	*(55.6)*
Belgique	A	Francs	768 933	825 798	884 882	946 941	1 050 848	1 167 255	1 274 736	1 425 924	1 624 324
	B	»	406 094	444 692	475 835	505 628	560 597	629 040	714 772	819 887	937 017
	%		*(52.8)*	*(53.8)*	*(53.8)*	*(53.4)*	*(53.3)*	*(53.9)*	*(56.1)*	*(59.5)*	*(57.7)*
Denmark	A[1]	Kroner	*64 046*	*70 174*	*76 872*	*| 84 678*	*97 032*	*107 144*	*116 999*	*132 195*	*151 597*
	B[1]	»	*34 918*	*38 912*	*42 855*	*| 47 574*	*53 812*	*61 547*	*69 689*	*78 296*	*...*
	%		*(54.5)*	*(55.5)*	*(55.7)*	*(56.2)*	*(55.5)*	*(57.4)*	*(59.6)*	*(59.2)*	*...*
España	A	Pesetas	1 207 600	1 383 500	1 524 200	1 682 700	1 868 700	2 089 300	2 347 600	2 750 100	3 260 100
	B	»	602 600	706 500	807 300	877 100	988 800	1 118 000	1 290 900	1 540 100	1 848 100
	%		*(49.9)*	*(51.1)*	*(53.0)*	*(52.1)*	*(52.9)*	*(53.5)*	*(55.0)*	*(56.0)*	*(56.7)*
Finland	A	Markkaa	23 242	25 060	27 152	30 754	34 767	38 681	42 640	49 228	58 991
	B	»	12 724	13 972	15 327	17 083	19 115	21 656	24 697	28 828	34 832
	%		*(54.7)*	*(55.8)*	*(56.4)*	*(55.5)*	*(55.0)*	*(56.0)*	*(57.9)*	*(58.6)*	*(59.0)*
France	A[2]	Francs	*439 807*	*477 951*	*515 002*	*565 115*	*649 800*	*| 698 398*	*778 408*	*873 108*	*991 300*
	B[2]	»	*229 023*	*247 307*	*267 175*	*298 465*	*343 887*	*| 385 962*	*432 959*	*486 180*	*559 700*
	%		*(52.1)*	*(51.7)*	*(51.9)*	*(52.8)*	*(52.9)*	*(55.3)*	*(55.6)*	*(55.7)*	*(56.5)*
Germany, Fed. Rep. of △ .	A	Mark	414 190	440 020	441 700	482 600	541 250	610 820	676 790	741 050	827 090
	B	»	229 030	246 570	246 650	265 030	298 950	352 140	399 200	438 380	497 880
	%		*(55.3)*	*(56.0)*	*(55.8)*	*(54.9)*	*(55.2)*	*(57.7)*	*(59.0)*	*(59.2)*	*(60.2)*
Grèce	A	Drachmas	170 300	188 200	204 400	222 400	248 600	277 100	306 800	354 700	460 900
	B	»	53 600	60 900	67 900	75 500	84 300	93 900	105 200	121 300	...
	%		*(31.5)*	*(32.4)*	*(33.2)*	*(33.9)*	*(33.9)*	*(33.9)*	*(34.3)*	*(34.2)*	*...*
Ireland	A	Pounds	926.7	974.2	1 062.4	1 199.4	1 370.7	1 537.0	1 747.9	2 075.1	2 491.0
	B	»	471.6	511.8	553.9	619.3	712.9	829.8	961.9	1 108.4	1 332.0
	%		*(50.9)*	*(52.5)*	*(52.1)*	*(51.6)*	*(52.0)*	*(54.0)*	*(55.0)*	*(53.4)*	*(53.5)*
Italie	A	Lire	33 682 000	36 460 000	40 189 000	43 431 000	47 820 000	53 270 000	57 712 000	62 927 000	73 380 000
	B	»	16 681 000	17 839 000	19 732 000	21 456 000	23 641 000	27 644 000	31 825 000	35 434 000	42 613 000
	%		*(49.5)*	*(48.9)*	*(49.1)*	*(49.4)*	*(49.4)*	*(51.9)*	*(55.1)*	*(56.3)*	*(58.1)*
Luxembourg	A[1]	Francs	*29 078*	*30 158*	*29 961*	*32 580*	*37 715*	*44 544*	*45 934*	*51 073*	*61 236*
	B[1]	»	*17 564*	*18 781*	*19 222*	*20 465*	*22 123*	*25 905*	*29 398*	*33 333*	*38 160*
	%		*(60.4)*	*(62.3)*	*(64.2)*	*(62.8)*	*(58.7)*	*(58.2)*	*(64.0)*	*(65.3)*	*(62.3)*

EXPLANATORY NOTES: See p. 585.   NOTES EXPLICATIVES: Voir p. 589.   NOTAS EXPLICATIVAS: Véase pág. 594.

A: National income — *Revenu national* — Renta nacional.
B: Compensation of employees — *Rémunération des salariés* — Remuneracion de asalariados.

[1] New SNA. [2] Beginning 1970: new SNA.   [1] *Nouveau SCN.* [2] *A partir de 1970 : nouveau SCN.*   [1] Nuevo SCN. [2] A partir de 1970: nuevo SCN.

24 Compensation of employees and national income
Rémunération des salariés et revenu national
Remuneración de asalariados y renta nacional

(Millions — *Millions* — Millones)

Country — *Pays* — País	Code *Code* Clave	Currency *Monnaie* Moneda	1965	1966	1967	1968	1969	1970	1971	1972	1973
Malta	A	Pounds	54.8	60.7	65.8	74.0	85.7	99.2	101.9	106.8	119.2
	B	»	25.6	27.7	29.9	33.7	38.7	47.1	50.5	50.7	55.5
	%		(46.7)	(45.6)	(45.4)	(45.5)	(45.2)	(47.5)	(49.6)	(47.5)	(46.6)
Norway	A [1]	Kroner	43 893	47 755	| 51 247	54 257	59 309	68 131	76 049	82 829	93 623
	B [1]	»	25 359	28 007	| 32 059	34 674	37 650	41 795	48 717	54 647	61 612
	%		(57.8)	(58.6)	(62.6)	(63.9)	(63.5)	(61.3)	(64.1)	(66.0)	(65.8)
Pays-Bas	A [2]	Guilders	...	67 835	74 680	| 82 655	93 797	105 257	118 760	135 410	153 290
	B [2]	»	...	40 734	44 457	| 49 027	56 801	65 098	74 580	83 350	95 150
	%		...	(60.0)	(59.5)	(59.3)	(60.6)	(61.8)	(62.8)	(61.5)	(62.1)
Portugal	A	Escudos	102 207	111 580	125 071	139 403	153 234	170 330	189 743	221 724	262 835
	B	»	44 317	48 807	55 285	60 335	65 997	76 387	90 239	104 678	120 763
	%		(43.4)	(43.7)	(44.2)	(43.3)	(43.1)	(44.8)	(47.6)	(47.2)	(45.9)
Suisse	A	Francs	53 935	58 025	61 705	66 320	72 230	...	...	...	...
	B	»	32 335	34 580	36 895	39 160	42 545	...	...	...	...
	%		(60.0)	(59.6)	(59.8)	(59.0)	(58.9)	...	...	...	...
Sweden	A [2]	Kronor	*102 231*	*111 075*	*120 090*	*127 417*	*139 067*	*154 896*	*166 048*	*179 872*	*198 326*
	B [2]	»	*65 218*	*72 466*	*78 490*	*84 593*	*92 218*	*103 107*	*112 753*	*123 132*	*133 265*
	%		*(63.8)*	*(65.2)*	*(65.4)*	*(66.4)*	*(66.3)*	*(66.6)*	*(67.9)*	*(68.5)*	*(67.2)*
United Kingdom	A [2]	£	*32 882*	*34 921*	*36 847*	*39 649*	*42 238*	*46 198*	*51 355*	*56 789*	*64 274*
	B [2]	»	*21 350*	*22 855*	*23 777*	*25 427*	*27 158*	*30 337*	*33 578*	*37 579*	*43 007*
	%		*(64.9)*	*(65.4)*	*(64.5)*	*(64.1)*	*(64.3)*	*(65.7)*	*(65.4)*	*(66.2)*	*(66.9)*
OCEANIA — OCÉANIE OCEANÍA											
Australia [3]	A [2]	Dollars	*18 463*	*20 277*	*21 548*	*24 313*	*26 874*	*29 672*	*33 105*	*37 895*	*46 519*
	B [2]	»	*10 669*	*11 626*	*12 630*	*13 956*	*15 633*	*17 912*	*20 061*	*22 443*	*27 455*
	%		*(57.8)*	*(57.3)*	*(58.6)*	*(57.4)*	*(58.2)*	*(60.4)*	*(60.6)*	*(59.2)*	*(59.0)*
Fiji	A [4]	Dollars	119.2	124.2	134.3	| *132.1*	*143.2*	*174.6*	*191.9*	*239.4*	*286.9*
	B [4]	»	66.3	70.0	76.4	| *56.1*	*66.1*	*73.3*	*82.4*	*108.6*	*129.1*
	%		*(55.6)*	*(56.4)*	*(56.9)*	*(42.5)*	*(46.2)*	*(42.0)*	*(42.9)*	*(45.4)*	*(45.0)*
New Zealand [5]	A	Dollars	3 511	3 632	3 763	3 974	4 389	5 039	5 896	6 822	8 074
	B	»	1 926	2 081	2 169	2 285	2 540	3 060	3 623	4 024	4 900
	%		(54.9)	(57.3)	(57.6)	(57.5)	(57.9)	(60.7)	(61.4)	(59.0)	(60.7)
Papua New Guinea [3] . . .	A [2]	Dollars	*310.1*	*363.1*	*396.1*	*432.6*	*499.7*	*566.3*	*574.7*	*681.5*	*860.8*
	B [2]	»	*157.1*	*169.8*	*187.8*	*198.9*	*240.7*	*296.9*	*311.5*	*322.4*	*372.0*
	%		*(50.7)*	*(46.8)*	*(47.4)*	*(46.0)*	*(48.2)*	*(52.4)*	*(54.2)*	*(47.3)*	*(43.2)*

EXPLANATORY NOTES: See p. 585.   NOTES EXPLICATIVES: Voir p. 589.   NOTAS EXPLICATIVAS: Véase pág. 594.

A: National income   — *Revenu national*   — Renta nacional.
B: Compensation of employees — *Rémunération des salariés* — Remuneración de asalariados.

[1] Beginning 1967: new SNA. [2] New SNA. [3] Twelve months beginning 1 July of year indicated. [4] Beginning 1968: new SNA. [5] Twelve months beginning 1 April of year indicated.

[1] *A partir de 1967: nouveau SCN.* [2] *Nouveau SCN.* [3] *Douze mois commençant le 1er juillet de l'année indiquée.* [4] *A partir de 1968: nouveau SCN.* [5] *Douze mois commençant le 1er avril de l'année indiquée.*

[1] A partir de 1967: nuevo SCN. [2] Nuevo SCN. [3] Doce meses que comienzan el 1.º de julio del año indicado. [4] A partir de 1968: nuevo SCN. [5] Doce meses que comienzan el 1.º de abril del año indicado.

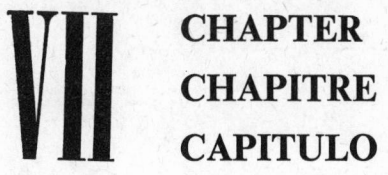

VII CHAPTER
CHAPITRE
CAPITULO

Consumer prices

Prix à la consommation

Precios del consumo

Consumer prices

Table 25

Consumer prices

Part A of this table contains general consumer price indices for all groups of consumption items combined. Parts B through E contain group indices respectively for " Food " (incl. drinks), " Fuel and light ", " Clothing " and " Rent ".

The consumer price indices are designed to show changes over time in the price level of certain goods and services which are selected as representative of the consumption patterns of the population concerned. Prices of items included in the index are collected at regular intervals in shops and markets and from service establishments in the area covered. The method employed in calculating the indices varies somewhat from one country to another. Usually the indices are calculated in the form of weighted arithmetic averages of price ratios between the base period and the period of reference (price relatives), using fixed weights corresponding to the base period (Laspeyres formula). The weights, which represent the relative importance of each item, are usually derived from family expenditure surveys conducted to obtain the pattern of consumer expenditure and the relative importance of each item for a particular population group.[1] Where data on family expenditures are not available, or are insufficient for a system of weights, supplementary calculations are commonly made for the purpose of establishing theoretical budgets; in a few cases weights are based on estimated total consumption, in the country, of the items considered.

Owing to differences in scope and in methods used for the compilation of the indices, the statistics for the different countries shown in the table are not uniformly representative of changes in price levels and vary in reliability from one country to another.[2]

As the original base period of the series also varies, a uniform base period (1970) has been adopted for the presentation of the data and as many as possible of the series have been recalculated by dividing the index for each date shown by the index for the year 1970 and multiplying the quotient by 100. Where data are available only for periods subsequent to 1970, the indices are generally presented with the first available calendar year as base. This operation does not involve any change in the weighting systems, etc., used by the countries.

In several cases, indicated by footnotes, where a series has been discontinued and has been replaced by a new series sufficiently comparable with the former, the two have been spliced.

The general consumer price index (Part A of this table) covers, in most cases, all the main categories of expenditure such as food (incl. drinks), fuel and light, clothing, rent and miscellaneous. Indices relating to this latter group are not shown separately in the *Year Book*, on account of the important variations in the composition of such group from one country to another.[3]

The consumer price indices are often used as deflators of nominal wage indices in the calculation of crude indicators of trends of real wages. Although such a deflation of nominal wages by consumer prices provides a useful measure of the relative purchasing power (with regard to consumer goods and services), the results may be misleading, in particular when the wage data correspond to a population group whose social and economic characteristics are very different from the population group to which the consumer price index corresponds.[4]

---

[1] In addition to the series presented in this table, readers will find in national publications of various countries (see Appendix, " References and Sources ") series referring to other localities, regions or population groups.

[2] For a detailed discussion of consumer price indices and techniques used in their compilation, see ILO: *Cost-of-living Statistics*, Studies and Reports, New Series, No. 7 (Part 2) (Geneva, 1948), and *Computation of Consumer Price Indices* (Special Problems), Tenth

International Conference of Labour Statisticians, Report IV (Geneva, 1970) (mimeographed).

[3] For the descriptions of the various national series, their scope, methods of compilation used, etc., see ILO: *Technical Guide 1972* (descriptions of series published in the *Bulletin* and the *Year Book of Labour Statistics*), Vol. I, " Consumer Prices " (Geneva, 1973).

[4] For an analysis of some of the problems involved, see ILO: *International Comparisons of Real Wages*, Studies and Reports, New Series, No. 45 (Geneva, 1956).

Prix à la consommation

Tableau 25

Prix à la consommation

La partie A de ce tableau présente les indices généraux des prix à la consommation pour tous les groupes d'articles de consommation combinés. Les parties B à E présentent les indices concernant respectivement les groupes suivants: « Alimentation » (y compris les boissons), « Combustible et éclairage », « Habillement » et « Loyer ».

Les indices des prix à la consommation ont pour objet de mettre en évidence les variations, au cours du temps, des prix de certains biens et services choisis de façon à représenter les habitudes de consommation de la population considérée. Les prix des articles retenus dans l'indice sont relevés à intervalles réguliers dans des magasins, des marchés et auprès de prestataires de services situés dans la zone à laquelle se rapporte la série. Les méthodes suivies lors du calcul des indices varient d'un pays à un autre. En général, les indices sont calculés sous forme de moyennes arithmétiques pondérées des rapports de prix entre la période de base et la période considérée (formule de Laspeyres). Les coefficients de pondération, qui permettent de tenir compte de l'importance relative des dépenses de consommation, sont généralement fondés sur les résultats d'enquêtes sur les dépenses familiales reflétant la structure des dépenses de consommation et leur importance relative pour un groupe de population donné [1]. Si l'on ne dispose pas de données sur les dépenses des familles ou si ces données sont insuffisantes pour qu'on puisse établir un système de coefficients de pondération, on effectue généralement des calculs supplémentaires en vue d'établir des budgets théoriques; dans quelques cas, les coefficients de pondération sont fondés sur une estimation de la consommation totale, dans le pays, des articles considérés.

Vu les différences existant dans la portée des indices et dans les méthodes utilisées pour les établir, les statistiques figurant dans le tableau pour les différents pays ne sont pas uniformément représentatives des variations des niveaux de prix et elles n'ont pas la même précision d'un pays à un autre [2].

Comme la période de base originale des séries varie elle aussi, on a adopté une période de base uniforme (1970) pour la présentation des données et le plus grand nombre possible des séries ont été recalculées en divisant l'indice se rapportant à chacune des dates indiquées par l'indice pour l'année 1970 et en multipliant le quotient par 100. Lorsqu'on ne dispose de données que pour des périodes postérieures à 1970, les indices sont généralement présentés en prenant pour période de base la première année civile pour laquelle existent des données. Ces opérations n'impliquent aucune modification des systèmes de pondération utilisés par les pays intéressés.

Dans plusieurs cas, indiqués en note, lorsqu'une série a été interrompue et remplacée par une nouvelle série suffisamment comparable à la première, les deux séries ont été raccordées.

L'indice général des prix à la consommation (partie A) couvre, dans la majeure partie des cas, toutes les catégories importantes de dépenses telles que l'alimentation (y compris les boissons), le combustible et l'éclairage, l'habillement, le loyer et les dépenses diverses. Des indices relatifs à ce dernier groupe ne sont pas présentés séparément dans l'*Annuaire*, en raison des variations importantes dans la composition de ce groupe d'un pays à un autre [3].

---

[1] En plus des séries figurant dans ce tableau, le lecteur trouvera dans les publications nationales des différents pays des séries concernant d'autres localités, d'autres régions ou d'autres groupes de population (voir annexe, « Références et sources »).

[2] Pour une étude détaillée des indices des prix à la consommation et des méthodes utilisées pour établir ces indices, voir BIT: *Statistiques du coût de la vie*, Etudes et documents, nouvelle série, n° 7 (partie 2) (Genève, 1948), et *Calcul des indices des prix à la consommation* (Problèmes particuliers), dixième Conférence internationale des statisticiens du travail, rapport IV (Genève, 1970) (document ronéoté).

[3] Pour la description des diverses séries nationales, de leur portée, des méthodes d'établissement de ces séries, etc., voir BIT: *Guide technique 1972* (descriptions des séries publiées dans le *Bulletin* et l'*Annuaire des statistiques du travail*), vol. I, « Prix à la consommation » (Genève, 1973).

On se sert fréquemment des indices des prix à la consommation pour corriger les indices des salaires nominaux lorsqu'on calcule les indicateurs approximatifs des tendances des salaires réels. Bien que cette correction des salaires nominaux au moyen des prix à la consommation permette de mesurer utilement le pouvoir d'achat relatif (en ce qui concerne les biens de consommation et les services), les résultats peuvent prêter à des interprétations erronées, notamment lorsque les données relatives aux salaires se rapportent à un groupe de population dont les caractéristiques sociales et économiques sont très différentes de celles du groupe de population auquel se rapporte l'indice des prix à la consommation [1].

[1] Pour une analyse de certains des problèmes relatifs à cette question, voir BIT: *Les comparaisons internationales des salaires réels*, Etudes et documents, nouvelle série, n° 45 (Genève, 1956).

Precios del consumo

Cuadro 25

Precios del consumo

La parte A de este cuadro presenta los índices generales de los precios del consumo de todos los grupos de artículos de consumo en su conjunto. Las partes B a E presentan los índices para los grupos siguientes: « Alimentación » (inclusive las bebidas), « Combustible y alumbrado », « Vestido » y « Alquiler ».

Los índices de los precios del consumo tienen por objeto medir los cambios que sufre, con el transcurso del tiempo, el nivel de los precios de un conjunto de bienes y servicios que se considera representativo de los hábitos del consumo de una población determinada. Los precios de los artículos incluidos en el índice se obtienen a intervalos regulares en almacenes, mercados y establecimientos de suministro de servicios ubicados en la zona abarcada por la serie. Los métodos utilizados para calcular los índices varían de un país a otro. Por lo general, dichos índices se calculan en forma de promedios aritméticos ponderados de los relativos de precios entre el período de base y el período considerado (fórmula de Laspeyres). Los coeficientes de ponderación, que permiten tener en cuenta la importancia relativa de los gastos del consumo, se basan generalmente en los resultados de encuestas sobre los gastos de las familias que reflejan la estructura de los gastos del consumo y su importancia relativa para un grupo dado de población [1]. Cuando no se dispone de informaciones sobre gastos de las familias, o cuando son insuficientes para establecer un sistema de ponderaciones, se efectúan ordinariamente cálculos adicionales con el fin de establecer presupuestos teóricos; en unos pocos casos, las ponderaciones se basan en el consumo total estimado de los artículos que se consideran en un determinado país.

Dadas las diferencias en el alcance de los índices y en los métodos que se utilizan para calcularlos, las estadísticas que se presentan en este cuadro para los diferentes países no representan de modo uniforme las variaciones de los niveles de los precios, y la exactitud de los datos varía de un país a otro [2].

En vista de que también varía el período escogido como base en las diferentes series, se ha adoptado un período de base uniforme (1970) para la presentación de los datos, y, en la medida de lo posible, se han calculado nuevamente en su mayor parte estas series dividiendo el índice de cada fecha indicada por el índice del año 1970 y multiplicando el cociente por 100. Cuando se dispone de datos sólo para los años posteriores a 1970, generalmente se presentan los índices escogiendo como base el primer año civil accesible. Esta operación no implica ninguna modificación en el procedimiento de ponderación, etc., utilizado por los distintos países.

En algunos casos que se indican en las notas de pie de página, cuando ha habido interrupción en una serie, y ha sido reemplazada por otra serie que puede compararse satisfactoriamente con la primera, se ha procedido a enlazar las dos series.

El índice general de los precios del consumo (parte A de este cuadro) comprende, en la mayoría de los casos, todas las principales categorías de gastos, a saber, la alimentación (inclusive las bebidas), el combustible y el alumbrado, el vestido, el alquiler y los gastos varios. Los índices relativos a este último grupo no se presentan por separado en el *Anuario*, a causa de las variaciones importantes, en la composición de este grupo, de un país a otro [3].

---

[1] Además de las series que se presentan en este cuadro, el lector encontrará en las publicaciones nacionales de los diversos países series que se refieren a otras localidades, zonas y grupos de población (véase anexo, « Referencias y fuentes »).

[2] Para un estudio detallado de los índices de precios del consumo y de los métodos que se utilizan en su cálculo, véanse OIT: *Estadísticas del costo de la vida*, nueva serie, núm. 7 (parte 2) (Ginebra, 1948), y *Cálculo de los índices de los precios del consumo* (Problemas especiales), décima Conferencia Internacional de Estadígrafos del Trabajo, Informe IV (Ginebra, 1970) (mimeografiado).

[3] Para las descripciones de las diversas series nacionales, su alcance, los métodos de compilación utilizados, etc., véase OIT: *Guía Técnica 1972* (descripciones de las series publicadas en el *Boletín* y el *Anuario de Estadísticas del Trabajo*), vol. I, « Precios del consumo » (Ginebra, 1973).

Los índices de los precios del consumo se utilizan a menudo para corregir los índices de salarios nominales cuando se calculan los indicadores aproximados de las tendencias de los salarios reales. Aunque esta corrección de los salarios nominales mediante los precios del consumo proporciona una medida del poder de compra relativo (con respecto a los bienes de consumo y a los servicios), los resultados pueden inducir en error, sobre todo cuando las informaciones sobre salarios corresponden a un grupo de población cuyas características económicas y sociales son muy diferentes de las del grupo de población a que corresponde el índice de los precios del consumo [1].

---

[1] Para el estudio de algunos de los problemas conexos, véase OIT: *Les comparaisons internationales des salaires éels*, Etudes et documents, nouvelle série, núm. 45 (Ginebra, 1956; en inglés y francés solamente).

25 Consumer prices / Prix à la consommation / Precios del consumo — A General indices / Indices généraux / Indices generales

(1970 = 100)

Country — *Pays* — País	1965	1966	1967	1968	1969	1970	1971	1972	1973	1974	1975 (VI)
AFRICA — AFRIQUE / AFRICA											
Botswana (Gaborone)	.	.	.	.	94.3	**100.0**	.	.	120.2[1]	136.0	...
Burundi (Bujumbura)[2,3]	87.9	91.8	90.8	96.3	100.3	**100.0**	103.9	107.9	114.3	132.2	151.1[20]
Cameroun (Yaoundé) . . . . . . *Afric.*	.	.	.	93.6	94.6	**100.0**	104.2	112.5	124.3	145.7	162.8
» » [4] . . . . . *Europ.*	89.0	91.1[5]	94.0	95.9	97.3	**100.0**	103.8	110.2	117.5	137.1	158.2
Cap-Vert (Praya)[6]	93.0	90.1	93.7	93.0	97.2	**100.0**	118.3	130.3	148.6	225.4	...
République centrafricaine (Bangui)[4] . *Europ.*	85.7	88.2	89.8	94.1	95.6	**100.0**	106.8	114.5	120.9	132.4	153.4
Congo (Brazzaville)[4] . . . . . . *Europ.*	87.7	92.4	95.7	99.3	98.6	**100.0**	104.1	114.2	118.2	124.8	145.5
Côte-d'Ivoire (Abidjan) . . . . . . *Afric.*	78.6	81.9	83.7	88.2	92.1	**100.0**	99.2	99.5	110.2	129.8	142.0[21]
» » » [4] . . *Europ.*	86.6	88.8	89.7	93.0	95.2	**100.0**	104.1	107.9	112.3	130.5	156.3[21]
Egypt[7]	*91.1*	*99.3*	**100.0**	93.2[8]	96.3	**100.0**	103.1	105.3	109.8	121.7	131.9
Ethiopia (Addis Ababa)[4]	.	88.7	89.4	89.5	90.8	**100.0**	100.5	94.4	102.8	111.7	119.1
Gabon (Libreville)[4] . . . . *Afric.*	*83.4*	*86.4*	*88.5*	*90.3*	*92.7*	*96.7[9]*	**100.0**	*104.8*	*110.0*	*123.0*	*161.2*
» » [4] . . . . [10]	81.8	86.8	89.4	92.8	96.6	**100.0**	103.8	111.2	123.7[5]	138.3	152.0
Ghana (Accra)	84.5	89.1	83.6	91.9	96.4	**100.0**	104.9	114.8	127.9	163.3	220.8[21]
Kenya (Nairobi)[11]	91.9	95.9	97.6	98.0	97.8	**100.0**	101.9[12]	**100.0**[8]	*108.2*	*124.3*	*150.8*
Lesotho[13]	.	.	.	.	.	.	.	93.5[14]	100.0	*114.6*	...
Liberia (Monrovia)	80.7	83.2	87.8	90.1	99.3	**100.0**	100.2	104.2	124.6	148.9	168.3
Libyan Arab Republic (Tripoli)	*78.8*	85.2	88.3	*92.1*	**100.0**	**100.0**[8]	97.3	97.0	104.5	...	...
Madagascar (Tananarive)[4] . . . . . . [15]	89.3	92.0	92.8	93.6	97.2	**100.0**	105.4	111.4	118.2[5]	144.2	156.3
» » [4] . . . . *Europ.*	79.7	81.9	84.1	86.4	95.0	**100.0**	106.2	113.0	115.5[5]	127.7	145.3
Malawi (Blantyre)[4,13]	.	.	.	90.5	91.3	**100.0**	108.2	112.1	117.8	135.9	152.9
» » [4,10]	.	.	.	.	.	**100.0**	108.3	112.5	119.7	139.5	163.2[20]
Maroc[16]	97.3	96.3	95.5	96.0	98.8	**100.0**	104.2	108.1	112.5	*122.0[17]*	129.5
Mauritanie (Nouakchott)[4] . . . . . *Europ.*	81.0	84.6	87.9	91.0	93.8	**100.0**	107.6	116.4	124.8	140.4[18]	152.1[21]
Mauritius	86.2	88.4	90.0	96.3	98.5	**100.0**	100.3	105.7	120.0	154.9	175.7
Mozambique (Lourenço Marques)	83.6	86.6	89.6	93.3	95.5	**100.0**	115.7	123.9	130.6	159.0	...
Niger (Niamey)[4] . . . . *Afric.*	82.9	91.7	92.1	89.7	98.9	**100.0**	104.3	114.4	127.8	132.2	145.3
» » [4] . . . . *Europ.*	79.4	82.4	90.5	94.0	95.9	**100.0**	103.6	105.7	108.1	116.4	129.2
Nigeria (Lagos)[13]	76.1	82.6	79.5	80.3	88.3	**100.0**	113.5	116.8	121.0[19]	141.4	195.4
Réunion (Saint-Denis)	.	90.8	92.3	92.9	95.2	**100.0**	106.4	114.6[5]	128.0	146.5	165.1

EXPLANATORY NOTES AND CODES: See p. 741.

1 April-Dec. 2 Government officials. 3 Incl. income taxes. 4 Excl. " Rent ". 5 Series linked to former series. 6 Excl. " Clothing " and " Rent ". 7 Prior to 1968: Cairo only. 8 Series replacing former series. 9 Jan.-June and Aug.-Dec. 10 High income group. 11 Middle income group; prior to 1972: low income group excl. " Rent ". 12 Jan.-Aug. 13 Low income group. 14 Oct. 15 Madagascans. 16 Prior to 1974: Casablanca only. 17 Series (base May 1972-April 1973 = 100) replacing former series. 18 Jan.-July and Sep.-Dec. 19 Jan.-Sep. and Dec. 20 April. 21 May.

NOTES EXPLICATIVES ET CODES: Voir p. 742.

1 *Avril-déc.* 2 *Fonctionnaires.* 3 *Y compris les impôts sur le revenu.* 4 *Non compris le groupe « Loyer ».* 5 *Série enchaînée à la précédente.* 6 *Non compris les groupes « Habillement » et « Loyer ».* 7 *Avant 1968: Le Caire seulement.* 8 *Série remplaçant la précédente.* 9 *Janv.-juin et août-déc.* 10 *Familles à revenu élevé.* 11 *Familles à revenu moyen; avant 1972: familles à revenu modique, non compris le groupe « Loyer ».* 12 *Janv.-août.* 13 *Familles à revenu modique.* 14 *Oct.* 15 *Malgaches.* 16 *Avant 1974: Casablanca seulement.* 17 *Série (base mai 1972-avril 1973 = 100) remplaçant la précédente.* 18 *Janv.-juillet et sept.-déc.* 19 *Janv.-sept. et déc.* 20 *Avril.* 21 *Mai.*

NOTAS EXPLICATIVAS Y CLAVES: Véase pág. 744.

1 Abril-dic. 2 Funcionarios. 3 Incl. los impuestos sobre los ingresos. 4 Excl. el grupo « Alquiler ». 5 Serie enlazada con la anterior. 6 Excl. los grupos « Vestido » y « Alquiler ». 7 Antes de 1968: El Cairo solamente. 8 Serie que substituye a la anterior. 9 Enero-junio y agosto-dic. 10 Familias de ingresos elevados. 11 Familias de ingresos medios; antes de 1972: familias de ingresos módicos, excl. el grupo « Alquiler ». 12 Enero-agosto. 13 Familias de ingresos módicos. 14 Oct. 15 Malgaches. 16 Antes de 1974: Casablanca solamente. 17 Serie (base mayo de 1972-abril de 1973 = 100) que substituye a la anterior. 18 Enero-julio y sept.-dic. 19 Enero-sept. y dic. 20 Abril. 21 Mayo.

25 Consumer prices / Prix à la consommation / Precios del consumo

A General indices / Indices généraux / Indices generales

(1970 = 100)

Country — Pays — País	1965	1966	1967	1968	1969	1970	1971	1972	1973	1974	1975 (VI)
Sénégal (Dakar) [1]	91.3	94.2	93.7	94.1	97.8	❙100.0 [2]	103.8	110.0	123.4	144.1	.
Seychelles (Victoria)	.	.	.	.	.	100.0	114.9	139.1	164.4	❙204.5 [3]	238.3
Sierra Leone (Freetown)	81.1	84.6	❙89.4 [3]	90.9	93.6	100.0	98.4	103.8	109.7	125.5	137.5 [18]
Somalia (Mogadishu)	.	90.5	90.0	93.2	99.3	100.0	99.4	96.5	102.7	121.5	148.1
South Africa, Rep. of [4]	84.7	87.8	90.7	92.3	95.0	❙100.0 [3]	106.1	113.0	123.7	138.1	156.2
Sudan	87.4	88.9	98.7	88.8	100.0	❙100.0 [2]	101.3	113.3	132.6	167.2	212.0
Swaziland (Mbabane-Manzini) [5, 6]	87.3	90.0	91.8	95.1	97.8	100.0	102.0	104.4	116.5	139.0	153.8
Tanzania [7]	86.3	90.7	92.9	96.1	❙96.6 [2]	100.0	104.7	112.8	124.5	148.9	189.6 [18]
Tchad (Ndjamena) [5, 8]	80.2	85.0	87.8	88.7	92.0	100.0	106.0	109.1	115.0	❙127.9 [3]	149.9
Togo (Lomé)	.	92.4	90.3	90.5	96.0	100.0	108.9	113.6	119.3	134.2	160.0
Tunisie (Tunis) [9]	86.7	90.0	92.7	95.0	98.9	❙100.0 [3]	106.0	108.0	113.1	117.7	129.0
Uganda (Kampala) [5, 6]	82.2	81.5	84.2	81.5	91.1	100.0	115.8	112.3	139.7	233.6	271.9 [18]
Zaïre (Kinshasa) [10]	35.1	40.6	55.6	85.4 [11]	97.0	100.0	104.9	❙137.5 [12]	159.4	206.3	257.6
Zambia [6, 13]	76.1	83.9	88.1	97.6	❙95.5 [2]	100.0	106.0	111.7	118.8	128.8	...
AMERICA — AMÉRIQUE AMÉRICA											
Antigua	.	.	.	.	93.5	100.0	108.6	118.3	134.2	167.6	184.0 [19]
Antilles néerlandaises [14, 15]	92.0	93.0	93.8	95.1	96.6	100.0	❙100.0 [2]	104.0	112.5	134.5	153.7 [19]
Argentina (Buenos Aires)	41.3	54.5	70.4	81.8	88.0	100.0	134.7	213.5	342.2	425.0	872.3
Bahamas (Nassau)	.	78.5	82.7	86.5	94.2	100.0	104.6	❙100.0 [2]	105.3	119.1	130.9
Barbados	.	79.0	81.9	88.0	92.7	100.0	107.5	120.2	140.5	195.1	231.3
Bermuda	76.6	78.5	81.1	88.7	94.0	100.0	109.4	120.0	135.5	157.7	168.9 [19]
Bolivia (La Paz)	75.1	80.3	89.3	94.2	96.3	100.0	103.7	110.4	145.2	236.5	253.3
Brésil (São Paulo)	28.9	42.3	54.9	68.1	84.0	100.0	121.1	❙100.0 [2]	115.5	144.3	185.3
Canada	82.8	85.9	89.0	92.6	96.8	100.0	102.9	107.8	❙116.0 [3]	128.6	141.9
Colombia (Bogotá)	61.9	74.2	80.3	85.0	93.6	100.0	109.0	124.6	152.9	190.3	246.1
Costa Rica (San José) [9]	88.2	88.4	89.4	93.0	95.6	100.0	103.1	107.8	124.2 [16]	161.6 [17]	188.0
Chile (Santiago)	31	39	46	58	75	❙100 [3]	120	213	967	5 846	27260
Dominica	76.9	80.3	81.0	85.4	89.1	100.0	103.7	107.6	120.6	164.2	195.0

EXPLANATORY NOTES AND CODES: See p. 741.

[1] Prior to 1970: Europeans; excl. "Rent". [2] Series replacing former series. [3] Series linked to former series. [4] White population. [5] Excl. "Rent". [6] Low income group. [7] Prior to 1969: Dar-es-Salaam only; excl. "Rent". [8] High income group. [9] Metropolitan area. [10] Prior to 1972: excl. "Rent". [11] Jan.-March and May-Dec. [12] Series (base 1969 = 100) replacing former series. [13] Prior to 1969: base 1969 = 100, excl. "Rent". [14] Excl. Bonaire and Windward Is.; prior to 1971: Curaçao only. [15] Excl. compulsory social security; prior to 1971: incl. direct taxes. [16] June and Dec. [17] June, Aug. and Oct.-Dec. [18] Second quarter. [19] April.

NOTES EXPLICATIVES ET CODES: Voir p. 742.

[1] Avant 1970 : Européens ; non compris le groupe « Loyer ». [2] Série remplaçant la précédente. [3] Série enchaînée à la précédente. [4] Population blanche. [5] Non compris le groupe « Loyer ». [6] Familles à revenu modique. [7] Avant 1969 : Dar es-Salaam seulement ; non compris le groupe « Loyer ». [8] Familles à revenu élevé. [9] Région métropolitaine. [10] Avant 1972 : non compris le groupe « Loyer ». [11] Janv.-mars et mai-déc. [12] Série (base 100 en 1969) remplaçant la précédente. [13] Avant 1969 : base 100 en 1969, non compris le groupe « Loyer ». [14] Non compris Bonaire et les îles Windward ; avant 1971 : Curaçao seulement. [15] Non compris la sécurité sociale obligatoire ; avant 1971 : y compris les impôts directs. [16] Juin et déc. [17] Juin, août et oct.-déc. [18] Deuxième trimestre. [19] Avril.

NOTAS EXPLICATIVAS Y CLAVES: Véase pág. 744.

[1] Antes de 1970: europeos; excl. el « grupo Alquiler ». [2] Serie que substituye a la anterior. [3] Serie enlazada con la anterior. [4] Población blanca. [5] Excl. el grupo « Alquiler ». [6] Familias de ingresos módicos. [7] Antes de 1969: Dar es-Salaam solamente; excl. el grupo « Alquiler ». [8] Familias de ingresos elevados. [9] Area metropolitana. [10] Antes de 1972: excl. el grupo « Alquiler ». [11] Enero-marzo y mayo-dic. [12] Serie (base 1969 = 100) que substituye a la anterior. [13] Antes de 1969: base 1969 = 100, excl. el grupo « Alquiler ». [14] Excl. Bonaire y las Islas Windward; antes de 1971: Curazao solamente. [15] Excl. la seguridad social obligatoria; antes de 1971: incl. los impuestos directos. [16] Junio y dic. [17] Junio, agosto y oct.-dic. [18] Segundo trimestre. [19] Abril.

PRICES

25 Consumer prices / Prix à la consommation / Precios del consumo

A General indices / Indices généraux / Indices generales

(1970 = 100)

Country — Pays — País	1965	1966	1967	1968	1969	1970	1971	1972	1973	1974	1975 (VI)
República Dominicana (Santo Domingo) [1]	92.1	90.8	92.5	94.1	92.3	97.1[2]	100.0	107.8	124.1	140.4	159.7
Ecuador (Quito)	79.4	82.6	85.8	89.5	95.2	100.0	108.4	117.0	132.1	163.0	188.5
El Salvador [3]	94.8	93.7	95.1	97.5	97.3	100.0	100.3[4]	102.0	108.5	126.8	153.2
Falkland Is. (Malvinas) (Stanley)	78.9	82.3	86.6	91.4	95.7	100.0	108.1	∣84.6[5]	100.0	119.4	...
Greenland	69.5	73.4	78.8	86.7	91.1	100.0	∣101.5[6]	107.6	118.1	137.1	163.4[26]
Grenada	77.9	81.2	86.1	93.8	100.0	.	.	.	.	.	.
Guadeloupe (Basse-Terre)	.	.	85.4	90.3	94.4	100.0	106.4	114.9	122.7	142.3	165.9
Guatemala (Guatemala)	92.8	93.4	93.9	95.6	97.7	100.0	99.5	100.1	114.4	132.7	154.0
Guyana [7]	88.1	89.9	92.6	95.4	96.7	100.0	102.0	106.6	116.1	∣133.9[8]	141.2
Guyane française (Cayenne)	.	.	.	.	96.2	100.0	106.9[9]	112.7	120.6	140.4	156.2[27]
Haïti (Port-au-Prince) [10]	92.0	99.4[11]	96.7	98.0	99.3	100.0	110.4	113.9	139.8	160.8	193.9
Honduras (Tegucigalpa)	91.8	92.0	93.1	95.5	97.2	100.0	103.1	108.7	113.2	127.5	134.9
Jamaica (Kingston) [12, 13]	95.2	97.2	∣80.9[14]	85.8	91.1	100.0	106.7	112.9	135.4	∣171.2[8]	203.2
Martinique (Fort-de-France)	.	82.9	85.9	89.0	93.7	100.0	106.6	112.8	121.5	144.4	164.1
México (México) [15]	84.1	87.7	90.3	92.5	95.1	100.0	103.2	109.8	127.9	167.8	198.5
Panamá (Panamá)	92.3	92.5	93.7	95.3	97.0	100.0	102.0	107.4	114.8	134.1	141.8
Paraguay (Asunción)	93.9	96.7	98.0	98.6	100.9	100.0	105.0	114.7	129.3	161.9	170.0
Perú (Lima) [12]	63.0	68.6	75.3	89.6	95.2	100.0	106.8	114.5	125.4	146.5	178.3
Puerto Rico	85.0	87.6	91.2	93.8	96.7	100.0	104.3	107.6	115.5	138.4	148.5
St. Kitts	.	.	.	.	86.3	100.0	98.4	104.5	115.2	148.0	164.2
St. Lucia	78.4	80.4	82.9	86.2	88.2	100.0	108.4	116.9	132.7	178.0	211.8
Surinam (Paramaribo) [16]	74.2	77.5	84.0	84.0	∣97.5[14]	100.0	100.2	103.4	116.9	136.6	148.0
Trinidad and Tobago	82.7	86.1	87.9	95.2	97.5	100.0	103.5	113.1	129.9	158.5	183.5
United States	81.3	83.6	86.0	89.6	94.4	100.0	104.3	107.7	114.4	127.0	138.1
Uruguay (Montevideo)	9.6	16.7	31.5	71.1	85.9	100.0	123.9	218.7	∣430.8[8]	763.3	1 338.0
Venezuela (Caracas) [12]	92.4	94.0	94.0	95.2	97.5	100.0	103.2	106.2	110.6	120.0	131.8
Virgin Is. (Brit.) [17]	.	.	82.7	88.5	94.6	100.0	104.3	∣94.4[18]	100.0	115.8	128.1
ASIA — ASIE / ASIA											
Afghanistan (Kabul) [15, 19]	.	.	.	86.7[20]	84.6	100.0	125.6	109.9	98.7	110.0	115.5
Bangladesh (Dacca) [21]	78.7	85.5	89.9	92.0	96.6	100.0	112.4[22]	144.5	209.1	∣330[23]	409
Brunei	91.9	92.7	96.1	103.3	101.9	102.7	103.7	100.0	111.9	135.7	141.4[28]
Burma (Rangoon)	83.5	106.4	103.9	110.1	104.3	100.0	102.2	109.9	135.8	172.4	...
Cambodge (Phnom-Penh) [24]	80.1	79.6	79.1	83.9	89.2	100.0	171.3	214.9	554.2	...	...
Cyprus [13]	98.8	99.3	∣91.9[14]	95.4	97.7	100.0	104.1	109.2	117.7	∣134.2[25]	
Hong Kong	80.3	82.7	87.4	89.8	92.9	100.0	103.1	109.4	129.1	148.0	

EXPLANATORY NOTES AND CODES: See p. 741.

[1] Incl. direct taxes. [2] Nov. [3] San Salvador, Mejicanos and Villa Delgado. [4] Jan.-May and Aug.-Dec. [5] April-Dec.; series replacing former series. [6] Series (base Jan. 1971 = 100) replacing former series. [7] Urban areas. [8] Series linked to former series. [9] Jan.-July and Sep.-Dec. [10] Excl. " Miscellaneous ". [11] Jan.-May and July-Dec. [12] Metropolitan area. [13] Prior to 1967: base 1967 = 100. [14] Series replacing former series. [15] Excl. " Rent " and Miscellaneous. [16] Prior to 1969: incl. direct taxes. [17] Prior to 1972: Dec. of each year. [18] May-Dec.; series replacing former series. [19] Provisional index. [20] April-Dec. [21] Government officials. [22] Jan., Feb. and April-Dec. [23] Series (base July 1969-June 1970 = 100) replacing former series. [24] Working class. [25] Jan.-July; series linked to former series. [26] July. [27] May. [28] April.

NOTES EXPLICATIVES ET CODES: Voir p. 742.

[1] Y compris les impôts directs. [2] Nov. [3] San Salvador, Mejicanos et Villa Delgado. [4] Janv.-mai et août-déc. [5] Avril-déc.; série remplaçant la précédente. [6] Série (base 100 en janv. 1971) remplaçant la précédente. [7] Régions urbaines. [8] Série enchaînée à la précédente. [9] Janv.-juillet et sept.-déc. [10] Non compris le groupe « Divers ». [11] Janv.-mai et juillet-déc. [12] Région métropolitaine. [13] Avant 1967: base 100 en 1967. [14] Série remplaçant la précédente. [15] Non compris les groupes « Loyer » et « Divers ». [16] Avant 1969: y compris les impôts directs. [17] Avant 1972: déc. de chaque année. [18] Mai-déc.; série remplaçant la précédente. [19] Indice provisoire. [20] Avril-déc. [21] Fonctionnaires. [22] Janv., fév. et avril-déc. [23] Série (base juillet 1969-juin 1970 = 100) remplaçant la précédente. [24] Classe ouvrière. [25] Janv.-juillet; série enchaînée à la précédente. [26] Juillet. [27] Mai. [28] Avril.

NOTAS EXPLICATIVAS Y CLAVES: Véase pág. 744.

[1] Incl. los impuestos directos. [2] Nov. [3] San Salvador, Mejicanos y Villa Delgado. [4] Enero-mayo y agosto-dic. [5] Abril-dic.; serie que substituye a la anterior. [6] Serie (base enero de 1971 = 100) que substituye a la anterior. [7] Areas urbanas. [8] Serie enlazada con la anterior. [9] Enero-julio y sept.-dic. [10] Excl. el grupo « Varios ». [11] Enero-mayo y julio-dic. [12] Area metropolitana. [13] Antes de 1967: base 1967 = 100. [14] Serie que substituye a la anterior. [15] Excl. los grupos « Alquiler » y « Varios ». [16] Antes de 1969: incl. los impuestos directos. [17] Antes de 1972: dic. de cada año. [18] Mayo-dic.; serie que substituye a la anterior. [19] Indice provisional. [20] Abril-dic. [21] Funcionarios. [22] Enero, febr. y abril-dic. [23] Serie (base julio de 1969-junio de 1970 = 100) que substituye a la anterior. [24] Clase obrera. [25] Enero-julio; serie enlazada con la anterior. [26] Julio. [27] Mayo. [28] Abril.

25 Consumer prices / Prix à la consommation / Precios del consumo

A General indices / Indices généraux / Indices generales

(1970 = 100)

Country — Pays — País	1965	1966	1967	1968	1969	1970	1971	1972	1973	1974	1975 (VI)
India	77.5	85.8	97.2	100.0	| 95.1[1]	100.0	103.3	109.8	128.3	165.2	178.3
» (Bombay)	.	79.4	87.8	92.2	96.1	100.0	104.4	110.0	124.4	152.8	171.7
» (Delhi)	68.7	75.4	86.2	91.3	93.3	100.0	107.2	111.8	128.2	166.2	174.9
» (Jamshedpur)	73.5	84.0	100.0	96.1	92.8	100.0	102.2	108.8	128.2	169.1	167.4
Indonesia (Djakarta)	1.1	12.5	33.6	75.8	89.0	100.0	104.3	111.1	145.6	204.8	239.4
Iran	93.2	92.8	94.3	95.0	| 98.3[2]	100.0	104.2	110.9	121.8	138.9	163.8
Iraq (Baghdad)	84.2	85.9	88.7	90.7	95.8	100.0	103.6	109.0	114.3	123.8	134.8
Israel	82.1	88.6	90.1	92.0	| 94.3[2]	100.0	112.0	126.4	151.6	211.9	289.4
Japan[3]	76.7	80.6	83.8	88.3	92.9	| 100.0[2]	106.1	110.9	123.9	154.2	172.4
Jordan (Amman)	.	.	87.1	86.8	93.6	100.0	104.4	112.6	124.5	149.4	164.8
Korea, Rep. of	56.0	62.5	69.1	76.6	86.2	100.0	113.5	126.8	130.8	162.6	203.9
Kuwait	.				.	.	.	100.0	107.9	122.7	143.2
Laos (Vientiane)	74.8	85.1	92.0	96.5	99.6	100.0	101.3	126.8	165.7	248.1	414.5
Liban (Beyrouth)	.	92.9	96.3	95.6	100.0	100.0	101.6	106.6	113.0	125.5	127.4
Malaysia:											
East Malaysia:											
Sarawak	.	.	100.7	99.8	99.1	100.0	99.4	102.9	111.2	127.1	...
West Malaysia	94.2	95.5	| 98.7[1]	98.5	98.1	100.0	101.6	104.8	115.9	136.0	141.2
Nepal (Katmandu)[4]	82.1	83.9	82.8	86.1	95.3	100.0	101.3	112.7	119.3	142.9	166.8
Pakistan[5]	80.2	86.0	91.8	92.0	94.9	100.0	104.7	| 105.2[6]	126.9	164.0	197.2
Philippines (Manila)[7]	82.2	85.9	91.8	92.2	94.8	| 100.0[1]	123.3	142.7	152.8	214.9	233.5
Singapore	94.2	96.1	99.2	99.9	99.6	100.0	101.9	104.0	127.9	| 122.3[8]	125.0
Sri Lanka (Colombo)	81.4	81.3	83.1	87.9	94.4	100.0	102.7	109.2	119.7	134.4	143.7
Sud Viet-Nam, Rép. du (Saigon)[9]	20.3	32.9	47.3	60.0[10]	73.1	100.0	118.2	| 148.1[2]	213.9	331.7	...
République arabe syrienne (Damas)	84.6	89.4	93.5	96.7	95.9	100.0	104.9	105.7	126.8	146.3	162.6
Thailand (Bangkok-Metropolis)	88.2	91.5	95.2	97.2	99.2	100.0	102.0	106.1	118.5	146.1	150.7
EUROPE — EUROPE EUROPA											
Austria	85.1	| 87.0[2]	90.4	93.0	95.8	100.0	104.7	111.3	119.7	131.1	142.3
Belgique[11]	84.2	| 87.8[2]	90.3	92.8	96.2	100.0	104.3	| 110.0[2]	117.7	132.6	148.5
Bulgarie	96.7	96.5	96.7	100.5	100.4	100.0	99.9	99.9	100.0	100.3	.
Czechoslovakia	91.0	91.5	93.3	94.5	98.3	100.0	99.7	99.5	99.7	100.2	100.7[13]
Denmark	72.6	77.6	84.0	90.7	93.9	100.0	105.8	112.8	123.3	142.1	156.7
España	78.1	82.9	88.3	| 92.6[2]	94.6	100.0	108.2	117.2	130.6	151.1	174.7
Finland[12]	91.1	94.7	| 87.3[1]	95.3	97.4	100.0	106.5	114.1	127.5	| 149.7[2]	174.5
France	81.0	83.2	85.4	89.3	95.0	| 100.0[2]	105.5	112.0	120.2	136.7	151.7

EXPLANATORY NOTES AND CODES: See p. 741.

[1] Series replacing former series. [2] Series linked to former series. [3] Excl. Okinawa Prefecture. [4] Excl. "Rent". [5] Prior to 1972: Karachi only; industrial workers. [6] Series (base 1971 = 100) replacing former series. [7] Middle income group; prior to 1970: low income group. [8] Series (base 1973 = 100) replacing former series. [9] Working class. [10] Jan., March.-Dec. [11] Excl. "Rent" and "Miscellaneous; prior to 1972: excl. "Rent" only. [12] Prior to 1967: base 1967 = 100. [13] Second quarter.

NOTES EXPLICATIVES ET CODES: Voir p. 742.

[1] Série remplaçant la précédente. [2] Série enchaînée à la précédente. [3] Non compris la préfecture d'Okinawa. [4] Non compris le groupe « Loyer ». [5] Avant 1972: Karachi seulement; travailleurs de l'industrie. [6] Série (base 100 en 1971) remplaçant la précédente. [7] Familles à revenu moyen; avant 1970: familles à revenu modique. [8] Série (base 100 en 1973) remplaçant la précédente. [9] Classe ouvrière. [10] Janv., mars-déc. [11] Non compris les groupes « Loyer » et « Divers »; avant 1972: non compris le groupe « Loyer » seulement. [12] Avant 1967: base 100 en 1967. [13] Deuxième trimestre.

NOTAS EXPLICATIVAS Y CLAVES: Véase pág. 744.

[1] Serie que substituye a la anterior. [2] Serie enlazada con la anterior. [3] Excl. la prefectura de Okinawa. [4] Excl. el grupo « Alquiler ». [5] Antes de 1972: Karachi solamente; trabajadores de la industria. [6] Serie (base 1971 = 100) que substituye a la anterior. [7] Familias de ingresos medios; antes de 1970: familias de ingresos módicos. [8] Serie (base 1973 = 100) que substituye a la anterior. [9] Clase obrera. [10] Enero, marzo-dic. [11] Excl. los grupos « Alquiler » y « Varios »; antes de 1972: excl. el grupo « Alquiler » solamente. [12] Antes de 1967: base 1967 = 100. [13] Segundo trimestre.

25 Consumer prices / Prix à la consommation / Precios del consumo

A General indices / Indices généraux / Indices generales

(1970 = 100)

Country — Pays — País	1965	1966	1967	1968	1969	1970	1971	1972	1973	1974	1975 (VI)
German Democratic Republic △	100.2	100.1	100.1	100.3	100.1	100.0	99.8	99.3	98.9	98.3	.
Germany, Fed. Rep. of △	88.7	91.9	93.4	94.9	96.7	100.0	105.3	111.1	118.8	127.1	135.4
Gibraltar	78.1	80.3 [1]	82.4	87.8	91.8	100.0	109.9	121.7	135.2 [1]	157.4	186.9 [10]
Grèce	88.5	92.9	94.5	94.8	97.2	100.0	103.0	107.5	124.2	157.6	179.8
Hongrie	.	.	97.7	97.4	98.7	100.0	102.0	104.9	108.4	110.5	*113.8* [11]
Iceland (Reykjavik) [2]	54.8	60.6	62.6	72.6 [1]	88.4	100.0	106.4	117.4	143.5	205.2	293.3
Ireland	77.3	79.6	82.1	86.0	92.4 [1]	100.0	108.9	118.4	131.8	154.2	188.5 [12]
Italie	86.3	88.3	91.6 [1]	92.8	95.3	100.0	104.8 [1]	110.8	122.8	146.3	170.7 [12]
Luxembourg [3]	86.2	89.1	91.0	93.4	95.6	100.0	104.7	110.1	116.8	128.0	141.1
Malta	91.2	91.7	92.4	94.2	96.4	100.0	102.3	105.8	113.9	122.2	130.5
Norway	78.6	81.1	84.7	87.7	90.4	100.0	106.2	113.9	122.4	133.9 [1]	148.7
Pays-Bas	79	83	86.0 [1]	89.1	95.8	100.0	107.6 [1]	116.0	125.2	137.3	150.4
Pologne	93.4	94.5	96.0	97.6	98.9	100.0	99.9	99.8	100.3	106.5	*107.8* [13]
Portugal (Lisbonne)	73.5	77.2	81.5	86.4	94.0	100.0	112.0	124.0	140.0	175.1	202.8
Roumanie	98.1	98.1	97.7	98.9	99.9	100.0	100.8	100.8	101.5	102.6	.
Suisse	84.4	88.4	91.9 [1]	94.1	96.5	100.0	106.6	113.7	123.6	135.7	145.3
Sweden	80.4	85.6	89.3	91.0	93.4	100.0	107.4	113.8	121.5	133.5	145.6
Turquie (Ankara) [4,5]	*89.8*	*93.7*	*100.0*	86.9 [6]	92.5	100.0	116.3	131.4	153.2	181.8	217.6
United Kingdom	80.0	83.1	85.2	89.2	94.0	100.0	109.4	117.2	128.0	148.4	187.6
Yugoslavia	60.7	74.5	79.7	83.7	90.4	100.0	115.6	134.8	161.3	195.3	250.2
OCEANIA — OCÉANIE OCEANÍA											
Australia	85.7	88.3	91.1	93.6	96.2	100.0	106.1	112.3	122.9	141.5	161.2 [14]
Cook Is. (Rarotonga)	.	.	87.7	92.8	95.8	100.0	110.6	123.2	135.1	152.6	172.6 [14]
Fiji	*95.4*	*95.0*	*96.3*	*100.0*	96.2 [6]	100.0	106.5	116.2	129.2	147.9 [1]	166.3
Gilbert and Ellice Is. (Tarawa)	.	.	.	.	.	95.5 [7]	100.0	*104.6*	*118.0*	*133.6*	...
New Zealand	78.7	80.9	85.8	89.5	93.9	100.0	110.4	118.0	127.7	141.9	159.6 [15]
Nouvelle-Calédonie (Nouméa)	81.9	83.3	85.7	87.9	92.0 [1]	100.0	108.2	116.6	124.0	139.8	158.3
Papua New Guinea	90.8	95.2	97.7	98.8	98.4	100.0	106.5	106.1 [8]	*114.9*	*141.6*	*154.1* [14]
Polynésie française (Tahiti) (Papeete)	69.9	80.3	84.1	86.9	88.9	100.0	103.5	108.8	117.6 [1]	138.8	160.9 [12]
Solomon Is. (Brit.) (Honiara)	.	80.2	81.2	86.5	92.2	100.0	102.8 [1]	106.9	110.2	130.6	144.9 [14]
Tonga (Nuku'alofa) [3]	.	.	.	.	100.1	100.0	102.1	108.7	131.2	150.5	...
Western Samoa (Apia)	89.7	92.6	92.0	93.7	97.1	100.0	104.6	112.6	...	...	...
URSS [9]	100.3	99.6	99.6	99.7	99.9	100.0	99.9	99.7	99.7	99.6	
RSS de Biélorussie	100.4	99.7	99.7	99.8	100.0	100.0	99.6	99.4	99.4	99.3	.
RSS d'Ukraine	99.7	99.2	99.3	99.6	99.8	100.0	99.8	99.7	99.7	99.8	.

EXPLANATORY NOTES AND CODES: See p. 741.

[1] Series linked to former series. [2] Prior to 1968: incl. direct taxes. [3] Excl. "Rent". [4] Prior to 1968: government officials. [5] Beginning 1968: excl. "Rent". [6] Series replacing former series. [7] Oct.-Dec. [8] Series (base 1971 = 100) replacing former series. [9] Incl. Byelorussian SSR and Ukrainian SSR, shown separately in this table. [10] April. [11] Base: corresponding month of 1970 = 100. [12] May. [13] Second quarter (base: corresponding quarter of 1970 = 100). [14] Second quarter. [15] Second quarter; series linked to former series.

NOTES EXPLICATIVES ET CODES: Voir p. 742.

[1] Série enchaînée à la précédente. [2] Avant 1968 : y compris les impôts directs. [3] Non compris le groupe « Loyer ». [4] Avant 1968 : fonctionnaires. [5] A partir de 1968 : non compris le groupe « Loyer ». [6] Série remplaçant la précédente. [7] Oct.-déc. [8] Série (base 100 en 1971) remplaçant la précédente. [9] Y compris les RSS de Biélorussie et d'Ukraine, figurant séparément dans ce tableau. [10] Avril. [11] Base : mois correspondant de 1970 = 100. [12] Mai. [13] Deuxième trimestre (base : trimestre correspondant de 1970 = 100). [14] Deuxième trimestre. [15] Deuxième trimestre ; série enchaînée à la précédente.

NOTAS EXPLICATIVAS Y CLAVES: Véase pág. 744.

[1] Serie enlazada con la anterior. [2] Antes de 1968: incl. los impuestos directos. [3] Excl. el grupo « Alquiler ». [4] Antes de 1968: funcionarios. [5] A partir de 1968: excl. el grupo « Alquiler ». [6] Serie que substituye a la anterior. [7] Oct.-dic. [8] Serie (base 1971 = 100) que substituye a la anterior. [9] Incl. las RSS de Bielorrusia y de Ucrania, que figuran separadamente en este cuadro. [10] Abril. [11] Base: mes correspondiente de 1970 = 100. [12] Mayo. [13] Segundo trimestre (base: trimestre correspondiente de 1970 = 100). [14] Segundo trimestre. [15] Segundo trimestre; serie enlazada con la anterior.

25

Consumer prices
Prix à la consommation
Precios del consumo

B **Food indices**
Indices de l'alimentation
Indices de la alimentación

(1970 = 100)

Country — *Pays* — País	1965	1966	1967	1968	1969	1970	1971	1972	1973	1974	1975 (VI)
AFRICA — AFRIQUE AFRICA											
Botswana (Gaborone)	.	.	.	.	95.6	**100.0**	99.6	106.9	122.9	143.7	...
Burundi (Bujumbura)[1]	90.2	94.5	91.4	99.8	102.9	**100.0**	104.9	106.9	113.2	135.5	159.0[17]
Cameroun (Yaoundé) . . . . *Afric.*	.	.	.	91.4	91.5	**100.0**	106.3	119.1	129.9	148.2	163.6
» » . . . . *Europ.*	94.8	|96.7[2]	98.2	98.3	97.5	**100.0**	106.1	114.5	122.8	146.1	168.8
Cap-Vert (Praya)	88.5	85.9	89.7	88.5	94.9	**100.0**	125.6	141.0	160.9	246.2	...
République centrafricaine (Bangui) . *Europ.*	91.4	92.8	92.3	98.0	98.5	**100.0**	108.1	118.4	125.3	137.4	157.5
Congo (Brazzaville) . . . . *Europ.*	89.1	95.2	98.4	101.4	99.3	**100.0**	104.9	115.7	121.4	128.4	149.0
Côte-d'Ivoire (Abidjan) . . . . . . *Afric.*	75.1	78.3	77.7	82.7	88.7	**100.0**	98.2	97.1	114.3	135.0	146.0[18]
» » » . . . . . *Europ.*	89.3	92.3	92.5	93.3	95.7	**100.0**	105.3	110.5	114.7	134.6	171.1[18]
Egypt[3]	*91.4*	*101.1*	**100.0**	|*88.7[4]*	93.6	**100.0**	105.4	108.3	115.6	135.2	149.2
Ethiopia (Addis Ababa)	.	87.1	85.6	85.0	86.8	**100.0**	99.9	87.9	99.2	107.7	113.3
Gabon (Libreville) . . . . *Afric.*	*82.6*	*84.2*	*86.8*	*89.1*	*91.8*	*94.0[5]*	**100.0**	*106.1*	*113.3*	*121.8*	*163.6*
» » . . . . [6]	80.0	85.6	88.8	91.9	95.5	**100.0**	103.6	111.1	|125.2[2]	143.7	158.1
Ghana (Accra)	89.1	92.1	78.0	88.2	95.3	**100.0**	106.2	118.9	141.9	184.7	248.3[17]
Kenya (Nairobi)[7]	90.7	97.2	98.5	98.7	97.6	**100.0**	102.5[8]	|**100.0**[4]	*104.8*	*123.6*	*150.1*
Lesotho[9]	.	.	.	.	.	.	.	91.6[10]	**100.0**	*114.5*	...
Liberia (Monrovia)	84.6	88.8	90.1	88.3	98.8	**100.0**	90.8	90.8	118.2	149.4	174.7
Libyan Arab Republic (Tripoli)	*72.6*	*82.8*	*84.4*	*89.3*	**100.0**	|**100.0**[4]	88.9	80.9	74.1	...	...
Madagascar (Tananarive) . . . . [11]	89.8	93.6	93.2	92.8	97.1	**100.0**	105.3	111.9	|122.3[2]	159.1	170.2
» » . . . . . *Europ.*	80.2	81.8	83.4	86.0	94.8	**100.0**	107.1	114.4	|119.9[2]	138.6	159.1
Malawi (Blantyre)[9]	.	.	.	84.6	86.1	**100.0**	111.2	115.9	123.8	144.2	163.2
» » [6]	.	.	.	.	.	**100.0**	110.6	115.2	125.3	139.4	156.2[18]
Mali (Bamako)	84.0	92.5	99.0	98.8	98.7	**100.0**	121.1[12]	130.0	154.2	...	...
Maroc[13]	99.5	96.6	95.6	95.8	98.9	**100.0**	106.3	111.7	117.7	|*128.7*[14]	134.6
Mauritanie (Nouakchott) . . . . . *Europ.*	85.0	91.0	94.3	94.2	93.9	**100.0**	109.6	119.2	132.4	153.8[15]	164.7[18]
Mauritius	86.3	88.0	89.1	98.1	98.6	**100.0**	100.1	106.3	123.0	162.9	187.6
Mozambique (Lourenço Marques)	79.5	84.8	87.9	90.2	94.7	**100.0**	113.6	129.5	127.3	155.3	...
Niger (Niamey) . . . . *Afric.*	80.6	93.9	91.9	88.1	102.4	**100.0**	105.5	122.7	143.8	147.8	159.3
» » . . . . *Europ.*	82.4	85.8	92.3	93.6	95.9	**100.0**	104.6	108.6	113.2	124.2	140.8
Nigeria (Lagos)[9]	65.5	77.2	69.2	66.8	80.9	**100.0**	126.2	128.1	125.1[16]	150.0	230.9
Réunion (Saint-Denis)	.	88.0	90.7	92.0	94.0	**100.0**	103.1	|111.6[2]	132.5	155.7	175.0

EXPLANATORY NOTES AND CODES: See p. 741.

1 Government officials. 2 Series linked to former series. 3 Prior to 1968: Cairo only. 4 Series replacing former series. 5 Jan.-June and Aug.-Dec. 6 High income group. 7 Middle income group; prior to 1972: low income group. 8 Jan.-Aug. 9 Low income group. 10 Oct. 11 Madagascans. 12 Jan.-Nov. 13 Prior to 1974: Casablanca only. 14 Series (base May 1972-April 1973 = 100) replacing former series. 15 Jan.-July and Sep.-Dec. 16 Jan.-Sep. and Dec. 17 April. 18 May.

NOTES EXPLICATIVES ET CODES: Voir p. 742.

1 *Fonctionnaires.* 2 *Série enchaînée à la précédente.* 3 *Avant 1968: Le Caire seulement.* 4 *Série remplaçant la précédente.* 5 *Janv.-juin et août-déc.* 6 *Familles à revenu élevé.* 7 *Familles à revenu moyen; avant 1972: familles à revenu modique.* 8 *Janv.-août.* 9 *Familles à revenu modique.* 10 *Oct.* 11 *Malgaches.* 12 *Janv.-nov.* 13 *Avant 1974: Casablanca seulement.* 14 *Série (base mai 1972-avril 1973 = 100) remplaçant la précédente.* 15 *Janv.-juillet et sept.-déc.* 16 *Janv.-sept. et déc.* 17 *Avril.* 18 *Mai.*

NOTAS EXPLICATIVAS Y CLAVES: Véase pág. 744.

1 Funcionarios. 2 Serie enlazada con la anterior. 3 Antes de 1968: El Cairo solamente. 4 Serie que substituye a la anterior. 5 Enero-junio y agosto-dic. 6 Familias de ingresos elevados. 7 Familias de ingresos medios; antes de 1972: familias de ingresos módicos. 8 Enero-agosto. 9 Familias de ingresos módicos. 10 Oct. 11 Malgaches. 12 Enero-nov. 13 Antes de 1974: Casablanca solamente. 14 Serie (base mayo de 1972-abril de 1973 = 100) que substituye a la anterior. 15 Enero-julio y sept.-dic. 16 Enero-sept. y dic. 17 Abril. 18 Mayo.

25 B — Consumer prices / Prix à la consommation / Precios del consumo — Food indices / Indices de l'alimentation / Indices de la alimentación

(1970 = 100)

Country — Pays — País	1965	1966	1967	1968	1969	1970	1971	1972	1973	1974	1975 (VI)
Sénégal (Dakar)[1]	92.0	96.4	95.2	94.0	97.1	▌100.0[2]	106.1	113.0	135.7	153.6	.
Seychelles (Victoria)	.	.	.	.	.	100.0	118.4	152.3	188.3	▌100.0[2]	119.0
Sierra Leone (Freetown)	79.0	80.9	▌85.0[3]	84.5	88.7	100.0	96.2	104.6	114.0	135.2	146.9[15]
Somalia (Mogadishu)	.	89.8	87.7	90.3	97.6	100.0	99.3	96.9	107.2	127.9	162.3
South Africa, Rep. of[4]	86.5	89.6	92.8	94.3	95.8	▌100.0[3]	104.8	112.3	129.4	148.8	170.9
Sudan	89.8	92.2	106.5	89.5	100.0	▌100.0[2]	99.2	109.5	127.4	159.9	209.6
Swaziland (Mbabane-Manzini)[5]	86.9	90.7	92.5	95.7	98.9	100.0	101.3	102.8	118.8	142.5	155.8
Tanzania[6]	90.8	94.8	96.7	98.0	▌97.8[2]	100.0	105.8	115.4	128.5	173.8	232.7[15]
Tchad (Ndjamena)[7]	77.9	83.3	85.7	85.9	90.0	100.0	106.0	108.6	115.8	▌128.6[3]	152.3
Togo (Lomé)	.	90.1	85.0	84.3	96.2	100.0	110.4	119.0	121.4	135.6	172.9
Tunisie (Tunis)[8]	85.7	88.6	91.4	93.6	98.6	▌100.0[3]	110.3	113.0	120.5	121.5	134.0
Uganda (Kampala)[5]	84.2	81.5	87.0	80.8	88.4	100.0	124.7	117.8	139.7	245.2	292.5[15]
Zaïre (Kinshasa)	37.2	45.1	63.3	88.3[9]	96.9	100.0	110.5	▌146.2[10]	170.2	222.6	276.6
Zambia[5, 11]	76.4	86.4	90.8	98.4	▌97.9[2]	100.0	106.6	111.6	119.0	129.9	...
AMERICA — AMÉRIQUE AMÉRICA											
Antigua	.	.	.	.	92.6	100.0	110.1	121.2	146.2	192.0	218.7[16]
Antilles néerlandaises[12]	88.0	90.4	91.9	93.8	96.3	100.0	▌100.0[2]	106.8	123.2	168.5	203.9[16]
Argentina (Buenos Aires)	43.2	54.2	69.8	80.9	85.9	100.0	141.7	231.2	358.7	412.8	828.7
Bahamas (Nassau)	.	79.2	86.1	91.2	95.5	100.0	104.8	▌100.0[2]	105.4	125.1	137.9
Barbados	.	80.3	82.8	89.4	93.9	100.0	108.2	126.3	148.7	214.6	258.2
Bermuda	72.1	75.9	79.2	87.7	93.9	100.0	109.1	122.5	147.6	180.8	191.4[16]
Bolivia (La Paz)	68.8	75.1	87.2	93.7	95.6	100.0	104.0	110.6	149.3	271.2	283.2
Brésil (São Paulo)	31.0	45.9	56.6	68.3	85.3	100.0	123.9	▌100.0[2]	120.1	153.7	191.4
Canada	84.3	89.7	90.8	93.8	97.8	100.0	101.1	108.8	▌124.6[3]	144.9	164.1
Colombia (Bogotá)	64.2	78.7	82.5	86.0	95.0	100.0	107.5	128.1	168.9	214.6	296.1
Costa Rica (San José)[8]	83.1	83.7	84.3	89.0	92.9	100.0	103.7	104.9	127.6[13]	165.0[14]	190.0
Chile (Santiago)	32	39	45	57	74	▌100 [3]	124	267	1 270	7 793	33839
Dominica	76.6	80.8	81.8	84.9	87.1	100.0	102.0	104.6	118.5	163.2	195.6

EXPLANATORY NOTES AND CODES: See p. 741.

1 Prior to 1970: Europeans. 2 Series replacing former series. 3 Series linked to former series. 4 White population. 5 Low income group. 6 Prior to 1969: Dar-es-Salaam only. 7 High income group. 8 Metropolitan area. 9 Jan.-March and May-Dec. 10 Series (base 1969 = 100) replacing former series. 11 Prior to 1969: base 1969 = 100. 12 Excl. Bonaire and Windwards Is.; prior to 1971: Curaçao only. 13 June and Dec. 14 June, Aug. and Oct.-Dec. 15 Second quarter. 16 April.

NOTES EXPLICATIVES ET CODES: Voir p. 742.

1 Avant 1970: Européens. 2 Série remplaçant la précédente. 3 Série enchaînée à la précédente. 4 Population blanche. 5 Familles à revenu modique. 6 Avant 1969: Dar es-Salaam seulement. 7 Familles à revenu élevé. 8 Région métropolitaine. 9 Janv.-mars et mai-déc. 10 Série (base 100 en 1969) remplaçant la précédente. 11 Avant 1969: base 100 en 1969. 12 Non compris Bonaire et les îles Windward; avant 1971: Curaçao seulement. 13 Juin et déc. 14 Juin, août et oct.-déc. 15 Deuxième trimestre. 16 Avril.

NOTAS EXPLICATIVAS Y CLAVES: Véase pág. 744.

1 Antes de 1970: europeos. 2 Serie que substituye a la anterior. 3 Serie enlazada con la anterior. 4 Población blanca. 5 Familias de ingresos módicos. 6 Antes de 1969: Dar es-Salaam solamente. 7 Familias de ingresos elevados. 8 Area metropolitana. 9 Enero-marzo y mayo-dic. 10 Serie (base 1969 = 100) que substituye a la anterior. 11 Antes de 1969: base 1969 = 100. 12 Excl. Bonaire y las Islas Windward: antes de 1971: Curazao solamente. 13 Junio y dic. 14 Junio, agosto y oct.-dic. 15 Segundo trimestre. 16 Abril.

25 B

Consumer prices
Prix à la consommation
Precios del consumo

Food indices
Indices de l'alimentation
Indices de la alimentación

(1970 = 100)

Country — *Pays* — País	1965	1966	1967	1968	1969	1970	1971	1972	1973	1974	1975 (VI)
República Dominicana (Santo Domingo) . . .	*94.9*	*93.2*	*93.8*	*96.1*	*90.2*	*95.1*[1]	**100.0**	*106.0*	*125.5*	*147.7*	*170.3*
Ecuador (Quito)	74.2	80.5	84.6	88.1	96.8	**100.0**	106.5	118.3	142.3	188.4	224.0
El Salvador [2]	89.6	88.0	91.9	95.9	95.3	**100.0**	100.2[3]	101.3	108.9	127.8	156.3
Falkland Is. (Malvinas) (Stanley)	88.6	88.7	89.6	95.2	97.5	**100.0**	105.4	.	.	.	.
Greenland	68.2	72.0	77.3	84.4	89.1	**100.0**	|*103*[4]	*110*	*126*	*149*	*177*[19]
Grenada	*75.5*	*78.5*	*84.5*	*94.7*	**100.0**	.	.	.	.	.	.
Guadeloupe (Basse-Terre)	.	.	84.0	89.5	93.3	**100.0**	107.8	117.0	126.2	149.9	175.0
Guatemala (Guatemala)	91.8	91.7	91.7	95.1	96.1	**100.0**	98.1	98.2	117.1	135.7	161.4
Guyana [5]	87.1	89.3	91.9	95.3	95.8	**100.0**	102.3	108.4	123.8	|155.9[6]	163.0
Guyane française (Cayenne)	.	.	.	.	95.3	**100.0**	107.8[7]	113.1	121.7	144.6	157.8[20]
Haïti (Port-au-Prince)	91.1	98.4[8]	94.9	97.3	99.6	**100.0**	107.2	117.9	150.2	168.2	208.9
Honduras (Tegucigalpa)	91.7	91.9	92.9	93.7	94.8	**100.0**	103.9	112.3	116.6	134.6	144.5
Jamaica (Kingston) [9, 10]	*94.8*	*96.6*	| 79.3[11]	84.6	90.1	**100.0**	107.9	111.3	140.0	|187.3[6]	223.6
Martinique (Fort-de-France)	.	81.2	86.1	89.4	92.8	**100.0**	107.8	112.4	121.3	148.4	163.6
México (México)	82.9	87.2	89.2	91.9	94.5	**100.0**	102.0	108.4	128.7	174.0	199.7
Panamá (Panamá)	91.2	90.9	92.3	95.2	97.2	**100.0**	102.4	107.1	117.7	144.5	155.6
Paraguay (Asunción)	99.0	101.8	100.1	100.3	102.2	**100.0**	108.6	120.7	146.8	183.2	185.5
Perú (Lima) [9]	66.0	69.1	76.8	88.5	94.5	**100.0**	106.8	114.7	126.3	150.0	198.7
Puerto Rico	81.7	84.5	89.1	92.7	96.4	**100.0**	105.7	109.5	123.3	160.2	170.8
St. Kitts	.	.	.	.	84.5	**100.0**	101.3	118.6	138.8	181.8	201.7
St. Lucia	81.8	83.1	86.7	90.0	91.3	**100.0**	111.8	121.5	144.1	202.4	241.7
Surinam (Paramaribo)	66.2	70.7	81.8	81.3	| 96.9[11]	**100.0**	98.8	102.3	125.8	147.0	157.5
Trinidad and Tobago	83.4	86.6	87.9	93.6	95.9	**100.0**	104.6	116.6	138.8	180.4	208.1
United States	82.2	86.2	87.0	90.2	94.8	**100.0**	103.0	107.5	123.1	140.7	151.8
Uruguay (Montevideo)	10.8	17.5	34.5	79.6	89.5	**100.0**	124.5	241.3	|489.3[6]	843.7	1 349.7
Venezuela (Caracas) [9]	95.5	95.8	94.7	95.9	98.7	**100.0**	103.5	108.5	116.8	132.9	151.1
Virgin Is. (Brit.) [12]	.	.	*83.1*	*88.3*	*94.3*	**100.0**	*108.3*	|*90.7*[13]	**100.0**	*126.4*	*145.8*
ASIA — ASIE **ASIA**											
Bangladesh (Dacca) [14]	81.5	88.1	93.1	93.4	97.8	**100.0**	110.1[15]	147.6	216.9	|*371*[16]	*440*
Brunei	.	.	.	.	.	.	.	**100.0**	*112.5*	*135.0*	*140.1*[21]
Burma (Rangoon)	81.6	112.0	110.9	113.6	107.9	**100.0**	102.4	114.8	150.0	187.4	...
Cambodge (Phnom-Penh) [17]	72.2	71.9	69.5	75.3	83.2	**100.0**	194.5	249.6	714.9	...	...
Cyprus [10]	*97.8*	*99.0*	| *90.9*[11]	94.8	98.7	**100.0**	104.9	111.9	121.4	|*140.6*[18]	.
Hong Kong	71.7	74.5	82.8	85.5	90.3	**100.0**	103.4	111.0	137.9	160.0	.

EXPLANATORY NOTES AND CODES: See p. 741.

[1] Nov. [2] San Salvador, Mejicanos and Villa Delgado. [3] Jan.-May and Aug.-Dec. [4] Series (base Jan. 1971 = 100) replacing former series. [5] Urban areas. [6] Series linked to former series. [7] Jan.-July and Sep.-Dec. [8] Jan.-May and July-Dec. [9] Metropolitan area. [10] Prior to 1967: base 1967 = 100. [11] Series replacing former series. [12] Prior to 1972: Dec. of each year. [13] May-Dec.; series replacing former series. [14] Government officials. [15] Jan., Feb. and April-Dec. [16] Series (base July 1969-June 1970 = 100) replacing former series. [17] Working class. [18] Jan.-July; series linked to former series. [19] July. [20] May. [21] April.

NOTES EXPLICATIVES ET CODES: Voir p. 742.

[1] *Nov.* [2] *San Salvador, Mejicanos et Villa Delgado.* [3] *Janv.-mai et août-déc.* [4] *Série (base 100 en janv. 1971) remplaçant la précédente.* [5] *Régions urbaines.* [6] *Série enchaînée à la précédente.* [7] *Janv.-juillet et sept.-déc.* [8] *Janv.-mai et juillet-déc.* [9] *Région métropolitaine.* [10] *Avant 1967: base 100 en 1967.* [11] *Série remplaçant la précédente.* [12] *Avant 1972: déc. de chaque année.* [13] *Mai-déc.; série remplaçant la précédente.* [14] *Fonctionnaires.* [15] *Janv., fév. et avril-déc.* [16] *Série (base juillet 1969-juin 1970 = 100) remplaçant la précédente.* [17] *Classe ouvrière.* [18] *Janv.-juillet; série enchaînée à la précédente.* [19] *Juillet.* [20] *Mai.* [21] *Avril.*

NOTAS EXPLICATIVAS Y CLAVES: Véase pág. 744.

[1] Nov. [2] San Salvador, Mejicanos y Villa Delgado. [3] Enero-mayo y agosto-dic. [4] Serie (base enero de 1971 = 100) que substituye a la anterior. [5] Areas urbanas. [6] Serie enlazada con la anterior. [7] Enero-julio y sept.-dic. [8] Enero-mayo y julio-dic. [9] Area metropolitana. [10] Antes de 1967: base 1967 = 100. [11] Serie que substituye a la anterior. [12] Antes de 1972: dic. de cada año. [13] Mayo-dic.; serie que substituye a la anterior. [14] Funcionarios. [15] Enero, febr. y abril-dic. [16] Serie (base julio de 1969-junio de 1970 = 100) que substituye a la anterior. [17] Clase obrera. [18] Enero-julio; serie enlazada con la anterior. [19] Julio. [20] Mayo, [21] Abril.

25 B

Consumer prices	Food indices
Prix à la consommation	Indices de l'alimentation
Precios del consumo	Indices de la alimentación

(1970 = 100)

Country — *Pays* — País	1965	1966	1967	1968	1969	1970	1971	1972	1973	1974	1975 (VI)
India	*75.5*	*83.7*	*97.5*	**100.0**	| *95.0* [1]	**100.0**	101.5	108.0	131.0	171.0	184.0
» (Bombay)	.	75.8	86.4	92.4	96.0	**100.0**	102.0	107.1	126.3	156.1	175.3
» (Delhi)	66.8	74.8	89.3	93.9	94.4	**100.0**	103.3	107.9	129.0	164.0	166.8
» (Jamshedpur)	68.6	81.4	102.9	97.1	91.4	**100.0**	100.0	107.6	130.0	177.6	167.1
Indonesia (Djakarta)	1.2	13.2	37.1	88.8	91.5	**100.0**	102.6	113.2	162.4	229.4	267.4
Iran	96.1	95.2	96.9	96.8	| 99.4 [2]	**100.0**	106.7	116.0	123.9	143.6	171.6
Iraq (Baghdad)	85.9	87.3	89.6	90.0	96.3	**100.0**	104.2	109.5	115.7	128.8	146.4
Israel	85.5	89.7	92.2	94.1	| 96.8 [2]	**100.0**	113.6	123.4	149.0	215.2	310.5
Japan [3]	74.6	77.5	81.3	86.5	91.7	|**100.0** [2]	106.0	110.1	124.4	158.9	177.4
Jordan (Amman)	.	.	78.1	76.3	92.7	**100.0**	106.2	118.0	140.3	189.1	213.5
Korea, Rep. of	55.3	59.5	64.5	70.9	82.3	**100.0**	118.9	134.7	138.2	176.3	231.9
Kuwait	.	.	.		.	.	.	**100.0**	*114.9*	*135.9*	*125.8*
Laos (Vientiane)	79.7	94.1	99.8	105.5	107.5	**100.0**	100.6	135.8	190.7	289.9	514.2
Liban (Beyrouth)	.	90.1	97.1	93.3	100.4	**100.0**	102.6	111.5	122.3	142.7	141.7
Malaysia:											
East Malaysia:											
Sarawak	.	.	102.0	100.0	99.0	**100.0**	99.0	104.1	119.4	146.9	...
West Malaysia	95.4	96.3	| 101.0 [1]	99.0	98.0	**100.0**	102.0	105.1	121.2	153.5	156.6
Nepal (Katmandu)	63.2	82.8	81.8	84.6	93.0	**100.0**	98.9	111.0	117.8	140.9	161.4
Pakistan [4]	79.2	84.8	91.1	90.3	93.1	**100.0**	105.2	| *104.5* [5]	*131.4*	*171.1*	*209.4*
Philippines (Manila) [6]	74.4	82.7	93.8	89.8	91.0	|**100.0** [1]	133.4	157.4	164.4	237.1	253.3
Singapore	94.5	97.4	102.5	102.7	100.6	**100.0**	102.5	105.3	142.7	| *125.6* [7]	*126.6*
Sri Lanka (Colombo)	78.6	79.9	82.5	88.7	93.7	**100.0**	101.9	108.0	121.7	138.9	150.6
Sud Viet-Nam, Rép. du (Saigon) [8]	16.3	30.0	46.0	57.8 [9]	73.9	**100.0**	113.8	| *146.9* [2]	216.0	321.3	...
République arabe syrienne (Damas)	79.4	84.7	93.1	96.2	96.2	**100.0**	103.8	103.8	126.7	145.8	164.9
Thailand (Bangkok-Metropolis)	81.3	86.6	92.8	96.0	99.8	**100.0**	100.6	107.1	122.5	157.4	162.6
Yemen, People's Dem. Rep. of	.	.	.	.	.	**100.0**	105.4	116.7	120.5	144.5	.
EUROPE — EUROPE EUROPA											
Austria	.	87.8	91.3	92.4	95.5	**100.0**	103.8	109.8	118.4	128.3	137.2
Belgique	84.4	| 88.6 [2]	90.8	92.4	96.6	**100.0**	101.9	| *108.6* [2]	117.3	128.3	140.9
Bulgarie	93.2	92.9	93.2	100.2	100.3	**100.0**	100.2	100.2	101.2	...	.
Czechoslovakia	98.9	98.5	98.5	98.7	99.8	**100.0**	99.6	99.4	99.5	99.7	99.5 [11]
Denmark	69.9	73.9	80.4	87.6	92.2	**100.0**	105.9	115.7	131.4	147.1	164.1
España	83.5	87.2	90.5	| 94.6 [2]	96.5	**100.0**	107.8	117.7	132.5	151.5	174.3
Finland [10]	*92.1*	*95.3*	| *86.0* [1]	95.6	98.5	**100.0**	104.4	114.1	128.3	| *148.8* [2]	177.5
France	82.5	84.8	86.2	88.8	94.4	|**100.0** [2]	106.4	114.8	125.6	141.4	155.3

EXPLANATORY NOTES AND CODES: See p. 741.

NOTES EXPLICATIVES ET CODES: Voir p. 742.

NOTAS EXPLICATIVAS Y CLAVES: Véase pág. 744.

[1] Series replacing former series. [2] Series linked to former series. [3] Excl. Okinawa Prefecture. [4] Prior to 1972: Karachi only; industrial workers. [5] Series (base 1971 = 100) replacing former series. [6] Middle income group; prior to 1970: low income group. [7] Series (base 1973 = 100) replacing former series. [8] Working class. [9] Jan., March-Dec. [10] Prior to 1967: base 1967 = 100. [11] Second quarter.

[1] *Série remplaçant la précédente.* [2] *Série enchaînée à la précédente.* [3] *Non compris la préfecture d'Okinawa.* [4] *Avant 1972: Karachi seulement; travailleurs de l'industrie.* [5] *Série (base 100 en 1971) remplaçant la précédente.* [6] *Familles à revenu moyen; avant 1970: familles à revenu modique.* [7] *Série (base 100 en 1973) remplaçant la précédente.* [8] *Classe ouvrière.* [9] *Janv., mars-déc.* [10] *Avant 1967: base 100 en 1967.* [11] *Deuxième trimestre.*

[1] Serie que substituye a la anterior. [2] Serie enlazada con la anterior. [3] Excl. la prefectura de Okinawa. [4] Antes de 1972: Karachi solamente; trabajadores de la industria. [5] Serie (base 1971 = 100) que substituye a la anterior. [6] Familias de ingresos medios; antes de 1970: familias de ingresos módicos. [7] Serie (base 1973 = 100) que substituye a la anterior. [8] Clase obrera. [9] Enero, marzo-dic. [10] Antes de 1967: base 1967 = 100. [11] Segundo trimestre.

25 Consumer prices / Prix à la consommation / Precios del consumo

B Food indices / Indices de l'alimentation / Indices de la alimentación

(1970 = 100)

Country — Pays — País	1965	1966	1967	1968	1969	1970	1971	1972	1973	1974	1975 (VI)
German Democratic Republic △	98.2	98.5	99.1	99.8	99.9	**100.0**	100.6	99.6	98.9	98.6	.
Germany, Fed. Rep. of △	93.6	96.4	96.4	95.5	97.7	**100.0**	103.8	109.7	118.0	123.6	132.7
Gibraltar	83.6	83.6 [1]	84.1	89.7	93.2	**100.0**	110.5	124.0	150.2 [1]	186.6	224.3
Grèce	88.1	93.1	93.8	93.8	97.0	**100.0**	105.1	109.2	132.6	169.2	191.0
Hongrie	.	.	98.8	98.3	99.1	**100.0**	102.0	103.1	107.9	108.4	*108.5* [7]
Iceland (Reykjavik)	*85.8*	*98.5*	**100.0**	68.7 [2]	86.3	**100.0**	101.9	118.8	154.5	224.3	322.0 [8]
Ireland	80.9	81.3	82.9	87.6	92.9 [1]	**100.0**	107.4	120.1	139.8	160.3	200.7 [8]
Italie	89.6	91.4	93.0 [1]	93.2	95.9	**100.0**	104.0 [1]	110.6	123.9	145.9	171.8
Luxembourg	84.0	87.2	88.4	91.7	95.1	**100.0**	103.5	110.5	118.3	129.0	142.8
Malta	89.4	89.8	90.4	93.3	97.1	**100.0**	100.7	105.0	119.6	128.6	137.8
Norway	77.3	79.1	82.5	85.2	88.7	**100.0**	106.1	113.7	121.6	131.8 [1]	149.7
Pays-Bas	81	86	87.8 [1]	89.9	95.8	**100.0**	104.2 [1]	111.1	119.9	128.5	138.6
Pologne	92.5	91.7	92.8	95.3	97.8	**100.0**	101.9	101.8	102.1	112.5	109.4 [9]
Portugal (Lisbonne)	77.5	83.1	84.6	88.1	95.3	**100.0**	108.8	119.6	130.5	173.0	212.8
Roumanie	96.2	96.6	96.5	98.8	98.7	**100.0**	101.5	101.9	103.2	104.9	.
Suisse	*95.4*	**100.0**	95.9 [2]	95.9	97.6	**100.0**	106.5	113.4	120.2	133.2	142.0
Sweden	80.3	85.3	88.2	89.1	92.2	**100.0**	109.2	119.1	126.0	133.8	148.1
Turquie (Ankara) [3]	*89.8*	*93.0*	**100.0**	84.6 [2]	92.7	**100.0**	114.0	126.5	151.8	180.8	232.6
United Kingdom	79.7	82.5	84.6	87.9	93.5	**100.0**	111.1	120.9	139.1	164.1	210.2
Yugoslavia	65.0	77.9	80.1	82.7	89.2	**100.0**	116.6	138.8	169.1	195.9	257.4
OCEANIA — OCÉANIE OCEANÍA											
Australia	87.7	89.4	92.9	95.3	96.5	**100.0**	103.9	107.9	124.3	143.3	152.9 [10]
Cook Is. (Rarotonga)	.	.	85.9	92.0	94.6	**100.0**	114.1	127.0	140.5	156.3	178.2 [10]
Fiji	*101.6*	*95.0*	*95.0*	**100.0**	95.9 [2]	**100.0**	109.1	121.8	146.4	169.3 [1]	190.9
Gilbert and Ellice Is. (Tarawa)	.	.	.	.	.	*94.9* [4]	**100.0**	*106.2*	*124.0*	*145.0*	...
New Zealand	79.5	80.9	86.8	89.5	93.8	**100.0**	109.1	114.3	127.1	141.8	154.2 [1]
Nouvelle-Calédonie (Nouméa)	81.9	82.1	84.9	86.6	90.9 [1]	**100.0**	108.1	117.0	124.8	150.5	170.5
Papua New Guinea	92.6	97.0	98.0	99.3	98.6	**100.0**	107.7	106.8 [5]	*117.4*	*155.9*	*166.6* [10]
Polynésie française (Tahiti) (Papeete)	70.4	82.8	85.5	88.9	91.0	**100.0**	103.2	104.8	117.9 [1]	143.5	160.0 [8]
Solomon Is. (Brit.) (Honiara)	.	.	.	.	100.3	**100.0**	103.5 [1]	112.6	116.7	146.9	164.9 [10]
Tonga (Nuku'alofa)	.	.	.	.	100.8	**100.0**	101.4	110.4	144.2	168.8	...
Western Samoa (Apia)	88.4	92.1	90.5	92.6	97.4	**100.0**	105.8	117.5	...	...	...
URSS [6]	99.7	99.3	99.2	99.4	99.7	**100.0**	100.3	100.3	100.5	100.8	.
RSS de Biélorussie	100.0	99.4	99.3	99.5	99.8	**100.0**	100.0	100.1	100.2	100.5	.
RSS d'Ukraine	98.8	98.6	98.7	99.2	100.0	**100.0**	100.4	100.6	100.7	101.2	.

EXPLANATORY NOTES AND CODES: See p. 741.

NOTES EXPLICATIVES ET CODES: Voir p. 742.

NOTAS EXPLICATIVAS Y CLAVES: Véase pág. 744.

[1] Series linked to former series. [2] Series replacing former series. [3] Prior to 1968: governments officials. [4] Oct.-Dec. [5] Series (base 1971 = 100) replacing former series. [6] Incl. Byelorussian SSR and Ukrainian SSR, shown separately in this table. [7] Base: corresponding month of 1970 = 100. [8] May. [9] Second quarter (base: corresponding quarter of 1970 = 100). [10] Second quarter.

[1] Série enchaînée à la précédente. [2] Série remplaçant la précédente. [3] Avant 1968: fonctionnaires. [4] Oct.-déc. [5] Série (base 100 en 1971) remplaçant la précédente. [6] Y compris les RSS de Biélorussie et d'Ukraine, figurant séparément dans ce tableau. [7] Base: mois correspondant de 1970 = 100. [8] Mai. [9] Deuxième trimestre (base: trimestre correspondant de 1970 = 100). [10] Deuxième trimestre.

[1] Serie enlazada con la anterior. [2] Serie que substituye a la anterior. [3] Antes de 1968: funcionarios. [4] Oct.-dic. [5] Serie (base 1971 = 100) que substituye a la anterior. [6] Incl. las RSS de Bielorrusia y de Ucrania, que figuran separadamente en este cuadro. [7] Base: mes correspondiente de 1970 = 100. [8] Mayo. [9] Segundo trimestre (base: trimestre correspondiente de 1970 = 100). [10] Segundo trimestre.

PRICES

25 C

25 Consumer prices
Prix à la consommation
Precios del consumo

C Fuel and light indices
Indices du combustible et éclairage
Indices del combustible y alumbrado

(1970 = 100)

Country — *Pays* — País	1965	1966	1967	1968	1969	1970	1971	1972	1973	1974
AFRICA — AFRIQUE AFRICA										
Cameroun (Yaoundé)[1] . . . . . . *Europ.*	.	108.2[2]	107.8	107.7	107.0	**100.0**	...	...	...	...
Cap-Vert (Praya)[3]	104.4	100.9	105.3	104.4	101.8	100.0	99.1	100.0	115.8	...
République centrafricaine (Bangui)[1] *Europ.*	85.1	87.4	91.8	94.2	96.2	100.0	107.7	113.4	113.4	...
Congo (Brazzaville)[4] . . . . . *Europ.*	*92.8*	*93.1*	*94.2*	...	*95.7*	...	**100.0**	*101.5*	*101.5*	*100.9*
Côte-d'Ivoire (Abidjan)[3] . . . . . *Afric.*	82.7	77.2	81.1	82.5	85.9	**100.0**	104.4	109.2	116.2	139.1
» » » [4] . . . . . *Europ.*	99.9	97.3	96.4	96.3	98.0	**100.0**	101.3	106.9	106.7	120.8
Egypt	.	.	.	100.5	100.3	**100.0**	98.2	93.3	88.6	90.5
Ethiopia (Addis Ababa)[5]	.	92.1	98.8	100.8	98.3	**100.0**	101.3	107.2	108.3	119.1
Gabon (Libreville) . . . . *Afric.*	*90.8*	*91.4*	*93.4*	*94.3*	*94.7*	*97.4*[6]	**100.0**	*106.7*	*108.1*	*111.3*
» » . . . . [7]	89.4	91.1	91.9	91.7	94.4	**100.0**	101.9	107.2	❙106.2[8]	116.1
Ghana (Accra)	88.9	96.7	90.5	96.5	99.4	**100.0**	98.0	111.3	127.6	170.9
Kenya (Nairobi)[9]	*97.0*	*97.1*	**100.0**	...	...	...	...	❙**100.0**[10]	*105.7*	*117.7*
Lesotho[11]	.	.	.	.	.	.	.	*96.5*[12]	**100.0**	*144.6*
Liberia (Monrovia)	99.4	97.9	...	...	102.7	**100.0**	104.3	103.1	115.7	151.5
Libyan Arab Republic (Tripoli)	.	.	.	.	.	**100.0**	97.0	76.9	79.8	...
Madagascar (Tananarive) . . . . [13]	92.2	93.7	94.6	94.8	96.6	**100.0**	100.9	101.3	❙103.6[8]	115.0
» » . . . . . *Europ.*	90.5	90.5	90.9	90.9	94.3	**100.0**	100.4	102.3	❙104.5[8]	114.5
Malawi (Blantyre)[11, 14]	.	.	.	96.8	96.4	**100.0**	107.0	110.3	113.0	137.8
» » [7, 11]	.	.	.	.	.	**100.0**	108.0	111.4	117.2	124.4
Mauritanie (Nouakchott)[1] . . . . *Europ.*	83.9	80.9	82.7	94.2	100.8	**100.0**	109.6	119.8	123.8	...
Mauritius	93.4	93.4	93.9	100.0	100.0	**100.0**	99.9	99.9	106.9	125.2
Mozambique (Lourenço Marques)	93.7	92.6	96.8	97.9	98.9	**100.0**	108.4	114.7	115.8	144.2
Niger (Niamey)[4] . . . . *Europ.*	98.0	100.0	100.0	99.4	100.0	**100.0**	100.0	97.8	97.1	103.9
Nigeria (Lagos)[11]	81.3	83.0	84.1	85.6	87.9	**100.0**	96.5	99.4	87.1[15]	88.1
Sénégal (Dakar)[1, 16]	95.9	96.3	96.7	97.0	98.0	❙**100.0**[10]	100.2	103.1	105.7	...
Seychelles (Victoria)	.	.	.	.	.	**100.0**	137.0	144.1	150.6	
Sierra Leone (Freetown)	79.2	92.4	❙96.1[8]	98.5	98.5	**100.0**	104.3	103.7	104.7	116.9
Somalia (Mogadishu)	.	101.8	100.4	101.9	112.3	**100.0**	102.8	101.0	74.1	78.3
South Africa, Rep. of[17]	91.1	93.6	94.6	97.0	98.8	❙**100.0**[8]	103.2	111.0	122.7	132.4

EXPLANATORY NOTES AND CODES: See p. 741.

NOTES EXPLICATIVES ET CODES: Voir p. 742.

NOTAS EXPLICATIVAS Y CLAVES: Véase pág. 744.

[1] Incl. water and cleaning products (Senegal: prior to 1970). [2] May-Dec. [3] Incl. water and soap. [4] Incl. water. [5] Incl. soap and certain kitchen utensils. [6] Jan.-June and Aug.-Dec. [7] High income group. [8] Series linked to former series. [9] Middle income group; prior to 1972: low income group. [10] Series replacing former series. [11] Low income group. [12] Oct. [13] Madagascans [14] Incl. certain household items. [15] Jan.-Sep. and Dec. [16] Prior to 1970: Europeans. [17] White population.

[1] *Y compris l'eau et les produits d'entretien (Sénégal: avant 1970).* [2] *Mai-déc.* [3] *Y compris l'eau et le savon.* [4] *Y compris l'eau.* [5] *Y compris le savon et certains ustensiles de cuisine.* [6] *Janv.-juin et août-déc.* [7] *Familles à revenu élevé.* [8] *Série enchaînée à la précédente.* [9] *Familles à revenu moyen ; avant 1972: familles à revenu modique.* [10] *Série remplaçant la précédente.* [11] *Familles à revenu modique.* [12] *Oct.* [13] *Malgaches.* [14] *Y compris certains articles de ménage.* [15] *Janv.-sept. et déc.* [16] *Avant 1970: Européens.* [17] *Population blanche.*

[1] Incl. el agua y los productos de limpieza (Senegal: antes de 1970). [2] Mayo-dic. [3] Incl. el agua y el jabón. [4] Incl. el agua. [5] Incl. el jabón y ciertos utensilios de cocina. [6] Enero-junio y agosto-dic. [7] Familias de ingresos elevados. [8] Serie enlazada con la anterior. [9] Familias de ingresos medios; antes de 1972: familias de ingresos módicos. [10] Serie que substituye a la anterior. [11] Familias de ingresos módicos. [12] Oct. [13] Malgaches. [14] Incl. ciertos artículos domésticos. [15] Enero-sept. y dic. [16] Antes de 1970: europeos. [17] Población blanca.

25 Consumer prices / Prix à la consommation / Precios del consumo — C Fuel and light indices / Indices du combustible et éclairage / Indices del combustible y alumbrado

(1970 = 100)

Country — Pays — País	1965	1966	1967	1968	1969	1970	1971	1972	1973	1974
Sudan [1]	*97.4*	*97.4*	*97.4*	*98.0*	*100.0*	.	.	.	.	.
Swaziland (Mbabane-Manzini) [2]	94.4	96.8	97.0	97.0	98.1	100.0	108.9	112.8	117.7	171.8
Tanzania [1, 3]	66.9	73.5	82.5	92.0	|90.7[4]	100.0	103.8	104.5	117.6	115.5
Tchad (Ndjamena) [1, 5, 6]	98.6	98.6	98.9	100.0	99.6	100.0	99.2	100.3	108.0	|135.2[7]
Togo (Lomé) [8]	.	93.5	89.8	97.2	98.4	100.0	111.1	112.8	118.5	...
Tunisie (Tunis) [1, 9]	89.9	90.5	87.5	89.5	96.9	|100.0[7]	101.9	103.9	105.1	106.7
Uganda (Kampala) [2, 10]	98.4	105.7	95.1	86.9	98.4	100.0	96.7	96.7	125.4	...
Zaïre (Kinshasa) [11]	34.1	43.7	68.6	84.9[12]	97.3	100.0	115.6	| ...	*124.0[13]*	*170.8*
AMERICA — AMÉRIQUE AMÉRICA										
Antilles néerlandaises [1, 14]	.	.	.	.	.	.	100.0	*100.9*	*101.0*	*112.2*
Argentina (Buenos Aires) [15]	47.5	60.7	80.2	88.9	93.4	100.0	139.0	220.0	345.4	460.6
» » » [16]	44.9	62.1	78.2	100.5	100.0	100.0	125.9	134.3	187.9	205.5
Bahamas (Nassau) [17]	.	88.3	89.2	90.9	95.7	100.0	107.5	.	.	.
Bermuda	92.0	92.0	92.0	96.9	97.7	100.0	106.7	117.3	131.0	...
Brésil (São Paulo)	30.2	44.0	63.1	76.0	90.9	100.0	125.9	.	.	.
Canada	86.5	86.5	89.7	93.3	95.5	100.0	106.0	110.1	|120.8[7]	137.4
Costa Rica (San José) [9]	98.0	95.7	94.9	95.7	97.1	100.0	100.3	102.5	109.4	206.0
Dominica	.	89.7	92.6	90.6	92.2	100.0	101.6	105.0	112.6	152.4
República Dominicana (Santo Domingo)	*110.0*	*92.3*	*93.6*	*95.6*	*97.4*	*96.4[18]*	*100.0*	*107.0*	*110.8*	*149.4*
Ecuador (Quito)	98.1	98.1	98.1	98.7	98.7	100.0	107.6	113.2	113.2	114.3
El Salvador [11, 19]	101.0	92.8	99.9	118.0	115.4	100.0	90.2[20]	98.7	118.7	148.5
Falkland Is. (Malvinas) (Stanley)	89.6	90.9	94.6	94.4	97.1	100.0	99.3	.	.	.
Greenland	68.8	68.1	74.4	85.0	85.0	100.0	|102[21]	*111*	*116*	*152*
Grenada	91.5	94.3	94.7	94.7	100.0	.	.	.	.	.
Guatemala (Guatemala)	94.1	95.7	96.1	100.7	101.3	100.0	101.4	103.0	114.1	175.5
Honduras (Tegucigalpa)	94.7	94.7	98.3	99.2	99.2	100.0	98.4	113.3	125.7	187.5
Jamaica (Kingston) [11, 15, 22]	*99.6*	*100.0*	|79.0[4]	80.2	88.3	100.0	105.4	109.3	125.3	|159.3[7]
México (México) [23]	86.4	89.3	94.7	95.1	95.3	100.0	110.2	133.9	135.4	165.1
Panamá (Panamá)	102.1	102.1	102.1	102.1	100.8	100.0	102.6	104.4	105.9	142.7

EXPLANATORY NOTES AND CODES: See p. 741.

1 Incl. water (Tanzania: beginning 1969). 2 Low income group. 3 Prior to 1969: Dar-es-Salaam only. 4 Series replacing former series. 5 Beginning 1974: electricity and water only. 6 High income group. 7 Series linked to former series. 8 Incl. cleaning products and certain kitchen utensils. 9 Metropolitan area. 10 Fuel and soap. 11 Fuel only (Zaire: beginning 1972; Jamaica: beginning 1967). 12 Jan.-March and May-Dec. 13 Series (base 1969 = 100) replacing former series. 14 Excl. Bonaire and Windward Is. 15 Fuel and cleaning products (Jamaica: prior to 1967). 16 Electricity only. 17 Incl. certain household items. 18 Nov. 19 San Salvador, Mejicanos and Villa Delgado. 20 Jan.-May and Aug.-Dec. 21 Series (base Jan. 1971 = 100) replacing former series. 22 Prior to 1967; base 1967 = 100. 23 Incl. soap.

NOTES EXPLICATIVES ET CODES: Voir p. 742.

1 Y compris l'eau (Tanzanie : à partir de 1969). 2 Familles à revenu modique. 3 Avant 1969 : Dar-es-Salaam seulement. 4 Série remplaçant la précédente. 5 A partir de 1974 : électricité et eau seulement. 6 Familles à revenu élevé. 7 Série enchaînée à la précédente. 8 Y compris les produits d'entretien et certains ustensiles de cuisine. 9 Région métropolitaine. 10 Combustible et savon. 11 Combustible seulement (Zaïre : à partir de 1972 ; Jamaïque : à partir de 1967). 12 Janv.-mars et mai-déc. 13 Série (base 1969 = 100) remplaçant la précédente. 14 Non compris Bonaire et les îles Windward. 15 Combustible et produits d'entretien (Jamaïque : avant 1967). 16 Electricité seulement. 17 Y compris certains articles de ménage. 18 Nov. 19 San Salvador, Mejicanos et Villa Delgado. 20 Janv.-mai et août-déc. 21 Série (base 100 en janv. 1971) remplaçant la précédente. 22 Avant 1967 : base 100 en 1967. 23 Y compris le savon.

NOTAS EXPLICATIVAS Y CLAVES: Véase pág. 744.

1 Incl. el agua (Tanzania: a partir de 1969). 2 Familias de ingresos módicos. 3 Antes de 1969: Dar-es-Salaam solamente. 4 Serie que substituye a la anterior. 5 A partir de 1974: electricidad y agua solamente. 6 Familias de ingresos elevados. 7 Serie enlazada con la anterior. 8 Incl. los productos de limpieza y ciertos utensilios de cocina. 9 Area metropolitana. 10 Combustible y jabón. 11 Combustible solamente (Zaire: a partir de 1972; Jamaica: a partir de 1967). 12 Enero-marzo y mayo-dic. 13 Serie (base 1969 = 100) que substituye a la anterior. 14 Excl. Bonaire y las Islas Windward. 15 Combustible y productos de limpieza (Jamaica: antes de 1967). 16 Electricidad solamente. 17 Incl. ciertos artículos domésticos. 18 Nov. 19 San Salvador, Mejicanos y Villa Delgado. 20 Enero-mayo y agosto-dic. 21 Serie (base enero de 1971 = 100) que substituye a la anterior. 22 Antes de 1967: base 1967 = 100. 23 Incl. el jabón.

25 Consumer prices / Prix à la consommation / Precios del consumo — C Fuel and light indices / Indices du combustible et éclairage / Indices del combustible y alumbrado

25 Consumer prices
Prix à la consommation
Precios del consumo

C Fuel and light indices
Indices du combustible et éclairage
Indices del combustible y alumbrado

(1970 = 100)

Country — Pays — País	1965	1966	1967	1968	1969	1970	1971	1972	1973	1974
Perú (Lima) [1]	.	57.4	58.8	78.7	79.9	**100.0**	100.0	100.3	105.0	106.7
Puerto Rico	96.3	98.5	98.2	98.5	99.4	**100.0**	104.8	108.7	110.7	134.5
St. Kitts	.	.	.	.	89.2	**100.0**	99.8	103.7	109.2	176.0
St. Lucia	.	94.8	97.0	97.5	95.0	**100.0**	101.6	105.3	109.6	177.9
Surinam (Paramaribo) [2]	96.3	99.4	100.0	100.0	❙100.0 [3]	**100.0**	100.8	101.0	103.9	...
Trinidad and Tobago	89.0	90.0	91.8	94.3	97.6	**100.0**	102.8	109.4	116.2	133.1
United States [4]	85.9	88.1	90.8	93.6	95.9	**100.0**	106.7	107.6	123.5	194.9
» » [5]	92.6	92.8	93.2	94.0	95.8	**100.0**	106.9	112.3	117.8	135.9
Venezuela (Caracas) [1]	107.0	100.0	100.0	100.0	100.0	**100.0**	100.0	100.0	100.0	100.0

ASIA — ASIE / ASIA

Country — Pays — País	1965	1966	1967	1968	1969	1970	1971	1972	1973	1974
Bangladesh (Dacca) [6]	70.4	74.8	78.2	90.1	97.1	**100.0**	108.4 [7]	158.2	213.5	❙311 [8]
Burma (Rangoon)	99.8	99.0	98.3	98.3	98.7	**100.0**	101.1	102.2	108.9	175.8
Cyprus [9]	*100.1*	*100.0*	❙97.5 [3]	101.6	101.6	**100.0**	99.8	100.3	101.0	.
Hong Kong	100.0	99.0	102.0	101.0	97.0	**100.0**	103.0	104.0	111.0	160.0
India	.	.	.	.	95.8	**100.0**	106.6	115.0	126.9	170.1
» (Bombay)	.	86.5	88.8	89.9	96.6	**100.0**	103.4	113.5	120.2	174.2
» (Delhi)	71.0	75.4	79.2	91.8	97.8	**100.0**	119.7	121.3	127.3	165.0
» (Jamshedpur)	74.4	80.2	91.3	95.3	96.5	**100.0**	103.5	102.9	122.7	156.4
Iran	93.8	90.5	91.8	95.2	❙100.5 [10]	**100.0**	99.4	101.7	104.4	...
Iraq (Baghdad)	88.3	88.8	91.5	95.2	98.5	**100.0**	91.3	92.3	90.4	82.8
Israel	93.8	95.5	99.8	99.9	❙100.0 [10]	**100.0**	109.8	123.1	135.9	246.6
Japan [11]	96.3	97.4	96.9	97.8	98.3	❙**100.0** [10]	103.7	105.3	111.0	142.1
Jordan (Amman)	.	.	97.7	97.7	98.4	**100.0**	104.3	105.8	109.0	109.8
Korea, Rep. of	56.5	68.3	80.2	86.9	92.4	**100.0**	108.2	119.1	126.0	173.7
Liban (Beyrouth)	.	89.4	93.7	98.9	100.0	**100.0**	100.2	100.5	100.7	101.0
Nepal (Katmandu)	109.9	102.2	102.3	93.8	102.3	**100.0**	101.7	107.2	116.9	124.4
Philippines (Manila) [12]	90.8	91.2	92.4	94.9	95.1	❙**100.0** [3]	107.7	111.3	117.8	195.0
Singapore	95.4	95.6	97.3	98.8	101.0	**100.0**	101.4	101.8	107.0	❙141.2 [13]
Sri Lanka (Colombo)	74.0	70.5	70.9	75.8	91.8	**100.0**	103.5	107.2	120.8	162.4
République arabe syrienne (Damas)	99.1	99.1	99.1	100.0	100.0	**100.0**	101.9	102.8	106.6	105.7
Yemen, People's Dem. Rep. of	.	.	.	.	.	**100.0**	103.1	110.7	115.1	155.6

EXPLANATORY NOTES AND CODES: See p. 741.

[1] Metropolitan area. [2] Beginning 1969: fuel only. [3] Series replacing former series. [4] Fuel oil and coal. [5] Gas and electricity. [6] Government officials. [7] Jan., Feb. and April-Dec. [8] Series (base July 1969-June 1970 = 100) replacing former series. [9] Prior to 1967: base 1967 = 100. [10] Series linked to former series. [11] Excl. Okinawa Prefecture. [12] Middle income group; prior to 1970: low income group. [13] Series (base 1973 = 100) replacing former series.

NOTES EXPLICATIVES ET CODES: Voir p. 742.

[1] Région métropolitaine. [2] A partir de 1969 : combustible seulement. [3] Série remplaçant la précédente. [4] Combustibles solides et mazout. [5] Gaz et électricité. [6] Fonctionnaires. [7] Janv., fév. et avril-déc. [8] Série (base juillet 1969-juin 1970 = 100) remplaçant la précédente. [9] Avant 1967 : base 100 en 1967. [10] Série enchaînée à la précédente. [11] Non compris la préfecture d'Okinawa. [12] Familles à revenu moyen ; avant 1970 : familles à revenu modique. [13] Série (base 100 en 1973) remplaçant la précédente.

NOTAS EXPLICATIVAS Y CLAVES: Véase pág. 744.

[1] Area metropolitana. [2] A partir de 1969: combustible solamente. [3] Serie que substituye a la anterior. [4] Combustibles sólidos y líquidos. [5] Gas y electricidad. [6] Funcionarios. [7] Enero, febr. y abril-dic. [8] Serie (base julio de 1969-junio de 1970 = 100) que substituye a la anterior. [9] Antes de 1967: base 1967 = 100. [10] Serie enlazada con la anterior. [11] Excl. la prefectura de Okinawa. [12] Familias de ingresos medios; antes de 1970: familias de ingresos módicos. [13] Serie (base 1973 = 100) que substituye a la anterior.

25 C

| | Consumer prices
Prix à la consommation
Precios del consumo | | | Fuel and light indices
Indices du combustible et éclairage
Indices del combustible y alumbrado | | | | | |

(1970 = 100)

Country — Pays — País	1965	1966	1967	1968	1969	1970	1971	1972	1973	1974
EUROPE — EUROPE EUROPA										
Austria	.	89.4	90.4	92.2	93.6	**100.0**	106.7	111.0	117.5	135.7
Belgique	92.2	❘ 93.0 [1]	93.1	93.9	95.3	**100.0**	104.9	❘ 106.8 [1]	109.2	142.0
Denmark	71.4	74.8	81.0	88.4	89.8	**100.0**	113.6	114.3	130.6	206.1
España [2]	83.0	86.4	90.2	❘ 93.2 [1]	94.1	**100.0**	107.5	114.0	122.6	146.9
Finland [3].	88.2	91.8	❘ 82.9 [4]	89.6	90.4	**100.0**	116.8	121.8	132.7	❘ 193.9 [1]
France	80.1	82.0	84.0	88.1	94.8	❘ 100.0 [1]	106.7	109.7	114.1	156.8
German Democratic Republic [5] △	100.0	100.0	100.0	100.0	100.0	**100.0**	100.0	100.0	100.0	100.0
Germany, Fed. Rep. of △	88.2	89.3	90.5	95.8	95.7	**100.0**	105.4	110.1	128.2	149.8
Gibraltar	80.3	❘ 80.3 [1]	80.3	86.6	87.3	**100.0**	99.9	99.9	❘ 111.4 [1]	...
Grèce	96.6	98.2	98.5	99.7	100.5	**100.0**	99.6	100.5	107.1	157.8
Hongrie	.	.	107.4	106.2	101.8	**100.0**	99.1	97.1	95.1	100.6
Iceland (Reykjavik) [5] . .	78.1	89.8	**100.0**	❘ 68.3 [4]	84.5	**100.0**	106.6	107.2	127.6	196.0
Ireland	80.2	81.4	84.2	87.2	❘ 91.7 [1]	**100.0**	111.7	122.8	131.6	198.7
Italie	94.2	94.7	❘ 100.0 [1]	98.8	96.6	**100.0**	❘ 103.9 [1]	103.9	104.7	149.2
Luxembourg	82.7	83.8	88.1	89.9	93.0	**100.0**	104.6	106.7	109.2	120.5
Malta	100.0	100.0	100.0	100.0	100.0	**100.0**	100.0	100.6	100.9	142.8
Norway	71.8	74.3	79.4	82.4	84.5	**100.0**	105.2	111.1	118.2	❘ 137.6 [1]
Pays-Bas	87	88	❘ 88.0 [1]	89.3	95.0	**100.0**	❘ 107.1 [1]	111.6	116.7	133.8
Portugal (Lisbonne)	100.0	99.3	99.4	99.4	99.4	**100.0**	103.5	103.5	110.4	132.3
Roumanie	78.6	78.6	78.6	88.5	101.2	**100.0**	100.5	99.7	99.8	99.9
Suisse	96.1	100.0	❘ 87.4 [4]	89.7	90.4	**100.0**	109.7	106.8	137.8	160.4
Sweden	92.7	94.7	93.3	98.6	94.2	**100.0**	110.6	111.4	136.0	194.6
United Kingdom	78.6	83.0	85.3	91.8	94.6	**100.0**	110.4	119.0	122.4	143.3
Yugoslavia	70.8	85.7	85.5	87.7	88.0	**100.0**	125.8	150.6	182.2	252.6
OCEANIA — OCÉANIE OCEANÍA										
Fiji [2, 6]	93.9	98.3	99.0	**100.0**	❘ 97.0 [4]	**100.0**	105.2	109.0	109.6	❘ 133.0 [1]
New Zealand	84.8	86.5	91.9	98.4	99.5	**100.0**	103.1	106.1	109.8	117.1
Nouvelle-Calédonie (Nouméa) [7]	82.5	85.2	85.6	86.5	❘ 91.5 [1]	**100.0**	101.4	104.4	114.4	140.6
Tonga (Nuku'alofa)	.	.	.	.	98.2	**100.0**	100.7	101.1	107.4	127.0
Western Samoa (Apia)	102.9	100.0	99.0	99.0	100.0	**100.0**	116.2	121.0	...	...

EXPLANATORY NOTES AND CODES: See p. 741.

[1] Series linked to former series. [2] Incl. certain household items. [3] Prior to 1967: base 1967 = 100. [4] Series replacing former series. [5] Incl. water (Iceland: prior to 1968). [6] Beginning 1974: incl. cleaning products. [7] Prior to 1969: incl. cleaning products and certain household expenditures.

NOTES EXPLICATIVES ET CODES: Voir p. 742.

[1] *Série enchaînée à la précédente.* [2] *Y compris certains articles de ménage.* [3] *Avant 1967: base 100 en 1967.* [4] *Série remplaçant la précédente.* [5] *Y compris l'eau (Islande: avant 1968).* [6] *A partir de 1974: y compris les produits d'entretien.* [7] *Avant 1969: y compris les produits d'entretien et certaines dépenses de ménage.*

NOTAS EXPLICATIVAS Y CLAVES: Véase pág. 744.

[1] Serie enlazada con la anterior. [2] Incl. ciertos artículos domésticos. [3] Antes de 1967: base 1967 = 100. [4] Serie que substituye a la anterior. [5] Incl. el agua (Islandia: antes de 1968). [6] A partir de 1974: incl. los productos de limpieza. [7] Antes de 1969: incl. los productos de limpieza y ciertos gastos domésticos.

PRICES

25 D Consumer prices / Prix à la consommation / Precios del consumo — Clothing indices / Indices de l'habillement / Indices del vestido

(1970 = 100)

Country — Pays — País	1965	1966	1967	1968	1969	1970	1971	1972	1973	1974
AFRICA — AFRIQUE AFRICA										
Botswana (Gaborone)	.	.	.	.	82.4	**100.0**	.	.	117.1	140.3
Burundi (Bujumbura)[1]	84.5	87.3	90.7	92.8	96.2	**100.0**	105.5	108.6	111.5	123.9
Cameroun (Yaoundé) . . . . *Afric.*	.	.	.	95.7	98.8	**100.0**	100.4	110.4	122.4	134.8
» » . . . . . . *Europ.*	.	89.3[2]	92.5	96.5	97.7	**100.0**	100.8	107.3	120.3	141.1
Rép. centrafricaine (Bangui) . . . . *Europ.*	70.8	73.1	74.2	83.3	91.7	**100.0**	101.8	107.0	116.6	...
Congo (Brazzaville) . . . . *Europ.*	*95.3*	*93.8*	*97.0*	...	*101.1*	...	**100.0**	*142.9*	*138.9*	*134.6*
Côte-d'Ivoire (Abidjan) . . . . . . *Afric.*	90.9	93.7	91.5	93.8	94.7	**100.0**	96.6	96.7	97.6	114.2
» » »[3,4] . . . . . *Europ.*	86.4	88.6	92.4	95.7	96.9	**100.0**	102.2	102.4	107.8	121.3
Egypt	.	.	.	99.0	99.8	**100.0**	99.9	104.1	110.8	121.4
Ethiopia (Addis Ababa)	.	85.3	89.9	89.7	93.9	**100.0**	103.3	107.1	119.8	128.1
Gabon (Libreville)[3] . . . . *Afric.*	*85.2*	*91.1*	*93.0*	*94.5*	*95.1*	*102.6*[5]	**100.0**	*102.7*	*101.6*	*126.6*
» »[6] . . . .[7]	90.4	94.4	95.0	97.4	99.5	**100.0**	100.5	106.1	❙117.9[8]	139.5
Ghana (Accra)	81.4	86.1	88.6	100.4	101.6	**100.0**	107.4	111.8	127.1	160.4
Kenya (Nairobi)[9]	*99.8*	*100.8*	**100.0**	...	...	...	...	❙*100.0*[10]	*115.5*	*149.5*
Lesotho[11]	.	.	.	.	.	.	.	*95.7*[12]	**100.0**	*109.9*
Liberia (Monrovia)	70.5	71.4	...	...	100.7	**100.0**	96.4	104.4	117.5	143.1
Libyan Arab Republic (Tripoli)	100.5	102.7	104.0	100.5	100.0	❙**100.0**[10]	95.6	92.9	92.1	...
Malawi (Blantyre)[11]	.	.	.	94.8	97.1	**100.0**	100.3	103.2	109.4	120.8
» »[7]	.	.	.	.	.	**100.0**	108.9	111.6	118.5	132.1
Maroc[13]	94.4	99.0	98.7	98.2	99.2	**100.0**	101.6	102.0	105.5	❙*119.4*[14]
Mauritanie (Nouakchott) . . . . . *Europ.*	84.0	87.4	92.0	102.7	100.8	**100.0**	103.7	118.2	124.7	...
Mauritius	81.3	83.9	85.4	91.7	99.9	**100.0**	100.8	103.3	120.6	161.7
Mozambique (Lourenço Marques)	92.7	92.7	91.1	99.2	99.2	**100.0**	121.8	135.5	146.0	193.5
Niger (Niamey) . . . . *Afric.*	84.8	87.5	92.2	90.5	92.1	**100.0**	99.3	89.5	89.5	90.9
» »[3] . . . . *Europ.*	80.9	83.4	88.9	95.1	95.6	**100.0**	109.2	107.0	107.0	109.5
Nigeria (Lagos)[11]	80.2	82.6	83.7	87.7	92.2	**100.0**	107.0	110.5	135.1[15]	167.1
Réunion (Saint-Denis)[3]	.	105.7	99.2	98.6	99.3	**100.0**	107.9	❙122.1[8]	128.8	141.9
Sénégal (Dakar)[16]	100.0	100.0	100.0	100.0	100.0	❙**100.0**[10]	102.2	106.2	111.3	120.6
Seychelles (Victoria)	.	.	.	.	.	**100.0**	104.5	114.3	140.3	.

EXPLANATORY NOTES AND CODES: See p. 741.

[1] Government officials. [2] May-Dec. [3] Incl. household linen (Réunion: beginning 1972). [4] Incl. certain household items. [5] Jan.-June and Aug.-Dec. [6] Prior to 1973: incl. household linen. [7] High income group. [8] Series linked to former series. [9] Middle income group; prior to 1972: low income group. [10] Series replacing former series. [11] Low income group. [12] Oct. [13] Prior to 1974: Casablanca only. [14] Series (base May 1972-April 1973 = 100) replacing former series. [15] Jan.-Sep. and Dec. [16] Prior to 1970: Europeans.

NOTES EXPLICATIVES ET CODES: Voir p. 742.

[1] *Fonctionnaires.* [2] *Mai-déc.* [3] *Y compris le linge de maison (Réunion: à partir de 1972).* [4] *Y compris certains articles de ménage.* [5] *Janv.-juin et août-déc.* [6] *Avant 1973: y compris le linge de maison.* [7] *Familles à revenu élevé.* [8] *Série enchaînée à la précédente.* [9] *Familles à revenu moyen; avant 1972: familles à revenu modique.* [10] *Série remplaçant la précédente.* [11] *Familles à revenu modique.* [12] *Oct.* [13] *Avant 1974: Casablanca seulement.* [14] *Série (base mai 1972-avril 1973 = 100) remplaçant la précédente.* [15] *Janv.-sept. et déc.* [16] *Avant 1970: Européens.*

NOTAS EXPLICATIVAS Y CLAVES: Véase pág. 744.

[1] Funcionarios. [2] Mayo-dic. [3] Incl. la ropa de casa (Reunión: a partir de 1972). [4] Incl. ciertos artículos domésticos. [5] Enero-junio y agosto-dic. [6] Antes de 1973: incl. la ropa de casa. [7] Familias de ingresos elevados. [8] Serie enlazada con la anterior. [9] Familias de ingresos medios; antes de 1972: familias de ingresos módicos. [10] Serie que substituye a la anterior. [11] Familias de ingresos módicos. [12] Oct. [13] Antes de 1974: Casablanca solamente. [14] Serie (base mayo de 1972-abril de 1973 = 100) que substituye a la anterior. [15] Enero-sept. y dic. [16] Antes de 1970: europeos.

25 Consumer prices / Prix à la consommation / Precios del consumo

D Clothing indices / Indices de l'habillement / Indices del vestido

(1970 = 100)

Country — Pays — País	1965	1966	1967	1968	1969	1970	1971	1972	1973	1974
Sierra Leone (Freetown)	79.7	82.1	87.6[1]	94.4	98.6	**100.0**	100.6	100.6	100.6	105.3
Somalia (Mogadishu)	.	76.9	81.5	92.3	99.6	**100.0**	103.7	104.9	110.1	126.5
South Africa, Rep. of [2]	95.5	96.3	96.7	97.6	98.5	**100.0**[1]	102.3	107.6	116.3	133.2
Sudan	*84.2*	*84.2*	*91.5*	*93.6*	100.0	**100.0**[3]	100.0	100.0	129.9	183.4
Swaziland (Mbabane-Manzini) [4]	86.6	87.0	88.2	98.2	97.7	**100.0**	97.7	100.4	108.6	135.1
Tanzania [5]	63.0	68.3	71.8	83.0	96.2[3]	**100.0**	104.7	116.3	132.5	147.5
Tchad (Ndjamena) [6]	94.1	103.3	102.9	96.1	95.3	**100.0**	110.4	111.5	126.6	155.2[1]
Togo (Lomé)	.	88.1	90.2	91.5	92.3	**100.0**	108.2	113.3	114.6	134.5
Tunisie (Tunis) [7]	92.3	96.6	97.6	98.5	98.8	**100.0**[1]	101.1	102.7	105.3	115.2
Uganda (Kampala) [4]	59.4	60.6	60.0	72.8	93.3	**100.0**	100.0	105.6	161.1	...
Zaïre (Kinshasa)	34.2	37.9	48.4	78.0[8]	95.6	**100.0**	102.4	...	*150.8*[9]	*199.6*
Zambia [4]	.	.	.	.	97.4	**100.0**	105.8	114.5	122.9	133.5
AMERICA — AMÉRIQUE AMÉRICA										
Antigua	.	.	.	.	92.1	**100.0**	108.0	125.8	142.9	...
Antilles néerlandaises [10]	96.3	96.3	96.6	97.8	98.9	**100.0**	100.0[3]	*102.1*	*107.0*	*116.2*
Argentina (Buenos Aires)	41.9	56.1	72.3	82.7	91.4	**100.0**	117.8	183.4	287.8	445.1
Bahamas (Nassau)	.	88.9	91.3	96.1	99.6	**100.0**	103.6	100.0[3]	*106.0*	*119.2*
Barbados	.	83.6	84.7	87.0	94.3	**100.0**	107.0	116.7	132.9	165.3
Bermuda	72.6	73.8	76.5	86.9	94.6	**100.0**	107.3	113.2	122.3	...
Bolivia (La Paz)	89.1	91.6	91.9	93.6	96.4	**100.0**	104.7	114.1	158.1	230.9
Brésil (São Paulo)	29.6	40.5	52.4	69.6	86.6	**100.0**	117.5	...	...	...
Canada	85.1	88.3	92.7	95.5	98.2	**100.0**	101.5	104.1	109.3[1]	119.8
Colombia (Bogotá)	54.9	70.6	77.7	83.2	91.1	**100.0**	111.6	126.3	158.6	203.3
Costa Rica (San José) [7]	96.9	94.7	95.7	99.2	99.9	**100.0**	101.1	103.6	117.7[11]	145.9[12]
Chile (Santiago)	33	40	49	61	78	**100**[1]	126	200	1 074	3 927
Dominica	.	71.6	65.6	79.5	86.9	**100.0**	104.1	105.4	107.6	153.8
República Dominicana (Santo Domingo) . . .	*101.7*	*94.7*	*98.4*	*99.6*	*101.5*	*98.3*[13]	**100.0**	*116.6*	*137.0*	*154.3*
Ecuador (Quito)	82.4	83.4	84.8	87.1	91.4	**100.0**	111.2	118.3	127.6	155.4
El Salvador [14]	116.8	113.2	100.7	97.6	98.0	**100.0**	102.1[15]	105.4	108.5	118.4
Falkland Is. (Malvinas) (Stanley)	98.0	98.1	98.5	99.4	98.7	**100.0**	101.1	.	.	.

EXPLANATORY NOTES AND CODES: See p. 741.

[1] Series linked to former series. [2] White population. [3] Series replacing former series. [4] Low income group. [5] Prior to 1969: Dar-es-Salaam only. [6] High income group. [7] Metropolitan area. [8] Jan.-March and May-Dec. [9] Series (base 1969 = 100) replacing former series. [10] Excl. Bonaire and Windward Is; prior to 1971: Curaçao only. [11] June and Dec. [12] June, August and Oct.-Dec. [13] Nov. [14] San Salvador, Mejicanos and Villa Delgado. [15] Jan.-May and Aug.-Dec.

NOTES EXPLICATIVES ET CODES: Voir p. 742.

[1] *Série enchaînée à la précédente.* [2] *Population blanche.* [3] *Série remplaçant la précédente.* [4] *Familles à revenu modique.* [5] *Avant 1969 : Dar es-Salaam seulement.* [6] *Familles à revenu élevé.* [7] *Région métropolitaine.* [8] *Janv.-mars et mai-déc.* [9] *Série (base 100 en 1969) remplaçant la précédente.* [10] *Non compris Bonaire et les iles Windward ; avant 1971: Curaçao seulement.* [11] *Juin et déc.* [12] *Juin, août et oct.-déc.* [13] *Nov.* [14] *San Salvador, Mejicanos et Villa Delgado.* [15] *Janv.-mai et août-déc.*

NOTAS EXPLICATIVAS Y CLAVES: Véase pág. 744.

[1] Serie enlazada con la anterior. [2] Población blanca. [3] Serie que substituye a la anterior; antes de 1971: Curazao solamente. [4] Familias de ingresos módicos. [5] Antes de 1969: Dar-es-Salaam solamente. [6] Familias de ingresos elevados. [7] Area metropolitana. [8] Enero-marzo y mayo-dic. [9] Serie (base 1969 = 100) que substituye a la anterior. [10] Excl. Bonaire y las Islas Windward; antes de 1971: Curazao solamente. [11] Junio y dic. [12] Junio, agosto y oct.-dic. [13] Nov. [14] San Salvador, Mejicanos y Villa Delgado. [15] Enero-mayo y agosto-dic.

25 Consumer prices / Prix à la consommation / Precios del consumo

D Clothing indices / Indices de l'habillement / Indices del vestido

(1970 = 100)

Country — *Pays* — País	1965	1966	1967	1968	1969	1970	1971	1972	1973	1974
Greenland	81.5	84.6	88.3	92.0	95.7	**100.0**	| *101* [1]	*107*	*120*	*138*
Grenada	*75.1*	*76.6*	*83.2*	*91.2*	*100.0*	.	.	.	.	.
Guadeloupe (Basse-Terre)	.	.	91.1	94.1	97.0	**100.0**	104.9	111.6	116.8	125.3
Guatemala (Guatemala)	97.9	101.9	100.2	87.6	98.9	**100.0**	101.3	105.0	121.7	135.4
Guyana [2]	87.0	88.3	90.5	93.2	96.4	**100.0**	103.5	107.6	113.9	| 138.8 [3]
Guyane française (Cayenne)	.	.	.	.	99.9	**100.0**	108.7 [4]	119.6	127.6	163.2
Haïti (Port-au-Prince)	74.1	72.3	77.2	89.7	97.3	**100.0**	100.1	99.4	101.7	140.6
Honduras (Tegucigalpa)	86.6	87.1	91.3	97.5	100.4	**100.0**	101.9	107.1	117.9	129.4
Jamaica (Kingston) [5, 6, 7]	*94.1*	*97.3*	| 88.3 [8]	90.2	94.5	**100.0**	108.2	114.8	123.7	| 142.7 [3]
Martinique (Fort-de-France)	.	94.3	94.7	95.2	97.3	**100.0**	102.3	106.5	113.4	128.7
México (México)	89.1	89.5	93.2	93.6	98.0	**100.0**	104.8	107.6	117.1	134.6
Panamá (Panamá)	96.9	97.8	98.9	98.8	99.5	**100.0**	102.6	106.4	110.9	121.9
Paraguay (Asunción)	91.3	93.6	93.6	94.2	98.6	**100.0**	101.0	104.5	110.4	133.3
Perú (Lima) [5]	70.1	73.0	79.1	89.4	93.7	**100.0**	109.5	121.7	133.5	155.8
Puerto Rico	93.8	94.3	95.3	96.2	98.2	**100.0**	102.0	103.9	106.0	111.1
St. Kitts	.	.	.	.	90.7	**100.0**	116.2	135.8	132.9	148.8
St. Lucia	.	81.8	81.4	83.3	87.2	**100.0** [9]	111.6	123.0	128.7	148.2
Surinam (Paramaribo)	94.5	95.5	96.4	100.9	| 101.5 [8]	**100.0**	98.3	98.7	109.4	123.1
Trinidad and Tobago	88.4	89.7	91.9	96.9	99.8	**100.0**	101.9	108.6	120.1	136.4
United States	80.7	82.8	86.1	90.8	96.0	**100.0**	103.2	105.3	109.2	117.3
Uruguay (Montevideo)	7.0	15.7	24.2	54.2	78.0	**100.0**	129.6	209.4	| 392.9 [3]	640.2
Venezuela (Caracas) [5]	92.6	92.5	93.7	94.9	96.5	**100.0**	100.4	102.8	111.3	133.8
ASIA — ASIE **ASIA**										
Bangladesh (Dacca) [10]	77.9	83.4	88.4	90.5	98.2	**100.0**	103.6 [11]	160.1	291.0	| 394 [12]
Burma (Rangoon)	77.6	88.1	99.2	113.3	94.7	**100.0**	102.3	100.0	108.1	132.7
Cambodge (Phnom-Penh) [13]	94.2	96.5	90.8	95.4	95.4	**100.0**	217.9	253.8	507.5	...
Cyprus [7]	*100.0*	*100.0*	| 96.0 [8]	97.5	98.3	**100.0**	102.7	107.0	115.2	.
Hong Kong	97.1	95.1	97.1	100.0	100.0	**100.0**	101.0	104.9	115.5	126.2
India	.	.	.	.	93.7	**100.0**	113.2	122.6	140.9	189.3
» (Bombay)	.	82.8	89.8	91.1	95.5	**100.0**	115.3	122.9	136.3	166.9
» (Delhi)	69.4	74.6	82.7	85.5	90.2	**100.0**	114.5	117.3	131.8	187.3
» (Jamshedpur)	81.9	87.5	95.8	90.3	94.4	**100.0**	111.8	120.8	146.5	196.5

EXPLANATORY NOTES AND CODES: See p. 741.

[1] Series (base Jan. 1971 = 100) replacing former series. [2] Urban areas. [3] Series linked to former series. [4] Jan.-July and Sep.-Dec. [5] Metropolitan area. [6] Prior to 1967: incl. household linen. [7] Prior to 1967: base 1967 = 100. [8] Series replacing former series. [9] Jan.-April and June-Dec. [10] Government officials. [11] Jan., Feb. and April-Dec. [12] Series (base July 1969-June 1970 = 100) replacing former series. [13] Working class.

NOTES EXPLICATIVES ET CODES: Voir p. 742.

[1] *Série (base 100 en janv. 1971) remplaçant la précédente.* [2] *Régions urbaines.* [3] *Série enchaînée à la précédente.* [4] *Janv.-juillet et sept.-déc.* [5] *Région métropolitaine.* [6] *Avant 1967: y compris le linge de maison.* [7] *Avant 1967: base 100 en 1967.* [8] *Série remplaçant la précédente.* [9] *Janv.-avril et juin-déc.* [10] *Fonctionnaires.* [11] *Janv., fév. et avril-déc.* [12] *Série (base juillet 1969-juin 1970 = 100) remplaçant la précédente.* [13] *Classe ouvrière.*

NOTAS EXPLICATIVAS Y CLAVES: Véase pág. 744.

[1] Serie (base enero de 1971 = 100) que substituye a la anterior. [2] Areas urbanas. [3] Serie enlazada con la anterior. [4] Enero-julio y sept.-dic. [5] Area metropolitana. [6] Antes de 1967: incl. la ropa de casa. [7] Antes de 1967: base 1967 = 100. [8] Serie que substituye a la anterior. [9] Enero-abril y junio-dic. [10] Funcionarios. [11] Enero, febr. y abril-dic. [12] Serie (base julio de 1969-junio de 1970 = 100) que substituye a la anterior. [13] Clase obrera.

25 Consumer prices / Prix à la consommation / Precios del consumo

D Clothing indices / Indices de l'habillement / Indices del vestido

(1970 = 100)

Country — Pays — País	1965	1966	1967	1968	1969	1970	1971	1972	1973	1974
Indonesia (Djakarta)	1.2	15.2	27.4	64.3	91.2	**100.0**	109.5	109.5	128.4	175.7
Iran	96.0	96.2	96.0	96.1	| 97.8 [1]	**100.0**	103.3	107.4	122.8	138.9
Iraq (Baghdad)	75.0	74.5	76.9	87.9	94.0	**100.0**	108.4	114.2	122.9	135.4
Israel	85.3	92.2	94.3	96.0	| 97.8 [1]	**100.0**	109.3	125.0	146.3	187.9
Japan [2]	78.9	81.7	84.0	87.7	92.0	| **100.0** [1]	109.0	115.0	139.7	172.3
Jordan (Amman)	.	.	93.3	92.8	94.5	**100.0**	104.4	111.5	124.2	140.3
Korea, Rep. of	64.8	73.3	82.4	88.2	94.7	**100.0**	106.3	115.6	129.7	158.6
Kuwait	.	.	.	.	.	.	.	100.0	*106.4*	*116.7*
Laos (Vientiane)	81.6	86.7	90.0	93.7	97.2	**100.0**	101.4	121.9	146.5	228.4
Liban (Beyrouth) [3]	.	87.0	84.3	90.6	98.2	**100.0**	108.2	115.0	126.3	143.8
Malaysia:										
East Malaysia:										
Sarawak	.	.	99.0	100.0	101.0	**100.0**	100.0	104.0	120.8	133.7
West Malaysia	96.2	98.1	| 98.0 [4]	99.0	99.0	**100.0**	101.0	103.9	126.5	141.2
Nepal (Katmandu)	84.4	75.8	86.5	93.9	107.4	**100.0**	116.6	141.2	181.9	245.4
Pakistan [5]	79.2	82.9	88.8	92.1	95.8	**100.0**	105.7	| *104.2* [6]	*137.3*	*185.0*
Philippines (Manila) [7]	78.3	79.9	85.2	85.8	87.5	| **100.0** [4]	117.9	138.3	165.3	284.1
Singapore	95.1	93.9	96.9	97.5	99.5	**100.0**	102.7	104.6	124.9	| *110.1* [8]
Sri Lanka (Colombo)	92.3	85.4	85.0	87.5	95.3	**100.0**	105.6	119.1	135.5	149.0
Sud Viet-Nam, Rép. du (Saigon) [9]	29.4	43.7	51.7	59.9 [10]	74.9	**100.0**	119.3	| 131.5 [1]	174.6	...
République arabe syrienne (Damas)	98.2	103.5	86.7	92.0	91.2	**100.0**	101.8	104.4	138.1	150.4
Thailand (Bangkok-Metropolis)	97.5	98.0	98.0	98.3	98.1	**100.0**	100.8	101.8	116.3	137.1
Yemen, People's Dem. Rep. of	.	.	.	.	.	**100.0**	109.8	135.1	143.3	...
EUROPE — EUROPE EUROPA										
Austria	.	93.7	95.4	96.5	97.6	**100.0**	103.4	108.5	116.6	127.4
Belgique	88.3	| 90.7 [1]	93.4	95.3	97.7	**100.0**	105.2	| 109.8 [1]	116.4	130.4
Denmark	85.1	88.4	91.7	95.9	96.7	**100.0**	102.5	107.4	117.4	131.4
España	70.1	76.9	85.8	| 89.3 [1]	91.5	**100.0**	108.6	118.1	134.9	159.2
Finland [11]	*94.4*	*96.4*	| *91.4* [4]	97.1	99.1	**100.0**	102.5	108.2	118.6	| 136.7 [1]
France [3]	87.4	88.8	90.6	92.2	96.4	| **100.0** [1]	104.3	109.8	118.1	134.3
German Democratic Republic △ [3, 12]	104.9	103.3	102.7	102.2	101.3	**100.0**	95.6	94.1	93.2	90.4
Germany, Fed. Rep. of △	91.6	94.0	95.2	95.2	96.2	**100.0**	105.9	112.3	120.7	129.7

EXPLANATORY NOTES AND CODES: See p. 741.

[1] Series linked to former series. [2] Excl. Okinawa Prefecture. [3] Incl. household linen. [4] Series replacing former series. [5] Prior to 1972: Karachi only; industrial workers. [6] Series (base 1971 = 100) replacing former series. [7] Middle income group; prior to 1970: low income group. [8] Series (base 1973 = 100) replacing former series. [9] Working class. [10] Jan. and March-Dec. [11] Prior to 1967: base 1967 = 100. [12] Excl. footwear.

NOTES EXPLICATIVES ET CODES: Voir p. 742.

[1] Série enchaînée à la précédente. [2] Non compris la préfecture d'Okinawa. [3] Y compris le linge de maison. [4] Série remplaçant la précédente. [5] Avant 1972: Karachi seulement; travailleurs de l'industrie. [6] Série (base 100 en 1971) remplaçant la précédente. [7] Familles à revenu moyen; avant 1970: familles à revenu modique. [8] Série (base 100 en 1973) remplaçant la précédente. [9] Classe ouvrière. [10] Janv. et mars-déc. [11] Avant 1967: base 100 en 1967. [12] Non compris la chaussure.

NOTAS EXPLICATIVAS Y CLAVES: Véase pág. 744.

[1] Serie enlazada con el anterior. [2] Excl. la prefectura de Okinawa. [3] Incl. la ropa de casa. [4] Serie que substituye a la anterior. [5] Antes de 1972: Karachi solamente; trabajadores de la industria. [6] Serie (base 1971 = 100) que substituye a la anterior. [7] Familias de ingresos medios; antes de 1970: familias de ingresos módicos. [8] Serie (base 1973 = 100) que substituye a la anterior. [9] Clase obrera. [10] Enero y marzo-dic. [11] Antes de 1967: base 1967 = 100. [12] Excl. el calzado.

25 Consumer prices / Prix à la consommation / Precios del consumo   D Clothing indices / Indices de l'habillement / Indices del vestido

(1970 = 100)

Country — Pays — País	1965	1966	1967	1968	1969	1970	1971	1972	1973	1974
Gibraltar	71.7	75.8 [1]	83.4	88.3	89.0	**100.0**	108.0	121.9	130.0 [1]	145.8
Grèce	90.0	94.0	97.5	97.5	98.1	**100.0**	101.2	105.3	120.0	146.4
Hongrie	.	.	95.3	94.9	97.8	**100.0**	102.5	106.6	108.4	110.7
Iceland (Reykjavik)	*92.0*	*96.0*	**100.0**	72.1 [2]	89.8	**100.0**	110.1	121.1	144.2	191.0
Ireland	85.2	86.4	87.7	89.1	92.2 [1]	**100.0**	109.5	120.3	139.4	167.9
Italie [3]	88.0	89.1	90.4 [1]	91.5	93.7	**100.0**	106.2 [1]	112.7	126.3	151.7
Luxembourg	91.4	92.4	93.8	95.4	96.9	**100.0**	105.5	111.0	119.4	130.8
Malta	96.2	96.1	96.4	96.6	97.8	**100.0**	101.7	103 6	106.5	109.8
Norway	83.6	86.2	88.9	91.1	92.5	**100.0**	105.3	114.1	124.1	137.0 [1]
Pays-Bas	77	81	85.9 [1]	88.9	95.8	**100.0**	110.7 [1]	118.9	130.8	148.0
Portugal (Lisbonne)	86.9	89.2	96.6	97.7	98.0	**100.0**	106.1	115.7	145.4	191.8
Roumanie	101.2	101.1	100.9	100.6	100.5	**100.0**	99.8	99.8	99.8	99.6
Suisse	*97.6*	**100.0**	96.6 [2]	97.0	97.5	**100.0**	105.9	114.2	125.9	138.2
Sweden	90.3	94.3	97.6	97.6	97.3	**100.0**	108.8	114.7	118.0	125.7
Turquie (Ankara) [4]	*86.5*	*94.1*	**100.0**	83.3 [2]	88.5	**100.0**	118.4	139.0	174.3	218.6
United Kingdom	86.4	88.8	90.2	91.6	95.1	**100.0**	106.8	114.5	125.3	147.2
Yugoslavia	56.9	71.4	79.2	83.7	91.2	**100.0**	113.0	129.9	157.1	193.7
OCEANIA — OCÉANIE OCEANÍA										
Australia	89.1	90.4	92.6	94.4	96.7	**100.0**	105.5	111.3	121.8	144.4
Cook Is. (Rarotonga)	.	.	95.0	96.4	98.6	**100.0**	105.7	118.8	137.0	173.8
Fiji	*91.9*	*97.0*	*98.4*	**100.0**	90.5 [2]	**100.0**	103.3	110.3	120.2	138.0 [1]
New Zealand	83.4	84.7	87.1	89.3	93.3	**100.0**	113.1	120.4	128.8	144.0
Nouvelle-Calédonie (Nouméa)	74.0	75.8	79.5	82.2	89.3 [1]	**100.0**	105.6	109.9	115.8	120.6
Papua New Guinea [5]	.	.	.	.	.	.	**100.0**	*104.2*	*108.6*	*124.9*
Polynésie française (Tahiti) (Papeete)	65.8	69.9	72.9	73.8	74.9	**100.0**	101.9	110.6	111.2 [1]	...
Solomon Is. (Brit.) (Honiara)	.	.	.	.	97.2	**100.0**	101.9 [1]	102.9	109.1	123.9
Tonga (Nuku'alofa)	.	.	.	.	98.0	**100.0**	102.4	105.6	108.9	113.4
Western Samoa (Apia)	79.2	84.7	90.3	92.4	93.7	**100.0**	104.9	111.1	...	...
URSS [6]	101.4	100.0	100.0	100.0	100.0	**100.0**	99.7	99.6	99.3	98.6
RSS de Biélorussie	101.1	100.0	100.0	100.0	100.0	**100.0**	99.6	99.6	99.2	98.2
RSS d'Ukraine	101.0	100.0	100.0	100.0	100.0	**100.0**	99.7	99.9	99.7	99.3

EXPLANATORY NOTES AND CODES: See p. 741.   NOTES EXPLICATIVES ET CODES: Voir p. 742.   NOTAS EXPLICATIVAS Y CLAVES: Véase pág. 744.

[1] Series linked to former series. [2] Series replacing former series. [3] Prior to 1967: incl. household linen. [4] Prior to 1968: government officials. [5] Incl. household linen. [6] Incl. Byelorussian SSR and Ukrainian SSR, shown separately in this table.

[1] Série enchaînée à la précédente. [2] Série remplaçant la précédente. [3] Avant 1967: y compris le linge de maison. [4] Avant 1968: fonctionnaires. [5] Y compris le linge de maison. [6] Y compris les RSS de Biélorussie et d'Ukraine, figurant séparément dans ce tableau.

[1] Serie enlazada con la anterior. [2] Serie que substituye a la anterior. [3] Antes de 1967: incl. la ropa de casa. [4] Antes de 1968: funcionarios. [5] Incl. la ropa de casa. [6] Incl. las RSS de Bielorrusia y de Ucrania, que figuran separadamente en este cuadro.

25 Consumer prices / Prix à la consommation / Precios del consumo

E Rent indices / Indices du loyer / Indices del alquiler

(1970 = 100)

Country — Pays — País	1965	1966	1967	1968	1969	1970	1971	1972	1973	1974
AFRICA — AFRIQUE AFRICA										
Burundi (Bujumbura) [1, 2, 3]	86.7	90.5	93.2	94.2	97.6	**100.0**	100.7	114.7	127.0	136.4
Cameroun (Yaoundé) [1] . . . . . . *Afric.*	.	.	.	100.0	100.0	**100.0**	103.1	114.2	121.7	137.9
Côte-d'Ivoire (Abidjan) . . . . . *Afric.*	95.8	96.6	103.3	106.8	106.9	**100.0**	95.8	95.9	96.2	103.0
Egypt	.	.	.	98.5	99.7	**100.0**	100.0	100.0	100.0	100.0
Ghana (Accra)	98.7	100.6	100.0	100.0	100.0	**100.0**	100.0	100.0	100.0	100.0
Kenya (Nairobi) [4]	.	.	.	.	.	.	.	**100.0**	*116.4*	*127.8*
Lesotho [5, 6].	.	.	.	.	.	.	.	*93.5* [7]	**100.0**	*105.8*
Liberia (Monrovia)	86.4	89.4	...	...	98.8	**100.0**	100.9	110.3	140.3	140.8
Libyan Arab Republic (Tripoli) [8]	*76.2*	*80.0*	*85.9*	*93.7*	**100.0**	|**100.0** [9]	108.0	124.8	172.4	...
Maroc (Casablanca) [1, 10]. . .	94.8	95.5	94.5	96.9	98.8	**100.0**	101.1	105.8	108.3	.
Mauritius	100.0	100.0	100.0	100.0	100.0	**100.0**	100.0	100.0	100.0	100.0
Mozambique (Lourenço Marques)	72.7	72.7	83.0	88.5	90.9	**100.0**	114.5	124.2	132.7	135.2
Nigeria (Lagos) [5, 6]	83.9	86.9	90.0	93.2	96.7	**100.0**	103.0	105.8	108.0 [11]	110.0
Réunion (Saint-Denis) [1, 12] . .	.	94.5	94.3	94.0	95.7	**100.0**	111.6	|*117.9* [13]	128.3	145.9
Sénégal (Dakar) [6]	.	.	.	.	.	**100.0**	102.2	111.2	112.6	...
Seychelles (Victoria)	.	.	.	.	.	**100.0**	109.3	130.0	138.4	.
Sierra Leone (Freetown)	81.7	87.2	|93.4 [13]	96.6	99.0	**100.0**	100.3	100.4	101.1	101.7
Somalia (Mogadishu) [14] . . .	.	104.0	103.7	105.1	111.1	**100.0**	89.1	74.9	76.3	74.7
South Africa, Rep. of [10, 15]	76.5	80.5	83.7	86.1	89.9	|**100.0** [13]	107.2	113.7	122.1	133.4
Sudan [1]	*67.7*	*67.7*	*67.7*	*70.2*	**100.0**	|**100.0** [9]	115.5	130.9	153.7	199.1
Tanzania	.	.	.	.	100.0	**100.0**	103.9	103.9	105.0	...
Togo (Lomé)	.	93.9	92.9	92.7	93.3	**100.0**	108.0	116.1	117.8	131.8
Tunisie (Tunis) [16]	93.3	98.7	98.7	101.4	104.7	|**100.0** [13]	100.0	100.0	104.6	107.4
Zambia [5]	.	.	.	.	94.4	**100.0**	103.1	105.9	110.0	114.0
AMERICA — AMÉRIQUE AMÉRICA										
Antigua [1]	.	.	.	.	93.9	**100.0**	107.3	114.1	119.7	...
Antilles néerlandaises [17]	100.0	100.0	100.0	100.0	100.0	**100.0**	|**100.0** [9]	*102.4*	*104.7*	*107.1*
Argentina (Buenos Aires)	21.3	68.3	75.1	82.6	90.9	**100.0**	155.7	210.3	673.4	751.3
Bahamas (Nassau) [7]	.	72.0	72.3	74.6	91.6	**100.0**	104.6	|**100.0** [9]	*103.4*	*111.6*
Barbados [10]	.	69.9	75.2	82.1	90.0	**100.0**	102.8	106.1	126.5	167.1

EXPLANATORY NOTES AND CODES: See p. 741.

[1] Incl. " Fuel and light " (Sudan: beginning 1970). [2] Incl. certain household items. [3] Government officials. [4] Middle income group. [5] Low income group. [6] Incl. expenditure on maintenance and repairs of dwelling. [7] Oct. [8] Incl. " Fuel and light " and certain household equipment (Libyan Arab Rep.: prior to 1970; Bahamas: beginning 1972). [9] Series replacing former series. [10] Incl. kitchen utensils. [11] Jan.-Sep. and Dec. [12] Incl. certain household equipment. [13] Series linked to former series. [14] Incl. water. [15] White population. [16] Metropolitan area. [17] Excl. Bonaire and Windward Is.; prior to 1971: Curaçao only.

NOTES EXPLICATIVES ET CODES: Voir p. 742.

[1] *Y compris le groupe « Combustible et éclairage » (Soudan : à partir de 1970).* [2] *Y compris certains articles de ménage.* [3] *Fonctionnaires.* [4] *Familles à revenu moyen.* [5] *Familles à revenu modique.* [6] *Y compris les dépenses pour l'entretien et la réparation du logement.* [7] *Oct.* [8] *Y compris le groupe « Combustible et éclairage » et certains biens d'équipement de ménage (Rép. arabe libyenne : avant 1970 ; Bahamas : à partir de 1972).* [9] *Série remplaçant la précédente.* [10] *Y compris les ustensiles de cuisine.* [11] *Janv.-sept. et déc.* [12] *Y compris certains biens d'équipement de ménage.* [13] *Série enchaînée à la précédente.* [14] *Y compris l'eau.* [15] *Population blanche.* [16] *Région métropolitaine.* [17] *Non compris Bonaire et les îles Windward ; avant 1971 : Curaçao seulement.*

NOTAS EXPLICATIVAS Y CLAVES: Véase pág. 744.

[1] Incl. el grupo « Combustible y alumbrado » (Sudán: a partir de 1970). [2] Incl. ciertos artículos domésticos. [3] Funcionarios. [4] Familias de ingresos medios. [5] Familias de ingresos módicos. [6] Incl. los gastos de conservación y reparación de la vivienda. [7] Oct. [8] Incl. el grupo « Combustible y alumbrado » y ciertos enseres domésticos (Rep. Arabe Libia: antes de 1970; Bahamas: a partir de 1972). [9] Serie que substituye a la anterior. [10] Incl. los utensilios de cocina. [11] Enero-sept. y dic. [12] Incl. ciertos enseres domésticos. [13] Serie enlazada con la anterior. [14] Incl. el agua. [15] Población blanca. [16] Area metropolitana. [17] Excl. Bonaire y las Islas Windward; antes de 1971: Curazao solamente.

25 | Consumer prices / Prix à la consommation / Precios del consumo | E | Rent indices / Indices du loyer / Indices del alquiler

(1970 = 100)

Country — Pays — País	1965	1966	1967	1968	1969	1970	1971	1972	1973	1974
Bermuda	83.5	83.7	84.8	88.2	92.9	**100.0**	108.5	116.4	121.5	...
Brésil (São Paulo).	31.3	46.6	62.5	77.6	88.8	**100.0**	113.7	...	...	...
Canada [1]	76.7	79.1	82.9	87.9	93.9	**100.0**	105.6	111.4	❘ 119.0 [2]	127.4
Colombia (Bogotá) [3, 4].	55.7	62.1	68.2	73.2	81.2	**100.0**	111.6	121.9	136.5	163.2
Costa Rica (San José) [5]	91.4	92.2	93.1	95.3	97.1	**100.0**	102.7	105.6	110.9 [6]	136.7 [7]
Chile (Santiago) [3, 4].	35	42	51	63	80	❘ 100 [2]	116	148	471	2 989
Dominica	.	85.0	79.2	88.4	91.7	**100.0**	104.2	117.6	132.7	170.4
República Dominicana (Santo Domingo) . . .	*99.0*	*93.6*	*94.3*	*94.3*	*94.3*	*97.0* [8]	**100.0**	*110.7*	*118.4*	*122.2*
Ecuador (Quito)	88.3	89.4	91.1	94.3	96.1	**100.0**	104.4	108.2	112.2	124.7
El Salvador [9, 10, 11]	95.4	98.0	99.8	96.7	97.7	**100.0**	101.3 [12]	102.7	108.7	128.2
Falkland Is. (Malvinas) (Stanley)	95.3	97.4	99.4	100.4	102.3	**100.0**	96.0	.	.	.
Greenland	78.5	80.1	81.2	84.8	90.1	**100.0**	❘ *100* [13]	*110*	*141*	*176*
Grenada [1]	*82.6*	*84.7*	*86.4*	*88.6*	*100.0*	.	.	.	.	.
Guadeloupe (Basse-Terre) [3, 4, 14]. . .	.	.	89.0	93.4	96.7	**100.0**	105.1	111.9	118.7	135.4
Guatemala (Guatemala)	100.0	100.0	100.0	100.0	100.0	**100.0**	100.0	100.0	100.0	100.0
Guyana [3, 15]	91.4	92.9	94.6	95.8	97.3	❘ **100.0** [2]	100.4	100.5	100.8	107.3
Guyane française (Cayenne) [3, 10].	.	.	.	.	98.4	**100.0**	106.6 [16]	109.7	112.6	123.1
Haïti (Port-au-Prince)	106.9	121.8	115.8	104.4	97.8	**100.0**	125.5	110.9	135.7	151.3
Honduras (Tegucigalpa)	95.1	95.1	96.5	96.5	99.0	**100.0**	113.2	116.4	118.8	121.5
Jamaica (Kingston) [5, 10, 11, 17]	*95.3*	*97.2*	❘ *86.5* [18]	90.2	93.4	**100.0**	106.0	110.5	127.2	❘ 149.4 [2]
Martinique (Fort-de-France) [3, 4, 14]	.	85.2	86.5	87.9	92.9	**100.0**	107.2	112.9	120.4	141.8
Panamá (Panamá)	93.9	95.1	96.4	97.8	99.6	**100.0**	102.0	106.6	109.5	111.6
Paraguay (Asunción) [1, 3, 4, 10, 14]	96.0	97.7	96.9	97.5	100.3	**100.0**	101.6	104.2	111.4	139.2
Perú (Lima) [3, 5]	54.0	72.6	75.7	88.3	99.2	**100.0**	108.3	118.0	132.8	154.4
Puerto Rico	97.8	98.4	98.8	99.4	99.5	**100.0**	100.3	100.5	100.7	101.1
St. Lucia [1]	66.3	66.3	66.3	66.3	73.5	**100.0**	102.1	111.5	119.9	150.0
Surinam (Paramaribo) [10, 11]	100.0	100.0	100.0	100.0	❘ 99.8 [18]	**100.0**	100.4	100.4	101.6	...
Trinidad and Tobago	84.5	88.4	94.1	96.6	98.8	**100.0**	101.8	105.4	116.3	119.5

EXPLANATORY NOTES AND CODES: See p. 741.

[1] Incl. expenditure on maintenance and repairs of dwelling. [2] Series linked to former series. [3] Incl. "Fuel and light". [4] Incl. certain household equipment. [5] Metropolitan area. [6] June and Dec. [7] June, Aug. and Oct.-Dec. [8] Nov. [9] San Salvador, Mejicanos and Villa Delgado. [10] Incl. water (Jamaica: prior to 1967). [11] Incl. electricity (Jamaica: prior to 1967; Surinam: beginning 1969). [12] Jan.-May and Aug.-Dec. [13] Series (base Jan. 1971 = 100) replacing former series. [14] Incl. cleaning products. [15] Urban areas. [16] Jan.-July and Sep.-Dec. [17] Prior to 1967: base 1967 = 100. [18] Series replacing former series.

NOTES EXPLICATIVES ET CODES: Voir p. 742.

[1] Y compris les dépenses pour l'entretien et la réparation du logement. [2] Série enchaînée à la précédente. [3] Y compris le groupe « Combustible et éclairage ». [4] Y compris certains biens d'équipement de ménage. [5] Région métropolitaine. [6] Juin et déc. [7] Juin, août et oct.-déc. [8] Nov. [9] San Salvador, Mejicanos et Villa Delgado. [10] Y compris l'eau (Jamaïque : avant 1967). [11] Y compris l'électricité (Jamaïque : avant 1967; Surinam : à partir de 1969). [12] Janv.-mai et août-déc. [13] Série (base 100 en janv. 1971) remplaçant la précédente. [14] Y compris les produits d'entretien. [15] Régions urbaines. [16] Janv.-juillet et sept.-déc. [17] Avant 1967 : base 100 en 1967. [18] Série remplaçant la précédente.

NOTAS EXPLICATIVAS Y CLAVES: Véase pág. 744.

[1] Incl. los gastos de conservación y reparación de la vivienda. [2] Serie enlazada con la anterior. [3] Incl. el grupo « Combustible y alumbrado ». [4] Incl. ciertos enseres domésticos. [5] Area metropolitana. [6] Junio y dic. [7] Junio, agosto y oct.-dic. [8] Nov. [9] San Salvador, Mejicanos y Villa Delgado. [10] Incl. el agua (Jamaica: antes de 1967). [11] Incl. la electricidad (Jamaica: antes de 1967; Surinam: a partir de 1969). [12] Enero-mayo y agosto-dic. [13] Serie (base enero de 1971 = 100) que substituye a la anterior. [14] Incl. los productos de limpieza. [15] Areas urbanas. [16] Enero-julio y sept.-dic. [17] Antes de 1967: base 1967 = 100. [18] Serie que substituye a la anterior.

25 Consumer prices / Prix à la consommation / Precios del consumo — E Rent indices / Indices du loyer / Indices del alquiler

(1970 = 100)

Country — Pays — País	1965	1966	1967	1968	1969	1970	1971	1972	1973	1974
United States	88.0	89.2	90.8	93.0	96.0	**100.0**	104.6	108.3	112.9	118.6
Uruguay (Montevideo) [1]	10.5	15.0	23.8	49.0	76.7	**100.0**	120.8	172.8	❘315.4 [2]	562.8
Venezuela (Caracas) [3]	95.3	96.7	97.3	97.5	98.7	**100.0**	100.9	101.7	103.1	105.2
ASIA — ASIE / ASIA										
Bangladesh (Dacca) [4,5]	89.1	90.7	92.7	94.6	98 7	**100.0**	103.1 [6]	118.5	147.3	...
Burma (Rangoon) [7]	93.0	98.3	96.6	102.3	100.3	**100.0**	104.0	90.1	102.0	124.8
Cambodge (Phnom-Penh) [5,8,9,10]	89.2	90.7	96.2	99.6	101.1	**100.0**	100.4	111.3	172.0	...
Cyprus [7,11]	*101.1*	99.9	❘94.2 [12]	94.0	95.2	**100.0**	105.0	112.9	119.6	...
Hong Kong	96.2	96.2	96.2	96.2	96.2	**100.0**	102.9	107.7	116.3	128.8
India	.	.	.	.	97.0	**100.0**	101.5	104.5	109.1	113.6
» (Bombay)	.	94.6	95.5	95.5	97.3	**100.0**	104.5	105.4	106.3	108.1
» (Delhi)	74.2	75.5	80.6	82.6	85.2	**100.0**	103.2	107.7	111.0	116.1
» (Jamshedpur)	99.1	98.1	99.1	99.1	99.1	**100.0**	100.0	102.8	104.7	107.5
Indonesia (Djakarta) [8,9]	0.7	8.7	31.2	50.8	69.3	**100.0**	107.2	108.0	121.7	147.5
Iran	91.9	92.2	93.0	94.3	❘96.3 [2]	**100.0**	105.1	112.0	122.7	...
Iraq (Baghdad)	92.0	92.0	97.4	92.1	94.8	**100.0**	101.7	102.3	103.8	108.4
Israel	78.5	84.4	82.8	86.7	❘88.9 [2]	**100.0**	112.9	136.6	180.4	258.4
Japan [13]	68.9	76.1	81.8	85.7	92.1	❘**100.0** [2]	108.4	117.1	127.0	136.7
Jordan (Amman)	.	.	93.2	95.9	99.0	**100.0**	106.0	118.1	122.0	126.7
Korea, Rep. of	45.6	62.9	83.7	88.3	92.8	**100.0**	110.1	119.2	123.4	135.4
Kuwait [9]	.	.	.	.	.	.	.	100.0	*100.5*	*102.2*
Laos (Vientiane) [9]	83.3	85.9	87.9	89.2	94.2	**100.0**	102.5	108.6	128.6	185.4
Liban (Beyrouth)	.	100.0	100.0	100.0	100.0	**100.0**	100.0	100.0	100.0	100.0
Malaysia: East Malaysia: Sarawak [9]	.	.	101.0	100.0	100.0	**100.0**	100.0	103.0	103.0	106.1
West Malaysia [7,9]	85.0	85.8	❘99.0 [12]	99.0	99.0	**100.0**	101.0	102.0	103.0	109.9
Pakistan [5,9,14]	85.5	90.9	99.1	99.5	99.8	**100.0**	102.3	❘*104.7* [15]	*116.8*	*149.6*
Philippines (Manila) [7,16]	84.8	87.7	92.3	93.0	96.1	❘**100.0** [12]	112.6	136.8	151.1	186.9
Singapore	92.5	91.8	94.0	94.9	97.1	**100.0**	101.8	103.7	109.5	❘*104.7* [17]

EXPLANATORY NOTES AND CODES: See p. 741.

[1] Incl. electricity. [2] Series linked to former series. [3] Metropolitan area. [4] Government officials. [5] Incl. certain household equipment (Pakistan: beginning 1972). [6] Jan., Febr. and April-Dec. [7] Incl. expenditure on maintenance and repairs of dwelling (Cyprus and West Malaysia: prior to 1967; Philippines: beginning 1970). [8] Incl. water. [9] Incl. " Fuel and light " (West Malaysia: beginning 1967). [10] Working class. [11] Prior to 1967: base 1967 = 100. [12] Series replacing former series. [13] Excl. Okinawa Prefecture. [14] Prior to 1972: Karachi only; industrial workers. [15] Series (base 1971 = 100) replacing former series. [16] Middle income group; prior to 1970: low income group. [17] Series (base 1973 = 100) replacing former series.

NOTES EXPLICATIVES ET CODES: Voir p. 742.

[1] Y compris l'électricité. [2] Série enchaînée à la précédente. [3] Région métropolitaine. [4] Fonctionnaires. [5] Y compris certains biens d'équipement de ménage (Pakistan : à partir de 1972). [6] Janv., fév. et avril-déc. [7] Y compris les dépenses pour l'entretien et la réparation du logement (Chypre et Malaisie occidentale : avant 1967; Philippines : à partir de 1970). [8] Y compris l'eau. [9] Y compris le groupe « Combustible et éclairage » (Malaisie occidentale : à partir de 1967). [10] Classe ouvrière. [11] Avant 1967 : base 100 en 1967. [12] Série remplaçant la précédente. [13] Non compris la préfecture d'Okinawa. [14] Avant 1972 : Karachi seulement ; travailleurs de l'industrie. [15] Série (base 100 en 1971) remplaçant la précédente. [16] Familles à revenu moyen; avant 1970 : familles à revenu modique. [17] Série (base 100 en 1973) remplaçant la précédente.

NOTAS EXPLICATIVAS Y CLAVES: Véase pág. 744.

[1] Incl. la electricidad. [2] Serie enlazada con la anterior. [3] Area metropolitana. [4] Funcionarios. [5] Incl. ciertos enseres domésticos (Pakistán: a partir de 1972). [6] Enero, febr. y abril-dic. [7] Incl. los gastos de conservación y reparación de la vivienda (Chipre y Malasia occidental: antes de 1967; Filipinas: a partir de 1970). [8] Incl. el agua. [9] Incl. el grupo « Combustible y alumbrado » (Malasia occidental: a partir de 1967). [10] Clase obrera. [11] Antes de 1967: base 1967 = 100. [12] Serie que substituye a la anterior. [13] Excl. la prefectura de Okinawa. [14] Antes de 1972: Karachi solamente; trabajadores de la industria. [15] Serie (base 1971 = 100) que substituye a la anterior. [16] Familias de ingresos medios; antes de 1970: familias de ingresos módicos. [17] Serie (base 1973 = 100) que substituye a la anterior.

25 Consumer prices / Prix à la consommation / Precios del consumo — E Rent indices / Indices du loyer / Indices del alquiler

(1970 = 100)

Country — Pays — País	1965	1966	1967	1968	1969	1970	1971	1972	1973	1974
Sri Lanka (Colombo)	92.5	92.5	92.5	92.5	98.8	**100.0**	100.0	100.0	100.0	100.0
Sud Viet-Nam, Rép. du (Saigon) [1,2]	32.5	39.7	46.5	52.7 [3]	70.8	**100.0**	136.2	❙164.7 [4]	234.2	...
Thailand (Bangkok-Metropolis) [5]	86.9	90.7	91.6	92.8	95.8	**100.0**	102.0	102.7	105.6	117.2
Yemen, People's Dem. Rep. of	.		.		.	**100.0**	100.0	89.6	75.0	75.0
EUROPE — EUROPE EUROPA										
Austria [5]	.	74.2	79.7	85.1	90.7	**100.0**	112.3	124.5	141.7	155.4
Denmark	65.2	71.4	77.5	86.4	93.1	**100.0**	109.6	117.5	126.3	137.2
España	75.1	81.0	88.1	❙94.1 [4]	95.4	**100.0**	105.9	111.3	122.7	138.6
Finland [6]	92.3	96.0	❙86.7 [7]	93.1	96.5	**100.0**	108.0	113.2	132.8	❙165.3 [4]
France [5]	65.4	71.2	78.7	85.2	93.1	❙**100.0** [4]	105.4	110.3	118.9	127.3
German Democratic Republic △	98.9	99.0	99.5	100.0	100.0	**100.0**	100.0	100.0	100.0	100.0
Germany, Fed. Rep. of △	72.9	78.7	84.0	90.1	95.8	**100.0**	106.1	112.5	119.2	125.1
Gibraltar	79.5	❙79.5 [4]	79.5	81.4	95.0	**100.0**	103.2	103.2	❙103.8 [4]	...
Grèce [5,8]	88.1	89.1	92.1	96.6	99.0	**100.0**	101.4	103.1	110.2	127.4
Hongrie	.	.	100.0	100.0	100.0	**100.0**	157.5	215.0	215.0	215.0
Iceland (Reykjavik)	83.8	91.9	100.0	❙88.8 [7]	94.5	**100.0**	105.5	119.5	137.7	172.1
Ireland [5]	68.4	72.8	77.2	82.5	❙91.5 [4]	**100.0**	110.4	123.2	131.6	143.3
Italie [8]	81.1	84.4	❙86.8 [4]	90.5	94.5	**100.0**	❙103.6 [4]	107.8	115.4	121.8
Malta [5,8]	94.6	95.7	97.1	98.0	98.7	**100.0**	101.1	102.1	103.1	105.1
Norway [5]	80.7	83.4	86.3	89.7	92.1	**100.0**	106.2	112.2	120.8	❙131.6 [4]
Pays-Bas [5]	74	79	❙82.5 [4]	88.7	94.9	**100.0**	❙109.4 [4]	119.3	130.6	141.4
Portugal (Lisbonne)	56.6	57.1	67.5	78.1	93.3	**100.0**	130.9	156.5	185.1	202.9
Roumanie	41.6	41.6	41.6	70.8	100.0	**100.0**	100.0	100.0	100.0	100.0
Suisse	92.5	**100.0**	❙82.2 [7]	88.3	93.9	**100.0**	108.6	117.7	125.5	134.9
Sweden [5]	70.0	76.0	80.7	83.6	90.9	**100.0**	101.8	106.7	114.0	125.5
United Kingdom [5]	76.2	81.3	85.1	89.4	93.0	**100.0**	109.2	120.6	134.8	150.6
Yugoslavia	41.7	54.6	67.1	81.2	96.3	**100.0**	103.7	112.4	129.6	151.8

EXPLANATORY NOTES AND CODES: See p. 741.

NOTES EXPLICATIVES ET CODES: Voir p. 742.

NOTAS EXPLICATIVAS Y CLAVES: Véase pág. 744.

[1] Working class. [2] Incl. "Fuel and light". [3] Jan. and March-Dec. [4] Series linked to former series. [5] Incl. expenditure on maintenance and repairs of dwelling (France: prior to 1970). [6] Prior to 1967: base 1967 = 100. [7] Series replacing former series. [8] Incl. water (Italy: prior to 1967).

[1] Classe ouvrière. [2] Y compris le groupe « Combustible et éclairage ». [3] Janv. et mars-déc. [4] Série enchaînée à la précédente. [5] Y compris les dépenses pour l'entretien et la réparation du logement (France: avant 1970). [6] Avant 1967 : base 100 en 1967. [7] Série remplaçant la précédente. [8] Y compris l'eau (Italie : avant 1967).

[1] Clase obrera. [2] Incl. el grupo « Combustible y alumbrado ». [3] Enero y marzo-dic. [4] Serie enlazada con la anterior. [5] Incl. los gastos de conservación y reparación de la vivienda (Francia: antes de 1970). [6] Antes de 1967: base 1967 = 100. [7] Serie que substituye a la anterior. [8] Incl. el agua (Italia: antes de 1967).

25

Consumer prices
Prix à la consommation
Precios del consumo

E

Rent indices
Indices du loyer
Indices del alquiler

(1970 = 100)

Country — *Pays* — País	1965	1966	1967	1968	1969	1970	1971	1972	1973	1974
OCEANIA — OCÉANIE OCEANÍA										
Australia [1]	78.6	82.1	85.7	89.3	93.9	**100.0**	107.3	115.3	124.7	143.5
Cook Is. (Rarotonga) [1,2]	.	.	90.6	94.0	96.3	**100.0**	106.6	118.9	127.8	141.5
Fiji [2]	85.2	95.4	96.9	100.0	∣ 96.7 [3]	**100.0**	106.4	120.5	129.5	∣ 140.4 [4]
New Zealand [1]	73.4	79.4	84.2	88.7	93.8	**100.0**	107.6	117.6	130.7	149.5
Nouvelle-Calédonie (Nouméa)	.	.	.	.	95.3 [5]	**100.0**	111.6	123.9	138.1	137.4
Polynésie française (Tahiti) (Papeete)	68.5	81.4	84.0	92.8	100.0	**100.0**	106.5	121.0	...	...
Solomon Is. (Brit.) (Honiara) [2,6]	.	.	.	.	46.6	**100.0**	∣ 102.6 [4]	74.6	75.4	77.7
Western Samoa (Apia)	97.5	97.5	97.5	97.5	100.0	**100.0**	100.0	100.0	...	
URSS [7]	100.0	100.0	100.0	100.0	100.0	**100.0**	100.0	100.0	100.0	100.0
RSS d'Ukraine	100.0	100.0	100.0	100.0	100.0	**100.0**	100.0	100.0	100.0	100.0

EXPLANATORY NOTES AND CODES: See p. 741.

[1] Incl. expenditure on maintenance and repairs of dwelling. [2] Incl. water. [3] Series replacing former series. [4] Series linked to former series. [5] March-Dec. [6] Incl. "Fuel and light". [7] Incl. Ukrainian SSR, shown separately in this table.

NOTES EXPLICATIVES ET CODES: Voir p. 742.

[1] *Y compris les dépenses pour l'entretien et la réparation du logement.* [2] *Y compris l'eau.* [3] *Série remplaçant la précédente.* [4] *Série enchaînée à la précédente.* [5] *Mars-déc.* [6] *Y compris le groupe « Combustible et éclairage ».* [7] *Y compris la RSS d'Ukraine, figurant séparément dans ce tableau.*

NOTAS EXPLICATIVAS Y CLAVES: Véase pág. 744.

[1] Incl. los gastos de conservación y reparación de la vivienda. [2] Incl. el agua. [3] Serie que substituye a la anterior. [4] Serie enlazada con la anterior. [5] Marzo-dic. [6] Incl. el grupo « Combustible y alumbrado ». [7] Incl. la RSS de Ucrania, que figura separadamente en este cuadro.

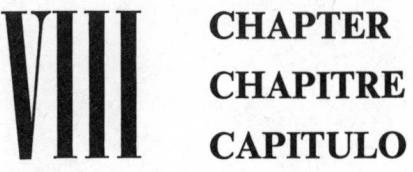

CHAPTER
CHAPITRE
CAPITULO

VIII

Industrial accidents

Accidents du travail

Accidentes del trabajo

Industrial accidents

Table 26 (Parts A to E) gives industrial accident *frequency* or *incidence rates* for a number of divisions of economic activities. In each case only *fatal* accident rates are given. As a rule deaths resulting from occupational diseases or commuting accidents (accidents on the way to or from work) are not included. The minimum duration of incapacity to which an accident must give rise in order to be included in the statistics varies greatly from one country to another; bearing in mind that the number of minor accidents is relatively high, data on non-fatal accidents do not lend themselves easily to international comparison and have therefore been excluded from these tables.

An accident frequency or incidence rate is the ratio of the number of cases of accident occurring during a given period to a number representing "exposure to risk" during the same period.

The number of cases of accident is generally based on industrial accident compensation data or on a compulsory accident reporting system. To indicate the basis of the rate for each country a series of symbols is used in the table headings and explained beneath each table.

The "exposure to risk" may be expressed in terms of the number of full-time workers, of persons insured or of hours of work. The industrial accident *frequency rate* is computed on the basis of hours worked, by dividing the number of accidents (multiplied by 1,000,000) occurring during the period covered by the statistics by the number of hours worked by all persons exposed to risk during the same period. Where the number of hours worked is unknown it may be estimated from the number of persons exposed to risk and average hours of work. The frequency rate is the best way of measuring accident risk as it is not affected by differences in working hours from one industry to another or from one country to another. In practice, however, such data are available in only a few countries. The majority of countries calculate the *incidence rate* of industrial accidents, which is the ratio of the number of industrial accidents (multiplied by 1,000) occurring during the period covered by the statistics to the average number of workers exposed to risk during that same period. As a rule information on the average number of workers may be obtained from returns of undertakings or from accident or other insurance data.

In an international comparison of industrial accident frequency and incidence rates full account must be taken of the effect on the figures of differences in the economic scope of the data or lack of uniformity in the definitions used or the methods of computation and estimation.

Variations in a series of accident frequency or incidence rates for a single country over a period of time will, in general, reflect changes in the conditions of accident risk within that country, though they may on occasion be affected by alterations in methods of reporting or computation. [1]

Table 26 A

Fatal accident rates for mining and quarrying

In so far as data are available, this table gives the rates for fatal accidents occurring in the mining industry in general, including quarrying. In comparing these rates from one country to another account must be taken of differences in the relative importance of the various types of mining covered (coal mining, iron mining, gold mining, etc.).

Table 26 B

Fatal accident rates for coal mining

This table shows separately the rates for coal mining, in view of the importance of this industry and the relatively high risk of accident involved. As with mining in general, the accident risk varies from country to country and from mine to mine, depending on the type of coal

---

[1] For further information on accident statistics, definitions, sources and methods of classification and with respect to Resolution No. II of the Tenth International Conference of Labour Statisticians concerning statistics of employment injuries, see ILO: *Statistics of Industrial Injuries* (Geneva, 1970), document D.17.1970/X.CIST/II/SAT.

extracted (anthracite, bituminous or lignite), the mineral formation, the depth, and the presence of water or fire-damp.

Table 26 C

Fatal accident rates for manufacturing

This table indicates the fatal industrial accident rates for all manufacturing industries. In comparing these figures from one country to another it should be borne in mind that the accident risk is not the same in every industry and that the predominant divisions of economic activities in a given country may be those with a high accident risk (such as woodworking or iron and steel) or those with a low accident risk (such as textiles, printing or tobacco); differences in rates from one country to another are thus influenced by differences in the industrial structure of the countries compared.

Table 26 D

Fatal accident rates for construction

In so far as data are available, this table shows the rates for fatal accidents occurring to construction workers.

Table 26 E

Fatal accident rates for railways

This table gives the fatal accident frequency or incidence rates among railway workers. Unless otherwise indicated, the figures shown exclude railway construction and railway workshops.

Accidents du travail

Les données présentées dans le tableau 26 (parties A à E) se rapportent aux *taux de fréquence* ou *d'incidence* des accidents du travail dans plusieurs branches d'activité économique. Pour chacune de ces branches, les taux de fréquence ou d'incidence ne sont donnés que pour les accidents *mortels* du travail. En règle générale, les cas mortels résultants de maladies professionnelles ou d'accidents de trajet (accidents survenus sur le chemin que parcourt le travailleur pour se rendre à son lieu de travail et en revenir) ne sont pas compris. La durée minimum de l'incapacité que doit entraîner un accident pour que celui-ci soit compté dans les statistiques varie beaucoup d'un pays à un autre; compte tenu du fait que le nombre des accidents peu graves est relativement élevé, les données se rapportant aux accidents non mortels ne se prêtent donc guère aux comparaisons sur le plan international. En conséquence les taux de ces accidents ne figurent pas dans les tableaux.

Le taux de fréquence ou le taux d'incidence des accidents du travail traduit le rapport du nombre des cas d'accidents survenus au cours d'une certaine période à un autre nombre représentant l'« exposition au risque » durant la même période.

Le nombre des cas d'accidents est généralement tiré des données du régime d'indemnisation ou d'un système de déclaration obligatoire. Pour préciser la méthode utilisée par chaque pays, on s'est servi, dans les en-têtes des tableaux, d'un certain nombre de symboles dont la signification est donnée en dessous de chaque tableau.

L'« exposition au risque » peut être mesurée par le nombre de travailleurs occupés à plein temps, par le nombre de personnes assurées ou par le nombre d'heures de travail. Le *taux de fréquence* des accidents du travail est calculé sur la base des heures de travail. Il est obtenu en divisant le nombre des accidents (multiplié par 1 000 000) survenus au cours de la période couverte par les statistiques par le nombre des heures de travail effectuées par toutes les personnes exposées au risque pendant la même période. Lorsque le nombre d'heures de travail est inconnu, il peut être évalué à partir du nombre de personnes exposées au risque et de la durée moyenne du travail. Le taux de fréquence est la meilleure mesure du risque d'accident, car il n'est pas influencé par les différences de la durée du travail d'une industrie à une autre ou d'un pays à un autre. En pratique, cependant, on ne dispose de ces données que pour un petit nombre de pays. La majorité des pays calcule le *taux d'incidence* des accidents du travail, qui est le rapport entre le nombre des accidents du travail (multiplié par 1 000) survenus au cours de la période couverte par les statistiques et le nombre moyen des travailleurs exposés au risque pendant la même période. Les informations relatives au nombre moyen des travailleurs proviennent généralement des rapports d'établissements ou sont obtenus à partir des données de l'assurance-accident ou d'une autre assurance.

Lors de la comparaison internationale des taux de fréquence et d'incidence des accidents du travail, il faut tenir pleinement compte de l'influence qu'exercent sur les chiffres les différences dans la portée économique des données ainsi que le manque d'uniformité des définitions utilisées et des méthodes d'élaboration et d'estimation.

Pour un pays donné, les variations des taux de fréquence ou d'incidence des accidents du travail durant une certaine période reflètent en général les changements dans les risques d'accidents dans ce pays, mais peuvent à l'occasion être influencés par des modifications des méthodes de rassemblement et de calcul des données [1].

Tableau 26 A

Taux des accidents mortels dans les industries extractives

Ce tableau fournit les taux des accidents mortels survenus dans les industries extractives

---

[1] Pour de plus amples détails sur les statistiques des accidents du travail, les définitions, les sources et les méthodes de classification, et pour la résolution II sur les statistiques des lésions professionnelles adoptée par la dixième Conférence internationale des statisticiens du travail, voir BIT: *Statistiques des accidents du travail* (Genève, 1970), document D.17.1970/X.CIST/II/SAT.

en général, y compris les carrières. Il faut tenir compte, lors de la comparaison de ces taux d'un pays à un autre, des différences dans l'importance respective des divers genres de mines (de charbon, de fer, d'or, etc.) couvertes par ces statistiques.

Tableau 26 B

Taux des accidents mortels dans les mines de charbon

Ce tableau présente séparément les taux pour les mines de charbon, étant donné l'importance de cette industrie et les risques d'accidents relativement élevés qu'elle comporte. Comme c'est le cas pour les industries extractives en général, les risques d'accidents ne sont pas identiques de pays à pays; ils varient d'un charbonnage à un autre en fonction de la qualité du charbon extrait (anthracite, charbon bitumineux ou lignite), de la structure minéralogique, de la profondeur, de la présence d'eau ou de grisou.

Tableau 26 C

Taux des accidents mortels dans les industries manufacturières

Ce tableau indique les taux des accidents mortels du travail dans l'ensemble des industries manufacturières. Dans la comparaison de ces chiffres d'un pays à un autre, il y a lieu de tenir compte de ce que les différentes industries ne présentent pas toutes les mêmes risques d'accidents et que les branches d'activité économique qui dominent dans un pays donné peuvent être celles à risques d'accidents élevés, comme l'industrie du bois ou l'industrie du fer et de l'acier, ou au contraire des secteurs à risques faibles comme l'industrie textile, les arts graphiques ou l'industrie du tabac; les différences de taux observées d'un pays à un autre sont donc influencées par les différences dans la structure industrielle des pays comparés.

Tableau 26 D

Taux des accidents mortels dans la construction

Ce tableau présente, dans la mesure où elles sont disponibles, les données se rapportant aux taux des accidents mortels survenus aux travailleurs du bâtiment et des travaux publics.

Tableau 26 E

Taux des accidents mortels dans les chemins de fer

Ce tableau donne les taux de fréquence ou d'incidence des accidents mortels survenus aux travailleurs des chemins de fer. Sauf indication contraire, les chiffres présentés excluent les accidents survenus dans la construction des lignes de chemin de fer et dans les ateliers de réparation.

Accidentes del trabajo

Los datos que se presentan en las partes A a E del cuadro 26 se refieren a las *tasas de frecuencia* o de *incidencia* de los accidentes del trabajo en varias ramas de actividades económicas. En cada una de estas ramas, las tasas de frecuencia o de incidencia se presentan sólo para los accidentes *mortales* del trabajo. Por regla general, no se incluyen los casos mortales que provienen de las enfermedades profesionales o de los accidentes ocurridos en el trayecto que efectúa el trabajador para ir a su sitio de trabajo o para regresar. La duración mínima de la incapacidad que debe ocasionar un accidente para que pueda incluirse en las estadísticas varía mucho de un país a otro; puesto que el número de accidentes poco graves es relativamente alto, los datos referentes a accidentes no mortales no se prestan a comparaciones internacionales. Por ello, las tasas de estos accidentes no figuran en los cuadros.

La tasa de frecuencia o de incidencia de los accidentes del trabajo indica la razón entre el número de los casos de accidentes ocurridos durante un período determinado y un número que representa la «exposición al riesgo» durante el mismo período.

El número de los casos de accidentes se obtiene generalmente de las informaciones sobre el régimen de indemnización o de un sistema de notificación obligatoria de los accidentes. A fin de precisar el método utilizado en cada país, en los encabezamientos del cuadro se ha empleado una serie de símbolos cuya explicación aparece al pie de cada cuadro.

La «exposición al riesgo» puede medirse ya sea por el número de trabajadores ocupados a tiempo completo o por el número de personas aseguradas, o por el número de horas de trabajo. La *tasa de frecuencia* de los accidentes del trabajo se calcula sobre la base de las horas de trabajo. Se la obtiene dividiendo el número de los accidentes (multiplicado por 1 000 000) ocurridos durante el período comprendido en las estadísticas por el número de las horas de trabajo efectuadas por todas las personas expuestas al riesgo durante el mismo período. Cuando se desconoce el número de horas de trabajo, la tasa de frecuencia puede ser calculada sobre la base del número de personas expuestas al riesgo y de la duración

media del trabajo. La tasa de frecuencia es la mejor medida del riesgo del accidente, ya que no se halla influida por las diferencias en la duración del trabajo de una industria a otra o de un país a otro. Sin embargo, en la práctica se dispone de estos datos sólo para un reducido número de países. La mayor parte de los países calculan la *tasa de incidencia* de los accidentes del trabajo, que es la razón entre el número de los accidentes del trabajo (multiplicado por 1 000) ocurridos durante el período comprendido en las estadísticas y el promedio de los trabajadores expuestos al riesgo durante dicho período. Las informaciones relativas al promedio de los trabajadores proceden generalmente de los informes de los establecimientos o se las obtiene a partir de los datos de los seguros de accidentes o de otras clases de seguros.

Al efectuar comparaciones internacionales de las tasas de frecuencia y de incidencia de los accidentes del trabajo hay que tener plenamente en cuenta la influencia que ejerce sobre las cifras la diferencia del alcance económico de los datos, así como la falta de uniformidad de las definiciones y de los métodos de elaboración y de estimación que se utilizan.

En un país dado, las variaciones de las tasas de frecuencia o de incidencia de los accidentes del trabajo durante un período determinado reflejan de ordinario los cambios de los riesgos de accidentes en dicho país, pero pueden hallarse influidas a veces por las modificaciones en los métodos de recolección y de cálculo de los datos [1].

Cuadro 26 A

Tasas de los accidentes mortales en minas y canteras

Este cuadro proporciona, en la medida en que se dispone de datos, las tasas de los accidentes

---

[1] Para mayores detalles sobre las estadísticas de los accidentes del trabajo, definiciones, fuentes y métodos de clasificación, véase OIT: *Estadísticas de los accidentes del trabajo*, décima Conferencia Internacional de Estadígrafos del Trabajo, Informe II (Ginebra, 1962). Respecto de la resolución II sobre las estadísticas de las lesiones profesionales, adoptada por la décima Conferencia Internacional de Estadígrafos del Trabajo, véase OIT: *Boletín Oficial*, vol. XLVI, núm. 1, 1963.

mortales ocurridos en las minas y canteras en general. Al efectuar comparaciones de estas tasas de un país a otro, hay que tener en cuenta las diferencias de la respectiva importancia de los diversos tipos de minas (de carbón, de hierro, de oro, etc.) comprendidas por estas estadísticas.

Cuadro 26 B

Tasas de los accidentes mortales en las minas de carbón

Este cuadro presenta por separado las tasas en las minas de carbón, considerando la importancia de esta industria y los riesgos de accidentes relativamente elevados que ella comporta. Como ocurre en las minas y canteras en general, los riesgos de accidentes en las minas de carbón varían según los países, y aun de una mina a otra, en función del tipo de carbón extraído (antracita, carbón bituminoso o lignito), la estructura mineralógica, la profundidad, la presencia de agua o de grisú.

Cuadro 26 C

Tasas de los accidentes mortales en las industrias manufactureras

Este cuadro presenta las tasas de los accidentes mortales del trabajo para el conjunto de las industrias manufactureras. Al efectuar la comparación de estas cifras de un país a otro hay que tener en cuenta que las diversas industrias no tienen todas el mismo riesgo de accidentes, y que las ramas de actividades económicas que predominan en un país determinado pueden ser aquellas que comportan riesgos de accidentes elevados, tal como sucede en la industria de la madera, del hierro o del acero, o, al contrario, pueden existir sectores de riesgos bajos, como ocurre en la industria textil, las artes gráficas o la industria del tabaco. Las diferencias de las tasas que se observan en los distintos países se hallan, pues, influidas por las diferencias en la estructura industrial de los países que se comparan.

Cuadro 26 D

Tasas de los accidentes mortales en la construcción

Este cuadro proporciona, en la medida en que se dispone de datos, las tasas de los accidentes mortales ocurridos entre los trabajadores de la construcción.

Cuadro 26 E

Tasas de los accidentes mortales en los ferrocarriles

Este cuadro proporciona las tasas de frecuencia o de incidencia de los accidentes ocurridos entre los trabajadores ferroviarios. Salvo indicación en contrario, las cifras que se presentan excluyen los accidentes que se producen en la construcción de las líneas de ferrocarriles y en los talleres de reparación.

26 Industrial accident rates
(Fatal accidents)

Taux des accidents du travail
(Accidents mortels)

Tasas de frecuencia de los accidentes del trabajo
(Accidentes mortales)

A Mining and quarrying
Industries extractives
Minas y canteras

Country — Pays — País	Code Code Clave	1965	1966	1967	1968	1969	1970	1971	1972	1973	1974
AFRICA — AFRIQUE AFRICA											
Egypt [1]	I/c	.	.	0.85	0.31	0.30	0.35	0.49	—	0.12	...
Kenya	II/c	1.30	—	—	...	...	...	...	...	0.80	...
Libyan Arab Republic	II/c	0.34	0.30	0.42	0.28	0.32	0.42	0.42	...	...	...
Mali	I/c	0.40	—	—	0.10	—	—	—	...	...	...
Maroc	I/b	1.16	0.67	0.73	1.19	0.75	0.79	1.01	...	...	...
Niger	II/b	.	.	1.00	0.96	—	2.60	0.95	—	0.62	...
Tanzania (Tanganyika)	II/b	1.25	1.13	0.92	—	—	0.74	0.54	...	...	...
Tunisie	I/d	1.13	1.73	1.17	0.62	0.71	0.96	1.16	1.03	0.73	0.16
Uganda	I/c	1.56	2.55	1.56	1.01	1.28	0.76	1.08	1.74	1.40 *	...
Zambia	I/c	0.55	0.78	0.76	0.80	1.01	2.92	0.91	0.45	0.71	0.53 *
AMERICA — AMÉRIQUE AMÉRICA											
Canada	I/b	2.26	1.83	3.09	1.73	2.17	1.11	1.90	1.82	2.08	1.31
Guatemala	I/b	1.68	1.72	1.09	2.49	1.85	1.17	1.73	2.97	3.64	1.38
Guyana [2]	I/c	1.00	❘ 0.72	0.52	❘ 0.19	0.90	0.49	...	...	...	...
Jamaica	I/c	0.20	0.11	0.51	—	0.02	0.04	0.05	—	0.04	...
Perú	I/d	0.83	0.82	0.92	0.92	0.67	0.86	0.87	...	...	...
Surinam	II/a	1.80	0.60	0.40	0.30	0.40	0.20	0.10	—	0.10	...
United States	I/d	0.53	0.52	0.51	0.66	0.48	0.53	0.44	0.54	0.49 *	0.40 *

EXPLANATORY NOTES: See p. 773.

I: Reported accidents.
II: Compensated accidents.

a: Rates per 1 000 man-years of 300 days each.
b: Rates per 1 000 wage earners (average numbers).
c: Rates per 1 000 persons employed (average numbers).
d: Rates per 1 000 000 man-hours worked.

[1] Year ending in June of the following year. [2] Bauxite mines; 1965: incl. manganese and columbite mines; 1966-67: incl. manganese mines.

NOTES EXPLICATIVES: Voir p. 775.

I: *Accidents signalés.*
II: *Accidents indemnisés.*

a: *Taux pour 1 000 années-homme de 300 jours.*
b: *Taux pour 1 000 ouvriers (effectif moyen).*
c: *Taux pour 1 000 personnes occupées (effectif moyen).*
d: *Taux pour 1 000 000 d'heures-homme effectuées.*

[1] *Année se terminant en juin de l'année suivante.* [2] *Mines de bauxite ; 1965 : y compris les mines de manganèse et de colombite ; 1966-67 : y compris les mines de manganèse.*

NOTAS EXPLICATIVAS: Véase pág. 777.

I: Accidentes declarados.
II: Accidentes indemnizados.

a: Tasas por 1 000 años-hombre de 300 días cada uno.
b: Tasas por 1 000 obreros (ocupación media).
c: Tasas por 1 000 personas ocupadas (ocupación media).
d: Tasas por 1 000 000 de horas-hombre efectuadas.

[1] Año que termina en junio del año siguiente. [2] Minas de bauxita; 1965: incl. las misnas de manganeso y colombita; 1966-67: incl. las minas de manganeso.

26 Industrial accident rates
(Fatal accidents)

Taux des accidents du travail
(Accidents mortels)

Tasas de frecuencia de los accidentes del trabajo
(Accidentes mortales)

A Mining and quarrying
Industries extractives
Minas y canteras

Country — Pays — País	Code Code Clave	1965	1966	1967	1968	1969	1970	1971	1972	1973	1974
ASIA — ASIE ASIA											
Cyprus	I/c	0.65	0.20	0.58	—	—	—	0.24	—	0.28	0.59
Hong Kong	I/c	4.56	2.23	1.72	0.65	3.33	3.70	0.77	4.30	4.65	1.07
India	I/c	0.79	0.45	0.43	0.52	0.50	0.43	0.48	0.44	0.44 *	...
Israel	II/b [1]	0.29	0.48	0.25	1.25	0.50	0.53	0.81	0.43	0.93	...
Japan	I/d [2]	1.26	0.72	0.59	0.74	0.57	0.69	0.43	0.63	0.51	0.62
Korea, Rep. of	II/c	1.67	4.88	3.71	.	1.34	4.72	4.41	3.64	5.98	4.50
Malaysia:											
East Malaysia (Sarawak) . . .	II/c	.	.	.	.	—	0.05	0.04	0.07	0.05	0.09
West Malaysia	II/c	0.48	0.61	0.79	1.35	1.18	0.94	0.87	1.19	0.92	0.75
Pakistan	I/b	2.17	1.76	1.06	1.45	0.70	1.07	0.93	...	...	...
République arabe syrienne	II/c	.	0.69	0.58	0.41	1.23	—	1.43	1.01	4.20 *	0.90 *
EUROPE — EUROPE EUROPA											
Austria	I/c [3]	0.78	0.66	0.50	0.39	0.42	0.61	0.99	0.58	0.87	...
Belgique	II/a	.	.	0.89	0.86	0.44	...	...	...	...	...
Czechoslovakia	I/b	0.68	0.59	0.43	0.36	0.47	0.43	0.35	0.47	0.35	0.31
España	I/a	0.73	0.29	0.50	0.72	0.41	0.50	1.20	0.49	0.57	0.62
Finland	II/a	0.28	1.01	0.36	0.55	0.95	0.63	0.33	...	...	...
France [4]	I/a	0.74	0.77	0.57	0.68	0.72	0.78	0.74	0.51	0.69	...
Germany, Fed. Rep. of △	II/a	0.82	0.88	0.82	0.73	0.71	0.68	0.71	0.62	0.69	0.56
Grèce	I/b	.	0.47	0.48	0.73	1.54	1.00	1.13	0.42	...	...
Hongrie [5]	I/a	0.67	0.46	0.56	0.44	0.48	0.32	0.45	0.45	0.44	0.36
Ireland	I/b	1.30	1.11	1.08	1.02	0.47	0.67	0.65	0.65	0.85	0.43
Italie	II/a	0.44	0.50	0.45	0.45	0.47	0.43	0.33	0.35	0.24	...

EXPLANATORY NOTES: See p. 773.   NOTES EXPLICATIVES: Voir p. 775.   NOTAS EXPLICATIVAS: Véase pág. 777.

I: Reported accidents.
II: Compensated accidents.

a: Rates per 1 000 man-years of 300 days each.
b: Rates per 1 000 wage earners (average numbers).
c: Rates per 1 000 persons employed (average numbers).
d: Rates per 1 000 000 man-hours worked.

I: Accidents signalés.
II: Accidents indemnisés.

a: Taux pour 1 000 années-homme de 300 jours.
b: Taux pour 1 000 ouvriers (effectif moyen).
c: Taux pour 1 000 personnes occupées (effectif moyen).
d: Taux pour 1 000 000 d'heures-homme effectuées.

I: Accidentes declarados.
II: Accidentes indemnizados.

a: Tasas por 1 000 años-hombre de 300 días cada uno.
b: Tasas por 1 000 obreros (ocupación media).
c: Tasas por 1 000 personas ocupadas (ocupación media).
d: Tasas por 1 000 000 de horas-hombre efectuadas.

[1] Incl. accidents on the way to and from work. Year ending in March of the following year. [2] Establishments employing 100 or more workers. [3] Insured persons only. [4] Excl. quarrying. [5] State industry.

[1] Y compris les accidents de trajet. Année se terminant en mars de l'année suivante. [2] Etablissements employant 100 ouvriers et plus. [3] Personnes assurées seulement. [4] Non compris les carrières. [5] Industrie d'Etat.

[1] Incl. accidentes en el trayecto de ida al trabajo o vuelta del mismo. Año que termina en marzo del año siguiente. [2] Establecimientos que emplean 100 obreros y más. [3] Sólo las personas aseguradas. [4] Excl. las canteras. [5] Industria de Estado.

26 Industrial accident rates
(Fatal accidents)

Taux des accidents du travail
(Accidents mortels)

Tasas de frecuencia de los accidentes del trabajo
(Accidentes mortales)

A Mining and quarrying
Industries extractives
Minas y canteras

Country — *Pays* — País	Code *Code* Clave	1965	1966	1967	1968	1969	1970	1971	1972	1973	1974
Luxembourg	II/d	0.22	0.27	—	0.50	1.18	—	—	2.17	—	...
Norway	I/b[1]	0.77	0.52	1.18	1.01	1.39	0.64	0.67	1.33	I 0.45	...
Pays-Bas	I/a	0.27	.	.	0.28	.	0.37	0.15	0.29	—	...
Pologne	I/c	0.42	0.38	0.34	0.36	0.37	0.41	...	...	...	...
Sweden	II/d	0.30	0.40	0.31	0.59	0.44	0.24	0.40	0.28	...	...
Turquie	II/a	3.90	4.80	2.80	2.90	3.50	3.20	2.40	3.10	4.10	3.10
United Kingdom [2]	I/a	0.63	0.50	0.52	0.45	0.44	0.45	0.36	0.39	0.47	0.30 *
Yugoslavia [3]	I/c	0.81	0.23	0.21	0.36	0.24	0.50	0.39	0.19	0.18	0.20
OCEANIA — OCÉANIE OCEANÍA											
Australia [4]	I/c	1.11	1.24	0.79	0.93	0.63	1.34	0.96	0.90	1.11	0.64
New Zealand	I/c	0.51	1.54	3.37	0.69	0.99	0.78	0.91	1.13	0.90 *	...
Nouvelle-Calédonie	I/b	1.84	0.58	1.80	1.71	0.10	0.12	0.12	0.33	0.34	1.02

EXPLANATORY NOTES: See p. 773.

NOTES EXPLICATIVES: Voir p. 775.

NOTAS EXPLICATIVAS: Véase pág. 777.

I: Reported accidents.
II: Compensated accidents.

a: Rates per 1 000 man-years of 300 days each.
b: Rates per 1 000 wage earners (average numbers).
c: Rates per 1 000 persons employed (average numbers).
d: Rates per 1 000 000 man-hours worked.

I: *Accidents signalés.*
II: *Accidents indemnisés.*

a: *Taux pour 1 000 années-homme de 300 jours.*
b: *Taux pour 1 000 ouvriers (effectif moyen).*
c: *Taux pour 1 000 personnes occupées (effectif moyen).*
d: *Taux pour 1 000 000 d'heures-homme effectuées.*

I: Accidentes declarados.
II: Accidentes indemnizados.

a: Tasas por 1 000 años-hombre de 300 días cada uno.
b: Tasas por 1 000 obreros (ocupación media).
c: Tasas por 1 000 personas ocupadas (ocupación media).
d: Tasas por 1 000 000 de horas-hombre efectuadas.

[1] 1965-72: code II/a. [2] Excl. Northern Ireland. Excl. quarrying. [3] Incl. processing of minerals and basic metal industries. [4] Excl. uranium mining. June of each year.

[1] *1965-1972 : code II/a.* [2] *Non compris l'Irlande du Nord. Non compris les carrières.* [3] *Y compris le traitement des minéraux et les industries métallurgiques de base.* [4] *Non compris l'extraction d'uranium. Juin de chaque année.*

[1] 1965-1972: clave II/a. [2] Excl. Irlanda del Norte. Excl. las canteras. [3] Incl. el tratamiento de los minerales y las industrias metalúrgicas básicas. [4] Excl. la extracción de uranio. Junio de cada año.

ACCIDENTS

26 Industrial accident rates
(Fatal accidents)

Taux des accidents du travail
(Accidents mortels)

Tasas de frecuencia de los accidentes del trabajo
(Accidentes mortales)

B Coal mining
Mines de charbon
Minas de carbón

Country — Pays — País	Code Code Clave	1965	1966	1967	1968	1969	1970	1971	1972	1973	1974
AFRICA — AFRIQUE **AFRICA**											
Maroc	I/b	0.94	0.98	0.96	2.15	1.41	0.69	1.38	...	...	...
AMERICA — AMÉRIQUE **AMÉRICA**											
Canada	I/b	1.86	2.07	4.06	1.32	3.03	1.81	1.70	1.69	2.26	1.78
Perú	I/d	—	0.98	1.06	0.52	1.18	—	0.84	...	...	...
United States	I/d	1.02	0.93	0.90	1.30	0.84	0.98	0.70	0.58	0.48	0.45
ASIA — ASIE **ASIA**											
India	I/c	1.10	0.52	0.52	0.64	0.58	0.54	0.60	0.53	0.50	...
Japan	I/d[1]	1.70	0.91	0.67	0.89	0.67	0.85	0.45	0.87	0.59	0.72
Pakistan	I/b	2.77	1.64	0.91	1.28	0.99	0.90	0.95	...	...	...
EUROPE — EUROPE **EUROPA**											
Czechoslovakia	I/b	0.76	0.67	0.42	0.39	0.48	0.43	0.36	0.54	0.38	0.32
France	I/a	0.78	0.79	0.58	0.63	0.64	0.76	0.70	0.41	0.64	...
Hongrie [2]	I/a	0.57	0.39	0.57	0.43	0.38	0.34	0.47	0.40	0.54	0.36
Ireland	I/b	—	1.00	—	—	—	—	—	—	—	—

EXPLANATORY NOTES: See p. 773.

I: Reported accidents.
II: Compensated accidents.

a: Rates per 1 000 man-years of 300 days each.
b: Rates per 1 000 wage earners (average numbers).
c: Rates per 1 000 persons employed (average numbers).
d: Rates per 1 000 000 man-hours worked.

[1] Establishments employing 100 or more workers.
[2] State industry.

NOTES EXPLICATIVES: Voir p. 775.

I: *Accidents signalés.*
II: *Accidents indemnisés.*

a: *Taux pour 1 000 années-homme de 300 jours.*
b: *Taux pour 1 000 ouvriers (effectif moyen).*
c: *Taux pour 1 000 personnes occupées (effectif moyen).*
d: *Taux pour 1 000 000 d'heures-homme effectuées.*

[1] *Etablissements employant 100 ouvriers et plus.* [2] *Industrie d'Etat.*

NOTAS EXPLICATIVAS: Véase pág. 777.

I: Accidentes declarados.
II: Accidentes indemnizados.

a: Tasas por 1 000 años-hombre de 300 días cada uno.
b: Tasas por 1 000 obreros (ocupación media).
c: Tasas por 1 000 personas ocupadas (ocupación media).
d: Tasas por 1 000 000 de horas-hombre efectuadas.

[1] Establecimientos que emplean 100 obreros y más.
[2] Industria de Estado.

26 Industrial accident rates
(Fatal accidents)

Taux des accidents du travail
(Accidents mortels)

Tasas de frecuencia de los accidentes del trabajo
(Accidentes mortales)

B Coal mining
Mines de charbon
Minas de carbón

Country — Pays — País	Code / Code / Clave	1965	1966	1967	1968	1969	1970	1971	1972	1973	1974
Pologne [1]	I/c	0.48	0.39	0.38	0.38	0.41	0.47	0.45	...	...	...
Turquie	II/a	4.90	3.90	3.50	3.50	4.90	4.00	3.00	3.7	5.50	4.40
United Kingdom [2]	I/a	0.62	0.50	0.50	0.44	0.43	0.43	0.34	0.36	0.43	0.30 *
Yugoslavia	I/c	1.94	0.40	0.31	0.59	0.35	1.21	0.69	0.28	0.25	0.38
OCEANIA — OCÉANIE OCEANÍA											
Australia [3]	I/c	1.11	1.24	0.76	0.80	0.10	1.40	0.87	0.97	1.69	0.51
New Zealand	I/c	—	0.89	...	0.33	1.90	0.38	1.03	1.21	0.64	...

EXPLANATORY NOTES: See p. 773.

NOTES EXPLICATIVES: Voir p. 775.

NOTAS EXPLICATIVAS: Véase pág. 777.

I: Reported accidents.
II: Compensated accidents.

a: Rates per 1 000 man-years of 300 days each.
b: Rates per 1 000 wage earners (average numbers).
c: Rates per 1 000 persons employed (average numbers).
d: Rates per 1 000 000 man-hours worked.

I: *Accidents signalés.*
II: *Accidents indemnisés.*

a: *Taux pour 1 000 années-homme de 300 jours.*
b: *Taux pour 1 000 ouvriers (effectif moyen).*
c: *Taux pour 1 000 personnes occupées (effectif moyen).*
d: *Taux pour 1 000 000 d'heures-homme effectuées.*

I: Accidentes declarados.
II: Accidentes indemnizados.

a: Tasas por 1 000 años-hombre de 300 días cada uno.
b: Tasas por 1 000 obreros (ocupación media).
c: Tasas por 1 000 personas ocupadas (ocupación media).
d: Tasas por 1 000 000 de horas-hombre efectuadas.

[1] Incl. auxiliary enterprises. [2] Excl. Northern Ireland.
[3] Incl. extraction of crude oil and natural gas.

[1] *Y compris les entreprises auxiliaires.* [2] *Non compris l'Irlande du Nord.* [3] *Y compris l'extraction de pétrole brut et de gaz naturel.*

[1] Incl. las empresas auxiliares. [2] Excl. Irlanda del Norte. [3] Incl. la extracción de petróleo crudo y gas natural.

26 Industrial accident rates
(Fatal accidents)
Taux des accidents du travail
(Accidents mortels)
Tasas de frecuencia de los accidentes del trabajo
(Accidentes mortales)

C Manufacturing
Industries manufacturières
Industrias manufactureras

Country — *Pays* — País	Code *Code* Clave	1965	1966	1967	1968	1969	1970	1971	1972	1973	1974
AFRICA — AFRIQUE AFRICA											
Cameroun	II/c	0.28	0.38	0.87	0.37	0.24	0.16	0.34	—	—	—
Egypt [1]	I/c	.	.	0.13	0.13	0.12	0.09	0.08	0.02	0.02	...
Ghana	I/c	.	.	.	0.74	0.58	0.64	0.02	0.13	...	...
Kenya	II/c	0.40	0.40	0.20	...	...	...	...	...	0.20	...
Libyan Arab Republic	II/c	0.04	0.07	—	0.06	0.06	0.07	0.07	...	...	...
Malawi	I/b	.	.	.	.	0.34	0.05	0.05	0.09	0.05	0.26
Mali	I/c	0.10	—	—	—	—	—	0.30	—	...	...
Maroc	I/b	0.10	0.09	0.10	...	1.47	2.20	2.88	3.29	1.70	...
Mauritius	I/b	.	.	.	.	.	.	.	0.13	—	0.06
Nigeria	I/b	0.25	0.09	0.05	0.07	0.07	0.12	0.10	0.21	0.06	0.18
Tanzania (Tanganyika)	II/b	0.12	0.10	0.06	0.17	0.16	0.13	0.15	...	...	...
Tunisie	I/d	0.21	0.22	0.18	...	...	0.05	0.05	0.08	0.07	0.07
Uganda	I/c	0.14	0.06	0.16	0.14	0.13	0.09	0.05	0.09	0.10 *	...
Zambia	I/c	0.07	0.26	0.10	0.12	0.11	0.03	0.92	0.12 *	0.08 *	...
AMERICA — AMÉRIQUE AMÉRICA											
Canada	I/c	0.16	0.15	0.12	0.12	0.13	0.12	0.11	0.14	0.15	0.14
Guadeloupe	I/b	—	0.25	0.25	0.20	0.25	0.28	—	0.33	0.25	0.25
Guatemala	I/b	0.21	0.19	0.10	0.28	0.26	0.17	0.23	0.23	0.30	0.31
Jamaica	I/c	0.07	0.05	—	0.10	0.05	—	0.04	0.15	0.09	...
Martinique	I/b	—	0.07	0.24	0.24	0.49	...	...	...	...	...
Panamá	II/c	.	.	.	.	.	0.14	0.74	0.14	0.07	0.07 *
Puerto Rico [2]	II/a	0.40	0.15	0.13	0.18	0.18	0.16	0.10	0.13	0.54	...
Surinam	II/a	0.40	0.60	...	0.10	0.10	0.10	0.20	—	0.10	...
Trinidad and Tobago	I/c	—	0.13	0.31	0.17	0.10	0.20	...	...	...	...
United States	I/d [3]	0.04	0.04	0.03	0.03	0.04	0.03	0.04	0.04	0.03	...

EXPLANATORY NOTES: See p. 773.

I: Reported accidents.
II: Compensated accidents.

a: Rates per 1 000 man-years of 300 days each.
b: Rates per 1 000 wage earners (average numbers).
c: Rates per 1 000 persons employed (average numbers).
d: Rates per 1 000 000 man-hours worked.

[1] Year ending in June of the following year. [2] Year ending in Feb. of the following year. [3] Based on sample surveys.

NOTES EXPLICATIVES: Voir p. 775.

I: *Accidents signalés.*
II: *Accidents indemnisés.*

a: *Taux pour 1 000 années-homme de 300 jours.*
b: *Taux pour 1 000 ouvriers (effectif moyen).*
c: *Taux pour 1 000 personnes occupées (effectif moyen).*
d: *Taux pour 1 000 000 d'heures-homme effectuées.*

[1] *Année se terminant en juin de l'année suivante.* [2] *Année se terminant en fév. de l'année suivante.* [3] *Fondé sur des enquêtes par sondage.*

NOTAS EXPLICATIVAS: Véase pág. 777.

I: Accidentes declarados.
II: Accidentes indemnizados.

a: Tasas por 1 000 años-hombre de 300 días cada uno.
b: Tasas por 1 000 obreros (ocupación media).
c: Tasas por 1 000 personas ocupadas (ocupación media).
d: Tasas por 1 000 000 de horas-hombre efectuadas.

[1] Año que termina en junio del año siguiente. [2] Año que termina en febr. del año siguiente. [3] Basado en encuestas por muestra.

26 Industrial accident rates
(Fatal accidents)

Taux des accidents du travail
(Accidents mortels)

Tasas de frecuencia de los accidentes del trabajo
(Accidentes mortales)

C Manufacturing
Industries manufacturières
Industrias manufactureras

Country — *Pays* — País	Code *Code* Clave	1965	1966	1967	1968	1969	1970	1971	1972	1973	1974
ASIA — ASIE ASIA											
Bangladesh	I/*b*	0.14	0.47	0.03	0.24	0.18	0.07	0.13	0.06	0.02	0.03
Burma	I/*c*	→	—	0.02	—	0.08	0.08	0.11	0.02	0.05	0.04
Cyprus [1]	I/*c*	0.12	0.15	—	0.05	—	0.03	0.05	0.10	0.05	0.06
Hong Kong	I/*c*	0.07	0.07	0.07	0.07	0.09	0.06	0.12	0.07	0.07	0.09
India [1, 2]	I/*c*	0.14	0.15	0.13	0.14	0.15	0.14	0.15 *	0.15 *	...	...
Israel	II/*b* [3]	0.18	0.10	0.15	0.13	0.14	0.14	0.17	0.14	0.16	...
Japan	I/*d* [4]	0.04	0.04	0.04	0.04	0.04	0.04	0.03	0.03	0.03	0.02
Jordan	I/*c*	0.20	0.35	0.22	0.53	—	—	—	0.01	0.02	0.22
Korea, Rep. of	II/*c*	0.32	0.28	0.16	.	0.10	0.26	0.25	0.24	0.19	0.25
Malaysia:											
East Malaysia (Sarawak) . . .	II/*c*	.	.	.	.	0.02	0.08	—	—	—	0.04
West Malaysia	II/*c*	0.28	0.99	0 48	0.67	0.39	0.45	0.23	0.29	0.25	0.21
Pakistan	I/*b*	0.26	0.33	0.12	0.25	0.15	0.16	0.24	...	...	...
Sri Lanka	II/*c*	1.55	1.65	1.67	1.68	1.66	1.68	1.67	1.65	1.66	1.68
Sud Viet-Nam, Rép. du	I/*c*	0.43	0.40	0.42	0.56	0.92	0.66	0.46	0.23	0.41	...
République arabe syrienne	II/*c*	.	0.12	0.17	0.17	0.16	0.17	0.15	0.18	0.35	0.32
Thailand	II/*c*	.	0.03	0.04	0.02	0.02	0.03	0.02	0.03	0.04	0.04
EUROPE — EUROPE EUROPA											
Austria [5]	I/*c* [6]	0.37	0.31	0.36	0.33	0.28	0.29	0.23	0.20	0.20	...
Belgique	II/*a*	.	.	0.13	0.14	0.13	...	...	...	...	...
Czechoslovakia	I/*b*	0.09	0.10	0.09	0.09	0.09	0.09	0.10	0.08	0.08	0.08
España	I/*a*	0.10	0.05	0.06	0.09	0.08	0.07	0.12	0.05	0.06	0.05

EXPLANATORY NOTES: See p. 773.

NOTES EXPLICATIVES: Voir p. 775.

NOTAS EXPLICATIVAS: Véase pág. 777.

I: Reported accidents.
II: Compensated accidents.

a: Rates per 1 000 man-years of 300 days each.
b: Rates per 1 000 wage earners (average numbers).
c: Rates per 1 000 persons employed (average numbers).
d: Rates per 1 000 000 man-hours worked.

I: *Accidents signalés.*
II: *Accidents indemnisés.*

a: *Taux pour 1 000 années-homme de 300 jours.*
b: *Taux pour 1 000 ouvriers (effectif moyen).*
c: *Taux pour 1 000 personnes occupées (effectif moyen).*
d: *Taux pour 1 000 000 d'heures-homme effectuées.*

I: Accidentes declarados.
II: Accidentes indemnizados.

a: Tasas por 1 000 años-hombre de 300 días cada uno.
b: Tasas por 1 000 obreros (ocupación media).
c: Tasas por 1 000 personas ocupadas (ocupación media).
d: Tasas por 1 000 000 de horas-hombre efectuadas.

[1] Incl. electricity, gas, water and sanitary services. [2] The number of states covered by the series varies according to the years. [3] Incl. accidents on the way to and from work. Year ending in March of the following year. [4] Establishments employing 100 or more workers. [5] 1965-1970: Incl. construction. [6] Insured persons only.

[1] *Y compris l'électricité, le gaz, l'eau et les services sanitaires.* [2] *Le nombre d'Etats couverts par la série varie selon les années.* [3] *Y compris les accidents de trajet. Année se terminant en mars de l'année suivante.* [4] *Etablissements employant 100 ouvriers et plus.* [5] *1965-1970: y compris la construction.* [6] *Personnes assurées seulement.*

[1] Incl. la electricidad, el gas, el agua y los servicios sanitarios. [2] El número de Estados cubiertos por la serie varía según los años. [3] Incl. accidentes en el trayecto de ida al trabajo o vuelta del mismo. Año que termina en marzo del año siguiente. [4] Establecimientos que emplean 100 obreros y más. [5] 1965-1970: Incl. la construcción. [6] Sólo las personas aseguradas.

26 Industrial accident rates
(Fatal accidents)
Taux des accidents du travail
(Accidents mortels)
Tasas de frecuencia de los accidentes del trabajo
(Accidentes mortales)

C Manufacturing
Industries manufacturières
Industrias manufactureras

Country — Pays — País	Code Code Clave	1965	1966	1967	1968	1969	1970	1971	1972	1973	1974
Finland	II/a	0.13	0.12	0.13	0.06	0.10	0.10	0.07	...	...	...
France	II/c	.	.	0.12	0.11	0.12	0.12	0.12	0.13	...	...
German Democratic Republic △[1]	.		0.07	0.07	0.06	0.08	0.06	0.06	0.06	0.06	0.05	0.05
Germany, Fed. Rep. of △	II/a	0.18	0.20	0.20	0.16	0.17	0.18	0.19	0.18	0.17	0.16
Grèce	I/b	.	0.08	0.13	0.12	0.13	0.13	...	...	...	...
Hongrie[2]	I/a[3]	0.09	0.10	0.10	0.11	0.10	0.10	0.13	0.09	0.10	0.08
Ireland	I/b	0.06	0.05	0.09	0.09	0.08	0.06	0.09	0.07	0.10	0.08
Italie	II/a	0.15	0.11	0.10	0.10	0.10	0.11	0.09	0.08	0.08	...
Luxembourg[4]	II/d	0.19	0.46	0.26	0.22	0.17	0.14	0.15	0.08	0.15	...
Malta	II/c	0.50	0.21	—	0.10	—	0.13	—	0.11	...	...
Norway	I/b[5]	0.12	0.08	0.08	0.09	0.08	0.11	0.06	0.09	0.08	...
Pays-Bas	I/a	0.19	.	.	0.04	.	0.03	0.04	0.04	0.04	...
Pologne	I/c	0.08	0.08	0.08	0.07	0.08	0.08	...	...	...	...
Roumanie[6]	I/c	0.25	0.21	0.21	0.18	0.20	0.22	0.18	...	...	...
Suisse	II/a	0.19	0.17	0.18	0.18	0.18	0.18	0.17	0.14	0.13	...
Sweden	II/d	0.05	0.06	0.04	0.05	0.05	0.05	0.04	0.04	...	...
Turquie	II/a	0.17	0.23	0.19	0.19	0.22	0.16	0.17	0.17	0.19	0.23
United Kingdom[7]	I/c	0.04	0.04	0.04	0.04	0.04	0.04	0.04	0.04	0.04	0.04
Yugoslavia	I/c	0.06	0.07	0.12	0.11	0.10	0.12	0.11	0.10	0.09 *	0.07
OCEANIA — OCÉANIE OCEANÍA											
Fiji	I/b	.	.	0.12	0.22	0.10	—	0.23	...	...	...
New Zealand	II/a	0.07	0.06	...	0.08	0.06	0.04	...	...	...	...
Nouvelle-Calédonie[8]	I/b	—	0.68	0.76	1.35	0.05	0.02	0.03	0.36	1.36	0.19
Polynésie française	I/c	0.50	1.00	0.12	0.10	0.15	...	...	...	...	...

EXPLANATORY NOTES: See p. 773.

NOTES EXPLICATIVES: Voir p. 775.

NOTAS EXPLICATIVAS: Véase pág. 777.

I: Reported accidents.
II: Compensated accidents.

a: Rates per 1 000 man-years of 300 days each.
b: Rates per 1 000 wage earners (average numbers).
c: Rates per 1 000 persons employed (average numbers).
d: Rates per 1 000 000 man-hours worked.

I: *Accidents signalés.*
II: *Accidents indemnisés.*

a: *Taux pour 1 000 années-homme de 300 jours.*
b: *Taux pour 1 000 ouvriers (effectif moyen).*
c: *Taux pour 1 000 personnes occupées (effectif moyen).*
d: *Taux pour 1 000 000 d'heures-homme effectuées.*

I: Accidentes declarados.
II: Accidentes indemnizados.

a: Tasas por 1 000 años-hombre de 300 días cada uno.
b: Tasas por 1 000 obreros (ocupación media).
c: Tasas por 1 000 personas ocupadas (ocupación media).
d: Tasas por 1 000 000 de horas-hombre efectuadas.

[1] Incl. mining, electricity and gas. [2] State industry. Incl. electricity and gas. [3] Beginning 1971: Excl. railway workshops. [4] Iron and steel industries only. [5] 1965-72: code II/a. [6] Incl. mining and quarrying. [7] Excl. Northern Ireland. [8] Nickel basic industries only.

[1] *Y compris les mines, l'électricité et le gaz.* [2] *Industrie d'Etat. Y compris l'électricité et le gaz.* [3] *A partir de 1971 : non compris les ateliers de réparation des chemins de fer.* [4] *Industrie sidérurgique seulement.* [5] *1965-1972 : code II/a.* [6] *Y compris les industries extractives.* [7] *Non compris l'Irlande du Nord.* [8] *Industries de transformation du minerai de nickel seulement.*

[1] Incl. las minas, la electricidad y el gas. [2] Industria de Estado. Incl. la electricidad y el gas. [3] A partir de 1971: excl. los talleres de ferrocarriles. [4] Sólo industrias del hierro y del acero. [5] 1965-1972: clave II/a. [6] Incl. las minas y canteras. [7] Excl. Irlanda del Norte. [8] Industrias básicas de níquel solamente.

26

Industrial accident rates
(Fatal accidents)
Taux des accidents du travail
(Accidents mortels)
Tasas de frecuencia de los accidentes del trabajo
(Accidentes mortales)

D

Construction
Construction
Construcción

Country — Pays — País	Code Code Clave	1965	1966	1967	1968	1969	1970	1971	1972	1973	1974
AFRICA — AFRIQUE AFRICA											
Burundi	II/c	0.10	—	0.11	0.25	0.10	0.11	...	...	...	...
Cameroun	II/c	.	0.49	1.00	0.61	1.42	1.07	0.89	0.24	1.04	1.01
Egypt [1]	I/c	.	.	0.62	0.22	0.64	0.50	0.18	0.03	0.10	...
Libyan Arab Republic	II/c	0.22	0.80	0.31	0.36	0.38	0.38	0.35	...	...	...
Malawi	I/b	.	.	.	.	0.81	0.38	0.23	0.16	0.23	0.26
Mali	I/c	0.40	0.10	0.30	0.20	0.10	0.10	0.40	0.20	...	...
Maroc	I/b	0.62	0.35	0.55	...	1.13	1.89	0.92	1.23	2.55	...
Mauritius	II/b	.	.	.	.	.	.	.	—	1.50	0.47
Niger [2]	II/b	0.61	1.03	1.52	ǀ 1.90	1.59	4.33	4.00	1.71	2.13	...
Tanzania (Tanganyika)	II/b	0.35	0.13	0.05	0.13	0.19	0.12	0.10	...	...	...
Tchad	I/c	.	1.82	2.42	1.92	0.82	...	...	...	...	...
Tunisie	I/d	0.60	0.80	0.70	0.25	0.43	0.16	0.13	0.26	0.18	0.21
Uganda	I/c	0.56	0.20	0.20	0.17	0.05	0.02	0.14	0.16	0.08	...
Zambia	I/c	0.03	0.21	0.05	0.14	1.18	0.19	0.13	0.10	0.10	...
AMERICA — AMÉRIQUE AMÉRICA											
Canada	I/c	1.25	1.20	0.96	0.95	1.03	0.81	1.00	0.90	0.96	0.96
Guadeloupe	I/b	0.50	0.33	0.50	0.15	0.30	0.50	0.40	0.66	0.40	0.35
Guatemala	I/b	2.08	3.65	3.45	4.73	3.28	2.78	3.47	3.47	4.31	3.67
Guyane française	II/c	0.66	0.54	.	.	0.56	.	0.14	0.13	—	1.00
Martinique	I/b	0.62	1.00	0.12	0.12	0.93	...	...	...	...	...
Panamá	II/c	.	.	.	.	.	0.21	0.42	0.47	0.26	1.44 *
Puerto Rico [3]	II/a	1.18	1.44	1.63	0.82	1.56	1.15	1.09	1.42	0.07	...
Trinidad and Tobago	I/c	—	0.87	0.44	0.03	0.08	—	...	...	...	...
United States	I/d [4]	0.28	0.18	0.19	0.16	0.19	0.20	0.25	0.23	0.13	...
ASIA — ASIE ASIA											
Cyprus	I/c	0.09	0.30	0.08	0.40	0.32	0.16	0.15	0.19	0.20	0.05
Israel	II/b [5]	0.31	0.30	0.20	0.26	0.46	0.24	0.30	0.31	0.27	...
Japan	I/d [6]	0.39	0.38	0.29	0.31	0.21	0.23	0.17	0.19	0.21	0.16
Jordan	I/c	0.50	0.88	0.62	0.96	0.02	0.03	0.01	0.01	0.05	0.31

EXPLANATORY NOTES: See p. 773.

I: Reported accidents.
II: Compensated accidents.

a: Rates per 1 000 man-years of 300 days each.
b: Rates per 1 000 wage earners (average numbers).
c: Rates per 1 000 persons employed (average numbers).
d: Rates per 1 000 000 man-hours worked.

[1] Year ending in June of the following year. [2] 1965-67: private sector. [3] Year ending in Feb. of the following year. [4] Based on sample surveys. [5] Incl. accidents on the way to and from work. Year ending in March of the following year. [6] Establishments employing 100 or more workers.

NOTES EXPLICATIVES: Voir p. 775.

I: *Accidents signalés.*
II: *Accidents indemnisés.*

a: *Taux pour 1 000 années-homme de 300 jours.*
b: *Taux pour 1 000 ouvriers (effectif moyen).*
c: *Taux pour 1 000 personnes occupées (effectif moyen).*
d: *Taux pour 1 000 000 d'heures-homme effectuées.*

[1] *Année se terminant en juin de l'année suivante.* [2] *1965-1967: secteur privé.* [3] *Année se terminant en fév. de l'année suivante.* [4] *Fondé sur des enquêtes par sondage.* [5] *Y compris les accidents de trajet. Année se terminant en mars de l'année suivante.* [6] *Etablissements employant 100 ouvriers et plus.*

NOTAS EXPLICATIVAS: Véase pág. 777.

I: Accidentes declarados.
II: Accidentes indemnizados.

a: Tasas por 1 000 años-hombre de 300 días cada uno.
b: Tasas por 1 000 obreros (ocupación media).
c: Tasas por 1 000 personas ocupadas (ocupación media).
d: Tasas por 1 000 000 de horas-hombre efectuadas.

[1] Año que termina en junio del año siguiente. [2] 1965-1967: sector privado. [3] Año que termina en febr. del año siguiente. [4] Basado en encuestas por muestra. [5] Incl. accidentes en el trayecto de ida al trabajo o vuelta del mismo. Año que termina en marzo del año siguiente. [6] Establecimientos que emplean 100 obreros y más.

26 Industrial accident rates
(Fatal accidents)

Taux des accidents du travail
(Accidents mortels)

Tasas de frecuencia de los accidentes del trabajo
(Accidentes mortales)

D Construction
Construction
Construcción

Country — Pays — País	Code Code Clave	1965	1966	1967	1968	1969	1970	1971	1972	1973	1974
Malaysia:											
East Malaysia (Sarawak) . . .	II/c	.	.	.	.	0.05	0.13	0.09	0.04	0.18	0.14
République arabe syrienne	II/c	.	0.11	0.23	0.25	0.13	0.84	0.52	0.42	0.57	0.76
Thailand	II/c	.	0.01	0.01	0.03	0.02	0.01	0.02	0.01	0.02	0.02
EUROPE — EUROPE EUROPA											
Austria	I/c	.	.	.	.	.	.	0.77	0.84	0.76	...
Czechoslovakia	I/b	0.23	0.27	0.20	0.22	0.19	0.20	0.23	0.31	0.23	0.16
España	I/a	0.36	0.18	0.18	0.21	0.26	0.24	0.44	0.33	0.35	0.34
Finland	II/a	0.33	0.05	0.63	0.26	0.37	0.54	0.31	...	...	...
France	II/c	.	.	0.48	0.46	0.48	0.49	0.50	0.47	...	...
German Democratic Republic △ [1] .	.	0.23	0.27	0.23	0.24	0.24	0.19	0.19	0.13	0.15	0.14
Germany, Fed. Rep. of △	II/a	0.51	0.46	0.50	0.47	0.40	0.40	0.44	0.39	0.37	0.33
Hongrie [2]	I/a	0.27	0.33	0.30	0.38	0.33	0.37	0.28	0.27	0.24	.
Ireland	I/b	0.09	0.20	0.14	0.09	0.09	0.16	0.25	0.14	0.15	0.15
Italie	II/a	0.82	0.69	0.74	0.73	0.70	0.65	0.53	0.55	0.51	...
Malta	II/c	0.15	0.43	0.41	0.30	—	0.08	0.09	...	...	...
Norway	I/b [3]	0.44	0.47	0.43	0.27	0.23	0.41	0.20	0.15	| 0.11	...
Pays-Bas	I/a	0.33	.	.	0.15	.	0.07	0.13	0.13	0.12	...
Pologne	I/c	0.18	0.20	0.22	0.24	0.20	0.20	0.22	...	...	...
Roumanie	I/c	0.40	0.35	0.29	0.27	0.28	0.26	0.27	...	...	...
Suisse [4]	II/a	0.84	0.79	0.61	0.65	0.72	0.63	0.56	0.66 *	0.63 *	...
Sweden	II/d	0.11	0.09	0.12	0.09	0.10	0.07	0.06	0.08	...	...
United Kingdom [5]	I/c	0.14	0.21	0.16	0.19	0.22	0.19	0.19	0.18	0.21	0.15
Yugoslavia	I/c	0.17	0.15	0.18	0.26	0.20	0.24	0.22	0.26	0.20	0.18
OCEANIA — OCÉANIE OCEANÍA											
Fiji	I/b	.	.	0.44	—	0.40	0.44	0.26	...	...	...
New Zealand	II/a	0.17	0.24	...	0.19	0.25	0.26	...	...	...	...
Nouvelle-Calédonie	I/b	2.71	0.56	0.53	—	0.65	0.03	0.03	0.83	0.34	1.01
Polynesie française	I/c	1.30	0.60	0.04	0.02	0.50	...	...	...	...	...

EXPLANATORY NOTES: See p. 773. NOTES EXPLICATIVES: Voir p. 775. NOTAS EXPLICATIVAS: Véase pág. 777.

I: Reported accidents.
II: Compensated accidents.

a: Rates per 1 000 man-years of 300 days each.
b: Rates per 1 000 wage earners (average numbers).
c: Rates per 1 000 persons employed (average numbers).
d: Rates per 1 000 000 man-hours worked.

I: *Accidents signalés.*
II: *Accidents indemnisés.*

a: *Taux pour 1 000 années-homme de 300 jours.*
b: *Taux pour 1 000 ouvriers (effectif moyen).*
c: *Taux pour 1 000 personnes occupées (effectif moyen).*
d: *Taux pour 1 000 000 d'heures-homme effectuées.*

I: Accidentes declarados.
II: Accidentes indemnizados.

a: Tasas por 1 000 años-hombre de 300 días cada uno.
b: Tasas por 1 000 obreros (ocupación media).
c: Tasas por 1 000 personas ocupadas (ocupación media).
d: Tasas por 1 000 000 de horas-hombre efectuadas.

[1] Incl. quarrying. [2] State industry. Beginning 1969: excl. construction of railway lines. [3] 1965-72: code II/a. [4] Beginning 1969: incl. quarrying. [5] Excl. Northern Ireland.

[1] *Y compris les carrières.* [2] *Industrie d'Etat. A partir de 1969 : non compris la construction de lignes de chemin de fer.* [3] *1965-1972 : code II/a.* [4] *A partir de 1969 : y compris les carrières.* [5] *Non compris l'Irlande du Nord.*

[1] Incl. las canteras. [2] Industria de Estado. A partir de 1969: excl. la construcción de vías férreas. [3] 1965-1972: clave II/a. [4] A partir de 1969: incl. las canteras. [5] Excl. Irlanda del Norte.

26 Industrial accident rates
(Fatal accidents)

Taux des accidents du travail
(Accidents mortels)

Tasas de frecuencia de los accidentes del trabajo
(Accidentes mortales)

E Railways
Chemins de fer
Ferrocarriles

Country — Pays — País	Code Code Clave	1965	1966	1967	1968	1969	1970	1971	1972	1973	1974
AFRICA — AFRIQUE **AFRICA**											
Cameroun	II/c	0.50	0.84	0.64	0.29	0.55	—	—	—	0.35	0.78
Egypt [1,2]	I/c	.	.	0.77	0.43	0.44	0.34	0.23	—	0.07	...
Kenya [3]	II/c	0.16	0.40	0.10	...	...	...	...	—	0.05	...
Malawi [1]	I/b	.	.	.	.	0.84	0.59	0.55	1.02	0.29	1.05
Mali	I/c	—	—	—	0.10	0.10	0.30	—	...	...	
Maroc [3]	I/b	0.80	0.78	0.65	—	0.51	0.63	0.86	...	...	...
Tanzania (Tanganyika) [4]	II/b	0.49	0.07	0.38	0.13	—	0.15	0.12	...	...	...
Tunisie [3]	I/d	0.64	0.11	0.13	0.90	0.24	0.06	0.06	0.06	0.50	0.56
Zambia [5]	I/c	0.03	0.15	0.42	0.48	0.24	0.12	0.35	0.12	2.98	—
AMERICA — AMÉRIQUE **AMÉRICA**											
Canada	I/c	0.27	0.31	0.30	0.31	0.34	0.23	0.28	0.30	0.33	0.40
Guatemala	I/b	1.18	1.08	0.77	1.63	1.54	2.38	1.83	1.83	2.38	2.28
Jamaica [3]	I/c	0.66	0.67	1.33	0.67	—	—	—	...	...	...
Perú	I/d	0.29	0.08	0.39	0.16	0.33	0.80	0.28	0.18	...	...
Puerto Rico [3,6]	II/a	2.03	2.09	—	—	—	—	...	...	...	...
United States [4]	I/d	0.15	0.14	0.15	0.14	0.16	0.16	0.13	0.12	0.14	0.13
ASIA — ASIE **ASIA**											
India [7]	I/c	0.28	0.29	0.26	0.25	0.25	0.28	0.24	0.25	0.20	0.19
Japan [4]	I/d [8]	0.06	0.07	0.06	0.07	0.06	0.04	0.04	0.04	0.02	0.04
Malaysia:											
East Malaysia (Sarawak) [9]	II/c	.	.	.	.	—		—	—	—	0.02
West Malaysia [3]	II/c	0.32	0.08	0.16	0.32	0.24	...	1.30	0.86	1.10	0.92
Sri Lanka [3]	II/c	0.23	0.29	0.28	0.27	0.26	0.27	0.26	0.25	0.26	0.28
Sud Viet-Nam, Rép. du	I/c	1.12	1.22	1.33	3.13	1.62	0.61	0.63	0.22	2.52	...
République arabe syrienne	II/c	.	0.65	0.20	0.87	0.41	0.60	1.27	0.48	0.80	2.84
Thailand [1]	II/c	.	0.01	0.01	0.01	0.01	—	—	—	0.01	0.03

EXPLANATORY NOTES: See p. 773.　　　NOTES EXPLICATIVES: Voir p. 775.　　　NOTAS EXPLICATIVAS: Véase pág. 777.

I: Reported accidents.
II: Compensated accidents.

a: Rates per 1 000 man-years of 300 days each.
b: Rates per 1 000 wage earners (average numbers).
c: Rates per 1 000 persons employed (average numbers).
d: Rates per 1 000 000 man-hours worked.

I: *Accidents signalés.*
II: *Accidents indemnisés.*

a: *Taux pour 1 000 années-homme de 300 jours.*
b: *Taux pour 1 000 ouvriers (effectif moyen).*
c: *Taux pour 1 000 personnes occupées (effectif moyen).*
d: *Taux pour 1 000 000 d'heures-homme effectuées*

I: Accidentes declarados.
II: Accidentes indemnizados.

a: Tasas por 1 000 años-hombre de 300 días cada uno.
b: Tasas por 1 000 obreros (ocupación media).
c: Tasas por 1 000 personas ocupadas (ocupación media).
d: Tasas por 1 000 000 de horas-hombre efectuadas.

[1] Transport and communications. [2] Year ending in June of the following year. [3] Incl. railway workshops and construction of railway lines. [4] Incl. railway workshops. [5] Transport, storage and communications. [6] Year ending in Feb. of the following year. [7] Year ending in March of the year indicated. [8] Establishments employing 100 or more workers. [9] Road transport.

[1] *Transports et communications.* [2] *Année se terminant en juin de l'année suivante.* [3] *Y compris les ateliers de réparation des chemins de fer et la construction de lignes de chemin de fer.* [4] *Y compris les ateliers de réparation des chemins de fer.* [5] *Transports, entrepôts et communications.* [6] *Année se terminant en fév. de l'année suivante.* [7] *Année se terminant en mars de l'année indiquée.* [8] *Etablissements employant 100 ouvriers et plus.* [9] *Transport routier.*

[1] Transportes y comunicaciones. [2] Año que termina en junio del año siguiente. [3] Incl. los talleres de ferrocarriles y la construcción de vías férreas. [4] Incl. los talleres de ferrocarriles. [5] Transportes, almacenaje y comunicaciones. [6] Año que termina en febr. del año siguiente. [7] Año que termina en marzo del año indicado. [8] Establecimientos que emplean 100 obreros y más. [9] Transporte por carretera.

Industrial accident rates
(Fatal accidents)

26 Taux des accidents du travail
(Accidents mortels)

Tasas de frecuencia de los accidentes del trabajo
(Accidentes mortales)

E Railways
Chemins de fer
Ferrocarriles

Country — Pays — País	Code Code Clave	1965	1966	1967	1968	1969	1970	1971	1972	1973	1974
EUROPE — EUROPE EUROPA											
Austria [1]	I/c [2]	0.32	0.35	0.32	0.25	0.33	0.39	0.39	0.43	0.33	...
Belgique [3]	II/b	0.14	0.07	0.11	0.34	0.13	0.24	0.20	0.23	0.17	0.13
Czechoslovakia	I/b	0.42	0.49	0.44	0.48	0.39	0.41	0.28	0.27	0.36	0.23
Finland	I/a	0.05	0.28	0.10	0.20	...	...	...	...	...	...
France [1]	I/c	0.25	0.23	0.21	0.19	0.13	...	...	...	...	...
German Democratic Republic △ [4] .	.	—	—	0.20	0.15	0.19	0.17	0.16	0.17	0.15	0.15
Germany, Fed. Rep. of △ [5] . . .	II/a	0.30	0.29	0.26	0.27	0.38	0.31	0.33	0.38	0.26	0.26
Hongrie [6, 7]	I/a	0.30	0.30	0.29	0.29	0.30	0.32	0.32	0.30	0.23	0.22
Ireland	I/c	0.38	0.59	0.19	0.19	—	0.40	0.20	—	0.19	—
Italie [8]	II/c	0.26	0.18	0.13	0.10	0.21	0.20	0.18	0.10	0.18	0.14
Norway	I/c	0.10	0.34	0.20	0.15	0.34	0.30	0.06	0.18	0.12	...
Pays-Bas [1]	I/a	0.14	0.25	0.33	0.19	0.27	0.44	0.11	—	0.15	...
Pologne [7]	I/c	0.41	0.31	0.40	0.39	0.35	0.33	0.41	...	...	...
Roumanie [9]	I/c	0.38	0.34	0.33	0.26	0.25	0.26	0.17	...	...	...
Suisse [1]	II/a	0.34	0.47	0.44	0.43	0.46	0.61	0.68	0.39	0.42	...
Sweden [6]	II/d	0.08	0.06	0.09	0.16	0.09	0.10	0.06	0.14	...	...
United Kingdom [10]	I/b	0.31	0.23	0.27	0.21	0.28	0.28	0.27	0.22	0.25	0.21
Yugoslavia [6]	I/c	0.42	0.40	0.47	0.36	0.39	0.49	0.41	0.36	0.31	0.34
OCEANIA — OCÉANIE OCEANÍA											
New Zealand	I/a	0.50	0.67	0.16	0.24	0.08	0.69	0.51	0.17	0.42	...

EXPLANATORY NOTES: See p. 773.

NOTES EXPLICATIVES: Voir p. 775.

NOTAS EXPLICATIVAS: Véase pág. 777.

I: Reported accidents.
II: Compensated accidents.

a: Rates per 1 000 man-years of 300 days each.
b: Rates per 1 000 wage earners (average numbers).
c: Rates per 1 000 persons employed (average numbers).
d: Rates per 1 000 000 man-hours worked.

I: Accidents signalés.
II: Accidents indemnisés.

a: Taux pour 1 000 années-homme de 300 jours.
b: Taux pour 1 000 ouvriers (effectif moyen).
c: Taux pour 1 000 personnes occupées (effectif moyen).
d: Taux pour 1 000 000 d'heures-homme effectuées.

I: Accidentes declarados.
II: Accidentes indemnizados.

a: Tasas por 1 000 años-hombre de 300 días cada uno.
b: Tasas por 1 000 obreros (ocupación media).
c: Tasas por 1 000 personas ocupadas (ocupación media).
d: Tasas por 1 000 000 de horas-hombre efectuadas.

[1] Incl. railway workshops. [2] Insured persons only. [3] State railways; incl. daily workers. [4] Transport and communications. [5] Incl. railway workshops and accidents involving road vehicles operated by federal railways. [6] Incl. railway workshops and construction of railway lines. [7] State industry. [8] Regular staff only: incl. railway workshops. [9] Transport. [10] Excl. Northern Ireland.

[1] Y compris les ateliers de réparation des chemins de fer. [2] Personnes assurées seulement. [3] Chemins de fer de l'Etat, y compris les travailleurs à la journée. [4] Transports et communications. [5] Y compris les ateliers de réparation des chemins de fer et les accidents survenus à des véhicules routiers des chemins de fer fédéraux. [6] Y compris les ateliers de réparation des chemins de fer et la construction de lignes de chemin de fer. [7] Industrie d'Etat. [8] Personnel permanent seulement ; y compris les ateliers de réparation des chemins de fer. [9] Transports. [10] Non compris l'Irlande du Nord.

[1] Incl. los talleres de ferrocarriles. [2] Sólo las personas aseguradas. [3] Ferrocarriles del Estado; incl. los jornaleros. [4] Transportes y comunicaciones. [5] Incl. los talleres de ferrocarriles y los accidentes sufridos por vehículos de carretera de los ferrocarriles federales. [6] Incl. los talleres de ferrocarriles y la construcción de vías férreas. [7] Industria de Estado. [8] Sólo personal de plantilla; incl. los talleres de ferrocarriles. [9] Transportes. [10] Excl. Irlanda del Norte.

Industrial disputes

Conflits du travail

Conflictos del trabajo

Industrial disputes

Industrial disputes

This table shows the total number of *industrial disputes which resulted in a stoppage of work, and the numbers of workers involved and working days lost*. No differentiation between strikes and lockouts has been possible, since in most countries the distinction is not observed in the compilations. In a few cases, however, the data relate to strikes only. Disputes of small importance and political strikes are frequently not included in the statistics. In some cases the data do not cover workers "indirectly affected", i.e. workers who, though not parties in the dispute, are thrown out of work *within the* establishment directly affected by the stoppage of work. As far as possible such cases are indicated by footnotes.

Various methods are used for calculating the number of working days lost, and these data, as well as the statistics of workers involved, are often approximations only. Nevertheless, the statistics indicate in a general way the extent of industrial disputes in the different countries. [1]

An additional table, providing a breakdown by major divisions of economic activity of the data on industrial disputes published in Table 27, is released, generally every three years, in the *Year Book* (see 1973 edition, Table 27 B).

---

[1] For references concerning the methods on statistics of industrial disputes, see ILO: *International Recommendations on Labour Statistics* (Geneva, 1976).

Conflits du travail

Tableau 27

Conflits du travail

Ce tableau fournit le nombre total des *conflits du travail ayant entraîné un arrêt du travail, le nombre des travailleurs impliqués et le nombre des journées de travail perdues* dans ces conflits. Il n'a pas été possible de distinguer entre les grèves et les lock-out, la plupart des pays n'établissant pas de statistiques séparées pour ces deux groupes. Toutefois, dans quelques cas, les données ne se réfèrent qu'aux grèves. Les conflits de peu d'importance et les grèves ayant un caractère politique sont fréquemment exclus des statistiques. Dans certains cas, les données ne couvrent pas les travailleurs « indirectement atteints », c'est-à-dire ceux qui, sans être parties au conflit, sont mis par celui-ci dans l'impossibilité de travailler *dans* l'établissement directement atteint par l'arrêt du travail. Dans la mesure du possible, ces cas sont indiqués dans les notes de bas de page.

Les méthodes utilisées pour le calcul du nombre des journées perdues varient aussi selon les pays. Ces chiffres, ainsi que le nombre des travailleurs impliqués, ne sont souvent que des approximations. Toutefois, ces données permettent de comparer dans une certaine mesure l'étendue et l'importance des conflits du travail dans les différents pays [1].

Un tableau complémentaire, fournissant la ventilation par branches principales d'activité économique des données sur les conflits du travail présentées au tableau 27, est publié en général tous les trois ans dans l'*Annuaire* (voir édition de 1973, tableau 27 B).

---

[1] Pour des références concernant les méthodes relatives aux statistiques des conflits du travail, voir BIT: *Recommendations internationales sur les statistiques du travail*, (Genève, 1975).

Conflictos del trabajo

Cuadro 27

Conflictos del trabajo

Este cuadro presenta el número total de *conflictos del trabajo que provocaron interrupciones de labores, el número de trabajadores afectados y los días de trabajo perdidos*. No ha sido posible distinguir entre huelgas y cierres a causa de que la mayoría de los países no hacen esa distinción en sus compilaciones. En unos pocos casos, las informaciones se refieren a huelgas solamente. Los conflictos de poca importancia y las huelgas políticas frecuentemente no se incluyen en las estadísticas. En algunos casos, las informaciones no se aplican a los trabajadores « indirectamente afectados », es decir, a los que, sin tomar parte en el conflicto, deben cesar en sus labores ante la imposibilidad de trabajar *dentro* del establecimiento directamente afectado por el conflicto. En la medida de lo posible, estos casos se indican en notas de pie de página.

El cálculo del número de días de trabajo perdidos se hace utilizando varios métodos, y este dato, así como las estadísticas del número de trabajadores afectados, es sólo aproximado. Sin embargo, las estadísticas indican de un modo general la magnitud de los conflictos del trabajo en los distintos países [1].

Un cuadro complementario, en que los datos sobre conflictos del trabajo presentados en el cuadro 27 aparecen clasificados según divisiones mayores de la actividad económica, se publica por lo general cada tres años en el *Anuario* (vease edición de 1973, cuadro 27 B).

---

[1] Para referencias relativas a los métodos sobre las estadísticas de los conflictos del trabajo, véase OIT: *Recomendaciones internacionales sobre estadísticas del trabajo* (Ginebra, 1975).

27 Industrial disputes
Conflits du travail
Conflictos del trabajo

Country — *Pays* — País	Code *Code* Clave	1965	1966	1967	1968	1969	1970	1971	1972	1973	1974
AFRICA — AFRIQUE AFRICA											
Algérie	D/C	.	.	.	.	42	57	70	100	99	...
	W/T	.	.	.	.	5 349	6 363	12 276	10 706	12 079	...
	D/J	.	.	.	.	25 142	25 771	52 161	40 588	5 321	...
Burundi	D/C	.	2	4	10	8	1	...	10	11	11
	W/T	.	378	1 340	1 027	1 003	110	...	3 712	2 382	3 372
	D/J	.	.	5 375	1 621	4 475	330	...	9 620	7 690	6 014
Cameroun	D/C	13	3	3	11	9	4	32	5	7	...
	W/T	2 534	179	53	5 591	10 216	1 857	2 530	3 901	8 124	...
	D/J	7 509	591	538	10 206	12 736	999	17 810	94	509	...
Egypt	D/C	.	.	.	.	214	45	90	537	13	6
	W/T	.	.	.	.	15 470	1 311	11 425	11 864	4 222	13 172
	D/J	.	.	.	.	...	...	...	22 275	4 907	71 321
Ghana	D/C	13	32	27	36	51	56	79	10	13	43
	W/T	7 052	15 027	6 326	37 625	28 369	21 378	41 052	2 336	3 917	32 371
	D/J	23 839	25 712	6 758	100 017	148 416	123 050	116 041	3 198	3 109	64 408
Haute-Volta	D/C	3	3	3	2	2	3	2	2	...	...
	W/T	220	162	123	286	1 496	287	252	21	...	...
	D/J	419	231	23	375	11 472	674	328	1 890	...	...
Kenya	D/C	200	155	138	93	124	84	246	466	83	...
	W/T	105 602	42 967	29 985	20 426	37 641	18 941	14 398	28 056	14 125	...
	D/J	345 855	127 632	109 128	47 979	87 816	49 517	32 681	42 462	42 267	...
Malawi	D/C	34	22	20	22	8	8	17	14	11	18
	W/T	9 670	2 201	2 385	2 611	1 091	601	1 696	1 575	1 661	1 234
	D/J	20 248	3 221	4 862	4 863	301	369	1 396	940	3 213	536
Mali	D/C	—	—	—	1	1	—	—	—	—	—
	W/T	—	—	—	1 146	19	—	—	—	—	—
	D/J	—	—	—	1 146	152	—	—	—	—	—
Maroc	D/C	192	173	159	90	74	97	259	479	462	367
	W/T	19 142	25 728	41 323	29 825	17 029	17 211	82 027	100 767	52 320	65 463
	D/J	207 785	91 486	134 459	162 883	151 474	81 274	589 334	785 860	353 499	320 631

EXPLANATORY NOTES: See p. 793.　　　　NOTES EXPLICATIVES: Voir p. 794.　　　　NOTAS EXPLICATIVAS: Véase pág. 795.

D/C : Number of disputes — *Nombre de conflits* — Número de conflictos.
W/T : Workers involved — *Travailleurs impliqués* — Trabajadores afectados.
D/J : Working days lost — *Journées de travail perdues* — Días de trabajo perdidos.

27 Industrial disputes
Conflits du travail
Conflictos del trabajo

Country — Pays — País	Code Code Clave	1965	1966	1967	1968	1969	1970	1971	1972	1973	1974
Mauritius [1]	D/C	11	15	1	7	13	8	19	1	9	26
	W/T	1 660	2 974	194	13 636	1 605	2 073	25 845	150	29 738	8 449
	D/J	3 862	3 514	1 050	15 845	3 774	5 214	142 916	150	88 588	17 847
Nigeria [2]	D/C	164	87	89	29	49	34	116	84	69	163
	W/T	78 992	40 449	40 785	11 551	20 624	20 065	79 598	29 628	43 504	62 693
	D/J	276 175	76 704	92 373	18 444	81 268	52 630	232 536	65 215	106 387	159 613
Seychelles	D/C	.	.	.	.	8	—	3	2	2	2
	W/T	.	.	.	.	1 131	—	117	2 150	100	159
	D/J	.	.	.	.	4 965	—	2 392	12 446	100	195
Sierra Leone	D/C	3	9	7	9	12	7	5	4	3	4
	W/T	1 320	781	1 951	1 714	6 864	903	2 711	860	612	438
	D/J	3 245	542	1 163	2 574	14 659	474	5 708	965	4 851	1 026
South Africa, Rep. of	D/C	84	98	76	56	78	76	69	71	370	...
	W/T	6 228	5 115	3 531	1 953	4 434	4 168	4 451	9 224	98 378	...
	D/J	16 570	15 751	13 871	4 746	4 596	5 158	3 485	14 959	246 071	...
Sudan	D/C	41	24	21	106	2	—	—	...	...	...
	W/T	59 407	17 341	26 206	43 099	283	—	—	...	...	...
	D/J	223 170	194 570	58 016	58 010	1 014	—	—	...	...	...
Tanzania (Tanganyika) [3]	D/C	13	16	25	13	4	3	3	...	...	...
	W/T	884	2 062	3 224	1 906	874	357	654	...	...	...
	D/J	1 825	8 845	7 224	5 757	2 141	726	3 026	...	...	...
Tunisie	D/C	.	5	—	1	1	25	32	150	49	131
	W/T	.	306	—	350	400	5 887	2 623	18 458	18 473	21 000
	D/J	.	469	—	88	1 200	6 104	3 587	31 589	49 653	65 572 [4]
Uganda	D/C	99	54	34	57	87	...	44	64	34	...
	W/T	17 707	5 658	5 305	7 498	32 032	...	23 245	23 301	5 834	...
	D/J	60 000	12 917	12 864	11 787	68 675	...	55 162	56 896	15 031	...
Zambia	D/C	114	241	222	206	159	128	127	74	68	60
	W/T	10 149	307 167	24 006	30 770	16 944	17 040	14 964	10 453	9 892	7 725
	D/J	22 493	579 280	46 088	65 898	20 773	122 951	18 894	20 874	6 453	38 334

EXPLANATORY NOTES: See p. 793.   NOTES EXPLICATIVES: Voir p. 794.   NOTAS EXPLICATIVAS: Véase pág. 795.

D/C : Number of disputes — *Nombre de conflits* — Número de conflictos.
W/T : Workers involved — *Travailleurs impliqués* — Trabajadores afectados.
D/J : Working days lost — *Journées de travail perdues* — Días de trabajo perdidos.

[1] Excl. workers indirectly affected.   [2] Excl. workers indirectly affected; year ending in March of the year indicated.   [3] Excl. disputes lasting less than one day.   [4] Computed on the basis of eight-hour working days.

[1] *Non compris les travailleurs indirectement atteints.*   [2] *Non compris les travailleurs indirectement atteints; année se terminant en mars de l'année indiquée.*   [3] *Non compris les conflits dont la durée est inférieure à une journée.*   [4] *Calculées sur la base de journées de travail de huit heures.*

[1] Excl. los trabajadores indirectamente afectados.   [2] Excl. los trabajadores indirectamente afectados; año que termina en marzo del año indicado.   [3] Excl. los conflictos de menos de un día de duración.   [4] Calculados a base de días de trabajo de ocho horas.

27 Industrial disputes
Conflits du travail
Conflictos del trabajo

Country — Pays — País	Code Code Clave	1965	1966	1967	1968	1969	1960	1971	1972	1973	1974
AMERICA — AMÉRIQUE AMÉRICA											
Antigua	D/C	8	8	4	9	2	2	3	5	4	...
	W/T	550	684	137	668	334	25	218	...	574	...
	D/J	4 174	1 770	773	3 573	5 577	87	272	2 612	1 322	...
Argentina [1]	D/C	32	27	6	7	8	5	16	12	.	| 543*
	W/T	203 596	235 913	547	1 609	6 697	2 912	68 632	61 259	.	| 271 697*
	D/J	590 511	1 003 710	2 702	15 502	150 256	32 849	159 277	153 047	.	| 651 555*
Bahamas	D/C	1	—	3	4	2	1	...	...	...	...
	W/T	190	—	234	1 685	330	153	...	...	...	...
	D/J	760	—	1 700	2 470	2 400	1 224	...	...	...	...
Barbados	D/C	3	6	5	—	3	—	3 [2]	7	71	2
	W/T	366	1 969	411	—	489	—	415	1 353	2 549	550
	D/J	1 342	4 328	2 248	—	2 753	—	54 065	1 450	4 147	2 400
Belize	D/C	6	2	2	1	4	2	...	...	...	...
	W/T	900	1050	42	629	1 709	44	...	...	...	...
	D/J	1 900	1 850	258	6 919	40 853	439	...	...	...	...
Bermuda	D/C	2	3	5	4	1	5	6	13	1	5
	W/T	173	144	303	922	87	518	672	1 485	494	556
	D/J	742	196	1 424	5 464	1 392	6 098	6 107	36 006	3 613	8 444
Canada [3]	D/C	501	617	522	582	595	542	569	598	724	1 216
	W/T	171 870	411 459	252 018	223 562	306 799	261 706	239 631	706 474	348 470	592 220
	D/J	2 349 870	5 178 170	3 974 760	5 082 732	7 751 880	6 539 560	2 866 590	7 753 530	5 776 080	9 255 120
Chile [4]	D/C	723	1 073	1 114	1 124	1 277	1 819	2 696	3 325	2 050	...
	W/T	182 359	195 435	225 470	292 794	362 010	656 170	298 677	393 954	711 028	...
	D/J	...	2 015 253	1 989 534	3 651 569	1 178 706	2 814 517	1 387 505	1 678 124	2 503 356	...
El Salvador	D/C	.	.	.	.	.	.	12	23	6	73
	W/T	.	.	.	.	.	.	10 614	3 919	618	...
	D/J	.	.	.	.	.	.	196 595	42 021	7 118	...
Guadeloupe	D/C	5	2	18	3	3	4	6	8	8	3
	W/T	310	89	4 900	3 127	236	121	12 818	1 485	4 277	249
	D/J	1 255	89	39 334	30 050	836	866	145 557	66 567	16 589	466

EXPLANATORY NOTES: See p. 793.   NOTES EXPLICATIVES: Voir p. 794.   NOTAS EXPLICATIVAS: Véase pág. 795.

D/C : Number of disputes — *Nombre de conflits* — Número de conflictos.
W/T : Workers involved — *Travailleurs impliqués* — Trabajadores afectados.
D/J : Working days lost — *Journées de travail perdues* — Días de trabajo perdidos.

[1] 1965-72: Buenos Aires City. Strikes only; excl. strikes lasting less than one day. Excl. workers indirectly affected. Beginning 1974: new series covering Great Buenos Aires. Excl. general strikes. [2] Excl. a general strike in the distributive trade, for which no information is available on the number of workers involved and working days lost. [3] Excl. disputes in which the time lost is less than ten man-days. Excl. workers indirectly affected. [4] Strikes only.

[1] *1965-1972: ville de Buenos Aires. Grèves seulement; non compris les grèves dont la durée est inférieure à une journée. Non compris les travailleurs indirectement atteints. A partir de 1974: nouvelle série couvrant le grand Buenos Aires. Non compris les grèves générales.* [2] *Non compris une grève générale dans le commerce, pour laquelle il n'y a pas d'informations sur le nombre des travailleurs impliqués et des journées de travail perdues.* [3] *Non compris les conflits pour lesquels moins de dix journées-homme sont perdues. Non compris les travailleurs indirectement atteints.* [4] *Grèves seulement.*

[1] 1965-1972: Buenos Aires. Huelgas solamente; excl. las huelgas de menos de un día de duración. Excl. los trabajadores indirectamente afectados. A partir de 1974: nueva serie que abarca el Gran Buenos Aires. Excl. las huelgas generales. [2] Excl. una huelga general en el comercio, por no disponerse del número de trabajadores afectados y días de trabajo perdidos. [3] Excl. los conflictos en los que se pierden menos de diez días-hombre. Excl. los trabajadores indirectamente afectados. [4] Huelgas solamente.

27 Industrial disputes
Conflits du travail
Conflictos del trabajo

Country — Pays — País	Code Code Clave	1965	1966	1967	1968	1969	1970	1971	1972	1973	1974
Guatemala [1]	D/C	.	.	8	4	3	36	1	4	16	53
	W/T	.	.	4 000	7 505	3 117	27 067	92	4 868	22 711	43 934
	D/J	.	.	50 723	323 764	15 753	50 934	460	33 238	257 089	526 593
Guyana [1]	D/C	146	172	170	136	126	159	198	175	...	...
	W/T	48 341	37 637	30 505	56 489	17 878	84 056	41 447	44 597	...	...
	D/J	137 098	108 638	152 421	306 009	38 660	453 928	141 816	135 199	...	...
Guyane française	D/C	.	.	2	5	—	—	20	25	3	—
	W/T	.	.	310	...	—	—	1 288	1 485	89	—
	D/J	.	.	2 600	...	—	—	14 480	28 305	4 136	—
Jamaica [2]	D/C	37	69	95	94	46	70	77	55	90	46*
	W/T	25 316	29 563	17 849	22 550	8 622	23 181	18 623	30 286	18 726	20 517*
	D/J	290 162	180 628	173 587	224 781	91 489	335 432	76 079	266 369	236 805	127 234*
Martinique	D/C	6	7	8	5	4	4	9	...	...	...
	W/T	12 530	1 983	5 563	3 106	2 369	2 332	3 968	...	...	...
	D/J	36 600	8 173	55 143	11 928	18 228	16 162	...	...	...	...
México [1,3]	D/C	67	91	78	156	144	206	204	207	...	...
	W/T	610[4]	500[4]	8 457	4 420[4]	4 442[4]	14 329	9 299	8 395	...	...
Panamá	D/C	.	.	.	3	9	6	280	...	...	...
	W/T	.	.	.	1 075	1 835	17 510	15 606	...	...	...
	D/J [5]	.	.	.	609	968	13 148	...	...	...	...
Paraguay	D/C	3	2	1	—	—	—	—	...	...	...
	W/T	780	637	233	—	—	—	—	...	...	...
	D/J	540	1 274	233	—	—	—	—	...	...	...
Perú	D/C	397	394	414	364	372	345	377	409	788	570
	W/T	135 582	126 706	142 282	107 809	91 531	110 990	161 415	130 643	416 251	362 737
	D/J [5]	802 576	1 461 087	1 046 596	422 225	486 163	722 732	1 360 244	791 377	1 961 086	1 676 630
Puerto Rico [6]	D/C	40	64	52	49	73	93	77	107	76	95
	W/T	9 638	12 511	7 022	9 012	12 270	19 454	14 296	23 779	17 757	22 109
	D/J	98 261	136 511	48 382	54 729	114 044	191 293	232 106	222 624	140 703	289 397
St. Lucia	D/C	2	1	—	—	—	5	5	6	4	6
	W/T	210	50	—	—	—	583	720	490	560	1 271
	D/J	145	800	—	—	—	1 339	1 020	674	1 432	9 651

EXPLANATORY NOTES: See p. 793. NOTES EXPLICATIVES: Voir p. 794. NOTAS EXPLICATIVAS: Véase pág. 795.

D/C: Number of disputes — *Nombre de conflits* — Número de conflictos.
W/T: Workers involved — *Travailleurs impliqués* — Trabajadores afectados.
D/J : Working days lost — *Journées de travail perdues* — Días de trabajo perdidos.

[1] Excl. workers indirectly affected. [2] Excl. disputes concerning less than ten workers and those for which less than 100 working days have been lost (except for 1965: ten working days). [3] Strikes only. [4] Figures for a smaller number of disputes than those indicated. [5] Computed on the basis of eight-hour working days. [6] Excl. workers indirectly affected; year ending in June of the year indicated.

[1] *Non compris les travailleurs indirectement atteints.* [2] *Non compris les conflits touchant moins de dix travailleurs ni ceux pour lesquels moins de 100 journées de travail sont perdues (sauf pour 1965 : dix journées de travail).* [3] *Grèves seulement.* [4] *Les chiffres se rapportent à un nombre de conflits inférieur à celui qui est indiqué.* [5] *Calculées sur la base de journées de travail de huit heures.* [6] *Non compris les travailleurs indirectement atteints; année se terminant en juin de l'année indiquée.*

[1] Excl. los trabajadores indirectamente afectados. [2] Excl. los conflictos que implican a menos de diez trabajadores y aquellos para los cuales se han perdido menos de 100 días de trabajo (salvo para 1965: diez días de trabajo). [3] Huelgas solamente. [4] Cifras correspondientes a un número de conflictos menor que el indicado. [5] Calculados a base de días de trabajo de ocho horas. [6] Excl. los trabajadores indirectamente afectados; año que termina en junio del año indicado.

27 Industrial disputes
Conflits du travail
Conflictos del trabajo

Country — Pays — País	Code Code Clave	1965	1966	1967	1968	1969	1970	1971	1972	1973	1974
Saint-Pierre-et-Miquelon .	D/C	.	1	1	—	2	—	—	...	...	...
	W/T	.	64	163	—	174	—	—	...	...	...
	D/J	.	64	6 520	—	348	—	—	...	...	...
Surinam	D/C	4	2	4	4	26	7	49	15	30	...
	W/T	578	196	727	1 919	5 063	420	6 641	2 826	5 073	...
	D/J	1 137	675	3 199	24 962	62 428	1 469	21 774	43 701	31 840	...
Trinidad and Tobago . . .	D/C	4	—	5	9	9	64	75	34	74	80
	W/T	7 160	—	648	681	2 767	11 280	18 008	8 740	15 543	54 698
	D/J	88 051	—	3 070	17 568	19 972	99 600	135 867	23 754	95 098	271 823
United States [1]	D/C	3 963	4 405	4 595	5 045	5 700	5 716	5 138	5 010	5 353	6 074
	W/T	1 550 000	1 960 000	2 870 000	2 650 000	2 481 000	3 305 200	3 279 600	1 713 600	2 251 000	2 778 100
	D/J	23 300 000	25 400 000	42 100 000	49 000 000	42 869 000	66 413 800	47 589 100	27 066 400	27 948 400	48 044 600
Venezuela	D/C	24	12	29	14	83	64	106	172[3]	250	116
	W/T	4 690	3 184	2 973	6 539	21 015	23 934	39 094	24 654	45 508	17 463
	D/J [2]	17 800	7 961	5 165	10 889	...	234 349	519 919	146 186	144 671	129 978
ASIA — ASIE ASIA											
Bangladesh	D/C	.	.	.	.	.	.	9	40	23*	19*
	W/T	.	.	.	.	.	.	35 324	43 655	26 590*	24 103*
	D/J	.	.	.	.	.	.	70 333	126 000	96 299*	86 919*
Cyprus	D/C	20	18	17	24	36	35	28	46	26	36
	W/T	1 013	1 468	4 015	6 557	13 406	4 725	6 867	21 431	2 790	8 498
	D/J	1 073	2 708	19 180	42 598	17 602	5 938	23 629	142 427	12 874	14 349
Hong Kong	D/C	.	14	13	25	27	47	41	46	54	19
	W/T	.	3 177	2 744	2 018	5 451	8 624	10 781	13 039	19 788	4 462
	D/J	.	24 355	22 525	8 432	39 911	47 243	24 600	41 834	56 691	10 708
India [4]	D/C	1 910	2 556	2 815	2 776	2 627	2 889	2 752	3 243	3 370	2 601*
	W/T	1 028 609	1 410 056	1 490 346	1 669 294	1 826 866	1 827 752	1 615 140	1 736 737	2 545 602	2 346 657*
	D/J	6 903 523	13 846 329	17 147 951	17 243 679	19 048 288	20 563 381	16 545 636	20 543 916	20 626 253	31 642 627*

EXPLANATORY NOTES: See p. 793. NOTES EXPLICATIVES: Voir p. 794. NOTAS EXPLICATIVAS: Véase pág. 795.

D/C : Number of disputes — *Nombre de conflits* — Número de conflictos.
W/T : Workers involved — *Travailleurs impliqués* — Trabajadores afectados.
D/J : Working days lost — *Journées de travail perdues* — Días de trabajo perdidos.

[1] Excl. disputes involving less than six workers and those lasting less than a full day or shift. [2] Computed on the basis of eight-hour working days. [3] Incl. 57 disputes for which data relating to workers involved and working days lost are not available. [4] Disputes involving ten or more workers; excl. political strikes.

[1] *Non compris les conflits touchant moins de six travailleurs et ceux dont la durée est inférieure à une journée ou à un poste de travail.* [2] *Calculées sur la base de journées de travail de huit heures.* [3] *Y compris 57 conflits pour lesquels les données concernant les travailleurs impliqués et les journées de travail perdues ne sont pas disponibles.* [4] *Conflits dans lesquels dix travailleurs ou plus sont impliqués ; non compris les grèves de caractère politique.*

[1] Excl. los conflictos que afectan a menos de seis trabajadores y los de una duración menor de un día o turno completo. [2] Calculados a base de días de trabajo de ocho horas. [3] Incl. 57 conflictos en los cuales los datos concernientes a los trabajadores afectados y los días de trabajo perdidos no están disponibles. [4] Se refiere a conflictos que afectan a diez o más trabajadores; excl. las huelgas políticas.

27 **Industrial disputes**
Conflits du travail
Conflictos del trabajo

Country — *Pays* — País	Code *Code* Clave	1965	1966	1967	1968	1969	1970	1971	1972	1973	1974
Indonesia	D/C	4	2	6	2	—	—	1	1	3	6
	W/T	470	24	1 172	575	—	—	27	70	624	672
	D/J [1]	1 046	103	1 555	267	—	—	56	70	282	426
Iraq	D/C	—	—	17	—	6	7	—	—	—	—
	W/T	—	—	4 788	—	1 020	1 124	—	—	—	—
	D/J	—	—	14 282	—	18 524	14 000	—	—	—	—
Israel [2]	D/C	288	282	142	100	114	163	169	168	96	71
	W/T	90 210	88 616	25 058	42 146	44 496	114 941	88 265	87 309	122 338	22 141
	D/J	207 561	155 975	58 286	71 789	102 162	390 344	178 612	235 058	375 020	51 333
Japan [3]	D/C	1 542	1 252	1 214	1 546	1 783	2 260	2 527	2 498	3 326	5 211
	W/T	1 682 342	1 132 406	732 505	1 163 357	1 411 898	1 720 135	1 896 252	1 543 557	2 236 119	3 621 049
	D/J	5 669 362	2 741 711	1 829 965	2 840 866	3 633 564	3 914 807	6 028 746	5 146 668	4 603 821	9 662 945
Jordan	D/C	.	.	.	4	1	2	—	—	2	5
	W/T	.	.	.	288	500	700	—	—	240	215
	D/J	.	.	.	288	2 500	2 600	—	—	240	...
Korea, Rep. of [4]	D/C	12	12	18	16	7	4	10	—	—	58
	W/T	3 852	30 690	2 787	18 437	30 499	541	832	—	—	22 609
	D/J	18 827	40 592	10 004	62 945	163 353	9 013	11 323	—	—	16 831
Malaysia:											
East Malaysia:											
Sabah	D/C	6	3	15	2	1	8	7	7	4	7
	W/T	388	130	1 129	407	26	302	361	532	823	658
	D/J	1 584	272	4 204	407	156	446	564	567	1 530	1 459
Sarawak	D/C	1	1	—	2	2	1	—	1	4	3
	W/T	22	24	—	93	398	80	—	28	864	61
	D/J	3	2 784	—	184	748	30	—	28	1 038	214
West Malaysia	D/C	46	60	45	103	49	17	45	66	66	85
	W/T	14 684	14 673	9 452	31 062	8 750	1 216	5 311	9 701	14 003	21 830
	D/J	152 666	109 915	157 980	280 417	76 779	1 867	20 265	33 455	40 866	103 884
Pakistan [5]	D/C	132	157	172	138	339	356	141	341	229	...
	W/T	125 241	144 489	257 180	116 576	298 137	272 387	107 962	125 588	126 930	...
	D/J	621 947	494 566	2 491 954	417 428	1 782 592	3 114 850	815 211	611 908	409 317	...
Philippines [6]	D/C	107	108	86	121	122	104	157	69	...	...
	W/T	54 944	61 496	46 928	46 445	62 803	36 852	62 138	33 396	...	...
	D/J	794 185	756 257	673 398	584 498	980 863	994 689	1 429 195	1 003 646	...	...

EXPLANATORY NOTES: See p. 793.   NOTES EXPLICATIVES: Voir p. 794.   NOTAS EXPLICATIVAS: Véase pág. 795.

D/C : Number of disputes — *Nombre de conflits* — Número de conflictos.
W/T : Workers involved — *Travailleurs impliqués* — Trabajadores afectados.
D/J : Working days lost — *Journées de travail perdues* — Días de trabajo perdidos.

[1] Computed on the basis of seven hour working days. [2] Excl. disputes where less than ten working days were lost. 1965-71: excl. disputes lasting two hours or less. [3] Excl. workers indirectly affected and disputes lasting less than four hours. [4] Excl. workers indirectly affected. [5] Disputes involving ten or more workers; excl. political strikes. Beginning 1971: geographical scope revised. [6] Excl. disputes involving less than six workers and those lasting less than a full day or shift. Excl. workers indirectly affected.

[1] *Calculées sur la base de journées de travail de sept heures.* [2] *Non compris les conflits dans lesquels moins de dix journées de travail ont été perdues. 1965-1971 : non compris les conflits d'une durée est inférieure à quatre moins.* [3] *Non compris les travailleurs indirectement atteints et les conflits dont la durée est inférieure à quatre heures.* [4] *Non compris les travailleurs indirectement atteints.* [5] *Conflits dans lesquels dix ouvriers ou plus sont impliqués : non compris les grèves de caractère politique. A partir de 1971 : portée géographique révisée.* [6] *Non compris les conflits touchant moins de six travailleurs et ceux dont la durée est inférieure à une journée ou à un poste de travail. Non compris les travailleurs indirectement atteints.*

[1] Calculados a base de días de trabajo de siete horas. [2] Excl. los conflictos que causaron una pérdida menor de diez días de trabajo. 1965-1971: excl. los conflictos de una duración de dos horas o menos. [3] Excl. los trabajadores indirectamente afectados y los conflictos de menos de cuatro horas de duración. [4] Excl. los trabajadores indirectamente afectados. [5] Se refiere a conflictos que afectan a diez o más trabajadores; excl. las huelgas políticas. A partir de 1971: alcance geográfico revisado. [6] Excl. los conflictos que afectan a menos de seis trabajadores y los de una duración menor de un día o turno completo. Excl. los trabajadores indirectamente afectados.

27 Industrial disputes
Conflits du travail
Conflictos del trabajo

Country — *Pays* — País	Code *Code* Clave	1965	1966	1967	1968	1969	1970	1971	1972	1973	1974
Singapore	D/C	30	14	10	4	—	5	2	10	5	10
	W/T	3 374	1 288	4 491	172	—	1 749	1 380	3 168	1 312	1 901
	D/J	45 800	44 762	41 322	11 447	8 512[1]	2 514	5 449	18 233	2 295	5 380
Sri Lanka[2]	D/C	230	164	230	197	189	340	165	187	448	91
	W/T	79 603	142 851	89 851	77 217	63 178	149 018	91 619	55 037	260 602	27 073
	D/J	574 707	4 151 615	699 345	988 416	464 165	1 314 563	568 161	298 898	1 170 042	105 744
Sud Viet-Nam, Rép. du . .	D/C	28	84	83	41	43	94	79	27	8	...
	W/T	12 267	33 095	32 111	15 110	19 356	60 653	35 623	9 138	2 927	...
	D/J	17 243	106 087	81 962	43 676	51 790	230 415	374 877	25 001	2 893	...
Thailand	D/C	17	17	5	14	16	22	27	34	501	357
	W/T	3 753	5 413	1 060	1 867	4 672	2 482	5 153	7 803	177 896	105 883
	D/J	6 484	18 764	678	3 217	20 070	7 670	12 646	...	296 887	507 607
Yemen, People's Dem. Rep. of (Aden)	D/C	17	12	6	9	5	4	—	—	—	—
	W/T	59 392	2 701	2 121	1 892	1 627	594	—	—	—	—
	D/J	59 418	9 669	1 858	20 769	50 267	5 589	—	—	—	—
EUROPE — EUROPE EUROPA											
Austria	W/T	146 009	120 922	7 496	3 129	17 449	7 547	2 431	7 096	78 251	7 295
	D/J	151 261	71 356	16 411	6 671	18 517	26 616	3 702	15 104	160 138	7 243
Belgique[3]	D/C	43	74	58	71	88	151	184	191	172	235
	W/T	18 774	41 629	37 621	29 338	24 691	107 670	86 979	66 622	62 281	55 747
	D/J	70 131	533 239	181 713	364 363	162 898	1 432 274	1 240 472	354 086	871 872	580 032
Denmark[4]	D/C	37	22	22	17	48	77	31	35	205	134
	W/T	14 194	10 369	10 442	28 772	35 856	55 585	6 379	7 601	337 100	142 352
	D/J	242 100	15 400	9 900	33 600	56 200	102 000	20 600	21 800	3 901 200	184 200
España	D/C	183	132	372	309	491	1 547	542	853	731	1 730
	W/T	58 591	36 977	198 740	130 742	205 325	440 114	196 665	236 421	303 132	426 037
	D/J[5]	189 548	184 760	235 962	240 659	559 591	1 092 364	859 693	586 616	1 081 158	1 534 047

EXPLANATORY NOTES: See p. 793.　　　　NOTES EXPLICATIVES: Voir p. 794.　　　　NOTAS EXPLICATIVAS: Véase pág. 795.

D/C : Number of disputes — *Nombre de conflits* — Número de conflictos.
W/T : Workers involved — *Travailleurs impliqués* — Trabajadores afectados.
D/J : Working days lost — *Journées de travail perdues* — Días de trabajo perdidos.

[1] Working days lost on account of a dispute which began in 1968. [2] Strikes only. Excl. political strikes and workers indirectly affected as well as strikes involving less than five workers or lasting less than one day except in cases where the aggregate number of man-days lost exceeds 50. [3] Excl. workers indirectly affected. [4] Excl. political strikes. Excl. disputes where less than 100 working days were lost. [5] Computed on the basis of eight-hour working days.

[1] *Journées de travail perdues par suite d'un conflit qui a commencé en 1968.* [2] *Grèves seulement. Non compris les grèves de caractère politique et les travailleurs indirectement atteints, ni les grèves touchant moins de cinq travailleurs ou durant moins d'une journée, sauf dans les cas où plus de 50 journées-homme sont perdues.* [3] *Non compris les travailleurs indirectement atteints.* [4] *Non compris les grèves de caractère politique. Non compris les conflits dans lesquels moins de 100 journées de travail sont perdues.* [5] *Calculées sur la base de journées de travail de huit heures.*

[1] Días de trabajo perdidos a causa de un conflicto que comenzó en 1968. [2] Huelgas solamente. Excl. las huelgas políticas y los trabajadores indirectamente afectados, así como las huelgas que afectan a menos de cinco trabajadores o las de duración menor de un día, salvo los casos en que el total de días-hombre perdidos exceda de 50. [3] Excl. los trabajadores indirectamente afectados. [4] Excl. las huelgas políticas. Excl. los conflictos que causaron una pérdida menor de 100 días de trabajo. [5] Calculados a base de días de trabajo de ocho horas.

27 Industrial disputes
Conflits du travail
Conflictos del trabajo

Country — Pays — País	Code Code Clave	1965	1966	1967	1968	1969	1970	1971	1972	1973	1974
Finland [1]	D/C	29	150	43	68	158	240	838	849	1 010	1 795
	W/T	6 959	66 051	26 591	26 843	83 207	201 556	403 297	239 732	678 193	370 700
	D/J	16 047	122 092	320 665	282 287	161 083	233 173	2 711 100	473 100	2 496 929	434 790
France [2]	D/C	1 674	1 711	1 675	.	2 480	3 319	4 358	3 464	3 731	3 381
	W/T	1 237 071	3 341 003	2 823 619	.	1 443 600	1 159 619	3 234 500	2 721 348	2 245 973	1 563 540
	D/J	979 861	2 523 488	4 203 509	.	2 223 568	1 742 175	4 387 781	3 755 343	3 914 598	3 379 977
Germany, Fed. Rep. of △ [3]	W/T	6 250	196 013	59 604	25 167	89 571	184 269	536 303	22 908	185 010	250 352
	D/J	48 520	27 086	389 581	25 249	249 184	93 203	4 483 740	66 045	563 051	1 051 290
Gibraltar	D/C	—	2	1	—	3	3	2	1	10	7
	W/T	—	284	20	—	130	1 500	118	20	252	4 960
	D/J	—	338	20	—	220	4 500	314	2	1 873	7 800
Grèce	D/C	434	609	89	—	—	—	—	—	—	...
	W/T	255 899	348 738	90 750	—	—	—	—	—	—	...
	D/J [4]	453 874	711 928	113 891	—	—	—	—	—	—	...
Iceland	D/C	66	23	60	67	137	66	7	5	...	...
	W/T	15 727	1 866	9 371	20 083	33 739	15 855	1 790	1 100	...	...
	D/J	84 131	5 233	18 044	216 169	139 478	298 242	31 985	12 037	...	...
Ireland	D/C	88	112	79	126	134	134	133	131	182	219
	W/T	38 917	52 238	20 925	38 880	61 760	28 752	43 783	22 274	31 761	43 459
	D/J	552 351	783 635	182 645	405 686	935 900	1 007 714	273 770	206 955	206 725	551 833
Italie [5]	D/C	3 191	2 387	2 658	3 377	3 788	4 162	5 598	4 765	3 769	5 174
	W/T	2 309 980	1 887 992	2 244 203	4 862 201	7 506 983	3 721 919	3 891 253	4 405 251	6 132 747	7 824 397
	D/J	6 992 856	14 473 551	8 568 433	9 239 793	37 824 573	20 887 459	14 798 589	19 497 143	23 419 285	19 466 714
Malta	D/C	3	9	8	19	17	35	23	42	...	...
	W/T	687	615	7 838	21 220	5 892	23 794	2 103	11 999	...	...
	D/J	4 154	11 599	27 314	58 333	41 445	148 499	24 070	14 677	...	...
Norway [6]	D/C	7	7	7	6	4	15	10	9	12	13
	W/T	591	1 392	436	486	824	3 133	2 519	1 185	2 380	22 149
	D/J	8 927	5 207	4 720	13 514	21 636	47 204	9 105	12 402	11 382	318 433

EXPLANATORY NOTES: See p. 793.   NOTES EXPLICATIVES: Voir p. 794.   NOTAS EXPLICATIVAS: Véase pág. 795.

D/C : Number of disputes — *Nombre de conflits* — Número de conflictos.
W/T : Workers involved — *Travailleurs impliqués* — Trabajadores afectados.
D/J : Working days lost — *Journées de travail perdues* — Días de trabajo perdidos.

[1] 1965-70: excl. workers indirectly affected but incl. working days lost by these workers. Excl. disputes lasting less than four hours, except when a loss of more than 100 working days is involved. [2] Excl. agriculture and public administration. [3] Excl. disputes lasting less than one day except when a loss of more than 100 working days is involved. [4] Computed on the basis of eight-hour working days. [5] Excl. political strikes and workers indirectly affected. [6] Excl. workers indirectly affected and disputes lasting less than one day.

[1] *1965-1970 : non compris les travailleurs indirectement atteints, mais y compris les journées de travail perdues par ces travailleurs. Non compris les conflits dont la durée est inférieure à quatre heures, sauf dans les cas où plus de 100 journées de travail sont perdues.* [2] *Non compris l'agriculture et l'administration publique.* [3] *Non compris les conflits dont la durée est inférieure à une journée, sauf dans les cas où plus de 100 journées de travail sont perdues.* [4] *Calculées sur la base de journées de travail de huit heures.* [5] *Non compris les grèves de caractère politique et les travailleurs indirectement atteints.* [6] *Non compris les travailleurs indirectement atteints et les conflits dont la durée est inférieure à une journée.*

[1] 1965-1970: excl. los trabajadores indirectamente afectados, pero incl. los días de trabajo perdidos por éstos. Excl. los conflictos de menos de cuatro horas de duración, salvo los casos que implican una pérdida de más de 100 días de trabajo. [2] Excl. agricultura y administración pública. [3] Excl. los conflictos de menos de un día de duración, salvo los casos que implican una pérdida de más de 100 días de trabajo. [4] Calculados a base de días de trabajo de ocho horas. [5] Excl. las huelgas políticas y los trabajadores indirectamente afectados. [6] Excl. los trabajadores indirectamente afectados y los conflictos de menos de un día de duración.

27 Industrial disputes
Conflits du travail
Conflictos del trabajo

Country — Pays — País	Code Code Clave	1965	1966	1967	1968	1969	1970	1971	1972	1973	1974
Pays-Bas	D/C	60	20	8	11	28	99	15	31	7	14
	W/T	23 213	11 188	1 564	4 599	12 403	52 333	35 560	19 548	58 113	2 979
	D/J	54 607	12 647	6 165	13 698	21 697	262 810	96 846	134 187	583 783	6 854
Suisse	D/C	2	2	1	1	1	3	11	5	—	3
	W/T	23	38	65	70	33	320	2 267	526	—	299
	D/J	163	62	1 690	1 785	231	2 623	7 491	2 002	—	2 777
Sweden	D/C	8	26	7	7	41	134	60	44	48	85
	W/T	248	29 436	90	379	9 023	26 669	62 919	7 145	4 252	17 470
	D/J	4 100	351 600	400	1 200	112 400	155 700	839 000	10 507	11 802	57 604
Turquie	D/C	43	36	100	54	81	112	96	121	55	105
	W/T	6 546	9 937	9 463	5 259	15 134	21 150	10 916	13 437	12 286	22 922
	D/J	304 920	333 645	344 480	176 448	267 863	241 226	475 456	628 246	677 345	741 397
United Kingdom [1]	D/C	2 354	1 937	2 116	2 378	3 116	3 906	2 228	2 497	2 873	2 922
	W/T	876 400	543 900	733 700	2 257 600	1 665 000	1 800 700	1 178 200	1 734 400	1 527 600	1 626 400
	D/J	2 925 000	2 398 000	2 787 000	4 690 000	6 846 000	10 980 000	13 551 000	23 909 000	7 197 000	14 750 000
OCEANIA — OCÉANIE OCEANÍA											
Australia [2]	D/C	1 346	1 273	1 340	1 713	2 014	2 738	2 404	2 298	2 538	2 809
	W/T	475 044	394 851	483 274	720 321	1 285 198	1 367 400	1 326 500	1 113 800	803 000	2 004 800
	D/J	815 869	732 084	705 315	1 079 464	1 957 957	2 393 700	3 068 600	2 010 300	2 634 700	6 292 500
Fiji [3]	D/C	4	2	12	17	27	8	28	...	...	...
	W/T	194	35	1 421	2 438	1 521	887	5 163	...	...	...
	D/J	331	101	6 855	4 110	4 526	752	13 312	...	...	...
New Zealand [4].	D/C	105	145	89	153	169	323	313	266	394	380
	W/T	15 267	33 132	28 490	37 458	44 041	110 096	86 009	60 429	115 865	70 904
	D/J	21 814	99 095	139 490	130 267	138 675	277 348	162 563	134 505	271 706	183 688
Nouvelle-Calédonie	D/C	—	5	4	4	2	23	25	...	9	21
	W/T	—	2 791	987	2 348	16	4 708	5 846	...	4 064	3 811
	D/J	—	14 343	259	8 522	150	18 263	...	...	2 597	14 817
Solomon Is. (Brit.)	D/C	.	.	1	5	9	2	10	9	3	5
	W/T	.	.	174	560	641	381	600	425	145	317
	D/J	.	.	457	3 536	1 310	2 149	8 301	2 601	292	192

EXPLANATORY NOTES: See p. 793.   NOTES EXPLICATIVES: Voir p. 794.   NOTAS EXPLICATIVAS: Véase pág. 795.

D/C: Number of disputes — *Nombre de conflits* — Número de conflictos.
W/T: Workers involved — *Travailleurs impliqués* — Trabajadores afectados.
D/J : Working days lost — *Journées de travail perdues* — Días de trabajo perdidos.

[1] Excl. disputes not connected with terms of employment or conditions of labour. Disputes involving less than ten workers or lasting less than one day are not included unless a loss of more than 100 working days is involved. [2] Excl. disputes where less than ten working days were lost. [3] Excl. workers indirectly affected. [4] Excl. political strikes.

[1] *Non compris les conflits dus à des causes autres que les conditions d'emploi ou les conditions de travail. Les conflits touchant moins de dix travailleurs ou durant moins d'une journée ne sont pas compris, sauf dans les cas ou plus de 100 journées de travail sont perdues.* [2] *Non compris les conflits dans lesquels moins de dix journées de travail sont perdues.* [3] *Non compris les travailleurs indirectement atteints.* [4] *Non compris les grèves de caractère politique.*

[1] Excl. los conflictos que no resulten del contrato de empleo o de las condiciones de trabajo. Excl. los conflictos que afectan a menos de diez trabajadores o aquellos cuya duración es menor de un día, salvo cuando implican una pérdida de más de 100 días de trabajo. [2] Excl. los conflictos que causaron una pérdida de menos de diez días de trabajo. [3] Excl. los trabajadores indirectamente afectados. [4] Excl. las huelgas políticas.

Exchange rates

Cours des changes

Tipos de cambio

Exchange rates

Table 28

The exchange rates given in this table are those reported by the International Monetary Fund in *International Financial Statistics* (monthly). They are uniformly stated in units of national currency per US dollar.

The table consists of two parts:

Part A shows end-of-year exchange rates from 1965 through 1974 and end-of-month rate for June 1975. The types of rates quoted are indicated in the column under the following headings:

I. *Selling rates:* rates at which the central bank or the commercial banks sell foreign currency for domestic currency.

II. *Buying rates:* rates at which the central bank or the commercial banks buy foreign currency for domestic currency.

III. *Mid-point rates:* average of buying and selling rates.

Part B shows the par value, central rates or official rates in respect of those countries for which it is sufficient to indicate the dates of change in rates and the corresponding new rates.

For more detailed information on exchange rates, see International Monetary Fund: *International Financial Statistics* (monthly) and *Annual Report on Exchange Restrictions*.

Cours des changes

Tableau 28

Les taux de change indiqués dans ce tableau sont ceux que présente le Fonds monétaire international dans sa publication mensuelle *International Financial Statistics*. Ils sont exprimés en unités de monnaie nationale par dollar des Etats-Unis.

Le tableau comprend deux parties:

La **partie A** indique les taux de change en vigueur en fin de période pour les années 1965 à 1974 et en juin 1975. Les taux présentés dans ce tableau se rapportent aux types de cours suivants:

I. *Cours de vente :* taux auxquels les banques centrales ou les banques commerciales vendent les devises étrangères contre la monnaie nationale.

II. *Cours d'achat :* taux auxquels les banques centrales ou les banques commerciales achètent les devises étrangères contre la monnaie nationale.

III. *Cours moyen :* moyennes des cours de vente et d'achat.

La **partie B** indique les parités, taux des banques centrales ou cours officiels, des pays pour lesquels il suffit d'indiquer les dates de changement des taux et les nouveaux taux correspondants.

Pour des renseignements plus détaillés sur les cours des changes, voir Fonds monétaire international: *International Financial Statistics* (publication mensuelle) et *Annual Report on Exchange Restrictions*.

Tipos de cambio

Cuadro 28

Los tipos de cambio incluidos en este cuadro son los que presenta el Fondo Monetario Internacional en la publicación mensual *International Financial Statistics*. Estos tipos se dan en forma de unidades de moneda nacional por dólar de Estados Unidos.

El cuadro comprende dos partes:

La **parte A** proporciona los tipos de cambio vigentes al final del año desde 1965 hasta 1974, y el de fines de junio de 1975. Los tipos de cambio que figuran en este cuadro corresponden a las siguientes clases:

I. *Tipos de venta:* tipos de cambio aplicados por los bancos centrales o los bancos comerciales en sus operaciones de venta de divisas extranjeras a cambio de moneda nacional.

II. *Tipos de compra:* tipos de cambio aplicados por los bancos centrales o los bancos comerciales en sus operaciones de compra de divisas extranjeras a cambio de moneda nacional.

III. *Tipos medios:* promedio de los tipos de venta y de compra.

La **parte B** presenta las paridades y los tipos de cambio oficiales o de los bancos centrales, respecto de aquellos países para los que es suficiente indicar las fechas de modificación de esos tipos, y los nuevos que, como consecuencia, se establezcan.

Para informes más detallados sobre los tipos de cambio, véase Fondo Monetario Internacional: *International Financial Statistics* (mensual) y *Annual Report on Exchange Restrictions*.

28 Exchange rates / Cours des changes / Tipos de cambio — A Fluctuating exchange rates / Taux de change fluctuants / Tipos de cambio fluctuantes

Units of national currency per US dollar *(end of period)*
Unités de la monnaie nationale par dollar des Etats-Unis *(fin de période)*
Unidades de moneda nacional por dólar de Estados Unidos *(fin del período)*

Date / Date / Fecha	AFRICA — AFRIQUE — AFRICA	AMERICA — AMÉRIQUE — AMÉRICA				
	South Africa, Rep. of	Argentina	Bolivia	Brésil	Canada	Colombia
	Rand/$US	Pesos [1]/$US	Pesos/$US	Cruzeiros [2]/$US	Dollars/$US	Pesos/$US
	I	I	III	I	III	I
1965	0.7144	188.50	11.88	2 220.00	1.075	18.29
1966	0.7177	247.30	11.88	2 220.00	1.084	16.30 [3]
1967	0.7134	350.00	11.88	2.715	1.081	16.30
1968	0.7196	350.00	11.88	3.830	1.073	16.95 [4]
1969	0.7149	350.00	11.88	4.350	1.073	17.93
1970	0.7172	4.00	11.88	4.950	1.011	19.17
1971	0.7653	5.00	11.88	5.635	1.002	21.00
1972	0.7828	5.00	20.00	6.215	0.996	22.88
1973	0.6712	5.00	20.00	6.220	0.996	24.89
1974	0.6896	5.00	20.00	7.435	0.991	28.69
1975: VI	0.7143	26.00	20.00	8.070	1.0306	31.10

Date / Date / Fecha	AMERICA — AMÉRIQUE — AMÉRICA					
	Costa Rica	Chile	Ecuador	Nicaragua	Paraguay	Perú
	Colones/$US	Escudos/$US	Sucres/$US	Córdobas/$US	Guaraníes/$US	Soles/$US
	II	I	I	III	I	III
1965	6.64	3.47	18.00	7.03	126.0	26.82
1966	6.64	4.37	18.00	7.03	126.0	26.82
1967	6.64	5.79	18.00	7.03	126.0	38.70 [5]
1968	6.64	7.67	18.00	7.03	126.0	38.70
1969	6.64	9.98	18.00	7.03	126.0	38.70
1970	6.64	12.23	25.00	7.03	126.0	38.70
1971	6.64	15.80	25.00	7.03	126.0	38.70
1972	6.64	25.00	25.00	7.03	126.0	38.70
1973	6.65	360.00	25.00	7.03	126.0	38.70
1974	8.57	1 870.00	25.00	7.03	126.0	38.70
1975: VI	8.57	5 000.00	25.00	7.03	126.0	38.70

EXPLANATORY NOTES: See p. 807. NOTES EXPLICATIVES: Voir p. 808. NOTAS EXPLICATIVAS: Véase pág. 809.

I :	Selling rates	— *Cours de vente*	— Tipos de venta.
II :	Buying rates	— *Cours d'achat*	— Tipos de compra.
III :	Mid-point rates	— *Cours moyens*	— Tipos medios.

[1] Beginning 1 Jan. 1970: 1 new peso = 100 old pesos. [2] Beginning 13 Feb. 1967: 1 new cruzeiro = 1,000 old cruzeiros. [3] Beginning 29 Nov. 1966: Capital Market rates. [4] Beginning 2 June 1968: Exchange certificate market rate. [5] Beginning 5 Oct. 1967: Exchange certificate market rate.

[1] *A partir du 1er janv. 1970 : 1 nouveau peso = 100 anciens pesos.* [2] *A partir du 13 fév. 1967 : 1 nouveau cruzeiro = 1 000 anciens cruzeiros.* [3] *A partir du 29 nov. 1966 : cours pour le marché des capitaux.* [4] *A partir du 2 juin 1968 : cours du marché pour les certificats de devises.* [5] *A partir du 5 oct. 1967 : cours du marché pour les certificats de devises.*

[1] A partir del 1.º de enero de 1970: 1 nuevo peso = 100 antiguos pesos. [2] A partir del 13 de febr. de 1967: 1 nuevo cruzeiro = 1 000 antiguos cruzeiros. [3] A partir del 29 de nov. de 1966: tipos por el mercado de capitales. [4] A partir del 2 de junio de 1968: tipos del mercado por los certificados de divisas. [5] A partir del 5 de oct. de 1967: tipos del mercado por los certificados de divisas.

28 Exchange rates / Cours des changes / Tipos de cambio

A Fluctuating exchange rates / Taux de change fluctuants / Tipos de cambio fluctuantes

Units of national currency per US dollar *(end of period)*
Unités de la monnaie nationale par dollar des Etats-Unis *(fin de période)*
Unidades de moneda nacional por dólar de Estados Unidos *(fin del período)*

Date / Date / Fecha	AMERICA — AMÉRIQUE — AMÉRICA		ASIA — ASIE — ASIA			
	Uruguay	Venezuela	Afghanistan	Burma	Hong Kong	India
	Pesos/$US	Bolívares/$US	Afghanis/$US	Kyats/$US	Dollars/$US	Rupees/$US
	I	I	I	III	I [2]	I [3]
1965	59.90	4.450	73.85	4.782	5.71	4.733
1966	76.20	4.450	74.15	4.805	5.73	7.509
1967	200.00	4.450	74.99	4.800	6.04	7.480
1968	250.00	4.450	73.67	4.810	6.10	7.560
1969	250.00	4.450	75.82	4.792	6.06	7.492
1970	250.00	4.450	85.18	4.802	6.08	7.509
1971	370.00	4.350	79.26	5.469	5.70	7.214
1972	732.00	4.350	77.94	5.402	5.65	8.008
1973	937.00	4.285	57.44	4.862	5.09	8.130
1974	1 616.50	4.285	56.02 [1]	4.810	4.93	8.078
1975: VI	2 315.00 [5]	4.285	.	6.306	4.95	8.354

Date / Date / Fecha	ASIA — ASIE — ASIA					
	Japan	Korea, Rep. of	Liban	Malaysia	Pakistan	Philippines
	Yen/$US	Won/$US	Livres/$US	Dollars/$US	Rupees/$US	Pesos/$US
	III	II [4]	I	III	III	I
1965	360.9	271	3.07	3.06	4.782	3.89
1966	362.5	270	3.17	3.07	4.805	3.88
1967	361.9	274	3.13	3.06	4.774	3.91
1968	357.7	281	3.18	3.06	4.809	3.91
1969	357.8	304	3.25	3.08	4.791	3.91
1970	357.6	316	3.25	3.08	4.803	6.44
1971	314.8	373	3.16	2.89	4.793	6.44
1972	302.0	399	3.01	2.82	11.031	6.69
1973	280.0	398	2.51	2.45	9.931	6.74
1974	301.0	484	2.30	2.31	9.931	7.07
1975: VI	296.4	484	2.22	2.31	9.931	7.02

EXPLANATORY NOTES: See p. 807.   NOTES EXPLICATIVES: Voir p. 808.   NOTAS EXPLICATIVAS: Véase pág. 809.

I : Selling rates — *Cours de vente* — Tipos de venta.
II : Buying rates — *Cours d'achat* — Tipos de compra.
III : Mid-point rates — *Cours moyens* — Tipos medios.

[1] June. [2] Beginning 1968: selling rates of the authorised banks. [3] Selling rates except from Dec. 1971 through May 1972: central rate, and from June 1972 through Jan. 1973: cross rates based on closing sterling-dollar rates in London. [4] Official buying rates of the banks. [5] April.

[1] *Juin.* [2] *A partir de 1968 : cours des ventes des établissements bancaires autorisés.* [3] *Cours de vente, sauf de déc. 1971 à mai 1972 : cours central, et de juin 1972 à janv. 1973 : cours croisés basés sur les cours de clôture livre sterling-dollar à Londres.* [4] *Cours d'achat officiel des établissements bancaires.* [5] *Avril.*

[1] Junio. [2] A partir de 1968: tipos de venta de los establecimientos bancarios autorizados. [3] Tipos de venta, salvo de dic. de 1971 a mayo de 1972: tipo intermedio, y de junio de 1972 a enero de 1973: tipos cruzados basados en la equivalencia libra esterlina-dólar al cierre en Londres. [4] Tipos de compra oficial de los establecimientos bancarios. [5] Abril.

28 Exchange rates / Cours des changes / Tipos de cambio   A   Fluctuating exchange rates / Taux de change fluctuants / Tipos de cambio fluctuantes

Units of national currency per US dollar *(end of period)*
Unités de la monnaie nationale par dollar des Etats-Unis *(fin de période)*
Unidades de moneda nacional por dólar de Estados Unidos *(fin del período)*

Date / Date / Fecha	ASIA — ASIE — ASIA				EUROPE — EUROPE — EUROPA	
	Sri Lanka	Sud Viet-Nam, Rép. du	République arabe syrienne	Thailand	Austria	Belgique
	Rupees/$US	Piastres/$US	Pounds/$US	Baht/$US	Schilling/$US	Francs/$US
	III	III	I [1]	I	III	III
1965	4.775	60.0	3.82	20.76	25.84	49.64
1966	4.775	118.0	3.82	20.68	25.85	50.05
1967	5.928	118.0	3.82	20.73	25.82	49.63
1968	5.928	118.0	3.82	20.78	25.82	50.14
1969	5.928	118.0	3.82	20.93	25.82	49.67
1970	5.928	118.0	3.82	20.93	25.82	49.68
1971	5.928	118.0	3.82	20.93	23.66	44.76
1972	6.698	465.0	3.82	20.93	23.14	44.06
1973	6.748	550.0	3.80	20.38	19.85	41.32
1974	6.693	685.0	3.70	20.38	17.13	36.12
1975: VI	6.872	755.0 [2]	3.70	20.38	16.64	35.25

Date / Date / Fecha	EUROPE — EUROPE — EUROPA					
	Denmark	España	Finland	France	Germany, Fed. Rep. of	Iceland
	Kroner/$US	Pesetas/$US	Markkaa/$US	Francs/$US	Mark/$US	Kronur/$US
	I	I	I	III	III	I
1965	6.891	59.88	3.21	4.902	4.006	42.96
1966	6.916	59.89	3.21	4.952	3.977	42.96
1967	7.462	69.57	4.19	4.908	3.999	56.94
1968	7.501	69.69	4.19	4.948	4.000	87.90
1969	7.492	69.93	4.19	5.558	3.690	87.90
1970	7.489	69.59	4.17	5.520	3.648	87.90
1971	7.062	65.90	4.14	5.224	3.268	87.22
1972	6.847	63.45	4.17	5.125	3.202	97.68
1973	6.294	56.85	3.85	4.708	2.703	83.81
1974	5.650	56.11	3.55	4.445	2.410	118.50
1975: VI	5.475	56.09	3.55	4.040	2.355	154.30

EXPLANATORY NOTES: See p. 807.   NOTES EXPLICATIVES: Voir p. 808.   NOTAS EXPLICATIVAS: Véase pág. 809.

I :   Selling rates   — *Cours de vente*   — Tipos de venta.
II :   Buying rates   — *Cours d'achat*   — Tipos de compra.
III :   Mid-point rates   — *Cours moyens*   — Tipos medios.

[1] Official selling rates.   [2] April.   [1] *Cours de vente officiel.*   [2] *Avril.*   [1] Tipos de venta oficial.   [2] Abril.

28 Exchange rates
Cours des changes
Tipos de cambio

A Fluctuating exchange rates
Taux de change fluctuants
Tipos de cambio fluctuantes

Units of national currency per US dollar *(end of period)*
Unités de la monnaie nationale par dollar des Etats-Unis *(fin de période)*
Unidades de moneda nacional por dólar de Estados Unidos *(fin del período)*

Date *Date* Fecha	EUROPE — EUROPE — EUROPA					
	Italie	Luxembourg	Norway	Pays-Bas	Portugal	Suisse
	Lire/$US	Francs/$US	Kroner/$US	Guilders/$US	Escudos/$US	Francs/$US
	III	III	III	III	I	II
1965	624.70	49.64	7.14	3.611	28.83	4.318
1966	624.45	50.05	7.15	3.614	28.98	4.327
1967	623.86	49.63	7.14	3.596	28.86	4.325
1968	623.50	50.14	7.14	3.606	28.77	4.302
1969	625.50	49.67	7.14	3.624	28.65	4.318
1970	623.00	49.68	7.13	3.597	28.75	4.316
1971	594.00	44.76	6.70	3.254	27.56	3.915
1972	582.50	44.06	6.64	3.226	27.00	3.774
1973	607.92	41.32	5.73	2.824	25.96	3.244
1974	649.43	36.12	5.21	2.507	24.71	2.550
1975: VI	630.43	35.25	4.95	2.440	24.54	2.502

Date *Date* Fecha	EUROPE — EUROPE — EUROPA				OCEANIA — OCÉANIE — OCEANÍA	
	Sweden	Turquie	United Kingdom	Yugoslavia	Australia	New Zealand
	Kronor/$US	Liras/$US	£/$US	Dinars/$US	Dollars/$US	Dollars/$US
	III	II	III	III	III	III
1965	5.174	9.04	0.3568	12.5	0.8941	0.7188
1966	5.174	9.04	0.3584	12.5	0.8977	0.7220
1967	5.156	9.04	0.4156	12.5	0.8921	0.8907
1968	5.174	9.04	0.4194	12.5	0.9009	0.8992
1969	5.164	9.04	0.4165	12.5	0.8945	0.8930
1970	5.164	14.92	0.4178	12.5	0.8969	0.8960
1971	4.859	14.15	0.3918	17.0	0.8396	0.8367
1972	4.743	14.15	0.4259	17.0	0.7843	0.8367
1973	4.588	14.15	0.4304	15.6	0.6720	0.7001
1974	4.081	13.99	0.4258	17.1	0.7536	0.7602
1975: VI	3.940	13.99	0.4550	17.0	0.7543	0.7718

EXPLANATORY NOTES: See p. 807.   NOTES EXPLICATIVES: Voir p. 808.   NOTAS EXPLICATIVAS: Véase pág. 809.

I : Selling rates — *Cours de vente* — Tipos de venta.
II : Buying rates — *Cours d'achat* — Tipos de compra.
III : Mid-point rates — *Cours moyens* — Tipos medios.

EXCHANGE RATES

28 B

Exchange rates	Cours des changes	Tipos de cambio	
Single exchange rates	Taux de change uniques	Tipos de cambio únicos	

Units of national currency per US dollar (a)
Unités de la monnaie nationale par dollar des Etats-Unis (a)
Unidades de moneda nacional por dólar de Estados Unidos (a)

Country / Pays / País	Currency / Monnaie / Moneda	Date / Date / Fecha	Exchange rate / Taux de change / Tipo de cambio
AFRICA — AFRIQUE AFRICA			
Algérie	Dinars	31 XII 1965	4.937
	»	XII 1971	4.547
	»	II 1973	4.093
	»	31 XII 1974	3.997
Cameroun	Fr. (CFA)[1]	31 XII 1965	246.85
	»	10 VIII 1969	277.71
	»	XII 1971	255.79
	»	II 1973	230.21[2]
	»	31 XII 1974	222.22
Rép. centrafricaine . . .	Fr. (CFA)[1]	31 XII 1965	246.85
	»	10 VIII 1969	277.71
	»	XII 1971	255.79
	»	II 1973	230.21[2]
	»	31 XII 1974	222.22
Congo	Fr. (CFA)[1]	31 XII 1965	246.85
	»	10 VIII 1969	277.71
	»	XII 1971	255.79
	»	II 1973	230.21[2]
	»	31 XII 1974	222.22
Côte-d'Ivoire	Fr. (CFA)[1]	31 XII 1965	246.85
	»	10 VIII 1969	277.71
	»	XII 1971	255.79
	»	II 1973	230.21[2]
	»	31 XII 1974	222.22
Egypt	Pounds	31 XII 1965	0.4348
	»	II 1973	0.3906
	»	31 XII 1974	0.3913
Gabon	Fr. (CFA)[2]	31 XII 1965	246.85
	»	10 VIII 1969	277.71
	»	XII 1971	255.79
	»	II 1973	230.21[2]
	»	31 XII 1974	222.22

Country / Pays / País	Currency / Monnaie / Moneda	Date / Date / Fecha	Exchange rate / Taux de change / Tipo de cambio
Ghana	Cedis[3]	19 VII 1965	0.8571
	» [4]	23 II 1967	0.7143
	»	8 VII 1967	1.0204
	»	XII 1971	1.8182
	»	7 II 1972	1.2821
	»	II 1973	1.1538
Guinée	Francs	31 XII 1965	246.85
	»	1 I 1972	227.36
	Syli[5]	2 X 1972	22.737
	»	II 1973	20.463
	»	31 XII 1974	20.650
Haute-Volta	Fr. (CFA)[1]	31 XII 1965	246.85
	»	10 VIII 1969	277.71
	»	XII 1971	255.79
	»	II 1973	230.21[2]
	»	31 XII 1974	222.22
Kenya	Shillings[6]	14 IX 1966	7.143
	»	VI 1973	6.9
	»	I 1974	7.143
Libyan Arab Republic . .	Pounds	31 XII 1965	0.3571
	»	XII 1971	0.3289
	»	II 1973	0.2961
Madagascar	Francs	31 XII 1965	246.85
	»	10 VIII 1969	277.71
	»	XII 1971	255.79
	»	II 1973	230.21[2]
	»	31 XII 1974	222.22
Malawi	Pounds	20 XI 1967	0.4167
	Kwacha[7]	15 II 1971	0.8333
	»	XII 1971	0.7675
	»	31 XII 1973	0.8475[8]
	»	31 XII 1974	0.8405
Mali	Francs	5 V 1967	493.71
	»	10 VIII 1969	555.42
	»	XII 1971	511.57
	»	II 1973	460.41
	»	31 XII 1974	444.45[2]

EXPLANATORY NOTES: See p. 807. NOTES EXPLICATIVES: Voir p. 808. NOTAS EXPLICATIVAS: Véase pág. 809.

(a) Par values, central rates, or official rates.

(a) Parités, taux des banques centrales ou cours officiels.

(a) Paridades, tipos de los bancos centrales o tipos oficiales.

[1] Franc of the " Communauté financiere africaine ". [2] Beginning 19 March 1973: the currency has been floating with the French franc. [3] New currency introduced on 19 July 1965: 1 cedi = five-twelfths of the old Ghanaian pound. [4] Beginning 23 Feb. 1967: 1 new cedi = 1.2 old cedis. [5] New currency introduced on 2 Oct. 1972: 1 syli = 10 old Guinean francs. [6] New currency introduced on 14 Sept. 1966: 1 shilling = 1 old East African shilling. [7] New currency introduced on 15 Feb. 1971: 2 Malawi kwacha = 1 old Malawi pound. [8] Beginning 23 June 1972: the currency has been floating with the pound sterling.

[1] Franc de la Communauté financière africaine. [2] A partir du 19 mars 1973 : la monnaie flotte avec le franc français. [3] Nouvelle monnaie introduite le 19 juillet 1965 : 1 cedi = cinq douzièmes de l'ancienne livre ghanéenne. [4] A partir du 23 fév. 1967 : 1 nouveau cedi = 1.2 ancien cedi. [5] Nouvelle monnaie introduite le 2 oct. 1972 : 1 syli = 10 anciens francs guinéens. [6] Nouvelle monnaie introduite le 14 sept. 1966 : 1 shilling = 1 ancien shilling est-africain. [7] Nouvelle monnaie introduite le 15 fév. 1971 : 2 kwacha du Malawi = 1 ancienne livre du Malawi. [8] A partir du 23 juin 1972 : la monnaie flotte avec la livre sterling.

[1] Franco de la « Communauté financiere africaine ». [2] A partir del 19 de marzo de 1973: la moneda fluctúa con el franco francés. [3] Nueva moneda adoptada el 19 de julio de 1965: 1 cedi = cinco dozavos de la antigua libra ghanesa. [4] A partir del 23 de febr. de 1967: 1 nuevo cedi = 1.2 antiguos cedis. [5] Nueva moneda adoptada el 2 de oct. de 1972: 1 syli = 10 antiguos francos guineos. [6] Nueva moneda adoptada el 14 de sept. de 1966: 1 chelín = 1 antiguo chelín de Africa Oriental. [7] Nueva moneda adoptada el 15 de febr. de 1971: 2 kwacha del Malawi = 1 antigua libra del Malawi. [8] A partir del 23 de junio de 1972: la moneda fluctúa con la libra esterlina.

28 B

28 Exchange rates
Cours des changes
Tipos de cambio

B Single exchange rates
Taux de change uniques
Tipos de cambio únicos

Units of national currency per US dollar *(a)*
Unités de la monnaie nationale par dollar des Etats-Unis (a)
Unidades de moneda nacional por dólar de Estados Unidos *(a)*

Country / Pays / País	Currency / Monnaie / Moneda	Date / Date / Fecha	Exchange rate / Taux de change / Tipo de cambio
Maroc	Dirhams	31 XII 1965	5.06
	»	XII 1971	4.66
	»	II 1973	4.19
	»	31 XII 1974	4.15
Mauritanie.	Fr. (CFA) [1]	31 XII 1965	246.85
	»	10 VIII 1969	277.71
	»	XII 1971	255.79
	Ouguiyas [2]	31 XII 1973	46.04 [3]
	»	31 XII 1974	43.30
Mauritius	Rupees	31 XII 1965	4.762
	»	18 XI 1967	5.556
	»	XII 1971	5.117
	»	31 XII 1973	5.739 [4]
	»	31 XII 1974	5.677
Mozambique	Escudos	31 XII 1965	28.75
	»	XII 1971	27.25
	»	II 1973	25.50
Niger	Fr. (CFA) [1]	31 XII 1965	246.85
	»	10 VIII 1969	277.71
	»	XII 1971	255.79
	»	II 1973	230.21 [3]
	»	31 XII 1974	222.22
Nigeria	Pounds	31 XII 1965	0.3571
	»	XII 1971	0.3289
	Nairas [5]	III 1973	0.6579
	»	31 XII 1974	0.6162 [6]
Réunion	Fr. (CFA) [1]	31 XII 1965	246.85
	»	10 VIII 1969	277.71
	»	XII 1971	255.79
	»	II 1973	230.21 [3]
	»	31 XII 1974	222.22
Sénégal	Fr. (CFA) [1]	31 XII 1965	246.85
	»	10 VIII 1969	277.71
	»	XII 1971	255.79
	»	II 1973	230.21 [3]
	»	31 XII 1974	222.22

Country / Pays / País	Currency / Monnaie / Moneda	Date / Date / Fecha	Exchange rate / Taux de change / Tipo de cambio
Sierra Leone	Leones [6]	31 XII 1965	0.7143
	»	22 XI 1967	0.8333
	»	XII 1971	0.7675 [4]
	»	31 XII 1974	0.8516
Somalia	Shillings	31 XII 1965	7.143
	»	XII 1971	6.579
	»	9 I 1972	6.925
	»	II 1973	6.233
	»	31 XII 1974	6.295
Sudan	Pounds	31 XII 1965	0.3482
Tanzania	Shillings [7]	14 VI 1966	7.143
	»	VII 1973	6.9
	»	I 1974	7.143
Tchad	Fr (CFA) [1]	31 XII 1965	246.85
	»	10 VIII 1969	277.71
	»	XII 1971	255.79
	»	II 1973	230.21 [3]
	»	31 XII 1974	222.22
Tunisie	Dinars	31 XII 1965	0.525
	»	XII 1971	0.484
	»	II 1973	0.435
	»	31 XII 1974	0.407
Uganda	Shillings [8]	15 VIII 1966	7.143
	»	VII 1973	6.9
	»	I 1974	7.143
Zaïre	Francs	9 XI 1965	180.00 [9]
	Zaïre [10]	23 VI 1967	0.50
Zambia	Kwacha [11]	16 I 1968	0.7143
	»	II 1973	0.643

EXPLANATORY NOTES: See p. 807. NOTES EXPLICATIVES: Voir p. 808. NOTAS EXPLICATIVAS: Véase pág. 809.

(a) Par values, central rates, or official rates.

(a) *Parités, taux des banques centrales ou cours officiels.*

(a) Paridades, tipos de los bancos centrales o tipos oficiales.

[1] Franc of the " Communauté financiere africaine ". [2] New currency introduced on 29 June 1973: 1 ouguiya = 5 old CFA francs. [3] Beginning 19 March 1973: the currency has been floating with the French franc. [4] Beginning 23 June 1972: the currency has been floating with the pound sterling. [5] New currency introduced on 1 Jan. 1973: 2 nairas = 1 old Nigerian pound. [6] Beginning 19 April 1974: the currency has been floating. [7] New currency introduced on 14 June 1966: 1 shilling = 1 old East African shilling. [8] New currency introduced on 15 Aug. 1966: 1 shilling = 1 old East African shilling. [9] Official selling rates. [10] New currency introduced on 23 June 1967: 1 zaire = 1,000 old Congolese francs. [11] New currency introduced on 16 Jan. 1968: 2 kwacha = 1 old Zambian pound.

[1] *Franc de la Communauté financière africaine.* [2] *Nouvelle monnaie introduite le 29 juin 1973 : 1 ouguiya = 5 anciens francs CFA.* [3] *A partir du 19 mars 1973 : la monnaie flotte avec le franc français.* [4] *A partir du 23 juin 1972 : la monnaie flotte avec la livre sterling.* [5] *Nouvelle monnaie introduite le 1er janv. 1973 : 2 naïras = 1 ancienne livre nigériane.* [6] *A partir du 19 avril 1974 : la monnaie flotte.* [7] *Nouvelle monnaie introduite le 14 juin 1966 : 1 shilling = 1 ancien shilling est-africain.* [8] *Nouvelle monnaie introduite le 15 août 1966 : 1 shilling = 1 ancien shilling est-africain.* [9] *Cours officiels de vente.* [10] *Nouvelle monnaie introduite le 23 juin 1967 : 1 zaïre = 1 000 anciens francs congolais.* [11] *Nouvelle monnaie introduite le 16 janv. 1968 : 2 kwacha = 1 ancienne livre zambienne.*

[1] Franco de la « Communauté financiere africaine ». [2] Nueva moneda adoptada el 29 de junio de 1973: 1 ouguiya = 5 antiguos francos CFA. [3] A partir del 19 de marzo de 1973: la moneda fluctúa con el franco francés. [4] A partir del 23 de junio de 1972: la moneda fluctúa con la libra esterlina. [5] Nueva moneda adoptada el 1.º de enero de 1973: 2 nairas = 1 antigua libra nigeriana. [6] A partir del 19 de abril de 1974: la moneda fluctúa. [7] Nueva moneda adoptada el 14 de junio de 1966: 1 chelín = 1 antiguo chelín del Africa Oriental. [8] Nueva moneda adoptada el 15 de agosto de 1966: 1 chelín = 1 antiguo chelín del Africa Oriental. [9] Tipos oficiales de venta. [10] Nueva moneda adoptada el 23 de junio de 1967: 1 zaire = 1 000 antiguos francos congoleños. [11] Nueva moneda adoptada el 16 de enero de 1968: 2 kwacha = 1 antigua libra zambiana.

28 Exchange rates / Cours des changes / Tipos de cambio — B Single exchange rates / Taux de change uniques / Tipos de cambio únicos

Units of national currency per US dollar [a]
Unités de la monnaie nationale par dollar des Etats-Unis [a]
Unidades de moneda nacional por dólar de Estados Unidos [a]

Country / Pays / País	Currency / Monnaie / Moneda	Date / Date / Fecha	Exchange rate / Taux de change / Tipo de cambio
AMERICA — AMÉRIQUE AMÉRICA			
Antilles néerlandaises . .	Guilders	31 XII 1965	1.886
	»	XII 1971	1.790
	»	31 XII 1974	1.786
Barbados	Dollars	6 X 1965	1.714
	»	22 XI 1967	2.000
	»	XII 1971	1.842
	»	31 XII 1973	2.066 [1]
	»	31 XII 1974	2.044
Belize	Dollars	31 XII 1965	1.429
	»	18 XI 1967	1.667
	»	XII 1971	1.535
	»	31 XII 1973	1.382 [1]
	»	31 XII 1974	1.361
República Dominicana . .	Pesos	31 XII 1965	1.00
El Salvador	Colones	31 XII 1965	2.50
Grenada	Dollars	6 X 1965	1.714
	»	18 XI 1967	2.000
	»	31 XII 1973	2.243 [1]
	»	31 XII 1974	2.219
Guatemala	Quetzales	31 XII 1965	1.00
Guyana	Dollars	15 XI 1965	1.714
	»	20 XI 1967	2.000
	»	31 XII 1973	2.243 [1]
	»	31 XII 1974	2.2190
Haïti	Gourdes	31 XII 1965	5.00
Honduras	Lempiras	31 XII 1965	2.00
Jamaica	Pounds	21 XI 1967	0.4167
	Dollars [2]	8 IX 1969	0.8333
	»	XII 1971	0.7675
	»	II 1973	0.9091
México	Pesos	31 XII 1965	12.49

Country / Pays / País	Currency / Monnaie / Moneda	Date / Date / Fecha	Exchange rate / Taux de change / Tipo de cambio
Panamá	Balboas	31 XII 1965	1.00
Surinam	Guilders	31 XII 1965	1.881
	»	31 XII 1971	1.695
	»	31 XII 1973	1.789
	»	31 XII 1974	1.785
Trinidad and Tobago . .	Dollars	10 II 1965	1.714
	»	23 XI 1967	2.000
	»	XII 1971	1.842
	»	31 XII 1973	2.066 [1]
	»	31 XII 1974	2.044
ASIA — ASIE ASIA			
Cyprus	Pounds	31 XII 1965	0.3571
	»	20 XI 1967	0.4167
	»	XII 1971	0.3838
	»	31 XII 1973	0.3610 [3]
	»	31 XII 1974	0.3576
Iran	Rials	31 XII 1965	75.75
	»	II 1973	68.17
	»	31 XII 1974	67.63
Iraq	Dinars	31 XII 1965	0.3571
	»	XII 1971	0.3289
	»	II 1973	0.2961
Israel	Pounds	31 XII 1965	3.00
	»	19 XI 1967	3.50
	»	XII 1971	4.20
	»	31 XII 1974	6.00
Laos	Kips	31 XII 1965	240.00
	»	IV 1972	600.00
Yemen People's Dem. Rep. of	Dinars	1 IV 1965	0.3571
	»	22 XI 1967	0.4167
	»	12 I 1972	0.3838
	»	II 1973	0.3454

EXPLANATORY NOTES: See p. 807.   NOTES EXPLICATIVES: Voir p. 808.   NOTAS EXPLICATIVAS: Véase pág. 809.

(a) Par values, central rates, or official rates.

(a) *Parités, taux des banques centrales ou cours officiels.*

(a) Paridades, tipos de los bancos centrales o tipos oficiales.

[1] Beginning 23 June 1972: the currency has been floating with the pound sterling. [2] New currency introduced on 8 Sep. 1969: 2 new Jamaican dollars = 1 old Jamaican pound. [3] Beginning 9 July 1973: the currency has been floating.

[1] *A partir du 23 juin 1972 : la monnaie flotte avec la livre sterling.* [2] *Nouvelle monnaie introduite le 8 sept. 1969 : 2 nouveaux dollars jamaïquains = 1 ancienne livre jamaïquaine.* [3] *A partir du 9 juillet 1973 : la monnaie flotte.*

[1] A partir del 23 de junio: la moneda fluctúa con la libra esterlina. [2] Nueva moneda adoptada el 8 de sept. de 1969: 2 nuevos dólares jamaicanos = 1 antigua libra jamaicana. [3] A partir del 9 de julio de 1973: la moneda fluctúa.

28 **Exchange rates**
Cours des changes
Tipos de cambio

B **Single exchange rates**
Taux de change uniques
Tipos de cambio únicos

Units of national currency per US dollar (a)
Unités de la monnaie nationale par dollar des Etats-Unis (a)
Unidades de moneda nacional por dólar de Estados Unidos (a)

Country / Pays / País	Currency / Monnaie / Moneda	Date / Date / Fecha	Exchange rate / Taux de change / Tipo de cambio
EUROPE — EUROPE EUROPA			
Gibraltar	Pounds	31 XII 1965	0.3571
	»	18 XI 1967	0.4167
	»	XII 1971	0.3838
	»	31 XII 1973	0.4305 [1]
	»	31 XII 1974	0.4258
Grèce	Drachmas	31 XII 1965	30.00
	»	31 XII 1973	29.70
	»	31 XII 1974	30.00
Ireland	Pounds	31 XII 1965	0.3571
	»	18 XI 1967	0.4167
	»	XII 1971	0.3838
	»	31 XII 1973	0.4305 [1]
	»	31 XII 1974	0.4263
Malta	Pounds	31 XII 1965	0.3571
	»	20 XI 1967	0.4167
	»	XII 1971	0.3744
	»	31 XII 1973	0.3867
	»	31 XII 1974	0.3745

Country / Pays / País	Currency / Monnaie / Moneda	Date / Date / Fecha	Exchange rate / Taux de change / Tipo de cambio
OCEANIA — OCÉANIE OCEANÍA			
Fiji	Pounds	26 XI 1967	0.4354
	Dollars [2]	13 I 1969	0.8708
	»	XII 1971	0.8021
	»	31 XII 1973	0.8092 [1]
	»	II 1974	0.8000
Nouvelle-Calédonie . . .	Fr. (CFP) [3]	31 XII 1965	89.76
	»	10 VIII 1969	100.98
	»	XII 1971	93.01
	»	II 1973	83.71
	»	31 XII 1974	80.81
Polynésie française . . .	Fr. (CFP) [3]	31 XII 1965	89.76
	»	10 VIII 1969	100.98
	»	XII 1971	93.01
	»	II 1973	83.71
	»	31 XII 1974	80.81

EXPLANATORY NOTES: See p. 807. NOTES EXPLICATIVES: Voir p. 808. NOTAS EXPLICATIVAS: Véase pág. 809.

(a) Par values, central rates, or official rates.

(a) Parités, taux des banques centrales ou cours officiels.

(a) Paridades, tipos de los bancos centrales o tipos oficiales.

[1] Beginning 23 June 1972: the currency has been floating with the pound sterling. [2] New currency introduced on 13 Jan. 1969: 2 new Fiji dollars = 1 old Fiji pound. [3] Franc of the " Communauté française du Pacifique ".

[1] A partir du 23 juin 1972 : la monnaie flotte avec la livre sterling. [2] Nouvelle monnaie introduite le 13 janv. 1969 : 2 nouveaux dollars fidjiens = 1 ancienne livre fidjienne. [3] Franc de la Communauté française du Pacifique.

[1] A partir del 23 de junio: la moneda fluctúa con la libra esterlina. [2] Nueva moneda adoptada el 13 de enero de 1969: 2 nuevos dólares de Fiji = 1 antigua libra de Fiji. [3] Franco de la « Communauté française du Pacifique ».

APPENDIX

ANNEXE

APENDICE

Classifications used in the "Year Book"
Classifications utilisées dans l'« Annuaire »
Clasificaciones empleadas en el « Anuario »

References and sources
Références et sources
Referencias y fuentes

International standard industrial classification of all economic activities (ISIC–1968)[1]

Major Division 1. — Agriculture, hunting, forestry and fishing:

11. Agriculture and hunting.
12. Forestry and logging.
13. Fishing.

Major Division 2. — Mining and quarrying:

21. Coal mining.
22. Crude petroleum and natural gas production.
23. Metal ore mining.
29. Other mining.

Major Division 3. — Manufacturing:

31. Manufacture of food, beverages and tobacco.

   311-12. Food manufacturing.
     313. Beverage industries.
     314. Tobacco manufactures.

32. Textile, wearing apparel and leather industries.

     321. Manufacture of textiles.
     322. Manufacture of wearing apparel, except footwear.
     323. Manufacture of leather and products of leather, leather substitutes and fur, except footwear and wearing apparel.
     324. Manufacture of footwear, except vulcanized or moulded rubber or plastic footwear.

33. Manufacture of wood and wood products, including furniture.

     331. Manufacture of wood and wood and cork products, except furniture.
     332. Manufacture of furniture and fixtures, except primarily of metal.

34. Manufacture of paper and paper products, printing and publishing.

     341. Manufacture of paper and paper products.
     342. Printing, publishing and allied industries.

35. Manufacture of chemicals and chemical, petroleum, coal, rubber and plastic products.

     351. Manufacture of industrial chemicals.
     352. Manufacture of other chemical products.
     353. Petroleum refineries.
     354. Manufacture of miscellaneous products of petroleum and coal.
     355. Manufacture of rubber products.
     356. Manufacture of plastic products not elsewhere classified.

36. Manufacture of non-metallic mineral products, except products of petroleum and coal.

     361. Manufacture of pottery, china and earthenware.
     362. Manufacture of glass and glass products.
     369. Manufacture of other non-metallic mineral products.

---

[1] For full details see United Nations: *Statistical Papers*, Series M, No. 4, rev. 2 (New York, 1968).

37. Basic metal industries.
    - 371. Iron and steel basic industries.
    - 372. Non-ferrous metal basic industries.

38. Manufacture of fabricated metal products, machinery and equipment.
    - 381. Manufacture of fabricated metal products, except machinery and equipment.
    - 382. Manufacture of machinery except electrical.
    - 383. Manufacture of electrical machinery apparatus, appliances and supplies.
    - 384. Manufacture of transport equipment.
    - 385. Manufacture of professional and scientific and measuring and controlling equipment not elsewhere classified, and of photographic and optical goods.

39. Other manufacturing industries.

Major Division 4. — Electricity, gas and water:

41. Electricity, gas and steam.
42. Water works and supply.

Major Division 5. — Construction:

50. Construction.

Major Division 6. — Wholesale and retail trade, restaurants and hotels:

61. Wholesale trade.
62. Retail trade.
63. Restaurants and hotels.

Major Division 7. — Transport, storage and communication:

71. Transport and storage.
72. Communication.

Major Division 8. — Financing, insurance, real estate and business services:

81. Financial institutions.
82. Insurance.
83. Real estate and business services.

Major Division 9. — Community, social and personal services:

91. Public administration and defence.
92. Sanitary and similar services.
93. Social and related community services.
94. Recreational and cultural services.
95. Personal and household services.
96. International and other extra-territorial bodies.

Major Division 0. — Activities not adequately defined:

0. Activities not adequately defined.

Classification internationale type, par industrie, de toutes les branches d'activité économique (CITI–1968)[1]

Branche 1. — Agriculture, chasse, sylviculture et pêche:

11. Agriculture et chasse.
12. Sylviculture et exploitation forestière.
13. Pêche.

Branche 2. — Industries extractives:

21. Extraction du charbon.
22. Production de pétrole brut et de gaz naturel.
23. Extraction des minerais métalliques.
29. Extraction d'autres minéraux.

Branche 3. — Industries manufacturières:

31 Fabrication de produits alimentaires, boissons et tabacs.

311-12. Industries alimentaires.
313. Fabrication des boissons.
314. Industrie du tabac.

32. Industries des textiles, de l'habillement et du cuir.

321. Industrie textile.
322. Fabrication d'articles d'habillement, à l'exclusion des chaussures.
323. Industrie du cuir, des articles en cuir et en succédanés du cuir, et de la fourrure, à l'exclusion des chaussures et des articles d'habillement.
324. Fabrication des chaussures, à l'exclusion des chaussures en caoutchouc vulcanisé ou moulé et des chaussures en matière plastique.

33. Industrie du bois et fabrication d'ouvrages en bois, y compris les meubles.

331. Industrie du bois et fabrication d'ouvrages en bois et en liège, à l'exclusion des meubles.
332. Fabrication de meubles et d'accessoires, à l'exclusion des meubles et accessoires faits principalement en métal.

34. Fabrication de papier et d'articles en papier; imprimerie et édition.
341. Fabrication de papier et d'articles en papier.
342. Imprimerie, édition et industries annexes.

35. Industrie chimique et fabrication de produits chimiques, de dérivés du pétrole et du charbon, et d'ouvrages en caoutchouc et en matière plastique.
351. Industrie chimique.
352. Fabrication d'autres produits chimiques.
353. Raffineries de pétrole.
354. Fabrication de divers dérivés du pétrole et du charbon.
355. Industrie du caoutchouc.
356. Fabrication d'ouvrages en matière plastique non classés ailleurs.

---

[1] Pour de plus amples détails, voir Nations Unies: *Etudes statistiques*, série M, nº 4, rév. 2 (New York, 1969).

36. Fabrication de produits minéraux non métalliques, à l'exclusion des dérivés du pétrole et du charbon.

    361. Fabrication des grès, porcelaines et faïences.
    362. Industrie du verre.
    369. Fabrication d'autres produits minéraux non métalliques.

37. Industrie métallurgique de base.

    371. Sidérurgie et première transformation de la fonte, du fer et de l'acier.
    372. Production et première transformation des métaux non ferreux.

38. Fabrication d'ouvrages en métaux, de machines et de matériel.

    381. Fabrication d'ouvrages en métaux, à l'exclusion des machines et du matériel.
    382. Construction de machines, à l'exclusion des machines électriques.
    383. Fabrication de machines, appareils et fournitures électriques.
    384. Construction de matériel de transport.
    385. Fabrication de matériel médico-chirurgical, d'instruments de précision, d'appareils de mesure et de contrôle, non classés ailleurs, de matériel photographique et d'instruments d'optique.

39. Autres industries manufacturières.

Branche 4. — Electricité, gaz et eau:

41. Electricité, gaz et vapeur.
42. Installations de distribution d'eau et distribution publique de l'eau.

Branche 5. — Bâtiment et travaux publics [1]:

50. Bâtiment et travaux publics.

Branche 6. — Commerce de gros et de détail; restaurants et hôtels:

61. Commerce de gros.
62. Commerce de détail.
63. Restaurants et hôtels.

Branche 7. — Transports, entrepôts et communications:

71. Transports et entrepôts.
72. Communications.

Branche 8. — Banque, assurances, affaires immobilières et services fournis aux entreprises:

81. Etablissements financiers.
82. Assurances.
83. Affaires immobilières et services fournis aux entreprises.

---

[1] Dans le but de faciliter la présentation des tableaux du présent *Annuaire*, les données relatives à cette branche figurent sous la dénomination « Construction ».

Classification internationale type, par industrie, de toutes les branches d'activité économique (CITI – 1968) *(fin)*

Branche 9. — Services fournis à la collectivité, services sociaux et services personnels:

91. Administration publique et défense nationale.
92. Services sanitaires et services analogues.
93. Services sociaux et services connexes fournis à la collectivité.
94. Services récréatifs et services culturels annexes.
95. Services fournis aux particuliers et aux ménages.
96. Organisations internationales et autres organismes extra-territoriaux.

Branche 0. — Activités mal désignées:

00. Activités mal désignées.

Clasificación industrial internacional uniforme de todas las actividades económicas (CIIU–1968)[1]

Gran división 1. — Agricultura, caza, silvicultura y pesca:

11. Agricultura y caza.
12. Silvicultura y extracción de madera.
13. Pesca.

Gran división 2. — Explotación de minas y canteras:

21. Explotación de minas de carbón.
22. Producción de petróleo crudo y gas natural.
23. Extracción de minerales metálicos.
29. Extracción de otros minerales.

Gran división 3. — Industrias manufactureras:

31. Productos alimenticios, bebidas y tabaco.

   311-12. Fabricación de productos alimenticios.
      313. Industrias de bebidas.
      314. Industria del tabaco.

32. Textiles, prendas de vestir e industrias del cuero.

      321. Fabricación de textiles.
      322. Fabricación de prendas de vestir, excepto calzado.
      323. Industria del cuero y productos de cuero y sucedáneos de cuero y pieles, excepto el calzado y otras prendas de vestir.
      324. Fabricación de calzado, excepto el de caucho vulcanizado o moldeado o de plástico.

33. Industria de la madera y productos de la madera, incluidos muebles.

      331. Industria de la madera y productos de madera y de corcho, excepto muebles.
      332. Fabricación de muebles y accesorios, excepto los que son principalmente metálicos.

34. Fabricación de papel y productos de papel; imprentas y editoriales.

      341. Fabricación de papel y productos de papel.
      342. Imprentas, editoriales e industrias conexas.

35. Fabricación de sustancias químicas y de productos químicos, derivados del petróleo y del carbón, de caucho y plásticos.

      351. Fabricación de sustancias químicas industriales.
      352. Fabricación de otros productos químicos.
      353. Refinerías de petróleo.
      354. Fabricación de productos diversos derivados del petróleo y del carbón.
      355. Fabricación de productos de caucho.
      356. Fabricación de productos plásticos, n.e.p.

---

[1] Para más amplios detalles, véase Naciones Unidas: *Informes estadísticos*, serie M, núm. 4, rev. 2 (Nueva York, 1969).

36. Fabricación de productos minerales no metálicos, exceptuando los derivados del petróleo y del carbón.

   361. Fabricación de objetos de barro, loza y porcelana.
   362. Fabricación de vidrio y productos de vidrio.
   369. Fabricación de otros productos minerales no metálicos.

37. Industrias metálicas básicas.

   371. Industrias básicas de hierro y acero.
   372. Industrias básicas de metales no ferrosos.

38. Fabricación de productos metálicos, maquinaria y equipo.

   381. Fabricación de productos metálicos, exceptuando maquinaria y equipo.
   382. Construcción de maquinaria, exceptuando la eléctrica.
   383. Construcción de maquinaria, aparatos, accesorios y suministros eléctricos.
   384. Construcción de material de transporte.
   385. Fabricación de equipo profesional y científico, instrumentos de medida y de control n.e.p., y de aparatos fotográficos e instrumentos de óptica.

39. Otras industrias manufactureras.

Gran división 4. — Electricidad, gas y agua:

41. Electricidad, gas y vapor.
42. Obras hidráulicas y suministro de agua.

Gran división 5. — Construcción:

50. Construcción.

Gran división 6. — Comercio al por mayor y al por menor y restaurantes y hoteles:

61. Comercio al por mayor.
62. Comercio al por menor.
63. Restaurantes y hoteles.

Gran división 7. — Transportes, almacenamiento y comunicaciones:

71. Transporte y almacenamiento.
72. Comunicaciones.

Gran división 8. — Establecimientos financieros, seguros, bienes inmuebles y servicios prestados a las empresas:

81. Establecimientos financieros.
82. Seguros.
83. Bienes inmuebles y servicios prestados a las empresas.

Clasificación industrial internacional uniforme de todas las actividades económicas (CIIU – 1968) *(fin)*

Gran división 9. — Servicios comunales, sociales y personales:

91.   Administración pública y defensa.
92.   Servicios de saneamiento y similares.
93.   Servicios sociales y otros servicios comunales conexos.
94.   Servicios de diversión y esparcimiento y servicios culturales.
95.   Servicios personales y de los hogares.
96.   Organizaciones internacionales y otros organismos extraterritoriales.

Gran división 0. — Actividades no bien especificadas:

00.   Actividades no bien especificadas.

International standard classification of occupations (ISCO-1968)[1]

Major Group 0/1. — Professional, technical and related workers:

0-1. Physical scientists and related technicians.
0-2/3. Architects, engineers and related technicians.
0-4. Aircraft and ships' officers.
0-5. Life scientists and related technicians.
0-6/7. Medical, dental, veterinary and related workers.
0-8. Statisticians, mathematicians, systems analysts and related technicians.
0-9. Economists.
1-1. Accountants.
1-2. Jurists.
1-3. Teachers.
1-4. Workers in religion.
1-5. Authors, journalists and related writers.
1-6. Sculptors, painters, photographers and related creative artists.
1-7. Composers and performing artists.
1-8. Athletes, sportsmen and related workers.
1-9. Professional, technical and related workers not elsewhere classified.

Major Group 2. — Administrative and managerial workers:

2-0. Legislative officials and government administrators.
2-1. Managers.

Major Group 3. — Clerical and related workers:

3-0. Clerical supervisors.
3-1. Government executive officials.
3-2. Stenographers, typists and card- and tape-punching machine operators.
3-3. Bookkeepers, cashiers and related workers.
3-4. Computing machine operators.
3-5. Transport and communications supervisors.
3-6. Transport conductors.
3-7. Mail distribution clerks.
3-8. Telephone and telegraph operators.
3-9. Clerical related workers not elsewhere classified.

Major Group 4. — Sales workers:

4-0. Managers (wholesale and retail trade).
4-1. Working proprietors (wholesale and retail trade).
4-2. Sales supervisors and buyers.
4-3. Technical salesmen, commercial travellers and manufacturers' agents.
4-4. Insurance, real estate, securities and business services salesman and auctioneers.
4-5. Salesmen, shop assistants and related workers.
4-9. Sales workers not elsewhere classified.

---

[1] Major and minor groups only; for full details see ILO: *International Standard Classification of Occupations, revised edition 1968* (Geneva, 1969).

Major Group 5. — Service workers:

5-0. Managers (catering and lodging services).
5-1. Working proprietors (catering and lodging services).
5-2. Housekeeping and related service supervisors.
5-3. Cooks, waiters, bartenders and related workers.
5-4. Maids and related housekeeping service workers not elsewhere classified.
5-5. Building caretakers, charworkers, cleaners and related workers.
5-6. Launderers, dry-cleaners and pressers.
5-7. Hairdressers, barbers, beauticians and related workers.
5-8. Protective service workers.
5-9. Service workers not elsewhere classified.

Major Group 6. — Agriculture, animal husbandry and forestry workers, fishermen and hunters:

6-0. Farm managers and supervisors.
6-1. Farmers.
6-2. Agriculture and animal husbandry workers.
6-3. Forestry workers.
6-4. Fishermen, hunters and related workers.

Major Group 7/8/9. — Production and related workers, transport equipment operators and labourers:

7-0. Production supervisors and general foremen.
7-1. Miners, quarrymen, well drillers and related workers.
7-2. Metal processers.
7-3. Wood preparation workers and paper makers.
7-4. Chemical processers and related workers.
7-5. Spinners, weavers, knitters, dyers and related workers.
7-6. Tanners, fellmongers and pelt dressers.
7-7. Food and beverage processers.
7-8. Tobacco preparers and tobacco product makers.
7-9. Tailors, dressmakers, sewers, upholsterers and related workers.

8-0. Shoemakers and leather goods makers.
8-1. Cabinetmakers and related woodworkers.
8-2. Stone cutters and carvers.
8-3. Blacksmiths, toolmakers and machine-tool operators.
8-4. Machinery fitters, machine assemblers and precision instrument makers (except electrical).
8-5. Electrical fitters and related electrical and electronics workers.
8-6. Broadcasting station and sound equipment operators and cinema projectionists.
8-7. Plumbers, welders, sheet metal and structural metal preparers and erectors.
8-8. Jewellery and precious metal workers.
8-9. Glass formers, potters and related workers.

9-0. Rubber and plastics product makers.
9-1. Paper and paperboard products makers.
9-2. Printers and related workers.

9-3.   Painters.
9-4.   Production and related workers not elsewhere classified.
9-5.   Bricklayers, carpenters and other construction workers.
9-6.   Stationary engine and related equipment operators.
9-7.   Material-handling and related equipment operators, dockers and freight handlers.
9-8.   Transport equipment operators.
9-9.   Labourers not elsewhere classified.

Major Group X. — Workers not classifiable by occupation:

X-1.   New workers seeking employment.
X-2.   Workers reporting occupations unidentifiable or inadequately described.
X-3.   Workers not reporting any occupation.

Armed Forces. — Members of the armed forces.

Classification internationale type des professions (CITP–1968)[1]

Grand groupe 0/1. — Personnel des professions scientifiques, techniques, libérales et assimilées:

0-1. Spécialistes des sciences physico-chimiques et techniciens assimilés.
0-2/3. Architectes, ingénieurs et techniciens assimilés.
0-4. Pilotes, officiers de pont et officiers mécaniciens (marine et aviation).
0-5. Biologistes, agronomes et techniciens assimilés.
0-6/7. Médecins, dentistes, vétérinaires et travailleurs assimilés.
0-8. Statisticiens, mathématiciens, analystes de systèmes et techniciens assimilés.
0-9. Economistes.
1-1. Comptables.
1-2. Juristes.
1-3. Personnel enseignant.
1-4. Membres du clergé et assimilés.
1-5. Auteurs, journalistes et écrivains assimilés.
1-6. Sculpteurs, peintres, photographes et artistes créateurs assimilés.
1-7. Musiciens, acteurs, danseurs et artistes assimilés.
1-8. Athlètes, sportifs et assimilés.
1-9. Personnel des professions scientifiques, techniques, libérales et assimilés non classé ailleurs.

Grand groupe 2. — Directeurs et cadres administratifs supérieurs:

2-0. Membres des corps législatifs et cadres supérieurs de l'administration publique.
2-1. Directeurs et cadres dirigeants.

Grand groupe 3. — Personnel administratif et travailleurs assimilés:

3-0. Chefs de groupe d'employés de bureau.
3-1. Agents administratifs (administration publique).
3-2. Sténographes dactylographes et opérateurs sur machines perforatrices de cartes et de rubans.
3-3. Employés de comptabilité, caissiers et travailleurs assimilés.
3-4. Opérateurs sur machines à traiter l'information.
3-5. Chefs de services de transports et de communications.
3-6. Chefs de train et receveurs.
3-7. Facteurs et messagers.
3-8. Opérateurs des téléphones et télégraphes.
3-9. Personnel administratif et travailleurs assimilés non classés ailleurs.

Grand groupe 4. — Personnel commercial et vendeurs:

4-0. Directeurs (commerces de gros et de détail).
4-1. Propriétaires-gérants de commerces de gros et de détail.
4-2. Chefs des ventes et acheteurs.
4-3. Agents commerciaux techniciens et voyageurs de commerce.
4-4. Agents d'assurances, agents immobiliers, courriers en valeurs, agents de vente de services aux entreprises et vendeurs aux enchères.
4-5. Commis vendeurs, employés de commerce et travailleurs assimilés.
4-9. Personnel commercial et vendeurs non classés ailleurs.

---

[1] Grands et sous-groupes seulement; pour de plus amples détails, voir BIT: *Classification internationale type des professions, édition révisée, 1968* (Genève, 1969).

Grand groupe 5. — Travailleurs spécialisés dans les services:

5-0. Directeurs d'hôtels, de cafés ou de restaurants.
5-1. Propriétaires-gérants d'hôtels, de cafés ou de restaurants.
5-2. Chefs de groupe d'employés de maison et travailleurs assimilés.
5-3. Cuisiniers, serveurs, barmen et travailleurs assimilés.
5-4. Employés de maison et travailleurs assimilés non classés ailleurs.
5-5. Gardiens d'immeubles, nettoyeurs et travailleurs assimilés.
5-6. Blanchisseurs, dégraisseurs et presseurs.
5-7. Coiffeurs, spécialistes des soins de beauté et travailleurs assimilés.
5-8. Personnel des services de protection et de sécurité.
5-9. Travailleurs spécialisés dans les services non classés ailleurs.

Grand groupe 6. — Agriculteurs, éleveurs, forestiers, pêcheurs et chasseurs:

6-0. Directeurs et chefs d'exploitations agricoles.
6-1. Exploitants agricoles.
6-2. Travailleurs agricoles.
6-3. Travailleurs forestiers.
6-4. Pêcheurs, chasseurs et travailleurs assimilés.

Grand groupe 7/8/9. — Ouvriers et manœuvres non agricoles et conducteurs d'engins de transport:

7-0. Agents de maîtrise et assimilés.
7-1. Mineurs, carriers, foreurs de puits et travailleurs assimilés.
7-2. Ouvriers de la production et du traitement des métaux.
7-3. Ouvriers de la première préparation des bois et de la fabrication du papier.
7-4. Conducteurs de fours et d'appareils chimiques.
7-5. Ouvriers du textile.
7-6. Tanneurs, peaussiers, mégissiers et ouvriers de la pelleterie.
7-7. Ouvriers de l'alimentation et des boissons.
7-8. Ouvriers des tabacs.
7-9. Tailleurs, couturiers, couseurs, tapissiers et ouvriers assimilés.

8-0. Bottiers, ouvriers de la chaussure et du cuir.
8-1. Ebénistes, menuisiers et travailleurs assimilés.
8-2. Tailleurs et graveurs de pierres.
8-3. Ouvriers du façonnage et de l'usinage des métaux.
8-4. Ajusteurs-monteurs, installateurs de machines et mécaniciens de précision (électriciens exceptés).
8-5. Electriciens, électroniciens et travailleurs assimilés.
8-6. Opérateurs de stations d'émissions de radio et de télévision, opérateurs d'appareils de sonorisation et projectionnistes de cinéma.
8-7. Plombiers soudeurs, tôliers-chaudronniers, monteurs de charpentes et de structures métalliques.
8-8. Joailliers et orfèvres.
8-9. Verriers, potiers et travailleurs assimilés.

9-0. Ouvriers de la fabrication d'articles en caoutchouc et en matières plastiques.
9-1. Confectionneurs d'articles en papier et en carton.
9-2. Compositeurs typographes et travailleurs assimilés.
9-3. Peintres.
9-4. Ouvriers à la production et assimilés non classés ailleurs.
9-5. Maçons, charpentiers et autres travailleurs de la construction.
9-6. Conducteurs de machines et d'installations fixes.
9-7. Conducteurs d'engins de manutention et de terrassement, dockers et manutentionnaires.
9-8. Conducteurs d'engins de transport.
9-9. Manœuvres non classés ailleurs.

Grand groupe X. — Travailleurs ne pouvant être classés selon la profession:

X-1. Personnes en quête de leur premier emploi.
X-2. Travailleurs ayant fait au sujet de leur profession une déclaration imprécise ou insuffisante.
X-3. Travailleurs n'ayant déclaré aucune profession.

Forces armées: Membres des forces armées.

Clasificación internacional uniforme de ocupaciones (CIUO–1968) [1]

Gran grupo 0/1. — Profesionales, técnicos y trabajadores asimilados:

0-1. Especialistas en ciencias físico-químicas y técnicos asimilados.
0-2/3. Arquitectos, ingenieros y técnicos asimilados.
0-4. Pilotos y oficiales de cubierta y oficiales maquinistas (aviación y marina).
0-5. Biólogos, agrónomos y técnicos asimilados.
0-6/7. Médicos, odontólogos, veterinarios y trabajadores asimilados.
0-8. Estadígrafos, matemáticos, analistas de sistemas y técnicos asimilados.
0-9. Economistas.
1-1. Contadores.
1-2. Juristas.
1-3. Profesores.
1-4. Miembros del clero y asimilados.
1-5. Autores, periodistas y escritores asimilados.
1-6. Escultores, pintores, fotógrafos y artistas asimilados.
1-7. Músicos, artistas, empresarios y productores de espectáculos.
1-8. Atletas, deportistas y trabajadores asimilados.
1-9. Profesionales, técnicos y trabajadores asimilados no clasificados bajo otros epígrafes.

Gran grupo 2. — Directores y funcionarios públicos superiores:

2-0. Miembros de los cuerpos legislativos y personal directivo de la administración pública.
2-1. Directores y personal directivo.

Gran grupo 3. — Personal administrativo y trabajadores asimilados:

3-0. Jefes de empleados de oficinas.
3-1. Agentes administrativos (administración pública).
3-2. Taquígrafos, mecanógrafos y operadores de máquinas perforadoras de tarjetas y cintas.
3-3. Empleados de contabilidad, cajeros y trabajadores asimilados.
3-4. Operadores de máquinas para cálculos contables y estadísticos.
3-5. Jefes de servicios de transportes y de comunicaciones.
3-6. Jefes de tren, controladores de coches-cama y cobradores.
3-7. Carteros y mensajeros.
3-8. Telefonistas y telegrafistas.
3-9. Personal administrativo y trabajadores asimilados no clasificados bajo otros epígrafes.

Gran grupo 4. — Comerciantes y vendedores:

4-0. Directores (comercio al por mayor y al por menor).
4-1. Comerciantes propietarios (comercio al por mayor y al por menor).
4-2. Jefes de ventas y compradores.
4-3. Agentes técnicos de ventas, viajantes de comercio y representantes de fábrica.
4-4. Agentes de seguros, agentes inmobiliarios, agentes de cambio y bolsa, agentes de venta de servicios a las empresas y subastadores.
4-5. Vendedores, empleados de comercio y trabajadores asimilados.
4-9. Comerciantes y vendedores no clasificados bajo otros epígrafes.

---

[1] Grandes grupos y subgrupos solamente; para más amplios detalles, véase OIT: *Clasificación internacional uniforme de ocupaciones, edición revisada, 1968* (Ginebra, 1970).

Gran grupo 5. — Trabajadores de los servicios:

5-0. Directores (servicios de hostelería, bares y similares).
5-1. Gerentes propietarios (servicios de hostelería, bares y similares).
5-2. Jefes de personal de servidumbre.
5-3. Cocineros, camareros, bármanes y trabajadores asimilados.
5-4. Personal de servidumbre no clasificado bajo otros epígrafes.
5-5. Guardianes de edificios, personal de limpieza y trabajadores asimilados.
5-6. Lavanderos, limpiadores en seco y planchadores.
5-7. Peluqueros, especialistas en tratamientos de belleza y trabajadores asimilados.
5-8. Personal de los servicios de protección y de seguridad.
5-9. Trabajadores de los servicios no clasificados bajo otros epígrafes.

Gran grupo 6. — Trabajadores agrícolas y forestales, pescadores y cazadores:

6-0. Directores y jefes de explotaciones agrícolas.
6-1. Explotadores agrícolas.
6-2. Obreros agrícolas.
6-3. Trabajadores forestales.
6-4. Pescadores, cazadores y trabajadores asimilados.

Gran grupo 7/8/9. — Obreros no agrícolas, conductores de máquinas y vehículos de transporte y trabajadores asimilados:

7-0. Contramaestres y capataces mayores.
7-1. Mineros, canteros, sondistas y trabajadores asimilados.
7-2. Obreros metalúrgicos.
7-3. Obreros del tratamiento de la madera y de la fabricación de papel.
7-4. Obreros de los tratamientos químicos y trabajadores asimilados.
7-5. Hilanderos, tejedores, tintoreros y trabajadores asimilados.
7-6. Obreros de la preparación, curtido y tratamiento de pieles.
7-7. Obreros de la preparación de alimentos y bebidas.
7-8. Obreros del tabaco.
7-9. Sastres, modistos, peleteros, tapiceros y trabajadores asimilados.

8-0. Zapateros y guarnicioneros.
8-1. Ebanistas, operadores de máquinas de labrar madera y trabajadores asimilados.
8-2. Labrantes y adornistas.
8-3. Obreros de la labra de metales.
8-4. Ajustadores-montadores e instaladores de maquinaria e instrumentos de precisión, relojeros y mecánicos (excepto electricistas).
8-5. Electricistas, electronicistas y trabajadores asimilados.
8-6. Operadores de estaciones emisoras de radio y televisión y de equipos de sonorización y de proyecciones cinematográficas.
8-7. Fontaneros, soldadores, chapistas, caldereros y preparadores y montadores de estructuras metálicas.
8-8. Joyeros y plateros.
8-9. Vidrieros, ceramistas y trabajadores asimilados.

9-0. Obreros de la fabricación de productos de caucho y plástico.

9-1. Confeccionadores de productos de papel y cartón.

9-2. Obreros de las artes gráficas.

9-3. Pintores.

9-4. Obreros manufactureros y trabajadores asimilados no clasificados bajo otros epígrafes.

9-5. Obreros de la construcción.

9-6. Operadores de máquinas fijas y de instalaciones similares.

9-7. Obreros de la manipulación de mercancías y materiales y de movimiento de tierras.

9-8. Conductores de vehículos de transporte.

9-9. Peones no clasificados bajo otros epígrafes.

Gran grupo X. — Trabajadores que no pueden ser clasificados según la ocupación:

X-1. Personas en busca de su primer empleo.

X-2. Trabajadores que han declarado ocupaciones no identificables o insuficientemente descritas.

X-3. Trabajadores que no han declarado ninguna ocupación.

Fuerzas armadas. — Miembros de las fuerzas armadas.

References and sources
Références et sources
Referencias y fuentes

The references given in **Part A** are a selected list of International Labour Office publications on methodology and practice in the field of labour statistics.

Part B lists the *principal* sources of current national statistics on labour topics, generally those cited by governments forwarding data for the *Year Book of Labour Statistics*. They often contain more detailed statistics than the Office has been able to use in the *Year Book*. Readers making investigations covering an extended period should also refer to previous issues of the *Year Book* and the sources listed therein.

Countries are grouped by continents in the alphabetical order, as presented in page xix. So far as possible the title of each publication is given in the respective national language. Where a publication contains translations into English (or French) the official English (or French) title is given in parentheses.

Les références présentées dans la **partie A** fournissent une liste sélectionnée de publications du Bureau international du Travail traitant des pratiques et des méthodes utilisées en matière de statistiques du travail.

La **partie B** contient les sources *principales* dans lesquelles sont publiées les statistiques nationales courantes sur les divers aspects du travail; en général, ces sources sont celles qui ont été transmises par les gouvernements en annexe aux données fournies pour l'*Annuaire des statistiques du travail*. On y trouvera souvent des statistiques plus détaillées que celles que le Bureau a pu utiliser dans l'*Annuaire*. Il est recommandé aux lecteurs qui se livrent à des recherches portant sur une période assez longue de consulter les éditions précédentes de l'*Annuaire* et les sources qui y sont indiquées.

Les pays sont groupés par continents, suivant l'ordre alphabétique tel qu'il est présenté à la page xix. Dans la mesure du possible, le titre de chaque publication est donné dans la langue nationale respective. Lorsque la publication contient des traductions en français (ou en anglais), le titre officiel français (ou anglais) est indiqué entre parenthèses.

Las referencias dadas en la **parte A** comprenden una selección de publicaciones de la Oficina Internacional del Trabajo sobre la metodología y la práctica en materia de estadísticas del trabajo.

La **parte B** contiene las *principales* fuentes de las estadísticas nacionales de la actualidad sobre temas del trabajo; en general, aquellas que los propios gobiernos citan al proporcionar los datos para el *Anuario de Estadísticas del Trabajo*. A menudo contienen estadísticas más detalladas que las que la Oficina ha podido usar en el *Anuario*. Los lectores que deseen practicar investigaciones que abarquen un período más extenso deben consultar, además, las ediciones anteriores del *Anuario* y las fuentes allí indicadas.

Los países se agrupan por continentes, en el orden alfabético tal como se presenta en la página xx. En la medida de lo posible, el título de cada publicación aparece en el idioma nacional respectivo. Cuando una publicación contiene traducciones al francés (o al inglés), su título oficial en francés (o en inglés) se indica entre paréntesis.

References and sources Références et sources Referencias y fuentes	A	References Références Referencias

Subject — *Sujet* — Sujeto	Publications — *Publications* — Publicaciones
General **Général** **General**	*International Recommendations on Labour Statistics* (Geneva, 1976) *Recommandations internationales sur les statistiques du travail* (Genève, 1975) *Recomendaciones internacionales sobre estadísticas del trabajo* (Ginebra, 1975) *International Standard Classification of Occupations (Revised 1968)* (Geneva, 1969) *Classification internationale type des professions (révisée 1968)* (Genève, 1969) *Clasificación internacional uniforme de ocupaciones (revisada, 1968)* (Ginebra, 1970) *Revision of the International Standard Classification of Occupations*, Eleventh International Conference of Labour Statisticians, Report III (Geneva, 1966) *Révision de la Classification internationale type des professions*, onzième Conférence internationale des statisticiens du travail, rapport III (Genève, 1966) *Revisión de la Clasificación internacional uniforme de ocupaciones*, undécima Conferencia Internacional de Estadígrafos del Trabajo, Informe III (Ginebra, 1966)
Employment and unemployment **Emploi et chômage** **Empleo y desempleo**	*Employment, Unemployment and Labour Force Statistics, A Study of Methods*, Studies and Reports, New Series, No. 7, Part 1 (Geneva, 1948) *Statistiques de l'emploi, du chômage et de la main-d'œuvre, Etude méthodologique*, Etudes et documents, nouvelle série, n° 7, partie 1 (Genève, 1948) *Estadísticas del empleo, del desempleo y de la mano de obra, Estudio metodológico*, Estudios y documentos, nueva serie, núm. 7, parte 1 (Ginebra, 1948) *Employment and Unemployment Statistics*, Eighth International Conference of Labour Statisticians, Report IV (Geneva, 1954) *Statistiques de l'emploi et du chômage*, huitième Conférence internationale des statisticiens du travail, rapport IV (Genève, 1954) *Estadísticas del empleo y del desempleo*, octava Conferencia Internacional de Estadígrafos del Trabajo, Informe IV (Ginebra, 1954) *Measurement of Underemployment*, Ninth International Conference of Labour Statisticians, Report IV (Geneva, 1957) *Mesure du sous-emploi*, neuvième Conférence internationale des statisticiens du travail, rapport IV (Genève, 1957) *Medición del subempleo*, novena Conferencia Internacional de Estadígrafos del Trabajo, Informe IV (Ginebra, 1957) *Measurement of Underemployment, Concepts and Methods*, Eleventh International Conference of Labour Statisticians, Report IV (Geneva, 1966) *Mesure du sous-emploi, concepts et méthodes*, onzième Conférence internationale des statisticiens du travail, rapport IV (Genève, 1966) *Medición del subempleo, conceptos y métodos*, undécima Conferencia Internacional de Estadígrafos del Trabajo, Informe IV (Ginebra, 1966) *Labour Force Projections, 1965-1985* (Geneva, 1971) Part I: Asia—Part II: Africa—Part III: Latin America—Part IV: Europe, Northern America, Oceania and USSR—Part V: World Summary—Part VI: Methodological Supplement *Projections de la main-d'œuvre, 1965-1985* (Genève, 1971) Partie I: Asie — Partie II: Afrique — Partie III: Amérique latine — Partie IV: Europe, Amérique du Nord, Océanie et URSS — Partie V: Monde (résumé) — Partie VI: Supplément méthodologique *Proyecciones de la fuerza de trabajo, 1965-1985* (Ginebra, 1971) Parte I: Asia — Parte II: Africa — Parte III: América latina — Parte IV: Europa, América del Norte, Oceanía y URSS — Parte V: Mundo (resumen) — Parte VI: Suplemento metodológico

REFERENCES

References and sources
Références et sources
Referencias y fuentes

A
References
Références
Referencias

Subject — *Sujet* — Sujeto	Publications — *Publications* — Publicaciones
Employment and unemployment (concl.) **Emploi et chomage** (fin) **Empleo y desempleo** (fin)	*Technical Guide 1976*, Descriptions of general series published in the *Bulletin of Labour Statistics*, Vol. II, Employment—Unemployment—Hours of work—Wages (Geneva, 1976) *Guide technique 1976*, descriptions des séries générales publiées dans le *Bulletin des statistiques du travail*, vol. II, Emploi — Chômage — Durée du travail — Salaires (Genève, 1976) *Guía Técnica 1976*, descripciones de las series generales publicadas en el *Boletín de Estadísticas del Trabajo*, vol. II, Empleo — Desempleo — Horas de trabajo — Salarios (Ginebra, 1976)
Hours of work **Durée du travail** **Horas de trabajo**	*Statistics of Hours of Work*, Tenth International Conference of Labour Statisticians, Report III (Geneva, 1962) *Statistiques de la durée du travail*, dixième Conférence internationale des statisticiens du travail, rapport III (Genève, 1962) *Estadísticas de la duración del trabajo*, décima Conferencia Internacional de Estadígrafos del Trabajo, Informe III (Ginebra, 1962) *Technical Guide 1976*, Descriptions of general series published in the *Bulletin of Labour Statistics*, Vol. II, Employment—Unemployment—Hours of work—Wages (Geneva, 1976) *Guide technique 1976*, descriptions des séries générales publiées dans le *Bulletin des statistiques du travail*, vol. II, Emploi — Chômage — Durée du travail — Salaires (Genève, 1976) *Guía Técnica 1976*, descripciones de las series generales publicadas en el *Boletín de Estadísticas del Trabajo*, vol. II, Empleo — Desempleo — Horas de trabajo — Salarios (Ginebra, 1976)
Labour productivity **Productivité du travail** **Productividad del trabajo**	*Methods of Statistics of Labour Productivity*, Studies and Reports, New Series, No. 18 (Geneva, 1951) *Méthodes d'établissement des statistiques de la productivité du travail*, Etudes et documents, nouvelle série, nº 18 (Genève, 1951) *Métodos para las estadísticas de la productividad del trabajo*, Estudios y documentos, nueva serie, núm. 18 (Ginebra, 1951) *International Productivity Comparisons: A brief survey of some methodological and statistical considerations.* Conf.Eur.Stats/WG.21/2 (Geneva, 1964) *Comparaisons internationales de la productivité : Etude sommaire de quelques aspects méthodologiques et statistiques.* Conf.Eur.Stats/WG.21/2 (Genève, 1964) *Measuring Labour Productivity*, Studies and Reports, New Series, No. 75 (Geneva, 1969) *La mesure de la productivité du travail*, Etudes et documents, nouvelle série, nº 75 (Genève, 1969)
Wages **Salaires** **Salarios**	*Wages and Payroll Statistics*, Studies and Reports, New Series, No. 16 (Geneva, 1949) *Statistiques des bordereaux des salaires et des gains*, Etudes et documents, nouvelle série, nº 16 (Genève, 1949) *Estadísticas de nóminas de salarios y de ganancias*, Estudios y documentos, nueva serie, núm. 16 (Ginebra, 1949) *International Comparisons of Real Wages*, Studies and Reports, New Series, No. 45 (Geneva, 1956) *Les comparaisons internationales des salaires réels*, Etudes et documents, nouvelle série, nº 45 (Genève, 1956) *Statistics of Labour Cost*, Eleventh International Conference of Labour Statisticians, Report II (Geneva, 1966) *Statistiques du coût de la main-d'œuvre*, onzième Conférence internationale des statisticiens du travail, rapport II (Genève, 1966) *Estadísticas del costo de la mano de obra*, undécima Conferencia Internacional de Estadígrafos del Trabajo, Informe II (Ginebra, 1966)

References and sources
Références et sources
Referencias y fuentes

A **References**
Références
Referencias

Subject — *Sujet* — Sujeto	Publications — *Publications* — Publicaciones
Wages (concl.) **Salaires** (fin) **Salarios** (fin)	*Statistics of Wages and Employee Income*, Twelth International Conference of Labour Statisticians, Report II (Geneva, 1973) *Statistiques des salaires et du revenu salarial*, douzième Conférence internationale des statisticiens du travail, rapport II (Genève, 1973) *Estadísticas de salarios e ingresos de los trabajadores*, duodécima Conferencia Internacional de Estadígrafos del Trabajo, Informe II (Ginebra, 1973) *Technical Guide 1976*, Descriptions of general series published in the *Bulletin of Labour Statistics*, Vol. II, Employment—Unemployment—Hours of work—Wages (Geneva, 1976) *Guide technique 1976*, descriptions des séries générales publiées dans le *Bulletin des statistiques du travail*, vol. II, Emploi — Chômage — Durée du travail — Salaires (Genève, 1976) *Guía Técnica 1976*, descripciones de las series generales publicadas en el *Boletín de Estadísticas del Trabajo*, vol. II, Empleo — Desempleo — Horas de trabajo — Salarios (Ginebra, 1976)
Consumer prices **Prix à la consommation** **Precios del consumo**	*A Contribution to the Study of International Comparisons of Cost of Living*, Studies and Reports, Series N, No. 17 (Geneva, 1932) *Contribution à l'étude de la comparaison internationale du coût de la vie*, Etudes et documents, série N, nº 17 (Genève, 1932) *International Comparisons of Cost of Living*, Studies and Reports, Series N, No. 20 (Geneva, 1934) *La comparaison internationale du coût de la vie*, Etudes et documents, série N, nº 20 (Genève, 1934) *Cost-of-Living Statistics*, Studies and Reports, New Series, No. 7, Part 2 (Geneva, 1948) *Statistiques du coût de la vie*, Etudes et documents, nouvelle série, nº 7, partie 2 (Genève, 1948) *Estadísticas del costo de la vida*, Estudios y documentos, nueva serie, núm. 7, parte 2 (Ginebra, 1948) *Computation of Consumer Price Indices (Special Problems)*, Tenth International Conference of Labour Statisticians, Report IV (Geneva, 1970) *Calcul des indices des prix à la consommation (Problèmes particuliers)*, dixième Conférence internationale des statisticiens du travail, rapport IV (Genève, 1970) *Cálculo de los índices de los precios del consumo (Problemas especiales)*, décima Conferencia Internacional de Estadígrafos del Trabajo, Informe IV (Ginebra, 1970) *Technical Guide 1976*, Descriptions of series published in the *Bulletin of Labour Statistics*, Vol. I, Consumer Prices (Geneva, 1976) *Guide technique 1976*, descriptions des séries publiées dans le *Bulletin des statistiques du travail*, vol. I, Prix à la consommation (Genève, 1976) *Guía Técnica 1976*, descripciones de las series publicadas en el *Boletín de Estadísticas del Trabajo*, vol. I, Precios del consumo (Ginebra, 1976)
Household budgets **Budgets de ménage** **Presupuestos del hogar**	*Methods of Family Living Studies*, Studies and Reports, Series N, No. 23 (Geneva, 1940) *Méthodes d'enquête sur les conditions de vie des familles*, Etudes et documents, série N, nº 23 (Genève, 1941) *Métodos de encuesta sobre las condiciones de vida de las familias*, Estudios y documentos, serie N, núm. 23 (Montreal, 1942) *Methods of Family Living Studies*, Studies and Reports, New Series, No. 17 (Geneva, 1949) *Méthodes d'enquête sur les conditions de vie des familles*, Etudes et documents, nouvelle série, nº 17 (Genève, 1949) *Métodos de encuesta sobre las condiciones de vida de las familias*, Estudios y documentos, nueva serie, núm. 17 (Ginebra, 1949)

References and sources
Références et sources
Referencias y fuentes

A

References
Références
Referencias

Subject — *Sujet* — Sujeto	Publications — *Publications* — Publicaciones
Household budgets (concl.) **Budgets de ménage** (fin) **Presupuestos del hogar** (fin)	*Family Living Studies—A Symposium*, Studies and Reports, New Series, No. 63 (Geneva, 1961) *Enquêtes sur les conditions de vie des familles : Recueil de monographies*, Etudes et documents, nouvelle série, n° 63 (Genève, 1961) *Encuestas sobre las condiciones de vida de las familias : Recopilación de monografías*, Estudios y documentos, nueva serie, núm. 63 (Ginebra, 1961) *Household Income and Expenditure Statistics*, No. 1, 1950-1964 (Geneva, 1967) *Statistiques du revenu et des dépenses des ménages*, n° 1, 1950-1964 (Genève, 1967) *Scope, Methods and Uses of Family Expenditure Surveys*, Twelth International Conference of Labour Statisticians, Report III (Geneva, 1971) *Portée, méthodes et utilisation des enquêtes sur les dépenses des familles*, douzième Conférence internationale des statisticiens du travail, rapport III (Genève, 1973) *Alcance, métodos y utilización de las encuestas sobre gastos familiares*, duodécima Conferencia Internacional de Estadígrafos del Trabajo, Informe III (Ginebra, 1971) *Household Income and Expenditure Statistics* No. 2—1960-1972 —Africa, Asia, Latin America (Geneva, 1974) —Northern America, Europe, USSR and Oceania (to be issued early 1976) *Statistiques des revenus et des dépenses des ménages* N°. 2 — 1960-1972 — Afrique, Amérique latine, Asie (Genève, 1974) — Amérique du Nord, Europe, URSS et Océanie (à paraître début 1976) *Estadísticas de ingresos y gastos de los hogares* núm. 2 — 1960-1972 — Africa, América latina, Asia (Ginebra, 1974) — América del Norte, Europa, URSS y Oceanía (aparecerá a principios de 1976)
Industrial accidents **Accidents du travail** **Accidentes del trabajo**	*Statistics of Industrial Injuries*, Geneva 1970 (document D17/1970/XCIST/II/SAT) *Statistiques des accidents du travail*, Genève, 1970 (document D17/1970/XCIST/II/SAT) *Estadísticas de los accidentes del trabajo*, décima Conferencia Internacional de Estadígrafos del Trabajo, Informe II (Ginebra, 1962) (documento mimeografiado)

References and sources
Références et sources
Referencias y fuentes

B Sources
Sources
Fuentes

Country — *Pays* — País	Author — *Auteur* — Autor	Publications — *Publications* — Publicaciones
AFRICA — AFRIQUE AFRICA		
Algérie	Secrétariat d'Etat au plan. Direction des statistiques	*Bulletin de statistiques générales*
Angola	Instituto Nacional de Estatística (Portugal)	*Boletim mensal de estatística* *Anuário estatístico, Provincias Ultramarinas, vol. II (Annuaire statistique, Provinces d'Outre-mer, vol. II)*
	Direcção Provincial dos Serviços de Estatística	*Boletim mensal*
Burundi	Département des statistiques	*Bulletin de statistique* (trimestriel)
Cameroun	Direction de la statistique et de la comptabilité nationale	*Bulletin mensuel de statistique* *Note trimestrielle de statistique, série B*
	Department of Statistics and National Accounts	*Monthly Digest of Statistics*
Cap-Vert	Instituto Nacional de Estatística (Portugal)	*Boletim mensal de estatística* *Anuário estatístico, Provincias Ultramarinas, vol. II (Annuaire statistique, Provinces d'Outre-mer, vol. II)*
	Serviços de Estatística	*Boletim trimestral de estatística (Bulletin trimestriel de statistique)*
Rép. centrafricaine	Direction de la statistique générale et des études économiques	*Bulletin mensuel de statistique*
Congo	Direction de la statistique et de la comptabilité économique	*Bulletin mensuel des statistiques*
Côte-d'Ivoire	Ministère de l'Economie et des Finances. Direction de la statistique	*Bulletin mensuel de statistique*
Egypt	Central Agency for Public Mobilisation and Statistics	*Statistical Abstract of the UAR* *Monthly Bulletin of Consumer Price Index* *Statistical Handbook*
	Central Bank of Egypt	*Economic Review*
Ethiopia	Central Statistical Office	*Statistical Abstract*
	National Bank of Ethiopia	*Quarterly Bulletin*
Gabon	Direction de la statistique et des études économiques	*Bulletin mensuel de statistique* *Situation économique, financière et sociale de la République gabonaise*
	Ministry of Labour. National Employment Service	*Employment Market Report*
Ghana	Central Bureau of Statistics	*Quarterly Digest of Statistics* *Labour Statistics* *Statistical Year Book*
	Ministry of Labour. National Employment Service	*Employment Market Report*
Haute-Volta	Ministère du Plan et des Travaux publics. Direction de la statistique et de la mécanographie	*Bulletin mensuel d'information statistique et économique*
Kenya	Central Bureau of Statistics. Ministry of Finance and Planning	*Kenya Statistical Digest* *Statistical Abstract*
	Office of the Registrar General	*Annual Report of the Registrar General*
Liberia	Bureau of Statistics. National Planning Agency	*Statistical Newsletter*
Libyan Arab Republic	Technical Planning Body. Census and Statistical Department	*Monthly Cost-of-Living Index for Tripoli Town* *Quarterly Bulletin of Statistics*
	Central Bank of Libya. Economic Research Division	*Economic Bulletin*
Madagascar	Direction générale du gouvernement. Direction de l'Institut national de la statistique et de la recherche économique	*Bulletin mensuel de statistique*
	Ministère du Travail et des Lois sociales	*Rapport statistique*
Malawi	National Statistical Office	*Monthly Statistical Bulletin*
Mali	Service de la statistique générale et de la comptabilité économique nationale	*Bulletin mensuel de statistique*
Maroc	Premier ministre. Secrétariat d'Etat au plan et au développement régional. Division des statistiques	*Bulletin mensuel de statistique* *Indice du coût de la vie*
	Société d'études économiques, sociales et statistiques	*Bulletin économique et social du Maroc*
Mauritanie	Ministère de la Santé et du Travail. Direction du travail	*Bulletin statistique et économique*
	Ministère de la Planification et de la Recherche. Direction de la statistique	*Bulletin mensuel statistique*

SOURCES

References and sources
Références et sources
Referencias y fuentes

B

Sources
Sources
Fuentes

Country — *Pays* — País	Author — *Auteur* — Autor	Publications — *Publications* — Publicaciones
Mauritius	Ministry of Labour Government Central Statistical Office	*Annual Report* *The Government Gazette of Mauritius* *Survey of Employment and Earnings in Large Establishments* *Bi-annual Digest of Statistics*
Mozambique	Instituto Nacional de Estatística (Portugal) Direcção Provincial dos Serviços de Estatística	*Boletim mensal de estatística* *Anuário estatístico, Provincias Ultramarinas, vol. II (Annuaire statistique, Provinces d'outre-mer, vol. II)* *Boletim mensal de estatística (Bulletin mensuel de statistique)*
Niger	Commissariat général au développement. Service de la statistique	*Bulletin de statistique*
Nigeria	Ministry of Labour Federal Office of Statistics	*Quarterly Review* *Annual Abstract of Statistics* *Digest of Statistics* *Retail Prices and Consumer Price Indices for Selected Urban Centres* *Economic Indicators*
Réunion	Institut national de la statistique et des études économiques (INSEE) INSEE. Service départemental de la Réunion	*Annuaire statistique de la Réunion* *Bulletin de statistique des départements et territoires d'outre-mer* *Bulletin de statistiques* *Informations statistiques rapides*
Sénégal	Ministère des Finances et des Affaires économiques. Direction de la statistique	*Bulletin statistique et économique mensuel*
Sierra Leone	Labour Division Government Central Statistics Office	*Annual Report* *The Sierra Leone Gazette* *Statistical Bulletin*
Somalia	Ministry of Planning and Co-ordination. Central Statistical Department	*Compendio Statistico (Statistical Abstract)* *Monthly Statistical Bulletin*
South Africa, Rep. of	Department of Labour Department of Statistics	*Annual Report* *Bulletin van Statistiek (Bulletin of Statistics)* *Short-Term Economic Indicators* *Suid-Afrikaanse Statistieke (South African Statistics)*
Sudan	H.Q. Council of Ministers. Department of Statistics	*Foreign Trade and Internal Statistics*
Swaziland	Central Statistical Office	*Annual Statistical Bulletin* *Employment and Wages* *Quarterly Digest of Statistics*
Tanzania (Tanganyika)	Department of Labour Central Statistical Bureau	*Annual Report* *Monthly Statistical Bulletin* *Statistical Abstract*
Tchad	Ministère du Plan et des Aides extérieures. Direction du plan et du développement. Sous-direction de la statistique	*Bulletin de statistique*
Togo	Direction de la statistique	*Bulletin mensuel de statistique*
Tunisie	Ministère du Plan. Institut national de la statistique	*Bulletin mensuel de statistique* *Bulletin de statistique et d'études économiques*
Uganda	Labour Department Government East African Statistical Department Ministry of Planning and Economic Development. Statistics Division	*Annual Report* *The Uganda Gazette* *Economic and Statistical Review* *Statistical Abstract* *Enumeration of Employees* *Quarterly Economic and Statistical Bulletin*

References and sources
Références et sources
Referencias y fuentes

B

Sources
Sources
Fuentes

Country — *Pays* — País	Author — *Auteur* — Autor	Publications — *Publications* — Publicaciones
Zaïre	Office national de la recherche et du développement. Institut national de la statistique	*Bulletin trimestriel des statistiques générales*
		Prix et indice des prix à la consommation familiale
	Banque du Zaïre	*Bulletin trimestriel*
Zambia	Department of Labour	*Annual Report*
	Central Statistical Office	*Monthly Digest of Statistics*
	Ministry of Rural Development. Statistics Section	*Statistical Bulletin*
AMERICA — AMÉRIQUE AMÉRICA		
Antilles néerlandaises	Departement Sociale en Economische Zaken. Bureau voor de Statistiek	*Statistische Mededelingen*
Argentina	Ministerio de Economía. Secretaría de Estado, de Programación y Coordinación Económica. Instituto Nacional de Estadística y Censos	*Boletín estadístico trimestral*
		Indices de precios al consumidor
Bahamas	Ministry of Labour	*Annual Report*
	Department of Statistics	*Quarterly Statistical Summary*
Barbados	Department of Labour	*Annual Report*
	Statistical Service	*Quarterly Digest of Statistics*
		Selected Monthly Indicators
		Abstract of Statistics
Belize	The Labour Department	*Annual Report*
		Manpower Report
	Government	*Government Gazette*
Brésil	Fundação IBGE. Instituto Brasileiro de Estatística	*Boletim estatístico*
		Anuário estatístico do Brasil
	IPE Universidade de São Paulo	*Indice de custo de vida*
	Instituto Brasileiro de Economía. Fundação Getulio Vargas	*Conjuntura económica*
Canada	Statistics Canada	*Employment Earnings and Hours*
		The Labour Force
		Canada Yearbook
		Prices and Price Indexes
		Price Movements
		Canadian Statistical Review
	Department of Labour	*Labour Gazette (Gazette du travail)*
	Bank of Canada	*Statistical Summary*
Colombia	Departamento Administrativo Nacional de Estadística	*Anuario general de estadística*
		Indicadores socioeconómicos
		Boletín mensual de estadística
	Banco de la República	*Revista*
Costa Rica	Ministerio de Economía, Industria y Comercio. Dirección General de Estadística y Censos	*Anuario estadístico*
		Indice de precios al por menor
	Banco Central de Costa Rica	*Boletín estadístico mensual*

SOURCES

References and sources
Références et sources
Referencias y fuentes

B

Sources
Sources
Fuentes

Country — *Pays* — País	Author — *Auteur* — Autor	Publications — *Publications* — Publicaciones
Chile	Instituto Nacional de Estadísticas	*Boletín* *Indice de precios al consumidor* *Serie de investigaciones muestrales. Muestra nacional de hogares* *Síntesis estadística*
	Banco Central de Chile	*Boletín mensual*
República Dominicana	Banco Central de la República Dominicana	*Boletín mensual*
Ecuador	Junta Nacional de Planificación y Coordinación. Departamento técnico. División de Estadística y Censos	*Estadísticas de precios. Indice de precios al consumidor de las familias de ingresos bajos y medios de Quito*
	Instituto Nacional de Estadística	*Indice de precios al consumidor* *Estadísticas del trabajo : Indices de empleo y remuneraciones*
	Banco Central del Ecuador	*Boletín*
El Salvador	Ministerio de Economía. Dirección General de Estadística y Censos	*Boletín estadístico* *Indice de precios al consumidor obrero para San Salvador, Mejicanos y Villa Delgado*
	Ministerio de Trabajo y Previsión Social. Sección de Estadística	*Estadísticas de trabajo*
	Consejo Nacional de Planificación y Coordinación Económica. Casa Presidencial	*Indicadores económicos y sociales*
Greenland	Danmarks Statistik	*Statistiske Efterretninger* *Statistisk Aarbog (Statistical Yearbook)*
Grenada	Government	*Grenada Government Gazette*
Guadeloupe	Institut national de la statistique et des études économiques	*Bulletin de statistique des départements et territoires d'outre-mer*
Guatemala	Banco de Guatemala	*Boletín estadístico*
	Ministerio de Economía. Dirección General de Estadística	*Informador estadístico*
Guyana	Ministry of Finance. The Statistical Bureau	*Quarterly Statistical Digest*
	Department of Labour	*Annual Report*
	Government	*The Official Gazette*
Guyane française	Institut national de la statistique et des études économiques	*Bulletin de statistique des départements et territoires d'outre-mer* *Bulletin statistique. Guyane*
Haïti	Département du Travail	*Revue du travail*
	Département des Finances et des Affaires économiques. Institut haïtien de statistique	*Bulletin trimestriel de statistique*
Honduras	Secretaría de Economía y Hacienda. Dirección General de Estadística y Censos	*Investigación industrial* *Honduras en cifras* *Anuario estadístico*
	Secretaría de Trabajo y Previsión Social. Departamento Nacional de Investigaciones y Estudios Sociales	*Estadísticas del trabajo*
	Banco Central	*Boletín Estadístico Mensual*
Jamaica	Department of Statistics	*Statistical Abstract* *Consumer Prices Indices, Urban and Rural* *The Labour Force*
Martinique	Institut national de la statistique et des études économiques	*Bulletin de statistique des départements et territoires d'outre-mer*
México	Secretaría de Industria y Comercio. Dirección General de Estadística	*Revista de estadística* *Anuario estadístico compendiado*
Nicaragua	Banco Central de Nicaragua	*Revista trimestral*
Panamá	Contraloría General de la República. Dirección de Estadística y Censo	*Estadística panameña* *Estadística del trabajo (Mano de obra)*
Paraguay	Ministerio de Hacienda. Dirección General de Estadística y Censos	*Boletín estadístico del Paraguay*
	Banco Central de Paraguay. Departamento de Estudios Económicos	*Boletín estadístico mensual*

References and sources
Références et sources
Referencias y fuentes

B

Sources
Sources
Fuentes

Country — *Pays* — País	Author — *Auteur* — Autor	Publications — *Publications* — Publicaciones
Perú	Servicio del Empleo y Recursos Humanos	*SERH Sueldos y salarios*
	Oficina Nacional de Estadística y Censos	*Indices de precios al consumidor*
	Banco Central	*Boletín*
Puerto Rico	Department of Labor. Bureau of Labor Statistics	*Employment, Hours and Earnings in the Manufacturing Industries in Puerto Rico*
		Employment and Unemployment in Puerto Rico
		Consumer Price Index for Wage Earners' Families in Puerto Rico
	Puerto Rico Planning Board	*Monthly Economic Indicators of Puerto Rico*
Surinam	Algemeen Bureau voor de Statistiek	*Prijsindexcijfers van de Gezinsconsumptie (Consumer Price Index)*
	Ministerie van Arbeid en Volkshuisvesting	*Arbeidsvoorzieningen*
St. Lucia	Government	*St. Lucia Gazette*
Trinidad and Tobago	Central Statistical Office	*Quarterly Economic Report*
		CSSP Labour Force
	Government	*Trinidad and Tobago Gazette (extraordinary)*
United States	Department of Labor. Bureau of Labor Statistics	*News*
		Employment and Earnings
		Monthly Labor Review
	Department of Agriculture. Statistical Reporting Service	*Farm Labor*
	Department of Commerce. Bureau of the Census	*Annual Report on the Labor Force*
		Statistical Abstract of the United States
	Economic Statistics Bureau	*The Handbook of Basic Economic Statistics*
Uruguay	Ministerio de Economía y Finanzas. Dirección General de Estadística y Censos	*Boletín estadístico*
		Indice de los precios del consumo
	Banco de la República Oriental del Uruguay. Departamento de Investigaciones Económicas	*Suplemento estadístico*
Venezuela	Ministerio de Fomento. Dirección General de Estadística y Censos Nacionales	*Boletín mensual de estadística*
	Banco Central de Venezuela	*Revista*
		Boletín mensual
	Ministerio del Trabajo. Dirección de Estadística Laboral	*Boletín de estadística del trabajo*
Asia — Asie Asia		
Bangladesh	Bangladesh Bureau of Statistics	*Monthly Statistical Bulletin*
Brunei	State and Labour Department	*Annual Report*
Burma	Labour Directorate	*People's Workers' Gazette*
	The Revolutionary Government of the Union of Burma. Central Statistical and Economics Department	*Quarterly Bulletin of Statistics*
Cambodge	Ministère du Plan. Institut national de la statistique et des recherches économiques	*Bulletin statistique*

SOURCES

References and sources
Références et sources
Referencias y fuentes

B
Sources
Sources
Fuentes

Country — *Pays* — País	Author — *Auteur* — Autor	Publications — *Publications* — Publicaciones
Cyprus	Ministry of Finance. Statistics and Research Department	*Statistical Summary*
		Statistical Abstract
	Ministry of Labour and Social Insurance	*Monthly Bulletin*
		Annual Report
		Report on the unemployment situation
Hong Kong	Commisioner of Labour	*Annual Departmental Report*
	Government Press	*Hong Kong Report for the Year*
	Census and Statistics Department	*Hong Kong Monthly Digest of Statistics*
India	Central Statistical Organisation. Government of India	*Monthly Abstract of Statistics*
	The Cabinet Secretariat, Central Statistical Organisation. Department of Statistics	*Indian Labour Journal*
		Annual Report of the Chief Inspector of Mines of India
	Labour Bureau. Ministry of Labour, Employment and Rehabilitation	*Indian Labour Statistics*
	Reserve Bank	*Bulletin*
Indonesia	Biro Pusat Statistik	*Monthly Statistical Bulletin*
		Statistik Indonesia (Statistical Pocketbook of Indonesia)
Iran	Bank Markazi. Economic Research Department	*Bulletin*
Iraq	Ministry of Planning. Central Statistical Organisation. Publication and Public Relations	*Annual Abstract of Statistics*
		Quarterly Bulletin of Statistics
		Price and Index Numbers
Israel	Central Bureau of Statistics	*Monthly Bulletin of Statistics*
		Israel Economic Indicators
		Statistical Abstract of Israel
	Bank of Israel	*Economic Review*
Japan	Minister's Secretariat. Ministry of Labour. Statistics and Information Department	*Monthly Labor Statistics and Research Bulletin*
	Economic Planning Agency	*Economic Statistics*
	Office of the Prime Minister. Bureau of Statistics	*Monthly Report on the Labor Force Survey*
		Monthly Report on the Retail Price Survey
		Consumer Price Index
		Statistical Yearbook
		Monthly Statistics of Japan
	The Bank of Japan. Statistics Department	*Monthly Economic Statistics*
	Japan Productivity Center	
Jordan	The Hashemite Kingdom of Jordan. Department of Statistics	*Amman and Zarka Consumer Price Index and Civil Servants' Price Index*
	Central Bank of Jordan	*Monthly Statistical Bulletin*

References and sources
Références et sources
Referencias y fuentes

B

Sources
Sources
Fuentes

Country — *Pays* — País	Author — *Auteur* — Autor	Publications — *Publications* — Publicaciones
Korea, Rep. of	Economic Planning Board. Bureau of Statistics Bank of Korea	*Monthly Statistics of Korea* *Monthly Economic Statistics* *Monthly Economic Review*
Laos	Ministère du Plan et de la Coopération. Service national de la statistique	*Bulletin de statistiques*
Liban	Ministère du Plan. Direction centrale de la statistique	*Bulletin statistique mensuel*
Malaysia	Ministry of Health, Labour and Social Welfare Department of Statistics Ministry of Labour	*Annual Report* *Monthly Statistical Bulletin of West Malaysia* *Monthly Newsletter*
Pakistan	Ministry of Health, Labour and Social Welfare Central Statistical Office State Bank of Pakistan. Department of Public Relations	*Pakistan Labour Gazette* *Monthly Statistical Bulletin* *Key Economic Indicators* *Bulletin*
Philippines	Department of Commerce and Industry. Bureau of the Census and Statistics Department of Commerce and Industry. Bureau of Commerce Office of Statistical Coordination and Standards. National Economic Council Central Bank of the Philippines. Department of Economic Research	*Monthly Bulletin of Statistics* *Yearbook of Philippine Statistics* *Journal of Philippine Statistics* *Consumers' Price Index for Low Income Families in Manila* *The BCS Survey of Households Bulletin—Labour Force* *Daily Market Report* *The Statistical Reporter* *Statistical Bulletin* *Central Bank New Digest*
Singapore	Department of Statistics Ministry of Labour and National Statistical Commission	*Monthly Digest of Statistics* *Report on the Labour Force Survey of Singapore*
Sri Lanka	Department of Labour Department of Census and Statistics Central Bank of Ceylon	*Sri Lanka Labour Gazette* *Statistical Abstract of Ceylon* *Bulletin*
République du Sud Viet-Nam	Bô Ké-Hoach Và Phât-Triên Quôc-Gia. Viên Quôc-Gia Thóng-Kê (National Institute of Statistics. Ministry of National Planning and Development)	*Niên giám Thong-Kê Viet-Nam (Statistical Yearbook/Annuaire statistique)* *Thong-kê Nguyêt-San (Monthly Bulletin of Statistics/Bulletin mensuel de statistique)*
République arabe syrienne	Ministry of Planning. Directorate of Statistics Office of the Prime Minister. Central Bureau of Statistics Centre d'études et de documentations économiques, financières et sociales Central Bank of Syria Ministry of Social Affairs and Labour. Statistics Division	*General Bulletin of Current Statistics* *Statistical Abstract* *Etude mensuelle sur l'économie et les finances des pays arabes* *Quarterly Bulletin* *The Annual Statistical Bulletin of the Ministry of Social Affairs and Labour*
Thailand	National Statistical Office. Office of the Prime Minister Bank of Thailand	*Quarterly Bulletin of Statistics* *Monthly Bulletin* *Final Report of the Labor Force Survey*
Yemen, People's Dem. Rep. of	Department of Labour and Welfare Government	*Annual Report* *People's Republic, Official Gazette*

SOURCES

References and sources
Références et sources
Referencias y fuentes

B

Sources
Sources
Fuentes

Country — *Pays* — País	Author — *Auteur* — Autor	Publications — *Publications* — Publicaciones
EUROPE — EUROPE EUROPA		
Austria	Österreichisches Statistisches Zentralamt	*Statistisches Handbuch für die Republik Österreich* *Statistische Nachrichten*
	Österreichisches Institut für Wirtschaftsforschung	*Monatsberichte* *Statistische Übersichten*
	Bundesministerium für Soziale Verwaltung	*Amtliche Nachrichten des Bundesministeriums für Soziale Verwaltung*
	Bundeskammer der gewerblichen Wirtschaft. Sektion Industrie (Bundessektion Industrie)	*Monatliche Beschäftigtenstatistik*
Belgique	Banque nationale de Belgique	*Bulletin*
	Ministère des Affaires économiques. Institut national de statistique	*Bulletin de statistique* *Statistiques sociales* *Annuaire statistique de la Belgique*
	Ministère de l'Emploi et du Travail	*Revue du travail* *Informations statistiques. Etudes*
	Ministère de l'Emploi et du Travail. Office national de l'emploi.	*Bulletin mensuel* *Rapport annuel*
	Office national de sécurité sociale	*Les gains des travailleurs assujettis à la Sécurité sociale*
	Ministère des Affaires économiques et de l'Energie	*Aperçu de l'évolution économique*
Bulgarie	Министерство на информацията и съобщенията. Централно статистическо управление (Ministère de l'Information et des Communications. Office central de statistique)	*Промышленность Народной Республики Болгария (L'industrie de la République populaire de Bulgarie)* *Статистика* *Статистически годишник на НР България* *Статистически известия (Statistical Bulletin)*
Czechoslovakia	Office fédéral de la statistique	*Statistická ročenka Československé socialistické republiky (Annuaire statistique de la République socialiste tchécoslovaque)*
	Federálni Statistický Úřad	*Statistické Přehledy*
Denmark	Danmarks Statistiks	*Statistiske Efterretninger* *Statistisk Aarbog (Statistical Yearbook)*
	Dansk Arbejdsgiverforenings Lønstatistik	*Statistikken*
España	Instituto Nacional de Estadística	*Boletín mensual de estadística* *Anuario estadístico* *Salarios*
	Servicio nacional de colocación de la Organización sindical española. Departamento de Estadística	*Estadísticas de demandas y ofertas de trabajo, colocaciones y desempleo*
Finland	Tilastokeskus Statistikcentralen (Central Statistical Office)	*Suomen Tilastollinen Vuosikirja — Statistisk Årsbok för Finland (Statistical Yearbook of Finland)* *Tilastokatsauksia — Statistiska Översikter (Bulletin of Statistics)*
	Sosiaaliministeriö — Socialministeriet	*Sosiaalinen Aikakauskirja — Social Tidskrift (Social Review)*
	Bank of Finland	*Monthly Bulletin*
	Työvoimaministeriö (Ministry of Labour)	*Työvoimakatsaus (Labour Reports)*
	Suomen Virallinen Tilasto	*Teollisuustilasto OSA I Industristatistik DELI,*
France	Ministère du Travail	*Bulletin mensuel des statistiques du travail* *Enquête trimestrielle sur l'activité et les conditions d'emploi de la main-d'œuvre* *Revue française des affaires sociales*
	Ministère de l'Economie et des Finances. Institut national de la statistique et des études économiques	*Bulletin mensuel de statistique* *Annuaire statistique de la France* *Economie et statistique* *Informations rapides*

References and sources
Références et sources
Referencias y fuentes

B

Sources
Sources
Fuentes

Country — *Pays* — País	Author — *Auteur* — Autor	Publications — *Publications* — Publicaciones
German Democratic Republic	Staatliche Zentralverwaltung für Statistik	*Statistisches Jahrbuch der Deutschen Demokratischen Republik*
Germany, Fed. Rep. of	Statistisches Bundesamt, Wiesbaden	*Wirtschaft und Statistik* *Statistischer Wochendienst* *Statistisches Jahrbuch für die Bundesrepublik Deutschland* *Preise, Löhne, Wirtschaftsrechnungen* *Industrie und Handwerk (Beschäftigung und Umsatz, Brennstoff-* *und Energieversorgung) Reihe 1*
	Bundesanstalt für Arbeit	*Amtliche Nachrichten der Bundesanstalt für Arbeit*
	Bundesministerium für Arbeit und Sozialordnung	*Arbeits- und sozialstatistische Mitteilungen* *Hauptergebnisse der Arbeits- und Sozialstatistik*
Gibraltar	Government	*Gibraltar Gazette*
Grèce	National Statistical Service	*Monthly Statistical Bulletin* *Statistical Yearbook of Greece*
	Bank of Greece. Economic Research Department	*Monthly Statistical Bulletin*
Hongrie	Központi statisztikai hivatal (Central Statistical Office)	*Statisztikai havi közlemények (Monthly Bulletin of Statistics)* *Statisztikai szemle (Statistical Review)* *Statisztikai Évkönyv (Statistical Yearbook)*
Iceland	The Statistical Bureau of Iceland and the Central Bank of Iceland	*Statistical Bulletin*
	Gefin út af Hagstofu Islands	*Hagtídindi*
Ireland	Central Statistics Office	*Irish Statistical Bulletin* *Statistical Abstract of Ireland* *The Trend of Employment and Unemployment*
	Central Bank of Ireland	*Quarterly Bulletin*
Italie	Ministero del Lavoro e della Previdenza Sociale	*Statistiche del lavoro* *Supplemento al Bollettino statistiche del lavoro*
	Istituto Centrale di Statistica	*Annuario statistico italiano* *Bollettino mensile di statistica* *Rilevazione nazionale delle forze di lavoro* *Compendio statistico italiano* *Notiziario ISTAT*
	Confederazione Generale della Industria Italiana	*Notiziario* *Rassegna di statistiche del lavoro*
Luxembourg	Ministère de l'Economie nationale. Service central de la statistique et des études économiques	*Bulletin du Statec* *Annuaire statistique*
	Inspection du travail et des mines	*Rapport annuel*
Malta	Minister of Labour, Employment and Welfare	*Report on the Working of the Department of Labour and Emigration*
	Government	*The Malta Government Gazette*
	Central Office of Statistics	*Annual Abstract of Statistics* *Quarterly Digest of Statistics*

SOURCES

References and sources
Références et sources
Referencias y fuentes

B

Sources
Sources
Fuentes

Country — *Pays* — País	Author — *Auteur* — Autor	Publications — *Publications* — Publicaciones
Norway	Statistisk Sentralbyrå (Central Bureau of Statistics)	*Statistisk Månedshefte (Monthly Bulletin of Statistics)* *Statistik Årbok (Statistical Yearbook)* *Statistisk Ukehefte* *Arbeidsmarked-statistikk (Labour Market Statistics)*
	Arbeidsdirektoratet	*Særtrykk fra Statistisk Ukehefte* *Månedsrapport om utviklingen på arbeidsmarkedet*
Pays-Bas	Centraal Bureau voor de Statistiek (Central Bureau of Statistics)	*Maandschrift* *Sociale Maandstatistiek* *Statistisch bulletin* *Jaarcijfers voor Nederland (Statistical Yearbook of the Netherlands)* *Maandstatistiek van de industrie (Monthly Statistical Bulletin of Manufacturing)*
Pologne	Główny Urzad Statystyczny. Central Statistical Office	*Biuletyn statystyczny* *Rocznik Statystyczny (Statistical Yearbook)*
Portugal	Instituto Nacional de Estatística. Serviços Centrais	*Boletim mensal de estatística (Bulletin mensuel de statistique)* *Anuário estatístico (Annuaire statistique)* *Estatísticas industriais (Statistiques industrielles)* *Estatística agrícola y alimentares*
	Serviço de Estatística, Ministério do Trabalho	*Estatísticas do Trabalho*
Roumanie	Directia Centralá de Statisticá	*Buletin Statistic Trimestrial* *Anuarul Statistic al RSR*
Suisse	Département fédéral de l'Economie publique Bureau fédéral de statistique	*La Vie économique* *Annuaire statistique de la Suisse*
Sweden	Arbetsmarknadsstyrelsen Kommerskollegium Statistika Centralbyran (National Central Bureau of Statistics)	*Arbetsmarknadsstatistik* *Sveriges Officiella Statistik, Olycksfall i arbete (Industrial Accidents)* *Statistisk Årsbok för Sverige (Statistical Abstract of Sweden)* *Sveriges Officiella Statistik (Official Statistics of Sweden), Industri (Manufacturing)* *Allmän Månadsstatistik (Monthly Digest of Swedish Statistics)* *Statistiska Meddelanden (Statistical Reports)*
Turquie	Türkiye Cumhuriyet Merkez Bankasi (Banque centrale de la République de Turquie) Devlet İstatístik Enstitüsu (State Institute of Statistics) Tícaret Bakanligi (Ministère du Commerce)	*Aylik Bülten (Bulletin mensuel)* *Aylik İstatístik Bülteni (Monthly Bulletin of Statistics)* *İstatístik Yilligí (Annuaire statistique)* *Aylik Fiyat Indeksleri Bülteni* *Konjonktür (Conjoncture)*
United Kingdom	Board of Trade Central Statistical Office Department of Employment	*Board of Trade Journal* *Monthly Digest of Statistics* *Annual Abstract of Statistics* *Economic Trends* *Department of Employment Gazette* *British Labour Statistics, Year Book*

References and sources
Références et sources
Referencias y fuentes

B Sources
Sources
Fuentes

Country — *Pays* — País	Author — *Auteur* — Autor	Publications — *Publications* — Publicaciones
Yugoslavia	Savezni Zavod za Statistiku	*Statist#k Godišnjak FNRJ (Annuaire statistique de la République fédérative socialiste de Yougoslavie)* *Statistički bilten (Bulletin statistique)* *Indeks, Mesečni Pregled Privredne Statistike SFR Jugoslavije (L'Indice, revue mensuelle des statistiques économiques de la RSF de Yougoslavie)*
	Jugoslovenski nacionalni odbor za socijalni rad	*Socijalna politika*
OCEANIA — OCÉANIE OCEANÍA		
Australia	Commonwealth Bureau of Census and Statistics	*Quarterly Summary of Australian Statistics* *Digest of Current Economic Statistics* *Monthly Review of Business Statistics* *Employment and Unemployment* *Wage Rates and Earnings* *Labour Report* *Year Book of the Commonwealth of Australia* *The Labour Force*
Fiji	Department of Labour Government Bureau of Statistics	*Annual Report* *Fiji Royal Gazette* *Current Economic Statistics*
New Zealand	Department of Statistics Department of Labour Social Security Department	*Monthly Abstract of Statistics* *Report on Industrial Accidents Statistics* *Prices, Wages, Labour* *Monthly Statistics of Employment* *Labour and Employment Gazette* *Annual Reports*
Nouvelle-Calédonie	Institut national de la statistique et des études économiques Commissariat général de la République française dans l'océan Pacifique	*Bulletin de statistique des départements et territoires d'outre-mer* *Journal officiel de la Nouvelle-Calédonie et dépendances*
Polynésie française	Institut national de la statistique et des études économiques	*Bulletin de statistique des départements et territoires d'outre-mer*
Solomon Is. (Brit.)	Statistical Office	*Quarterly Digest of Statistics*
Western Samoa	Department of Statistics	*Quarterly Statistical Bulletin*
URSS	Центральное статистическое управление при Совете Министров СССР (Central Statistical Board under the Council of Ministers of the USSR; Office central de statistique près le Conseil des ministres de l'URSS)	*Народное хозяйство СССР, статистический ежегодник* *Страна Советов за 50 лет, статистический сборник,* Москва, 1967 (*Soviet Union, 50 years: Statistical returns,* Moscow, 1969; *Le pays des Soviets en 50 ans: Recueil de statistiques,* Moscou, 1968) *Труд в СССР, статистический сборник,* Москва, 1968
RSS de Biélorussie	Центральное статистическое управление при Совете Министров Белорусской ССР	*Народное хозяйство Белорусской ССР. Статистический сборник*
RSS d'Ukraine	Центральне статистичне управління при Раді Міністрів УРСР	*Народне господарство Української РСР*

INDEX
INDEX
INDICE

Countries and territories included in each table

Pays et territoires compris dans chaque tableau

Países y territorios incluidos en cada cuadro

INDEX

Countries and territories included in each table (with corresponding page number)
Pays et territoires compris dans chaque tableau (avec numéro de page correspondant)
Países y territorios incluidos en cada cuadro (con número de página correspondiente)

| | | I POPULATION / POPULATION / POBLACIÓN | | | II EMPLOYMENT / EMPLOI / EMPLEO | | | | | | | | | III UNEMPL. / CHÔMAGE / DESEMPL. | | IV HOURS OF WORK / DURÉE DU TRAVAIL / HORAS DE TRABAJO | | | | | | |
| Code / Code / Clave | Country / Pays / País | By sex & age group | By industry | By occupation | By economic activity | General level | Non-agr. sectors | All industries (Manufact.) | By industry (Manufact.) | Tot. hours work. (Manufact.) | Mining & quarrying | Construction | Transport | General level | By industry/occup. | Non-agr. sectors | All industries (Manufact.) | By industry (Manufact.) | Distribution (%) (Manufact.) | Mining & quarrying | Construction | Transport |
		1	2 A	2 B	3	4	5	6 A	6 B	6 C	7	8	9	10	11	12	13 A	13 B	13 C	14	15	16
	AFRICA — AFRIQUE / AFRICA																					
1	Algérie	9	50	160												489	491	494		557	560	563
2	Angola	9																				
3	Botswana	9	50	160																		
4	Burundi	9																				
5	Cameroun	9				337	340	343				418	421	436	440							
6	Cap-Vert	9																				
7	République centrafricaine	9												436								
8	Congo																					
9	Côte-d'Ivoire	10	50																			
10	Dahomey	10																				
11	Egypt	10	52	162	306	337	340	343				418	421	436	441	489	491	495		557	560	563
12	Ethiopia	10						343	346													
13	Gabon	10	52		306	337	340	343			415	418	421									
14	Ghana	10		162		337	340	343	347		415	418	421	436	442							
15	Guinée																					
16	Haute-Volta	11												436								
17	Kenya				307	337	340	343	348		415	418	421									
18	Lesotho	11																				
19	Liberia	11																				
20	Libyan Arab Republic	11	52	164					349					436								
21	Madagascar	11												436								
22	Malawi				307	337	340	343	349	413	415	418	421	436	443							
23	Mali													436		489	491				560	563
24	Maroc	11	54	164										436								
25	Mauritanie																					
26	Mauritius	12	54	166	308	337	340	343	350				421	436	443							
	» (Rodrigues)	12																				
27	Mozambique	12	54						351					436								
28	Namibia	12																				
29	Niger	12												436								
30	Nigeria	12		166				343	352		415			436	444							
31	Réunion	13	56																			
32	St. Helena	13																				
33	Sénégal	13												436								
34	Seychelles	13	56	168																		
35	Sierra Leone	13	56	168			340	343			415	418	421	436	444	489	491			557	560	563
36	Somalia																				560	
37	South Africa, Rep. of	14	58	170			340	343	353		415	418	421	436	445		491	496			560	
38	Sudan													436								

V PRODUCTIVITY PRODUCTIVITÉ PRODUCTIVIDAD			VI WAGES SALAIRES SALARIOS								VII PRICES PRIX PRECIOS					VIII ACCIDENTS ACCIDENTS ACCIDENTES					IX DISP. CONF. CONF.	EXCHANGE CHANGE CAMBIO		Code Code Clave
National economy — Economie nationale	Industrial sector — Secteur industriel	Manufacturing — Industries manufact.	Non-agr. sectors — Secteurs non agricoles	All industries — Ensemble industries	By industry — Par industrie	Mining & quarrying — Indust. extractives	Construction — Construcción	Transport — Transports	Agriculture — Agricultura	Compens. of empl. — Rémun. des salariés	General indices — Indices généraux	Food — Alimentation	Fuel & light — Combustible et éclairage	Clothing — Habillement	Rent — Loyer	Mining & quarrying — Indust. extractives	Coal mines — Mines de charbon	Manufacturing — Industries manufact.	Construction — Construcción	Railways — Chemins de fer	Industrial disputes — Conflits du travail	Exchange rates — Cours des changes		
17 A	17 B	17 C	18	19 A	19 B	20	21	22	23	24	25 A	25 B	25 C	25 D	25 E	26 A	26 B	26 C	26 D	26 E	27	28 A	28 B	
·	·	·	598	605	614	697	704	711	·	·	·	·	·	·	·	·	·	·	·	·	796	·	814	1
·	·	·	·	·	·	·	·	·	·	·	·	·	·	·	·	·	·	·	·	·	·	·	·	2
·	·	·	·	·	·	·	·	·	·	·	746	751	·	760	·	·	·	·	·	·	·	·	·	3
·	·	·	·	·	·	·	·	·	·	·	746	751	·	760	765	·	·	·	787	·	796	·	·	4
·	·	·	·	·	·	·	704	711	717	733	746	751	756	760	765	·	·	784	787	789	796	·	814	5
·	·	·	·	·	·	·	·	·	·	·	746	751	756	·	·	·	·	·	·	·	·	·	·	6
·	·	·	·	·	·	·	·	·	·	·	746	751	756	760	·	·	·	·	·	·	·	·	814	7
·	·	·	·	·	·	·	·	·	·	·	746	751	756	760	·	·	·	·	·	·	·	·	814	8
·	·	·	·	·	·	·	·	·	·	·	746	751	756	760	765	·	·	·	·	·	·	·	814	9
·	·	·	·	·	·	·	·	·	·	733	·	·	·	·	·	·	·	·	·	·	·	·	·	10
·	·	·	598	605	615	697	704	711	·	733	746	751	756	760	765	779	·	784	787	789	796	·	814	11
·	·	·	·	·	·	·	·	·	·	·	746	751	756	760	·	·	·	·	·	·	·	·	·	12
·	·	·	·	·	·	·	·	·	·	·	746	751	756	760	·	·	·	·	·	·	·	·	814	13
·	576	579	598	605	616	697	704	711	717	·	746	751	756	760	765	·	·	784	·	·	796	·	814	14
·	·	·	·	·	·	·	·	·	·	·	·	·	·	·	·	·	·	·	·	·	·	·	814	15
·	·	·	·	605	·	697	704	711	717	·	·	·	·	·	·	·	·	·	·	·	796	·	814	16
·	·	·	·	·	·	·	·	·	·	733	746	751	756	760	765	779	·	784	·	789	796	·	814	17
·	·	·	·	·	·	·	·	·	·	·	746	751	756	760	765	·	·	·	·	·	·	·	·	18
·	·	·	·	·	·	·	·	·	·	·	746	751	756	760	765	·	·	·	·	·	·	·	·	19
·	·	·	·	·	·	·	·	·	·	733	746	751	756	760	765	779	·	784	787	·	·	·	814	20
·	·	·	·	·	·	·	·	·	·	733	746	751	756	·	·	·	·	·	·	·	·	·	814	21
·	·	·	598	605	617	697	704	711	717	733	746	751	756	760	·	·	·	784	787	789	796	·	814	22
·	·	·	598	605	·	697	704	711	·	·	·	751	·	·	·	779	·	784	787	789	796	·	814	23
·	·	·	·	605	·	697	·	·	718	·	746	751	·	760	765	779	782	784	787	789	796	·	815	24
·	·	·	·	·	·	·	·	·	·	·	746	751	756	760	·	·	·	·	·	·	·	·	815	25
·	·	·	598	605	618	697	704	711	718	733	746	751	756	760	765	·	·	784	787	·	797	·	815	26
·	·	·	·	·	·	·	·	·	·	·	746	751	756	760	765	·	·	·	·	·	·	·	815	27
·	·	·	·	·	·	·	·	·	·	·	·	·	·	·	·	·	·	·	·	·	·	·	·	28
·	·	·	·	·	·	·	·	·	·	733	746	751	756	760	·	779	·	·	787	·	·	·	815	29
·	·	·	·	·	·	·	·	·	·	·	746	751	756	760	765	·	·	784	·	·	797	·	815	30
·	·	·	·	·	·	·	·	·	·	·	746	751	·	760	765	·	·	·	·	·	·	·	815	31
·	·	·	·	·	·	·	·	·	·	·	·	·	·	·	·	·	·	·	·	·	·	·	·	32
·	·	·	·	·	·	·	·	·	·	·	747	752	756	760	765	·	·	·	·	·	·	·	815	33
·	·	·	·	·	·	·	·	·	·	·	747	752	756	760	765	·	·	·	·	·	797	·	·	34
·	·	·	598	605	·	697	704	711	·	733	747	752	756	761	765	·	·	·	·	·	797	·	·	35
·	·	·	·	605	·	·	704	711	·	733	747	752	756	761	765	·	·	·	·	·	·	·	815	36
·	·	·	·	605	·	·	704	711	·	733	747	752	756	761	765	·	·	·	·	·	797	810	·	37
·	·	·	·	·	·	·	·	·	·	733	747	752	757	761	765	·	·	·	·	·	797	·	815	38

858

V — PRODUCTIVITY / PRODUCTIVITÉ / PRODUCTIVIDAD			VI — WAGES / SALAIRES / SALARIOS								VII — PRICES / PRIX / PRECIOS					VIII — ACCIDENTS / ACCIDENTES					IX DISP. CONF.	EXCHANGE / CHANGE / CAMBIO		Code / Clave
National economy — Economía nacional	Industrial sector — Sector industrial	Manufacturing — Industrias manufact.	Non-agr. sectors — Sectores no agrícolas	All industries — Todas las industrias	By industry — Por industria	Mining & quarrying — Minas y canteras	Construction — Construcción	Transport — Transportes	Agriculture — Agricultura	Compens. of empl. — Remuneración de asalariados	General indices — Indices generales	Food — Alimentación	Fuel & light — Combustible y alumbrado	Clothing — Vestido	Rent — Alquiler	Mining & quarrying — Minas y canteras	Coal mines — Minas de carbón	Manufacturing — Industrias manufact.	Construction — Construcción	Railways — Ferrocarriles	Industrial disputes — Conflictos del trabajo	Exchange rates — Tipos de cambio	Exchange rates — Tipos de cambio	
17 A	17 B	17 C	18	19 A	19 B	20	21	22	23	24	25 A	25 B	25 C	25 D	25 E	26 A	26 B	26 C	26 D	26 E	27	28 A	28 B	
·	·	·	·	·	·	·	·	·	·	733	747	752	757	761	·	·	·	·	·	·	·	·		39
·	·	·	·	·	·	·	·	·	·	·	747	752	757	761	765	·	·	·	·	·	·	·	815	40
·	·	·	598	606	·	697	704	711	718	734	·	·	·	·	·	779	·	784	787	789	797	·	·	
·	·	·	·	·	·	·	·	·	·	·	747	752	757	761	·	·	·	·	787	·	·	·	815	41
·	·	·	·	·	·	·	·	·	·	734	747	752	757	761	765	·	·	·	·	·	·	·	·	42
·	576	·	·	·	·	·	·	·	718	·	747	752	757	761	765	779	·	784	787	789	797	·	815	43
·	·	·	·	·	·	·	·	·	·	734	747	752	757	761	·	779	·	784	787	·	797	·	815	44
·	·	·	·	·	·	·	·	·	·	734	747	752	757	761	·	·	·	·	·	·	·	·	815	45
573	576	579	598	606	619	697	705	712	718	734	747	752	·	761	765	779	·	784	787	789	797	·	815	46
·	·	·	·	·	·	·	·	·	·	·	747	752	·	761	765	·	·	·	·	·	798	·	·	47
·	·	·	599	·	·	·	·	·	·	734	747	752	757	761	765	·	·	·	·	·	·	·	816	48
·	·	·	·	606	621	697	705	712	719	734	747	752	757	761	765	·	·	·	·	·	798	810	·	49
·	·	·	·	·	·	·	·	·	·	·	747	752	757	761	765	·	·	·	·	·	798	·	·	50
·	·	·	599	606	·	697	705	712	719	·	747	752	·	761	765	·	·	·	·	·	798	·	816	51
·	·	·	·	·	·	697	705	712	719	·	·	·	·	·	·	·	·	·	·	·	798	·	816	52
·	·	·	·	·	·	·	·	712	719	·	747	752	757	761	766	·	·	·	·	·	798	·	·	53
573	576	579	599	606	622	697	705	712	·	734	747	752	·	761	·	·	·	·	·	·	·	810	·	54
·	·	579	·	606	623	698	·	·	·	·	747	752	757	761	766	·	·	·	·	·	·	810	·	55
573	·	579	599	606	625	698	705	712	720	734	747	752	757	761	766	779	782	784	787	789	798	810	·	56
·	·	·	·	·	·	·	·	·	·	·	·	·	·	·	·	·	·	·	·	·	·	·	·	57
·	·	579	·	606	626	698	·	·	720	734	747	752	·	761	766	·	·	·	·	·	·	810	·	58
·	·	·	·	·	·	·	·	·	720	734	747	752	757	761	766	·	·	·	·	·	·	810	·	59
·	·	·	·	·	·	·	·	·	·	·	·	·	·	·	·	·	·	·	·	·	·	·	·	60
573	576	579	·	606	627	698	·	·	721	734	747	752	·	761	766	·	·	·	·	·	798	810	·	61
·	·	·	·	·	·	·	·	·	·	·	747	752	757	761	766	·	·	·	·	·	·	·	·	62
·	·	·	·	607	628	698	·	·	·	·	748	753	757	761	766	·	·	·	·	·	·	·	816	63
573	576	579	·	607	630	698	·	·	·	734	748	753	757	761	766	·	·	·	·	·	·	810	·	64
·	·	·	·	607	631	·	705	·	·	·	748	753	757	761	766	·	·	·	·	·	798	·	816	65
·	·	·	·	·	·	·	·	·	·	·	748	753	757	761	766	·	·	·	·	·	·	·	·	66
·	·	·	·	·	·	·	·	·	·	·	748	753	757	762	766	·	·	·	·	·	·	·	·	67
·	·	·	·	·	·	·	705	712	721	·	748	753	757	762	766	·	·	·	·	·	·	·	816	68
·	·	·	·	·	·	·	·	·	·	·	748	753	·	762	766	·	·	784	787	·	798	·	·	69
·	·	·	·	607	632	·	·	·	·	735	748	753	757	762	766	779	·	784	787	789	799	·	816	70
·	·	·	599	607	·	698	705	712	721	735	748	753	·	762	766	779	·	·	·	·	799	·	816	71
·	·	·	·	·	·	·	·	·	·	·	748	753	·	762	766	·	·	·	787	·	799	·	·	72
·	·	·	·	·	·	·	·	·	·	·	748	753	·	762	766	·	·	·	·	·	·	·	816	73
·	·	·	·	·	·	·	·	·	·	735	748	753	757	762	766	·	·	·	·	·	·	·	816	74

INDEX

Countries and territories included in each table (with corresponding page number)
Pays et territoires compris dans chaque tableau (avec numéro de page correspondant)
Países y territorios incluidos en cada cuadro (con número de página correspondiente)

Column groups and headings:

- **I — POPULATION / POPULATION / POBLACIÓN**
  - 1: By sex & age group — Par sexe et gr. d'âge — Por sexo y grupo de edad
  - 2 A: By industry — Par activité économique — Por actividad económica
  - 2 B: By occupation — Par profession — Por ocupación
- **II — EMPLOYMENT / EMPLOI / EMPLEO**
  - 3: By economic activity — Par activité écon. — Por actividad económica
  - 4: General level — Niveau général — Nivel general
  - 5: Non-agr. sectors — Secteurs non agricoles — Sectores no agrícolas
  - Manufact.: 6 A All industries — Ensemble industries — Todas las industrias; 6 B By industry — Par industrie — Por industria; 6 C Tot. hours work. — Tot. heures effect. — Total horas efectuadas
  - 7: Mining & quarrying — Indust. extractives — Minas y canteras
  - 8: Construction — Construction — Construcción
  - 9: Transport — Transports — Transportes
- **III — UNEMPL. / CHÔMAGE / DESEMPL.**
  - 10: General level — Niveau général — Nivel general
  - 11: By industry/occup. — Par act. écon./profess. — Por actividad económica/ocupaciones
- **IV — HOURS OF WORK / DURÉE DU TRAVAIL / HORAS DE TRABAJO**
  - 12: Non-agr. sectors — Secteurs non agricoles — Sectores no agrícolas
  - Manufact.: 13 A All industries — Ensemble industries — Todas las industrias; 13 B By industry — Par industrie — Por industria; 13 C Distribution (%) — Répartition (%) — Repartición (%)
  - 14: Mining & quarrying — Indust. extractives — Minas y canteras
  - 15: Construction — Construcción
  - 16: Transport — Transports

Code	Country	1	2 A	2 B	3	4	5	6 A	6 B	6 C	7	8	9	10	11	12	13 A	13 B	13 C	14	15	16
75	Jamaica	22	78	.	312	337	340	.	.	.	.	.	.	437	448	.	.	.	.	.	.	.
76	Martinique	23	78	190	.	.	.	.	.	.	.	.	.	.	.	.	.	.	.	.	.	.
77	México	23	80	192	.	.	.	.	.	.	.	.	.	.	.	.	491	503	554	557	560	56
78	Montserrat	23	.	.	.	.	.	.	.	.	.	.	.	.	.	.	.	.	.	.	.	.
79	Nicaragua	24	80	194	.	.	.	.	.	.	.	.	.	.	.	.	.	.	.	.	.	.
80	Panamá	24	82	194	312	337	340	343	360	.	.	.	421	437	449	.	491	504	.	.	.	.
81	Panama Canal Zone	24	.	.	.	.	.	.	.	.	.	.	.	.	.	.	.	.	.	.	.	.
82	Paraguay	24	82	196	.	.	.	.	.	.	.	.	.	.	.	.	.	.	.	.	.	.
83	Perú	25	84	196	.	.	.	343	361	.	415	.	.	437	.	489	491	.	.	.	560	56
84	Puerto Rico	25	84	198	313	337	340	343	362	413	415	418	421	437	449	489	491	505	554	557	.	.
85	St. Kitts	25	.	.	.	.	.	.	.	.	.	.	.	.	.	.	.	.	.	.	.	.
86	St. Lucia	25	.	.	.	.	.	.	.	.	.	.	.	.	.	.	.	.	.	.	.	.
87	Saint-Pierre-et-Miquelon	26	84	.	.	.	.	.	.	.	.	.	.	.	.	.	.	.	.	.	.	.
88	St. Vincent	26	.	.	.	.	.	.	.	.	.	.	.	.	.	.	.	.	.	.	.	.
89	Surinam	26	86	198	.	.	.	.	.	.	.	.	.	437	.	.	.	.	.	.	.	.
90	Trinidad and Tobago	26	86	200	313	337	340	344	.	.	415	418	421	437	451	.	.	.	.	.	.	.
91	Turks and Caicos Is.	26	.	.	.	.	.	.	.	.	.	.	.	.	.	.	.	.	.	.	.	.
92	United States	27	88	200	314	337	340	344	363	413	416	418	421	437	452	489	491	507	554	557	560	56
93	Uruguay	27	88	202	.	.	.	.	.	.	.	.	.	437	453	.	.	.	554	.	.	.
94	Venezuela	27	90	204	.	.	.	344	365	413	416	.	.	437	454	489	491	509	.	557	.	.
95	Virgin Is. (Brit.)	28	90	204	.	.	.	.	.	.	.	.	.	.	.	.	.	.	.	.	.	.
96	Virgin Is. (US)	28	.	.	.	.	.	.	.	.	.	.	.	.	.	.	.	.	.	.	.	.
	ASIA — ASIE / ASIA																					
97	Afghanistan	.	.	.	.	.	.	.	.	.	.	.	.	.	.	.	.	.	.	.	.	.
98	Bahrain	29	92	206	.	.	.	.	.	.	.	.	.	.	.	.	.	.	.	.	.	.
99	Bangladesh	29	.	.	.	.	.	.	.	.	.	.	.	.	.	.	.	.	.	.	.	.
100	Brunei	29	92	206	315	338	341	344	.	.	416	419	422	.	.	.	.	.	.	.	.	.
101	Burma	.	94	.	.	.	.	.	.	.	.	.	.	437	.	.	491	510	.	557	.	56
102	Cambodge	29	.	.	.	.	.	.	.	.	.	.	.	.	.	.	.	.	.	.	.	.
103	Cyprus	29	94	.	315	338	341	344	366	.	416	419	422	437	455	489	491	511	554	558	560	56
104	Hong Kong	30	94	208	.	.	.	344	367	.	416	.	422	.	.	.	.	.	.	558	560	56
105	India	30	96	208	.	.	341	344	368	413	416	.	422	437	456	.	.	.	.	558	.	.
106	Indonesia	30	96	210	.	.	.	.	.	.	.	.	.	437	457	.	.	.	.	.	.	.
107	Iran	30	98	210	.	.	.	.	.	.	.	.	.	.	.	.	.	.	.	.	.	.
108	Iraq	.	.	.	.	.	.	.	.	.	.	.	.	437	.	.	.	.	.	.	.	.
109	Israel	31	98	212	316	338	341	344	370	413	416	419	422	437	458	489	491	512	554	.	.	.
110	Japan	31	100	214	316	338	341	344	371	413	416	419	422	437	.	489	492	513	554	.	560	56
111	Jordan	31	.	.	.	.	.	344	.	.	416	.	.	.	.	.	.	513	.	558	561	56
112	Korea, Rep. of	32	102	216	317	338	341	344	372	413	416	419	422	437	459	489	492	515	555	558	561	56

V PRODUCTIVITY · PRODUCTIVITÉ · PRODUCTIVIDAD			VI WAGES · SALAIRES · SALARIOS								VII PRICES · PRIX · PRECIOS					VIII ACCIDENTS · ACCIDENTES					IX DISP. CONF.	EXCHANGE · CHANGE · CAMBIO		Code Clave
National economy — Economie nationale	Industrial sector — Secteur industriel	Manufacturing — Industries manufact.	Non-agr. sectors — Secteurs non agricoles	All industries — Ensemble industries (Manufact.)	By industry — Par industrie (Manufact.)	Mining & quarrying — Indust. extractives	Construction — Construcción	Transport — Transports	Agriculture — Agricultura	Compens. of empl. — Rémun. des salariés	General indices — Indices généraux	Food — Alimentation	Fuel & light — Combustible et éclairage	Clothing — Habillement	Rent — Loyer	Mining & quarrying — Indust. extractives	Coal mines — Mines de charbon	Manufacturing — Industries manufact.	Construction — Construcción	Railways — Chemins de fer	Industrial disputes — Conflits du travail	Exchange rates — Cours des changes		Code · Clave
17 A	17 B	17 C	18	19 A	19 B	20	21	22	23	24	25 A	25 B	25 C	25 D	25 E	26 A	26 B	26 C	26 D	26 E	27	28 A	28 B	
.	.	.	.	.	.	.	.	.	.	735	748	753	757	762	766	779	.	784	.	789	799	.	816	75
.	.	.	.	.	.	.	.	.	.	.	748	753	.	762	766	.	.	784	787	.	799	.	.	76
573	576	579	.	607	633	698	706	712	721	735	748	753	757	762	.	.	.	.	.	.	799	.	816	77
.	.	.	.	.	.	.	.	.	.	.	.	.	.	.	.	.	.	.	.	.	.	.	.	78
573	.	.	.	607	.	698	.	.	.	735	.	.	.	.	.	.	.	.	.	.	.	810	.	79
573	.	.	.	607	634	.	.	.	.	735	748	753	757	762	766	.	.	784	787	.	799	.	816	80
.	.	.	.	.	.	.	.	.	.	735	748	753	.	762	766	.	.	.	.	.	799	.	.	81
.	.	.	599	607	.	.	706	712	.	735	748	753	.	762	766	.	.	.	.	.	799	810	.	82
.	.	.	.	608	635	698	.	.	.	735	748	753	758	762	766	779	782	.	.	789	799	810	.	83
.	.	.	.	.	.	.	.	.	.	735	748	753	758	762	766	.	.	784	787	789	799	.	.	84
.	.	.	.	.	.	.	.	.	.	.	748	753	758	762	.	.	.	.	.	.	.	.	.	85
.	.	.	.	.	.	.	.	.	.	.	748	753	758	762	766	.	.	.	.	.	799	.	.	86
.	.	.	.	.	.	.	.	.	.	.	.	.	.	.	.	.	.	.	.	.	800	.	.	87
.	.	.	.	.	.	.	.	.	.	.	.	.	.	.	.	.	.	.	.	.	.	.	.	88
.	.	.	.	608	.	698	706	712	721	.	748	753	758	762	766	779	.	784	.	.	800	.	816	89
.	.	.	599	.	.	698	706	713	.	.	748	753	758	762	766	.	.	784	787	.	800	.	816	90
.	.	.	.	.	.	.	.	.	.	.	.	.	.	.	.	.	.	.	.	.	.	.	.	91
573	576	579	599	608	637	699	706	713	722	735	748	753	758	762	767	779	782	784	787	789	800	.	.	92
.	.	.	599	608	639	.	706	713	722	735	748	753	.	762	767	.	.	.	.	.	.	811	.	93
.	.	.	599	608	640	699	.	.	.	736	748	753	758	762	767	.	.	.	.	.	800	811	.	94
.	.	.	.	.	.	.	.	.	.	.	748	753	.	.	.	.	.	.	.	.	.	.	.	95
.	.	.	.	.	.	.	.	.	.	.	.	.	.	.	.	.	.	.	.	.	.	.	.	96
.	.	.	.	.	.	.	.	.	.	.	748	.	.	.	.	.	.	.	.	.	.	811	.	97
.	.	.	.	.	.	.	.	.	.	.	.	.	.	.	.	.	.	.	.	.	.	.	.	98
.	.	.	.	.	641	.	706	.	.	.	748	753	758	762	767	.	.	785	.	.	800	.	.	99
.	.	.	.	.	.	.	.	.	.	.	748	753	.	.	.	.	.	.	.	.	.	.	.	100
.	.	.	.	608	642	699	.	713	722	.	748	753	758	762	767	.	.	785	.	.	.	811	.	101
.	.	.	.	.	.	.	.	.	.	.	748	753	.	762	767	.	.	.	.	.	.	.	.	102
.	.	579	599	608	643	699	706	713	723	.	748	753	758	762	767	780	.	785	787	.	800	.	816	103
.	.	.	.	608	.	.	.	.	.	.	748	753	758	762	767	780	.	785	.	.	800	811	.	104
.	.	.	.	608	644	700	.	.	723	.	749	754	758	762	767	780	782	785	.	789	800	811	.	105
.	.	.	.	.	.	.	.	.	.	.	749	754	.	763	767	.	.	.	.	.	801	.	.	106
.	.	.	.	.	.	.	.	.	.	736	749	754	758	763	767	.	.	.	.	.	.	.	816	107
573	576	.	599	608	645	700	706	713	723	736	749	754	758	763	767	780	.	785	787	.	801	.	816	108
573	576	579	599	609	646	700	706	713	723	736	749	754	758	763	767	780	782	785	787	789	801	811	.	109
.	.	.	.	.	.	.	.	.	.	736	749	754	758	763	767	780	.	785	787	.	801	811	.	110
.	.	.	.	.	.	.	.	.	.	736	749	754	758	763	767	.	.	785	787	.	801	811	.	111
.	576	579	600	609	648	700	707	713	723	736	749	754	758	763	767	780	.	785	.	.	801	811	.	112

INDEX

Countries and territories included in each table (with corresponding page number)

Pays et territoires compris dans chaque tableau (avec numéro de page correspondant)

Países y territorios incluidos en cada cuadro (con número de página correspondiente)

Column groups and headings

V — PRODUCTIVITY / PRODUCTIVITÉ / PRODUCTIVIDAD
- 17 A — National economy / Économie nationale / Economía nacional
- 17 B — Industrial sector / Secteur industriel / Sector industrial
- 17 C — Manufacturing — Industries manufact. / Industrias manufactureras

VI — WAGES / SALAIRES / SALARIOS
- 18 — Non-agr. sectors — Secteurs non agricoles / Sectores no agrícolas
- 19 A — All industries — Ensemble industries / Todas las industrias (Manufact.)
- 19 B — By industry — Par industrie / Por industria (Manufact.)
- 20 — Mining & quarrying — Indust. extractives / Minas y canteras
- 21 — Construction / Construcción
- 22 — Transport / Transportes
- 23 — Agriculture / Agricultura
- 24 — Compens. of empl. — Rémun. des salariés / Remuneración de asalariados

VII — PRICES / PRIX / PRECIOS
- 25 A — General indices — Indices généraux / Indices generales
- 25 B — Food / Alimentation / Alimentación
- 25 C — Fuel & light — Combustible et éclairage / Combustible y alumbrado
- 25 D — Clothing / Habillement / Vestido
- 25 E — Rent / Loyer / Alquiler

VIII — ACCIDENTS / ACCIDENTS / ACCIDENTES
- 26 A — Mining & quarrying — Indust. extractives / Minas y canteras
- 26 B — Coal mines — Mines de charbon / Minas de carbón
- 26 C — Manufacturing — Industries manufact. / Industrias manufactureras
- 26 D — Construction / Construcción
- 26 E — Railways — Chemins de fer / Ferrocarriles

IX — DISP. CONF. CONF.
- 27 — Industrial disputes — Conflits du travail / Conflictos del trabajo

EXCHANGE / CHANGE / CAMBIO
- 28 A, 28 B — Exchange rates — Cours des changes / Tipos de cambio

17A	17B	17C	18	19A	19B	20	21	22	23	24	25A	25B	25C	25D	25E	26A	26B	26C	26D	26E	27	28A	28B	Code
										736	749	754		763	767									113
											749	754		763	767								816	114
											749	754	758	763	767							811		115
																					801	811		116
											749	754		763	767	780		785	788	789	801	811		
						700		714	724	736	749	754		763	767	780		785		789	801	811		117
											749	754	758	763										118
				609	649				724		749	754		763	767	780	782	785			801	811		119
673		579	600	609	650	700		714	724		749	754	758	763	767	780		785			801	811		120
73			600	609	651	700	707	714			749	754	758	763	767						802			121
			600	609			707	714	724	736	749	754	758	763	768			785		789	802	812		122
			600						725	736	749	754		763	768			785		789	802	812		123
			600	609	652	700	707	714	725		749	754	758	763		780		785	788	789		812		124
			600	609			707	714		736	749	754		763	768			785	788	789	802	812		125
												754	758	763	768						802		816	126
																								127
74	576		601	609	654	701	707	714	725	737	749	754	759	763	768	780		785	788	790	802	812		128
74	576	580	601	609	655	701	707	714	726	737	749	754	759	763		780		785		790	802	812		129
	577		601	609	657	701	707	714	726		749	754												130
																								131
74	577	580	601	609	658	701	707	714	726		749	754				780	782	785	788	790				132
74		580	601	610	660		708		727	737	749	754	759	763	768						802	812		133
	577	580	601	610	661	701	708		727	737	749	754	759	763	768	780		785	788		802	812		134
																								135
74	577	580		610	662	701	708		727	737	749	754	759	763	768	780		786	788	790	803	812		136
74	577		601	610	663	701	708	714	728	737	749	754	759	763	768	780	782	786	788	790	803	812		137
	577		602	610			708	715	728		750	755	759	763	768			786	788	790				138
74	577	580	602	610	664	701	708		728	737	750	755	759	763	768	780		786	788	790	803	812		139
			602				708	715			750	755	759	764	768						803		817	140
				610	666					737	750	755	759	764	768	780		786			803		817	141
	577	580	602	611	667	702	708	715	729		750	755	759	764	768	780	782	786	788	790				142
			602								750	755	759	764	768						803	812		143
	577	580	602	611	669	702	708		729	737	750	755	759	764	768	780	782	786	788	790	803		817	144
																								145
74	577	580	603	611	670	702	708	715	729	737	750	755	759	764	768	780		786	788	790	803	813		146
																								147

	V PRODUCTIVITY / PRODUCTIVITÉ / PRODUCTIVIDAD			VI WAGES / SALAIRES / SALARIOS								VII PRICES / PRIX / PRECIOS					VIII ACCIDENTS / ACCIDENTS / ACCIDENTES					IX DISP. CONF.	EXCHANGE CHANGE CAMBIO		Code / Code / Clave
	National economy — Economía nacional	Industrial sector — Sector industrial	Manufacturing — Industrias manufactureras	Non-agr. sectors — Sectores no agrícolas	All industries — Todas las industrias (Manufact. Ensemble)	By industry — Por industria	Mining & quarrying — Minas y canteras	Construction — Construcción	Transport — Transportes	Agriculture — Agricultura	Compens. of empl. — Remuneración de asalariados	General indices — Indices generales	Food — Alimentación	Fuel & light — Combustible y alumbrado	Clothing — Vestido	Rent — Alquiler	Mining & quarrying — Minas y canteras	Coal mines — Minas de carbón	Manufacturing — Industrias manufactureras	Construction — Construcción	Railways — Ferrocarriles	Industrial disputes — Conflictos del trabajo	Exchange rates — Tipos de cambio		
	17 A	17 B	17 C	18	19 A	19 B	20	21	22	23	24	25 A	25 B	25 C	25 D	25 E	26 A	26 B	26 C	26 D	26 E	27	28 A	28 B	
	674	577	.	603	611	671	702	708	.	.	737	750	755	759	764	.	781	.	786	.	.	.	813	.	148
	674	577	580	.	.	672	702	709	715	.	738	750	755	759	764	768	.	.	786	788	.	803	.	817	149
	.	.	.	.	.	.	.	.	.	.	.	.	.	.	.	.	.	.	.	.	.	.	.	.	150
	674	577	580	.	611	674	702	709	715	730	738	750	755	759	764	768	781	.	786	788	790	803	813	.	151
	675	578	580	603	611	677	702	709	715	730	738	750	755	759	764	768	781	.	786	788	790	804	813	.	152
	675	578	580	603	612	678	702	709	715	730	.	750	755	.	.	.	781	783	786	788	790	.	813	.	153
	.	578	.	.	.	680	702	709	.	730	738	750	755	759	764	768	.	.	.	.	.	.	813	.	154
	675	578	.	603	612	681	.	709	715	731	.	750	755	759	764	768	.	.	786	788	790	.	813	.	155
	.	.	.	603	612	682	702	709	715	.	738	750	755	759	764	768	.	.	786	788	790	804	813	.	156
	675	578	581	.	612	684	703	709	715	731	738	750	755	759	764	768	781	.	786	788	790	804	813	.	157
	675	578	.	603	612	686	703	709	715	731	.	750	755	.	764	.	781	783	786	.	.	804	812	.	158
	675	578	581	604	613	687	703	709	716	731	738	750	755	759	764	768	781	783	786	788	790	804	813	.	159
	.	578	.	604	613	690	703	710	716	731	.	750	755	759	764	768	781	783	786	788	790	.	813	.	160
	.	.	.	.	.	.	.	.	.	.	.	.	.	.	.	.	.	.	.	.	.	.	.	.	161
	.	.	.	604	613	692	703	710	716	.	738	750	755	.	764	769	781	783	.	.	.	804	813	.	162
	.	.	.	.	.	.	.	.	.	.	.	.	.	.	.	.	.	.	.	.	.	.	.	.	163
	.	.	.	.	.	.	.	.	.	.	.	.	.	.	.	.	.	.	.	.	.	.	.	.	164
	.	.	.	.	.	.	.	.	.	.	.	750	755	.	764	769	.	.	.	.	.	.	.	.	165
	.	.	.	604	613	693	703	710	716	732	738	750	755	759	764	769	.	.	786	788	.	804	.	817	166
	.	.	.	.	.	.	.	.	.	.	.	750	755	.	.	.	.	.	.	.	.	.	.	.	167
	.	.	.	.	.	.	.	.	.	.	.	.	.	.	.	.	.	.	.	.	.	.	.	.	168
	.	.	.	.	.	.	.	.	.	.	.	.	.	.	.	.	.	.	.	.	.	.	.	.	169
	.	.	.	.	.	.	.	.	.	.	.	.	.	.	.	.	.	.	.	.	.	.	.	.	170
	75	.	581	604	613	694	703	710	716	732	738	750	755	759	764	769	781	783	786	788	790	804	813	.	171
	.	.	.	.	.	.	.	.	.	.	.	.	.	.	.	.	.	.	.	.	.	.	.	.	172
	.	.	.	.	.	.	.	.	.	.	.	.	.	.	.	.	.	.	.	.	.	.	.	.	173
	.	.	.	.	613	.	703	710	716	.	.	750	755	759	764	769	781	.	786	788	.	804	.	817	174
	.	.	.	.	.	.	.	.	.	.	.	.	.	.	.	.	.	.	.	.	.	.	.	.	175
	.	.	.	.	.	.	.	.	.	.	738	750	755	.	764	.	.	.	.	.	.	.	.	.	176
	.	.	.	.	.	.	.	.	.	732	.	750	755	.	764	769	.	.	786	788	.	.	.	817	177
	.	.	.	.	.	.	.	.	.	.	.	750	755	.	764	769	.	.	.	.	.	804	.	.	178
	.	.	.	.	.	.	.	.	.	.	.	.	.	.	.	.	.	.	.	.	.	.	.	.	179
	.	.	.	.	.	.	.	.	.	.	.	750	755	759	764	.	.	.	.	.	.	.	.	.	180
	.	.	.	.	.	.	.	.	.	.	.	750	755	759	764	769	.	.	.	.	.	.	.	.	181
	75	578	581	604	613	695	703	710	716	732	.	750	755	.	764	769	.	.	.	.	.	.	.	.	182
	.	578	581	604	613	696	703	710	716	732	.	750	755	.	764	.	.	.	.	.	.	.	.	.	183
	.	578	581	604	613	.	703	710	716	732	.	750	755	.	764	769	.	.	.	.	.	.	.	.	184

Publications of the International Labour Office

Bulletin of Labour Statistics

Published quarterly in trilingual form, this *Bulletin* supplements the annual data given in the *Year Book*, with monthly or quarterly series on the following:

Indices of the general level of employment and of employment in non-agricultural sectors — Indices of numbers employed and total hours worked in manufacturing — Numbers and percentages unemployed — Average number of hours worked in non-agricultural sectors and in manufacturing — Average earnings or wage rates in non-agricultural sectors and in manufacturing — General indices and food indices of consumer prices.

In addition, the results of the ILO October inquiry on hourly wages of adult wage earners in 41 occupations, monthly salaries and normal hours of work per week in selected occupations, and on retail prices of selected consumer goods, are included in each second quarterly issue.

Annual subscription (four main issues and eight supplements): **40 Swiss frs.**
Price per each of four main issues: 12 Swiss frs.

Technical Guide

Descriptions of general series published in the *Bulletin* and the *Year Book of Labour Statistics* (5th edition, 1976).

Volume I: **Consumer prices** (about 300 pp.)
Volume II: **Employment — Unemployment — Hours of work — Wages** (about 350 pp.)

Both volumes available early 1976.

This publication presents summary descriptions of the methods used by national statistical offices in the computation of the series published by the ILO in both the *Bulletin of Labour Statistics* and the *Year Book of Labour Statistics*; it provides useful basic information on the coverage of the series, their definition, methods of computation and other characteristics which determine the international comparability of these statistics.

Changes introduced in the methodological descriptions of the series published in the *Bulletin* (introduction of new series or revision of existing series) appear in an annex to the *Bulletin* and are subsequently incorporated in the next edition of the *Technical Guide*.

Household Income
and Expenditure Statistics, 1960-1972

Africa, Asia, Latin America
Covering 45 countries. On sale now.
ISBN 92-2-101179-8. 17.50 Swiss frs.

Northern America, Europe and USSR, Oceania
Covering 32 countries. To be issued early 1976.
ISBN 92-2-101434-7.

These publications present, on a uniform basis, data on the level, components and size distribution of household income and expenditure based on surveys conducted during the period 1960-1972.

The data presented in the various tables of these publications for urban and rural sectors, social and occupational groups and households of different sizes supply the basis for a comparative analysis of household income and expenditure distributions.

Publications du Bureau international du Travail

Bulletin des statistiques du travail

Publié tous les trois mois en édition trilingue, ce *Bulletin* complète les données contenues dans l'*Annuaire des statistiques du travail* et présente des séries mensuelles ou trimestrielles sous les rubriques suivantes:

Indices du niveau général de l'emploi et de l'emploi dans les secteurs non agricoles — Indices des effectifs employés et du total des heures de travail effectuées dans les industries manufacturières — Chiffres absolus et pourcentages du chômage — Durée hebdomadaire moyenne du travail dans les secteurs non agricoles et dans les industries manufacturières — Gains ou taux de salaire moyens dans les secteurs non agricoles et dans les industries manufacturières — Prix à la consommation: indices généraux et indices de l'alimentation.

En outre, les résultats de l'enquête d'octobre du BIT sur les salaires horaires des ouvriers adultes dans 41 professions, sur les traitements et la durée normale du travail des employés dans certaines professions et sur les prix de détail de certains biens de consommation figurent chaque année dans le numéro du deuxième trimestre.

Abonnement annuel (quatre numéros principaux et huit suppléments): **40 fr. suisses**
Prix de chaque numéro principal: **12 fr. suisses**

Guide technique

Descriptions des séries générales publiées dans le *Bulletin* et l'*Annuaire des statistiques du travail* (cinquième édition, 1976).

Volume I: **Prix à la consommation** (env. 300 pp.)

Volume II: **Emploi — Chômage — Durée du travail — Salaires** (env. 350 pp.)

Les deux volumes à paraître début 1976.

Cette publication présente un résumé descriptif des méthodes utilisées par les services statistiques nationaux lors de l'établissement des séries qui sont publiées par le BIT dans le *Bulletin des statistiques du travail* et dans l'*Annuaire des statistiques du travail*; elle fournit des renseignements de base très utiles sur la portée des statistiques, leur définition, les méthodes de calcul employées et d'autres caractéristiques permettant de déterminer la comparabilité des séries sur le plan international.

Les modifications apportées aux descriptions méthodologiques des séries publiées dans le *Bulletin* (introduction de nouvelles séries ou révision de séries existantes), qui sont indiquées dans une annexe du *Bulletin*, sont incorporées dans l'édition suivante du *Guide technique*.

Statistiques des revenus et des dépenses des ménages, 1960-1972

Afrique, Amérique latine, Asie

Englobant 45 pays. En vente.
ISBN 92-2-201179-1. 17,50 fr. suisses.

Amérique du Nord, Europe et URSS, Océanie

Englobant 32 pays. A paraître début 1976.
ISBN 92-2-201434-0.

Ces publications présentent, sur une base uniformisée, des données sur le niveau, les composantes et la répartition des revenus et des dépenses des ménages fondées sur des enquêtes effectuées pendant la période 1960-1972.

Les statistiques présentées dans les divers tableaux de ces volumes portent sur les secteurs urbains et ruraux, sur des groupes sociaux et professionnels et sur des ménages de tailles différentes, et permettent une analyse comparative de la répartition des revenus et des dépenses des ménages.

Publicaciones de la Oficina Internacional del Trabajo

Boletín de Estadísticas del Trabajo

Este *Boletín*, que se publica trimestralmente en edición trilingüe, completa los datos anuales proporcionados en el *Anuario* con series mensuales o trimestrales sobre las siguientes cuestiones:

Indices del nivel general del empleo y del empleo en los sectores no agrícolas — Indices del total de trabajadores ocupados y del total de horas de trabajo efectuadas en las industrias manufactureras — Cantidades y porcentajes de desempleados — Promedio de las horas de trabajo en los sectores no agrícolas y en las industrias manufactureras — Promedios de las ganancias o de las tarifas de salarios en los sectores no agrícolas y en las industrias manufactureras — Indices generales de los precios del consumo, e índices de los precios de los alimentos.

Además, el número del segundo trimestre de cada año incluye los resultados de la encuesta de la OIT ejecutada en octubre del año precedente sobre los salarios por hora de obreros adultos en cuarenta y una ocupaciones, y sobre los precios al por menor de ciertos bienes de consumo.

Suscripción anual (cuatro números y ocho suplementos): **40 frs. suizos**
Número suelto: 12 frs. suizos

Guía Técnica

Descripciones de las series generales publicadas en el *Boletín* y el *Anuario de Estadísticas del Trabajo* (quinta edición, 1976).

Volumen I: **Precios del consumo** (aprox. 300 páginas)

Volumen II: **Empleo — Desempleo — Horas de trabajo — Salarios** (aprox. 350 páginas)

Los dos volúmenes aparecerán a principios de 1976.

Esta publicación contiene un resumen detallado de los métodos utilizados por los servicios nacionales de estadística para establecer las series publicadas por la OIT en el *Boletín de Estadísticas del Trabajo* y en el *Anuario de Estadísticas del Trabajo* ; proporciona datos básicos muy útiles sobre el alcance de las estadísticas, su definición, los métodos de cálculo utilizados y demás características que permiten determinar la comparabilidad de las series en el plano internacional.

Las modificaciones efectuadas en las descripciones metodológicas de las series publicadas en el *Boletín* (introducción de nuevas series o revisión de las existentes) figuran en un anexo al *Boletín* y se incorporan a la próxima edición de la *Guía Técnica*.

Estadísticas de ingresos y gastos de los hogares, 1960-1972

Africa, América latina, Asia

Abarca 45 países. En venta.
ISBN 92-2-301179-5. 17,50 frs. suizos.

América del Norte, Europa y URSS, Oceanía

Abarca 32 países. Aparecerá a principios de 1976.
ISBN 92-2-301434-4.

Estas publicaciones presentan de manera uniforme los datos sobre el nivel, la composición y la distribución de los ingresos y gastos de los hogares basados en encuestas realizadas entre 1960 y 1972.

Los datos presentados en los diferentes cuadros de las publicaciones, referentes a las áreas urbanas o rurales y a distintos grupos sociales, de ocupación o de tamaño de los hogares, suministran bases para un análisis comparativo de la distribución de los ingresos y gastos de los hogares.